Property of Simpson

P9-AFH-885

HOLT Science Spectrum®

Physical Science

TEACHER'S EDITION

<table>
<tr><td>

Teacher's Edition Walk-Through

</td><td>

Student Edition Contents In Brief

</td></tr>
</table>

HOLT, RINEHART AND WINSTON

A Harcourt Education Company

Orlando • **Austin** • New York • San Diego • London

HOLT Science Spectrum®

Physical Science

Interactive
Online Edition

National Science
Teachers Association

with Standardized
Test Preparation

v=d/t
speed=distance divided by time

Learn to think like a scientist...

This introductory high school physical science program integrates chemistry, physics, Earth science, space science, and applied mathematics. The program emphasizes the connections between these subjects and cross-disciplinary applications, and helps students think analytically, like scientists.

UNRIVALED SUPPORT FOR BOTH TEACHERS AND STUDENTS

In the pages that follow, we will illustrate exactly how Holt addresses the key challenges science teachers tell us they face most. A few highlights include:

- Interactive teacher resources that allow you to easily edit or adapt templates to suit your needs. Everything is at your fingertips, located on both the *Teacher's One-Stop Planner*® and online in our *Interactive Online Edition.*

- Our convenient *Chapter Resource Files,* in print format, contain masters of student worksheets and laboratory data sheets, along with teacher answer keys. The key resources for each chapter are together in one easy-to-use booklet.

- **Holt Calendar Planner, Puzzle Pro**®**,** and the *Lab Generator* with **Lab Materials QuickList** allow you to be more productive during your valuable after-school hours.

- Address your need for differentiating instruction by providing the **Interactive Reader,** ability-leveled worksheets and lab data sheets, materials translated into Spanish, MP3 audio readings of the textbook, or our exclusive **Live Ink**® **Online Reading Help** technology, to students who need extra help or greater challenges.

- Provide formative assessment before leaving the lesson. Tailor your assessments to provide diagnoses by mastery of standards or by performance improvement. The **ExamView**® **Version 5 Assessment Suite** works seamlessly with **Holt Online Assessment** and **MindPoint**® **Quiz Show** to make this all possible.

What's new and notable about this edition

- A new student **Interactive Reader** provides more active engagement. Designed for struggling or reluctant readers, it contains the same content as the textbook, but lowered in reading level.

- A redesigned **Teacher's One-Stop Planner®** with nearly every Holt resource is now completely editable, allowing you to customize and repurpose.

- A comprehensive **Student One Stop** includes not only the textbook, but also other valuable student resources on one easy-to-use CD-ROM.

- **Lab Videos on DVD** show the actual performance of the chapter labs, so you can prepare your students before the lab or replace the lab if needed.

- A **Math Skills Workbook** provides remedial help where needed.

- A revamped **Interactive Online Edition** makes it easier to find all the resources in the program online.

- A best-in-class **Lab Generator** helps manage all your laboratory needs, allowing you to search, edit, and add your own labs.

- **Virtual Investigations** contain over twenty simulations, offering your students interactive experiences that make key science principles both understandable and engaging.

Teach with Digital Resources

Holt provides you with a wealth of technology tools that combine functionality with content, allowing you to customize, organize, and adapt to your students' changing needs.

FOR THE TEACHER

- Holt Calendar Planner
- Lab Materials Quick-List
- One-Stop Planner® with editable worksheets
- Lab Generator

- PowerPoint® Resources
- Visual Concepts
- Virtual Investigations
- Transparencies on CD and One-Stop Planner®

PLAN → **PRESENT**

FOR THE STUDENT

Teach with Print Resources

If you prefer the familiarity of print resources, or if you're not able to make full use of our digital resources, we also provide a wide variety of traditional print materials for both students and teachers.

FOR THE TEACHER

- Teacher's Edition Planning Guide
- Strategies for English Language Learners
- Science Skills Workshop: Reading in the Content Area
- Professional Reference for Teachers

- Teaching Transparencies
- Teaching Masters of tables, graphs, and more
- Concept Mapping Transparencies
- Chapter Resource File blackline masters

PLAN → **PRESENT**

FOR THE STUDENT

- Physical Science Lab Generator
- Lab Videos DVD
- Virtual Investigations
- Holt PuzzlePro®

- MindPoint® Quiz Show
- ExamView® Version 5 Assessment Suite worksheets
- Holt Online Assessment
- Support for "clicker" response systems

STUDY

- Interactive Online Edition with Live Ink® and MP3 audio
- Student One Stop with Interactive Reader, Study Guide, and more
- Guided Reading Audio CD program (also in Spanish)
- Visual Concepts

HANDS-ON

- Virtual Investigations
- Interactive Tutor
- CBL™ Probeware Labs
- Interactive Concept Maps

ASSESS

- Holt Online Assessment
- Online Section Reviews
- Online Chapter Reviews
- Online Standardized Test Prep Practice

- Laboratory Manager's Professional Reference
- Chapter Resource File Lab Data Sheets (leveled)
- Forensics and Applied Science Experiments Workbook Teacher's Edition

- ExamView® Version 5 Assessment Suite worksheets
- Chapter Resource File Assessments
- Spanish Assessments

STUDY

- Interactive Reader
- Study Guide (also in Spanish)
- Science Skills Workshop: Reading in the Content Area
- Spanish Resources
- Math Skills Workbook

HANDS-ON

- Forensics and Applied Science Experiments Workbook Student Edition
- Inquiry Lab Datasheets
- Quick Lab Datasheets
- Chapter Lab Datasheets

ASSESS

- Pretests
- Section Quizzes
- Chapter Tests A & B
- Standardized Test Prep Practice

T5

Unparalleled Reading and Comprehension Tools

Learning physical science requires students to absorb a multitude of concepts and build a strong vocabulary. Providing students with tools that will help them organize concepts and understand terms is essential to a well-rounded science program.

READING TOOLBOX

Visual Literacy Students may have difficulty interpreting the rapid series of events that cause an air bag to inflate. Ask students to describe what happens in each step in the illustration. If possible, have a volunteer sketch the steps on the board and use force arrows to identify the forces involved. **LS Visual**

- **Reading Toolbox:** Every chapter starts with helpful tools such as a **Graphic Concept Organizer** or a **Word Problems Chart.** These valuable student tools are suggested again at point-of-use within the chapter. The *Teacher's Edition* provides additional toolbox suggestions in the margin wrap. Also, the first question in every **Chapter Review** provides practice using a **Reading Toolbox** application.

- **Key Ideas:** Each section begins with questions that students will learn to answer within the chapter and emphasizes (with vibrant red icons) key ideas to remember. Important points are reinforced with speed-bump **Reading Check** questions.

Key **Ideas**

❯ How is work calculated?

❯ What is the relationship between work and power?

❯ How do machines make work easier?

Power

Running up a flight of stairs does not require more work than walking up slowly does, but running is more exhausting than walking. The amount of time that a given amount of work takes is an important... machines. The quan... is **power.** ❯ **Power is... much work is done**

 Power equation

power (POW uhr) a quantity that measures the rate at which work is done or energy is transformed

Academic Vocabulary

factor (FAK tuhr) a condition or event that brings about a result

- **Key Terms:** Scientific vocabulary is highlighted in context, and defined in the margin for quick reference. Other terms that are used frequently in science are also defined in **Academic Vocabulary** margin notes.

Additionally you'll find:

- The **Interactive Reader** to help struggling or reluctant readers.
- The **Guided Reading Audio CD Program** that provides a direct read of the textbook. Files are also available in MP3 format.
- **Visual Concepts** animations and videos online and on CD.

Why It Matters

Capturing student interest occurs when you demonstrate how science relates to their everyday lives and can shape their future careers.

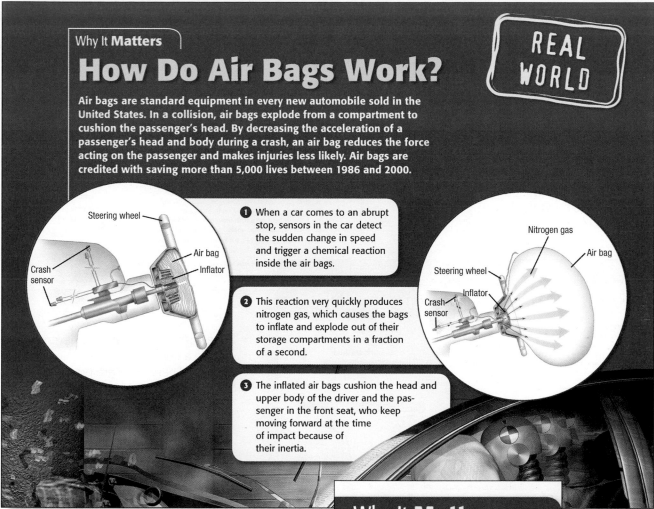

Why It **Matters**

How Do Air Bags Work?

REAL WORLD

Air bags are standard equipment in every new automobile sold in the United States. In a collision, air bags explode from a compartment to cushion the passenger's head. By decreasing the acceleration of a passenger's head and body during a crash, an air bag reduces the force acting on the passenger and makes injuries less likely. Air bags are credited with saving more than 5,000 lives between 1986 and 2000.

Steering wheel
Air bag
Inflator
Crash sensor

❶ When a car comes to an abrupt stop, sensors in the car detect the sudden change in speed and trigger a chemical reaction inside the air bags.

❷ This reaction very quickly produces nitrogen gas, which causes the bags to inflate and explode out of their storage compartments in a fraction of a second.

❸ The inflated air bags cushion the head and upper body of the driver and the passenger in the front seat, who keep moving forward at the time of impact because of their inertia.

Nitrogen gas
Air bag
Steering wheel
Inflator
Crash sensor

- **Why It Matters:** Designed more like a museum exhibit than a textbook page, **Why it Matters Articles** evoke the visual dynamics of physical science in the context of real-world science, weird science, or science and society.

- **Section Openers:** Each section begins by emphasizing **Why it Matters**—that is, how lesson content is of practical value in students' lives.

Why It **Matters**

Knowing how compounds are named can help you recognize them in food ingredients.

- **Online projects:** You and your students have access to **NSTA's SciLinks®,** a library of approved Web links. As a teacher, you also have access to **New Scientist Online®,** the world's most popular weekly science digest.

Developing Math and Science Skills

Being able to do things like convert units, create a graph, make a scientific prediction, and find reputable Web sources, are all skills fundamental to science. Holt offers exceptional support to target these skills.

- **Worked examples** are presented in two columns, reflecting how you teach. The right column is what students would see on the chalkboard, and the left column is what they would hear. Every example is followed by stepped practice problems, along with a directed hint or two.

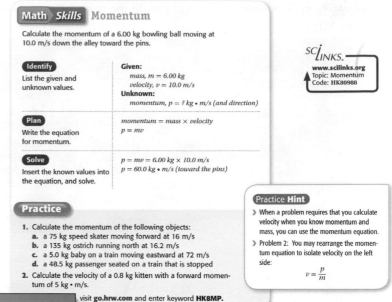

Math *Skills* Momentum

Calculate the momentum of a 6.00 kg bowling ball moving at 10.0 m/s down the alley toward the pins.

Identify
List the given and unknown values.

Given:
mass, $m = 6.00$ kg
velocity, $v = 10.0$ m/s
Unknown:
momentum, $p = ?$ kg • m/s (and direction)

Plan
Write the equation for momentum.

momentum = mass × velocity
$p = mv$

Solve
Insert the known values into the equation, and solve.

$p = mv = 6.00$ kg × 10.0 m/s
$p = 60.0$ kg • m/s (toward the pins)

www.scilinks.org
Topic: Momentum
Code: HK80988

Practice Hint
➤ When a problem requires that you calculate velocity when you know momentum and mass, you can use the momentum equation.
➤ Problem 2: You may rearrange the momentum equation to isolate velocity on the left side:
$$v = \frac{p}{m}$$

Practice

1. Calculate the momentum of the following objects:
   a. a 75 kg speed skater moving forward at 16 m/s
   b. a 135 kg ostrich running north at 16.2 m/s
   c. a 5.0 kg baby on a train moving eastward at 72 m/s
   d. a 48.5 kg passenger seated on a train that is stopped
2. Calculate the velocity of a 0.8 kg kitten with a forward momentum of 5 kg • m/s.

..., visit go.hrw.com and enter keyword **HK8MP.**

Graphing Motion

Science Skills

Problem

The graph shown here contains data about a runner. What information is being graphed? What can be determined from the graph about the runner's speed? Is the speed constant during the run? Explain.

Technology
Math
Scientific Methods
Graphing

Solution

❶ Examine the graph. Determine what the x-axis and y-axis are to find out what is being graphed.

The x-axis is time, measured in seconds. The y-axis is distance, measured in meters. This is a graph of the runner's distance from some arbitrary starting point as a function of time.

❷ Speed is equal to the slope of a distance vs. time graph.

The runner's average speed at various times can be determined from the graph.

❸ A horizontal line indicates zero speed and acceleration. A straight line has a constant speed and zero acceleration.

The slope of the graph is different at different times. The runner's speed is not constant but varies from time to time.

Distance Vs. Time

- **Science Skills** features in every chapter provide a concentrated refresher for a key skill. These skills are practiced in the **Section** and **Chapter Reviews.**

Math Skills Workbook

HOLT Science Spectrum®
Physical Science

HOLT, RINEHART AND WINSTON

- Offer students unlimited practice with assignments that you've created with **ExamView® Version 5 Assessment Suite** and posted to **Holt Online Assessment.**

- The **Math Skills Workbook** provides more remediation and practice for students who need additional support.

Labs, Scientific Inquiry, and Hands-On Learning

Thinking like a scientist means learning how to conduct scientific inquiry, especially in a hands-on setting. *Holt Science Spectrum* provides many opportunities to gain lab experience, ranging from ten-minute activities with minimal equipment to full-scale labs with a discovery focus.

 **20 min**

Matter and Chemical Reactions

Place about **5 g (1 tsp) of baking soda** into a **sealable plastic bag.** Place about **5 mL (1 tsp) of vinegar** into a **plastic film canister.** Secure the lid. Place the canister into the bag. Squeeze the air out of the bag, and tightly seal the bag.

Use a **balance** to determine the total mass of the bag and its contents. Make a note of this value. Open the canister without opening the bag, and allow the vinegar and baking soda to mix. When the reaction has stopped, measure and record the total mass of the bag and its contents.

Questions to Get You Started

1. What evidence shows that a chemical reaction has taken place?
2. Compare the masses of the bag and its contents before and after the reaction. What does this result demonstrate about chemical reactions?

- **Inquiry Opener:**
  Chapters start with an inquiry-driven activity to get students asking the right questions about the lab topic.

- **Demonstrations:**
  "Show and Tell" suggestions for things you can show your students are located in the margin of the *Teacher's Edition*.

QuickLab **Making Butter** **10 min**

Procedure

1. Pour 250 mL (about 1/2 pint) of **heavy cream** into an empty **500 mL container.**
2. Add a clean **marble,** and then seal the container tightly so that it will not leak.
3. Take turns shaking the container. When the cream becomes very thick, you will no longer hear the marble moving.
4. Record your observations of the substance that formed.

Analysis

1. Cream is an emulsion of fats in water. If joined fat droplets make up butter, what must make up most of the remaining liquid?
2. Why does butter form when you shake the cream?

Application Lab **50 min**

Lenses and Images

As an optical engineer for a camera company, you have been given a lens for which your job is to figure out the focal length. Based on the specifications you obtain by doing an experiment, a new model of camera will be designed that uses that lens.

Procedure

Preparing for Your Experiment

1. The shape of a lens determines the size, position, and types of images that it may form. When parallel rays of light from a distant object pass through a converging lens, they come together to form an image at a point called the *focal point*. The distance from this point to the lens is called the *focal length*. In this experiment, you will find the focal length of a lens. Then, verify this value by forming images, measuring distances, and using the lens formula below.

$$\frac{1}{d_o} + \frac{1}{d_i} = \frac{1}{f}$$

where d_o = object distance,

d_i = image distance, and

f = focal length

2. On a clean sheet of paper, make a data table like the one shown.
3. Set up the equipment as illustrated in the figure below. Make sure the lens and screen are securely fastened to the meterstick.

What You'll Do

> **Observe** images formed by a convex lens.
> **Measure** the distance of objects and images from the lens.
> **Analyze** your results to determine the focal length of the lens.

What You'll Need

cardboard screen, 10 cm × 20 cm
convex lens, 10 cm to 15 cm focal length
lens holder
light box with light bulb
meterstick
ruler, metric
screen holder
supports for meterstick

Safety

- **Quick Labs:** Incorporate a short, hands-on activity every day to underscore a point, with few demands on time and equipment.

- **Chapter Labs:** Major labs that focus on either a key experimental skill or test a scientific principle in a manner that promotes use of scientific methods. Additional labs are available in the ancillary package and are also provided in a searchable, editable, and expandable format on the ***Holt Lab Generator CD-ROM.***

You'll find additional support with:

- **Lab Videos on DVD** that can help you prepare your students for labs or replace hands-on labs with virtual labs as needed.

- Simulated experiments, which allow you to change parameters that will affect outcomes on our **Virtual Investigations CD.**

Lab Videos
HOLT Science Spectrum
Physical Science

Virtual Investigations CD-ROM
HOLT Science Spectrum
Physical Science

Differentiating Instruction

Today's classroom is comprised of students with widely different abilities and learning styles. That's why **Holt Science Spectrum** provides you with resources targeted to meet special needs and to challenge advanced learners.

Differentiated Instruction	Differentiated Instruction
Special Education Students **Mass Judgments** Gather 15 or 20 different-sized, solid-mass items, such as marbles, books, or heavy backpacks. Randomly pair the items. Select two pairs. Ask students which of the two pairs has greater gravitational force. Continue until all pairs are addressed. Then, choose two items and ask a volunteer to choose two other items that have more or less gravitational force. **LS Kinesthetic**	**Advanced Learners** **Terminal Velocity** The acceleration due to gravity is the same for all objects, regardless of weight (disregarding air resistance). Ask students to explain whether terminal velocity for an object falling in air depends on the object's weight. (Yes. Terminal velocity is the point where air resistance equals weight, so if weight changes, a different amount of air resistance will be needed to balance the force of gravity. Therefore, a different terminal velocity will be achieved.) **LS Logical**

- The *Teacher's Edition* wrap-around margin provides tips and strategies for differentiated instruction, always in the same easy-to-find place on the page, and referenced again in the **Chapter Planning Guide** for each chapter.

- For struggling readers, provide the **Interactive Reader,** written to a lower reading level and designed to engage the student more frequently. The same students can take advantage of **Live Ink® Online Reading Help** technology in the *Interactive Online Edition,* or listen to an audio read of each section on their MP3 player or computer.

- The **Teacher's One-Stop Planner®** and the Physical Science Lab Generator have worksheets and lab data sheets in three versions — Basic, General, and Advanced — so all your students can be doing the same lesson, but at their own levels.

- **Support for English-language learners** is vast, with everything from the *Student Edition in Spanish,* to audio in Spanish and assessment bank questions translated into Spanish, located on **ExamView® Version 5 Assessment Suite.**

Complete Technology Solutions

There are many digital components of *Holt Science Spectrum,* but three in particular are designed to make your life easier.

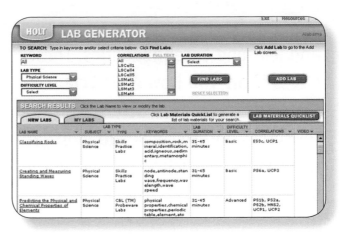

TEACHER'S ONE-STOP PLANNER®

An indispensable collection of resources, all in one place.

- Printable and editable worksheets, lab sheets, assessments, and more.
- Digital transparencies of images from the textbook.
- Pre-built and editable **PowerPoint®** presentations, complete with embedded animations and figures.
- Installers for teacher productivity software, such as **ExamView® Version 5 Assessment Suite, Calendar Planner,** and **Puzzle Pro.**
- A link to download state-specific resources.

HOLT LAB GENERATOR

Our entire lab database on one CD.

- Contains every lab from **Quick Labs** to **Inquiry Labs,** all searchable by criteria you choose, including ability level (basic, general, advanced).
- Every lab is editable to suit your needs.
- The database is expandable, so you can add labs you've received from your colleagues or found on the Web.
- **Lab Materials QuickList,** allows you to create an adaptable order sheet, suited to the size of your classes and the number of workgroups, complete with part numbers.

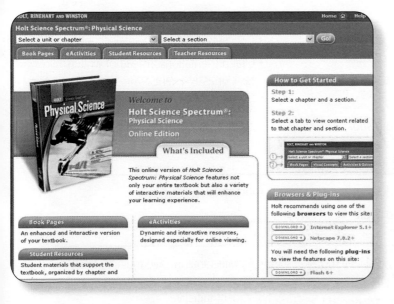

INTERACTIVE ONLINE EDITION

Newly redesigned, **http://my.hrw.com** lets you and your students communicate online.

- Loaded with interactive **eActivities,** it is much more than an online textbook.
- Students have access to ancillary resources with one click, and teachers have their own access to additional resources.
- **ExamView® Version 5 Assessment Suite** and **Holt Online Assessment** let you create custom assignments, control how they are delivered to students, and analyze their progress quickly and easily before you leave the lesson.

Meeting Individual Needs

Students have a wide range of abilities and learning exceptionalities. These pages show you how *Holt Science Spectrum: Physical Science* provides resources and strategies to help you tailor your instruction to engage every student in your classroom.

Learning exceptionality	Resources and strategies	
Learning Disabled and Slow Learners Students who have dyslexia or dysgraphia, students reading below grade level, students having difficulty understanding abstract or complex concepts, and slow learners	• Inclusion Strategies labeled *Learning Disabled* • Activities labeled *Basic* • Activities labeled *Visual* or *Kinesthetic*	• Hands-on activities or projects • Oral presentations instead of written tests or assignments
Developmental Delays Students who are functioning far below grade level because of mental retardation, autism, or brain injury; goals are to learn or retain basic concepts	• Inclusion Strategies labeled *Developmentally Delayed* • Activities labeled *Basic*	• Project-based activities • Observation Labs
Attention Deficit Disorders Students experiencing difficulty completing a task that has multiple steps, difficulty handling long assignments, or difficulty concentrating without sensory input from physical activity	• Inclusion Strategies labeled *Attention Deficit Disorder* • Activities labeled *Basic* • *Group Activities* • Activities labeled *Visual* or *Kinesthetic*	• Concepts broken into small chunks • Oral presentations instead of written tests or assignments
English as a Second Language Students learning English	• Activities labeled *Visual* • Activities labeled *Basic*	• Observation Labs
Gifted and Talented Students who are performing above grade level and demonstrate aptitude in crosscurricular assignments	• Inclusion Strategies labeled *Gifted and Talented* • Activities labeled *Advanced* • *Connection* activities	• Activities that involve multiple tasks, a strong degree of independence, and student initiative

General Strategies The following strategies can help you modify instruction to help students who struggle with common classroom difficulties.

A student experiencing difficulty with . . .	May benefit if you . . .	
Beginning assignments	• Assign work in small amounts • Have the student use cooperative or paired learning • Provide varied and interesting activities	• Allow choice in assignments or projects • Reinforce participation • Seat the student closer to you
Following directions	• Gain the student's attention before giving directions • Break up the task into small steps • Give written directions rather than oral directions • Use short, simple phrases • Stand near the student when you are giving directions	• Have the student repeat directions to you • Prepare the student for changes in activity • Give visual cues by posting general routines • Reinforce improvement in or approximation of following directions
Keeping track of assignments	• Have the student use folders for assignments • Have the student use assignment notebooks	• Have the student keep a checklist of assignments and highlight assignments when they are turned in
Reading the textbook	• Provide outlines of the textbook content • Reduce the length of required reading • Allow extra time for reading • Have the students read aloud in small groups	• Have the student use peer or mentor readers • Have the student use books on tape or CD • Discuss the content of the textbook in class after reading
Staying on task	• Reduce distracting elements in the classroom • Provide a task-completion checklist • Seat the student near you	• Provide alternative ways to complete assignments, such as oral projects taped with a buddy
Behavioral or social skills	• Model the appropriate behaviors • Establish class rules, and reiterate them often • Reinforce positive behavior • Assign a mentor as a positive role model to the student • Contract with the student for expected behaviors • Reinforce the desired behaviors or any steps toward improvement	• Separate the student from any peer who stimulates the inappropriate behavior • Provide a "cooling off" period before talking with the student • Address academic/instructional problems that may contribute to disruptive behaviors • Include parents in the problem-solving process through conferences, home visits, and frequent communication
Attendance	• Recognize and reinforce attendance by giving incentives or verbal praise • Emphasize the importance of attendance by letting the student know that he or she was missed when he or she was absent	• Encourage the student's desire to be in school by planning activities that are likely to be enjoyable, giving the student a preferred responsibility to be performed in class, and involving the student in extracurricular activities • Schedule problem-solving meeting with parents, faculty, or both
Test-taking skills	• Prepare the student for testing by teaching ways to study in pairs, such as using flashcards, practice tests, and study guides, and by promoting adequate sleep, nourishment, and exercise • During testing, allow the student to respond orally on tape or to respond using a computer; to use	notes; to take breaks; to take the test in another location; to work without time constraints; or to take the test in several short sessions • Decrease visual distraction by improving the visual design of the test through use of larger type, spacing, consistent layout, and shorter sentences

Pacing Guide

Today's science classroom often requires a more flexible curriculum than ever before. *Holt Science Spectrum: Physical Science* can help you meet a variety of needs and challenges you and your students face in the classroom. The **Pacing Guide** below shows a number of ways to adapt the program to your teaching schedule.

This **Guide** can be further adapted, allowing you to mix and match or compress the material so you can spend more time on select topics, or to allow for special projects and activities.

- **General** provides the recommended course of study as indicated in the *Teacher's Edition,* found in the individual chapter guides preceding each chapter. (This adds up to more than a year because of the advanced topics provided later in the book, which you may choose to omit, as indicated below.)

- **Compressed** indicates how you can still cover the essentials of physical science, even in the face of time constraints.

- **Basic** gives more time for the foundations of physical science, especially mathematical problem-solving, with less emphasis on some advanced topics from later in the course.

- **Advanced** moves quickly through the foundations of physical science for students who may be comfortable with the basics, to provide additional time for advanced topics.

- **Heavy Lab/Activity** indicates ways to streamline "lecture" time to provide hands-on experience for more than a third of the blocks in the school year. (Note: even this approach does not cover all of the labs and activities that are available with *Holt Science Spectrum: Physical Science* and its *Chapter Resource Files.*)

	General	Compressed	Basic	Advanced	Heavy Lab/Activity
Chapter 1 Introduction to Science	9	6	11	6	9
Chapter Intro	1	–	1	–	1
1 The Nature of Science	2	1	2	1	1
2 The Way Science Works	2	2	3	2	2
3 Organizing Data	2	2	3	2	2
Resource File Labs	–	–	–	–	2
Chapter Review and Assessment	2	1	2	1	1
Chapter 2 Matter	9	6	10	7	9
Chapter Intro	1	–	1	–	1
1 Classifying Matter	2	1	2	2	1
2 Properties of Matter	2	2	3	2	2
3 Changes of Matter	2	2	2	2	2
Resource File Labs	–	–	–	–	2
Chapter Review and Assessment	2	1	2	1	1
Chapter 3 States of Matter	11	6	12	9	9
Chapter Intro	1	–	1	–	1
1 Matter and Energy	2	2	2	2	2
2 Changes of State	2	2	4	2	2
3 Fluids	2	–	–	3	–
4 Behavior of Gases	2	1	3	2	1
Resource File Labs	–	–	–	–	2
Chapter Review and Assessment	2	1	2	–	1

	General	Compressed	Basic	Advanced	Heavy Lab/Activity
Chapter 4 *Atoms*	9	5	8	6	8
Chapter Intro	1	–	1	–	1
1 The Development of Atomic Theory	2	2	2	2	2
2 The Structure of Atoms	2	1	2	2	1
3 Modern Atomic Theory	2	1	1	1	1
Resource File Labs	–	–	–	–	2
Chapter Review and Assessment	2	1	2	1	1
Chapter 5 *The Periodic Table*	9	4	9	9	6
Chapter Intro	1	–	1	–	1
1 Organizing the Elements	2	1	2	2	1
2 Exploring the Periodic Table	2	1	2	3	2
3 Families of Elements	2	1	2	3	1
Resource File Labs	–	–	–	–	–
Chapter Review and Assessment	2	1	2	1	1
Chapter 6 *The Structure of Matter*	11	6	10	11	9
Chapter Intro	1	–	1	1	1
1 Compounds and Molecules	2	1	2	2	1
2 Ionic and Covalent Bonding	2	2	2	2	2
3 Compound Names and Formulas	2	2	3	2	2
4 Organic and Biochemical Compounds	2	–	–	3	–
Resource File Labs	–	–	–	–	2
Chapter Review and Assessment	2	1	2	1	1
Chapter 7 *Chemical Reactions*	11	5	11	10	8
Chapter Intro	1	–	1	–	1
1 The Nature of Chemical Reactions	2	1	2	2	1
2 Chemical Equations	2	2	3	2	2
3 Reaction Types	2	1	3	2	1
4 Reaction Rates and Equilibrium	2	–	–	3	
Resource File Labs	–	–	–	–	2
Chapter Review and Assessment	2	1	2	1	1
Chapter 8 *Solutions*	9	6	10	7	9
Chapter Intro	1	–	1	–	1
1 Solutions and Other Mixtures	2	2	2	2	2
2 How Substances Dissolve	2	2	2	2	2
3 Solubility and Concentration	2	1	3	2	1
Resource File Labs	–	–	–	–	2
Chapter Review and Assessment	2	1	2	1	1

	General	Compressed	Basic	Advanced	Heavy Lab/Activity
Chapter 9 *Acids, Bases, and Salts*	9	6	11	7	9
Chapter Intro	1	–	1	–	1
1 Acids, Bases, and pH	2	2	4	2	2
2 Reactions of Acids with Bases	2	2	2	2	2
3 Acids, Bases, and Salts in the Home	2	1	2	2	1
Resource File Labs	–	–	–	–	2
Chapter Review and Assessment	2	1	2	1	1
Chapter 10 *Nuclear Changes*	9	6	9	7	9
Chapter Intro	1	–	1	–	1
1 What is Radioactivity?	2	2	2	2	2
2 Nuclear Fission and Fusion	2	2	4	2	2
3 Nuclear Radiation Today	2	1	2	2	1
Resource File Labs	–	–	–	–	2
Chapter Review and Assessment	2	1	–	1	1
Chapter 11 *Motion*	9	5	11	7	8
Chapter Intro	1	–	1	–	1
1 Measuring Motion	2	1	3	2	1
2 Acceleration	2	1	3	2	1
3 Motion and Force	2	2	2	2	2
Resource File Labs	–	–	–	–	2
Chapter Review and Assessment	2	1	2	1	1
Chapter 12 *Forces*	9	5	10	7	8
Chapter Intro	1	–	1	–	1
1 Newton's First and Second Laws	2	2	4	2	2
2 Gravity	2	1	2	2	1
3 Newton's Third Law	2	1	1	2	1
Resource File Labs	–	–	–	–	2
Chapter Review and Assessment	2	1	2	1	1
Chapter 13 *Work and Energy*	11	7	13	9	10
Chapter Intro	1	–	1	–	1
1 Work, Power, and Machines	2	2	3	2	2
2 Simple Machines	2	1	2	2	1
3 What is Energy?	2	2	3	2	2
4 Conservation of Energy	2	1	2	2	1
Resource File Labs	–	–	–	–	2
Chapter Review and Assessment	2	1	2	1	1

	General	Compressed	Basic	Advanced	Heavy Lab/Activity
Chapter 14 *Heat and Temperature*	9	6	10	6	8
Chapter Intro	1	–	–	–	–
1 Temperature	2	2	3	2	2
2 Energy Transfer	2	2	3	2	2
3 Using Heat	2	1	2	1	1
Resource File Labs	–	–	–	–	2
Chapter Review and Assessment	2	1	2	1	1
Chapter 15 *Waves*	9	6	10	6	9
Chapter Intro	1	–	1	–	1
1 Types of Waves	2	1	2	1	1
2 Characteristics of Waves	2	2	3	2	2
3 Wave Interactions	2	2	2	2	2
Resource File Labs	–	–	–	–	2
Chapter Review and Assessment	2	1	2	1	1
Chapter 16 *Sound and Light*	11	4	11	8	9
Chapter Intro	1	–	1	–	1
1 Sound	2	1	2	2	1
2 The Nature of Light	2	1	2	2	1
3 Reflection and Color	2	1	2	1	1
4 Refraction, Lenses, and Prisms	2	–	2	2	2
Resource File Labs	–	–	–	–	2
Chapter Review and Assessment	2	1	2	1	1
Chapters 17 *Electricity*	9	5	10	9	8
Chapter Intro	1	–	1	–	1
1 Electric Charge and Force	2	1	2	2	1
2 Current	2	2	3	3	2
3 Circuits	2	1	3	3	1
Resource File Labs	–	–	–	–	2
Chapter Review and Assessment	2	1	1	1	1
Chapter 18 *Magnetism*	9	3	4	9	5
Chapter Intro	1	–	1	–	1
1 Magnets and Magnetic Fields	2	2	2	2	2
2 Magnetism from Electric Currents	2	–	–	3	–
3 Electric Currents from Magnetism	2	–	–	3	–
Resource File Labs	–	–	–	–	1
Chapter Review and Assessment	2	1	1	1	1
Total	172	97	180	140	150

Correlation to the National Science Education Standards

The following list shows the chapter correlation of *Holt Science Spectrum* with the National Science Education Standards (grades 9–12) for Physical Science content. For further detail, see the interleaf pages before each chapter.

UNIFYING CONCEPTS AND PROCESSES

Standard	Code
Systems, order, and organization	UCP 1
Evidence, models, and explanation	UCP 2
Change, consistency, and measurements	UCP 3
Evolution and equilibrium	UCP 4
Form and function	UCP 5

SCIENCE AS INQUIRY

Standard	Code
Abilities to do scientific inquiry	SAI 1
Understanding about scientific inquiry	SAI 2

SCIENCE AND TECHNOLOGY

Standard	Code
Abilities of technological design	ST 1
Understanding about science and technology	ST 2

HISTORY AND NATURE OF SCIENCE

Standard	Code
Science as a human endeavor	HNS 1
Nature of science	HNS 2
History of science	HNS 3

SCIENCE IN PERSONAL AND SOCIAL PERSPECTIVES

Standard	Code
Personal health	SPSP 1
Populations, resources, and environments	SPSP 2
Natural hazards	SPSP 3
Risks and benefits	SPSP 4
Science and technology in society	SPSP 5

PHYSICAL SCIENCE CONTENT STANDARDS

Standard	Code	Chapter Correlation
Structure of Atoms		
Matter is made of minute particles called atoms, and atoms are composed of even smaller components. These components have measurable properties, such as mass and electrical charge. Each atom has a positively charged nucleus surrounded by negatively charged electrons. The electric force between the nucleus and electrons holds the atom together.	**PS 1a**	Chapter 2 Chapter 4 Chapter 17
The atom's nucleus is composed of protons and neutrons, which are much more massive than electrons. When an element has atoms that differ in the number of neutrons, these atoms are called different isotopes of the element.	**PS 1b**	Chapter 4
The nuclear forces that hold the nucleus of an atom together, at nuclear distances, are usually stronger than the electric forces that would make it fly apart. Nuclear reactions convert a fraction of the mass of interacting particles into energy, and they can release much greater amounts of energy than atomic interactions. Fission is the splitting of a large nucleus into smaller pieces. Fusion is the joining of two nuclei at extremely high temperature and pressure, and is the process responsible for the energy of the sun and other stars.	**PS 1c**	Chapter 10 Chapter 13
Radioactive isotopes are unstable and undergo spontaneous nuclear reactions, emitting particles and/or wavelike radiation. The decay of any one nucleus cannot be predicted, but a large group of identical nuclei decay at a predictable rate. This predictability can be used to estimate the age of materials that contain radioactive isotopes.	**PS 1d**	Chapter 4 Chapter 10
Structure and Properties of Matter		
Atoms interact with one another by transferring or sharing electrons that are furthest from the nucleus. These outer electrons govern the chemical properties of the element.	**PS 2a**	Chapter 5 Chapter 6
An element is composed of a single type of atom. When elements are listed in order according to the number of protons (called the atomic number), repeating patterns of physical and chemical properties identify families of elements with similar properties. This "Periodic Table" is a consequence of the repeating pattern of outermost electrons and their permitted energies.	**PS 2b**	Chapter 2 Chapter 5

PHYSICAL SCIENCE CONTENT STANDARDS, *continued*

Standard	Code	Chapter Correlation
Bonds between atoms are created when electrons are paired up by being transferred or shared. A substance composed of a single kind of atom is called an element. The atoms may be bonded together into molecules or crystalline solids. A compound is formed when two or more kinds of atoms bind together chemically.	**PS 2c**	Chapter 2 Chapter 6
The physical properties of compounds reflect the nature of the interactions among its molecules. These interactions are determined by the structure of the molecule, including the constituent atoms and the distances and angles between them.	**PS 2d**	Chapter 3 Chapter 6 Chapter 8
Solids, liquids, and gases differ in the distances and angles between molecules or atoms and therefore the energy that binds them together. In solids the structure is nearly rigid; in liquids molecules or atoms move around each other but do not move apart; and in gases molecules or atoms move almost independently of each other and are mostly far apart.	**PS 2e**	Chapter 3 Chapter 6 Chapter 15 Chapter 16
Carbon atoms can bond to one another in chains, rings, and branching networks to form a variety of structures, including synthetic polymers, oils, and the large molecules essential to life.	**PS 2f**	Chapter 6

Chemical Reactions

Standard	Code	Chapter Correlation
Chemical reactions occur all around us, for example in health care, cooking, cosmetics, and automobiles. Complex chemical reactions involving carbon-based molecules take place constantly in every cell in our bodies.	**PS 3a**	Chapter 2 Chapter 6 Chapter 7 Chapter 9
Chemical reactions may release or consume energy. Some reactions such as the burning of fossil fuels release large amounts of energy by losing heat and by emitting light. Light can initiate many chemical reactions such as photosynthesis and the evolution of urban smog.	**PS 3b**	Chapter 7 Chapter 13

PHYSICAL SCIENCE CONTENT STANDARDS, *continued*

Standard	Code	Chapter Correlation
A large number of important reactions involve the transfer of either electrons (oxidation/reduction reactions) or hydrogen ions (acid/base reactions) between reacting ions, molecules, or atoms. In other reactions, chemical bonds are broken by heat or light to form very reactive radicals with electrons ready to form new bonds. Radical reactions control many processes such as the presence of ozone and greenhouse gases in the atmosphere, burning and processing of fossil fuels, the formation of polymers, and explosions.	**PS 3c**	Chapter 7 Chapter 9
Chemical reactions can take place in time periods ranging from the few femtoseconds (10^{-15} seconds) required for an atom to move a fraction of a chemical bond distance to geologic time scales of billions of years. Reaction rates depend on how often the reacting atoms and molecules encounter one another, on the temperature, and on the properties–including shape–of the reacting species.	**PS 3d**	Chapter 7
Catalysts, such as metal surfaces, accelerate chemical reactions. Chemical reactions in living systems are catalyzed by protein molecules called enzymes.	**PS 3e**	Chapter 7
Motion and Forces		
Objects change their motion only when a net force is applied. Laws of motion are used to calculate precisely the effects of forces on the motion of objects. The magnitude of the change in motion can be calculated using the relationship $F = ma,$ which is independent of the nature of the force. Whenever one object exerts force on another, a force equal in magnitude and opposite in direction is exerted on the first object.	**PS 4a**	Chapter 11 Chapter 12
Gravitation is a universal force that each mass exerts on any other mass. The strength of the gravitational attractive force between two masses is proportional to the masses and inversely proportional to the square of the distance between them.	**PS 4b**	Chapter 12

PHYSICAL SCIENCE CONTENT STANDARDS, *continued*

Standard	Code	Chapter Correlation
The electric force is a universal force that exists between any two charged objects. Opposite charges attract while like charges repel. The strength of the force is proportional to the charges, and, as with gravitation, inversely proportional to the square of the distance between them.	**PS 4c**	Chapter 11 Chapter 17
Between any two charged particles, electric force is vastly greater than the gravitational force. Most observable forces such as those exerted by a coiled spring or friction may be traced to electric forces acting between atoms and molecules.	**PS 4d**	Chapter 11 Chapter 17
Electricity and magnetism are two aspects of a single electromagnetic force. Moving electric charges produce magnetic forces, and moving magnets produce electric forces. These effects help students to understand electric motors and generators.	**PS 4e**	Chapter 18

Conservation of Energy and the Increase in Disorder

The total energy of the universe is constant. Energy can be transferred by collisions in chemical and nuclear reactions, by light waves and other radiations, and in many other ways. However, it can never be destroyed. As these transfers occur, the matter involved becomes steadily less ordered.	**PS 5a**	Chapter 3 Chapter 7 Chapter 13 Chapter 14 Chapter 15 Chapter 18
All energy can be considered to be either kinetic energy, which is the energy of motion; potential energy, which depends on relative position; or energy contained by a field, such as electromagnetic waves.	**PS 5b**	Chapter 3 Chapter 13 Chapter 14 Chapter 15 Chapter 18
Heat consists of random motion and the vibrations of atoms, molecules, and ions. The higher the temperature, the greater the atomic or molecular motion.	**PS 5c**	Chapter 3 Chapter 14
Everything tends to become less organized and less orderly over time. Thus, in all energy transfers, the overall effect is that the energy is spread out uniformly. Examples are the transfer of energy from hotter to cooler objects by conduction, radiation, or convection and the warming of our surroundings when we burn fuels.	**PS 5d**	Chapter 3 Chapter 14 Chapter 17

PHYSICAL SCIENCE CONTENT STANDARDS, *continued*

Standard	Code	Chapter Correlation
Interactions of Energy and Matter		
Waves, including sound and seismic waves, waves on water, and light waves, have energy and can transfer energy when they interact with matter.	**PS 6a**	Chapter 13 Chapter 14 Chapter 15 Chapter 16
Electromagnetic waves result when a charged object is accelerated or decelerated. Electromagnetic waves include radio waves (the longest wavelength), microwaves, infrared radiation (radiant heat), visible light, ultraviolet radiation, x-rays, and gamma rays. The energy of electromagnetic waves is carried in packets whose magnitude is inversely proportional to the wavelength.	**PS 6b**	Chapter 15 Chapter 16 Chapter 18
Each kind of atom or molecule can gain or lose energy only in particular discrete amounts and thus can absorb and emit light only at wavelengths corresponding to these amounts. These wavelengths can be used to identify the substance.	**PS 6c**	Chapter 4
In some materials, such as metals, electrons flow easily, whereas in insulating materials such as glass they can hardly flow at all. Semiconducting materials have intermediate behavior. At low temperatures some materials become superconductors and offer no resistance to the flow of electrons.	**PS 6d**	Chapter 5 Chapter 17

Safety in Your Laboratory

Risk Assessment

MAKING YOUR LABORATORY A SAFE PLACE TO WORK AND LEARN

Concern for safety must begin before any activity in the classroom and before students enter the lab. A careful review of the facilities should be a basic part of preparation for each school term. You should investigate the physical environment, identify any safety risks, and inspect your work areas for compliance with safety regulations.

The review of the lab should be thorough, and all safety issues must be addressed immediately. Keep a file of your review, and add to the list each year. This will allow you to continue to raise the standard of safety in your lab and classroom.

Many classroom experiments, demonstrations, and other activities are classics that have been used for years. This familiarity may lead to a comfort that can obscure inherent safety concerns. Review all experiments, demonstrations, and activities for safety concerns before presenting them to the class. Identify and eliminate potential safety hazards.

1. Identify the Risks

Before introducing any activity, demonstration, or experiment to the class, analyze it and consider what could possibly go wrong. Carefully review the list of materials to make sure they are safe. Inspect the equipment in your lab or classroom to make sure it is in good working order. Read the procedures to make sure they are safe. Record any hazards or concerns you identify.

2. Evaluate the Risks

Minimize the risks you identified in the last step without sacrificing learning. Remember that no activity you perform in the lab or classroom is worth risking injury. Thus, extremely hazardous activities, or those that violate your school's policies, must be eliminated. For activities that present smaller risks, analyze each risk carefully to determine its likelihood. If the pedagogical value of the activity does not outweigh the risks, the activity must be eliminated.

3. Select Controls to Address Risks

Even low-risk activities require controls to eliminate or minimize the risks. Make sure that in devising controls you do not substitute an equally or more hazardous alternative. Some control methods include the following:

- Explicit verbal and written warnings may be added or posted.

- Equipment may be rebuilt or relocated, have parts replaced, or be replaced entirely by safer alternatives.

- Risky procedures may be eliminated.

- Activities may be changed from student activities to teacher demonstrations.

4. Implement and Review Selected Controls

Controls do not help if they are forgotten or not enforced. The implementation and review of controls should be as systematic and thorough as the initial analysis of safety concerns in the lab and laboratory activities.

SOME SAFETY RISKS AND PREVENTATIVE CONTROLS

The following list describes several possible safety hazards and controls that can be implemented to resolve them. This list is not complete, but it can be used as a starting point to identify hazards in your laboratory.

Identified risk	Preventative control
Facilities and Equipment	
Lab tables are in disrepair, room is poorly lighted and ventilated, faucets and electrical outlets do not work or are difficult to use because of their location.	Work surfaces should be level and stable. There should be adequate lighting and ventilation. Water supplies, drains, and electrical outlets should be in good working order. Any equipment in a dangerous location should not be used; it should be relocated or rendered inoperable.
Wiring, plumbing, and air circulation systems do not work or do not meet current specifications.	Specifications should be kept on file. Conduct a periodic review of all equipment, and document compliance. Damaged fixtures must be labeled as such and must be repaired as soon as possible.
Eyewash fountains and safety showers are present but no one knows anything about their specifications.	Ensure that eyewash fountains and safety showers meet the requirements of the ANSI standard (Z358.1).
Eyewash fountains are checked and cleaned once at the beginning of each school year. No records are kept of routine checks and maintenance on the safety showers and eyewash fountains.	Flush eyewash fountains for 5 min. every month to remove any bacteria or other organisms from pipes. Test safety showers (measure flow in gallons per min) and eyewash fountains every 6 months and keep records of the test results.
Labs are conducted in multipurpose rooms, and equipment from other courses remains accessible.	Only the items necessary for a given activity should be available to students. All equipment should be locked away when not in use.
Students are permitted to enter or work in the lab without teacher supervision.	Lock all laboratory rooms whenever a teacher is not present. Supervising teachers must be trained in lab safety and emergency procedures.
Safety equipment and emergency procedures	
Fire and other emergency drills are infrequent, and no records or measurements are made of the results of the drills.	Always carry out critical reviews of fire or other emergency drills. Be sure that plans include alternate routes. Don't wait until an emergency to find the flaws in your plans.
Emergency evacuation plans do not include instructions for securing the lab in the event of an evacuation during a lab activity.	Plan actions in case of emergency: establish what devices should be turned off, which escape route to use, and where to meet outside the building.
Fire extinguishers are in out-of-the-way locations, not on the escape route.	Place fire extinguishers near escape routes so that they will be of use during an emergency.
Fire extinguishers are not maintained. Teachers are not trained to use them.	Document regular maintenance of fire extinguishers. Train supervisory personnel in the proper use of extinguishers. Instruct students not to use an extinguisher but to call for a teacher.
Teachers in labs and neighboring classrooms are not trained in CPR or first aid.	Teachers should receive training. The American Red Cross and other groups offer training. Certifications should be kept current with frequent refresher courses.

Identified risk	Preventative control
Teachers are not aware of their legal responsibilities in case of an injury or accident.	Review your faculty handbook for your responsibilities regarding safety in the classroom and laboratory. Contact the legal counsel for your school district to find out the extent of their support and any rules, regulations, or procedures you must follow.
Emergency procedures are not posted. Emergency numbers are kept only at the switchboard or main office. Instructions are given verbally only at the beginning of the year.	Emergency procedures should be posted at all exits and near all safety equipment. Emergency numbers should be posted at all phones, and a script should be provided for the caller to use. Emergency procedures must be reviewed periodically, and students should be reminded of them at the beginning of each activity.
Spills are handled on a case-by-case basis and are cleaned up with whatever materials happen to be on hand.	Have the appropriate equipment and materials available for cleaning up; replace them before expiration dates. Make sure students know to alert you to spilled chemicals, blood, and broken glass.

Work habits and environment

Identified risk	Preventative control
Safety wear is only used for activities involving chemicals or hot plates.	Aprons and goggles should be worn in the lab at all times. Long hair, loose clothing, and loose jewelry should be secured.
There is no dress code established for the laboratory; students are allowed to wear sandals or open-toed shoes.	Open-toed shoes should never be worn in the laboratory. Do not allow any footwear in the lab that does not cover feet completely.
Students are required to wear safety gear but teachers and visitors are not.	Always wear safety gear in the lab. Keep extra equipment on hand for visitors.
Safety is emphasized at the beginning of the term but is not mentioned later in the year.	Safety must be the first priority in all lab work. Students should be warned of risks and instructed in emergency procedures for each activity.
There is no assessment of students' knowledge and attitudes regarding safety.	Conduct frequent safety quizzes. Only students with perfect scores should be allowed to work in the lab.
You work alone during your preparation period to organize the day's labs.	Never work alone in a science laboratory or a storage area.
Safety inspections are conducted irregularly and are not documented. Teachers and administrators are unaware of what documentation will be necessary in case of a lawsuit.	Safety reviews should be frequent and regular. All reviews should be documented, and improvements must be implemented immediately. Contact legal counsel for your district to make sure your procedures will protect you in case of a lawsuit.

Purchasing, storing, and using chemicals

Identified risk	Preventative control
The storeroom is too crowded, so you decide to keep some equipment on the lab benches.	Do not store reagents or equipment on lab benches and keep shelves organized. Never place reactive chemicals (in bottles, beakers, flasks, wash bottles, etc.) near the edges of a lab bench.
You prepare solutions from concentrated stock to save money.	Reduce risks by ordering diluted instead of concentrated substances.

Identified risk	Preventative control
You purchase plenty of chemicals to be sure that you won't run out or to save money.	Purchase chemicals in class-size quantities. Do not purchase or have on hand more than one year's supply of each chemical.
You don't generally read labels on chemicals when preparing solutions for a lab, because you already know about a chemical.	Read each label to be sure it states the hazards and describes the precautions and first aid procedures (when appropriate) that apply to the contents in case someone else has to deal with that chemical in an emergency.
You never read the Material Safety Data Sheets (MSDSs) that come with your chemicals.	Always read the Material Safety Data Sheet (MSDS) for a chemical before using it and follow the precautions described. File and organize MSDSs for all chemicals where they can be found easily in case of an emergency.
The main stockroom contains chemicals that haven't been used for years.	Do not leave bottles of chemicals unused on the shelves of the lab for more than one week or unused in the main stockroom for more than one year. Dispose of or use up any leftover chemicals.
No extra precautions are taken when flammable liquids are dispensed from their containers.	When transferring flammable liquids from bulk containers, ground the container, and before transferring to a smaller metal container, ground both containers.
Students are told to put their broken glass and solid chemical wastes in the trash can.	Have separate containers for trash, for broken glass, and for different categories of hazardous chemical wastes.
You store chemicals alphabetically instead of by hazard class. Chemicals are stored without consideration of possible emergencies (fire, earthquake, flood, etc.), which could compound the hazard.	Use MSDSs to determine which chemicals are incompatible. Store chemicals by the hazard class indicated on the MSDS. Store chemicals that are incompatible with common fire-fighting media like water (such as alkali metals) or carbon dioxide (such as alkali and alkaline-earth metals) under conditions that eliminate the possibility of a reaction with water or carbon dioxide if it is necessary to fight a fire in the storage area.
Corrosives are kept above eye level, out of reach from anyone who is not authorized to be in the storeroom.	Always store corrosive chemicals on shelves below eye level. Remember, fumes from many corrosives can destroy metal cabinets and shelving.
Chemicals are kept on the stockroom floor on the days that they will be used so that they are easy to find.	Never store chemicals or other materials on floors or in the aisles of the laboratory or storeroom, even for a few minutes.

HOLT Science Spectrum®

Physical Science

HOLT, RINEHART AND WINSTON

A Harcourt Education Company

Orlando • **Austin** • New York • San Diego • London

About the cover: The cover image shows a racing bicycle's back wheel in motion. The chain running through the gear assembly (derailleur) is labeled with the basic equation for speed. By convention, speed is indicated by the letter "v" (velocity) even when the only component being considered is the magnitude.

Copyright © 2008 by Holt, Rinehart and Winston

All rights reserved. No part of this publication may be reproduced or transmitted in any form or by any means, electronic or mechanical, including photocopy, recording, or any information storage and retrieval system, without permission in writing from the publisher.

Requests for permission to make copies of any part of the work should be mailed to the following address: Permissions Department, Holt, Rinehart and Winston, 10801 N. MoPac Expressway, Building 3, Austin, Texas 78759.

CBL is a trademark of Texas Instruments Incorporated.

ExamView is a registered trademark of FSCreations, Inc.

HOLT, ONE-STOP PLANNER, and the **"Owl Design"** are trademarks licensed to Holt, Rinehart and Winston, registered in the United States of America and/or other jurisdictions.

LIVE INK is a registered trademark of Walker Reading Technologies, Inc., licensed for use by Holt, Rinehart and Winston.

The trademark **SCIENCE SPECTRUM**® is used under license from Science Spectrum, Inc., Lubbock, Texas.

SCILINKS is a registered trademark owned and provided by the National Science Teachers Association. All rights reserved.

Printed in the United States of America

If you have received these materials as examination copies free of charge, Holt, Rinehart and Winston retains title to the materials and they may not be resold. Resale of examination copies is strictly prohibited.

Possession of this publication in print format does not entitle users to convert this publication, or any portion of it, into electronic format.

ISBN 13: 978-0-03-093636-4

ISBN 10: 0-03-093636-5

3 4 5 6 0914 10 09

Acknowledgments

Authors

Ken Dobson, MSc FInstP
Former Head of Science
Thurston Upper School
Suffolk, United Kingdom

Professor John Holman
Director, The National Science Learning Centre
University of York
York, United Kingdom

Michael Roberts, Ph.D.
Science Writer
Bristol, United Kingdom

Contributing Authors

Robert Davisson
Science Writer
Albuquerque, New Mexico

Doug Jenkins
Adjunct Professor
Department of Physics and Astronomy
Western Kentucky University
Bowling Green, Kentucky

William G. Lamb, Ph.D.
Winningstad Chair in the Physical Sciences
Oregon Episcopal School
Portland, Oregon

Lab Writer/Reviewer

Marlin L. Simon, Ph.D.
Associate Professor of Physics
Department of Physics
Auburn University
Auburn, Alabama

Reading Specialist

Robin Scarcella, Ph.D.
*Director and Professor, Academic English
  and English as a Second Language*
University of California, Irvine
Irvine, California

Reviewers

Thomas J. M. Connolly, Ph.D.
Assistant Professor
Department of Mechanical Engineering
The University of Texas at San Antonio
San Antonio, Texas

Hima S. Joshi, Ph.D.
Assistant Professor
Department of Chemistry and Biochemistry
California Polytechnic State University, San Luis Obispo
San Luis Obispo, California

James L. Pazun, Ph.D.
Professor and Chair, Chemistry and Physics
Department of Chemistry and Physics
Pfeiffer University
Charlotte, North Carolina

H. Michael Sommermann, Ph.D.
Professor
Department of Physics
Westmont College
Santa Barbara, California

Larry Stookey, P.E.
Physics and Chemistry Teacher
Antigo High School
Antigo, Wisconsin

Raymond Turner, Ph.D.
Professor Emeritus of Physics
Department of Physics and Astronomy
Clemson University
Clemson, South Carolina

Inclusion Specialist

Joan Altobelli
Special Education Director
Austin Independent School District
Austin, Texas

Contents in Brief

Contents

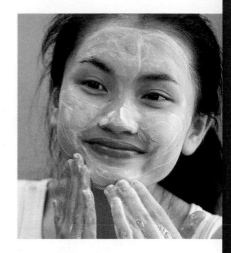

Physics 361

Chapter 13: Work and Energy

Chapter 14: Heat and Temperature

Chapter 17: Electricity

Chapter 18: Magnetism

Reference   649

Why It **Matters**

Have you ever wondered why you need to learn science? Check out these short, interesting articles to learn how science relates to the world around you.

Science Skills

Science Skills will help you succeed in your science class by allowing you to practice a variety of skills used in science.

READING TOOLBOX

Reading a textbook is different from reading a novel. The *Reading ToolBoxes* suggest ways to help you organize the concepts in each chapter to get the most out of your reading.

Labs

Short Labs

These short *Inquiry Labs* and *QuickLabs* are designed to be done quickly during any class period (or at home!) with simple materials.

Inquiry Labs

QuickLabs

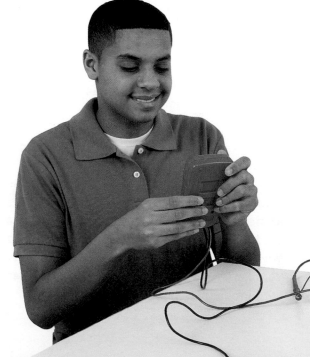

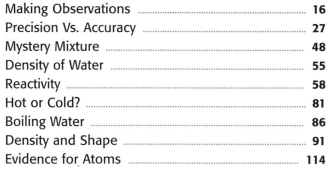

Chapter Labs

Each chapter includes an in-depth, hands-on lab that lets you experience science first-hand.

Skills Practice Labs

Application Labs

Inquiry Labs

Lab Safety

In the laboratory or in the field, you can engage in hands-on explorations, test your scientific hypotheses, and build practical lab skills. However, while you are working, it is your responsibility to protect yourself and your classmates by conducting yourself in a safe manner. You will avoid accidents by following directions, handling materials carefully, and taking your work seriously. Read the following safety guidelines before working in the lab or field. Make sure that you understand all safety guidelines before entering the lab or field.

Before You Begin

- **Read the entire activity before entering the lab.** Be familiar with the instructions before beginning an activity. Do not start an activity until you have asked your teacher to explain any parts of the activity that you do not understand.

- **Wear the right clothing for lab work.** Before beginning work, tie back long hair, roll up loose sleeves, and put on any required personal protective equipment as directed by your teacher. Remove your wristwatch and any necklaces or jewelry that could get caught in moving parts or contact electrical connections. Avoid or confine loose clothing that could knock things over, catch on fire, get caught in moving parts, contact electrical connections, or absorb chemical solutions. Wear pants rather than shorts or skirts. Nylon and polyester fabrics burn and melt more readily than cotton does. Protect your feet from chemical spills and falling objects. Do not wear open-toed shoes, sandals, or canvas shoes in the lab.

- **Know the location of all safety and emergency equipment used in the lab.** Know proper fire-drill procedures and the location of all fire exits. Ask your teacher where the nearest eyewash stations, safety blankets, safety shower, fire extinguisher, first-aid kit, and chemical spill kit are located. Be sure that you know how to operate the equipment safely.

While You Are Working

- **Always wear a lab apron and safety goggles.** Wear these items while in the lab, even if you are not working on an activity. Labs contain chemicals that can damage your clothing, skin, and eyes. Aprons and goggles also protect against many physical hazards. If your safety goggles cloud up or are uncomfortable, ask your teacher for help. Lengthening the strap slightly, washing the goggles with soap and warm water, or using an anti-fog spray may help the problem.

- **NEVER work alone in the lab.** Work in the lab only when supervised by your teacher.

- **NEVER leave equipment unattended while it is in operation.**

- **Perform only activities specifically assigned by your teacher.** Do not attempt any procedure without your teacher's direction. Use only materials and equipment listed in the activity or authorized by your teacher. Steps in a procedure should be performed only as described in the activity or as approved by your teacher.

- **Keep your work area neat and uncluttered.** Have only books and other materials that are needed to conduct the activity in the lab. Keep backpacks, purses, and other items in your desk, locker, or other designated storage areas.

- **Always heed safety symbols and cautions listed in activities, listed on handouts, posted in the room, provided on equipment or chemical labels (whether provided by the manufacturer or added later), and given verbally by your teacher.** Be aware of the potential hazards of the required materials and procedures, and follow all precautions indicated.

- **Be alert, and walk with care in the lab.** Be aware of others near you and your equipment and be aware of what they are doing.

- **Do not take food, drinks, chewing gum, or tobacco products into the lab.** Do not store or eat food in the lab. Either finish these items or discard them before coming into the lab or beginning work in the field.

- **NEVER taste chemicals or allow them to contact your skin.** Keep your hands away from your face and mouth, even if you are wearing gloves. Only smell vapors as instructed by your teacher and only in the manner indicated.

- **Exercise caution when working with electrical equipment.** Do not use electrical equipment with frayed or twisted wires. Check that insulation on wiring is intact. Be sure that your hands are dry before using electrical equipment. Do not let electrical cords dangle from work stations. Dangling cords can catch on apparatus on tables, can cause you to trip and can cause an electrical shock. The area under and around electrical equipment should be dry; cords should not lie in puddles of spilled liquid, under sink spigots, or in sinks themselves.

- **Use extreme caution when working with hot plates and other heating devices.** Keep your head, hands, hair, and clothing away from the flame or heating area. Remember that metal surfaces connected to the heated area will become hot by conduction. Gas burners should be lit only with a spark lighter, not with matches. Make sure that all heating devices and gas valves are turned off before you leave the lab. Never leave a heating device unattended when it is in use. Metal, ceramic, and glass items do not necessarily look hot when they are hot. Allow all items to cool before storing them.

- **Do not fool around in the lab.** Take your lab work seriously, and behave appropriately in the lab. Lab equipment and apparatus are not toys; never use lab time or equipment for anything other than the intended purpose. Be considerate and be aware of the safety of your classmates as well as your safety at all times.

Emergency Procedures

- **Follow standard fire-safety procedures.** If your clothing catches on fire, do not run; WALK to the safety shower, stand under it, and turn it on. While doing so, call to your teacher. In case of fire, alert your teacher and leave the lab.

- **Report any accident, incident, or hazard—no matter how trivial—to your teacher immediately.** Any incident involving bleeding, burns, fainting, nausea, dizziness, chemical exposure, or ingestion should also be reported immediately to the school nurse or to a physician. If you have a close call, tell your teacher so that you and your teacher can find a way to prevent it from happening again.

- **Report all spills to your teacher immediately.** Call your teacher rather than trying to clean a spill yourself. Your teacher will tell you whether it is safe for you to clean up the spill; if it is not safe, your teacher will know how to clean up the spill.

- **If you spill a chemical on your skin, wash the chemical off in the sink and call your teacher.** If you spill a solid chemical onto your clothing, using an appropriate container, brush it off carefully without scattering it onto somebody else and call your teacher. If you spill corrosive substances on your skin or clothing, use the safety shower or a faucet to rinse. Remove affected clothing while you are under the shower, and call to your teacher. (It may be temporarily embarrassing to remove clothing in front of your classmates, but failure to thoroughly rinse a chemical off your skin could result in permanent damage.)

- **If you get a chemical in your eyes, walk immediately to the eyewash station, turn it on, and lower your head so your eyes are in the running water.** Hold your eyelids open with your thumbs and fingers, and roll your eyeballs around. You have to flush your eyes continuously for at least 15 minutes. Call your teacher while you are doing this.

When You Are Finished

- **Clean your work area at the conclusion of each lab period as directed by your teacher.** Broken glass, chemicals, and other waste products should be disposed of in separate, special containers. Dispose of waste materials as directed by your teacher. Put away all material and equipment according to your teacher's instructions. Report any damaged or missing equipment or materials to your teacher.

- **Even if you wore gloves, wash your hands with soap and hot water after each lab period.** To avoid contamination, wash your hands at the conclusion of each lab period, and before you leave the lab.

Safety Symbols

Before you begin working on an activity, familiarize yourself with the following safety symbols, which are used throughout your textbook, and the guidelines that you should follow when you see these symbols.

Eye Protection

- **Wear approved safety goggles as directed.** Safety goggles should be worn in the lab at all times, especially when you are working with a chemical or solution, a heat source, or a mechanical device.

- **If chemicals get into your eyes, flush your eyes immediately.** Go to an eyewash station immediately, and flush your eyes (including under the eyelids) with running water for at least 15 minutes. Use your thumb and fingers to hold your eyelids open and roll your eyeballs around. While doing so, call your teacher or ask another student to notify your teacher.

- **Do not wear contact lenses in the lab.** Chemicals can be drawn up under a contact lens and into the eye. If you must wear contacts prescribed by a physician, tell your teacher. In this case, you must also wear approved eye-cup safety goggles to help protect your eyes.

- **Do not look directly at the sun or any intense light source or laser.** Do not look at these through any optical device or lens system. Do not reflect direct sunlight to illuminate a microscope. Such actions concentrate light rays to an intensity that can severely burn your retinas, causing blindness.

Clothing Protection

- **Wear an apron or lab coat at all times in the lab to prevent chemicals or chemical solutions from contacting skin or clothes.**

- **Tie back long hair, secure loose clothing, and remove loose jewelry so that they do not knock over equipment, get caught in moving parts, or come into contact with hazardous materials or electrical connections.**

- **Do not wear open-toed shoes, sandals, or canvas shoes in the lab.** Splashed chemicals directly contact skin or quickly soak through canvas. Hard shoes will not allow chemicals to soak through as quickly and they provide more protection against dropped or falling objects.

Hand Safety

- **Do not cut an object while holding the object in your hand.** Cut objects on a suitable work surface. Always cut in a direction away from your body.

- **Wear appropriate protective gloves when working with an open flame, chemicals, solutions, or wild or unknown plants.** Your teacher will provide the type of gloves necessary for a given activity.

- **Use a heat-resistant mitt to handle resistors, light sources, and other equipment that may be hot.** Allow all equipment to cool before storing it.

Hygienic Care

- **Keep your hands away from your face; hair and mouth while you are working on any activity.**

- **Wash your hands thoroughly before you leave the lab or when you finish any activity.**

- **Remove contaminated clothing immediately.** If you spill corrosive substances on your skin or clothing, use the safety shower or a faucet to rinse. Remove affected clothing while you are under the shower, and call to your teacher. (It may be temporarily embarrassing to remove clothing in front of your classmates, but failure to thoroughly rinse a chemical off your skin could result in permanent damage.)

Sharp-Object Safety

- **Use extreme care when handling all sharp and pointed instruments, such as scalpels, sharp probes, and knives.**

- **Do not cut an object while holding the object in your hand.** Cut objects on a suitable work surface. Always cut in a direction away from your body.

- **Do not use double-edged razor blades in the lab.**

- **Be aware of sharp objects or protrusions on equipment or apparatus.**

Glassware Safety

- **Inspect glassware before use; do not use chipped or cracked glassware.** Use heat-resistant glassware for heating materials or storing hot liquids, and use appropriate tongs or a heat-resistant mitt to handle this equipment.

- **Notify immediately your teacher if a piece of glassware or a light bulb breaks.** Do not attempt to clean up broken glass or remove broken bulbs unless your teacher directs you to do so.

 ## Proper Waste Disposal

- **Clean and sanitize all work surfaces and personal protective equipment after each lab period as directed by your teacher.**

- **Dispose of contaminated materials (biological or chemical) in special containers only as directed by your teacher.** Never put these materials into a regular waste container or down the drain.

- **Dispose of sharp objects (such as broken glass) in the appropriate sharps or broken glass container as directed by your teacher.**

 ## Electrical Safety

- **Do not use equipment with frayed electrical cords or loose plugs.** Do not attempt to remove a plug tine if it breaks off in the socket. Notify your teacher and stay away from the outlet.

- **Fasten electrical cords to work surfaces by using tape.** Doing so will prevent tripping and will ensure that equipment will not be pulled or fall off the table.

- **Do not use electrical equipment near water or when your clothing or hands are wet.**

- **Hold the plug housing when you plug in or unplug equipment.** Do not touch the metal prongs of the plug, and do not unplug equipment by pulling on the cord.

- **Wire coils in circuits may heat up rapidly.** If heating occurs, open the switch immediately and use a hot mitt to handle the equipment.

 ## Heating Safety

- **Be aware of any source of flames, sparks, or heat (such as open flames, electric heating coils, or hot plates) before working with flammable liquids or gases.**

- **Avoid using open flames.** If possible, work only with hot plates that have an on/off switch and an indicator light. Do not leave hot plates unattended. Do not use alcohol lamps. Turn off hot plates and open flames when they are not in use.

- **Never leave a hot plate unattended while it is turned on or while it is cooling off.**

- **Know the location of lab fire extinguishers and fire-safety blankets.**

- **Use tongs or appropriate insulated holders when handling heated objects.** Heated objects often do not appear to be hot. Do not pick up an object with your hand if it could be warm.

- **Keep flammable substances away from heat, flames, and other ignition sources.**

- **Allow all equipment to cool before storing it.**

 ## Fire Safety

- **Know the location of lab fire extinguishers and fire-safety blankets.**

- **Know your school's fire-evacuation routes.** Always evacuate the building when the fire alarm is activated.

- **If your clothing catches on fire, walk (do not run) to the emergency lab shower to put out the fire.** If the shower is not working, STOP, DROP, and ROLL! Smother the fire by stopping immediately, dropping to the floor, and rolling until the fire is out.

 ## Safety with Gases

- **Do not inhale any gas or vapor unless directed to do so by your teacher.** Never inhale pure gases.

- **Handle materials that emit vapors or gases in a well-ventilated area.** This work should be done in an approved chemical fume hood. Always work at least four to six inches inside the front edge of the hood.

 ## Caustic Substances

- **If a chemical gets on your skin, on your clothing, or in your eyes, rinse it immediately (shower, faucet or eyewash fountain) and alert your teacher.**

- **If you spill a chemical on the floor or lab bench, alert your teacher, but do not clean it up yourself unless your teacher directs you to do so.**

How to Use Your Textbook

This textbook might seem confusing to you when you first look through it. But by reading the next few pages, you will learn how the different parts of this textbook will help you to become a successful science student. You may be tempted to skip this section, but you should read it. This textbook is an important tool in your exploration of science. Like any tool, the more you know about how to use this textbook, the better your results will be.

Step into Science

The beginning of each chapter is designed to get you involved with science. You will immediately see that science matters!

Chapter Outline You can get a quick overview of the chapter by looking at the chapter's outline. In the outline, the section titles and the topics within that section are listed.

Why It Matters The photo that starts each chapter was selected not only to be interesting but also to relate to the content you will learn about in the chapter. The photo caption lets you know how this content applies to the real world.

Inquiry Lab This lab gives you a chance to get some hands-on experience right away. It is designed to help focus your attention on the concepts that you will learn in the chapter.

Read for Meaning

At the beginning of each chapter you will find tools that will help you grasp the meaning of what you read. Each section also introduces what is important in that section and why.

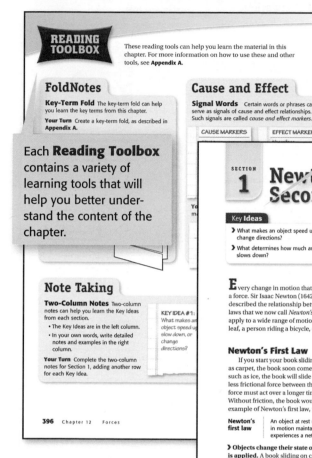

The **Key Ideas** ask the important questions that you will be able to answer after learning about the science in each section.

Each **Reading Toolbox** contains a variety of learning tools that will help you better understand the content of the chapter.

The **Key Terms** are science words that you may not be familiar with but that are important to understanding the section. Pay special attention when you see them highlighted in the pages that follow.

Why It Matters This gives at least one reason that you might be interested in the subject of the section. Often, this topic is covered in more detail with an article later in the section.

Keep an Eye on Headings

Notice that the headings in this textbook are different sizes and different colors. The headings help you organize your reading and form a simple outline, as shown below.

Blue: Section titles

Red: Key-idea heading

Blue: Topic sentences

The paragraph under each red heading contains an answer to a **Key Idea** question from the section opener. These key-idea answers are indicated with a red arrow and are printed in bold.

Science Is Doing

You will get many opportunities throughout this textbook to actually do science. After all, doing is what science is about.

Almost every section in the textbook has at least one **Quick Lab** or slightly more-involved **Inquiry Lab** to help you get real experience doing science.

SciLinks lets you use the Internet to link to interesting topics and activities related to the section.

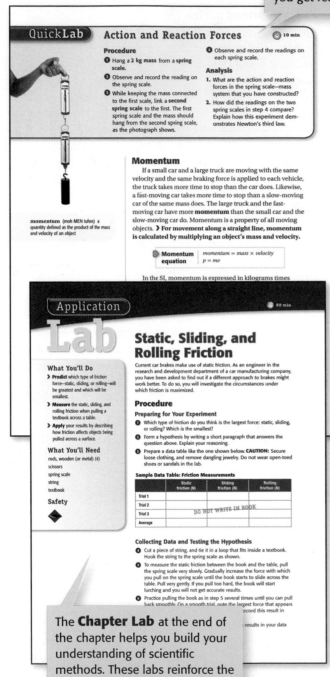

QuickLab — Action and Reaction Forces ⏱ 10 min

Procedure

❶ Hang a **2 kg mass** from a **spring scale.**

❷ Observe and record the reading on the spring scale.

❸ While keeping the mass connected to the first spring scale, link a **second spring scale** to the first. The first spring scale and the mass should hang from the second spring scale, as the photograph shows.

❹ Observe and record the readings on each spring scale.

Analysis

1. What are the action and reaction forces in the spring scale–mass system that you have constructed?

2. How did the readings on the two spring scales in step 4 compare? Explain how this experiment demonstrates Newton's third law.

Momentum

If a small car and a large truck are moving with the same velocity and the same braking force is applied to each vehicle, the truck takes more time to stop than the car does. Likewise, a fast-moving car takes more time to stop than a slow-moving car of the same mass does. The large truck and the fast-moving car have more **momentum** than the small car and the slow-moving car do. Momentum is a property of all moving objects. ❯ **For movement along a straight line, momentum is calculated by multiplying an object's mass and velocity.**

momentum (moh MEN tuhm) a quantity defined as the product of the mass and velocity of an object

> **Momentum equation**
> $momentum = mass \times velocity$
> $p = mv$

In the SI, momentum is expressed in kilograms times

Application Lab ⏱ 80 min

Static, Sliding, and Rolling Friction

Current car brakes make use of static friction. As an engineer in the research and development department of a car manufacturing company, you have been asked to find out if a different approach to brakes might work better. To do so, you will investigate the circumstances under which friction is maximized.

What You'll Do

❯ **Predict** which type of friction force—static, sliding, or rolling—will be greatest and which will be smallest.

❯ **Measure** the static, sliding, and rolling friction when pulling a textbook across a table.

❯ **Apply** your results by describing how friction affects objects being pulled across a surface.

What You'll Need

rods, wooden (or metal) (4)
scissors
spring scale
string
textbook

Safety

◆

Procedure

Preparing for Your Experiment

❶ Which type of friction do you think is the largest force: static, sliding, or rolling? Which is the smallest?

❷ Form a hypothesis by writing a short paragraph that answers the question above. Explain your reasoning.

❸ Prepare a data table like the one shown below. **CAUTION:** Secure loose clothing, and remove dangling jewelry. Do not wear open-toed shoes or sandals in the lab.

Sample Data Table: Friction Measurements

	Static friction (N)	Sliding friction (N)	Rolling friction (N)
Trial 1			
Trial 2		DO NOT WRITE IN BOOK	
Trial 3			
Average			

Collecting Data and Testing the Hypothesis

❹ Cut a piece of string, and tie it in a loop that fits inside a textbook. Hook the string to the spring scale as shown.

❺ To measure the static friction between the book and the table, pull the spring scale very slowly. Gradually increase the force with which you pull on the spring scale until the book starts to slide across the table. Pull very gently. If you pull too hard, the book will start lurching and you will not get accurate results.

❻ Practice pulling the book as in step 5 several times until you can pull back smoothly. On a smooth trial, note the largest force that appears [...] record this result in [...] results in your data

The **Chapter Lab** at the end of the chapter helps you build your understanding of scientific methods. These labs reinforce the chapter with hands-on activity.

Force is related to change in momentum.

To catch a baseball, you must apply a force on the ball to make the ball stop moving. When you force an object to change its motion, you force it to change its momentum. In fact, you are changing the momentum of the ball over a period of time.

As the period of time of the momentum's change becomes longer, the force needed to cause this change in momentum becomes smaller. So, if you pull your glove back while you are catching a ball, as shown in **Figure 4,** you increase the time for changing the ball's momentum. Increasing the time causes the ball to put less force on your hand. As a result, the sting to your hand is less than it would be otherwise.

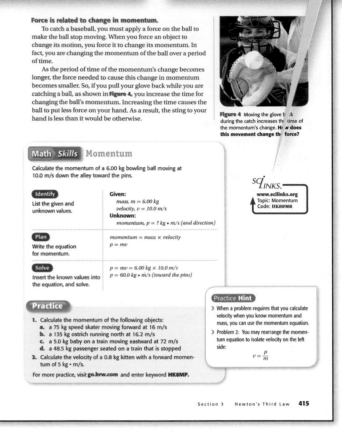

Figure 4 Moving the glove back during the catch increases the time of the momentum's change. How does this movement change the force?

Math Skills — Momentum

Calculate the momentum of a 6.00 kg bowling ball moving at 10.0 m/s down the alley toward the pins.

Identify List the given and unknown values.	**Given:** $mass, m = 6.00 kg$ $velocity, v = 10.0 m/s$ **Unknown:** $momentum, p = ? kg \cdot m/s$ (and direction)
Plan Write the equation for momentum.	$momentum = mass \times velocity$ $p = mv$
Solve Insert the known values into the equation, and solve.	$p = mv = 6.00 kg \times 10.0 m/s$ $p = 60.0 kg \cdot m/s$ (toward the pins)

Practice

1. Calculate the momentum of the following objects:
   a. a 75 kg speed skater moving forward at 16 m/s
   b. a 135 kg ostrich running north at 16.2 m/s
   c. a 5.0 kg baby on a train moving eastward at 72 m/s
   d. a 48.5 kg passenger seated on a train that is stopped

2. Calculate the velocity of a 0.8 kg kitten with a forward momentum of 5 kg · m/s.

For more practice, visit **go.hrw.com** and enter keyword **HK8MP.**

Practice Hint

❯ When a problem requires that you calculate velocity when you know momentum and mass, you can use the momentum equation.

❯ Problem 2: You may rearrange the momentum equation to isolate velocity on the left side:
$$v = \frac{p}{m}$$

sciLINKS
www.scilinks.org
Topic: Momentum
Code: HK80988

Work the Practice Problems

Build your reasoning and problem-solving skills by following the example problems in **Math Skills.** Then, you can practice those skills in the Practice problems that follow.

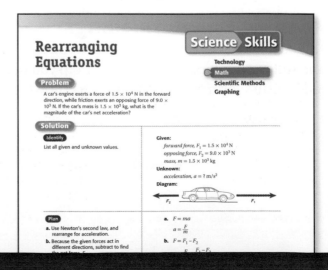

Rearranging Equations

Science Skills
Technology
Math
Scientific Methods
Graphing

Problem

A car's engine exerts a force of 1.5×10^4 N in the forward direction, while friction exerts an opposing force of 9.0×10^3 N. If the car's mass is 1.5×10^3 kg, what is the magnitude of the car's net acceleration?

Solution

Identify
List all given and unknown values.

Given:
$forward force, F_1 = 1.5 \times 10^4$ N
$opposing force, F_2 = 9.0 \times 10^3$ N
$mass, m = 1.5 \times 10^3$ kg

Unknown:
$acceleration, a = ? m/s^2$

Diagram:

$F_2 \leftarrow \quad \rightarrow F_1$

Plan

a. Use Newton's second law, and rearrange for acceleration.

b. Because the given forces act in different directions, subtract to find [...]

a. $F = ma$
   $a = \frac{F}{m}$

b. $F = F_1 - F_2$

Review What You Have Learned

You can't review too much when you are learning science. To help you review, a **Section Review** appears at the end of every section and a **Chapter Summary** and **Chapter Review** appear at the end of every chapter. These reviews not only help you study for tests but also help further your understanding of the content.

Just a few clicks away, each **Super Summary** gives you even more ways to review and study for tests using a computer and the Internet.

Be sure to read the **Key Ideas** to see how they all fit together. If you need to recall any of the **Key Terms,** the page number on which they appear is given.

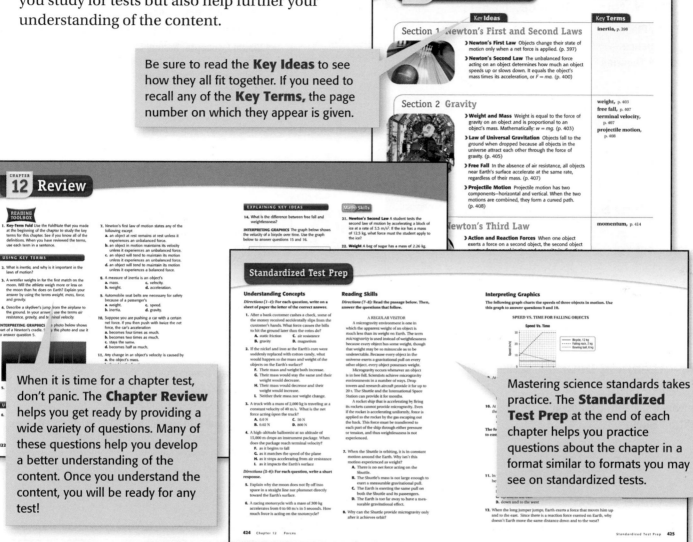

When it is time for a chapter test, don't panic. The **Chapter Review** helps you get ready by providing a wide variety of questions. Many of these questions help you develop a better understanding of the content. Once you understand the content, you will be ready for any test!

Mastering science standards takes practice. The **Standardized Test Prep** at the end of each chapter helps you practice questions about the chapter in a format similar to formats you may see on standardized tests.

◢ Be Resourceful—Use the Web!

More Practice

Each Math Skills example is followed by Practice problems. However, you may want more practice than you find in this book. You can find more practice online at **go.hrw.com.** There, type in the keyword **HK8MP,** and find more practice problems for your chapter.

Your Online Textbook

If your teacher gives you a special password to log onto the **Holt Online Learning** site, you will find your complete textbook on the Web. In addition, you will find some great learning tools and interactive materials. You can now access your textbook anywhere and anytime via the Internet.

Take a Test Drive

How well can you use this book now? Take Chapter 1 out for a spin and see how you do. Log onto **go.hrw.com** and enter the keyword **HK8 TEST DRIVE** for a short list of questions that will test your ability to navigate this book.

CHAPTER OPENER, pp. 2–4 `50 min.`

	Standards	Teach Key Ideas

SECTION 1 The Nature of Science, pp. 5–13 `50 min.`
> How Science Takes Place
> The Branches of Science
> Scientific Laws and Theories

Standards: UCP 1, UCP 2, SAI 2, ST 2, HNS 1, HNS 2, HNS 3

Teach Key Ideas:
- **Bellringer Transparency**
- **Teaching Transparency** TM1 Branches of Science
- **Visual Concepts** Natural Science • Biology • Physics • Earth Sciences • Comparing Theories and Laws • Models • Physical, Mathematical, and Conceptual Models

SECTION 2 The Way Science Works, pp. 14–21 `50 min.`
> Science Skills
> Units of Measurement

Standards: UCP 2, UCP 3, SAI 2, ST 2, HNS 1, HNS 2

Teach Key Ideas:
- **Bellringer Transparency**
- **Teaching Transparencies** TM2 Scientific Method • TM3 SI Base Units • TM4 SI Prefixes • TM69 Other Commonly Used Units
- **Visual Concepts** Hypothesis • SI • Volume • Scientific Method

SECTION 3 Organizing Data, pp. 22–29 `50 min.`
> Presenting Scientific Data
> Writing Numbers in Scientific Notation
> Using Significant Figures

Standards: UCP 2, UCP 3, SAI 1

Teach Key Ideas:
- **Bellringer Transparency**
- **Teaching Transparencies** G1 Line Graph • G2 Bar Graph • G3 Accuracy and Precision
- **Visual Concepts** Scientific Notation • Significant Figures • Accuracy and Precision • Controlled Experiment and Variable

See also PowerPoint® Resources

Chapter Review and Assessment Resources

- **SE** Science Skills: Forming a Hypothesis, p. 34
- **SE** Chapter Summary, p. 35
- **SE** Chapter Review, pp. 36–37
- **SE** Standardized Test Prep, pp. 38–39
- Concept Review Worksheets ■
- Chapter Tests A and B ■
-  Holt Online Assessment

CHAPTER
Fast Track *To shorten instruction because of time limitations, omit Section 2 and the chapter lab.*

Basic Learners
- **TE** Applying Scientific Methods, p. 15
- **TE** Standard Units of Measure, p. 18
- **TE** Significant Digits, p. 27
- Science Skills Worksheets
- Differentiated Datasheets A for Labs and Activities ■
- Study Guide A ■

Advanced Learners
- **TE** Revised Scientific Theories, p. 10
- **TE** Making Predictions, p. 10
- **TE** Evaluating Advertising Claims, p. 16
- **TE** Using a Spreadsheet, p. 23
- Cross-Disciplinary Worksheets
- Differentiated Datasheets C for Labs and Activities ■

Key

SE Student Edition
TE Teacher's Edition

🗀 Chapter Resource File
📓 Workbook
🖼 Transparency

💿 CD or CD-ROM
* Datasheet or blackline master available

■ Also available in Spanish

All resources listed below are also available on the Teacher's One-Stop Planner.

Why It Matters	Hands-On	Skills Development	Assessment
Build student motivation with resources about high-interest applications.	**SE Inquiry Lab** Measuring Area, p. 3* ■	**TE Reading Toolbox** Assessing Prior Knowledge, p. 2 **SE Reading Toolbox** p. 4	🗀 **Pretest** ■
TE Technology and Experimental Equipment, p. 6 **TE Biology,** p. 6 **TE The International Space Station,** p. 8 **TE Revised Theories and Laws,** p. 10 **SE Millennium Bridge,** p. 11 **SE Leonardo da Vinci,** p. 13 🗀 **Cross-Disciplinary Worksheets** Integrating Biology—Serendipity and Science • Integrating Chemistry—The Chemistry Connection • Integrating Mathematics—Using Quantitative Statements to Solve Problems	**TE Demonstration** Making Observations and Testing Ideas, p. 5	**SE Reading Toolbox** Spider Map, p. 6 **TE Science Skills** Interpreting Visuals, p. 7 **TE Reading Toolbox** Visual Literacy, p. 8 **TE Science Skills** Interpreting Visuals, p. 8 **TE Reading Toolbox** Interpreting Visuals, p. 9 **TE Science Skills** Models, p. 11 **TE Reading Toolbox** Visual Literacy, p. 13	**TE Reteaching Key Ideas** Scientific Law or Theory, p. 12 **TE Formative Assessment,** p. 12 🗀 **Spanish Assessment*** ■ 🗀 **Section Quiz** ■
TE A Surprising Discovery, p. 16 **TE Exploring Space,** p. 17 **TE A Costly Mistake,** p. 18 **TE Kelvins and Amperes,** p. 19 🗀 **Cross-Disciplinary Worksheet** Connection to Language Arts—The Structure of Medical Terminology	**TE Demonstration** Are They the Same? p. 14 **SE Quick Lab** Making Observations, p. 16* ■ 🗀 **Observation Lab** Comparing the Densities of Pennies 🗀 **CBL™ Probeware Lab** Designing a Pendulum Clock	**SE Reading Toolbox** Spider Map, p. 15 **SE Math Skills** Conversions Within SI, p. 19	**TE Reteaching Key Ideas** Tools, p. 21 **TE Formative Assessment,** p. 21 🗀 **Spanish Assessment*** ■ 🗀 **Section Quiz** ■
TE Graphs Convey Information, p. 23 **TE Big and Small,** p. 25 **TE Amazing Accuracy,** p. 26 **SE How Was The Gateway Arch Built?** p. 29 🗀 **Cross-Disciplinary Worksheet** Integrating Physics—Observing and Experimenting to Find Relationships	**TE Demonstration** Daily Life Activity, p. 22 **SE Quick Lab** Precision vs. Accuracy, p. 27* ■ **SE Skills Practice Lab** Making Measurements, pp. 30–33* ■	**TE Reading Toolbox** Visual Literacy, p. 24 **SE Reading Toolbox** Everyday Words Used in Science, p. 25 **SE Math Skills** Writing Scientific Notation, p. 25 **TE Math Skills** Using Calculators, p. 25 **SE Math Skills** Using Scientific Notation, p. 26 **SE Math Skills** Using Significant Figures, p. 28	**TE Reteaching Key Ideas** Converting, p. 28 **TE Formative Assessment,** p. 28 🗀 **Spanish Assessment*** ■ 🗀 **Section Quiz** ■

See also Lab Generator

See also Holt Online Assessment Resources

Resources for Differentiated Instruction

English Learners

TE Deciphering Words, p. 17
🗀 Differentiated Datasheets A, B, and C for Labs and Activities ■
📓 Study Guide A ■

Struggling Readers

TE Paired Learning, p. 6
📓 Interactive Reader

Special Education Students

TE What's the Measure? p. 20
TE Pie Charts, p. 24

Alternative Assessment

TE Planning an Experiment, p. 7
TE Distinguishing Between Theories and Laws, p. 9
TE Understanding Science, p. 35

CHAPTER 1 Introduction to Science

Overview

This chapter explores the nature of science, the scientific method of discovery, and the difference between scientific theories and laws. This chapter also describes how scientists use models and mathematics. Science skills, math skills, and units of measurement are taught next, followed by organization and presentation of data. The knowledge and skills gained in this chapter will serve as a foundation for the study of science.

READING TOOLBOX

Assessing Prior Knowledge Students should understand the following concepts:
• problem identification
• basic problem-solving skills
• everyday physical phenomena

MISCONCEPTION ALERT

Science education research has identified the following misconceptions about science:
• Most students believe learning is passive and is, in fact, the canonical transfer of knowledge. (Learning is dynamic and involves continuously questioning information.)
• Some students and teachers view science as a static, faithful copy of the world. (Science is a tentative human construction based on the most logical interpretation of experiment and theory.)

Chapter Outline

❶ The Nature of Science
How Science Takes Place
The Branches of Science
Scientific Laws and Theories

❷ The Way Science Works
Science Skills
Units of Measurement

❸ Organizing Data
Presenting Scientific Data
Writing Numbers in Scientific Notation
Using Significant Figures

Why It **Matters**

Many inventions, such as cars, would not exist today if scientists did not understand how to use scientific methods and how to perform experiments. For example, a model of a car can be tested in a wind tunnel to perfect the car's design.

Chapter Correlations   *National Science Education Standards*

The following correlations show the National Science Standards that relate to this chapter. For the full text of the standards, see the National Science Education Standards at the front of the book.

UCP1 Systems, order, and organization (Section 1)

UCP 2 Evidence, models, and explanation (Sections 1–3)

UCP 3 Constancy, change, and measurement (Section 2, Skills Practice Lab: Making Measurements)

SAI 1 Abilities necessary to do scientific inquiry (Section 3, Skills Practice Lab: Making Measurements)

SAI 2 Understandings about scientific inquiry (Sections 1, 2)

ST 2 Understandings about science and technology (Sections 1, 2)

HNS 1 Science as a human endeavor (Sections 1, 2)

HNS 2 Nature of scientific knowledge (Sections 1, 2)

HNS 3 Historical perspectives (Section 1)

InquiryLab ⏱ 10 min

Measuring Area

Using a **meterstick,** measure the length and width of the top surface of a rectangular **table.** Multiply your two measurements to calculate the surface area of the table. Compare your results with those of other students.

Questions to Get You Started

1. To what fraction of a unit can you reliably measure?

2. How can you explain any differences between your results and those of your classmates?

InquiryLab

Teacher's Notes Students should use SI units (centimeters or millimeters) to measure their desks so that results can be easily shared among students. If available desks are of varying sizes, choose one and have several different groups measure it.

Materials per Group
- meterstick
- desk

Answers

1. Answers may depend on the meterstick used, but should be in SI units (centimeters or millimeters). Most students will be able to make measurements to one-tenth of a unit.

2. The results differed because we used different measuring tools.

Key Resources

📋 **Datasheet**
   Measuring Area

Science Terms

Answers may vary. Terms in the chapter containing the word "scientific" include *scientific law, scientific theory,* and *scientific notation.* Students should give both the common and scientific meanings for the words "law," "theory," and "notation."

Classification

Answers may vary. The following branches of science and their respective subjects are mentioned in Section 1 and are included in the table below:

Branch of science	Area of study
social science	human behavior
natural science	how the whole universe behaves
biology	living things
botany	plants
zoology	animals
ecology	balance in nature
physical science	matter and energy
chemistry	matter and its changes
physics	forces and energy
geology	Earth's physical nature and history
meteorology	the atmosphere and weather
biochemistry	the matter of living things
geophysics	forces that affect Earth

These reading tools can help you learn the material in this chapter. For more information on how to use these and other tools, see **Appendix A.**

Science Terms

Everyday Words Used in Science All of the key terms that you will learn in this book are used by scientists. Many words used in science are also words used in everyday speech. You should pay attention to the definitions of such words so that you use them correctly in scientific contexts.

Your Turn As you read the chapter, make a table like the one below for the terms *scientific law, scientific theory,* and *scientific notation.* Include the everyday meaning of the word that comes after the word *scientific.*

TERM	SCIENTIFIC CONTEXT	EVERYDAY MEANING
scientific method	a series of steps used to solve problems or answer questions in a scientific way	method—a way of doing something

Classification

Branches of Science Classification is a logical tool for organizing ideas. Classification involves grouping things into categories. The example below shows that you do a lot of classifying without even realizing it.

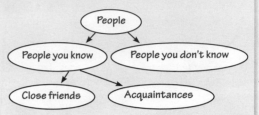

Your Turn Figure 3 in Section 1 shows how branches of science can be classified. Write down the definitions of the branches of science included in the figure. Explain why astronomy, geology, and meteorology are classified as types of Earth science, and explain why physics and chemistry are classified as types of physical science.

Graphic Organizers

Spider Maps Graphic Organizers are drawings that you can make to help you organize the concepts that you learn. A spider map is a Graphic Organizer that shows how details are organized into categories that relate to a main idea.

Your Turn As you read Section 2, complete a spider map like the one started here to organize the ideas that you learn about SI units. You may also create more spider maps to organize the science skills that you learn in this chapter.

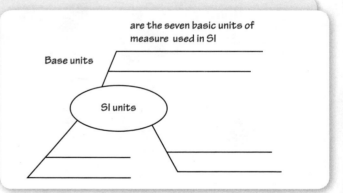

Graphic Organizers

Answers may vary. Students should include topics related to SI units, such as base units, derived units, prefixes, and conversions.

The Nature of Science

Key Ideas

> How do scientists explore the world?

> How are the many types of science organized?

> What are scientific theories, and how are they different from scientific laws?

Key Terms

science
technology
law
theory

Why It Matters

Science is applied to the technologies that are used to build many important things, such as bridges and vehicles.

When you have a question about how something works, how do you find the answer? Generally, scientists describe the universe by using basic rules, which can be discovered by careful, methodical study.

How Science Takes Place

> **A scientist may perform experiments to find a new aspect of the natural world, to explain a known phenomenon, to check the results of other experiments, or to test the predictions of current theories.**

Imagine that it is 1895 and you are experimenting with mysterious rays known as cathode rays. These rays were discovered almost 40 years earlier, but in 1895 no one knows that they are composed of electrons. To produce the rays, you pump the air out of a sealed glass tube, which creates a vacuum. An early version of this type of tube is shown in **Figure 1.** You then connect rods inside the tube to an electrical source. Electric charges flow through the empty space between the rods and produce the rays.

Figure 1 An early cathode-ray tube is shown on the left. A television picture tube, on the right, is a form of the same cathode-ray tube.

Cathode-ray tube

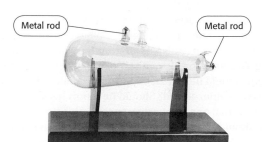

Metal rod

Metal rod

Key Resources

Teaching Transparency
TM1 Branches of Science

Visual Concepts
Natural Science
Biology
Physics
Earth Sciences
Comparing Theories and Laws
Models
Physical, Mathematical, and
 Conceptual Models

Science Skills Worksheets
Creating a Concept Map
Compiling and Weighing Evidence

Cross-Disciplinary Worksheets
Integrating Biology—Serendipity and
 Science
Integrating Chemistry—The Chemistry
 Connection
Integrating Mathematics—Using
 Quantitative Statements to Solve
 Problems

> Focus

This section introduces students to the main branches of natural science. Students learn about confirming results by designing and repeating experiments. Scientific theories and laws are discussed, along with the role of models in both.

Bellringer

Use the Bellringer transparency to prepare students for this section.

Demonstrate

Making Observations and Testing Ideas Before class, cut a piece of paper into five pieces as shown.

Tell the students that the pieces can be arranged to look like a fish. Have the students observe the diagram. Then have them predict how to put the pieces together to form a fish.

Test their ideas by taping the pieces to the chalkboard. Emphasize that scientists solve problems by making observations and testing their ideas.

LS Interpersonal

Why It **Matters**

Technology and Experimental Equipment Scientists at the turn of the twentieth century had to design and build most of their own experimental equipment. For example, a scientist studying cathode rays may have had to be a glass blower to make the tube, an electrician to build the batteries and connect the rods in the tube to the batteries, and a mechanic to build and maintain the vacuum pump used to evacuate the cathode-ray tube. The need for scientific equipment often drives the invention of new technologies. Although scientists today still build prototypes of new instruments, they can get assistance from specialists in technologies that were not previously available.

Why It **Matters**

Biology Fleming, who treated soldiers in France during World War I, was well aware of the lack of an effective treatment for many infections. After discovering penicillin, he learned that it could effectively treat many kinds of bacteria, including anthrax and the bacteria that caused meningitis. Although he published his results, penicillin's potential for treating infections was not well understood until about a decade later. World War II hastened the development of penicillin, which was quickly produced in large quantities by the United States, Britain, and later Russia. By 1944, there was enough penicillin to treat all of the Allied soldiers wounded on D-Day.

Academic Vocabulary

conduct (kuhn DUHKT) to do

Integrating **Biology**

Penicillin In 1928, the Scottish scientist Alexander Fleming was investigating disease-causing bacteria. He saw that one of his cultures contained an area where no bacteria were growing. An unknown organism was growing in that area. Rather than discard the culture as a failure, Fleming investigated the unfamiliar organism and found that it was a type of mold. This mold produced a substance that prevented the growth of many disease-causing bacteria. What he found by questioning the results of a "failed" experiment became the first modern antibiotic, penicillin. Major discoveries are often made by accident when scientists are trying to find something else.

READING TOOLBOX

Spider Map
Create a spider map that explains the steps that happen when science takes place. Use the blue heads in the section as the branches of your map.

Scientists answer questions by investigating.

As a scientist, you have learned from the work of other scientists and have <u>conducted</u> your own experiments. You know that when certain minerals are placed inside the tube, the cathode rays make them glow. Cardboard pieces coated with powder made from these minerals are used to detect the rays. If a very high voltage is used, even the glass tube glows.

Other scientists have found that cathode rays can pass through thin metal foil, but the rays travel in our atmosphere for only 2 or 3 cm. You wonder if the rays could pass through the glass tube. Other experiments have shown that cathode rays do not go through glass. You think that scientists may not have been able to see the weak glow from the mineral-coated cardboard because the glass tube glowed too brightly. So, you decide to cover the glass tube with heavy black paper.

Scientists plan experiments.

Before experimenting, you write your plan in a laboratory notebook and sketch the equipment that you are using. You make a table in which you can record your observations and your variables—the electric voltage used, the distance from the tube to the cathode-ray detector, and the air temperature. You state the idea that you are going to test: At a high voltage, cathode rays will be strong enough to be detected outside the tube by causing the mineral-coated cardboard to glow.

Scientists observe.

You are ready to start your experiment but want to be sure that the black-paper cover does not have any gaps. So, you darken the room and turn on the tube. The cover blocks all of the light from the tube. Just before you switch off the tube, you glimpse a light nearby. When you turn on the tube again, the light reappears.

You realize that this light is coming from the mineral-coated cardboard that you planned to use to detect cathode rays. The detector is already glowing even though it is almost 1 m away from the tube. You know that cathode rays cannot travel 1 m in air. You suspect that the tube is giving off a new type of ray that no one has seen before. What do you do now?

Wilhelm Roentgen (RENT guhn) pondered this question in Würzburg, Germany, on November 8, 1895, when he did this experiment. Should he call the experiment a failure because the results were unexpected? Should he report his findings in a scientific journal or ask reporters to cover this news story? Maybe he should send letters about his discovery to famous scientists and invite them to come see his experiment.

READING TOOLBOX

Spider Map Sample spider map:

Scientists answer questions by investigating.

Scientists plan experiments.

How science takes place

Scientists always confirm results.

Scientists observe.

Differentiated Instruction

Struggling Readers

Paired Learning Have students silently read the paragraphs under the heading *Scientists observe*. Instruct students to mark on self-adhesive notes those portions of the text that they do not understand. Group students together in pairs, and have one student in each pair discuss with the other student those parts of the passage that he or she found difficult. The listener should either clarify the difficult passages or help frame a common question for later explanation. **LS** Verbal/Interpersonal

Scientists always confirm results.

Because Roentgen was a scientist, he first repeated his experiment to be sure of his observations. His results caused him to think of new questions and to do more experiments to find the answers to these questions.

He found that the rays passed through almost everything, but dense materials absorbed some of the rays. When he held his hand in the path of the rays, the bones were visible as shadows on the detector, as **Figure 2** shows. When Roentgen published his findings in December, he still did not know what the rays were. He called them *X rays* because *x* represents an unknown in a mathematical equation.

Within three months of Roentgen's discovery, a doctor in Massachusetts used X rays to help set the broken bones in a boy's arm. After a year, more than a thousand scientific papers about X rays had been published. In 1901, Roentgen received the first Nobel Prize in physics for his discovery.

✔️ **Reading Check** How did Roentgen confirm his observation? (See Appendix E for answers to Reading Checks.)

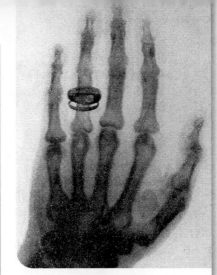

Figure 2 Roentgen included this X ray of his wife's hand in one of the first papers that he wrote about X rays.

science (SIE uhns) the knowledge obtained by observing natural events and conditions in order to discover facts and formulate laws or principles that can be verified or tested

The Branches of Science

Roentgen's work with X rays shows how scientists work, but what is science about? **Science** is observing, studying, and experimenting to find the nature of things. You can think of science as having two main branches: social science, which deals with individual and group human behavior, and natural science. Natural science tries to understand how "nature," or "the whole universe," behaves. ❭ **Most of the time, natural science is divided into biological science, physical science, and Earth science. Figure 3** shows how science is divided.

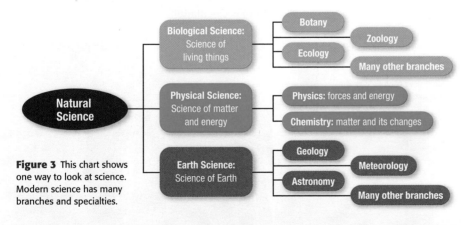

Figure 3 This chart shows one way to look at science. Modern science has many branches and specialties.

Natural Science
- **Biological Science:** Science of living things
  - Botany
  - Zoology
  - Ecology
  - Many other branches
- **Physical Science:** Science of matter and energy
  - Physics: forces and energy
  - Chemistry: matter and its changes
- **Earth Science:** Science of Earth
  - Geology
  - Meteorology
  - Astronomy
  - Many other branches

Science Skills

Interpreting Visuals Have students examine **Figure 2.** Group students in pairs, and have them create an explanation of why the bones are dark and the surrounding areas are bright. (The bones block the X rays and create a shadow.) **LS Visual**

Teaching Key Ideas

The Activity of Science After students have read this section, have them work together as a group to brainstorm examples of how science occurs through the steps listed here (investigating, planning experiments, observing, and testing results). Ask a student volunteer to create a list on the board of all student contributions. Then have students create a diagram that summarizes the results of their brainstorming activity. **LS Verbal**

Teaching Key Ideas

Classification of the Sciences Have students look at **Figure 3** and consider where they would place astronomy, analytical chemistry, archeology, geophysics, organic chemistry, paleontology, nuclear physics, and biochemistry. **LS Logical**

Differentiated Instruction

Alternative Assessment

Planning an Experiment Ask students to imagine that they are Wilhelm Roentgen, and have them write their own plan for investigating cathode rays. Students should include a specific question to investigate, a diagram of their equipment set-up, a data table for any information they plan to collect, and a detailed description of each step of the experiment.

Some students may have trouble coming up with their own plan. Tell these students that Roentgen's plan was to see if the cathode rays would pass through glass if the electric voltage applied to the rods was high enough. Use the following criteria to assess students' plans:
- Did students pose thoughtful questions?
- Did they explain each step of the experiment they designed?
- Did they include a diagram and a data table?
- Is their design a reasonable approach for answering the proposed question? **LS Logical**

READING TOOLBOX

Visual Literacy Explain to students that the computer model shown in **Figure 4** uses four different colors to show the locations and chemical compositions of the four different molecules that make up human DNA. **LS** **Visual**

MISCONCEPTION ALERT

Science and Technology Be sure students understand the distinction between science and technology. The goal of science is to gain knowledge about the natural world. The goal of technology is to apply scientific understanding to solve problems.

Science Skills

Interpreting Visuals Have students examine **Figure 5.** Allow students to brainstorm explanations for how computers became both smaller and faster over time. **LS** **Logical**

Answer to caption question

Answers may vary. Possible answers include portable music or video game players, cell phones, digital cameras, programmable appliances such as microwaves or DVD players, and calculators.

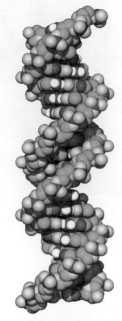

Figure 4 This model shows the structure of DNA (deoxyribonucleic acid), which makes each of us unique.

The branches of science work together.

The classification of science seems to be very simple. For example, life science is *biology*. Biology has many branches, such as *botany,* the science of plants, and *ecology,* the science of balance in nature. Medicine and agriculture are also branches of biology.

Physical science has two main branches—chemistry and physics. *Chemistry* is the science of matter and its changes. *Physics* is the science of forces and energy. Both depend greatly on mathematics.

Two branches of Earth science are *geology,* the science of the physical nature and history of Earth, and *meteorology,* the science of the atmosphere and weather.

But the branches of science have become more mixed. For example, some chemists study chemicals that make up living things, such as the DNA shown in **Figure 4.** This branch of science is *biochemistry,* the study of the matter of living things. It is both a life science and a physical science. Other branches of science are also mixed. For example, *geophysics*—the study of the forces that affect Earth, is both an Earth science and a physical science.

Science and technology work together.

Scientists who do experiments to learn more about the world are doing *pure science.* **Technology** is the application of science for practical uses. Engineers apply scientific knowledge and methods to design products people use. Advances in science and technology depend on one another. The first computers, such as the one shown in **Figure 5,** often filled up a whole room. But advances in science have led to smaller computers that are both faster and cheaper. Modern computers also help scientists. For example, computers help scientists make complex calculations quickly.

Figure 5 Advances in science have greatly reduced the size of and increased the availability of computers. **What devices that use computer technology do you use?**

Why It Matters

The International Space Station One recent example of the mutually beneficial relationship between science and technology is the international space station (ISS). The technology used to build the space station makes new scientific experiments possible. Scientists use the ISS to conduct both pure and practical research in many branches of science and engineering, including gravity and microgravity research (physical science), life science, space science, earth science, space product development, and engineering research and technology. To learn more about the experiments on the ISS, you can check NASA's web site.

Scientific Laws and Theories

People sometimes say things like, "My theory is that we'll see Jaime on the school bus," when they really mean, "I'm guessing that we'll see Jaime on the school bus." People use the word *theory* in everyday speech to refer to a guess about something. In science, a theory is much more than a guess. ❯ **Theories explain why something happens, and laws describe how something works.**

Experimental results support laws and theories.

When you place a hot cooking pot in a cooler place, does the pot become hotter as it stands? No, it will always get cooler. This example illustrates a scientific law that states that warm objects always become cooler when they are placed in cooler surroundings. A scientific **law** describes a process in nature that can be tested by repeated experiments. A law allows predictions to be made about how a system will behave under a wide range of conditions.

However, a law does not *explain* how a process takes place. In the example of the hot cooking pot, nothing in the law tells why hot objects become cooler in cooler surroundings. Such an explanation of how a natural process works must be provided by a scientific **theory.**

Scientific theories are always being questioned and examined. To be valid, a theory must continue to pass several tests.

- A theory must explain observations clearly and consistently. For example, the theory that heat is the energy of particles in motion explains why the hot cooking pot gets cooler when it is placed in cooler surroundings.

- Experiments that illustrate the theory must be repeatable. A cooking pot always gets warmer when placed on a hot stove and always gets cooler when placed in cooler surroundings, whether the pot is moved for the first time or the 31st time.

- You must be able to predict results from the theory. You might predict that anything that makes the particles in an object move faster will make the object hotter. Sawing a piece of wood, as shown in **Figure 6,** will make the metal particles in the saw move faster. If you saw rapidly, the saw will get hot to the touch. The theory can explain both why the saw gets warmer and why the cooking pot gets cooler.

✔ Reading Check How does a scientific law differ from a scientific theory?

technology (tek NAHL uh jee) the application of science for practical purposes

law (LAW) a descriptive statement or equation that reliably predicts events under certain conditions

theory (THEE uh ree) a system of ideas that explains many related observations and is supported by a large body of evidence acquired through scientific investigation

Figure 6 The kinetic theory of energy explains many things that you can observe, such as why a saw blade gets hot when used.

Teaching Key Ideas

Theories and Laws The distinction between scientific theories and laws can be confusing to students. Stress that a scientific law is an observation about nature—a summary of a natural event. Many laws can be stated as mathematical formulas. A scientific law does not explain how or why something happens, but a scientific theory does. A scientific theory is a wide-ranging idea that explains many different laws. In some cases, the laws explained by a theory appeared to be unrelated before the theory was developed. Theories are always open to challenges and testing.

READING TOOLBOX

Interpreting Visuals Have students examine **Figure 6.** Explain that some of the effort of sawing is used to overcome friction—the saw does not slide smoothly through the wood. Friction results in the higher temperatures of both the saw and the wood. **LS Visual**

Differentiated Instruction

Alternative Assessment

Distinguishing Between Theories and Laws To help students understand the distinction between scientific theories and laws, have them analyze some theories and laws that they have studied in previous science courses. Instruct them to make a three-column chart with the column headings "Example," "Theory or Law?" and "Reasons." Tell them to list all of their examples in the first column and to classify each example as either a theory or a law in the second column. They should explain the reasons for their classification in the third column. Possible responses could include: Newton's laws of motion (laws); gas laws (laws); conservation of energy (law); universal law of gravitation (law); atomic theory (theory); theory of evolution (theory); kinetic theory (theory); plate tectonics (theory); relativity (theory). Be sure their reasons for each classification are accurate and logical. **LS Logical**

MISCONCEPTION ///ALERT\\\

Laws as Approximations Tell students that many laws that are not correct under all circumstances are still used because they represent easy-to-understand models of things that we observe in the natural world. One example is the relationship between the current, resistance, and voltage in an electric circuit (*resistance = voltage/current*), commonly called Ohm's Law. This equation does not apply to all materials and, when it does apply, it is only valid for a given range of voltages. But even though the "law" is not absolute, it is a very useful tool for many particular situations.

Why It **Matters**

Revised Theories and Laws Some theories and laws that have been revised still have great practical value. For example, Newton's laws of motion are learned and used by many students and scientists. Under ordinary conditions, these laws provide approximations that are accurate enough for all practical purposes. But we know now that they do not apply to subatomic particles or to moving particles approaching the speed of light.

Figure 7 The gravitational force of attraction between Earth and these sky divers varies depending on the mass of the sky divers and their distance from Earth.

Mathematics can describe physical events.

How would you state the law of gravitation? You could say that something you are holding will fall to Earth when you let go. This *qualitative* statement describes with words something that you have seen many times. But many scientific laws and theories can be stated as mathematical equations, which are *quantitative* statements.

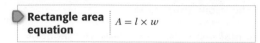

> **Rectangle area equation** $\quad A = l \times w$

The rectangle area equation works for all rectangles, whether they are short, tall, wide, or thin.

> **Universal gravitation equation** $\quad F = G \dfrac{m_1 m_2}{d^2}$

In the same way, the universal gravitation equation describes how large the force will be between two galaxies or between Earth and the sky divers shown falling to Earth in **Figure 7.** Quantitative expressions of the laws of science make communicating about science easier. Scientists around the world speak and read many different languages, but mathematics, the language of science, is the same everywhere.

Theories and laws are always being tested.

Sometimes, theories must be changed or replaced when new discoveries are made. More than 200 years ago, scientists used the *caloric theory* to explain how objects become warmer and cooler. Heat was thought to be an invisible fluid, called *caloric,* that flowed from a warm object to a cool one. People thought that fires were fountains of caloric, which flowed into surrounding objects and made them warmer. The caloric theory could explain all that people knew about heat.

During the 1800s, after doing many experiments, some scientists presented a new theory based on the idea that heat was a result of the motion of particles. Like many new ideas, this new theory was strongly criticized and was not accepted at first by other scientists. But the caloric theory could not explain why rubbing two rough surfaces together made them warmer. This new theory, the *kinetic theory,* could be used to explain why the surfaces became warmer—rubbing the surfaces together caused the particles in the surfaces to move faster. The kinetic theory was accepted because it explained both the old and new observations, and the caloric theory was no longer used.

Differentiated Instruction

Advanced Learners

Revised Scientific Theories Have students research a scientific theory that is no longer accepted, such as the fluid theory of electricity or the phlogiston theory of combustion. Ask them to write a few paragraphs explaining why the theory was originally accepted, why it was later replaced, and what it was replaced by. They may wish to use the discussion of caloric theory on this page as a model. **LS** Verbal

Advanced Learners

Making Predictions Scientific laws and theories can be used to make predictions about what will happen in different situations. If the results of an experiment match a prediction based on a scientific law or theory, the experiment supports that law or theory.

Challenge students to pose examples of hypothetical situations or experiments where a scientific law or theory may explain a given outcome. **LS** Logical

Models can represent physical events.

When you see the word *model,* you may think of a small copy of an airplane or a person who shows off clothing. Scientists use models, too. A scientific model is a representation of an object or event that can be studied to understand the real object or event. Sometimes, models represent things that are too small, too big, or too complex to study easily.

A model of a water molecule is shown in **Figure 8.** Chemists use models to study how water molecules form ice crystals, such as snowflakes. Models can be drawings on paper. Real objects can also be used as models to help us picture things that we cannot see. For example, a spring can be used as a model of a sound wave. A model can also be a mental "picture" or a set of rules that describes how something works. After you have studied atoms, you will be able to picture atoms in your mind. You can use these pictures to figure out what will happen in chemical reactions.

Reading Check What are three types of models?

Figure 8 Models can be used to describe a water molecule (top right) and to study how water molecules are arranged in a snowflake.

Science Skills

Models Point out to students that they probably use models every day without even realizing that they are doing so. When they plan a route to their next class via their locker, they are using a mental map that is a model of the school. A paper map is also a model of the real world. Any set of instructions on how to build something or put something together is a model of that object. If a student explains to a friend how to use a computer, that student is using a mental model of the operating rules of the computer. Have students work in small groups to brainstorm as many commonly used models as they can. Then have a volunteer from each group share their list with the class.
LS Interpersonal

MISCONCEPTION ALERT

The Nature of Science Some students believe that science is simply an accumulation of facts. Use the discussion of theories and laws in this section to dispel this notion. Point out that science includes both the accumulation of observations and the ever-changing interpretations of those observations. Remind them that a scientific theory can never be proved absolutely; there is always the possibility that it will be revised or even replaced by a new theory that explains additional observations or laws.

Why It **Matters**
Millennium Bridge

SCIENCE & SOCIETY

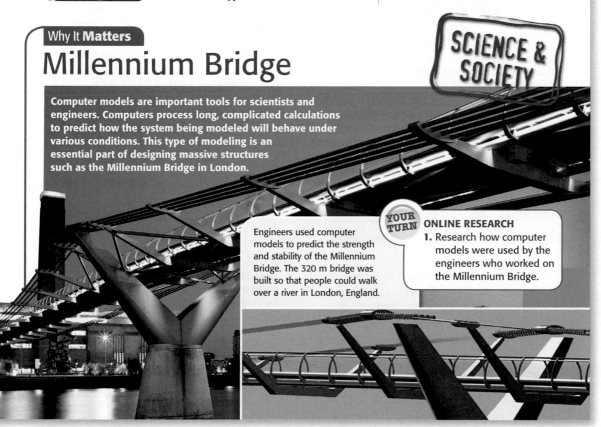

Computer models are important tools for scientists and engineers. Computers process long, complicated calculations to predict how the system being modeled will behave under various conditions. This type of modeling is an essential part of designing massive structures such as the Millennium Bridge in London.

Engineers used computer models to predict the strength and stability of the Millennium Bridge. The 320 m bridge was built so that people could walk over a river in London, England.

YOUR TURN

ONLINE RESEARCH
1. Research how computer models were used by the engineers who worked on the Millennium Bridge.

Why It **Matters**

Millennium Bridge The Millennium Bridge is the first pedestrian bridge over the River Thames in more than 100 years. It connects St. Paul's Cathedral in central London with the Tate Modern Gallery. One of the goals for building the bridge was to engineer a pedestrian walkway with unimpeded views of the river and the skyline. This vision included building a suspension bridge with very minimal sag and supporting the bridge with balustrades below eye-level. When the bridge opened on June 10, 2000, between 80,000 and 100,000 people walked across. This resulted in a side-to-side sway of about 70 mm, much more than expected. Engineers built models to understand the reason for the motion.

These models showed that sideways forces exerted from the walking motion of people in a crowd matched the resonant frequency of the bridge. In order to counteract this behavior, engineers attached dampers to the bridge, which absorb the energy of the sideways forces.

Answer to Your Turn
1. Answers may vary. Students should discuss how computer models helped engineers predict the strength, stiffness, and safety of the bridge under various loading conditions. Students may also discuss what factors were not included in the computer models of the bridge.

Reteaching Key Ideas

Scientific Law or Theory? Lift up a textbook and tell the students that they need to design an experiment that allows them to determine the volume of the textbook. Have them discuss different ways that they might measure the volume. Ask how the students would check if their experiments led to correct results. Ask if their experiments led to scientific laws or scientific theories. **LS Interpersonal**

Formative Assessment

What are the two main branches of physical science?

A. biological science and earth science (Incorrect. These are two of the major branches of natural sciences, but not part of physical science.)

B. botany and ecology (Incorrect. These are branches of biological science.)

C. geology and astronomy (Incorrect. These are branches of earth science.)

D. physics and chemistry (Correct. Physics is the study of energy and forces and chemistry is the study of matter and its changes. Both are considered branches of physical science.)

Projected path on August 26, 2005

Projected path on August 27, 2005

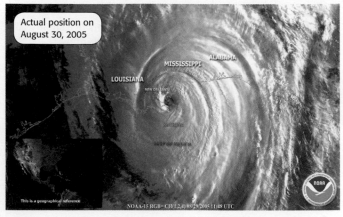

Actual position on August 30, 2005

Figure 9 Models help forecast the weather. The black lines in these models indicate the projected path of Hurricane Katrina days before the eye of the storm made landfall. The satellite image shows the actual location where the eye of the storm hit land.

We use models in our everyday lives.

Computer models have many uses. For example, they can be used by *meteorologists* to help forecast the weather. Meteorologists use computer models that use information about wind speed and direction, air temperature, moisture levels, and ground shape. **Figure 9** shows how a model was used to predict the path of a hurricane.

The outcome of a model depends on the information that is put into the model. Notice that in the first model of the hurricane path, the predicted area where the eye of the hurricane would hit land is very large. As the hurricane got closer to land, more data were collected and added to the model, and the area of the potential landfall was smaller. The satellite image of the actual hurricane shows that this model did a very good job predicting where the hurricane would hit land.

Section 1 Review

KEY IDEAS

1. **Compare** the two branches of physical science.
2. **Explain** how science and technology depend on each other and how they differ from each other.
3. **Define** *scientific law,* and give an example.
4. **Compare** a scientific law and a scientific theory.
5. **Explain** why a scientific theory might be changed.
6. **Describe** how a scientific model is used, and give an example of a scientific model.

CRITICAL THINKING

7. **Applying Ideas** How may Roentgen's training as a scientist have affected the way that he responded to his discovery?
8. **Analyzing Ideas** Explain how a scientific theory differs from a guess or an opinion.
9. **Forming Hypotheses** Pick a common occurrence, develop an explanation for it, and describe an experiment that you could perform to test your explanation.

Answers to Section Review

1. Chemistry is the study of matter and its changes. Physics is the study of forces and energy and their interaction with matter.

2. Science is knowledge about the nature of things that is obtained by doing experiments. Technology is the application of science. Improving technology involves finding a use for a scientific discovery. However, some scientific discoveries cannot be made until a certain technology exists.

3. A scientific law describes how things work based on experimental observations. Examples may vary, but could include the laws of gravitation and the conservation of matter.

4. A law summarizes an observation; a theory explains observations.

5. A scientific theory may change if new discoveries are found that cannot be explained by the theory, but are supported by experimental evidence. A new theory that can explain both the new and the old observations would take the place of the old theory.

6. A model is used to study or make predictions about an object or situation the model represents. One example of a model is a computer model that is used to design bridges and buildings.

Answers continued on p. 39A

Leonardo da Vinci

Science and technology depend on each other. Basic scientific research is needed to obtain the knowledge to develop technology. However, technology is also needed to advance scientific ideas. Sometimes, great thinkers use their knowledge of science to invent new things that are "ahead of their time." Leonardo da Vinci was such a thinker. He designed many things, including a forerunner to the modern-day helicopter. But in the 15th century he did not have the technology available to make his ideas work. For example, he did not have the engine technology that would give his machine enough lift to get it off the ground.

HISTORY IN SCIENCE

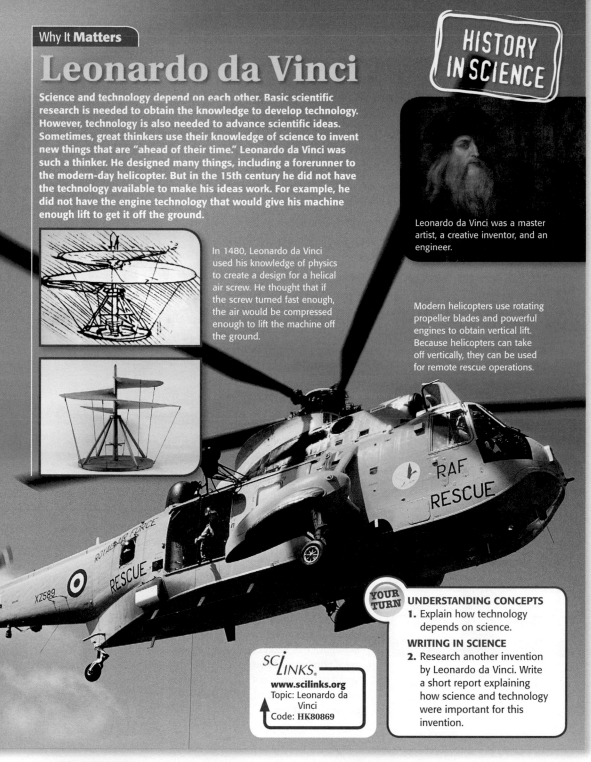

Leonardo da Vinci was a master artist, a creative inventor, and an engineer.

In 1480, Leonardo da Vinci used his knowledge of physics to create a design for a helical air screw. He thought that if the screw turned fast enough, the air would be compressed enough to lift the machine off the ground.

Modern helicopters use rotating propeller blades and powerful engines to obtain vertical lift. Because helicopters can take off vertically, they can be used for remote rescue operations.

Leonardo da Vinci (April 15, 1452 – May 2, 1519) was a man of exceptional genius and talent. His skills included the fields of architecture, physiology, anatomy, sculpting, painting, engineering, and music. Leonardo's approach to design was unique in that he carefully studied the individual parts of machines and then considered how these parts could be modified or placed together in new ways to create new inventions.

Leonardo had a fascination with designing machines that would allow people to fly. He spent significant effort studying birds in order to better understand how they fly. The helicopter pictured in the drawing would have required four men to power it. Unfortunately, it would not have flown because the body of the machine would have rotated in the opposite direction from the screw. Modern helicopters counteract the rotation of the overhead propellers using the rotation of the propeller in the rear. Leonardo also developed plans for a hang glider, which theoretically could have flown.

It is suggested that Leonardo was planning to compile his scientific inventions into a set of treatises before his death, but this never occurred. Most of his surviving technical ideas are known from journals, which are dispersed in collections throughout the world.

YOUR TURN

UNDERSTANDING CONCEPTS
1. Explain how technology depends on science.

WRITING IN SCIENCE
2. Research another invention by Leonardo da Vinci. Write a short report explaining how science and technology were important for this invention.

SCILINKS.

www.scilinks.org
Topic: Leonardo da Vinci
Code: **HK80869**

READING TOOLBOX

Visual Literacy Have students examine Leonardo's drawings. Ask them to brainstorm why the design could not be built until the twentieth century. **LS** Logical

Answers to Your Turn
1. Without science, we would not have the knowledge needed to make technological advances.
2. Answers may vary. Possible topics students may choose include parachutes, military weapons, swing bridges, other flying machines, and an underwater diving device.

SECTION 2

The Way Science Works

❯Focus

This section introduces critical thinking skills, steps of scientific methods, scientific tools, and the SI system of measurement.

Bellringer

Use the Bellringer transparency to prepare students for this section.

Demonstrate

Are They the Same? For this demonstration you will need distilled water, isopropyl alcohol (70%), stick lighter or long matches, and beakers (200 mL). Allow 15 minutes.

Safety Caution: Wear gloves and safety goggles before lighting the isopropyl alcohol. Be sure to perform this demonstration a safe distance away from students.

Before class, pour a small amount of isopropyl alcohol into a 200 mL heat-resistant beaker. Pour an equal amount of distilled water into another beaker.

Review the steps of scientific methods with students. Ask students to think of ways to test the hypothesis that the two liquids differ even though they look the same. Then dim the lights. Place the beakers on a safe, flat surface. Using a stick lighter or a long match, try to set the water on fire. Then carefully set the alcohol on fire. Students will see that it burns with a blue flame. Ask students: What conclusion can be drawn from this demonstration? (Careful observation and testing was the only way to distinguish between the two liquids.) **LS Visual**

Key Ideas

> ❯ How can I think and act like a scientist?
> ❯ How do scientists measure things?

Key Terms

critical thinking
scientific methods
variable
length
mass
volume
weight

Why It Matters

Thinking logically, like a scientist, can help you solve problems that you face in your daily life. For example, you can use critical thinking to help you find the best deals when shopping.

In our society, riding a bicycle or driving a car is considered almost a survival skill. The skills that we think are important, however, change over time, as society and technology change.

Science Skills

Pouring liquid into a test tube without spilling it may be a useful skill in the lab, but other skills are more important in science. **❯ Identifying problems, planning experiments, recording observations, and correctly reporting data are some of the most important science skills.** The most important skill is learning to think creatively and critically.

Critical thinking helps you solve problems logically.

Imagine that you and a friend want to buy some popcorn but also want to save money. Would you buy the large container of popcorn, shown in **Figure 1**, and share? Or would you buy two small containers of popcorn? We often assume that products in larger packages are a better value than products in smaller packages. However, we need to make observations and compare data to see if this assumption is true.

How many ounces are in each container of popcorn? What is the price of each container? How many ounces would you get if you bought two small containers? How much would two small containers cost? If you approach the problem by asking questions, making observations, and using logic, you are using **critical thinking.**

Figure 1 Logical decision making is important in scientific processes and in everyday life. **Which size of popcorn is the better deal?**

Key Resources

** Teaching Transparencies**
TM2 Scientific Method
TM3 SI Base Units
TM4 SI Prefixes
TM69 Other Commonly Used Units

Visual Concepts
Hypothesis
SI
Volume
Scientific Method

Datasheet
Making Observations

Science Skills Worksheets
Classifying Items
Understanding Symbols
Testing a Hypothesis
Reading to Evaluate and Identify Bias
Dimensional Analysis
SI Units and Conversions Between
    Them

Math Skills Worksheet
Conversions

Cross-Disciplinary Worksheet
Connection to Language Arts—The
    Structure of Medical Terminology

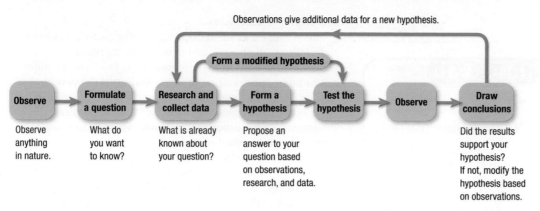

Observations give additional data for a new hypothesis.

Form a modified hypothesis

Observe → **Formulate a question** → **Research and collect data** → **Form a hypothesis** → **Test the hypothesis** → **Observe** → **Draw conclusions**

Observe anything in nature.

What do you want to know?

What is already known about your question?

Propose an answer to your question based on observations, research, and data.

Did the results support your hypothesis? If not, modify the hypothesis based on observations.

Scientists use scientific methods to solve problems.

Critical thinking is used to solve scientific problems as part of scientific methods. **Scientific methods** are general ways to help organize your thinking about questions. Using scientific methods helps you find and evaluate possible answers. Scientific methods are sets of procedures that scientists use, as **Figure 2** shows, but the steps can vary.

Although the set of procedures used depends on the nature of the question to be answered, most scientific questions begin with observations—simple things that you notice. For example, you may notice that when you open a door, you hear a squeak. You ask the question, "Why does this door make noise?" You may gather data by checking other doors. You form a hypothesis, a possible answer that you can test. For example, you may think that the doorknob is the source of the squeak. Your hypothesis might then be: The doorknob makes this door squeak.

✓ Reading Check Do you have to use exactly the same steps every time that you use a scientific method?

Scientists test hypotheses.

Scientists test a hypothesis by doing a *controlled experiment*. In a controlled experiment, **variables** that can affect the outcome of the experiment are kept constant, or controlled, except the one(s) that you want to measure. Only the results of changing the given variables are observed.

The more things that you change at a time, the harder it is to make reliable conclusions. You may stop the squeak if you remove the knob and oil the hinges, but you will not find the cause of the squeak. You may not find the answer on the first try, even if you test one thing at a time. If the door makes noise after you take the knob off, was your experiment a failure?

Figure 2 A scientific method is a general description of scientific thinking rather than an exact path for scientists to follow.

READING TOOLBOX

Spider Map
Create a spider map for scientific methods. Label the center "Scientific methods," and create a branch for each step.

critical thinking (KRIT i kuhl THINGK ing) the ability and willingness to assess claims critically and to make judgments on the basis of objective and supported reasons

scientific methods (SIE uhn TIF ik METH uhdz) a series of steps followed to solve problems including collecting data, formulating a hypothesis, testing the hypothesis, and stating conclusions

variable (VER ee uh buhl) a factor that changes in an experiment in order to test a hypothesis

Answer to caption question

The smaller container of popcorn is the better deal. If you buy two small containers, you spend $4.00 for 160 oz. of popcorn. If you buy the large container, you get the same amount of popcorn for $4.50. (Note that ounces are used here to describe the volume of the containers rather than the weight of the popcorn.)

Teaching Key Ideas

Thinking Like a Scientist After the students are settled in class, quickly turn out the lights. Ask the students what they think they should do to figure out what's going on with the lights. Do they think you should call the electrical company? Do they think you should check if the lights are on in other classrooms in the building? Suppose all the lights are off in the building, can they see other lights on in other buildings nearby? What does that mean? Students' thoughts should be directed toward asking questions, collecting data and making observations, and drawing conclusions.
LS Verbal/Logical

READING TOOLBOX

Spider Map Sample spider map:

observe
formulate a question
research and collect data

Scientific Methods

form a hypothesis
test the hypothesis
draw conclusions

Differentiated Instruction

Basic Learners

Applying Scientific Methods Point out to students that scientists may use different scientific-method steps in different situations. Have students work independently or in small groups to design a way to apply scientific methods to buying peanut butter, a CD, or a book. Ask volunteers to share their examples with the class, and discuss the differences between them. Point out that there can be more than one valid approach for any given problem. You could also emphasize that thinking like a scientist is a valuable skill in any profession. **LS** Logical

MISCONCEPTION ///ALERT\\\

Scientific Methods Your students may think of scientific methods as a set of rigid steps for solving problems. When teaching this section, emphasize that there is no single scientific method. Scientific methods are ways of thinking critically about a question and testing possible answers to that question by collecting data and making unbiased observations. Scientists approach problems from a variety of viewpoints. They conduct their research using available tools, data, time, and people. Research often leads to new problems and new hypotheses, which require further research and testing.

QuickLab

Teacher's Notes Place the candles in a fireproof container, such as an aluminum pie plate, before lighting them. Encourage students to observe the changes as they occur.

Materials per Group
• candle
• fireproof container
• matches

Answers

2. Answers may vary. Students should note the color of the wax and the wick. Students should also record the length and/or thickness of the candle.

4. Answers may vary. Students may make qualitative assessments of the heat and light produced, the height of the flame, the color of the flame, changes in the wick, the rate of consumption of the wax, and any color change as the solid wax melts. They may also note that the wax changes from a solid to a liquid near the flame.

Teaching Key Ideas

Learning Through Failure With experiments such as the discovery of X rays, it is easy to see that an unexpected result is not a failure. Point out to students that even experiments that do not work can be learning experiences. For example, when a chemical reaction fails to occur and the student or scientist can determine why the reaction did not occur, he or she will have learned more about the reaction being tested.

QuickLab 10 min

Making Observations

❶ Get an ordinary **candle** of any shape and color.

❷ Record all the observations that you can make about the candle.

❸ Light the candle, and watch it burn for 1 min. Use caution around open flame.

❹ Record as many observations about the burning candle as you can.

❺ Share your results with your class, and find out what other types of observations were made.

Experiments test ideas.

Even if an experiment does not give the desired results, it is not a failure. All observations of events in the natural world can be used to revise a hypothesis and to plan tests of a different variable. For example, once you know that the doorknob did not cause the squeak, you can change your hypothesis, "Will oiling the hinges stop the noise?" Often, as with Roentgen's X rays, experimental results are surprising and lead scientists in new directions.

Scientists always keep in mind the question to be tested. To keep from making false conclusions, they must carefully search for bias in the way that they plan and analyze their experiments. Scientists who work together tend to see things the same way. So, it is important for them to publish their results in scientific journals, where other experts can review the work. Research that has been examined by other scientists is said to have been *peer reviewed.*

Scientists should keep in mind their personal bias and report conflicts of interest. Government agencies, private foundations, and industrial interests often fund scientific research. Scientists must guard against reaching false conclusions that may be desired by the groups that give them money.

Some questions, such as how Earth's climate has changed over millions of years, cannot be answered by doing experiments in the laboratory. Instead, geologists make observations all over Earth. As **Figure 3** shows, scientists collect many samples to study so that they can form conclusions based on a convincing amount of data.

✓ **Reading Check** Why should scientists publish their results?

Figure 3 Researchers can analyze the chemicals that are trapped inside the many ice-core samples they collect to learn about past climates on Earth.

Why It **Matters**

A Surprising Discovery Experiments do not always turn out as expected. In 1856, William Henry Perkin was experimenting to synthesize the antimalarial drug quinine from coal tar. He didn't succeed, but he accidentally made aniline purple (mauve), the first synthetic dye.

Differentiated Instruction

Advanced Learners

Evaluating Advertising Claims Have students bring in advertisements for products and services that contain claims that can be verified by measurement. Challenge students to identify the claim, describe the types of measurements that could verify or discredit the claim, and indicate which units they would use for the measurements. In addition, students should provide examples of sample data that would verify the claim and examples of sample data that would call the claim into question.
LS Logical

Figure 4 Kitt Peak National Observatory in Arizona has a large assortment of telescopes that can be used to study distant galaxies or the sun. This photograph of the Fireworks galaxy (NGC 6946) was taken with an optical telescope. This spiral galaxy is almost 20 million light-years from Earth.

Scientists use special tools.

Logical thinking is not the only skill used in science. Sometimes, scientists make observations by using tools made through advancements in technology. Scientists must know how to use these tools, what the limits of the tools are, and how to interpret data from them.

Astronomers, for example, use *telescopes* with lenses and mirrors. Some of the observatories shown in **Figure 4** hold telescopes that magnify objects that appear small because they are far away, such as distant galaxies. Other observatories contain telescopes that do not form pictures from visible light. *Radio telescopes* <u>detect</u> the radio waves given off by distant objects. Some of the oldest, most distant objects in the universe have been found with radio telescopes.

Chemists use *spectroscopes* to separate light into a rainbow of colors. By using this tool, chemists can learn about a substance from the light that it absorbs or gives off. Physicists use *particle accelerators* to make fragments of atoms move very fast. Then, they let the pieces smash into atoms or parts of atoms. Scientists learn about the structure of atoms from the data that they collect.

Units of Measurement

Mathematics is the language of science, and mathematical models rely on accuracy. ❯ **Scientists use standard units of measure that together form the International System of Units, or SI.** *SI* stands for the French term *le Système Internationale d'Unités*. This system allows scientists around the world to compare observations and calculations.

Academic Vocabulary

bias (BIE uhs) a way of thinking that favors one outcome or interpretation

detect (dee TEKT) to discover the presence of

SCINKS.
www.scilinks.org
Topic: SI Units
Code: HK81390

Why It **Matters**

Exploring Space Kitt Peak National Observatory (KPNO) operates a diverse collection of optical, infrared, and radio telescopes. While optical telescopes are used primarily at night, or in the daytime to study the sun, some infrared telescopes and almost all radio telescopes can be used around the clock to study all types of astronomical objects. Since it was founded in 1958, KPNO has been involved with several major discoveries about the universe. For example, scientists studying spiral galaxy rotation curves first discovered dark matter at KPNO. Dark matter may be more common than the more familiar matter in the universe. Measurements of radio emissions led to the discovery of ancient high redshift galaxies. Research at KPNO has helped explain how the environment influences the evolution of galaxies, how fast the universe is expanding, and how stars are formed. KPNO is located about 56 miles southwest of Tucson, AZ.

Differentiated Instruction

English Learners

Deciphering Words The word *scope* comes from the Greek word *skopein*, meaning "to see." Tell the students that scientists use many different scopes to see things that can't be seen with unaided eyes. For example, a telescope gets its name from the Greek prefix *tele-*, meaning "distant." So, a telescope is a tool for seeing far. Have the students use a dictionary to find out what is seen by a microscope (small objects), a retinoscope (the retina of the eye), a kaleidoscope (varied patterns formed by glass and plastic reflected off mirrors) and a hygroscope (changes in atmospheric humidity). **LS** **Verbal**

Teaching Key Ideas

Units of Measurement Be sure students understand the need to use appropriate units when measuring. Many, but not all, scientists use SI units. Pose a question to students, such as "How far is it to the nearest bathroom?" Help them realize there is a big difference between 15 m (about 49 ft) and 15 ft, especially for the person who needs the information. Another possibility might be, "How far is it to the sun?" The answer could be 8.3, but 8.3 what? Meters? Kilometers? Actually, it is 8.3 light-minutes. A light-minute is the distance that light travels in 1 min—18,000,000,000 m (about 11 million miles). **LS** **Logical**

Why It **Matters**

A Costly Mistake A $125-million space probe, the Mars Climate Observer, crashed on Mars in 1999 because key numbers were calculated by one group in English units while another group used metric units. The difference was not clearly communicated between the groups. Because critical maneuvers necessary to place the spacecraft in a proper Mars orbit relied on calculations involving numbers from both groups, and conversions between the two systems were not applied, the probe crashed and was destroyed.

Figure 5 SI Base Units

Quantity	Unit	Abbreviation
Length	meter	m
Mass	kilogram	kg
Time	second	s
Temperature	kelvin	K
Electric current	ampere	A
Amount of substance	mole	mol
Luminous intensity	candela	cd

Figure 6 Prefixes for Large Measurements

Prefix	Symbol	Meaning	Multiple of base unit
kilo-	k	thousand	1,000
mega-	M	million	1,000,000
giga-	G	billion	1,000,000,000

Figure 7 Prefixes for Small Measurements

Prefix	Symbol	Meaning	Multiple of base unit
deci-	d	tenth	0.1
centi-	c	hundredth	0.01
milli-	m	thousandth	0.001
micro-	μ	millionth	0.000001
nano-	n	billionth	0.000000001

SI units are used for consistency.

Suppose that one of your classmates estimates that she drinks three gallons of water in a week. Another classmate thinks that he drinks about 350 ounces of water in a week. Who drinks more water? When all scientists use the same system of measurement, sharing data and results is easier. SI is based on the metric system and uses the seven SI base units that are listed in **Figure 5.**

You may have noticed that the base units do not include area, volume, pressure, weight, force, speed, and other familiar quantities. Combinations of the base units are called *derived units* and are used for these measurements.

For example, suppose that you want to order carpet for a floor that measures 8.0 m long and 6.0 m wide. You know that the area of a rectangle is its length times its width.

$$A = l \times w$$

The area of the floor can be calculated as shown below.

$$A = 8.0 \text{ m} \times 6.0 \text{ m} = 48 \text{ m}^2 \quad \text{(or 48 square meters)}$$

The SI unit of area, m^2, is a derived unit.

SI prefixes are used for very large and very small measurements.

Look at a meterstick. How would you express the length of a bird's egg or the distance you traveled on a trip in meters? The bird's egg might be 5/100 m, or 0.05 m, long. The distance of your trip could have been 800,000 m. To avoid writing a lot of decimal places and zeros, you can use SI prefixes to express very small or very large numbers. These prefixes are all *multiples* of 10, as **Figure 6** and **Figure 7** show.

If you use the prefixes, you can say that the bird's egg is 5 cm (1 *centi*meter equals 0.01 m) long and your trip was 800 km (1 *kilo*meter equals 1,000 m) long. Note that the base unit of mass is the kilogram, which is a multiple of the gram.

It is easy to convert SI units to smaller or larger units. Remember that for the same measurement, you need to use more of a small unit or less of a large unit. For example, if a person's height is 1.75 m, the same height in centimeters would be 175 cm, a larger number. But 1.75 m and 175 cm express the same quantity.

✔ **Reading Check** Why are SI prefixes used?

Differentiated Instruction

Basic Learners

Standard Units of Measure Separate students into small groups. Ask each group to pick an object to use as a unit of measurement. Allow students to use anything, including their hands, feet, or a pencil. Have each group find the length of the classroom in their chosen unit of measure. Ask each group to share their result with the class. Then list all the units of measurements used on the chalkboard. Lead a discussion about why it is so important to use standard units of measure. **LS** **Interpersonal/Kinesthetic**

You can convert between smaller and larger numbers.

To convert to a smaller unit, multiply the measurement by the ratio of units so that you get a larger number. For example, to change 1.85 m to centimeters, multiply by 100.

$$1.85 \text{ m} \times \frac{100 \text{ cm}}{1 \text{ m}} = 185 \text{ cm}$$

To convert to a larger unit, as in the question in **Figure 8,** divide the measurement by the ratio of units so that you get a smaller number. To change 185 cm to meters, divide by 100.

$$185 \text{ cm} \times \frac{1 \text{ m}}{100 \text{ cm}} = 1.85 \text{ m}$$

Figure 8 The size of bat that a player uses depends on his or her height. If a bat is 0.81 m long, it is 81 cm long. **If you use a bat that is 76 cm long, how long is your bat in meters?**

Math Skills Conversions Within SI

The width of a soccer goal is 7 m. What is the width of the goal in centimeters?

Identify
List the given and unknown values.
	Given:
	    length in meters (l) = 7 m
	Unknown:
	    length in centimeters = ? cm

Plan Determine the relationship between units.	Look at **Figure 5** through **Figure 7.** You can find that 1 cm = 0.01 m. So, 1 m = 100 cm. You must multiply by 100 because you are converting from meters, a larger unit, to centimeters, a smaller unit.
Solve Write the equation for the conversion. Insert the known values into the equation, and solve.	*length in cm* = m $\times \dfrac{100 \text{ cm}}{1 \text{ m}}$ *length in cm* = 7 m $\times \dfrac{100 \text{ cm}}{1 \text{ m}}$ *length in cm* = 700 cm

Practice

1. Write 55 *deci*meters as meters.
2. Convert 1.6 *kilo*grams to grams.
3. Change 2,800 *milli*moles to moles.
4. Change 6.1 amperes to *milli*amperes.

For more practice, visit **go.hrw.com** and enter keyword **HK8MP.**

Practice **Hint**

➤ If you have done the conversions properly, all the units above and below the fraction will cancel except the units that you need.

Math Skills

Answers to Practice

1. 55 dm × (1 m/10 dm) = 5.5 m
2. 1.6 kg × (1,000 g/1 kg) = 1,600 g
3. 2,800 mmol × (1 mol/1,000 mmol) = 2.8 mol
4. 6.1 A × (1,000 mA/1 A) = 6,100 mA

Additional Examples
Convert 15 m into:
a. mm
Answer: 15,000 mm
b. km
Answer: 0.015 km
LS Logical

Answer to caption question
0.76 m

Why It **Matters**

Kelvins and Amperes The SI unit of temperature is called the kelvin and the unit of electric current is called the ampere. The kelvin was selected to honor William Thomson (later Lord Kelvin), a Scottish engineer, mathematician, and physicist. Lord Kelvin was a major contributor to the development of the laws of thermodynamics. The ampere was named to honor André-Marie Ampère, a French physicist, who by 1825 had laid the foundation of electromagnetic theory.

MISCONCEPTION
ALERT

Weight and Mass Some students confuse weight and mass, believing that "felt weight" is a characteristic property of an object and that mass is something that "presses down." Emphasize that mass is how much matter an object has, while weight is how hard gravity is pulling on it. Tell students that when astronauts travel to the moon, they have the same mass. However, they weigh less because the moon is smaller (both in size and mass) than Earth. The change in weight is due to a change in gravitational attraction between the astronaut and Earth and the astronaut and the moon.

Figure 9 Quantitative Measurements

	SI unit	Other units	Examples
Time	second (s) 	millisecond (ms) minute (min) hour (h)	Stopwatches measure time precisely. 
Length	meter (m) 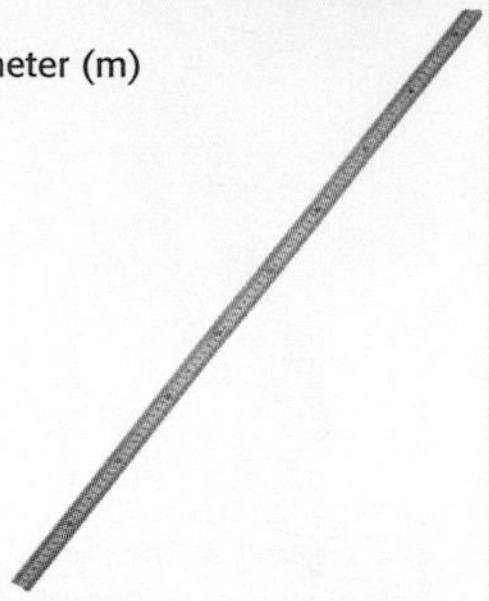	millimeter (mm) centimeter (cm) kilometer (km)	Many diving boards are as long as 4.9 m. 
Mass	kilogram (kg) 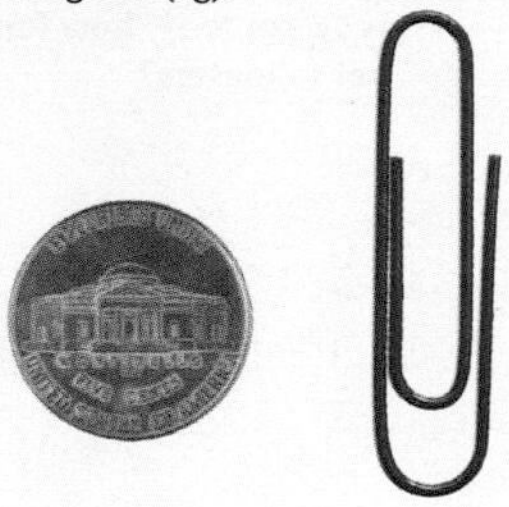	milligram (mg) gram (g)	A CD in its case has a mass of about 100 g.  Mass can be measured by using a triple-beam balance. 
Volume	cubic meter (m^3) 	cubic centimeter (cm^3) milliliter (mL) liter (L)	A liquid's volume can be measured by using a graduated cylinder.   You can find the volume of a dresser by multiplying the length, width, and height.

Differentiated Instruction

Special Education Students

What's the Measure? Ask students to cut pictures of common objects out of magazines. The objects should include solid objects, liquids, small objects, and large objects. Students may glue each picture to a piece of construction paper. Students can determine what properties of the object are to be measured, such as length, mass, volume or weight. They may also choose a unit of measure that would be appropriate for measuring that property of the object. Students can label each picture with the property and unit of measure they chose. This activity can be done individually, in small groups, or with help from a teaching assistant. **LS** Visual

Measurements quantify your observations.

Many observations rely on quantitative measurements. Basic scientific measurements usually answer questions such as "How much time did it take?" and "How big is it?"

Often, you will measure time, **length, mass,** and **volume.** The SI units for these quantities, examples of each quantity, and some of the tools that you may use to measure them are shown in **Figure 9.**

Although someone may say that he or she is "weighing" an object with a balance, **weight** is not the same as mass. Mass is the quantity of matter, and weight is the force with which Earth's gravity pulls on that quantity of matter. Your weight would be less on Mars than it is on Earth, but your mass would be the same on both planets.

In the lab, you will use a graduated cylinder to measure the volume of liquids. The volume of a solid that has a specific geometric shape can be calculated from the measured lengths of its surfaces. Small volumes are usually expressed in cubic centimeters (cm³). One cubic centimeter is equal to one milliliter (mL).

Scientific instruments can measure quantities that are very small. You cannot see the tiny guitar shown in **Figure 10** with the unaided eye. But by using an electron microscope, the width of the strings on the tiny guitar can be measured. At only about 50 nanometers (nm) wide, these strings are more than 1,000 times as thin as one of your hairs.

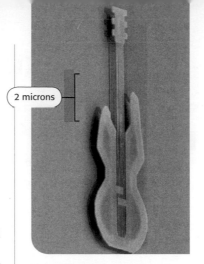

2 microns

Figure 10 This tiny guitar is made of silicon and is only about 10 micrometers long.

length (LENGKTH) a measure of the straight-line distance between two points

mass (MAS) a measure of the amount of matter in an object

volume (VAHL yoom) a measure of the size of a body or region in three-dimensional space

weight (WAYT) a measure of the gravitational force exerted on an object

---

Section 2 Review

KEY IDEAS

1. **Describe** a hypothesis and how it is used. Give an example of a hypothesis.

2. **Explain** why you should not call any experiment a failure.

3. **Explain** the difference between SI base units and SI derived units. Give an example of each.

4. **List** three examples each of objects that are commonly measured by mass, by volume, and by length.

CRITICAL THINKING

5. **Applying Concepts** Explain why scientific methods are said to involve critical thinking.

6. **Summarizing Information** Why do you think that it is a good idea to limit an experiment to test only one variable at a time whenever possible?

7. **Understanding Relationships** Using scientists' tools as an example, explain how science and technology depend on each other.

8. **Drawing Conclusions** An old riddle asks, "Which weighs more, a pound of feathers or a pound of lead?" Answer the question, and explain why you think that people sometimes answer incorrectly.

Math *Skills*

9. Convert the following measurements to grams.
   a. 50 kilograms
   b. 4,630 micrograms

10. Convert 0.42 kilometers to meters.

› Close

Reteaching Key Ideas

Tools Have students consider some of the tools used for measuring time, length, mass, and volume and suggest other tools for those quantities. (An hourglass, a sundial, and an atomic clock can be used for measuring time. Length can also be measured with a surveyor's wheel or a car odometer. A double-pan balance and a single-beam balance that students may have seen in medical offices are both used to measure mass. Volume can be measured with pipettes and syringes.) **LS** **Logical**

Formative Assessment

Which of the following quantities is measured using an SI base unit?

A. weight (Incorrect. The unit of weight is a derived unit, the Newton, which is equal to 1 kg m/s².)

B. force (Incorrect. The unit of force is a derived unit, the Newton, which is equal to 1 kg m/s².)

C. mass (Correct. The unit of mass is kg, which is an SI base unit.)

D. work (Incorrect. The unit of work is the Joule, which is equivalent to 1 kg m²/s² and is a derived unit.)

Answers to Section Review

1. A hypothesis is a possible answer to a question that can be tested. An example would be, "I can pass the test if I study at least 5 hours."

2. No experiment should be called a failure since an experiment that produces unexpected results provides a chance to learn something new.

3. An SI base unit is a single unit while a derived unit is a combination of base units. Base units include: seconds, meters, kilograms, kelvins, amperes, moles, and candelas. Examples of derived units include meters squared (m²) and milliliters (mL, cm³).

4. Answers may vary. Sample answers: mass: solid food items, people, and mail; volume: liquid food items, gasoline, shampoo; length: rope, distance, height

5. The scientific method involves critical thinking in that it entails thinking about a problem and making objective judgments about results.

6. It is much easier to determine which factor your experiment depends on if you only check one factor at a time. If you change more than one thing and something unexpected happens, you will not know what caused the result.

7. There are still scientific theories that have not been verified because the tools needed to test these theories do not yet exist.

Answers continued on p. 39A

Organizing Data

⟩ Focus

This section introduces students to techniques for organizing and interpreting data. They learn how to analyze line graphs, bar graphs, and pie charts, and how to use scientific notation and significant figures in problem solving. The difference between precision and accuracy is also covered.

🔊 Bellringer

Use the Bellringer transparency to prepare students for this section.

Demonstrate

Daily Life Activity Ask students to think of something in their daily life that they do each day and to estimate how much time they spend on it. For example, they could estimate how many hours a day they spend on homework, how many hours they sleep every night, what percentage of their free time is spent watching television, or how much they weigh each day. Have them create a data table for the information. After they read this section, have students determine the appropriate type of graph and use it to display their data. They may wish to analyze their graphs for patterns and trends. **LS Intrapersonal**

Key Ideas

⟩ Why is organizing data an important science skill?

⟩ How do scientists handle very large and very small numbers?

⟩ How can you tell the precision of a measurement?

Key Terms

scientific notation

precision

significant figure

accuracy

Why It Matters

Measurements must be reported correctly when building structures such as the Gateway Arch in St. Louis, Missouri.

Being able to read about the experiments that other scientists had performed with the cathode-ray tube helped Roentgen discover X rays. He was able to learn from the data.

Presenting Scientific Data

Suppose that you are trying to determine the speed of a chemical reaction that produces a gas. You could let the gas push water out of a graduated cylinder, as **Figure 1** shows. You read the volume of gas in the cylinder every 20 s from the start of the reaction until there is no change in volume for three readings. You make a table to organize the data that you collect in the experiment. ⟩ **Because scientists use written reports and oral presentations to share their results, organizing and presenting data are important science skills.**

Because you did the experiment, you saw how the volume changed over time. But how can someone who reads your report see how the volume changed? To show the results, you can make a graph.

Experimental Data

Time (s)	Volume of gas (mL)
0	0
20	6
40	25
60	58
80	100
100	140
120	152
140	156
160	156
180	156

Figure 1 You can find the volume of gas that a chemical reaction produces by measuring the volume of water that a gas displaces in a graduated cylinder.

Gas

Water

Chemical reaction

Key Resources

 Teaching Transparencies
G1 Line Graph
G2 Bar Graph
G3 Accuracy and Precision

💿 **Visual Concepts**
Scientific Notation
Significant Figures
Accuracy and Precision
Controlled Experiment and Variable

📋 **Datasheet**
Precision Vs. Accuracy

📋 **Science Skills Worksheets**
Basic Exercises in Logic

Deciding Which Type of Graph Is Appropriate
Evaluating Data
How to Round Numbers
Making a Line Graph
Scientific Notation
Significant Figures

📋 **Math Skills Worksheets**
Writing Scientific Notation
Using Scientific Notation
Using Significant Figures

📋 **Cross-Disciplinary Worksheet**
Integrating Physics—Observing and Experimenting to Find Relationships

Line graphs show continuous changes.

There are many types of graphs that you could use, but which one best shows how the volume changed over time? A *line graph* is a good choice for displaying data that change continuously. Our example experiment has two variables, time and volume. Time is the *independent variable*—you chose the time intervals to take the measurements. The volume of gas is the *dependent variable*—its value depends on what happens in the experiment.

When you make line graphs, you should put the independent variable on the *x*-axis and the dependent variable on the *y*-axis. **Figure 2** is a graph of the data that is in the table in **Figure 1.**

Line graphs clearly show how the data changed during an experiment. A person who has not seen your experiment can look at this graph and know how much the volume of gas increased over time. The graph shows that gas was produced slowly for the first 20 s. From 40 s to 100 s, the rate increased until it became constant. The reaction then slowed down and stopped after about 140 s.

✓ **Reading Check** When should you use a line graph?

Bar graphs compare the values of items.

A *bar graph* is useful when you want to compare similar data for several individual items or events. If you measured the melting temperatures of some metals, your data could be presented in a table. **Figure 3** shows the melting temperatures of five metals presented in a table and as a bar graph. The bar graph clearly shows how large or small the differences in individual values are. A bar graph is a better choice than a line graph for showing single values for many items.

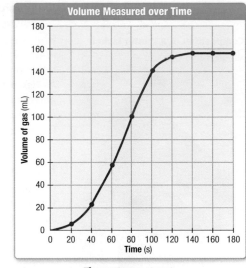

Volume Measured over Time

Figure 2 Data that change are best represented by a line graph. Notice that many in-between volumes can be estimated.

Figure 3 Data that have specific values for various items or events should be represented by a bar graph.

Melting Points of Some Common Metals

Element	Melting temperature (K)
Aluminum	933
Gold	1,337
Iron	1,808
Lead	601
Silver	1,235

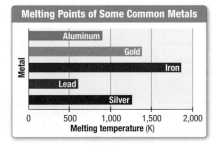

❯Teach

Why It **Matters**

Graphs Convey Information Point out that graphs are used in many fields, not just science. Ask students to look through their social studies or history textbooks to find examples of graphs. Have each student choose one graph to analyze. Instruct them to reproduce the graph and to write a paragraph explaining in words what the graph shows. Their paragraphs should include both specific data and general trends. For example, for a bar or line graph that shows the percent of the U.S. workforce unemployed from 1929 to 1935, a student's paragraph could explain that unemployment levels rose sharply each year until 1933, and then slowly began decreasing. In 1935, the unemployment rate was still much higher than it had been in 1929. Students could also mention the percent of unemployment in 1929 and at its height in 1933. **LS Verbal**

Differentiated Instruction

Advanced Learners

Using a Spreadsheet Have students use a spreadsheet program to create graphs for the data shown in **Figure 1.** Print the graphs, and have students label important points on the graph. Ask students if they have ever seen powers of ten, i.e., exponents, displayed in spreadsheet software or scientific calculators as E values. **LS Logical**

READING TOOLBOX

Visual Literacy As students examine the pie chart in **Figure 4,** ask them the following questions: Which type of fabric makes up the greatest percentage? (Nylon) About what fraction of the sample consists of this element? (2/3) To what value must the sum of percentages in a pie chart always add up? (100) **LS Visual**

Answer to caption question
The total of all the percentages equals 100%.

Teaching Key Ideas
Scientific Notation Scientific notation is a shorthand way to represent where the decimal point is located in a measurement or value. Tell students that a positive exponent, such as 10^4, means to move the decimal point to the right. So $5.4 \text{ m} \times 10^4$ is the same as 54,000 m (move the decimal point four places to the right). A negative exponent means move the decimal point to the left, so 2.54×10^{-3} cm is the same as 0.00254 cm (move the decimal point three places to the left and fill in with zeros). **LS Logical**

Composition of a Winter Jacket

Polyester 30%
Nylon 66%
Spandex 4%

Figure 4 A pie graph is best for data that represent parts of a whole. This pie graph shows the composition of a winter jacket and gives the percentage of each type of fabric in a jacket. **If you add the percentages of each material, what is the total?**

scientific notation (SIE uhn TIF ik noh TAY shuhn) a method of expressing a quantity as a number multiplied by 10 to the appropriate power

www.scilinks.org
Topic: Presenting Scientific Data
Code: HK81213

Pie graphs show the parts of a whole.
A *pie graph* is ideal for displaying data that are parts of a whole. Winter jackets, such as the one shown in **Figure 4,** are made of various fabrics that help keep you warm and dry. A jacket may contain 66% nylon, 30% polyester, and 4% spandex. As **Figure 4** shows, you can draw a pie graph that shows these percentages as a portion of the whole pie. In this case, the pie represents the jacket. To construct a pie graph, refer to Graphing Skills in Appendix B.

Writing Numbers in Scientific Notation
Sometimes, the value of a measurement is very large or very small. For example, the speed of light in space is about 300,000,000 m/s. Suppose that you wanted to calculate the time required for light to travel from Neptune to Earth when Earth and Neptune are 4,500,000,000,000 m apart. To calculate this time, you would divide the distance between Earth and Neptune by the speed of light, as shown in the equations below.

$$t = \frac{\text{distance from Earth to Neptune (m)}}{\text{speed of light (m/s)}}$$

$$t = \frac{4,500,000,000,000 \text{ m}}{300,000,000 \text{ m/s}}$$

There are a lot of zeros to keep track of when performing this calculation. ❯**To reduce the number of zeros in very big and very small numbers, you can express the values as simple numbers multiplied by a power of 10, a method called scientific notation.** Some powers of 10 and their decimal equivalents are shown below.

$$
\begin{aligned}
10^3 &= 1{,}000 \\
10^2 &= 100 \\
10^1 &= 10 \\
10^0 &= 1 \\
10^{-1} &= 0.1 \\
10^{-2} &= 0.01 \\
10^{-3} &= 0.001
\end{aligned}
$$

In scientific notation, 4,500,000,000,000 m can be written as 4.5×10^{12} m. The speed of light in space is 3.0×10^8 m/s. Refer to Math Skills in Appendix B for more information on scientific notation.

✔ **Reading Check** When should you use scientific notation to express a quantity?

Social Studies Connection
Ancient Number Systems Numbers were expressed as powers during the Old Babylonian Empire almost 4,000 years ago. Ancient Babylonians used squares and square roots to solve geometric problems. They expressed large numbers by positions with values of 60^0, 60^1, 60^2, and 60^3 just as we use 10^0, 10^1, 10^2, and 10^3 for ones, tens, hundreds, and thousands.

Differentiated Instruction

Special Education Students
Pie Charts To help students understand the concept of a pie chart, ask them to construct a pie chart that depicts the percentage of students of different ages in the class. Students' pie charts can be constructed of colored paper or colored on white paper. You may wish to have students try other pie charts as well, such as one showing the percentage of ingredients on a food product label. **LS Kinesthetic**

Use scientific notation to make calculations.

When you use scientific notation in calculations, you should follow the math rules for powers of 10. For example, when you multiply two values, you add the powers of 10. When you divide two values, you subtract the powers of 10.

Using these rules can help you calculate more easily the time required for light to travel from Earth to Neptune.

$$t = \frac{4.5 \times 10^{12}\,\text{m}}{3.0 \times 10^{8}\,\text{m/s}}$$

$$t = \left(\frac{4.5}{3.0} \times \frac{10^{12}}{10^{8}}\right) \frac{\text{m}}{\text{m/s}}$$

$$t = (1.5 \times 10^{(12-8)})\,\text{s}$$

$$t = 1.5 \times 10^{4}\,\text{s}$$

READING TOOLBOX

Everyday Words Used in Science

As you read this section, make a list of scientific words that you have heard before, such as *precision*. Then, compare the familiar meaning of the word with the scientific meaning.

READING TOOLBOX

Everyday Words Used in Science

Students may include words such as "precise" or "precision," "accuracy," "significant figures," and "rounding" on their list.

Math **Skills**

Answers to Practice

1. **a.** 8×10^{8} m
   b. 1.5×10^{-3} kg
2. **a.** 4,500 g
   b. 0.0000000199 cm

Additional Examples

Write the following quantities in scientific notation and then convert them to the specified units.

a. 0.0254 m to cm
Answer: 2.54×10^{-2} m; 2.54 cm

b. 6,210 m to km
Answer: 6.21×10^{3} m; 6.21 km

Convert the following quantities to the units specified and then write them in scientific notation.

a. 2.71 µg to kg
Answer: 0.00000000271 kg; 2.71×10^{-9} kg

b. 62,800 km to m
Answer: 62,800,000 m; 6.28×10^{7} m
LS Logical

Math **Skills** **Writing Scientific Notation**

The adult human heart pumps about 18,000 L of blood each day. Write this value in scientific notation.

Identify	**Given:**
List the given and unknown values.	$volume\ (V) = 18{,}000$ L **Unknown:** $volume\ (V) = ? \times 10^{?}$ L
Plan	$V = ? \times 10^{?}$ L
Write the form for scientific notation.	
Solve	Divide 18,000 L by 10,000. The result is 1.8, leaving one digit before the decimal point. So, 18,000 L can be written as $(1.8 \times 10{,}000)$ L. Because $10{,}000 = 10^{4}$, you can write 18,000 L as 1.8×10^{4} L. $V = 1.8 \times 10^{4}$ L
First, find the largest power of 10 that will divide into the known value. Then, write that number as a power of 10. Insert the values that you obtained into the form.	

Practice

1. Write the following measurements in scientific notation.
   a. 800,000,000 m   **b.** 0.0015 kg
2. Write the following measurements in long form.
   a. 4.5×10^{3} g   **b.** 1.99×10^{-8} cm

For more practice, visit **go.hrw.com** and enter keyword **HK8MP**.

Practice Hint

> To use a shortcut for scientific notation, move the decimal point and count the number of places it is moved. To change 18,000 to 1.8, move the decimal point four places to the left. The number of places that the decimal is moved is the correct power of 10.

$$18{,}000\ L = 1.8 \times 10^{4}\ L$$

> When a quantity smaller than 1 is converted to scientific notation, the decimal moves to the right and the power of 10 is *negative*. To express 0.0000021 m in scientific notation, move the decimal point to the right.

$$0.0000021\ m = 2.1 \times 10^{-6}\ m$$

Why It Matters

Big and Small The mass of the sun is about 2,000,000,000,000,000,000,000,000,000,000 kg. In contrast, the mass of a single electron is 0.000000000000000000000000000911 kg.

These examples can be used to illustrate the value of scientific notation. In scientific notation, the electron's mass is expressed as 9.11×10^{-25} kg, and the sun's mass is expressed as 2×10^{30} kg.

Math **Skills**

Using Calculators If your students use calculators, you may need to review the procedures for dealing with exponents. Ask volunteers to demonstrate this for the class with both regular and graphing calculators. **LS** Logical

Math ❯ Skills

Answers to Practice

1. a. $(5.5 \times 10^4 \text{ cm}) \times (1.4 \times 10^4 \text{ cm}) =$
$(5.5 \times 1.4)(10^{4+4})(\text{cm} \times \text{cm}) =$
$7.7 \times 10^8 \text{ cm}^2$
b. $(4.34 \text{ g/mL}) \times (8.22 \times 10^6 \text{ mL}) =$
$3.57 \times 10^7 \text{ g}$
c. $(3.8 \times 10^{-2} \text{ cm}) \times (4.4 \times 10^{-2} \text{ cm})$
$\times (7.5 \times 10^{-2} \text{ cm}) = (3.8 \times 4.4 \times$
$7.5)(10^{-2+-2+-2})(\text{cm} \times \text{cm} \times \text{cm}) =$
$1.2 \times 10^{-4} \text{ cm}^3$

2. a. $\dfrac{5.2 \times 10^8 \text{ cm}^3}{9.5 \times 10^2 \text{ cm}} = 5.5 \times 10^5 \text{ cm}^2$

b. $\dfrac{6.05 \times 10^7 \text{ g}}{8.8 \times 10^6 \text{ cm}^3} = 6.9 \text{ g/cm}^3$

Additional Examples

Perform the following calculations:

a. $\dfrac{(5.2 \times 10^3 \text{ kg})(4.3 \times 10^3 \text{ m})}{(3.5 \times 10^2 \text{ s})(3.5 \times 10^2 \text{ s})}$

Answer: $1.8 \times 10^2 \text{ kg} \bullet \text{m/s}^2$ (or N)

b. $\dfrac{(3.6 \times 10^3 \text{ kg})(6.5 \text{ m})}{1.5 \times 10^2 \text{ m}^2}$

Answer: $1.6 \times 10^2 \text{ kg/m}$

LS Logical

Math ❯ Skills **Using Scientific Notation**

Your county plans to buy a rectangular tract of land measuring 5.36×10^3 m by 1.38×10^4 m to establish a nature preserve. What is the area of this tract in square meters?

Identify List the given and unknown values.	**Given:** $length\ (l) = 1.38 \times 10^4$ m $width\ (w) = 5.36 \times 10^3$ m **Unknown:** $area\ (A) = ?$ m^2
Plan Write the equation for area.	$A = l \times w$
Solve Insert the known values into the equation, and solve.	$A = (1.38 \times 10^4 \text{ m})\ (5.36 \times 10^3 \text{ m})$ Regroup the values and units as follows. $A = (1.38 \times 5.36)\ (10^4 \times 10^3)\ (\text{m} \times \text{m})$ When multiplying, add the powers of 10. $A = (1.38 \times 5.36)\ (10^{4+3})(\text{m} \times \text{m})$ $A = 7.3968 \times 10^7 \text{ m}^2$ Round the answer. $A = 7.40 \times 10^7 \text{ m}^2$

Practice Hint

❯ Because some scientific calculators and computer math software cannot display superscript numbers, they use E values to display numbers in scientific notation. A calculator may show the number 3.12×10^4 as 3.12 E4. Very small numbers are shown with negative values. For example, 2.637×10^{-5} may be shown as 2.637 E–5. The letter *E* signifies exponential notation. The E value is the exponent (power) of 10. When writing this number on paper, be sure to use the form 2.637×10^{-5}.

Practice

1. Perform the following calculations.
   a. $(5.5 \times 10^4 \text{ cm}) \times (1.4 \times 10^4 \text{ cm})$
   b. $(4.34 \text{ g/mL}) \times (8.22 \times 10^6 \text{ mL})$
   c. $(3.8 \times 10^{-2} \text{ cm}) \times (4.4 \times 10^{-2} \text{ cm}) \times (7.5 \times 10^{-2} \text{ cm})$

2. Perform the following calculations.
   a. $\dfrac{5.2 \times 10^8 \text{ cm}^3}{9.5 \times 10^2 \text{ cm}}$ **b.** $\dfrac{6.05 \times 10^7 \text{ g}}{8.8 \times 10^6 \text{ cm}^3}$

For more practice, visit **go.hrw.com** and enter keyword **HK8MP**.

Using Significant Figures

The **precision,** or exactness, of measurements can vary. What would you use to measure the distances of two long jumps that are very close? If you use a tape measure that is marked every 0.1 m, you could report that both measurements were 4.1 m. But if you use a tape measure that is marked every 0.01 m, you could report more precise values—one jump was 4.11 m, and the other was 4.14 m.

❯ **Scientists use significant figures to show the precision of a measured quantity.** The distance of 4.1 m has two significant figures because the measured value has two digits.

Why It **Matters**

Amazing Accuracy In April of 1999, scientists reported measuring the acceleration due to gravity with an accuracy of three parts in one billion. This is equivalent to measuring the width of Ireland with an accuracy within one millimeter! Scientists measured the acceleration by observing the effect of gravity on extremely cold cesium atoms falling in an "atom fountain." To prevent the atoms' thermal motion from interfering with the measurement, the atoms were cooled to ten billionths of a degree above absolute zero.

Good accuracy (near post) and good precision (close together)

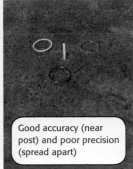
Good accuracy (near post) and poor precision (spread apart)

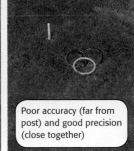
Poor accuracy (far from post) and good precision (close together)

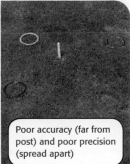
Poor accuracy (far from post) and poor precision (spread apart)

Figure 5 This ring toss can help you visualize how accuracy differs from precision.

Accuracy differs from precision.

Precision and **accuracy** do not have the same meaning, as **Figure 5** shows. If you measure the long jump with a tape measure that has a broken tip, you can still read 4.14 m precisely. But that number is not accurate because it is not the actual distance of the jump. A measured quantity is only as accurate and precise as the tool used to make the measurement. Significant figures tell you how precise a measurement is, but they do not tell you how accurate the measurement is.

Round your answers to the correct significant figures.

When you use measurements in calculations, the answer is only as precise as the least precise measurement used in the calculation—the measurement with the fewest significant figures. For example, suppose that you are going to paint a mural on a wall. To figure out how much paint you will need for your project, you need to know the area of the wall. The measured dimensions are reported to be 8.871 m by 9.14 m.

If you use a calculator to multiply 8.871 by 9.14, the display may show 81.08094 as an answer. But you do not know the area of the room to the nearest 0.00001 m^2, as the calculator showed. To have the correct number of significant figures, you must round off your results. The answer should have the same number of significant figures as the least precise value in the calculation. In this case, the value of 9.14 had three significant figures, so the correct rounded result is $A = 81.1$ m^2.

When adding or subtracting, use this rule: The answer cannot have more decimal places than the least number of decimal places in the calculation. A calculator will add 6.3421 and 12.1 to give 18.4421 as a result. The least precise value was known to 0.1, so round the answer to 18.4.

✔ **Reading Check** When you add measurements, how many significant figures should the result have?

precision (pree SIZH uhn) the exactness of a measurement

significant figure (sig NIF uh kuhnt FIG yuhr) a prescribed decimal place that determines the amount of rounding off to be done based on the precision of the measurement

accuracy (AK yur uh see) a description of how close a measurement is to the true value of the quantity measured

QuickLab ⏱ 10 min

Precision Vs. Accuracy

❶ Crunch **five pieces of paper** into five paper balls.

❷ Try to throw the balls into a **trash bin** that is 2 m in front of you.

❸ Move the trash bin 2 m farther away, and try to throw the balls into the bin.

❹ How accurate were your throws when the bin was 2 m away? How precise were your throws?

❺ When the bin was moved farther away, were your accuracy and precision better or worse?

Teaching Key Ideas
Accuracy Differs from Precision
Students often have difficulty understanding the difference between accuracy and precision. In common speech, these terms are often used inaccurately or interchangeably, which makes it a greater burden for a student to understand the differences. Stress the differences with students using simple examples like a ring toss game or estimating the number of people in a crowd. When discussing accuracy, is "about 2,000" more accurate than "1,383?" If the true value is 1,826, then about 2,000 is more accurate than 1,383 even though 1,383 is a more precise number. **LS Logical**

QuickLab

Teacher's Notes If trash bins are not available have students put a notebook on the floor and aim for it.

Materials per Group
• 5 pieces of paper
• trash bin

Answers
4. Answers may vary. Students should say their throws were accurate if most of the balls made it into or close to the basket, and precise if all of their throws landed in or near the same place.
5. Answers may vary. It is likely that the accuracy and precision will be worse the farther away the student is from the basket.

Differentiated Instruction

Basic Learners

Significant Digits Students may have trouble understanding significant digits. It may be hard for them to remove digits because they feel they are "losing information" or "taking information away." Explain that the extra digits are not accurate and so they do not actually provide real information. Have the students practice the following problems to practice working with significant digits:

Round the following numbers to two significant figures.

a. 13,589
b. 889
c. 0.000241949
d. 0.725

Answers
a. 14,000
b. 890
c. 0.00024
d. 0.72
LS Logical

Answers to Practice

1. **a.** $12.65 \text{ m} \times 42.1 \text{ m} = 5.33 \times 10^2 \text{ m}^2$

   b. $\dfrac{3.244 \text{ m}}{1.4 \text{ s}} = 2.3 \text{ m/s}$

〉Close

Reteaching Key Ideas

Converting Tell the students that they have received data from a colleague about the salinity of water measured from a ship moving from the ocean into a river. After the measurements were taken, the researcher found that the accuracy of the instrument used for the measurements was too low by 0.3% and that only 2 significant units were reliable. Have the students convert the measurements so that they reflect the correct accuracy and precision and plot the data on a line graph. **LS** Visual/Logical

distance from initial measurement (km)	salinity (%)
0	3.22
2	3.05
4	2.57
6	1.15
8	0.81
10	0.20

Answer on p. 39A

Practice Hint

〉 When rounding to get the correct number of significant figures, do you round up or down if the last digit is a 5? The correct way is to round to get an even number. For example, 3.25 is rounded to 3.2, and 3.35 is rounded to 3.4. Using this simple rule, you will generally round up half the time and will round down half the time. See Math Skills in Appendix B for more about significant figures and rounding.

Math **Skills** Significant Figures

Calculate the volume of a room that is 3.125 m high, 4.25 m wide, and 5.75 m long. Write the answer with the correct number of significant figures.

Identify	**Given:**
List the given and unknown values.	$length\ (l) = 5.75 \text{ m}$ $width\ (w) = 4.25 \text{ m}$ $height\ (h) = 3.125 \text{ m}$ **Unknown:** $volume\ (V) = ? \text{ m}^3$
Plan	$volume\ (V) = l \times w \times h$
Write the equation for volume.	
Solve	$V = 5.75 \text{ m} \times 4.25 \text{ m} \times 3.125 \text{ m}$ $V = 76.3671875 \text{ m}^3$ The value with the fewest significant figures has three significant figures, so the answer should have three significant figures. $V = 76.4 \text{ m}^3$
Insert the known values into the equation, and solve.	

Practice

1. Perform the following calculations, and write the answer with the correct number of significant figures.
   a. $12.65 \text{ m} \times 42.1 \text{ m}$
   b. $3.244 \text{ m} \div 1.4 \text{ s}$

For more practice, visit **go.hrw.com** and enter keyword **HK8MP**.

Section 3 Review

KEY IDEAS

1. **Describe** the kind of data that you would display in a line graph.
2. **Describe** the kind of data that you would display in a pie graph. Give an example of data from everyday experiences that could be placed in a pie graph.
3. **Explain** in your own words why scientists use significant figures.

CRITICAL THINKING

4. **Applying Concepts** You throw three darts at a dartboard. The darts all hit the board near the same spot close to the edge but far away from the bull's-eye. Were your throws accurate or precise? Explain.

Math **Skills**

5. Convert the following measurements to scientific notation.
   a. $15{,}400 \text{ mm}^3$
   b. $2{,}050 \text{ mL}$
6. Make the following calculations.
   a. $3.16 \times 10^3 \text{ m} \times 2.91 \times 10^4 \text{ m}$
   b. $1.85 \times 10^{-3} \text{ cm} \times 5.22 \times 10^{-2} \text{ cm}$
7. Make the following calculations, and round the answer to the correct number of significant figures.
   a. $54.2 \text{ cm}^2 \times 22 \text{ cm}$
   b. $23{,}500 \text{ m} \div 89 \text{ s}$

Formative Assessment

Write 0.000065 m in scientific notation.

A. 6.5×10^5 m (Incorrect. The numbers are to the right of the decimal so the exponent must be negative.)

B. 6.5×10^{-5} m (Correct. If you divide 10^{-5} into 0.000065 you end up with 6.5, which has one number in front of the decimal place. You can also think about moving the decimal to the right 5 times to get the exponent –5.)

C. 65 μm (Incorrect. This converts the unit (meters to micrometers), but does not change the measurement into scientific notation.)

D. 6.5×10^{-6} μm (Incorrect. This number is equal to 0.0000000000065 m.)

Answers to Section Review

1. Line graphs are best for continuous changes.
2. Pie charts show the parts of a whole. An example is the percentages of the different types of music that make up a CD collection.
3. Scientists use significant figures because they indicate how precise their calculations really are.
4. The throws were precise because they all hit the dartboard near the same spot. However, they were not accurate because they were not close to the bull's eye.

Answers continued on p. 39A

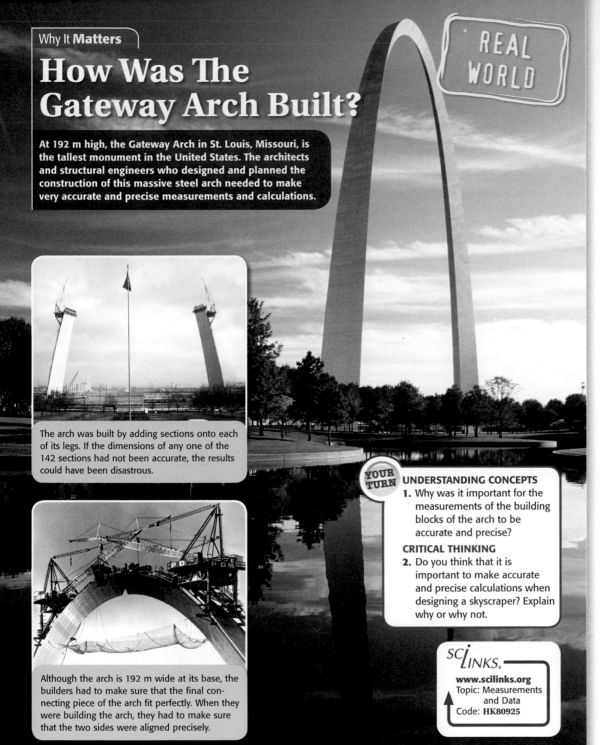

How Was The Gateway Arch Built?

At 192 m high, the Gateway Arch in St. Louis, Missouri, is the tallest monument in the United States. The architects and structural engineers who designed and planned the construction of this massive steel arch needed to make very accurate and precise measurements and calculations.

REAL WORLD

The arch was built by adding sections onto each of its legs. If the dimensions of any one of the 142 sections had not been accurate, the results could have been disastrous.

Although the arch is 192 m wide at its base, the builders had to make sure that the final connecting piece of the arch fit perfectly. When they were building the arch, they had to make sure that the two sides were aligned precisely.

YOUR TURN

UNDERSTANDING CONCEPTS
1. Why was it important for the measurements of the building blocks of the arch to be accurate and precise?

CRITICAL THINKING
2. Do you think that it is important to make accurate and precise calculations when designing a skyscraper? Explain why or why not.

SCILINKS.

www.scilinks.org
Topic: Measurements and Data
Code: HK80925

Why It **Matters**

How Was the Gateway Arch Built?
Completed in 1965, the Gateway Arch was built to commemorate the westward expansion of the United States during the 1800s. Because Lewis and Clark began their historic journey from the banks of the Mississippi River near St. Louis, St. Louis was chosen for the location. The architect was Eero Saarinen. The shape is an inverted catenary curve, which is the same shape a chain makes when it is held at the ends between two supports. Each of the sections is made up of equilateral triangles made of steel that taper in size from the base to the top. The Arch's width is identical to its height.

The final section at the top of the Arch was put in place on a hot fall day. The southern leg was exposed to more heat from the sun than the northern leg, causing it to expand and move away from the northern leg. Several fire trucks were called to hose the southern leg down with water to cool it off. Eventually, the steel contracted enough to maneuver the final piece into place and bolt the Arch together.

Answers to Your Turn

1. If the measurements of the building blocks of the arch were not accurate and precise, the curve or alignment of the arch could have been inaccurate and the pieces at the top might not have matched up.
2. Sample answer: I think it is important for the calculations to be accurate and precise. If they are not, the pieces of the skyscraper might not fit together the way they should and the building could be unstable.

Skills Practice Lab

Teacher's Notes

You may want to use salt and baking soda purchased through a supply company or a grocery store instead of reagent-grade sodium chloride and sodium hydrogen carbonate.

Time Required

1 lab period

Lab Ratings

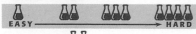

EASY ——————→ HARD

Teacher Prep 🝪🝪
Student Set-Up 🝪🝪
Concept Level 🝪
Clean Up 🝪🝪

Skills Acquired

- Collecting data
- Communicating
- Experimenting
- Identifying/recognizing patterns
- Interpreting
- Measuring
- Organizing and analyzing data
- Predicting

Scientific Methods

In this lab, students will:
- Make observations
- Analyze the results
- Draw conclusions
- Communicate results

Skills Practice

What You'll Do

➤ **Measure** temperature, length, mass, and volume.

➤ **Organize** data into tables and graphs.

What You'll Need

balance, platform or triple-beam

basketball, volleyball, or soccer ball

beaker, small

block or box, small

graph paper

graduated cylinder, 100 mL

meterstick or metric ruler, marked with centimeters and millimeters

rock or irregularly shaped object, small

sodium chloride (table salt)

sodium hydrogen carbonate (baking soda)

string

test tubes (and test-tube holder)

thermometer, wall

Safety

Making Measurements

In scientific investigations, you must collect data accurately so that you can reach valid conclusions. In this laboratory exercise, you will practice this skill by using laboratory tools to measure familiar objects.

Procedure

Preparing for Your Experiment

1 In this laboratory exercise, you will use a thermometer to measure temperature, a meterstick to measure length, a balance to measure mass, and a graduated cylinder to measure volume. You will then determine volume by liquid displacement.

Measuring Temperature

2 At a convenient time during the lab, go to the wall thermometer, and read the temperature. Be sure that no one else is recording the temperature at the same time. On the board, record your reading and the time at which you read the temperature. After you have finished taking your lab measurements, you will make a graph of the temperature readings made by the class.

Measuring Length

3 Measure the length, width, and height of a block or box in centimeters. Record the measurements in a table like the one below. Using the equation below, calculate the volume of the block in cubic centimeters (cm^3), and write the volume in the table.

$$volume = length\ (cm) \times width\ (cm) \times height\ (cm)$$
$$V = l \times w \times h$$
$$V = ?\ cm^3$$

4 Repeat the measurements two more times, and record the data in your table. Find the average of your measurements and the average of the volume that you calculated.

Sample Data Table: Dimensions of a Rectangular Block

	Length (cm)	Width (cm)	Height (cm)	Volume (cm³)
Trial 1				
Trial 2		DO NOT WRITE		
Trial 3		IN BOOK		
Average				

Sample Data: Dimensions of a Rectangular Block

	Length (cm)	Width (cm)	Height (cm)	Volume (cm³)
Trial 1	8.15	4.25	2.20	76.2
Trial 2	8.20	4.25	2.25	78.4
Trial 3	8.15	4.20	2.20	75.3
Average	8.17	4.23	2.22	76.7

5 To measure the circumference of a ball, wrap a piece of string around the ball and mark the end point. Use the meterstick or metric ruler to measure the length of the string. Record your measurements in a table like the one shown below. Using a different piece of string each time, make two more measurements of the circumference of the ball, and record your data in the table.

6 Find the average of the three values, and calculate the difference, if any, of each of your measurements from the average.

Sample Data Table: Circumference of a Ball

	Circumference (cm)	Difference from average (cm)
Trial 1		
Trial 2	DO NOT WRITE	
Trial 3	IN BOOK	
Average		

Measuring Mass

7 Place a small beaker on the balance, and measure the beaker's mass. Record the value in a data table like the one below. Measure to the nearest 0.01 g if you are using a triple-beam balance and to the nearest 0.1 g if you are using a platform balance.

8 Move the balance rider to a setting that will give a value 5 g more than the mass of the beaker. Add sodium chloride (table salt) to the beaker a little at a time until the balance just begins to swing. You now have about 5 g of salt in the beaker. Wait until the balance stops moving, and record in your table the total mass of the beaker and the sodium chloride (to the nearest 0.01 g or 0.1 g). Subtract the mass of the beaker from the total mass to find the mass of the sodium chloride.

9 Repeat steps 7 and 8 two times, and record your data in your table. Find the averages of your measurements, and record them in your data table.

10 Make another data table like the one below, but change the name of the substance to "sodium hydrogen carbonate." Repeat steps 7, 8, and 9 using sodium hydrogen carbonate (baking soda), and record your data.

Sample Data Table: Mass of Sodium Chloride

	Mass of beaker and sodium chloride (g)	Mass of beaker (g)	Mass of sodium chloride (g)
Trial 1			
Trial 2	DO NOT WRITE		
Trial 3	IN BOOK		
Average			

Tips and Tricks

Use this lab as an opportunity to discuss significant figures and how they are estimated. Students are instructed to repeat the measuring process three times. This will help students become familiar with the measuring process and will also allow students to better understand the concepts of accuracy, precision, bias, and reproducibility.

Show students how to measure volume properly by reading the bottom of the meniscus. The concept of parallax can also be introduced with a discussion or demonstration of how it affects measurement.

Measuring Temperature

When students are ready to measure temperature, make sure they read the thermometer to the nearest 0.1 °C or 0.5 °C. Placing the thermometer near a window or a heating/cooling vent may produce greater variability.

Measuring Length

Students should be asked to vary the sequence of measurements of the block. The uncertainty of error in measuring each dimension of the block is multiplied when the volume of the block is calculated.

The ball should be kept in a box or otherwise contained so that it is not a hazard. Remind students that while in the lab, everything used is a scientific tool, not a toy. Do not allow students to roll or throw the ball to each other.

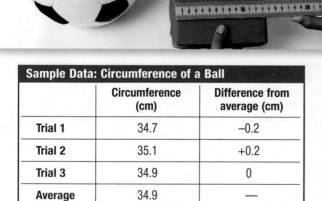

Sample Data: Circumference of a Ball

	Circumference (cm)	Difference from average (cm)
Trial 1	34.7	−0.2
Trial 2	35.1	+0.2
Trial 3	34.9	0
Average	34.9	—

Sample Data: Mass of Sodium Chloride

	Mass of beaker and sodium chloride (g)	Mass of beaker (g)	Mass of sodium chloride
Trial 1	60.10	55.20	4.90
Trial 2	59.90	55.20	4.70
Trial 3	60.45	55.20	5.25
Average	60.15	55.20	4.95

Skills Practice Lab

Measuring Mass

The differences in behavior between the granular salt and the powdery baking soda may cause differences in students' ability to measure 5 g of each solid.

Measuring Volume

A demonstration or discussion of how to read a meniscus should be incorporated into this step.

Measuring Volume by Liquid Displacement

Caution students to dry the cylinder so that it does not slip from their hands. If a small rock or mineral sample is used for liquid displacement, encourage students to tilt the cylinder and gently slide the object down the cylinder's side instead of dropping the rock into the cylinder.

Disposal Information

The salt and soda can be rinsed down the sink with water.

Sample Data: Liquid Volume

	Volume (mL)
Test tube 1	16.5
Test tube 2	15.8
Test tube 3	16.0
Average	16.1

Measuring Volume

11 Fill one of the test tubes with tap water. Pour the water into a 100 mL graduated cylinder.

12 The top of the column of water in the graduated cylinder will have a downward curve. This curve is called a *meniscus* and is shown in the figure below. Take your reading at the bottom of the meniscus. Record the volume of the test tube in a data table like the one below. Measure the volumes of the other test tubes, and record their volumes. Find the average volume of the three test tubes.

Sample Data Table: Liquid Volume

	Volume (mL)
Test tube 1	
Test tube 2	DO NOT WRITE
Test tube 3	IN BOOK
Average	

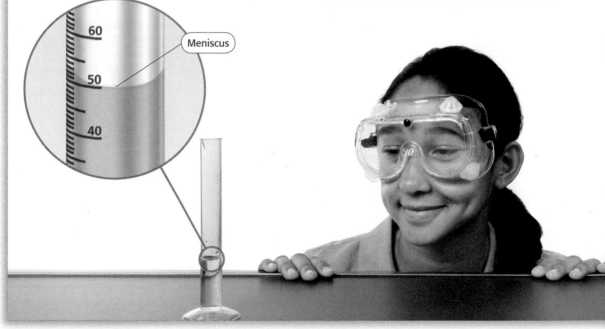

Meniscus

Measuring Volume by Liquid Displacement

13 Pour about 20 mL of tap water into the 100 mL graduated cylinder. Record the volume as precisely as you can in a data table like the one below.

14 Gently drop a small object, such as a rock, into the graduated cylinder. Be careful not to splash any water out of the cylinder. To prevent splashing, you may tilt the cylinder slightly and let the object slide down the side. Measure the volume of the water and the object. Record the volume in your data table. Determine the volume of the object by subtracting the volume of the water from the total volume.

Sample Data Table: Volume of a Solid

	Total volume (mL)	Volume of water only (mL)	Volume of object (mL)
Trial 1		DO NOT WRITE	
Trial 2		IN BOOK	
Trial 3			
Average			

Sample Data: Volume of an Irregular Solid

	Total volume (mL)	Volume of water only (mL)	Volume of object (mL)
Trial 1	17.5	10.5	7.0
Trial 2	14.5	9.0	5.5
Trial 3	21.5	10.0	11.5
Average	17.8	9.8	8.0

Sample Data (additional): Mass of Sodium Hydrogen Carbonate

	Mass of beaker and sodium hydrogen carbonate (g)	Mass of beaker (g)	Mass of sodium hydrogen carbonate (g)
Trial 1	60.35	55.20	5.15
Trial 2	60.20	55.20	5.00
Trial 3	59.90	55.20	4.70
Average	60.15	55.20	4.95

Analysis

1. **Graphing Data** On a sheet of graph paper, make a line graph of the temperatures that were measured with the wall thermometer during the class. Did the temperature change during the class period? If so, find the average temperature, and determine the greatest number of degrees above and below the average.

Communicating Your Results

2. **Drawing Conclusions** On a sheet of graph paper, make a bar graph using the data from the three calculations of the mass of sodium chloride. Indicate the average value of the three calculations by drawing a line across the individual bars that represents the average value. Do the same for the sodium hydrogen carbonate masses. Using the information in your graphs, determine whether you measured the sodium chloride or the sodium hydrogen carbonate more precisely.

3. **Applying Concepts** Suppose that one of your test tubes has a capacity of 23 mL. You need to use about 5 mL of a liquid. Describe how you could estimate 5 mL.

4. **Analyzing Methods** Why is it better to align the meterstick with the edge of the object at the 1 cm mark than at the end of the stick?

5. **Analyzing Methods** Why do you think that using string to measure the circumference of the ball is better than using a flexible metal measuring tape?

Extension

In this lab, you did not investigate time, another basic measurement of science. Design an accurate and precise method for measuring the time required for a certain pendulum to swing back and forth once.

Answer to Analysis

1. Students' graphs should accurately represent their given data. It is unlikely that temperature will vary more than a few degrees during the lab period.

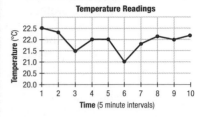

Answers to Communicating Your Results

2. The precision of the measurements for salt and baking soda may vary because of the behavior of the solids. This is an opportunity to reinforce the difference between precision and accuracy.

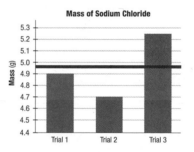

Answers continued on p. 39A

Key Resources

 Virtual Investigation

Classroom Lab Video/DVD

Holt Lab Generator CD-ROM
Search for any lab by type, standard, difficulty level, or time. Edit any lab to fit your needs, or create your own labs. Use the Lab Materials QuickList software to customize your lab materials list.

Differentiated Datasheets
Making Measurements

Observation Lab
Comparing the Densities of Pennies

CBL™ Probeware Lab
Designing a Pendulum Clock

Reteaching Key Ideas

Forming a Hypothesis Remind students that scientists use scientific methods to solve problems that they encounter in the world around them. Scientific methods can just as easily be used to solve problems that students encounter. In fact, they probably use many of the steps of a scientific method without realizing it. Use the exercise on this page to demonstrate how forming a hypothesis can help answer all types of questions about the world, from simple to complex.

Answers to Practice

1. Sample answer: I observed that the printer was plugged in and connected to my computer. However, the ink on the last page that the printer printed before it stopped working was faint. I hypothesize that the printer is not working because it ran out of ink. I can test my hypothesis by changing the ink cartridge in the printer and then testing the printer to see if it will print.

Answers continued on p. 39A

Forming a Hypothesis

One important step of any scientific method is forming a hypothesis. A *hypothesis* is a possible answer to a question. A hypothesis is an educated guess that can be tested with experiments. A good hypothesis attempts to account for any known data and observations. The steps below show you how to form a hypothesis.

❶ **Making Observations**
Suppose that you baked some bread, but it did not rise. You want to form a hypothesis about what happened. First, you need to make observations.

Observations
- The kitchen is drafty.
- The dough was left to rise in a covered, porcelain bowl.
- The oven was set to 350 degrees.
- The yeast is several months old.

❷ **Evaluating Observations**
Think about which observations from step 1 may offer clues to the cause of the problem.

> You have heard that bread dough must rise in a warm room, so the draft could be one reason the bread did not rise.

> Old yeast may not work very well.

Observations
- The kitchen is drafty.
- The dough was left to rise in a covered, porcelain bowl.
- The oven was set to 350 degrees.
- The yeast is several months old.

❸ **Forming Explanations**
Use the list of observations that you made in step 2, and think of some possible explanations about why the bread did not rise.

Possible hypotheses
- The temperature in the room was not warm enough to allow the bread to rise.
- The yeast was too old to work properly.

❹ **Determining Which Explanations Are Hypotheses**
Examine the possible solutions that you listed in step 3. A hypothesis can be tested by an experiment. Because both of these explanations can be tested with experiments, both are valid hypotheses.

Testing my hypotheses
- Experiment 1: Turn up the thermostat, and block any drafts in the kitchen.
- Experiment 2: Use new yeast.

Practice

1. Suppose that your computer printer is not able to print. Make a list of the observations that you might make. Then, follow the steps above to form a hypothesis about what is wrong with the printer.

2. Think of a question that you can investigate by using a scientific method. Follow the steps above to form a hypothesis that may help answer the question.

Key Resources

📁 **Science Skills Worksheets**
Creating a Concept Map
Compiling and Weighing Evidence
Forming a Hypothesis
Testing a Hypothesis
Reading to Evaluate and Identify Bias
Dimensional Analysis
SI Units and Conversions Between Them
Converting Between U.S. Conventional and SI Measurements
Making a Line Graph
Making and Interpreting Bar Graphs and Pie Charts
Scientific Notation

go.hrw.com
SUPER SUMMARY
KEYWORD: HK8INTS

SUMMARY

SUPER SUMMARY

Have students connect the major concepts in this chapter through an interactive Super Summary. Visit **go.hrw.com** and type in the keyword **HK8INTS** to access the Super Summary for this chapter.

Key Ideas

Key Terms

Section 1 The Nature of Science

❯ **How Science Takes Place** A scientist may perform experiments to find a new aspect of the natural world, to explain a known phenomenon, to check the results of other experiments, or to test the predictions of current theories. (p. 5)

❯ **The Branches of Science** Most of the time, natural science is divided into biological science, physical science, and Earth science. (p. 7)

❯ **Scientific Laws and Theories** Theories explain why something happens, and laws describe how something works. Theories and laws are supported by scientific experiments. (p. 9)

science, p. 7
technology, p. 8
law, p. 9
theory, p. 9

Section 2 The Way Science Works

❯ **Science Skills** Identifying problems, planning experiments, recording observations, and correctly reporting data are some of the most important skills in science. Scientists use scientific methods to find answers to their questions. (p. 14)

❯ **Units of Measurement** Scientists use standard units of measure that together form the International System of Units, or SI. (p. 17)

critical thinking, p. 14
scientific methods,
  p. 15
variable, p. 15
length, p. 21
mass, p. 21
volume, p. 21
weight, p. 21

Section 3 Organizing Data

❯ **Presenting Scientific Data** Because scientists use written reports and oral presentations to share their results, organizing and presenting data are important science skills. (p. 22)

❯ **Writing Numbers in Scientific Notation** To reduce the number of zeros in very big and very small numbers, you can express the values as simple numbers multiplied by a power of 10, a method called *scientific notation*. (p. 24)

❯ **Using Significant Figures** Scientists use significant figures to show the precision of a measured quantity. Precision is the degree of exactness of a measurement. (p. 26)

scientific notation,
  p. 24
precision, p. 26
significant figure,
  p. 26
accuracy, p. 27

Differentiated Instruction

Alternative Assessment

Understanding Science Organize students into small groups. Ask them to think of the greatest challenge they see facing science today. Ideas might include increasing energy efficiency, containing waste, space exploration, etc. Ask them to come up with a list of observations about the issue. They should brainstorm about what kind of experiments might be useful for meeting these challenges. Finally, the groups should identify what kind of data might be collected from these experiments and how it might be presented. **LS Interpersonal**

Key Resources

🔲 **Interactive Concept Map**

📁 **Review Resources**
Concept Review Worksheets

📁 **Assessment Resources**
Chapter Tests A and B
Performance-Based Assessment

CHAPTER

1 Review

Reading Toolbox

1. In scientific contexts, precision is the exactness of a measurement, while accuracy is a description of how close a measurement is to the true value of the measured quantity. These two terms are not interchangeable as they are used in science.

Using Key Terms

2. Physical science is no longer the study of only the nonliving world. As knowledge has increased, scientists have learned that the discoveries in one area are applicable to another. For example, chemistry, a physical science, applies to living beings. This field of study is called biochemistry.

3. It has been observed repeatedly, and it does not attempt to explain why the sun sets in the west.

4. The rotation of Earth causing the sun to set could be considered a scientific theory because it is a tested, possible explanation of why the sun sets in the west.

5. Mass is a quantity of matter, whereas weight is the force with which Earth's gravity pulls on that quantity of matter.

6. Scientific notation would be used to express 35 nanometers in terms of meters because it is 0.000000035 m. Using scientific notation decreases the number of zeros that need to be written and decreases the possibility of errors in calculations.

7. The measured mass of the elephant is accurate because it is very close to the actual weight of the elephant.

Understanding Key Ideas

8. d
9. b
10. a
11. d
12. c
13. a
14. c
15. b
16. b
17. b

READING TOOLBOX

1. **Everyday Words Used in Science** In everyday speech, the words *precision* and *accuracy* are often used interchangeably. When these terms are used in science, are their meanings the same as their everyday meanings?

USING KEY TERMS

2. *Physical science* was once defined as "the science of the nonliving world." Explain why that definition is no longer sufficient.

3. Explain why the observation that the sun sets in the west could be called a *scientific law*.

4. Explain why the following statement could be considered a *scientific theory:* The rotation of Earth causes the sun to set.

5. What is *mass,* and how does it differ from *weight*?

6. Some features on computer chips can be as small as 35 nm. Explain why you would use *scientific notation* to express this quantity in meters.

7. The mass of a certain elephant is 3,476 kg. A zoologist who measures the mass of that elephant finds that the mass is 3,480 kg. Is the mass measured by the zoologist *accurate*?

UNDERSTANDING KEY IDEAS

8. Which branch of science is not included in physical science?
   a. physics
   b. chemistry
   c. astronomy
   d. zoology

9. Which science deals most with energy and forces?
   a. biology
   b. physics
   c. botany
   d. agriculture

10. Using superconductors to build computers is an example of
    a. technology.
    b. applied biology.
    c. pure science.
    d. an experiment.

11. A balance is a scientific tool used to measure
    a. temperature.
    b. time.
    c. volume.
    d. mass.

12. Which unit is an SI base unit?
    a. liter
    b. cubic meter
    c. kilogram
    d. centimeter

13. The composition of the mixture of gases that makes up our air is best represented on what kind of graph?
    a. pie graph
    b. bar graph
    c. line graph
    d. variable graph

14. In a controlled experiment,
    a. the outcome is controlled.
    b. one variable remains fixed, and the other variables are changed.
    c. you change one variable throughout the experiment, and the other variables remain fixed.
    d. results are obtained by computer models.

15. Written in scientific notation, 0.000060 s is
    a. 60 s.
    b. 6.0×10^{-5} s.
    c. 6.0×10^{-6} s.
    d. 6.0×10^{4} s.

16. When studying a molecule, a chemist might make a model of the molecule to
    a. know the outcome of the experiment.
    b. help visualize the molecule.
    c. measure the mass of the molecule.
    d. observe the results of a chemical reaction.

17. The maximum depth of a certain lake is 244 m. What is the depth of the lake in kilometers?
    a. 0.0244 km
    b. 0.244 km
    c. 24,400 km
    d. 244,000 km

18. Do scientific laws ever change? Explain.

19. Explain whether or not scientific methods are sets of procedures that scientists follow.

INTERPRETING GRAPHICS The graph below shows how temperature changes during a chemical reaction. Use the graph to answer questions 20–21.

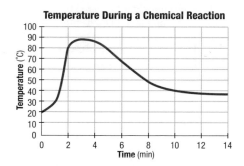

Temperature During a Chemical Reaction

20. Which variable is the dependent variable, and which variable is the independent variable?

21. Why was this data presented in a line graph?

CRITICAL THINKING

22. Applying Ideas Today, scientists must search through scientific journals before performing an experiment or making methodical observations. Where would this step take place in a diagram of scientific methods?

23. Evaluating Assumptions At an air show, you are watching a group of sky divers when a friend says, "We learned in science class that things fall to Earth because of the law of gravitation." What is wrong with your friend's statement? Explain your reasoning.

24. Applying Concepts You report that a friend can go exactly 500 m on a bicycle in 39.46 s. But your stopwatch runs 2 s fast. Explain how your stopwatch affects the accuracy and precision of your measurement.

Graphing Skills

25. Bar Graphs The bar graph below summarizes how a consumer magazine has rated several stereos by price and sound quality. Use the graph to answer the following questions.

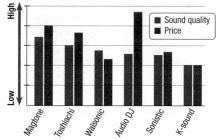

Quality and Price of Portable Stereos

a. Which brand do you think has the best sound for the price?

b. Do you think that sound quality is truly related to price? Explain your answer.

26. Pie Graph The composition of silver solder is 40% silver, 40% tin, 14% copper, and 6% zinc. Show this composition in a pie graph.

Math Skills

27. Writing Scientific Notation Write the following measurements in scientific notation.
   a. 22,000 mg   **b.** 0.0000037 kg

28. Using Scientific Notation Write the answers to the following calculations in scientific notation.
   a. 37,000,000 A × 7,100,000 s
   b. 0.000312 m^3 ÷ 486 s

29. Significant Figures Round the following measurements to the number of significant figures shown in parentheses.
   a. 7.376 m (2)   **b.** 362.00306 s (5)

30. Significant Figures Write the answers to the following calculations. Be sure to use the correct number of significant figures.
   a. 15.75 m × 8.45 m   **b.** 5,650 L ÷ 27 min

Assignment Guide

Section	Items
1	2–4, 8–10, 18, 23
2	5–7, 11, 12, 14, 16, 17, 19, 22
3	1, 13, 15, 20, 21, 24–30

26. Sample pie graph:

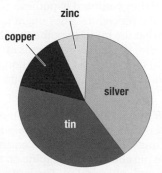

Answers continued on p. 39A

Explaining Key Ideas

18. Scientific laws can change. Scientific laws are based on the results of many experiments and observations. If a new discovery that cannot be predicted by a law is confirmed by repeated experiments, the law may need to be modified to explain the new discovery.

19. Scientific methods are not exact sets of procedures that scientists follow. They are guidelines that describe the process of finding answers in a scientific way, but the exact procedure may vary depending on the questions to be answered.

20. Temperature is the dependent variable because its value depends on what happens in the experiment, and it is on the y-axis. Time is the independent variable because its value does not depend on what happens in the experiment, and it is on the x-axis.

21. A line graph was used because the temperature changed continuously with time during the experiment.

Critical Thinking

22. This step would take place in the research and data collection step.

23. The law of gravitation states that objects fall to Earth; it even shows how to calculate the force. It does not explain why.

24. Because my stopwatch runs 2 s fast, the time that I measured is not accurate. However, the watch can measure to one hundredth of a second, so my measurement is precise.

Graphing Skills

25. a. Walsonic has the sound for the best price.

b. No. If sound quality and price were equal for all of the companies, then sound quality and price would be related. The graph shows that these two properties change relative to one another depending on the company; so sound quality and price are not truly related.

Standardized Test Prep

 TEST DOCTOR

Question 1 Answer C is correct. To find the correct answer, students must divide one kilowatt, or 1.0×10^3 watts, by one milliwatt, or 1.0×10^{-3} watts, to get 1.0×10^6, or one million. Students struggling with this problem should review the SI prefixes.

Question 2 Answer I is correct. Biochemistry combines biology, which is the study of living things with chemistry, which is the study of the way that molecules interact. G is not the best choice because it focuses on living things on a more macroscopic scale than biochemistry. Answer F, botany, focuses on the biology of plants. Answer H, geophysics, is concerned with physical phenomena of the planet Earth.

Question 3 Answer C is correct. Students might answer A if they did not realize that it is important to use SI units in scientific measurement; B if they were confusing the units of volume and distance; or D if they were confusing units of mass and distance. Answers B and D also indicate that students do not understand the system of prefixes used in SI measurements.

Question 4 Answer G is correct. The description is an observed event, not an explanation. Answers F and H both involve an explanation of phenomena. Answer I is incorrect because the universal gravitation equation is a general equation, not a specific result.

Question 5 Full-credit answers should include the following point:
• The result will have three significant figures.

Question 6 Full-credit answers should include the following point:
• A bar graph would best suit this purpose.

Understanding Concepts

Directions (1–4): **For each question, write on a sheet of paper the letter of the correct answer.**

1. How many milliwatts are there in a kilowatt?
   A. 100
   B. 1,000
   C. 1,000,000
   D. 1,000,000,000

2. A student is trying to decide what subject to study. The student is most interested in the way that molecules of living things interact. What should the student study?
   F. botany
   G. biology
   H. geophysics
   I. biochemistry

3. An astronomer is measuring the distance between a comet and the sun. What units of measurement should the astronomer use?
   A. miles
   B. centiliters
   C. kilometers
   D. micrograms

4. The universal gravitation equation describes how the gravitational attraction between two masses is inversely proportional to the distance between them squared. What is the universal gravitation equation?
   F. a hypothesis
   G. a scientific law
   H. a scientific theory
   I. an experimental result

Directions (5–6): **For each question, write a short response.**

5. Density equals mass divided by volume. If a chemist is calculating the density of a substance with a known mass of 23.523 g and a known volume of 17.5 L, how many significant figures will the result have?

6. A demographics researcher needs a graph comparing the populations of the 10 largest cities in the world. What would be the best type of graph to use?

Reading Skills

Directions (7): **Read the passage below. Then, answer the question that follows.**

AIR MAY BE HEAVIER THAN YOU THINK

In 1642, the Italian scientists Rafael Magiotti and Gasparo Berti attempted to produce a vacuum. They filled a long tube with water and plugged both ends. Then, they placed the tube upright into a basin of water and opened the bottom end of the tube. Only a portion of the water in the tube flowed out, and the water still inside the tube stayed at the level of 10.4 m. Air could not have filled the empty space in the tube because no air had been in contact with that space. This result seemed to suggest that a vacuum existed in the space above the water. Magiotti and Berti theorized that the attractive power of that vacuum caused some water to stay in the tube.

Evangelista Torricelli had a different opinion. He hypothesized that air must have weight and that the weight of the air pressing down on the water in the basin kept all of the water in the tube from draining out. He performed the same experiment using mercury, which is 14 times as heavy as water. Mercury stopped flowing out of the tube when the level in the tube reached a height 14 times lower than the height at which water stopped. Thus, Torricelli's idea seemed to be confirmed.

7. What was the initial hypothesis of Magiotti and Berti?
   A. A long tube filled with water, with both ends plugged, was placed in a basin of water.
   B. The weight of air on the basin kept all of the water from flowing out of the tube.
   C. The attractive force of the vacuum drew the water up the tube.
   D. A vacuum can exist.

Question 7 Answer D is correct. Students might answer A if they confused hypothesis with experimental procedure. They might answer B if they confused the initial hypothesis of Magiotti and Berti with the initial hypothesis of Torricelli. They might have chosen C if they thought a hypothesis was an explanation of experimental results.

Question 8 Answer H is correct. To find the correct answer, students must first recognize that since the question deals with percentages of the whole, the pie chart, or the graphic on the left is the one under discussion. The largest wedge in the pie is just under half of the total area, so answer H is most reasonable.

Question 9 Full-credit answers should contain the following points:
• One fertilizer did not work best on every plant.
• The bar graph shows the results of this experiment.
• The vertical axis represents growth. The four clusters of bars represent the four plants. The three different shading patterns represent the three types of fertilizer.
• In the first plant the fertilizer represented by the dark grey bar worked best. In the other three plants the fertilizer represented by the dotted fertilizer worked best.

Interpreting Graphics

The graphs below show two sets of data. Use these graphs to answer questions 8–9.

UNDERSTANDING TYPES OF GRAPHS

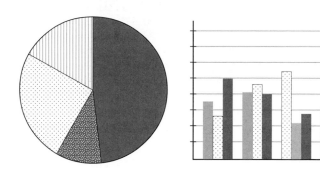

8. One of the graphs shows the percentage of the total mass of each of four compounds in a mixture. If there is more water than any other compound in the mixture, what is the percentage of water in the mixture?

   F. 100%   **H.** 48%

   G. 83%   **I.** 25%

9. One of the graphs shows the results of a fertilization experiment in which four types of fertilizers were applied to groups of three kinds of plants. The plants' average height increase was measured. Was there a single fertilizer that worked best on every plant? How do you know?

The graphic below displays the projected world population in the year 2012, along with the average number of cells in the human body. Use this graphic to answer question 10.

PROJECTED WORLD POPULATION

Estimated world population	👤👤👤👤👤👤👤	👤 1 billion people
Average number of cells in the human body	🦠🦠🦠🦠🦠 🦠🦠🦠🦠🦠	🦠 10 trillion cells

10. In the year 2012, how many human cells will there be in the world?

    A. 7.0×10^7 **C.** 1.43×10^7

    B. 7.0×10^{22} **D.** 1.43×10^{22}

Answers

1. C
2. I
3. C
4. G
5. Answers may vary; see Test Doctor for a detailed scoring rubric.
6. Answers may vary; see Test Doctor for a detailed scoring rubric.
7. D
8. H
9. Answers may vary; see Test Doctor for a detailed scoring rubric.
10. B

Test Tip

When answering short-response or extended-response questions, be sure to write in complete sentences. When you have finished writing your answer, be sure to proofread for errors in spelling, grammar, and punctuation.

Question 10 Answer B is correct. To find the correct answer, students must multiply 7 billion (or 7×10^9) people by 10 trillion (or 1.0×10^{13}) cells per person, to get 7×10^{22} total cells. Students may choose Answer C if they divided 10 trillion by 7 billion. Answer A would result from correctly multiplying the 10 by 7 and incorrectly handling exponents, subtracting them instead of adding them. Answer D results from dividing the number 10 by 7 and then adding the exponents as if using multiplication.

State Resources

For specific resources for your state, visit **go.hrw.com** and type in the keyword **HSHSTR**.

📖 **Test Practice with Guided Reading Development**

Continuation of Answers

Answers continued from p. 12

7. He did not give up after his experiment did not give the results he expected. Instead, he asked more questions and performed more experiments to learn what was causing the glow.

8. A guess or opinion is usually an unsupported statement. A scientific theory uses repeatedly tested results to explain observed events.

9. Answers may vary.

Answers continued from p. 21

8. The correct answer is that both weigh the same. A reason for an incorrect answer might be that mass is confused with volume or density, and a given volume of feathers would be much lighter than the same volume of lead.

9. **a.** 50 kg × (1,000 g/1 kg) = 50,000 g

   b. 4,630 µg × (1 g/1,000,000 µg) = 0.00463 g

10. 0.42 km × (1,000 m/km) = 420 m

Answers continued from p. 28

Answer to Reteaching Key Ideas

distance from initial measurement (km)	salinity (%)
0	3.5
2	3.4
4	2.9
6	1.4
8	1.1
10	0.50

Answers to Section Review, cont.

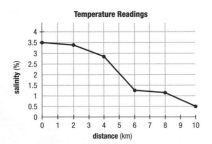

Temperature Readings

5. **a.** 1.54×10^4 mm³

   b. 2.05×10^3 mL

6. **a.** 9.20×10^7 m²

   b. 9.66×10^{-5} cm²

7. **a.** 1.2×10^3 cm³

   b. 2.6×10^2 m/s

Answers continued from p. 33

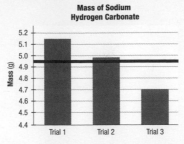

Mass of Sodium Hydrogen Carbonate

3. Answers may vary. One option is to estimate the length of the test tube, divide it into five equal parts, and then fill it 1/5 full.

4. Metersticks may get damaged at the ends and not be accurate.

5. The circumference is more easily measured with the string because it makes contact all around the ball. Most flexible metal tapes do not conform to the surface well enough to make contact and stay in place easily.

Answers to Extension

Answers may vary. Students may suggest using the sound of the pendulum hitting an object as a signal to stop timing when they are looking at a watch. More sophisticated experiments may suggest using the motion of the pendulum itself to stop a timer or using a beam of light to signal the return of the pendulum.

Answers continued from p. 34

2. Sample answer: Will I get to school faster if I take a different route? Observations: I walk to school. The route that I take now is shorter than the other route. There is a park along the route that I currently take to school. The other route has less traffic and fewer streets that I need to cross. Evaluating observations: The distance of the route and the number of streets that I have to cross are most likely to affect the time that it takes me to get to school. Possible hypotheses: 1. The route I take to school now is the fastest because it is the shortest. 2. The other route will be faster because I will not have to wait as long to cross the street. Testing my two hypotheses: For one week, I will time how long it takes me to get to school walking along my current route each day. The following week I will take the other route and time myself each day. I will compare the times to see which route is faster.

Answers continued from p. 37

Math Skills

27. **a.** 2.2×10^4 mg

   b. 3.7×10^{-6} kg

28. **a.** 2.6×10^{14} A•s

   b. 6.42×10^{-7} m³/s

29. **a.** 7.4 m

   b. 362.00 s

30. **a.** 133 m²

   b. 210 L/min

Chemistry

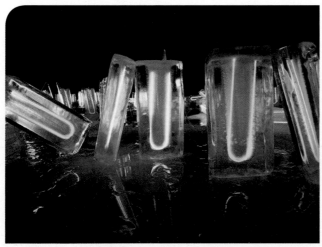

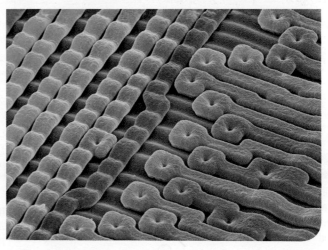

	Standards	Teach Key Ideas

CHAPTER OPENER, pp. 42–44 [50 min.]

SECTION 1 Classifying Matter, pp. 45–50 [50 min.]

> What Is Matter?
> Elements
> Compounds
> Pure Substances and Mixtures

Standards: PS 1a, PS 2b, PS 2c, UCP 1

Teach Key Ideas:
- Bellringer Transparency
- Teaching Transparencies C1 Elements in the Human Body • TM5 Chemical Formula • C2 Types of Mixtures
- Visual Concepts Matter • Element • Atom • Compounds • Molecule • Chemical Formula • Comparing Miscible and Immiscible Liquids

---

SECTION 2 Properties of Matter, pp. 51–58 [50 min.]

> Physical Properties
> Chemical Properties

Standards: PS 3a, UCP 2, UCP 3, SAI 1, SAI 2, ST 2

Teach Key Ideas:
- Bellringer Transparency
- Teaching Transparency TM6 Physical and Chemical Properties
- Visual Concepts Comparing Physical and Chemical Properties • Reactivity • Equation for Density

---

SECTION 3 Changes of Matter, pp. 59–65 [50 min.]

> Physical Changes
> Chemical Changes
> Breaking Down Mixtures and Compounds

Standards: PS 3a, UCP 2, UCP 3, SAI 1

Teach Key Ideas:
- Bellringer Transparency
- Teaching Transparencies C3 Chemical Changes • TM7 Dissolving as a Physical Change
- Visual Concepts Liquid • Heat • Melting • Comparing Physical and Chemical Changes

See also PowerPoint® Resources

Chapter Review and Assessment Resources

- **SE** Science Skills: Converting Units, p. 68
- **SE** Chapter Summary, p. 69
- **SE** Chapter Review, pp. 70–71
- **SE** Standardized Test Prep, pp. 72–73
- Concept Review Worksheets ■
- Chapter Tests A and B ■
- Holt Online Assessment

Basic Learners
- **TE** Presenting Information, p. 46
- **TE** Measuring Volume, p. 53
- **TE** Comparing Densities, p. 55
- Science Skills Worksheets
- Differentiated Datasheets A for Labs and Activities ■
- Study Guide A ■

Advanced Learners
- **TE** Investigating Alloys, p. 48
- **TE** Applying Concepts, p. 49
- **TE** Comparing Planet Densities, p. 53
- **TE** Desalination, p. 60
- Cross-Disciplinary Worksheets
- Differentiated Datasheets C for Labs and Activities ■

CHAPTER Fast Track To shorten instruction because of time limitations, omit Section 3 and the chapter lab.

Key
SE Student Edition
TE Teacher's Edition

🗋 Chapter Resource File
📓 Workbook
🖨 Transparency

💿 CD or CD-ROM
* Datasheet or blackline master available

■ Also available in Spanish

All resources listed below are also available on the Teacher's One-Stop Planner.

Why It Matters	Hands-On	Skills Development	Assessment
Build student motivation with resources about high-interest applications.	**SE Inquiry Lab** Finding Density, p. 43* ■	**TE Reading Toolbox** Assessing Prior Knowledge, p. 42 **SE Reading Toolbox** p. 44	🗋 **Pretest** ■
🗋 **Cross-Disciplinary Worksheets** Real World Applications—Glassmaking • Integrating Biology—What's Special about Indigo? • Science and the Consumer—Is Dry Cleaning Dangerous? • Integrating Earth Science—Uses of Pumice	**TE Demonstration** Comparing Substances, p. 45 **SE Quick Lab** Mystery Mixture, p. 48* ■	**TE Reading Toolbox** Visual Literacy, p. 47 **SE Reading Toolbox** Finding Examples, p. 50	**TE Reteaching Key Ideas** Venn Diagrams, p. 50 **TE Formative Assessment,** p. 50 🗋 **Spanish Assessment*** ■ 🗋 **Section Quiz** ■
SE Aerogel, p. 53 **TE Choosing Materials,** p. 54 **TE Blimps and Dirigibles,** p. 55 **TE Flammability of the *Hindenburg,*** p. 56 **SE Identifying Mystery Substances,** p. 57 🗋 **Cross-Disciplinary Worksheets** Real World Applications—Characteristic Properties • Real World Applications—Choosing Materials for Bicycle Frames • Integrating Environmental Science—Ozone Depletion	**TE Demonstration** Mass of Gaseous Matter, p. 51 **SE Quick Lab** Density of Water, p. 55* ■ **SE Quick Lab** Reactivity, p. 58* ■ **SE Application Lab** Physical Properties of Metals, pp. 66–67* ■ 🗋 **Observation Lab** Measuring Density with a Hydrometer 🗋 **CBL™ Probeware Lab** Comparing the Buoyancy of Different Objects	**SE Reading Toolbox** Finding Examples, p. 52 **SE Math Skills** Density, p. 54 **TE Reading Toolbox** Connecting to Personal Experience, p. 56	**TE Reteaching Key Ideas** Concept Map, p. 58 **TE Formative Assessment,** p. 58 🗋 **Spanish Assessment*** ■ 🗋 **Section Quiz** ■
TE Acid Precipitation, p. 62 **TE Separating Mixtures,** p. 63 **TE Refining Crude Oil,** p. 63 **SE How Is Glass Made?** p. 65 🗋 **Cross-Disciplinary Worksheet** Connection to Language Arts—Hidden Meanings	**TE Demonstration** Observing Changes in Matter, p. 59 **TE Demonstration** Identifying a Physical or Chemical Change, p. 61 **SE Inquiry Lab** Can You Separate a Mixture? p. 63* ■	**TE Reading Toolbox** Paired Reading, p. 60 **TE Science Skills** Comparing and Contrasting, p. 62 **SE Reading Toolbox** Two-Column Notes, p. 64	**TE Reteaching Key Ideas** Comparing and Contrasting, p. 64 **TE Formative Assessment,** p. 64 🗋 **Spanish Assessment*** ■ 🗋 **Section Quiz** ■

See also Lab Generator

See also Holt Online Assessment Resources

Resources for Differentiated Instruction

English Learners
TE Rocks as Mixtures, p. 48
TE Using Charts Physical Properties, p. 52
TE Comparing Different Changes, p. 61
🗋 Differentiated Datasheets A, B, and C for Labs and Activities ■
📓 Study Guide A ■

Struggling Readers
TE Words That Have Multiple Meanings, p. 46
TE Generalizing, p. 49
TE Decoding Word Problems, p. 54
TE Predicting, p. 61
📓 Interactive Reader

Special Education Students
TE Chemical Changes, p. 62

Alternative Assessment
TE Making Models, p. 47
TE Physical Change, p. 60
TE Identifying Materials, p. 69

CHAPTER 2 Matter

Overview

This chapter covers matter, atoms, and elements and distinguishes between elements and compounds. Molecules and chemical formulas are also discussed, as well as the differences between pure substances and mixtures. It also covers physical and chemical properties and characteristic properties. The concept of density and calculations involving density are introduced. Finally, the chapter covers the physical and chemical changes of matter and explains how chemical changes can be detected.

READING TOOLBOX

Assessing Prior Knowledge Students should understand the following concepts:
- scientific laws
- units of measurement
- using significant figures

MISCONCEPTION /// ALERT \\\

Science education research has identified the following misconceptions about matter.
- Students confuse *pure substances* with commercial products that have no additives or that are clean or uncontaminated. (*Pure substance* refers to matter that has only one type of particle, such as an atom in elements, a molecule in covalent compounds, or a formula unit in ionic compounds.)
- Students confuse mass with weight, size, density, or volume. (Mass is the measure of the amount of matter in a sample. The unit for mass is the kilogram (kg).)
- Students confuse changes of state with chemical changes. (Changes of state are physical changes; the composition of the substance before and after a change of state remains the same.)

Chapter Outline

❶ Classifying Matter
  What Is Matter?
  Elements
  Compounds
  Pure Substances and Mixtures

❷ Properties of Matter
  Physical Properties
  Chemical Properties

❸ Changes of Matter
  Physical Changes
  Chemical Changes
  Breaking Down Mixtures and Compounds

Why It **Matters**

This glass is part of a sculpture by artist Dale Chihuly. He blows the glass while it is hot and nearly liquid. Then, he controls its shape as it cools and becomes solid.

Chapter Correlations   *National Science Education Standards*

The following correlations show the National Science Standards that relate to this chapter. For the full text of the standards, see the National Science Education Standards at the front of the book.

PS 1a Matter is made of minute particles called atoms, and atoms are composed of even smaller components. (Section 1)

PS 2b An element is composed of a single type of atom. (Section 1)

PS 2c A substance composed of a single kind of atom is called an element. The atoms may be bonded together into molecules or crystalline solids. A compound is formed when two or more kinds of atoms bind together chemically. (Section 1)

PS 3a Chemical reactions occur all around us, for example in health care, cooking, cosmetics, and automobiles. (Sections 2, 3)

UCP 1 Systems, order, and organization (Section 1)

UCP 2 Evidence, models, and explanation (Sections 2, 3)

UCP 3 Constancy, change, and measurement (Sections 2, 3)

SAI 1 Abilities necessary to do scientific inquiry (Section 3, Application Lab: Physical Properties of Metals)

SAI 2 Understandings about scientific inquiry (Section 2)

ST 2 Understandings about science and technology (Section 2)

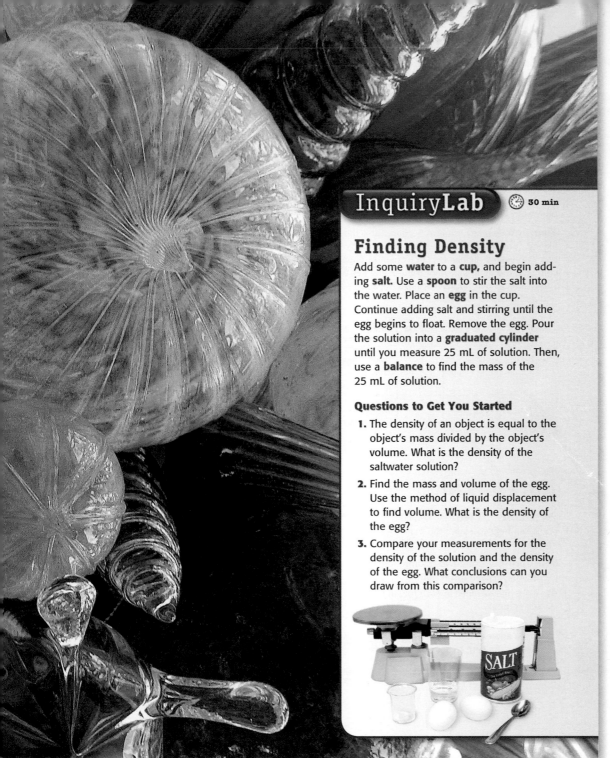

InquiryLab ⏱ 30 min

Finding Density

Add some **water** to a **cup,** and begin adding **salt.** Use a **spoon** to stir the salt into the water. Place an **egg** in the cup. Continue adding salt and stirring until the egg begins to float. Remove the egg. Pour the solution into a **graduated cylinder** until you measure 25 mL of solution. Then, use a **balance** to find the mass of the 25 mL of solution.

Questions to Get You Started

1. The density of an object is equal to the object's mass divided by the object's volume. What is the density of the saltwater solution?

2. Find the mass and volume of the egg. Use the method of liquid displacement to find volume. What is the density of the egg?

3. Compare your measurements for the density of the solution and the density of the egg. What conclusions can you draw from this comparison?

InquiryLab

Teacher's Notes This activity introduces students to the physical property of density.

Materials per Group
- balance
- cup
- egg
- graduated cylinder, 100 mL
- salt
- spoon
- water

Answers

1. Answers may vary. Students should calculate density as mass divided by volume for the solution.

2. Answers may vary. Students should calculate the density of the egg as the mass of the egg divided by the volume of water displaced by the egg.

3. The density of the solution changes as salt is added. At the point when the egg just barely floats in the solution, its density is equal to that of the solution.

Key Resources

📋 **Datasheet**
   Finding Density

READING TOOLBOX

Word Parts

Reactivity, reactive, -ity, the capacity of a substance to combine chemically with another substance. Sample answer: attractiveness, attractive, -ness, the quality or condition of being attractive; hardness, hard, -ness, the state or quality of being firm, solid, and compact

Finding Examples

Students should create 3-column tables. The first column should include the key terms from Section 1. The second column should include examples for each key term. The third column should include words or phrases signaling examples in the text. Sample entry: compound, water; homogeneous mixture, vinegar.

Note Taking

Answers may vary. Students' notes should appear similar to the example shown. The Key Ideas in the first column may correspond to the Key Ideas listed at the beginning of Section 1, but they do not have to match exactly. The detailed notes in the second column should be written in students' own words. Sample entry: How are elements related to compounds? A molecule of a compound is composed of atoms of two or more elements.

READING TOOLBOX These reading tools can help you learn the material in this chapter. For more information on how to use these and other tools, see **Appendix A.**

Word Parts

Suffixes The suffixes *–ity* and *–ness* usually change adjectives into nouns that denote a state, condition, or property. The root can help you understand the word's meaning.

Your Turn Two key terms in Section 2 use the suffix *–ity*. (Key terms in sections are indicated by bold text with yellow highlights.) On a sheet of paper, complete the table below for the missing key term. Then, think of two nouns that have the suffix *–ness*, and add those to your table.

WORD	ROOT	SUFFIX	DEFINITION
density	dense	-ity	the quality of being dense; the ratio of mass to volume
		-ity	

Finding Examples

Words that Signal Examples Examples can help you picture an idea or concept. Certain words or phrases can serve as signals that an example is about to be introduced. Such signals include

- *for example*
- *such as*
- *for instance*

Your Turn Make a list of the key terms from Section 1. See the sample list below. As you read Section 1, add examples that correspond to each key term. If a word or phrase in the text signals the example, add that word or phrase:

KEY TERM	EXAMPLES	SIGNAL WORDS
• element	• carbon • copper	(none)

Note Taking

Two-Column Notes Two-column notes can help you learn the main ideas from each section.

Your Turn Complete two-column notes for the Key Ideas in this chapter.

❶ Write one Key Idea in each row in the left column.

❷ As you read the chapter, add detailed notes and examples in the right column. Be sure to put these details and examples in your own words.

KEY IDEA	DETAIL NOTES
How can matter be classified?	• Matter is either an element, a compound, or a mixture. • Every sample of matter can be classified into one of these three groups.
Why are carbon and copper classified as elements?	• Each element is made of one kind of atom. • Diamonds are made up of carbon atoms.

Classifying Matter

Key Ideas

❭ How can matter be classified?

❭ Why are carbon and copper classified as elements?

❭ How are elements related to compounds?

❭ What is the difference between a pure substance and a mixture?

Key Terms

matter
element
atom
molecule
compound
pure substance
mixture

Why It Matters

By letting a charcoal grill rust outside, you are making a compound. By making a glass of iced tea, you are making a mixture. Understanding matter helps you understand your world.

What do you have in common with this textbook? You are made of matter, and so is this textbook. Your pencil and paper are also made of matter.

What Is Matter?

All of the materials that you can hold or touch are matter. **Matter** is anything that has mass and takes up space. The air that you are breathing is matter even though you cannot see it. Light and sound are not matter. Unlike air, they have no mass or volume.

The study of matter and its changes is what chemistry is about. When chemists study matter, they explore the makeup, properties, changes, and interactions of matter. Chemistry is an important part of your daily life. Many items that you use each day, from soaps to foods and from carbonated drinks to gasoline, are chosen in part for their chemical properties.

One important part of chemistry is classification. The compact discs in **Figure 1** are easy to find because they are classified into groups. All classical music is grouped. Likewise, all pop music is together. Matter can be classified into groups in a similar way. One useful way to classify matter is based on what makes up the matter. ❭ **Every sample of matter is either an element, a compound, or a mixture.** For instance, gold is an element, water is a compound, and a vegetable salad is a mixture. You will learn more about each of these types of matter in this section.

matter (MAT uhr) anything that has mass and takes up space

Figure 1 Compact discs are classified by music type. **What is one way to classify matter?**

Key Resources

Teaching Transparencies
C1 Elements in the Human Body
TM5 Chemical Formula
C2 Types of Mixtures

Visual Concepts
Matter
Element
Atom
Compounds
Molecule
Chemical Formula
Comparing Miscible and Immiscible
Liquids

Datasheet
Mystery Mixture

Science Skills Worksheets
Making and Interpreting Bar Graphs
and Pie Charts
Ratios and Proportions

Cross-Disciplinary Worksheets
Real World Applications—Glassmaking
Integrating Biology—What's Special
about Indigo?
Science and the Consumer—Is Dry
Cleaning Dangerous?
Integrating Earth Science—Uses of
Pumice

❭Focus

This section discusses the composition of matter and the relationship between matter, atoms, and elements. Students learn the differences between elements and compounds, and how molecules are formed. Chemical formulas and symbols are also introduced. The section concludes by comparing pure substances and mixtures, and by classifying mixtures as homogeneous or heterogeneous.

Bellringer

Use the Bellringer transparency to prepare students for this section.

Demonstrate

Comparing Substances You will need charcoal, granulated sugar, and two vials with lids, one labeled "hydrogen" and one "oxygen." Show students the four substances, then tell them that the sugar is made from the other three substances. Ask students how sugar is like the substances that form it, and how it differs. (Few similarities exist. There are differences in appearance, state, and solubility.) Ask students if they think sugar would form if you mixed charcoal, oxygen, and hydrogen. (No.) **LS Visual**

Answer to caption question

Matter can be classified by what it is made of. With this classification system, every sample of matter is either an element, a compound, or a mixture.

Teaching Key Ideas

Elements vs. Compounds Show students the derivation of the word *atom* from its Greek roots, and ask them what idea about matter is conveyed by that meaning.

a–: not

tomos: cutting

The literal meaning: *indivisible*. The idea, which also originated in ancient Greece, is that matter can be subdivided only as small as the elemental particle, the atom. Have students contrast the terms *element* and *compound* given their understanding of the word parts described above. **LS Verbal**

MISCONCEPTION
///ALERT

Elements Students may not realize that the human body is composed of the elements shown in **Figure 3.** They often think that animals are composed only of "skin, bones, and muscle." Clarify that the human body is composed of living cells, which in turn are made of molecules and compounds. Have students identify which element is most prevalent in the human body. (Oxygen) **LS Verbal**

Answer to caption question
Oxygen makes up the largest percentage.

---

element (EL uh muhnt) a substance that cannot be separated or broken down into simpler substances by chemical means

atom (AT uhm) the smallest unit of an element that maintains the chemical properties of that element

molecule (MAHL i KYOOL) a group of atoms that are held together by chemical forces; a molecule is the smallest unit of matter that can exist by itself and retain all of a substance's chemical properties

compound (KAHM POWND) a substance made up of atoms of two or more different elements joined by chemical bonds

Figure 2 Every element is made up of a single kind of atom. Both copper and carbon are elements.

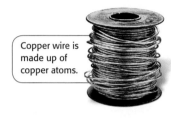

Copper wire is made up of copper atoms.

Diamonds are made up of carbon atoms.

Elements

When wood gets too hot, it chars—its surface turns black. Its surface breaks down to form carbon, whose properties differ from the properties of wood. The carbon will not decompose further by normal chemical processes. Carbon is an **element,** a substance that cannot be broken down into simpler substances by chemical means.

The smallest unit of an element that keeps the element's chemical properties is an **atom. ❯ Each element is made of one kind of atom.** As a result, every known element is unique. The elements carbon and copper are shown in **Figure 2.** Carbon has multiple forms, including diamond and graphite, but each form is made of carbon atoms.

✓ Reading Check **Can elements be broken down into simpler substances?** (See Appendix E for answers to Reading Checks.)

Elements are represented by symbols.

Each element is represented by a one- or two-letter symbol that is used worldwide. Symbols for elements are always a single capital letter or a capital letter followed by a lowercase letter. For example, the symbol for carbon is C, and the symbol for aluminum is Al. The periodic table on the inside back cover of this textbook shows all of the elements and the symbols used to represent them. The elements that make up the human body are shown in **Figure 3.** For example, nitrogen, N, makes up 2.4% of the total weight of the human body.

Elements in the Human Body

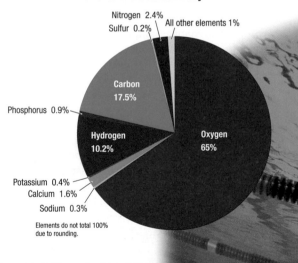

Nitrogen 2.4%
Sulfur 0.2%
All other elements 1%
Carbon 17.5%
Phosphorus 0.9%
Hydrogen 10.2%
Oxygen 65%
Potassium 0.4%
Calcium 1.6%
Sodium 0.3%

Elements do not total 100% due to rounding.

Figure 3 The human body is made up of many elements. **Which element makes up the largest percentage of the total weight of the body?**

Differentiated Instruction

Struggling Readers

Words That Have Multiple Meanings Ask students the difference between asking "What is matter?" and "What's the matter?" (The first question asks about substances, and the second question asks about a problem.) Tell students to search this section for other words that have multiple meanings. (element, compound) Ask students to write the definitions for these words and for their alternate meanings. (Sample answer: element, a distinct group within a larger group; compound, a word made up of other words) **LS Verbal**

Basic Learners

Presenting Information Using **Figure 3** and the periodic table, have students construct a class poster showing the percentages of elements that make up Earth. Students should include the symbols for each element, the percentage of the element found on Earth, and definitions for matter, atom, element, and compound. The students may present the information to the class. They may tape record the information as though they were reporting the information on an educational television channel. **LS Visual**

Atoms that make up a molecule act as a unit.

Atoms can join to make millions of molecules just as letters of the alphabet combine to form different words. A **molecule** is the smallest unit of a substance that behaves like the substance. The atoms of some elements, such as neon, are found uncombined in nature. Other elements, such as oxygen, form molecules that have more than one atom. **Figure 4** shows some molecules that are made of atoms of the same element.

Compounds

One substance that you are familiar with is water. When oxygen and hydrogen atoms combine to form a molecule of water, the atoms act as a unit. Water is an example of a compound. A **compound** is a substance made up of atoms of different elements. **❯ Each molecule of a compound contains two or more elements that are chemically combined.**

When elements combine to make a certain compound, they always combine in the same proportions. For example, a water molecule is always made of two hydrogen atoms and one oxygen atom, as **Figure 5** shows. The compound iron (III) oxide, which is often seen as rust, always has two atoms of iron for every three atoms of oxygen.

Compounds have unique properties.

Every compound differs from the elements that it contains. For example, the elements hydrogen, oxygen, and nitrogen are colorless gases. But they combine with carbon to form nylon, a flexible solid. Likewise, the properties of water differ from those of hydrogen and oxygen, which make up water.

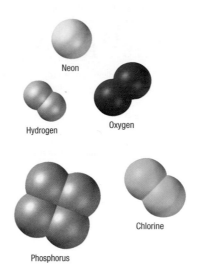

Neon

Hydrogen   Oxygen

Chlorine

Phosphorus

Figure 4 Each of these molecules is made of atoms of the same element. **How many atoms are in one phosphorus molecule?**

Oxygen atom

Hydrogen atoms

Figure 5 Water is an example of a compound. Each water molecule is made up of two hydrogen atoms and one oxygen atom.

Teaching Key Ideas

Element Ratios in Compounds and Mixtures If students do not understand what is meant by "combine in the same proportions," illustrate this concept with substances whose formulas are already familiar to them. For example, water exists in a ratio represented by the formula H_2O: two atoms of hydrogen to every one atom of oxygen. Explain that it is a definite ratio because all water molecules, regardless of their source, consist of these elements in the same ratio. Have students compare the compositions of compounds and mixtures. For example, describe the composition of water and the composition of a mixture of hydrogen and oxygen gases. (Compounds, such as water, are made up of elements combined in fixed proportions, while the elements in mixtures, which can have variable composition, are not combined in fixed proportions.) **LS Verbal**

Answer to caption question

Each phosphorus molecule is made up of four atoms.

READING TOOLBOX

Visual Literacy Make sure students understand that a molecule may consist of two or more atoms of *different* elements or atoms of the *same* element. Tell them that examples of molecular elements other than those mentioned in the text and **Figure 4** include ozone, O_3, and several different molecules formed from carbon. Have students write a chemical formula for each particle in **Figure 4.** (Ne, H_2, O_2, P_4, Cl_2) **LS Visual**

Differentiated Instruction

Alternative Assessment

Making Models Provide students with several ball-and-stick models of compounds. Model kits or gumdrops and toothpicks can be used. (Remind students to never taste anything in the laboratory.) Be sure that different-colored balls represent different elements. Have students use the models to write formulas for each of the compounds. (Students may not list the elements in the proper order in the compound; accept any formula that indicates the correct number of each type of atom.) **LS Visual**

MISCONCEPTION ALERT

Polyatomic Forms of Elements Students may think that only single atoms are true "elements." As shown in **Figure 4,** explain that the atoms of some elements (e.g., neon) occur singly in nature, and the atoms of other elements combine to form polyatomic molecules (as in O_2 or H_2). Have students compare the particle in **Figure 5** with those in **Figure 4.** Ask them to explain how the models are different. (The model for water has atoms of different colors, while the other molecules are each made up of atoms of a single color.) **LS Visual**

QuickLab

Teacher's Notes The size of the strips can be adjusted to better fit the cups that students will be using. You might want students to wear lab aprons during this activity. This activity works best if students are given a variety of brands of markers. Brands that are known to work include Mr. Sketch®, Vis-à-vis®, Crayola Washable®, and Flair®. Test the markers for suitability. This procedure (called chromatography) can be used to identify a sample. Students can determine the type of marker you used by comparing the pattern of colors on your paper with the pattern on theirs.

Materials per Group
• coffee filter
• cup, clear plastic
• marker, black and water soluble
• pencil
• tape
• water

Answers to Analysis
1. The ink in the dot separated into several colors and moved up the paper.
2. Answers may vary. If several varieties of markers are used, differences in the order and colors of ink can be seen.
3. The process involved is a physical change. The colors of ink can be separated without changing their chemical makeup.

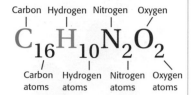

Carbon   Hydrogen   Nitrogen   Oxygen

$$C_{16}H_{10}N_2O_2$$

Carbon   Hydrogen   Nitrogen   Oxygen
atoms   atoms   atoms   atoms

Figure 6 The chemical formula for a molecule of indigo shows that it is made of four elements. **How many atoms are in a molecule of indigo?**

pure substance (PYOOR SUHB stuhns) a sample of matter, either a single element or a single compound, that has definite chemical and physical properties

mixture (MIKS chuhr) a combination of two or more substances that are not chemically combined

Chemical formulas represent compounds.

Indigo is the dye first used to turn blue jeans blue. The *chemical formula* for a molecule of indigo, $C_{16}H_{10}N_2O_2$, is shown in **Figure 6.** A chemical formula shows how many atoms of each element are in a unit of a substance. The number of atoms of each element is written as a *subscript* after the element's symbol. If only one atom of an element is present, no subscript number is used.

Numbers placed in front of a chemical formula show the number of molecules. So, three molecules of table sugar are written as $3C_{12}H_{22}O_{11}$. Each molecule of sugar contains 12 carbon atoms, 22 hydrogen atoms, and 11 oxygen atoms.

Pure Substances and Mixtures

The word *pure* often means "not mixed with anything." For example, pure grape juice contains the juice of grapes and nothing else. In chemistry, the word *pure* has another meaning. A **pure substance** is matter that has a fixed composition and definite properties.

The composition of grape juice is not fixed. Grape juice is a mixture of pure substances, such as water and sugars. A **mixture** is a combination of substances that are not chemically combined. ❯**Elements and compounds are pure substances, but mixtures are not.** A mixture can be physically separated into its parts. The parts of a pure substance are chemically combined and cannot be physically separated.

✔ **Reading Check** Why are compounds classified as pure substances?

QuickLab   **Mystery Mixture**   ⏱ 10 min

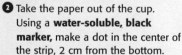

Procedure
❶ Place a **pencil** on a **clear plastic cup.** Use **scissors** to cut a strip of paper (3 cm × 15 cm) from a **coffee filter.** Wrap one end around the pencil. Attach the paper with **tape.**
❷ Take the paper out of the cup. Using a **water-soluble, black marker,** make a dot in the center of the strip, 2 cm from the bottom.
❸ Pour **water** in the cup to a depth of 1 cm.

❹ Lower the paper into the cup. Keep the dot above the water.
❺ Remove the paper when the water is 1 cm from the top of the paper. Record your observations.

Analysis
1. What happened as the paper soaked up the water?
2. Which colors make up the black ink?
3. Is the ink-making process a physical change, or is it a chemical change? Explain.

Differentiated Instruction

English Learners
Rocks as Mixtures Explain that granite is a mixture of solids. Give students a hands-on opportunity to study the different mixtures of granite and see how they have different compositions. Ask a granite retailer for a variety of granite samples. Have students arrange the samples according to visible amounts of mica, then by amounts of feldspar, and finally by amounts of quartz. (Samples should be arranged from darkest to lightest.) **LS Kinesthetic**

Advanced Learners
Investigating Alloys Have students learn about solid-in-solid solutions of metals by asking them to research an alloy, such as brass. Encourage students to investigate how the alloy is manufactured and used. Then, have students write a research paper or create a computer presentation about the alloy. **LS Verbal**

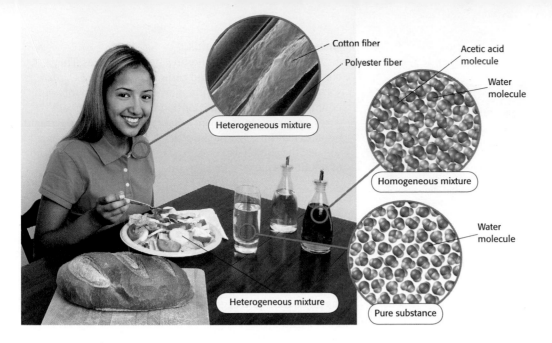

Cotton fiber
Polyester fiber
Heterogeneous mixture

Acetic acid molecule
Water molecule
Homogeneous mixture

Water molecule
Pure substance

Heterogeneous mixture

Mixtures are classified by how well the substances mix.

There are several examples of mixtures in **Figure 7.** Mixtures are defined by how well their substances are mixed. The salad is a mixture of lettuce and vegetables. The shirt is a mixture of cotton and polyester fibers. The vinegar in the dressing is a mixture of water and acetic acid. The water is not a mixture. Water is a pure substance because it has a fixed composition and definite properties.

The vegetables in the salad are not evenly distributed. One spoonful may contain tomatoes. Another spoonful may have cucumber slices. A mixture such as a salad is a *heterogeneous mixture*. The substances in a heterogeneous mixture are not evenly distributed. Some heterogeneous mixtures are harder to recognize. The shirt is a heterogeneous mixture because the cotton and polyester fibers are not evenly distributed.

In a *homogeneous mixture*, the components are evenly distributed. The mixture is the same throughout. For example, vinegar is a homogeneous mixture of evenly-distributed water molecules and acetic acid molecules.

Gasoline is a homogeneous mixture of at least 100 liquids. The liquids in gasoline are *miscible,* or able to be mixed. On the other hand, if you shake a mixture of oil and water, the oil and water will not mix well. The water will settle out. Oil and water are *immiscible*. You can see two layers in the mixture.

Figure 7 Mixtures are all around you. **What is the difference between the mixtures and the pure substance shown? What is the difference between the two types of mixtures?**

Integrating **Biology**

Indigo The pure substance indigo is a natural dye made from plants of the genus *Indigofera*, which are in the pea family. Before synthetic dyes were developed, indigo plants were widely grown in Indonesia, in India, and in the Americas. Most species of indigo are shrubs that are 1 to 2 m tall and often have small flowers in spikes or clusters. The dye is made from the leaves and branches of the shrubs. Today, most indigo dye is synthetic rather than natural.

Teaching Key Ideas

Classifying Mixtures *Solution* and *homogeneous mixture* are synonymous. Homogeneous mixtures are mixed completely, all the way down to the particles—atoms, molecules, or ions—of the mixed substances. However, *heterogeneous* mixtures are not completely mixed. The words *homogeneous* and *heterogeneous* have the following Greek prefixes:
homo–: same
hetero–: different
So a homogeneous mixture is one that appears the same throughout, and a heterogeneous mixture is one in which differences can be seen.

Answer to caption question

The pure substance, water, has a fixed composition, while each mixture is made up of pure substances in various proportions. The heterogeneous mixtures (salad and shirt) are not mixed uniformly, while the homogeneous mixture (vinegar) contains evenly-distributed water and acetic acid molecules.

MISCONCEPTION ALERT

Miscibility Many students believe that all liquids can "mix together." Clarify that only miscible liquids (e.g., ethylene glycol and water) can dissolve in each other. Such substances form a homogeneous liquid mixture called a *solution*. Other pairs of liquids, such as oil and vinegar, are immiscible. This means they form two layers, with the denser liquid on the bottom.

Differentiated Instruction

Advanced Learners

Applying Concepts Explain that dry cleaning isn't really dry. That is, it involves liquid solvents instead of water to dissolve stains. A very simple form of dry cleaning involves dipping fabrics in kerosene and then in gasoline to clean them. While both substances are excellent degreasers, they are also dangerous because of their flammability. Ask students to infer why it is difficult to remove greasy stains from fabrics with water-based cleaners. (Fats, greases, and oils are insoluble in water, so it is difficult to remove them from fabrics with water-based washing.) **LS** Logical

Struggling Readers

Generalizing After reading this section, have groups defend or reject one of these generalizations: *All solutions are mixtures. All mixtures are solutions.* Have students find headings, main ideas, and examples in the text to strengthen their position. (Sample answer: The substances in a mixture are not chemically combined. A homogeneous mixture is a solution. A salad is a mixture, but not a homogeneous mixture.) Explain that readers and scientists make generalizations based on evidence. **LS** Logical

Finding Examples Examples are specific things that illustrate ideas. Have students list four examples of gas-liquid mixtures. (Carbonated drinks, cold water, foam, raw meringue) **LS** Logical

Close

Reteaching Key Ideas

Venn Diagrams Make a Venn diagram using the following terms: compounds, elements, heterogeneous mixtures, homogeneous mixtures, matter, mixtures, and pure substances. **LS** Visual

Formative Assessment

What can chemical formulas tell you about the compounds they represent?

A. They tell what state the compound is at room temperature. (Incorrect. State cannot be determined by a chemical formula.)

B. They give the number and kinds of atoms in a molecule of the compound. (Correct. The chemical symbols represent the kinds of elements, and the subscripts represent the number of atoms.)

C. They indicate what kinds of substances can undergo a chemical change to produce the compound. (Incorrect. Chemical formulas don't indicate reactants that form the products they represent.)

D. They provide safety information for properly handling chemicals. (Incorrect. A safety or hazard label will provide this information.)

READING TOOLBOX

Finding Examples
Make a list of all of the examples given on this page. Use signal words such as *for example,* but also look for unmarked examples. Next to each example, write the general idea that the example represents.

Gases can mix with liquids.

Carbonated drinks are homogeneous mixtures. They contain sugar, flavorings, and carbon dioxide gas, CO_2, dissolved in water. This example shows that gases can mix with liquids. Liquids that are not carbonated can also contain gases. For example, if you let a glass of cold water sit overnight, bubbles may form inside the glass. The bubbles form when some of the air that was dissolved in the cold water comes out of solution as the water warms up.

Carbonated drinks often have a foam on top. The foam is a gas-liquid mixture. The gas is not dissolved in the liquid but forms tiny bubbles in the liquid. The bubbles join to form bigger bubbles that escape from the foam and cause it to collapse.

Some foams are stable and last for a long time. For example, if you whip egg whites with air, as shown in the photograph on the left in **Figure 8,** you get a foam. When you bake the foam, the liquid egg white dries and hardens, as shown in the photograph on the right. The solid foam is meringue.

Figure 8 The meringue in this pie is a mixture of air and liquid egg white that has been beaten and then heated to form a solid foam.

Section 1 Review

KEY IDEAS

1. **Describe** matter, and explain why light is not classified as matter.

2. **State** the relationship between atoms and elements. Are atoms and elements matter?

3. **Define** *molecule,* and give examples of molecules formed by one element and molecules formed by two elements.

4. **State** the chemical formula of water.

5. **List** the two types of pure substances.

CRITICAL THINKING

6. **Classifying** Classify each of the following as an element or a compound.
   a. sulfur, S_8 c. carbon monoxide, CO
   b. methane, CH_4 d. cobalt, Co

7. **Making Comparisons** How are mixtures and pure substances alike? How are they different?

8. **Drawing Conclusions** David says, "Pure honey has nothing else added." Susan says, "The honey is not really pure. It is a mixture of many substances." Who is right? Explain your answer.

Answers to Section Review

1. Matter has mass and occupies space. Light has neither mass nor volume, nor is it made up of atoms.

2. An atom is the smallest unit of an element that has that element's properties. Both atoms and elements are matter.

3. A molecule is the smallest unit of a substance that keeps all of the physical and chemical properties of that substance. Oxygen (O_2) is an example of a molecule formed by atoms of one element. Water (H_2O) is an example of a molecule formed by atoms of two elements.

4. H_2O

5. elements, compounds

6. a. element
   b. compound
   c. compound
   d. element

7. Both can contain atoms of more than one element. A pure substance, such as water, has the same composition throughout and definite properties. The composition of a mixture, such as air, can vary because a mixture contains more than one pure substance.

8. David's statement reflects the common meaning of "pure." Susan's use of the word "pure" is more correct scientifically because honey is a mixture of several different compounds.

Properties of Matter

Key **Ideas**

❯ Why are color, volume, and density classified as physical properties?

❯ Why are flammability and reactivity classified as chemical properties?

Key **Terms**

melting point

boiling point

density

reactivity

Why It **Matters**

Properties determine uses. For instance, the properties of a substance called *aerogel* enable it to trap fast-moving comet particles.

❯Focus

In this section, students learn about the physical and chemical properties of matter, and how materials are suited for different uses based on these properties. They also perform calculations involving the physical property of density. The section concludes with an explanation of characteristic properties.

When playing sports, you choose a ball that has the shape and mass suitable for your game. It would be hard to play soccer with a football or to play softball with a bowling ball. The properties of the balls make the balls useful for different activities.

Physical Properties

Shape and mass are examples of *physical properties*. Some other physical properties are color, volume, and texture. The balls in **Figure 1** have different physical properties. ❯**Physical properties are characteristics that can be observed without changing the identity of the substance.** For example, you can determine the color, mass, and shape of a ball without changing the substance that makes up the ball.

Physical properties are often very easy to observe. For instance, you can easily observe that a tennis ball is yellow, round, and fuzzy. Matter can also be described in terms of physical properties that are not as obvious. For example, a physical property of air is that it is colorless.

Physical properties can help identify substances.

Because many physical properties remain constant, you can use your observations or measurements of these properties to identify substances. For example, you recognize your friends by their physical properties, such as height and hair color. At room temperature and under atmospheric pressure, all samples of pure water are colorless and liquid. Pure water is never a powdery green solid. The physical properties of water help you identify water.

Figure 1 The physical properties of these balls make the balls useful in different sports. **How many physical properties can you observe?**

Bellringer

Use the Bellringer transparency to prepare students for this section.

Demonstrate

Mass of Gaseous Matter Disprove the misconception that air and gases have no mass by comparing the mass of an inflated balloon and a deflated balloon. First, have a pair of students measure the mass of a deflated balloon and record the mass on the board. Next, have one student blow up and tie the balloon. Then, ask students to measure the mass of the inflated balloon and record the mass on the board. Discuss the discrepancy between the numbers. Ask students to explain where the extra mass of the inflated balloon came from. (The extra mass is the mass of the air inside the balloon.) Explain that mass is a physical property because you can determine it without having to change the substance. **LS** Logical

Answer to caption question

Answers could include size, shape, color, texture, and density.

Key Resources

 Teaching Transparency
TM6 Physical and Chemical Properties

Visual Concepts
Comparing Physical and Chemical Properties
Reactivity
Equation for Density

Datasheets
Finding Density
Reactivity

Science Skills Worksheet
Rearranging Algebraic Equations

Math Skills Worksheet
Density

Cross-Disciplinary Worksheets
Real World Applications—Characteristic Properties
Real World Applications—Choosing Materials for Bicycle Frames
Integrating Environmental Science—Ozone Depletion

Finding Examples Review with students the words that can signal an example: *for example, such as,* and *for instance.* Have students skim the first paragraph on this page for one of these signal words and indicate what property is exemplified. (For example, states of matter for water.)

MISCONCEPTION ALERT

Specific Temperatures of Phase Changes Students often have the misconception that changes of state such as freezing, melting, or vaporizing are not connected to a specific temperature. Clarify the terms *melting point* and *boiling point*, explaining that they are physical properties that are constant for specific pure substances. Use the chart below for examples of the melting and boiling points of some common substances.

Substance	Melting Point (°C)	Boiling Point (°C)
Gold	1064	3080
Iron	1535	2750
Mercury	−39	357
Nitrogen	−210	−196
Oxygen	−218	−183
NaCl	801	1413
Water	0	100

Finding Examples
As you read this section, find examples for each property that is discussed. Don't forget to use signal words as clues. Make a table of properties and examples.

melting point (MELT ing POYNT) the temperature and pressure at which a solid becomes a liquid

boiling point (BOYL ing POYNT) the temperature and pressure at which a liquid becomes a gas

Academic Vocabulary

durable (DUR uh buhl) able to withstand wear or damage

flexible (FLEK suh buhl) capable of bending easily without breaking

Figure 2 Aluminum is light, strong, and durable, which makes it ideal for use in foil.

Physical properties can be observed or measured.

You can use your senses to observe some of the basic physical properties of a substance: shape, color, odor, and texture. Another physical property that you can observe is *state*—the physical form of a substance. Solid, liquid, and gas are three common states of matter. For example, water can be in the form of solid ice, liquid water, or gaseous steam.

Other physical properties, such as melting point and boiling point, can be measured. The temperature at which a substance changes from a solid to a liquid is the **melting point.** The temperature at which a liquid changes to a gas is the **boiling point.** A characteristic of any pure substance is that its boiling point and its melting point are constant if the pressure remains the same. At sea level, water boils at 100 °C and freezes at 0 °C. At constant pressure, pure water always has the same boiling point and the same melting point. Regardless of the mass or volume of water, the physical properties of the water are the same. This principle is true for all pure substances.

Other physical properties that can be measured are strength, hardness, and magnetism. The ability to conduct electricity or heat is also a physical property. For instance, copper conducts electricity well, while plastic does not.

✓ Reading Check Name five examples of physical properties.

Physical properties help determine uses.

Every day, you use physical properties to recognize substances. Physical properties help you decide whether your socks are clean (odor), whether your books will fit in your backpack (volume), or whether your clothes match (color).

Physical properties are often used to select substances that may be useful. Copper is used in power lines, telephone lines, and electric motors because it conducts electricity well. As **Figure 2** shows, aluminum is used in foil because it is lightweight yet durable and flexible. Car frames are made of steel, which is a strong solid that provides structure. Tires are made of a flexible solid that cushions your ride. Antifreeze is used in car radiators because it remains a liquid at temperatures that would freeze or boil water.

Can you think of other physical properties that help us determine how we can use a substance? Some substances have the ability to conduct heat, while others do not. Plastic-foam cups do not conduct heat well, so they are often used for holding hot drinks. What would happen if you poured hot tea into a metal cup?

Differentiated Instruction

English Learners

Using Charts Physical Properties Have students copy the following chart in their notebooks:

	Object 1	Object 2	Object 3
Color			
Odor			
Texture			
Size			
Shape			
State			

Let students examine several objects that have different physical properties. Ask them to take notes on the color, odor, texture, size, shape, and state of each object. Students may ask for help in describing the objects; encourage them to develop their vocabulary by allowing them to ask you or other students for words. Then, ask each student to describe aloud the physical properties of one of the objects. **LS Visual**

Aerogel

Aerogel, nicknamed "solid blue smoke," is a substance with unique physical properties. For instance, aerogel has the lowest density of any known solid. Air makes up 99.8% of one form of aerogel. Glass is 1,000 times as dense as aerogel! NASA's *Stardust* mission, shown below, used aerogel to trap thousands of tiny, fast-moving comet particles. Aerogel's unique properties enabled it to capture the particles without damaging or vaporizing them.

WEIRD SCIENCE

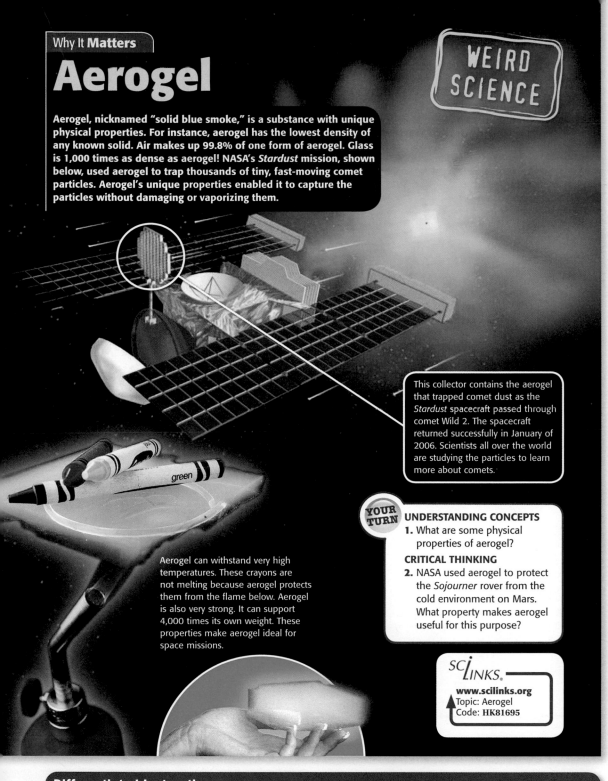

This collector contains the aerogel that trapped comet dust as the *Stardust* spacecraft passed through comet Wild 2. The spacecraft returned successfully in January of 2006. Scientists all over the world are studying the particles to learn more about comets.

Aerogel can withstand very high temperatures. These crayons are not melting because aerogel protects them from the flame below. Aerogel is also very strong. It can support 4,000 times its own weight. These properties make aerogel ideal for space missions.

green

YOUR TURN

UNDERSTANDING CONCEPTS
1. What are some physical properties of aerogel?

CRITICAL THINKING
2. NASA used aerogel to protect the *Sojourner* rover from the cold environment on Mars. What property makes aerogel useful for this purpose?

SCI**LINKS**.

www.scilinks.org
Topic: Aerogel
Code: HK81695

Aerogel Gels are materials that contain a solid molecular network (a skeleton) surrounded by a liquid. Gelatin dessert is a type of gel. The solid skeleton is made of protein and the surrounding liquid contains water. A type of gel known as aerogel has been used in NASA's Stardust mission. It is made from a material called silica alcogel. Silica alcogel is made up of a silica network surrounded by an ethanol solvent. To make aerogel, chemists carefully remove the surrounding liquid, leaving only the intricate silica skeleton. The resulting aerogel is clear, has a very low density, and is an excellent thermal insulator.

Answers to Your Turn

1. very low density, ability to withstand high temperatures, strong
2. It protected the rover from the cold Martian environment because it is a very poor thermal conductor.

Teaching Key Ideas

Characterizing Objects Before students read about physical and chemical properties, have them choose items in the classroom and then identify and classify the properties of each item. Have students share and compare their classifications in a class discussion, which should include a justification for each classification. After students have completed this section, ask them to revisit their answers and to correct any that were inaccurate.
LS Interpersonal

Differentiated Instruction

Advanced Learners

Comparing Planet Densities Using a reference book or the Internet, have the students create a Planet Notebook by listing the planets of the solar system on individual sheets of paper. Each page of this notebook should have a list of the elements or compounds found on each planet. Students can then identify the density of each planet, indicating whether the density is greater or less than that of water. **LS** Visual

Basic Learners

Measuring Volume Review the concept of volume with students. Display several items and have students discuss in groups how the volume of each item can be determined. Some items should be regular in shape so that dimensions can be measured and the volume calculated. Other items should be irregular in shape so that students must estimate or use displacement to find the volume. **LS** Interpersonal

Choosing Materials Explain that some false teeth are made from white plastic, which is relatively inexpensive. False teeth have also been made from gold, animal bone, and composite materials. Composite materials are those in which one material is embedded in another. The resulting material can be stronger than either material by itself. The material chosen for false teeth must have properties that make them suitable for withstanding the physical force of chewing and the chemical stresses resulting from corrosive saliva. Have students do research to identify some physical and chemical properties of different materials used to make false teeth. (Gold is easily shaped and nonreactive. Animal bone is similar in strength and composition to human teeth. Acrylic plastic is nontoxic, hard and durable, waterproof, and noncorrosive.) **LS** Verbal

Math **Skills**

Answers to Practice
1. $D = 16.52 \text{ g}/2.26 \text{ cm}^3 = 7.31 \text{ g/cm}^3$
2. $D = 163 \text{ g}/50.0 \text{ cm}^3 = 3.26 \text{ g/cm}^3$
3. $m = 11.3 \text{ g/cm}^3 \times 6.7 \text{ cm}^3 = 76 \text{ g}$

Additional Examples
The density of oak wood is generally 0.7 g/cm³. If a 35 cm³ piece of wood has a mass of 25 g, is the wood likely to be oak?
Answer: Wood with a density of 0.71 g/cm³ is probably oak.
The density of silver is 10.5 g/cm³. A bracelet made of silver has a volume of 1.12 cm³. What is the bracelet's mass?
Answer: 11.8 g
LS Logical

---

density (DEN suh tee) the ratio of the mass of a substance to the volume of the substance

SCLINKS.
www.scilinks.org
Topic: Density
Code: HK80388

Density is a physical property.

Another physical property is *density*. **Density** is a measurement of how much matter is contained in a certain volume of a substance. The density of an object is calculated by dividing the object's mass by the object's volume.

| **Density equation** | $D = \dfrac{m}{V}$ | $density = \dfrac{mass}{volume}$ |

The density of a liquid or a solid is usually expressed in grams per cubic centimeter (g/cm³). For example, 10.0 cm³ of water has a mass of 10.0 g. Thus, the water's density is 10.0 g for every 10.0 cm³, or 1.00 g/cm³. A cubic centimeter has the same volume as a milliliter (mL).

✔ **Reading Check** What is the density of water in grams per milliliter?

Math **Skills** Density

If 10.0 cm³ of ice has a mass of 9.17 g, what is the density of ice?

Identify	**Given:**
List the given and the unknown values.	mass, $m = 9.17$ g volume, $V = 10.0$ cm³ **Unknown:** density, $D = ?$ g/cm³
Plan	
Write the equation for density.	$density = \dfrac{mass}{volume}$ $D = \dfrac{m}{V}$
Solve	
Insert the known values into the equation, and solve.	$D = \dfrac{9.17 \text{ g}}{10.0 \text{ cm}^3}$ $D = 0.917 \text{ g/cm}^3$

Practice **Hint**

> Problem 3: You can solve for mass by multiplying both sides of the density equation by volume.

$$D = \frac{m}{V}$$

$$DV = \frac{m\cancel{V}}{\cancel{V}}$$

$$m = DV$$

Practice

1. A piece of tin has a mass of 16.52 g and a volume of 2.26 cm³. What is the density of tin?

2. A man has a 50.0 cm³ bottle completely filled with 163 g of a slimy, green liquid. What is the density of the liquid?

3. A piece of metal has a density of 11.3 g/cm³ and a volume of 6.7 cm³. What is the mass of this piece of metal?

For more practice, visit **go.hrw.com** and enter keyword **HK8MP**.

Differentiated Instruction

Struggling Readers

Decoding Word Problems When students are doing word problems, remind them to read the equations like phrases. For example, the equation $D = m/V$ is read as *density is equal to mass divided by volume.* Tell them to find numbers in problems that correspond to the terms in an equation. Then, have students substitute the numbers into the equation phrase and solve the problem. **LS** Verbal

Density of Water

 20 min

Procedure

❶ Find the mass of an empty **100 mL graduated cylinder.**

❷ Pour 10 mL of **water** from a **250 mL beaker** into the graduated cylinder. Use a **balance** to find the mass of the graduated cylinder that contains the water.

❸ Repeat Step 2 for several different volumes of water.

❹ Use **graph paper** or a **graphing calculator** to plot volume (on the *x*-axis) versus mass (on the *y*-axis).

Analysis

1. Estimate the mass of 55 mL of water and 85 mL of water.

2. Predict the volume of 25 g of water and 75 g of water.

3. Use your graph to determine the density of water.

QuickLab

Teacher's Notes Remind students that an accurate measurement of volume requires reading the level of the bottom of the meniscus. Explain that the slope of the line of the graph that shows mass (g) as a function of volume (mL) will be the density in g/mL.

Materials per Group

- balance
- beaker, 250 mL
- graduated cylinder, 100 mL
- graph paper or graphing calculator
- water

Answers to Analysis

1. Predictions should be approximately 55 g and 85 g.
2. Predictions should be approximately 25 mL and 75 mL.
3. Students should choose two points on the graph, and divide the difference in the *x* values by the difference in the *y* values.

Answer to caption questions

Figure 3 hot air

Figure 4 The brick would have less volume.

Density is different from weight.

A substance that has a low density is "light" in comparison with something else of the same volume. The balloons in **Figure 3** float because the denser air sinks around them. A substance that has a high density is "heavy" in comparison with another object of the same volume. A stone sinks to the bottom of a pond because the stone is denser than the water.

The brick and sponge shown in **Figure 4** have similar volumes, but the brick is more massive than the sponge. Because the brick has more mass per unit of volume than the sponge does, the brick is denser. If you held the brick in one hand and the sponge in the other hand, you would know instantly that the brick is denser than the sponge.

Although the denser brick feels heavier than the sponge, weight and density are different. In the example of a brick and sponge, both objects have about the same volume. But compare two objects that have different volumes. Two pounds of feathers are heavier than one pound of steel. But the feathers are less dense than the steel, so two pounds of feathers have a greater volume than one pound of steel does.

Figure 3 Helium-filled balloons float because helium is less dense than air. Hot-air balloons rise for a similar reason. **Which is less dense: hot air or cool air?**

More mass   Denser

Less mass   Less dense

Figure 4 This brick is denser than this sponge because the brick has more matter in a similar volume. **If a brick and a sponge have equal masses, which has less volume?**

Differentiated Instruction

Basic Learners

Comparing Densities To help students understand the concept of density, display two objects of obviously different densities, such as a table-tennis ball and a golf ball. Ask students to describe the objects in terms of relative mass, volume, and density. Then, ask students to formulate a definition of density in their own words. Help them understand that density relates to how heavy something is for its size. **LS Logical**

Why It **Matters**

Blimps and Dirigibles Explain that blimps and dirigibles are types of airships. Airships float in air because the gases they contain are less dense than air. In the early 1900s, airships were commonly used for travel, including trans-Atlantic flights. Airships containing flammable hydrogen were used much less frequently after the 1937 explosion of the *Hindenburg* in New Jersey. Airships in use today contain helium, which is nonflammable. Have students describe the properties of hydrogen and helium that make them suitable or unsuitable for use in airships. (Both gases are less dense than air, which helps the airship float. Because hydrogen is flammable, it is unsuitable.) **LS Verbal**

Teaching Key Ideas

Demonstrating the Properties of Iron You will need a magnet, some rusted steel wool, and some steel wool that is not rusted. Show students both pieces of steel wool. Then show them the effect a magnet has on both pieces of steel wool. Ask students the following questions:

1. Does steel wool have the same composition after it has rusted? (no)

2. Is the ability to rust a chemical or a physical property? (chemical)

3. Does steel wool have the same composition after it is checked with the magnet? (yes)

4. Is attraction to a magnet a chemical or a physical property? (physical)

LS Visual

Answer to caption question

Iron reacts most easily with oxygen.

READING TOOLBOX

Connecting to Personal Experience

Before students read this page, ask them: What is one unfavorable chemical property of iron?

a. its high melting point
b. its nonreactivity with oil and gasoline
c. its reactivity with oxygen to form rust
d. its nonflammability

(Answer: c)

LS Verbal

reactivity (REE ak TIV uh tee) the capacity of a substance to combine chemically with another substance

Figure 5 One chemical property is reactivity. **Which reacts more easily with oxygen: iron, paint, or chromium?**

This hole started as a small chip in the paint, which exposed the iron in the car to oxygen. The iron rusted and crumbled away.

Paint does not react with oxygen, so paint provides a barrier between oxygen and the iron in the car's steel.

This bumper is rust free because it is coated with chromium, which does not react with oxygen.

Chemical Properties

Some elements react very easily with other elements. For example, because magnesium is very reactive, it is used to make emergency flares. Reactive elements are usually found as compounds in nature. Other elements, such as gold, are much less reactive. These elements are often found uncombined. Light bulbs are filled with argon gas because it is not very reactive.

These properties are examples of *chemical properties*. ❯ **A chemical property describes how a substance changes into a new substance, either by combining with other elements or by breaking apart into new substances.** Chemical properties are related to the specific elements that make up substances. Chemical properties are generally not as easy to observe as physical properties.

Flammability is a chemical property.

One chemical property is *flammability*—the ability to burn. For example, wood can be burned to form new substances that have new properties. So, one chemical property of wood is flammability. Even when wood is not burning, it is flammable. A substance always has its chemical properties, even when you cannot observe them. A substance that does not burn, such as gold, has the chemical property of nonflammability.

Reactivity is a chemical property.

Another chemical property is the reactivity of elements or compounds with oxygen, water, or other substances. **Reactivity** is the capacity of a substance to combine with another substance. For example, although iron has many useful properties, its reactivity with oxygen is one property that can cause problems. When exposed to oxygen, iron rusts. You can see rust on the old car shown in **Figure 5.** Why does rust occur? The steel parts of a car rust when iron atoms in the steel react with oxygen in air to form iron(III) oxide. The painted and chromium parts of the car do not rust because they do not react with oxygen. In other words, the elements in steel, paint, and chrome have different chemical properties.

✅ **Reading Check** Name two chemical properties.

Why It Matters

Flammability of the *Hindenburg* The German zeppelin *Hindenburg*, which was filled with hydrogen, caught fire upon landing in 1937. The entire airship was engulfed in flames and crashed to the ground. For decades, most people believed the fire started when a spark ignited the flammable hydrogen. But hydrogen burns with a near-colorless flame, not one that would produce a fireball. Scientists now think that the spark actually ignited the airship's highly flammable outer covering. Have interested students find out about and carry out flame tests in which the color of the flame produced by a burning substance can help identify it. **LS** Visual

Identifying Mystery Substances

FORENSICS

Forensic scientists use physical and chemical properties to identify substances, such as paint, glass, or fibers. For instance, paint chips from an accident can be analyzed to learn about the car from which the paint came. Although this method does not always provide conclusive evidence, it can be used to support further investigation.

1 The first step is to collect the paint chips. This forensic investigator is using a scraping tool to collect paint from a car.

2 This scientist is studying a sample under a microscope to look for small traces of paint left by another car.

3 The next step is to study the collected sample's physical and chemical properties. Physical properties include color, layer sequence, and layer thickness. Chemical properties include pigments and additives.

4 The physical and chemical properties can then be compared with a database of paint properties for different makes and models of automobiles. The investigators can use this information to determine from what kind of car the paint sample most likely came.

YOUR TURN

UNDERSTANDING CONCEPTS
1. Why is layer thickness a physical property?

CRITICAL THINKING
2. What is one situation in which the database of automobile paint would not provide information about the unknown car?

Identifying Mystery Substances
Samples of materials at crime scenes are often collected as evidence. Some tests used to identify these materials can destroy the samples. If only a small amount of material, such as a few tiny chips of paint, is collected from a crime scene, investigators will try non-destructive tests first, including examining the physical properties of paint chips under a microscope. Only when those are found to be inconclusive do they perform the destructive tests. Destructive tests might include dissolving the paint chips in various solvents and testing their reactivity with various chemicals. Determining the chemical properties of materials often involves destructive tests because the chemicals must be chemically changed into other materials during the test.

Answers to Your Turn

1. Layer thickness is a physical property because it can be observed without changing the identity of the substance.
2. If a car had been repainted, the database would not provide accurate information.

QuickLab

Teacher's Notes Label the baking soda and sugar **A** and **B**, respectively.

Materials per Group
- baking soda
- clear plastic cups (2)
- graduated cylinder
- powdered sugar
- vinegar

Answer

4. Baking soda is **A**; powdered sugar is **B**.

❯ Close

Reteaching Key Ideas

 Concept Map Have students make a concept map that organizes the following concepts: properties of matter, physical properties, and chemical properties. Have them include examples of each type of property and the definitions of those examples. **LS Visual**

Formative Assessment

What term describes the mass per unit volume of a substance?

A. melting point (Incorrect. Melting point is the temperature at which a substance changes from a solid to a liquid.)

B. reactivity (Incorrect. Reactivity is the ability of a substance to undergo a chemical change.)

C. density (Correct. Density often has units of grams (mass) divided by liters (volume).)

D. weight (Incorrect. Weight is a measure of the force of gravity on matter.)

QuickLab ⏱ 10 min

Reactivity

❶ Measure 4 g each of **compounds A** and **B.** Place them in separate **clear plastic cups.**

❷ Observe the color and texture of each compound. Record your observations.

❸ Add 5 mL of **vinegar** to each cup. Record your observations.

❹ Baking soda reacts with vinegar, but powdered sugar does not. Which of these two substances is compound A, and which is compound B?

Physical and chemical properties are different.

It is important to remember the differences between physical and chemical properties. You can observe physical properties without changing the identity of the substance. But you can observe chemical properties only in situations in which the identity of the substance changes.

Figure 6 summarizes the physical and chemical properties of a few common substances. Some substances have similar physical properties but different chemical properties. Other substances have similar chemical properties but different physical properties. For example, wood and rubbing alcohol both have the chemical property of flammability, but they have different physical properties.

Figure 6 Comparison of Physical and Chemical Properties

Substance	Wood	Iron	Red dye
		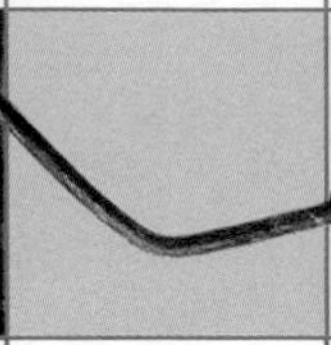	
Physical property	has a grainy texture	bends without breaking	has red color
Chemical property	is flammable	reacts with oxygen to form rust	reacts with bleach; loses color

Section 2 Review

KEY IDEAS

1. **List** two physical properties and two chemical properties.

2. **Identify** the following as physical properties or chemical properties.
   - **a.** reacts with water
   - **b.** is red
   - **c.** is shiny and silvery
   - **d.** melts easily
   - **e.** boils at 100 °C
   - **f.** is nonflammable
   - **g.** has a low density
   - **h.** tarnishes in moist air

CRITICAL THINKING

3. **Applying Concepts** Describe several uses for plastic, and explain why plastic is a good choice for these purposes.

4. **Making Inferences** Suppose that you need to build a raft. Write a paragraph describing the physical and chemical properties of the raft that would be important to ensure your safety.

Math Skills

5. Calculate the density of a rock that has a mass of 454 g and a volume of 100.0 cm³.

6. Calculate the density of a substance in a sealed 2,500 cm³ flask that is full to capacity with 0.36 g of a substance.

7. A sample of copper has a volume of 23.4 cm³. If the density of copper is 8.9 g/cm³, what is the copper's mass?

Answers to Section Review

1. Answers may vary. Two physical properties are melting point and density. Two chemical properties are flammability and reactivity.

2. **a.** chemical
   b. physical
   c. physical
   d. physical
   e. physical
   f. chemical
   g. physical
   h. chemical

3. Answers may vary, but could include use of strong, rigid plastic in cases for delicate objects, such as compact discs, and use of flexible, transparent plastic as plastic food wrap. Plastic is a good choice for these purposes because it can be hard, flexible, durable, opaque, or transparent.

4. Answers may vary. Physical properties could include a density less than that of water, enough strength to not bend or break when a load is placed on it, and insolubility in water. Chemical properties could include not reacting with water or not burning.

5. $D = 454 \text{ g}/100.0 \text{ cm}^3 = 4.54 \text{ g/cm}^3$

6. $D = 0.36 \text{ g}/2500 \text{ cm}^3 = 1.4 \times 10^{-4} \text{ g/cm}^3$

7. $m = 23.4 \text{ cm}^3 \times 8.9 \text{ g/cm}^3 = 208 \text{ g}$

Changes of Matter

❯Focus

In this section, students learn about physical and chemical changes. They also learn how mixtures can be separated by physical changes, how compounds are broken down through chemical changes, and how chemical changes can be detected.

Bellringer

Use the Bellringer transparency to prepare students for this section.

Demonstrate

Observing Changes in Matter Have students organize into small groups and perform the following activity. Each group will need a paper towel, a pie plate, vinegar, and 2 or 3 shiny pennies. First, have students place a folded paper towel in a small pie plate. Then, have them pour vinegar into the pie plate until the paper towel is damp. Next, have them place 2 or 3 shiny pennies on top of the paper towel. Ask students if they think a physical or chemical change will occur. (chemical) Finally, have them put the plate aside for 24 hours. After 24 hours, have students observe the pennies and describe the change that occurred. (The shiny copper surface became coated with a dull, green substance.) Ask them to identify the type of change that occurred. (The change in the appearance of the coins indicates a chemical change.) **LS** Visual

Key Ideas

❯ Why is a getting a haircut an example of a physical change?

❯ Why is baking bread an example of a chemical change?

❯ How can mixtures and compounds be broken down?

Key Terms

physical change
chemical change

Why It Matters

The process of making glass—for practical applications or as art—involves both physical and chemical changes.

Leaves change color in the fall, an ice cube melts in your glass, and bread dough turns into bread when it bakes in the oven. Such changes occur in matter as a result of physical or chemical changes.

Physical Changes

If you break a piece of chalk, you change its physical properties of size and shape. But no matter how many times you break the chalk, its chemical properties remain unchanged. The chalk is still chalk, and each piece of chalk would produce bubbles if you placed it in vinegar. Breaking chalk is an example of a **physical change. ❯A physical change affects one or more physical properties of a substance without changing the identity of the substance.**

Figure 1 shows several examples of physical changes. Some other examples of physical changes are dissolving sugar in water, sanding a piece of wood, and mixing oil and vinegar.

physical change (FIZ i kuhl CHAYNJ) a change of matter from one form to another without a change in chemical properties

Figure 1 Examples of Physical Changes

Melting changes the state of matter of a substance.

Cutting changes the size of a substance.

Crushing changes the shape of a substance.

Key Resources

📦 **Teaching Transparencies**
C3 Chemical Changes
TM7 Dissolving as a Physical Change

💿 **Visual Concepts**
Liquid
Heat
Melting
Comparing Physical and Chemical Changes

📁 **Datasheet**
Can You Separate a Mixture?

📁 **Cross-Disciplinary Worksheet**
Connection to Language Arts—Hidden Meanings

READING
TOOLBOX

Paired Reading Have students read to the end of this section. Pair students. Each student should point to an object and ask their partner to describe its physical properties and the physical changes that might occur. Students should ask each other to point out three materials that undergo chemical changes. Have students evaluate whether their choices meet the criteria for physical and chemical changes.
LS Interpersonal

Answer to caption question
Changes that occur include shape, size, and state.

MISCONCEPTION ALERT

Physical and Chemical Changes
Students may think that changes of state are chemical changes. Because solid ice and liquid water have some different properties, students may think they are different substances and that melting is a chemical change. Students may confuse the combustion of a substance (e.g., alcohol) with the physical change of evaporation. In changes of state, the identity of the substance does not change.

go.hrw.com
★ interact online

Students can interact with the figure by going to **go.hrw.com** and typing in the keyword **HK8MATF3.**

Gold nugget

Molten gold

Gold rings

Figure 2 One way to form gold rings is to melt the gold and then pour it into a mold. **What physical properties of gold change during this process?**

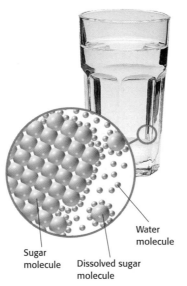

Sugar molecule

Dissolved sugar molecule

Water molecule

Figure 3 When sugar dissolves in water, the water molecules attract the sugar molecules and pull them apart. As a result, the sugar molecules spread out in the water.

go.hrw.com
★ interact online
Keyword: HK8MATF3

Physical changes do not change a substance's identity.

Melting a gold nugget to form a gold ring involves several physical changes, as **Figure 2** shows. The gold changes from solid to liquid and then back to solid. The shape of the gold also changes. The gold nugget becomes a ring of gold. But these physical changes do not change all of the properties of the gold. For example, the gold's color, melting point, and density do not change.

During a physical change, energy is absorbed or released. After a physical change, a substance may look different, but the arrangement of atoms that make up the substance is not changed. A gold nugget, molten gold, and gold rings are all made of gold atoms.

Dissolving is a physical change.

When you stir sugar into water, the sugar dissolves and seems to disappear. But the sugar is still there. You can taste the sweetness when you drink the water. What happened to the sugar?

Figure 3 shows sugar molecules dissolving in water. (The sugar and water molecules are represented as spheres to simplify the diagram.) When sugar dissolves, the sugar molecules become spread out between the water molecules. The molecules of the sugar do not change. So, dissolving is an example of a physical change.

Differentiated Instruction

Alternative Assessment

Physical Change Ask students to bring in different brands and types of plastic sandwich bags, along with packaging, ads, and other promotional materials. Have them design and perform an experiment to test how much mass each bag can hold before breaking. Pool the data and have students answer the following questions: What inferences can be drawn from the data? (Some claims of strength will be upheld, and others may not.) Was this a test of physical or chemical changes? (physical)
LS Logical

Advanced Learners

Desalination Have students investigate why desalination is expensive, and determine under what conditions it should be used on a large scale. (Desalination is best used in locations where it is less expensive than piping or shipping fresh water from distant sources.) Have students summarize their findings in a brief written report.
LS Verbal

Chemical Changes

Some materials are useful because of their ability to change and combine to form new substances. For example, the compounds in gasoline burn in the presence of oxygen to form carbon dioxide and water. The burning of the compounds is a **chemical change.** ❯**A chemical change happens when one or more substances are changed into entirely new substances that have different properties.** The chemical properties of a substance describe which chemical changes can happen. You can learn about chemical properties by observing chemical changes.

✓ **Reading Check** What is the difference between a physical change and a chemical change?

Chemical changes happen everywhere.

You see chemical changes happening more often than you may think. When a battery dies, the chemicals inside the battery have changed, so the battery can no longer supply energy. The oxygen that you inhale when you breathe is used in a series of chemical reactions in your body. After the oxygen reacts with molecules containing carbon, the oxygen is then exhaled as part of the compound carbon dioxide. Chemical changes occur when fruits and vegetables ripen and when the food you eat is digested. **Figure 4** shows some other examples of chemical changes.

chemical change (KEM i kuhl CHAYNJ) a change that occurs when one or more substances change into entirely new substances with different properties

www.scilinks.org
Topic: Physical/
Chemical
Changes
Code: HK81145

Figure 4 Examples of Chemical Changes

Chemical reactions produce pigments that give leaves their colors. In the fall, green leaves change colors as different reactions take place.

When effervescent tablets are added to water, the citric acid and baking soda in them react to produce carbon dioxide, which forms bubbles.

The shiny, orange-brown copper of the Statue of Liberty has reacted with carbon dioxide and water to form green copper compounds.

Teaching Key Ideas

Chemical Change You will need a beaker, copper sulfate ($CuSO_4$) solution, and a large iron nail. Place the iron nail in a $CuSO_4$ solution and leave it there overnight. Observe the nail and solution the next day. Ask students what change in the nail indicates that a chemical change occurred. (Copper from the solution appears on the nail as copper metal.) How do they know that this change was not physical? (The copper was initially in a compound. It changed to a free element, which is a different substance.) **LS** Visual

Demonstrate

Identifying a Physical or Chemical Change You will need 3% hydrogen peroxide (H_2O_2) solution, a self-sealing plastic bag, a small plastic pill bottle, and steel wool. (**Safety Caution:** *If students perform this, they should wear safety goggles, gloves, and an apron; they should handle the hydrogen peroxide carefully.*) Fill the pill bottle halfway with hydrogen peroxide. Then place a small piece of steel wool and the pill bottle into a plastic bag, being careful not to spill the hydrogen peroxide. Force the air out of the bag and seal it tightly. Tip the bottle over so that the hydrogen peroxide comes in contact with the steel wool. Invite students to feel the bag; ask them how they know a chemical change has occurred. (A gas was formed that inflated the bag, and the bag's contents became warm.) **LS** Kinesthetic

Differentiated Instruction

Struggling Readers

Predicting Explain that good readers predict what they will read about by using headings, images, and prior knowledge. Ask students to read the heads on pp. 59–60 and to look at the images. Give students objects, such as a lump of clay or a lemon. Tell the students to make physical changes to the objects. Finally, ask students if they still have the same object after making the changes. **LS** Kinesthetic

English Learners

Comparing Different Changes Have students work in small groups. Ask each group to create a poster that illustrates the differences between physical and chemical changes. Remind them to focus on the composition of a substance. Have the students present their posters to the class. Then, as a final activity, have students use the charts as a guide as they write a paragraph comparing physical and chemical changes. **LS** Interpersonal

Science Skills

Comparing and Contrasting Ask students to describe several methods of causing a sugar cube to undergo a physical change. (crush it, grind it, dissolve it in water) Then ask how they would cause the sugar cube to undergo a chemical change. (burn it, eat it, cause it to react with another chemical) Have students make a concept map that compares physical changes to chemical changes for sugar. **LS Logical**

Why It Matters

Acid Precipitation When fossil fuels are burned, a chemical change takes place involving sulfur (a substance in fossil fuels) and oxygen (from the air). This chemical change produces sulfur dioxide, a gas. When sulfur dioxide enters the atmosphere, it undergoes another chemical change by interacting with water and oxygen. This chemical change produces sulfuric acid, a contributor to acid precipitation. Acid precipitation can kill trees and make ponds and lakes unable to support life. As an extension, have interested students research acid precipitation and present their findings in an oral or written report, or as a "TV News Bulletin." **LS Verbal**

Figure 5 These ingredients are combined and baked to make French bread. **What evidence shows that chemical changes occurred?**

Water / Flour / Salt / Yeast

Academic Vocabulary

interaction (IN tuhr AK shuhn) the action or influence between things

Figure 6 Table sugar is a compound made of carbon, hydrogen, and oxygen. When table sugar is heated, it caramelizes.

Chemical changes form new substances.

When you bake French bread, you combine the ingredients shown in **Figure 5:** water, flour, yeast, and salt. Each ingredient has its own set of properties. When you mix the ingredients and heat them in an oven, the heat of the oven and the interaction of the ingredients cause chemical changes. These changes result in bread, whose properties differ from the properties of the ingredients. This is an example of how new substances are formed by chemical changes.

Chemical changes can be detected.

When a chemical change takes place, clues often suggest that a chemical change has happened. A change in odor or color is a good clue that a substance is changing chemically. When food burns, you can often smell the gases given off by the chemical changes. When paint fades, you can observe the effects of chemical changes in the paint. Chemical changes often cause color changes, fizzing or foaming, or the production of sound, heat, light, or odor.

Figure 6 shows table sugar being heated on a dessert to form a thin caramel layer. How do you know a chemical change is taking place? The sugar has changed color, bubbles are forming, and a caramel smell is filling the air.

Chemical changes cannot be reversed by physical changes.

Because new substances are formed in a chemical change, a chemical change cannot be reversed by physical changes. Most of the chemical changes that you observe in your daily life, such as bread baking, milk turning sour, or iron rusting, are impossible to reverse. Imagine trying to unbake a loaf of bread! However, under the right conditions, some chemical changes can be reversed by other chemical changes. For example, the water that forms in a space shuttle's rockets can be split into hydrogen and oxygen by using an electric current to start a reaction.

Differentiated Instruction

Special Education Students

Chemical Changes Students find it difficult to identify with phrases they do not personally use, such as "chemical changes." Help students understand this phrase by displaying examples of common substances that undergo chemical changes, such as effervescent tablets, milk, etc. For example, they can see effervescent tablets bubble when put in water; they can smell milk after it becomes sour. Have volunteers name other common items that undergo chemical changes. (Sample answer: eggs and other food when they are cooked; wood when it is burned; fireworks when they explode) **LS Intrapersonal**

Breaking Down Mixtures and Compounds

You know that a mixture is a combination of substances that are not chemically combined. A compound, on the other hand, is made up of atoms that are chemically combined. As a result of this difference, mixtures and compounds must be separated in different ways. ❯ **Mixtures can be separated by physical changes, but compounds must be broken down by chemical changes.**

Reading Check Why must mixtures and compounds be separated in different ways?

Mixtures can be physically separated.

Because mixtures are not chemically combined, each part of a mixture has the same chemical makeup that it had before the mixture was formed. Each substance keeps its identity. Thus, mixtures can be separated by physical means.

In some mixtures, such as a pizza, you can see the components. You can remove the mushrooms on a pizza. The removal results in a physical change. Not all mixtures are this easy to separate. For example, you cannot pick salt out of saltwater. But you can separate saltwater into its parts by heating it. When the water evaporates, the salt remains.

If components of a mixture have different boiling points, you can heat the mixture in a distillation device. The component that boils and evaporates first separates from the mixture. Another technique for separating mixtures is to use a centrifuge, which spins a mixture rapidly until the components separate. **Figure 7** shows blood separated by a centrifuge.

Figure 7 You can see layers in this blood sample because it has been separated into its components by the centrifuge. **Is blood a mixture or a compound?**

Answer to caption question
Blood is a mixture because it can be separated by physical means.

InquiryLab

Teacher's Notes The mixture should contain 5 g samples of salt, sand, iron filings, and poppy seeds. Students should devise a procedure that uses solubility, density, and magnetism to separate the mixture. Give them another sample of the mixture without telling them the exact masses of each component. Students can then run their procedures and determine the mass of each component.

Materials per Group
- clear plastic cup
- distilled water
- filter funnel
- filter paper
- magnet
- paper towels
- plastic spoon
- sample mixture (5 g salt, 5 g sand, 5 g iron filings, and 5 g poppy seeds)

Answers to Analysis
1. solubility, magnetism, low density
2. Salt is separated by solubility, poppy seeds by density, and iron filings by magnetism.
3. Sand, poppy seeds, and iron filings are insoluble; only the iron filings are magnetic.
4. salt, sand, iron filings, poppy seeds

InquiryLab **Can You Separate a Mixture?** 30 min

Procedure

❶ Study the **sample mixture** provided by your teacher.

❷ Design an experiment in which the following materials are used to separate the components of the mixture: **distilled water, filter funnel, filter paper, magnet, paper towels, clear plastic cup,** and **plastic spoon.** Consider physical properties such as density, magnetism, and the ability to dissolve.

Analysis

1. What properties did you observe in each of the components of the mixture?
2. How did these properties help you to separate the components of the sample?
3. Did any of the components share similar properties?
4. Based on your observations, what items do you think made up the mixture?

Why It Matters

Refining Crude Oil Explain that crude oil is separated into its different components by distillation, which involves separating crude oil into different components by heating the oil. As the different components reach their boiling points, they vaporize and are separated. Have students prepare posters that illustrate how the components of crude oil are separated by distillation. Encourage students to be creative. **LS Visual**

Why It Matters

Separating Mixtures The property of density is observed when farmers harvest ripe cranberries. Ripe cranberries float in water. During harvesting, cranberry bogs are flooded, and the floating cranberries are skimmed from the water. Ask students what they can infer about the relative densities of water and ripe cranberries. (The density of water is greater than that of ripe cranberries.) **LS Logical**

Teaching Key Ideas

Demonstrating Decomposition Note that the experiment shown in **Figure 8** is not done in the classroom because mercury is toxic. You can demonstrate a similar experiment in the lab with potassium chlorate or calcium carbonate.

Answer to caption question

This is a chemical change.

Two-Column Notes Point out that the Key Ideas for this section are questions whose answers can be found in the text under the red headings within the section. Have students use these red headings and the blue subheadings to organize their notes.

›Close

Reteaching Key Ideas

Comparing and Contrasting Have students make a chart that compares and contrasts physical and chemical changes and gives examples of each. **LS Logical**

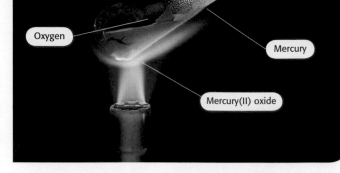

Oxygen · Mercury · Mercury(II) oxide

Figure 8 Heating the compound mercury(II) oxide breaks it down into the elements mercury and oxygen. **Is this change a physical change or a chemical change?**

READING TOOLBOX

Two-Column Notes
Create two-column notes to review the Key Ideas for this section. Put the Key Ideas in the left column, and add details and examples in your own words in the right column.

Some compounds can be broken down through chemical changes.

Some compounds can be broken down into elements through chemical changes. For instance, when the compound mercury(II) oxide is heated, it breaks down into the elements mercury and oxygen. This process is shown in **Figure 8.** Electric currents can be used to separate some compounds. For example, if a current is passed through melted table salt, which is a compound, the elements sodium and chlorine are produced.

Other compounds undergo chemical changes to form simpler compounds. When you open a bottle of soda, compounds in the soda break down into carbon dioxide and water. The carbon dioxide escapes as bubbles. The escaping carbon dioxide is the reason that a soda bubbles when you open it. Through additional chemical changes, the carbon dioxide and water can be further broken down into the elements carbon, oxygen, and hydrogen.

Section 3 Review

KEY IDEAS

1. **Define** *physical change* and *chemical change,* and give examples of each type of change.
2. **Explain** why changes of state are physical changes.
3. **Describe** how you would separate the components of a mixture of sugar and sand. Would your methods result in physical or chemical changes?
4. **Explain** why physical changes can easily be reversed but why chemical changes cannot.
5. **Identify** two ways to break down a compound into simpler substances.
6. **List** three clues that indicate a chemical change.

CRITICAL THINKING

7. **Classifying** Classify each of the following as a chemical change or a physical change.
   a. sugar being added to lemonade
   b. plants using carbon dioxide and water to form oxygen and sugar
   c. water boiling
   d. an egg frying
   e. rust forming on metal
   f. fruit rotting
   g. salt being removed from water by evaporation
8. **Making Inferences** Describe the difference between physical and chemical changes in terms of what happens to the molecules.

Formative Assessment

Which of the following statements is true?

A. Water turning into steam and gasoline into a gas are both physical changes. (Correct. Both changes are examples of a substance in its liquid form to its gaseous form.)

B. Dissolving is a chemical change. (Incorrect. Dissolving involves the distribution of a solid or a gas into a liquid. When substances form a solution in this way, it is a physical change.)

C. In a chemical change, the identity of the substances stays the same. (Incorrect. In a chemical change the identities of the substances change. No new substances are formed in a physical change.)

D. In a physical change, the energy absorbed goes into changing the identity of the substance. (Incorrect. The identity of the substance does not change in a physical change.)

Answers to Section Review

1. Physical changes alter the physical properties of a substance without changing its identity. Physical changes include pounding, breaking, and melting. Chemical changes form new substances that have new properties. Chemical changes include baking, rotting, and oxidation.

2. The composition of the substances does not change in a change of state.

Answers continued on p. 73A

How Is Glass Made?

People have been making glass for thousands of years. The raw materials of sand, limestone, and soda ash are heated and turned into glass through chemical changes. Several physical changes, including changes in state, shape, and size, also occur. There are different ways to shape the glass once it has been made. One method, called *glass blowing,* is illustrated below.

1 Glassmakers often purchase the raw ingredients—sand, limestone, and soda ash—mixed together in a form called *batch*. When the batch is heated to about 1,500 °C, the mixture becomes transparent and flows like honey.

2 A glass blower dips a hollow iron blowpipe into the hot mixture and picks up a gob of molten glass. The blower occasionally reheats the glass to keep it soft.

3 By turning the sticky glob and blowing into the tube, the glass blower creates a hollow bulb that can be pulled, twisted, and blown into different shapes. When the finished shape is broken from the tube, a work of art has been created.

YOUR TURN

UNDERSTANDING CONCEPTS

1. After the molten glass has been shaped, it cools and solidifies. Is this a physical change or a chemical change?

WRITING IN SCIENCE

2. Research another method of shaping glass, such as pressing, drawing, or casting. Write a paragraph describing this method.

SC**i**NKS.

www.scilinks.org
Topic: Glass
Code: **HK80678**

How Is Glass Made? There are many types of glass found in nature. Natural glasses include obsidian, tektites, and fulgurites. They form when rocky material containing silica, such as sand, is heated to very high temperatures and then cooled quickly. Obsidian is a glass that forms when the heat from a volcano melts silica. Impurities in the silica cause the obsidian to be black, red, or green. Tektites are a type of natural glass that forms from meteorites, which are heated to very high temperatures as they pass through the atmosphere. When the meteorites strike the Earth, they melt Earth materials, forming glass. Fulgurites are natural glass formations caused when lightning strikes sand.

Answers to Your Turn

1. physical change
2. Answers may vary.

ApplicationLab

Teacher's Notes

Students can measure heat conductivity in one of two ways. They could place the metal sample on a hot plate, add a drop of hardened wax, and then heat. (The wax on the metal with the greatest heat conductivity will melt first.) Students could also add hot melted wax to metals at room temperature. (The wax on the metal with the greatest heat conductivity will harden first.)

Time Required

1 lab period

Lab Ratings

EASY ———————→ HARD

Teacher Prep 🧪🧪
Student Set-Up 🧪🧪
Concept Level 🧪
Clean Up 🧪🧪

Skills Acquired

- Classifying
- Collecting data
- Communicating
- Designing experiments
- Experimenting
- Identifying/Recognizing patterns
- Inferring
- Measuring
- Organizing and analyzing data

Scientific Methods

In this lab, students will:
- Make observations
- Form a hypothesis
- Analyze the results
- Draw conclusions
- Communicate results

Application

Lab

What You'll Do

> **Measure** the physical properties of various metals.

> **Compare** possible applications for the metals that you test based on the properties of the metals.

What You'll Need

balance
beakers (several)
graduated cylinder
hot plate
ice
magnet
metal samples: aluminum, iron, nickel, tin, and zinc
ruler, metric
stopwatch
water
wax

Safety

Physical Properties of Metals

Some properties are shared by all metals, but not all metals are exactly alike. As a materials engineer at a tool manufacturing company, you have been asked to determine which of several metals would be the best to use as plating on heavy-duty drill bits. The main requirements are that the metal be dense and hard. It is also desirable for the metal not to conduct too much heat and not to be affected by magnetism.

Procedure

Testing the Properties of Different Metals

❶ You will be comparing the four properties of the five metals in the sample data table below. You will be able to measure some of the properties directly. For other properties, you will rank the metals from most to least (1 through 5).

Sample Data Table: Physical Properties of Some Metals

Metal	Density (g/mL)	Hardness (1–5)	Heat conductivity (1–5)	Affected by magnetism (yes/no)
Aluminum, Al				
Iron, Fe				
Nickel, Ni		DO NOT WRITE IN BOOK		
Tin, Sn				
Zinc, Zn				

❷ Density is the mass per unit volume of a substance. If the metal is box shaped, you can measure its length, width, and height, and then use these measurements to calculate the metal's volume. If the shape of the metal is irregular, you can add the metal to a known volume of water and determine what volume of water is displaced.

❸ Relative hardness indicates how easy it is to scratch a metal. A metal that is harder can scratch a metal that is less hard, but not vice versa.

❹ Relative heat conductivity indicates how quickly a metal heats or cools. A metal that conducts heat well will heat up or cool down faster than other metals.

❺ If a magnet placed near a metal attracts the metal, the metal is affected by magnetism.

Safety Cautions

Students should wash their hands immediately and avoid touching their eyes if they accidentally touch a tin sample. This element poses a health risk if it enters the body. Have students review safety guidelines before working in the lab. Caution students not to touch the hot beaker containing the melted wax.

Designing Your Experiment

6 With your lab partner(s), decide how you will use the materials provided to determine the properties of each of the metals to be tested. There is more than one way to measure some of the physical properties that are listed, so you might not use all of the materials that are provided.

7 In your lab report, list each step that you will perform in your experiment.

8 Have your teacher approve your plan before you carry out your experiment.

Performing Your Experiment

9 After your teacher approves your plan, carry out your experiment. Keep in mind that repeating your measurements will help ensure that your data are accurate.

10 Record all of the data you collect and any observations you make.

Analysis

1. **Making Comparisons** Which physical properties were the easiest for you to measure and compare? Which properties were the most difficult to measure and compare? Explain why.

2. **Describing Events** What happens when you try to scratch aluminum with zinc?

3. **Applying Ideas** Suppose you find a metal fastener and determine that its density is 7 g/mL. What are two ways that you could determine whether the metal in the fastener is tin or zinc?

4. **Applying Concepts** Suppose someone gives you an alloy that is made of both zinc and nickel. In general, how do you think the physical properties of the alloy would be similar to or different from those of the individual metals?

Communicating Your Results

5. **Organizing Data** In a data table like the one provided in this lab, list the physical properties that you compared and the data that you collected for each of the metals.

6. **Evaluating Methods** What are some possible sources of error in the measurements that you made? What could you have done differently to minimize those sources of error?

Application

Which of these metals would you recommend as the best one to use as plating on heavy-duty drill bits? Justify your answer.

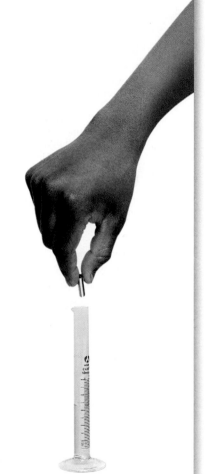

Answers to Analysis

1. Student answers may vary but should include a discussion of the measurement and comparison of each property.

2. Nothing. Neither aluminum nor zinc should be able to scratch the other one since they have such similar hardness.

3. Measuring the relative hardness and the relative heat conductivity of the metal fastener are two ways to determine whether the metal is tin or zinc.

4. The physical properties of an alloy of zinc and nickel would have intermediate values compared with the values of the properties of the metals alone.

Answers to Communicating Your Results

5. See Sample Data Table

6. Sample answer: Density measurements may have been affected by a few drops of water splashing out of the graduated cylinder of water when metal samples were placed in it to find their volume. To prevent this, more care could have been taken to prevent any water from splashing out.

Answer to Application

Zinc is somewhat dense and hard, so it would be the best metal (among those tested) for plating heavy-duty drill bits. It is also not magnetic and has only moderate heat conductivity.

Sample Data Table

Metal	Density (g/mL)	Hardness (1–6)	Heat conductivity (1–6)	Affected by magnetism? (yes/no)
Aluminum (Al)	2.7	4 or 5	1	no
Iron (Fe)	7.9	3	5	yes
Nickel (Ni)	8.9	2	4	yes
Tin (Sn)	7.3	6	6	no
Zinc (Zn)	7.1	4 or 5	3	no

Key Resources

 Virtual Investigation

 Classroom Lab Video/DVD

 Holt Lab Generator CD-ROM
Search for any lab by type, standard, difficulty level, or time. Edit any lab to fit your needs, or create your own labs. Use the Lab Materials QuickList software to customize your lab materials list.

 Differentiated Datasheets
Physical Properties of Metals

 Observation Lab
Measuring Density with a Hydrometer

 CBL™ Probeware Lab
Comparing the Buoyancy of Different Objects

Converting Units

Science Skills

Math Skills

Solving Formulas Review with students how to solve for a variable in a formula. Work through several examples of formulas, such as the area formula, $A = l \times w$. Show students how the same principles apply to the formula for density and for conversion factors. Conversion factors are equal to one because when you rearrange the equation that shows how two values are equivalent, you get the number one on one side of the equation. When you multiply by a conversion factor, you are multiplying by one. Emphasize to students that this multiplication does not change the value of the measurement, only the units in which it is expressed.

LS Logical

Answers to Practice

1. **a.** 0.000 001 29 g/mm³
   b. 1,290 g/m³
2. 0.001 g/mm³
3. 180 g/m³
4. greater; 700,000 g/m³
5. 7,860,000 g/m³

Technology

 Math

Scientific Methods

Graphing

Problem

Density can be expressed in grams per cubic centimeter (g/cm³). The density of lead is 11.3 g/cm³. What is the density of lead in grams per cubic millimeter (g/mm³)?

Solution

Identify

List the given and unknown values.

Given:
$density, d = 11.3 \text{ g/cm}^3$

Unknown:
$density, d = ? \text{ g/mm}^3$

Plan

a. Determine the relationship between units. Because cm is cubed, the conversion value must also be cubed.

a. $1 \text{ cm} = 10 \text{ mm}$
   $1 \text{ cm}^3 = (10 \text{ mm})^3 = 1,000 \text{ mm}^3$

b. Write the equation for the conversion. Use the units as a guide. If the units don't cancel properly, you may have the conversion equation backwards.

b. $\text{density in g/mm}^3 = \text{density in } \dfrac{\text{g}}{\text{cm}^3} \times \dfrac{1 \text{ cm}^3}{1,000 \text{ mm}^3}$

Solve

Insert the known values into the equation, and solve.

$\text{density in g/mm}^3 = \dfrac{11.3 \text{ g}}{\text{cm}^3} \times \dfrac{1 \text{ cm}^3}{1,000 \text{ mm}^3}$

$d = 0.0113 \text{ g/mm}^3$

Practice

Use the table to answer the following questions.

1. Find the density of dry air in the following units:
   a. grams per cubic millimeter (g/mm³)
   b. grams per cubic meter (g/m³)
2. What is the density of water in grams per cubic millimeter?
3. Find the density of helium in grams per cubic meter.
4. Will the density of gasoline in grams per cubic meter be greater than or less than the value given in the table? To see if you are correct, convert the value given in the table to grams per cubic meter.
5. What is the density of iron in grams per cubic meter?

Substance	Density (g/cm³)
Air (dry)	0.00129
Brick (common)	1.9
Gasoline	0.7
Helium	0.00018
Ice	0.92
Iron	7.86
Lead	11.3
Nitrogen	0.00125
Steel	7.8
Water	1.00

Key Resources

Science Skills Worksheets
Making and Interpreting Bar Graphs and Pie Charts
Ratios and Proportions
Rearranging Algebraic Equations

go.hrw.com
SUPER SUMMARY
KEYWORD: HK8MATS

Key **Ideas**

Section 1 Classifying Matter

> **What Is Matter?** Every sample of matter is either an element, a compound, or a mixture. (p. 45)

> **Elements** Each element is made of one kind of atom. (p. 46)

> **Compounds** Each molecule of a compound contains two or more elements that are chemically combined. (p. 47)

> **Pure Substances and Mixtures** Elements and compounds are pure substances, but mixtures are not. (p. 48)

Section 2 Properties of Matter

> **Physical Properties** Physical properties are characteristics that can be observed without changing the identity of the substance. Examples include color, mass, melting point, boiling point, and density. (p. 51)

> **Chemical Properties** A chemical property describes how a substance changes into a new substance, either by combining with other elements or by breaking apart into new substances. Examples include flammability and reactivity. (p. 56)

Section 3 Changes of Matter

> **Physical Changes** A physical change affects one or more physical properties of a substance without changing the identity of the substance. (p. 59)

> **Chemical Changes** A chemical change happens when one or more substances are changed into entirely new substances that have different properties. (p. 61)

> **Breaking Down Mixtures and Compounds** Mixtures can be separated by physical changes, but compounds must be broken down by chemical changes. (p. 63)

Key **Terms**

matter, p. 45
element, p. 46
atom, p. 46
molecule, p. 47
compound, p. 47
pure substance, p. 48
mixture, p. 48

melting point, p. 52
boiling point, p. 52
density, p. 54
reactivity, p. 56

physical change, p. 59
chemical change,
p. 61

SUPER SUMMARY

Have students connect the major concepts in this chapter through an interactive Super Summary. Visit **go.hrw.com** and type in the keyword **HK8MATS** to access the Super Summary for this chapter.

Differentiated Instruction

Alternative Assessment

Identifying Materials Have students imagine they are given a piece of a material that is painted black so that they cannot tell its normal appearance. Have them work in small groups to plan tests they would do on the material to decide whether it is metal, glass, plastic, or wood. (Student answers may vary but may include testing to see if the material conducts electricity (metal), burns (wood), has a low melting point (plastic), or can be crushed and has a high melting point (glass).) **LS** Intrapersonal

Key Resources

 **Interactive Concept Map**

 **Review Resources**
Concept Review Worksheets

Assessment Resources
Chapter Tests A and B
Performance-Based Assessment

Reading Toolbox

1. Answers may vary. Sample answer: Physical changes—breaking a piece of chalk, cutting hair, dissolving sugar, melting ice, and crushing a metal can. Chemical changes—burning gasoline, fruits and vegetables ripening, digesting food, baking bread, and paint fading.

Using Key Terms

2. **a.** An atom is the smallest unit of an element that has the properties of the element; a molecule is the smallest unit of a substance that exhibits all the properties characteristic of that substance.

   b. A molecule is a group of atoms that are held together by chemical forces; a compound is a substance that is composed of atoms of two or more elements.

   c. A compound is made of two or more different elements that are chemically combined in the same proportions; a mixture is a combination of two or more pure substances physically mixed together.

3. Wood has the chemical property of flammability, meaning it burns in the presence of oxygen. This is a chemical change, not a physical change, because new substances with properties that are different from wood and oxygen are created; also heat (a sign of a chemical change) is given off.

4. They form a mixture, because dissolving (a physical change) has occurred; it can be separated into its components, the sugar and water are mixed physically, it does not have a fixed composition or definite properties, and it is formed from two pure substances (sugar and water).

5. They are miscible; two or more liquids that are able to dissolve are miscible, while two or more liquids that do not dissolve are immiscible.

6. Energy is released from the magnesium as heat and light.

7. physical properties: color, density, magnetism, melting point, boiling point, dissolving, conducting electricity; chemical properties: reactivity, corrosion, flammability

---

CHAPTER 2 Review

READING TOOLBOX

1. **Finding Examples** Review Section 3. As you review, list at least five examples of a physical change and at least five examples of a chemical change.

USING KEY TERMS

2. For each pair of terms, explain how the meanings of the terms differ.
   a. *atom* and *molecule*
   b. *molecule* and *compound*
   c. *compound* and *mixture*

3. When wood is burned, new substances are produced. Describe this reaction, and explain what type of change occurs. Use the terms *flammability, chemical property,* and *physical change* or *chemical change.*

4. When sugar is added to water, the sugar dissolves and the resulting liquid is clear. Do the sugar and water form a *pure substance,* or do they form a *mixture*? Explain your answer.

5. When water is mixed with rubbing alcohol, the two liquids completely dissolve. Are the two liquids *miscible,* or are they *immiscible*? Explain the difference between the two terms.

6. The photograph shows magnesium burning in the presence of oxygen. Give some evidence that a *chemical change* is occurring.

7. Make a table that has two columns. Label one column "Physical properties" and the other "Chemical properties." Put each of the following terms in the correct column: *color, density, reactivity, magnetism, melting point, corrosion, flammability, dissolving, conducting electricity,* and *boiling point.*

UNDERSTANDING KEY IDEAS

8. What is matter?
   a. any visible solid that has mass
   b. any liquid that takes up space and has mass
   c. anything that takes up space and has mass
   d. any liquid or solid that takes up space

9. What is the chemical formula for iron(III) oxide?
   a. Fe^{2+}
   b. NaCl
   c. I_2
   d. Fe_2O_3

10. Which of the following is a mixture?
    a. air
    b. salt
    c. water
    d. sulfur

11. Compounds and elements are
    a. always solids.
    b. mixtures.
    c. pure substances.
    d. dense.

12. Which of the following is an example of a physical change?
    a. melting ice cubes
    b. burning paper
    c. rusting iron
    d. burning gasoline

13. Which of the following is a pure substance?
    a. grape juice
    b. saltwater
    c. table salt
    d. gasoline

14. If you add oil to water and shake the liquid, you will form a
    a. pure substance.
    b. miscible liquid.
    c. heterogeneous mixture.
    d. homogeneous mixture.

EXPLAINING KEY IDEAS

15. List four properties that can be used to classify elements.

16. Describe a procedure to separate a mixture of salt, finely ground pepper, and pebbles.

INTERPRETING GRAPHICS The graph below shows mass versus volume for two metals. Use the graph to answer questions 17–19.

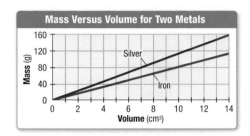

Mass Versus Volume for Two Metals

17. What does the slope of each line represent?

18. Which has a greater density: silver or iron? Explain how you can answer this question without doing any calculations.

19. What is the density of silver?

CRITICAL THINKING

20. Analyzing Data A jar contains 30 mL of glycerin (mass = 37.8 g) and 60 mL of corn syrup (mass = 82.8 g). Which liquid is the top layer? Explain your answer.

21. Applying Concepts A light green powder is heated in a test tube. A gas is given off while the solid becomes black. What type of change is occurring? Explain your reasoning.

22. Making Inferences Suppose you are planning a journey to the center of Earth in a self-propelled tunneling machine. List properties of the special materials that would be needed to build the machine, and explain why each property would be important.

Assignment Guide	
SECTION	**ITEMS**
1	2–5, 8–11, 13, 14
2	7, 15–20, 22–27
3	1, 6, 12, 21

Graphing Skills

23. Constructing Graphs Use the data below to make a graph that shows the relationship between the mass and volume of aluminum samples of different sizes. Plot mass on the y-axis, and plot volume on the x-axis. What does the shape of the graph tell you about the density of aluminum?

Block number	Mass (g)	Volume (cm³)
1	1.20	0.443
2	3.59	1.33
3	5.72	2.12
4	12.4	4.60
5	15.3	5.66
6	19.4	7.17
7	22.7	8.41
8	24.1	8.94
9	34.0	12.6
10	36.4	13.5

Math Skills

24. Calculating Density A piece of titanium metal has a mass of 67.5 g and a volume of 15 cm³. What is the density of titanium?

25. Calculating Density A sample of a substance that has a mass of 85 g has a volume of 110 cm³. What is the density of the substance? Will the substance float in water? Explain your answer.

26. Calculating Volume The density of a piece of brass is 8.4 g/cm³. If the mass of the brass is 510 g, find the volume of the brass.

27. Calculating Mass What mass of water will fill a tank that is 100.0 cm long, 50.0 cm wide, and 30.0 cm high? Express the answer in grams.

Math Skills

24. $D = 67.5 \text{ g}/15 \text{ cm}^3 = 4.5 \text{ g/cm}^3$

25. $D = 85 \text{ g}/110 \text{ cm}^3 = 0.77 \text{ g/cm}^3$
It will float because its density is less than that of water (1.00 g/cm³).

26. $V = 510 \text{ g}/(8.4 \text{ g/cm}^3) = 61 \text{ cm}^3$

27. $m = 1.00 \text{ g/cm}^3 = (100.0 \text{ cm} \times 50.0 \text{ cm} \times 30.0 \text{ cm})$
$m = 1.50 \times 10^5 \text{ g}$

Understanding Key Ideas

8. c
9. d
10. a
11. c
12. a
13. c
14. c

Explaining Key Ideas

15. Answers may vary. Student answers may include: melting point, boiling point, density, reactivity with acid, color, hardness, texture, flammability, malleability, thermal conductivity, and solubility.

16. Sample answer: Pass the mixture through a filter that allows the salt and pepper to pass through but traps the pebbles. Mix the salt and pepper with water to dissolve the salt. Filter the mixture to trap the pepper. Evaporate the water to recover the salt.

17. density

18. silver; by comparing the slopes

19. about 10.5 g/cm³

Critical Thinking

20. glycerin (because it is less dense); density of glycerin = 37.8 g/30.0 mL = 1.26 g/mL; density of corn syrup = 82.8 g/60.0 mL = 1.38 g/mL

21. It is a chemical change; the change in color and the formation of a gas imply that a chemical change took place.

22. Answers could include high melting point to endure the heat at Earth's core, as well as hardness and strength to bore through different materials in Earth's crust.

Graphing Skills

23. The density of these aluminum samples fluctuates somewhat, as volume and mass increase. These aluminum samples may not be pure aluminum, as density should remain constant in an element.

TEST DOCTOR

Question 1 Answer C is correct. Answer A is incorrect because evaporation is a physical change. Answer B is incorrect because dissolving is physical change. Answer D is incorrect because mixtures are not combined through chemical means.

Question 2 Answer G is correct. Answer F is incorrect because carbon and oxygen are chemically combined to form the compound carbon dioxide. Answer H is incorrect because the elements in a mixture are not chemical combined. Answer I is incorrect because the particles in a solution are not chemically combined.

Question 3 Answer C is correct. Answer A results from incorrectly converting kilograms to grams before determining the volume (10 g/13.57 cm³). Answer B results from dividing the density by the volume in kilograms (13.57 cm³/1 kg). Answer D results from incorrectly converting kilograms to grams and then multiplying the density by the volume (13.57 cm³ × 100 g).

Question 4 Full-credit answers should include the following points:
- The density of water at 4 °C is 15 g/15 cm³, or 1 g/cm³.
- The density of water at 20 °C is 15 g/15.03 cm³, or 0.998 g/cm³.
- Thus, the density decreased.

Question 5 Full-credit answers should include the following points:
- The change in density is a physical change.
- Water has the same chemical and physical properties before and after the change in temperature, so it is a physical change.

Question 6 Full-credit answers should include the following points:
- Water has a greater density than gasoline.
- The slope of the line in the graph of mass as a function of volume is density.
- The slope for water is greater than the slope for gasoline in the graph shown.

Question 7 Answer H is correct. Bronze is an alloy of copper and tin.

Understanding Concepts

Directions (1–3): For *each* question, write on a sheet of paper the letter of the correct answer.

1. Which of the following is an example of a chemical change?
   - **A.** gasoline evaporating
   - **B.** sugar dissolving in water
   - **C.** a metal surface rusting
   - **D.** a mixture separating into its components

2. Which of the following terms most accurately describes carbon dioxide?
   - **F.** element
   - **G.** compound
   - **H.** mixture
   - **I.** solution

3. An experiment shows that the element mercury has a density of 13.57 g/cm³. What is the volume of 1.000 kg of pure mercury?
   - **A.** 0.7369 cm³
   - **B.** 13.57 cm³
   - **C.** 73.69 cm³
   - **D.** $1,357$ cm³

Directions (4–6): For *each* question, write a short response.

4. At 4 °C, the volume of 15 g of water was 15 cm³. At 20 °C, the volume of the same 15 g of water was 15.03 cm³. What effect did the increase in temperature have on the water's density?

5. If the density of water changes because the temperature of the water changes, is this change a physical change or a chemical change?

6. Study the graph below. Which has a greater density: water or gasoline?

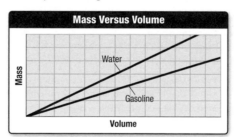

Mass Versus Volume

Mass — Volume; Water; Gasoline

Reading Skills

Directions (7–8): Read the passage below. Then, answer the questions that follow.

METAL ALLOYS

When a metallic element is combined with one or more other elements and the resulting combination has metallic properties, that combination is known as an *alloy*. Metals are most often alloyed with other metals, but other elements and compounds can also be included in an alloy to give it particular properties. For example, blending small amounts of manganese and carbon with iron creates a substance known as *carbon steel*. Carbon steel is harder and more corrosion-resistant than pure iron.

Some alloys are compounds. One example is cementite, Fe_3C. Other alloys, such as bronze and brass, are solutions of two or more metals dissolved in one another. Alloys that are mixtures of several compounds may not have a single melting point. Instead, they may have a melting range, in which the material is a combination of a solid and a liquid.

7. Which of the following is an alloy?
   - **F.** iron
   - **G.** carbon
   - **H.** bronze
   - **I.** manganese

8. An alloy of aluminum is observed to have a melting range instead of a single melting point. What can be concluded from this observation?
   - **A.** The alloy is a compound.
   - **B.** The alloy is probably a mixture of different compounds.
   - **C.** The other components in the alloy have higher melting points.
   - **D.** Each individual molecule of the aluminum alloy has all of the properties of the alloy.

Answers F, G, and I are incorrect because iron, carbon, and manganese are all elements.

Question 8 Answer B is correct: alloys that are mixtures of several compounds display a melting range. Answer A is incorrect because if the alloy were a single compound, it would not display a melting range. Answer C is incorrect because it cannot be concluded that the other components of the alloy have higher melting points. Answer D is incorrect because the melting range of the alloy is different than the melting point of aluminum.

Question 9 Answer F is correct. Answer G is incorrect because ozone molecules (O_3) contain one kind of atom. Answer H is incorrect because

hydrogen gas molecules (H_2) contain one kind of atom. Answer I is incorrect because sulfur molecules (S_8) contain one kind of atom.

Question 10 Answer C is correct. There are 1×30 [baking soda] $+ 6 \times 20$ [ethanol] $+ 2 \times 10$ [water] $= 170$ atoms of hydrogen. Answer A is incorrect because there are 130 atoms of sodium. Answer B is incorrect because there are 120 atoms of oxygen. Answer D is incorrect because there are 70 atoms of carbon.

Question 11 300 molecules of water (H_2O) have 600 atoms H and 300 atoms O. 100 molecules of O_3 have 300 atoms O, and 300 molecules H_2 have 600 atoms H. Thus, 100 molecules of ozone are needed, and 300 molecules of hydrogen gas are needed.

Interpreting Graphics

The tables below give the chemical formulas for some common substances. Use the tables to answer questions 9–11.

Substance	Chemical formula
Ethanol	C_2H_6O
Baking soda	$NaHCO_3$
Hydrogen gas	H_2
Oxygen gas	O_2

Substance	Chemical formula
Ozone	O_3
Table salt	$NaCl$
Solid sulfur	S_8
Water	H_2O

9. Which of the following substances is classified as a compound?

    F. water   **H.** hydrogen gas

    G. ozone   **I.** solid sulfur

10. A mixture contains 100 molecules of table salt, 30 molecules of baking soda, 20 molecules of ethanol, and 10 molecules of water. Atoms from which of the following elements make up most of the mixture?

    A. sodium, Na   **C.** hydrogen, H

    B. oxygen, O   **D.** carbon, C

11. A scientist discovers a way to easily combine molecules of ozone and molecules of hydrogen gas to make molecules of water. To create 300 molecules of water, how many molecules of ozone and how many molecules of hydrogen gas would the scientist need?

A geologist who is studying rocks found on an expedition places a 25 g graduated cylinder on a scale and adds 100 cm³ of water to the cylinder. Then, the geologist places the rocks in the cylinder one at a time, as shown below. Use the graphic to answer questions 12 and 13.

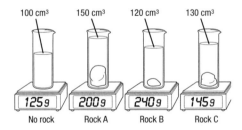

12. Which rock or rocks have the greatest density?

13. Which rock or rocks will float to the surface of the water in the cylinder? Why?

Test Tip

On a standardized test, take time to read completely each question, including all of the answer choices. Consider each answer choice before determining which one is correct.

Question 12 Rock B is the densest. Rock A has a density of 75 g/50 cm³ = 1.5 g/cm³. Rock B has a density of 115 g/20 cm³ = 5.75 g/cm³. Rock C has a density of 20 g/30 cm³ = 0.67 g/cm³.

Question 13 Full-credit answers should include the following points:
- Rock C would float.
- The density of Rock C, 20 g/30 cm³ = 0.67 g/cm³, is less than the density of water, 1 g/cm³.

State Resources

For specific resources for your state, visit go.hrw.com and type in the keyword **HSHSTR**.

 Test Practice with Guided Reading Development

Answers

1. C
2. G
3. C
4. Answers may vary; see Test Doctor for a detailed scoring rubric.
5. Answers may vary; see Test Doctor for a detailed scoring rubric.
6. Answers may vary; see Test Doctor for a detailed scoring rubric.
7. H
8. B
9. F
10. C
11. 100 molecules of ozone and 300 molecules of hydrogen gas
12. Rock B
13. Answers may vary; see Test Doctor for a detailed scoring rubric.

Continuation of Answers

Answers continued from p. 64

3. Dissolve the sugar in water and filter out the sand. Then evaporate the water from the sugar. The changes would be physical changes.

4. Physical changes do not change the identity of substances and, therefore, are easy to undo. In chemical changes, new substances are formed that cannot be reversed using physical means.

5. heating, using an electric current

6. color change; bubbling; fizzing or foaming; production of heat, light, or sound

7. **a.** physical

   b. chemical

   c. physical

   d. chemical

   e. chemical

   f. chemical

   g. physical

8. In a physical change, the material's particles do not change; in a chemical change, the particles recombine, so they have different properties.

	Standards	Teach Key Ideas

CHAPTER OPENER, pp. 74–76 **50 min.**

SECTION 1 Matter and Energy, pp. 77–81 **50 min.**

> Kinetic Theory
> States of Matter
> Energy's Role

Standards: PS 2d, PS 2e, PS 5b, PS 5c, UCP 1, UCP 2, SAI 2

Teach Key Ideas:
- 🔲 **Bellringer Transparency**
- 🔲 **Teaching Transparencies** C4 Three States of Matter • C5 Kinetic Energy and States of Matter
- 💿 **Visual Concepts** Kinetic Molecular Theory • Gas • Solid, Liquid, and Gas • Liquid

---

SECTION 2 Changes of State, pp. 84–88 **50 min.**

> Energy and Changes of State
> Conservation of Mass and Energy

Standards: PS 5a, PS 5d, UCP 1, UCP 2, UCP 3, SAI 1, SAI 2

Teach Key Ideas:
- 🔲 **Bellringer Transparency**
- 🔲 **Teaching Transparencies** TM8 Changes in State for Water • C6 Changes in State
- 💿 **Visual Concepts** Law of Conservation of Mass • Law of Conservation of Energy • Vaporization and Condensation

---

SECTION 3 Fluids, pp. 89–94 **50 min.**

> Pressure
> Buoyant Force
> Pascal's Principle
> Fluids in Motion

Standards: PS 2e, UCP 1, UCP 2, UCP 3, UCP 4, SAI 2, ST 2, HNS 3

Teach Key Ideas:
- 🔲 **Bellringer Transparency**
- 🔲 **Teaching Transparencies** TM9 Archimedes' Principle • C7 Density
- 💿 **Visual Concept** Pressure

SECTION 4 Behavior of Gases, pp. 96–101 **50 min.**

> Properties of Gases
> Gas Laws

Standards: PS 2e, UCP 1, UCP 2, UCP 3, SAI 2

Teach Key Ideas:
- 🔲 **Bellringer Transparency**
- 🔲 **Teaching Transparencies** TM10 Boyle's Law • TM11 Charles's Law
- 💿 **Visual Concepts** Barometer • Comparing Real and Ideal Gases • Properties of Gases • Boyle's Law • Dalton's Law of Partial Pressures • Combined Gas Law • Equation for Pressure • Charles's Law • Graham's Law of Effusion • Comparing Diffusion and Effusion

See also PowerPoint® Resources

Chapter Review and Assessment Resources

- **SE** Science Skills: Making Graphs, p. 104
- **SE** Chapter Summary, p. 105
- **SE** Chapter Review, pp. 106–107
- **SE** Standardized Test Prep, pp. 108–109
- 🗀 Concept Review Worksheets ■
- 🗀 Chapter Tests A and B ■
- 🔳 Holt Online Assessment

Basic Learners
- **TE** Reading Skills, p. 86
- **TE** Will It Float? p. 91
- 🗀 Science Skills Worksheets
- 🗀 Differentiated Datasheets A for Labs and Activities ■
- 📙 Study Guide A ■

Advanced Learners
- **TE** Forms of Solids, p. 78
- **TE** Lifejacket Buoyancy, p. 91
- **TE** Hydraulic Devices, p. 92
- 🗀 Cross-Disciplinary Worksheets
- 🗀 Differentiated Datasheets C for Labs and Activities ■

CHAPTER Fast Track To shorten instruction because of time limitations, omit Section 4 and the chapter lab.

Key

SE Student Edition
TE Teacher's Edition

📁 Chapter Resource File
📓 Workbook
🗄 Transparency

💿 CD or CD-ROM
* Datasheet or blackline master available

■ Also available in Spanish

All resources listed below are also available on the Teacher's One-Stop Planner.

Why It Matters	Hands-On	Skills Development	Assessment
Build student motivation with resources about high-interest applications.	**SE Inquiry Lab** Changes in Density, p. 75*■	**TE Reading Toolbox** Assessing Prior Knowledge, p. 74 **SE Reading Toolbox** p. 76	📁 **Pretest** ■
TE Trees and Water, p. 79 **SE Plasma,** pp. 82–83 **TE Fusion on Earth,** p. 83 📁 **Cross-Disciplinary Worksheet** Integrating Physics—Plasma	**TE Demonstration** Motion of Particles, p. 77 **TE Demonstration** Visualizing Particles, p. 79 **SE Quick Lab** Hot or Cold? p. 81*■	**SE Reading Toolbox** Comparison Table, p. 78	**TE Reteaching Key Ideas** Adding Energy, p. 81 **TE Formative Assessment,** p. 81 📁 **Spanish Assessment***■ 📁 **Section Quiz** ■
SE Why Do People Sweat? p. 85 **TE Condensation,** p. 85 📁 **Cross-Disciplinary Worksheets** Science and the Consumer—Dry Ice • Integrating Space Science—Our Changing Universe • Science and the Consumer—Refrigerants	**TE Demonstration** Changes in Energy, p. 84 **SE Quick Lab** Boiling Water, p. 86*■ **SE Inquiry Lab** Boiling and Freezing, pp. 102–103*■	**SE Reading Toolbox** Comparison Table, p. 86	**TE Reteaching Key Ideas** Adding Energy, p. 88 **TE Formative Assessment,** p. 88 📁 **Spanish Assessment***■ 📁 **Section Quiz** ■
TE Motor Oil, p. 93 **TE Floating Continents,** p. 93 **SE How Do Submarines Work?** p. 95 📁 **Cross-Disciplinary Worksheets** Real World Applications—Submarines • Integrating Biology—Density and Swim Bladders	**TE Demonstration** Floating in Layers, p. 89 **SE Quick Lab** Density and Shape, p. 91*■	**TE Science Skills** Making Models, p. 91 **SE Reading Toolbox** Laws and Principles, p. 92 **SE Math Skills** Pascal's Principle, p. 93	**TE Reteaching Key Ideas** Changing Forces, p. 94 **TE Formative Assessment,** p. 94 📁 **Spanish Assessment***■ 📁 **Section Quiz** ■
TE Internal Combustion Engine, p. 97 📁 **Cross-Disciplinary Worksheet** Real World Applications—Gas Laws	**TE Demonstration** Gas Flow, p. 96 **TE Demonstration** Gas Pressure, p. 97 **SE Inquiry Lab** How Are Temperature and Volume Related? p. 99*■ 📁 **Observation Lab** Boyle's Law 📁 **CBL™ Probeware Lab** Investigating the Relationship Between Pressure and Volume	**SE Reading Toolbox** Laws and Principles, p. 97 **SE Math Skills** Boyle's Law, p. 98 **TE Science Skills** Interpreting Diagrams, p. 100 **TE Science Skills** Kelvins, p. 100	**TE Reteaching Key Ideas** Gas Laws, p. 101 **TE Formative Assessment,** p. 101 📁 **Spanish Assessment***■ 📁 **Section Quiz** ■

See also Lab Generator

See also Holt Online Assessment Resources

Resources for Differentiated Instruction

English Learners
TE Change of State, p. 87
📁 Differentiated Datasheets A, B, and C for Labs and Activities ■
📓 Study Guide A ■

Struggling Readers
TE Testing Surface Tension, p. 90
TE Behavior of Gases, p. 98
📓 Interactive Reader

Special Education Students
TE Heat Transfer, p. 80

Alternative Assessment
TE Thermal Energy, p. 80
TE Relating Pressure and Temperature, p. 105

Overview

This chapter covers the kinetic theory of matter, changes of state, the law of conservation of mass, and the law of conservation of energy. This chapter then introduces the characteristics and behavior of fluids. This chapter ends with the properties and behavior of gases, as well as Boyle's, Charles's, and Gay-Lussac's laws.

READING TOOLBOX

Assessing Prior Knowledge Students should understand the following concepts:

- scientific laws
- units of measurement
- using significant figures
- mass versus weight
- density

MISCONCEPTION ///ALERT\\\

Science education research has identified the following misconceptions about matter:

- Students interpret the statement "energy is neither created nor destroyed" to mean that energy is stored up and released in its original form. (Energy can change from one form to another.)
- Students believe light objects float and heavy objects sink, and that mass is the factor determining whether an object sinks or floats. (An object floats or sinks based on its density.)
- Students believe that matter is continuous, rather than particulate; they don't recognize intermolecular forces in solids, liquids, and gases. (When water boils, forming a gas, and then condenses, forming a liquid again, the forces between particles change but the matter remains the same. The forces between the particles of a liquid are stronger than the forces between particles of a gas.)

CHAPTER 3 States of Matter

Chapter Outline

❶ Matter and Energy
Kinetic Theory
States of Matter
Energy's Role

❷ Changes of State
Energy and Changes of State
Conservation of Mass and Energy

❸ Fluids
Pressure
Buoyant Force
Pascal's Principle
Fluids in Motion

❹ Behavior of Gases
Properties of Gases
Gas Laws

Why It **Matters**

This temporary art exhibit, called "100,000 Pounds of Ice and Neon," was on display for a weekend at an ice rink in Tacoma, Washington. Colorful gases inside solid blocks of ice illustrate two states of matter.

Chapter Correlations *National Science Education Standards*

The following correlations show the National Science Standards that relate to this chapter. For the full text of the standards, see the National Science Education Standards at the front of the book.

PS 2d The physical properties of compounds reflect the nature of the interactions among its molecules. (Section 1)

PS 2e Solids, liquids, and gases differ in the distances and angles between molecules or atoms and therefore the energy that binds them together. In solids the structure is nearly rigid; in liquids molecules or atoms move around each other but do not move apart; and in gases molecules or atoms move almost independently of each other and are mostly far apart. (Sections 1, 3, 4)

PS 5a The total energy of the universe is constant. Energy can be transferred by collisions in chemical and nuclear reactions, by light waves and other radiations, and in many other ways. However, it [energy] can never be destroyed. (Section 2)

PS 5b All energy can be considered to be either kinetic energy, which is the energy of motion; potential energy, which depends on relative position; or energy contained by a field, such as electromagnetic waves. (Section 1)

PS 5c The higher the temperature, the greater the atomic or molecular motion. (Section 1)

PS 5d Thus, in all energy transfers, the overall effect is that the energy is spread out uniformly. Examples are the transfer of energy from hotter to cooler objects by conduction, radiation, or convection and the warming of our surroundings when we burn fuels. (Section 2)

UCP 1 Systems, order, and organization (Sections 1–4)

UCP 2 Evidence, models, and explanation (Sections 1–4)

UCP 3 Constancy, change, and measurement (Sections 2–4)

UCP 4 Evolution and equilibrium (Section 3)

SAI 1 Abilities necessary to do scientific inquiry (Inquiry Lab: Boiling and Freezing)

SAI 2 Understandings about scientific inquiry (Sections 1–4)

ST 2 Understandings about science and technology (Section 3)

HNS 3 Historical perspectives (Section 3)

Teacher's Notes By Pascal's principle, pressure on the wall of the bottle is transmitted to all parts of the fluid contents. This increases the pressure inside the dropper. The increased pressure decreases the volume of air in the bulb so it decreases the amount of water displaced by the air. As the buoyant force decreases, the dropper sinks. Before pressure is placed on the bottle, part of the bulb should extend above the surface of the water. If not, check the dropper for leaks.

Materials per Group
- bottle, plastic, with cap, 2 L
- dropper with rubber bulb
- water

Answers
1. When the water level inside the dropper rises, the dropper starts sinking. When the water level inside the dropper decreases, the dropper floats.
2. Higher water level in the dropper corresponds to higher density. Adding more water to the dropper results in more mass for the same volume, so density is higher and the dropper sinks.
3. Submarines control the amount of water inside them to change density, allowing them to move up or down in the water.

Key Resources

📋 **Datasheet**
Changes in Density

InquiryLab ⏱ **20 min**

Changes in Density

Fill an **empty, 2 L plastic bottle** with **water**. Fill a **medicine dropper** halfway with water, and place it in the bottle. The dropper should float with part of the rubber bulb above the surface of the water. (If the dropper floats too high, remove it and add more water. If it sinks, try less water.) Place the cap tightly on the bottle, and gently squeeze the bottle. Watch the water level inside the dropper as you squeeze and release the bottle. Try to make the dropper rise, sink, or stop at any level.

Questions to Get You Started

1. How do changes inside the dropper affect its position in the water?

2. What is the relationship between the dropper's density and the dropper's position in the water?

3. How could a submarine use changes in density to move up and down?

FoldNotes

Students' key-term folds should look similar to the example shown, and should contain definitions for each of the key terms from the chapter (Section 1: *plasma, energy, thermal energy, evaporation, sublimation, condensation*. Section 2: *fluid, buoyant force, pressure, Archimedes' principle, pascal, Pascal's principle, viscosity*. Section 3: *Boyle's law, Charles' law, Gay-Lussac's law*.)

Fact, Hypothesis, or Theory?

Law of conservation of energy: When energy exists, it continues to exist. Archimedes' principle: When an object displaces a fluid, an upward buoyant force equal to the weight of the displaced fluid acts on the object. Boyle's law: For a fixed amount of gas at a constant temperature, when the pressure of the gas increases the volume of the gas decreases, and when the pressure of the gas decreases the volume of the gas increases. Charles' law: For a fixed amount of gas at a constant pressure, when the temperature of the gas increases the volume of the gas increases, and when the temperature of the gas decreases the volume of the gas decreases. Gay-Lussac's law: For a gas at a constant volume, when the pressure of the gas increases the temperature of the gas increases, and when the pressure of the gas decreases the temperature of the gas decreases.

These reading tools can help you learn the material in this chapter. For more information on how to use these and other tools, see **Appendix A.**

FoldNotes

Key-Term Fold A key-term fold can help you learn the key terms in this chapter.

Your Turn Make a key-term fold, as described in **Appendix A.**

① Write the key terms from the summary page on the front of each tab. The first few terms are shown on the right.

② As you read the chapter, write the definitions under the tabs for each term.

③ Use this FoldNote to study the key terms.

fluid

plasma

energy

Fact, Hypothesis, or Theory?

Laws and Principles A scientific law or principle describes how nature works. The following describe laws and principles:

- They are general descriptions of what happens in nature.
- They differ from theories.
- They have been confirmed by experiments.
- They can be mathematical equations.

Below is a common form of laws and principles.

Law or principle	"If *X* happens, then *Y* happens."

Your Turn As you read Sections 3 and 4, add to the list of laws and principles below. Include the conditions under which the law or principle is true.

Pascal's principle	A change in pressure at any point in an enclosed fluid will be transmitted equally to all parts of the fluid.

Note Taking

Comparison Table You can use a comparison table to organize your notes as you compare related topics. A table that compares the states of matter described in Section 1 has been started for you. It includes the following:

- topics that you are going to compare
- specific characteristics that you are going to compare

Your Turn As you read Section 1, complete the table. Add columns and rows as needed.

	SOLIDS	LIQUIDS
Shape and volume	have definite shape and volume	have definite volume; shape changes to fit container
Behavior of particles	vibrate around fixed positions	

Note Taking

Answers may vary. Three or four states of matter should be listed across the top of the table: solids, liquids, gases, (plasmas). Characteristics listed down the side of the table might include shape and volume, behavior of particles, thermal energy, and examples. Information in the table should be consistent with information in the chapter.

Matter and Energy

Key **Ideas**

❯ What makes up matter?

❯ What is the difference between a solid, a liquid, and a gas?

❯ What kind of energy do all particles of matter have?

Key **Terms**

fluid

plasma

energy

temperature

thermal energy

Why It **Matters**

When you can see your breath on a cold day, you are watching gaseous water turn into liquid water.

W hen food is cooking, energy is transferred from the stove to the food. As the temperature increases, some particles in the food move very fast and spread through the air in the kitchen. The *state,* or physical form, of a substance is determined partly by how the substance's particles move.

Kinetic Theory

If you visit a restaurant kitchen, such as the one in **Figure 1,** you can smell the food cooking even if you are a long way from the stove. One way to explain this phenomenon is to make some assumptions. First, assume that the atoms and molecules within the food substances are always in motion and are colliding with each other. Second, assume that the atoms and molecules move faster as the temperature increases.

A theory based on these assumptions is called the *kinetic theory of matter.* ❯ **According to the kinetic theory of matter, matter is made of atoms and molecules. These atoms and molecules act like tiny particles that are always in motion.** The following are observations of particles in motion.

- The higher the temperature of the substance is, the faster the particles move.

- At the same temperature, more massive particles move slower than less massive ones.

For example, consider a cup of hot tea. At first, the particles move very quickly. As the tea cools, its particles begin to slow down. As you will see, the kinetic theory can help you understand the differences between the three common states of matter: solid, liquid, and gas.

Figure 1 The ingredients in foods are chemicals. A skilled chef understands how the chemicals in foods interact and how changes of state affect cooking.

❯ Focus

This section introduces the kinetic theory of matter and compares the physical properties of solids, liquids, gases, and plasmas. The role of energy in changes of state is explained, as is temperature as a measure of average kinetic energy.

Bellringer

Use the Bellringer transparency to prepare students for this section.

Demonstrate

Motion of Particles You will need a balloon, an eyedropper, and some vanilla extract. Before class, place five drops of vanilla extract into a balloon. Inflate the balloon and tie it shut. Have students smell the balloon. Ask the students to describe what they notice when they smell the balloon and what this smell tells them about the particles of vanilla extract. (The students will smell vanilla, which demonstrates that particles of vanilla extract move through the walls of the balloon.)
LS Kinesthetic

Key Resources

Teaching Transparencies
C4 Three States of Matter
C5 Kinetic Energy and States of Matter

Visual Concepts
Kinetic Molecular Theory
Gas
Solid, Liquid, and Gas
Liquid

Datasheet
Hot or Cold?

Cross-Disciplinary Worksheet
Integrating Physics—Plasma

Teaching Key Ideas

States of Matter The drawings in **Figure 2** are two-dimensional models of the three principal states of matter. Ask students to compare the space between particles for the three states of matter illustrated. (The particles of a liquid and the particles of a solid are about the same distance apart. The particles of a gas are much farther apart than the particles of a liquid or solid are.) Have students compare the shape and volume of the states of matter illustrated. (Solids have definite shape and volume. Liquids have definite volume, but not definite shape. Gases have neither definite shape nor definite volume. Gases will expand to fill the container they are in.)
LS **Visual/Verbal**

READING TOOLBOX

Comparison Table If students have trouble getting started with their comparison tables, have them think about specific solids, liquids, and gases and the state-related properties that make various items useful. Ask students: "Why does a desk have to be made of a solid material?" "How would a basketball be different if it were filled with liquid instead of gas?" (Accept all reasonable answers.) **LS** **Verbal**

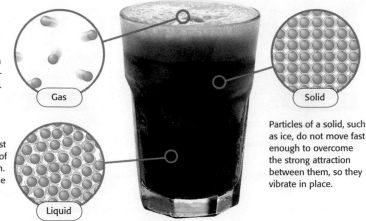

Particles of a gas, such as carbon dioxide, move fast enough to overcome nearly all of the attraction between them. The particles move independently of one another.

Gas

Solid

Particles of a solid, such as ice, do not move fast enough to overcome the strong attraction between them, so they vibrate in place.

Particles of a liquid move fast enough to overcome some of the attraction between them. The particles are able to slide past one another.

Liquid

Figure 2 Three Familiar States of Matter

READING TOOLBOX

Comparison Table
Complete a comparison table for the three common states of matter as you read these pages. See the Reading Toolbox on p. 76 if you need help getting started.

States of Matter

Three familiar states of matter are solid, liquid, and gas, as **Figure 2** shows. Notice the differences in the atomic models for each state. Particles in a solid vibrate in place. In a liquid, the particles are closely packed, but they can slide past each other. Gas particles are in constant motion and do not usually stick together. ❯ **You can classify matter as a solid, a liquid, or a gas by determining whether the shape and volume are definite or variable.** Most matter found naturally on Earth is either a solid, a liquid, or a gas, although matter can also be in other states.

Solids have a definite shape and volume.

An ice cube removed from an ice tray has the same volume and shape that it had in the ice tray. The structure of a solid is rigid, and the particles cannot easily change position. The particles are held closely together by strong attractions, and they vibrate in place. Because of the strong attractions between the particles, solids have a definite shape and volume.

Liquids change shape, not volume.

The particles in a liquid move more rapidly than the particles in a solid do. The particles move fast enough to overcome some of the forces of attraction between them. Thus, liquids flow freely. And liquids are able to take the shape of their containers. Although liquids change shape, they do not easily change volume. The particles of a liquid are close together and are in contact most of the time. Thus, the volume of a liquid remains constant.

MISCONCEPTION /// **ALERT** \\\

Amorphous Solids A common misconception is that all solids are rigid, hard substances. Therefore, students may have difficulty understanding that amorphous solids, such as rubber bands, are solids. Students may think that because many amorphous solids do not hold their shape, amorphous solids are not solids. Explain that although the particles in an amorphous solid are not arranged in a definite pattern, each particle remains in position relative to the surrounding particles.

Differentiated Instruction

Advanced Learners

Forms of Solids Provide students with a hand lens and samples of salt, sugar, margarine or butter, and a rubber band. Give students time to observe and compare all of the samples. Encourage them to investigate and describe the differences between an amorphous solid and a crystalline solid, and then have them make a chart of other solid materials, classifying each material as an amorphous or crystalline solid. (Salt and sugar are crystalline solids. Margarine, butter, and rubber bands are amorphous solids.) **LS** **Visual/Logical**

Gases change both shape and volume.

Like liquids, gases do not have fixed shapes. Liquids and gases both can flow. Because the particles in liquids and gases can move past each other, liquids and gases are **fluids.**

But gases change more than shape—they change volume, too. If you leave a bottle of perfume open, particles of the liquid perfume will escape as gas, and you will smell it around the room. The particles of a gas move fast enough to break away from each other. So, the amount of empty space between the particles changes, and the gas expands to fill the space.

For example, consider the cylinder of helium shown in **Figure 3.** It can fill about 700 balloons. The helium atoms in the cylinder have been forced close together, or *compressed.* But as the helium fills a balloon, the atoms spread out, and the amount of empty space between gas particles increases.

✓ **Reading Check** What is one difference between liquids and gases? (See Appendix E for answers to Reading Checks.)

Plasma is the most common state of matter.

Scientists estimate that 99% of the known matter in the universe, including the sun and other stars, is made of plasma. **Plasma** is a state of matter that does not have a definite shape or volume. Particles in plasma are electrically charged, or *ionized.* Natural plasmas are found in lightning, fire, and the aurora borealis shown in **Figure 4.** The glow of fluorescent light is caused by artificial plasma, which is formed by passing electric currents through gases.

Plasmas are similar to gases but have some properties that are different from the properties of gases. For instance, plasmas conduct electric current, while gases do not.

Figure 3 The particles of helium gas in the cylinder are much closer together than the particles of the gas in the balloons.

fluid (FLOO id) a nonsolid state of matter in which the atoms or molecules are free to move past each other, as in a gas or liquid

plasma (PLAZ muh) a state of matter that consists of free-moving ions and electrons

Figure 4 Auroras form when high-energy plasma collides with gas particles in the upper atmosphere. **What other states of matter do you see in the photograph?**

Why It **Matters**

Trees and Water The tallest living organism is the giant sequoia tree, which grows primarily in California and can reach a height of 100 m. As water evaporates from the leaves, a thin column of liquid water molecules travels up through the tissues of the trunk and limbs. Ask students why many plants are dormant in winter. (Water is frozen, so there is no liquid water available for the plants. The plants become dormant during the winter because they cannot replace the water needed for growth.) **LS** **Verbal/Logical**

MISCONCEPTION ALERT

Gas Mass A common misconception is that gases do not have mass. Clarify that all gases have mass because all matter has mass. For example, a cubic kilometer of air at sea level has a mass of about 1×10^9 kg. Ask students: "What is the mass of 10 grams of liquid water when it evaporates?" (10 grams)

Teaching Key Ideas

Particles of Matter Ask students to describe helium (think of a helium balloon). (a clear colorless gas that is less dense than air) Then have students look at **Figure 3.** Point out that the helium gas inside the tank and the balloons is matter, so it is made of small particles. What evidence in the picture indicates that helium is a form of matter? (It fills the balloon and pushes against the inside wall of the balloon.) **LS** **Visual**

Demonstrate

Visualizing Particles Divide the class into three groups. Have one group enact the behavior of a solid, have another group enact the behavior of a liquid, and have the third group enact the behavior of a gas. Tell students that each member of the group represents a particle. For the liquid and gas groups, you might want to define a boundary to represent a container. Have each group perform for the class. After each performance, have groups explain why they chose the specific behaviors they exhibited to represent that state of matter. **LS** **Interpersonal/Kinesthetic**

Answer to caption question

Sample answer: The trees and snow are solids, and the air is a gas.

Teaching Key Ideas

Energetic Particles Have students hold one hand in front of them, flat with palm up, and then place a sheet of paper on the palm. What happens to the paper when the hand is held as motionless as possible? (The paper still moves with small vibrations.) Explain that all matter is in motion all the time. The motion of the paper is due to tiny motions of the hand muscles even if the movement of the hand is too slight to detect. Particles of matter, including solids, are constantly in motion, even if an object does not appear to be moving. This energy of motion is kinetic energy. **LS** Verbal

QuickLab

Teacher's Notes Students should observe that the warm water felt warmer to the hand that had been in cold water, and cooler to the hand that had been in hot water.

Materials per Group
• bucket of warm water
• bucket of cold water
• bucket of hot water

Answer to Analysis

1. Hands are unreliable temperature indicators. The warm water felt warmer because it was the initial exposure to water temperature on the skin surface. The warm water felt cooler at first than it did after I put my hand in the cold water.

Energy's Role

What sources of energy would you use if the electricity were off? You might use candles for light and batteries to power a clock. Electricity, candles, and batteries are sources of energy. The food you eat is also a source of energy. **Energy** is the ability to change or move matter, or to do *work*. The energy of motion is called *kinetic energy*.

According to kinetic theory, all matter is made of particles—atoms and molecules—that are constantly in motion. ❯ **Because they are in motion, all particles of matter have kinetic energy. Figure 5** compares the kinetic energy of the particles in a solid, a liquid, and a gas.

Temperature is a measure of average kinetic energy.

Do you think of temperature as a measure of how hot or cold something is? Specifically, **temperature** is a measure of the average kinetic energy of the particles in an object. Particles of matter are <u>constantly</u> moving, but they do not all move at the same speed. As a result, some particles have more kinetic energy than others have. When you measure an object's temperature, you measure the average kinetic energy of the particles in the object. The more kinetic energy the particles of an object have, the higher the temperature of the object is.

✔ **Reading Check** What does temperature measure?

Academic Vocabulary
constant (KAHN stuhnt) without interruption; continual

Figure 5 Kinetic Energy of Solids, Liquids, and Gases

Solid

The particles in an ice cube vibrate in place. Compared to the particles in liquids and gases, they have the least kinetic energy.

Liquid

The particles in ocean water move around. They have more kinetic energy than the particles in a solid but less than those in a gas.

Gas

The particles in steam move around rapidly. Compared to the particles in solids and liquids, they have the most kinetic energy.

Differentiated Instruction

Alternative Assessment

Thermal Energy Explain to students that the thermal energy of Earth's oceans has a profound effect on climate and weather. An example of this is the phenomenon known as El Niño and its counterpart La Niña. Have students research these two phenomena and describe in a report or a poster how thermal energy is responsible for each. **LS** Verbal/Visual

Special Education Students

Heat Transfer Have students place a piece of butter into a glass of cold water and another piece of butter in a glass of hot water. Ask the students to predict what will happen before they perform the experiment. (Although the butter does not dissolve in the water, the hot water will transfer energy to the butter, causing it to melt.) **LS** Kinesthetic/Verbal

QuickLab

Hot or Cold?

⏱ 10 min

Procedure

❶ You will need **three buckets**: one with **warm water,** one with **cold water,** and one with **hot water.** CAUTION: Test a drop of the hot water to make sure that it is not too hot to put your hands into.

❷ Put both of your hands into the bucket of warm water, and note how the water feels.

❸ Now, put one hand into the bucket of cold water and the other into the bucket of hot water.

❹ After a minute, take your hands out of the hot and cold water, and put them back in the warm water.

Analysis

1. Can you rely on your hands to determine temperature? Explain your observations.

Thermal energy depends on particle speed and number of particles.

The temperature of a substance is not determined by how much of the substance you have. For example, a teapot holds more tea than a mug does. But the temperature, or average kinetic energy, of the particles in the tea is the same in both containers. However, the total kinetic energy of the particles in each container is different. The total kinetic energy of the particles that make up a substance is **thermal energy.**

Because particles of matter move faster at higher temperatures than they do at lower temperatures, the faster the particles in a substance move, the more kinetic energy they have. However, the *total* kinetic energy (thermal energy) of a substance depends on the number of particles in that substance. Look back at **Figure 5.** Although the individual particles in the steam have the most kinetic energy, the ocean has the greatest thermal energy because it contains so many more particles.

energy (EN uhr jee) the capacity to do work

temperature (TEM puhr uh chuhr) a measure of how hot (or cold) something is; specifically, a measure of the average kinetic energy of the particles in an object

thermal energy (THUHR muhl EN uhr jee) the total kinetic energy of a substance's atoms

Section 1 Review

KEY IDEAS

1. **List** three main points of the kinetic theory of matter.
2. **State** two examples for each of the four states of matter.
3. **Compare** the shape and volume of solids, liquids, and gases.
4. **Describe** the relationship between temperature and kinetic energy.

CRITICAL THINKING

5. **Compare and Contrast** Compare the temperature and thermal energy of hot soup in a small mug and that of hot soup in a large bowl.
6. **Applying Concepts** Which particles have the strongest attraction between them: the particles of a gas, the particles of a liquid, or the particles of a solid?
7. **Making Inferences** Use the kinetic theory to explain how a dog could find you by your scent.

❯ Close

Reteaching Key Ideas

Adding Energy Place a handful of small rubber balls in a shallow box so that they form a single layer on the bottom of the box. Have students shake the box back and forth gently and observe the motion of the balls. Then, have students shake the box vigorously, adding more energy to the balls. Discuss how this model illustrates a change of state as energy is added to a substance. (The balls represent atoms or molecules. As energy is added, the balls move faster and may eventually escape the box, moving far apart. This represents the change of state from liquid to gas.)

LS **Visual/Kinesthetic**

Formative Assessment

Which of the following statements describes a solid, liquid, and a gas?

A. They have definite volume, but variable shape. (Incorrect. Only solids and liquids have definite volume. Gases expand to fill the container they are in.)

B. They have variable volume and shape, but the distance between particles remains constant. (Incorrect. Gases have particles that are very far apart while solids have particles that are very close together.)

C. They can be classified based on their shape and volume. (Correct. Solids have definite shape and volume. Liquids have variable shape and definite volume. Gases have variable shape and variable volume.)

D. They change state only when energy is added to the material. (Incorrect. The addition of energy causes a change in state, but these changes also occur when energy is removed.)

Answers to Section Review

1. Atoms and molecules are always in motion. Particles move faster at higher temperatures. At any temperature, heavier particles move slower than lighter particles do.

2. Sample answers: solid—marble and brass; liquid—water and mercury; gas—oxygen and nitrogen; plasma—fire and lightning

3. Solids have definite volume and shape; liquids have definite volume but no definite shape; gases have neither definite volume nor definite shape.

4. Temperature is a direct measure of average kinetic energy.

5. Both have the same temperature, but the large bowl of soup has more thermal energy than the small mug of soup does because there is more matter present in the bowl.

6. Sample answer: The particles of a solid have a stronger attraction to one another than the particles of a liquid or a gas has.

7. Gas particles can move freely in all directions. The traces of chemicals that a person leaves when he or she touches something absorb energy, vaporize, and spread outward, so that a dog can detect them.

Plasma A plasma is a fourth state of matter, similar to a gas, except that the electrons are not bound to particular atoms, but are instead free to flow throughout the plasma. Plasmas form when a gas absorbs enough energy to ionize the atoms and free the electrons. A plasma can often be recognized because it tends to emit light.

Although plasmas are relatively rare on Earth, 99% of all visible matter in the universe is in the plasma state. The sun and other stars, as well as glowing interstellar matter, are all primarily plasma. Inside the sun, particles have so much energy that the electrons are completely removed from atoms. The electrons form much of the solar wind, a flow of particles from the sun.

Plasmas on Earth include lightning, the mercury plasma in fluorescent lights, and the aurora borealis. Plasma televisions contain small bubbles of neon or xenon that are enclosed within small chambers between two sheets of glass. When electric currents excite these gases, they ionize to become plasmas and emit ultraviolet (UV) light. This UV light in turn excites red, green, or blue phosphors that produce one part (one pixel) of the visible image on the TV screen. The plasma can only exist as long as there is enough energy added to it to keep the oppositely charged ions apart.

Plasma

We are surrounded by matter in one of three states: solid, liquid, and gas. But 99.9% of all matter in the universe, including the sun and all other stars, is plasma. Matter in the plasma state is a collection of free-moving electrons and ions, or atoms that have lost electrons. Plasmas conduct electricity and are affected by magnets. They require an energy source to exist. This energy may be a heat source, such as the heat of the sun; an electric current; or a strong light, such as a laser.

The sun is a giant ball of superheated plasma. On its surface, violent eruptions send waves of plasma streaming out into space at high speeds. Earth is bathed in waves of plasma known as solar wind. After periods of disturbance on the surface of the sun, strong solar winds can disrupt radio and telephone communications, damage orbiting satellites, and cause electrical blackouts. Scientists are working to understand the forces behind solar wind and hope to better forecast damaging solar wind that is headed toward Earth.

Some plasmas, including lightning and fire, occur naturally on Earth. Artificial plasmas, including fluorescent and neon lights, are created by running an electric current through a gas to change the gas into a plasma that emits light. When the current is removed, the plasma becomes a gas again.

WEIRD SCIENCE

Scientists hope to someday harness nuclear fusion—the process that powers the sun and other stars. Fusion occurs at very high temperatures, so the fuel for fusion is a plasma. In the Tokamak Fusion Reactor, shown here, the plasma is heated in a ring-shaped vessel. Strong magnetic fields keep the plasma from touching the walls. Scientists study the plasma to learn more about fusion as a possible future energy source on Earth.

SCI LINKS.
www.scilinks.org
Topic: Plasma
Code: HK81169

YOUR TURN

CRITICAL THINKING
1. Why do you think scientists want to predict solar winds in Earth's atmosphere?

ONLINE RESEARCH
2. Research the Tokamak Fusion Reactor, and answer the following questions: What do scientists hope to achieve with this research? What challenges do scientists face when studying plasma?

Why It Matters

Fusion on Earth Controlled fusion reactions, which are needed to produce power by fusion, have only occurred on Earth in lab experiments. Uncontrolled fusion reactions have taken place when nuclear weapons have been detonated as part of a test. Neither lab experiments nor bomb tests have resulted in a fusion reaction that could be harnessed as an economically efficient and practical source of energy.

MISCONCEPTION
ALERT

Energy in the Sun Because people sometimes talk about the sun as "burning out," students may believe that the source of solar energy is similar to combustion. Explain that fusion reactions are very different from chemical reactions, such as burning. Fusion reactions involve the formation of larger nuclei from the combining of two or more smaller nuclei, which releases energy. Burning involves the breakdown of materials to release energy. Burning releases far less energy than fusion does.

Answers to Your Turn

1. Scientists would like to predict solar winds because solar winds can disrupt radio and telephone communications, damage satellites, and cause electrical blackouts.

2. Answers may vary. Students should recognize that scientists are trying to harness the energy of fusion reactions. Students should also recognize that because of its high temperature, plasma is a difficult material to contain and manipulate.

Changes of State

This section reviews the role of energy in changes of state and describes specific changes of state in terms of the flow of energy as heat. The section concludes with an explanation of the law of conservation of mass and the law of conservation of energy.

 Bellringer

Use the Bellringer transparency to prepare students for this section.

Demonstrate

Changes in Energy You will need a bottle of rubbing alcohol for the class and a cotton swab for each student. Have each student dip the swab in the alcohol and then make a streak across the palms of his or her hand or wrist. Then, have students describe what happened to their hand and the alcohol. (Sample answer: My hand felt cooler, and the alcohol evaporated.) Ask students: "How can you tell that there was a change of energy and what was the source of the heat energy?" (Sample answer: The alcohol changed from the liquid state to the gas state. The change needed an input of energy. Energy was transferred as heat from the student's body to the alcohol, causing a sensation of coldness.)
Safety Caution: Do not let students handle the bottle of rubbing alcohol. **LS Kinesthetic/Visual**

Key Ideas

❯ What happens when a substance changes from one state of matter to another?

❯ What happens to mass and energy during physical and chemical changes?

Key Terms

evaporation

sublimation

condensation

Why It Matters

The evaporation that occurs when you sweat helps to keep your body cool in warm weather.

What causes dew drops to form or causes ice to melt? These changes of state—conversions of a substance from one physical form to another—are caused by energy transfers.

Energy and Changes of State

Five changes of state of water are shown in **Figure 1.** The ice, liquid water, and steam are all the same substance—water, H_2O. But they all have different amounts of energy. ❯ **The identity of a substance does not change during a change of state, but the energy of a substance does change.**

If energy is added to a substance, its particles move faster. If energy is removed, the substance's particles move slower. For instance, the particles in steam have more energy than the particles in liquid water. A transfer of energy known as *heat* causes the temperature of a substance to change. If enough energy is added or removed, the substance will change state.

evaporation (ee VAP uh RAY shuhn) the change of state from a liquid to a gas

sublimation (SUHB luh MAY shuhn) the process in which a solid changes directly into a gas

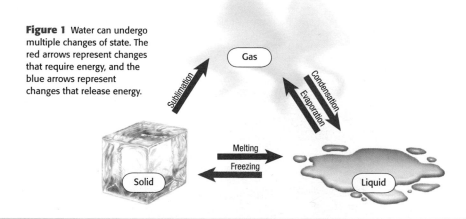

Figure 1 Water can undergo multiple changes of state. The red arrows represent changes that require energy, and the blue arrows represent changes that release energy.

Gas

Sublimation

Condensation

Evaporation

Melting

Freezing

Solid

Liquid

Key Resources

Teaching Transparencies
TM8 Changes in State for Water
C6 Changes in State

Visual Concepts
Law of Conservation of Mass
Law of Conservation of Energy
Vaporization and Condensation

Datasheet
Boiling Water

Cross-Disciplinary Worksheets
Science and the Consumer—Dry Ice
Integrating Space Science—Our
    Changing Universe
Science and the Consumer—
    Refrigerants

Some changes of state require energy.

A solid changes to a liquid by melting. Heating a solid transfers energy to the particles, which vibrate faster as they gain energy. Eventually, they break from their fixed positions, and the solid melts. The *melting point* is the temperature at which a substance changes from solid to liquid. Melting point depends on the pressure.

Evaporation is the change of a substance from a liquid to a gas. Boiling is evaporation that occurs throughout a liquid at a specific temperature and pressure. The temperature at which a liquid boils is the liquid's *boiling point*.

Solids can also change directly into gases in a process called **sublimation**. In **Figure 2**, solid carbon dioxide (dry ice) changes into gaseous carbon dioxide. Ice cubes in a freezer will eventually get smaller, as the ice sublimes. Note that melting, evaporation, and sublimation all require energy.

✅ **Reading Check** What is one example of sublimation?

Figure 2 Solid dry ice changes directly into a gas. **Which change of state is shown here?**

❯Teach

Teaching Key Ideas

Interpreting Visuals Have students look at **Figure 1.** Ask them: "During which changes of state are the substances gaining energy?" (melting, sublimation, and evaporation) Ask students to explain how they are able to determine this. (Sample answer: In melting, a substance is changed from a solid to a liquid, the latter of which is more energetic. Sublimation is the change of a solid to a gas. A gas has more energy than a solid does. Evaporation occurs when a liquid becomes a gas. Gases have more energy than either liquids or solids do.) **LS** **Logical**

Answer to caption question
sublimation

Why It **Matters**

Why Do People Sweat?

REAL WORLD

You can feel the effects of an energy change when you sweat. Energy is needed to separate the particles of a liquid to form a gas. As you sweat, energy from your body is transferred to sweat molecules as heat. This energy transfer cools your body.

Nitrogen molecule in air

Water vapor in air

The molecules in sweat on your skin gain energy from your body and move faster. Eventually, the fastest-moving particles break away, and the sweat evaporates. This loss of energy by the body makes the body feel cooler.

Sweat droplet

Oxygen molecule in air

YOUR TURN
CRITICAL THINKING
1. Does your body take in energy or give off energy during sweating? Explain.

Why It **Matters**

Why Do People Sweat? Converting water from a liquid to a vapor takes a certain amount of heat energy. The added heat energy makes water molecules move faster and then they escape from the skin. The amount of evaporation is affected by the relative humidity of the air around you. If humidity is high, then the air has a lot of water vapor in it and cannot hold much more water vapor. Ask students to predict how this affects sweating. (In very humid climates, sweating does not cool the body very effectively.) Ask students to predict the effectiveness of sweating in low humidity. (More water vapor can enter the air, so sweating is more effective in dry climates.) Relate to students that they may not even recognize that they are sweating in dry climates because sweat evaporates so quickly. **LS** **Verbal/Logical**

Why It **Matters**

Condensation There is always some water vapor in air but when the amount of water vapor exceeds a temperature-based limit, some of the water vapor changes state. Usually, human breath is warmer than the surrounding air is and has more water vapor than the surrounding air does. As the air released from human lungs cools, water may change state to make tiny drops of liquid water. If a person breathes on a very cold window, the water vapor may change to ice. Ask students how this concept relates to water forming on a glass containing a cold drink on a warm day. (Sample answer: Water vapor cools against the side of the glass, forming droplets on the glass.) **LS** **Logical**

Answer to Your Turn
1. My body gives off energy during sweating. Sweat gains energy from my body and evaporates. This energy transfer is how sweat cools the body.

>Teach, continued

QuickLab

Teacher's Notes Because the boiling temperature of the water depends on the size of the syringes used, determine in advance the necessary temperature.

Materials per Group
- syringe
- warm water

Answers to Analysis

1. I am not burned because the water is boiling at a lower temperature than its normal boiling point of 100 °C.
2. A decrease in pressure lowers the boiling point.

READING TOOLBOX

Comparison Table On the board, create a table that includes the following heads: "Changes that absorb energy" (melting, evaporation, and sublimation) and "Changes that release energy" (freezing and condensation). Ask students to add the changes of state under the appropriate heading. Explain to students that it is also possible for matter to go directly from the gas state to the solid state, as when frost forms on a very cold window. Ask students: "Does a substance that changes state from a gas to a solid absorb or release energy?" (release) **LS Logical**

Answer to caption question
condensation

QuickLab Boiling Water

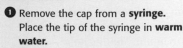

⏱ 10 min

Procedure

❶ Remove the cap from a **syringe.** Place the tip of the syringe in **warm water.**

❷ Pull the plunger out until you have 10 mL of water in the syringe.

❸ Tighten the cap on the syringe. Hold the syringe, and slowly pull the plunger out. This decreases the pressure inside the syringe.

❹ Observe any changes you see in the water. Record your observations.

Analysis

1. Water usually boils at 100 °C. Why are you not burned by the boiling water in the syringe?

2. What effect does a decrease in pressure have on the boiling point of the water?

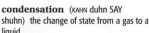

condensation (KAHN duhn SAY shuhn) the change of state from a gas to a liquid

READING TOOLBOX

Comparison Table
Make a comparison table for five changes of state that water may undergo. Include information about the states of matter involved and about the direction of energy transfer.

Figure 3 Dew drops can form overnight. Water vapor from the air turns into a liquid when it contacts a cool surface such as grass or a dragonfly's wings. **Which change of state is shown here?**

Energy is released in some changes of state.

When water vapor in the air becomes a liquid, as **Figure 3** shows, energy is released from the water to its surroundings. This process is an example of **condensation,** which is the change of state from a gas to a liquid. For a gas to become a liquid, large numbers of gas particles clump together. Energy is released from the gas, and the particles slow down.

Condensation sometimes takes place when a gas comes in contact with a cool surface. For instance, drops of water form on the outside of a glass that contains a cool drink. The *condensation point* of a gas is the temperature at which the gas becomes a liquid.

Energy is also released during freezing, which is the change of state from a liquid to a solid. The temperature at which a liquid changes into a solid is the substance's *freezing point.* Freezing and melting occur at the same temperature. For example, liquid water freezes at the same temperature that ice melts: 0 °C. For a liquid to freeze, the attractions between the particles must overcome their motion.

✔ **Reading Check** What is the relationship between the freezing point and the melting point of a substance?

Teaching Key Ideas

Water Vapor Water is the only substance that can be found as a solid, a liquid, and a gas at the various surface temperatures on Earth. Students might think that when they see a cloud, they see water vapor. Emphasize that water vapor cannot be seen. Relate to students that clouds are made up of small droplets of water that have condensed from water vapor around a particle of dust or dirt. Ice and snow sometimes sublime directly to water vapor. If the air is dry after a snowstorm, a thin layer of ice on a street may disappear in a few hours, even though the temperature never rises above freezing.

Differentiated Instruction

Basic Learners

Reading Skills Write the following on the board: "The temperature of boiling water is 100° on the Celsius scale and 212° on the Fahrenheit scale. The temperature in the room is about 22° on the Celsius scale and 70° on the Fahrenheit scale." Then, have students decide whether they think that the following temperatures are hot or cold: 65 °F, 65 °C, 27 °F, 27 °C, 0 °F, 0 °C, 100 °F, and 100 °C. **LS Logical**

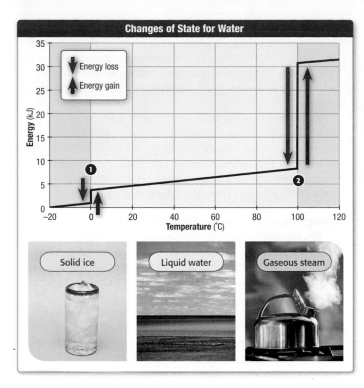

Changes of State for Water

Energy loss
Energy gain

Energy (kJ) / Temperature (°C)

Solid ice | Liquid water | Gaseous steam

Figure 4 Temperature remains constant when matter changes state. **Why are the arrows on each side the same length?**

❶ Energy is released when water freezes and is absorbed when ice melts.

❷ Energy is released when water vapor condenses and is absorbed when water vaporizes.

Temperature is constant during changes of state.

When a substance loses or gains energy, either its temperature changes or its state changes. But the temperature of a substance does not change during a change of state, as **Figure 4** shows. For example, if you add energy to ice at 0 °C, the temperature will not rise until all of the ice has melted.

Conservation of Mass and Energy

Look back at the changes of state shown in **Figure 4.** When an ice cube melts, the mass of the liquid water is the same as the mass of the ice cube. This change of state is an example of a physical change. Mass is conserved for all physical and chemical changes.

Likewise, energy can change forms during physical and chemical changes, but the total amount of energy present before and after a change is the same. The amount of energy in a substance can change, but this added energy must come from another source. ❯ **Mass and energy are both conserved. Neither mass nor energy can be created or destroyed.** These principles are fundamental laws of physical science.

Integrating Space Science

The Mass of the Universe Studies of the chemical changes that stars and nebulae undergo are constantly adding to our knowledge. Current estimates are that hydrogen makes up more than 90% of the atoms in the universe and makes up about 75% of the mass of the universe. Helium atoms make up most of the remainder of the mass of the universe. The total mass of all of the other elements is a very small part of the total mass of the universe.

Answer to caption question
The arrows are the same length because the same amount of energy is needed for each change of state; the energy is transferred in opposite directions.

Teaching Key Ideas

Interpreting Visuals Draw students' attention to the vertical segments of the graph in **Figure 4.** Ask students: "What is happening to the energy if it is not causing an increase in temperature?" (The energy is being absorbed or released by the material during a change of state.) **LS Visual**

MISCONCEPTION ALERT

Freezing Points Students may think that two different substances with the same mass and same initial temperature release the same amount of energy when they freeze, and that freezing only occurs at very cold temperatures. Point out that the amount of energy released by a substance during freezing and the substance's freezing point are physical properties unique to that substance. Depending on the substance, freezing can occur at high or low temperatures. For example, ammonia freezes at –77.7 °C, and magnesium freezes at 650 °C.

Differentiated Instruction

English Learners

Change of State Have students draw a sequence of changes of state, from solid to liquid to gas or vice versa. After completing their drawings, ask students to create a concept map that shows the changes of state and whether each change of state requires energy or releases energy. **LS Visual**

Social Studies Connection

Frederick McKinley Jones Frederick McKinley Jones (1892–1961) was an African-American inventor who had more than 60 patents to his name. One of his most important inventions was a compact, automatic-refrigeration unit for trucks that were transporting produce. His invention, later adapted for trains, is still in use. **LS Verbal**

Reteaching Key Ideas

Adding Energy Discuss with the class the conservation of mass and energy that occurs when a candle burns. Ask students: "Where does the energy come from and where does it go?" (Energy comes from the chemical changes that occur as the candle burns, and it is released into the surroundings as light and heat.) "How is mass conserved as the candle disappears?" (Mass is conserved but all of the products of the reaction cannot be seen because some of the products are gases.) **LS** **Logical/Verbal**

Formative Assessment

How are mass and energy affected by a physical and chemical change?

A. The amount of mass and energy remains constant in an open system. (Incorrect. Mass and energy will remain constant in a closed system, but some mass and energy may be lost in an open system.)

B. Mass and energy can be converted to other forms. (Correct. Mass and energy are neither created nor destroyed, but they can be converted to other forms.)

C. Some mass and energy are destroyed. (Incorrect. Mass and energy are never destroyed; instead, they are converted to other forms.)

D. Mass and energy are created. (Incorrect. Mass and energy cannot be created. They are converted from other forms.)

www.scilinks.org
Topic: Conservation of Energy
Code: **HK80345**

Figure 5 Energy is conserved when gasoline is burned to power a lawn mower.

Mass cannot be created or destroyed.

In chemical changes, as well as in physical changes, the total mass of the substances undergoing the change stays the same before and after the change. In other words, mass cannot be created or destroyed, which is the *law of conservation of mass*.

For instance, when you burn a match, it seems to lose mass. The ash has less mass than the match. But the oxygen that reacts with the match, the tiny smoke particles, and the gases formed in the reaction also have mass. The total mass of the reactants (the match and oxygen) is the same as the total mass of the products (the ash, smoke, and gases).

Energy cannot be created or destroyed.

Energy may be changed to another form during a physical or chemical change, but the total amount of energy present before and after the change is the same. In other words, energy cannot be created or destroyed, which is the *law of conservation of energy*.

Starting a lawn mower, as **Figure 5** shows, may seem to violate the law of conservation of energy, but that is not the case. It is true that for the small amount of energy needed to start the mower, a lot of energy results. But the mower needs gasoline to run. Gasoline has stored energy that is released when it is burned. When the stored energy is considered, the energy present before you start the lawn mower is equal to the energy that is produced.

Some of the energy from the gasoline is transferred to the surroundings as heat, which is why the lawn mower gets hot. The total amount of energy released by the gasoline is equal to the energy used to power the lawn mower plus the energy transferred to the surroundings as heat.

Section 2 Review

KEY IDEAS

1. **Describe** the following changes of state, and explain how particles behave in each state.
   a. freezing   **c.** sublimation
   b. boiling   **d.** melting
2. **State** whether energy is released or whether energy is required for the following changes of state to take place.
   a. melting   **c.** sublimation
   b. evaporation   **d.** condensation
3. **Describe** the role of energy when ice melts and when water vapor condenses to form liquid water.
4. **State** the law of conservation of mass and the law of conservation of energy, and explain how they apply to changes of state.

CRITICAL THINKING

5. **Drawing Conclusions** If you used dry ice in your holiday punch, would it become watery after an hour? Why or why not?

Answers to Section Review

1. **a.** During freezing (liquid to solid), particles slow down.

   b. During boiling (liquid to gas), particles speed up.

   c. During sublimation (solid to gas), particles speed up.

   d. During melting (solid to liquid), particles speed up.

2. **a.** Energy is required.

   b. Energy is required.

   c. Energy is required.

   d. Energy is released.

3. Sample answer: As energy is transferred to ice, the attraction between water molecules is broken and the ice melts. As water vapor releases energy, attraction between molecules increases, and liquid water condenses.

4. Mass cannot be created or destroyed. Energy cannot be created or destroyed. During a change of state, the total mass and total energy of the system remain constant.

5. Sample answer: No. Dry ice is solid carbon dioxide, which undergoes sublimation and turns directly from a solid into a gas.

Fluids

Key **Ideas**

❯ How do fluids exert pressure?

❯ What force makes a rubber duck float in a bathtub?

❯ What happens when pressure in a fluid changes?

❯ What affects the speed of a fluid in motion?

Key **Terms**

pressure

pascal

buoyant force

viscosity

Why It **Matters**

A submarine crew knows how to change the density of its boat, and this is how the crew controls the submarine's depth.

As you have learned, liquids and gases are classified as fluids. The properties of fluids allow huge ships to float, divers to explore the ocean depths, and jumbo jets to soar across the skies.

Pressure

You probably have heard the terms *air pressure, water pressure,* and *blood pressure.* **Pressure** is the amount of force exerted on a given area of surface. ❯ **Fluids exert pressure evenly in all directions.**

For instance, when you add air to a bicycle tire, you push air into the tire. Inside the tire, tiny air particles push against each other and against the walls of the tire, as **Figure 1** shows. The more air you pump into the tire, the greater the number of air particles pushing against the inside of the tire and the greater the pressure is. Pressure can be calculated by dividing force by the area over which the force is exerted.

❯ **Pressure**

$$pressure = \frac{force}{area} \qquad P = \frac{F}{A}$$

The SI unit of pressure is the **pascal.** One pascal (1 Pa) is the force of one newton exerted over an area of one square meter (1 N/m²). The newton is the SI unit of force.

pressure (PRESH uhr) the amount of force exerted per unit area of a surface

pascal (pas KAL) the SI unit of pressure; equal to the force of 1 N exerted over an area of 1 m² (symbol, Pa)

Figure 1 The force of air particles inside the tire creates pressure, which keeps the tire inflated. **How does the pressure change if you remove some of the air?**

Key Resources

 Teaching Transparencies
TM9 Archimedes' Principle
C7 Density

Visual Concept
Pressure

 Datasheet
Density and Shape

 Math Skills Worksheet
Pascal's Principle

Cross-Disciplinary Worksheets
Real World Applications—Submarines
Integrating Biology—Density and Swim
Bladders

❯**Focus**

In this section, students will learn about buoyant force and the relationship between an object's mass and its buoyant force. The role of density in an object's ability to float and the concepts of fluid pressure and viscosity are explained. Students also will learn three basic principles pertaining to fluids: Archimedes', Pascal's, and Bernoulli's principles.

Bellringer

Use the Bellringer transparency to prepare students for this section.

Demonstrate

Floating in Layers Add 20 mL each of molasses, cooking oil, and water to a 100 mL graduated cylinder. Either before students enter the classroom or while they observe the liquid layers, insert several objects that will float on the layers (for example, cork, marbles, jacks, and small plastic toys). You might also try adding droplets of alcohol to the liquids. Use the results of the demonstration to start a discussion about buoyant force. Ask students to identify what property of the liquids causes some objects to float on a particular layer while others do not. (density) **LS Visual**

Answer to caption question
If some air is removed, the pressure will decrease.

Teaching Key Ideas

Effects of Air Pressure Use a hand pump to inflate a small balloon. Keep pumping until the balloon bursts. Discuss with students what caused the balloon to explode. (As more air was pumped into the balloon, the increase in the number of molecules caused more pressure to be exerted on the inside of the balloon. When the pressure was greater than the strength of the rubber wall, the balloon exploded. **LS Logical/Verbal**

MISCONCEPTION ALERT

Buoyancy Students may think that all light objects will float, that all heavy objects will sink, and that objects that float on water will float on any fluid. Clarify that whether or not an object floats depends on its density and the density of the fluid in which it is immersed. Only objects that are less dense than the fluid will float. Objects that are more dense than the fluid will sink. Ask students to think of something that floats in water but does not float in air. (Sample answers: cork, wood, and paper)

---

buoyant force (BOY uhnt FAWRS) the upward force that keeps an object immersed in or floating on a fluid

Figure 2 Archimedes' Principle

An object is lowered into a container of water.

When the object is completely submerged, the weight of the displaced fluid equals the buoyant force acting on the object.

Buoyant Force

If you push a rubber duck to the bottom of a bathtub, the duck pops to the surface when you release it. A **buoyant force** pushes the duck up. **> All fluids exert an upward buoyant force on matter.** When you float on an air mattress in a swimming pool, the buoyant force keeps you afloat.

Buoyant force results from the fact that pressure increases with depth. The forces pushing up on an object in a fluid are greater than the forces pushing it down. Thus, there is a net upward force: the buoyant force.

Archimedes' principle is used to find buoyant force.

Archimedes, a Greek mathematician in the third century BCE, discovered a method for determining buoyant force.

Archimedes' principle | The buoyant force on an object in a fluid is an upward force equal to the weight of the fluid that the object displaces.

For example, imagine that you put a brick in a container of water, as **Figure 2** shows. The total volume of water that collects in the smaller container is the displaced volume of water from the larger container. The weight of the displaced fluid is equal to the buoyant force acting on the brick.

You can determine whether an object will float or sink by comparing the buoyant force on the object with the object's weight, as **Figure 3** shows. Note that the seagull is only partly underwater. The seagull's feet, legs, and stomach displace a weight of water that is equal to the seagull's total weight. So, the seagull is *buoyed up* and floats on the water's surface.

Figure 3 Comparing Weight and Buoyant Force

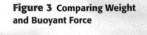

The buoyant force acting on the seagull is equal to the weight of the displaced fluid, so the seagull floats on the surface.

The buoyant force equals the fish's weight, so the fish is suspended in the water.

The weight of the shell is greater than the buoyant force, so the shell sinks.

Teaching Key Ideas

Buoyant Forces Bring in several rubber ducks and large bowls of water. Have students experiment with the amount of force needed to hold a duck underwater and the effects of releasing it underwater. Ask them to identify and describe the force that opposes submerging the duck. (The buoyant force of water pushes upward on the duck. When the duck is held underwater, the buoyant force is equal to the force pushing downward. When that force is released, the buoyant force pushes the duck to the surface.) **LS Logical/Kinesthetic**

Differentiated Instruction

Struggling Readers

Testing Surface Tension Have students fill a small, clear plastic cup to the brim with water. Next, have students predict how many paperclips can be placed in the cup before the water overflows. Have students record their prediction, and test their prediction by adding paperclips one-by-one to the cup of water. Have students record the actual number of paperclips that causes the water to overflow. **LS Kinesthetic**

QuickLab

Density and Shape

⏱ 10 min

Procedure

❶ Roll **two equal pieces of clay** into two balls (the size of golf balls). Drop the first ball into a **container of water.** Record your observations.

❷ Flatten the second ball until it is thinner than your little finger, and press it into the shape of a canoe.

❸ Place the clay boat gently into the water. Record your observations.

Analysis

1. How does the change of shape affect the buoyant force?

2. How is the change of shape related to the overall density of the boat?

An object will float or sink based on its density.

You can also determine if a substance will float or sink by comparing densities. For example, the density of a brick is about 2 g/cm³, and the density of water is 1.00 g/cm³. The brick will sink in water because it is denser than the water. On the other hand, helium has about one-seventh the density of air. A given volume of helium in a balloon displaces a volume of air that is much heavier than helium, so the balloon floats.

Steel is almost eight times denser than water. And yet huge steel ships cruise the oceans with ease. They even carry very heavy loads. But substances that are denser than water will sink in water. Given this, how does a steel ship float?

The shape of the ship allows the ship to float. Imagine a ship that was just a big block of steel, as shown on the left in **Figure 4.** If you put that steel block into water, it would sink. But ships are built with a hollow shape. The amount of steel is the same, but the hollow shape decreases the ship's density. Water is denser than the hollow ship, so the ship floats.

✔ **Reading Check** How can you use density to determine if an object will float?

Integrating Biology

Swim Bladders Some fish can adjust their density so that they can stay at a certain depth in the water. Most fish have an organ called a *swim bladder*, which is filled with gases. The inflated swim bladder increases the fish's volume, decreases the fish's overall density, and keeps the fish from sinking. The fish's nervous system controls the amount of gas in the bladder based on the fish's depth. Some fish, such as sharks, do not have a swim bladder. So, they must swim constantly to keep from sinking.

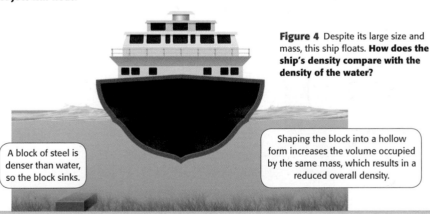

A block of steel is denser than water, so the block sinks.

Shaping the block into a hollow form increases the volume occupied by the same mass, which results in a reduced overall density.

Figure 4 Despite its large size and mass, this ship floats. **How does the ship's density compare with the density of the water?**

QuickLab

Materials per Group
- bowl or pail, medium
- clay, modeling, golf-ball sized piece
- water

Answers to Analysis

1. Forming the clay into a boat shape causes the clay to displace more water, which increases the buoyant force.

2. The change in shape causes the overall density of the clay boat to decrease so that the boat is less dense than the water. Therefore, the clay boat floats.

Science Skills

Making Models Have groups of students design models of a hot-air balloon. Beforehand, discuss how heating the air inside the balloon reduces the balloon's overall density. For their models, provide students with tissue paper, tape, glue, string, and other materials. To evaluate their models, have students hold the balloons in place over a hair dryer while another member of the group turns on the hair dryer. After the air in the balloon warms up, students should then release the balloon to see if it will fly. **Safety Caution:** Students should not hold their balloons close to the hair dryer. **LS Kinesthetic**

Answer to caption question

The ship's density is less than the water's density.

Differentiated Instruction

Advanced Learners

Lifejacket Buoyancy Ask students to apply what they have learned to explain how a lifejacket helps prevent boaters who fall out of a boat from sinking. (Most lifejackets are made from porous material that is filled with air, which greatly increases the wearer's overall volume without greatly increasing his or her mass. Thus, the wearer's overall density decreases, enabling him or her to float.) Challenge students to design a life jacket that provides the greatest amount of buoyancy using the smallest amount of material. **LS Logical**

Basic Learners

Will It Float? Place the following objects on a table: a rock, an orange, a screw, a quarter, a candle, a plastic-foam packing peanut, and a chalkboard eraser. Have students examine each object, and then write down which object or objects they think will float in water. Let students place each object in an aquarium or large bowl containing water, then have them compare their results to their predictions. Ask students to write a hypothesis for why an aircraft carrier does not sink. **LS Kinesthetic**

Teaching Key Ideas

Pascal's Principle Each time you squeeze a tube of toothpaste, you experience Pascal's principle in action. The pressure you apply by squeezing the sides of the tube is transmitted throughout the toothpaste, and is equal at all points on the tube. Because one end is open, the increased pressure forces the paste out and onto the toothbrush. Suggest that students experiment pressure at different places and different forces the next time they squeeze a toothpaste tube.

READING TOOLBOX

Laws and Principles Students should list the following principles along with a restatement of the principle: Archimedes' principle—true when any object is in a fluid; Pascal's principle—true when a fluid is enclosed; Bernoulli's principle—true when the speed of any moving fluid changes.

Connection to Social Studies

Pascal's Achievements Blaise Pascal (1623–1662) published a geometry book when he was 16 and invented a mechanical calculator at the age of 19. Working with the mathematician Pierre Fermat, Pascal laid the foundation for the study of probability and statistics. In physics, he pioneered the study of fluid mechanics. Pascal eventually abandoned mathematics and physics for meditation and religious writing. He died at the age of 39.

SCLINKS.
www.scilinks.org
Topic: Pascal's Principle
Code: HK81116

READING TOOLBOX

Laws and Principles
Write down all of the scientific laws or principles that are covered in this section. State each one in your own words, and list the conditions under which the law or principle is true.

Pascal's Principle

What happens when you squeeze one end of a tube of toothpaste? Toothpaste usually comes out the opposite end because the pressure you apply is transmitted throughout the toothpaste. So, the increased pressure near the open end of the tube forces the toothpaste out. This phenomenon is explained by Pascal's principle, which was discovered by the French scientist Blaise Pascal in the 17th century.

Pascal's principle	A change in pressure at any point in an enclosed fluid will be transmitted equally to all parts of the fluid.

> **In other words, if the pressure in a container is increased at any point, the pressure increases at all points by the same amount.** Mathematically, Pascal's principle is stated as $P_1 = P_2$. Because $P = F/A$, Pascal's principle can be expressed $F_1/A_1 = F_2/A_2$.

Hydraulic devices are based on Pascal's principle.

Hydraulic devices use liquids to transmit pressure from one point to another. Because liquids cannot be compressed into a much smaller space, they can transmit pressure more efficiently than gases can. Hydraulic devices can multiply forces. For example, in **Figure 5,** a small downward force is applied to a small area. This force exerts pressure on the liquid in the device, such as oil. According to Pascal's principle, this pressure is transmitted equally to a larger area, where the pressure creates a larger force. Note that the plunger travels through a larger distance on the side that has the smaller area.

✓ **Reading Check** How does a hydraulic device multiply force?

Figure 5 Because the pressure is the same on both sides of the enclosed fluid in a hydraulic lift, a small force on the smaller area (left) produces a much larger force on the larger area (right).

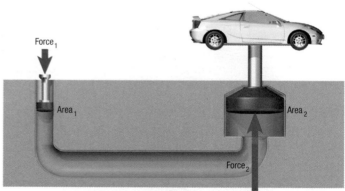

Force₁

Area₁

Area₂

Force₂

MISCONCEPTION ALERT

Pressure Students may assume that calculations involving pressure only involve the force of a fluid. Explain that because weight is a measure of gravitational force, anything that has weight exerts pressure. Thus, a crate or other object on a floor exerts pressure on the floor beneath it.

Differentiated Instruction

Advanced Learners

Hydraulic Devices Have students research the similarity between the hydraulic lifts used in auto repair shops and the power brakes used in automobiles. Ask students to make a diagram or a flow chart that illustrates the operation of a hydraulic lift and a brake system.
LS Visual

Math Skills — Pascal's Principle

A hydraulic lift uses Pascal's principle to lift a 19,000 N car. If the area of the small piston (A_1) equals 10.5 cm² and the area of the large piston (A_2) equals 400 cm², what force needs to be exerted on the small piston to lift the car?

Identify

List the given and unknown values.

Given:
$$F_2 = 19,000 \text{ N}$$
$$A_1 = 10.5 \text{ cm}^2$$
$$A_2 = 400 \text{ cm}^2$$

Unknown:
$$F_1 = ? \text{ N}$$

Plan

Start with Pascal's principle, and substitute the equation for pressure. Then, rearrange the equation to isolate the unknown value.

$$P_1 = P_2$$
$$\frac{F_1}{A_1} = \frac{F_2}{A_2}$$
$$F_1 = \frac{(F_2)(A_1)}{A_2}$$

Solve

Insert the known values into the equation, and solve.

$$F_1 = \frac{(19,000 \text{ N})(10.5 \text{ cm}^2)}{400 \text{ cm}^2}$$
$$F_1 = 500 \text{ N}$$

Practice

1. In a car's liquid-filled, hydraulic brake system, the master cylinder has an area of 0.5 cm², and the wheel cylinders each have an area of 3.0 cm². If a force of 150 N is applied to the master cylinder by the brake pedal, what force does each wheel cylinder exert on its brake pad?

For more practice, visit **go.hrw.com** and enter keyword **HK8MP**.

Practice **Hint**

❭ The pressure equation
$$pressure = \frac{force}{area}$$
can be used to find pressure or can be rearranged to find force or area.
$$force = (pressure)(area)$$
$$area = \frac{force}{pressure}$$

Fluids in Motion

Examples of moving fluids include liquids flowing through pipes, air moving as wind, or honey dripping, as **Figure 6** shows. Fluids in motion have some properties in common. Have you ever used a garden hose? When you place your thumb over the end of the hose, your thumb blocks some of the area through which the water flows out of the hose. Because the area is smaller, the water exits at a faster speed. ❭ **Fluids move faster through small areas than through larger areas, if the overall flow rate remains constant. Fluids also vary in the rate at which they flow.**

Figure 6 Dripping honey is an example of a fluid in motion.

Math Skills

Answer to Practice

1. $F_1/A_1 = F_2/A_2$, so $F_2 = F_1A_2/A_1 = $ 150 N × 3.0 cm²/0.5 cm² = 900 N

Additional Example

The pistons of a hydraulic lift have areas of 1.55 m² and 0.0065 m². How much force must be applied to the smaller piston if the larger piston is to lift a 45,000 N vehicle?
Answer: $F_1/A_1 = F_2/A_2$, so, $F_2 = F_1A_2/A_1 = $ 45,000 N × 0.0065 m²/1.55 m² = 190 N
LS Logical

Why It **Matters**

Motor Oil Bring in containers of several different types of motor oil. Have students read what the labels say about viscosity. Then, ask students to research the relationship between types of engines and driving conditions and the viscosity of the motor oil used. (The viscosity index on motor oil containers consists of an SAE, or Society of Automotive Engineers, number, typically from 5 to 50, followed by the letter W. The higher the SAE number, the more viscous the oil is. Low-viscosity oils are used in cold-weather climates because they flow more easily in cold temperatures. For hot climates or high-speed driving conditions, a high-viscosity oil is used because heat thins the oil, decreasing viscosity.)
LS Verbal

Why It **Matters**

Floating Continents The rock that makes up the Earth's continents is about 15 percent less dense than the molten mantle rock below it. Because of this difference in densities, the continents are "floating" on the mantle. How does the buoyant force on a continent compare to the force of gravity on that continent? (The buoyant force is greater.)

Teach, continued

Teaching Key Ideas

Bernoulli's Principle Ask students how a sheet of paper will move if you blow across its upper surface. (A common misconception is that it will move downward because of air pressure.) Have each student hold a sheet of paper so that it bends downward and then blow a steady stream of air above the paper. Ask how Bernoulli's principle explains their observations. (The air moving above the paper causes a decrease in pressure. The higher air pressure below the paper pushes it upward.)
LS Logical/Verbal

Answer to caption question

Because the pressure is reduced, the speed of the air (a fluid) increases.

Close

Reteaching Key Ideas

Changing Forces Place a table tennis ball and a hard ball that is denser than water in a bowl of water. When putting the balls in the water, initially push each ball to the bottom and release. Ask the students to explain the difference in the actions of the balls. (For the table tennis ball, the buoyant force is greater than the gravitational force. When the force that is holding it down is removed, the table tennis ball comes to the surface rapidly. For the other ball, the buoyant force is less than the force of gravity, so the ball remains at the bottom of the bowl when the force of the hand is removed.) **LS** Visual/Kinesthetic

viscosity (vis KAHS uh tee) the resistance of a gas or liquid to flow

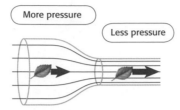

Figure 7 This leaf speeds up when it enters the narrow part of the pipe, where there is less pressure. **How does this example illustrate Bernoulli's principle?**

Viscosity depends on particle attraction.

Honey dripping from a spoon flows more slowly than lemonade poured from a pitcher. A liquid's resistance to flow is called **viscosity.** In general, the stronger the attraction between a liquid's particles is, the more viscous the liquid is. Honey flows more slowly than lemonade because honey has a higher viscosity than lemonade.

Fluid pressure decreases as speed increases.

Imagine a waterlogged leaf being carried along by water in a pipe, as **Figure 7** shows. The water will move faster through the narrow part of the pipe than through the wider part. Therefore, as the water carries the leaf into the narrow part of the pipe, the leaf moves faster.

If you measure the pressure at different points, you would find that the water pressure in front of the leaf is less than the pressure behind the leaf. The pressure difference causes the leaf and the water around it to accelerate as the leaf enters the narrow part of the tube. This behavior illustrates a general principle, known as *Bernoulli's principle,* which states that as the speed of a moving fluid increases, the pressure of the moving fluid decreases. This property of moving fluids was first described in the 18th century by Daniel Bernoulli, a Swiss mathematician.

Section 3 Review

KEY IDEAS

1. **Explain** how differences in fluid pressure create buoyant force on an object.
2. **State** Archimedes' principle, and give an example of how you could determine a buoyant force.
3. **State** Pascal's principle. Give an example of its use.
4. **Compare** the viscosity of milk and the viscosity of molasses.

CRITICAL THINKING

5. **Applying Concepts** An object weighs 20 N. It displaces a volume of water that weighs 15 N.
   a. What is the buoyant force on the object?
   b. Will the object float or sink? Explain.
6. **Drawing Conclusions** Iron has a density of 7.9 g/cm³. Mercury has a density of 13.6 g/cm³. Will iron float or sink in mercury? Explain.
7. **Making Inferences** Two boats in a flowing river are sailing side-by-side with only a narrow space between them.
   a. What happens to the fluid speed and the pressure between the two boats?
   b. How could the changes in fluid speed and pressure lead to a collision of the boats?

Math *Skills*

8. A water bed that has an area of 3.75 m² weighs 1,025 N. Find the pressure that the water bed exerts on the floor.
9. The small piston of a hydraulic lift has an area of 0.020 m². A car weighing 12,000 N is mounted on the large piston (area = 0.90 m²). What force must be applied to the small piston to support the car?

Formative Assessment

Why does a rubber duck float in your bathtub?
A. The rubber duck exerts an upward force on the water. (Incorrect. The rubber duck exerts a downward, not upward, force on the water.)
B. The rubber duck is denser than the water is. (Incorrect. If the duck were denser than the water, it would sink.)
C. The rubber duck is less dense than the water is. (Correct. The rubber duck is less dense than water is, and the weight of the water displaced is equal to the weight of the duck. As a result, the duck is buoyed up.)
D. The water exerts a downward force on the duck. (Incorrect. The water exerts an upward, not downward, force on the duck.)

Answers to Section Review

1. Sample answer: Fluid pressure is exerted on all sides of an object. The horizontal pressures cancel each other out. The pressure exerted at the bottom is greater than the pressure exerted at the top because pressure increases with depth. This creates an overall upward, or buoyant, force.
2. Archimedes' principle states that the buoyant force on an object in a fluid equals the weight of the fluid that the object displaces. To find buoyant force, weigh the fluid displaced by an object.
3. Pascal's principle states that pressure applied to a fluid in a closed container is transmitted equally throughout the fluid. The principle is used in hydraulic lifts.

Answers continued on p. 109A

How Do Submarines Work?

A submarine is a type of ship that can travel both on the surface of the water and underwater. Submarines have special ballast tanks that control their buoyancy. The crew can control the amount of water in the tanks to control the submarine's depth, as shown below.

The first submarine was used in 1776 during the American Revolution. It was a one-person, hand-powered, wooden vessel. Most modern submarines are built of metals and use nuclear power, which enables them to remain submerged almost indefinitely.

REAL WORLD

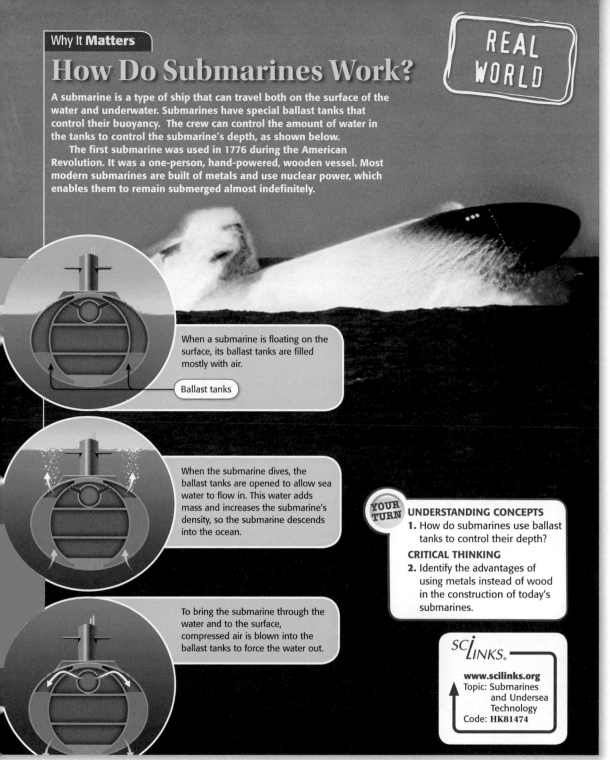

When a submarine is floating on the surface, its ballast tanks are filled mostly with air.

Ballast tanks

When the submarine dives, the ballast tanks are opened to allow sea water to flow in. This water adds mass and increases the submarine's density, so the submarine descends into the ocean.

To bring the submarine through the water and to the surface, compressed air is blown into the ballast tanks to force the water out.

YOUR TURN

UNDERSTANDING CONCEPTS
1. How do submarines use ballast tanks to control their depth?

CRITICAL THINKING
2. Identify the advantages of using metals instead of wood in the construction of today's submarines.

SCI LINKS.

www.scilinks.org
Topic: Submarines and Undersea Technology
Code: HK81474

How Do Submarines Work?

Submarines are just one type of underwater vehicle, or submersible. One type of submersible, the bathyscaphe, is like an underwater balloon. Large tanks are filled with gasoline, which is less dense than sea water, so that the bathyscaphe can float upward. Metal bearings are used to make the bathyscaphe sink.

Answers to Your Turn

1. A submarine crew changes the amount of water in the ballast tanks to change the submarine's density. The change in density causes the submarine to rise or sink in the ocean.

2. Sample answer: Some woods are less dense than water, so it would be difficult to keep a submersible made of wood under water. Wood can absorb water, which will uncontrollably increase density of the wood and affect the buoyancy of the submarine. Metal does not absorb water. Also, wood breaks down in water easier than metal does.

Behavior of Gases

›Focus

This section begins by reviewing the properties of gases and the ways in which gases differ from solids and liquids. Students will learn the three basic gas laws: Boyle's law, Charles's law, and Gay-Lussac's law. Finally, students will perform calculations using Boyle's Law.

Bellringer

Use the Bellringer transparency to prepare students for this section.

Answer to caption question

If the pressure becomes too great, the balloon will pop.

Demonstrate

Gas Flow You will need a 1-L beaker, a candle, dry ice, a flask, matches, paper, and warm water. Demonstrate the fluid property of a gas using CO_2. Place a small piece of dry ice and a little warm water in a flask. As the flask fills with CO_2, place a candle in the bottom of the large beaker, and light the candle. Form a trough from a folded sheet of paper, and pour the CO_2 gas down the trough into the beaker. The candle should extinguish. If the gas seems foggy, remind students that CO_2 cannot be seen. Water droplets suspended in CO_2 gas create the cloudy appearance.
LS Visual

Key Ideas
› What are some properties of gases?
› How can you predict the effects of pressure, temperature, and volume changes on gases?

Key Terms
gas laws

Why It Matters
The expanding gas in a car engine's cylinder provides the energy for motion.

Figure 1 Gas particles exert pressure by hitting the walls of a balloon. **What happens if the pressure becomes too great?**

Because many gases are colorless and odorless, it is easy to forget that they exist. But every day, you are surrounded by gases. Some examples of gases in Earth's atmosphere are nitrogen, oxygen, argon, helium, and carbon dioxide, as well as methane, neon, and krypton. In chemistry, as in everyday life, gases are very important.

Properties of Gases

As you have learned, gases are fluids, and their particles move rapidly in all directions. Many properties of gases are unique. › **Gases expand to fill their containers. They spread out easily and mix with one another. They have low densities and are compressible. Unlike solids and liquids, gases are mostly empty space.** All gases share these properties.

Gases exert pressure on their containers.

A balloon that is filled with helium gas is under pressure. Helium atoms in the balloon are moving rapidly. They are constantly hitting each other and the walls of the balloon, as **Figure 1** shows. Each gas particle's effect on the balloon wall is small, but the battering by millions of particles adds up to a steady force. If too many gas particles are in the balloon, the battering overcomes the force of the balloon that is holding the gas in, and the balloon pops.

If you let go of a balloon that you have pinched at the neck, most of the gas inside rushes out and causes the balloon to shoot through the air. The balloon shoots through the air because a gas under pressure will escape its container if possible. For this reason, gases in pressurized containers, such as propane tanks for gas grills, can be dangerous and must be handled carefully.

Key Resources

Teaching Transparencies
TM10 Boyle's Law
TM11 Charles's Law

Visual Concepts
Boyle's Law
Charles's Law

Datasheet
How Are Temperature and Volume Related?

Math Skills Worksheet
Boyle's Law

Cross-Disciplinary Worksheet
Real World Applications—Gas Laws

Gas Laws

You can easily measure the volume of a solid or liquid, but how do you measure the volume of a gas? The volume of a gas is the same as the volume of the gas's container. But there are other factors, such as pressure, to consider. Gases behave differently than solids and liquids. The **gas laws** describe how the behavior of gases is affected by pressure, volume, and temperature. ❯ **The gas laws will help you understand and predict the behavior of gases in specific situations.**

Boyle's law relates the pressure of a gas to its volume.

A diver at a depth of 10 m blows a bubble of air. As the bubble rises, its volume increases. When the bubble reaches the water's surface, the volume of the bubble will have doubled because of the decrease in pressure.

The relationship between the volume and pressure of a gas is known as Boyle's law. Boyle's law is stated as follows:

Boyle's law	For a fixed amount of gas at a constant temperature, the volume of a gas increases as the gas's pressure decreases. Likewise, the volume of a gas decreases as the gas's pressure increases.

Boyle's law is illustrated in **Figure 2.** Each illustration shows the same piston and the same amount of gas at the same temperature. These examples show that pressure and volume have an inverse relationship: one increases when the other decreases. Note that the temperature is not changing.

✓ Reading Check What two variables are related by Boyle's law?

gas laws (GAS LAWZ) the laws that state the mathematical relationships between the volume, temperature, pressure, and quantity of a gas

READING TOOLBOX

Laws and Principles
Write down all of the laws in this section. If possible, write the law in the form "If X happens, then Y happens," and state the conditions under which the law is true.

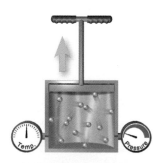 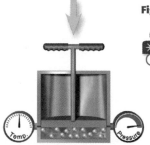

Figure 2 Boyle's Law

go.hrw.com
✳ **interact online**
Keyword: HK8STAF2

Lifting the piston decreases the pressure. The gas particles spread farther apart, and the volume increases.

Pushing the piston increases the pressure. The gas particles are pushed closer together, and the volume decreases.

Why It Matters

Internal Combustion Engine In a car engine, gasoline and air are mixed and then compressed by a piston. Combustion of the gasoline forms gases which are under high pressure because of the small volume. The pressure of the gases forces the piston to move, providing energy for the car to move.

go.hrw.com
✳ **interact online**

Students can interact with the figure by going to **go.hrw.com** and typing in the keyword **HK8STAF2**.

❯ **Teach**

Demonstrate

Gas Pressure Be sure to wear safety goggles and an apron when doing this demonstration. You will need 4 teaspoons of baking soda, two different sizes of small plastic containers with lids, and 4 tablespoons of vinegar. Place two teaspoonfuls of baking soda and two tablespoonfuls of vinegar into the smaller container. Quickly snap the lid in place. Shake the container once, and then leave it on the desk. The lid should pop off within seconds. Ask students why this happens. (Pressure from the gas caused the lid to pop off.) Repeat the demonstration using the larger container, but use the same amount of reactants. It should take longer for the lid to pop off. Have students discuss why this is the case. (More gas molecules are needed to create enough pressure to pop off the lid in the larger volume. Also, the two different containers have different characteristics, so the pressure required to pop off the lids may differ.) **LS** Visual/Logical

READING TOOLBOX

Laws and Principles Answers should include Boyle's law (applies when temperature is constant), Gay-Lussac's law (applies when volume is constant), and Charles's law (applies when pressure is constant). **LS** Logical

Teaching Key Ideas

Properties of Gases Have students squeeze two thin-walled water bottles—one unopened and filled with water and the other emptied of water and tightly recapped. Ask them to describe the differences between the bottles in terms of the properties of gases, using the words *density* and *compressible*. (The bottle filled with air is lighter because gases are mostly empty space, so they have low density. The air-filled bottle compresses but the water-filled bottle does not, because gases are compressible and liquids are not.)
LS Verbal/Kinesthetic

Math Skills

Answers to Practice

1. $P_2 = P_1V_1/V_2 = (22.5 \text{ kPa} \times 155 \text{ cm}^3)/90.0 \text{ cm}^3 = 38.8 \text{ kPa}$

2. $V_2 = P_1V_1/P_2 = (0.500 \text{ atm} \times 300.0 \text{ mL})/0.750 \text{ atm} = 200 \text{ mL}$

3. $V_2 = P_1V_1/P_2 = (0.947 \text{ atm} \times 150 \text{ mL})/1.000 \text{ atm} = 142 \text{ mL}$

Additional Example

A cylinder that has a volume of 0.15 L contains a gas at a pressure of 150 kPa. If a piston compresses the gas at constant temperature to a volume of 0.025 L, what is the new pressure of the gas?
Answer: $P_2 = P_1V_1/V_2 = 150 \text{ kPa} \times 0.15 \text{ L}/0.025 \text{ L} = 9.0 \times 10^2 \text{ kPa}$
LS Logical

Academic Vocabulary
initial (i NISH uhl) first
final (FIEN uhl) last

*SC*LINKS.
www.scilinks.org
Topic: Gas Laws
Code: HK80637

Practice Hint

❯ Problems 2 and 3: The equation for Boyle's law can be rearranged to solve for volume in the following way.

Start with the equation for Boyle's Law:
$$P_1V_1 = P_2V_2$$
Divide both sides by P_2:
$$\frac{P_1V_1}{P_2} = \frac{P_2V_2}{P_2}$$
After you cancel like terms, you are left with the final volume.
$$\frac{P_1V_1}{P_2} = V_2$$

The product of pressure and volume is constant.

Boyle's law tells you that when pressure increases, volume decreases, and vice versa. In mathematical terms, pressure multiplied by volume is constant (if temperature is constant). This is expressed as follows:

▷ **Boyle's law** | $(pressure_1)(volume_1) = (pressure_2)(volume_2)$
$P_1V_1 = P_2V_2$

P_1 and V_1 represent the <u>initial</u> volume and pressure, while P_2 and V_2 represent the <u>final</u> volume and pressure.

Math Skills Boyle's Law

The gas in a balloon has a volume of 7.5 L at 100.0 kPa. In the atmosphere, the gas expands to a volume of 11 L. Assuming a constant temperature, what is the final pressure in the balloon?

Identify List the given and unknown values.	**Given:** $V_1 = 7.5 \text{ L}$ $P_1 = 100.0 \text{ kPa}$ $V_2 = 11 \text{ L}$ **Unknown:** $P_2 = ? \text{ kPa}$
Plan Write the equation for Boyle's law, and rearrange to solve for P_2.	$P_1V_1 = P_2V_2$ $P_2 = \dfrac{P_1V_1}{V_2}$
Solve Insert the known values into the equation, and solve.	$P_2 = \dfrac{(100.0 \text{ kPa})(7.5 \text{ L})}{11 \text{ L}}$ $P_2 = 68 \text{ kPa}$

Practice

1. A flask contains 155 cm³ of hydrogen at a pressure of 22.5 kPa. Under what pressure would the gas have a volume of 90.0 cm³ at the same temperature? (Recall that 1 cm³ = 1 mL.)

2. If the pressure exerted on a 300.0 mL sample of hydrogen gas at constant temperature is increased from 0.500 kPa to 0.750 kPa, what will be the final volume of the sample?

3. A sample of oxygen gas has a volume of 150 mL at a pressure of 0.947 kPa. If the temperature remains constant, what will the volume of the gas be at a pressure of 1.000 kPa?

For more practice, visit **go.hrw.com** and enter keyword **HK8MP**.

Differentiated Instruction

Struggling Readers

Behavior of Gases Distribute a three-column chart to students with the following headings: "Observed behavior of gas," "Property of gas," and "Kinetic-molecular explanation." Then, as a class, have students list several behaviors of gases in the first column. In small groups, have students complete the other columns of the table. **LS** Logical/Interpersonal

Gay-Lussac's law relates gas pressure to temperature.

What would you predict about the relationship between the pressure and temperature of a gas at constant volume? Remember that pressure is the result of collisions of gas molecules against the walls of their containers. As temperature increases, the kinetic energy of the gas particles increases. The energy and frequency of the collision of gas particles against their containers increases. For a fixed quantity of gas at constant volume, the pressure increases as the temperature increases. This property of gases is sometimes known as Gay-Lussac's law.

Gay-Lussac's law	The pressure of a gas increases as the temperature increases, if the volume of the gas does not change. The pressure decreases as the temperature decreases.

If you often measure the pressure in your bicycle tire, as **Figure 3** shows, you may notice that the tire pressure in the winter is lower than it is in the summer. As the temperature outside decreases, the tire pressure also decreases. When the temperature outside rises, the tire pressure rises. Notice that in this example, the volume is constant.

If pressurized containers that hold gases, such as spray cans, are heated, the containers may explode. You should always be careful to keep containers of pressurized gas away from heat sources.

✅ **Reading Check** If volume is constant and temperature decreases, how does pressure change?

Figure 3 The pressure in a bicycle tire increases when temperature increases. **Which gas law does this illustrate?**

Teaching Key Ideas

Ideal Gas Law Explain to students that each of the gas laws studied are special cases of a more general law called the ideal gas law. Write the mathematical form of this law on the chalkboard:

$$\frac{P_1 V_1}{T_1} = \frac{P_2 V_2}{T_2}$$

Point out that by holding any one variable constant (temperature, pressure, or volume), the ideal gas law reduces to either Boyle's law (constant temperature), Charles's law (constant pressure), or Gay-Lussac's law (constant volume).

Answer to caption question

Gay-Lussac's law

InquiryLab

How Are Temperature and Volume Related?

🕐 **30 min**

Procedure

❶ Fill an **aluminum pan** with 5 cm of **water.** Put the pan on a **hot plate.**

❷ Fill a second **aluminum pan** with 5 cm of **ice water.**

❸ Blow up a **balloon** inside a **250 mL beaker.** The balloon should fill the beaker but should not extend outside it. Tie the balloon at its opening.

❹ Place the beaker and balloon in the ice water. Record your observations.

❺ Remove the balloon and beaker from the ice water. Observe the balloon for several minutes, and record any changes.

❻ Next, put the beaker and balloon in the hot water. Record your observations.

Analysis

1. How did changing the temperature affect the volume of the balloon?

2. Is the density of a gas affected by temperature? Explain.

InquiryLab

Teacher's Notes Remind students to wear goggles and aprons. They must also wear heat-resistant gloves when handling the hot beaker. Tell students to keep all power cords away from beakers and pans. Warn students that hot plates may remain hot for a long time.

Materials per Group
• balloon
• beaker, 250 mL
• pan, aluminum
• water, ice

Answers to Analysis
1. When the balloon cooled, it contracted. When the balloon was heated, it expanded.

2. Yes. As temperature increases, the volume increases and the mass remains constant. Therefore, density decreases. Conversely, density increases when the temperature decreases.

Students can interact with the figure by going to **go.hrw.com** and typing in the keyword **HK8STAF4**.

Science Skills

Interpreting Diagrams Remind students that gas law calculations must always be done using absolute temperatures (in K). If the calculated result is temperature, kelvins can be converted to other temperature units, such as degrees Celsius (°C). Explain that the temperature and volume of a gas are proportional, and that they are directly proportional when the temperature is measured in kelvins. When the temperature in kelvins in **Figure 4** is doubled, the volume of the gas is also doubled. Have students predict what might happen to solids or liquids in a closed container when the temperature is changed. (Depending on the temperature, the solid may melt or the liquid might evaporate. If the temperature change does not cause a change of state, then there will be little to no change in pressure.)
LS Visual/Logical

Figure 4 Charles's Law

When the temperature is decreased, the gas particles move more slowly and hit the sides of the piston with less force. As a result, the volume decreases.

When the temperature is increased, the gas particles move faster and hit the sides of the piston with more force. As a result, the volume increases.

Charles's law relates temperature to volume.

Another gas law, Charles's law, is shown by the model in **Figure 4.** Each illustration shows the same piston and the same amount of gas at the same pressure.

Charles's law	For a fixed amount of gas at a constant pressure, the volume of the gas increases as the gas's temperature increases. Likewise, the volume of the gas decreases as the gas's temperature decreases.

Because of Charles's law, an inflated balloon will pop when it gets too hot. Or, as **Figure 5** shows, if the gas in an inflated balloon is cooled (at constant pressure), the volume of gas will decrease and cause the volume of the balloon to shrink. You can observe another example by putting an inflated balloon in the freezer and waiting about 10 minutes to see what happens.

Figure 5 This experiment illustrates Charles's law.

Air-filled balloons are exposed to liquid nitrogen.

The low temperature of the liquid nitrogen makes the balloons shrink in volume.

When the balloons are removed from the liquid nitrogen and warmed, they expand to their original volume.

Science Skills

Kelvins After students have finished reading this section, ask them why kelvins must be used when measuring temperature for gas law calculations. (Even though one degree on the Celsius scale is equal to one degree on the Kelvin scale, Celsius temperatures can have negative values, unlike kelvins, which have only positive values.) Point out how the use of negative temperature values in gas law calculations can lead to answers in which gas volume is negative, an impossible condition. **LS Verbal/Logical**

Teaching Key Ideas

Applying Charles's Law Ask students the following question: "If one of your friends overinflated the tires on a bicycle, how would Charles's Law help you to explain why your friend should let out some of the air before going for a ride on a hot day?" (Sample answer: On a hot day, the gas in the tire will heat up and expand. If some of the air is not let out of the tire before going for a ride, the tire may burst due to the increased gas pressure.)
LS Logical

The top graph shows volume versus temperature for a gas at a constant pressure. What can be determined from this graph about the relationship between volume and temperature?

❶ Determine whether the relationship is direct or inverse.	In a *direct* relationship, the two variables change in the same direction. In an *inverse* relationship, they change in opposite directions. In this graph, temperature increases as volume increases, so the relationship is *direct*.
❷ Study the shape of the line.	If a graph is a straight line, one variable is directly or inversely *proportional* to the other. If a graph is a curve, the relationship is more complex. Because this graph is a straight line, temperature is *directly proportional* to volume.

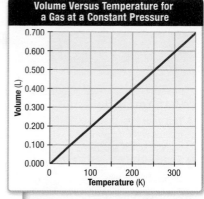

Volume Versus Temperature for a Gas at a Constant Pressure

Practice

1. Which gas law does the straight-line graph represent?
2. Is the relationship shown by the curve in the bottom graph a direct relationship or an inverse relationship?
3. Is this relationship proportional?
4. Which gas law is represented by the curved graph?

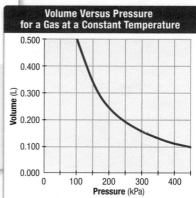

Volume Versus Pressure for a Gas at a Constant Temperature

Section 4 Review

KEY IDEAS

1. **List** four properties of gases.
2. **Explain** why the volume of a gas can change.
3. **Describe** how gases are different from solids and liquids, and give examples.
4. **Identify** what causes the pressure exerted by gas molecules on their container.
5. **Restate** Boyle's law, Charles's law, and Gay-Lussac's law in your own words.

CRITICAL THINKING

6. **Applying Concepts** Identify a real-life example for each of the three gas laws.
7. **Making Inferences** Why do gases have low densities?

8. **Relating Concepts** When scientists record the volume of a gas, why do they also record the temperature and the pressure?
9. **Making Predictions** Predict what would happen to the volume of a balloon left on a sunny windowsill. Which gas law predicts this result?

Math Skills

10. A partially inflated weather balloon has a volume of 1.56×10^3 L and a pressure of 98.9 kPa. What is the volume of the balloon when the balloon is released to a height where the pressure is 44.1 kPa?

Graphing Skills

Answers to Practice

1. The graph shows Charles's law because the line illustrates a linear relationship in which volume increases as temperature increases.
2. The slope of the curve is downward, so it shows an inverse relationship.
3. No, the relationship is not proportional because the graph is not a straight line.
4. Boyle's Law is illustrated because the curve shows that pressure increases as volume decreases.

❯ Close

Reteaching Key Ideas

Gas Laws On the board, draw three columns with the following headings: "Boyle's law," "Charles's law," and "Gay-Lussac's law." Ask student volunteers to fill what they know about each law under each heading. Then, ask students to perform a sample calculation based on each law. **LS Logical**

Formative Assessment

Which law relates the effect of temperature on the volume of a gas?

A. Boyle's law (Incorrect. Boyle's law describes the relationship between volume and pressure.)
B. Gay-Lussac's law (Incorrect. Gay-Lussac's law describes the relationship between temperature and pressure.)
C. Charles's law (Correct. Charles's law describes the relationship between temperature and volume.)
D. All of the above (Incorrect. Only Charles's law describes the relationship between temperature and volume.)

Answers to Section Review

1. Gases flow, have low density, are compressible, and expand to fill their containers.
2. Sample answer: Attraction between gas particles is not strong, so the volume of a gas can easily change.
3. Unlike solids and liquids, gases have very low densities and can easily change volume. This makes them suitable for filling tires, balloons, and scuba tanks.
4. The pressure exerted on a container by a gas is caused by the gas particles colliding with the walls of the container.

Answers continued on p. 109A

InquiryLab

Teacher's Notes

Boiling less water will take less time, but increases the chance of thermometer breakage due to contact between the thermometer and the beaker, so these considerations should be balanced. A plastic stirring rod is an acceptable substitute for a wire-loop stirrer.

Time Required

1 lab period

Lab Ratings

EASY ————————→ HARD

Teacher Prep 🧪🧪
Student Set-Up 🧪🧪
Concept Level 🧪🧪
Clean Up 🧪🧪

Skills Acquired

- Collecting data
- Communicating
- Identifying/recognizing patterns
- Interpreting
- Measuring
- Organizing and analyzing data
- Predicting

Scientific Methods

In this lab, students will:
- Make observations
- Form a hypothesis
- Analyze the results
- Draw conclusions
- Communicate results

Inquiry Lab

 50 min

What You'll Do

❯ **Test your hypothesis** by measuring the temperature of water as it boils and freezes.

❯ **Graph** data, and interpret the slopes of the graphs.

What You'll Need

beaker, 250 mL or 400 mL
clamp
coffee can, large
gloves, heat-resistant
graduated cylinder, 100 mL
hot plate
ice, crushed
paper, graph
ring stand
rock salt
stirring device, wire loop
stopwatch
thermometer
water

Safety

Boiling and Freezing

Adding or removing energy from a substance often causes its temperature to change. But does the temperature of a substance always change when the substance's energy changes? In this lab, you will investigate this question with a common substance—water.

Ask a Question

When you add or remove energy from water, does its temperature always change?

Forming and Testing a Hypothesis

1 Make some predictions. What happens to the temperature of boiling water as the boiling process continues? What happens to the temperature of freezing water as the freezing process continues?

Boiling Water

2 Prepare two data tables like the one below. (Note that you can also use Time and Temperature as column headings, to create a vertical table.) You will need to add additional cells for the time measurements.

Sample Data Table: Temperature of Water

Time (s)	30	60	90	120	150	180	etc.
Temperature (°C)	DO NOT	WRITE IN	BOOK				

3 Fill the beaker about one-third to one-half full with water.

4 Put on heat-resistant gloves. Turn on the hot plate, and put the beaker on the plate. Put the thermometer in the beaker. Use the clamp on the ring stand to hold the thermometer so that it does not touch the bottom of the beaker. **CAUTION:** Be careful not to touch the hot plate. Also, be careful not to break the thermometer.

5 In your first data table, record the temperature of the water every 30 s. Continue doing this until about one-fourth of the water boils away. Note the first temperature reading at which the water is steadily boiling.

6 Turn off the hot plate. Let the beaker cool for a few minutes. Then, use heat-resistant gloves to pick up the beaker. Pour the warm water out in the sink, and rinse the warm beaker with cool water. **CAUTION:** Even after rinsing the beaker with cool water, the beaker may still be too hot to handle without gloves.

Safety Cautions

Review glassware and heating safety before students begin the experiment. Remind students to wear heat-resistant gloves when handling glassware that may be hot. Caution students to handle thermometers carefully. Students should gently place thermometers into glassware, and they should not use the thermometers for stirring.

Answer to Forming and Testing a Hypothesis

1. Sample answer: Temperature will remain constant while the water absorbs energy as it vaporizes. The temperature remains constant during freezing as well.

Freezing Water

7 Put approximately 20 mL of water in the graduated cylinder.

8 Put the graduated cylinder in the coffee can, and fill in around the graduated cylinder with three to four alternating layers of crushed ice and rock salt.

9 Slide the tip of the thermometer through the loop on the wire-loop stirring device, and put the thermometer and the wire-loop stirring device in the graduated cylinder.

10 As the ice melts and mixes with the rock salt, the level of ice will decrease. Add ice and rock salt to the can as needed.

11 In your second data table, record the temperature of the water in the graduated cylinder every 30 s. Stir the water occasionally by moving the wire-loop stirring device up and down along the thermometer. **CAUTION:** Do not stir in a circular motion with the thermometer.

12 Once the water begins to freeze, stop stirring. Do not try to pull the thermometer out of the solid ice in the graduated cylinder.

13 Note the temperature when you first notice ice crystals forming in the water. Continue taking temperature readings until the water in the graduated cylinder is frozen.

14 After you record the final reading, pour warm water into the can. Wait until the ice in the graduated cylinder melts. Remove the thermometer. Pour the water out of the cylinder, and rinse the cylinder with water. Pour out the contents of the can. Rinse the can with water.

Analysis

1. Graphing Data Make a graph of temperature (*y*-axis) versus time (*x*-axis) for the data on boiling water from the first table. Indicate the temperature at which the water started to boil.

2. Graphing Data Make a graph of temperature (*y*-axis) versus time (*x*-axis) for the data on freezing water from the second table. Indicate the temperature at which the water started to freeze.

3. Interpreting Graphs What does the slope of the line on each graph represent?

4. Analyzing Data In your first graph, compare the slope when the water is boiling with the slope before the water starts to boil.

5. Analyzing Data In your second graph, compare the slope when the water is freezing with the slope before the water starts to freeze.

Communicating Your Results

6. Drawing Conclusions What happened to the temperature of water while the water was boiling or freezing?

7. Interpreting Graphs Explain what happens to the energy that is added to the water while the water is boiling.

Extension

When water freezes, energy is removed from the water. How do you think this energy affected the water before the energy was removed? What happens to the energy when it is removed?

Answers to Analysis

1. The graphs will vary according to the data obtained. Graphs should show an increase in temperature with time (positive slope) until 100 °C is reached, at which point the line becomes nearly horizontal with increasing time.

2. The graphs will vary according to the data obtained. Graphs should show a decrease in temperature with time (negative slope) until 0 °C is reached, at which point the line becomes nearly horizontal with increasing time.

3. The slope represents change in water's temperature with time.

4. Sample answer: The slope of the line becomes flat (zero) once the water starts to boil. Before the water boils, the slope of the line is positive (increasing).

5. Sample answer: The slope of the line becomes flat (zero) once the water starts to freeze. Before the water freezes, the slope of the line is negative (decreasing).

Answers to Communicating Your Results

6. Sample answer: The temperature stayed the same during the process. Temperature does not change during a change of state.

7. Sample answer: The energy added to the water during boiling overcomes the attraction between liquid water molecules, so that they can move freely as water vapor.

Answer to Extension

Sample answer: Before it was removed, the energy kept the liquid water molecules moving enough so that they were not strongly attracted to each other, as they are in ice. This energy, once removed from the water, is transferred to the surrounding air, causing the air's temperature to increase.

Key Resources

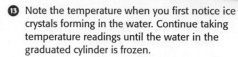

Virtual Investigation

Classroom Lab Video/DVD

Holt Lab Generator CD-ROM
Search for any lab by type, standard, difficulty level, or time. Edit any lab to fit your needs, or create your own labs. Use the Lab Materials QuickList software to customize your lab materials list.

Differentiated Datasheets
Boiling and Freezing

Observation Lab
Boyle's Law

CBL™ Probeware Lab
Investigating the Relationship Between Pressure and Volume

Tell students that data can be presented in different graphical forms. Ask them what the advantage is to presenting this kind of information in the form of a line graph. (Change over time is clearly represented by a sloped line, and an interval of time in which no change occurs is represented by a flat line.) **LS** **Logical/Visual**

Answers to Practice

1. Energy is absorbed.

2. Changes of state are occurring between 1 and 7 min and after 14 min.

3. Between 1 and 7 min, ice is melting. After 14 min, water is evaporating.

4. The temperature is constant when changes of state are occurring.

5. Answers may vary. Graphs should look roughly similar to the graph in this example, but the data trends are reversed. The temperature should start at 100 °C and decrease steadily to 0 °C. The temperature should then remain constant at 0 °C for several minutes before descending to –25 °C.

6. The part of the graph in which the temperature is constant at 0 °C should be labeled "Freezing."

7. Energy is released.

Making Graphs

Problem

Suppose that 100 g of ice is heated in a pan on a stove. The initial temperature of the ice is –25 °C. The temperature rises steadily to 0 °C in 1 min. The temperature then remains at 0 °C for 6 min as the ice melts. The temperature of the water then steadily rises to 100 °C in another 7 min. After that, the temperature remains constant. Make a graph that shows the temperature of the water as a function of time.

Solution

❶	Determine the *x*-axis and *y*-axis of the graph.	The *x*-axis is time in minutes. The *y*-axis is temperature in degrees Celsius.
❷	Determine the range of each axis, and add tick marks.	The time ranges from 0 to 14 min. Add and label marks on the *x*-axis for 0, 5, 10, and 15. The temperature ranges from –25 °C to 100 °C. Add and label marks on the *y*-axis for –25, 0, 25, 50, 75, 100, and 125.
❸	Mark all of the key points described in the problem.	The key points are (0, –25), (1, 0), (7, 0), and (14, 100).
❹	Fill in the lines between the points.	Because the temperature changes were steady, straight lines connect the points. Add a horizontal line after the last point.

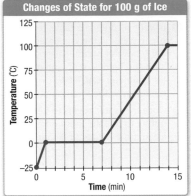

Changes of State for 100 g of Ice

Practice

Use the graph to answer questions 1–4.

1. Was energy released or absorbed during the process shown in the graph?

2. During what time intervals did changes of state happen?

3. What changes of state happened during those time intervals?

4. Describe what happened to the temperature during those time intervals.

Based on what you have learned, answer questions 5–7.

5. Suppose the hot water at the end of this process is put in a freezer with a temperature of –25 °C. Sketch a graph that shows the temperature of the water as a function of time until it reaches –25 °C.

6. Identify and label any changes of state that are represented on your graph.

7. Is energy released or absorbed during the process shown in your graph?

go.hrw.com
SUPER SUMMARY
KEYWORD: HK8STAS

SUMMARY

Key **Ideas**

Section 1 **Matter and Energy**

❯ **Kinetic Theory** All matter is made of atoms and molecules that are always in motion. (p. 77)

❯ **States of Matter** You can classify matter as a solid, a liquid, or a gas by determining whether the shape and volume are definite or variable. (p. 78)

❯ **Energy's Role** Because they are in motion, all particles of matter have kinetic energy. (p. 80)

Section 2 **Changes of State**

❯ **Energy and Changes of State** The identity of a substance does not change during a change of state, but the energy of a substance does change. (p. 84)

❯ **Conservation of Mass and Energy** Mass and energy are both conserved. Neither mass nor energy can be created or destroyed. (p. 87)

Section 3 **Fluids**

❯ **Pressure** Fluids exert pressure evenly in all directions. (p. 89)

❯ **Buoyant Force** All fluids exert an upward buoyant force on matter. (p. 90)

❯ **Pascal's Principle** If the pressure in a container is increased at any point, the pressure increases at all points by the same amount. (p. 92)

❯ **Fluids in Motion** Fluids move faster through small areas than through larger areas, if the overall flow rate remains constant. (p. 93)

Section 4 **Behavior of Gases**

❯ **Properties of Gases** Gases expand to fill their containers. They have low densities, are compressible, and are mostly empty space. (p. 96)

❯ **Gas Laws** The gas laws will help you understand and predict the behavior of gases in specific situations. (p. 97)

Key **Terms**

fluid, p. 79
plasma, p. 79
energy, p. 80
temperature, p. 80
thermal energy, p. 81

evaporation, p. 85
sublimation, p. 85
condensation, p. 86

pressure, p. 89
pascal, p. 89
buoyant force, p. 90
viscosity, p. 94

gas laws, p. 97

SUMMARY

SUPER SUMMARY

Have students connect the major concepts in this chapter through an interactive Super Summary. Visit **go.hrw.com** and type in the keyword **HK8STAS** to access the Super Summary for this chapter.

Differentiated Instruction

Alternative Assessment

Relating Pressure and Temperature Have students use the Internet or the library to find out how a pressure cooker can be used to shorten cooking time. Instruct them to make a drawing that compares the pressure, temperature, and volume to an open pan and a pressure cooker that is the same size. **LS Logical**

Key Resources

🖧 **Interactive Concept Map**

📁 **Review Resources**
Concept Review Worksheets

📁 **Assessment Resources**
Chapter Tests A and B
Performance-Based Assessment

REVIEW

Reading Toolbox

1. Answers may vary. The five changes of state covered in the chapter should be listed across the top of the table: melting, freezing, evaporation, condensation, and sublimation. Characteristics listed in the rows of the table might include starting state, ending state, and energy change (endothermic or exothermic). Information in the table should be consistent with information in the chapter.

Using Key Terms

2. In a solid, particles are held closely together and vibrate. In a liquid, particles are close together but slide past one another. In a gas, particles spread apart to fill available space. In a plasma, particles spread apart to fill space, and the particles have broken apart.

3. Fluids exert pressure evenly in all directions.

4. Buoyant force is the upward force exerted on an object immersed in or floating on a fluid. Archimedes' principle states that the buoyant force on an object is equal to the weight of the volume of fluid that the object displaces.

Understanding Key Ideas

5. d
6. c
7. b
8. b
9. d
10. c
11. d

Explaining Key Ideas

12. The law of conservation of energy states that energy cannot be created or destroyed. The law of conservation of mass states that mass cannot be created or destroyed. In a change of state, energy and mass may be transformed, but they are not destroyed.

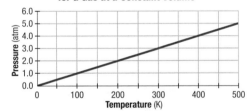

READING TOOLBOX

1. **Comparison Table** Make a comparison table to compare the five changes of state that are described in this chapter.

USING KEY TERMS

2. Describe four states of matter by using the terms *solid, liquid, gas,* and *plasma.* Describe the behavior of particles in each state.

3. Describe how *pressure* is exerted by fluids.

4. Describe the *buoyant force,* and explain how it relates to *Archimedes' principle.*

UNDERSTANDING KEY IDEAS

5. Which of the following assumptions is *not* part of the kinetic theory?
   a. All matter is made up of tiny, invisible particles.
   b. The particles are always moving.
   c. Particles move faster at higher temperatures.
   d. Particles are smaller at lower pressure.

6. Three common states of matter are
   a. solid, water, and gas.
   b. ice, water, and gas.
   c. solid, liquid, and gas.
   d. solid, liquid, and air.

7. During which of the following changes of state do atoms or molecules become more ordered?
   a. boiling   c. melting
   b. condensation   d. sublimation

8. Which of the following describes what happens as the temperature of a gas in a balloon increases?
   a. The speed of the particles decreases.
   b. The volume of the gas increases.
   c. The volume of the gas decreases.
   d. The pressure decreases.

9. Fluid pressure is always directed
   a. up.   c. sideways.
   b. down.   d. in all directions.

10. Matter that flows to fit its container includes
    a. gases.   c. gases and liquids.
    b. liquids.   d. liquids and solids.

11. If an object that weighs 50 N displaces a volume of water that weighs 10 N, what is the buoyant force on the object?
    a. 60 N   c. 40 N
    b. 50 N   d. 10 N

EXPLAINING KEY IDEAS

12. State the law of conservation of energy and the law of conservation of mass. Explain what happens to energy and mass in a change of state.

13. For each pair, explain the difference in meaning.
    a. *solid* and *liquid*
    b. *Boyle's law* and *Charles's law*
    c. *Gay-Lussac's law* and *Pascal's principle*

INTERPRETING GRAPHICS Use the graph below to answer questions 14 and 15.

Pressure Versus Temperature for a Gas at a Constant Volume

14. What type of relationship does the graph represent: direct or inverse?

15. To which law or principle does the graph apply?

16. Inferring Relationships Explain what happens to the pressure of a gas if the volume of the gas is tripled. Assume that the temperature remains constant.

17. Drawing Conclusions Why are liquids instead of gases used in hydraulic brakes?

18. Applying Concepts After taking a shower, you notice that the mirror is foggy and covered with very small droplets of water. Explain how this happens by describing where the water comes from and the changes the water goes through.

19. Making Inferences An iceberg is partially submerged in the ocean. At what part of the iceberg is the water pressure the greatest?

20. Applying Concepts Use Boyle's Law to explain why bubbled packing wrap pops when you squeeze it.

21. Making Predictions Will a ship loaded with plastic-foam balls float higher or lower in the water than an empty ship? Explain.

22. Applying Concepts All vacuum cleaners have a high-speed fan. Explain how this fan allows the vacuum cleaner to pick up dirt.

Graphing Skills

23. Graphing Data Kate placed 100 mL of water in each of five different pans. She then placed the pans on a windowsill for a week and measured how much water evaporated. Graph her data, which are shown in the table below. Place surface area on the *x*-axis.
a. Is the graph linear or nonlinear?
b. What does this answer tell you?

Pan number	1	2	3	4	5
Surface area (cm^2)	44	82	20	30	65
Volume evaporated (mL)	42	79	19	29	62

24. Interpreting Graphs The graph below shows the effects of heating on ethylene glycol, the liquid commonly used as antifreeze. Before the temperature is 197 °C, is the temperature increasing or decreasing? What physical change is taking place when the ethylene glycol is at 197 °C? Describe what is happening to the ethylene glycol molecules at 197 °C. How do you know this is happening?

Heating of Ethylene Glycol

Math Skills

25. Pressure Calculate the area of a 1,500 N object that exerts a pressure of 500 Pa. Then, calculate the pressure exerted by the same object over twice that area. Express your answer in the correct SI unit.

26. Pascal's Principle One of the largest helicopters in the world weighs 1.0×10^6 N. If you were to place this helicopter on a large piston of a hydraulic lift, what force would need to be applied to the small piston to lift the helicopter? The area of the small piston is 0.7 m^2, and the area of the large piston is 140 m^2.

27. Boyle's Law A sample of neon gas occupies a volume of 2.8 L at 180 kPa. What will its volume be at 120 kPa?

28. Boyle's Law At a pressure of 650 kPa, 2.2 L of hydrogen is used to fill a balloon to a final pressure of 115 kPa. What is the balloon's final volume?

Assignment Guide

Section	Items
1	2, 5, 6, 8, 10, 23
2	1, 7, 9, 12, 18, 24
3	3, 4, 11, 19, 21, 25, 26
4	13–17, 20, 22, 27, 28

22. The fan causes the air inside the vacuum cleaner to move faster, which decreases pressure. The higher air pressure outside of the vacuum then pushes dirt into the vacuum cleaner.

Answers continued on p. 109A

13. a. Solid is the state of matter in which the substance has a definite shape and volume. Liquid is the state of matter in which the substance takes the shape of its container but has a definite volume.

b. Boyle's law states that when the pressure of a gas at constant temperature increases, its volume decreases. Charles's law states that when the temperature of a gas at constant pressure increases, its volume increases.

c. Gay-Lussac's law states that when the temperature of a gas at constant volume increases, its pressure increases. Pascal's principle states that pressure applied to a fluid in a closed container is transmitted equally throughout the fluid.

14. Because the slope of the line is positive, the relationship is direct.

15. Because it relates pressure and temperature, the graph illustrates Gay-Lussac's law.

Critical Thinking

16. Boyle's law states that the volume of a gas is inversely proportional to its pressure. If the volume is tripled, the pressure of the gas would drop to one-third of the original pressure.

17. Liquids are used in hydraulic brakes because liquids cannot be compressed easily. Gases are easily compressible.

18. As you take a shower, some of the liquid water evaporates and becomes a gas. When the gaseous water touches the mirror, the water releases energy to the mirror and condenses into drops of liquid water on the mirror.

19. The pressure on the iceberg is greatest at the lowest depth.

20. As the bubble is squeezed to a smaller volume, the pressure of the gas inside the bubble increases until it is high enough to burst the bubble.

21. The ship will float lower in the water because the plastic-foam balls will add to the ship's total mass, but will not increase its volume. Therefore, the overall density of the ship will increase, causing it to sink a little.

TEST DOCTOR

Question 1 Answer D is correct. The pressure is determined by dividing the force (400 N) by the area (200 cm² = 0.02 m²). Answer B is obtained through an incorrect conversion of cm² to m². Answers A and C may be obtained by multiplying force and area with incorrect conversion of units.

Question 2 Answer G is correct. The internal pressure increases. Choice F assumes the relationship between temperature and pressure is inverse; Choice H assumes that there is no relationship, and Choice I shows a misunderstanding of the concept of gas pressure.

Question 3 Answer C is correct. Sublimation is the change of state from solid to gas. The other answers refer to different state changes: evaporation is liquid to gas; condensation is gas to liquid; and melting is solid to liquid.

Question 4 Full-credit answers should include the following points:
- Plastic should be liquid when it is placed in the mold.
- As a liquid, it will flow to the shape of the mold.
- When the liquid cools, it forms a solid that retains the shape of the mold.

Question 5 Full-credit answers should include the following points:
- Mass is conserved in the chemical reaction.
- The original mass is 105.0 g (5.0 g baking soda + 100.0 g vinegar), so the final mass must also be 105.0 g.
- Subtracting the mass of the liquid (102.4 g) from 105.0 g gives the mass of the gas as 2.6 g.

Question 6 Answer H is correct. Because the ship floats, the mass of the water it displaces is equal to the mass of the ship. The mass of the ship can be calculated by multiplying its volume by its specific gravity (100,000 m³ × 0.4 g/cm³ × 1 metric ton/1,000,000 g × 1,000,000 cm³/1 m³). Choice F does not correctly convert units. Choices G and I use incorrect calculations.

Understanding Concepts

Directions (1–3): **For each question, write on a sheet of paper the letter of the correct answer.**

1. An industrial thermometer is heated until the mercury inside it is exerting 400 N of force against the inner surface. That surface has a total area of 200 cm². How much pressure is the mercury exerting against the inner surface of the thermometer? Note that 1 Pa = 1 N/m².
   - **A.** 800 Pa
   - **B.** 2,000 Pa
   - **C.** 8,000 Pa
   - **D.** 20,000 Pa

2. A sealed refuse container is buried near a fault line, and seismic activity brings the container close to an underground source of geothermal energy. As the container gets warmer, what happens to the internal air pressure of the container?
   - **F.** The internal air pressure decreases.
   - **G.** The internal air pressure increases.
   - **H.** There is no effect on internal air pressure.
   - **I.** There is no air pressure inside a sealed container.

3. In the year 2032, a space probe investigating Neptune scoops up a load of solid frozen oxygen from the planet's atmosphere. Upon re-entry into Earth's atmosphere, some of the solid oxygen immediately changes into a gas. Which of the following processes happened?
   - **A.** evaporation
   - **B.** condensation
   - **C.** sublimation
   - **D.** melting

Directions (4–5): **For each question, write a short response.**

4. Plastic is put into molds to create specific shapes. In what state of matter should the plastic be when it is put in the mold, and why?

5. A kitchen scientist combines 5.0 g of baking soda with 100.0 g of vinegar, which causes a gas (carbon dioxide) to be given off. After all of the gas has escaped, the liquid has a mass of 102.4 g. What is the mass of the escaped gas?

Reading Skills

Directions (6–8): **Read the passage below. Then, answer the questions that follow.**

SPECIFIC GRAVITY

Buoyancy makes a piece of wood float in water. It also makes a battleship float on the high seas and makes a block of steel float in a pool of liquid mercury. The first principle of buoyancy is simple: if a solid immersed in a fluid weighs less than an equal volume of the fluid, the solid will float. Another way of saying the same thing is the following: if a solid has a lower specific gravity than a fluid, then the solid will float in that fluid. Specific gravity is defined as the weight of a substance divided by the weight of an equal volume of pure water.

If an immersed solid floats, the level at which the solid floats is determined by the second principle of buoyancy: a floating object will displace its own weight in a fluid. The percentage of the volume of the solid immersed in the fluid will be equal to the specific gravity of the solid divided by the specific gravity of the fluid. If a block of wood that has a specific gravity of 0.3 floats in water (specific gravity = 1.0), 30% of the volume of the block will be below the water's surface.

6. A cruise ship has a volume of 100,000 m³ and possesses an overall specific gravity of 0.4. If the density of sea water is 1,000 kg/m³, what is the mass of the sea water displaced by the cruise ship? Note that 1,000 kg = 1 metric ton.
   - **F.** 40,000 kg
   - **G.** 60,000 kg
   - **H.** 40,000 metric tons
   - **I.** 60,000 metric tons

7. If 90% of a floating iceberg is underwater, what is the specific gravity of the ice?
   - **A.** 0.2
   - **B.** 0.9
   - **C.** 20
   - **D.** 90

8. If a substance is compressed, what happens to its specific gravity?

Question 7 Answer B is correct. The part of the iceberg that is underwater has the same mass as the water displaced. If 90% is below water, the specific gravity of the ice is 90% of 1.0 or 0.9. Choice A is incorrect because a specific gravity of 0.2 would indicate 20% of the mass is below the water line. Choices C and D represent densities much higher than the density of water.

Question 8 Full-credit answers should include the following points:
- Specific gravity is calculated by dividing the mass by the volume.
- Specific gravity increases because the ratio of mass to volume increases.

Question 9 Answer I is correct. Evaporation is the change of state from liquid to gas. Answers F, G, and H are incorrect because they all refer to different changes of state: F (gas to liquid), G (gas to solid), and H (solid to liquid).

Question 10 Answer D is correct. Sublimation is the change of state from solid to gas. The other choices represent different changes: A (gas to solid), B (solid to liquid), C (liquid to gas).

Question 11 Full-credit answers should include the following points:
- The phase change between solid and liquid occurs at 0 °C.
- Phase change between solid and gas can occur at 0 °C.

Interpreting Graphics

The graphic below shows the water cycle. Note that the water in the clouds is in liquid form. Use this diagram to answer questions 9–11.

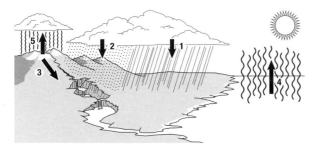

9. Which arrow indicates evaporation?

   F. 1   **H.** 3

   G. 2   **I.** 4

10. Which arrow indicates sublimation?

   A. 2   **C.** 4

   B. 3   **D.** 5

11. Which three arrows indicate a phase change that occurs at 0 °C?

The following graphic shows a full tank of helium, the same tank after it has filled 10 balloons, and then the same tank after it has filled 20 balloons. Use this graphic to answer questions 12 and 13.

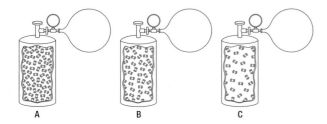

12. In which tank is the greatest pressure being exerted on the tank's inner surface?

13. As more helium is released from the tank, the person who is inflating the balloons notices that the tank has become cold to the touch. Why does this happen?

Test Tip

When answering short-response questions, be sure to write in complete sentences. When you finish, proofread for errors in spelling, grammar, and punctuation.

• Arrows 2, 3, and 5, indicate changes that can occur at 0 °C.

Question 12 Full-credit answers should include the following points:

• Pressure is exerted on the tank by collisions of gas particles.

• Tank A has the most gas particles.

• Tank A has the greatest pressure.

Question 13 Full-credit answers should include the following points:

• As particles leave the tank, the pressure decreases.

• Temperature and pressure are proportional at constant volume.

• The decrease in pressure causes a decrease in temperature.

Answers

1. D
2. G
3. C
4. Answers may vary; see Test Doctor for a detailed scoring rubric.
5. Answers may vary; see Test Doctor for a detailed scoring rubric.
6. H
7. B
8. Answers may vary; see Test Doctor for a detailed scoring rubric.
9. I
10. D
11. Answers may vary; see Test Doctor for a detailed scoring rubric.
12. Answers may vary; see Test Doctor for a detailed scoring rubric.
13. Answers may vary; see Test Doctor for a detailed scoring rubric.

State Resources

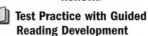

For specific resources for your state, visit **go.hrw.com** and type in the keyword **HSHSTR**.

📖 **Test Practice with Guided Reading Development**

Continuation of Answers

Answers continued from p. 94

4. Molasses has a higher viscosity than milk does.

5. a. 15 N

   b. The object would sink because weight exceeds buoyant force.

6. The iron will float because it is less dense than mercury.

7. a. Fluid speed increases because fluid pressure decreases.

   b. As fluid speed between the boats increases, fluid pressure decreases. If the pressure on the outer sides of the boats exceeds the pressure between them, the boats are pushed together.

8. $P = F/A = 1{,}025 \text{ N}/3.75 \text{ m}^2 = 273 \text{ Pa}$

9. $F_2 = F_1/A_1 \times A_2 = 12{,}000 \text{ N}/0.90 \text{ m}^2 \times 0.020 \text{ m}^2 = 270 \text{ N}$

Answers continued from p. 101

5. Sample answer: Boyle's law states that the volume of a gas increases as pressure decreases at constant temperature. Charles's law states that the volume of a gas increases as temperature increases at constant pressure. Gay-Lussac's law states that gas pressure increases as temperature increases at constant volume.

6. Sample answer: Boyle's law: If you let air out of a tire, the air will expand outside of the tire, because pressure on the air decreases. Charles's law: When pressure is constant, the air in a balloon will expand if the balloon is exposed to heat. Gay-Lussac's law: If you heat a spray can, which has constant volume, it may explode due to the increase in pressure.

7. Gases have low densities because their particles are so far apart.

8. The volume of a gas can be changed by changing either the temperature or pressure.

9. Sample answer: Leaving the balloon on a sunny windowsill will cause the temperature of the gas in the balloon to increase. According to Charles's law, the volume will increase as the temperature increases at constant pressure.

10. $V_2 = V_1 P_1/P_2 = (1.56 \times 10^3 \text{ L}) \times 98.9 \text{ kPa}/44.1 \text{ kPa} = 3.50 \times 10^3 \text{ L}$

Answers continued from p. 107

Graphing Skills

23. Sample graph:

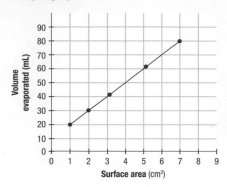

a. The graph is linear.

b. A linear line indicates that an increase in surface area causes an increase in evaporation.

24. The temperature is increasing. Ethylene glycol undergoes a change of state at 197 °C; it is changing from a liquid to a gas. At 197 °C, ethylene glycol molecules are absorbing energy to vaporize, so there is no increase in temperature.

Math Skills

25. $1{,}500 \text{ N}/500 \text{ Pa} = 3 \text{ m}^2$; $500 \text{ Pa}/2 = 250 \text{ Pa}$

26. $\dfrac{(1.0 \times 10^6 \text{ N})(0.7 \text{ m}^2)}{140 \text{ m}^2} = 5 \times 10^3 \text{ N}$

27. $\dfrac{1.8 \text{ kPa} \times 2.8 \text{ L}}{1.2 \text{ kPA}} = 4.2 \text{ L}$

28. $\dfrac{6.5 \text{ kPa} \times 2.2 \text{ L}}{1.15 \text{ kPa}} = 12 \text{ L}$

		Standards	**Teach Key Ideas**

CHAPTER OPENER, pp. 110–112 · 50 min.

SECTION 1 The Development of Atomic Theory, pp. 113–118 · 50 min.

> The Beginnings of Atomic Theory
> Dalton's Atomic Theory
> Thomson's Model of the Atom
> Rutherford's Model of the Atom

Standards: PS 1a, UCP 1, UCP 2, SAI 1, SAI 2, ST 2, HNS 1, HNS 2, HNS 3

Teach Key Ideas:
- **Bellringer Transparency**
- **Visual Concepts** Atom • Parts of the Atom • Comparing Models of the Atom

SECTION 2 The Structure of Atoms, pp. 119–127 · 50 min.

> What Is in an Atom?
> Atomic Number and Mass Number
> Isotopes
> Atomic Masses

Standards: PS 1a, PS 1b, PS 1d, UCP 1, SAI 1, SAI 2, ST 2

Teach Key Ideas:
- **Bellringer Transparency**
- **Teaching Transparencies** C8 Nucleus • TM12 Subatomic Particles • C9 Isotopes • TM13 Mole-Mass Conversion
- **Visual Concepts** Atomic Number • Mass Number • Isotopes and Nuclides • Average Atomic Mass • The Mole

SECTION 3 Modern Atomic Theory, pp. 128–133 · 50 min.

> Modern Models of the Atom
> Electron Energy Levels
> Electron Transitions

Standards: PS 6c, UCP 1, UCP 2, SAI 1, SAI 2, ST 2, HNS 1, HNS 2, HNS 3

Teach Key Ideas:
- **Bellringer Transparency**
- **Teaching Transparencies** C10 Elevator Model • TM14 The s and p Orbitals
- **Visual Concepts** Electron Energy Levels • s Orbital • p Orbital • Orbital

See also PowerPoint® Resources

Chapter Review and Assessment Resources

- **SE** Science Skills: Testing a Hypothesis, p. 136
- **SE** Chapter Summary, p. 137
- **SE** Chapter Review, pp. 138–139
- **SE** Standardized Test Prep, pp. 140–141
- 🗋 Concept Review Worksheets ■
- 🗋 Chapter Tests A and B ■
- Holt Online Assessment

CHAPTER FastTrack *To shorten instruction because of time limitations, omit Section 1 and the chapter lab.*

Basic Learners
- **TE** Identifying Preconceptions, p. 114
- **TE** Small to Large, p. 121
- **TE** Conversion Factors, p. 126
- 🗋 Science Skills Worksheets
- 🗋 Differentiated Datasheets A for Labs and Activities ■
- 🗋 Study Guide A ■

Advanced Learners
- **TE** Electron Charge and Mass, p. 115
- **TE** Wave-Particle Duality, p. 129
- **TE** Filled Energy Levels, p. 130
- 🗋 Cross-Disciplinary Worksheets
- 🗋 Differentiated Datasheets C for Labs and Activities ■

Key

SE Student Edition
TE Teacher's Edition

📁 Chapter Resource File
📒 Workbook
🖨 Transparency

💿 CD or CD-ROM
* Datasheet or blackline master available

■ Also available in Spanish

All resources listed below are also available on the Teacher's One-Stop Planner.

Why It Matters	Hands-On	Skills Development	Assessment
Build student motivation with resources about high-interest applications.	**SE Inquiry Lab** Making a Model, p. 111*■	**TE Reading Toolbox** Assessing Prior Knowledge, p. 110 **SE Reading Toolbox** p. 112	📁 **Pretest** ■
TE Nanotechnology, p. 113 **SE How Do Televisions Work?** p. 116 📁 **Cross-Disciplinary Worksheets** Integrating Physics—Atomic Fingerprints • Integrating Technology—Seeing Atoms: The STM	**SE Quick Lab** Evidence for Atoms, p. 114*■	**TE Reading Toolbox** Visual Literacy, p. 115 **SE Reading Toolbox** Pyramid FoldNote, p. 117	**TE Reteaching Key Ideas** Clay Models, p. 118 **TE Formative Assessment,** p. 118 📁 **Spanish Assessment***■ 📁 **Section Quiz** ■
TE Quarks and Leptons, p. 120 **TE Deuterium as a Fuel for Fusion,** p. 122 **TE Avogadro's Contribution,** p. 125 **SE Nuclear Medicine,** p. 123 📁 **Cross-Disciplinary Worksheet** Connection to Fine Arts—Carbon-Dating Masterpieces	**TE Demonstration** Counting Large Numbers by Mass, p. 119 **SE Quick Lab** Modeling Isotopes, p. 122*■ **SE Skills Practice Lab** Building Isotopes, pp. 134–135*■	**TE Reading Toolbox** Visual Literacy, p. 120 **SE Reading Toolbox** Pyramid FoldNote, p. 121 **TE Reading Toolbox** Visual Literacy, p. 121 **TE Reading Toolbox** Visual Literacy, p. 122 **TE Reading Toolbox** Visual Literacy, p. 124 **TE Math Skills** Counting with Isotopes, p. 124 **TE Math Skills** Conversion Factors, p. 125 **SE Math Skills** Converting Moles to Grams, p. 126 **TE Reading Toolbox** Visual Literacy, p. 126	**TE Reteaching Key Ideas** Concept Mapping, p. 127 **TE Formative Assessment,** p. 127 📁 **Spanish Assessment***■ 📁 **Section Quiz** ■
TE Spectra and Light Emission, p. 130 **SE How Do Fireworks Work?** p. 133	**TE Demonstration** Gaining and Losing Energy, p. 128 **SE Quick Lab** Electron Levels, p. 131*■ 📁 **Observation Lab** Drawing Atomic Models	**SE Reading Toolbox** Making Comparisons, p. 129 **TE Reading Toolbox** Revising Preconceptions, p. 132	**TE Reteaching Key Ideas** Making Analogies, p. 132 **TE Formative Assessment,** p. 132 📁 **Spanish Assessment***■ 📁 **Section Quiz** ■

See also Lab Generator

See also Holt Online Assessment Resources

Resources for Differentiated Instruction

English Learners
TE Organizing and Narrating Past Events, p. 116
📁 Differentiated Datasheets A, B, and C for Labs and Activities ■
📒 Study Guide A ■

Struggling Readers
TE Scanning for Specific Information, p. 116
TE Meaning of New Words, p. 123
📒 Interactive Reader

Special Education Students
TE Demonstrating Relative Size, p. 117

Alternative Assessment
TE Weighted Average, p. 124
TE Modeling Atoms, p. 137

CHAPTER 4 Atoms

Overview

In this chapter, students learn what atoms are, what they are made up of, and how they can be represented by models. This chapter covers atomic number, mass number, isotopes, and average atomic mass. Students also learn how to use moles to count atoms. Finally, students will learn about electron energy levels and photon absorption and emission.

READING TOOLBOX

Assessing Prior Knowledge Students should understand the following concepts:
• units of measurement
• scientific notation
• significant figures
• atoms
• elements

MISCONCEPTION ///ALERT\\\

Science education research has identified the following misconceptions about atoms:
• Students believe that atoms possess macro properties such as hardness, color, shape, or stickiness. (Atomic structure, in particular electron arrangement, dictate macro properties, but atoms themselves do not possess those properties.)
• Students believe that atoms contain no empty space and are static. (The densest part of the atom is its nucleus, and tiny electrons occupy the vast space surrounding the nucleus).
• Students do not understand how small molecules and atoms truly are. (Show students a mole of sulfur powder, 32 g, and explain that it contains 6.022×10^{23} atoms)
• Students confuse molar mass with atomic mass. (Molar mass is expressed in grams, g, while atomic mass is expressed in unified atomic mass units, u.)

Chapter Outline

❶ The Development of Atomic Theory
The Beginnings of Atomic Theory
Dalton's Atomic Theory
Thomson's Model of the Atom
Rutherford's Model of the Atom

❷ The Structure of Atoms
What Is in an Atom?
Atomic Number and Mass Number
Isotopes
Atomic Masses

❸ Modern Atomic Theory
Modern Models of the Atom
Electron Energy Levels
Electron Transitions

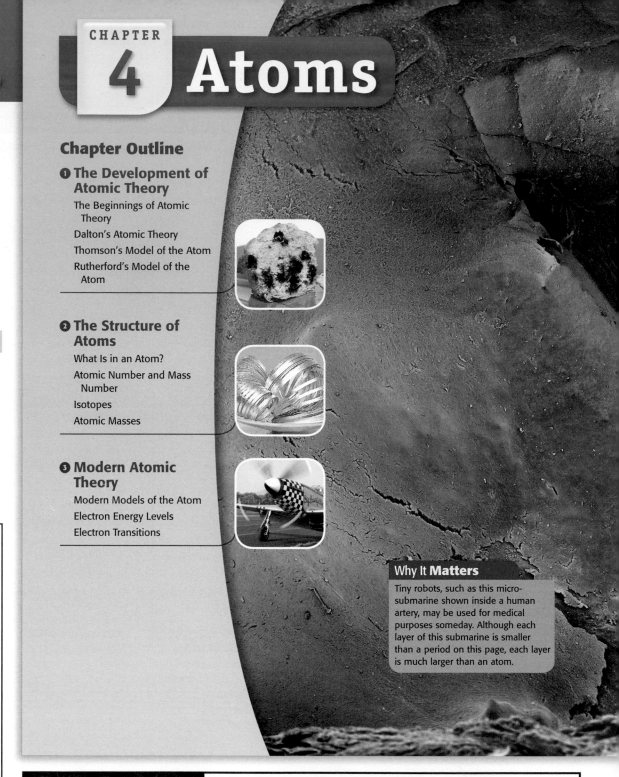

Why It Matters
Tiny robots, such as this micro-submarine shown inside a human artery, may be used for medical purposes someday. Although each layer of this submarine is smaller than a period on this page, each layer is much larger than an atom.

Chapter Correlations *National Science Education Standards*

The following correlations show the National Science Standards that relate to this chapter. For the full text of the standards, see the National Science Education Standards at the front of the book.

PS 1a Matter is made of minute particles called atoms, and atoms are composed of even smaller components. These components have measurable properties, such as mass and electrical charge. Each atom has a positively charged nucleus surrounded by negatively charged electrons. The electric force between the nucleus and electrons holds the atom together. (Sections 1, 2)

PS 1b The atom's nucleus is composed of protons and neutrons, which are much more massive than electrons. When an element has atoms that differ in the number of neutrons, these atoms are called different isotopes of the element. (Section 2, Skills Practice Lab: Building Isotopes)

PS 1d Radioactive isotopes are unstable and undergo spontaneous nuclear reactions, emitting particles and/or wavelike radiation. (Section 2)

PS 6c Each kind of atom or molecule can gain or lose energy only in particular dis-

crete amounts and thus can absorb and emit light only at wavelengths corresponding to these amounts. These wavelengths can be used to identify the substance. (Section 3)

UCP 1 Systems, order, and organization (Sections 1–3)

UCP 2 Evidence, models, and explanation (Sections 1, 3)

SAI 1 Abilities necessary to do scientific inquiry (Sections 1–3, Skills Practice Lab: Building Isotopes)

SAI 2 Understandings about scientific inquiry (Sections 1–3)

ST 2 Understandings about science and technology (Sections 1–3)

HNS 1 Science as a human endeavor (Sections 1, 3)

HNS 2 Nature of scientific knowledge (Sections 1, 3)

HNS 3 Historical perspectives (Sections 1, 3)

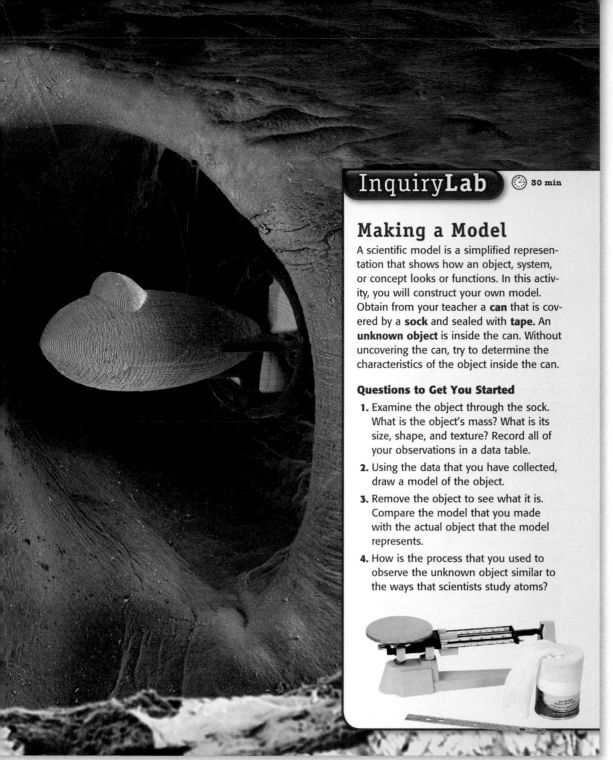

InquiryLab ⏱ 30 min

Making a Model

A scientific model is a simplified representation that shows how an object, system, or concept looks or functions. In this activity, you will construct your own model. Obtain from your teacher a **can** that is covered by a **sock** and sealed with **tape**. An **unknown object** is inside the can. Without uncovering the can, try to determine the characteristics of the object inside the can.

Questions to Get You Started

1. Examine the object through the sock. What is the object's mass? What is its size, shape, and texture? Record all of your observations in a data table.

2. Using the data that you have collected, draw a model of the object.

3. Remove the object to see what it is. Compare the model that you made with the actual object that the model represents.

4. How is the process that you used to observe the unknown object similar to the ways that scientists study atoms?

InquiryLab

Teacher's Notes Be sure students know that a model is used to represent an item or event that is too small, too large, or too dangerous to view directly. Models can include any representation of that item or event and can take the form of drawings, computer models, and three-dimensional physical models. Remind students that they use models such as maps and globes regularly in daily life. Have students list other models they commonly use.

Materials per Group
- can
- mystery object
- sock
- tape

Answers

3. Discuss with students how close their model is to the actual object. Have them explain why the model might not match the object exactly.

4. Sample answer: This process is similar to how scientists study atoms because very often scientists cannot directly observe the atoms they are studying.

Key Resources

📁 **Datasheet**
Making a Model

💿 **Interactive Tutor**
Disc One, Module 2: Models of the Atom

Word Origins

Answers may vary. Sample answer: *pro-* means positive and *neut-* means neutral. Actual etymology: *pro-* comes from Greek *protos,* which means *first; neut-* comes from *neutral.*

Analogies

Sample answer: A blueberry muffin is similar to Thomson's atomic model. A blueberry muffin and Thomson's atomic model are alike in that they both contain smaller objects (blue-berries or electrons) that are spread throughout. The two things are different in that the blueberry muffin is large, while the atom is very small.

FoldNotes

Students' pyramids should look similar to the example shown. On the three sides of the pyramid students should write 1) Atomic number—the number of protons in the nucleus of an atom, 2) Mass number—the sum of the numbers of protons and neutrons in an atom, and 3) Average atomic mass—the weighted average of all commonly found isotopes of an element.

These reading tools can help you learn the material in this chapter. For more information on how to use these and other tools, see **Appendix A.**

Word Origins

Subatomic Particles Before atoms were understood, people discovered that they could generate static electricity by rubbing fur against amber (tree resin). This is where the word *electron* comes from:

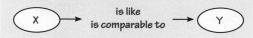

- The word *electricity* is derived from the ancient Greek word *elektron,* which means *amber.*
- The word *electron* was later formed by combining this same root (*electr-*) with the suffix *–on,* which means *particle.*

Your Turn When you learn about protons and neutrons in this chapter, guess at the root meanings of the words *proton* and *neutron.* Look up the etymology (word origin) of the words in a diction-ary to see if you guessed right.

Analogies

Making Comparisons An analogy compares two things that may seem quite different. Analogies are often formed by using the word *like,* as in "*X* is like *Y.*" Other words or phrases that signal analogies include *as, just as, is comparable to,* and *resembles.* An analogy can be modeled as follows:

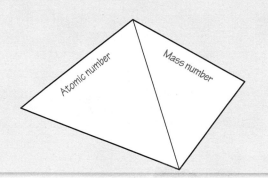

Your Turn In this chapter, you will learn about sev-eral models of the structure of atoms. Analogies are often used to describe these models. Make a list of analogies as you come across them. For each anal-ogy, write down ways in which the two things com-pared are alike, and ways in which the two things are different.

FoldNotes

Pyramid Pyramid FoldNotes help you compare words or ideas in sets of three.

Your Turn Create a Pyramid FoldNote as described in **Appendix A.**

① Along one edge of one side of the note, write "Atomic number."

② On another side, write "Mass number."

③ On the third side, write "Average atomic mass."

As you read Section 2, fill in for each term the definition and an example. Use this FoldNote to review these terms.

The Development of Atomic Theory

Key Ideas

❯ Who came up with the first theory of atoms?

❯ What did Dalton add to the atomic theory?

❯ How did Thomson discover the electron?

❯ What is Rutherford's atomic model?

Key Terms

electron
nucleus

Why It Matters

The electrons stripped from atoms are used in television tubes to help create the images on a television screen.

SECTION 1

❯ Focus

This section discusses the atomic theories of Democritus, Dalton, Thomson, and Rutherford. Through these discussions, students learn about the nucleus and electrons of atoms.

🔔 Bellringer

Use the Bellringer transparency to prepare students for this section.

Why It Matters

Nanotechnology Explain that the micro-submarine shown in the scanning electron micrograph on the chapter opener page is very small, but it is much larger than an atom. It was constructed one layer at a time. Each layer of the submarine was made when lasers guided by a computer polymerized specific regions in a bath of liquid acrylic. The hardened layers, each 10 micrometers thick—10,000 times the diameter of a hydrogen atom—were built one layer on top of the other, producing the final three-dimensional shape seen here. Nanotechnology, a branch of chemical engineering or materials science, involves building particles and machines that are similar in scale to atoms, having sizes of about 0.1 to 10 nanometers. One nanometer (1 nm) is equal to 10^{-9} m. Have students search the Internet or library for examples of nanotechnology in the news. **LS Visual**

Atoms are everywhere. They make up the air you are breathing, the chair you are sitting in, and the clothes you are wearing. Atoms determine the properties of matter. For example, the aluminum containers shown in **Figure 1** are lightweight because of the properties of the atoms that make up the aluminum.

The Beginnings of Atomic Theory

Today, it is well known that matter is made up of particles called atoms. But atomic theory was developed slowly over a long period of time. The first theory of atoms was proposed more than 2,000 years ago. ❯ **In the fourth century BCE, the Greek philosopher Democritus suggested that the universe was made of indivisible units.** He called these units *atoms.* "Atom" comes from *atomos,* a Greek word that means "unable to be cut or divided." Democritus thought that movements of atoms caused the changes in matter that he observed.

Democritus did not have evidence for his atomic theory.

Although his theory of atoms explained some observations, Democritus did not have the evidence needed to convince people that atoms existed. Throughout the centuries that followed, some people supported Democritus's theory. But other theories were also proposed.

As the science of chemistry was developing in the 1700s, the emphasis on making careful and repeated measurements in experiments increased. Because of this change, more-precise data were collected and were used to favor one theory over another.

Figure 1 The properties of aluminum containers come from the properties of aluminum atoms, shown magnified here in an image from a scanning tunneling electron microscope.

Key Resources

💿 **Visual Concepts**
Atom
Parts of the Atom
Comparing Models of the Atom

📁 **Datasheets**
Making a Model
Evidence for Atoms

📁 **Cross-Disciplinary Worksheets**
Integrating Physics—Atomic Fingerprints
Integrating Technology—Seeing Atoms: The STM

▶ Teach

QuickLab

Teacher's Notes Each student or group of students needs two cups that contain marbles and pennies. The cups should have different overall amounts of marbles and pennies, but the same ratio of marbles to pennies (such as two marbles to one penny).

Materials per Group
- balance
- cups, 2
- marbles
- pennies

Answers

4. Yes, they contain the same "compound," although in different amounts.

5. Because each compound has the same percentage of pennies and marbles by mass, you can conclude that each basic unit of the compound is made up of the same number of pennies and marbles.

Teaching Key Ideas

Definite Proportions Draw students' attention to the pie chart in **Figure 2.** Explain that the pie chart shows the proportions (or the relative amounts) of each element in the compound. This means that when hydrogen and oxygen react completely to form 100 grams of water, 11 grams of hydrogen and 89 grams of oxygen are used. This represents a proportion of 2 hydrogen atoms for every oxygen atom. Ask students to infer why the pie chart does not show a 2:1 ratio. (Hydrogen has a smaller mass, so two atoms of hydrogen have less mass than one oxygen atom.) **LS Visual**

QuickLab ⏱ 10 min

Evidence for Atoms

1. Your teacher will provide **two cups** that contain a mixture of **pennies** and **marbles.**

2. Use a **balance** to find the total mass of the pennies in the first cup. Then, find the mass of the marbles.

3. Repeat step 2 for the second cup.

4. Compare the composition of the "compounds" in the two cups in terms of the proportions of marbles and pennies by mass. Do the cups contain the same "compound"?

5. What can you deduce from your results?

Dalton's Atomic Theory

In 1808, an English schoolteacher named John Dalton proposed a revised atomic theory. Dalton's theory was developed on a scientific basis, and some parts of his theory still hold true today. Like Democritus, Dalton proposed that atoms could not be divided. **❯ According to Dalton, all atoms of a given element were exactly alike, and atoms of different elements could join to form compounds.**

✔ **Reading Check** How are Dalton's and Democritus's atomic theories similar? (See Appendix E for answers to Reading Checks.)

Dalton used experimental evidence.

Unlike Democritus, Dalton based his theory on experimental evidence. For instance, scientists were beginning to observe that some substances combined together in consistent ways. According to the *law of definite proportions,* a chemical compound always contains the same elements in exactly the same proportions by weight or mass. For example, any sample of water contains the same proportions of hydrogen and oxygen by mass, as **Figure 2** shows. This and other evidence supported Dalton's theory.

Dalton's theory did not fit all observations.

Today, Dalton's theory is considered the foundation for modern atomic theory. Some parts of Dalton's work turned out to be correct. However, as experiments continued, Dalton's theory could not explain all of the experimental evidence. Like many scientific theories, the atomic theory changed gradually over many years as scientists continued to do experiments and acquire more information.

Figure 2 The Law of Definite Proportions

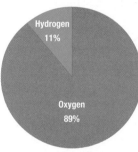

Water Composition by Mass

Hydrogen 11%

Oxygen 89%

For any given water sample, the proportions of hydrogen and oxygen by mass are constant.

This fact suggests that water molecules are made up of atoms that combine in simple whole-number ratios to form compounds.

▨▨ MISCONCEPTION ALERT ▨▨

Properties Atoms are responsible for properties, but the atoms themselves do not possess them. For example, silver is shiny, but silver atoms are not shiny. (Electron arrangement in atoms is the largest determining factor of properties.) Discuss other properties of matter that are not shared between samples of different sizes. Have students compare a single bead and a jar of beads. (For example, the jar of beads makes a rattling sound when you shake it, while the single bead makes a bouncing sound when you drop it.) **LS Kinesthetic**

Differentiated Instruction

Basic Learners

Identifying Preconceptions Before students read the chapter, write the following statements on the chalkboard:
- An atom cannot be broken down into smaller parts.
- An atom is the same throughout.
- An atom is made up of several different, smaller parts.

Ask students their opinions of the statements. Have them discuss the opinions and try to justify their own opinions. Save a list of the opinions for discussion after completing the section. **LS Verbal**

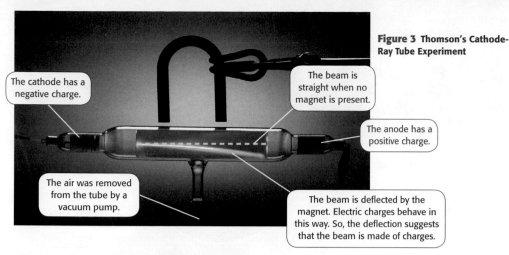

Figure 3 Thomson's Cathode-Ray Tube Experiment

The cathode has a negative charge.

The beam is straight when no magnet is present.

The anode has a positive charge.

The air was removed from the tube by a vacuum pump.

The beam is deflected by the magnet. Electric charges behave in this way. So, the deflection suggests that the beam is made of charges.

Thomson's Model of the Atom

In 1897, J. J. Thomson, a British scientist, conducted an experiment that suggested that atoms were not indivisible. Thomson wasn't planning to learn about the atom. Instead, he was experimenting with electricity. He was studying *cathode rays,* mysterious rays in vacuum tubes. ❯ **Thomson's cathode-ray tube experiment suggested that cathode rays were made of negatively charged particles that came from inside atoms.** This result revealed that atoms could be divided into smaller parts.

Thomson developed the plum-pudding model.

An experiment similar to Thomson's is shown in **Figure 3.** The two metal plates at the ends of the vacuum tube are called the *cathode* and the *anode.* The cathode has a negative charge, and the anode has a positive charge. When a voltage is applied across the plates, a glowing beam comes from the cathode and strikes the anode.

Thomson knew that magnets deflected charges. He reasoned that because all of the air was removed from the tube, the beam must have come from the cathode or from the anode. The direction of the deflection confirmed that the beam was made of negative charges and thus came from the cathode. Thomson had discovered **electrons,** negatively charged particles inside the atom.

Thomson proposed a new model of the atom based on his discovery. In this model, electrons are spread throughout the atom, just as blueberries are spread throughout the muffin in **Figure 4.** Thomson's model, often called the *plum-pudding model,* was named after a dessert that was popular in his day.

electron (ee LEK TRAHN) a subatomic particle that has a negative charge

Figure 4 This blueberry muffin is similar to Thomson's atomic model. **What do the blueberries represent?**

READING TOOLBOX

Visual Literacy Help students understand that electricity and magnetism are related. Make an electric circuit by connecting a battery, a flashlight bulb, and a switch with insulated wires. Explain that a compass needle is a small magnet. Hold a small compass near one of the wires in the circuit. Have students observe how the compass needle moves when the switch in the circuit is turned on and off. Have students compare this movement to the deflection of the beam by a magnet as shown in **Figure 3.**
LS Visual

Teaching Key Ideas

Scientific Theories and Laws

Because of the way the word *theory* is used in everyday speech, many students have the idea that all theories are just unproved notions. In science, however, a theory explains a law and is supported by scientific evidence. Laws are simple statements of the behavior of nature. They can be demonstrated to be true at any time or place.

Dalton was confident in proposing his atomic theory because it accounted for many observed laws, including the law of definite composition, the law of multiple proportions, and the law of the conservation of mass. Have students conduct research to find out what each of these laws states. Then ask them to describe how each law can be explained by Dalton's theory.
LS Verbal

Answer to caption question

The blueberries represent electrons.

Differentiated Instruction

Advanced Learners

Electron Charge and Mass Tell students that Thomson did not know the magnitude of an electron's charge, nor the mass. Thomson showed the ratio of the charge, *e,* to the mass, *m,* to be $e/m = 1.76 \times 10^{11}$ C/kg, Coulombs per kilogram. In 1909, Robert Millikan determined the charge of the electron, *e,* to be -1.6×10^{-19} C. Have students use these two values to calculate the mass of the electron. (1.6×10^{-19} C $\div 1.76 \times 10^{11}$ C/kg $= 9.1 \times 10^{-31}$ kg)
LS Logical

Why It **Matters**

How Do Televisions Work? A picture on a television screen is composed of pixels in much the same way that color comics in the newspaper are composed of tiny dots of color. However, the colors of light emitted from the phosphors in pixels combine in a different way than the inks that make up newsprint. When an electron beam hits the red phosphor of a pixel, it glows red. Likewise, when the electron beams light up the blue and green phosphors, they glow blue and green. To make the pixel light up white, all three electron beams must light up the red, blue, and green phosphors of the pixel. To make a black pixel, all three electron beams turn off. Allow students to experiment with red, green, and blue gels (slides) on an overhead projector to understand how primary colors of light combine to make secondary colors. **LS** Visual

Answers to Your Turn

1. Both use combinations of colored pixels to create images.
2. Students' posters should illustrate one type of flat-screen technology.

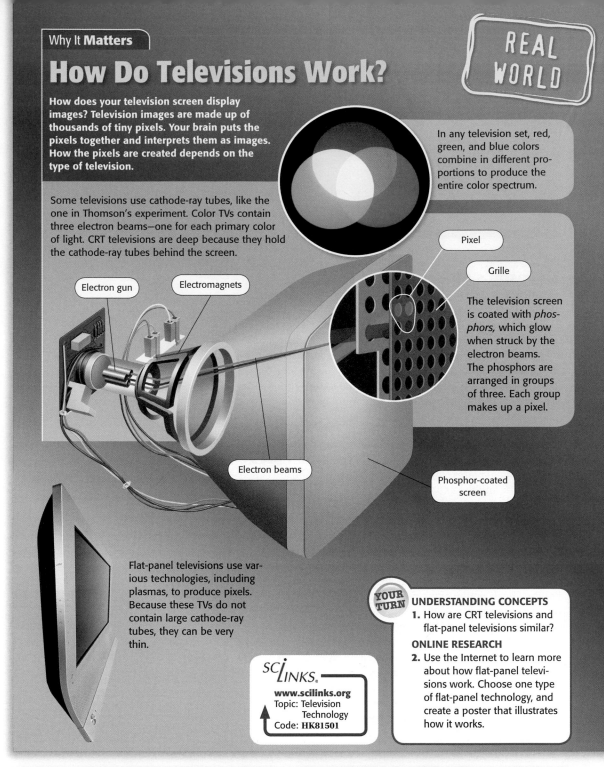

Why It **Matters**

How Do Televisions Work?

REAL WORLD

How does your television screen display images? Television images are made up of thousands of tiny pixels. Your brain puts the pixels together and interprets them as images. How the pixels are created depends on the type of television.

Some televisions use cathode-ray tubes, like the one in Thomson's experiment. Color TVs contain three electron beams—one for each primary color of light. CRT televisions are deep because they hold the cathode-ray tubes behind the screen.

In any television set, red, green, and blue colors combine in different proportions to produce the entire color spectrum.

Pixel

Grille

The television screen is coated with *phosphors,* which glow when struck by the electron beams. The phosphors are arranged in groups of three. Each group makes up a pixel.

Electron gun

Electromagnets

Electron beams

Phosphor-coated screen

Flat-panel televisions use various technologies, including plasmas, to produce pixels. Because these TVs do not contain large cathode-ray tubes, they can be very thin.

SCLINKS
www.scilinks.org
Topic: Television Technology
Code: HK81501

YOUR TURN

UNDERSTANDING CONCEPTS
1. How are CRT televisions and flat-panel televisions similar?

ONLINE RESEARCH
2. Use the Internet to learn more about how flat-panel televisions work. Choose one type of flat-panel technology, and create a poster that illustrates how it works.

Differentiated Instruction

Struggling Readers

Scanning for Specific Information Scanning is an important skill for answering questions or taking notes. Encourage students to use their fingers to move quickly over the text to look for key words, checking for capital letters for names and bold letters for new terms. Ask them to scan the pages in this section to find the person who matches a description you provide. **LS** Visual

English Learners

Organizing and Narrating Past Events Give students a list of facts on the development of atomic theories, and ask them to fill in the information on a chart in chronological order. They should put the year, scientist, and discovery in columns. Students should then use the chart as a guide for writing a paragraph, using the past tense to narrate the way each scientist's discovery helped the next scientist develop his or her theory. **LS** Verbal

Rutherford's Model of the Atom

Shortly after Thomson proposed his new atomic model, Ernest Rutherford, another British scientist, developed an experiment to test Thomson's model. Rutherford found that Thomson's model needed to be revised. **❭ Rutherford proposed that most of the mass of the atom was concentrated at the atom's center.** To understand why Rutherford came to this conclusion, you need to learn about his experiment.

Rutherford conducted the gold-foil experiment.

In Rutherford's experiment, shown in **Figure 5,** two of Rutherford's students aimed a beam of positively charged alpha particles at a very thin sheet of gold foil. In Thomson's model of the atom, the mass and positive charge of an atom are evenly distributed, and electrons are scattered throughout the atom. The positive charge at any location would be too small to affect the paths of the incoming particles. Rutherford predicted that most particles would travel in a straight path and that a few would be slightly deflected.

The observations from the experiment did not match Rutherford's predictions. As **Figure 5** shows, most particles did pass straight through the gold foil, but some were deflected by a large amount. A few particles came straight back. Rutherford wrote, "It was quite the most incredible event that has ever happened to me in my life. It was almost as incredible as if you fired a 15-inch shell at a piece of tissue paper and it came back and hit you."

✅ **Reading Check** Why were Rutherford's results surprising?

Figure 5 Rutherford's Gold-Foil Experiment

go.hrw.com
✳ **interact online**
Keyword: HK8ATSF5

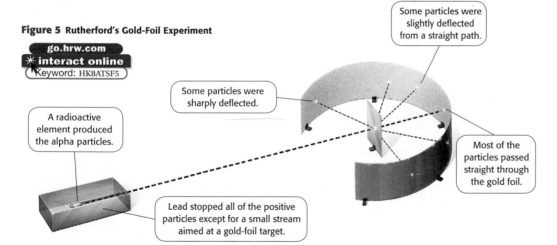

Some particles were slightly deflected from a straight path.

Some particles were sharply deflected.

A radioactive element produced the alpha particles.

Lead stopped all of the positive particles except for a small stream aimed at a gold-foil target.

Most of the particles passed straight through the gold foil.

READING TOOLBOX

Pyramid FoldNote
Create a Pyramid FoldNote to compare the atomic models of Dalton, Thomson, and Rutherford. Be sure to note the similarities and differences between the models.

www.scilinks.org
Topic: Atomic Theory
Code: HK80120

READING TOOLBOX

Pyramid FoldNote Students' pyramids should look similar to the example shown at the beginning of the chapter. Have students include on their pyramids an illustration of each model or experiment to help them distinguish each scientist's contribution.

Teaching Key Ideas

Modeling Rutherford's Experiment Have groups of students model Rutherford's experiment by placing a piece of plywood over four soup cans at each of its corners. Have one student place a can of tuna underneath the board while the others are not looking. Then have students shoot marbles underneath the board and determine the location of the can of tuna by measuring the angles of the deflections of the marbles. **LS Kinesthetic**

go.hrw.com
✳ **interact online**

Students can interact with the figure by going to **go.hrw.com** and typing in the keyword **HK8ATSF5.**

Differentiated Instruction

Special Education Students

Demonstrating Relative Size Help students understand how much smaller a nucleus is than an atom by pointing out the model in **Figure 6.** Go to a football field as a group. Stand in the center of the field and have a student place a marble on the ground. Explain that the marble and football field just shows the relationship between the sizes of a nucleus and the whole atom, not the actual size. Point out that an actual whole atom is much smaller than the marble. Billions and billions of atoms make up the marble. **LS Kinesthetic**

Reteaching Key Ideas

Clay Models Have students use clay to make models of each of the atomic models described in the section. Call on volunteers to demonstrate how their models represent Dalton's, Thomson's, and Rutherford's models of the atom.
LS Visual

Formative Assessment

Which of the following is unique to Rutherford's model of the atom?

A. The atom cannot be divided. (Incorrect. Both Democritus and Dalton said that atoms could not be divided.)

B. The atom has negative charges. (Incorrect. Both Thomson's and Rutherford's atomic models had negative charges.)

C. The atom has a positive nucleus. (Correct. Rutherford's experiment suggested that an atom's positive charge is concentrated in the center of the atom, at its nucleus.)

D. The atom contains negative charges evenly distributed throughout. (Incorrect. Thomson's plum-pudding model had electrons distributed throughout.)

Answer to caption question

The nucleus is positive.

Figure 6 If the nucleus of an atom were the size of a marble, the whole atom would be the size of a football stadium!

nucleus (NOO klee uhs) an atom's central region, which is made up of protons and neutrons

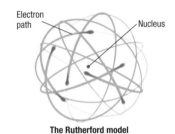

Figure 7 In Rutherford's model, electrons orbit the nucleus. (This figure does not accurately represent sizes and distances.) **Is the nucleus positive, negative, or neutral?**

Electron path

Nucleus

The Rutherford model of the atom

Rutherford discovered the nucleus.

Rutherford's experiment suggested that an atom's positive charge is concentrated in the center of the atom. This positively charged, dense core of the atom is called the **nucleus.** In the gold-foil experiment, incoming positive charges that passed close to the nucleus were deflected sharply. Incoming positive charges that were aimed directly at the nucleus bounced straight back. Data from Rutherford's experiment suggested that compared with the atom, the nucleus was very small, as **Figure 6** shows.

Rutherford's results led to a new model of the atom, shown in **Figure 7.** In Rutherford's model, negative electrons orbit the positively charged nucleus in much the same way that planets orbit the sun. Today, we understand that the nucleus contains particles called *protons* and *neutrons.* Protons have a positive charge, and neutrons have no charge. You will learn more about these particles in the next section.

Section 1 Review

KEY IDEAS

1. **Describe** Democritus's atomic theory.
2. **Summarize** the main ideas of Dalton's theory.
3. **Explain** why Dalton's theory was more successful than Democritus's theory.
4. **Compare** Thomson's atomic model with Rutherford's atomic model.

CRITICAL THINKING

5. **Analyzing Experiments**
   a. How did the cathode-ray tube experiment lead to the conclusion that atoms contain electrons?
   b. How did the gold-foil experiment lead to the conclusion that the atom has a nucleus?
6. **Making Inferences** Does the term *indivisible* still describe the atom? Explain.

Answers to Section Review

1. Everything in the universe is made up of indivisible units called atoms.

2. Elements are made of tiny, unique particles called atoms. Atoms cannot be divided. Atoms of the same element are identical. Atoms of different elements can join to form molecules.

3. Dalton had experimental evidence to support his theory, while Democritus did not.

4. In Thomson's model, electrons are embedded in a sphere of positive charge. In Rutherford's model, positive charge is concentrated in the nucleus (the dense core of the atom), and electrons surround the nucleus.

5. **a.** Because air was removed from the tube, the beam of negative particles observed by Thomson most likely came from the atoms of the cathode. This suggests that atoms are made up of smaller units, including negative charges.

   b. The observation that positive particles were deflected at large angles suggested that positive charge is concentrated at the center of the atom, in the nucleus.

6. No, the atom is not indivisible. It is made up of smaller parts, such as the electron.

SECTION 2 The Structure of Atoms

Key Ideas

> What is the difference between protons, neutrons, and electrons?

> What do atoms of an element have in common with other atoms of the same element?

> Why do isotopes of the same element have different atomic masses?

> What unit is used to express atomic mass?

Key Terms

proton
neutron
atomic number
mass number
isotope
unified atomic mass unit
mole

Why It Matters

Radioisotopes emit energy when they decay. To diagnose and treat diseases, doctors use this property of radioisotopes to track where in the body certain atoms go.

Less than 100 years after Dalton published his atomic theory, scientists determined that atoms consisted of smaller particles, such as the electron. In this section, you will learn more about the particles inside the atom.

What Is in an Atom?

Atoms are made up of various subatomic particles. To understand the chemistry of most substances, however, we need to study only three of these particles. > **The three main subatomic particles are distinguished by mass, charge, and location in the atom. Figure 1** compares these particles.

At the center of each atom is a small, dense *nucleus.* The nucleus is made of **protons,** which have a positive charge, and **neutrons,** which have no charge. Protons and neutrons are almost identical in size and mass. Moving around outside the nucleus is a cloud of very tiny, negatively charged *electrons.* The mass of an electron is much smaller than that of a proton or neutron.

proton (PROH TAHN) a subatomic particle that has a positive charge and that is located in the nucleus of an atom

neutron (NOO TRAHN) a subatomic particle that has no charge and that is located in the nucleus of an atom

Figure 1 Subatomic Particles

Particle	Charge	Mass (kg)	Location in the atom
Proton	+1	1.67×10^{-27}	in the nucleus
Neutron	0	1.67×10^{-27}	in the nucleus
Electron	−1	9.11×10^{-31}	outside the nucleus

Key Resources

Teaching Transparencies
C8 Nucleus
TM12 Subatomic Particles
C9 Isotopes
TM13 Mole-Mass Conversion

Visual Concepts
Atomic Number
Mass Number
Isotopes and Nuclides
Average Atomic Mass
The Mole

Datasheet
Modeling Isotopes

Science Skills Worksheets
Scientific Notation
Significant Figures
Dimensional Analysis

Math Skills Worksheets
Conversion Factors
Converting Amount to Mass
Converting Mass to Amount

Cross-Disciplinary Worksheets
Connection to Fine Arts–Carbon-Dating Masterpieces

> Focus

In this section, students compare the three basic subatomic particles (protons, electrons, neutrons). They learn how atomic number, mass number, and molar mass are used to represent properties of atoms.

Bellringer

Use the Bellringer transparency to prepare students for this section.

Demonstrate

Counting Large Numbers by Mass
Put students into groups. Each group will need a large container, identical items to fill the container (such as beans), and a balance. Ask students to find the following: the mass of the empty container (m_{cont}), the mass of a few (x) of the items ($m_{x\,items}$), and the mass of the container with all of the items in it (m_{tot}). Tell each group to use their data to calculate the number of small items without counting them. (First, find the mass of one item by dividing the mass of a given number of items by that number. Then find the mass of all of the items by subtracting the mass of the container from the total mass. Finally, the number of unknown items (n) equals the mass of all of the items divided by the mass of one item.) Tell students that in this section they will see how this method can be used to "count atoms." **Kinesthetic**

Teaching Key Ideas

Neutral Atoms On the chalkboard, write a number line that contains both positive and negative numbers. Use the number line to show students that adding equal numbers of positive and negative charges results in no charge—zero on the number line. **LS** Visual

Answer to caption question

The number of protons (two) defines the element as helium.

READING TOOLBOX

Visual Literacy Students might ask why the protons in the nucleus, shown in **Figure 2,** stay together since positive charges repel each other. Tell students that even though the protons in the nucleus do electrically repel each other, they are held together by a stronger force known as the *strong nuclear force.* This force is unique to the nucleus and exists only over very short distances. Gravity also attracts nuclear particles to each other. But gravity is not the main force that holds together the nucleus because it is not strong enough to overcome the electrical repulsion. Ask students to compare atomic forces to the forces at work in a tug of war. (As in a tug of war, a stronger force wins out even if it is opposed by a weaker force.) **LS** Logical

Figure 2 Helium atoms, including the ones in this helium blimp, are made up of two protons, two neutrons, and two electrons. **Which of these particles defines the element as helium?**

Academic Vocabulary

overall (OH vuhr AWL) total; net

Each element has a unique number of protons.

A hydrogen atom has one proton. A helium atom, shown in **Figure 2,** has two protons. Lithium has three protons. As you move through the periodic table of the elements, this pattern continues. Each element has a unique number of protons. In fact, an element is defined by the number of protons in an atom of that element.

Unreacted atoms have no overall charge.

Even though the protons and electrons in atoms have electric charges, most atoms do not have an <u>overall</u> charge. The reason is that most atoms have an equal number of protons and electrons, whose charges exactly cancel. For example, a helium atom has two protons and two electrons. The atom is neutral because the positive charge of the two protons exactly cancels the negative charge of the two electrons, as shown below.

Charge of two protons:	+2
Charge of two neutrons:	0
Charge of two electrons:	−2
Total charge of a helium atom:	0

If an atom gains or loses electrons, it becomes charged. A charged atom is called an *ion.*

The electric force holds the atom together.

Positive and negative charges attract each other with a force known as the *electric force.* Because protons are positive and electrons are negative, protons and electrons are attracted to one another by the electric force. In fact, the electric force between protons in the nucleus and electrons outside the nucleus holds the atom together. On a larger scale, this same force holds solid and liquid materials together. For instance, electric attractions hold water molecules together.

Why It Matters

Quarks and Leptons Most matter, including protons and neutrons, is made up of smaller particles, called quarks. There are six types of quarks: up, down, charm, strange, top (or truth), and bottom (or beauty). Protons and neutrons both consist of up and down quarks. The proton, for example, is made of two up quarks and one down quark. Electrons belong to a class of fundamental particles called leptons, which are different than quarks. Other leptons are the muon, the tau, and three types of neutrinos. Have interested students find out more about fundamental particles of matter and present their findings in a poster. **LS** Visual

Atomic Number and Mass Number

Atoms of different elements have their own unique structures. Because these atoms have different structures, they have different properties. Atoms of the same element can vary in structure, too. ❯ **Atoms of each element have the same number of protons, but they can have different numbers of neutrons.**

The atomic number equals the number of protons.

The **atomic number** of an element, Z, tells you how many protons are in an atom of the element. Remember that most atoms are neutral because they have an equal number of protons and electrons. Thus, the atomic number also equals the number of electrons in the atom. Because each element is defined by its unique number of protons, each element has a unique atomic number. Hydrogen has only one proton, so $Z = 1$ for hydrogen. The largest naturally occurring element, uranium, has 92 protons, so $Z = 92$ for uranium. The atomic number of a given element never changes.

The mass number equals the total number of subatomic particles in the nucleus.

The **mass number** of an element, A, equals the number of protons plus the number of neutrons in an atom of the element. A fluorine atom has 9 protons and 10 neutrons, so $A = 19$ for fluorine. Oxygen has 8 protons and 8 neutrons, so $A = 16$ for oxygen. The mass number reflects the number of protons and neutrons (and not the number of electrons) because protons and neutrons provide most of the atom's mass. Although atoms of an element have the same atomic number, they can have different mass numbers because the number of neutrons can vary. **Figure 3** shows which subatomic particles in the nucleus of an atom contribute to the atomic number and which contribute to the mass number.

✓ **Reading Check** Which defines an element: the atomic number of the element or the mass number of the element?

atomic number (uh TAHM ik NUHM buhr) the number of protons in the nucleus of an atom

mass number (MAS NUHM buhr) the sum of the numbers of protons and neutrons in the nucleus of an atom

READING TOOLBOX

Pyramid FoldNote
Create a Pyramid FoldNote for the terms *proton, neutron,* and *electron,* and describe which can vary for a given element. Also include the terms *atomic number* and *mass number* in your notes.

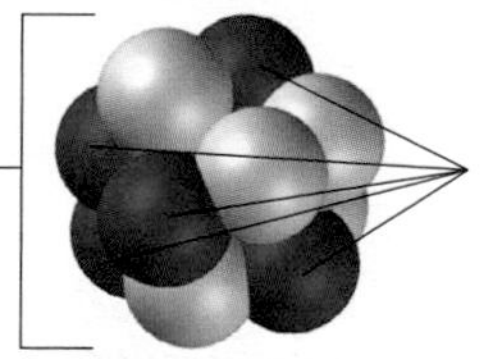

Nucleus

Mass number, $A =$ number of protons + number of neutrons

Atomic number, $Z =$ number of protons

Figure 3 Atoms of the same element have the same number of protons and thus the same atomic number. But because the number of neutrons may vary, atoms of the same element may have different mass numbers.

Teaching Key Ideas

Mass Number Students may find it hard to tell mass number from the average atomic masses given in the periodic table. Point out that the mass number is not an actual atomic mass, but rather a way of stating the total number of particles in the nucleus. Ask students to explain why mass number is so similar to actual atomic mass for a given atom. (Protons and neutrons each have a mass close to 1 u.)
LS Logical

READING TOOLBOX

Pyramid FoldNote Students' pyramids should look similar to the example shown at the beginning of the chapter. Students' answers should explain that neutrons can vary for neutral isotopes of the same element. Have students include on their pyramids an illustration similar to that in **Figure 2** that labels each subatomic particle.

Teaching Key Ideas

Protons and Neutrons Group students in pairs. List the symbols and mass numbers of 20 elements on the chalkboard. Have students create a table that lists the number of protons (atomic number) and number of neutrons (mass number–atomic number) for all of the elements listed. Then, ask them to summarize the information in their table. (For light elements, the number of protons and the number of neutrons are approximately equal. For heavier elements, the number of neutrons increases faster than the number of protons in an atom.) **LS Verbal**

Differentiated Instruction

Basic Learners

Small to Large Help students keep the details straight by putting the following items in order from smallest to greatest mass: electron, atom, proton, nucleus. (electron, proton, nucleus, atom) To make the activity more concrete, have students also create a diagram with the relative sizes for each part of the atom. **LS Logical**

READING TOOLBOX

Visual Literacy After students examine **Figure 3,** ask the following: Which colored spheres would you count to find the atomic number of this element? (pink) Which would you count to find the mass number? (gray and pink) Which color would increase or decrease for a different isotope of this same element? (gray) Are the number of pink and gray spheres necessarily the same? (No; the number of protons does not always equal the number of neutrons.) **LS Visual**

Teacher's Notes Remind students not to eat any materials used in the laboratory. The activity also works with colored marshmallows or balls of clay.

Materials per Group
• gumdrops of three different colors
• toothpicks

Answers to Analysis

1. The hydrogen isotopes each have one proton and one electron, but different numbers of neutrons (0, 1, or 2).

2. The hydrogen and helium isotopes have different numbers of protons and electrons. Each hydrogen isotope has one of each, while each helium isotope has two of each. Some of the helium and hydrogen isotopes have the same number of neutrons.

3. Tritium and helium-3 have the same mass number ($A = 3$). The hydrogen isotopes share the same atomic number ($Z = 1$), as do the helium isotopes ($Z = 2$).

READING TOOLBOX

Visual Literacy Ask students to draw a nucleus diagram like the one shown in **Figure 3** for the three isotopes of hydrogen shown in **Figure 4**. Tell them to include a key that distinguishes between protons and neutrons. (Student diagrams should illustrate the following: protium: 1 proton; deuterium: 1 proton, 1 neutron; tritium: 1 proton, 2 neutrons) **LS Visual**

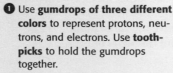

QuickLab **Modeling Isotopes** ⏱ **20 min**

Procedure

❶ Use **gumdrops of three different colors** to represent protons, neutrons, and electrons. Use **toothpicks** to hold the gumdrops together.

❷ Create atomic models for the three isotopes of hydrogen: protium ($A = 1$), deuterium ($A = 2$), and tritium ($A = 3$).

❸ Create atomic models for helium-3 ($A = 3$) and helium-4 ($A = 4$).

Analysis

1. How do the isotopes of hydrogen compare to one another?

2. How do the hydrogen isotopes differ from the helium isotopes?

3. Which isotopes have the same mass number? Which isotopes have the same atomic number?

SC**LINKS**.

www.scilinks.org
Topic: Isotopes
Code: HK80820

isotope (IE suh TOHP) an atom that has the same number of protons (or the same atomic number) as other atoms of the same element do but that has a different number of neutrons (and thus a different atomic mass)

Isotopes

As you have learned, atoms of a single element can have different numbers of neutrons and thus different mass numbers. An **isotope** is an atom that has the same number of protons but a different number of neutrons relative to other atoms of the same element. Because they have the same number of protons and electrons, isotopes of an element have the same chemical properties. However, isotopes have different masses. ❯ **Isotopes of an element vary in mass because their numbers of neutrons differ.**

Each of the three isotopes of hydrogen, shown in **Figure 4,** has one proton and one electron. The most common hydrogen isotope, protium, does not have any neutrons. Because it has one proton in its nucleus, its mass number, A, is 1. Deuterium, a second isotope of hydrogen, has one neutron as well as one proton in its nucleus. Its mass number, A, is 2. A third isotope, tritium, has two neutrons. Because its nucleus contains two neutrons and one proton, tritium has a mass number of 3.

✓ **Reading Check** Which hydrogen isotope has the most mass?

Isotopes of Hydrogen

Figure 4 Each isotope of hydrogen has one proton, but the number of neutrons varies. **What is the atomic number, Z, of each isotope?**

| Protium | Deuterium | Tritium |
| $A = 1$ | $A = 2$ | $A = 3$ |

Answer to caption question

Each hydrogen isotope has an atomic number of $Z = 1$.

Why It Matters

Deuterium as a Fuel for Fusion Deuterium is the fuel required for nuclear fusion, a potential energy source. The amount of energy released by fusing two deuterium atoms is greater than the energy released by an equal mass of uranium during a nuclear fission reaction. Another advantage of fusion is that the waste products of certain fusion reactions are not radioactive. Scientists have not yet been able to create the conditions required for fusion in a laboratory, but many are working in this area with the hope of one day making fusion a practical energy source. Have students research fusion and fission and make a poster comparing the two types of reactions as energy sources. **LS Visual**

Some isotopes are more common than others.

Hydrogen is present on Earth and on the sun. In both places, protium is most common. Only a small fraction of the hydrogen found on Earth and on the sun is deuterium. For instance, only 1 out of every 6,000 hydrogen atoms in Earth's crust is a deuterium isotope. Similarly, on the sun, protium isotopes outnumber deuterium isotopes 50,000 to 1.

Tritium is an unstable isotope that decays over time. Thus, tritium is the least common isotope of hydrogen. Unstable isotopes, called *radioisotopes,* emit radiation and decay into other isotopes. A radioisotope continues to decay until the isotope reaches a stable form. Each radioisotope decays at a fixed rate, which can vary from a fraction of a second to millions of years.

SCILINKS.
www.scilinks.org
Topic: Radioisotopes
Code: HK81260

Why It **Matters**

Nuclear Medicine

Radioactive isotopes, or radioisotopes, are widely used in medicine. They are used to diagnose and treat certain conditions. Some isotopes are used to create images similar to X-ray images. Doctors interpret the images to study organ structures and functions. Radioisotopes are also used to study organ metabolisms and to identify and treat cancer.

In the full-body image shown here, the radioisotope *technetium-99m*, along with a biological agent that localizes the radioactivity in the bones, was injected into the body. The image, called a *colored gamma scan* or *scintigram,* shows a healthy human skeleton.

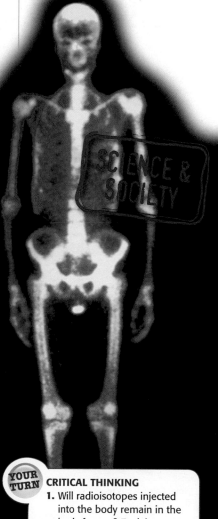

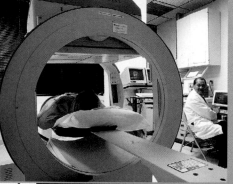

A radioisotope that has been injected into the body emits small amounts of radiation. A special camera, such as the one shown here, detects the radiation. A computer uses the information from the camera to create the image. The image is often interpreted by a radiologist, a doctor who specializes in imaging technologies.

YOUR TURN

CRITICAL THINKING

1. Will radioisotopes injected into the body remain in the body forever? Explain.

Differentiated Instruction

Struggling Readers

Meaning of New Words Readers need opportunities to monitor understanding of new terms by using them in structured ways. Have students fill in blanks using key words from a word bank of terms from this section. Example: Atoms are made of protons, (neutrons), and electrons. The protons and neutrons are particles in the (nucleus). The (protons) are positively charged. The (electrons) are negatively charged particles outside the nucleus. The (atomic number) of an element is the number of protons in an atom of that element. **LS Verbal**

Teaching Key Ideas

Isotopes Make it clear to students that the identity of an atom is determined entirely by the number of protons in its nucleus. Atoms of the same element (same number of protons) may have varying numbers of neutrons, thus creating different isotopes. When an atom forms an ion, it may have more or fewer electrons than protons. Have students look through a chemistry handbook to see the different isotopes of carbon and their relative abundance. Have them determine the number of protons in an atom of each isotope of carbon. (6) **LS Logical**

Why It **Matters**

Nuclear Medicine Radioisotopes are not only used to diagnose diseases. They are sometimes used to treat diseases, such as cancer. The radioactive source may be sealed in a capsule and placed directly in a patient's body near cancerous cells. Treatment in which a radioisotope is surgically placed inside the body is called internal radiation therapy. Because radiation can pass through the body, a person undergoing internal radiation therapy must stay in the hospital away from others. Have students find out more about internal and external radiation therapies and present their findings to the class. **LS Verbal**

Answer to Your Turn

1. Accept all reasonable answers. Sample answer: Provided the atoms decay at a relatively fast rate, they will not remain in the body forever. They will either be excreted from the body or decay until they reach a stable form.

READING TOOLBOX

Visual Literacy Ask students to summarize orally the calculations shown in **Figure 5** and the example provided. Be sure students show understanding of atomic number and mass number and of how to use them to find the number of neutrons in an atom. **LS** Verbal

Math Skills

Counting with Isotopes Have students calculate the number of neutrons there are in the following isotopes. Show them how to use a periodic table to find the atomic numbers. To calculate the number of neutrons in the isotopes, students should subtract the atomic numbers from the given mass numbers.

1. carbon-14 $(14 - 6 = 8)$
2. nitrogen-15 $(15 - 7 = 8)$
3. sulfur-35 $(35 - 16 = 19)$
4. calcium-45 $(45 - 20 = 25)$
5. iodine-131 $(131 - 53 = 78)$

LS Logical

Answer to caption question

The isotope with a mass of 35 u is more common.

35
17 Cl

17 protons
17 electrons
$35 - 17 =$ **18 neutrons**

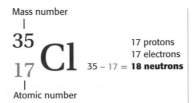

37
17 Cl

17 protons
17 electrons
$37 - 17 =$ **20 neutrons**

Figure 5 One isotope of chlorine has 18 neutrons, while the other isotope has 20 neutrons.

Figure 6 The average atomic mass of chlorine is closer to 35 u than it is to 37 u. **Which chlorine isotope is more common?**

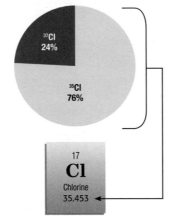

Isotopes of Chlorine

^{37}Cl 24%

^{35}Cl 76%

17
Cl
Chlorine
35.453

Note: Calculations using the values from the pie graph do not give a result of exactly 35.453 u because of rounding.

The number of neutrons can be calculated.

To represent different isotopes, you can write the mass number and atomic number of the isotope before the symbol of the element. The two isotopes of chlorine are represented this way in **Figure 5**. (Sometimes the atomic number is omitted because it is always the same for any given element.)

If you know the atomic number and mass number, you can calculate the number of neutrons that an atom has. For example, the isotope of uranium that is used in nuclear reactors is uranium-235, or $^{235}_{92}$U. Like all uranium atoms, this isotope has an atomic number of 92, so it has 92 protons. Its mass number is 235, so there are a total of 235 protons and neutrons. The number of neutrons can be found by subtracting the atomic number from the mass number, as shown below.

Mass number (A):	235
Atomic number (Z):	$- 92$
Number of neutrons:	143

Atomic Masses

The mass of a single atom is very small. The mass of a single fluorine atom is less than one trillionth of a billionth of a gram. ❭ **Because working with such tiny masses is difficult, atomic masses are usually expressed in unified atomic mass units.** A **unified atomic mass unit** (u) is equal to one-twelfth of the mass of a carbon-12 atom. (This unit is sometimes called the atomic mass unit, amu.) Carbon-12, an isotope of carbon, has six protons and six neutrons, so each individual proton and neutron has a mass of about 1.0 u. Recall that electrons contribute very little mass to an atom.

Average atomic mass is a weighted average.

Often, the atomic mass listed for an element in the periodic table is an average atomic mass for the element as found in nature. The *average atomic mass* for an element is a weighted average. In other words, commonly found isotopes have a greater effect on the average atomic mass than rarely found isotopes do.

For example, **Figure 6** shows how the natural abundance of chlorine's two isotopes affects chlorine's average atomic mass, which is 35.453 u. This mass is closer to 35 u than it is to 37 u. The reason is that the atoms of chlorine that have a mass of nearly 35 u are more common in nature. Thus, they make a greater contribution to chlorine's average atomic mass.

Differentiated Instruction

Alternative Assessment

Weighted Average Tell students that a weighted average is based on both the number of items and the value of each.

Step 1 Provide students with the following example: a student received four As, ten Bs, three Cs, and one F as grades. Using a 4-point grading scale, what is the student's average grade? $\{(4 \times 4) + (10 \times 3) + (3 \times 2) + (1 \times 0)\} \div (4 + 10 + 3 + 1) = 52/18 = 2.9$

Step 2 Have students work the following problem, then write problems of their own and share them. Juan had four quarters, six dimes, nine nickels, and 15 pennies. What is the average value of the coins? $\{(4 \times 25) + (6 \times 10) + (9 \times 5) + (15 \times 1)$ cents$\} \div (4 + 6 + 9 + 15) = 220$ cents$/34 \times 6.5$ cents

LS Logical

The mole is useful for counting small particles.

Because chemists often deal with large numbers of small particles, they use a large counting unit called the **mole** (mol). A mole is a collection of a very large number of particles.

1 mol = 602, 213, 670, 000, 000, 000, 000, 000 particles

This number is usually written as 6.022×10^{23} and is called *Avogadro's number*. The number is named for Italian scientist Amedeo Avogadro. Why is 6.022×10^{23} the number of particles in one mole? The mole has been defined as the number of atoms in 12.00 grams of carbon-12. Experiments have shown this value to be 6.022×10^{23}. So, one mole of a substance contains 6.022×10^{23} particles of that substance.

The following example demonstrates the magnitude of Avogadro's number: 6.022×10^{23} popcorn kernels would cover the United States to form a pile about 500 km (310 mi) tall! So, Avogadro's number is not useful for counting items such as popcorn kernels but is useful for counting atoms or molecules.

✔ **Reading Check** How many particles are in 1 mol of iron?

Moles and grams are related.

The mass in grams of one mole of a substance is called *molar mass.* For example, 1 mol of carbon-12 atoms has a mass of 12.00 g, so the molar mass of carbon-12 is 12.00 g/mol. **Figure 7** shows the molar mass of magnesium.

In nature, elements often occur as mixtures of isotopes. So, a mole of an element usually contains several isotopes. As a result, an element's molar mass in grams per mole equals its average atomic mass in unified atomic mass units, u. The average atomic mass of carbon is 12.01 u. So, one mole of carbon has a mass of 12.01 g. Because this mass is a weighted average of the masses of several isotopes of carbon, it differs from the molar mass of carbon-12, which is a single isotope.

Integrating Space Science

Counting Stars How many stars are in the universe? In 2003, a group of astronomers estimated that the visible universe—the portion that our telescopes can reach—contains 70,000,000,000,000,000,000,000 stars, or 7×10^{22} stars. This quantity is about one-tenth of Avogadro's number! Of course, this estimate is based on observations from existing telescopes. As improvements in telescopes occur, the estimate could increase. Perhaps the estimate will reach Avogadro's number someday.

unified atomic mass unit (YOON uh FIED uh TAHM ik MAS YOON it) a unit of mass that describes the mass of an atom or molecule; it is exactly 1/12 the mass of a carbon atom with mass number 12 (symbol, u)

mole (MOHL) the SI base unit used to measure the amount of a substance whose number of particles is the same as the number of atoms of carbon in exactly 12 g of carbon-12

Figure 7 One mole of magnesium (6.022×10^{23} Mg atoms) has a mass of 24.3050 g. Note that the balance is accurate only to one-tenth of a gram, so it reads 24.3 g.

**MISCONCEPTION /// ALERT **

Atomic Masses Some students believe that subatomic particles have no mass. Explain that although atomic and subatomic masses are very small, they are significant at the atomic level. Point out that the masses of the proton and neutron are very large compared to the mass of the electron. Thus, electron mass is negligible in ordinary mass calculations. Have students revisit **Figure 1** to reinforce this concept. **LS** Logical

Why It Matters

Avogadro's Contribution Have interested students find out more about the scientist Amedeo Avogadro. (Although Avogadro did not develop Avogadro's constant, he made many important contributions that dealt with particles of matter. For example, he hypothesized that equal volumes of gases at the same temperature and pressure contain equal numbers of particles.) Have students present their findings in a written or oral report. **LS** Verbal

Teaching Key Ideas

Counting Units Draw an analogy between a mole and a dozen, as counting units. Explain that just as eggs are counted by the dozens, atoms are counted by moles. Have students think of another counting unit. (Sample answer: Paper is sold in reams, or 500-sheet bundles.) **LS** Verbal

Teaching Key Ideas

Moles Emphasize that moles are a measure of the number of particles, not the mass. For example, 16.00 g of oxygen is the mass of 1 mol, or 6.022×10^{23} of oxygen atoms. Have students identify how they can tell if a measurement is mass. (Look at the units. If they are a form of grams, the measurement is mass.) **LS** Logical

Math Skills

Conversion Factors Explain that equations that compare units can be rearranged to become a conversion factor equal to 1. You can convert numbers from one unit to another by multiplying by a conversion factor that has both units. Have students use conversion factors to solve the following problems.

1. What is the mass of exactly 150 gumballs if the mass of 10 gumballs is 21.4 g? (150 gumballs $\times$ (21.4 g/10 gumballs) = 321 g)
2. If a football player is tackled 1.7 ft short of the end zone, how many more yards does the team need to get a touchdown? (1.7 ft $\times$ (1 yd/3 ft) = 0.57 yd)
3. A bicycle travels at a speed of 30.0 km/h. How fast does the bicycle travel in m/s? (More than one conversion factor must be used.) (8.33 m/s)

LS Logical

Teaching Key Ideas

Counting Groups On the chalk-board, make a table that has one column labeled *Counting unit* and another column labeled *Number of units*. Have students brainstorm and record counting units that could be used for grouping students in the class. (Possible units include basketball teams (5), baseball teams (9), dozens (12), and pairs (2).) **LS Logical**

READING TOOLBOX

Visual Literacy Point out that **Figure 8** illustrates how to convert between the amount of an element and its mass. Tell students to look at the periodic table to determine an element's average atomic mass, then arrange the conversion factor in the correct orientation. **LS Visual**

Math Skills

Answer to Practice

1. **a.** (2.50 mol S)(32.07 g S /1 mol S) = 80.2 g S
   b. (1.80 mol Ca)(40.08 g Ca /1 mol Ca) = 72.1 g Ca
   c. (0.50 mol C)(12.01 g C /1 mol C) = 6.0 g C
   d. (3.20 mol Cu)(63.55 g Cu /1 mol Cu) = 203.4 g Cu

Additional Example

What is the mass in grams of 1.93 mol of cobalt, Co?
Answer: 114 g Co
LS Logical

You can convert between moles and grams.

Converting between the amount of an element in moles and the mass of an element in grams is outlined in **Figure 8**. For example, to determine the mass of 5.50 mol of iron, first you must find iron, Fe, in the periodic table. The average atomic mass of iron, rounded to the hundredths place, is 55.84 u. So, the molar mass of iron is 55.84 g/mol. Next, you must set up the problem by using the molar mass as if it were a conversion factor, as shown below.

Figure 8 The molar mass of an element allows you to convert between the amount of the element in moles and the mass of the element in grams.

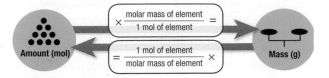

Math Skills Converting Moles to Grams

Determine the mass in grams of 5.50 mol of iron.

Identify	**Given:**
List the given and unknown values.	amount of iron = 5.50 mol molar mass of iron = 55.84 g/mol **Unknown:** mass of iron = ? g

Plan	
Write down the conversion factor that converts moles to grams.	The conversion factor you choose should have what you are trying to find (grams of Fe) in the numerator and what you want to cancel (moles of Fe) in the denominator. $\dfrac{55.84 \text{ g Fe}}{1 \text{ mol Fe}}$

Solve	
Multiply the amount of iron by this conversion factor, and solve.	$5.50 \text{ mol Fe} \times \dfrac{55.84 \text{ g Fe}}{1 \text{ mol Fe}} = 307 \text{ g Fe}$

Practice **Hint**

> Remember to use the periodic table to find molar masses. The average atomic mass of an element is equal to the molar mass of the element. For consistency, this book rounds values to the hundredths place.

> Follow the procedure shown in the sample to convert grams to moles, but be sure to reverse the conversion factor, as shown in Figure 8. You can convert grams to moles to check your answers to the practice questions.

Practice

1. What is the mass in grams of each of the following?
   a. 2.50 mol of sulfur, S
   b. 1.80 mol of calcium, Ca
   c. 0.50 mol of carbon, C
   d. 3.20 mol of copper, Cu

For more practice, visit **go.hrw.com** and enter keyword **HK8MP**.

Differentiated Instruction

Basic Learners

Conversion Factors To give students practice with conversion factors, divide the class into four groups. Assign one of the following to each group: length, mass and weight, volume, and area. Have students in each group make a set of cards of units that can be used to measure that property. For example, length cards can include inches, feet, meters, kilometers, and so on.

Have one student in each group shuffle the cards, and have another student draw two of them. Have students place those cards side-by-side. Ask students to figure out the conversion factors needed to change from the unit on the left to the unit on the right. Tell students that sometimes more than one conversion factor is needed. Have them repeat the activity for additional cards. **LS Interpersonal**

Compounds also have molar masses.

Recall that compounds are made up of atoms joined together in specific ratios. To find the molar mass of a compound, you can add up the molar masses of all of the atoms in a molecule of the compound. For example, to find the molar mass of water, H_2O, first you must find the masses of hydrogen and oxygen in the periodic table. Oxygen's average atomic mass is 16.00 u, so its molar mass is 16.00 g/mol. The molar mass of hydrogen is 1.01 g/mol. You must multiply this value by 2 because a water molecule contains two hydrogen atoms. Thus, the molar mass of H_2O can be calculated as follows:

$$\text{molar mass of } H_2O = (2 \times 1.01 \text{ g/mol}) + 16.00 \text{ g/mol} = 18.02 \text{ g/mol}$$

What does this value tell you? As you learned earlier, molar mass equals the mass in grams of 1 mol of a substance. Thus, the mass of 1 mol of water is 18.02 g. In other words, the total mass of 6.022×10^{23} water molecules is 18.02 g. Take a look at **Figure 9.** Then use information in the caption to find the molar mass of carbon monoxide, another common compound.

Figure 9 Burning charcoal produces carbon dioxide and carbon monoxide, CO, which is a colorless, odorless gas. **What is the molar mass of CO?**

Answer to caption question
CO has a molar mass of 12.01 + 16.00 = 28.01.

> **Close**

Reteaching Key Ideas

Concept Mapping Have students read the section and then organize the ideas presented in the section in the form of a concept map. Concept maps might show how to convert from moles to grams or grams to moles. Have students share their maps after you have checked them for accuracy. **LS** Visual

Formative Assessment

How are isotopes of an element different from one another?

A. Isotopes have the same number of neutrons but different numbers of protons. (Incorrect. Atoms that have different numbers of protons are different elements.)

B. Isotopes have the same number of protons but different numbers of neutrons. (Correct. Atoms that have different numbers of neutrons but the same number of protons are of the same element.)

C. Isotopes have the same number of protons but different numbers of electrons. (Incorrect. Atoms that have different numbers of electrons but the same number of protons are different ions of the same element.)

D. Isotopes have the same number of electrons but different numbers of protons. (Incorrect. Atoms that have different numbers of protons are different elements.)

Section 2 Review

KEY IDEAS

1. **List** the charge, mass, and location of each of the three subatomic particles found in atoms.

2. **Explain** how you can use an atom's mass number and atomic number to determine the number of protons, electrons, and neutrons in the atom.

3. **Identify** the subatomic particle used to define an element, and explain why this particle is used.

4. **Explain** why the masses of atoms of the same element may differ.

5. **Calculate** the number of neutrons that each of the following isotopes contains. Use the periodic table to find the atomic numbers.
   a. carbon-14
   b. nitrogen-15
   c. sulfur-35
   d. calcium-45

6. **Identify** the unit that is used for atomic masses.

7. **Define** Avogadro's number, and describe how it relates to a mole of a substance.

8. **Determine** the molar mass of each of the following elements:
   a. manganese, Mn
   b. cadmium, Cd
   c. arsenic, As
   d. strontium, Sr

CRITICAL THINKING

9. **Making Inferences** If an atom loses electrons, will it have an overall charge?

10. **Making Predictions** Predict which isotope of nitrogen is more common in nature: nitrogen-14 or nitrogen-15. (Hint: What is the average atomic mass listed for nitrogen in the periodic table?)

11. **Applying Concepts** Which has a greater number of atoms: 3.0 g of iron, Fe, or 2.0 g of sulfur, S?

12. **Drawing Conclusions** A graph of the amount of a particular element in moles versus the mass of the element in grams is a straight line. Explain why.

> **Math** *Skills*

13. What is the mass in grams of 0.48 mol of platinum, Pt?

14. What is the mass in grams of 3.1 mol of mercury, Hg?

15. How many moles does 11 g of silicon, Si, contain?

16. How many moles does 205 g of helium, He, contain?

Answers to Section Review

1. The proton is positive, the electron is negative, and the neutron is neutral. Protons and neutrons are found in the nucleus and are massive ($m = 1.67 \times 10^{-27}$ kg) compared to the electrons ($m = 9.11 \times 10^{-31}$ kg), which are found outside the nucleus.

2. Atomic number is the number of protons only. The number of electrons equals the number of protons in a neutral atom. Mass number is the total number of protons and neutrons. The number of neutrons is found by subtracting the atomic number from the mass number.

3. The proton defines the element because each element always has the same number of protons, while the number of neutrons and electrons can vary.

4. Atoms of the same element can have different masses because they can have different numbers of neutrons. These "versions" of each element are called isotopes.

5. a. $14 - 6 = 8$
   b. $15 - 7 = 8$
   c. $35 - 16 = 19$
   d. $45 - 20 = 25$

6. The unified atomic mass unit (u)

Answers continued on p. 141A

❯Focus

The section introduces modern models of the atom, such as Bohr's model and the wave-particle model. It concludes with a discussion of electron orbitals, electron energy levels, valence electrons, and photon absorption and emission.

🔔 Bellringer

Use the Bellringer transparency to prepare students for this section.

Demonstrate

Gaining and Losing Energy
Demonstrate how location can affect the energy of an object by placing a table-tennis ball on a table. Explain that the ball has potential energy due to its location. If you let it fall to the ground, it will bounce and make a noise. This is similar to an electron moving from a higher energy level to a lower energy level and giving off a photon. Now place the table-tennis ball on the floor. In order to raise it to the tabletop, you have to lift the ball, which requires you to exert energy. This is similar to an electron moving from a lower energy level to a higher energy level by absorbing an electron. **LS** Visual

SECTION
3 **Modern Atomic Theory**

Key Ideas

❯ What is the modern model of the atom?

❯ How are the energy levels of an atom filled?

❯ What makes an electron jump to a new energy level?

Key Terms

orbital

valence electron

photon

Why It Matters

Modern atomic theory explains why different elements produce different colors in fireworks.

Dalton's theory that the atom could not be split had to be modified after the discovery that atoms are made of protons, neutrons, and electrons. Like most scientific models and theories, the model of the atom has been revised many times to explain new discoveries.

Modern Models of the Atom

The modern model of the atom, which accounts for many new discoveries in the early 20th century, is very different from the model proposed by Rutherford. ❯ **In the modern atomic model, electrons can be found only in certain energy levels, not between levels. Furthermore, the location of electrons cannot be predicted precisely.** This model is not as easy to visualize as the earlier models that you have studied.

Electron location is limited to energy levels.

In 1913, Niels Bohr, a Danish physicist, suggested that the energy of each electron was related to the electron's path around the nucleus. Electrons can be in only certain energy levels. They must gain energy to move to a higher energy level or must lose energy to move to a lower energy level. Bohr's description of energy levels is still used by scientists today.

One way to imagine Bohr's model is to compare an atom to the stairless building shown in **Figure 1.** Imagine that the nucleus is in a deep basement. The energy levels begin on the first floor, above the basement. Electrons can be on any floor, but they cannot be between floors. Electrons gain energy by riding up the elevator and lose energy by riding down.

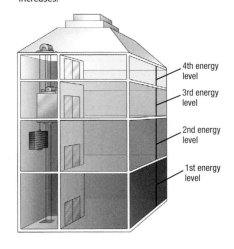

Figure 1 The energy levels of an atom are like the floors of the building shown here. The energy difference between energy levels decreases as the energy level increases.

4th energy level

3rd energy level

2nd energy level

1st energy level

Key Resources

 Teaching Transparencies
C10 Elevator Model
TM14 The s and p Orbitals

Visual Concepts
Electron Energy Levels
s Orbital
p Orbital
Orbital

Datasheet
Electron Levels

Electrons act like waves.

By 1925, Bohr's model of the atom no longer explained all aspects of electron behavior. A new model, which no longer assumed that electrons orbited the nucleus along definite paths in the same way that planets orbit the sun, was proposed. According to this new atomic model, electrons behave more like waves on a vibrating string than like particles.

✓ Reading Check How does the electron-wave model of the atom differ from earlier atomic models?

The exact location of an electron cannot be determined.

Imagine the moving propeller of a plane, such as the one shown in **Figure 2.** If you were asked to identify the location of any of the blades at a certain instant, you would not be able to give an exact answer. Knowing the exact location of any of the blades is very difficult because the blades are moving so quickly. All you know is that each blade could be anywhere within the blurred area that you see as the blades turn.

Similarly, determining the exact location of an electron in an atom and the speed and direction of the electron is impossible. The best that scientists can do is to calculate the chance of finding an electron in a certain place within an atom. One way to show visually the likelihood of finding an electron in a given location is by shading. The darker the shading, the better the chance of finding an electron at that location. The shaded region is called an **orbital.**

Academic Vocabulary

assume (uh SOOM) to accept without proof

READING TOOLBOX

Making Comparisons

As you read this section, make a list of comparisons that you find. For each pair of items, write down ways in which the two items are alike and ways in which they differ.

orbital (AWR buh tuhl) a region in an atom where there is a high probability of finding electrons

Figure 2 The exact location of any of the blades of this airplane is difficult to determine. Likewise, pinpointing the location of an electron in an atom is difficult.

The shaded region, or orbital, shows where electrons are most likely to be.

›Teach

Teaching Key Ideas

Waves and Particles Scientists have discovered that particles act as waves, and waves act as particles. This concept is called the *wave-particle duality of nature.* The smaller the particle, the greater its wavelike nature. Demonstrate a wave property by showing how light passing through a slit is diffracted. Explain that beams of electrons can also be diffracted when passing through a slit. **LS Visual**

READING TOOLBOX

Making Comparisons Students may find it useful to make comparisons in chart form. For example, students may make a chart with the headings "Bohr's atomic model" and "Modern atomic model." Categories could be "how alike" and "how different." **LS Visual**

Differentiated Instruction

Advanced Learners

Wave-Particle Duality In 1923, Louis de Broglie, a French physicist, made a hypothesis that led to a statement of the wave-particle duality of nature and the present theory of how atoms are structured. De Broglie used research done by Albert Einstein and Max Planck to develop a mathematical equation that relates the mass and velocity of a particle to its wavelength. Have students find out more about the lives and work of these scientists and present their findings in a written report. **LS Verbal**

MISCONCEPTION ///ALERT

The Bohr Model The Bohr model leads some students to believe that the distance of an electron from the nucleus of an atom is directly proportional to the electron's energy. Be sure to emphasize that there is no direct proportion between the distance of a given level from the nucleus and the amount of energy needed to reach that energy level. Show students **Figure 2** to remind them that electrons are located in orbitals, which do not represent set distances from the nucleus. **LS Visual**

MISCONCEPTION
////ALERT

Orbitals Some students believe that electrons reside in rings around the nucleus. Point out that energy levels aren't ring shaped; they consist of orbital shapes, as illustrated in **Figure 2** and **Figure 4.** Be sure students understand that the ringed atom diagrams often used to show electron configuration (as, for example, shown in **Figure 3**) do not reflect reality. Ringed atom diagrams are used because, like many models, they provide a simple, useful way to represent a phenomenon—in this case, electron levels—provided their limitation is kept in mind. Also explain to students that an orbital exists as a physical entity only when it is occupied by an electron. **LS Visual**

Answer to caption question

The first four levels can hold $2 + 8 + 18 + 32 = 60$ electrons total.

Electron Energy Levels

Within the atom, electrons that have various amounts of energy exist in different energy levels. There are many possible energy levels that an electron can occupy. **Figure 3** shows how the first four energy levels of an atom are filled. ❯ **The number of energy levels that are filled in an atom depends on the number of electrons.** For example, a lithium atom has three electrons: two in the first energy level and one in the second.

The electrons in the outer energy level of an atom are called **valence electrons.** Valence electrons determine the chemical properties of an atom. Because lithium has one electron in its outer energy level, it has one valence electron.

There are four types of orbitals.

Within each energy level, electrons occupy orbitals that have the lowest energy. There are four kinds of orbitals: s, p, d, and f orbitals. **Figure 4** shows the s and p orbitals.

The s orbital is the simplest kind of orbital. An s orbital has only one possible orientation in space because it is shaped like a sphere, as the figure shows. An s orbital has the lowest energy and can hold two electrons.

A p orbital, on the other hand, is shaped like a dumbbell and can be oriented in space in one of three ways. The axes on the graphs in **Figure 4** can help you picture how these orbitals look in three dimensions. Imagine that the y-axis is flat on the page. Imagine that the dotted lines on the x- and z-axes are going into the page and the darker lines are coming out of the page. Because each p orbital can hold two electrons, the three p orbitals can hold a total of six electrons.

The d and f orbitals are much more complex. There are five possible d orbitals and seven possible f orbitals. Although all of these orbitals are very different in shape, each can hold a maximum of two electrons.

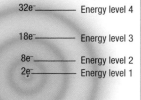

Electron Energy Levels

32e⁻	Energy level 4
18e⁻	Energy level 3
8e⁻	Energy level 2
2e⁻	Energy level 1

Figure 3 Each energy level holds a certain number of electrons. **How many total electrons can the first four energy levels hold?**

SCILINKS.

www.scilinks.org
Topic: Atomic Orbitals
Code: HK80118

Figure 4 The s and p Orbitals

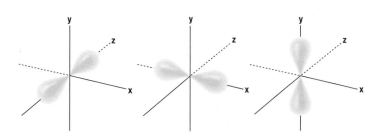

An s orbital is shaped like a sphere, so it has only one possible orientation in space. An s orbital can hold a maximum of two electrons.

Each of these p orbitals can hold a maximum of two electrons, so all three p orbitals can hold a total of six electrons.

Why It Matters

Spectra and Light Emission Have interested students find out more about spectral analysis and the type of light emitted by different elements. Have them present their findings in a poster display. (Posters may include examples of different spectra from different elements or list colors of light associated with lighted signs made up of tubes of gases. For example, the following gases produce distinct colors: mercury (blue), carbon dioxide (white), helium (gold), and neon (red).) **LS Visual**

Differentiated Instruction

Advanced Learners

Filled Energy Levels Explain that one way to determine the total amount of electrons that each energy level can hold is to use the following equation: $x = 2n^2$. Have students use the equation to confirm the numbers given in the table for the first four energy levels. Then have students determine the total number of electrons that the $n = 5$ energy level can hold. $(2 \times 5^2 = 50)$ **LS Logical**

Orbitals determine the number of electrons that each level can hold.

You have seen that each energy level contains a certain number of electrons. The orbitals in each energy level determine the total number of electrons that the level can hold, as **Figure 5** shows. For instance, you learned earlier that the second energy level can hold eight electrons. The reason is that this level contains four orbitals: one s orbital and three p orbitals. Because each orbital can hold two electrons, the second energy level holds $4 \times 2 = 8$ electrons.

Figure 5 Orbitals and Electrons for Energy Levels 1–4

Energy level	Number of orbitals by type				Total number of orbitals		Number of electrons
	s	p	d	f			
1	1				1 = 1	×2 =	2
2	1	3			1 + 3 = 4		8
3	1	3	5		1 + 3 + 5 = 9		18
4	1	3	5	7	1 + 3 + 5 + 7 = 16		32

Electron Transitions

As you have learned, the modern model of the atom limits the location of electrons to specific energy levels. An electron is never found between these levels. Instead, it "jumps" from one level to the next. What makes an electron move from one level to another? ❯ **Electrons jump between energy levels when an atom gains or loses energy.**

The lowest state of energy of an electron is called the *ground state.* At normal temperatures, most electrons are in the ground state. However, if an electron gains energy, it moves to an *excited state.* It gains energy by absorbing a particle of light, called a **photon.** The electron may then fall back to a lower level. In doing so, the electron releases a photon.

Photons of light have different energies. The energy of a photon determines to which level the electron will jump. Think back to the elevator analogy. When an electron absorbs a photon, it gains energy and "rides up the elevator." The energy of the photon determines the level up to which the electron rides. When the electron loses energy and "rides down the elevator," a photon is released. In this case, the change in levels determines the energy of the emitted photon. Electrons can move between any two levels of the atom.

✓ **Reading Check** What makes an electron jump from the ground state to an excited state?

QuickLab ⏱ 20 min

Electron Levels

❶ Make a table that has 10 columns and 4 rows. Label the first cell "Energy level." Label the remaining cells in the first row "s" (1 cell), "p" (3 cells), and "d" (5 cells). Label the remaining cells in the first column "1," "2," and "3."

❷ For each energy level, place an *X* in cells that correspond to orbitals that are not found in that level.

❸ Place **pennies** in empty cells to represent electrons. Each "orbital" can hold two "electrons."

❹ Draw Bohr models of atoms whose atomic numbers are 3, 5, 10, and 20. For each model, fill in the cells with the correct number of pennies (in order) to see how the electrons are located in the energy levels.

valence electron (VAY luhns ee LEK TRAHN) an electron that is found in the outermost shell of an atom and that determines the atom's chemical properties

photon (FOH TAHN) a unit or quantum of light

QuickLab

Teacher's Notes Point out that in this model of electron levels in atoms, each cell in the table represents an orbital. Each orbital holds two electrons.

Materials per Group
• pennies, 38

Answer

4. The model of $Z = 3$ (lithium) has 2 electrons in the level 1 s orbital and 1 electron in the level 2 s orbital.
The model of $Z = 5$ (boron) has 2 electrons in the level 1 s orbital, 2 electrons in the level 2 s orbital, and 1 electron in the level 2 p orbitals.
The model of $Z = 10$ (neon) has 2 electrons in the level 1 s orbital, 2 electrons in the level 2 s orbital, and 6 electrons in the level 2 p orbitals.
The model of $Z = 20$ (calcium) has 2 electrons in the level 1 s orbital, 2 electrons in the level 2 s orbital, 6 electrons in the level 2 p orbitals, 2 electrons in the level 3 s orbital, 6 electrons in the level 3 p orbitals, and 2 electrons in the level 4 s orbital.

Teaching Key Ideas

Levels and Sublevels Students may have trouble keeping track of levels and sublevels. Levels are represented by numbers and sublevels are represented by letters. Explain that a sublevel consists of all the s, p, d, or f orbitals for an electron energy level. The first energy level—the one closest to the nucleus—contains only one sublevel, the s. Thus, this level contains only one orbital and can contain only two electrons. The second energy level has one s orbital and three p orbitals, so it can hold eight electrons. The third energy level contains s, p, and d sublevels for a maximum of 2 + 6 + 10, or 18, electrons. The fourth energy level has s, p, d, and f sub-levels for a maximum of 2 + 6 + 10 + 14, or 32, electrons.

Revising Preconceptions Have students revisit their opinions from the beginning of the chapter. Have them discuss whether their opinions have changed or remained the same. Have them cite passages in the text that account for the change in or reinforcement of their opinions. **LS** Verbal

Answer to caption question

The electrons are jumping down from an excited state to the ground state, releasing energy as photons.

>Close

Reteaching Key Ideas

Making Analogies Have students come up with an analogy for what happens when atoms absorb or emit light. For example, they might compare the electron to a monetary deposit. To make an electron go up an energy level, the environment must make a deposit by allowing a photon to be absorbed. When the electron goes back down an energy level, the "deposit" is returned to the environment. Have students explain their analogies to a partner. **LS** Interpersonal

---

Integrating Space Science

Spectral Analysis Astronomers use the principle that every element emits a unique set of wavelengths to learn about elements in space. This method, called *spectral analysis,* has been used to identify elements in stars. The element helium was discovered through spectral analysis of light from the sun. It was named *helium* because the Greek word for "sun" is *helios.* Helium was later found on Earth.

Figure 6 This neon sign lights up because atoms first gain energy from electricity and then release this energy in the form of light. **What happens to the electrons as the light is released?**

Atoms absorb or emit light at certain wavelengths.

You have learned that photons are particles of light. The energy of a photon is related to the wavelength of the light. High-energy photons have short wavelengths, and low-energy photons have long wavelengths. Because atoms gain or lose energy in certain amounts, they can absorb or emit only certain wavelengths.

Because each element has a unique atomic structure, the wavelengths emitted depend on the particular element. For instance, the set of wavelengths emitted by hydrogen differs from the set of wavelengths emitted by any other element. For this reason, the wavelengths can be used to identify the substance. They are a type of "atomic fingerprint."

The emission of photons produces the light in neon signs. The wavelength of visible light determines the color of the light. For instance, the wavelengths emitted in neon gas produce the red color shown in **Figure 6.** Gases of other elements produce other colors.

Section 3 **Review**

KEY IDEAS

1. **State** two key features of the modern model of the atom.
2. **Explain** what determines how the energy levels in an atom are filled.
3. **Describe** what happens when an electron jumps from one energy level to another.
4. **Identify** how many electrons the third energy level can hold, and explain why this is the case.

CRITICAL THINKING

5. **Analyzing Models** Compare an atom's structure to a ladder. Identify one way in which a ladder is not a good model for the atom.
6. **Making Comparisons** Explain how Bohr's model and the modern model of the atom differ in terms of the path of an electron.
7. **Applying Concepts** How many valence electrons does nitrogen ($Z = 7$) have?

Formative Assessment

Which describes the location of electrons in the modern atomic model?

A. They are located within the nucleus. (Incorrect. Only protons and neutrons are found in an atom's nucleus.)

B. They are evenly distributed throughout the atom? (Incorrect. In Thomson's atomic model, electrons are spread throughout the atom.)

C. They orbit in fixed paths around the nucleus of the atom? (Incorrect. In Bohr's model electrons have energy determined by their fixed path around the nucleus.)

D. Electrons are found in orbitals and cannot be located precisely. (Correct. The orbitals describe the most likely electron locations.)

Answers to Section Review

1. Electrons can be found only in certain energy levels. Electron location cannot be predicted precisely because electrons act more like waves than like particles.

Answers continued on p. 141A

How Do Fireworks Work?

REAL WORLD

Today's firework displays often feature complex patterns and vivid colors. The colors in fireworks are produced by the emission of photons. The photon wavelength—and thus the color—depends on the compounds that are used. Just as neon gas produces red light, various compounds create specific firework colors. For instance, sodium salts produce yellow, and magnesium and aluminum produce white. These coloring agents are packed into the "stars" inside the shell, often by hand.

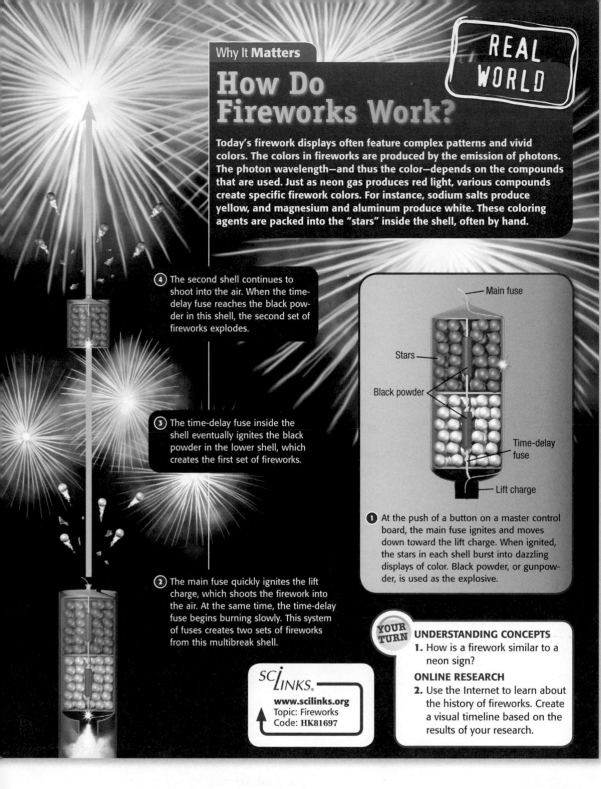

④ The second shell continues to shoot into the air. When the time-delay fuse reaches the black powder in this shell, the second set of fireworks explodes.

③ The time-delay fuse inside the shell eventually ignites the black powder in the lower shell, which creates the first set of fireworks.

② The main fuse quickly ignites the lift charge, which shoots the firework into the air. At the same time, the time-delay fuse begins burning slowly. This system of fuses creates two sets of fireworks from this multibreak shell.

Main fuse

Stars

Black powder

Time-delay fuse

Lift charge

❶ At the push of a button on a master control board, the main fuse ignites and moves down toward the lift charge. When ignited, the stars in each shell burst into dazzling displays of color. Black powder, or gunpowder, is used as the explosive.

SC**I**LINKS®

www.scilinks.org
Topic: Fireworks
Code: **HK81697**

YOUR TURN

UNDERSTANDING CONCEPTS

1. How is a firework similar to a neon sign?

ONLINE RESEARCH

2. Use the Internet to learn about the history of fireworks. Create a visual timeline based on the results of your research.

Why It **Matters**

How Do Fireworks Work? Fireworks that you may see in the sky at a holiday fireworks show are called aerial fireworks. The shells used to produce these shows are much larger than the ones you can buy at a fireworks stand. Some can be larger than a cantaloupe! Fireworks technicians launch the shells from short lengths of pipe called mortars that contain a bit of fuel that explodes when ignited, sending the shell out the end of the pipe and into the air. Spheres of fuel mixed with different chemicals cause the fireworks to produce different colors when ignited. Fireworks technicians design fireworks to produce explosions of different colors and shapes by varying the type of chemicals in the stars and the way that the stars are packed in the shells.

Have interested students find out which substances in fireworks produce the different colors that they see in a fireworks display. Have them present their findings in a poster. (Sample answer: yellow—sodium; orange—$CaCl$; red—$SrCO_3$; green—$BaCl$; blue—$CuCl$) **LS** Visual

Answers to Your Turn

1. Fireworks and neon signs produce colored light when electrons jump between levels in the atom, emitting photons (light particles).

2. Students' timelines should visually display information about the history of the development of fireworks.

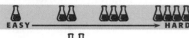

Teacher's Notes

Show students how to use a periodic table to determine an element's atomic number. Remind them that the name of the isotope comes from the mass number, not from the molar mass listed in the periodic table.

Time Required

1 lab period

Ratings

⚗	⚗⚗	⚗⚗⚗	⚗⚗⚗⚗
EASY		→	HARD

Teacher Prep ⚗⚗

Student Set-Up ⚗⚗

Concept Level ⚗

Clean Up ⚗

Skills Acquired

- Classifying
- Communicating
- Identifying/Recognizing patterns
- Inferring
- Making models
- Organizing and analyzing data

Scientific Methods

In this lab, students will:
- Make observations
- Analyze the results
- Draw conclusions
- Communicate results

Safety Caution

Be sure that students use caution with sharp objects.

Skills Practice

Lab

What You'll Do

❯ **Build** models of nuclei of certain isotopes.

❯ **Use** the periodic table to determine the composition of atomic nuclei.

What You'll Need

periodic table

plastic-foam balls, blue, 2–3 cm in diameter (6)

plastic-foam balls, white, 2–3 cm in diameter (4)

toothpicks (20)

Building Isotopes

Imagine that you are an employee at the Elements-4-U Company, which custom builds models of elements. Your job is to construct a model of the atomic nucleus for each element ordered by your clients. You were hired for the position because of your knowledge about what a nucleus is made of and your understanding of how isotopes of an element differ from each other. Now, it's time to put that knowledge to work!

Procedure

Making the Simplest Nucleus

❶ Copy the sample data table onto another sheet of paper.

❷ Your first assignment is the nucleus of hydrogen-1. Pick up one proton (a white plastic-foam ball). Congratulations! You have built a hydrogen-1 nucleus, the simplest nucleus possible.

❸ The atomic number of an element is the number of protons in an atom of the element. In your data table, record the atomic number and the number of neutrons for hydrogen-1.

❹ Add the atomic number and the neutron number together to determine the mass number of hydrogen-1. Record this information in your table.

❺ Draw a picture of your hydrogen-1 model.

Building More-Complicated Nuclei

❻ For the next part of the lab, you will need to use information from the periodic table of the elements. You can find the atomic number of any element at the top of the element's entry on the periodic table. For example, the atomic number of carbon is 6. Find the atomic number for each remaining isotope in the data table, and add this information to your table.

❼ The name of the isotope tells you the mass number. For instance, the mass number of hydrogen-2 is 2, and the mass number of helium-4 is 4. Determine the mass number for each remaining isotope in the data table, and add this information to your table.

❽ Subtract the atomic number from the mass number to find the number of neutrons for each remaining isotope in the table.

Tips and Tricks

This lab can also be done using modeling clay, marshmallows, or gumdrops in place of the plastic-foam balls. Students can use colored markers to distinguish between the particles.

Sample Data Table: Nuclei of Various Isotopes

	Hydrogen-1	Hydrogen-2	Helium-3	Helium-4	Beryllium-9	Beryllium-10
Atomic number (*Z*)						
Number of neutrons			DO NOT WRITE IN BOOK			
Mass number (*A*)						

9 In a nucleus, the protons and neutrons are held together by the strong nuclear force, which is represented in this activity by toothpicks. Protons and neutrons always form the smallest arrangement possible because the strong nuclear force pulls them together. Using a toothpick, build a model of the nucleus of hydrogen-2.

10 Draw a picture of your hydrogen-2 model.

11 Repeat steps 9–10 for the remaining isotopes in your table. Remember to put the protons and neutrons as close together as possible—each particle should attach to at least two other particles.

Analysis

1. **Interpreting Data** Why do different isotopes of the same element have the same atomic number?

2. **Applying Concepts** If you know the mass number and the number of neutrons of an isotope, how can you determine the atomic number?

Communicating Your Results

3. **Applying Conclusions** Look up uranium on the periodic table. What is the atomic number of uranium? How many neutrons does the isotope uranium-235 have?

4. **Evaluating Models** Compare your model with the models of your classmates. How are the models similar? How are they different?

Extension

Create a new nucleus by combining your model with another student's model. Identify the new element (and isotope) that you have created.

Answers to Analysis

1. The atomic number of an atom is equal to the number of protons in its nucleus. This number defines the element. Thus, isotopes of the same element always have the same atomic number.

2. The atomic number can be determined by subtracting the number of neutrons from the mass number.

Answers to Communicating Your Results

3. atomic number = 92; 235 − 92 = 143 neutrons

4. Sample answer: They differ in the way the protons and neutrons are connected to each other. They are the same in the number of protons and neutrons that each of the same isotope has.

Answer to Extension

If all of the protons and neutrons are used, the isotope created will be oxygen-20.

Sample Data Table: Nuclei of Different Isotopes

	Hydrogen-1	Hydrogen-2	Helium-3	Helium-4	Beryllium-9	Beryllium-10
Atomic number (*Z*)	1	1	2	2	4	4
Number of neutrons	0	1	1	2	5	6
Mass number (*A*)	1	2	3	4	9	10

Key Resources

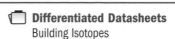 Virtual Investigation

 Classroom Lab Video/DVD

 Holt Lab Generator CD-ROM
Search for any lab by type, standard, difficulty level, or time. Edit any lab to fit your needs, or create your own labs. Use the Lab Materials QuickList software to customize your lab materials list.

 Differentiated Datasheets
Building Isotopes

 Observation Lab
Drawing Atomic Models

Testing A Hypothesis

Science > Skills

Testing a Hypothesis Remind students that a hypothesis is a like an intelligent guess at what will happen. However, a hypothesis must be testable. Scientists design experiments so that the data that results will either support or refute the hypothesis. Have students imagine what kind of data would have resulted from Rutherford's experiment if his hypothesis were correct. (The positive charges would not have been deflected very much by the atoms in the foil.) **LS Logical**

Answers to Practice

1. Sample answer: You could test this hypothesis by putting fresh batteries in the flashlight. If the hypothesis is correct, the flashlight should work with new batteries. If the hypothesis is incorrect, the flashlight probably won't work after replacing the batteries.

2. Sample answer: My first hypothesis is that the chili is causing my stomachache. To test this hypothesis, I will eat a hotdog without eating the chili. If my hypothesis is correct, I will not get a stomachache. If my hypothesis is incorrect, I will get a stomachache anyway.

Once you have formed a hypothesis, the next step is to test it. To test a hypothesis, you need to create an experiment that will clearly show whether the hypothesis is true or false. The steps below show you how to test a hypothesis.

Technology
Math
Scientific Methods
Graphing

1 State the hypothesis.
A hypothesis is formed from observations that you have made or data that you have already collected. Sometimes, scientists test a hypothesis that was formed by another scientist.

Ernest Rutherford wanted to test J. J. Thomson's model of the atom. Rutherford's hypothesis was: Atoms consist of negative electrons embedded in a cloud of positive charge.

2 Design an experiment.
To think of an experiment that will test the hypothesis, you can start by asking yourself, "What can I do that will give me one result if the hypothesis is true and a different result if the hypothesis is false?"

In Rutherford's experiment, positively charged alpha particles were fired at a thin sheet of gold foil. A detector showed the angles at which the particles left the foil.

3 Make predictions.
Your predictions should state what the outcomes of the experiment would be if the hypothesis were true. You may also want to state what the outcomes would be if the hypothesis were false.

If positive charges are spread throughout the atom, then most alpha particles would pass straight through the foil. A few would be deflected, but not at very large angles.

4 Do the experiment, analyze the results, and draw conclusions.
Analyze the results of the experiment to see how they compare to your predictions. If your original hypothesis was false, you may need to form a new hypothesis and begin the testing process again.

A few particles were deflected at large angles, and some even came straight back. This result did not match the prediction. Thus, the hypothesis was incorrect.

Practice

1. Suppose that you have a flashlight that does not work. You form the hypothesis that the batteries are dead. Describe an experiment that you could do to test this hypothesis. Predict what the results of the experiment will be if the hypothesis is true and what they will be if it is false.

2. Suppose that you get a stomachache every time you eat a hot dog with chili. Form a hypothesis to explain this observation. Then, describe an experiment to test the hypothesis. Predict what the results of the experiment will be if the hypothesis is true and what they will be if it is false.

Key Resources

Science Skills Worksheets
Scientific Notation
Significant Figures
Dimensional Analysis

go.hrw.com
SUPER SUMMARY
KEYWORD: HK8ATSS

SUMMARY

Key Ideas

Section 1 The Development of Atomic Theory

> **The Beginnings of Atomic Theory** Democritus suggested that the universe was made of indivisible units called *atoms*. (p. 113)

> **Dalton's Atomic Theory** According to Dalton, all atoms of a given element were exactly alike, and atoms of different elements could join to form compounds. (p. 114)

> **Thomson's Model of the Atom** Thomson's cathode-ray tube experiment suggested that cathode rays were made of negatively-charged particles that came from inside atoms. (p. 115)

> **Rutherford's Model of the Atom** Rutherford proposed that most of the mass of the atom was concentrated at the atom's center. (p. 117)

Section 2 The Structure of Atoms

> **What Is in an Atom?** The three main subatomic particles are distinguished by mass, charge, and location in the atom. (p. 119)

> **Atomic Number and Mass Number** Atoms of an element have the same number of protons, but they can have different numbers of neutrons. (p. 121)

> **Isotopes** Isotopes of an element vary in mass because their numbers of neutrons differ. (p. 122)

> **Atomic Masses** Atomic masses are usually expressed in unified atomic mass units. (p. 124)

Section 3 Modern Atomic Theory

> **Modern Models of the Atom** Electrons can be found only in certain energy levels. The location of electrons cannot be predicted precisely. (p. 128)

> **Electron Energy Levels** The number of energy levels that are filled in an atom depends on the number of electrons. (p. 130)

> **Electron Transitions** Electrons jump between levels when an atom gains or loses energy. (p. 131)

Key Terms

electron, p. 115
nucleus, p. 118

proton, p. 119
neutron, p. 119
atomic number, p. 121
mass number, p. 121
isotope, p. 122
unified atomic mass unit, p. 124
mole, p. 125

orbital, p. 129
valence electron, p. 130
photon, p. 131

SUPER SUMMARY

Have students connect the major concepts in this chapter through an interactive Super Summary. Visit **go.hrw.com** and type in the keyword **HK8ATSS** to access the Super Summary for this chapter.

Differentiated Instruction

Alternative Assessment

Modeling Atoms Ask students to create three-dimensional models of an atom of their choice. Encourage them to create more than one model of their atom, corresponding to different versions of the atomic theory throughout history. Instruct them to include information about which historical theories they are representing in each model, and which parts of those theories are no longer accepted today. Also ask them to include information about the limitations of their models. **LS Kinesthetic**

Key Resources

⊡ **Interactive Concept Map**

🗍 **Review Resources**
Concept Review Worksheets

🗍 **Assessment Resources**
Chapter Tests A and B
Performance-Based Assessment

Reading Toolbox

1. Answers may vary. Possible answers include: electric, electrical, electricity, electrocution, electromagnetic, electronic.

Using Key Terms

2. In the nucleus, a silicon atom has 14 protons, and it usually has 14 neutrons. A silicon atom has 14 electrons, four of which are valence electrons.

3. Atomic number tells the number of protons in the atom. All atoms of the same element have the same number of protons, so they have the same atomic number. The mass number is the total number of protons and neutrons in an atom. The number of neutrons can vary, so the mass number can vary among atoms of the same element. These different atoms are called isotopes.

4. The molar mass is the mass of one mole, or 6.022×10^{23} particles, of the element.

5. An orbital is a region in the atom where there is a high probability of finding electrons.

Understanding Key Ideas

6. a

7. b

8. d

9. c

10. a

11. b

12. b

13. c

Explaining Key Ideas

14. Deflection *A* was a surprise because Rutherford didn't expect the positive charge in the atom to be concentrated enough to deflect a positive charge back at such a large angle.

READING TOOLBOX

1. Word Origins The word electron was formed by combining the root *electr-*, meaning amber, with the suffix *–on*. List at least three other words that include the root *electr-*.

USING KEY TERMS

2. How many *protons* and *neutrons* does a silicon, Si, atom have, and where are these two types of subatomic particles located? How many *electrons* does a silicon atom have?

3. Explain why different atoms of the same element always have the same *atomic number* but can have different *mass numbers*. What are these different atoms called?

4. What does an element's *molar mass* tell you about the element?

5. What is an *orbital*?

UNDERSTANDING KEY IDEAS

6. Which of Dalton's statements about the atom was proven false by J. J. Thomson?
a. Atoms cannot be subdivided.
b. Atoms are tiny.
c. Atoms of different elements are not identical.
d. Atoms join to form molecules.

7. What did Rutherford learn about the atom from his gold-foil experiment?
a. Atoms have electrons.
b. Atoms have a nucleus.
c. Atoms have negative charge embedded in a sphere of positive charge.
d. The nucleus is most of the atom's volume.

8. If an atom has a mass of 11 u and contains five electrons, its atomic number must be
a. 55.
b. 16.
c. 6.
d. 5.

9. Which statement is not true of Bohr's model of the atom?
a. Electrons cannot be between energy levels.
b. Electrons orbit the nucleus.
c. An electron's path is not known exactly.
d. Electrons exist in energy levels.

10. According to the modern model of the atom,
a. moving electrons form an electron cloud.
b. electrons and protons circle neutrons.
c. neutrons have a positive charge.
d. the number of protons for a given element varies.

11. Carbon has six protons. How many valence electrons does carbon have?
a. 2
b. 4
c. 6
d. 12

12. The second energy level has 1 s orbital and 3 p orbitals. How many electrons can this energy level hold?
a. 2
b. 8
c. 18
d. 32

13. An electron moves from the ground state to an excited state when it absorbs
a. a proton.
b. a neutron.
c. a photon.
d. an isotope.

EXPLAINING KEY IDEAS

14. Study the graphic below of Rutherford's gold-foil experiment. Which of the deflections, A or B, was a surprise to Rutherford? Why?

15. Identify the particles that make up an atom. How do these particles relate to the identity of an atom?

16. Determine the atomic number and mass number of an isotope that has 56 electrons and 82 neutrons.

17. Why do most atoms have no charge even though they are made up of positively charged protons and negatively charged electrons?

INTERPRETING GRAPHICS The diagrams below show three atoms. Use the diagrams to answer questions 18–20.

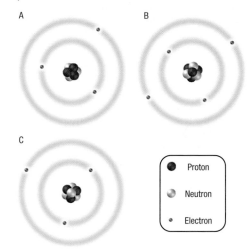

A   B

C

● Proton
◐ Neutron
• Electron

18. Which diagrams represent the same element?

19. What is the atomic number for atom A?

20. What is the mass number for atom B?

CRITICAL THINKING

21. Applying Ideas Particle accelerators are devices that speed up charged particles in order to smash them together. Scientists use the devices to make atoms. How can scientists determine whether the atoms formed are a new element or a new isotope of a known element?

---

22. Making Inferences Why is measuring the size of an atom difficult?

23. Drawing Conclusions Are hydrogen-3 and helium-3 isotopes of the same element? Explain.

24. Making Inferences Some forces push atoms apart, and other forces pull atoms together. Describe how the subatomic particles in each atom interact to produce these forces.

25. Analyzing Methods If scientists had tried to repeat Thomson's experiment and found that they could not, would Thomson's conclusion still have been valid? Explain your answer.

Graphing Skills

26. Interpreting Graphs Study the graph of mass (g) versus amount (mol) for iron.
  a. Is the relationship between the two variables direct or inverse?
  b. How many particles are there in 111.6 g of iron?

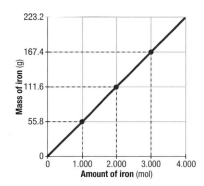

Math Skills

27. Converting Grams to Moles For an experiment you have been asked to do, you need 1.5 g of iron. How many moles of iron do you need?

28. Converting Moles to Grams Robyn recycled 15.1 mol of aluminum last month. What was the mass in grams of the aluminum she recycled?

Assignment Guide	
SECTION	**ITEMS**
1	1, 6, 7, 14, 22, 25
2	2, 3, 4, 8, 15–21, 23, 24, 26–28
3	5, 9, 10–13

Math Skills

27. 1.5 g Fe × 1 mol Fe/55.85 g Fe = 0.027 mol Fe

28. 15.1 mol Al × 26.98 g Al/1 mol Al = 407 g Al

---

15. The particles that make up an atom are protons, neutrons, and electrons. The number of protons determines the atom's atomic number. In a neutral atom, this number also equals the number of electrons.

16. $Z = 56$, $A = 138$

17. Most atoms have no overall charge because they have equal numbers of protons and electrons, so the positive and negative charges exactly cancel one another.

18. a and c

19. $Z = 3$ for a

20. $A = 7$ for b

Critical Thinking

21. Scientists must determine the atomic number, or the number of protons, in the newly formed nucleus. The nucleus is that of a new element only if the number of protons is different from all known elements.

22. It is difficult to measure the size of an atom because atoms are very small. In addition, some atoms do not exist for very long due to their radioactivity.

23. No, they are not isotopes of the same element. They have the same mass number, but different numbers of protons. It is the number of protons that defines the element.

24. Because like charges repel each other and unlike charges attract, protons repel each other and attract electrons. Electrons repel each other and attract protons. Since protons in the nucleus repel each other, there must be a stronger force that holds them together in the nucleus.

25. No, the results of an experiment must be repeatable to be considered valid.

Graphing Skills

26. a. direct
  b. The graph shows that 111.6 g corresponds to 2 mol: 2 mol × $(6.022 \times 10^{23}$ particles/mol) = 1.204×10^{24} particles

Standardized Test Prep

 TEST DOCTOR

Question 1 Answer A is correct. Students might answer B if they thought of orbitals as objects, instead of regions of probable location; C if they thought that a proton must be emitted to balance the photon, or if they thought that they were the same thing; or D if they thought the photon had a negative charge.

Question 2 Answer G is correct. Other answers indicate that students do not know that atoms of a particular element all have the same number of protons.

Question 3 Answer B is correct. To find the correct answer, students must first divide 100 grams by the molar mass of 196.97 grams/mole, giving a total of 0.50769 moles. They must then multiply that number by Avogadro's number to find the number of atoms, 3.0573×10^{23}.

Question 4 Answer H is correct. Other answers indicate that students are not familiar with the modern understanding of the structure of atoms. Students might answer F or G if they did not know that protons and neutrons are found in the nucleus, or I if they were confusing electrons with photons.

Question 5 The atom has 54 protons and 77 neutrons. The atomic number of an element equals the number of protons each atom of the element possesses. Xenon's atomic number, and therefore its number of protons, is 54. To find the number of neutrons, the atomic number must be subtracted from the atomic mass number; $131 - 54 = 77$.

Question 6 To find the correct answer, students must take the weighted average of the two mass numbers. The average atomic mass would be 207.2 u. One way to answer this question is to multiply 207 by 80%, or 0.8, and 208 by 20%, or 0.2. Then add the two products together to get 207.2.

Understanding Concepts

Directions (1–4): **For each question, write on a sheet of paper the letter of the correct answer.**

1. When electricity is connected to a neon sign, an atom of neon inside the sign emits a photon. What has happened within the atom to allow the emission of light energy?
   - **A.** An electron has moved to a lower energy level.
   - **B.** Two electron orbitals have collided.
   - **C.** A proton has been lost from the nucleus.
   - **D.** The atom has gained a positive charge.

2. After a single subatomic particle is removed from an atom of helium, the helium atom becomes an atom of hydrogen. What subatomic particle was removed?
   - **F.** an electron
   - **G.** a proton
   - **H.** a quark
   - **I.** a neutron

3. Gold has an average atomic mass of 196.97 u. Approximately how many atoms of gold are there in 100 g of gold? Note: there are 6.022×10^{23} atoms in a mole.
   - **A.** 3.0573×10^{19}
   - **B.** 3.0573×10^{23}
   - **C.** 1.1862×10^{24}
   - **D.** 1.1862×10^{28}

4. What subatomic particles can be found in regions called *orbitals*?
   - **F.** protons
   - **G.** neutrons
   - **H.** electrons
   - **I.** photons

Directions (5–6): **For each question, write a short response.**

5. Xenon has an atomic number of 54. A particular isotope of xenon has a mass number of 131. How many protons and how many neutrons does each atom of that isotope have?

6. Suppose that a team of chemists discovered that lead has the following composition: 80% of lead is an isotope whose mass number is 207, and 20% of lead is an isotope whose mass number is 208. What would they determine the average atomic mass of lead to be?

Reading Skills

Directions (7–8): **Read the passage below. Then, answer the questions that follow.**

THE BOHR MODEL OF THE ATOM
In the Bohr model of the atom, electrons can be found only in certain energy levels. Electrons "jump" directly from one level to the next level; they are never found between levels. When an electron moves from one level to another, it gains or loses energy, depending on the direction of its jump.

Bohr's model explained an unusual event. When electric charges pass through atoms of a gaseous element, the gas produces a glowing light, like in a neon sign. If this light is passed through a prism, a pattern of lines appears. Each line has a different color. The pattern depends on the element—neon has one pattern, and helium has another. In Bohr's model, the lines are caused by electron jumps from higher to lower energy levels. Because only certain jumps are possible, electrons release energy only in certain quantities. These "packets" of energy produce the lines that are seen.

7. In the Bohr model of the atom, which of the following characteristics of electrons is limited?
   - **A.** the number of electrons in an atom
   - **B.** the location of the electrons
   - **C.** the size of electrons
   - **D.** the speed of electrons

8. What causes the colored lines that appear when the light from a gas is passed through a prism?
   - **F.** packets of energy released by electron jumps
   - **G.** electrons changing color
   - **H.** atoms of the gas exchanging electrons
   - **I.** There is not enough information to determine the answer.

Question 7 Answer B is correct. To find the correct answer, students should examine the first sentence of the passage, which indicates that there is a limit on where electrons can be found in the Bohr model.

Question 8 Answer F is correct. To find the correct answer, students should examine the last sentence of the passage, which describes the "packets" of energy that produce spectral lines.

Question 9 Answer D is correct. To find the correct answer, students must count the number of orbitals and multiply by 2, $(1 + 3 + 5 + 7) \times 2 = 32$.

Question 10 To find the correct answer, students must first find the number of electrons in each level by adding up the orbitals and multiplying by 2; $1 \times 2 = 2$ and $4 \times 2 = 8$, so there are a total of 10 electrons in the first two energy levels. Students must subtract this number from the total number of electrons in a neutral sulfur atom, 16. There are 6 electrons in the $n = 3$ energy level.

Question 11 For every energy level n, there are a number of orbitals equal to the sum of the first n odd numbers. $1 + 3 + 5 + 7 + 9 + 11 + 13 = 49$ orbitals. Alternatively, the number of orbitals in an energy level is the square of the number of that energy level. For level 7, there are 7^2, or 49 orbitals, that can hold a total of 98 electrons.

Interpreting Graphics

The graphic below shows how electron orbitals around the nucleus of an atom are organized into energy levels. Each orbital holds 2 electrons. Use this graphic to answer questions 9–11.

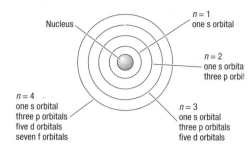

Nucleus

$n = 1$
one s orbital

$n = 2$
one s orbital
three p orbital

$n = 3$
one s orbital
three p orbitals
five d orbitals

$n = 4$
one s orbital
three p orbitals
five d orbitals
seven f orbitals

9. If every orbital of an atom's $n = 4$ energy level was full of electrons, how many electrons would there be in that energy level?

   A. 7   **C.** 16

   B. 14   **D.** 32

10. The atomic number of sulfur is 16. If energy levels are filled with electrons from the innermost level to the outermost level, how many electrons are in the $n = 3$ energy level of a neutral sulfur atom?

11. Every known element has seven or fewer energy levels. How many orbitals would there be room for in energy level $n = 7$?

The table below gives information about the subatomic particles in six atoms. Use this table to answer questions 12–13.

	Protons	Electrons	Neutrons
Mystery atom #1	15	15	15
Mystery atom #2	17	16	15
Mystery atom #3	23	23	23
Mystery atom #4	23	24	22
Mystery atom #5	42	43	52
Mystery atom #6	51	51	41

12. Which two atoms are isotopes of the same element?

   F. #1 and #2   **H.** #3 and #4

   G. #2 and #3   **I.** #4 and #5

13. What is the mass of one mole of the heaviest atom in the table?

Test Tip

For multiple-choice questions, try to eliminate any answer choices that are obviously incorrect, and then consider the remaining answer choices.

Question 12 Answer H is correct. Other answers indicate that students may not realize that every atom of an element has the same number of protons, but not necessarily the same number of electrons or neutrons.

Question 13 The heaviest atom can be identified by adding the number of protons and neutrons for each mystery atom listed. #5 is the heaviest, with an atomic mass of 94. One mole of #5 would have a mass of 94 grams.

State Resources

For specific resources for your state, visit **go.hrw.com** and type in the keyword **HSHSTR**.

📖 **Test Practice with Guided Reading Development**

Answers

1. A

2. G

3. ~~A~~ B

4. H

5. 54 protons and 77 neutrons

6. 207.2 u

7. B

8. F

9. D

10. 6 electrons

11. 49 orbitals

12. H

13. 94 grams

Continuation of Answers

Answers continued from p. 127

7. Avogadro's constant is 6.022×10^{23}/mol. It is the number of particles in one mole of a substance.

8. **a.** 54.94 g/mol Mn
   b. 112.41 g/mol Cd
   c. 74.92 g/mol As
   d. 87.62 g/mol Sr

9. Yes. The atom is normally neutral because the protons and electrons are balanced. If an atom loses electrons, it will have a net positive charge.

10. The average atomic mass for nitrogen is 14.01 u, so nitrogen-14 is more commonly found.

11. 3.0 g Fe $\times$ 1 mol Fe/55.85 g Fe = 0.054 mol Fe; 2.0 g S $\times$ 1 mol S/32.07 g S = 0.062 mol S. Because the number of moles of sulfur is greater, the number of atoms of sulfur is greater.

12. The graph is a straight line because a direct relationship exists between the amount of an element in moles and the element's mass in grams.

13. 0.48 mol Pt $\times$ 195.08 g Pt/1 mol Pt = 94 g Pt

14. 3.1 mol Hg $\times$ 200.59 g Hg/1 mol Hg = 620 g Hg

15. 11 g Si $\times$ 1 mol Si/28.09 g Si = 0.39 mol Si

16. 205 g He $\times$ 1 mol He/4.00 g He = 51.3 mol He

Answers continued from p. 132

2. Each energy level can hold a certain number of electrons, depending on the number of orbitals in that level. The energy levels are filled in order, from the inner to the outer levels. Each orbital can hold a maximum of two electrons.

3. When an electron jumps between levels, the atom either gains or loses energy in the form of photons.

4. The third energy level can hold 18 electrons: 2 in the s orbital, 2 in each of 3 p orbitals (for 6 total), and 2 in each of 5 d orbitals (for 10 total).

5. Each rung of the ladder represents an energy level. Electrons can be only on the rungs, not between rungs. A ladder is not a good model for an atom because electrons exist in three-dimensional orbitals.

6. In Bohr's model, the electrons travel along fixed paths. In the modern model, electrons behave more like waves on a string than like particles.

7. Nitrogen has 7 electrons, so there are 2 in the first level and 5 in the second level. Thus, nitrogen has 5 valence electrons.

CHAPTER OPENER, pp. 142–144 — **50 min.**

	Standards	Teach Key Ideas

SECTION 1 Organizing the Elements, pp. 145–150 — 50 min.

> Recognizing a Pattern
> Changing the Arrangement
> The Periodic Table of the Elements

Standards: PS 2b, UCP 1, UCP 2, SAI 2, HNS 1, HNS 2, HNS 3, SPSP 3

Teach Key Ideas:
- Bellringer Transparency
- Teaching Transparencies C11 The Periodic Table • TM15 The Periodic Table
- Visual Concept Periodic Table Overview

SECTION 2 Exploring the Periodic Table, pp. 151–155 — 50 min.

> The Role of Electrons
> Ion Formation
> How Are Elements Classified?

Standards: PS 2a, PS 2b, PS 6d, UCP 1, UCP 2

Teach Key Ideas:
- Bellringer Transparency
- Teaching Transparencies C12 Ion Formation • TM16 Elements and Orbitals
- Visual Concept Valence Electrons

SECTION 3 Families of Elements, pp. 156–165 — 50 min.

> Classifying Elements Further
> Metals
> Nonmetals
> Semiconductors

Standards: PS 2a, PS 2b, PS 6d, UCP 1, ST 2

Teach Key Ideas:
- Bellringer Transparency
- Teaching Transparency TM17 Element Families

See also PowerPoint® Resources

Chapter Review and Assessment Resources

- **SE** Science Skills: Reading Web Addresses, p. 168
- **SE** Chapter Summary, p. 169
- **SE** Chapter Review, pp. 170–171
- **SE** Standardized Test Prep, pp. 172–173
- Concept Review Worksheets ■
- Chapter Tests A and B ■
- Holt Online Assessment

CHAPTER Fast Track
To shorten instruction because of time limitations, omit Section 3 and the chapter lab.

Basic Learners
- **TE** Metallic Properties, p. 154
- **TE** Periodic Table's Big Ideas, p. 157
- **TE** Abbreviations, p. 159
- **TE** Chlorine Gas, p. 162
- Science Skills Worksheets
- Differentiated Datasheets A for Labs and Activities ■
- Study Guide A ■

Advanced Learners
- **TE** Early Periodic Tables, p. 146
- **TE** Mendeleev's Competition, p. 149
- **TE** Colorful Gems, p. 159
- **TE** The First Noble Gas, p. 161
- **TE** Fluorine, p. 162
- Cross-Disciplinary Worksheets
- Differentiated Datasheets C for Labs and Activities ■

Key

SE Student Edition
TE Teacher's Edition

📁 Chapter Resource File
📓 Workbook
🗂 Transparency

💿 CD or CD-ROM
* Datasheet or blackline master available

■ Also available in Spanish

All resources listed below are also available on the Teacher's One-Stop Planner.

Why It Matters	Hands-On	Skills Development	Assessment
Build student motivation with resources about high-interest applications.	**SE Inquiry Lab** A Periodic Table, p. 143*■	**TE Reading Toolbox** Assessing Prior Knowledge, p. 142 **SE Reading Toolbox** p. 144	📁 **Pretest** ■
SE Mercury in Fish, p. 147 **TE Elements' Diverse Histories,** p. 149 📁 **Cross-Disciplinary Worksheet** Connection to Language Arts—Chemical Symbols	**TE Demonstration** Periodic Calendar, p. 145	**SE Reading Toolbox** Spider Maps, p. 146 **TE Reading Toolbox** Previewing, p. 146 **TE Reading Toolbox** Visual Literacy, p. 148 **TE Reading Toolbox** Bookmarking Important References, p. 148 **TE Science Skills** Interpreting the Periodic Table, p. 149	**TE Reteaching Key Ideas** Predicting Element Properties, p. 150 **TE Formative Assessment,** p. 150 📁 **Spanish Assessment***■ 📁 **Section Quiz** ■
📁 **Cross-Disciplinary Worksheet** Integrating Biology—The Elements in Your Body	**TE Demonstration** Conductivity, p. 151 📁 **CBL™ Probeware Lab** Predicting the Physical and Chemical Properties of Elements	**SE Reading Toolbox** Root Words, p. 152 **TE Reading Toolbox** Vocabulary, p. 153 **TE Reading Toolbox** Vocabulary, p. 154	**TE Reteaching Key Ideas** Ions of Metals and Nonmetals, p. 155 **TE Formative Assessment,** p. 155 📁 **Spanish Assessment***■ 📁 **Section Quiz** ■
TE Metal Coins, p. 156 **TE Nutritional Sodium,** p. 157 **TE Magnesium Uses,** p. 158 **TE Uses of Gold,** p. 159 **TE Uses of Synthetic Elements,** p. 160 **TE Noble Gas Compounds,** p. 161 **TE Organic Chemistry,** p. 163 **TE Silicon Microchip,** p. 163 **SE How Are Silicon Chips Made?** p. 165 📁 **Cross-Disciplinary Worksheets** Connection to Architecture—Buckyball • Integrating Earth Science—Magnesium: From Sea Water to Fireworks • Real World Applications—How Do Scientists Find Cures for Diseases?	**SE Quick Lab** Elements in Food, p. 158*■ **SE Quick Lab** The Cost of Metals, p. 160*■ **SE Inquiry Lab** Exploring Periodic Trends, pp. 166–167*■	**TE Reading Toolbox** Summarizing, p. 157 **TE Reading Toolbox** Visual Literacy, p. 159 **TE Reading Toolbox** Vocabulary, p. 160 **TE Reading Toolbox** Vocabulary, p. 162 **SE Reading Toolbox** Spider Maps, p. 163 **TE Reading Toolbox** Visual Literacy, p. 163	**TE Reteaching Key Ideas** Periodic Flashcards, p. 164 **TE Formative Assessment,** p. 164 📁 **Spanish Assessment***■ 📁 **Section Quiz** ■

See also Lab Generator

See also Holt Online Assessment Resources

Resources for Differentiated Instruction

English Learners
TE Multiple Meanings, p. 152
TE Focus on Information, p. 158
📁 Differentiated Datasheets A, B, and C for Labs and Activities ■
📓 Study Guide A ■

Struggling Readers
TE Converting Table to Text, p. 148
📓 Interactive Reader

Special Education Students
TE Assembling the Periodic Table, p. 152
TE Mixed Groups of Elements, p. 161

Alternative Assessment
TE Group Characteristics, p. 153
TE Mapping the Periodic Table, p. 169

CHAPTER 5

Overview

In this chapter, students learn how elements in the periodic table were arranged historically and how they are arranged now. This chapter also covers valence electrons, ionization, and periodicity. There is a guided tour of the periodic table, including organization of the table into periods and groups. Finally, this chapter covers the classification of elements as metals (alkali, alkaline-earth, and transition) and nonmetals (halogens, noble gases, and semiconductors) and provides examples and properties of each type of element.

READING TOOLBOX

Assessing Prior Knowledge Students should understand the following concepts:

- atoms
- elements
- reactivity
- chemical and physical properties
- chemical changes

MISCONCEPTION ///ALERT\\\

Science education research has identified the following misconceptions about elements and the periodic table:

- Students are intimidated by the complexity of the periodic table. They may think they will have to memorize the entire table. (Tell students they will learn how to navigate through the table to find information about the elements.)
- Students think that elements with similar chemical properties also have similar physical properties. (As an example, have students compare the properties of chlorine and bromine. Both are halogens of Group 17 and exist elementally as diatomic molecules, but chlorine is a yellowish-green gas, and bromine is a reddish-brown liquid.)

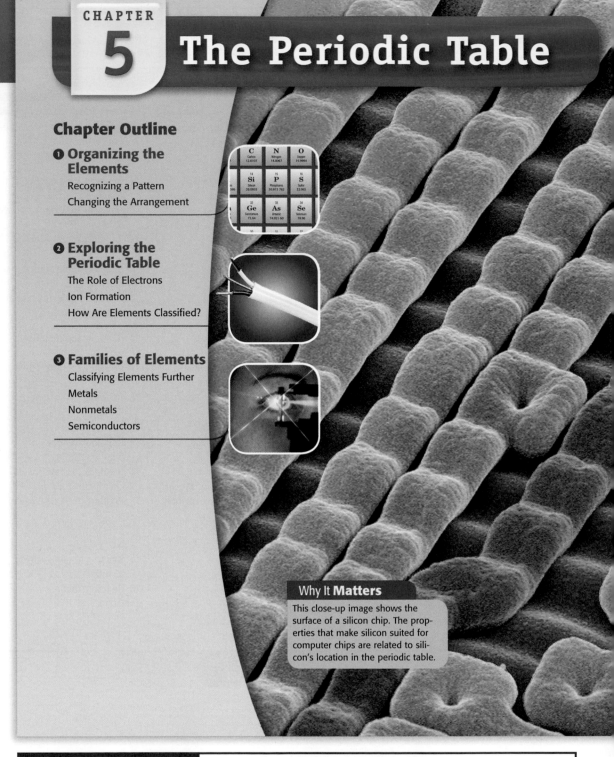

The Periodic Table

Chapter Outline

❶ Organizing the Elements
Recognizing a Pattern
Changing the Arrangement

❷ Exploring the Periodic Table
The Role of Electrons
Ion Formation
How Are Elements Classified?

❸ Families of Elements
Classifying Elements Further
Metals
Nonmetals
Semiconductors

Why It **Matters**

This close-up image shows the surface of a silicon chip. The properties that make silicon suited for computer chips are related to silicon's location in the periodic table.

Chapter Correlations   *National Science Education Standards*

The following correlations show the National Science Standards that relate to this chapter. For the full text of the standards, see the National Science Education Standards at the front of the book.

PS 2a Atoms interact with one another by transferring or sharing electrons that are furthest from the nucleus. These outer electrons govern the chemical properties of the element. (Sections 2, 3)

PS 2b When elements are listed in order according to the number of protons (called the atomic number), repeating patterns of physical and chemical properties identify families of elements with similar properties. This "Periodic Table" is a consequence of the repeating pattern of outermost electrons and their permitted energies. (Sections 1, 2; Inquiry Lab: Exploring Periodic Trends)

PS 6d In some materials, such as metals, electrons flow easily, whereas in insulating materials such as glass they can hardly flow at all. Semiconducting materials have intermediate behavior. (Sections 2, 3)

UCP1 Systems, order, and organization (Sections 1–3)

UCP 2 Evidence, models, and explanation (Sections 1, 2)

SAI 1 Abilities necessary to do scientific inquiry (Inquiry Lab: Exploring Periodic Trends)

SAI 2 Understandings about scientific inquiry (Section 1)

ST 2 Understandings about science and technology (Section 3)

HNS 1 Science as a human endeavor (Section 1)

HNS 2 Nature of scientific knowledge (Section 1)

HNS 3 Historical perspectives (Section 1)

SPSP 3 Natural resources (Section 1)

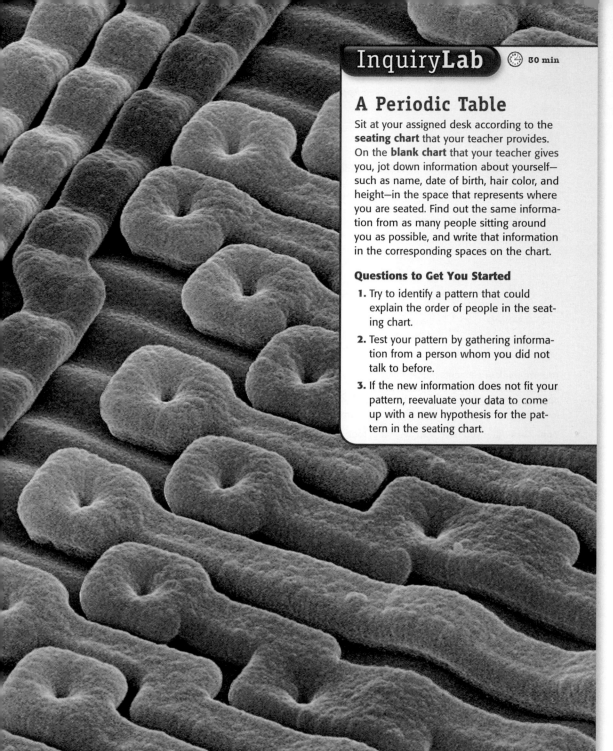

InquiryLab ⏱ 50 min

A Periodic Table

Sit at your assigned desk according to the **seating chart** that your teacher provides. On the **blank chart** that your teacher gives you, jot down information about yourself—such as name, date of birth, hair color, and height—in the space that represents where you are seated. Find out the same information from as many people sitting around you as possible, and write that information in the corresponding spaces on the chart.

Questions to Get You Started

1. Try to identify a pattern that could explain the order of people in the seating chart.

2. Test your pattern by gathering information from a person whom you did not talk to before.

3. If the new information does not fit your pattern, reevaluate your data to come up with a new hypothesis for the pattern in the seating chart.

InquiryLab

Teacher's Notes Before class, make a seating chart sorting students by two characteristics, one in rows and the other in columns; for instance, alphabetical by last name in columns, and by date of birth in rows. You might want to list specific types of information for students to gather in order to avoid students asking one another uncomfortable questions. If individual students have difficulty coming up with a pattern, have pairs of students combine information and collectively come up with a pattern.

Materials per Group
- seating chart
- blank charts, one per student

Key Resources

📁 **Datasheet**
A Periodic Table

💿 **Interactive Tutor**
Disc One, Module 3: Periodic Properties

Word Parts

Sample answer: *hal-* and *halo-* mean "salt." The elements in Group 17 are likely to be found in salts.

Generalizations

Answers may vary. Students should list generalizations from the text. For some examples, students may list words or phrases that signal the generalization.

Graphic Organizers

Answers may vary. Students should draw one or more spider maps to organize their notes about different groups of elements in the periodic table. For example, one oval could be for metals, with individual legs for alkali metals, alkaline-earth metals, transition metals, and synthetic elements. Details about each group could then be added on lines coming off each leg.

These reading tools can help you learn the material in this chapter. For more information on how to use these and other tools, see **Appendix A.**

Word Parts

Root Words Many scientific words are made up of word parts derived from ancient or foreign languages. Understanding the meanings of these word parts can help you understand new scientific terms. Here are two examples from this chapter:

WORDS	alkali metal alkaline earth metal
ROOT	alkali
SOURCE OF ROOT	Arabic "al-qali"
MEANING	ashes of plants grown in salty soil

You can think of elements in these groups as elements that are likely to be found in ashes. Alkaline-earth metals have low solubility, so they are more likely to be found in solid—or earthy—form.

Your Turn After you have read Section 3, look up the roots *hal-* and *halo-* in a dictionary. Then, explain why you think the word *halogen* is appropriate for the elements in Group 17 of the periodic table.

Generalizations

Properties of Groups Generalizations are general statements or principles applied to a large set or group of things (or people).

- Generalizations are sometimes signaled by words such as *most, mostly,* or *generally,* or by phrases such as *in general* or *for the most part.*
- Most generalizations, however, are not signaled by any telltale phrases.

> **Example of a generalization:**
> For the most part, pure metals are solid at room temperature.

This example statement is a generalization because

- the statement applies to most but not all metals.
- mercury, which is a liquid at room temperature, is an exception.

Your Turn As you read about the properties of groups of elements, make a list of generalizations that you find in the text. If there is a word or phrase that signals the generalization, underline that word or phrase in the generalization.

Graphic Organizers

Spider Maps Spider maps show how details are organized into categories, which in turn are related to a main idea.

To make a spider map, follow the steps.

1. Write a main topic title, and draw an oval around it.

2. From the oval, draw legs. Each leg represents a category of the main topic.

3. From each leg, draw horizontal lines. Write details about each category on these lines.

Your Turn As you read Section 3, use a spider map to organize the information that you learn about families of elements in the periodic table.

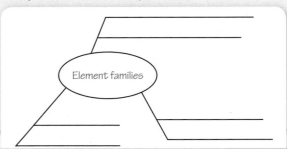

SECTION 1 Organizing the Elements

Key **Ideas**

❯ How did Mendeleev arrange the elements in his periodic table?

❯ How are elements arranged in the modern periodic table?

Key **Terms**

periodic law

period

group

Why It **Matters**

Gold and silver—both used in jewelry—have similar properties and are, therefore, located in the same column of the periodic table.

Scientists in the 1860s knew some of the chemical and physical properties of more than 60 elements. However, there was no general system of organizing the elements. To find a way to organize the elements, scientists studied the elements and the properties of the elements.

Recognizing a Pattern

Dmitri Mendeleev, a Russian chemist, was one of the first scientists to design a way of organizing the elements. He studied the properties of the elements and looked for patterns among the properties. He found that if the elements were listed by in-creasing atomic mass, certain properties appeared at certain intervals within the list.

In 1869, Mendeleev published the first periodic table of the elements. ❯ **In this periodic table, Mendeleev arranged elements in rows by increasing atomic mass.** He started a new row each time the chemical properties of the elements repeated. So, for any column, all of the elements in that column had similar properties. **Figure 1** shows Mendeleev's hand-written list of the elements and a copy of his published table.

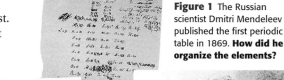

Figure 1 The Russian scientist Dmitri Mendeleev published the first periodic table in 1869. **How did he organize the elements?**

Key Resources

Teaching Transparencies
C11 The Periodic Table
TM15 The Periodic Table

Visual Concept
Periodic Table Overview

Cross-Disciplinary Worksheet
Connection to Language Arts—
Chemical Symbols

❯ Focus

In this section, students study the organization of the periodic table. They learn about how Mendeleev first arranged elements in order of increasing atomic mass and observed periodic trends in their properties. Also, they learn how the modern periodic table is arranged by atomic number and demon-strates periodic law.

Bellringer

Use the Bellringer transparency to prepare students for this section.

Demonstrate

Periodic Calendar Show students a large, one-month calendar and ask them to make a list of things that they put on their calendars at home. Ask volunteers to read their lists and, as they do so, write the items on the calendar each time they occur. Ask students: "What types of items did you list?" (Answers will vary but could include appointments, weekly music lessons, and daily practices.) "What items appear in a regular pattern, or are periodic?" (Answers should include items that recur on a monthly, weekly, or daily basis.) **LS** **Intrapersonal**

Answer to caption question

Mendeleev organized the elements in rows by increasing atomic mass, start-ing a new row each time the chemical properties repeated.

READING TOOLBOX

Spider Maps Have students highlight the smaller legs that are similar for each larger leg on the spider map. For example, both Mendeleev's and the modern periodic table show a pattern in element properties. **LS Visual**

READING TOOLBOX

Previewing Before students read this section, have them examine a copy of the periodic table and see what they can discover about its arrangement. Ask them to make a list of their observations. After reading the section, have students look over their lists again, correct any errors, and add new information. (Students' initial lists could include the following: elements are grouped into categories; elements in columns are often in the same category; elements are arranged horizontally in order of atomic number.) **LS Verbal/Visual**

READING TOOLBOX

Spider Maps
Create a spider map that has two legs and several lines on each leg. Use the map to compare Mendeleev's periodic table with the modern periodic table.

Figure 2 Mendeleev's periodic table left a question mark for germanium, which was discovered in 1886. Germanium's properties are similar to those predicted by Mendeleev, as shown in the table.

Mendeleev was able to predict new elements.

When Mendeleev arranged the elements in a list, he left gaps in the list. When he used his list to construct a table, he included these gaps in the table. **Figure 2** shows that he put question marks in these gaps. The question marks indicate places where there was no known element whose properties fit the pattern. He predicted that new elements would be discovered that would fill those gaps. He used each new element's position in the periodic table to predict some of the properties of the element.

For example, Mendeleev left a space for an element after silicon. He predicted that this element would be a gray metal that has a high melting point. In 1886, the element germanium was discovered. As **Figure 2** shows, the properties of germanium are very similar to those predicted by Mendeleev. Also discovered were two other elements that closely matched Mendeleev's predictions: gallium and scandium.

Mendeleev was not the only person to develop a periodic table, but he was first to use the table to make predictions. Mendeleev is often considered to be the father of the periodic table. The element *mendelevium* was named in his honor.

✓ **Reading Check** Why did Mendeleev leave gaps in the periodic table? (See Appendix E for answers to Reading Checks.)

A few elements did not fit the pattern.

Mendeleev found that some elements did not quite fit the pattern. For example, he had to reverse the positions of the elements tellurium and iodine. When he did so, they were in columns with similar elements. However, they were no longer in order of increasing atomic mass. Mendeleev thought that perhaps the values of the masses were not accurate, but later experiments proved that the values were correct.

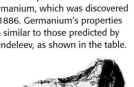

Properties of Germanium		
	Mendeleev's prediction	**Actual property**
Atomic mass	70	72.6
Density*	5.5 g/cm^3	5.3 g/cm^3
Appearance	Dark gray metal	Gray metalloid
Melting point*	High	937 °C

*at room temperature and pressure

Teaching Key Ideas

Mendeleev's Arrangement of Elements Show students tellurium and iodine on the modern periodic table and explain that Mendeleev placed these elements in this order in spite of the reverse order of their atomic masses. Have students find other pairs of elements in the modern periodic table that would not have fit Mendeleev's organization of the elements by increasing atomic mass. (Sg and Bh, Hs and Mt, Th and Pa, U and Np, Pu and Am) Point out that these elements were not known at Mendeleev's time. **LS Logical**

Differentiated Instruction

Advanced Learners

Early Periodic Tables Although the Russian chemist Dmitri Mendeleev is generally credited as being the "father" of the periodic table, his work was based on earlier versions of periodic tables by a number of scientists, including the French geologist Alexandre-Emile Béguyer de Chancourtois and the English chemist John Newlands. A German chemist, Lothar Meyer, developed a periodic table very similar to Mendeleev's around the same time. Have students conduct research and prepare a report detailing the contributions of these scientists and of Mendeleev. **LS Verbal**

Changing the Arrangement

As scientists learned more about the structure of the atom, they improved Mendeleev's table. About 40 years after Mendeleev published his table, the English chemist Henry Moseley arranged the elements by atomic number rather than by atomic mass. As you learned earlier, an element's atomic number is the number of protons in an atom of the element. Most elements did not change their location in the table, but a few elements did. This new arrangement fixed the discrepancies with elements such as tellurium and iodine.

Today's periodic table, which includes more than 100 elements, is shown on the next two pages. **❯ The modern periodic table organizes elements by atomic number. When the elements are arranged in this way, elements that have similar properties appear at regular intervals.** This principle is known as the **periodic law.** The periodic table in this book lists the atomic number, the symbol, the name, and the average atomic mass of each element.

Academic Vocabulary

discrepancy (di SKREP uhn see)
disagreement or difference between apparent facts

periodic law (PIR ee AHD ik LAW) the law that states that the repeating chemical and physical properties of elements change periodically with the atomic numbers of the elements

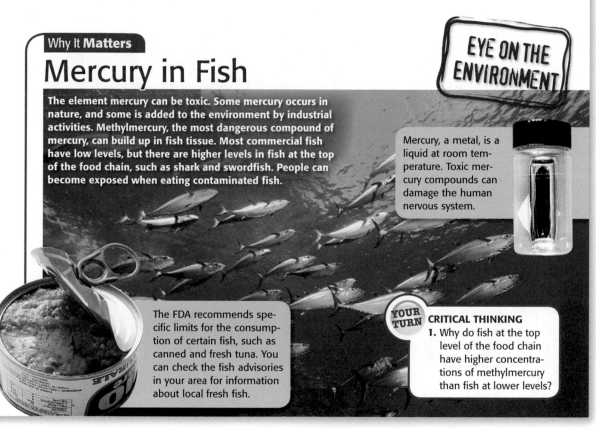

Why It Matters
Mercury in Fish

EYE ON THE ENVIRONMENT

The element mercury can be toxic. Some mercury occurs in nature, and some is added to the environment by industrial activities. Methylmercury, the most dangerous compound of mercury, can build up in fish tissue. Most commercial fish have low levels, but there are higher levels in fish at the top of the food chain, such as shark and swordfish. People can become exposed when eating contaminated fish.

Mercury, a metal, is a liquid at room temperature. Toxic mercury compounds can damage the human nervous system.

The FDA recommends specific limits for the consumption of certain fish, such as canned and fresh tuna. You can check the fish advisories in your area for information about local fresh fish.

YOUR TURN

CRITICAL THINKING
1. Why do fish at the top level of the food chain have higher concentrations of methylmercury than fish at lower levels?

Why It Matters

Mercury in Fish Because some pollutants do not leave the body when they are ingested, predators that eat other animals that have ingested pollutants will retain those pollutants in their own bodies. Over time, after eating many contaminated animals, the predators will have great amounts of pollutants built up in their bodies. Thus, even though the pollutants may enter a food chain through lower organisms, higher organisms will eventually become affected by them. The higher up on the food chain you go, the more pollutants the animals will have. This increase in concentration of pollutants from prey to predator is called *biological magnification*. Pollutants such as mercury and DDT can be biologically magnified in predators. Have students draw a food chain and demonstrate how mercury in water can affect organisms that do not drink or live in that water. **LS Visual**

Answer to Your Turn

1. Fish at the top of the food chain have higher levels of mercury because they eat animals that have already ingested mercury.

Teaching Key Ideas

Changing the Periodic Table When Mendeleev published his first table, scientists did not know about subatomic particles. Today, elements are arranged by atomic number (number of protons) instead of by atomic weight. This changed the order of a few elements, resolving some discrepancies between predicted and observed properties. Also, the modern periodic table has over 111 elements—many more than were known to scientists in Mendeleev's time. Have interested students find out about the work of Henry Moseley, whose characterization of atomic number led to the modern arrangement of the periodic table. Encourage students to present their findings in an oral report. **LS Verbal**

READING TOOLBOX

Visual Literacy At this stage, students should not worry if they do not understand the precise meaning of the periodic law. Assure them that its meaning will become clearer as they study the groups in the periodic table. To help students gain a better understanding, ask them to name some periodicals and to define the word *periodical*. Use this idea to point out the arrangement of the periodic table.

Inform students of the information available in the periodic table, including symbol, name, atomic number, average atomic mass, group number, period number, and whether the element is a metal or a nonmetal. Point out that the table exists as a scientific tool. The student's job is to learn to interpret the information on the table, not to memorize it. **LS Verbal**

READING TOOLBOX

Bookmarking Important References Have students place bookmarks in their texts to mark the periodic table on these two pages. Encourage students to familiarize themselves with the information listed in the table and to make frequent reference to these pages as they read the rest of the chapter. **LS Visual**

The Periodic Table of the Elements

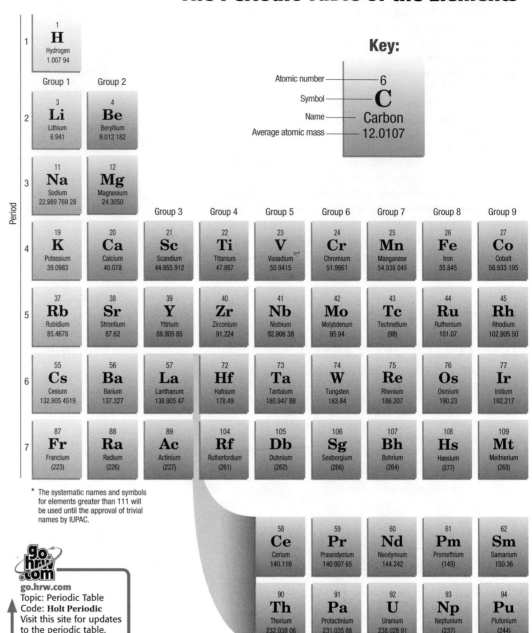

Key:

Atomic number — 6
Symbol — **C**
Name — Carbon
Average atomic mass — 12.0107

* The systematic names and symbols for elements greater than 111 will be used until the approval of trivial names by IUPAC.

go.hrw.com
Topic: Periodic Table
Code: **Holt Periodic**
Visit this site for updates to the periodic table.

Differentiated Instruction

Struggling Readers

Converting Table to Text Some readers will have trouble reading the information in the periodic table. Model sentences describing some elements. (Sample sentence: The chemical symbol C stands for carbon, which has an atomic number of 6 and an atomic mass of 12.01.) Then, have students work in pairs stating sentences aloud for each element and checking them against the table. **LS Interpersonal**

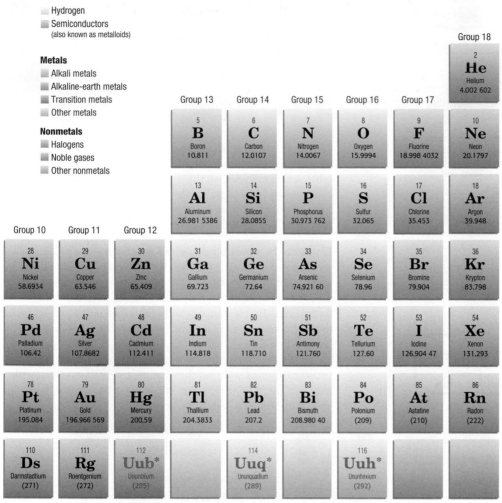

Hydrogen
Semiconductors
(also known as metalloids)

Metals
Alkali metals
Alkaline-earth metals
Transition metals
Other metals

Nonmetals
Halogens
Noble gases
Other nonmetals

Group 18

| 2 |
| He |
| Helium |
| 4.002 602 |

Group 13 Group 14 Group 15 Group 16 Group 17

5	6	7	8	9	10
B	C	N	O	F	Ne
Boron	Carbon	Nitrogen	Oxygen	Fluorine	Neon
10.811	12.0107	14.0067	15.9994	18.998 4032	20.1797

13	14	15	16	17	18
Al	Si	P	S	Cl	Ar
Aluminum	Silicon	Phosphorus	Sulfur	Chlorine	Argon
26.981 5386	28.0855	30.973 762	32.065	35.453	39.948

Group 10 Group 11 Group 12

28	29	30	31	32	33	34	35	36
Ni	Cu	Zn	Ga	Ge	As	Se	Br	Kr
Nickel	Copper	Zinc	Gallium	Germanium	Arsenic	Selenium	Bromine	Krypton
58.6934	63.546	65.409	69.723	72.64	74.921 60	78.96	79.904	83.798

46	47	48	49	50	51	52	53	54
Pd	Ag	Cd	In	Sn	Sb	Te	I	Xe
Palladium	Silver	Cadmium	Indium	Tin	Antimony	Tellurium	Iodine	Xenon
106.42	107.8682	112.411	114.818	118.710	121.760	127.60	126.904 47	131.293

78	79	80	81	82	83	84	85	86
Pt	Au	Hg	Tl	Pb	Bi	Po	At	Rn
Platinum	Gold	Mercury	Thallium	Lead	Bismuth	Polonium	Astatine	Radon
195.084	196.966 569	200.59	204.3833	207.2	208.980 40	(209)	(210)	(222)

110	111	112		114		116		
Ds	Rg	Uub*		Uuq*		Uuh*		
Darmstadtium	Roentgenium	Ununbium		Ununquadium		Ununhexium		
(271)	(272)	(285)		(289)		(292)		

The discoveries of elements with atomic numbers 112, 114, and 116 have been reported but not fully confirmed.

63	64	65	66	67	68	69	70	71
Eu	Gd	Tb	Dy	Ho	Er	Tm	Yb	Lu
Europium	Gadolinium	Terbium	Dysprosium	Holmium	Erbium	Thulium	Ytterbium	Lutetium
151.964	157.25	158.925 35	162.500	164.930 32	167.259	168.934 21	173.04	174.967

95	96	97	98	99	100	101	102	103
Am	Cm	Bk	Cf	Es	Fm	Md	No	Lr
Americium	Curium	Berkelium	Californium	Einsteinium	Fermium	Mendelevium	Nobelium	Lawrencium
(243)	(247)	(247)	(251)	(252)	(257)	(258)	(259)	(262)

The atomic masses listed in this table reflect the precision of current measurements. (Each value listed in parentheses is the mass number of that radioactive element's most stable or most common isotope.)

Teaching Key Ideas

The Modern Periodic Table Give students the names of several of the most common elements in the modern periodic table. Emphasize that while students should not try to memorize all of the chemical symbols, it is helpful to know the most common ones and their general locations in the periodic table. Have students make a flashcard for each element on your list. Each card should contain the name of the element on one side and its symbol on the other side. After students study their cards, quiz them orally on the symbols. Once they have mastered the symbols, have them memorize the atomic numbers and locations of the first 10 or 18 elements.
LS Visual

Science Skills

Interpreting the Periodic Table Group students in pairs. Ask one student in each pair to choose an element. The other student should use the periodic table to identify the element's symbol, atomic number, average atomic mass, group number, period number, and whether the element is a metal or a nonmetal, while the first student verifies their answers. Then have students switch roles and repeat the activity.
LS Interpersonal

Differentiated Instruction

Advanced Learners

Mendeleev's Competition At about the same time as Mendeleev was creating his table, John Newlands of England proposed an arrangement of elements. Have students research Newlands and prepare a report that answers the following questions: "What is Newlands' Law of Octaves?" (When elements were arranged in order of atomic mass, properties of elements repeated every eighth element.) "Why did Newlands' rows have only 7 elements?" (The eighth element would have been a noble gas, and noble gases were unknown at the time.) **LS Verbal**

Why It Matters

Elements' Diverse Histories Elements have connections to different cultures. Carbon, sulfur, tin, gold, and silver were named and used by many ancient civilizations. Platinum was first introduced to Europe from the Americas. The name for zirconium comes from the Persian word *zargûn,* which means "like gold." Vanadium was discovered in Mexico and was named after a Scandinavian goddess. Polonium was named after Poland to honor the birthplace of one of its discoverers, Marie Curie.

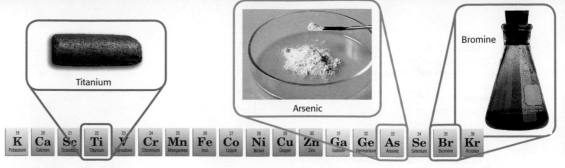

❯Close

Answer to caption question
Titanium is the most metallic and bromine is the least metallic.

Reteaching Key Ideas
Predicting Element Properties Have students use the periodic law to predict the properties of an atom of hypothetical element 118 and explain their reasoning. (It would be unreactive, because the elements above its spot in the same column are unreactive.) **LS** Logical

Formative Assessment
Suppose that elements A and B are located next to one another on a modern periodic table. If element A has a greater atomic mass than element B, which of the following would be true?

A. Element A must be to the right of element B. (Incorrect. An element with a greater atomic mass may or may not fall to the right on the periodic table.)

B. Element A must have a greater atomic number than element B. (Incorrect. An element with a greater atomic mass would usually, but not always, have a greater atomic number.)

C. The elements' order would be reversed on Mendeleev's periodic table. (Incorrect. An element with a greater atomic mass usually, but not always, would fall to the right on Mendeleev's periodic table.)

D. Given the information, you cannot draw conclusions about the relative atomic numbers of the two elements. (Correct. A greater atomic mass does not always mean a greater atomic number.)

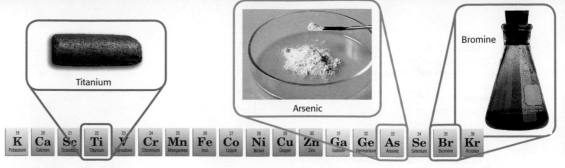

| 19 K Potassium | 20 Ca Calcium | 21 Sc Scandium | 22 Ti Titanium | 23 V Vanadium | 24 Cr Chromium | 25 Mn Manganese | 26 Fe Iron | 27 Co Cobalt | 28 Ni Nickel | 29 Cu Copper | 30 Zn Zinc | 31 Ga Gallium | 32 Ge Germanium | 33 As Arsenic | 34 Se Selenium | 35 Br Bromine | 36 Kr Krypton |

Figure 3 Titanium, arsenic, and bromine are in Period 4. **Which is most metallic, and which is least metallic?**

period (PIR ee uhd) a horizontal row of elements in the periodic table

group (GROOP) a vertical column of elements in the periodic table; elements in a group share chemical properties

www.scilinks.org
Topic: Origin of Elements
Code: HK81082

Elements become less metallic across each period.
Each row of the periodic table is a **period.** The periodic table, which is shown on the previous pages, has seven periods. **Figure 3** shows three elements in Period 4. As you move from left to right across a period, properties such as reactivity and conductivity change, and elements become less metallic.

Elements in a group have similar properties.
Each column of the periodic table is a **group.** For each group, all of the elements in that group have similar chemical properties. For example, helium and neon, in Group 18, are both unreactive elements. That is, under normal conditions, these elements do not join with atoms of other elements to form compounds.

The periodic table on the previous pages shows color-coded categories. Many of these categories are associated with a certain group or groups. You will learn more about specific groups of elements later in this chapter.

Section 1 Review

KEY IDEAS
1. **Describe** how Mendeleev organized his periodic table.
2. **Explain** why Mendeleev left a space for the unknown (at the time) element germanium in his periodic table.
3. **State** the property used to organize elements in the modern periodic table.
4. **Identify** the following on the periodic table.
   a. the chemical symbol for mercury
   b. the period and group of gold
   c. the atomic mass of iron
   d. the atomic number of neon
   e. the element represented by Cu

CRITICAL THINKING
5. **Applying Concepts** Metals conduct electricity well, while nonmetals do not. Which element should conduct electricity better: germanium, aluminum, or helium?
6. **Drawing Conclusions** Are the properties of sodium, Na, more like the properties of lithium, Li, or magnesium, Mg? Explain your answer.
7. **Making Inferences** Before 1937, all naturally occurring elements had been discovered, but no one had found a trace of element 43. Chemists predicted the chemical properties of this element, now called *technetium*. How were these predictions possible? Which elements would you expect to be similar to technetium?

Answers to Section Review
1. Mendeleev organized elements in order of increasing atomic mass.
2. Mendeleev left a space for germanium to keep elements with similar properties together.
3. atomic number
4. **a.** Hg
   b. period 6, group 11
   c. 55.845
   d. 10
   e. copper

5. aluminum
6. lithium; Sodium and lithium are in the same group so their properties should be more alike than the properties of sodium and magnesium.
7. Technetium's properties would be predicted from and similar to the properties of manganese or rhenium, which are in the same group.

Exploring the Periodic Table

Key **Ideas**

❯ Why do elements within a group of the periodic table have similar chemical properties?

❯ What happens to an atom that gains or loses electrons?

❯ What are the three main categories of elements?

Key **Terms**

ion

metal

nonmetal

semiconductor

Why It **Matters**

The properties of metals make metals useful for conducting electricity. For example, wires that carry electricity are made of metal.

Why is neon an unreactive element? Why is sodium so reactive that it reacts violently with moisture and oxygen in the air? These chemical properties are related to the number of electrons in each element.

The Role of Electrons

The periodic table is organized by atomic number, which is the number of protons in an atom. For a neutral atom, the number of protons equals the number of electrons. ❯ **The periodic trends in the periodic table are the result of electron arrangement.** Specifically, the chemical properties of each group are largely determined by the number of valence electrons. These electrons are closest to the outside of the atom and are sometimes considered part of an outer "shell" of electrons.

Valence electrons account for similar properties.

The number of valence electrons determines many of the chemical properties of an element. The diagrams in **Figure 1** show atoms of two elements from Group 1: lithium and sodium. Because they each have one valence electron, lithium and sodium have similar chemical properties. In general, elements in a group have chemical and physical properties in common because they have the same number of valence electrons. Of course, elements in a group are not exactly alike. They differ in numbers of protons in their nuclei and in numbers of electrons in their filled inner energy levels. As a result, the properties of elements in a group are not exactly the same.

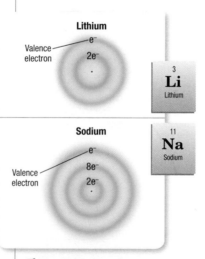

Figure 1 These two elements in Group 1 each have one valence electron. **What is the difference in the location of these electrons?**

SECTION 2

❯Focus

In this section, students learn about the process of ionization and how valence electrons account for the periodic properties of elements. The section concludes with a brief description of how elements are classified as metals, semiconductors, and nonmetals according to their properties and where, in general, these categories can be found in the periodic table.

Bellringer

Use the Bellringer transparency to prepare students for this section.

Demonstrate

Conductivity For this demonstration you will need a conductivity tester and samples of elements, such as a copper coin, an iron nail, and pieces of charcoal and sulfur. A conductivity tester can be made from insulated wire, a battery, and a flashlight bulb.

Use the conductivity tester to see which elements conduct an electric current. Ask students: "Which elements are metals?" "How do you know?" (Generally, elements that conduct a current under standard conditions are metals.) "Which elements are nonmetals?" "How do you know?" (Generally, elements that do not conduct a current under standard conditions are nonmetals.)
LS Logical

Answer to caption question

Lithium has one valence electron in the second level, while sodium has one valence electron in the third level.

Key Resources

Teaching Transparencies
C12 Ion Formation
TM16 Elements and Orbitals

Visual Concept
Valence Electrons

Cross-Disciplinary Worksheets
Integrating Biology—The Elements in Your Body

❯Teach

Teaching Key Ideas

Energy Levels Be sure students do not attempt to show how electrons are arranged in atoms past calcium in the periodic table. As electron energy levels increase, the difference in their energies decreases. Starting with the third energy level, the levels overlap and the order in which orbitals fill becomes irregular. The pattern of this overlap is beyond the scope of this course, but more information can be found in a high school chemistry textbook.

Root Words The word *hydrogen* comes from root words that mean "bringing forth water" because when hydrogen burns, water forms. The word *helium* comes from a root word that means "the Sun" because chemists first observed its characteristic spectrum when examining sunlight. The word *lithium* comes from a root word that means "stone" because it was first observed in a rock sample.

Teaching Key Ideas

Element Groups Be sure students understand that *physical* properties may or may not be similar among elements in a group. Have students examine **Figure 2.** Ask: "Why do elements in the same column have similar chemical properties?" (They have the same number of valence electrons, and the number of valence electrons determines how an element will chemically react with other elements) **LS Visual**

READING TOOLBOX

Root Words
Use a dictionary or the Internet to find the root words for *hydrogen, helium,* and *lithium*. Explain how each root is related to the properties of that element.

SCILINKS.
www.scilinks.org
Topic: Periodic Table
Code: HK81125

An element's location in the periodic table is related to electron arrangement.

You can find out how the electrons are arranged in the atoms of an element if you know where the element is located in the periodic table. Hydrogen and helium are in Period 1. **Figure 2** shows that a hydrogen atom has one electron in an s orbital and that a helium atom has two electrons in an s orbital. Lithium is located in Period 2. Like helium, lithium has two electrons in an s orbital. But lithium has a third electron, which is in an s orbital in the second energy level. The table below shows the electron arrangement of lithium.

Element	Energy level	Orbital	Number of electrons
Lithium	1	s	2
	2	s	1

As you move to the right in Period 2, electrons begin to fill the p orbitals. For instance, a carbon atom's six electrons are in two s orbitals and one p orbital, as shown in the table below.

Element	Energy level	Orbital	Number of electrons
Carbon	1	s	2
	2	s	2
	2	p	2

A nitrogen atom has three electrons in p orbitals, an oxygen atom has four, and a fluorine atom has five. **Figure 2** shows that a neon atom has six electrons in p orbitals. Each p orbital can hold two electrons, so neon's three p orbitals are filled.

Figure 2 The electronic arrangement of atoms becomes increasingly complex as you move to the right across a period and as you move down along a group.

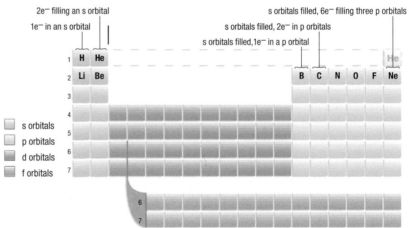

Differentiated Instruction

English Learners

Multiple Meanings For students having difficulty with familiar words, ask them to define the word *period*. (era, stage, cycle, punctuation) Point out that the definition in the text includes the words "periodic table," to distinguish it from other definitions. Also note the different forms of period. (period: noun; periodic: adjective; periodically: adverb) Ask students to find other words with multiple non-scientific meanings. (element: part, factor; property: land, possessions) **LS Verbal**

Special Education Students

Assembling the Periodic Table Ask each student to select several elements from the periodic table. Label the front side of an index card with atomic number, symbol, name, and atomic mass. On the back of the card, give two examples of compounds that include this element. Students may present their own elements and exchange element cards. All of the completed cards may be placed on a poster or bulletin board to construct parts of the entire periodic table. **LS Visual**

Ion Formation

Atoms whose outermost orbitals are not filled may undergo a process called *ionization*. That is, such atoms may gain or lose valence electrons so that they have a filled outermost orbital. **❯ If an atom gains or loses electrons, it no longer has an equal number of electrons and protons. Because the charges do not cancel completely, the atom has a net electric charge.** A charged atom is called an **ion.**

Group 1 elements form positive ions.

Lithium is a Group 1 element. Lithium is reactive in air, in water, and especially in acid. The atomic structure of lithium explains lithium's reactivity. A lithium atom has three electrons, as shown in the upper left diagram in **Figure 3**. Two of these electrons occupy the first energy level in the s orbital, but only one electron occupies the second energy level. This single valence electron is easily removed, which makes lithium very reactive. Removing this electron forms a positive ion, or *cation,* as shown in the upper right diagram in **Figure 3**. A lithium ion, written as Li$^+$, has a filled outer s orbital.

Atoms of other Group 1 elements also have one valence electron. These elements are reactive and behave similarly to lithium.

Group 17 elements form negative ions.

Like lithium, fluorine is very reactive. Each fluorine atom has nine electrons. Two of these electrons occupy the first energy level. The other seven electrons—the valence electrons—are in the second energy level. A fluorine atom needs only one more electron to have a filled outermost energy level. An atom of fluorine easily gains this electron to form a negative ion, or *anion,* as the bottom diagram in **Figure 3** shows. Because an ion of fluorine has a filled outer energy level, the ion is more stable and less reactive than a fluorine atom.

Ions of fluorine, which have a 1– charge, are called *fluoride ions*. The symbol for the fluoride ion is F$^-$. Because atoms of other Group 17 elements have seven valence electrons, other Group 17 elements are reactive and behave like fluorine, too.

✔ Reading Check Why do Group 1 and Group 17 elements easily form ions?

ion (IE AHN) an atom, radical, or molecule that has gained or lost one or more electrons and has a negative or positive charge

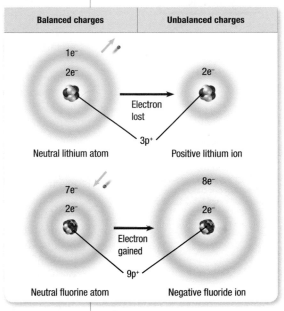

Balanced charges	Unbalanced charges

1e$^-$

2e$^-$

Electron lost

3p$^+$

Neutral lithium atom — Positive lithium ion

2e$^-$

7e$^-$

2e$^-$

Electron gained

9p$^+$

8e$^-$

2e$^-$

Neutral fluorine atom — Negative fluoride ion

Figure 3 The valence electron of a lithium atom may be removed to form a lithium ion, Li$^+$, which has a 1+ charge. A fluorine atom easily gains one valence electron to form a fluoride ion, F$^-$, which has a 1– charge.

go.hrw.com
✷ interact online
Keyword: HK8PTAF3

Teaching Key Ideas

Ions Have Charge Students are sometimes confused by how the sign of an ion's charge is related to the loss and gain of electrons. Remind them that the gain of an electron means the gain of a negative charge, producing a negatively charged ion. Conversely, the loss of an electron means the loss of a negative charge, which leaves a positively charged ion. Have students model ionization in a single atom using balls of modeling clay to represent protons and electrons. Point out that they cannot add or remove protons, but they can remove or add electrons to change the charge.
LS Kinesthetic

READING TOOLBOX

Vocabulary Inform students that because anions and cations are types of ions, they are pronounced accordingly. Anion is pronounced "an-ion," and cation is pronounced "cat-ion." Students who are familiar with batteries might relate these terms to the negative pole of a battery, the anode, which attracts cations, and the positive pole of a battery, the cathode, which attracts anions.

go.hrw.com
✷ interact online

Students can interact with the figure by going to **go.hrw.com** and typing in the keyword **HK8PTAF3**.

Differentiated Instruction

Alternative Assessment

Group Characteristics Have students perform the following group research activity.
Step 1 Divide the class into four groups. Assign each student group one of the following: Group 1, Group 2, Group 17, or Group 18 from the periodic table.
Step 2 Have students find out the properties and uses of the elements in their assigned group and what they have in common.
Step 3 Have each student group prepare a poster that shows what they learned so that they can present this information to the class.
LS Interpersonal/Visual

Teaching Key Ideas

Sometimes Called Metalloids Semiconductors are sometimes called *metalloids* because they share some properties with metals and others with nonmetals. Show students a photograph of silicon and lead them to understand that silicon has some metallic properties and some properties that are similar to that of nonmetals. Ask students what visual property silicon shares with metals. (silicon is shiny) **LS** **Visual**

READING TOOLBOX

Vocabulary Make sure students distinguish between the scientific and everyday meanings of the word *metal.* The scientific term metal applies only to individual elements with certain properties. Point out that in common speech, the term *metal* is often applied to metallic objects, which are almost always alloys, i.e., homogeneous mixtures of metals with other metals and/or nonmetals.

Teaching Key Ideas

Categorizing Elements Have students draw a cartoon of the periodic table that summarizes the properties and general locations of metals, semiconductors, and nonmetals. Encourage students to use fun illustrations, such as common metal objects or balloons full of gas, to give them a visual reminder of where each category of element is typically located on the periodic table. **LS** **Visual**

www.scilinks.org
Topic: Metals/
Nonmetals
Code: HK80948

metal (MET′l) an element that is shiny and that conducts heat and electricity well

nonmetal (nahn MET′l) an element that conducts heat and electricity poorly

semiconductor (SEM i kuhn DUK tuhr) an element or compound that conducts electric current better than an insulator does but not as well as a conductor does

How Are Elements Classified?

As you have learned, elements within a group have similar chemical properties. In addition to being organized into groups, the elements in the 18 groups in the periodic table are further classified into three main categories. These three categories are based on general properties that the elements in the categories have in common, as shown in **Figure 4.** > **All elements are either metals, nonmetals, or semiconductors.**

Elements in each category have similar properties.

As shown in **Figure 4,** most elements are **metals.** Most metals are shiny solids that can be stretched and shaped. They are also good conductors of heat and electricity. Some examples of metals are gold, platinum, and copper.

Figure 4 shows that all **nonmetals,** except for hydrogen, are found on the right side of the periodic table. Examples of nonmetals include carbon, oxygen, and helium. Nonmetals may be solids, liquids, or gases at room temperature. Solid nonmetals are often dull and brittle. They are poor conductors of heat and electricity. Materials that do not conduct heat or electricity well are sometimes called *insulators.*

Some elements can conduct electricity under certain conditions. These six elements, shown in **Figure 4,** are called **semiconductors**. Semiconductors are also sometimes called *metalloids.* Two common semiconductors are silicon and germanium. The main properties of metals, nonmetals, and semiconductors are summarized in **Figure 5** on the next page.

✓ **Reading Check** Which category contains the most elements, and which category contains the fewest elements?

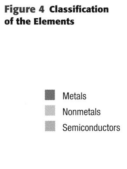

Figure 4 Classification of the Elements

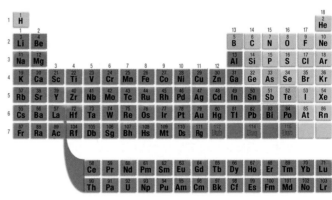

■ Metals
■ Nonmetals
■ Semiconductors

Differentiated Instruction

Basic Learners

Metallic Properties Ask students to bring in small objects made of metal. Also select samples from classroom and lab supplies. Allow students to evaluate the physical properties of the samples, such as electrical conductivity, thermal conductivity, and attraction to a magnet. Supply students with a magnet and a battery-powered conductivity tester, if available. Students should use hot tap water as a heat source for thermal conductivity tests. **LS** **Kinesthetic**

Figure 5 Three Categories of Elements

	Metals	Nonmetals	Semiconductors
Properties	• Metals are good conductors of electricity. • Metals are good conductors of heat. • Metals are ductile (easily drawn into thin wires) and malleable (easily shaped or formed). • Most metals are shiny.	• Nonmetals are poor conductors of electricity. • Nonmetals are poor conductors of heat. • Nonmetals are not malleable or ductile. • Most nonmetals are not shiny.	• Semiconductors share properties with metals and nonmetals. • Semiconductors can conduct electricity under certain conditions. • Semiconductors are the main components of chips in computers and in other electronic devices.
Examples	Copper Lead	Carbon Sulfur	Tellurium Silicon

Section 2 Review

KEY IDEAS

1. **Explain** why elements in a group on the periodic table have similar chemical properties.

2. **Compare** the number of valence electrons in an atom of oxygen, O, with the number of valence electrons in an atom of selenium, Se. Are oxygen and selenium in the same period or group?

3. **Explain** why some atoms gain or lose electrons to form ions.

4. **Describe** why lithium and other Group 1 elements usually form positive ions, while fluorine and other Group 17 elements form negative ions.

5. **List** the three main categories of elements, and give an example of each.

CRITICAL THINKING

6. **Making Predictions** Predict which ions cesium forms: Cs^+ ions or Cs^{2+} ions.

7. **Drawing Conclusions** Determine whether elements that fit the following descriptions are more likely to be metals or nonmetals:
   a. a shiny substance used to make flexible bed springs
   b. a yellow powder from underground mines
   c. a gas that does not react
   d. a conducting material used within flexible wires
   e. a brittle substance that does not conduct heat

8. **Making Predictions** Predict the charge of a beryllium ion.

Answers to Section Review

1. The chemical properties of each group are related to the number of valence electrons.

2. Each atom has six valence electrons; they are in the same group.

3. Atoms with unfilled outer *s* and *p* orbitals often form ions by gaining or losing electrons. The resulting ions have a filled outer energy level.

4. Group 1 elements form positive ions because they have a single outer electron which is easily lost. Group 17 elements form negative ions because they have a nearly filled outer energy level, which is easily filled.

5. Sample answer: Metal: gold, Nonmetal: neon, Semiconductor: silicon.

6. Cesium is in Group 1, so its atom loses one valence electron to form a Cs^+ ion.

7. **a.** metal
   b. nonmetal
   c. nonmetal
   d. metal
   e. nonmetal

8. Beryllium is a Group 2 metal. Therefore, its atom has two valence electrons that can be removed to form a Be^{2+} ion.

❯Close

Reteaching Key Ideas

Ions of Metals and Nonmetals Have students review the section and predict whether, in general, metals or nonmetals would tend to form cations. Have them explain their answers. (Metals, rather than non-metals, tend to form cations because they tend to be located on the left side of the periodic table where elements have fewer valence electrons.)
LS Logical

Formative Assessment

Elements in the same _____ of the periodic table have the same number of valence electrons and similar chemical properties?

A. group (Correct. Valence electrons determine bonding, which determines the chemical properties of elements.)

B. period (Incorrect. Elements within a period have increasing numbers of valence electrons and therefore different chemical properties.)

C. side (Incorrect. While, in general, the metals on the left side of the periodic table have many similar properties, which differ from nonmetals on the right side of the periodic table, they do not all have the same number of valence electrons.)

D. version (Incorrect. The different versions of the periodic table show periodic differences in their properties according to group location.)

SECTION 3

Families of Elements

> Focus

In this section, students learn how metals and nonmetals can be grouped into families with similar properties: alkali metals, alkaline-earth metals, transition metals, semiconductors, halogens, and noble gases. They learn about the general properties of each family of elements and also study specific examples.

 Bellringer

Use the Bellringer transparency to prepare students for this section.

Why It **Matters**

Metal Coins To get students thinking about the similar properties of groups of elements, have students form small research groups. Supply each group with samples of pennies, nickels, dimes, and quarters. Have students in each group list the metals that they think are used in each of the coins. Tell them to observe the edges of several coins. Discuss how a combination of value and properties determines what metals are used to make coins. Then have students in each group conduct research to find out more about the metals used in U.S. coins today and throughout history. You may wish to ask each group to research one particular type of coin and then have them share their results with the class.

LS Interpersonal

Key **Ideas**

> What does each element family have in common?

> What are the families of metals?

> What are some of the families of nonmetals?

> What are semiconductors?

Key **Terms**

alkali metal

alkaline-earth metal

transition metal

noble gas

halogen

Why It **Matters**

The tiny chips in electronic devices contain semiconductors, such as silicon. Semiconductors give chips properties that allow computers to work.

Sometimes, one or more groups in the periodic table are categorized as being members of a unit called a *family*. Consider your own family. Each member is unique, but you all share some features. For example, family members often have a similar appearance, as **Figure 1** shows. Likewise, members of a family in the periodic table have properties in common.

Classifying Elements Further

You learned earlier that elements can be classified as metals, nonmetals, and semiconductors. **Figure 2** shows how elements are further categorized into five families. **> The elements in a family have the same number of valence electrons**. This section explores some of the shared physical and chemical properties of elements in each family.

Figure 1 Just as the members of this family have similarities, elements in a family on the periodic table have similarities.

Figure 2 Element Families

Group number	Number of valence electrons	Name of family
Group 1	1	alkali metals
Group 2	2	alkaline-earth metals
Groups 3–12	varied	transition metals
Group 17	7	halogens
Group 18	8*	noble gases

*except helium, which has two electrons

Key Resources

Teaching Transparency
TM17 Element Families

Datasheets
Elements in Food
The Cost of Metals

Cross-Disciplinary Worksheets
Real World Applications—How Do Scientists Find Cures for Diseases?
Connection to Architecture—Buckyball
Integrating Earth Science—Magnesium: From Sea Water to Fireworks

Metals

Many elements are classified as metals. All metals conduct heat and electricity. Most metals can also be stretched and shaped into flat sheets, or pulled into wires. ❭ **Families of metals include the alkali metals, the alkaline-earth metals, and the transition metals.**

The alkali metals are very reactive.

Sodium is found in Group 1 of the periodic table, as shown in **Figure 3.** Like other **alkali metals**, it is soft and shiny and reacts violently with water. Alkali metals are often stored in oil to prevent them from reacting with moisture in the air.

An atom of an alkali metal is very reactive because it has one valence electron that can easily be removed to form a positive ion. You have already seen how lithium forms positive ions that have a 1+ charge. Similarly, when its valence electron is removed, a sodium atom forms the positive ion Na^+.

Because alkali metals such as sodium are very reactive, they are not found in nature as uncombined elements. Instead, they are found combined with other elements in the form of compounds. For example, the salt that you use to season your food is the compound sodium chloride, NaCl. In addition to having similar reactivity, many alkali metals have similar melting points, boiling points, and densities.

✔️ **Reading Check** Why are alkali metals very reactive?

SCILINKS.
www.scilinks.org
Topic: Element Families
Code: HK80494

alkali metal (AL kuh LIE MET'l) one of the elements of Group 1 of the periodic table

Potassium is an alkali metal.
Which property of alkali metals is illustrated here?

Group 1

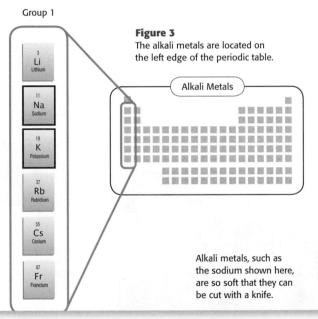

Figure 3
The alkali metals are located on the left edge of the periodic table.

Alkali Metals

Alkali metals, such as the sodium shown here, are so soft that they can be cut with a knife.

❭ Teach

READING TOOLBOX

Summarizing As students read each passage about a family of elements, ask for a volunteer to summarize the passage for the class. Then have the class, as listeners, ask for clarification of parts of the summary. All students may consult the text during the clarification process. **LS Interpersonal/Verbal**

Teaching Key Ideas

Uses of Alkali Metals Explain that compounds of alkali metals are used extensively, especially those of sodium and of potassium. Sodium hydroxide is an important industrial compound that is used in the manufacture of paper, soap, and synthetic fabrics as well as in petroleum refining. Sodium chloride is common table salt, and potassium chloride is a table salt substitute. Other potassium compounds are important components of chemical fertilizers. Have students perform research to find various uses for alkali metals and present their findings in a chart. **LS Visual**

Answer to caption question
The photo illustrates how alkali metals react violently with water.

Differentiated Instruction

Basic Learners

Periodic Table's Big Ideas For students who have difficulty with the large amount of information in the periodic table, share a list of the key concepts that they need to know: The large letters in the squares of the periodic table are the chemical symbols of the elements; O is the symbol for oxygen. The elements in a vertical group have similar properties; lithium (Li) and sodium (Na) are silvery metals that are very reactive. The periodic table groups metals, nonmetals, and semiconductors. **LS Verbal**

Why It **Matters**

Nutritional Sodium Too much sodium in one's diet can be unhealthy, but sodium ions and potassium ions are important for the proper functioning of nerves in the human body. They allow electrical impulses to pass from one nerve to another via axons. Have students research the functions of sodium and potassium ions in nerve impulses and make a poster illustrating their findings. **LS Visual**

QuickLab

Teacher's Notes If students need help performing this activity, give them the following hints: Ingredients that are not named as elements are probably compounds; ingredients that are plant or animal products probably contain carbon, hydrogen, and oxygen; commas separate ingredients (for example, if an ingredient is sodium citrate, it is a compound by that name, not the element sodium and then a compound).

Answers
Student lists will vary according to their diets.

Teaching Key Ideas

Comparing Reactivity Ionization energy is the amount of energy needed to remove an electron from an atom. The ionization energy for an alkali metal is low because one electron is easy to remove.

The first electron in an alkaline-earth atom is easy to remove also. However, the second electron requires more energy to remove. It must be removed from a positively charged ion, which does not lose an electron as easily as a neutral atom does. This is why alkaline-earth metals are less reactive than alkali metals. To reinforce this concept, have volunteers act out a skit that represents the differences in removing the first and second electrons from alkali and alkaline-earth metals. **LS Interpersonal/Verbal**

QuickLab ⏱ 20 min

Elements in Food

❶ For 1 day, make a list of the ingredients in all of the foods and drinks that you consume in that day.

❷ Identify which ingredients on your list are compounds.

❸ For each compound on your list, try to figure out which elements make up the compound.

Group 2

Be Beryllium (4)
Mg Magnesium (12)
Ca Calcium (20)
Sr Strontium (38)
Ba Barium (56)
Ra Radium (88)

Alkaline-earth metals form compounds that are found in limestone and in the human body.

Calcium is in Group 2 of the periodic table, as shown in **Figure 4**. Calcium is an **alkaline-earth metal.** In general, alkaline-earth metals are harder, denser, stronger, and have higher melting points than alkali metals.

Atoms of alkaline-earth metals, such as calcium, have two valence electrons. Alkaline-earth metals are less reactive than alkali metals, but alkaline-earth metals still react to form positive ions. These ions have a 2+ charge. When a calcium atom loses its two valence electrons, the resulting ion, Ca^{2+}, has a filled outer energy level. Alkaline-earth metals, such as calcium, combine with other elements to form compounds.

Calcium compounds make up the hard shells of many sea animals. When the animals die, their shells settle to form large deposits that eventually become limestone or marble, both of which are very strong materials used in construction. Coral is one example of a limestone structure. The limestone skeletons of millions of tiny animals combine to form sturdy coral reefs that are the habitats of many fish. Your bones and teeth also get their strength from calcium compounds.

Magnesium, another alkaline-earth metal, is the lightest of all structural metals, or metals used as part of a structure. Magnesium is used to build some airplanes. Magnesium, as Mg^{2+}, activates many of the enzymes that speed up processes in the human body. Two magnesium compounds are commonly used in medicines—milk of magnesia and Epsom salts.

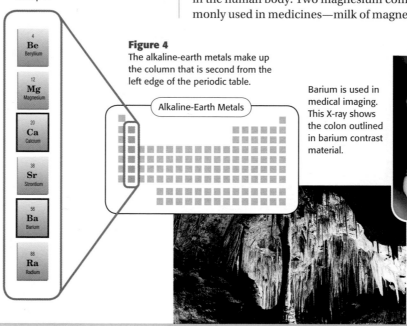

Figure 4
The alkaline-earth metals make up the column that is second from the left edge of the periodic table.

Alkaline-Earth Metals

Barium is used in medical imaging. This X-ray shows the colon outlined in barium contrast material.

The stalagmites and stalactites in limestone caves contain calcium carbonate deposits.

Why It **Matters**

Magnesium Uses Magnesium is very flammable and produces a bright white flash when ignited. For this reason, old photography flash systems relied on burning magnesium. Magnesium and magnesium alloys are vital to the aerospace industry because of their low densities. But because of its flammability, magnesium is often machined in an inert atmosphere. Have interested students do research and make a poster displaying the uses of magnesium throughout history. **LS Visual**

Differentiated Instruction

English Learners
Focus on Information Draw students' attention to calcium under the Group 2 heading. Have students fill in the blanks of the following paragraph with the correct information: The atomic number for calcium is _____. (20) The chemical symbol for calcium is _____. (Ca) The name of the element is _____. (calcium) The element is in the second column, so calcium is a(n) _____. (alkaline-earth metal) Have students practice with other elements. **LS Logical**

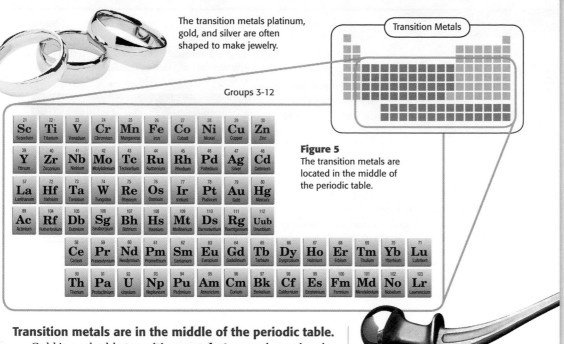

The transition metals platinum, gold, and silver are often shaped to make jewelry.

Groups 3-12

Transition Metals

Figure 5
The transition metals are located in the middle of the periodic table.

This artificial hip component is made of titanium, which is light, strong, and nonreactive.

Transition metals are in the middle of the periodic table.

Gold is a valuable **transition metal. Figure 5** shows that the transition metals are located in Groups 3–12 of the periodic table. Unlike most other transition metals, gold is not found in nature combined with other elements.

Transition metals, such as gold, are much less reactive than sodium or calcium. But transition metals can lose electrons to form positive ions, too. There are two possible cations that a gold atom can form. If an atom of gold loses only one electron, it forms Au^+. If the atom loses three electrons, it forms Au^{3+}. Some transition metals can form as many as four differently charged cations because of their complex arrangement of electrons. With the exception of mercury, transition metals are harder, more dense, and have higher melting points than alkali metals and alkaline-earth metals.

Because gold, silver, and platinum are shiny metals, they are often molded into various kinds of jewelry, as shown in **Figure 5.** There are many other useful transition metals. Copper is often used for plumbing or electrical wiring. Light-bulb filaments are made of tungsten. Iron, cobalt, copper, and manganese play important roles in your body chemistry. Mercury, the only metal that is a liquid at room temperature, is sometimes used in thermometers.

✔ **Reading Check** What are some examples of transition metals?

alkaline-earth metal (AL kuh LIEN UHRTH MET'l) one of the elements of Group 2 of the periodic table

transition metal (tran ZISH uhn MET'l) one of the metals that can use the inner shell before using the outer shell to bond

READING TOOLBOX

Visual Literacy The metals in the photograph in **Figure 5** are grouped together because of a common use. Other groups of transition elements are also grouped by use. Copper, silver, and gold, which are in the same family, are called coinage metals. Iron, cobalt, and nickel, which are in the same period, are often called the "iron triad" and are the only elements that can be magnetized. Have students find these groups of elements in the figure. **LS Visual**

Teaching Key Ideas

Variable Charges Because transition elements can gain or lose different numbers of electrons, many of them can form more than one kind of ion. Illustrate this by pointing out common transition element ions, such as Cu^+, Cu^{2+}, Fe^{2+}, Fe^{3+}, Hg_2^{2+}, Hg^{2+}, Sn^{2+}, Sn^{4+}, Pb^{2+}, and Pb^{4+}.

Why It **Matters**

Uses of Gold Gold, platinum, and silver are often used in jewelry because of their pleasing appearance and durability. Although silver is a better conductor, gold is also a very good conductor and has the advantage of not corroding or tarnishing under ordinary conditions. For this reason, gold is widely used on connectors in computers and other electronic devices. Have students infer from its properties why gold might be more valuable than other similar metals. (Sample answer: Gold is less reactive than many other metals, so it does not tarnish.) **LS Logical**

Differentiated Instruction

Advanced Learners

Colorful Gems The transition elements frequently form colorful compounds. Traces of transition elements provide the color in many gems, such as rubies and emeralds. Have interested students do research to find out what elements give gems their different colors and present their findings in a poster or visual display. **LS Verbal**

Basic Learners

Abbreviations Explain to students that most elements have abbreviations that are similar to the element names. Explain that this makes it easier to remember the names that correspond to the abbreviations. Tell students that a few elements do not match their abbreviations. Have students use the periodic table to find the following abbreviations and to write down the full names of these elements: Na, K, W, Fe, Cu, Ag, Au, Hg, Sn, Pb, Sb. **LS Visual**

Teacher's Notes While aluminum is the most abundant metal, most of its cost is due to a necessary smelting process. Dividing $100 by the price per gram for each metal will give the number of grams of the metal. Because the prices listed in the table are given in dollars per kilogram, students should incorporate the conversion of kilograms to grams in their spreadsheets.

Answers to Procedure

1. Al, Fe, Cr, Zn, Cu, Sn, Ag, Au
2. Fe, Cr, Zn, Al, Cu, Sn, Ag, Au

Answers to Analysis

1. The lists match perfectly, except for the price of aluminum compared with its abundance.
2. Aluminum is the most reactive metal on the list. While aluminum is also the most abundant, it must cost extra to purify it.
3. Dividing $100 by the price per gram for each metal will give the number of grams of the metal. Because the prices listed in the table are given in dollars per kilogram, students should incorporate the conversion of kilograms to grams in their spreadsheets.

QuickLab — The Cost of Metals

⏲ 20 min

Procedure

❶ The table gives the abundance of some metals in Earth's crust. List these metals in order of abundance, from most abundant to least abundant.

❷ List the metals in order of price, from cheapest to most expensive.

Analysis

1. If the price of a metal depends on the metal's abundance, you would expect the order to be the same on both lists. How well do the two lists match? Mention any mismatches.

2. A list of these metals in order from most reactive to least reactive is as follows: aluminum, zinc, chromium, iron, tin, copper, silver, and gold. Use this information to explain any mismatches that you noticed in item 1.

3. Create a spreadsheet that can be used to calculate the number of grams of each metal that you could buy with $100.

Metal	Abundance in Earth's crust (%)	Price ($/kg)
Aluminum, Al	8.2	1.55
Chromium, Cr	0.01	0.06
Copper, Cu	0.006 0	2.44
Gold, Au	0.000 000 4	11 666.53
Iron, Fe	5.6	0.03
Silver, Ag	0.000 007	154.97
Tin, Sn	0.000 2	6.22
Zinc, Zn	0.007	1.29

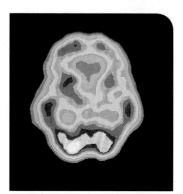

Figure 6 By using the radioactive isotope technetium-99, doctors are able to create brain scans, such as the one shown, that help confirm that a patient has a healthy brain.

Some elements are synthetic.

Technetium and promethium are two synthetic elements (elements made in a laboratory). They are both *radioactive*, which means the nuclei of their atoms are continually decaying to produce different elements. There are several isotopes of technetium. The most stable isotope is technetium-99, which has 56 neutrons. Technetium-99 was used to create the image shown in **Figure 6.** Doctors use scans such as this to diagnose cancer as well as other medical problems that occur in soft tissues of the body.

When looking at the periodic table, you might have wondered why part of the last two periods of the transition metals are placed toward the bottom. This arrangement keeps the periodic table narrow so that similar elements elsewhere in the table still line up. Promethium is one element found in this bottom-most area. Its most useful isotope is promethium-147, which is an ingredient in some glow-in-the-dark paints.

All elements that have atomic numbers greater than 92 are also synthetic and are similar to technetium and promethium. For example, americium, another element in the bottom-most area of the periodic table, is also radioactive. Tiny amounts of americium-241 are found in most household smoke detectors. Although even small amounts of radioactive material can affect you, americium-241 is safe when contained inside your smoke detector.

Why It **Matters**

Uses of Synthetic Elements Although a few synthetic elements have practical uses, many do not. The most common reason for this is that many synthetic elements have extremely short half-lives, sometimes measured in seconds. Explain that the half-life of a radioactive element is the amount of time it takes for half of the amount of the element present to break down into other elements. Have students find out about the recent history of some of the newly isolated elements, such as those whose atomic numbers are greater than 109. Students should present their findings to the class in an oral report. **LS Verbal**

READING TOOLBOX

Vocabulary Ask students what is meant by the common use of the term *decay.* (Student descriptions may include how plant and animal materials break down into other materials.) From this description, ask them to hypothesize what it means for an element to decay. (Student answers should indicate that these elements break down, forming other elements.) **LS Verbal**

Nonmetals

Except for hydrogen, nonmetals are found on the right side of the periodic table. Nonmetals include some elements in Groups 13–16 and all of the elements in Groups 17 and 18.

❯ **Families of nonmetals include the noble gases and the halogens.**

The noble gases are relatively inert.

Neon is one of the **noble gases** that make up Group 18 of the periodic table, as shown in **Figure 7.** Neon is responsible for the bright reddish orange light of neon signs. Mixing neon with other substances can change the color of a sign.

The noble gases are different from most elements that are gases because noble gases exist as single atoms instead of as molecules. Like other members of Group 18, neon is *inert,* or unreactive, because its s and p orbitals are filled. For this reason, neon and other noble gases do not gain or lose electrons to form ions. Also, under <u>normal</u> conditions, most noble gases do not join with other atoms to form compounds.

Helium and argon are other common noble gases. Helium is less dense than air and is used to give lift to blimps and balloons. Argon is used to fill light bulbs because its lack of reactivity prevents the bulbs' filaments from burning.

✔ **Reading Check** Why are the noble gases unreactive?

noble gas (NOH buhl GAS) one of the elements of Group 18 of the periodic table

Academic Vocabulary

normal (NAWR muhl) usual; typical

MISCONCEPTION ALERT

Nonmetals Some students believe that anything that is not a metal is classified as a nonmetal, such as sugar or wood. Remind students that the scientific definition of the term nonmetal refers only to elements. All elements are either metals or nonmetals, but no compounds are classified as nonmetals.

Teaching Key Ideas

Noble Nonmetals Have students look up the common definition of the word *noble* and discuss its meaning. Tell students that the noble gases were named for their "nobility" in keeping to themselves and not readily combining with other elements.

Why It **Matters**

Noble Gas Compounds Group 18 gases were always considered to be completely inert. However, in 1962, the first true Group 18 compound was formed from xenon. Currently, compounds of xenon, krypton, radon, and argon exist. More recently, chemists have made compounds between some of the noble gases and the elements uranium, fluorine, oxygen, and chlorine. Have students review by explaining to a partner why noble gases generally do not form compounds. **LS Interpersonal/Verbal**

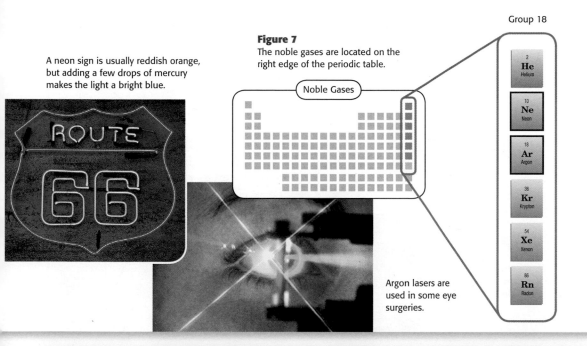

A neon sign is usually reddish orange, but adding a few drops of mercury makes the light a bright blue.

Figure 7
The noble gases are located on the right edge of the periodic table.

Noble Gases

Group 18

| 2 He Helium |
| 10 Ne Neon |
| 18 Ar Argon |
| 36 Kr Krypton |
| 54 Xe Xenon |
| 86 Rn Radon |

Argon lasers are used in some eye surgeries.

Differentiated Instruction

Special Education Students

Mixed Groups of Elements Give each student a periodic table with Groups 14, 15, and 16 blanked out. Groups 14–16 contain metals, nonmetals, and semiconductors. Give students an alphabetical list of the elements in the three groups. Have students fill in the empty spaces on the table, using crayons or pencils of three different colors to identify nonmetals, semiconductors, and metals. Have pairs of students quiz each other on classifying elements. **LS Interpersonal**

Advanced Learners

The First Noble Gas Argon was the first noble gas to be identified. Henry Cavendish proposed its existence in 1785 because he and other chemists could not account for all the major constituents of air. Argon makes up about 1 percent of air. It was not until 1894 that British chemists William Ramsay and Lord Raleigh identified it. Because of its chemical inertness, it was given the name *argon* from the Greek *argos,* which means "inactive." Have interested students find out more about the history of argon and present their findings in a written report. **LS Verbal**

Teaching Key Ideas

Halogens Point out to students that halogens all have the same number of valence electrons, seven. This configuration is one electron short of the complete octet found in the noble gas atoms. As a result, halogen elements react by gaining one electron to form ions with a 1– charge.

Integrating Earth Science

Elements in Seawater One common way that magnesium is recovered from seawater is by the use of electrolysis. Chloride ions release an electron to the anode of the electrolysis setup and free chlorine is formed. At the cathode, magnesium ions accept electrons and become metallic magnesium. Have students find out more about obtaining elements from seawater and present their findings in a poster. **LS Visual**

READING TOOLBOX

Vocabulary The term halogen comes from the roots *hal* (salt) and *gen* (to form), so halogen means "salt former." The root *hal* is also used in halite, or rock salt. *Gen* is a common root used in many words, including generate and generation. Explain that halogens were given this name because they form salts in compounds. Have students find examples of salts formed by halogens. (Sample answer: Examples include common table salt (NaCl) and silver salt (AgBr), used in photography.) **LS Verbal**

---

halogen (HAL oh juhn) one of the elements of Group 17 of the periodic table

Integrating **Earth Science**

Elements in Seawater Eighty-one elements—including magnesium and bromine—have been detected in seawater. To extract an element from a sample of seawater, you must evaporate some of the water in the sample. Evaporation causes sodium chloride (NaCl) to crystallize, which raises the concentration of bromide, magnesium, and other ions in the water that remains. The rise in concentration makes the extraction of the elements easier.

The halogens combine easily with metals to form salts.

Chlorine and other **halogens** belong to Group 17 of the periodic table, as **Figure 8** shows. The halogens are the most reactive nonmetals. Halogens have seven valence electrons. With the addition of a single electron, halogens become stable. For this reason, the halogens combine easily with alkali metals. Halogens can also combine with other metals. Compounds that result from such combinations are called *salts*.

You have probably noticed the strong smell of chlorine in swimming pools. Chlorine is widely used to kill bacteria in pools, as well as in drinking-water supplies. The chlorine in most swimming pools is added in the form of the compound calcium hypochlorite, $Ca(OCl)_2$. Elemental chlorine is a poisonous yellowish green gas made of pairs of joined chlorine atoms. A chlorine atom may gain an electron to form a negative chloride ion, Cl^-. The attraction between Na^+ ions and Cl^- ions forms sodium chloride, NaCl, which is table salt.

Fluorine, bromine, and iodine are also Group 17 elements. Fluorine is a poisonous yellowish gas, bromine is a dark red liquid, and iodine is a dark purple solid. Atoms of each of these elements can also form compounds by gaining an electron to become negative ions. A compound containing the negative fluoride ion, F^-, is used in some toothpastes and added to some water supplies to help prevent tooth decay. Adding a compound containing iodine in the form of the negative iodide ion, I^-, to table salt makes iodized salt. You need iodine in your diet for proper thyroid gland function.

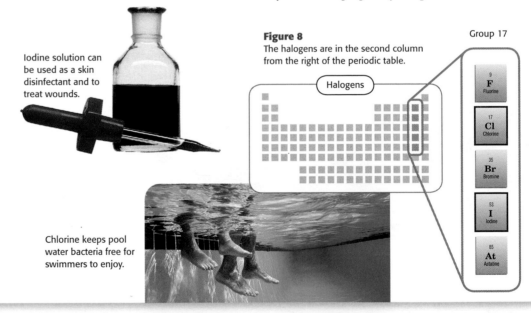

Iodine solution can be used as a skin disinfectant and to treat wounds.

Chlorine keeps pool water bacteria free for swimmers to enjoy.

Figure 8
The halogens are in the second column from the right of the periodic table.

Group 17

Halogens

| 9 **F** Fluorine |
| 17 **Cl** Chlorine |
| 35 **Br** Bromine |
| 53 **I** Iodine |
| 85 **At** Astatine |

Differentiated Instruction

Basic Learners

Chlorine Gas When certain cleaning agents are mixed together, toxic chlorine gas is released. The gas is quite hazardous to humans. This is one reason that different cleaning agents should never be mixed. Have students research some safety precautions to be used with chemical cleaning products and present their findings in an informative brochure. **LS Verbal**

Advanced Learners

Fluorine The halogen fluorine is the most reactive element known. Fluorine gas (F_2) is so reactive that it is hard to find containers to store it in; most metals burst into flames when they come in contact with it, and it attacks glass and quartz. A compound of fluorine and carbon is used to make Teflon, a nonstick coating commonly used in cookware. Have interested students find out more about useful compounds containing fluorine and present their findings in a written report. **LS Verbal**

Nonmetals and their compounds are plentiful on Earth.

In addition to the noble gases and the halogens, six other nonmetals are on the right side of the periodic table, as shown in **Figure 9.** Oxygen, nitrogen, and sulfur are common nonmetals. These three nonmetals may form compounds or may gain electrons to form negative ions. Oxygen forms oxide, O^{2-}, nitrogen forms nitride, N^{3-}, and sulfur forms sulfide, S^{2-}. The most plentiful gases in air are nitrogen and oxygen. Sulfur is an odorless yellow solid, but many sulfur compounds, such as those in rotten eggs and skunk spray, have a terrible smell.

Carbon can form many compounds.

In its pure state, carbon is usually found as graphite (pencil "lead") or as diamond. The existence of *fullerenes,* a third form of carbon, was confirmed in 1990. The most famous fullerene, a cluster of 60 carbon atoms, is called a *buckminsterfullerene.* It resembles a geodesic dome, which is a structure designed by the American engineer and inventor R. Buckminster Fuller.

Carbon can also combine with other elements to form millions of carbon-containing compounds. Carbon compounds are found in both living and nonliving things. Glucose, $C_6H_{12}O_6$, is a sugar in your blood. A type of chlorophyll, $C_{55}H_{72}O_5N_4Mg$, is found in all green plants. Many gasolines contain isooctane, C_8H_{18}, and rubber tires are made of large molecules that have many repeating C_5H_8 units.

✓ Reading Check What are some examples of carbon compounds?

Sulfur is a solid yellow powder at room temperature. Sulfur is found in meteorites, volcanoes, and hot springs.

READING TOOLBOX

Spider Maps
Create a spider map for element families that has one leg for each family. To each leg, add examples of the family and a description of the family's shared properties.

READING TOOLBOX

Spider Maps Students may wish to use colored highlighters to compare the types of properties displayed in each family. For example, they could use yellow to represent reactivity and pink to represent conductivity.

READING TOOLBOX

Visual Literacy One reason carbon has so many forms and can form so many compounds is that it has the ability to bond to up to four other carbon atoms. Carbon's ability to bond to itself is called *catenation.* Have students note the differences in properties of the two forms of carbon that are shown in **Figure 9.** In addition to diamond, graphite, and fullerenes, which are described in the text, carbon also exists as charcoal and amorphous carbon, which has no crystalline form.
LS Visual

Why It Matters

Organic Chemistry Organic chemistry is the study of carbon-containing compounds, called organic compounds. Carbon atoms have the ability to form molecule chains thousands of atoms long. There are over six million organic compounds, including all types of foods (carbohydrates, lipids, and proteins), plastics, synthetic and natural fibers, and petroleum products. Have students look through a chemistry textbook to find images of molecular models of organic compounds.

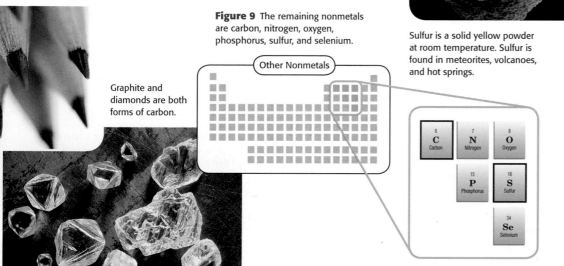

Figure 9 The remaining nonmetals are carbon, nitrogen, oxygen, phosphorus, sulfur, and selenium.

Graphite and diamonds are both forms of carbon.

Other Nonmetals

6 C Carbon	7 N Nitrogen	8 O Oxygen
15 P Phosphorus	16 S Sulfur	
	34 Se Selenium	

Why It Matters

Silicon Microchip Have students look at the image in the chapter opener of a colorized scanning electron micrograph (SEM) of a silicon microchip. Explain that silicon is a semiconductor, which means that it has properties similar to both metals and nonmetals. When combined (doped) with other elements, the thin tracks of silicon shown in the picture form microcircuits that conduct electricity. Silicon microchips are covered in an article at the end of this chapter.

Teaching Key Ideas

Semiconductor Greeting This activity requires several musical greeting cards and hand lenses (at least one of each per student group). Play the greeting cards, then divide students into groups. Let each group of students take their card apart and examine the mechanism. Tell students that semiconductors play a part in the mechanism. Ask each group to answer the following questions: What parts of the mechanism can you recognize? (Answers may vary, but students will probably locate the speaker.) What do you think a semiconductor is? (Answers might include that it conducts electricity but not as well as a metal does.) **LS** Interpersonal/Kinesthetic

Reteaching Key Ideas

Periodic Flashcards Have students make illustrated flashcards for the following groups of elements: alkali metals, alkaline-earth metals, halogens, noble gases, and transition metals. On each flashcard, have them list the group numbers associated with the group of elements, three properties shared by the elements in that group, and a picture that represents at least one element in that group. Then, have pairs of students quiz each other on the groups using their flashcards.
LS **Interpersonal**

Formative Assessment

Which group of elements is the most stable (rather than being reactive)?

A. Group 1: alkali metals (Incorrect. The alkali metals are the most reactive metals.)

B. Group 2: alkaline-earth metals (Incorrect. Most alkaline-earth metals readily react to give up two electrons.)

C. Group 17: halogens (Incorrect. The halogens are the most reactive nonmetals.)

D. Group 18: noble gases (Correct. Due to the complete set of 8 valence electrons, noble gases are relatively inert.)

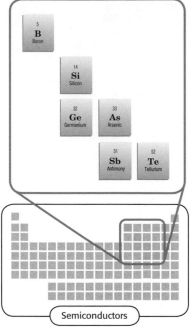

Figure 10
Semiconductors are located toward the right side of the periodic table.

Semiconductors

The six elements sometimes referred to as *semiconductors* or *metalloids* are shown in **Figure 10.** Although these elements are not metals, they have some properties of metals. ❯ **As their name suggests, semiconductors are elements that are able to conduct heat and electricity under certain conditions.**

Silicon atoms, usually in the form of compounds, account for 28% of the mass of Earth's crust. Sand is made of the most common silicon compound, called silicon dioxide, SiO_2. Small chips made of silicon are used in the parts of computers and other electronic devices.

Boron is an extremely hard element. It is often added to steel to increase steel's hardness and strength at high temperatures. Compounds of boron are often used to make heat-resistant glass. Arsenic is a shiny solid that tarnishes when exposed to air. Antimony is a bluish white, brittle solid that also shines like a metal. Some compounds of antimony are used as fire retardants. Tellurium is a silvery white solid whose ability to conduct increases slightly with exposure to light.

Hydrogen is in a class by itself.

Hydrogen, which has just one proton and one electron, does not behave like any of the other elements. As a result, hydrogen is in a class by itself in the periodic table. Hydrogen is the most abundant element in the universe. About three out of every four atoms in the universe are hydrogen atoms, mostly in the form of clouds of gas and stars. With its one electron, hydrogen can react with many other elements, including oxygen. The compound water, H_2O, is essential to life and is present in all living organisms.

Section 3 Review

KEY IDEAS

1. **Classify** the following elements as alkali, alkaline-earth, or transition metals based on their positions in the periodic table:
   a. iron, Fe
   b. potassium, K
   c. strontium, Sr
   d. platinum, Pt
2. **Describe** why chemists might sometimes store reactive chemicals in argon, Ar. To which family does argon belong?
3. **Describe** why atoms of bromine, Br, are very reactive. To which family does bromine belong?
4. **Identify** which element is more reactive: lithium, Li, or beryllium, Be.

CRITICAL THINKING

5. **Creative Thinking** Imagine that you are a scientist who is analyzing an unknown element. You have confirmed that the element is a metal, but you do not know which kind of metal it is: an alkali metal, an alkaline-earth metal, or a transition metal. Write a paragraph describing the additional tests that you can do to further classify this metal.

Answers to Section Review

1. **a.** transition metal
   b. alkali metal
   c. alkaline-earth metal
   d. transition metal
2. Reactive chemicals might react with oxygen or water vapor in the air. They will not react with argon because it is inert. Argon is a noble gas.
3. A bromine atom is one electron short of a complete valence energy level and will react with an element that can supply that electron. Bromine is a halogen.
4. Lithium is an alkali metal and is more reactive than an alkaline-earth metal such as beryllium.
5. Answers may vary, but one method is to check the reactivity of the metal against the reactivities of other alkali, alkaline-earth, and transition metals. The element belongs to the family that is most similar to the element chemically.

How Are Silicon Chips Made?

REAL WORLD

Silicon is an important component of semiconductor chips, which are used in computers, cell phones, and many other electronic devices. Each silicon chip is a tiny electronic circuit. Impurities such as boron, aluminum, phosphorus, and arsenic are added to the silicon to increase its ability to conduct electricity.

The most sophisticated chips, called *microprocessors*, can execute hundreds of millions of instructions per second. The chip-making process involves hundreds of steps. Some of the main steps are shown below.

1 First, pure silicon is melted down in a crucible. A large crystal cylinder of silicon is extracted, and thin discs called *wafers* are cut from it. The wafers are then ground, polished, and cleaned.

2 Materials are precisely added to, removed from, and shaped on the wafer through chemical and photographic processes. These processes create a complex set of layers, as shown in this side view. These layers make up the circuitry of a chip.

3 Silicon chips are made in the world's cleanest environment: clean rooms. Air in these clean rooms is highly filtered, and workers must wear clean-room suits, sometimes called "bunny suits."

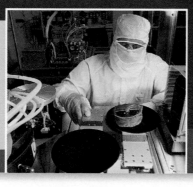

4 Several microprocessors are created from a single wafer. When the wafer is finished, the circuitry of each microprocessor is tested. Then, the wafer is cut with a diamond saw. The final result is a computer chip like this one.

YOUR TURN

UNDERSTANDING CONCEPTS

1. Why are impurities such as boron added to the silicon?

CRITICAL THINKING

2. Why must semiconductor chips be made in clean rooms?

SCiLINKS.

www.scilinks.org
Topic: Silicon
Code: HK81393

How Are Silicon Chips Made? The conductivity of semiconductors increases when certain impurities are added to them. This process is called *doping*. The most common doping process involves adding small amounts of arsenic or gallium to silicon. Because these elements contain different numbers of valence electrons, electrons flow more easily and conductivity increases.

Have students use the Internet, the library, or a high school chemistry textbook to find out more about silicon doping and how it allows silicon to conduct electricity. Have them present their findings in an illustrated poster display. **LS Visual**

Answers to Your Turn

1. The impurities increase silicon's ability to conduct electricity.
2. Unwanted impurities introduced in an unclean environment can affect the conductivity of the silicon chips.

Teacher's Notes

Have students identify periods and groups on the modified periodic table template. This will help them with the analysis and conclusion questions.

Also note that although the radius shrinks and grows along with the atomic number, it also changes as electronic subshells fill. This change is not linear.

Time Required

1 lab period

Lab Ratings

EASY ———————————➤ HARD

Teacher Prep ⚗
Student Set-Up ⚗
Concept Level ⚗⚗
Clean Up ⚗

Skills Acquired

- Communicating
- Identifying/Recognizing patterns
- Interpreting
- Measuring
- Organizing and analyzing data
- Predicting

Scientific Methods

In this lab, students will:
- Make observations
- Analyze the results
- Draw conclusions
- Communicate results

⏱ 50 min

What You'll Do:

❯ **Form a hypothesis** describing how the radius of an atom depends on the atomic number of that atom.

❯ **Graph** atomic radius as a function of atomic number on regular graph paper (data provided).

❯ **Create** a three-dimensional model of the periodic trend in the radius of atoms using the well tray, straws and the modified periodic table template.

What You'll Need

marker, permanent, fine point
paper, graph
ruler, metric
scissors
straws, 1/4 in. outer diameter (25)
well tray, transparent, 96-hole

Safety

Exploring Periodic Trends

Many element properties vary predictably according to the position of the element in the periodic table. In this lab, you will make a model that represents the periodic trends in the atomic radii of the elements.

Asking a Question

How do the atomic radii of the elements vary with atomic number?

Forming and Testing a Hypothesis

❶ Hypothesize about how atomic radius varies with atomic number.

Performing Your Experiment

❷ Using the data in the table below, graph the atomic radius (in picometers, pm; 1 pm = 10^{-12} m) versus atomic number on a sheet of graph paper. Use a ruler to help you scale the graph. Choose a scale for the largest radius that is less than the length of one straw.

Atomic Radii of the First 40 Elements

Atomic number	Element	Atomic radius (pm)	Atomic number	Element	Atomic radius (pm)
1	H	37	21	Sc	162
2	He	50	22	Ti	147
3	Li	152	23	V	134
4	Be	111	24	Cr	130
5	B	88	25	Mn	135
6	C	77	26	Fe	126
7	N	70	27	Co	125
8	O	66	28	Ni	124
9	F	64	29	Cu	128
10	Ne	70	30	Zn	138
11	Na	186	31	Ga	122
12	Mg	160	32	Ge	122
13	Al	143	33	As	121
14	Si	117	34	Se	117
15	P	110	35	Br	114
16	S	104	36	Kr	109
17	Cl	99	37	Rb	244
18	Ar	94	38	Sr	215
19	K	231	39	Y	178
20	Ca	197	40	Zr	160

3 Cut a straw to represent each element where the length of the straw represents the atomic radius of the element. To do this, place one end of the straw on the graph at the value of the radius plotted for that element and cut the straw where it crosses the graph's x-axis. (**Hint:** First, cut straws for the elements whose radii are largest, and then use the straw scraps for the elements that have smaller radii. This will allow you to represent 40 elements with just 25 straws.) With a fine point marker, label each straw with the element symbol.

4 Place the transparent well tray on top of the modified periodic table template below and insert each straw into the well that is over the symbol of the element that the straw represents.

H 1																	He 2
Li 3	Be 4											B 5	C 6	N 7	O 8	F 9	Ne 10
Na 11	Mg 12											Al 13	Si 14	P 15	S 16	Cl 17	Ar 18
K 19	Ca 20											Ga 31	Ge 32	As 33	Se 34	Br 35	Kr 36
Rb 37	Sr 38																
		Sc 21	Ti 22	V 23	Cr 24	Mn 25	Fe 26	Co 27	Ni 28	Cu 29	Zn 30						
		Y 39	Zr 40														

Analysis

1. **Analyzing Methods** What trends in atomic radius are more visible in the three-dimensional model that you built with straws than they are in the two-dimensional graph that you drew?

Communicating Your Results

2. **Drawing Conclusions** Does the model that you built confirm your hypothesis? Explain why or why not.

Extension

As you move down a group on the periodic table, each successive element has one more filled main energy level than the previous element has. Which trend that your model showed does this explain?

Tips and Tricks

The periodic trends for atomic radius can be observed once the regular graph of atomic radius is plotted; however, a very dramatic three-dimensional histogram results when the activity is complete. For a permanent display of the periodic trend of the atomic radius, have students put a little glue on the end of the straw before inserting it into the well tray.

Be sure students recognize both trends that the three-dimensional model illustrates: (1) atomic radius increases as you move down a group and (2) atomic radius decreases as you move across a period. The physical cause of this first trend is explored in the extension question. Students may also want to know the physical cause of the second trend. Explain that as you move across a period, the atoms gain protons and electrons, but the electrons are added to the same energy level. The positive charge of the nuclei increases as the number of protons increases. As a result, the nuclei attract the electrons with a greater force. Thus, the electrons are pulled closer to the nuclei. This reduces the size of the atoms.

Answer to Analysis

1. Trends among elements of the same group are more obvious on the three-dimensional model than on the two-dimensional graph.

Answer to Communicating Your Results

2. Sample answer: My hypothesis that atomic radius increases with atomic number was confirmed as a general trend by the model. The model showed that as you move down a group, the atomic radius increases. However, I did not expect the atomic radius to decrease across each period.

Answer to Extension

The addition of another level of electrons increases the atom's atomic radius. This is why the atomic radius increases as you move down a group.

Key Resources

 Virtual Investigation

 Classroom Lab Video/DVD

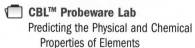 Holt Lab Generator CD-ROM
Search for any lab by type, standard, difficulty level, or time. Edit any lab to fit your needs, or create your own labs. Use the Lab Materials QuickList software to customize your lab materials list.

 Differentiated Datasheets
Exploring Periodic Trends

CBL™ Probeware Lab
Predicting the Physical and Chemical Properties of Elements

Reading Web Addresses When using the World Wide Web to do research, students may have difficulty judging when they can trust the information provided by an online source. Point out that, in general, *edu* and *gov* Web sites provide reliable information. However, remind students that they may produce their own Web sites for a school project, and these could have *edu* suffixes. As with reputable academic print sources, writers of reliable Web sites include links or references to their information sources. These references can help students judge whether the information provided can be trusted, and they also provide additional sources for information. Have students choose a topic for research and locate one trustworthy source and one less trustworthy source on the World Wide Web. Then, have students explain how they formed their judgment. **LS Logical**

Answers to Practice

1. a. The server name is *www.smithsonianeducation.org.*
b. The top-level domain is *org,* which tells me that the Web site is run by a non-profit organization.
c. This is a Web page written in hypertext markup language because the file's extension is *html.*

2. a. This Web site is run by the United States government.
b. The file is called CollegePlanGuide_WEB1, and it is a *pdf* document.

Reading Web Addresses

Technology

Math
Scientific Methods
Graphing

The World Wide Web is one of the most frequently used parts of the Internet. Every page on the Web has a unique address, called a *uniform resource locator* (URL). A URL locates a certain file.

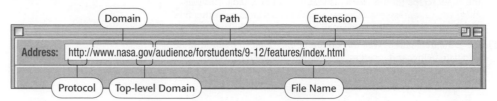

❶ Protocol The protocol tells you what method is used to transfer the information between computers on the Internet.

- The protocol for most Web pages is **http,** which stands for *hypertext transfer protocol.*
- The *file transfer protocol,* or **ftp,** is used for downloading files.

❷ Domain The domain specifies the computer or server on the Internet that contains the Web site. The domain often tells you the name of the company, organization, or institution that owns the Web site.

- The last part of the domain, called the *top-level domain,* is the broadest level of organization. Top-level domains include
  - **.com** (commercial sites)
  - **.net** (Internet service providers)
  - **.org** (nonprofit organizations)
  - **.edu** (educational institutions)
  - **.gov** (the U.S. government)

❸ Path The path specifies the file's location on the server.

- The path consists of directory and subdirectory names that are separated by one or more forward slashes (/).

❹ File Name and Extension The file name identifies the file, and the extension tells you the file type. If no file name is specified, most servers will look for index.html, default.html, or home.html.

- The extensions **html** and **htm** indicate that a Web page is written in HTML, which stands for *hypertext markup language.*
- Image files may have the extensions **jpg** or **gif.**
- Documents often have the extensions **pdf, doc,** or **txt.**
- Files with the extension **exe** are executable files that can install software, some of which may be unwanted, on your computer.

Practice

1. Consider the following Web address:
http://www.smithsonianeducation.org/students/index.html
  a. What is the server name?
  b. What does the top-level domain tell you about the Web site?
  c. What kind of file is this? How do you know?

2. Consider the following Web address:
http://www.science.doe.gov/feature/WFD/CollegePlanGuide_WEB1.pdf
  a. What does the top-level domain tell you about the Web site?
  b. What is the name of this file, and what type of file is it?

SUMMARY

Key Ideas

Key Terms

Section 1 Organizing the Elements

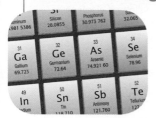

> **Recognizing a Pattern** Mendeleev arranged elements in rows by increasing atomic mass. He started a new row each time the chemical properties of the elements repeated. (p. 145)

> **Changing the Arrangement** The modern periodic table organizes elements by atomic number. When the elements are arranged in this way, elements with similar properties appear at regular intervals. (p. 147)

periodic law, p. 147
period, p. 150
group, p. 150

Section 2 Exploring the Periodic Table

> **The Role of Electrons** The periodic trends in the periodic table are the result of electron arrangement. (p. 151)

> **Ion Formation** If an atom gains or loses electrons, it no longer has an equal number of electrons and protons. Because the charges do not cancel completely, the atom—now called an ion—has a net electric charge. (p. 153)

> **How Are Elements Classified?** All elements are metals, nonmetals, or semiconductors. (p. 154)

ion, p. 153
metal, p. 154
nonmetal, p. 154
semiconductor, p. 154

Section 3 Families of Elements

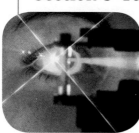

> **Classifying Elements Further** Elements can be grouped into families. The elements in each family have the same number of valence electrons. As a result, they have similar chemical properties. (p. 156)

> **Metals** Families of metals include the alkali metals, the alkaline-earth metals, and the transition metals. (p. 157)

> **Nonmetals** Families of nonmetals include the noble gases and the halogens. Other nonmetals are carbon, nitrogen, oxygen, phosphorus, sulfur, and selenium. (p. 161)

> **Semiconductors** As their name suggests, semiconductors are able to conduct heat and electricity under certain conditions. (p. 164)

alkali metal, p. 157
alkaline-earth metal, p. 158
transition metal, p. 159
noble gas, p. 161
halogen, p. 162

SUPER SUMMARY

Have students connect the major concepts in this chapter through an interactive Super Summary. Visit **go.hrw.com** and type in the keyword **HK8PTAS** to access the Super Summary for this chapter.

Differentiated Instruction

Alternative Assessment

Mapping the Periodic Table Provide students with colored pencils and a blank periodic table with no symbols on it. Have them label and draw color-coded circles around the regions of the periodic table that contains metals, nonmetals, and metalloids. Then have them label and draw circles around the following groups: alkali metals, alkaline-earth metals, halogens, noble gases, and transition metals. Finally, have them write within or next to each circle a brief list of the properties and electron configurations shared by the elements enclosed by each circle. **LS Visual**

Key Resources

⊞ **Interactive Concept Map**

▢ **Review Resources**
Concept Review Worksheets

▢ **Assessment Resources**
Chapter Tests A and B
Performance-Based Assessment

REVIEW

Reading Toolbox

1. Answers may vary. Sample answer: *Semi-* is an appropriate prefix because semiconductors are somewhat—but not entirely—like metals, which are conductors of heat and electricity.

Using Key Terms

2. a. An atom is the smallest unit of an element, and a molecule consists of two or more atoms.

b. A neutral atom has no net charge. An ion is a charged atom or molecule.

c. A cation has a positive charge, and an anion has a negative charge.

3. Answers may vary. Students may cite the following transition metals: gold, silver, platinum, copper, nickel, and zinc. Transition metals are often used in wiring, jewelry, and as conductors of heat and electricity.

4. All halogens have the same number of valence electrons (7) and similar chemical properties.

5. Semiconductors deserve their name because, under certain conditions, they can conduct heat or electricity the way that metals can.

6. Alkali metals are highly reactive, metallic elements. Alkaline-earth metals are less reactive. Alkali metals such as sodium are found in compounds such as sodium chloride. Alkaline-earth metals such as calcium are often found in limestone and other strong building materials and in the human body.

Understanding Key Ideas

7. a

8. c

9. b

10. b

11. c

Explaining Key Ideas

12. Magnesium has two valence electrons. To achieve a full outermost energy level, it will lose both electrons, forming Mg^{2+}.

1. Prefixes The prefix *semi-* means "half," "partially," or "somewhat." Explain why this prefix is appropriate for the term *semiconductor*.

USING KEY TERMS

2. Compare the following terms:
a. an *atom* and a *molecule*
b. an *atom* and an *ion*
c. a *cation* and an *anion*

3. List several familiar *transition metals* and their uses.

4. How is the *periodic law* demonstrated in the halogens?

5. Explain why the name *semiconductors* makes sense.

6. Distinguish between *alkali metals* and *alkaline-earth metals,* and give several examples of how they are used.

UNDERSTANDING KEY IDEAS

7. How did Mendeleev arrange atoms in the periodic table?
a. by atomic mass
b. by atomic number
c. by the number of electrons
d. by the number of neutrons

8. Which statement about atoms of elements in a group of the periodic table is true?
a. They have the same number of protons.
b. They have the same mass number.
c. They have similar chemical properties.
d. They have the same total number of electrons.

9. The majority of elements in the periodic table are
a. nonmetals.
b. conductors.
c. synthetic.
d. noble gases.

10. An atom of which of the following elements is unlikely to form a positively charged ion?
a. potassium, K
b. selenium, Se
c. barium, Ba
d. silver, Ag

11. Which of the following statements about krypton is not true?
a. Krypton's molar mass is 83.798 g/mol.
b. Krypton's atomic number is 36.
c. Krypton forms ions that have a 1+ charge.
d. Krypton is a noble gas.

EXPLAINING KEY IDEAS

12. Explain why magnesium forms ions that have the formula Mg^{2+}, not Mg^+ or Mg^-.

13. Why did Mendeleev leave a few gaps in his periodic table? What eventually happened to these gaps?

14. Compare the meanings of *period* and *group,* in terms of the periodic table.

INTERPRETING GRAPHICS The figure below shows a sodium atom and a chlorine atom. Use the figure to answer questions 15 and 16.

Neutral sodium atom   Neutral chlorine atom

15. What types of ions will sodium and chlorine each form? Explain.

16. Sodium ions bond with chlorine ions to form table salt, NaCl. Explain why one sodium ion bonds with one chlorine ion.

CRITICAL THINKING

17. Forming Hypotheses Why was Mendeleev unable to make any predictions about the noble gas elements?

18. Identifying Relationships When an element whose nucleus has 115 protons is synthesized, which type of element will it be: a metal, a nonmetal, or a metalloid? Explain your answer.

19. Making Comparisons How is the periodic table like a calendar?

20. Applying Concepts Your classmate offers to give you a piece of sodium that he found on a hiking trip. What is your response? Explain.

21. Making Inferences Identify each element described below.
   a. This metal is very reactive, has properties similar to those of magnesium, and is in the same period as bromine.
   b. This nonmetal is in the same group as lead.

22. Evaluating Data The figure shows relative sizes of ionic radii for ions of elements in Period 2 on the periodic table. Why do the negative ions have larger radii than the positive ions do?

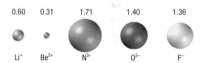

| 0.60 | 0.31 | 1.71 | 1.40 | 1.36 |
| Li^+ | Be^{2+} | N^{3-} | O^{2-} | F^- |

23. Analyzing Information You can keep your bones healthy by eating 1,200 to 1,500 mg of calcium a day. Use the table below to make a list of the foods that you might eat in a day to satisfy your body's need for calcium. How does your typical diet compare with your list?

Item, serving size	Calcium (mg)
Plain lowfat yogurt, 1 cup	415
Ricotta cheese, 1/2 cup	337
Skim milk, 1 cup	302
Cheddar cheese, 1 ounce	213
Cooked spinach, 1/2 cup	106
Vanilla ice cream, 1/2 cup	88

24. Problem Solving Suppose that the following alterations are made to poisonous chlorine gas. How will the identity and properties of the chlorine change in each case?
   a. A proton is added to each atom.
   b. An electron is added to each atom.
   c. A neutron is added to each atom.

25. Applying Knowledge You read a science fiction story about an alien race of silicon-based life-forms. Use the periodic table to hypothesize why the story's author chose silicon over other elements. (**Hint:** Life on Earth is carbon based.)

Graphing Skills

26. Interpreting Graphs The pie chart shows the elements in the Earth's crust. Examine the chart, and then answer the questions.
   a. What is the most abundant element in Earth's crust?
   b. Excluding the category *Other,* what percentage of Earth's crust is alkali metals, and what percentage is alkaline-earth metals?

Elements in Earth's Crust

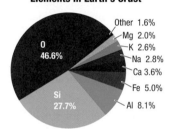

Other 1.6%
Mg 2.0%
K 2.6%
Na 2.8%
Ca 3.6%
Fe 5.0%
Al 8.1%
O 46.6%
Si 27.7%

27. Constructing Graphs Use a graphing calculator, a computer spreadsheet, or a graphing program to plot the atomic number on the *x*-axis and the average atomic mass in u on the *y*-axis for the transition metals in Period 4 (from scandium to zinc). Does the graph show a trend? Is there a break in the trend near cobalt? Explain why elements that have larger atomic numbers do not necessarily have larger atomic masses.

---

25. Silicon is in the same group as carbon, which is the basis of life forms on Earth. Thus, silicon could potentially be a life-forming element in alien environments.

Graphing Skills
26. a. oxygen

   b. 5.4% (sodium and potassium); 5.6% (magnesium and calcium)

27. Graphs should show increasing atomic mass with increasing atomic number, with one exception. The atomic number of Ni is higher than that of Co, but the atomic mass is less. Ni has more protons than Co does, but Co has more neutrons.

---

13. Mendeleev left gaps for elements whose existence he predicted based on the periodic arrangement of the elements. The gaps were filled in when the elements were discovered.

14. A period in the periodic table is a row of elements. A group is a column of elements.

15. Sodium atoms will form positive ions by losing one electron, and chlorine atoms will form negative ions by gaining one electron.

16. Sodium and chlorine bond together because the single electron from sodium's outer shell fills the outer shell of chlorine.

Critical Thinking

17. Mendeleev could make predictions only where there were gaps in his table. Because no noble gases were known at the time, there were no obvious gaps in the table and no way that he could have known that a whole column was missing.

18. Metal; it will be located below the metal bismuth.

19. Both are periodic. The periodic table has repeating properties of elements. The calendar has repeating days and months.

20. I would tell my classmate that he didn't find sodium. Sodium is very reactive and cannot be found uncombined in nature.

21. a. calcium
   b. carbon

22. All atoms in a period have the same number of electron energy levels. When an atom in that period becomes a positive ion, it loses that outer level and becomes smaller. An atom that becomes a negative ion keeps the outer level and becomes larger.

23. Answers may vary. Any combination of the listed foods that has a total of 1200–1500 mg Ca is acceptable.

24. a. Each atom would gain a positive charge and become an Ar ion. Ar is a noble gas.
   b. Each atom would form the negative chloride ion, Cl^-.
   c. Each atom would gain mass, forming a different isotope.

Assignment Guide

Section	Items
1	2, 7, 8, 13, 14, 17, 19
2	1, 5, 9, 10, 12, 15, 16, 18, 22, 24, 27
3	3, 4, 6, 11, 20, 21, 23, 25, 26

Standardized Test Prep

 TEST DOCTOR

Question 1 Answer C is correct. Other answers indicate that students do not know that the outer electron shells of noble gases are completely full.

Question 2 Answer H is correct. Students might answer F if they believed the + represented an extra neutron, G if they did not know that changing the number of electrons means the ion is no longer neutral, or I if they believed the + represented two joined lithium atoms.

Question 3 Answer A is correct. None of the other answers are relevant to the placement of elements on the periodic table.

Question 4 Answer G is correct. Students might answer F if they thought that carbon and sulfur had the same number of valence electrons, H if they thought that both columns and rows indicated extra valence electrons, or I if they thought all elements had exactly two fewer valence electrons than their atomic number (as carbon happens to).

Question 5 Full-credit answers should include the following points:
• Elements in Group 1 have exactly one valence electron.
• When an orbital only has one valence electron, that electron is easily shared with any element with a partially filled electron orbital, so it easily reacts.

Question 6 Full-credit answers should include the following points:
• The atomic number would be 118.
• Ununoctium would be a noble gas in the far right column of the periodic table.
• It would be nonreactive because all of its orbitals would be filled.

Question 7 Full-credit answers should include the following points:
• Semiconductors, or metalloids, are nonmetals with some of the properties of metals.
• Semiconductors are between the metals and the nonmetals on the periodic table.

Standardized Test Prep

Understanding Concepts

Directions (1–4): **For each question, write on a sheet of paper the letter of the correct answer.**

1. What group of elements is the least reactive?
   A. halogens   **C.** noble gases
   B. alkali metals   **D.** semiconductors

2. What does the symbol Li^+ represent?
   F. a lithium isotope
   G. a lithium atom
   H. a lithium ion
   I. a lithium molecule

3. What information about an element is most crucial for locating that element in the periodic table?
   A. the element's atomic number
   B. the element's electric charge
   C. the element's most common isotope
   D. the number of orbitals the element has

4. Carbon, whose atomic number is 6, has four valence electrons. Sulfur's atomic number is 16, and sulfur is located two columns to the right of carbon and one row down on the periodic table. How many valence electrons does sulfur have?
   F. 4   **H.** 7
   G. 6   **I.** 14

Directions (5–7): **For each question, write a short response.**

5. Why are the elements in Group 1 the most reactive?

6. If the element ununoctium is ever synthesized, it will be located directly under radon, xenon and krypton on the periodic table. What would ununoctium's atomic number be? Predict ununoctium's properties.

7. What group of elements has some properties of metals and some properties of nonmetals? How does the periodic table reflect this fact?

Reading Skills

Directions (8–10): **Read the passage below. Then, answer the questions that follow.**

MENDELEEV'S DISCOVERY

On March 6, 1869, Mendeleev made a formal presentation to introduce his new periodic table. He explained that elements that have similar chemical properties either have atomic masses that are nearly the same value (as have Os, Ir, and Pt) or have atomic masses that increase regularly (as have K, Rb, and Cs). Arranging the elements in rows, within which they are in order of their atomic masses, creates columns corresponding to electron valences. The elements whose particles are the most widely diffused—gases—have small atomic masses. Mendeleev told scientists that they should expect the discovery of some new elements. Two of the elements whose existence he predicted are gallium and germanium. Based on their location in the periodic table (directly below aluminum and silicon), he accurately predicted their atomic masses to be between 65 and 75.

8. Based on the passage, what does the word *diffused* mean?
   A. close together   **C.** a high temperature
   B. spread apart   **D.** a low temperature

9. What is one of the widely diffused elements Mendeleev was likely referring to in his presentation?
   F. bromine   **H.** helium
   G. iodine   **I.** uranium

10. When Mendeleev predicted the existence of the elements gallium and germanium, he temporarily named these elements *ekaaluminum* and *ekasilicon*. What does the prefix *eka-* mean, in terms of the layout of the periodic table?

Question 8 Answer B is correct; other answers indicate that students do not know that gas particles are spread far apart from one another compared to liquids and solids.

Question 9 Answer H is correct; other answers indicate that students do not know that hydrogen and helium have the lowest atomic numbers.

Question 10 Full-credit answers should include the following points:
• The elements predicted by Mendeleev are located just below aluminum and silicon in the same columns.

• The "eka-" prefix indicates these elements share properties with aluminum and silicon but have higher atomic numbers.

Question 11 Answer D is correct. Other answers indicate that students either do not know that valence electrons are those located in an atoms outermost shell or that they have not counted correctly.

Question 12 Answer G is correct. Students might answer F if they thought that only protons contributed to the mass of elements, or H or I if they were confusing the number of atoms in a mole with the mass in grams of a mole.

Interpreting Graphics

The graphic below shows the bonding of sodium and chlorine to form sodium chloride, NaCl. Use this graphic to answer questions 11–12.

SODIUM CHLORIDE

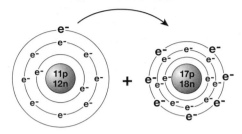

11. How many total valence electrons do the two atoms have?

A. 0

B. 1

C. 7

D. 8

12. What is the mass of one mole of NaCl molecules?

F. 28 g

G. 58 g

H. 1.68×10^{25} g

I. 3.49×10^{25} g

The graphic below shows the upper right segment of the periodic table. Use this graphic to answer questions 13–15.

SEGMENT OF THE PERIODIC TABLE

					18
					2 He 4.00
13	14	15	16	17	
5 B 10.81	6 C 12.01	7 N 14.01	8 O 16.00	9 F 19.00	10 Ne 20.18
13 Al 26.98	14 Si 28.09	15 P 30.97	16 S 32.06	17 Cl 35.45	18 Ar 39.95

13. Which pair of elements would most likely have a similar arrangement of outer electrons and have similar chemical behaviors?

A. boron and aluminum

B. helium and fluorine

C. carbon and nitrogen

D. chlorine and oxygen

14. What is the atomic mass of helium?

15. How many neutrons does the average helium atom contain?

Test Tip

For multiple-choice questions, try to eliminate any answer choices that are obviously incorrect, and then consider the remaining answer choices.

Answers

1. C
2. H
3. A
4. G
5. Answers may vary; see Test Doctor for a detailed scoring rubric.
6. Answers may vary; see Test Doctor for a detailed scoring rubric.
7. Answers may vary; see Test Doctor for a detailed scoring rubric.
8. B
9. H
10. Answers may vary; see Test Doctor for a detailed scoring rubric.
11. D
12. G
13. A
14. 4.00 u
15. 2 neutrons

Question 13 Answer A is correct. Other answers indicate that students do not understand that only elements within the same group have similar arrangements of outer electrons and therefore similar chemical behavior.

Question 14 For helium, He, the atomic mass given is 4.00 u. Atomic mass is located below the element symbol in this segment of the periodic table.

Question 15 The number of neutrons for an atom is approximately the atomic mass less the atomic number. For helium, He, the number of neutrons is $4.00 - 2 = 2$.

State Resources

For specific resources for your state, visit **go.hrw.com** and type in the keyword **HSHSTR**.

📖 **Test Practice with Guided Reading Development**

The Structure of Matter

	Standards	Teach Key Ideas

CHAPTER OPENER, pp. 174–176 — *50 min.*

SECTION 1 Compounds and Molecules, pp. 177–182 — *50 min.*
> Chemical Bonds
> Chemical Structure
> How Does Structure Affect Properties?

Standards: PS 2c, PS 2d, PS 2e, UCP 2, UCP 5

Teach Key Ideas:
- 🖳 **Bellringer Transparency**
- 🖳 **Teaching Transparency** C13 Water Bonding
- 💿 **Visual Concepts** Compounds • Chemical Bond • Bond Length • Bond Angle

---

SECTION 2 Ionic and Covalent Bonding, pp. 183–190 — *50 min.*
> Why Do Chemical Bonds Form?
> Ionic Bonds
> Covalent Bonds
> Metallic Bonds
> Polyatomic Ions

Standards: PS 2a, PS 2c, PS 2d, UCP 2, UCP 5, SAI 1

Teach Key Ideas:
- 🖳 **Bellringer Transparency**
- 🖳 **Teaching Transparencies** C14 Multiple Bonds • TM18 Polyatomic Anions
- 💿 **Visual Concepts** Ionic Bonding • Metallic Bonding • Covalent Bonding • Naming Compounds Containing Polyatomic Ions • Comparing Polar and Nonpolar Covalent Bonds

---

SECTION 3 Compound Names and Formulas, pp. 191–196 — *50 min.*
> Naming Ionic Compounds
> Naming Covalent Compounds
> Empirical Formulas

Standards: UCP 1, UCP 2, SAI 2

Teach Key Ideas:
- 🖳 **Bellringer Transparency**
- 🖳 **Teaching Transparencies** TM19 Common Cations • TM20 Common Anions • TM21 Naming Prefixes
- 💿 **Visual Concepts** Naming Ionic Compounds • Naming Covalently-Bonded Compounds • Comparing Molecular and Empirical Formulas

---

SECTION 4 Organic and Biochemical Compounds, pp. 197–204 — *50 min.*
> Organic Compounds
> Polymers
> Biochemical Compounds

Standards: PS 2d, PS 2f, PS 3a, UCP 2, UCP 5, SAI 1, ST 2

Teach Key Ideas:
- 🖳 **Bellringer Transparency**
- 🖳 **Teaching Transparency** C15 Six-Carbon Alkanes
- 💿 **Visual Concepts** Organic Compound • Hydrocarbon • Alkane • Alcohol • Naming Alcohols • Polymers • Carbohydrates • Proteins • Amino Acid • DNA Overview

---

See also PowerPoint® Resources

Chapter Review and Assessment Resources

SE Science Skills: Understanding Symbols, p. 208
SE Chapter Summary, p. 209
SE Chapter Review, pp. 210–211
SE Standardized Test Prep, pp. 212–213
🗀 Concept Review Worksheets ■
🗀 Chapter Tests A and B ■
📶 Holt Online Assessment

CHAPTER
FastTrack
To shorten instruction because of time limitations, omit Section 3 and the chapter lab.

Basic Learners
TE Interpreting Visuals, p. 178
TE Making Models, p. 179
TE Growing Salt Crystals, p. 181
TE Transition Metals, p. 192
TE Common Names, p. 194
TE Identifying Prefixes, p. 203
🗀 Science Skills Worksheets
🗀 Differentiated Datasheets A for Labs and Activities ■
📓 Study Guide A ■

Advanced Learners
TE Lewis Structures, p. 186
TE Nitrogen Fixation, p. 189
TE Creating Brochures, p. 199
TE Sugar Substitutes, p. 200
🗀 Cross-Disciplinary Worksheets
🗀 Differentiated Datasheets C for Labs and Activities ■

Key

SE Student Edition
TE Teacher's Edition

📁 Chapter Resource File
📄 Workbook
🎬 Transparency

💿 CD or CD-ROM
* Datasheet or blackline master available

■ Also available in Spanish

All resources listed below are also available on the Teacher's One-Stop Planner.

Why It Matters	Hands-On	Skills Development	Assessment
Build student motivation with resources about high-interest applications.	**SE Inquiry Lab** Melting Sugar and Salt, p. 175 *■	**TE Reading Toolbox** Assessing Prior Knowledge, p. 174 **SE Reading Toolbox** p. 176	📁 **Pretest** ■
SE How Is Clay Molded? p. 179 📁 **Cross-Disciplinary Worksheet** Connection to Fine Arts—What Happens in a Kiln?	**TE Demonstration** What Are Compounds? p. 177 **TE Demonstration** Forming Compounds, p. 178	**SE Reading Toolbox** Always, Sometimes, or Never? p. 180 **TE Science Skills** Modeling Network Structures, p. 180 **TE Reading Toolbox** Vocabulary, p. 181	**TE Reteaching Key Ideas** Forces in Molecules, p. 182 **TE Formative Assessment,** p. 182 📁 **Spanish Assessment** *■ 📁 **Section Quiz** ■
TE Table Salt, p. 184 📁 **Cross-Disciplinary Worksheets** Connection to Social Studies—Linus Pauling: A Life Well Spent • Integrating Space Science—Ion Propulsion in *Deep Space I*	**TE Demonstration** Modeling Molecules, p. 183 **SE Quick Lab** A Close-Packed Structure, p. 188 *■	**TE Science Skills** Modeling Double and Triple Bonds, p. 186 **SE Reading Toolbox** Always, Sometimes, or Never? p. 187 **TE Reading Toolbox** Vocabulary, p. 189	**TE Reteaching Key Ideas** Bonding, p. 190 **TE Formative Assessment,** p. 190 📁 **Spanish Assessment** *■ 📁 **Section Quiz** ■
	TE Demonstration Balancing Charges, p. 191 📁 **CBL™ Probeware Lab** Determining Which Household Solutions Conduct Electricity	**SE Math Skills** Writing Ionic Formulas, p. 193 **SE Reading Toolbox** Suffixes, p. 195 **SE Math Skills** Finding Empirical Formulas, p. 196	**TE Reteaching Key Ideas** Formulas of Covalent Compounds, p. 196 **TE Formative Assessment,** p. 196 📁 **Spanish Assessment** *■ 📁 **Section Quiz** ■
SE How Do Gas Grills Work? p. 198 **TE Substitutions,** p. 200 **TE Distinguishing Fibers,** p. 201 **SE DNA Fingerprinting,** p. 205 📁 **Cross-Disciplinary Worksheets** Connection to Engineering—Fractions of Crude Oil • Integrating Environmental Science—Plastics • Integrating Mathematics—Amino Acid Combinations	**TE Demonstration** Combustion of Organic Compounds, p. 197 **SE Quick Lab** Polymer Memory, p. 201 *■ **SE Application Lab** Comparing Polymers, pp. 206–207 *■	**TE Science Skills** Graphic Organizer, p. 199 **TE Science Skills** Interpreting Diagrams, p. 199 **SE Reading Toolbox** Layered Book, p. 202	**TE Reteaching Key Ideas** Organic Molecule Flashcards, p. 204 **TE Formative Assessment,** p. 204 📁 **Spanish Assessment** *■ 📁 **Section Quiz** ■

See also Lab Generator

See also Holt Online Assessment Resources

Resources for Differentiated Instruction

English Learners
TE Three-Dimensional Models, p. 187
TE Suffixes, p. 192
TE Prefixes, p. 195
📁 Differentiated Datasheets A, B, and C for Labs and Activities ■
📄 Study Guide A ■

Struggling Readers
TE Examples, p. 188
TE Reading Skills, p. 202
📄 Interactive Reader

Special Education Students
TE Poster Project, p. 180
TE Reactive Atoms, p. 185
TE Paper Backbones and Bonds, p. 198
TE Practical Polymers, p. 201

Alternative Assessment
TE Different Chemical Structures, p. 209

Overview

This chapter introduces chemical bonding in compounds, and discusses the use of models to visually represent compounds and the relationship between chemical structure and properties. The chapter also explores the differences between ionic, covalent, and metallic bonds. Formulas and naming conventions for both ionic and covalent compounds are discussed. Finally, the concepts of the chapter are applied to a study of organic and biochemical compounds.

READING TOOLBOX

Assessing Prior Knowledge Students should understand the following concepts:
- elements and compounds
- chemical and physical properties
- atomic structure
- periodic table
- families of elements
- metals and nonmetals
- ions
- atomic mass
- molar mass

**MISCONCEPTION /// ALERT **

Science education research has identified the following misconceptions about the structure of matter.
- Students fail to distinguish between mixtures and compounds and do not recognize that a compound is a new substance rather than a mixture of the elements that compose it. (When two elements are mixed, they can be separated by physical processes. When elements form a compound, they can be separated only by chemical processes.)
- Students confuse molecules and compounds. (A molecule is a group of atoms that are held together by covalent bonds. Compounds that form from ionic bonds, such as sodium chloride, do not consist of molecules.)

CHAPTER 6 The Structure of Matter

Chapter Outline

❶ Compounds and Molecules
Chemical Bonds
Chemical Structure
How Does Structure Affect Properties?

❷ Ionic and Covalent Bonding
Why Do Chemical Bonds Form?
Ionic Bonds
Covalent Bonds
Metallic Bonds
Polyatomic Ions

❸ Compound Names and Formulas
Naming Ionic Compounds
Naming Covalent Compounds
Empirical Formulas

❹ Organic and Biochemical Compounds
Organic Compounds
Polymers
Biochemical Compounds

Why It Matters

All properties of matter depend on the structure of the elements and compounds that make up matter. The patterns in this diamond crystal come from the bonding patterns of its carbon atoms.

Chapter Correlations   *National Science Education Standards*

The following correlations show the National Science Standards that relate to this chapter. For the full text of the standards, see the National Science Education Standards at the front of the book.

PS 2a Atoms interact with one another by transferring or sharing electrons that are furthest from the nucleus. (Section 2)

PS 2c Bonds between atoms are created when electrons are paired up by being transferred or shared. The atoms may be bonded together into molecules or crystalline solids. A compound is formed when two or more kinds of atoms bind together chemically. (Sections 1, 2)

PS 2d The physical properties of compounds reflect the nature of the interactions among its molecules. These interactions are determined by the structure of the molecule, including the constituent atoms and the distances and angles between them. (Sections 1, 2, 4)

PS 2e Solids, liquids, and gases differ in the distances and angles between molecules or atoms and therefore the energy that binds them together. In solids the structure is nearly rigid; in liquids molecules or atoms move around each other but

do not move apart; and in gases molecules or atoms move almost independently of each other and are mostly far apart. (Section 1)

PS 2f Carbon atoms can bond to one another in chains, rings, and branching networks to form a variety of structures, including synthetic polymers, oils, and the large molecules essential to life. (Section 4)

PS 3a Complex chemical reactions involving carbon-based molecules take place constantly in every cell in our bodies. (Section 4)

UCP1 Systems, order, and organization (Section 3)

UCP 2 Evidence, models, and explanation (Sections 1–4)

UCP 5 Form and function (Sections 1, 2, 4)

SAI 1 Abilities necessary to do scientific inquiry (Sections 2, 4; Application Lab: Comparing Polymers)

SAI 2 Understandings about scientific inquiry (Section 3)

ST 2 Understandings about science and technology (Section 4)

InquiryLab ⏱ 20 min

Melting Sugar and Salt

Sugar and salt are both white, granular substances. You know they taste different, but are their other properties different? Make a hypothesis about whether sugar or salt will melt more easily.

To test your hypothesis, place **1 mL of sugar** in a **test tube.** Use **tongs** to position the test tube over a **Bunsen burner** flame, as shown below. **CAUTION:** Tie back long hair and confine loose clothing. Use tongs and heat-resistant gloves to handle hot glassware. When heating a test tube, always point the open end of the test tube away from yourself and others.

Move the test tube back and forth slowly over the flame. Use a **stopwatch** to measure the time it takes for the sugar to melt. If the sample does not melt within 1 min, remove it from the flame. Next, place **1 mL of salt** in a test tube. Repeat the steps that you followed for the sugar.

Questions to Get You Started

1. Which compound melts more easily? Was your hypothesis right?

2. How can you relate your results to the structure of each compound?

InquiryLab

Teacher's Notes Have test tube racks available so students can place hot test tubes in the racks until the test tubes cool. Remind students that all factors except what is in the test tube should be constant. Be sure students heat the sugar only until it melts. If it burns, the test tube will be difficult to clean.

Materials per Group
• 2 test tubes
• tongs
• salt
• sugar
• Bunsen burner
• stopwatch

Answers

1. Sample answer: Sugar melts more easily than salt does. Because I hypothesized that salt would melt more easily than sugar would, my hypothesis is incorrect.

2. Sample answer: My results indicate that the chemical bonds of salt are stronger than the bonds in sugar.

Key Resources

📁 **Datasheet**
Melting Sugar and Salt

💿 **Interactive Tutor**
Disc One, Module 4: Chemical Bonding

Word Parts

Answers may vary. The three words from Section 2 are *ionic* (ion; pertaining to ions), *metallic* (metal; pertaining to metal), and polyatomic (poly + atom; having many atoms). Examples of other words and their related nouns include *conic* (cone), *comic* (comedy), *chaotic* (chaos), *periodic* (period), *tragic* (tragedy), *circular* (circle), *linear* (line), and *planar* (plane).

Frequency

Answers may vary. Students should list generalizations from the text. For the generalizations, students should list words or phrases that signal the generalization.

FoldNotes

Answers may vary. Students' layered books should look similar to the example shown and should contain notes about the material in the chapter.

These reading tools can help you learn the material in this chapter. For more information on how to use these and other tools, see **Appendix A.**

Word Parts

Suffixes The suffix *-ic* usually changes a noun to an adjective and adds the meaning "pertaining to" or "having characteristics of" to that noun. For example, *periodic* is an adjective formed from the noun *period*. It means "pertaining to a period." The suffixes *-al* and *-ar* affect a noun in much the same way. When you see a word that uses one of these suffixes, look at the noun at the root of the word. It can help you understand the word's meaning.

Your Turn In Section 2, there are three key terms that contain words with the suffix *-ic*. For each of these words, write the word, the noun the word is related to, and the word's definition. Then, do the same for three more words that you can think of that have the suffixes *-ic* or *-ar*. The example below is for the word *molecular*, which is in the key term *molecular formula* in Section 3.

WORD	RELATED NOUN	DEFINITION OF WORD
molecular	molecule	pertaining to molecules

Frequency

Always, Sometimes, or Never? Many statements include a word that tells you how often that statement is true. Examples include words such as *always, sometimes,* and *never*. Words such as *some, many,* and *most* tell you about frequency in number.

Your Turn As you read this chapter, make a list of statements that contain frequency words. For each statement in your list, underline the word or phrase that tells how frequently the statement is true. An example is given at right.

Frequency Statement: A compound is <u>always</u> made of the same elements in the same proportions.

FoldNotes

Layered Book FoldNotes are a fun way to help you learn and remember ideas that you encounter as you read.

Your Turn As you read the chapter, make a layered book, as described in **Appendix A.** Label the tabs of the layered book with "Chemical Bonding," "Naming Compounds," and "Organic Molecules." Write notes on the appropriate layer as you read the chapter.

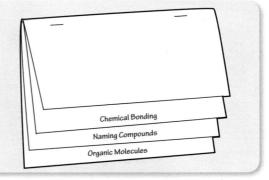

Compounds and Molecules

SECTION **1**

Key **Ideas**

> What holds a compound together?

> How can the structure of chemical compounds be shown?

> What determines the properties of a compound?

Key **Terms**

chemical bond

chemical structure

bond length

bond angle

Why It **Matters**

Understanding the structure of compounds can help you understand changes in matter, such as in molding clay.

If you step on a sharp rock with your bare foot, your foot will hurt. It hurts because rocks are hard substances. Many rocks are made of quartz. Table salt and sugar are both grainy, white solids. But they taste very different. Quartz, salt, and sugar are all compounds that are solids. Their similarities and differences partly come from the way their atoms or ions are joined.

Chemical Bonds

A compound is made of two or more elements that are chemically combined. **> The forces that hold atoms or ions together in a compound are called chemical bonds. Figure 1** shows that when a mixture of hydrogen gas and oxygen gas is heated, a fiery chemical reaction takes place. Chemical bonds are broken, and atoms are rearranged. New chemical bonds form water, a compound that has properties very different from the properties of the original gases.

chemical bond (KEM i kuhl BAHND) the attractive force that holds atoms or ions together

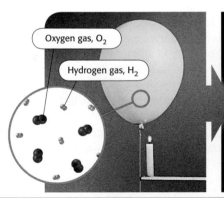
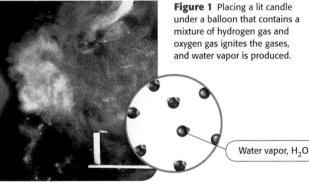

Oxygen gas, O$_2$

Hydrogen gas, H$_2$

Water vapor, H$_2$O

Figure 1 Placing a lit candle under a balloon that contains a mixture of hydrogen gas and oxygen gas ignites the gases, and water vapor is produced.

SECTION 1

❯ **Focus**

In this section, students learn that the atoms in a compound are bonded together chemically, and they learn how chemical bonds and structures are described and modeled. The section also explores how chemical structure affects the properties of compounds.

🔊 **Bellringer**

Use the Bellringer transparency to prepare students for this section.

Demonstrate

What Are Compounds? Have students list uses of the term *compound.* (Sample answers: compound sentences, chemical compounds, compound fracture, and compound interest rates.) Ask students to describe what the items on their lists have in common. Students should recognize that the definition of the word *compound* relates that more than one thing is involved.
LS Verbal

Key Resources

 Teaching Transparency
C13 Water Bonding

 Visual Concepts
Compounds
Chemical Bond
Bond Length
Bond Angle

 Cross-Disciplinary Worksheet
Connection to Fine Arts—What Happens in a Kiln?

Teaching Key Ideas

Structural Formulas Structural formulas are especially important in organic chemistry because many organic compounds have the same chemical formula but different structures. Compounds that have the same chemical formula but different structures are called *isomers*. Isomers are common in organic chemistry because carbon is able to form many different kinds of chemical bonds. The more carbon atoms in a molecule, the more isomers of that molecule there can be. For example, C_8H_{18} has 18 isomers, $C_{20}H_{42}$ has 366,319 isomers, and $C_{40}H_{82}$ has approximately 6.25×10^{13} isomers!

Demonstrate

Forming Compounds For a dramatic example of the formation of a compound, you can use the following demonstration. **Safety Caution:** This reaction gives off toxic fumes and heat. Do this demonstration outdoors or in a fume hood only. Wear safety goggles, protective gloves, and a lab apron. Students should stand at least 10 ft from the demonstration. Measure out 3 g of powdered zinc and 2 g of iodine crystals. Place them in a test tube. Stopper the tube and shake it to mix the elements. Attach the clamp to the ring stand, then clamp the test tube upright. Remove the stopper. Measure 1 mL of water and add it to the test tube. Have students observe the reaction. The shiny zinc metal and the dark purple iodine crystals will react vigorously, forming a black solid, zinc iodide.

Academic Vocabulary

structure (STRUHK chuhr) the arrangement of the parts of a whole

chemical structure (KEM i kuhl STRUHK chuhr) the arrangement of atoms in a substance

bond length (BAHND LENGKTH) the average distance between the nuclei of two bonded atoms

bond angle (BAHND ANG guhl) the angle formed by two bonds to the same atom

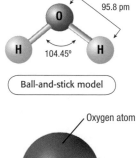

Ball-and-stick model

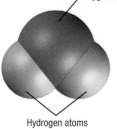

Oxygen atom

Hydrogen atoms

Space-filling model

Figure 2 The ball-and-stick model (top) shows the bond angle in a molecule of H_2O. A picometer (pm) is equal to 1×10^{-12} m. The space-filling model of water (bottom) shows that each hydrogen atom takes up less space than the oxygen atom.

Chemical Structure

Water's chemical formula tells us what atoms make up water, but it does not tell us anything about the way the atoms are connected. The structure of a building is the way the building's parts fit together. Similarly, a compound's **chemical structure** is the way the compound's atoms are bonded to make the compound. **❯ Just as the structure of buildings can be represented by blueprints, the structure of chemical compounds can be shown by various models. Different models show different aspects of compounds.**

Some models represent bond lengths and angles.

In the ball-and-stick model of water shown in **Figure 2**, the atoms are represented by balls. The bonds that hold the atoms together are represented by sticks. Although bonds between atoms are not as rigid as sticks, this model makes it easy to see the bonds and the angles they form in a compound.

Two terms are used to specify the positions of atoms in relation to one another in a compound. **Bond length** is the distance between the nuclei of two bonded atoms. When a compound has three or more atoms, a **bond angle,** the angle formed by two bonds to the same atom, tells which way these atoms point. A ball-and-stick model helps you understand a compound's structure by showing you how the atoms or ions are arranged in the compound. In **Figure 2,** you can see that the way hydrogen and oxygen atoms bond to form water looks more like a boomerang than a straight line.

Structural formulas can also show the structures of compounds. Notice that water's structural formula, shown here, is a lot like water's ball-and-stick model. But in the structural formula, chemical symbols are used to represent the atoms.

Structural formula

Space-filling models show the space occupied by atoms.

Another way that chemists represent a water molecule is shown in **Figure 2.** The model below the ball-and-stick model is called a *space-filling model* because it shows the space that the oxygen and hydrogen atoms take up, or fill. A space-filling model shows the relative sizes of atoms in a compound, but not bond lengths.

✔ Reading Check Name an advantage to each model: the ball-and-stick model and the space-filling model. (See Appendix E for answers to Reading Checks.)

MISCONCEPTION ALERT

Chemical Structures Students might think that when the same elements are present in a compound, the compounds are the same. Provide them with examples in which the same elements form different compounds. For example, both carbon dioxide, CO_2, and carbon monoxide, CO, contain carbon and oxygen molecules, but they are not the same compound. Carbon dioxide always has one carbon atom and two oxygen atoms in each molecule. On the other hand, carbon monoxide molecules always have one atom of carbon and one atom of oxygen.

Differentiated Instruction

Basic Learners

Interpreting Visuals Ask students to speculate why space-filling models, such as the model in **Figure 2,** look so different from structural formulas and from ball-and-stick models. Point out that the shape of the space-filling models represents the best estimation of the way the molecule would actually appear (but without the colors) if it could be seen. Students should not get the impression that atoms are balls at the ends of sticks. **LS Visual**

How Is Clay Molded?

Clay has a layered structure of silicon, oxygen, aluminum, and hydrogen atoms. Artists can mold wet clay into any shape because water molecules hold the clay together loosely, which allows layers of clay to slide over one another. After the artist has gotten the clay into just the right shape, a series of chemical changes have to be made to clay for it to harden. These changes to the chemical structure of the clay molecules make the molded clay into something durable and useful.

When clay dries, the water molecules that had kept the clay soft evaporate and leave the clay dry and crumbly. This is one step in finishing a clay pot, but you wouldn't want a crumbly pot!

The last step in making a clay pot is to fire it in a kiln. Heating the clay causes bonds to form between the molecules of the clay, which makes the pot hard so that you can use it.

YOUR TURN

UNDERSTANDING CONCEPTS

1. Name two other substances that can be shaped when they are wet and then set when they are dried or heated.

2. Suggest what happens to these substances when they dry and set.

How Is Clay Molded? Ensure that students realize the distinction between materials in which chemical bonds form when they dry and those materials that just dry. Have students think about each of their examples and answer the following question: "Will the dried material return to its original state if the original solvent were added to it, indicating that the change was not chemical?" (Sample answers: Yes, so the material probably just dried and did not change chemically. No, the clay in fired pottery has a different chemical structure after drying, so it won't return to its original state.) Concrete is another example of a material that changes its chemical structure as it dries.
LS Verbal/Logical

Answers to Your Turn

1. Sample answer: paint and glue
2. Answers may vary. Answers should mention the fact that the bonding changes within a substance as it sets.

Bonds can bend, stretch, and rotate without breaking.

Some chemical bonds are stronger than others. But bonds themselves are not really like the sticks in a ball-and-stick model. If the ball-and-stick model was more accurate, bonds would be represented by flexible springs, as **Figure 3** shows. Bonds can bend, stretch, and rotate without breaking. The atoms can move back and forth a little, and their nuclei do not always stay the same distance apart. In fact, most reported bond lengths are average distances. Although bonds are not rigid, they hold atoms together tightly.

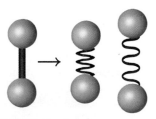

Figure 3 Chemists often use a solid bar to show a bond between two atoms, but bonds are actually flexible, like springs.

Differentiated Instruction

Basic Learners

Making Models Discuss with students other examples of how something can be represented in more than one way. In music, sounds can be represented as single notes on a staff or as letters that represent groups of notes called *chords*. In math, multiplication can be represented by several different symbols: a multiplication cross, a dot, parentheses, or just two symbols written side by side. Emphasize to students that molecules can be represented in many different ways as well. **LS** Musical/Logical

Science Skills

Interpreting Visuals Have students examine **Figure 3.** Ask students why chemists use a solid bar to represent atomic bonds, even though the bonds are actually flexible like springs. (The model on the left is simpler to draw and use, and can serve the same purpose of representing the structure of a compound and the bonds that make it up.) Remind students that, while models often represent things simply and quickly, it is important to keep in mind their limitations. **LS** Logical

Teaching Key Ideas

Structure and Properties Have students think of things that are made of wood, such as a box, house, or toy. Discuss the differences in the properties of the wooden objects. Ask students: "How can things made of wood be so different?" (The properties of the object depend on the type of wood, the size and shape of the pieces of wood, and how the pieces are arranged and assembled.) Tell students that the properties of a chemical compound depend on its structure: the type and number of atoms and how they are arranged.
LS **Verbal/Logical**

Science Skills

Modeling Network Structures Have students work in small groups. Provide students with gumdrops of two different colors and toothpicks. You can also use ball-and-stick model kits. Have students model two network solids—quartz and a one-to-one ionic solid, such as potassium bromide. Tell students to start the quartz model by making a tetrahedron of four oxygen atoms that surround a silicon atom in the center. Then, students should expand this basic unit until it shows the pattern of a network solid. The ionic solid should have alternating colors representing positive and negative ions in several layers. Challenge students to create a model of a network ionic solid in which the ions are in a 2:1 ratio.
Safety Caution: Never eat anything in a laboratory.
LS **Kinesthetic/Interpersonal**

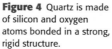

sci LINKS.
www.scilinks.org
Topic: Structures of Substances
Code: HK81470

READING TOOLBOX

Always, Sometimes, or Never?
As you read this section, make a list of frequency statements that describe the structure of various kinds of chemical compounds.

How Does Structure Affect Properties?

Some compounds, such as the quartz found in many rocks, form a large network of bonded atoms. Other compounds, such as table salt, are also large networks but are made of bonded positive and negative ions. Still other compounds, such as water and sugar, are made of many separate molecules. ❯**The chemical structure of a compound determines the properties of that compound.**

Compounds with network structures are strong solids.

Quartz is sometimes found in the form of beautiful crystals, as **Figure 4** shows. Quartz is made of silicon dioxide, SiO_2. Every silicon atom in quartz is bonded to four oxygen atoms. The bonds that hold these atoms together are very strong. All of the Si–O–Si and O–Si–O bond angles are the same—109.5°. This arrangement is the same everywhere in silicon dioxide and holds the silicon and oxygen atoms together in a strong, rigid structure.

The chemical structure of the silicon dioxide determines the properties of the quartz. Silicon dioxide has a very rigid structure, so rocks that contain quartz are hard and inflexible solids. It takes a lot of energy to break the strong bonds between silicon and oxygen atoms in quartz. The strong bonds also make the melting point and boiling point of quartz and other minerals very high, as the table in **Figure 4** shows.

✔ **Reading Check** How is the hardness of minerals explained by minerals' chemical structure?

Figure 4 Quartz is made of silicon and oxygen atoms bonded in a strong, rigid structure.

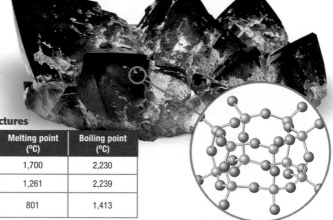

Some Compounds with Network Structures

Compound	State (at 25 °C)	Melting point (°C)	Boiling point (°C)
Silicon dioxide, SiO_2 (quartz)	solid	1,700	2,230
Magnesium fluoride, MgF_2	solid	1,261	2,239
Sodium chloride, NaCl (table salt)	solid	801	1,413

READING TOOLBOX

Always, Sometimes, or Never? Many statements include a word that tells how often something occurs. Words such as *generally, some, most,* and *usually* are examples that indicate frequency.

Differentiated Instruction

Special Education Students

Poster Project Provide students with reference material about table sugar from journals, books, or the Internet. Ask students to make a poster of the structural formula of a table sugar molecule, labeling each element and how many atoms of each element are found in the molecule. Have students explain why structural models are important. **LS** **Visual/Kinesthetic**

Some networks are made of bonded ions.

Table salt—sodium chloride—is found in the form of regularly shaped crystals. Crystals of sodium chloride are cube shaped. Sodium chloride is made of a repeating network connected by strong bonds. The network is made of tightly packed, positively charged sodium ions and negatively charged chloride ions, as **Figure 5** shows. The strong attractions between the oppositely charged ions give table salt and other similar compounds high melting points and high boiling points.

Some compounds are made of molecules.

Salt and sugar are both white solids that you can eat, but their structures are very different. Unlike salt, sugar is made of molecules. A molecule of sugar, as **Figure 6** shows, is made of carbon, hydrogen, and oxygen atoms that are joined by bonds. Molecules of sugar attract each other to form crystals. But these attractions are much weaker than the attractions that bond carbon, hydrogen, and oxygen atoms to make a sugar molecule.

We breathe nitrogen, N_2, oxygen, O_2, and carbon dioxide, CO_2, every day. All three substances are gases that you cannot see or smell, and are made of molecules. Within each molecule, the atoms are so strongly attracted to one another that they are bonded. But the molecules of each gas have very little attraction to one another. Because the molecules of these gases have weak attractions to one another, they spread out. Thus, gases can take up a lot of space.

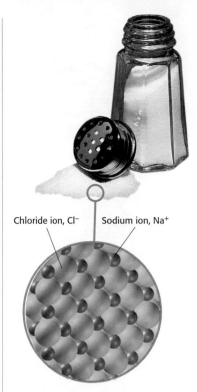

Chloride ion, Cl⁻   Sodium ion, Na⁺

Figure 5 Each grain of table salt, or sodium chloride, is made of a tightly packed network of Na⁺ ions and Cl⁻ ions.

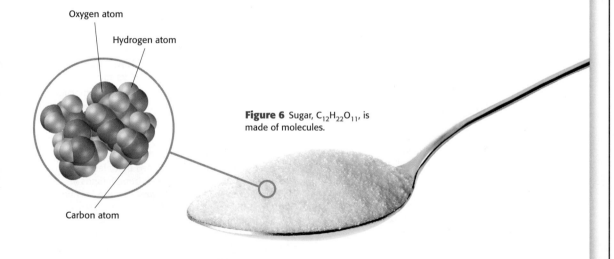

Oxygen atom

Hydrogen atom

Carbon atom

Figure 6 Sugar, $C_{12}H_{22}O_{11}$, is made of molecules.

Science Skills

Interpreting Visuals Sometimes, a crystal of a network solid reveals the pattern made by the ions in the solid. Have students use a hand lens to examine some granulated salt and compare what they see with the network structure shown in **Figure 5.** Students should see that the salt granules are cubic, as is the arrangement of its ions. **LS Visual**

READING TOOLBOX

Vocabulary Ask students to describe what they think of when they hear the term *network.* (Students likely will mention television networks or networked computers.) Help students recognize that a network takes many individual parts and joins them as a unit. Another name for a network solid is a *macromolecule.* **LS Verbal**

MISCONCEPTION ALERT

States of Matter Students might think that a compound is, by nature, either a solid, a liquid, or a gas. Emphasize that most substances can be in any state, depending on temperature and sometimes pressure. Explain that when a substance is classified as a solid, a liquid, or a gas, and no temperature is mentioned, the temperature is usually room temperature. Ask students to investigate various compounds, such as water, methane, and sugar. Have them identify the melting point and boiling point for the substances they study. **LS Logical**

Differentiated Instruction

Basic Learners

Growing Salt Crystals Have students use library or Internet resources to find out how to grow salt crystals. This can be done with basic materials in the home, over a period of a few days. Tell students that they can add food coloring to water to make salt crystals of different colors. Students can also try the same process with sugar, baking soda, and cream of tartar. Have students bring their crystals to class so everyone can observe them. Have students use a magnifying glass to observe the crystal structure in more detail. **LS Kinesthetic/Visual**

Reteaching Key Ideas

Forces in Molecules Molecules are affected by both intermolecular and intramolecular forces. Intramolecular forces are forces within the molecule, or chemical bonds. Intermolecular forces are forces between molecules, such as the attraction between the positive part of one molecule and the negative part of another molecule. Adding energy can break both types of attractions but, in general, much more energy is required to break intramolecular forces. Ask students to describe each of these forces in their own words.

Formative Assessment

Which of the following can give you the most information about a compound's properties?

A. type of chemical bonds (Incorrect. Chemical bonds are part of the structure of a compound but you need more information to determine all of the compound's properties.)

B. a list of its component elements (Incorrect. The list of elements does not tell you all of the properties of the compound because very different compounds can be made of the same elements. You also need to know how atoms are arranged.)

C. chemical structure (Correct. The chemical structure includes the number and types of atoms and how they are arranged.)

D. bond angle (Incorrect. Bond angles are part of the structural information but they are not enough information to determine all of the properties of the compound.)

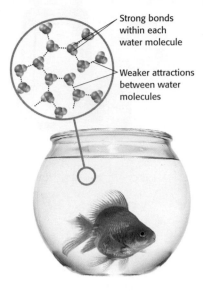

Strong bonds within each water molecule

Weaker attractions between water molecules

Figure 7 Water is a liquid at room temperature because of the attractions between water molecules.

Some Molecular Compounds

Compound	State (at 25 °C)	Melting point (°C)	Boiling point (°C)
Sugar, $C_{12}H_{22}O_{11}$	solid	185–186	–
Water, H_2O	liquid	0	100
Dihydrogen sulfide, H_2S	gas	−86	−61

The strength of attractions between molecules varies.

Compare sugar, water, and dihydrogen sulfide, H_2S, in the table in **Figure 7.** Although all three compounds are made of molecules, their properties are very different. Sugar is a solid, water is a liquid, and dihydrogen sulfide is a gas. Thus, sugar molecules have a stronger attraction for each other than water molecules do. And dihydrogen sulfide molecules have weaker attractions for each other than sugar or water molecules do. The fact that sugar and water have such different properties probably does not surprise you. Their chemical structures are not at all alike. But think about water and dihydrogen sulfide, which have similar chemical structures.

Because water has higher melting and boiling points than dihydrogen sulfide, we know that water molecules attract each other more than dihydrogen sulfide molecules do. **Figure 7** shows an oxygen atom of a water molecule attracted to a hydrogen atom of a nearby water molecule. This attraction is called a *hydrogen bond*. Water molecules attract each other, but these attractions are not as strong as the bonds holding oxygen and hydrogen atoms together within a molecule.

Section 1 Review

KEY IDEAS

1. **Classify** the following substances as mixtures or compounds:
   a. air **c.** SnF_2
   b. CO **d.** pure water

2. **Draw** a ball-and-stick model of a boron trifluoride, BF_3, molecule. In this molecule, a boron atom is attached to three fluorine atoms. Each F–B–F bond angle is 120°, and all B–F bonds are the same length.

3. **Explain** why silver iodide, AgI, a compound used in photography, has a much higher melting point than vanillin, $C_8H_8O_3$, a sweet-smelling compound used in flavorings.

4. **Explain** why glass, which is made of mostly SiO_2, is often used to make cookware. (**Hint:** What properties does SiO_2 have because of its structure?)

5. **Predict** which molecules have a greater attraction for each other: C_3H_8O molecules in liquid rubbing alcohol or CH_4 molecules in methane gas.

CRITICAL THINKING

6. **Analyzing Relationships** A picometer (pm) is equal to 1×10^{-12} m. The O–H bond lengths in water are 95.8 pm, while S–H bond lengths in dihydrogen sulfide are 135 pm. Why are S–H bonds longer than O–H bonds? (**Hint:** Which is larger: a sulfur atom or an oxygen atom?)

Answers to Section Review

1. **a.** mixture
   b. compound
   c. compound
   d. compound

2. Student drawings should show a boron atom surrounded by three equally spaced fluorine atoms in the same plane. A line from each fluorine atom to the boron atom represents a bond. Lines should be of equal length.

3. Sample answer: Silver iodide has a network structure of positive and negative ions. Vanillin consists of molecules. The attraction between particles in silver iodide is much stronger than the attraction between particles in vanillin.

4. Sample answer: SiO_2 has a network structure, resulting in a high melting point. So, it does not melt when heated to high cooking temperatures.

5. Sample answer: Molecules in a liquid, such as C_3H_8O, have a greater attraction for each other because they are closer together and are moving more slowly than the molecules in a gas, such as CH_4.

6. Sample answer: Sulfur atoms are larger than oxygen atoms by one electron energy level. The valence electrons of sulfur are farther from the nucleus, so the nucleus-to-nucleus distance is greater in molecules that contain sulfur than it is in molecules that contain oxygen.

Ionic and Covalent Bonding

Key Ideas

> Why do atoms form bonds?

> How do ionic bonds form?

> What do atoms joined by covalent bonds share?

> What gives metals their distinctive properties?

> How are polyatomic ions similar to other ions?

Key Terms

ionic bond

covalent bond

metallic bond

polyatomic ion

Why It Matters

Chemical structure explains matter's properties, such as why metals like copper conduct electricity.

In many of the models that you have seen so far, the bonds that hold atoms together are represented by sticks. But what bonds atoms in a real molecule?

Why Do Chemical Bonds Form?

Atoms bond when their valence electrons interact. You have learned that atoms with full outermost *s* and *p* orbitals are more stable than atoms with only partly filled outer *s* and *p* orbitals. **> Generally, atoms join to form bonds so that each atom has a stable electron configuration.** When this happens, each atom has an electronic structure similar to that of a noble gas.

There are two basic kinds of chemical bonding: ionic bonding and covalent bonding. **Figure 1** shows some differences between ionic and covalent compounds. The way that a compound bonds determines many of the properties of that compound.

SC*L*INKS.
www.scilinks.org
Topic: Chemical
Bonding
Code: **HK80264**

Figure 1 Comparing Ionic and Covalent Compounds

	Ionic compounds	Covalent compounds
Structure	network of bonded ions	molecules
Valence electrons	transferred	shared
Electrical conductivity	good (when melted or dissolved)	poor
State at room temperature	solid	solid, liquid, or gas
Melting and boiling points	generally high	generally low

SECTION 2

> Focus

This section explains why and how atoms bond together in ionic bonds, metallic bonds, covalent bonds, and polyatomic ions.

Bellringer

Use the Bellringer transparency to prepare students for this section.

Demonstrate

Modeling Molecules For this demonstration you will need the following materials: foam balls (3, one larger), pencil, protractor and copper wire (2 50-cm lengths). Wrap the wire around the pencil to make two springs, each approximately 3 cm long. Leave about 4 cm of wire unwound at each end. Stick one end of a spring into each small ball. Stick the other end of each wire into the large foam ball, forming a bond angle of 105°. Explain to students that this is a model of a water molecule. Ask students: "What element does the large ball represent?" (oxygen) "What element do the small balls represent?" (hydrogen) "Springs represent bonds better than sticks do. What do you suppose that says about chemical bonds?" (Chemical bonds bend and stretch.) **LS** **Visual**

Key Resources

 Teaching Transparencies
C14 Multiple Bonds
TM18 Polyatomic Anions

 Visual Concepts
Ionic Bonding
Metallic Bonding
Covalent Bonding
Naming Compounds Containing
Polyatomic Ions
Comparing Polar and Nonpolar
Covalent Bonds

 Datasheet
A Close-Packed Structure

 **Cross-Disciplinary Worksheets**
Connection to Social Studies—Linus
Pauling: A Life Well Spent
Integrating Space Science—Ion
Propulsion in *Deep Space 1*

Teaching Key Ideas

Electron Attraction and Bonding Tell students that in the periodic table, atoms' attraction for electrons generally *increases* from left to right across and *decreases* from top to bottom. Have students use the periodic table to determine the relationship between electron attraction and the number of valence electrons and compare this relationship to the number of valence electrons in a noble gas. (The extremes in electron attraction occur in elements that have one more or one fewer valence electron than a noble gas has.)
LS Visual/Verbal

MISCONCEPTION
ALERT

Networks of Ions Students may think of sodium chloride as a compound formed by bonding between one sodium ion and one chlorine ion. Emphasize that the ions in ionic compounds are attracted to all of the surrounding ions having the opposite charge. Provide students with various materials, such as gumballs, foam balls, pipe cleaners, and wire, and a diagram of a sodium chloride crystal. Have students model a sodium chloride crystal.
LS Kinesthetic

Answer to caption question
The chlorine ion is negatively charged, and the sodium ion is positively charged.

---

ionic bond (ie AHN ik BAHND) the attractive force between oppositely charged ions, which form when electrons are transferred from one atom to another

---

Integrating Social Studies

Achievements of Linus Pauling American scientist Linus Pauling studied how electrons are arranged within atoms. He also studied the ways that atoms share and transfer electrons. In 1954, he won the Nobel Prize in chemistry for his valuable research. Later, Pauling fought to ban nuclear weapons testing. Pauling won the Nobel Peace Prize in 1962 for his efforts. A year later, a treaty outlawing nuclear weapons testing in the atmosphere, in outer space, and underwater went into effect.

Figure 2 Ionic bonds form when one atom transfers one or more electrons to another atom. The result is two ions with opposite charges, which attract each other. **In sodium chloride, which ion is negatively charged and which ion is positively charged?**

go.hrw.com
✳ interact online
Keyword: HK8STRF2

Salt

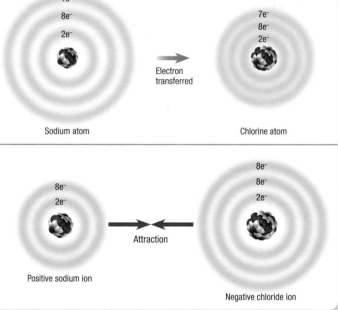

Sodium atom → Electron transferred → Chlorine atom

Positive sodium ion ← Attraction → Negative chloride ion

---

go.hrw.com
✳ interact online

Students can interact with the figure by going to **go.hrw.com** and typing in the keyword **HK8STRF2.**

Ionic Bonds

Atoms of metals, such as sodium and calcium, form positively charged ions. Atoms of nonmetals, such as chlorine and oxygen, form negatively charged ions. ❯**Ionic bonds form from the attractions between such oppositely charged ions.**

Ionic bonds are formed by the transfer of electrons.

Some atoms form bonds because they transfer electrons. One of the atoms gains the electrons that the other one loses. The result is a positive ion and a negative ion, such as the Na^+ ion and the Cl^- ion in sodium chloride shown in **Figure 2.**

Each positive sodium ion attracts several negative chloride ions. These negative chloride ions attract positive sodium ions, and so on. A crystal of table salt is made of a large network of oppositely charged ions. Two atoms tend to form an ionic bond when one atom has more attraction for electrons than the other. Chlorine has much more attraction for electrons than sodium. So, neutral chlorine atoms react with neutral sodium atoms to form sodium chloride.

✓ Reading Check What holds two ionically bonded atoms together?

Connection to Health Science

Salt in the Body The human body needs salt to regulate the balance of electrolytes in the body, both inside and outside of cells. Major salt deficiencies, such as a phenomenon known as "salt starvation" in India, can lead to serious health problems. In America, most people easily reach the minimum recommended daily amount of salt—500 mg. (This is an average value; the actual amount needed by an individual depends on many factors, including lifestyle and genetic makeup.) In fact, Americans consume an average of 3,500 mg of salt per day. Ask students to investigate the reaction of the body to a lack or excess of salt. Students should also describe ways to prevent either condition. **LS** Verbal

---

Ionic compounds are in the form of networks, not molecules.

Because sodium chloride is a network of ions, there is no such thing as "a molecule of NaCl." Sodium chloride is a network because every sodium ion is next to six chloride ions. Therefore, chemists talk about the smallest ratio of ions in ionic compounds. Sodium chloride's chemical formula, NaCl, tells us that there is one Na^+ ion for every Cl^- ion, or a 1:1 ratio of ions. Thus, the compound has a total charge of zero. One Na^+ ion and one Cl^- ion make up a *formula unit* of NaCl.

Not every ionic compound has the same ratio of ions as sodium chloride. An example is calcium fluoride, which is shown in **Figure 3**. The ratio of Ca^{2+} ions to F^- ions in calcium fluoride must be 1:2 to make a neutral compound. Thus, the chemical formula for calcium fluoride is CaF_2.

When melted or dissolved in water, ionic compounds conduct electricity.

Electric current is moving charges. Solid ionic compounds do not conduct electric current because the charged ions are locked into place. But if you dissolve an ionic compound in water or melt it, it can conduct electric current. This is because the ions are then free to move, as **Figure 4** shows.

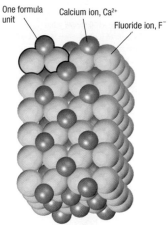

One formula unit — Calcium ion, Ca^{2+} — Fluoride ion, F^-

Figure 3 There are twice as many fluoride ions as calcium ions in a crystal of calcium fluoride, CaF_2. So, one Ca^{2+} ion and two F^- ions make up one formula unit of the compound.

Figure 4 Conductivity of an Ionic Compound

As a solid, an ionic compound's particles are fixed in place and cannot conduct electric current.

When an ionic compound is melted, ions can move more freely and conduct electric current.

Ions dissolved in water can move freely and conduct electricity.

Differentiated Instruction

Special Education Students

Reactive Atoms Have students create models of two atoms. Give each student three colors of dried beans and paper plates on which to place the beans. Ask students to use the beans to represent the electrons in the different energy levels. Have students add or remove electrons from their models to show positive or negative ions. **LS** Logical/Kinesthetic

Why It **Matters**

Table Salt Table salt from the store is usually not pure NaCl. It often contains small amounts of finely divided insoluble substances, such as silicates or complex salts of aluminum. Particles of these materials stick to the cubic NaCl crystals and keep the crystals from clumping together in high humidity. In addition, much table salt is iodized, so it contains small amounts of KI, which provides dietary iodine for proper thyroid function. Ask students to describe a way in which KI is chemically similar to NaCl. (They are both ionic compounds of an alkali metal and a halogen.) **LS** Verbal/Logical

READING TOOLBOX

Reading Skills Have students use the following table to organize the main ideas of this section. Write the table on the board and fill in the left column. Ask students to complete the other two columns as they read the section.

Ionic and Covalent Bonding		
Type of bonds in compounds	Ionic	Covalent
Basic unit	Ion	Molecule
Melting point	High	Low
Example	Sodium chloride	Water

LS Verbal/Logical

Science Skills

Graphing The table below shows the melting points of the potassium halides.

Compound	Melting point (°C)
KF	846
KCl	776
KBr	730
KI	686

Have students graph melting point versus the atomic mass of the potassium halides. Then, ask them to explain the relationship between the melting point and atomic mass based on the graph. (The graph shows that as the atomic mass increases, the melting point decreases.) **LS** Logical

› Teach, *continued*

Teaching Key Ideas

Energy and Covalent Bonds When atoms join together to form a covalent bond, energy is given off. The compound is more stable than the individual atoms were because the compound has less energy. To pull the atoms apart and break up the compound, energy must be added. For example, when two hydrogen atoms combine to form H_2, energy is given off. Energy must be added to split the compound H_2 back into hydrogen atoms.

Science Skills

Modeling Double and Triple Bonds Explain to students that in addition to forming single covalent bonds (as in H_2O), atoms can also form double (four shared electrons) or triple (six shared electrons) covalent bonds to complete their outer energy levels. Tell students that oxygen forms a double bond with another oxygen atom. On the board, draw the corresponding electron-dot diagram for O_2, and point out the double bond. Show how each oxygen atom has eight electrons in the outer energy level. Have students make electron-dot diagrams that show the triple bond in nitrogen, N_2, and the double bonds in carbon dioxide, CO_2.
LS Visual/Logical

covalent bond (koh VAY luhnt BAHND) a bond formed when atoms share one or more pairs of electrons

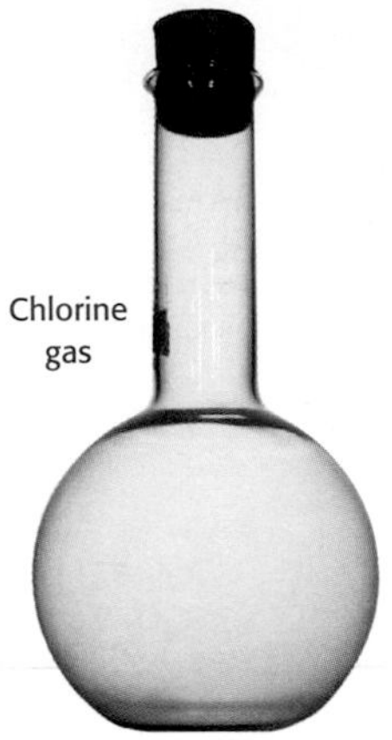

Covalent Bonds

Compounds that are made of molecules, such as water and sugar, have **covalent bonds. › Atoms joined by covalent bonds share electrons.** Compounds that are networks of bonded atoms, such as silicon dioxide, are also covalently bonded. Covalent bonds usually form between nonmetal atoms.

Covalent compounds can be solids, liquids, or gases. Most covalent compounds that are made of molecules have low melting points—usually below 300 °C. Molecules are free to move when the compound is dissolved or melted. But most of these molecules do not conduct electricity, because they are not charged. Chlorine, Cl_2, is a covalent compound that is a gas at room temperature. **Figure 5** shows how two chlorine atoms bond to form a chlorine molecule. Before bonding, each atom has seven electrons in its outermost energy level. If each atom shares one electron with the other atom, then both atoms have a full outermost energy level. That is, both atoms have eight valence electrons.

The structural formula in **Figure 5** shows how the chlorine atoms are connected in the molecule that forms. A single line drawn between two atoms shows that the atoms share two electrons and are joined by one covalent bond.

Reading Check What holds two covalently bonded atoms together?

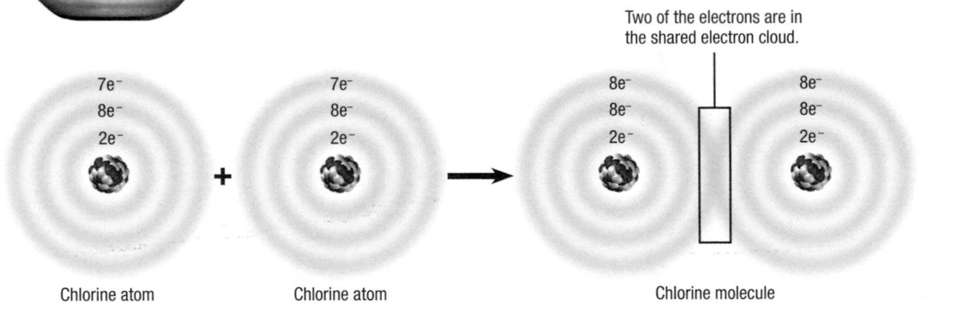

Figure 5 Two chlorine atoms (above) share electrons equally to form a *nonpolar covalent bond.* Covalent bonds are often shown as a single line drawn between two atoms. The model at right shows that the two chlorine atoms share two electrons. Dots represent electrons that are not involved in bonding.

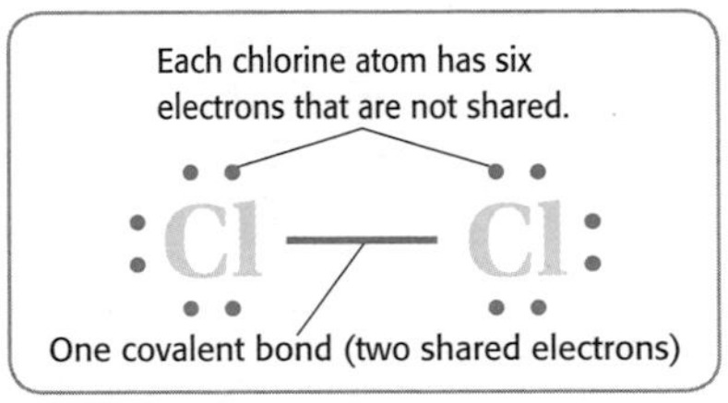

MISCONCEPTION ALERT

Electrons Some students may think that specific electrons belong with specific atoms in a compound. However, in a compound, electrons are shared between atoms. Have students model this for a water molecule using three colors of beads and three paper plates. Beads in each plate represent the number of electrons in the atom. Then, have students trade equal numbers of electrons between the atoms until the bead colors are mixed on each plate. **LS Kinesthetic/Visual**

Differentiated Instruction

Advanced Learners

Lewis Structures Have students conduct research to find out about the octet rule and the steps for drawing Lewis structures. Have them apply their research to draw Lewis structures for some simple ionic and covalent compounds. **LS Verbal/Visual**

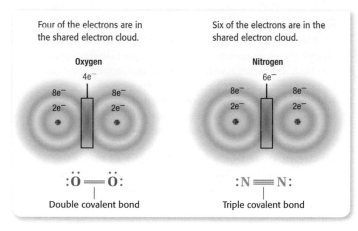

Four of the electrons are in the shared electron cloud.

Oxygen

$4e^-$

$8e^-$ $8e^-$

$2e^-$ $2e^-$

$:\ddot{O} = \ddot{O}:$

Double covalent bond

Six of the electrons are in the shared electron cloud.

Nitrogen

$6e^-$

$8e^-$ $8e^-$

$2e^-$ $2e^-$

$:N \equiv N:$

Triple covalent bond

Figure 6 Molecules of oxygen and nitrogen have covalent bonds. Electrons that are not involved in bonding are represented in these structural models by dots.

Atoms may share more than one pair of electrons.

Covalent bonding in oxygen gas, O_2, and nitrogen gas, N_2, is shown in **Figure 6**. Notice that the bond joining two oxygen atoms is represented by two lines. Two lines show that two pairs of electrons (a total of four electrons) are shared to form a double covalent bond.

The bond that joins two nitrogen atoms is represented by three lines. Two nitrogen atoms form a triple covalent bond by sharing three pairs of electrons (a total of six electrons). More energy is needed to break a triple bond than to break a double bond. So, the triple bond between two nitrogen atoms is stronger than the double bond between two oxygen atoms. Triple and double bonds are shorter than single bonds.

Atoms do not always share electrons equally.

Any two chlorine atoms are identical. When the atoms bond, electrons are equally attracted to the positive nucleus of each atom. Bonds, like this one, in which electrons are shared equally are called *nonpolar covalent bonds*.

When two atoms of different elements share electrons, the electrons are not shared equally. The shared electrons are attracted to the nucleus of one atom more than to the nucleus of the other. An unequal sharing of electrons forms a *polar covalent bond*.

Usually, electrons are more attracted to atoms of elements that are located farther to the right and closer to the top of the periodic table. An example is nitrogen in an ammonia molecule, NH_3, shown in **Figure 7**. The shared electrons in an ammonia molecule are more attracted to the nitrogen atom than they are to the hydrogen atoms.

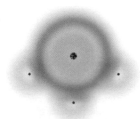

Figure 7 In a molecule of ammonia, NH_3, electrons are more attracted to nitrogen atoms than to hydrogen atoms. So, the bonds in ammonia are *polar covalent bonds*.

READING TOOLBOX

Always, Sometimes, or Never?
As you read this section, make a list of frequency statements that describe different ways that electrons can be shared within a chemical compound.

Teaching Key Ideas

Polar Covalent Bond Have students think of a situation that is analogous to a polar covalent bond and write a paragraph explaining their analogy. (Sample answer: A tug-of-war between ten students who have been lifting weights and ten students who have not been lifting weights is similar to a covalent bond because even though both groups have some pull on the rope, the pull will not be even.) **LS Logical/Verbal**

READING TOOLBOX

Always, Sometimes, or Never?
Explain to students that many statements include a word that tells how often something occurs. Words such as *generally*, *some*, *most* and *usually* are examples that indicate frequency.

MISCONCEPTION ALERT

Polar Bonds Many students believe that electrons are always shared equally between atoms in covalent bonds. Use the discussion of polar covalent bonds on this page to emphasize that electrons are not always shared equally. In nonpolar bonding, the sharing is equal, while in polar bonding, the shared electrons are attracted to the nucleus of one atom more than to the nucleus of the other atom. Have students draw an example of each type of bond. **LS Visual**

Differentiated Instruction

English Learners

Three-Dimensional Models Demonstrate how to make three-dimensional models of hydrogen sulfide molecules using gumdrops and toothpicks. One color gumdrop represents the sulfur atom; another color represents the two hydrogen atoms. Use toothpicks to "bond" the sulfur gumdrop to the hydrogen gumdrops. Have students work in pairs to repeat the demonstration and explain their process orally. Next, have pairs make models of ammonia (NH_3) and methane (CH_4). Tell one student in each pair to describe the model-making process for ammonia using past tense and transitions such as *first, next,* and *finally*. Tell the other student in the pair to describe the final model of ammonia using present tense and at least three adjectives. Have the partners reverse roles for methane. **LS Kinesthetic/Verbal**

Answer to caption question

Sample answers: The photo shows that copper can be stretched into thin wires, a characteristic of metals. Shininess is a characteristic of metals.

QuickLab

Teacher's Notes Be sure that the books are large enough to allow several balls to fit into the triangle. Students will not see the pattern if too few balls are used. As an alternate activity, have students use equal numbers of balls of two different sizes, alternating them in the pattern. Students can also use a rectangular frame instead of a triangle. Tell students that sometimes the arrangement of network ionic solids is called *closest packing*. Ask them to explain why this term is applicable. (The ions in upper layers fill in depressions in the lower levels. This arrangement is the closest the ions can be.)

Materials per Group
- balls, table tennis
- books (3)

Answers to Analysis

1. Sample answer: Each atom in a middle layer is touching 12 other atoms.

2. Sample answer: Yes; every available space between atoms is filled.

3. Sample answer: I have seen a similar arrangement in tomatoes stacked at the grocery store.

Academic Vocabulary

conduct (kuhn DUHKT) to be able to carry

Metallic Bonds

Metals, such as copper, shown in **Figure 8,** can <u>conduct</u> electricity when they are solid. Metals are also flexible, so they can bend and stretch without breaking. Copper, for example, can be pounded into thin sheets or drawn into very thin wire.

> Metals are flexible and conduct electric current well because their atoms and electrons can move freely throughout a metal's packed structure.

Electrons move freely between metal atoms.

The atoms in metals such as copper form **metallic bonds.** The attraction between an atom's nucleus and a neighboring atom's electrons packs the atoms together. This packing causes the outermost energy levels of the atoms to overlap, as **Figure 8** shows. Thus, electrons are free to move from atom to atom.

Figure 8 Copper is a flexible metal that melts at 1,083 °C and boils at 2,567 °C. Copper conducts electricity because electrons can move freely between atoms. **What is one property of metals that you can see in this picture?**

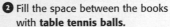
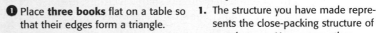

QuickLab

A Close-Packed Structure

⏱ 10 min

Procedure

❶ Place **three books** flat on a table so that their edges form a triangle.

❷ Fill the space between the books with **table tennis balls.**

❸ Adjust the books so that the table tennis balls, or atoms, make a one-layer, close-packed pattern.

❹ Build additional layers on top of the first layer. Each ball should be as close as possible to those around it.

Analysis

1. The structure you have made represents the close-packing structure of metal atoms. How many other atoms does each atom touch?

2. Is the structure that you have made packed as closely as it could be? Explain.

3. Where have you seen other patterns in daily life that are similar to this one?

Differentiated Instruction

Struggling Readers

Examples Explain that the text often uses examples. These examples provide one illustration of the topic being discussed but there are other examples. Examples are indicated by words or phrases including *such as, for example, like,* and *as.* Have students find two phrases on this page in which copper is used as an example. (Sample answer: "such as copper" and "copper, for example") **LS** Verbal

Polyatomic Ions

Until now, we have talked about compounds that have either ionic or covalent bonds. But some compounds have both ionic and covalent bonds. Such compounds are made of **polyatomic ions,** which are groups of covalently bonded atoms that have a positive or negative charge as a group. ❭ **A polyatomic ion acts as a single unit in a compound, just as ions that consist of a single atom do.**

There are many common polyatomic ions.

Many compounds that you use either contain or are made from polyatomic ions. For example, baking soda is a compound that has polyatomic ions. Another name for baking soda is sodium hydrogen carbonate, $NaHCO_3$. Hydrogen carbonate, HCO_3^-, is a polyatomic ion. Sodium carbonate, Na_2CO_3, is often used to make soaps and other cleaners. It contains the carbonate ion, CO_3^{2-}. Sodium hydroxide, $NaOH$, has hydroxide ions, OH^-, and is also used to make soaps. A few of these polyatomic ions are shown in **Figure 9.**

Oppositely charged polyatomic ions, like other ions, can bond to form compounds. For example, ammonium nitrate, NH_4NO_3, and ammonium sulfate, $(NH_4)_2SO_4$, both contain positively charged ammonium ions, NH_4^+. Ammonium nitrate contains one ammonium ion, and ammonium sulfate has two ammonium ions. Nitrate, NO_3^-, and sulfate, SO_4^{2-}, are both negatively charged polyatomic ions.

Parentheses group the atoms of a polyatomic ion.

You might be wondering why the chemical formula for ammonium sulfate is written as $(NH_4)_2SO_4$ instead of as $N_2H_8SO_4$. The parentheses remind us that ammonium, NH_4, acts like a single ion. Parentheses represent the group that the atoms of the ammonium ion form. The subscript 2 outside the parentheses applies to the whole ion. Parentheses are not needed in compounds such as ammonium nitrate, NH_4NO_3, because there is only one of each ion.

Always keep in mind that a polyatomic ion's charge applies not only to the last atom in the formula but to the whole ion. For example, the 2– charge of the carbonate ion, CO_3^{2-}, applies to carbonate, CO_3, not just the oxygen atom. A polyatomic ion acts as a single unit in a compound.

✔ **Reading Check** Why are parentheses used in a chemical formula for a compound that contains more than one of a particular polyatomic ion?

metallic bond (muh TAL ik BAHND) a bond formed by the attraction between positively charged metal ions and the electrons around them

polyatomic ion (PAHL ee uh TAHM ik IE ahn) an ion made of two or more atoms

Hydroxide ion, OH^-

Carbonate ion, CO_3^{2-}

Ammonium ion, NH_4^+

Figure 9 The hydroxide ion, OH^-, carbonate ion, CO_3^{2-}, and ammonium ion, NH_4^+, are all polyatomic ions.

READING TOOLBOX

Vocabulary The prefix *poly–* means "many." Ask students to think of other words with this prefix. (Sample answers: polyhedron, polygon, polyester, and polyglot) Emphasize to students that polyatomic ions are ions that contain many atoms. **LS Verbal**

Teaching Key Ideas

Polyatomic Ions Emphasize the difference between monatomic ions and polyatomic ions by writing the names and formulas of a series of compounds containing monatomic ions and a second series containing polyatomic ions. Lists could include the following:

Compounds that have monatomic ions

sodium oxide Na_2O
iron(III) fluoride FeF_3
barium iodide BaI_2
copper(II) oxide CuO

Compounds that have polyatomic ions

sodium sulfate Na_2SO_4
potassium carbonate K_2CO_3
calcium chlorate $Ca(ClO_3)_2$
tin(II) acetate $Sn(CH_3COO)_2$

Stress to students that each polyatomic ion is treated as a single unit. Have students infer the charge of the anions from what they already know about the cations.

Differentiated Instruction

Advanced Learners

Nitrogen Fixation Nitrogen is a component of proteins, nucleic acids, and other cellular materials, so it is an essential nutrient for all organisms, including plants. Most of the nitrogen in Earth's atmosphere is in the form of N_2, which plants and most other organisms are unable to use because of the triple bond between the nitrogen atoms. For nitrogen to be useful to plants, it must be in the form of ammonium (NH_4^+) or nitrate (NO_3^-) ions. This form of nitrogen is said to be *fixed,* and the process of converting N_2 to these ions is called *nitrogen fixation.* Nitrogen fixation occurs both naturally through bacterial activity and, to a lesser degree, lightning strikes and a commercial process called the Haber-Bosch process. Have students use library or Internet sources to learn more about these examples of nitrogen fixation. Ask students to create a poster that illustrates the process and explains why nitrogen fixation is so important to plants and other organisms. **LS Visual**

Reteaching Key Ideas

Bonding In pairs, have students refer back to **Figure 2** to explain ionic bonding, **Figures 5** and **6** to explain nonpolar covalent bonding, **Figure 7** to explain polar covalent bonding, and **Figure 8** to explain metallic bonding. You may wish to have students recreate the illustrations in a poster and add their own written explanations. You could then display the posters around the classroom. **LS Interpersonal/Visual**

Formative Assessment

Which of the following compounds includes both ionic and covalent bonds in its structure?

A. carbon dioxide (Incorrect. All of the bonds between carbon and oxygen atoms in this compound are covalent.)

B. sodium carbonate (Correct. Compounds that have polyatomic ions often have both covalent and ionic bonds. The polyatomic carbonate ion has covalent bonds and the sodium and carbonate ions are held together by ionic bonds.)

C. potassium iodide (Incorrect. The bonds are ionic.)

D. ammonia (Incorrect. All of the bonds in an ammonia molecule are covalent bonds.)

Integrating Space Science

Ions and Molecules in Space Most of the ions and molecules in space are not the same as the ions and molecules that are found on Earth or in Earth's atmosphere. C_3H, C_6H_2, and HCO^+ have all been found in space. So far, no one has been able to figure out how these unusual molecules and ions form in space.

Some names of polyatomic anions relate to the oxygen content of the anion.

You may have noticed that many polyatomic anions are made of oxygen. Most of their names end with *-ite* or *-ate*. An *-ate* ending is usually used to name an ion that has more oxygen atoms, while ions that have fewer oxygen atoms associated with the same positive group usually end in *-ite*. **Figure 10** lists several common polyatomic anions. Notice that hydroxide, OH^-, is a polyatomic ion that is not named in the way that other ions that contain oxygen are named. Hydroxide and cyanide, CN^-, are examples of polyatomic anions that have unique names and are not named according to any general rules.

Figure 10 Some Common Polyatomic Anions

Ion name	Ion formula	Ion name	Ion formula
Acetate ion	$CH_3CO_2^-$	Hydroxide ion	OH^-
Carbonate ion	CO_3^{2-}	Hypochlorite ion	ClO^-
Chlorate ion	ClO_3^-	Nitrate ion	NO_3^-
Chlorite ion	ClO_2^-	Nitrite ion	NO_2^-
Cyanide ion	CN^-	Phosphate ion	PO_4^{3-}
Hydrogen carbonate ion	HCO_3^-	Phosphite ion	PO_3^{3-}
Hydrogen sulfate ion	HSO_4^-	Sulfate ion	SO_4^{2-}
Hydrogen sulfite ion	HSO_3^-	Sulfite ion	SO_3^{2-}

Section 2 Review

KEY IDEAS

1. **Determine** if the following compounds are likely to have ionic or covalent bonds.
   a. magnesium oxide, MgO
   b. strontium chloride, $SrCl_2$
   c. ozone, O_3
   d. methanol, CH_3OH

2. **Draw** the structural formula for acetylene, C_2H_2. The atoms of acetylene bond in the order HCCH. Carbon and hydrogen atoms share two electrons, and each carbon atom must have a total of four bonds. How many electrons do the carbon atoms share?

3. **Identify** which two of the following substances will conduct electric current, and explain why.
   a. aluminum foil
   b. sugar, $C_{12}H_{22}O_{11}$, dissolved in water
   c. potassium hydroxide, KOH, dissolved in water

4. **Explain** why electrons are shared equally in oxygen, O_2, but not in carbon monoxide, CO.

5. **Predict** whether a silver coin can conduct electricity. What kind of bonds does silver have?

6. **Identify** which of the bonds in calcium hydroxide, $Ca(OH)_2$, are ionic and which are covalent.

CRITICAL THINKING

7. **Applying Concepts** Does dinitrogen tetroxide, N_2O_4, have covalent or ionic bonds? Explain how you reached your conclusion.

8. **Applying Ideas** An atom of the element iodine, I, has much more attraction for electrons than an atom of strontium, Sr, does. What kind of bonds are likely to form between atoms of the two elements?

9. **Compare and Contrast** How are metallic bonds similar to covalent bonds? How are they different?

Answers to Section Review

1. a. ionic
   b. ionic
   c. covalent
   d. covalent

2. H–C≡C–H; The carbon atoms share three pairs of electrons.

3. Sample answer: Aluminum foil will conduct electricity because it is a metal and its valence electrons are free to move. KOH dissolved in water will conduct electricity because its ions are free to move.

4. Sample answer: Because the atoms in a molecule of oxygen are the same, they attract and share electrons equally. Carbon and oxygen attract electrons differently, so electron sharing is unequal.

5. Sample answer: Silver has metallic bonds, so it has electrons that are free to move. The coin will conduct electricity.

6. The compound is composed of Ca^{2+} and OH^- ions, which are held together by ionic bonds. OH^- consists of covalently bonded oxygen and hydrogen atoms.

7. Sample answer: Dinitrogen tetroxide has covalent bonds because both nitrogen and oxygen are nonmetals.

8. Ionic bonds will form between strontium and iodine atoms.

Answers continued on p. 213A

Compound Names and Formulas

Key **Ideas**

> How are ionic compounds named?

> What do the numerical prefixes used in naming covalent compounds tell you?

> What does a compound's empirical formula indicate?

Key **Terms**

empirical formula

molecular formula

Why It **Matters**

Knowing how compounds are named can help you recognize them in food ingredients.

> **Focus**

This section explains how to name ionic and covalent compounds, how to determine the charge of a cation in an ionic compound, how to write formulas for simple ionic compounds, and how to distinguish between the empirical and molecular formulas of a covalent compound.

 Bellringer

Use the Bellringer transparency to prepare students for this section.

Demonstrate

Balancing Charges For this activity, you will need a double-pan balance, pennies, and two index cards. Use stacks of pennies to represent the amount of charge on ions. Place a card that has a plus sign in front of the left-hand pan of the balance and a card that has a minus sign in front of the right-hand pan. Choose several ionic compounds, and use the pennies to show that a correct formula balances charge. For example, if Fe^{3+} and S^{2-} ions are represented by stacks of three and two pennies, it will take two stacks of three pennies (two Fe^{3+} ions) to balance three stacks of two pennies (three S^{2-} ions). The final formula is Fe_2S_3. Have students use the balance and pennies to find the formulas for all compounds that would form from the following: Au^{3+}, Pb^{2+}, O^{2-}, and Cl^- ions. (Au_2O_3, $AuCl_3$, $PbCl_2$, and PbO)

 **Logical/Kinesthetic**

J ust like elements, compounds have names that distinguish them from other compounds. Although the compounds BaF_2 and BF_3 may seem to have similar chemical formulas, their names make it clear that they are different. BaF_2 is *barium fluoride*, and BF_3 is *boron trifluoride*. You can see that the names of these compounds come from the elements that make up the compounds.

Naming Ionic Compounds

Ionic compounds are formed by the strong attractions between oppositely charged particles, cations (positive ions) and anions (negative ions). Both ions are important to the compound's structure, so both ions are included in the name.
> **The names of ionic compounds consist of the names of the ions that make up the compounds.**

Names of cations include the elements of which they are composed.

In many cases, the name of the cation is just like the name of its element. For example, when an atom of the element *sodium* loses an electron, a *sodium ion*, Na^+, forms. Similarly, when a *calcium* atom loses two electrons, a *calcium ion*, Ca^{2+}, forms. And when an *aluminum* atom loses three electrons, an *aluminum ion*, Al^{3+}, forms. Common cations are listed in **Figure 1.** The periodic table can be used as a tool for figuring out what ions are formed by different elements. Notice that ions of Group 1 elements have a 1+ charge and that ions of Group 2 elements have a 2+ charge. In many cases, you can tell what charge an ion will have by looking at where the element is located on the periodic table.

Figure 1 Some Common Cations

Ion name and symbol	Ion charge
Cesium ion, Cs^+	1+
Lithium ion, Li^+	
Potassium ion, K^+	
Rubidium ion, Rb^+	
Sodium ion, Na^+	
Barium ion, Ba^{2+}	2+
Beryllium ion, Be^{2+}	
Calcium ion, Ca^{2+}	
Magnesium ion, Mg^{2+}	
Strontium ion, Sr^{2+}	
Aluminum ion, Al^{3+}	3+

Key Resources

 **Teaching Transparencies**
TM19 Common Cations
TM20 Common Anions
TM21 Naming Prefixes

Visual Concepts
Naming Ionic Compounds
Naming Covalently-Bonded
   Compounds
Comparing Molecular and Empirical
   Formulas

Math Skills Worksheet
Writing Ionic Formulas

Teaching Key Ideas

Order in Ionic Formulas Give examples, such as Einstein Albert, Marie Madame Curie, and Carver Washington George, to illustrate to students the importance of correct order and spelling of a name to accurately denote a person. Extend the discussion to include the naming of ionic compounds. Cations and anions can be thought of as the first and last names, respectively, of ionic compounds.

READING TOOLBOX

Abbreviations Ask students to list abbreviations for common terms. (Students might list abbreviations for units of measurement and abbreviations for phrases, such as *etc.* and *e.g.*) Relate the use of abbreviations in daily life to the use of chemical formulas to represent the composition of substances. **LS** **Verbal**

Math Skills

Adding Integers To help students determine the charge of an ion in a compound, review with them how to add positive and negative integers. Draw a number line on the board to help students who have difficulty with the concept. Have students determine the charge on the titanium ion in the ionic compound Ti_2O_3 if oxygen ions always have a 2– charge. (3+) **LS** **Logical**

Figure 2 Some Common Anions

Element	Ion	Ion charge
Fluorine, F	fluoride ion, F⁻	1–
Chlorine, Cl	chloride ion, Cl⁻	
Bromine, Br	bromide ion, Br⁻	
Iodine, I	iodide ion, I⁻	
Oxygen, O	oxide ion, O²⁻	2–
Sulfur, S	sulfide ion, S²⁻	
Nitrogen, N	nitride ion, N³⁻	3–

Figure 3 Some Transition Metal Cations

Ion name	Ion symbol
Copper(I) ion	Cu⁺
Copper(II) ion	Cu²⁺
Iron(II) ion	Fe²⁺
Iron(III) ion	Fe³⁺
Nickel(II) ion	Ni²⁺
Nickel(III) ion	Ni³⁺
Chromium(II) ion	Cr²⁺
Chromium(III) ion	Cr³⁺
Cadmium(II) ion	Cd²⁺
Titanium(II) ion	Ti²⁺
Titanium(III) ion	Ti³⁺
Titanium(IV) ion	Ti⁴⁺

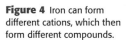

Figure 4 Iron can form different cations, which then form different compounds.

Names of anions are altered names of elements.

An anion of an element has a name similar to that element's name. The difference is the name's ending. **Figure 2** shows how some common anions are named. Like most cations, anions of elements in the same group of the periodic table have the same charge. NaF is made of sodium ions, Na⁺, and fluoride ions, F⁻. Therefore, its name is *sodium fluoride*.

An ionic compound must have a total charge of zero.

If an ionic compound is made up of ions that have different charges, the ratio of ions will not be 1:1. Calcium fluoride is made of calcium ions, Ca^{2+} and fluoride ions, F⁻. For calcium fluoride to have a total charge of zero, there must be two fluoride ions for every calcium ion: $(2 \times -1) + (+2) = 0$. So, the formula for calcium fluoride is CaF_2.

✅ **Reading Check** What determines the amounts of each ion in an ionic compound?

Some cation names must show their charge.

Iron is a transition metal. Transition metals may form several cations—each with a different charge. A few of these cations are listed in **Figure 3.** Think about the compounds FeO and Fe_2O_3. According to the rules you have learned so far, both of these compounds would be named *iron oxide*, even though they are not the same compound, as **Figure 4** shows. They are different compounds and should have different names.

The charge of the iron cation in Fe_2O_3 is different from the charge of the iron cation in FeO. In cases such as this, the cation name must be followed by a Roman numeral in parentheses. The Roman numeral shows the cation's charge. Fe_2O_3 is made of Fe^{3+} ions, so it is named *iron(III) oxide*. FeO is made of Fe^{2+} ions, so it is named *iron(II) oxide*.

Fe_2O_3, iron(III) oxide, is a component of rust.

FeO, iron(II) oxide, is a black powdery substance.

Differentiated Instruction

Basic Learners

Transition Metals On the chalkboard, write the following formulas for transition element compounds: CrO, CrCl₃, Cr(SO₄)₃, CoBr₂, Co₂O₃, KMnO₄, MnO₂, MnS, MnO₃, and MnN. Have students use the formulas to make a table that lists the charges on chromium, cobalt, and manganese in each compound. Review with students how to use the periodic table to find charges of elements in certain families. (The charges for chromium are 2+, 3+, and 6+. The charges for cobalt are 2+ and 3+. The charges for manganese are 2+, 3+, 4+, 6+, and 7+.) **LS** **Logical**

English Learners

Suffixes Explain that changing a suffix can change the meaning of a word. The simplest example the addition of *-s* to make many nouns plural. For example, the words *house* and *houses* have different meanings. Give examples of other suffixes, such as *-ed* for past tense. Point out that the same concept applies to naming ions; for example, *chlorine* and *chloride* have different meanings. Have students work in pairs to create a table that describes how suffixes influence the names of ions and compounds. **LS** **Verbal**

Determine the charge of a transition metal cation.

How can you tell that the iron ion in Fe_2O_3 has a charge of 3+? Three oxide ions, O^{2-}, have a total charge of 6–. Thus, the total positive charge in the formula must be 6+ so that the total charge can be zero. So, each of the two iron ions must have a charge of 3+.

Write formulas for ionic compounds using names.

You can find the charge of each ion in a compound if you are given the compound's formula. You can find the formula for a compound if you are given the compound's name.

www.scilinks.org
Topic: Naming Compounds
Code: HK81010

Math **Skills** Writing Ionic Formulas

What is the chemical formula for aluminum fluoride?

Identify List the given and unknown values.	**Given:** *Symbol for an aluminum ion from* **Figure 1:** Al^{3+} *Symbol for a fluoride ion from* **Figure 2:** F^- **Unknown:** *chemical formula*
Plan Write the symbols for the ions, with the cation first.	$Al^{3+}F^-$
Solve Find the least common multiple of the ions' charges. Write the chemical formula. Show with subscripts the number of each ion needed to make a neutral compound.	The least common multiple of 3 and 1 is 3. To make a neutral compound, you need a total of three positive charges and three negative charges. You need only one Al^{3+} ion because $1 \times (+3) = +3$. You need three F^- ions because $3 \times (-1) = -3$. AlF_3

Practice

Write formulas for the following ionic compounds.

1. lithium oxide
2. beryllium chloride
3. titanium(III) nitride

For more practice, visit **go.hrw.com** and enter the keyword **HK8MP.**

> **Practice Hint**
>
> ❯ Once you have determined a chemical formula, always check the formula to see if it makes a neutral compound. For this example, the aluminum ion has a charge of 3+. The fluoride ion has a charge of only 1–, but there are three of them for a total of 3–.
>
> $(3+) + (3-) = 0$, so the charges balance, and the formula is neutral.

Teaching Key Ideas

Cation-Anion Pairs To reinforce the idea of electrical neutrality, write the symbols of six cations and six anions on the board. The ions should have a variety of charges. Point to a cation-anion pair, and ask students how many of each ion will produce a net charge of 0. You may want to ask students to write or state the correct formula, but the main purpose of the exercise is to help students understand how to construct an electrically neutral combination. **LS** **Logical**

Math **Skills**

Teacher's Note Students might notice what they consider to be a shortcut in writing ionic formulas. The numerical value of the charge on one ion is usually the subscript of the other ion in the formula for the compound. For example, if Sn^{2+} and PO_4^{3-} form a compound, the 2 that describes the charge for Sn becomes the subscript of the PO_4 part of the formula, and 3 that describes the charge for PO_4 becomes the subscript for Sn. The final formula is $Sn_3(PO_4)_2$. However, this method does not work in all cases. For example, Mg^{2+} and O^{2-} form MgO, not Mg_2O_2. The procedure in the Math Skills activity on this page emphasizes the concept of balanced charges and is not just a manipulation of numbers.

Answers to Practice

1. Li_2O
2. $BeCl_2$
3. TiN

Teaching Key Ideas

Naming Covalent Compounds Have students work in groups of four. Provide two students in each group with flashcards that have the prefixes listed in **Figure 5** written on them. Give one of the other students flashcards that have the names of nonmetals, and give the remaining student flashcards that have *-ide* names based on nonmetals, such as *oxide.* Write the formula for a covalent compound on the chalkboard, and have students combine the flashcards to name it. Before starting the activity, remind students that the prefix *mono-* is used only with the second part of a chemical name, not the first. For example, CO is carbon monoxide, not monocarbon monoxide. Final *o*'s and *a*'s of prefixes can be dropped if it makes the name easier to pronounce. For example, *tetroxide* would be used, not *tetraoxide.*

LS **Interpersonal/Verbal**

READING TOOLBOX

Vocabulary Have students look up the meaning of the word *empirical* in the dictionary. Have them use the definition to explain where information is obtained about an empirical formula. (Student explanations should reflect that empirical formulas are determined from experimental data.) **LS** **Verbal**

Figure 5 Prefixes Used to Name Covalent Compounds

Number of atoms	Prefix
1	*mono-*
2	*di-*
3	*tri-*
4	*tetra-*
5	*penta-*
6	*hexa-*
7	*hepta-*
8	*octa-*
9	*nona-*
10	*deca-*

$$N_2O_4$$

Dinitrogen tetroxide

Figure 6 One molecule of diitrogen tetroxide has two nitrogen atoms and four oxygen atoms.

Naming Covalent Compounds

Covalent compounds, such as silicon dioxide, SiO_2 and carbon dioxide, CO_2, are named using rules that are different from rules used to name ionic compounds. The main difference from ionic compounds is the use of prefixes. **›For covalent compounds of two elements, numerical prefixes tell how many atoms of each element are in the molecule.**

Numerical prefixes are used to name covalent compounds of two elements.

Some prefixes used in naming covalent compounds are shown in **Figure 5.** If there is only one atom of the first element, the name does not get a prefix. The element farther to the right in the periodic table is named second and ends in *-ide*.

One boron atom and three fluorine atoms make up *boron trifluoride*, BF_3. *Dinitrogen tetroxide*, N_2O_4, is made of two nitrogen atoms and four oxygen atoms, as **Figure 6** shows. Notice that the *a* in *tetra* is dropped to make the name easier to say.

Empirical Formulas

Emeralds, shown in **Figure 7,** are made of a mineral called beryl. The chemical formula for beryl is $Be_3Al_2Si_6O_{18}$. But how did scientists determine this formula? It took some experiments. Chemical formulas that are unknown are determined by figuring out the mass of each element in the compound.

Once the mass of each element in a sample of the compound is known, scientists can calculate the compound's **empirical formula,** or simplest formula. **›An empirical formula tells us the smallest whole-number ratio of atoms that are in a compound.**

For most ionic compounds, the empirical formula is the same as the chemical formula. Covalent compounds have empirical formulas, too. The empirical formula for water is H_2O. The formula tells you that the ratio of hydrogen atoms to oxygen atoms is 2:1.

✓ Reading Check What is an empirical formula?

Figure 7 Emerald gemstones are cut from the mineral beryl. Very tiny amounts of chromium(III) oxide, Cr_2O_3, in the gemstones gives them their beautiful green color.

Differentiated Instruction

Basic Learners

Common Names In addition to a scientific name, some compounds also have a common name. For example, few people would refer to dihydrogen monoxide, H_2O, as anything but water. Other compounds that have common names include vinegar (acetic acid) and rubbing alcohol (isopropanol).

Common names have been known and used before the rules for chemical naming were standardized. For example, although many chemical salts exist, sodium chloride (NaCl) is commonly referred to as *salt.* Another example, dinitrogen monoxide (N_2O) is commonly referred to as both *nitrous oxide* and *laughing gas.* Have students research the common and standard names of some of the compounds with which they are familiar. Students should explain the origin of the common names when possible. You may wish to have students make a poster of common and scientific names that compiles all their research. **LS** **Verbal**

Different compounds can have the same empirical formula.

Empirical formulas show only a ratio of atoms, so it is possible for different compounds to have the same empirical formula. Formaldehyde, acetic acid, and glucose all have the empirical formula CH_2O, as **Figure 8** shows. However, these three compounds are not alike. Formaldehyde is sometimes used to keep dead organisms from decaying so that they can be studied. Acetic acid gives vinegar its sour taste and strong smell. And glucose is a sugar that plays a very important role in your body chemistry.

Molecular formulas are determined from empirical formulas.

Formaldehyde, acetic acid, and glucose are all covalent compounds that are made of molecules. They all have the same empirical formula, but each compound has its own molecular formula. A compound's **molecular formula** tells you how many atoms are in one molecule of the compound.

As **Figure 8** shows, formaldehyde's empirical formula is the same as the molecular formula. The molecular formula for acetic acid is two times the empirical formula, and the molecular formula of glucose is six times the empirical formula.

Masses can be used to determine empirical formulas.

You can find the empirical formula of a compound if you know the mass of each element present in a sample of the compound. Convert the masses to moles. Then, find the molar ratio, which will give you the empirical formula.

READING TOOLBOX

Suffixes
Find two adjectives on this page that end in the suffix *-ar.* For each one, tell what noun is its root, and give the meaning of the phrase in which it appears.

empirical formula (em PIR i kuhl FAWR myoo luh) the composition of a compound in terms of the relative numbers and kinds of atoms in the simplest ratio

molecular formula (moh LEK yoo lur FAWR myoo luh) a chemical formula that shows the number and kinds of atoms in a molecule, but not the arrangement of atoms

Figure 8 Empirical and Molecular Formulas for Some Compounds

Compound	Empirical formula	Molar mass	Molecular formula	Structure
Formaldehyde	CH_2O	30.03 g/mol	CH_2O	Oxygen — Carbon — Hydrogen
Acetic acid	CH_2O	60.06 g/mol	$2 \times CH_2O = C_2H_4O_2$	
Glucose	CH_2O	180.18 g/mol	$6 \times CH_2O = C_6H_{12}O_6$	

READING TOOLBOX

Suffixes For the term molecular, the root is "molecule." The phrase *molecular formula* describes the number of atoms in one molecule of the compound. For the term *molar,* the root is "mole." The phrase *molar ratio* describes the ratio of moles that can be used to find the empirical formula.

Teaching Key Ideas

Finding Molecular Formulas Show students how to find the molecular formula when given the empirical formula and the molar mass of a compound. Use the information in **Figure 8** as an example. The molar mass of the empirical formula is found by adding the molar mass of each atom, expressed in g/mol. For CH_2O, the molar mass is $(1 \times 12.01) + (2 \times 1.01) + (1 \times 16.00) = 30.03$ g/mol. The molecular formula will be a multiple of the empirical formula, so divide the molar mass of the molecule by the molar mass of the empirical formula. For glucose, 180.18 g/mol / 30.03 g/mol = 6. So, the molecule is made up of six units of the empirical formula. The molecular formula is $C_6H_{12}O_6$. Have students find the molecular formulas for the following molecules:

Empirical formula	Molar mass (g/mol)	Molecular formula
CH	78.12	C_6H_6
NH_2	32.06	N_2H_4
$C_3H_6N_2$	210.33	$C_9H_{18}N_6$

LS Logical

Differentiated Instruction

English Learners

Prefixes Ask students for examples of words that contain prefixes denoting a number. (Sample answers: *bicycle, tricycle, octopus, decade, triangle, pentagon, quadrilateral,* and *hexagon*) Tell students that such prefixes are also used to name molecular compounds.
LS Verbal

MISCONCEPTION ALERT

Chemical Formulas Some students interpret chemical formulas incorrectly. For example, they think that the chemical formula N_2O_4 represents an N_2 molecule bound to an O_4 molecule. Use examples in this section, including the structures illustrated in the last column of **Figure 8,** to emphasize that this interpretation is incorrect.

Answers to Practice

1. CH_2
2. BH_3

>**Close**

Reteaching Key Ideas

Formulas of Covalent Compounds
Have students write the formulas for the following compounds: carbon tetrachloride (CCl_4), sulfur hexafluoride (SF_6), and dihydrogen monoxide (H_2O). Ask students why scientists prefer to use the name *water* instead of *dihydrogen monoxide*. (Sample answer: The term *water* is common usage and easier to say.)
LS Logical

Formative Assessment

In which of the following compounds does the empirical formula describe one molecule of the compound?

A. carbon dioxide (Correct. Each molecule of carbon dioxide has one carbon atom and two oxygen atoms, so its empirical formula, CO_2, is also its molecular formula.)

B. dinitrogen tetroxide (Incorrect. The molecular formula of dinitrogen tetroxide is N_2O_4 but the empirical formula is NO_2.)

C. sodium chloride (Incorrect. Sodium chloride is an ionic compound, so it does not have a molecular formula.)

D. copper(II) chloride (Incorrect. Copper(II) chloride is an ionic compound, so it does not have a molecular formula.)

Practice Hint

> An empirical formula must have whole numbers of elements. If the molar ratio of elements has a decimal in it, you will need to multiply the ratio by a whole number to make the ratio consist of only whole numbers.

$1.5:1 \times 2 = 3:2$

> An empirical formula must represent the simplest possible molar ratio between the elements in the compound. If a molar ratio can be reduced to a simpler fraction, divide it by a whole number.

$10:4 \div 2 = 5:2$

Math *Skills* **Finding Empirical Formulas**

One mole of an unknown compound contains 62 g of phosphorus and 80 g of oxygen. What is the empirical formula of this compound?

Identify
List the given and unknown values.

Given:
62 g phosphorus, 80 g oxygen
Unknown:
empirical formula

Plan
Write the atomic masses.

phosphorus: 30.97 g/mol
oxygen: 16.00 g/mol

Solve
The molar ratio of elements in the compound will be the compound's empirical formula.

$\dfrac{62\,g\,P \times 1\,mol\,P}{30.97\,g} = 2.0\,mol\,P$

$\dfrac{80\,g\,O \times 1\,mol\,O}{16.00\,g\,O} = 5.0\,mol\,O$

empirical formula: P_2O_5

Practice

1. One mole of an unknown compound has 36.04 g of carbon and 6.04 g of hydrogen. What is the compound's empirical formula?

2. A sample of a compound contains 3.6 g of boron and 1.0 g of hydrogen. What is the compound's empirical formula?

For more practice, visit **go.hrw.com** and enter keyword **HK8MP**.

Section 3 Review

KEY IDEAS

1. **Name** the following ionic compounds, and specify the charge of any transition metal cations.
   a. FeI_2 **c.** $CrCl_2$
   b. MnF_3 **d.** CuS

2. **Find** the charge of the cadmium cation in cadmium bromide, $CdBr_2$. Explain your reasoning.

3. **Name** the following covalent compounds:
   a. SeO_2 **c.** As_2O_5
   b. SiI_4 **d.** P_4S_3

CRITICAL THINKING

4. **Analyzing Data** A mole of a certain compound contains 207.2 g of lead and 32.00 g of oxygen. Without doing any calculations, tell whether a formula unit of the compound contains more atoms of lead or more atoms of oxygen. Explain.

Math *Skills*

5. Determine the chemical formulas for the following ionic compounds:
   a. magnesium sulfate
   b. rubidium bromide
   c. chromium(II) fluoride
   d. nickel(I) carbonate

6. What is the empirical formula of a compound that contains 4.03 g of hydrogen per mole, 64.14 g of sulfur per mole, and 128.00 g of oxygen per mole?

7. A sample of a compound contains 160 g of oxygen and 20.2 g of hydrogen. What is the compound's empirical formula?

Answers to Section Review

1. **a.** iron(II) iodide
   b. manganese(III) fluoride
   c. chromium(II) chloride
   d. copper(II) sulfide

2. The charge of the cadmium ion is 2+ because there are two bromide ions, each of which is has a charge of 1–, and the total charge on the molecule must add up to zero.

3. **a.** selenium dioxide
   b. silicon tetriodide
   c. diarsenic pentoxide
   d. tetraphosphorus trisulfide

4. Sample answer: Looking at the atomic mass of lead and oxygen, I can see that there are about two moles of oxygen for each mole of lead. So, there must be more atoms of oxygen than there are of lead in each formula unit of the compound.

5. **a.** $MgSO_4$
   b. $RbBr$
   c. CrF_2
   d. Ni_2CO_3

6. H_2SO_4

7. H_2O

Organic and Biochemical Compounds

Key **Ideas**

❯ What is an organic compound?

❯ What is a polymer?

❯ What organic compounds are essential to life?

Key **Terms**

organic
  compound

polymer

carbohydrate

protein

amino acid

Why It **Matters**

Your body is made of organic compounds, which play important roles in keeping you alive.

❯Focus

In this section, students learn how carbon atoms bond covalently to form organic compounds, including alkanes, alkenes, and alcohols. Next, students study both man-made and natural polymers. The section concludes with a discussion of biochemical compounds, including carbohydrates, proteins, and DNA.

🔔Bellringer

Use the Bellringer transparency to prepare students for this section.

Demonstrate

Combustion of Organic Compounds
This demonstration requires notebook paper, a test tube, a test-tube holder, a Bunsen burner, a sparker to light the burner, ice, a beaker, and tongs. Place a strip of notebook paper into the test tube. Place ice in the beaker. Using the test-tube holder, hold the test tube over the lit burner. At the same time, use tongs to hold the beaker just above the mouth of the test tube. Ask students: "What change did you notice in the paper?" (The paper turned black.) "What element could you see after the paper was heated?" (carbon) "What did you notice on the bottom of the beaker?" (Water condensed on the bottom of the beaker.) "What other two elements must be present in the paper?" (hydrogen and oxygen) **LS Logical**

The word *organic* has many different meanings. Most people associate the word *organic* with living organisms. Perhaps you have heard of or eaten organically grown fruits or vegetables. They are grown using fertilizers and pesticides that come from plant and animal matter. In chemistry, the word *organic* is used to describe a type of compound.

Organic Compounds

❯**An organic compound is a covalently bonded compound that contains carbon.** Most organic compounds also contain hydrogen. Oxygen, nitrogen, sulfur, and phosphorus, can also be found in organic compounds.

Many ingredients of familiar substances are organic compounds. The active ingredient in aspirin is a form of the organic compound acetylsalicylic acid, $C_9H_8O_4$. Sugarless chewing gum also contains organic compounds. Two of its ingredients are the sweeteners sorbitol, $C_6H_{14}O_6$, and aspartame, $C_{14}H_{18}N_2O_5$, both of which are shown in **Figure 1.**

organic compound (awr GAN ik KAHM POWND) a covalently bonded compound that contains carbon, excluding carbonates and oxides

Figure 1 The organic compounds sorbitol and aspartame sweeten some sugarless chewing gums.

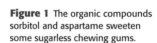

Sorbitol

Aspartame

Key Resources

Teaching Transparency
C15 Six-Carbon Alkanes

Visual Concepts
Organic Compound
Hydrocarbon
Alkane
Alcohol
Naming Alcohols
Polymers
Carbohydrates
Proteins
Amino Acid
DNA Overview

Datasheets
Polymer Memory
What Properties Does a Polymer
  Have?

**Cross-Disciplinary
Worksheets**
Connection to Engineering–
  Fractions of Crude Oil
Integrating Environmental
  Science–Plastics
Integrating Mathematics–Amino
  Acid Combinations

MISCONCEPTION
///ALERT

Inorganic Carbon Compounds
Not all covalently bonded carbon-containing molecules are organic compounds. Carbon dioxide, carbon monoxide, and carbon disulfide are inorganic covalent compounds. Other carbon-containing compounds that are not organic include carbonic acid, carbides, and carbonates. Ask students to investigate ways that they can differentiate between organic and inorganic carbon compounds.

Why It Matters

How Do Gas Grills Work? Grills use natural gas supplied by pipes or propane, supplied in tanks. Natural gas does not compress to form a liquid as easily as propane. Propane is compressed and stored in a tank at normal temperatures, but at normal pressure changes from a liquid to a gas at −43 °C. When the pressure drops as propane leaves the tank, it becomes a gas, which ignites at between 450 °C and 500 °C, the temperature generated by a match or an electric igniter.

Answer to Your Turn
Sample answer: Another outdoor grill fuel is natural gas, methane (CH_4). Methane, like propane, is a hydrocarbon, but it has only one carbon atom per molecule to propane's three carbon atoms.

www.scilinks.org
Topic: Organic Compounds
Code: HK81078

Methane   Ethane

Figure 2 Methane and ethane are the two simplest hydrocarbons.

Carbon atoms form four covalent bonds in organic compounds.

When a compound is made of only carbon and hydrogen atoms, it is called a *hydrocarbon*. Methane, CH_4, is the simplest hydrocarbon. Its structure is shown in **Figure 2.** Methane gas is formed when living matter, such as plants, decay, so it is often found in swamps and marshes. The natural gas used in stoves is also mostly methane. Carbon atoms have four valence electrons to use for bonding. In methane, each of these electrons participates in a C–H single bond.

A carbon atom may also share two of its electrons with two from another atom to form a double bond. Or a carbon atom may share three electrons to form a triple bond. However, a carbon atom can never form more than four bonds at a time.

Alkanes are hydrocarbons that have only single covalent bonds. Methane is the simplest alkane. It has only C–H bonds. But alkanes can also have C–C bonds. You can see from **Figure 2** that the two carbon atoms in ethane, C_2H_6, bond to each other. Note how each carbon atom in both of these compounds bonds to four other atoms.

Why It Matters

How Do Gas Grills Work?

REAL WORLD

Many gas grills are fueled by the alkane propane, C_3H_8. Propane is a gas that is stored in tanks at high pressure. When the valve to the tank is opened, the gas comes out in small amounts to the burner, where it is ignited. Like other hydrocarbons, propane undergoes combustion and releases a lot of energy as heat.

This man is preparing his dinner on a gas grill that is fueled by propane. Propane is an alkane that has two C–C bonds and eight C–H bonds.

YOUR TURN

ONLINE RESEARCH
1. Find one other compound besides propane that is used as a fuel for outdoor grills. What does it have in common with propane? How is it different from propane?

Differentiated Instruction

Special Education Students

Paper Backbones and Bonds Cut 60 blue and 30 yellow strips of paper, each 10 cm × 2 cm. Have students use the blue strips to represent hydrogen atoms, the yellow strips to represent carbon atoms, and staples to represent chemical bonds. Students can then staple the strips into paper chains to create models of different kinds of carbon backbones and carbon bonds.
LS Kinesthetic

Arrangements of carbon atoms in alkanes may vary.

The carbon atoms in methane, ethane, and propane are all bonded in a single line because that is their only possible arrangement. When there are more than three bonded carbon atoms in a molecule, the carbon atoms do not have to be in a single line. When they are, the alkane is called a *normal alkane*, or *n-alkane*. **Figure 3** shows chemical formulas for the *n*-alkanes that have up to 10 carbon atoms. *Condensed structural formulas* in the table show how the atoms bond.

The carbon atoms in any alkane that has more than three carbon atoms can have more than one possible arrangement. Carbon atom chains may have branches, and they can even form rings. **Figure 4** shows some of the ways that six-carbon atoms with only single bonds can be arranged.

✔ Reading Check What is the shortest chain of carbon atoms that can have more than one arrangement? Explain.

Alkane chemical formulas usually follow a pattern.

Except for cyclic alkanes, the chemical formulas for alkanes follow a special pattern. The number of hydrogen atoms is always two more than twice the number of carbon atoms. This pattern is represented by the general formula C_nH_{2n+2}. Look at the six-carbon alkanes shown in **Figure 4**. All of the alkanes except for cyclohexane have the chemical formula C_6H_{14}, which is what you get when you replace the variable *n* in the general formula C_nH_{2n+2} with the number 6.

Figure 3 The First 10 *n*-Alkanes

n-Alkane	Molecular formula	Condensed structural formula
Methane	CH_4	CH_4
Ethane	C_2H_6	CH_3CH_3
Propane	C_3H_8	$CH_3CH_2CH_3$
Butane	C_4H_{10}	$CH_3(CH_2)_2CH_3$
Pentane	C_5H_{12}	$CH_3(CH_2)_3CH_3$
Hexane	C_6H_{14}	$CH_3(CH_2)_4CH_3$
Heptane	C_7H_{16}	$CH_3(CH_2)_5CH_3$
Octane	C_8H_{18}	$CH_3(CH_2)_6CH_3$
Nonane	C_9H_{20}	$CH_3(CH_2)_7CH_3$
Decane	$C_{10}H_{22}$	$CH_3(CH_2)_8CH_3$

Figure 4 Hexane, 3-methylpentane, 2,3-dimethylbutane, and cyclohexane are some of the forms that six-carbon atoms with single covalent bonds may have.

Some Six-Carbon Alkanes

Hexane

3-Methylpentane

2,3-Dimethylbutane

Cyclohexane

Science Skills

Graphic Organizer The graphic organizer below may help students with alkane classification.

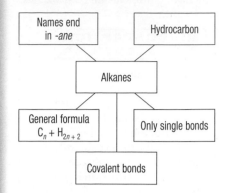

Teaching Key Ideas

Naming Organic Compounds
Although organic compounds are covalent, they are not named by the conventions used to name other covalent compounds. The prefixes used to name alkanes, as shown in **Figure 3,** are also used to name alkenes and alkynes. Naming becomes more complex when chains become branched or when other atoms or groups of atoms are substituted for hydrogen atoms on a hydrocarbon. Most high school chemistry books provide complete guidelines for naming organic compounds. In addition to these scientific names, many organic compounds have common names.

Differentiated Instruction

Advanced Learners

Creating Brochures Ask each student to choose one alkane to study in more detail. Instruct them to use library and Internet resources to learn about practical applications of the alkane. Have students use their results to create and design a brochure that illustrates information about their alkane and its uses. Brochures should include illustrations and text, designed by hand or with computer software.
LS Visual

Science Skills

Interpreting Diagrams Tell students that the numbers in the names of the organic compounds in **Figure 4** are used for locating branches. Carbon atoms in the longest chain in the molecule are numbered, starting with one. A number indicates where on the chain branches occur.

Answer to caption question
Ethene and propene are both alkenes.

MISCONCEPTION ALERT

Hydroxyl Group Be sure students understand that the hydroxyl group, –OH, found in alcohols is not the same as the hydroxide ion, OH⁻. The hydroxyl group is covalently bonded to an organic compound. The hydroxide ion is charged and is ionically bonded to a cation. Ask students to create a table that compares the hydroxyl group and hydroxide ion, including examples of compounds that contain each.
LS Logical/Visual

Why It Matters

Substitutions Compounds known as *substituted hydrocarbons* form when an atom or group of atoms substitutes for a hydrogen atom in a hydrocarbon. For example, a halogen atom can replace a hydrogen atom. An alcohol is a substituted hydrocarbon, as is an organic acid. Other substituted hydrocarbons include ethers, aldehydes, ketones, and esters. Depending on their structure, substituted hydrocarbons have many uses, including use as solvents, fuels, flavorings, and perfumes.

Figure 5 The peaches in this plastic container, which is made by joining propene molecules, release ethene gas as they ripen. **To what class of hydrocarbons do ethene and propene both belong?**

Figure 6 Many products, such as the sterno in a buffet heater, contain a mixture of the alcohols methanol and ethanol. This mixture is called *denatured alcohol.*

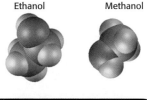

Ethanol   Methanol

Alkenes have double carbon-carbon bonds.

Alkenes are also hydrocarbons. Alkenes are different from alkanes because alkenes have at least one double covalent bond between carbon atoms. This bond is shown by C=C. Alkenes are named by replacing the *-ane* ending with *-ene*.

The simplest alkene is ethene (or ethylene), C_2H_4. Ethene is formed when fruit ripens. Propene (or propylene), C_3H_6, is used to make rubbing alcohol and some plastics. The structures of both compounds are shown in **Figure 5.**

Alcohols have hydroxyl groups.

Alcohols are organic compounds that are made of oxygen as well as carbon and hydrogen. Alcohols have *hydroxyl*, or –OH, groups. The alcohol methanol, CH_3OH, is sometimes mixed with another alcohol ethanol, CH_3CH_2OH, to make denatured alcohol. Denatured alcohol is found in some familiar products, as **Figure 6** shows. Isopropanol, which is found in rubbing alcohol, has the chemical formula C_3H_8O, or $(CH_3)_2CHOH$. You may have noticed how the names of these three alcohols end in *-ol*. This is true for most alcohols.

Alcohol and water molecules behave similarly.

A methanol molecule is like a methane molecule except that one of the hydrogen atoms is replaced by a hydroxyl group. Like water molecules, neighboring alcohol molecules are attracted to one another. Because of the attractions many alcohols are liquids at room temperature. Alcohols have much higher boiling points than alkanes of similar size.

Differentiated Instruction

Advanced Learners

Sugar Substitutes Have students find out more about the use of sugar substitutes, including sorbitol and aspartame. You may wish to assign different topics to different students or groups of students. Possible topics include: Why do some people use sugar substitutes? What are the health risks associated with excess sugar consumption? Are there any health risks associated with sugar substitutes? What are the differences in chemical makeup and structure between sugar and various sugar substitutes? Are some sugar substitutes better than others? Some students could also research individual sugar substitutes in more detail, including sorbitol, aspartame, saccharine, stevia, and the recently approved sucralose. Ask students to share their results with the class. You could also ask students to bring in examples of sugar substitutes to share with other students. **LS Verbal**

Polymers

What do rubber, wood, plastic milk jugs, and the DNA inside the cells of your body have in common? They are all made of large molecules called polymers. **> A polymer is a molecule that is a long chain made of smaller molecules.**

Polymers have repeating subunits.

Polyethene, which is also known as *polyethylene* or *polythene,* is the polymer that makes up plastic milk jugs. The name *polyethene* tells polyethene's structure. *Poly* means "many." *Ethene* is an alkene that has the formula C_2H_4. Thus, *polyethene* means "many ethenes," as **Figure 7** shows. The smaller molecule that makes up the polymer, in this case C_2H_4, is called a *monomer.*

Some polymers are natural, and others are artificial.

Rubber, wood, cotton, wool, starch, protein, and DNA are all natural polymers. Human-made polymers are usually either plastics or fibers. Most plastics are flexible and easily molded, whereas fibers form long, thin strands.

Some polymers can be used as both plastics and fibers. For example, polypropene (polypropylene) is molded to make plastic containers, such as the one shown in **Figure 5,** as well as some parts for cars and appliances. It is also used to make ropes, carpet, and artificial turf for athletic fields.

✓ Reading Check What is the relationship between a monomer and a polymer?

A polymer's structure determines its elasticity.

As with all substances, the properties of a polymer are determined by its structure. Polymer molecules are like long, thin chains. A small piece of plastic or a single fiber is made of billions of these chains. Polymer molecules can be compared to spaghetti. Like a bowl of spaghetti, the chains are tangled but can slide over each other. Milk jugs are made of polyethene, a plastic made of such long chains. You can crush or dent a milk jug because the plastic is flexible. Once the jug has been crushed, though, it does not return to its original shape. It cannot be reshaped because polyethene is not elastic.

When the chains are connected to each other, the polymer's properties are different. Some polymers are elastic, like a volleyball net. An elastic polymer can stretch. When the polymer is released, it returns to its original shape. Rubber bands are made of elastic polymers. As long as a rubber band is not stretched too far, it can go back to its original form.

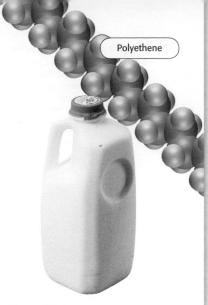

Polyethene

Figure 7 Polyethene is a polymer made of many repeating ethene units. It is used to make various plastics, such as the plastics in this milk jug.

polymer (PAHL uh muhr) a large molecule that is formed by more than five monomers, or small units

QuickLab ⏱ 10 min

Polymer Memory

❶ Polymers that return to their original shape after stretching can be thought of as having a "memory." Test the memory of a **rubber band** and that of the **plastic rings** from a six-pack of cans.

❷ Which polymer is easier to stretch?

❸ Which one has better memory?

❹ Warm the stretched six-pack holder over a **hot plate.** Be careful not to melt it. Will the six-pack holder return to the shape it had before it was heated? Explain.

Teaching Key Ideas

Polymers Show students different types of polymers. Examples might include plastic wrap; rubber tubing; polyester thread; nylon pantyhose; foam cups; trash bags; a plastic that is firm but flexible, such as a margarine container; and a rigid plastic, such as the material used to make a telephone. Tell students that all of the examples are made up of the same type of compound. Ask students to describe what property of the compound that makes up each item makes it a polymer. (All of the compounds are made of chains of smaller molecules.) **LS Logical**

QuickLab

Teacher's Notes Caution students about not touching the hot plate and not melting the plastic. If the plastic accidentally melts, tell students to leave the area and notify you immediately. They should not touch the melted plastic or breathe any of the fumes produced by melting plastic.

Materials per Group
• hot plate
• plastic rings from a six-pack of cans
• rubber band

Answers

2. The rubber band is easier to stretch than the plastic rings are.
3. The rubber band has better polymer memory than the plastic rings do.
4. No, the plastic rings change shape and do not return to their original shape.

Differentiated Instruction

Special Education Students

Practical Polymers Ask students to fold a piece of paper in half vertically. Label one side of the paper "Natural polymers" and the other side "Synthetic polymers." Under each title, write an example of each polymer to help students recognize each type. Then, have students look up and write a definition for each term. Finally, have students cut pictures from magazines that show objects made of polymers and paste the pictures under the appropriate heading.
LS Visual/Kinesthetic

Why It **Matters**

Distinguishing Fibers Sometimes, natural fibers such as wool and cotton are difficult to distinguish from synthetic fibers such as nylon or rayon. One way to tell them apart is to hold them in a flame. The natural fiber will char, and the synthetic fiber will melt.

**READING
TOOLBOX**

Layered Book Sample notes:
Hydrocarbons
- molecules composed of carbon and hydrogen
- covalently bonded
- can have single, double, or triple carbon bonds
- carbon atoms form a chain or branded chain

Carbohydrates
- molecules composed of carbon, hydrogen, and oxygen
- include sugars and starches
- provide energy to living things

Proteins
- molecules composed of carbon, hydrogen, oxygen, nitrogen, and sulfur
- made of long chains of amino acids
- structure is determined by the amino acids that it is made of

DNA
- molecules composed of carbon, hydrogen, oxygen, nitrogen, and phosphorus
- made of two linked strands of sugar molecules attached to phosphate units and DNA monomers
- provides information needed to make proteins

Teaching Key Ideas

Biology Have a biology or health teacher explain the importance of various compounds to the human body. Emphasize the importance of trace minerals and how to obtain needed substances by eating a balanced diet.

Figure 8 Athletes often eat a lot of foods that are high in carbohydrates the day before a big event. Carbohydrates provide them with a ready supply of stored energy.

**READING
TOOLBOX**

Layered Book
Make a layered book FoldNote, and label the tabs with "Hydrocarbons," "Carbohydrates," "Proteins," and "DNA." Write notes on the appropriate tab as you read this section.

carbohydrate (KAHR boh HIE drayt) a class of molecules that includes sugars, starches, and fiber; contains carbon, hydrogen, and oxygen

protein (PROH teen) an organic compound that is made of one or more chains of amino acids and that is a principal component of all cells

amino acid (uh MEE noh AS id) a compound of a class of simple organic compounds that contain a carboxyl group and an amino group and that combine to form proteins

Biochemical Compounds

Biochemical compounds are organic compounds that can be made by living things. **❯ Biochemicals, which are essential to life, include carbohydrates, proteins, and DNA.** Burning carbohydrates gives you energy. Proteins form important parts of your body, such as muscles, tendons, fingernails, and hair. The DNA inside your cells gives your body information about what proteins you need. Each of these biochemical compounds is a polymer.

Many carbohydrates are made of glucose.

Biochemicals called **carbohydrates,** which include sugars and starches, provide energy to living things. Sucrose, table sugar, is made of two simple carbohydrates, glucose and fructose, bonded together. Starch is made of a series of bonded glucose molecules, and is therefore a polymer. You get energy from the chains of starch stored in certain plants.

When you eat starchy foods, such as potatoes or pasta, enzymes in your body break down the starch. This process makes glucose available as a nutrient for your cells. Glucose that is not needed right away by the body is stored as *glycogen,* a polymer of glucose. When you become active, glycogen breaks apart into glucose molecules, which give you energy. Athletes often eat starchy foods so that they will have more energy when they exert themselves later on, as **Figure 8** shows.

✔ **Reading Check** Why do people need carbohydrates in their diets?

Demonstrate

Model a Polymer For this demonstration you will need clothespins. Attach one clothespin onto the leg of another one. Continue to form a chain of clothespins. Show students that the chain can bend and otherwise move, but still remains a chain. Discuss with students what each clothespin represents. (a monomer) What does the chain represent? (a polymer) If the chain represents a protein, what does each clothespin represent? (an amino acid) **LS** Visual

Differentiated Instruction

Struggling Readers

Reading Skills Have students read the section and, using self-adhesive notes, mark passages they do not understand. Be sure students study all tables and figures to help clarify relevant passages. After reading, have students work in pairs to discuss difficult passages. Have the entire class discuss the passages that pairs cannot figure out. **LS** Interpersonal

Proteins are complex polymers of amino acids.

Starch is made of only glucose. **Proteins,** which provide structure and function to parts of cells, are much more complex. Proteins are made of many different molecules that are called **amino acids.** Every amino acid contains an amino group (–NH$_2$), a carboxyl group (–COOH), and a side group that gives the amino acid its unique properties. There are 20 amino acids found in naturally occurring proteins. Each protein is made of a specific combination of a certain number of amino acids. The amino acids that make up a protein determine the protein's structure and function.

Proteins are long chains made of amino acids. A small protein, insulin, is shown in **Figure 9.** Many proteins are made of thousands of bonded amino acid molecules. Thus, millions of different proteins can be made. When you eat foods that contain proteins, such as cheese, your digestive system breaks down the proteins into individual amino acids. Later, your cells bond the amino acids in different ways to form the proteins that your body needs.

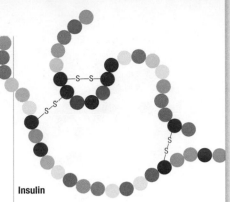

Insulin

Figure 9 The protein insulin controls the use and storage of glucose in your body. Each color in the chain represents a different amino acid. Disulfide bridges between certain amino acids link different chains and provide additional structure.

InquiryLab

Teacher's Notes If time allows, have students repeat the activity to find out what happens if less borax is used. Have students compare the result with their prediction in Analysis item 3.

Materials per Group
- bag, plastic sandwich
- beaker, 250 mL (2)
- borax, 4 g
- glue, white
- spoon, plastic

Answers to Analysis

1. The material stretches and bounces but keeps its shape.
2. Sample answer: Glue is a liquid that flows easily. The new material has properties that are more like that of a solid.
3. Sample answer: If less borax were used, the properties of the material would be closer to those of the glue. The material would flow more easily and would not hold its shape as well.
4. The new material has the properties of a polymer because it is elastic and can return to its original shape.

InquiryLab

What Properties Does a Polymer Have?

⏱ **30 min**

Procedure

❶ In one **250 mL beaker,** mix **4 g borax** with 100 mL **water,** and stir well.

❷ In a second **250 mL beaker,** mix equal parts of **white glue** and water. This solution will determine the amount of new material made. The volume of diluted glue should be between 100 mL and 200 mL.

❸ Pour the borax solution into the beaker containing the glue, and stir well using a **plastic spoon.**

❹ When the solution is too thick to stir, remove the material from the cup and knead it with your fingers. You can store this new material in a **plastic sandwich bag.**

Analysis

1. What happens to the new material when it is stretched or rolled into a ball and bounced?

2. Compare the properties of the glue with the properties of the new material.

3. The properties of the new material resulted from the bonds between the borax and the glue particles. If too little borax were used, in what way would the properties of the new material differ?

4. Does the new material have the properties of a polymer? Explain your conclusion.

Differentiated Instruction

Basic Learners

Identifying Prefixes Tell students that the suffix *-ose* is often added to a word to identify a carbohydrate. Inform students that glucose, cellulose, and lactose are all carbohydrates. Have students work in small groups to determine what the prefixes for *glucose, cellulose,* and *lactose* mean. Encourage students to use their textbook and a dictionary to find the answers. (The prefix *gluc-* means "sweet," *cell-* means "small room," and *lac-* means "milk.")

LS **Logical/Verbal**

Teaching Key Ideas

Essential Amino Acids Many of the 20 amino acids needed for protein synthesis are made by the human body. However, eight amino acids—called *essential amino acids*—are not made by the body. Relate to students that the essential amino acids are obtained from food. Emphasize the importance of eating foods that contain the essential amino acids so that the body has the raw materials needed to manufacture proteins. Have students research amino acids to find the names of the eight essential amino acids. (tryptophan, lysine, methionine, phenylalanine, threonine, valine, leucine, and isoleucine) **LS** **Verbal**

❯Close

Reteaching Key Ideas

Organic Molecule Flashcards Have each student create a set of flashcards using the key words and concepts presented in this section. Then, ask students to pair up and quiz each other using the flashcards. **LS Logical/Verbal**

Formative Assessment

Which of the following molecules is NOT a polymer?

A. DNA (Incorrect. DNA is a polymer that is made up of carbon, hydrogen, oxygen, nitrogen, and phosphorus, all of which form a very long chain.)

B. glucose (Correct. Glucose is a carbohydrate monomer. It is a component of some polymers, but it is not a polymer.)

C. cellulose (Incorrect. Cellulose is a carbohydrate polymer.)

D. protein (Incorrect. Protein is a polymer that is made up of amino acids.)

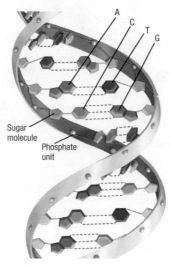

Figure 10 In DNA, cytosine, C, always pairs with guanine, G. Adenine, A, always pairs with thymine, T.

DNA is a polymer that stores genetic information.

All of your genes are made of DNA molecules. DNA is a very long molecule made of carbon, hydrogen, oxygen, nitrogen, and phosphorus.

Figuring out the complex structure of DNA was one of the greatest scientific challenges of the 20th century. Instead of forming one chain, like many proteins and polymers, DNA is in the form of paired chains, or strands. It has the shape of a twisted ladder known as a *double helix*.

Sugar molecules that are bonded to phosphate units correspond to the ladder's sides, as **Figure 10** shows. Attached to each sugar molecule is one of four DNA monomers—adenine, thymine, cytosine, or guanine. These DNA monomers pair with DNA monomers that are attached to the opposite strand in a predictable way, as **Figure 10** shows. Together, the DNA monomer pairs make up the rungs of the ladder.

Most cells in your body have a copy of your genetic material in the form of chromosomes made of DNA. When a cell in your body divides, copies of your chromosomes are made. This process happens when DNA strands separate and a new strand is made from of the old strands.

DNA is the information that the cell uses to make proteins.

The sequence of monomers in DNA determines the proteins that are made in a cell. Each group of three monomers represents a specific amino acid in a protein. The resulting proteins that are made determine all of the activities and characteristics of the cell.

Section 4 Review

KEY IDEAS

1. **Identify** which compound is an alkane: CH_2O, C_6H_{14}, or C_3H_4. Explain your reasoning.

2. **Determine** how many hydrogen atoms a compound has if it is a hydrocarbon and its carbon atom skeleton is C=C–C=C.

3. **Identify** the following compounds as alkanes, alkenes, or alcohols based on their names:
   a. 2-methylpentane   d. 2-butanol
   b. 3-methyloctane   e. 3-heptene
   c. 1-nonene   f. cyclohexanol

4. **Compare** the structures and properties of carbohydrates with those of proteins.

CRITICAL THINKING

5. **Analyzing Information** Why can there be no such compound as CBr_5? Give an acceptable chemical formula for a compound that is made of only carbon and bromine.

6. **Predicting Patterns** *Alkynes* are hydrocarbons that have carbon-carbon triple covalent bonds, or C≡C bonds. Draw the structure of the alkyne that has the chemical formula C_3H_4. Guess the name of this compound.

Answers to Section Review

1. An alkane has the general formula C_nH_{2n+2} and contains only hydrogen and carbon. C_6H_{14} is the alkane.

2. Sample answer: Each carbon atom can form four bonds. Each end carbon currently has two bonds, so each will bond to two hydrogen atoms. The two interior carbon atoms each have three bonds, so each can bond to one hydrogen atom. The total number of hydrogen atoms is six.

3. **a.** alkane
   b. alkane
   c. alkene
   d. alcohol
   e. alkene
   f. alcohol

4. Sample answer: Carbohydrates contain hydrogen, carbon, and oxygen and may or may not be polymers. Proteins contain hydrogen, carbon, oxygen, nitrogen, and sulfur and are polymers of amino acids. In the human body, carbohydrates provide energy, and proteins provide the amino acids that are used to make the proteins that the body needs. Polymers of both carbohydrates and proteins must be broken down into their monomers before they can be used.

Answers continued on p. 213A

DNA Fingerprinting

For over a century, detectives have solved crimes using fingerprint identification. But more recently, detectives have used DNA analysis to identify traces of evidence that contain human cells.

1 Detectives at a crime scene can often find items that have come into contact with a suspect's skin or hair. Every cell in a person's body has a complete set of that person's DNA, so it takes just a single cell left at a crime scene to get DNA evidence.

2 The DNA is isolated. Then, large numbers of copies of the DNA are made so that the DNA is easier to work with. Certain highly variable regions of DNA are analyzed and made into a *DNA profile* that has patterns that are distinctive to each individual.

3 DNA evidence is matched to an individual by comparing it to a DNA sample known to be from that individual. The chances that any two people's DNA profile will match is extremely small. However, the chances of laboratory error are much higher and may result in failure to match DNA profiles. However, matching DNA profiles are a very reliable indication that they came from the same person.

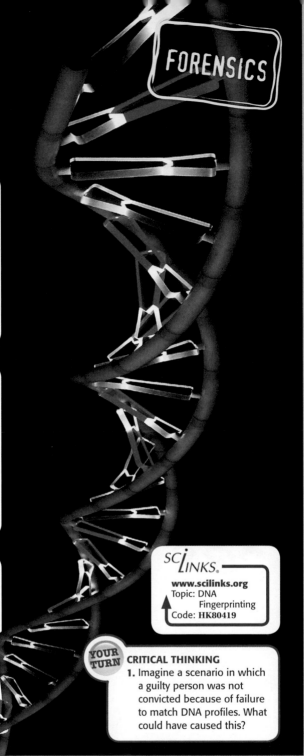

FORENSICS

SC*LINKS*.

www.scilinks.org
Topic: DNA Fingerprinting
Code: **HK80419**

YOUR TURN

CRITICAL THINKING

1. Imagine a scenario in which a guilty person was not convicted because of failure to match DNA profiles. What could have caused this?

DNA Fingerprinting James Watson, Francis Crick, and Maurice Wilkins deciphered the double helix structure of DNA using X-ray crystallographs of DNA taken by Rosalind Franklin. They were also able to correctly predict how DNA replicates. For their discovery, which has led to many genetic engineering applications, Watson, Crick, and Wilkins won the 1963 Nobel Prize for chemistry.

DNA fingerprinting uses a process called a *polymerase chain reaction* (PCR), which reproduces sections of the DNA molecule very rapidly. An enzyme copies a section of DNA in the sample millions of times. The replication is run over and over again. After 30 rounds, there are about one billion copies of the original DNA fragment. Because DNA in biological samples can last a long time, DNA fingerprinting can be used to solve mysteries tens, or even hundreds of years later. Scientists have even studied DNA from ancient Egyptian mummies.

Answer to Your Turn

1. If there is laboratory error in the analysis of the DNA sample, then DNA profiles might fail to match, even though they should.

Teacher's Notes

Use either deionized or distilled water when making the polymers. Have students roll the latex and the ethanol-silicate polymer into a ball. Students will have difficulty making a perfect sphere, but they should try to make it as regular as possible. The more irregular the shape is, the more difficulty students will have determining the bounce height because the ball will not bounce straight up.

Remind students to be patient with the ethanol-silicate polymer, which tends to crumble. If it crumbles too much, a few drops of water will rehydrate it so that it can be reshaped into a ball.

Time Required

1 lab period

Ratings

EASY ——————————→ HARD

Teacher Prep 🧪🧪

Student Set-Up 🧪🧪🧪

Concept Level 🧪

Clean Up 🧪🧪🧪

Skills Acquired

- Collecting data
- Communicating
- Interpreting
- Measuring
- Organizing and analyzing data

Scientific Methods

In this lab, students will:
- Make observations
- Analyze the results
- Draw conclusions
- Communicate results

Application Lab

TESTED & APPROVED

What You'll Do

❯ **Synthesize** two different polymers, shape each into a ball, and measure how high each ball bounces.

❯ **Draw conclusions** about which polymer would make a better toy ball.

What You'll Need

acetic acid solution (vinegar), 5%

container, 2 L

craft sticks, wooden (2)

cups, paper, medium-sized (2)

ethanol solution, 50%

graduated cylinder, 10 mL

graduated cylinder, 25 mL (2)

latex, liquid

meterstick

paper towels

sodium silicate solution

water, deionized

Safety

Comparing Polymers

You work in the research and development lab of a toys and novelties company. The company wants to manufacture bouncy toy balls. Such toy balls are made of polymers that bounce back after they are stretched, bent, or compressed. Your job is to review the bounce heights of the polymers and to make a recommendation about which of two polymers to use for the toy balls.

Procedure

① Prepare a data table like the sample data table shown.

Making Latex Rubber

CAUTION: Wear goggles, gloves, and an apron. If you get a chemical on your skin or clothing, wash it off with lukewarm water while calling to your teacher. If you get a chemical in your eyes, flush it out immediately at the eyewash station and alert your teacher.

② Pour 1 L of deionized water into a 2 L container.

③ Use a 25 mL graduated cylinder to pour 10 mL of liquid latex into one of the paper cups.

④ Clean the graduated cylinder thoroughly with soap and water. Then, rinse it with deionized water, and use it to add 10 mL of deionized water to the cup of liquid latex.

⑤ Use the same graduated cylinder to add 10 mL of acetic acid solution to the mixture of liquid latex and water.

⑥ Immediately begin stirring the mixture with a wooden craft stick. As you stir, a lump of the polymer will form around the stick.

⑦ Transfer the stick and the attached polymer to the 2 L container. While keeping the polymer underwater, gently pull it off the stick with your gloved hands.

⑧ Squeeze the polymer underwater to remove any unreacted chemicals, shape it into a ball, and remove the ball from the water.

⑨ Make the ball smooth by rolling it between your gloved hands. Set the ball on a paper towel to dry while you continue the lab.

⑩ Wash your gloved hands with soap and water, and then dispose of the gloves. Wash your hands again with soap and water.

Sample Data Table: Bounce Heights of Polymers

Polymer	Bounce height (cm)					
	Trial 1	Trial 2	Trial 3	Trial 4	Trial 5	Average
Latex rubber						
Ethanol-silicate			DO NOT WRITE IN BOOK			

Safety Caution

Ethanol is flammable, so make sure that no heat sources are present. Sodium silicate is a skin irritant. Caution students to tell you immediately if they spill any of the chemical on themselves. They should immediately flush any affected areas with water and remove contaminated clothing. If inhaled, sodium silicate can irritate the upper respiratory tract. If a student inhales sodium silicate, immediately get the student to fresh air. Seek medical attention if student has a severe reaction. Do not allow students to take any ethanol-silicate polymer from the laboratory.

Making an Ethanol-Silicate Polymer

CAUTION: Put on a new pair of disposable gloves. Ethanol is flammable, so make sure there are no flames or other heat sources anywhere in the laboratory.

⓫ Use a clean 25 mL graduated cylinder to pour 12 mL of sodium silicate solution into the clean paper cup.

⓬ Use a 10 mL graduated cylinder to add 3 mL of the ethanol solution to the sodium silicate solution.

⓭ Immediately begin stirring the mixture with a clean, wooden craft stick until a solid polymer forms.

⓮ Remove the polymer with your gloved hands, and gently press it between your palms until you form a ball that does not crumble. This activity may take some time. Dripping some tap water on the polymer might be helpful.

⓯ When the ball no longer crumbles, dry it very gently with a paper towel.

⓰ Repeat step 10, and put on a new pair of disposable gloves.

⓱ Examine both polymers closely. Record in your lab report how the two polymers are alike and how they are different.

⓲ Use a meterstick to measure the highest bounce height of each ball when each is dropped from a height of 1 m. Drop each ball five times, and record the highest bounce height each time in your data table.

Analysis

1. **Analyzing Data** Calculate the average bounce height for each ball by adding the five bounce heights and dividing by 5. Record the averages in your data table.

Communicating Your Results

2. **Evaluating Methods** What was the purpose of measuring the bounce heights of each polymer in five trials? If you had only measured the bounce height of each polymer once, how would the validity of your results compare with the validity of your results after several trials?

3. **Drawing Conclusions** On average, which polymer bounced higher?

4. **Applying Concepts** What chemical difference between the two polymers might cause the difference in bounce heights?

Application

Based on only their bounce heights, which polymer would make a better toy ball?

Disposal Information

Paper cups and towels, disposable gloves, latex, and ethanol-silicate polymer balls and fragments should be thrown in the trash can. Waste liquids from this lab can be poured down the drain.

Answer to Analysis

1. Answers may vary depending on observations. Data table should be complete.

Answers to Communicating Your Results

2. Sample answer: Repeated trials are necessary to ensure repeatable and valid results. If the bounce height was only measured once for each polymer, the results would not provide much assurance that they accurately reflected the properties of the polymers tested.

3. Answers may vary depending on the measured bounce heights, but the ethanol-silicate polymer tends to bounce higher than the latex rubber does.

4. Sample answer: The molecules of the polymer that bounces higher have a tendency to reform their intermolecular configuration more quickly when deformed than those of the other polymer do.

Answer to Application

Based only on bounce height, the ethanol-silicate polymer would make a better toy ball than the latex would.

Key Resources

 Virtual Investigation

 Classroom Lab Video/DVD

Holt Lab Generator CD-ROM
Search for any lab by type, standard, difficulty level, or time. Edit any lab to fit your needs, or create your own labs. Use the Lab Materials QuickList software to customize your lab materials list.

 **Differentiated Datasheets**
Comparing Polymers

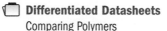 **Observation Lab**
Extracting Iron from Cereal

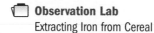 **CBL™ Probeware Lab**
Determining Which Household Solutions Conduct Electricity

Understanding Symbols

Technology

Math

Scientific Methods

Graphing

Interpreting Symbols Students should know how to use context to determine the type of symbol being used. For example, the letter *F* represents fluorine in the context of chemical symbols, but it represents force in the equation $F = ma$. If the meaning of a symbol is not clear, look for clues in the discussion before and after the appearance of the symbol.

Answers to Practice

1. **a.** chemical formula
   b. Two elements are represented: bromine and oxygen. There are two atoms: one atom of bromine and one atom of oxygen.
2. **a.** physical equation
   b. The quantity v (velocity) is squared.

Scientific symbols are a kind of shorthand that makes expressing scientific ideas easier. The meaning of a symbol depends on the context in which it is used. These tips will help you understand some of the most common kinds of scientific symbols.

❶ **Chemical symbols** represent chemical elements. The symbols stand alone when representing elements, but chemical symbols are combined in chemical formulas. To form a chemical equation, we combine chemical symbols and formulas with plus signs and an arrow (a yields sign).

- The symbol for each element can be found in the periodic table. There is a different symbol for each element. Each symbol starts with a capital letter.
- When chemical symbols are used in chemical formulas, subscripts are used to tell you how many atoms of that element are in one unit of the compound. If there is no subscript after an element symbol, that substance contains only one atom of the element per unit.
- The charge on an ion is given by a superscript after the chemical symbol or chemical formula.
- Subscripts and superscripts **before** an element's symbol tell you about a specific isotope of that element. The subscript is the atomic number (*Z*, the number of protons), and the superscript is the mass number (*A*, the number of protons + neutrons).

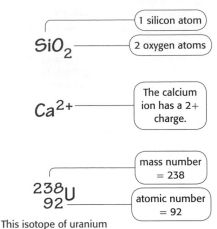

This isotope of uranium has 92 protons.

❷ **Physical symbols** are used to represent certain kinds of physical quantities. Equations are used to show the mathematical relationships between physical quantities.

- Physical quantities that are variable are represented by italic letters. When you learn about a physical quantity, take note of the symbol used to represent the quantity.
- Subscripts usually distinguish one variable from another variable of the same kind.
- Superscripts are powers of multiplication, just as in any mathematical equation.

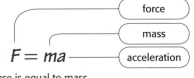

Force is equal to mass times acceleration.

Energy is equal to mass times the speed of light squared.

Practice

1. Consider the following: BrO^-
   a. Is this a chemical symbol, a chemical formula, or a chemical equation?
   b. How many elements are represented? What are they? How many atoms are represented?

2. Consider the following: $KE = \frac{1}{2}mv^2$
   a. Is this a physical quantity, a physical equation, or a unit of measurement?
   b. What does the superscript 2 tell you?

SUMMARY

Key Ideas

Section 1 Compounds and Molecules

> **Chemical Bonds** The forces that hold atoms or ions together in a compound are called *chemical bonds*. (p. 177)

> **Chemical Structure** The structure of chemical compounds can be shown by various models. (p. 178)

> **How Does Structure Affect Properties** The chemical structure of a compound determines the properties of that compound. (p. 180)

Section 2 Ionic and Covalent Bonding

> **Why Do Chemical Bonds Form?** Atoms join to form bonds so that each atom has a stable electron configuration. (p. 183)

> **Ionic, Covalent, and Metallic Bonds** Ionic bonds form between oppositely charged ions. (p. 184) Atoms joined by covalent bonds share electrons. (p. 186) Electrons in metal atoms have freedom of movement. (p. 188)

> **Polyatomic Ions** A polyatomic ion acts as a single unit in a compound. (p. 189)

Section 3 Compound Names and Formulas

> **Naming Ionic and Covalent Compounds** The names of ionic compounds consist of the names of the ions of which the compounds are made. (p. 191) Numerical prefixes tell how many atoms of each element are in a covalent compound. (p. 194)

> **Empirical Formulas** An empirical formula tells us the smallest whole-number ratio of atoms that are in a compound. (p. 194)

Section 4 Organic and Biochemical Compounds

> **Organic Compounds** An organic compound is a covalent compound that contains carbon. (p. 197)

> **Polymers** A polymer is a molecule that is a long chain made of smaller molecules. (p. 201)

> **Biochemical Compounds** Biochemicals include carbohydrates, proteins, and DNA. (p. 202)

Key Terms

chemical bond, p. 177

chemical structure, p. 178

bond length, p. 178

bond angle, p. 178

ionic bond, p. 184

covalent bond, p. 186

metallic bond, p. 188

polyatomic ion, p. 189

empirical formula, p. 194

molecular formula, p. 195

organic compound, p. 197

polymer, p. 201

carbohydrate, p. 202

protein, p. 203

amino acid, p. 203

SUPER SUMMARY

Have students connect the major concepts in this chapter through an interactive Super Summary. Visit **go.hrw.com** and type in the keyword **HK8STRS** to access the Super Summary for this chapter.

Differentiated Instruction

Alternative Assessment

Different Chemical Structures Have students use molecular model kits or colored marshmallows and toothpicks to make molecular models of chemical compounds that have 5 carbon atoms and 12 hydrogen atoms. Ask students to determine how many chemical structures are possible if each carbon atom is connected to 4 other atoms and each hydrogen atom is connected to one other atom. (There are three different structures possible.) **LS** **Logical**

Key Resources

🔲 **Interactive Concept Map**

🗂 **Review Resources**
Concept Review Worksheets

🗂 **Assessment Resources**
Chapter Tests A and B
Performance-Based Assessment

Reading Toolbox

1. Answers may vary. Sample answer: Salts are ionic compounds. The nature of metallic bonds enables metals to be shiny, malleable, and conduct electricity and heat. A polyatomic ion acts as a single unit in an ionic compound.

Using Key Terms

2. Proteins and some carbohydrates are made up of many smaller molecules, or monomers, that are joined together. The monomers for proteins are amino acids, and glucose is a monomer for carbohydrates.

3. Sample answer: In ionic bonds, electrons are transferred from one atom to another, whereas in covalent bonds electrons are shared between atoms. Ionic bonds form by the attraction of oppositely charged ions, whereas covalent bonds form in order to give each atom a stable octet.

4. Sample answer: Organic compounds contain carbon and usually hydrogen. Common organic compounds include acetylsalicyclic acid, sorbitol, methane, propane, and ethane.

5. A hydroxyl group, or –OH group, is made of oxygen and hydrogen. Alcohols contain hydroxyl groups.

6. A hydrocarbon is made of hydrogen and carbon. The simplest hydrocarbon is methane.

Understanding Key Ideas

7. d
8. b
9. a
10. c
11. b
12. c
13. b
14. d

Explaining Key Ideas

15. Sample answer: Both compounds have two identical atoms covalently bonded to a central atom of a different element. Carbon dioxide has the larger bond angle at 180°; oxygen difluoride has a bond angle of less than 180°.

READING TOOLBOX

1. Suffixes Refer to the word parts table that you made for the words in Section 2 containing the suffix *-ic*. Use each of the words in a sentence.

USING KEY TERMS

2. Explain why *proteins* and *carbohydrates* are *polymers*. What makes up these polymers?

3. List two differences between *ionic bonds* and *covalent bonds*.

4. What does an *organic compound* contain? List several organic compounds that can be found in your body or used in your daily life.

5. What is a *hydroxyl group*? What organic compound contains a hydroxyl group?

6. What makes up a *hydrocarbon*? Name the simplest hydrocarbon.

UNDERSTANDING KEY IDEAS

7. Compounds that are made of molecules
  a. never exist as liquids.
  b. never exist as solids.
  c. never exist as gases.
  d. tend not to have high melting points.

8. A chemical bond can be defined as a force that
  a. holds the parts of an atom together.
  b. joins atoms in a compound.
  c. causes electric repulsion.
  d. blends nuclei together.

9. A compound is different from a mixture because
  a. a compound is held together by chemical bonds.
  b. each substance in a compound maintains its own properties.
  c. each original substance in a compound remains chemically unchanged.
  d. a mixture is held together by chemical bonds.

10. Ionic solids
  a. are formed by networks of ions that have the same charge.
  b. melt at very low temperatures.
  c. have very regular structures.
  d. are sometimes found as gases at room temperature.

11. Crystals of table salt, sodium chloride, are
  a. made of molecules.
  b. made of a network of ions.
  c. chemically similar to sugar crystals.
  d. weak solids.

12. The compound _____ is an example of an ionic compound.
  a. H_2O
  b. CO_2
  c. KCl
  d. PCl_3

13. The chemical formula for calcium chloride is
  a. $CaCl$.
  b. $CaCl_2$.
  c. Ca_2Cl.
  d. Ca_2Cl_2.

14. All organic compounds
  a. come only from living organisms.
  b. contain only carbon and hydrogen.
  c. are biochemical compounds.
  d. have atoms connected by covalent bonds.

EXPLAINING KEY IDEAS

15. Compare the chemical structure of oxygen difluoride with that of carbon dioxide. Which compound has the larger bond angle?

Carbon dioxide

Oxygen difluoride

16. The figure below shows how atoms are bonded in a molecule of vitamin C. Which elements make up vitamin C? What is its molecular formula?

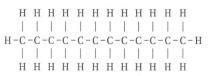

17. Name the following covalent compounds:
   a. SF$_4$ **c.** PCl$_3$
   b. N$_2$O   **d.** P$_2$O$_5$

CRITICAL THINKING

18. Recognizing Relationships Noble gases, such as helium and neon, have full, stable, outer-level electron configurations. How does this fact explain why atoms of noble gases usually do not form chemical bonds?

19. Analyzing Data A certain compound is a solid at room temperature. It is unable to conduct electricity as a solid but can conduct electricity as a liquid. This compound melts at 755 °C. What type of bonds would you expect this compound to have: ionic, metallic, or covalent bonds?

20. Applying Concepts Dodecane is a combustible organic compound that is used in research on jet fuel. It is an *n*-alkane made of 12 carbon atoms. How many hydrogen atoms does dodecane have? Draw the structural formula for dodecane.

21. Evaluating Assumptions A classmate claims that sodium gains a positive charge when it becomes an ion because it gains a proton. Explain what is wrong with the student's claim.

22. Predicting Outcomes Consider two atoms that form a chemical bond. One atom has a much stronger attraction for electrons than the other atom does. What kind of chemical bond is likely to form between the atoms? Explain.

Graphing Skills

23. The melting points of ionic compounds with cations in the same group follow a pattern. To see this, plot the melting point of each of the ionic compounds in the table below on the *y*-axis and the atomic number of the element from which the cation is made on the *x*-axis.
   a. What trend do you notice in the melting points as you move down Group 2?
   b. The compound BeCl$_2$ has a melting point of 405 °C. Is this likely to be an ionic compound? Explain. (**Hint:** Locate beryllium in the periodic table.)
   c. Predict the melting point of the ionic compound RaCl$_2$. (**Hint:** Check the periodic table, and compare radium's location with the location of magnesium, calcium, strontium, and barium.)

Melting Points of Some Ionic Compounds

Compound	Melting Point (°C)
MgCl$_2$	714
CaCl$_2$	782
SrCl$_2$	875
BaCl$_2$	963

Math Skills

24. Writing Ionic Formulas Determine the chemical formula for each of the following ionic compounds:
   a. strontium nitrate, an ingredient in some fireworks, signal flares, and matches
   b. sodium cyanide, a compound used in electroplating and treating metals
   c. chromium(III) hydroxide, a compound used to tan and dye substances

25. Finding Empirical Formulas A sample of a compound contains 111.7 g of iron and 64.1 g of sulfur. What is the compound's empirical formula?

16. Vitamin C is made of carbon, hydrogen, and oxygen atoms. Its formula is C$_6$H$_8$O$_6$.

17. a. sulfur tetrafluoride
   b. dinitrogen monoxide
   c. phosphorus trichloride
   d. diphosphorus pentoxide

Critical Thinking

18. Sample answer: Chemical bonds are formed by atoms to obtain a stable outer electron configuration. Noble gases tend not to form chemical bonds because they already have a stable outer electron configuration.

19. Because it is a solid at room temperature, is only able to conduct electricity in the liquid state, and has a high melting point, the compound probably has ionic bonds.

20. The general formula for n-alkanes is C$_n$H$_{2n+2}$. Because n = 12, dodecane must have 2(12) + 2 = 26 hydrogen atoms, as shown in the structural formula.

```
    H H H H H H H H H H H H
    | | | | | | | | | | | |
H - C-C-C-C-C-C-C-C-C-C-C-C - H
    | | | | | | | | | | | |
    H H H H H H H H H H H H
```

21. Sample answer: Sodium gains a positive charge when it ionizes because it loses a valence electron, not because it gains a proton. If it gained a proton, it would be a different element.

22. If one atom has a much higher attraction for electrons than another atom in the bond does, there is likely to be electron transfer between the atoms, forming an ionic bond.

Answers continued on p. 213A

Assignment Guide	
SECTION	**ITEMS**
1	1, 8, 9, 15, 18, 21
2	3, 7, 10–12, 19, 22, 23
3	13, 17, 24, 25
4	2, 4–6, 14, 16, 20

TEST DOCTOR

Question 1 Answer C is correct. Chemical bonds are formed by the interaction of valence electrons to form a stable configuration. Answer A is incorrect because atoms do not become more stable by losing electrons. Answer B is incorrect because atoms do not merge into one atom. Answer D is incorrect because the nuclei of atoms are positively charged, so they do not attract each other.

Question 2 Answer I is correct. To find the correct answer, students must multiply the 4 oxygen atoms in the SO_4 molecule by the number of SO_4 molecules, 3, to get 12 atoms of oxygen.

Question 3 Answer A is correct. To find the correct answer, students must first find the total negative charge of the nitride anions in the molecule by multiplying the charge of 3– by the number of nitride anions, 2, to get a total negative charge of 6–. Therefore, the total positive charge is 6+, which is then divided by the number of titanium cations, 3, to get a positive charge of 2+ per cation.

Question 4 Answer I is correct. To find the correct answer, students must know that n-alkanes are chains of CH_2 molecules that have CH_3 molecules on each end.

Question 5 Full-credit answers should include the following points:
- In a covalent bond, the electrons are shared between two atoms
- The atoms in an ionic bond form due to their opposite charges
- In a metallic bond, valence electrons move freely among positively charged nuclei.

Question 6 Full-credit answers should include the following point:
- The differences in the proteins that make up the seven types of silk result from variation in the amino acids that make up the silk.

Question 7 Answer C is correct. Answers A and D are incorrect because silk that is heavy would not have enough strength and would require a lot of work on the part of

Understanding Concepts

Directions (1–4): **For each question, write on a sheet of paper the letter of the correct answer.**

1. What causes atoms to form chemical bonds with other atoms?
   A. Atoms are more stable when they give away electrons.
   B. When two atoms get close together, they merge into one.
   C. The interaction of valence electrons forms a more stable configuration.
   D. The attraction of the nuclei for one another causes atoms to share electrons.

2. How many atoms of oxygen are in one formula unit of aluminum sulfate, $Al_2(SO_4)_3$?
   F. 3
   G. 4
   H. 8
   I. 12

3. A nitride anion, N^{3-}, has a charge of 3–. What is the charge of a titanium cation in the compound Ti_3N_2?
   A. 2+
   B. 2–
   C. 3+
   D. 3–

4. What is the condensed structural formula for the n-alkane heptane, which has a molecular formula of C_7H_{16}?
   F. C_7H_{16}
   G. $(CH_2)_6CH_4$
   H. $C_3H_4(CH_3)_4$
   I. $CH_3(CH_2)_5CH_3$

Directions (5): **For each question, write a short response.**

5. The difference between the three types of chemical bonds—covalent, ionic, and metallic—is what happens to valence electrons that are part of the bond. Compare the three types of bonds based on valence electrons.

Reading Skills

Directions (6–8): **Read the passage below. Then, answer the questions that follow.**

SPIDER SILK

Spider silk is one of the strongest known fibers. It is strong enough to support the spider and has enough elasticity to absorb the energy of the collision of a flying insect. The strength comes from the covalent bonds between units of the amino acid polymer of which spider silk, a protein, is made. The elasticity is the result of interactions between different parts of the molecule. Coils or folds in the protein expand on impact.

Spiders can make at least seven kinds of silk for different purposes by varying the amino acids that make up the silk. Scientists studying the structure of silk have identified some of the structures that account for silk's properties. They have even found ways to mimic the properties of spider silk in synthetic fibers. However, there is still much for scientists to learn from the amazing natural properties of spider silk.

6. How do the various kinds of spider silk differ based on their protein structures?

7. Which of the following describes the properties of spider silk?
   A. heavy and strong
   B. light and flimsy
   C. strong and elastic
   D. rigid and heavy

8. Which of the following best describes what scientists have learned about spider silk?
   F. All of its properties have been explained.
   G. Scientists have made synthetic fibers with properties similar to spider silk.
   H. All spider silk has the same chemical structure.
   I. The unique properties of spider silk remain a mystery.

the spider. Answer B is incorrect because flimsy silk would not have enough strength to be useful to the spider.

Question 8 Answer G is correct. Answer F is incorrect because the passage clearly states that scientists still have much to learn about silk. Answer H is incorrect because it clearly states that the seven kinds of silk have varying amino acid structure. Answer I is incorrect because the passage discusses the characteristics of silk that scientists have discovered.

Question 9 Full-credit answers should include the following points:
- The forces of attraction within a water mol-

ecule are covalent chemical bonds, which are very strong.
- The hydrogen bonds between water molecules are weaker than the covalent bonds within water molecules.

Question 10 Answer C is correct. Students must calculate the number of atoms of each element in the structural formula, and compare those to the number of balls of each letter in the molecular model. Answer A is incorrect because letter A represents oxygen. Answer B is incorrect because letter B represents nitrogen. Answer D is incorrect because letter D represents hydrogen.

Interpreting Graphics

The illustration below models how water molecules are arranged in the liquid state. Use this illustration to answer question 9.

INTERACTION OF WATER MOLECULES IN THE LIQUID STATE

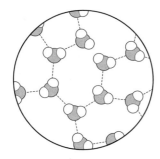

9. Compare the forces of attraction between the atoms of a water molecule to the forces of attraction between two water molecules.

The following graphic shows a model of one molecular unit of the amino acid alanine, which has a structural formula of CH_3CHNH_2COOH. Use this graphic to answer questions 10–11.

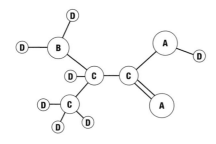

10. What letter represents carbon in the model?
   A. A
   B. B
   C. C
   D. D

11. Atoms of which two elements share a double covalent bond in alanine?

Test Tip

When possible, use the text in multiple-choice questions to help you "jump start" your thinking.

Question 11 Full-credit answers should include the following points:
- The letter C represents carbon atoms.
- The letter A represents oxygen.
- A double bond is represented by two lines.
- Carbon and oxygen share a double covalent bond.

State Resources

For specific resources for your state, visit **go.hrw.com** and type in the keyword **HSHSTR**.

 Test Practice with Guided Reading Development

Answers

1. C
2. I
3. A
4. I
5. Answers may vary; see Test Doctor for a detailed scoring rubric.
6. Answers may vary; see Test Doctor for a detailed scoring rubric.
7. C
8. G
9. Answers may vary; see Test Doctor for a detailed scoring rubric.
10. C
11. Answers may vary; see Test Doctor for a detailed scoring rubric.

Continuation of Answers

Answers continued from p. 190

9. Sample answer: Metallic bonds are similar to covalent bonds in that electrons are shared between atoms. Metallic bonds are different from covalent bonds in that electrons are free to move around in the space between the atoms.

Answers continued from p. 204

5. Carbon atoms form four bonds, not five. Bromine atoms form one bond, so a carbon-bromine compound would be CBr_4.

6.

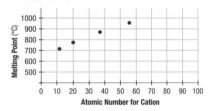

Because the compound has three carbon atoms (*prop-*) and is an alkyne (*-yne*), the compound is propyne.

Answers continued from p. 211

Graphing Skills

23. Sample graph:

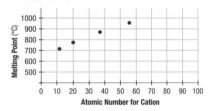

a. The melting point of the compound increases as the atomic mass of the cation increases.

b. $BeCl_2$ is an ionic compound because it is a compound of a metal and a nonmetal. therefore, it has a relatively high melting point.

c. Radium is in the same group as the other cations, and it has a larger atomic mass. Therefore, the melting point of $RaCl_2$ will be higher than the melting point of other Group 12 ionic compounds, at greater than 1000 °C.

Math Skills

24. a. $Sr(NO_3)_2$

  b. NaCN

  c. $Cr(OH)_3$

25. FeS

Ethnobotany and Drug Discovery

Many drugs that are used in Western medicine are derived from natural sources. For example, in ancient Greece the physician Hippocrates prescribed the bark and leaves of the willow tree as a treatment for pain. Ancient cultures in North America, Africa, and India also used the willow tree to alleviate pain. In the 1800s, chemists experimented with the substance salicin, which is found in the bark, and they formed salicylic acid. In the 1890s salicylic acid was modified into a more chemically stable form, acetylsalicylic acid, which is the active ingredient in aspirin. Today, salicylic acid is also used to treat skin disorders, including acne, psoriasis, and warts.

Careers Using Chemistry

When you think of a chemist, you may think of a lab-coated scientist surrounded by test tubes. But people use chemistry in hundreds of careers, not all of which require work in a lab. Whether designing fuel cells, preserving art, or investigating a crime scene, people use chemistry to get the job done. The careers listed here are examples of careers that use chemistry.

Medical Practitioner

Medical practitioners care for people who suffer from injuries or disease. Medical students study chemistry in order to understand the chemical properties of human body systems. For example, a doctor may have a patient's blood chemically analyzed. Chemical blood tests can detect the presence of compounds such as sugar and specific proteins, which can indicate the cause of illness. Medical practitioners must know the chemical properties of medications to avoid prescribing medicines that have harmful drug interactions.

Arson Investigator

Arson investigators help detectives interpret evidence at crime scenes that involve fire. Arson investigators examine the fire debris and try to determine how a fire was started, how it spread, and whether there are clues that might help identify suspects. The presence of an accelerant is an important indicator that a fire was set intentionally. The most common accelerants are hydrocarbon-based fuels, such as gasoline. Arson investigators use a technique called *gas chromatography-mass spectrometry* (GC-MS) to detect accelerants in fire debris.

Ethnobotanist

Ethnobotanists study how cultures use plants for specific purposes. Sometimes, the compounds that scientists find in plants can be used as medicines or other products. For example, ethnobotanist Paul Cox researched a tea made from a rain-forest tree in Samoa. Local healers used this tea to treat viral hepatitis, a disease of the liver. Chemical analysis showed that the plant contains the virus-fighting chemical prostratin, which is a potential treatment for AIDS.

Conservator

Conservators restore and preserve historical artifacts, such as coins, art, documents, and film. To be a conservator, you must understand how factors such as time, use, and humidity affect chemical reactions that damage artifacts. For example, many historic documents were written with iron gall ink. The ink was made by mixing ferrous sulfate with gallic acid extracted from oak trees that had parasitic infections, or galls. Over time, iron gall ink releases sulfuric acid, which destroys the paper on which the ink was printed. Conservators store historic documents in low-temperature, low-humidity environments to limit the rate of this reaction.

Perfumer

The recent discovery of a 4,000-year-old perfume factory in Cyprus suggests that human societies have valued perfumes for a very long time. Modern-day perfumers use analytic, synthetic, and organic chemistry to develop fragrances for everything from soaps and perfumes to food products and new cars. A perfumer must understand chemical properties, such as how gases diffuse, and must understand the chemical reactions that occur between various organic compounds. Perfumers must also understand how the human body detects and perceives fragrances. For example, simple changes in a compound's molecular structure can determine whether the compound has a wonderful smell or an offensive one.

Chef

Cooking—from grilling a steak to baking a cake—involves chemical reactions. Because they must know how to control these reactions, chefs and bakers find a knowledge of chemistry useful. For example, Louis Maillard, a chemist, discovered why all foods brown at temperatures higher than 154 °F (68 °C). He found that a chemical reaction, now called the *Maillard reaction,* occurs when sugars and amino acids are heated together. This reaction makes foods brown and produces many of the flavors and aromas of cooked foods. Understanding chemistry can make cooking more fun.

YOUR TURN

UNDERSTANDING CONCEPTS

1. Describe how understanding chemistry plays an important role in two of the careers described on these pages.

CRITICAL THINKING

2. How can ethnobotanical research benefit indigenous communities?

SCI LINKS.

www.scilinks.org
Topic: Careers in Chemistry
Code: HK81689

Why It Matters

Chef Many culinary education programs include a course on food science that includes chemistry. Chemistry can explain many interesting culinary phenomena. For example, chemistry can explain how gelatin forms a gel. Gelatin is a protein, but it is rarely used by itself to thicken sauces. The long gelatin molecules form only weak bonds with each other. When heated in water, the molecules spread throughout the water. Because the molecules are long, when the solution is cooled and the proteins reform bonds, the molecules can form a gel. The protein matrix interferes with the movement of water and makes a solid gel. Most gelatin desserts contain a relatively small amount of gelatin: about a 3% solution.

Chemistry can also explain how you can avoid crying when you chop onions. Try chewing parsley. The chemicals released from the parsley oxidize the sulfur compounds that are released by chopped onions. Thus, the compounds do not make you cry.

Answers to Your Turn

1. Answers may vary but should describe how chemistry is used by a medical practitioner, an arson investigator, an ethnobotanist, a conservator, a perfumer, or a chef.

2. Answers may vary. By showing that traditional healing practices and local resources are important, an ethnobotanist can help preserve some of the cultural practices of indigenous cultures.

		Standards	Teach Key Ideas
CHAPTER OPENER, pp. 216–218	50 min.		

SECTION 1 The Nature of Chemical Reactions, pp. 219–224 — *50 min.*

❭ Chemical Reactions
❭ Energy and Reactions

Standards: PS 3a, PS 3b, PS 5a, UCP 1, SAI 1

Teach Key Ideas:
- 📺 **Bellringer Transparency**
- 📺 **Teaching Transparencies** C16 Reaction Model • TM22 Exothermic and Endothermic
- 💿 **Visual Concepts** Chemical Reaction • Signs of a Chemical Reaction • Limiting Reactants and Excess Reactants

SECTION 2 Chemical Equations, pp. 225–229 — *50 min.*

❭ Describing Reactions
❭ Balanced Equations and Mole Ratios

Standards: UCP 2, UCP 3, SAI 1, SAI 2, SPSP 4, SPSP 6

Teach Key Ideas:
- 📺 **Bellringer Transparency**
- 📺 **Teaching Transparency** TM23 Balanced Equation
- 💿 **Visual Concepts** Chemical Equation • Reading a Chemical Equation • Symbols Used in Chemical Equations • Balancing a Chemical Equation by Inspection

SECTION 3 Reaction Types, pp. 230–237 — *50 min.*

❭ Classifying Reactions
❭ Electrons and Chemical Reactions

Standards: PS 3b, PS 3c, UCP 1, SAI 1

Teach Key Ideas:
- 📺 **Bellringer Transparency**
- 📺 **Teaching Transparency** C17 Single Displacement
- 💿 **Visual Concepts** Decomposition Reaction • Single Displacement Reaction • Double Displacement Reaction

SECTION 4 Reaction Rates and Equilibrium, pp. 238–247 — *50 min.*

❭ Factors Affecting Reaction Rates
❭ Catalysts
❭ Equilibrium Systems

Standards: PS 3a, PS 3d, PS 3e, UCP 1, UCP 3, UCP 4, SAI 1, SAI 2

Teach Key Ideas:
- 📺 **Bellringer Transparency**
- 📺 **Teaching Transparencies** C18 Equilibrium • TM24 Changing Equilibrium
- 💿 **Visual Concepts** Factors Affecting Reaction Rate • Catalyst • Enzyme • Equilibrium • Factors Affecting Equilibrium • Le Châtelier's Principle

See also PowerPoint® Resources

Chapter Review and Assessment Resources

SE Science Skills: Using Mole Ratios to Calculate Mass, p. 250
SE Chapter Summary, p. 251
SE Chapter Review, pp. 252–253
SE Standardized Test Prep, pp. 254–255
🗋 Concept Review Worksheets ■
🗋 Chapter Tests A and B ■
💻 Holt Online Assessment

CHAPTER
FastTrack *To shorten instruction because of time limitations, omit Section 4 and the chapter lab.*

Basic Learners

TE Concept Map, p. 222
TE Concept Map, p. 240
TE Chemical Equilibrium, p. 245
🗋 Science Skills Worksheets
🗋 Differentiated Datasheets A for Labs and Activities ■
📖 Study Guide A ■

Advanced Learners

TE Chemical Engineering, p. 227
🗋 Cross-Disciplinary Worksheets
🗋 Differentiated Datasheets C for Labs and Activities ■

Key

| SE | Student Edition |
| TE | Teacher's Edition |

📁 Chapter Resource File
📓 Workbook
🎨 Transparency

💿 CD or CD-ROM
* Datasheet or blackline master available

■ Also available in Spanish

All resources listed below are also available on the Teacher's One-Stop Planner.

Why It Matters	Hands-On	Skills Development	Assessment
Build student motivation with resources about high-interest applications.	**SE Inquiry Lab** Matter and Chemical Reactions, p. 217*■	**TE Reading Toolbox** Assessing Prior Knowledge, p. 216 **SE Reading Toolbox** p. 218	📁 **Pretest** ■
TE Activation Energy, p. 220 **SE Bioluminescence,** p. 223 📁 **Cross-Disciplinary Worksheets** Connection to Social Studies—Alchemists' Theory of the Elements • Real World Applications—Hot Meals on Hand • Integrating Biology—Organisms that Glow	**TE Demonstration** Electric Lemon, p. 219 **SE Quick Lab** An Endothermic Reaction, p. 222*■	**SE Reading Toolbox** Table Fold, p. 220 **TE Science Skills** Interpreting Graphs, p. 222	**TE Reteaching Key Ideas** Chemical Reactions at School, p. 224 **TE Formative Assessment,** p. 224 📁 **Spanish Assessment***■ 📁 **Section Quiz** ■
📁 **Cross-Disciplinary Worksheets** Science and the Consumer—The Right Fire Extinguisher for the Job • Connection to Fine Arts—The Chemistry of Art	**TE Demonstration** Equation Analogy, p. 225 **SE Quick Lab** Balancing Chemical Equations, p. 228*■ 📁 **Observation Lab** Combining Elements	**TE Science Skills** Equation Information, p. 226 **TE Reading Toolbox** Coefficients, p. 227 **SE Math Skills** Balancing Chemical Equations, p. 227 **SE Reading Toolbox** Table Fold, p. 228	**TE Reteaching Key Ideas** Balancing Equations, p. 229 **TE Formative Assessment,** p. 229 📁 **Spanish Assessment***■ 📁 **Section Quiz** ■
TE Chloralkali Cells, p. 231 **SE How Are Fires Extinguished?** p. 232 **SE Ozone,** p. 236 **TE Oxidation-Reduction Reactions,** p. 237 📁 **Cross-Disciplinary Worksheets** Connection to Social Studies—Fireworks • Integrating Earth Science—Limestone Reactions	**TE Demonstration** Synthesis Reaction, p. 230 **TE Demonstration** Electrolysis, p. 231 **SE Inquiry Lab** Determining the Products of a Reaction, p. 235*■	**SE Reading Toolbox** Reading Equations, p. 233 **TE Science Skills** Interpreting Visuals, p. 233 **TE Science Skills** Activity Series, p. 234	**TE Reteaching Key Ideas** Mnemonic Devices, p. 237 **TE Formative Assessment,** p. 237 📁 **Spanish Assessment***■ 📁 **Section Quiz** ■
TE Hydrogen Peroxide, p. 241 **SE What Kinds of Chemical Reactions Happen in the Human Body?** pp. 242–243 📁 **Cross-Disciplinary Worksheet** Integrating Environmental Science—Fertilizers: Friend or Foe?	**TE Demonstration** Surface Area, p. 238 **SE Quick Lab** Catalysts in Action, p. 241*■ **SE Inquiry Lab** Rate and Temperature of a Chemical Reaction, pp. 248–249*■	**TE Reading Toolbox** Vocabulary, p. 241 **TE Reading Toolbox** Visual Literacy, p. 242 **SE Reading Toolbox** Prefixes, p. 244 **TE Science Skills** Interpreting Visuals, p. 244 **TE Reading Toolbox** Mnemonics, p. 246	**TE Reteaching Key Ideas** Reaction Rates, p. 247 **TE Formative Assessment,** p. 247 📁 **Spanish Assessment***■ 📁 **Section Quiz** ■

See also Lab Generator

See also Holt Online Assessment Resources

Resources for Differentiated Instruction

English Learners
TE Reading Skills, p. 242
TE Changing Equilibrium, p. 246
📁 Differentiated Datasheets A, B, and C for Labs and Activities ■
📓 Study Guide A ■

Struggling Readers
TE Using Headings, p. 220
TE Learning Reactions, p. 233
TE Words in Context, p. 241
TE Recognizing Context Clues, p. 243
📓 Interactive Reader

Special Education Students
TE Acting and Reacting, p. 221
TE Balanced Chemical Equations, p. 226

Alternative Assessment
TE Researching Enzymes, p. 251

CHAPTER
7

Chemical Reactions

Overview

This chapter discusses chemical reactions, how to recognize chemical reactions, and how energy is involved in chemical reactions. It then discusses five general types of reactions and the role of the electron in chemical bonding. Then, it explains how to read and balance chemical equations, how to predict reaction amounts, and how to identify mole ratios. Finally, it covers reaction rates and chemical equilibrium.

READING TOOLBOX

Assessing Prior Knowledge Students should understand the following concepts:
- conservation of mass
- formulas
- chemical changes
- the periodic table
- moles
- ions
- atomic structure
- atomic mass
- chemical structure
- bonding
- compound names
- formulas

**MISCONCEPTION /// ALERT **

Science education research has identified the following misconceptions about chemical reactions.
- The failure to recognize products, especially gaseous ones, leads students to believe that reactants disappear. (Mass is conserved in all chemical reactions. If the total amount of mass appears to decrease, it is likely that at least one of the products is a gas.)
- Some students think chemical changes are irreversible. (Although some chemical reactions are irreversible, most chemical reactions occur in an equilibrium state in which the reaction can occur in either direction, and the products can become the reactants.)

Chapter Outline

❶ The Nature of Chemical Reactions
Chemical Reactions
Energy and Reactions

❷ Chemical Equations
Describing Reactions
Balanced Equations and Mole Ratios

❸ Reaction Types
Classifying Reactions
Electrons and Chemical Reactions

❹ Reaction Rates and Equilibrium
Factors Affecting Reaction Rates
Catalysts
Equilibrium Systems

Why It Matters

Chemical reactions are everywhere. They are especially important to living things. This sea anemone is an animal that produces its own light by special chemical reactions in its cells.

Chapter Correlations   National Science Education Standards

The following correlations show the National Science Standards that relate to this chapter. For the full text of the standards, see the National Science Education Standards at the front of the book.

PS 3a Chemical reactions occur all around us, for example in health care, cooking, cosmetics, and automobiles. Complex chemical reactions involving carbon-based molecules take place constantly in every cell in our bodies. (Sections 1, 4)

PS 3b Chemical reactions may release or consume energy. Some reactions such as the burning of fossil fuels release large amounts of energy by losing heat and by emitting light. Light can initiate many chemical reactions such as photosynthesis and the evolution of urban smog. (Sections 1, 3)

PS 3c A large number of important reactions involve the transfer of either electrons (oxidation/reduction reactions) or hydrogen ions (acid/base reactions) between reacting ions, molecules, or atoms. In other reactions, chemical bonds are broken by heat or light to form very reactive radicals with electrons ready to form new bonds. Radical reactions control many processes such as the presence of ozone and green-house gases in the atmosphere, burning and processing of fossil fuels, the formation of polymers, and explosions. (Section 3)

PS 3d Chemical reactions can take place in time periods ranging from the few femtoseconds (10-15 seconds) required for an atom to move a fraction of a chemical bond distance to geologic time scales of billions of years. Reaction rates depend on how often the reacting atoms and molecules encounter one another, on the temperature, and on the properties--including shape--of the reacting species. (Section 4, Inquiry Lab: Rate and Temperature of a Chemical Reaction)

PS 3e Catalysts, such as metal surfaces, accelerate chemical reactions. Chemical reactions in living systems are catalyzed by protein molecules called enzymes. (Section 4)

PS 5a Energy can be transferred by collisions in chemical and nuclear reactions, by light waves and other radiations, and in many other ways. However, it can never be destroyed. (Section 1)

UCP 1 Systems, order, and organization (Sections 1, 3, 4)

InquiryLab

Teacher's Notes Students should observe that the bag inflates as gas is produced. If the bag does not inflate, have students repeat the experiment, making sure that the bag is securely sealed and does not have any holes.

Materials per Group
- balance
- bag, plastic, sealable
- baking soda, 5 g (1 tsp)
- film canister, plastic
- vinegar, 5 mL (1 tsp)

Answers
1. Sample answer: Bubbles of gas formed. (Students may also note that the temperature changed.)
2. Sample answer: The mass of the bag and its contents before and after the reaction are the same. This demonstrates that no mass is lost or gained in a chemical reaction.

Key Resources

📋 **Datasheet**
Matter and Chemical Reactions

💿 **Interactive Tutor**
Disc One, Module 5: Chemical Equations

InquiryLab 🕐 20 min

Matter and Chemical Reactions

Place about **5 g (1 tsp) of baking soda** into a **sealable plastic bag.** Place about **5 mL (1 tsp) of vinegar** into a **plastic film canister.** Secure the lid. Place the canister into the bag. Squeeze the air out of the bag, and tightly seal the bag.

Use a **balance** to determine the total mass of the bag and its contents. Make a note of this value. Open the canister without opening the bag, and allow the vinegar and baking soda to mix. When the reaction has stopped, measure and record the total mass of the bag and its contents.

Questions to Get You Started
1. What evidence shows that a chemical reaction has taken place?
2. Compare the masses of the bag and its contents before and after the reaction. What does this result demonstrate about chemical reactions?

UCP 2 Evidence, models, and explanation (Section 2)

UCP 3 Constancy, change, and measurement (Sections 2, 4)

UCP 4 Evolution and equilibrium (Section 4)

SAI 1 Abilities necessary to do scientific inquiry (Sections 1–4, Inquiry Lab: Rate and Temperature of a Chemical Reaction)

SAI 2 Understandings about scientific inquiry (Sections 2, 4)

SPSP 4 Environmental quality (Section 2)

SPSP 6 Science and technology in local, national, and global challenges (Section 2)

Word Parts

Sample table:

Word	Prefix	Root	Definition
exothermic	exo-	therm (heat)	releasing heat
endothermic	endo-	therm (heat)	requiring or absorbing heat
exergonic	ex-	erg (energy)	releasing energy
endergonic	end-	erg (energy)	requiring or absorbing energy

Reading Equations

Sample answer: The reaction of two water molecules yields two hydrogen molecules and one oxygen molecule.

FoldNotes

Answers may vary. Students' table folds should look similar to the example shown (a page divided into a 4 cell by 3 cell table). Cells in the table should contain notes from Section 3 about different types of chemical reactions. Reaction types include synthesis, decomposition, combustion, single-displacement, double-displacement, and oxidation-reduction reactions.

These reading tools can help you learn the material in this chapter. For more information on how to use these and other tools, see **Appendix A.**

Word Parts

Prefixes Many scientific words are made up of word parts that come from other languages. These word parts can be prefixes, suffixes, or word roots. Understanding the meanings of these word parts can help you understand new scientific terms.

The prefix *endo-* means "within" or "inside," while the prefix *exo-* means "external" or "outside." If these prefixes are used before a vowel, they can be shortened to *end-* and *ex-*.

Your Turn The table below lists four words for describing chemical reactions based on changes in energy. After you have read Section 1, finish filling out a similar table. Look up the words in a dictionary to find out what the word parts mean.

TABLE OF WORD PARTS

WORD	PREFIX	ROOT	DEFINITION
Exothermic		therm (heat)	releasing energy as heat
Endothermic	endo-		
Exergonic	ex-	erg (energy)	
Endergonic			requiring or absorbing energy

Reading Equations

Chemical Equations Chemical equations are used to represent chemical reactions. Chemical equations are similar to mathematical equations in certain ways:

- The atoms in the substances on the left side are the same as the atoms in the substances on the right side but are rearranged.
- Instead of using an "equals" sign, a chemical equation uses an arrow that means "yields," or "gives." For example, the balanced chemical equation for a reaction between methane and oxygen is as follows:

$$CH_4 + 2O_2 \rightarrow CO_2 + 2H_2O$$

This equation means "The reaction of one methane molecule and two oxygen molecules yields one carbon dioxide molecule and two water molecules." The formulas of the molecules can be read out loud. For example, to read CH_4 aloud, say the letters *C* and *H* and the number 4 (SEE AYCH FAWR).

Your Turn As you read chemical equations in this chapter, practice writing them in words and saying them aloud.

FoldNotes

Table Fold FoldNotes are a fun way to help you learn ideas as you read. FoldNotes help you to organize concepts and to see the "big picture."

Your Turn Follow the instructions in **Appendix A** for making a table fold. As you read Section 3, fill in each section of the table with notes about a type of chemical reaction. Use the FoldNote to review the chapter.

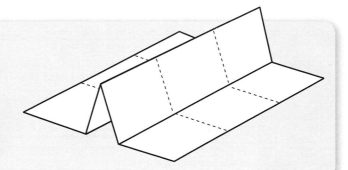

The Nature of Chemical Reactions

Key Ideas

> When do chemical reactions take place?

> What is the role of energy in chemical reactions?

Key Terms

reactant

product

chemical energy

exothermic reaction

endothermic reaction

Why It Matters

Many of the processes that you see every day—such as the starting of a car, the lighting of a match, or the ripening of a piece of fruit—are chemical reactions.

If you hear the words *chemical reaction,* you might think about scientists doing experiments in laboratories. But words such as *grow, ripen, decay,* and *burn* describe chemical reactions that you see every day. Many different chemical reactions take place inside your body all of the time. The food you eat and the oxygen you breathe change form during reactions inside your body. You breathe out the carbon dioxide that is formed in these reactions into the air.

Chemical Reactions

When sugar, water, and yeast are mixed into flour to make bread dough, a chemical reaction takes place. The yeast acts on the sugar to form new substances, including carbon dioxide and lactic acid. You know that a chemical reaction has happened because lactic acid and carbon dioxide differ from sugar. **> Chemical reactions occur when substances go through chemical changes to form new substances.** Often, you can tell that a chemical reaction is happening because you are able to see changes, such as the ones in **Figure 1.**

Figure 1 Easily visible signs of a chemical reaction include formation of a gas, formation of a solid, and release of energy.

Formation of a gas

Formation of a solid

Release of energy

Key Resources

Teaching Transparencies
C16 Reaction Model
TM22 Exothermic and Endothermic

Visual Concepts
Chemical Reaction
Signs of a Chemical Reaction
Limiting Reactants and Excess Reactants

Datasheet
An Endothermic Reaction

Cross-Disciplinary Worksheets
Connection to Social Studies—
  Alchemists' Theory of the Elements
Real World Applications—Hot Meals
  on Hand
Integrating Biology—Organisms that
  Glow

> Focus

This section introduces chemical reactions. Students learn how to recognize chemical reactions, what happens at the atomic level during a chemical reaction, and how energy is involved in chemical reactions.

Bellringer

Use the Bellringer transparency to prepare students for this section.

Demonstrate

Electric Lemon You will need a lemon, a piece of copper wire and a paper clip for this demonstration. Straighten the paper clip, and insert it and the copper wire into the lemon. Ask a volunteer to touch the ends of both wires to his or her tongue and describe what happens. The volunteer should feel a tingling sensation on the tongue. This is because saliva provides an electrolytic solution that conducts current. What must be contained in the lemon for it to conduct a current between the two metals? (ions) Hydrogen ions in a lemon are part of the chemical reaction that produces the electric current. Hydrogen ions are present in almost all acids and the strength of the acid increases as the hydrogen ion concentration does. Why can a lemon be used to make an electric cell and an orange cannot? (A lemon is more acidic than an orange. So, the lemon contains more hydrogen ions to react.) **LS Logical**

READING TOOLBOX

Table Fold Key terms should include *reactants, products, energy, exothermic,* and *endothermic.* If students are having trouble with important ideas, have them work in groups and discuss which terms are giving them trouble. Then, have students write the definitions of each term in their own words.

Teaching Key Ideas

Finding the Change Remind students that for a chemical change to occur, at least one substance must be changed into at least one other substance. Ask students to identify evidence of chemical change in everyday events, such as a burning candle, (Sample answer: Wax disappears, and heat is generated.) rusting of iron, (Sample answer: The hard, shiny iron changes to soft, reddish-brown rust.) cooking pancakes, (Sample answer: The texture of the batter changes and bubbles form in the cakes.) and a piece of fruit spoiling. (Sample answer: The fruit changes in color, texture, and odor.)
LS **Intrapersonal**

READING TOOLBOX

Table Fold
Make a table fold, and write some of the key terms about chemical reactions along the top row. Fill in the columns with the important ideas about each term.

Figure 2 Gasoline is a mixture of many different compounds, each of which contains 5 to 12 carbon atoms. Isooctane, C_8H_{18}, is one of the compounds of this mixture.

Chemical reactions rearrange atoms.

When gasoline burns in the engine of a car or boat, several reactions happen. In one of these reactions, two reactants—isooctane, C_8H_{18}, and oxygen, O_2—react to form two products—carbon dioxide, CO_2, and water, H_2O. A **reactant** is a substance that participates in a chemical reaction. A **product** is a substance that forms in a chemical reaction.

The products and reactants of a chemical reaction contain the same types of atoms. The reaction does not create the atoms of the products or destroy the atoms of the reactants. Instead, the reaction rearranges the bonds between the atoms. In all chemical reactions, mass remains the same.

Energy and Reactions

If isooctane and oxygen reacted whenever they were put in the same place, filling a car's tank with gasoline would be very dangerous. Like most chemical reactions, the isooctane-oxygen reaction needs energy to get started. A small spark gives enough energy to start this reaction. Therefore, having any spark or open flame near a gas pump is not allowed.
❯ **Chemical reactions always involve changes in energy.**

Energy must be added to break bonds.

In each isooctane molecule, such as the one shown in **Figure 2,** all of the bonds to carbon atoms are covalent. In an oxygen molecule, covalent bonds hold the two oxygen atoms together. For the atoms in isooctane and oxygen to react, all of these bonds must be broken. This process takes energy.

Many forms of energy can be used to break bonds. Sometimes, the energy is transferred as heat, as is the case when a spark starts the isooctane-oxygen reaction. Energy also can be transferred as electricity, sound, or light. When molecules collide and enough energy is transferred to separate the atoms, bonds can break.

Hydrogen, H

Carbon, C

Why It **Matters**

Activation Energy Even if a reaction is exothermic, energy must be added to start the reaction. This energy is called *activation energy.* An example of activation energy is the flame needed to start a newspaper burning. Materials that will burn vary greatly in the amount of activation energy needed to start the reaction. Materials such as gasoline, which has a low activation energy, are considered flammable. Other materials, such as paper, burn but require more energy to start burning. They are classified as combustible. Ask students to identify the source of energy that causes a match to start burning. (Sample answer: friction between the match and the striker strip) **LS** **Logical/Verbal**

Differentiated Instruction

Struggling Readers

Using Headings Remind students that section headings usually include important information that will be explained in the section. Have students copy each heading under the main heading *Energy and Reactions* on a sheet of paper. Point out that they now have a summary of the important points about energy and reactions. Have students scan the text under each B-head and find a sentence that gives more information about its statement. Have them copy this statement onto their paper under the appropriate heading. **LS** **Logical/Visual**

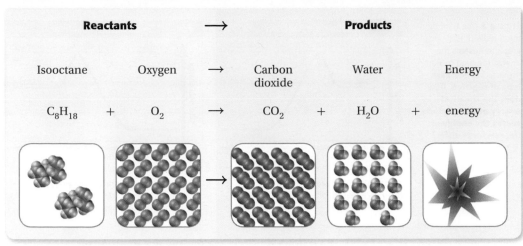

Reactants		→		Products	
Isooctane	Oxygen	→	Carbon dioxide	Water	Energy
C_8H_{18}	+	O_2	→	CO_2	+	H_2O	+	energy

Forming bonds releases energy.

When enough energy is added to start the isooctane-oxygen reaction, new bonds form to make the products, as **Figure 3** shows. Each carbon dioxide molecule consists of two oxygen atoms connected to one carbon atom by a double bond. A water molecule is made when two hydrogen atoms each form a single bond with an oxygen atom.

When new bonds form, chemical energy is released. When gasoline burns, energy in the form of heat and light is released as the products of the reaction form. Other chemical reactions can produce electrical energy.

Energy is conserved in chemical reactions.

Energy may not appear to be conserved in the isooctane-oxygen reaction. After all, a tiny spark can set off an explosion. This fact may suggest that a small amount of energy turns into a large amount of energy. However, the energy in that explosion comes from the bonds between atoms in the reactants.

Energy that is stored in the form of chemical bonds is called **chemical energy.** Molecules of isooctane and oxygen carry stored chemical energy. During the isooctane-oxygen reaction, the chemical energy changes form. But the total amount of energy of the reactants must always equal the total amount of energy of the products and their surroundings. Energy in a chemical reaction can change form, energy is never created or destroyed.

✔ **Reading Check** Where does the chemical energy released in a chemical reaction come from? (See Appendix E for answers to Reading Checks.)

Figure 3 The formation of carbon dioxide and water from isooctane and oxygen produces the energy used to power the engines in cars.

reactant (ree AK tuhnt) a substance or molecule that participates in a chemical reaction

product (PRAHD uhkt) a substance that forms in a chemical reaction

chemical energy (KEM i kuhl EN uhr jee) the energy released when a chemical compound reacts to produce new compounds

Teaching Key Ideas

Chemical Energy Emphasize that all chemical reactions involve a change in energy. The amount of energy released or absorbed during the reaction is equal to the difference in the energy of the chemical bonds of the reactants and products. Tell students that when trinitrotoluene (TNT) explodes, a large molecule breaks apart to form a number of smaller molecules. Ask students: What is the source of energy for the explosion? (Sample answer: The formation of chemical bonds in the small molecules releases more energy than was required to break the chemical bonds of the large molecule.)

MISCONCEPTION ALERT

Chemical Changes Some students believe that matter is destroyed in a chemical change. This misconception stems from the failure to recognize products, especially gaseous ones. Emphasize that matter is changed, not lost, in all reactions. You can use a simple chemical equation to clarify this point: $C + O_2 \rightarrow CO_2$. Write the terms "products" and "reactants" above the equation, and use differently colored spheres to visually illustrate the atoms in each molecule. Have students count the atoms on each side. (3 atoms on each side) Ask students to describe how solid carbon can "disappear" when it burns, even though the total number of atoms remains the same. (Carbon combines with oxygen to make carbon dioxide, a gas which is present but not visible.) **LS** **Logical/Visual**

Differentiated Instruction

Special Education Students

Acting and Reacting Divide the class into groups of 8 to 10 students. Have each group choose a chemical reaction in which a bond is broken and then a new bond is formed. Assign each student to be an atom in the reaction. Work with individual groups to make sure each student understands his or her role. Finally, have each group act out their chosen chemical reaction for the class and explain which part of the reaction requires adding energy and which part releases energy. **LS** **Kinesthetic/Verbal**

Science Skills

Interpreting Graphs Have students work in pairs or small groups. Ask students to write sentences that describe what is happening in the graphs shown in **Figure 4.** (Sample answer: The graph of the exothermic reaction in **Figure 4** shows that energy is released as the reactants form the products. The endothermic reaction graph in **Figure 4** shows that energy is absorbed as the reactants form the products.) [LS] **Logical/Visual**

Answer to caption question

The products of an exothermic reaction have lower energy than the reactants do. The products of an endothermic reaction have higher energy than the reactants do.

QuickLab

Teacher's Notes Students should observe a drop in the temperature of the solution. If there is no change, have them stir or swirl the solution gently.

Materials per Group
• calcium chloride solution
• cup, plastic
• sodium bicarbonate (baking soda), 5 g (1 tsp)
• thermometer

Answer

4. The temperature of the solution dropped, which indicates that an endothermic reaction took place.

Figure 4 The hump in the middle of each graph represents the energy required to start the reaction. **For each type of reaction, how does the chemical energy of the products versus the energy of the reactants differ?**

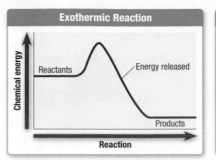
Exothermic Reaction
Chemical energy / Reaction
Reactants — Energy released — Products

In an exothermic reaction, chemical energy is released, often as heat.

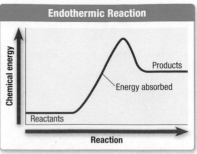
Endothermic Reaction
Chemical energy / Reaction
Products — Energy absorbed — Reactants

In an endothermic reaction, energy is absorbed by the reactants and stored in the products as chemical energy.

exothermic reaction (EK soh THUHR mik ree AK shuhn) a chemical reaction in which energy is released to the surroundings as heat

endothermic reaction (EN doh THUHR mik ree AK shuhn) a chemical reaction that requires energy input

QuickLab 10 min

An Endothermic Reaction

❶ Fill a **plastic cup** halfway with **calcium chloride solution,** and use a **thermometer** to measure the temperature of the solution.

❷ Carefully add **5 g (1 tsp)** of **baking soda** to the cup. Record your observations.

❸ When the reaction has stopped, record the temperature of the solution.

❹ What evidence of an endothermic reaction did you see?

Reactions that release energy are exothermic.

In the reaction between isooctane and oxygen, the amount of energy released as the products form is greater than the amount of energy absorbed to break the bonds in the reactants. This reaction is an **exothermic reaction,** a chemical reaction in which energy is released to the surroundings as heat. The released energy comes from the chemical energy of the reactants. All combustion reactions are exothermic.

Figure 4 shows an energy diagram for an exothermic reaction. This diagram shows what happens to the chemical energy in an exothermic reaction. In all exothermic reactions, the products have less energy than the reactants.

Reactions that absorb energy are endothermic.

If you put hydrated barium hydroxide and ammonium nitrate in a flask, the reaction between them takes so much energy from the surroundings that water in the air will condense and then freeze on the surface of the flask. This reaction is an **endothermic reaction,** a chemical reaction in which more energy is needed to break the bonds in the reactants than is given off by forming bonds in the products.

When an endothermic reaction happens, you may be able to notice a drop in temperature. Sometimes, endothermic reactions need more energy than they can get from their surroundings. In those cases, energy must be added as heat to cause the reaction to take place. The changes in chemical energy for an endothermic reaction are shown in an energy diagram in **Figure 4.**

✓ **Reading Check** What is the difference between an exothermic reaction and an endothermic reaction?

MISCONCEPTION /// ALERT \\\

Bond Energy Some students believe that a reaction that requires activation energy can't be exothermic. Stress that bond breaking always requires energy. The overall process of bond breaking (which requires energy) and bond formation (which releases energy) results in either an endothermic or an exothermic reaction. Use **Figure 4** to support your statement. Have students take note of the increase in energy that takes place during a chemical reaction, whether it is exothermic or endothermic.

Differentiated Instruction

Basic Learners

Concept Map Have students create a concept map that includes all of the key terms introduced in this section. Encourage students to include drawings on their concept maps to help them recognize each term. Students should also include information about recognizing chemical reactions and about what happens to atoms and molecules during chemical reactions. [LS] **Visual**

Why It **Matters**

Bioluminescence

Fireflies are not the only organisms that can make their own light. The fish shown in this photograph, as well as some kinds of bacteria, fungi, squid, and jellyfish, also give off light. This process, called *bioluminescence,* depends on a chemical reaction made possible by the enzyme *luciferase.* Scientists can use bacteria that contain luciferase to track the spread of infection in the human body.

Some living things, such as this firefly, produce light through a chemical process called *bioluminescence.*

The comb jelly (*Mnemiopsis leidyi*) is about 10 cm wide and is native to the Atlantic coast.

Some kinds of fungi, such as these members of the genus *Armillaria* that are growing on decaying wood, give off bioluminescence.

YOUR TURN

ONLINE RESEARCH
1. Find out more about the chemical process of bioluminescence. Describe one major way in which it differs from most artificial means of light production.

SCILINKS
www.scilinks.org
Topic: Bioluminescence
Code: HK80156

Why It **Matters**

Bioluminescence The fish in the background photo are sweeper fish (genus *Pempheridae*) from the Red Sea, near Egypt. Sweeper fish are small fish that congregate in caves during the day and then leave to feed on zooplankton during the night. They are found throughout the world.

Many organisms generate their own light, but bioluminescence can be generated by symbiotic organisms that are carried within a larger organism. Many marine animals, including fishes, use bioluminescence to attract prey or to confuse predators. Photophores, which are small organs that are found in benthic fishes and produce light, are as simple as spots under the skin or as complex as an organ such as the eye, including lenses, shutters, and filters that control wavelength. Most marine organisms that exhibit bioluminescence glow with a blue or green light because these colors are most visible deep in the ocean.

Chemical reactions that produce energy as light instead of heat are called *chemiluminescent reactions.* The glow produced by light sticks, when the capsule inside the liquid-filled plastic tube is broken, results from chemiluminescent reactions. Bioluminescence is a particular type of chemiluminescence that occurs in living organisms.

Answer to Your Turn

1. Sample answer: Bioluminescence does not produce heat the way the artificial lights do.

❯Close

Reteaching Key Ideas

Chemical Reactions at School Ask students to describe some chemical reactions they encounter at school. Have them consider reactions related to transportation, cooking in the cafeteria, cleaning, battery-powered equipment, and so on. List the responses on the board, and discuss the signs of a chemical reaction in each example. Identify the energy change in each reaction and whether the reaction is endothermic or exothermic. **LS** **Verbal**

Formative Assessment

What is the function of activation energy in an exothermic reaction?

A. Activation energy is a continuous source of energy for the reactants. (Incorrect. Activation energy starts an exothermic reaction, but after the reaction begins energy comes from the reaction itself.)

B. Activation energy provides energy to break chemical bonds in the reactants. (Correct. Exothermic reactions release energy, but they require energy to begin the breaking of the bonds that releases this energy.)

C. Activation energy provides the energy needed to form new chemical bonds in the products. (Incorrect. Forming new bonds releases energy, so additional energy does not need to be added.)

D. Activation energy causes the reaction to proceed faster. (Incorrect. Activation energy breaks chemical bonds and causes the reaction to start, but it does not affect how quickly it proceeds.)

Photosynthesis is an endothermic reaction.

Photosynthesis, like many reactions in living things, is endothermic. During photosynthesis, plants use energy from light to convert carbon dioxide and water into glucose and oxygen, as **Figure 5** shows. The energy from light is used to form the high-energy bonds that make sugars, from which the plant gets the energy that its cells need. You also get this energy, which originally came from the sun, when you eat fruits or vegetables. Another product of photosynthesis is oxygen, which plants release into the air. You make use of this product of photosynthesis every time you breathe!

Figure 5 Plant cells absorb light energy by photosynthesis and store the energy in the form of sugars.

Carbon dioxide, CO_2

Water, H_2O

Oxygen, O_2

Glucose, $C_6H_{12}O_6$

Section 1 Review

KEY IDEAS

1. List three signs that could indicate that a chemical reaction is taking place.

2. Identify whether each of the following is a chemical reaction:
 a. melting ice
 b. burning a candle
 c. rusting iron

3. Predict which atoms will be found in the products of the following reactions:
 a. Mercury(II) oxide, HgO, is heated and decomposes.
 b. Limestone, $CaCO_3$, reacts with hydrochloric acid, HCl.
 c. Table sugar, $C_{12}H_{22}O_{11}$, burns in air to form caramel.

4. List four forms of energy that may be absorbed or released during a chemical reaction.

5. Classify each of the following reactions as exothermic or endothermic:
 a. paper burning with a bright flame
 b. plastics becoming brittle after being left in the sun
 c. a firecracker exploding

CRITICAL THINKING

6. Applying Concepts Calcium oxide, CaO, is used in cement mixes. When water is added, energy is released as CaO forms calcium hydroxide, $Ca(OH)_2$. What signs indicate a chemical reaction? Draw an energy diagram to represent this reaction. Which has more chemical energy: the reactants or the products?

Answers to Section Review

1. Sample answer: formation of gas, formation of solid, and release of energy

2. a. not a chemical reaction
 b. chemical reaction
 c. chemical reaction

3. a. Hg, O
 b. Ca, C, O, H, Cl
 c. C, H, O

4. heat, light, electricity, and sound

5. a. exothermic
 b. endothermic
 c. exothermic

6. Sample answer: The reaction releases energy, so a chemical reaction has likely happened. Additionally, a new substance is formed. The energy diagram for this reaction would be similar to the one below. The reactants have more energy than the products do.

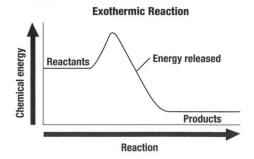

Exothermic Reaction

Chemical energy

Reactants

Energy released

Products

Reaction

SECTION 2 Chemical Equations

Key Ideas

❯ What is a chemical equation?

❯ What can a balanced chemical equation tell you?

Key Terms

chemical equation
mole ratio

Why It Matters

Chemical reactions are more effective for making the desired products, such as medicines, if the reactants are combined in the correct ratios.

❯Focus

In this section, students learn about reading and balancing chemical equations. The section also discusses mole ratios and the law of definite proportions.

Bellringer

Use the Bellringer transparency to prepare students for this section.

Demonstrate

Equation Analogy For this activity you will need 12 index cards and tape or thumbtacks. Divide the index cards into three sets of four cards. Write the term *center* on the cards of the first group, *guard* on the cards of the second group, and *forward* on the cards of the third group. Draw a diagram of the positions for a basketball team on the board. Fasten the cards to the board or a bulletin board. Have volunteers create as many basketball teams as they can from the cards. Can the leftover cards be used to make another team? (No; there are not enough of all the positions to form another basketball team.) Ask students to write an equation that shows the formula for a basketball team. (2 forwards + 1 center + 2 guards → 1 basketball team) Point out that the same number of people are represented on both sides of the arrows. They are just arranged differently. Discuss with students that the same principle applies to atoms represented in a chemical reaction.
LS Visual/Logical

W hen natural gas burns, methane reacts with oxygen gas to form carbon dioxide and water. Energy is also released as heat and light. You have seen this reaction at home if your kitchen has a gas stove.

Describing Reactions

You can describe the reaction between methane and oxygen in many ways, as **Figure 1** shows. One way is to write a word equation. A word equation shows the names of the products and reactants. Another way is to use molecular models, which can be used to show how the atoms are rearranged during the reaction. The clearest way is to write a chemical equation. ❯**A chemical equation uses symbols to represent a chemical reaction and shows the relationship between the reactants and products of a reaction.**

chemical equation (KEM i kuhl ee KWAY zhuhn) a representation of a chemical reaction that uses symbols to show the relationship between the reactants and the products

Figure 1 The natural gas that stoves burn is mostly made of the compound methane. Methane burns with oxygen gas to make carbon dioxide and water.

Word equation

methane   and   oxygen   yield   carbon dioxide   and   water

Molecular model

Chemical equation

$$CH_4 \quad + \quad 2O_2 \quad \rightarrow \quad CO_2 \quad + \quad 2H_2O$$

Key Resources

Teaching Transparency
TM23 Balanced Equation

Visual Concepts
Chemical Equation
Reading a Chemical Equation
Symbols Used in Chemical Equations
Balancing a Chemical Equation by Inspection

Datasheet
Balancing Chemical Equations

Cross-Disciplinary Worksheets
Science and the Consumer—The Right Fire Extinguisher for the Job
Connection to Fine Arts—The Chemistry of Art

Teaching Key Ideas

Chemical Equations Because students know that the order of elements in a formula is important, they might think that there is a specific order of reactants and products in a chemical equation. Tell them that a chemical equation is similar to a mathematical equation. Items that are added together in a mathematical equation can be listed in any order, as can the reactants in a chemical equation. Chemical equations are like mathematical equations because the two sides of the equation must be equal. Ask students how the two sides of the equation in **Figure 1** are equal. (Sample answer: Each side of the equation has the same number of each type of atom.)

Science ❯ Skills

Equation Information Students might notice that chemical equations from other sources contain more information than is presented in this chapter. The state of a substance is frequently indicated by *(s), (l), (g),* or *(aq)* written after a formula. Ask students what these abbreviations would indicate about a reactant or product. (solid, liquid, gas state, and aqueous solution) Explain to students that information provided above or below the arrow often indicates conditions such as required temperatures or pressure or the presence of a catalyst. **LS** Verbal

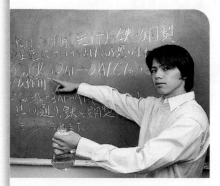
Figure 2 This student is giving a talk on reactions that use copper. You can read the chemical equations even if you cannot read Japanese.

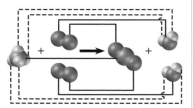
Figure 3 This diagram represents the balanced chemical equation discussed in the text. It shows how the atoms of each element balance. **How many atoms of each element are on each side of the equation?**

Chemical equations show products and reactants.

Look at the chemical equation below. The reactants, which are on the left side of the arrow, form the products, which are on the right side of the arrow. In a chemical equation, an arrow pointing to the right ($\longrightarrow$) means "yield," or "give." Chemical equations give chemists all over the world a common way to express chemical reactions, as **Figure 2** shows.

▷ **Chemical equation**	$\underset{\text{reactants}}{CH_4 + O_2}$	$\underset{\text{"yield"}}{\longrightarrow}$	$\underset{\text{products}}{CO_2 + H_2O}$

Balanced chemical equations account for the conservation of mass.

As written, the chemical equation above just tells you what compounds are involved in the reaction. When the number of atoms of each element on the right side of the equation matches the number of atoms of each element on the left side, the chemical equation is said to be *balanced.* By accounting for each atom that reacts, a balanced equation follows the law of conservation of mass.

For some of the elements in the equation above, the numbers of atoms on each side do not match. Carbon is balanced because each side of the equation contains one carbon atom. But four hydrogen atoms are on the left, and only two are on the right. Also, two oxygen atoms are on the left, and three are on the right. This cannot be correct, because atoms cannot be created or destroyed in a chemical reaction.

A chemical equation is balanced by adding coefficients in front of one or more of the formulas. A *coefficient* is a number that shows the relative amount of a compound in a reaction. Placing a coefficient of 2 in front of the formula for water means that for each methane molecule that reacted, two water molecules were formed. Thus, all four hydrogen atoms from each methane molecule reacted. Likewise, one must place a 2 in front of the formula for oxygen, one of the reactants.

▷ **Balanced chemical equation**	$CH_4 + 2O_2 \longrightarrow CO_2 + 2H_2O$

Now, for each element, the number of atoms on one side matches the number of atoms on the other side, so the equation is balanced. **Figure 3** shows how each atom is accounted for on both sides of the above balanced chemical equation.

✔ **Reading Check** Why should chemical equations be balanced?

Answer to caption question

Each side of the equation shows one atom of carbon, four atoms of hydrogen, and four atoms of oxygen.

Differentiated Instruction

Special Education Students

Balanced Chemical Equations Have students create a graphic that lists the steps necessary to write a balanced chemical equation. The graphic should include writing the formula for each reactant and product, using plus signs and an arrow where needed, and using coefficients to balance the number of each type of atom on each side of the equation. Encourage students to keep the graphics to refer to when working with chemical equations. **LS** Logical

Math **Skills** Balancing Chemical Equations

Write the balanced chemical equation that describes the burning of magnesium in air to form magnesium oxide.

Identify

List the given and unknown values.

Given:
Magnesium and oxygen gas are the reactants that form magnesium oxide, the product.

Unknown:
balanced chemical equation

Plan

Write a word equation for the reaction.

Write the chemical equation by using formulas for the elements and compounds in the word equation.

magnesium + oxygen $\longrightarrow$ magnesium oxide

Remember that some gaseous elements, such as oxygen, come in molecules of two atoms each. Oxygen in air is O_2.

$$Mg + O_2 \longrightarrow MgO$$

Solve

Balance the equation one element at a time.

1. **Count the atoms** of each element on each side. There are fewer oxygen atoms in the products than there are in the reactants.

Reactants		Products
$Mg + O_2$	$\longrightarrow$	MgO
$Mg = 1$ $O = 2$		$Mg = 1$ $O = 1$

2. **To balance the oxygen atoms,** place the coefficient 2 in front of MgO. But now too few magnesium atoms are in the reactants.

Reactants		Products
$Mg + O_2$	$\longrightarrow$	$2MgO$
$Mg = 1$ $O = 2$		$Mg = 2$ $O = 2$

3. **To balance the magnesium atoms,** place the coefficient 2 in front of Mg. Now, for each element, the number of atoms on each side is the same.

Reactants		Products
$2Mg + O_2$	$\longrightarrow$	$2MgO$
$Mg = 2$ $O = 2$		$Mg = 2$ $O = 2$

Practice

1. Hydrogen peroxide, H_2O_2, decomposes to give water and oxygen. Write a balanced equation for the decomposition reaction.

2. In a double-displacement reaction, sodium sulfide, Na_2S, reacts with silver nitrate, $AgNO_3$, to form sodium nitrate, $NaNO_3$, and silver sulfide, Ag_2S. Balance this equation.

For more practice, visit **go.hrw.com** and enter keyword **HK8MP**.

Practice Hint

> You cannot balance a chemical equation by changing the subscripts within a chemical formula. Changing a formula would indicate that a different substance participates in the reaction. An equation can be balanced only by putting coefficients in front of the chemical formulas.

> Sometimes, changing the coefficients to balance one element may cause another element in the equation to become unbalanced. So, check your work to ensure that all elements are balanced.

Answers to Practice
1. $2H_2O_2 \rightarrow 2H_2O + O_2$
2. $Na_2S + 2AgNO_3 \rightarrow 2NaNO_3 + Ag_2S$

Additional Examples
Write the following sentences on the board and have the class write balanced equations:
Potassium metal reacts violently with water to produce potassium hydroxide and hydrogen gas.
Answer: $(2K + 2H_2O \rightarrow 2KOH + H_2)$
Calcium oxide, an ingredient in cement, combines with water to produce calcium hydroxide.
Answer: $(CaO + H_2O \rightarrow Ca(OH)_2)$
Ethanol, C_2H_5OH, produces water and carbon dioxide when it burns.
Answer: $(C_2H_5OH + 3O_2 \rightarrow 2CO_2 + 3H_2O)$
LS Logical

Differentiated Instruction

Advanced Learners
Chemical Engineering Arrange for a student to interview a chemical engineer. The interview should include questions regarding the educational requirements to become a chemical engineer, the different types of work involved in chemical engineering, the different types of companies or agencies that hire chemical engineers, and a list of schools that offer a chemical engineering degree programs. Have the students present their findings to the class.
LS Verbal/Interpersonal

READING TOOLBOX

Coefficients Have students write a paragraph explaining why the sum of the coefficients on one side of a balanced equation doesn't necessarily equal the sum of the coefficients on the other side of the equation. (Paragraphs should include the idea that the number of each type of atom must be the same on both sides of the equation. That number is determined by the formulas, including subscripts, not just coefficients.)
LS Logical/Verbal

Teacher's Notes Review with students that each element in the exercise forms a characteristic number of chemical bonds. If necessary, use the periodic table to show that the substances in the examples actually exist. Point out that the reactions given are not balanced, but the model must be balanced.

Materials per Group
• toothpicks
• gumdrops, at least 3 colors

Answers to Analysis
1. **a.** $H_2 + Cl_2 \longrightarrow 2HCl$
   b. $Ca + 2H_2O \longrightarrow Ca(OH)_2 + H_2$
   c. $2C_2H_6 + 7O_2 \longrightarrow 4CO_2 + 6H_2O$

READING TOOLBOX

Table Fold Sample table:

reactants	substances present before the reaction
products	substance present after the reaction
chemical formula	indicates what atoms are in each reactant and product
coefficient	the amount of each reactant and product
arrow	shows direction of the reaction

QuickLab — Balancing Chemical Equations

Procedure
❶ Use **toothpicks** and **gumdrops of at least three different colors** (representing atoms of different elements) to make models of the reactants in each of the following chemical equations:
   a. $H_2 + Cl_2 \longrightarrow HCl$
   b. $Ca + H_2O \longrightarrow Ca(OH)_2 + H_2$
   c. $C_2H_6 + O_2 \longrightarrow CO_2 + H_2O$

❷ Rearrange the "atoms" of the reactants to form the products. (You may need different proportions of some of the reactant compounds.)

Analysis
1. On the basis of your experiment with the gumdrops and toothpicks, balance each of the chemical equations shown in step 1 of the Procedure.

READING TOOLBOX

Table Fold
Make a Table Fold, and write the names for the parts of a chemical equation along the top row. Fill in the columns with the information that is given by each part of a chemical equation.

Balanced Equations and Mole Ratios

Other ways of looking at the amounts in a chemical reaction are shown in **Figure 4.** Notice that the numbers of magnesium and oxygen atoms in the product equal the numbers of magnesium and oxygen atoms in the reactants.

❯A balanced equation tells you the mole ratio, or proportion of reactants and products, in a chemical reaction. The balanced equation tells you that for every 2 mol of magnesium, 1 mol of oxygen is needed. So, if you want 4 mol of magnesium to react, you will need 2 mol of oxygen. No matter how much magnesium and oxygen are combined or how the magnesium oxide is made, the balanced equation does not change. This follows *the law of definite proportions.*

Law of definite proportions	A compound always contains the same elements in the same proportions regardless of how the compound is made or how much of the compound is formed.

Figure 4 Information from a Balanced Equation

Equation:	2Mg	+	O_2	$\longrightarrow$	2MgO
Amount (mol)	2		1	$\longrightarrow$	2
Molar mass (g/mol)	24.3		32.0	$\longrightarrow$	40.3
Mass calculation	24.3 g/mol × 2 mol		32.0 g/mol × 1 mol	$\longrightarrow$	40.3 g/mol × 2 mol
Mass (g)	48.6		32.0	$\longrightarrow$	80.6
Model					

Teaching Key Ideas

Ratios of Substances A balanced chemical equation shows the ratio of each substance in the reaction. Remind students that coefficients in a balanced equation can represent either single units or moles. To illustrate this concept, write a simple balanced chemical equation on the chalkboard. Multiply all coefficients by a small integer, such as 3. Show that even though the coefficients are not as simple as they could be, the equation is still balanced. Then, relate that the coefficients can represent individual atoms or molecules or the number of moles of each substance.

Repeat this demonstration several times, using different integers. Emphasize that a chemical equation is like a mathematical equation, in that you can multiply through the entire equation by the same number without changing the relationship among the formulas. For coefficients to represent the number of atoms or molecules in moles, the number used to multiply the coefficients in a balanced equation is Avogadro's constant.

Mole ratios tell you the relative amounts of reactants and products.

The mole ratio of magnesium to oxygen in the reaction shown in **Figure 4** is 2:1. Thus, for every 2 mol of magnesium that reacts, 1 mol of oxygen will also react. If 4 mol of magnesium is present, 2 mol of oxygen is needed to react. This is a ratio of 4:2, which is the same as 2:1.

In the following equation for the electrolysis of water, the mole ratio for $H_2O:H_2:O_2$, according to the coefficients from the balanced equation, is 2:2:1.

$$2H_2O \longrightarrow 2H_2 + O_2$$

There are twice as many molecules of hydrogen gas produced in this reaction as there are molecules of oxygen gas. Thus, as **Figure 5** shows, the hydrogen gas produced in this reaction takes up twice as much space as the oxygen gas does.

Mole ratios can be converted to masses.

If you know the mole ratios of the substances in a reaction, you can determine the relative masses of the substances needed to react completely. Simply multiply the molecular mass of each substance by the mole ratio from the balanced equation.

For example, for the reaction shown in **Figure 4,** the molar mass of magnesium, 24.3 g/mol, is multiplied by 2 mol to get a total mass of 48.6 g for the magnesium. The molar mass of molecular oxygen, 32.0 g/mol, is multiplied by 1 mol. So, for the magnesium to react completely with oxygen, there must be 32.0 g of oxygen available for every 48.6 g of magnesium.

mole ratio (MOHL RAY shee OH) the relative number of moles of the substances required to produce a given amount of product in a chemical reaction

Figure 5 Electrical energy causes water to decompose into oxygen (in the test tube on the left) and hydrogen (on the right).

Section 2 Review

KEY IDEAS

1. **Identify** which of the following is a complete and balanced chemical equation:
   a. $H_2O \longrightarrow H_2 + O_2$
   b. $NaCl + H_2O$
   c. $Fe + S \longrightarrow FeS$
   d. $CaCO_3$

2. **Determine** balanced chemical equations for the following chemical reactions:
   a. $KOH + HCl \longrightarrow KCl + H_2O$
   b. $NaHCO_3 \longrightarrow H_2O + CO_2 + Na_2CO_3$
   c. $Pb(NO_3)_2 + KI \longrightarrow KNO_3 + PbI_2$

3. **Explain** why balancing an equation requires changing the coefficients in front of chemical formulas rather than the subscripts within chemical formulas.

4. **Describe** the information needed to calculate the mass of a reactant or product for the following balanced equation:

$$FeS + 2HCl \longrightarrow H_2S + FeCl_2$$

CRITICAL THINKING

5. **Applying Concepts** Chlorine gas is produced by the electrolysis of sodium chloride in water in the following reaction:

$$2NaCl + 2H_2O \longrightarrow Cl_2 + H_2 + 2NaOH$$

What mass of sodium chloride is needed to make 71 g of chlorine gas?

> **Close**

Reteaching Key Ideas

Balancing Equations Remind students that some elements are contained in more than one reactant or more than one product. For example, H is contained in both reactants in the reaction $NH_3 + HCl \longrightarrow NH_4Cl$. Both of the hydrogen-containing reactants must be considered in balancing the equation. Tell students that polyatomic ions in reactants, that remain the same in the products, can be balanced as units. For example, in $2Fe + 3H_2SO_4 \longrightarrow Fe_2(SO_4)_3 + 3H_2$, the sulfate ion is on both sides. It can be balanced as sulfate ions instead of as oxygen and sulfur atoms. If the ion is changed at all, it cannot be considered a unit. Write several equations on the board and ask students to fill in the coefficients. **LS Logical**

Formative Assessment

Which of the following chemical equations is balanced?

A. $3P_4 + 10KClO_3 \longrightarrow 10KCl + 6P_2O_5$ (Correct. There are the same number of atoms of each element on both sides of the equation.)

B. $H_2SO_4 + 2Al \longrightarrow Al_2(SO_4)_3 + H_2$ (Incorrect. There are 3 sulfate ions in the products, but only 1 sulfate ion in the reactants.)

C. $C_2H_6O + 3O_2 \longrightarrow 2CO_2 + 2H_2O$ (Incorrect. The coefficient for the product water should be 3.)

D. $CaBr_2 + NaOH \longrightarrow Ca(OH)_2 + NaBr$ (Incorrect. The bromide and the hydroxide ions are unbalanced in the equation.)

Answers to Section Review

1. c

2. **a.** $KOH + HCl \longrightarrow KCl + H_2O$
   b. $2NaHCO_3 \longrightarrow H_2O + CO_2 + Na_2CO_3$
   c. $Pb(NO_3)_2 + 2KI \longrightarrow 2KNO_3 + PbI_2$

3. Changing subscripts changes the identities of the substances in the reaction. Changing coefficients does not change the identity of a substance, just the amount of it.

4. Sample answer: You need to know the molar mass of the substance and the mass and molar mass of one other substance in the reaction.

5. molar mass of $Cl_2 = 2 \times 35.5$ g/mol $= 71.0$ g/mol Cl_2; molar mass of NaCl $= 35.5$ g/mol $+ 23$ g/mol $= 58.5$ g/mol NaCl

$$\frac{mass_1}{coefficient_1 \times molar\ mass_1} = \frac{mass_2}{coefficient_2 \times molar\ mass_2}$$

$x \div (2$ mol $\times 58.5$ g/mol$) = 71$ g $\div (1$ mol $\times 71.0$ g/mol$)$
$x = 117$ g NaCl

SECTION
3

Reaction Types

❯ Focus

This section covers six types of chemical reactions: synthesis, decomposition, combustion, single-displacement, double-displacement, and oxidation-reduction. The section concludes with a discussion of reactions as the transfer or sharing of electrons.

🔔 Bellringer

Use the Bellringer transparency to prepare students for this section.

Demonstrate

Synthesis Reaction You will need concentrated ammonia, concentrated hydrochloric acid, and two 25 mL beakers. **Safety Caution:** Wear safety goggles, protective gloves, and a lab apron. Perform demonstration in a well-ventilated area, and do not breathe fumes. Students should stand at least 10 ft from the demonstration. Neutralize all reactants before disposal.

   Place 5 mL of ammonia solution in one beaker and 5 mL of hydrochloric acid solution in the other beaker. Situate the beakers about 4 inches apart, in an area that has no breeze. Ask students: What do they observe? (A cloud forms.) What are the reactants? (ammonia and hydrogen chloride) What is the product? (ammonium chloride) Tell students that this is a *synthesis* reaction, a type of reaction that forms one substance out of two or more.

LS Visual

Key Ideas

❯ How does learning about reaction types help in understanding chemical reactions?

❯ In which kinds of chemical reactions do the numbers of electrons in atoms change?

Key Terms

synthesis reaction

decomposition reaction

combustion reaction

single-displacement reaction

double-displacement reaction

free radical

oxidation-reduction reaction

Why It Matters

Chemical reactions can create ozone (sometimes where ozone is not healthy) and can destroy ozone (sometimes where ozone is needed).

I n the last section, you saw what a chemical equation is and what it can tell you. Now that you are familiar with chemical equations, you will learn about the kinds of reactions that can be expressed by a chemical equation.

Classifying Reactions

   Even though there are millions of unique substances and millions of possible reactions, there are only a few general kinds of reactions. You have learned how to follow patterns to name compounds. ❯ **You also can use patterns to identify kinds of chemical reactions and to predict the products of the chemical reactions.** For example, look at the long molecule shown in **Figure 1.** A certain kind of reaction joins many small molecules to form a much larger molecule. Recognizing this kind of reaction can help you predict the products that the reaction will form.

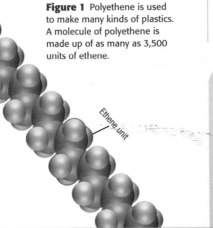

Figure 1 Polyethene is used to make many kinds of plastics. A molecule of polyethene is made up of as many as 3,500 units of ethene.

Ethene unit

Key Resources

📦 **Teaching Transparency**
C17 Single Displacement

💿 **Visual Concepts**
Decomposition Reaction
Single Displacement Reaction
Double Displacement Reaction

📁 **Datasheet**
Determining the Products of a
Reaction

📁 **Science Skills Worksheets**
Balancing Chemical Equations
Ratios and Proportions

📁 **Math Skills Worksheet**
Balancing Chemical Equations

📁 **Cross-Disciplinary Worksheets**
Connection to Social Studies—
Fireworks
Integrating Earth Science—Limestone
Reactions

Synthesis reactions combine substances.

Polyethene, shown in **Figure 1,** is a plastic that is often used to make trash bags and soda bottles. It is produced by polymerization, one kind of synthesis reaction. A **synthesis reaction** is a reaction in which multiple substances combine to form a new compound. In polymerization reactions, many small molecules join together in chains to make larger structures called *polymers*. Polyethene is a polymer made up of repeating ethene molecules.

Hydrogen gas reacts with oxygen gas to form water. In a synthesis reaction, at least two reactants join to form a product. Synthesis reactions have the following general form.

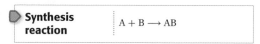

▷ **Synthesis reaction**	$A + B \longrightarrow AB$

In the synthesis reaction below, the metal sodium reacts with chlorine gas to form sodium chloride, or table salt.

$$2Na + Cl_2 \longrightarrow 2NaCl$$

Because a synthesis reaction joins substances, the product of such a reaction is a compound that is more complex than the reactants.

Decomposition reactions break substances apart.

Digestion is a series of reactions that break down complex foods into simple fuels that the body can use. A kind of reaction known as *cracking* is similar to digestion. In cracking, large molecules made of carbon and hydrogen within crude oil are broken down to make gasoline and other products, such as the ones shown in **Figure 2.** Digestion and cracking oil are **decomposition reactions,** reactions in which substances are broken apart. The general form for decomposition reactions is as follows.

▷ **Decomposition reaction**	$AB \longrightarrow A + B$

The following shows the decomposition of water.

$$2H_2O \longrightarrow 2H_2 + O_2$$

The *electrolysis* of water is a simple decomposition reaction. Water breaks down into hydrogen gas and oxygen gas when there is an electric current in the water.

✓ Reading Check How do decomposition reactions compare with synthesis reactions?

www.scilinks.org
Topic: Types of Reactions
Code: HK81570

synthesis reaction (SIN thuh sis ree AK shuhn) reaction in which two or more substances combine to form a new compound

decomposition reaction (DEE kahm puh ZISH uhn ree AK shuhn) a reaction in which a single compound breaks down to form two or more simpler substances

Figure 2 Crude oil is broken down in decomposition reactions to form plastics, which can be made into many kinds of products.

❯ Teach

Teaching Key Ideas

Classifying Point out to students that classifying things helps to make predictions about them. For example, if an animal is classified as a bird, what can you predict about its features? (Sample answer: It has feathers, has hollow bones, and is warm-blooded.) The classification does not tell you everything—hummingbirds and ostriches are both birds. Chemical reactions are classified by what happens to the reactants. For example, knowing that a reaction is a synthesis reaction tells you that the reactants will combine into a new substance. Knowing that a chemical reaction is a decomposition reaction tells you that a substance breaks apart. Have students look at the generic reactions for the four types of reactions shown in this section and describe the reactions in their own words.
LS Verbal

Why It **Matters**

Chloralkali Cells Chlorine and sodium hydroxide are two important industrial chemicals that can be produced simultaneously from salt water. Many industrial plants have been located near natural brine (saltwater) wells because chlorine and sodium hydroxide are readily available. In chloralkali manufacturing plants, a strong electric current is passed through the brine solution. Chlorine gas is produced at one electrode and sodium, which reacts with water to form sodium hydroxide, is produced at the other electrode.

Demonstrate

Electrolysis Sharpen both ends of two eraser-less hard-lead pencils. Place one end of each pencil into a beaker of water containing sodium carbonate. Using wires that have alligator clips, attach the lead at the other ends of the pencils to the two poles of a 9-volt battery. Have students observe what happens at the submerged ends of the pencils. Ask students to identify the bubbles at the two electrodes. (hydrogen and oxygen).

Ask students to predict how they can determine which electrode is producing hydrogen. (Sample answer: The reaction produces twice as much hydrogen as oxygen, so there will be more hydrogen bubbles at the electrode that produces hydrogen.) Metal electrodes can be used, but they may break down due to competing chemical reactions. Graphite electrodes do not break down. One or two tablespoons of sodium carbonate in 250 mL of water is necessary in order to provide ions to complete the circuit. **LS** Logical/Visual

Why It Matters

How Are Fires Extinguished? Have students determine where fire extinguishers are located in their school and home. Under adult supervision, have them check the codes found on these extinguishers. Are the extinguishers the correct type to put out the type of fire that might occur in the location? Some older extinguishers may have different codes than those shown on the student page. The old code style used a green triangle for type A, a red square for type B, a purple circle for type C, and a yellow star for type D.

Stress that a fire extinguisher is to be used only on the fire type or types specified by the extinguisher's code. In the case of chemical fires, it's important to know the properties of the burning chemicals. For example, a carbon dioxide fire extinguisher would not successfully extinguish burning magnesium because magnesium burns at a temperature high enough to decompose carbon dioxide.

Answers to Your Turn

1. Sample answer: A fire extinguisher stops a combustion reaction by separating the fuel and the oxygen.
2. Sample answer: There are also Class D fire extinguishers, which are for extinguishing metal fires. Class K (for kitchen) fire extinguishers, which are for grease fires, have also been introduced.

SC/LINKS.
www.scilinks.org
Topic: Combustion
Code: HK80315

Academic Vocabulary

undergo (UHN duhr GOH) to go through

Combustion reactions use oxygen as a reactant.

Methane forms carbon dioxide and water during combustion. Oxygen is a reactant in every **combustion reaction,** so at least one product of such a reaction will contain atoms of oxygen. Water is a common product of combustion reactions.

$$CH_4 + 2O_2 \longrightarrow CO_2 + 2H_2O$$

Other carbon compounds, such as those in gasoline and wax, <u>undergo</u> combustion reactions similar to the one above.

When there is not enough oxygen during a combustion reaction, not all fuels are converted completely into carbon dioxide. In that case, some carbon monoxide may form. Carbon monoxide, CO, is a poisonous gas that lowers the ability of the blood to carry oxygen. Carbon monoxide has no color or odor, so you cannot tell when it is present. In some combustion reactions, you can tell if the air supply is limited because the excess carbon is given off as small particles that make a dark, sooty smoke.

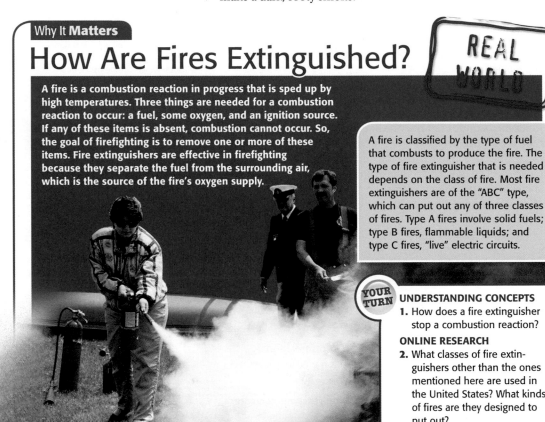

Why It Matters

How Are Fires Extinguished?

REAL WORLD

A fire is a combustion reaction in progress that is sped up by high temperatures. Three things are needed for a combustion reaction to occur: a fuel, some oxygen, and an ignition source. If any of these items is absent, combustion cannot occur. So, the goal of firefighting is to remove one or more of these items. Fire extinguishers are effective in firefighting because they separate the fuel from the surrounding air, which is the source of the fire's oxygen supply.

A fire is classified by the type of fuel that combusts to produce the fire. The type of fire extinguisher that is needed depends on the class of fire. Most fire extinguishers are of the "ABC" type, which can put out any of three classes of fires. Type A fires involve solid fuels; type B fires, flammable liquids; and type C fires, "live" electric circuits.

YOUR TURN

UNDERSTANDING CONCEPTS
1. How does a fire extinguisher stop a combustion reaction?

ONLINE RESEARCH
2. What classes of fire extinguishers other than the ones mentioned here are used in the United States? What kinds of fires are they designed to put out?

MISCONCEPTION ALERT

Combustion Some students think that the products of a combustion reaction will weigh less than the reactants do because the material is used up.
- Review the law of the conservation of mass and ask students to explain how this law applies to combustion. (The law of conservation of mass applies to all chemical reactions, so the mass of reactants and the mass of products in a combustion reaction are identical.)

- Ask students to name the reactants in the combustion of a candle. (wax and oxygen) Students often recognize that oxygen is required for combustion, but they do not consider it a reactant. Emphasize this point in your discussion of combustion reactions. Also emphasize that the reactant is oxygen, not air.

In single-displacement reactions, elements trade places.

Copper(II) chloride dissolves in water to make a bright blue solution. If you add a piece of aluminum foil to the solution, the color goes away and clumps of reddish brown material form. The reddish brown clumps are copper metal. Aluminum replaces copper in the copper(II) chloride to form aluminum chloride. Aluminum chloride does not make a colored solution, so the blue color goes away as the amount of blue copper(II) chloride decreases, as shown in **Figure 3.**

The copper(II) ions, as part of copper(II) chloride, become neutral copper metal. The aluminum metal atoms become aluminum ions. The chloride ions remain the same. Because the atoms of one element appear to move into a compound and atoms of the other element appear to move out, this reaction is called a **single-displacement reaction.** Single-displacement reactions have the following general form.

> **Single-displacement reaction** | $AX + B \longrightarrow BX + A$

The equation for the single-displacement reaction between copper(II) chloride and aluminum is as follows.

$$3CuCl_2 + 2Al \longrightarrow 2AlCl_3 + 3Cu$$

In general, a more reactive element will take the place of a less reactive one in a single-displacement reaction.

✔️ **Reading Check** What do all single-displacement reactions have in common?

READING TOOLBOX

Reading Equations
Pick out some of the chemical equations given in this section, and practice saying them aloud and writing them in the form of sentences.

combustion reaction (kuhm BUHS chuhn ree AK shuhn) the oxidation reaction of an organic compound, in which heat is released

single-displacement reaction (SING guhl dis PLAYS muhnt ree AK shuhn) a reaction in which one element or radical takes the place of another element or radical in a compound

Figure 3 Aluminum undergoes a single-displacement reaction with copper(II) chloride to form copper and aluminum chloride.

READING TOOLBOX

Reading Equations Sample answer: Three moles of copper-two (II) chloride react with two moles of aluminum to form two moles of aluminum chloride and three moles of copper. Alternatively, students can use molecules and atoms instead of moles to describe the reactants and products. **LS** Verbal

Science Skills

Interpreting Visuals After students have studied **Figure 3,** have them answer the following questions: "What are the reactants?" (aluminum and copper(II) chloride) "What are the products?" (copper and aluminum chloride) "Describe the reaction in words." (The chloride ions in the copper-two (II) chloride bond with the aluminum atoms, forming aluminum chloride. The reaction also produces copper atoms.) **LS** Visual

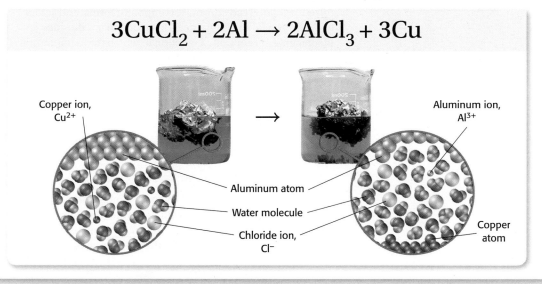

$$3CuCl_2 + 2Al \rightarrow 2AlCl_3 + 3Cu$$

Copper ion, Cu^{2+}

Aluminum atom

Water molecule

Chloride ion, Cl^-

Aluminum ion, Al^{3+}

Copper atom

Differentiated Instruction

Struggling Readers

Learning Reactions Have students write the types of chemical reactions on five note cards (one type per card). Then, have them write definitions for each of the chemical reactions on five additional note cards. Have students work individually or in pairs to match each type of reaction with its definition. To create a more difficult matching activity, make additional cards with examples of each type of reaction. **LS** Logical

go.hrw.com
✳ interact online

Students can interact with the figure by going to **go.hrw.com** and typing in the keyword **HK8REAF4.**

Answer to caption question
Sample answer: One atom of potassium trades places with one atom of hydrogen from each water molecule to form the reactants.

Why It Matters

Pain Relievers From the time of Hippocrates, an ancient Greek healer, people knew that chewing willow bark would relieve pain. Native Americans and the Chinese also used it. But with the pain relief of willow bark came a problem: stomach discomfort. In the 1800s, the active ingredient in the bark was isolated. It is salicylic acid, which causes stomach discomfort because of its acidity. Felix Hoffman, a German chemist, used a displacement reaction to make the acid less acidic without destroying its pain-relieving properties. He replaced the hydrogen atom of an –OH group on the molecule with an acetyl group, –OCCH$_3$. The result—acetylsalicylic acid—relieves pain with fewer stomach problems.

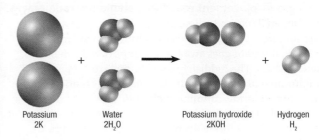

Potassium
2K

Water
2H$_2$O

Potassium hydroxide
2KOH

Hydrogen
H$_2$

Figure 4 Potassium reacts with water in a single-displacement reaction. **Which atoms of the reactants trade places to form the products?**

go.hrw.com
✳ interact online
Keyword: HK8REAF4

Alkali metals undergo single-displacement reactions.

Potassium metal is so reactive that it undergoes a single-displacement reaction with water, as **Figure 4** shows. The potassium and water reaction is so exothermic that the H$_2$ that is produced may explode and burn instantly. All alkali metals and some other metals undergo similar single-displacement reactions with water. All such reactions form hydrogen gas, metal ions, and hydroxide ions.

In double-displacement reactions, ions appear to be exchanged between compounds.

The yellow lines painted on roads are colored with lead chromate, PbCrO$_4$. This compound can be formed by mixing solutions of lead nitrate, Pb(NO$_3$)$_2$, and potassium chromate, K$_2$CrO$_4$. In solution, these compounds form the ions Pb^{2+}, NO$_3^-$, K$^+$, and CrO$_4^{2-}$. The lead ions and chromate ions are more attracted to one another than they are to the water molecules around them. Therefore, when the solutions are mixed, a yellow lead chromate compound forms, and settles to the bottom of the container. This reaction is a **double-displacement reaction,** a reaction in which two compounds appear to exchange ions. The general form of a double-displacement reaction appears below.

▷ **Double-displacement reaction** : AX + BY ⟶ AY + BX

The double-displacement reaction that forms lead chromate is as follows.

$$Pb(NO_3)_2 + K_2CrO_4 \longrightarrow PbCrO_4 + 2KNO_3$$

The lead and chromate ions form a compound. Potassium and nitrate ions are soluble together in water, so they do not form a compound. Instead, they stay in solution just as the lead and nitrate ions were before the reaction.

Science Skills

Activity Series In most single-displacement reactions, a more active element replaces a less active one. An *activity series,* which lists substances in order of relative activity, can be used to predict whether a replacement reaction will occur. An activity series lists the most active elements first (or at the top) and the least active ones last (or at the bottom). An activity series of common metals is as follows: Li, K, Ca, Na, Mg, Al, Mn, Zn, Fe, Ni, Sn, Pb, Cu, Ag, Pt, Au. In a solution, each element is able to displace those listed after it in the series. Usually, this series can be used to predict whether a single-displacement reaction will occur at room temperature in an aqueous solution, but there are some exceptions. Write this series on the board. Name two metals and ask students to rapidly determine which metal is most likely to displace the other.
LS Logical

InquiryLab — Determining the Products of a Reaction

⏱ **20 min**

Procedure

CAUTION: Wear safety goggles and an apron. Silver nitrate will stain your skin and clothes.

❶ With a **wax pencil**, label **three test tubes** "NaCl," "KBr," and "KI."

❷ Using a **10 mL graduated cylinder**, measure **5 mL each of sodium chloride, potassium bromide,** and **potassium iodide solutions** into the appropriate test tubes. Rinse the graduated cylinder between each use.

❸ Add **1 mL of silver nitrate** solution to each of the test tubes. Record your observations.

Analysis

1. What sign of a reaction did you observe?

2. Identify the reactants and products for each reaction.

3. Write the balanced equation for each reaction.

4. Which ion(s) produced a solid with silver nitrate?

5. Does this test let you identify all the ions? Why or why not?

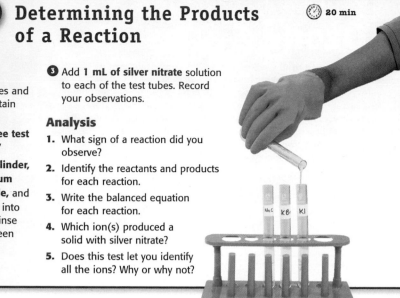

InquiryLab

Materials per Group

- graduated cylinder, 10 mL
- pencil, wax
- potassium bromide solution
- potassium iodide solution
- silver nitrate solution
- sodium chloride solution
- test tubes (3)
- test tube holder

Answers to Analysis

1. the formation of a precipitate

2. For sodium chloride and silver nitrate, the reactants are NaCl and $AgNO_3$, and the products are AgCl and $NaNO_3$. For potassium bromide and silver nitrate, the reactants are KBr and $AgNO_3$, and the products are AgBr and KNO_3. For potassium iodide and silver nitrate, the reactants are KI and $AgNO_3$ and the products are AgI and KNO_3.

3. $NaCl + AgNO_3 \rightarrow AgCl + NaNO_3$
   $KBr + AgNO_3 \rightarrow AgBr + KNO_3$
   $KI + AgNO_3 \rightarrow AgI + KNO_3$

4. Cl^-, Br^-, and I^- all form solids with $AgNO_3$.

5. Solid AgCl is white, AgBr is pale yellow, and AgI is also yellow. Although AgI is darker than AgBr, it might be difficult to distinguish the two by color.

Electrons and Chemical Reactions

The general classes of reactions described earlier in this section were used by early chemists, who knew nothing about the parts of the atom. After chemists learned about the presence of electrons in atoms, they developed another way to classify reactions. ❯ **Free-radical reactions and redox reactions can be understood as changes in the numbers of electrons that atoms have.**

Free radicals have electrons available for bonding.

Many synthetic fibers, as well as plastic bags and wraps, are made by polymerization reactions, which were discussed earlier. Often, these reactions involve free radicals. A **free radical** is an atom or a group of atoms that has one unpaired electron.

Sometimes, a covalent bond is broken such that an un-paired electron is left on each fragment of the molecule. These fragments are free radicals. Because an uncharged hydrogen atom has one electron available for bonding, it is a free radical. Electrons tend to form pairs with other electrons. So, free radicals react quickly to form covalent bonds with other substances. As a result, new compounds are made. Some free-radical reactions are very important in the environment.

✓ **Reading Check** Why are free radicals so reactive?

double-displacement reaction (DUHB uhl dis PLAYS muhnt ree AK shuhn) a reaction in which a gas, a solid precipitate, or a molecular compound forms from the apparent exchange of atoms or ions between two compounds

free radical (FREE RAD i kuhl) an atom or a group of atoms that has one unpaired electron

Teaching Key Ideas

Oxidation and Reduction Have students use a number line to explain why gaining electrons (adding a negative charge) during reduction results in a decrease in positive charge. Have them also explain why losing electrons (subtracting negative charge) during oxidation results in an increase in positive charge. Remind students that free elements have zero charge, and provide them with several examples of changes of charge. For each, have them identify the change as oxidation or reduction. Examples of oxidation include Fe to Fe^{2+}, Cr^{2+} to Cr^{3+}, and Cl^- to Cl. Examples of reduction include F to F^-, Pb^{4+} to Pb^{2+}, and Mg^{2+} to Mg. After mastering the concepts of oxidation and reduction, have groups of students create posters that use a number line to explain oxidation and reduction along with examples of each. **LS Logical/Visual**

Why It **Matters**

Ozone The ozone layer is essential to protect living things from ultraviolet radiation. However, ozone is also a toxic chemical that can cause lung problems and harm other living organisms. The difference between the protective ozone layer and harmful ozone lies only in where it occurs. The concentration of ozone in the stratosphere varies naturally depending on seasons, latitude, and variation in solar radiation. The atmosphere recovers from natural decreases in ozone. In the mid-20th century, however, scientists detected a decrease in the amount of ozone that was not followed by complete recovery.

After many experiments, atmospheric scientists determined that the additional loss of ozone was due to free radicals of chlorine in the upper atmosphere. Because they are so reactive, free radicals can be harmful. Ultraviolet radiation from the sun breaks down chemicals called chlorofluorocarbons (CFCs), forming chlorine free radicals. Each of these free radicals can destroy tens of thousands of ozone molecules in a chain reaction that destroys a molecule of ozone and produces another free radical. The ozone layer has recovered significantly following a ban on use of CFCs.

Answer to Your Turn

1. Ozone is helpful in the upper atmosphere because it absorbs the sun's radiation. It is harmful in the lower atmosphere because it is a pollutant and part of smog.

Why It **Matters**

Ozone

Ozone is a form of oxygen, but it consists of molecules of O_3 rather than O_2, the oxygen we breathe. When the sun's radiation strikes oxygen molecules in the upper atmosphere, some of them break apart into free radicals. The oxygen radicals react with other oxygen molecules to form the *ozone layer* in the upper atmosphere. Because of its unique properties, ozone is able to absorb much of the sun's radiation and protect Earth's surface. But ozone in the lower atmosphere, created by incomplete combustion, contributes to smog.

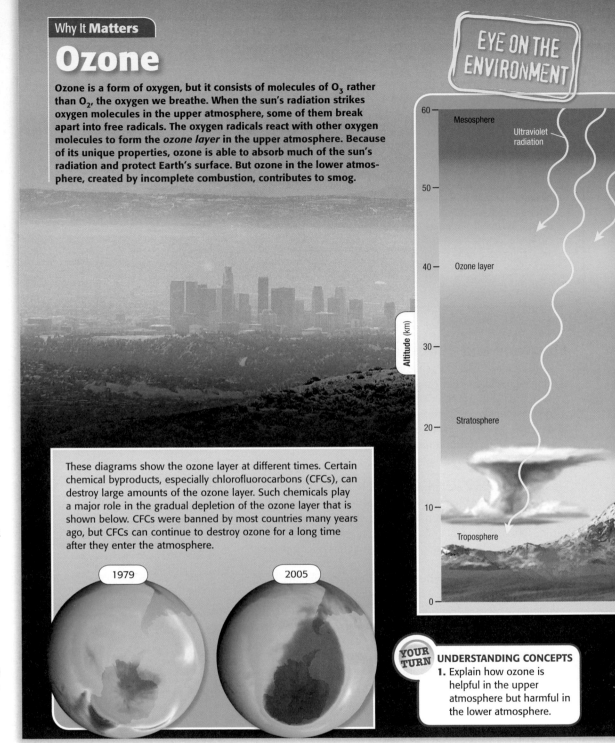

EYE ON THE ENVIRONMENT

These diagrams show the ozone layer at different times. Certain chemical byproducts, especially chlorofluorocarbons (CFCs), can destroy large amounts of the ozone layer. Such chemicals play a major role in the gradual depletion of the ozone layer that is shown below. CFCs were banned by most countries many years ago, but CFCs can continue to destroy ozone for a long time after they enter the atmosphere.

1979   2005

YOUR TURN **UNDERSTANDING CONCEPTS**
1. Explain how ozone is helpful in the upper atmosphere but harmful in the lower atmosphere.

Electrons are transferred in redox reactions.

A very common type of reaction involves the transfer of electrons. The formation of rust is an example of such a reaction. In the presence of water, atoms of iron metal, Fe, react with oxygen molecules, O_2, to form rust, Fe_2O_3. Each iron atom loses three electrons to form Fe^{3+} ions, and each oxygen atom gains two electrons to form O^{2-} ions.

Substances that accept electrons are said to be *reduced*. Substances that give up electrons are said to be *oxidized*. One way to remember which term is which is that the gain of electrons reduces the positive charge on an ion or makes an uncharged atom become a negative ion. Whenever reduction happens, oxidation happens, too. The reverse is also true. Reactions in which one substance loses electrons and another substance gains electrons are called **oxidation-reduction reactions.** These reactions are called *redox reactions* for short.

Some redox reactions do not involve ions. In these reactions, oxidation is a gain of oxygen or a loss of hydrogen, and reduction is the loss of oxygen or the gain of hydrogen. Respiration and combustion are redox reactions because oxygen gas reacts with carbon compounds to form carbon dioxide. Carbon atoms in CO_2 are oxidized, and oxygen atoms in O_2 are reduced. Scientists knew about redox reactions before they knew about electrons. They now know that oxidation does not necessarily require oxygen. But they still use the name *oxidation* to describe any reaction in which an atom loses electrons.

oxidation-reduction reaction
(AHKS i DAY shuhn ri DUHK shuhn ree AK shuhn) any chemical change in which one species is oxidized (loses electrons) and another species is reduced (gains electrons); also called *redox reaction*

Integrating Fine Arts

Redox Reactions and the Statue of Liberty Metal sculptures often corrode because of redox reactions. The Statue of Liberty, which is covered with 200,000 pounds of copper, was as bright as a new penny when it was first built. However, after more than 100 years, the statue had turned green. The copper reacted with the damp air of New York harbor. More important, oxidation reactions between the damp, salty air and the internal iron supports made the structure dangerously weak. The statue was closed for several years in the 1980s while the supports were cleaned and repaired.

Oxidation-Reduction Reactions
Different metals corrode different ways. Although the green coating, or *patina,* on the Statue of Liberty was caused by corrosion, the coating helped protect the copper from further corrosion. However, the rust that formed on the iron framework did not protect the remaining iron. The rust crumbled away, and the exposed iron corroded further.

When repairing the framework of the statue, materials resistant to corrosion were used. Two materials were chosen—an extremely strong iron-aluminum alloy called *ferallium* and a more flexible stainless steel alloy made from iron, chromium, and nickel. Sealants were also used to protect the structure from the environment and to separate the copper and iron-based parts of the statue.

❯ Close

Reteaching Key Ideas

Mnemonic Devices An easy mnemonic device for associating oxidation and reduction with electron transfer is **OIL RIG: O**xidation **I**s the **L**oss of electrons, **R**eduction **I**s the **G**ain of electrons. Some students may prefer **LEO** says **GER: L**oss of **E**lectrons is **O**xidation, **G**ain of **E**lectrons is **R**eduction. Ask students to develop mnemonic devices for the other chemical reactions. Have students share their ideas with the class. **LS Logical/Verbal**

Section 3 **Review**

KEY IDEAS

1. **Classify** each of the following reactions by type:
   a. $S_8 + 8O_2 \longrightarrow 8SO_2 + energy$
   b. $6CO_2 + 6H_2O \longrightarrow C_6H_{12}O_6 + 6O_2$
   c. $2NaHCO_3 \longrightarrow Na_2CO_3 + H_2O + CO_2$
   d. $Zn + 2HCl \longrightarrow ZnCl_2 + H_2$

2. **List** three possible results of a double-displacement reaction.

3. **Define** *free radical*.

4. **Identify** which element is oxidized and which element is reduced in the following reaction:
$$Zn + CuSO_4 \longrightarrow ZnSO_4 + Cu$$

CRITICAL THINKING

5. **Predicting Consequences** Explain why charcoal grills or charcoal fires should not be used to heat the inside of a house. (Hint: When it is cold, doors and windows are closed, so there is little fresh air.)

6. **Compare and Contrast** Compare and contrast single-displacement and double-displacement reactions based on the number of reactants. Use the terms *compound, atom* or *element,* and *ion.*

7. **Analyzing Ideas** Describe how a polymer is made, and explain how this process is an example of a synthesis reaction.

8. **Analyzing Processes** Explain why a reduction must take place whenever oxidation occurs.

Formative Assessment

Which of the following general reaction types illustrates a double-displacement reaction?

A. $XA + B \longrightarrow BA + X$ (Incorrect. This is a single-displacement reaction.)

B. $AB \longrightarrow A + B$ (Incorrect. This is a decomposition reaction.)

C. $A + B \longrightarrow AB$ (Incorrect. This is a synthesis reaction.)

D. $AX + BY \longrightarrow AY + BX$ (Correct. This is a double-displacement reaction.)

Answers to Section Review

1. **a.** synthesis
   b. synthesis
   c. decomposition
   d. single-displacement

2. Sample answer: formation of a gas, a precipitate, or a covalent molecule, such as water

3. an atom or molecule that has an unpaired electron

4. Zinc is oxidized, and copper is reduced.

Answers continued on p. 255A

Reaction Rates and Equilibrium

>Focus

In this section, students learn how temperature, surface area, concentration, pressure, molecule shape and size, and the use of catalysts can affect reaction rates. The section concludes with a discussion of equilibrium systems and Le Châtelier's principle.

 **Bellringer**

Use the Bellringer transparency to prepare students for this section.

Demonstrate

Surface Area For this demonstration you will need two 100 mL graduated cylinders, rock salt, table salt, weighing paper, a balance, and 1 can of carbonated soda. Label one graduated cylinder "rock salt" and the other cylinder "table salt." Pour 75 mL of carbonated soda into each graduated cylinder. Measure the mass of one large crystal of rock salt. Obtain an equivalent mass of table salt. Simultaneously dump each salt sample into the appropriately labeled graduated cylinder. Tell students that since the masses of the salt samples are identical, the only variable between the two samples is the amount of surface area. The increased surface area of the table salt provides many more reactive sites, resulting in a greater amount of foam being formed.

Key Ideas

> What kinds of things speed up a reaction?

> What does a catalyst do?

> What happens when a reaction goes backward as well as forward?

Key Terms

catalyst

enzyme

substrate

chemical
  equilibrium

Why It Matters

By raising some reaction rates in the body, a fever can help a person recover from an illness.

Chemical reactions can occur at different rates, or speeds. Some reactions, such as the explosion of nitroglycerin, shown in **Figure 1,** are very fast. Other reactions, such as the burning of carbon in charcoal, are much slower. But what happens if you slow down the nitroglycerin reaction to make it safer? What happens if you speed up the reaction by which yeast makes carbon dioxide in order to make bread rise in less time? If you think carefully, you may realize that you already know some ways to change reaction rates. In fact, you may use the factors that affect reaction rates every day.

Figure 1 Nitroglycerin, which is used as a rocket fuel, reacts very quickly.

Oxygen   Nitrogen

Hydrogen

Carbon

Factors Affecting Reaction Rates

Think about the following observations:

• A potato slice takes 5 minutes to cook at 200 °C but takes 10 minutes to cook at 100 °C. Therefore, potatoes cook faster at higher temperatures.

• Potato slices take 10 minutes to cook, but whole potatoes take about 30 minutes to cook. Therefore, potatoes cut into smaller pieces cook faster.

These observations have to do with the speed of chemical reactions. In each situation in which the potatoes cooked faster, the contact between particles was greater, so the cooking reaction went faster. This relationship reflects a general principle. **> Anything that increases contact between particles will increase the rate of a reaction.** Factors that affect the rate of a reaction include temperature, surface area, concentration, and pressure.

Key Resources

 Teaching Transparencies
C18 Equilibrium
TM24 Changing Equilibrium

Visual Concepts
Factors Affecting Reaction Rate
Catalyst
Enzyme
Equilibrium
Factors Affecting Equilibrium
Le Châtelier's Principle

Datasheets
What Affects the Rates of Chemical Reactions?
Catalysts in Action

Cross-Disciplinary Worksheet
Integrating Environmental Science—
Fertilizers: Friend or Foe?

Most reactions go faster at higher temperatures.

Heating food starts the chemical reactions that happen in cooking. Cooking at higher temperatures cooks food faster. Cooling food slows down the chemical reactions that result in spoiling, as shown in **Figure 2.** Particles move faster at higher temperatures. Faster-moving particles collide more often, so there are more chances for the particles to react. Therefore, reactions are faster at higher temperatures.

A large surface area speeds up reactions.

When a whole potato is placed in boiling water, only its surface touches the boiling water. The energy from the water has to go all the way through the potato. Cutting a potato into pieces exposes inner parts of the potato. Increasing the *surface area* of a reactant in this way speeds up a reaction.

Higher concentrations of reactants react faster.

Imagine building a bonfire. As you read above, a high temperature will get a reaction going. In this case, the energy released in the reaction also keeps the fire going. Small pieces of wood burn faster than thick logs because small pieces have more surface area. Increasing the concentration of the reactants also speeds up a reaction. So, another thing you can do to get a fire blazing is to put plenty of wood on it!

✔ Reading Check Why are reactions at high temperatures faster than at low temperatures?

Figure 2 Mold will grow on bread stored at room temperature. Bread stored in the freezer for the same length of time will be free of mold when you take the bread out of the freezer.

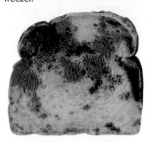

Bread stored at room temperature

Bread stored in the freezer

InquiryLab What Affects the Rates of Chemical Reactions?

⏱ **30 min**

Procedure

❶ Using **tongs,** hold a **paper clip** in the hottest part of a **burner** flame for 30 s. Repeat with a **ball of steel wool.** Record your observations.

❷ Label **three test tubes** "A," "B," and "C." Put **10 mL of vinegar** into test tube A, **5 mL of vinegar** and **5 mL of water** into test tube B, and **2.5 mL of vinegar** and **7.5 mL of water** into test tube C. Add a piece of **magnesium ribbon** to each test tube. Record your observations.

❸ Label **three more test tubes** "1," "2," and "3." Put **5 mL of vinegar** and **5 mL of water** into each test tube. Submerge the solution in test tube 1 in a **small beaker of ice-cold water.** Submerge the solution in test tube 3 in a **small beaker of hot water.** Add a piece of **magnesium ribbon** to the test tubes. Record your observations.

Analysis

1. Describe and interpret your results. For each step, list the factor(s) that influenced the rate of reaction.

> **Teach**

Teaching Key Ideas

Faster Reactions Point out to students that chemical reactions occur when reactant particles collide with each other with sufficient energy to cause a reaction. Ask students to suggest ways to increase the frequency of collisions, the energy of the collisions, or both, thus increasing the reaction rate. Lead students to realize that increasing concentration, temperature, or surface area will increase the reaction rate. Ask students to explain how each of these changes would lead to a change in the rate of a reaction. (Increasing concentration increases collisions; increasing temperature increases both collisions and energy; and increasing surface area increases collisions.) **LS Logical/Verbal**

InquiryLab

Teacher's Notes The reactions in steps 2 and 3 can be vigorous. Remind students to wear eye protection and to be sure that test tubes do not point toward themselves or classmates.

Materials per Group

- beakers (2)
- burner
- magnesium ribbon, 6 pieces
- paper clip
- steel wool
- test tubes (3)
- tongs
- vinegar
- water

Answer to Analysis

1. In step 1, the paper clip showed no evidence of reaction. The steel wool had rust, indicating a reaction with oxygen. The factor that influenced rate of reaction in this step was surface area. In step 2, Mg reacted the fastest in test tube A, slower in test tube B, and the slowest in test tube C. The rate of reaction decreased as the concentration of vinegar decreased. In step 3, Mg reacted slowest in test tube A, faster in test tube B, and fastest in test tube C. The reaction rate in this case varied directly with temperature.

Demonstrate

Increasing Concentration Model the effect of increasing concentration on reaction rate. Remove the plastic insert that holds the CD in a case, leaving a clear shallow box. Cover ¾ in. of the outer edge of the box so that students will not be distracted by BBs hitting the sides of the box. Place 25 to 50 metal BBs in the case, and place the case on an overhead projector. Swirl and jerk the case so that the frequency of collisions between the BBs can be seen. Next double the number of BBs in the box. This doubles the concentration of BBs. Swirl the box again; students should be able to see the increase in the frequency of collisions.
LS Visual

Teaching Key Ideas

Types of Catalysts There are two types of catalysts. Heterogeneous catalysts provide a surface on which reactants concentrate, increasing reaction rate. A heterogeneous catalyst is used in catalytic converters. Catalytic converters have one section in which nitrogen oxides are reduced to N_2 and O_2 using heterogeneous catalysts, such as platinum. The second section uses the same catalyst to completely oxidize hydrocarbons and carbon monoxide in exhaust gases. Homogeneous catalysts, such as enzymes, mix with the reactants and form an intermediate compound that reacts more readily. Many biological processes use homogeneous catalysts. For both types of catalysts, the catalyst remains unchanged by the reaction.

SCILINKS.
www.scilinks.org
Topic: Catalysts
Code: HK80231

catalyst (KAT uh LIST) a substance that changes the rate of a chemical reaction without being consumed or changed significantly

enzyme (EN ZIEM) a molecule, either protein or RNA, that acts as a catalyst in biochemical reactions

substrate (SUHB STRAYT) the reactant in reactions catalyzed by enzymes

Figure 3 An automobile's catalytic converter reduces pollution by helping pollutant molecules react to form harmless substances.

A metal surface, such as platinum or palladium, can act as a catalyst.

Reactions are faster at higher pressure.

The *concentration* of a gas is the number of particles in a certain volume. A gas at high pressure has a higher concentration than the same amount of the gas at a low pressure. The reason is that the gas at high pressure has been squeezed into a smaller space. Gases react faster at higher pressures. When the particles of a gas have less space in which to move, they have more collisions and thus more reactions.

Massive, bulky molecules react more slowly.

The mass of the reactant molecules affects the rate of the reaction. According to the kinetic theory of matter, massive molecules move more slowly than less massive molecules at the same temperature. So, for equal numbers of molecules whose masses differ but whose sizes are similar, the molecules that have more mass collide less often with other molecules.

The size and shape of reactant molecules also affect how fast the molecules react. Large, bulky molecules usually must be in a certain position relative to other molecules to react with the other molecules. Because of their size and their number of branching or bulky parts, large and bulky molecules may not reach the right position. Thus, these molecules tend not to react as readily as small and simple ones.

Catalysts

Why would one add a substance to a reaction if that substance may not react? One reason is to increase the rate of the reaction. A substance that changes the rate of a reaction is called a **catalyst. 》A catalyst speeds up or slows down a reaction but is not changed by the reaction.** Substances that slow reactions are also called *inhibitors*. Catalysts are used in various industries. For example, they are used to help make ammonia, to process crude oil, and to make plastics. Catalysts can be expensive yet profitable to use because they can be cleaned or renewed and reused. Sometimes, the presence of a catalyst is shown by writing the name of the catalyst over the reaction arrow of a chemical equation.

Catalysts work in various ways. Most solid catalysts, such as the ones in car exhaust systems, speed up reactions by providing a surface where the reactants can collect and react. Then, the reactants can form new bonds to make the products. Most solid catalysts are more effective if they have a large surface area, such as the area of the honeycomb-like metal surface of the catalytic converter in **Figure 3.**

Differentiated Instruction

Basic Learners

Concept Map Concept maps can help students clarify the relationships between ideas. Ask students to make a concept map for the main ideas in the section entitled "Factors Affecting Reaction Rates." You can use the following example to get students started. Students should add information that explains how each factor affects reaction rates. **LS** Visual/Logical

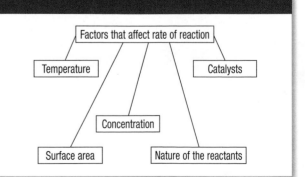

Enzymes are biological catalysts.

Enzymes are catalysts for chemical reactions in living things. Enzymes have very specific purposes. Each enzyme controls one reaction or one set of similar reactions. **Figure 4** lists some common enzymes and the reactions that they control. Most enzymes are fragile. If kept too cold or too warm, they tend to fall apart. Most stop working above about 45 °C.

Catalase, an enzyme in the cells of humans and most other living organisms, breaks down hydrogen peroxide. Hydrogen peroxide is the substrate for catalase. A **substrate** is the reactant that is catalyzed, or acted upon, by an enzyme.

$$2H_2O_2 \longrightarrow 2H_2O + O_2$$

For an enzyme to catalyze a reaction, the substrate and the enzyme must fit like a key in a lock. The location on the enzyme where the substrate fits is called the *active site,* as shown in **Figure 4.** The active site of an enzyme is suited for the particular shape of the substrate and the catalyzed reaction.

Enzymes are very efficient. In 1 min, one molecule of catalase can catalyze the decomposition of 6 million molecules of hydrogen peroxide. Without the enzyme, the reaction would go much more slowly.

✓ **Reading Check** What does an enzyme do?

Common Enzymes and Their Uses

Enzyme	Substrate	Role of the enzyme
Amylase	starch	to break down starch into smaller molecules
Cellulase	cellulose	to break down long cellulose molecules into sugars
DNA polymerase	nucleic acid	to build up DNA chains in cell nuclei
Lipase	fat	to break down fat into smaller molecules
Protease	protein	to break down proteins into amino acids

Enzymes have an active site that fits a particular substrate.

The enzyme catalyzes a reaction that the substrate undergoes.

The substrate then leaves the active site, and another substrate takes its place.

QuickLab ⏱ 20 min

Catalysts in Action

❶ Pour **2% hydrogen peroxide** into a **test tube** to a depth of 2 cm.

❷ Pour **water** into **another test tube** to a depth of 2 cm.

❸ Drop a **small piece of raw liver** into each test tube.

❹ Liver contains the enzyme catalase. Watch carefully, and describe what happens. Explain your observations.

❺ Using **a piece of liver that has been boiled for 3 min,** repeat steps 1–4. Explain your result.

❻ Using **iron filings** instead of liver, repeat steps 1–4 one more time. What happens?

❼ Describe some principles of catalysts that you observed in this experiment.

Figure 4 Each enzymes has a specific fit with its substrate. The substrate fits into the enzyme's active site, and then undergoes a particular reaction.

QuickLab

Teacher's Notes As an extension of this activity, students can use pieces of carrot or potato instead of liver. Although the results will not be as dramatic, these foods also contain catalytic enzymes.

Materials per Group
- hydrogen peroxide solution, 2%
- iron filings
- liver, boiled and not boiled
- test tubes (2)
- water

Answers

4. Liver had no effect on the water. The hydrogen peroxide bubbled after the addition of the liver, decomposing into water and oxygen. The liver contains an enzyme that acts as a catalyst for the reaction.

5. Boiled liver does not act as a catalyst because the heat destroyed the enzyme in liver.

6. Iron filings had no catalytic effect.

7. I observed that exposure of the hydrogen peroxide to the liver caused the peroxide to break down and release a gas. Boiling the liver caused the enzymes to no longer work.

Why It Matters

Hydrogen Peroxide Hydrogen peroxide bubbles when placed on a cut or scrape because blood and cells in the cut contain the enzyme catalase. The bubbles are oxygen gas created by the reaction that is stimulated by the enzyme. Because catalase is not found on the surface of skin, hydrogen peroxide does not react when placed directly on skin, and no foam is observed.

Differentiated Instruction

Struggling Readers

Words in Context Explain that a reader can sometimes figure out what a word means by looking at how it is used. Refer to the table in **Figure 4.** Ask students what the word *substrate* means, using the information on the table to provide clues. (Sample answer: The substrate is the substance that is affected by the enzyme.)
LS Verbal

READING TOOLBOX

Vocabulary Catalysts make a reaction proceed faster. Inhibitors make a reaction proceed slower. Although inhibitors appear to retard reactions, they actually bind reactants so that they are not available for other reactions. The term *inhibitor* comes from the Latin *in,* which means "in," and *habere,* which means "to have or to hold." Thus, an inhibitor is a substance that holds a reactant, keeping it from reacting with another substance.

Why It **Matters**

What Kinds of Chemical Reactions Happen in the Human Body? Few chemical reactions in the human body would occur at a rate fast enough to sustain life without the presence of enzymes. Not all enzymes break down large molecules. Some enzymes catalyze the formation of larger molecules, including large polymers such as starch and proteins. These enzymes carry out biosyntheses, which are usually endothermic. For this reason, the reactions require a large amount of energy stored in the form of ATP, adenosine triphosphate, to occur. This is one of the reasons why living things require a constant supply of energy.

READING TOOLBOX

Visual Literacy It may not be clear from these illustrations that the catalysts mentioned are individual molecules. Although cells, such as the red blood cells, are tiny, each cell contains thousands of enzymes, each involved in a different chemical reaction. Because enzymes are catalysts, they are not changed by the reaction. Some enzymes take part in as many as one million chemical reactions in one second.

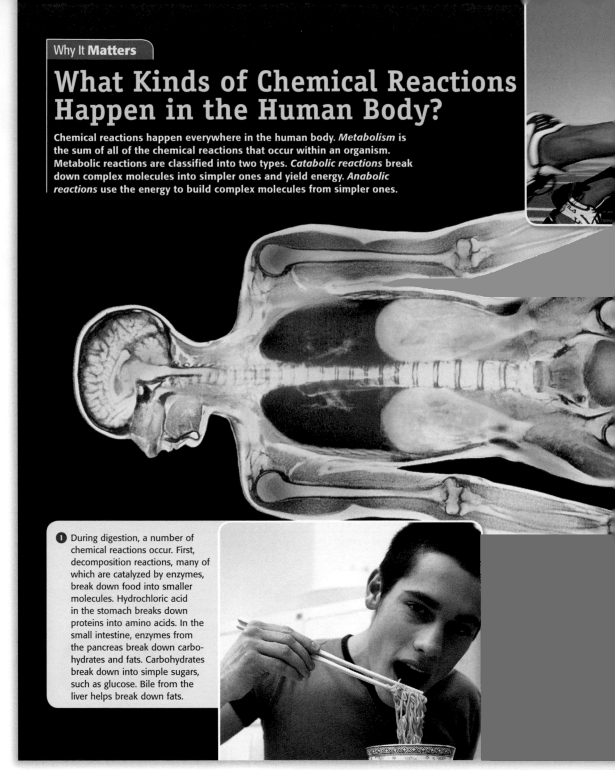

What Kinds of Chemical Reactions Happen in the Human Body?

Chemical reactions happen everywhere in the human body. *Metabolism* is the sum of all of the chemical reactions that occur within an organism. Metabolic reactions are classified into two types. *Catabolic reactions* break down complex molecules into simpler ones and yield energy. *Anabolic reactions* use the energy to build complex molecules from simpler ones.

❶ During digestion, a number of chemical reactions occur. First, decomposition reactions, many of which are catalyzed by enzymes, break down food into smaller molecules. Hydrochloric acid in the stomach breaks down proteins into amino acids. In the small intestine, enzymes from the pancreas break down carbohydrates and fats. Carbohydrates break down into simple sugars, such as glucose. Bile from the liver helps break down fats.

Differentiated Instruction

English Learners

Reading Skills Have students work in pairs or small groups. Make sure each student who is still learning English is paired with an English speaker. Give students progressively difficult equations to describe. Have students take turns describing each equation to their partner or group. Have students help each other through the descriptions until they feel comfortable.
LS Verbal

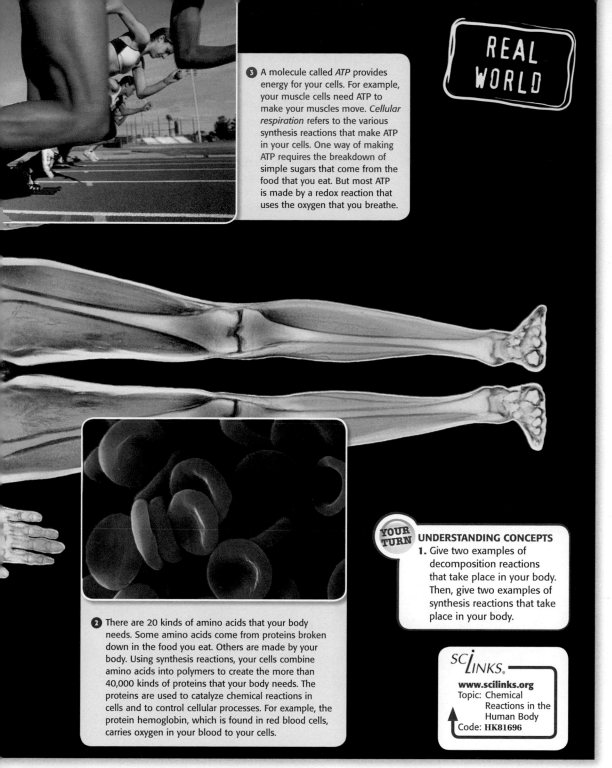

③ A molecule called *ATP* provides energy for your cells. For example, your muscle cells need ATP to make your muscles move. *Cellular respiration* refers to the various synthesis reactions that make ATP in your cells. One way of making ATP requires the breakdown of simple sugars that come from the food that you eat. But most ATP is made by a redox reaction that uses the oxygen that you breathe.

REAL WORLD

② There are 20 kinds of amino acids that your body needs. Some amino acids come from proteins broken down in the food you eat. Others are made by your body. Using synthesis reactions, your cells combine amino acids into polymers to create the more than 40,000 kinds of proteins that your body needs. The proteins are used to catalyze chemical reactions in cells and to control cellular processes. For example, the protein hemoglobin, which is found in red blood cells, carries oxygen in your blood to your cells.

YOUR TURN

UNDERSTANDING CONCEPTS

1. Give two examples of decomposition reactions that take place in your body. Then, give two examples of synthesis reactions that take place in your body.

SCI LINKS.

www.scilinks.org
Topic: Chemical Reactions in the Human Body
Code: **HK81696**

READING TOOLBOX

Vocabulary Ask students to describe what the terms *synthesis, decomposition,* and *displacement* mean to them. All are terms that have common usage. Students should associate synthesis with making something, decomposition with things breaking down, and displacement with movement from one place to another. Have students compare their descriptions and discuss any similarities and differences. **LS Verbal**

Answer to Your Turn

1. Decomposition reactions happen during digestion and during the break down of glucose that happens in the cells. Synthesis happens when proteins are made out of amino acids and when ATP is made during cellular respiration.

Differentiated Instruction

Struggling Readers

Recognizing Context Clues Remind students that writers often provide definitions of important terms in the sentence that introduces the term or in the sentence that follows. Ask students for words or phrases that indicate definitions. (Sample answers: *is, are,* and *called*) Have students scan the text under each head that describes a type of reaction for the phrase that helps them find the definition for that reaction. **LS Visual**

>Teach, continued

Teaching Key Ideas

Equilibrium Tell students that *chemical equilibrium* means that reaction rates are equal. It does not mean that amounts of reactants and products are equal. The percentage of reactants that produce products at equilibrium depends on the reaction itself and conditions, such as temperature, that affect the equilibrium. Ask students if a reaction at equilibrium has stopped. (No, the reaction has not stopped. It is going in both directions at the same rate.)
LS Logical

Connection to History

"Cracking" Molecules for Gasoline
In the early part of the twentieth century, a rapid increase in use of vehicles that contained internal combustion engines resulted in an equally rapid increase in demand for gasoline. Distillation of petroleum resulted in production of gasoline, but the amount of gasoline produced was not adequate to meet demand. Additionally, other heavier petroleum products were produced by the distillation, and few uses existed for them. In 1912, gasoline producers started using high temperatures to perform large-scale "cracking" of these larger molecules. The resulting smaller molecules were suitable for gasoline. In 1936, a cracking procedure that used catalysts instead of high temperatures was developed. This procedure was instrumental in providing Allied forces with gasoline during World War II.

READING TOOLBOX

Prefixes
Make a table of word parts that includes three of the unfamiliar words in this section, such as *catalyst, enzyme, substrate,* and *equilibrium.*

Equilibrium Systems

Reactions may happen slowly or quickly, but still go in the same direction. **›Some processes, however, may go in both directions, which results in an equilibrium system.** *Equilibrium* can be described as a balance that is reached by two opposing processes.

Some changes are reversible.

Some processes do not reach completion each time they occur. Some are reversible. A reversible physical process is shown in **Figure 5.** Carbonated drinks contain carbon dioxide. These drinks are made by dissolving carbon dioxide in water under pressure. While it is under pressure, carbon dioxide is constantly coming both into and out of solution.

Opening the bottle releases the pressurized air, which makes a hissing sound as it escapes. At this point, the process begins to go in only one direction. The carbon dioxide starts to come out of solution, and a stream of carbon dioxide bubbles appears.

$$CO_2 \text{ (gas above liquid)} \underset{\substack{\text{increase} \\ \text{pressure}}}{\overset{\substack{\text{decrease} \\ \text{pressure}}}{\rightleftharpoons}} CO_2 \text{ (gas dissolved in liquid)}$$

This change is reversible, as indicated by the $\rightleftharpoons$ sign in the chemical equation. The arrow usually seen in chemical reactions, $\rightarrow$, indicates a change that goes in one direction.

✓ Reading Check When you open a soda bottle, what change occurs that allows the dissolved carbon dioxide in the soda to come out of solution?

Figure 5 Equilibrium of Gas Dissolved in a Soda Bottle

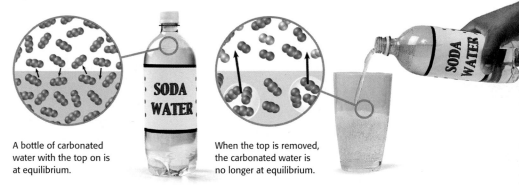

A bottle of carbonated water with the top on is at equilibrium.

When the top is removed, the carbonated water is no longer at equilibrium.

READING TOOLBOX

Prefixes Other words that may be listed in tables include *concentration, inhibitor,* and *continuous.*

Science Skills

Interpreting Visuals Have students look at **Figure 5.** Ask them: "What do the red and green spheres represent?" (The red spheres are oxygen atoms, and the green spheres are carbon atoms. Each group of spheres is one carbon dioxide molecule.) "What do the backgrounds represent?" (The white represents gas, and the blue represents liquid.) "Why does part B show white circles in the blue part?" (These represent gas bubbles of CO_2 in the liquid.) **LS Visual**

Equilibrium results when rates balance.

When a carbonated drink is in a closed bottle, you cannot see any changes. The system is in equilibrium—a balanced state. But if you could see individual molecules in the bottle, you would see <u>continuous</u> change. Molecules of CO_2 not only are coming out of solution constantly but also are dissolving back into the liquid at the same rate.

The result is that the amount of dissolved and undissolved CO_2 does not change even though individual CO_2 molecules are moving in and out of the solution. This situation is like the situation in which the number of players on a football field is constant. Although different players can be on the field, there are 11 players from each team on the field at any given time.

Systems in equilibrium respond to minimize change.

Chemical equilibrium is a state in which a reversible chemical reaction is proceeding in both directions equally. No net change happens, but if products or reactants are added or removed, the reaction will start going in one direction more than the other.

The conversion of limestone, $CaCO_3$, to lime, CaO, is a chemical reaction that can lead to equilibrium. Limestone and seashells, which are also made of $CaCO_3$, were used to make lime more than 2,000 years ago. Limestone was heated in an open pot, and the lime produced was used to make cement. The ancient buildings in Greece and Rome, such as the one shown in **Figure 6,** were built with cement that was probably made by the following reaction:

$$CaCO_3 + energy \longrightarrow CaO + CO_2$$

Because the CO_2 gas can escape from an open pot, the reaction continues until all of the limestone reacts. However, if some limestone is sealed in a closed container and heated, the result is different. As soon as some CO_2 builds up in the container, the reverse reaction starts. Once the concentrations of the $CaCO_3$, CaO, and CO_2 stabilize, equilibrium is reached.

$$CaCO_3 \rightleftharpoons CaO + CO_2$$

If the pressure or temperature does not change, the forward and reverse reactions take place at the same rate. As in the case of the carbonated drink, this equilibrium is reached because the products are not allowed to escape. Once some CO_2 is allowed to escape, the forward reaction goes faster until the forward and reverse reactions are happening at the same rate again. So, a system in equilibrium responds to change by doing whatever is required to go back to an equilibrium state.

Academic Vocabulary

continuous (kuhn TIN yoo uhs) going on without stopping

chemical equilibrium (KEM i kuhl EE kwi LIB ree uhm) a state of balance in which the rate of a forward reaction equals the rate of the reverse reaction and the concentrations of products and reactants remain unchanged

Figure 6 Cement in ancient buildings, such as this one in Limeni, Greece, contains lime that came from seashells.

READING TOOLBOX

Vocabulary The word *dynamic* comes from the Greek word *dunamis,* which means "power." Ask students to brainstorm related terms. (Lists will probably include such terms as *dynamite* and *dynamo.*) Tell students that the terms all relate to power and/or motion. *Dynamic,* as it relates to equilibrium, indicates that the situation is not static. Constant, opposite reactions occur at equal rates. **LS Verbal**

Demonstrate

Dissolving Gases and Pressure Have students bring in bottles of carbonated soft drinks. Discuss with students that there is carbon dioxide in the space above the liquid in the bottle and that there is carbon dioxide dissolved within the liquid. Explain that the carbon dioxide is in equilibrium. Ask students to identify whether an opened carbonated soft drink is at higher or lower pressure than a sealed one. (The opened bottle is at lower pressure than a sealed bottle of carbonated soft drink is.) Have students write a paragraph predicting how the amount of dissolved gas will be influenced by decreasing the pressure. When students have made predictions, they can demonstrate the influence of decreasing pressure on the dissolved gas by opening their bottles. In a second paragraph, ask students to discuss how well their observations match their predictions. **LS Kinesthetic/Verbal**

Differentiated Instruction

Basic Learners

Chemical Equilibrium Have students write a paragraph that explains why most reactions in the human body go to completion and don't reach equilibrium. If students have difficulty, allow them to discuss their ideas in small groups before writing their paragraphs. Paragraphs should include the idea that energy produced by exothermic reactions is used or released by the body, shifting the reaction toward completion. Also, for reactions such as cellular respiration, the circulatory system constantly supplies reactants of oxygen and glucose to cells and removes carbon dioxide, shifting the reaction to completion. **LS Verbal**

Connection to Environmental Science

Environmental Science Soil often lacks sufficient amounts of the organisms that change nitrogen gas to a form of nitrogen that can be used by living organisms, so fertilizers that contain usable nitrogen compounds are added to soil. To reduce the amount of chemical fertilizers needed for farming, agriculturists usually rotate crops, alternating a nitrogen-fixing legume crop, such as clover, beans, peas, or peanuts, with other crops. Nodules in the roots of legumes contain nitrogen-fixing bacteria that convert atmospheric nitrogen to usable nitrogen. Recently, researchers at the University of Sydney, in Australia, have succeeded in adding nitrogen-fixing bacteria to the roots of wheat plants. Similar research is ongoing with other crops, such as corn and rice.

READING TOOLBOX

Mnemonics Tell students that sometimes people create mnemonic, or memory, devices to help them remember information. Ask students to work in small groups to come up with a mnemonic device that helps them remember Le Châtelier's principle and the effects of temperature, pressure, and concentration on equilibrium. Have students share their ideas with the class. **LS Verbal/Interpersonal**

Integrating Biology

The Nitrogen Cycle All living things need nitrogen, which cycles through the environment. Nitrogen gas, N_2, is changed to ammonia by bacteria in the soil. Different bacteria in the soil change the ammonia to nitrites and nitrates. Plants need nitrogen in the form of nitrates to grow. Animals eat the plants and deposit nitrogen compounds back in the soil. When plants or animals die, nitrogen compounds are also returned to the soil. Additional bacteria change the nitrogen compounds back to nitrogen gas, and the cycle can start again.

Figure 7 The Effects of Change on Equilibrium

Condition	Effect
Temperature	Increasing temperature favors the reaction that absorbs energy.
Pressure	Increasing pressure favors the reaction that produces fewer molecules of gas.
Concentration	Increasing the concentration of one substance favors the reaction that produces less of that substance.

Le Châtelier's principle predicts changes in equilibrium.

Le Châtelier's principle is a general rule that describes how equilibrium systems respond to change.

> **Le Châtelier's principle** | If a change is made to a system in chemical equilibrium, the equilibrium shifts to oppose the change until a new equilibrium is reached.

The effects of various changes on an equilibrium system are listed in **Figure 7.**

Ammonia is a chemical building block used to make products such as fertilizers, dyes, plastics, cosmetics, cleaning products, and fire retardants, such as the ones being used in **Figure 8.** The Haber process, which is used to make ammonia industrially, is shown below.

$$\text{nitrogen and hydrogen} \rightleftarrows \text{ammonia and energy}$$
$$N_2(gas) + 3H_2(gas) \rightleftarrows 2NH_3(gas) + \text{energy}$$

At an ammonia-manufacturing plant, chemists must choose the conditions that favor the highest yield of ammonia gas, NH_3. In other words, the conditions of the chemical reaction need to be engineered such that the equilibrium favors the production of NH_3.

Figure 8 Ammonium sulfate and ammonium phosphate are being dropped from the airplane as fire retardants. The red dye that is used for identification fades away after a few days.

Ammonium sulfate, $(NH_4)_2SO_4$

Differentiated Instruction

English Learners

Changing Equilibrium The concept of a system responding to a change in equilibrium may be difficult to understand conceptually. Have two-thirds of the class stand on one side of the room and ask them to quickly divide into two groups that are about equal in numbers without any discussion. Initially, too many or two few students may move across the room. Students will move between groups to reach equilibrium. Have members occasionally switch groups, trying to keep the numbers about equal. This is an equilibrium condition. Now, have the remaining students join one of the groups. The groups are now out of equilibrium. Again, without discussion, have students move to make the groups equal in numbers. Students should move back and forth until another equilibrium is reached. **LS Kinesthetic/Logical**

Le Châtelier's principle can be used to control reactions.

A manufacturing plant that uses the Haber process to make ammonia is shown in **Figure 9**. The Haber process is one of the most important industrial reactions. Its invention about 100 years ago led to the ability to produce large amounts of artificial fertilizer, which is made from ammonia. A large percentage of the world's population today is fed by food grown with such artificial fertilizer. Many other important products are made from ammonia. It is estimated that 1% of the entire world's energy output is used to make ammonia by the Haber process!

The Haber process is a good example of balancing equilibrium conditions to make the most product. If you raise the temperature during the Haber process, Le Châtelier's principle predicts that the equilibrium will shift to the left, the process in which energy is absorbed and less ammonia is made. If you raise the pressure, the equilibrium will move to reduce the pressure, according to Le Châtelier's principle. One way to reduce the pressure is to decrease the number of gas molecules. As a result, the equilibrium moves to the right—more ammonia—because fewer gas molecules are on the right. So, getting the most ammonia requires running the reaction at a high pressure and a low temperature.

Figure 9 The Haber process is used to make ammonia in huge quantities in plants like this one.

Section 4 **Review**

KEY IDEAS

1. **State** one thing that must be done to particles in a chemical reaction to increase the reaction rate.

2. **List** five factors that may affect the rate of a chemical reaction.

3. **Compare** a catalyst and an inhibitor.

4. **Determine** which way an increase in pressure will shift the following equilibrium system: $2C_2H_6$(gas) + $7O_2$(gas) $\leftrightarrows$ $6H_2O$(liquid) + $4CO_2$(gas).

5. **Describe** the effect of the changes below on the system in which the following reversible reaction is taking place: $4HCl$(gas) + O_2(gas) $\leftrightarrows$ $2Cl_2$(gas) + $2H_2O$(gas) + energy.
   a. The pressure of the system increases.
   b. The pressure of the system decreases.
   c. The concentration of O_2 decreases.
   d. The temperature of the system increases.

CRITICAL THINKING

6. **Applying Concepts** All organisms need a certain amount of heat, which may be obtained from outside the body or generated by the body itself. In terms of chemical reactions, explain why.

7. **Evaluating Assumptions** A person claims that a reaction must have stopped because the overall amounts of reactants and products have not changed. Indicate what might be wrong with this person's reasoning.

8. **Analyzing Processes** Consider the decomposition of solid calcium carbonate to solid calcium oxide and carbon dioxide gas.

$$CaCO_3 + energy \leftrightarrows CaO + CO_2(gas)$$

What conditions of temperature and pressure would result in the most decomposition of $CaCO_3$? Explain your answer.

❯ Close

Reteaching Key Ideas

Reaction Rates Remind students that the rate of reaction can be increased by increasing the number and energy of collisions. Make a series of large flash cards that have the phrases *increase concentration, add a catalyst, add an inhibitor, increase temperature, lower concentration, increase pressure of a gas, increase volume of gas, grind a solid into a powder, lower the temperature,* and *lower the pressure of a gas.* Show each card and have the class quickly tell whether the change increases collisions or decreases collisions and why. Shuffle the cards and repeat, having the class tell whether the reaction rate will generally increase or decrease.
LS **Visual/Verbal**

Formative Assessment

Which of the following changes will increase the rate of a chemical reaction?

A. lowering the temperature of the reaction mixture (Incorrect. Reaction rates typically increase at higher temperature and decrease at lower temperature.)

B. increasing the size of the particles of one of the reactants (Incorrect. Larger particles have a smaller surface area, which decreases the reaction rate.)

C. doubling the concentration of the reactants (Correct. Increasing concentration of reactants causes an increase in reaction rate.)

D. adding an inhibitor (Incorrect. An inhibitor is a substance that causes a decrease in reaction rate.)

Answers to Section Review

1. Anything that will increase collisions and energy between reactant particles will increase the reaction rate of a chemical reaction.

2. Sample answers: surface area, concentration, temperature, presence of a catalyst, pressure, and the size of the reactant particles

3. A catalyst alters the rate of a reaction, usually by speeding it up. An inhibitor is a type of negative catalyst that ties up a reactant, slowing the rate of reaction.

4. Sample answer: Pressure changes affect the reactions of gases only. Because there are more moles of gas on the left side of the equation, increasing the pressure increases the reaction to the right.

5. a. The reaction will increase to the right.
   b. The reaction will increase to the left.
   c. The reaction will increase to the left.
   d. The reaction will increase to the left.

6. Sample answer: If there is too little heat, the chemical reactions necessary for life proceed too slowly.

7. Sample answer: The person has not considered that if the reaction is in equilibrium, it is proceeding in both directions at equal rates, so the overall amounts of the reactants and products would not change.

Answers continued on p. 255A

Teacher's Notes

Ask students to write and balance the equation for the reaction.
$Zn + 2HCl \rightarrow ZnCl_2 + H_2$
Sidearm flasks (filter flasks) are specified rather than test tubes to avoid the risk involved with asking students to insert glass tubing through a test-tube stopper.

Time Required

1 lab period

Ratings

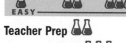

EASY —————————→ HARD

Teacher Prep 🧪🧪
Student Set-Up 🧪🧪🧪
Concept Level 🧪🧪🧪
Clean Up 🧪🧪🧪

Skills Acquired

- Collecting data
- Communicating
- Designing experiments
- Experimenting
- Identifying/recognizing patterns
- Inferring
- Interpreting
- Measuring
- Organizing and analyzing data

Scientific Methods

In this lab, students will:
- Make observations
- Ask a question
- Form a hypothesis
- Analyze the results
- Draw conclusions
- Communicate results

Inquiry Lab

What You'll Do

❯ **Measure** the volume of gas produced to determine the average rate of the reaction between zinc and hydrochloric acid.

❯ **Determine** how the rate of this reaction depends on the temperature of the reactants.

What You'll Need

balance

beaker to hold a 10 mL graduated cylinder

flasks, sidearm, with rubber stoppers (2)

graduated cylinder, 10 mL

graduated cylinder, 25 mL

hydrochloric acid, 1.0 M (25 mL)

ice

metric ruler

rubber tubing

scissors, heavy-duty

stopwatch

thermometer

water bath to hold a sidearm flask

zinc, mossy, about 0.5 g

Safety

Rate and Temperature of a Chemical Reaction

Many factors can influence the rate of a chemical reaction. In this lab, you will investigate how the rate of a chemical reaction varies with temperature.

Asking a Question

How does the rate of a chemical reaction vary with temperature?

Observing the Reaction Between Zinc and Hydrochloric Acid

CAUTION: Wear a lab apron, gloves, and safety goggles for this lab. Do not allow zinc to come in contact with your skin. If the zinc comes in contact with your skin, flush thoroughly with water. Hydrochloric acid can cause severe burns. If you get acid on your skin or clothing, wash it off at the sink while calling to your teacher. If you get acid in your eyes, immediately flush it out at the eyewash station while calling to your teacher. Continue rinsing for at least 15 min or until help arrives.

❶ On a blank sheet of paper, prepare a data table like the one shown in this lab activity.

❷ Fill a 10 mL graduated cylinder with water. Taking care to keep the cylinder full, turn the cylinder upside down in a beaker of water. Place one end of the rubber tubing under the spout of the graduated cylinder. Attach the other end of the tubing to the arm of one of the flasks. Place the flask in a water bath at room temperature. Record the initial gas volume of the cylinder and the temperature of the water bath in your data table.

❸ Collect and weigh about 0.2 g of mossy zinc. If necessary, break up larger pieces. Place the zinc in the sidearm flask that is in the water bath.

❹ Measure 25 mL of hydrochloric acid in a graduated cylinder.

❺ Carefully pour the acid from the graduated cylinder into the flask with the zinc. Start the stopwatch as you begin to pour. Stopper the flask as soon as the acid is transferred.

❻ Hydrogen gas should begin to be given off by the reaction, which will cause gas to flow through the tube and into the inverted graduated cylinder. Record the volume of gas in the graduated cylinder every minute for five minutes.

Safety Cautions

Polyethylene gloves must be worn when handling hydrochloric acid. Hydrogen gas is extremely flammable. Because of the risk of igniting the hydrogen, the second half of the experiment should be performed at an elevated temperature only if no spark source or open flame is present.

Forming and Testing a Hypothesis

7 Form a hypothesis about how the reaction that you just observed will differ if it is carried out at a different temperature.

Designing Your Experiment

8 With your lab partners, decide how you will test your hypothesis. By completing steps 1–6, you have half of the data needed to answer the question. How will you collect the rest of the data?

9 In your lab report, list each step that you will perform in your experiment. Because temperature is the variable that you are testing, the other variables in your experiment should be the same as they were in steps 1–6.

Performing Your Experiment

10 Have your teacher approve your plan, and carry out your experiment. Record your results in another similar data table.

Analysis

1. **Describing Events** How did the results of the two reactions differ?

2. **Interpreting Data** Plot the results of volume over time for both reactions on a graph. Which reaction was more rapid?

3. **Analyzing Data** For each time measurement in each experiment, calculate the amount of gas evolved for each time interval. For each experiment, did the reaction rate change over time? How can you tell?

4. **Analyzing Data** Calculate the rate of each reaction, expressed as milliliters of gas produced per minute.

5. **Analyzing Data** Divide the faster rate by the slower rate, and express the reaction rates as a ratio.

Communicating Your Results

6. **Drawing Conclusions** According to your results, how does changing the temperature affect the rate of a chemical reaction?

Extension

How would you design an experiment to test the effect of surface area on this reaction? How would your results be expressed?

Sample Data Table: Measuring Reaction Rate

Initial gas volume (mL)	
Temperature (°C)	
Mass of zinc (g)	
Gas volume at 1 min	DO NOT WRITE IN BOOK
Gas volume at 2 min	
Gas volume at 3 min	
Gas volume at 4 min	
Gas volume at 5 min	

Sample Data Table

	Reaction 1	Reaction 2
Mass of zinc (g)	0.2	0.2
Initial gas volume (mL)	0.4	0.2
Temperature (°C)	21	11
Gas volume at 1 min	3	2
Gas volume at 2 min	5.6	4
Gas volume at 3 min	9	6
Gas volume at 4 min	9	8
Gas volume at 5 min	9	10

Tips and Tricks

Review with students how to collect gas by volumetric displacement. In the second half of the experiment, students need to devise a way to conduct the same reaction at a different temperature. Although student procedures may vary, having ice available will point them toward conducting the experiment in an ice bath.

Disposal Information

Neutralize the acid with 0.1 M NaOH, and filter the solution. The filtrate may be poured down the drain. After the $Zn(OH)_2$ precipitate has dried, it may be wrapped in newspaper and discarded in the trash.

Answers to Analysis

1. The two reactions differ in that the reaction at room temperature gave off more hydrogen gas than the reaction at the lower temperature.

2. The reaction at room temperature was more rapid than the reaction at the lower temperature.

3. Sample answer: In each experiment, the reaction rate remained almost the same throughout. I could tell because the amount of gas produced for all the time intervals was the same or very similar.

4. Answer calculated from sample data: Reaction 1: (9 mL – 0.4 mL)/ 3 min = 2.9 mL/min; Reaction 2: (10 mL – 0.2 mL)/5 min = 2.0 mL/min

5. The ratio obtained from the sample data is (2.9 mL/min)/ (2.0 mL/min) = 1.5:1.

Answers continued on p. 255A

Key Resources

 Virtual Investigation

 Classroom Lab Video/DVD

 Holt Lab Generator CD-ROM
Search for any lab by type, standard, difficulty level, or time. Edit any lab to fit your needs, or create your own labs. Use the Lab Materials QuickList software to customize your lab materials list.

 Differentiated Datasheets
Rate and Temperature of a Chemical Reaction

 Observation Lab
Combining Elements

 CBL™ Probeware Lab
Investigating the Effect of Temperature on the Rate of a Reaction

Reteaching Key Ideas

Balancing Equations Remind students that calculating the mole ratio depends on having a balanced chemical equation. All chemical equations need to be checked to be sure that the number of all reactant atoms equals the number of all product atoms. If the equation is not balanced, point out that there are a few methods that can make the trial-and-error process of equation-balancing easier. As a rule, the atoms in complex compounds should be balanced first, followed by simpler compounds, and ending with the simplest compounds.

For example, consider the following reaction:

$$P_4 + KClO_3 \longrightarrow KCl + P_2O_5$$

The first step is to balance the oxygen atoms in $KClO_3$ and P_2O_5 with coefficients of 5 and 3, respectively. Further balancing indicates that 5 is the correct coefficient for KCl. However, the balancing coefficient for P_4 is 1.5, which is not a whole number:

$$1.5P_4 + 5KClO_3 \longrightarrow 5KCl + 3P_2O_5$$

By multiplying the equation by 2, the correct coefficients (3, 10, 10, and 6) are obtained:

$$3P_4 + 10KClO_3 \longrightarrow 10KCl + 6P_2O_5$$

Answers to Practice

1. 1 mol H_2O and 1 mol SO_3
   produces 1 mol H_2SO_4;
   1 mol H_2SO_4 = 1 mol ×
   98.0 g/mol = 98.0 g H_2SO_4
2. 2 mol Zn and 2 mol $CuSO_4$
   produces 2 mol $ZnSO_4$;
   2 mol $ZnSO_4$ = 2 mol ×
   161.5 g/mol = 323.0 g $ZnSO_4$

Using Mole Ratios to Calculate Mass

Technology

Math

Scientific Methods

Graphing

Problem

Determine the mass of hydrogen gas, H_2, and oxygen gas, O_2, produced by 4 mol of water, H_2O, in the following chemical reaction:

$$2H_2O \longrightarrow 2H_2 + O_2$$

Solution

Identify

Write the mole ratio for the balanced equation. Multiply the ratio by the factor that gives the number of moles of H_2O that are present.

There are 4 mol H_2O, so multiply each number in the ratio by 2.

Equation	$2H_2O$	$\longrightarrow$	$2H_2$	+	O_2
Mole ratio	2	:	2	:	1
Amount (mol)	4		4		2

Plan

Determine the molar mass of each substance.

Look up the molar mass of each element. There are two hydrogen atoms and one oxygen atom in each molecule of H_2O, so the molar mass of H_2O is 2×1 g/mol + 16 g/mol = 18 g/mol. Similarly, the molar mass of H_2 is 2 g/mol, and the molar mass of O_2 is 32 g/mol.

Solve

Multiply the number of moles of each substance by the molar mass of that substance.

The total mass of the reactants should match the total mass of the products.

Equation	$2H_2O$	$\longrightarrow$	$2H_2$	+	O_2
Mole ratio	2	:	2	:	1
Amount (mol)	4		4		2
Molar mass (g/mol)	18		2		32
Mass calculation	18 g/mol × 4 mol	=	2 g/mol × 4 mol	+	32 g/mol × 2 mol
Total mass (g)	72	=	8	+	64

Four moles (72 g) of water, H_2O, will produce 8 g H_2 and 64 g O_2.

Practice

1. Determine the mass of H_2SO_4 produced when 1 mol H_2O reacts with 1 mol SO_3 in the following reaction:

   $$H_2O + SO_3 \longrightarrow H_2SO_4$$

2. Determine the mass of $ZnSO_4$ produced in the following reaction if 2 mol Zn reacts with 2 mol $CuSO_4$.

   $$Zn + CuSO_4 \longrightarrow ZnSO_4 + Cu$$

Key Resources

📁 **Science Skills Worksheets**
Balancing Chemical Equations
Ratios and Proportions

go.hrw.com
SUPER SUMMARY
KEYWORD: HK8REAS

SUMMARY

Key Ideas

Section 1 The Nature of Chemical Reactions

❯ **Chemical Reactions** Chemical reactions occur when substances undergo chemical changes to form new substances. (p. 219)

❯ **Energy and Reactions** Chemical reactions involve changes in energy. (p. 220)

Section 2 Chemical Equations

❯ **Describing Reactions** A chemical equation uses symbols to represent a chemical reaction. (p. 225)

❯ **Balanced Equations and Mole Ratios** A balanced equation tells you the mole ratio, or proportion of reactants and products, in a chemical reaction. (p. 228)

Section 3 Reaction Types

❯ **Classifying Reactions** You can use patterns to identify kinds of chemical reactions and to predict the products of the chemical reactions. (p. 230)

❯ **Electrons and Chemical Reactions** Free-radical reactions and redox reactions can be understood as changes in the numbers of electrons that atoms have. (p. 235)

Section 4 Reaction Rates and Equilibrium

❯ **Factors Affecting Reaction Rates** Anything that increases contact between particles will increase the rate of a reaction. (p. 238)

❯ **Catalysts** A catalyst speeds up or slows down a reaction but is not changed by the reaction. (p. 240)

❯ **Equilibrium Systems** Processes that can go in both directions may result in equilibrium. (p. 244)

Key Terms

reactant, p. 220
product, p. 220
chemical energy, p. 221
exothermic reaction, p. 222
endothermic reaction, p. 222

chemical equation, p. 225
mole ratio, p. 228

synthesis reaction, p. 231
decomposition reaction, p. 231
combustion reaction, p. 232
single-displacement reaction, p. 233
double-displacement reaction, p. 234
free radical, p. 235
oxidation-reduction reaction, p. 237

catalyst, p. 240
enzyme, p. 241
substrate, p. 241
chemical equilibrium, p. 245

SUPER SUMMARY

Have students connect the major concepts in this chapter through an interactive Super Summary. Visit **go.hrw.com** and type in the keyword **HK8REAS** to access the Super Summary for this chapter.

Differentiated Instruction

Alternative Assessment

Researching Enzymes Have students choose one of the enzymes listed in the table "Common Enzymes and Their Uses" in Section 4. Have them use the library or the Internet to research the structure of the enzyme and how it works in living cells. Finally, have them make a poster showing a chemical reaction for which the enzyme is a catalyst. **LS** Verbal/Visual

Key Resources

 Interactive Concept Map

 Review Resources
Concept Review Worksheets

Assessment Resources
Chapter Tests A and B
Performance-Based Assessment

Reading Toolbox

1. Nitrogen and hydrogen react, forming ammonia and heat. Ammonia in the presence of heat reacts to form nitrogen and hydrogen.

Using Key Terms

2. Sample answer: Wood undergoes combustion in the presence of oxygen, which is an exothermic reaction. The total energy released in the reaction plus the chemical energy in the bonds of the products is the same as the chemical energy contained in the chemical bonds of the reactants. Energy was neither created nor destroyed.

3. Sample answer: One mole of methane reacts with two moles of oxygen gas to yield one mole of carbon dioxide gas and two moles of water.

4. Sample answer: A combustion reaction differs from other reactions in that oxygen is always a reactant in a combustion reaction.

5. Sample answer: An oxidation-reduction reaction is a reaction that involves an exchange of electrons between the reactants.

6. Sample answer: It means that a factor that favors formation of products has changed in the system. The system will shift to produce more products to regain equilibrium.

Understanding Key Ideas

7. c
8. c
9. b
10. b
11. d
12. a

Explaining Key Ideas

13. **a.** synthesis
    b. single-displacement
    c. decomposition
    d. combustion
    e. decomposition
    f. synthesis
    g. double-displacement

READING TOOLBOX

1. **Reading Equations** Equations for reversible chemical reactions use a double arrow instead of a single arrow. Such equations can be read as two separate equations. One goes from left to right, and the other goes from right to left. Write out in words the two separate equations for the Haber process, shown below.

$$N_2 + 3H_2 \leftrightarrows 2NH_3 + energy$$

USING KEY TERMS

2. When wood is burned, energy is released in the form of heat and light. Describe the reaction, and explain why this reaction does not violate the law of conservation of energy. Use the terms *combustion, exothermic,* and *chemical energy.*

3. Translate the following chemical equation into a sentence.

$$CH_4 + 2O_2 \longrightarrow CO_2 + 2H_2O$$

4. How does a *combustion reaction* differ from other types of chemical reactions?

5. What is an *oxidation-reduction reaction*?

6. Explain what it means when a system in *chemical equilibrium* shifts to favor the products.

UNDERSTANDING KEY IDEAS

7. When a chemical reaction occurs, atoms are never
   a. ionized.
   b. rearranged.
   c. destroyed.
   d. vaporized.

8. What happens during an exothermic reaction?
   a. Energy is lost.
   b. Energy is created.
   c. Energy is released.
   d. Energy is absorbed.

9. Which of the following statements about free radicals is true?
   a. Free radicals form ionic bonds with other ions.
   b. Free radicals result from broken covalent bonds.
   c. Free radicals usually break apart to form smaller components.
   d. Free radicals bind molecules together.

10. Hydrogen peroxide, H_2O_2, decomposes to produce water and oxygen gas. What is the balanced equation for this reaction?
    a. $H_2O_2 \longrightarrow H_2O + O_2$
    b. $2H_2O_2 \longrightarrow 2H_2O + O_2$
    c. $2H_2O_2 \longrightarrow H_2O + 2O_2$
    d. $2H_2O_2 \longrightarrow 2H_2O + 2O_2$

11. Most reactions speed up when
    a. the temperature decreases.
    b. equilibrium is achieved.
    c. the concentration of the products increases.
    d. the reactant is in small pieces.

12. A system in chemical equilibrium
    a. responds to oppose change.
    b. has particles that do not move.
    c. is undergoing visible change.
    d. is stable only when all of the reactants have been used.

EXPLAINING KEY IDEAS

13. Classify each of the following reactions as a synthesis reaction, a decomposition reaction, a single-displacement reaction, a double-displacement reaction, or a combustion reaction:
    a. $N_2 + 3H_2 \longrightarrow 2NH_3$
    b. $2Li + 2H_2O \longrightarrow 2LiOH + H_2$
    c. $2NaNO_3 \longrightarrow 2NaNO_2 + O_2$
    d. $2C_6H_{14} + 19O_2 \longrightarrow 12CO_2 + 14H_2O$
    e. $NH_4Cl \longrightarrow NH_3 + HCl$
    f. $BaO + H_2O \longrightarrow Ba(OH)_2$
    g. $AgNO_3 + NaCl \longrightarrow AgCl + NaNO_3$

14. Molecular models of some chemical reactions are pictured below. Copy the drawings, and add coefficients to reflect balanced equations.

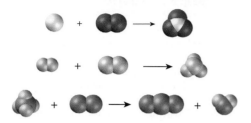

15. For each of the following changes to the equilibrium system below, predict which reaction will be favored—forward (to the right), reverse (to the left), or neither.

$$H_2(gas) + Cl_2(gas) \rightleftharpoons 2HCl(gas) + energy$$

a. addition of Cl_2
b. removal of HCl
c. increase in pressure
d. decrease in temperature
e. removal of H_2

CRITICAL THINKING

16. **Designing Experiments** Paper consists mainly of cellulose, a complex compound made up of simple sugars. Suggest a method for turning old newspapers into sugars by using an enzyme. What problems would there be? What precautions would need to be taken?

17. **Analyzing Processes** Explain why hydrogen gas is given off when a reactive metal undergoes a single-displacement reaction with water.

18. **Applying Concepts** Sulfur burns in air to form sulfur dioxide in the following reaction:

$$S + O_2 \longrightarrow SO_2$$

a. What mass of SO_2 forms from 64 g of sulfur?
b. What mass of sulfur is necessary to form 256 g of sulfur dioxide?

Assignment Guide

SECTION	ITEMS
1	2, 6–9
2	3, 10, 14, 18, 20–22
3	4, 13, 17
4	1, 5, 11, 12, 15, 16, 19

19. **Interpreting Graphs** A chemist carried out an experiment to study the effect of temperature on a certain reaction. Her results are shown in the graph below.

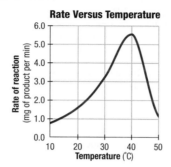

Rate Versus Temperature

a. Between which temperatures does the rate of the reaction rise?
b. Between which temperatures does the rate of the reaction slow down?
c. At what temperature is the rate of the reaction the fastest?

Math Skills

20. **Balancing Chemical Equations** In 1774, Joseph Priestley discovered oxygen when he heated solid mercury(II) oxide, HgO, and produced the element mercury and oxygen gas. Write and balance this equation.

21. **Balancing Chemical Equations** Write the balanced chemical equation for the reaction in which methane, CH_4, reacts with oxygen gas to produce water and carbon dioxide.

22. **Balancing Chemical Equations** Sucrose, $C_{12}H_{22}O_{11}$, is a sugar that is used to sweeten many foods. Inside the body, it is broken down to produce H_2O and CO_2.

$$C_{12}H_{22}O_{11} + 12O_2 \longrightarrow 12CO_2 + 11H_2O$$

List all of the mole ratios that can be determined from this equation.

14. Sample answer:
$$2A + 3B_2 \rightarrow 2AB_3$$
$$3A_2 + B_2 \rightarrow 2A_3B$$
$$AB_4 + 2C_2 \rightarrow C_2A + 2CB_2$$

15. a. forward
b. forward
c. no effect
d. forward
e. reverse

Critical Thinking

16. Answers may vary but might include adding water to shredded newspaper, then adding enzymes that break down cellulose. Problems might include interference from inks or other materials in the paper, using the wrong amount of enzyme, or being unable to separate the sugars from other materials. Precautions might include controlling the temperature so the enzyme stays active.

17. Sample answer: In single-displacement reactions, the more reactive element will take the place of the less reactive element. Thus, when a reactive metal reacts with water, the metal displaces hydrogen atoms in the water, and hydrogen is released as gas.

18. a. 64 g S ÷ 32.07 g/mol S × 1 mol SO_2/1 mol S × 64.07 g/mol SO_2 = 130 g SO_2

b. 256 g SO_2 ÷ 64.07 g/mol SO_2 × 1 mol S/1 mol SO_2 × 32.07 g/mol S = 128 g S

Graphing Skills

19. a. between 10 °C and about 40 °C
b. between about 40 °C to 50 °C
c. about 40 °C

Math Skills

20. $2HgO \rightarrow 2Hg + O_2$

21. $CH_4 + 2O_2 \rightarrow 2H_2O + CO_2$

22. 1:12 for $C_{12}H_{22}O_{11}$:O_2 and $C_{12}H_{22}O_{11}$:CO_2; 1:11 for $C_{12}H_{22}O_{11}$:H_2O; 1:1 for O_2:CO_2; 12:11 for O_2:H_2O and CO_2:H_2O

Standardized Test Prep

Standardized Test Prep

 TEST DOCTOR

Question 1 Answer D is correct. In this reaction, both positive and negative ions switch compound, so it is a double-displacement reaction. A synthesis reaction builds a product from two or more reactants; decomposition has only one reactant; combustion includes oxygen as a reactant.

Question 2 Answer G is correct. Photosynthesis is an endothermic reaction. The other examples are all exothermic reactions, which produce energy.

Question 3 Answer C is correct. Lowering the temperature, adding an inhibitor, or decreasing the surface area of the reactants would decrease the rate of the reaction.

Question 4 Answer G is correct. Systems at equilibrium respond to minimize a change. If energy is added, the equilibrium will shift in the direction of the reaction, requiring an input of energy. That is a change toward the left. Choice H would occur if energy is removed. Choices F and I describe non-existent situations.

Question 5 Full-credit answers should include the following points:
- The element that is reduced gains electrons.
- The element that is oxidized loses electrons.
- Electrons are transferred from hydrogen to fluorine in the reaction.
- Fluorine is reduced and hydrogen is oxidized.

Question 6 Answer A is correct. A synthesis reaction involves the combination of two or more simpler molecules to form a more complex molecule. In this case, hydrogen and nitrogen molecules combine to form an ammonia molecule.

Question 7 Full-credit answers should include the following point:
- the balanced chemical equation: $N_2 + 3H_2 \rightarrow 2NH_3$

Understanding Concepts

Directions (1–4): For each question, write on a sheet of paper the letter of the correct answer.

1. What type of reaction is $Pb(NO_3)_2 + 2KI \rightarrow PbI_2 + 2KNO_3$?
   - **A.** a synthesis reaction
   - **B.** a combustion reaction
   - **C.** a decomposition reaction
   - **D.** a double-displacement reaction

2. Which of the following describes an endothermic chemical reaction?
   - **F.** the explosion of fireworks in the sky
   - **G.** photosynthesis in plant cells
   - **H.** respiration in animal cells
   - **I.** the burning of wood in a fireplace

3. Which of the following changes will always increase the rate of a chemical reaction?
   - **A.** lowering the temperature
   - **B.** adding an inhibitor to the reaction mixture
   - **C.** increasing the concentration of the reactants
   - **D.** decreasing the surface area of the reactants

4. The equation $PCl_3 + Cl_2 \leftrightarrows PCl_5 + energy$ describes an equilibrium system. How would raising the temperature affect the system?
   - **F.** The equilibrium would move to the right to create more PCl_3 and Cl_2.
   - **G.** The equilibrium would move to the left to create more PCl_3 and Cl_2.
   - **H.** The equilibrium would move to the right to create more PCl_5.
   - **I.** The equilibrium would move to the left to create more PCl_5.

Directions (5): For this question, write a short response.

5. In the redox reaction $H_2 + F_2 \rightarrow 2HF$, which element is reduced, and which is oxidized?

Reading Skills

Directions (6–7): Read the passage below. Then, answer the questions that follow.

NITROGEN FIXATION
The element nitrogen makes up about 78% of Earth's atmosphere. It is also an essential component of many of the chemical compounds that are vital to all living things. However, atmospheric nitrogen is not directly accessible to living things; it is primarily in the form of N_2, a molecule composed of two atoms of nitrogen linked by a triple bond. Because of the strength of this bond, large amounts of energy are required to free up the nitrogen atoms so that they can become part of the organic molecules of life.

When sufficient energy is added to N_2 and hydrogen is present in the form of H_2, the result is the compound ammonia, NH_3. The nitrogen in ammonia is much more reactive than that in N_2 and thus is much more readily available to living systems. The process of combining nitrogen and hydrogen into ammonia is an oxidation-reduction reaction known as *nitrogen fixation*. Nitrogen fixation is accomplished by certain microorganisms, which then feed nitrogen-rich compounds into the rest of the ecosystem. Nitrogen fixation is also done artificially at chemical plants where ammonia is made.

6. In addition to being an oxidation-reduction reaction, what type of reaction is nitrogen fixation of N_2 and H_2 into NH_3?
   - **A.** a synthesis reaction
   - **B.** a decomposition reaction
   - **C.** a single-displacement reaction
   - **D.** a double-displacement reaction

7. Write the balanced chemical equation for nitrogen fixation.

Question 8 Answer A is correct. Some energy must be added to start the reaction, indicated by the "hill" on the graph. Choice B is incorrect because the rise represents an energy input, not release. Choice C is incorrect because the energies of the reactants and products are indicated by the flat portions of the graph. Choice D is incorrect because the total change is the difference in level between reactants and products.

Question 9 Answer B is correct. Each side of the equation has the same number of atoms of each element—4 hydrogen atoms and 2 oxygen atoms. Choice A has two oxygen atoms in the reactants but only one in the products; Choice C is incorrect because the only product of the reaction is water; Choice D is incorrect because there are four hydrogen atoms in the reactants but only two hydrogen atoms in the products and because the incorrect product is shown.

Interpreting Graphics

The graphics below plot energy changes during two types of chemical reactions. Use these graphics to answer question 8.

ENERGY CHANGES DURING CHEMICAL REACTIONS

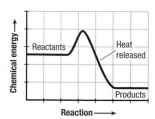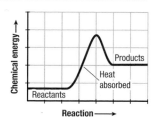

8. In each of these reactions, the chemical energy increases and then decreases during the course of the reaction. What does the height of the "hill" on each graph represent?

   A. energy that must be added to start the reaction

   B. energy released as reactant molecules approach one another

   C. the potential energy of the chemical bonds in the molecules of the reactants

   D. the change in total chemical energy between the reactants and the products

In hydrogen fuel cells, a catalyzed reaction between hydrogen and oxygen gases forms water. One of the diagrams below represents the balanced chemical equation for this reaction. Use these diagrams to answer question 9.

9. Which of the diagrams represents the balanced equation for the reaction?

   A. A   **C.** C

   B. B   **D.** D

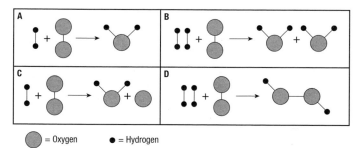

Test Tip

When using a diagram to answer a question, look in the image for evidence that supports your potential answer.

State Resources

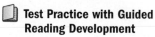

For specific resources for your state, visit **go.hrw.com** and type in the keyword **HSHSTR**.

Test Practice with Guided Reading Development

Answers

  1. D

  2. G

  3. C

  4. G

  5. Answers may vary; see Test Doctor for a detailed scoring rubric.

  6. A

  7. Answers may vary; see Test Doctor for a detailed scoring rubric.

  8. A

  9. B

Continuation of Answers

Answers continued from p. 237

5. Combustion consumes oxygen and produces carbon dioxide. In a closed room or house, the oxygen levels might become too low for people to breathe.

6. In single-displacement reactions, atoms of one element replace the atoms of another element in a compound. In a double-displacement reaction, positive ions in two compounds trade places, forming two different compounds.

7. A polymer is made by reactions that join several smaller molecules to make a long chain. Because this is an example of different substances combining to form a new molecule, it is a synthesis reaction.

8. Oxidation is a loss of one or more electrons. When one atom loses electrons in a reaction, another atom participating in the reaction must gain those electrons.

Answers continued from p. 247

8. Sample answer: CO_2 is the only substance in the reaction that is affected by pressure. Decreasing pressure would increase decomposition of $CaCO_3$. Because the reaction is endothermic, increasing temperature would also increase the rate of decomposition.

Answers continued from p. 249

Answer to Communicating Your Results

6. Decreasing the temperature slows the rate of a chemical reaction.

Answer to Extension

Sample answer: To test the effect of surface area, the reaction can be conducted with equal amounts of zinc but with one sample folded tightly in half so that volume is controlled. The rate of the reactions would be given in mL of hydrogen gas/mm^2 of zinc.

	Standards	**Teach Key Ideas**
CHAPTER OPENER, pp. 256–258 *50 min.*		
SECTION 1 Solutions and Other Mixtures, pp. 259–266 *50 min.* ❯ Heterogeneous Mixtures ❯ Homogeneous Mixtures	PS 2d, UCP 1, SAI 2, ST 2, SPSP 3	🖳 **Bellringer Transparency** 🖳 **Teaching Transparencies** C19 Suspension • C20 Homogeneous Mixture 💿 **Visual Concepts** Comparing Miscible and Immiscible Liquids • Suspensions • Colloids • Emulsions • Solutions
SECTION 2 How Substances Dissolve, pp. 267–273 *50 min.* ❯ Water: A Common Solvent ❯ The Dissolving Process	PS 2d, UCP 2, UCP 3, UCP 5, SAI 1, SAI 2, ST 2, SPSP 6	🖳 **Bellringer Transparency** 🖳 **Teaching Transparencies** C21 Hydrogen Bonding • C22 Surface Area 💿 **Visual Concepts** Hydrogen Bonding • Dissolving Process • Factors Affecting the Rate of Dissolution • Like Dissolves Like
SECTION 3 Solubility and Concentration, pp. 276–281 *50 min.* ❯ Solubility in Water ❯ Saturated Solutions ❯ Concentration of Solutions	PS 2d, UCP 2, SAI 2	🖳 **Bellringer Transparency** 🖳 **Teaching Transparency** TM25 Solubilities of Some Ionic Compounds 💿 **Visual Concepts** Comparing Molarity and Molality • Solution Equilibrium

See also PowerPoint® Resources

Chapter Review and Assessment Resources

SE Science Skills: Making Pie Graphs, p. 284
SE Chapter Summary, p. 285
SE Chapter Review, pp. 286–287
SE Standardized Test Prep, pp. 288–289
📄 Concept Review Worksheets ■
📄 Chapter Tests A and B ■
🌐 Holt Online Assessment

CHAPTER
Fast Track *To shorten instruction because of time limitations, omit Section 3 and the chapter lab.*

Basic Learners
TE Orange Juice Suspension, p. 260
TE The Advantages of Alloys, p. 264
TE Vocabulary, p. 278
📄 Science Skills Worksheets
📄 Differentiated Datasheets A for Labs and Activities ■
📖 Study Guide A ■

Advanced Learners
TE Bile, p. 262
TE Chromatography, p. 264
TE Electrolytes in the Body, p. 268
TE Mass Percent, p. 280
📄 Cross-Disciplinary Worksheets
📄 Differentiated Datasheets C for Labs and Activities ■

Key

SE Student Edition
TE Teacher's Edition

▭ Chapter Resource File
▯ Workbook
▱ Transparency

◉ CD or CD-ROM
* Datasheet or blackline master available

■ Also available in Spanish

All resources listed below are also available on the Teacher's One-Stop Planner.

Why It Matters	Hands-On	Skills Development	Assessment
Build student motivation with resources about high-interest applications.	**SE Inquiry Lab** Dissolving Salt and Sugar, p. 257* ■	**TE Reading Toolbox** Assessing Prior Knowledge, p. 256 **SE Reading Toolbox** p. 258	▭ **Pretest** ■
TE Colloid Classification, p. 261 **TE Stabilizing Emulsions,** p. 262 **SE How Is Crude Oil Turned into Gasoline?** p. 265 ▭ **Cross-Disciplinary Worksheets** Integrating Physics—The Centrifuge • Integrating Biology—Phospholipids • Connection to Engineering—Pigments in Paints • Real World Applications—What is Your Favorite Flavor?	**TE Demonstration** Types of Mixtures, p. 259 **TE Demonstration** Solution or Not? p. 261 **SE Quick Lab** Making Butter, p. 262* ■ ▭ **Observation Lab** Separating Substances in a Mixture	**TE Reading Skills,** p. 260 **SE Reading Toolbox** Examples of Mixtures, p. 263 **TE Visual Literacy,** p. 265	**TE Reteaching Key Ideas** Heterogeneous and Homogeneous Mixtures, p. 266 **TE Formative Assessment,** p. 266 ▭ **Spanish Assessment*** ■ ▭ **Section Quiz** ■
TE Brining, p. 271 **SE Blood Substitutes,** pp. 274–275 ▭ **Cross-Disciplinary Worksheet** Integrating Biology—Osmosis	**TE Demonstration** Electrolytes and Nonelectrolytes, p. 268 **SE Inquiry Lab** What Will Dissolve a Nonpolar Substance? p. 270* ■ **TE Demonstration** Effect of Stirring on Dissolving, p. 271 **TE Demonstration** Temperature and Solubility, p. 272	**TE Reading Toolbox** Reading Skills, p. 269 **TE Science Skills** Interpreting Visuals, p. 269 **TE Science Skills** Nonpolar Molecules, p. 270 **SE Reading Toolbox** Summarizing Ideas, p. 271	**TE Reteaching Key Ideas** Water as a Solvent, p. 273 **TE Formative Assessment,** p. 273 ▭ **Spanish Assessment*** ■ ▭ **Section Quiz** ■
TE Le Châtelier's Principle and Plumping Raisins, p. 277 **TE Treating Injuries with Oxygen,** p. 279 **TE Fluoride in Water,** p. 281	**SE Application Lab** How Temperature Affects Gas Solubility, pp. 282–283* ■ ▭ **CBL™ Probeware Lab** Determining the Concentration of an Ionic Solution	**TE Reading Toolbox** Interpreting Visuals, p. 278 **SE Reading Toolbox** Summarizing Ideas, p. 279 **TE Reading Toolbox** Interpreting Visuals, p. 279 **SE Math Skills** Molarity, p. 280 **SE Science Skills** Ions in Sea Water, p. 280	**TE Reteaching Key Ideas** Saturation, p. 281 **TE Formative Assessment,** p. 281 ▭ **Spanish Assessment*** ■ ▭ **Section Quiz** ■

See also Lab Generator

See also Holt Online Assessment Resources

Resources for Differentiated Instruction

English Learners
TE Prefixes, p. 270
▭ Differentiated Datasheets A, B, and C for Labs and Activities ■
▯ Study Guide A ■

Struggling Readers
TE Previewing, p. 268
TE Generalizing, p. 271
▯ Interactive Reader

Special Education Students
TE Rocks as Mixtures, p. 262

Alternative Assessment
TE Solubility Tables, p. 285

CHAPTER 8

Overview

This chapter describes the characteristics of heterogeneous and homogeneous mixtures. It also introduces water's utility as a solvent and the dissolving process. Finally, students learn about solubility and quantitative means of expressing concentration.

READING TOOLBOX

Assessing Prior Knowledge Students should understand the following concepts:
- moles
- equilibrium
- Le Châtelier's principle
- ions
- bonding
- chemical formulas

MISCONCEPTION ///ALERT\\\

Science education research has identified the following misconceptions about solutions.

- Students fail to recognize that dissolving involves two or more substances. (A glass of salt water looks like a glass of pure water but if a drop of the salt water is placed on a hot surface, water evaporates, leaving behind a residue of salt.)
- Students may believe that a solution has less mass than the masses of the uncombined solute and solvent because they can no longer see the solute. (A solution has the same mass as the sum of its components. Dissolving 5 g of sugar in 100 g of warm water yields 105 g of solution.)
- Students fail to recognize that the disappearance of the solute-solvent boundary implies a single phase and therefore think that a solution can still be filtered or settled. (Add salt and pepper to water and stir. Filter through paper and examine the solids removed. The salt solution is a single phase but the pepper does not dissolve.)

Chapter Outline

❶ Solutions and Other Mixtures
Heterogeneous Mixtures
Homogeneous Mixtures

❷ How Substances Dissolve
Water: A Common Solvent
The Dissolving Process

❸ Solubility and Concentration
Solubility in Water
Saturated Solutions
Concentration of Solutions

Why It **Matters**

Most of Earth's water is a solution of salts in water. This woman is floating easily on the surface of the Dead Sea because so much salt is dissolved in the water of the sea.

Chapter Correlations   *National Science Education Standards*

The following correlations show the National Science Standards that relate to this chapter. For the full text of the standards, see the National Science Education Standards at the front of the book.

PS 2d The physical properties of compounds reflect the nature of the interactions among its molecules. These interactions are determined by the structure of the molecule, including the constituent atoms and the distances and angles between them. (Sections 1–3)

UCP 1 Systems, order, and organization (Section 1)

UCP 2 Evidence, models, and explanation (Sections 2, 3)

UCP 3 Constancy, change, and measurement (Section 2)

UCP 5 Form and function (Section 2)

SAI 1 Abilities necessary to do scientific inquiry (Section 2, Application Lab: How Temperature Affects Gas Solubility)

SAI 2 Understandings about scientific inquiry (Sections 1–3)

ST 2 Understandings about science and technology (Sections 1, 2)

SPSP 3 Natural resources (Section 1)

SPSP 6 Science and technology in local, national, and global challenges (Section 2)

InquiryLab ⏱ 20 min

Dissolving Salt and Sugar

Fill a **clear plastic cup** with **water**. After the water settles, add **table salt** one **teaspoon** at a time to the water. Stir after you add each spoonful until all of the salt disappears. Continue adding salt and stirring until no more salt dissolves. Repeat this activity using sugar instead of salt.

Questions to Get You Started

1. How much salt are you able to add before it stops dissolving and settles to the bottom of the cup?

2. Does the same amount of sugar dissolve? If not, what might explain the difference?

InquiryLab

Teacher's Notes Students may notice the rate of dissolution decreases as more salt or sugar is added to the solution. You may want to tell students to set a stirring time, such as 15 seconds, before they decide that the solution is saturated. Students should observe that more sugar than salt dissolves in a given volume of water.

Materials per Group
- cup, clear plastic
- salt
- sugar
- teaspoon
- water

Answers

1. Answers may vary depending on how much water is in the glass and what size spoon was used. The solubility of sodium chloride is about 36 g per 100 g of water at 20 °C.

2. Sample answer: No, more sugar was able to dissolve after the salt stopped dissolving. Students may answer that both sugar and water are covalent compounds.

Key Resources

📋 **Datasheet**
Dissolving Salt and Sugar

💿 **Interactive Tutor**
Disc One, Module 8: Solutions

READING TOOLBOX

FoldNotes

Students' key-term folds should look similar to the example shown in Appendix A and should contain definitions for each of the key terms from the Summary page: *suspension, colloid, emulsion, solution, solute, solvent, alloy, polar, hydrogen bonding, nonpolar, solubility, concentration, saturated solution, unsaturated solution, supersaturated solution,* and *molarity.*

Finding Examples

Sample list:

Examples	Signals
granite	no signal
orange juice	no signal
latex paint	"an example"
gelatin	no signal
egg white	no signal
blood plasma	no signal
mayonnaise	no signal
cream	"for example"

Note Taking

Answers may vary. Summaries should build on the subheads and capture key points of each paragraph.

READING TOOLBOX

These reading tools can help you learn the material in this chapter. For more information on how to use these and other tools, see **Appendix A.**

FoldNotes

Key-Term Fold The key-term fold can help you learn the key terms from this chapter.

Your Turn Create a key-term fold as described in **Appendix A.**

1. Write the key terms from the Chapter Summary on the front of each tab.

2. As you read the chapter, write the definitions under the tabs for each term.

3. Use this FoldNote to study the key terms.

suspension

Finding Examples

Examples of Mixtures Examples can help you picture an idea or concept. Certain words or phrases can serve as signals that an example is about to be introduced. Such signals include

- *for example*
- *such as*
- *for instance*

Your Turn As you read Section 1, make a list like the one started below to organize the examples of heterogeneous mixtures. Some examples may not be signaled by a word or phrase.

HETEROGENEOUS MIXTURES

EXAMPLE	SIGNAL
1. fruit salad	"just as"
2. garden dirt	no signal

Note Taking

Summarizing Ideas Summarizing the content of each paragraph or set of paragraphs under a heading is a simple way to take notes. A few tips on summarizing are listed below.

1. Summary statements should be short but should fully express the idea.

2. Use the blue subheadings for guidance in forming summary statements.

3. Many paragraphs start or end with a sentence that summarizes the main idea of the paragraph.

Your Turn Use summarizing to take notes for Section 1. You may add structure to your notes by also writing the section titles and red headings in the appropriate places. The example below for Section 1 can help you get started.

Section 1—Solutions and Other Mixtures
 • All matter is either a pure substance or a mixture of pure substances.
Heterogeneous Mixtures
 • In heterogeneous mixtures, the amount of each substance varies.

Solutions and Other Mixtures

Key Ideas

❯ What is a heterogeneous mixture?
❯ What is a homogeneous mixture?

Key Terms

suspension
colloid
emulsion
solution
solute
solvent
alloy

Why It Matters

During oil refining, the components of a mixture called *crude oil* are separated to form gasoline and other products that we use on a daily basis.

SECTION 1

❯Focus

This section discusses heterogeneous and homogeneous mixtures, comparing the properties of suspensions, colloids, and solutions. The section concludes with a discussion of solutions that involve gases and solids as solvents.

🔔 Bellringer

Use the Bellringer transparency to prepare students for this section.

Demonstrate

Types of Mixtures Fill two glasses halfway with water. Add some vegetable oil to the first glass and a spoonful of sugar to the second glass. Vigorously stir each glass. Have students inspect the mixture in each glass. Ask students to draw what they think the mixture in each glass is like at the molecular level. Allow students to share their sketches with the class and have students compare the drawings. Allow the glasses to settle until the water and oil separate, and have the students draw both mixtures again and discuss their drawings. (The drawing should show droplets of oil in which molecules are completely isolated from the water and molecules of sugar that are surrounded by water molecules.) Point out that in this section students will learn about different types of mixtures and their properties. **LS** Visual/Kinesthetic

Any sample of matter is either a pure substance or a mixture of pure substances. You can easily tell that fruit salad is a mixture because you can see the various kinds of fruit. But some mixtures look like they are pure substances. For example, a mixture of salt dissolved in water looks the same as pure water. Air is a mixture of several gases, but you cannot see the gases that make up air.

Heterogeneous Mixtures

❯ **A heterogeneous mixture does not have a fixed composition.** The amount of each substance in different samples of a heterogeneous mixture varies, just as the amount of each kind of fruit varies in each spoonful of fruit salad, as **Figure 1** shows. If you compare two shovelfuls of dirt from a garden, they will not be exactly the same. The amounts of rock, sand, clay, and decayed matter in each shovelful vary.

Another naturally occurring heterogeneous mixture is granite, a type of igneous rock. Granite is a mixture of crystals of the minerals quartz, mica, and feldspar. Samples of granite from different locations can vary greatly in appearance because the samples have different proportions of minerals.

Figure 1 Fruit salad is a heterogeneous mixture. The composition of each spoonful of fruit varies because the fruits are not distributed evenly throughout the salad.

Key Resources

 Teaching Transparencies
C19 Suspension
C20 Homogenous Mixture

Visual Concepts
Comparing Miscible and Immiscible Liquids
Suspensions
Colloids
Emulsions
Solutions

Datasheet
Making Butter

Science Skills Worksheet
SI Units and Conversions Between Them

Cross-Disciplinary Worksheets
Integrating Physics—The Centrifuge
Integrating Biology—Phospholipids
Connection to Engineering—Pigments in Paints
Real World Applications—What is Your Favorite Flavor?

Reading Skills Have students read the section and then organize the ideas presented in the section in a concept map. Concept maps should start with the term *Mixtures* and list the two types of mixtures. Students' maps should also provide examples of the two types of mixtures.
Sample concept map:

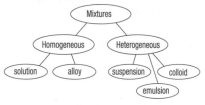

LS Verbal/Logical

Teaching Key Ideas

Suspensions Have students work in pairs. Give each pair paper cups, straws, a container of water, and small amounts of ground coffee, sand, sugar, vegetable oil, and vinegar. Ask students to determine how many suspensions they can make by mixing any two materials. Make a list of the suspensions. (Sample answers: water and oil, water and ground coffee, water and sand, sand and oil, ground coffee and oil.) Discuss how the mixtures of water and sugar or water and vinegar differed from the suspensions. (Sample answer: One of the two substances in the mixture was not visible and did not settle out.) Ask students to identify the materials that form a heterogeneous mixture with water. (coffee, sand, and vegetable oil)
LS Kinesthetic/Logical

Figure 2 Orange Juice: A Heterogeneous Mixture

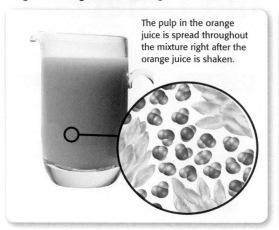

The pulp in the orange juice is spread throughout the mixture right after the orange juice is shaken.

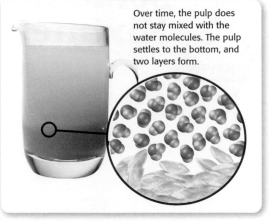

Over time, the pulp does not stay mixed with the water molecules. The pulp settles to the bottom, and two layers form.

suspension (suh SPEN shuhn) a mixture in which particles of a material are more or less evenly dispersed throughout a liquid or gas

colloid (KAHL oyd) a mixture consisting of tiny particles that are intermediate in size between those in solutions and those in suspensions and that are suspended in a liquid, solid, or gas

Particles in a suspension are large and settle out.

Have you ever forgotten to shake the orange juice carton before pouring yourself a glass of juice? The juice was probably thin and watery. Natural orange juice is a suspension of orange pulp in a clear liquid that is mostly water, as **Figure 2** shows. A property of a **suspension** is that the particles settle out when the mixture is allowed to stand. When the orange juice carton is not shaken, the top layer of the juice in the carton is mostly water because all of the pulp has settled to the bottom.

You can see that orange juice is a heterogeneous mixture. After the juice settles, the mixture near the top of the container differs from the mixture near the bottom. Shaking the container mixes the pulp and water, but the pulp pieces are large enough that they will eventually settle out again.

✔ **Reading Check** Over time, what happens to the particles in a suspension? (See Appendix E for answers to Reading Checks.)

Particles in a suspension may be filtered out.

Particles in suspensions are usually about the size of a bacterial cell, which has a diameter of about 1,000 nm. Particles of this size are large enough to be filtered out of the mixture. For example, you can use a filter made of porous paper to catch the suspended pulp in orange juice. That is, the pulp stays in the filter, and smaller particles, such as water molecules, pass through the filter easily. You can classify a mixture as a suspension if the particles settle out or can be filtered out.

Differentiated Instruction

Basic Learners

Orange Juice Suspension Have students pour a glass of orange juice from an orange juice container that has not been shaken. Next, have students shake a different orange juice container and pour a glass of juice from the container. Ask students to diagram the difference between the glasses. Have students use a stopwatch to time how long it takes for the two glasses of juice to look the same.
LS Visual/Kinesthetic

Some mixtures of two liquids will separate.

Oil, vinegar, and flavorings can be shaken together to make salad dressing. But the dressing is a heterogeneous mixture. When the dressing stands for a few minutes, two layers form, as **Figure 3** shows. The two liquids separate because they are *immiscible,* which means that they do not mix. Eventually, the oil, which is less dense, rises and floats on the vinegar, which is denser.

One way to separate two immiscible liquids is to carefully pour the less dense liquid off the top. Some cooks use this technique to separate melted fat from meat juices. The cook removes the fat by pouring or spooning it off the meat juices, which are denser than the fat. The process of pouring a less dense liquid off a denser liquid is called *decanting.*

Particles in a colloid are too small to settle out.

Latex paint is an example of another kind of heterogeneous mixture, a **colloid.** The color in latex paint comes from solid particles of colored pigments that are <u>dispersed</u> in water. Other substances in the paint make the pigment stick to a surface. The difference between colloids and suspensions is that the particles in colloids are smaller than those in suspensions. Particles in colloids range from only 1 to 1,000 nm in diameter. Because the particles in colloids are so small, they pass through most filters and stay spread throughout the mixture. Even though the colloid may look like clear water, the particles are large enough to scatter light that passes through the colloid, as **Figure 4** shows. This scattering of light is called the *Tyndall effect.*

Figure 3 Some salad dressings are made with oil and vinegar, which form a suspension when shaken. Because oil-and-vinegar mixtures are heterogeneous, they separate after standing for a few minutes.

Academic Vocabulary

disperse (di SPUHRS) to spread through evenly

www.scilinks.org
Topic: Colloids
Code: HK80312

Figure 4 The liquid in the jar on the right is a colloid. Colloids exhibit the Tyndall effect, in which light is scattered by the invisible particles.

Demonstrate

Solution or Not? You will need 2 beakers, a flashlight, gelatin, two spoons, sugar, and hot distilled water. Add equal amounts of hot water to the two beakers. To one beaker, add some dry gelatin and stir. To the other beaker, add the same quantity of table sugar and stir to dissolve. Darken the room and shine light through both beakers. Have students observe the beakers and describe what they see. Identify the gelatin mixture as a colloid and the sugar mixture as a solution. Let the beakers sit undisturbed until near the end of class. Then, shine the light through them, and have students make observations. Discuss with students: What did you observe? (Sample answer: The light beam could not be seen in the solution but could be seen in the colloid.) Particles can reflect light. In which mixture do you think the particles are larger? Explain. (Sample answer: Light was reflected from the gelatin and not from the sugar in the other tumbler, so the gelatin particles are larger.) Did anything settle out in either tumbler? (no) Describe the size of the particles in a colloid. (Sample answer: The particles are large enough to scatter light but also small enough to stay suspended.)
LS Visual

Why It **Matters**

Colloid Classifications A colloid is made up of a dispersed substance and a continuous substance. For example, in fog, the dispersed substance is liquid water and the continuous substance is air. The states of the dispersed and continuous substances determine the classification of the colloid. For example, fog is an aerosol because it consists of a liquid dispersed in a gas. Smog is also an aerosol, consisting of a solid dispersed in a gas. Foam is a gas dispersed in a liquid (whipped cream) and solid foam is a gas dispersed in a solid (packaging peanuts). A gel is a liquid dispersed in a solid (soft contact lenses).

⟩Teach, continued

QuickLab

Teacher's Notes Fresh or unhomogenized cream works best for this lab. Homogenization decreases the particle size, so it takes longer for the particles to agglomerate.

Students will find that the activity produces butter and a liquid that is mostly water and contains a few milk solids. Discuss with students that the lipids (fats) that formed the emulsion (cream) clumped together to form the butter.

Materials per Group
- jar with lid, 500 mL
- heavy cream, 250 mL
- marble

Answers to Analysis
1. water
2. Shaking the mixture causes the emulsion to separate, so that the fats come together to form butter.

Why It **Matters**

Stabilizing Emulsions An ingredient that stabilizes an emulsion, such as the egg yolk in mayonnaise, is called an emulsifier. One common emulsifier found in many foods is the mixture of compounds known as lecithin. Lecithin is found in egg yolks and soybeans. Have students check for lecithin on the ingredient labels of food items, such as salad dressings, cooking sprays, soft vegetable spreads, and pancake mix.

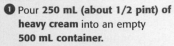

QuickLab   Making Butter   ⏱ 10 min

Procedure
1. Pour **250 mL** (about 1/2 pint) of **heavy cream** into an empty **500 mL container**.
2. Add a clean **marble**, and then seal the container tightly so that it will not leak.
3. Take turns shaking the container. When the cream becomes very thick, you will no longer hear the marble moving.
4. Record your observations of the substance that formed.

Analysis
1. Cream is an emulsion of fats in water. If joined fat droplets make up butter, what must make up most of the remaining liquid?
2. Why does butter form when you shake the cream?

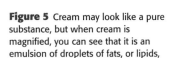

Figure 5 Cream may look like a pure substance, but when cream is magnified, you can see that it is an emulsion of droplets of fats, or lipids, dispersed in water.

Other familiar materials are also colloids.

Although the particles in most colloids are made up of many atoms, ions, or molecules, individual protein molecules are also large enough to form colloids. Gelatin, egg whites, and blood plasma are all protein colloids. They consist of protein molecules dispersed in a liquid.

Whipped cream is a colloid that is made by dispersing a gas in a liquid, and marshmallows are made by dispersing a gas in a solid. Fog is made of small droplets of water spread in air, and smoke contains small solid particles dispersed in air.

Some immiscible liquids can form colloids.

Mayonnaise is a colloid made up of tiny droplets of oil suspended in vinegar. Vinegar-and-oil salad dressings separate into two layers, but the egg yolk in mayonnaise keeps the oil and vinegar from separating. Egg yolk coats the oil droplets so that they do not join together and form a separate layer. Mayonnaise is an **emulsion**, a colloid in which liquids that usually do not mix are spread throughout each other. Emulsions are also found in your body. In the small intestine, bile salts cause fats to form an emulsion. Then, enzymes can break down the smaller fat particles more quickly.

Like other colloids, an emulsion has particles so small that it may appear to be uniform, but it is not. For example, cream does not form separate layers, so it looks like a pure substance. But cream is really a mixture of oily fats, proteins, and carbohydrates dispersed in water. The lipid droplets are coated with a protein that acts as an emulsifier. The protein keeps the lipid droplets dispersed in the water so that they can spread throughout the entire mixture, as **Figure 5** shows.

Differentiated Instruction

Advanced Learners

Bile Ask students to research bile and how it works in the body. Students should identify where bile is produced and stored, the function of bile, and why bile is considered to be an emulsifier. Students should also identify what health problems are related to the function or dysfunction of bile. Encourage students to interview a medical professional who specializes in the organs that produce and utilize bile.
LS Verbal

Special Education Students

Rocks as Mixtures Granite is a mixture of the minerals mica, feldspar, and quartz. Obtain granite samples and have students arrange the samples in order of increasing amount of a mineral. (Answers may vary depending on the granite samples. Students should be able to sort the rocks based on mineral color or shape.)
LS Visual/Kinesthetic

Homogeneous Mixtures

Homogeneous mixtures, such as salt water, are uniform. When you stir aquarium salt—pure sodium chloride—and water, the mixture soon looks like pure water. **> A homogeneous mixture looks uniform even when you examine it under a microscope because the individual components of the mixture are too small to be seen.** In the saltwater mixture, water molecules surround sodium ions and chloride ions, as **Figure 6** shows. The mixture is homogeneous because the number of ions is the same everywhere in the salt water.

Salt and water do not react when mixed. So, the two substances can be separated by evaporating the water. Salt crystals, like those that originally dissolved, form as the water evaporates. Only salt is left after the water has evaporated.

Homogeneous mixtures are solutions.

Mixtures are homogeneous when the smallest particles of one substance are uniformly spread among similar particles of another substance. This description is also true for **solutions,** so all homogeneous mixtures are also solutions. When you add salt to water and stir, the solid seems to disappear. The salt has *dissolved* in water to form a solution. In the saltwater solution, the salt (sodium chloride) is the substance that dissolves, the **solute.** Water is the substance in which the solute dissolves, so water is the **solvent.** When a solute dissolves in a solvent, the solute separates into the smallest particles of the substance—atoms, ions, or molecules.

✓ **Reading Check** What types of solute particles are present in a solution?

READING TOOLBOX

Examples of Mixtures
Create a list of the examples of solutions that you find as you read about homogeneous mixtures.

emulsion (ee MUHL shuhn) any mixture of two or more immiscible liquids in which one liquid is dispersed in the other

solution (suh LOO shuhn) a homogeneous mixture throughout which two or more substances are uniformly dispersed

solute (SAHL yoot) in a solution, the substance that dissolves in the solvent

solvent (SAHL vuhnt) in a solution, the substance in which the solute dissolves

READING TOOLBOX

Examples of Mixtures
Sample answers: salt water, rubbing alcohol, methanol and water, fingernail polish remover, paint stripper, gasoline, diesel fuel, kerosene, vinegar, air, soft drinks, amalgam of mercury and silver, brass, bronze, steel

Teaching Key Ideas

Interpreting Visuals Have students refer to **Figure 6.** Ask students: "What are the smallest particles that make up water?" (water molecules) "What are the smallest particles are that make up sodium chloride?" (sodium ions and chloride ions) "What are the smallest particles that make up a solution of sodium chloride and water?" (water molecules, sodium ions, and chloride ions) Finally, ask students if any new substances are formed when sodium chloride dissolves in water. (no) **LS** Visual/Verbal

Figure 6 Pure Water and Salt Water

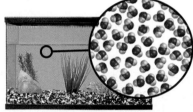

Plain water is homogeneous because it is a single substance.

Chloride ion, Cl⁻

Water

Sodium ion, Na⁺

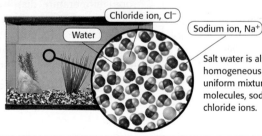

Salt water is also homogeneous because it is a uniform mixture of water molecules, sodium ions, and chloride ions.

Demonstrate

Conservation of Mass but not Volume Obtain four identical 100-mL graduated cylinders. Fill two graduated cylinders each with 50 mL of ethanol, and fill the other two graduated cylinders each with 50 mL of distilled water. Place one graduated cylinder of ethanol and one graduated cylinder of water on one pan of a double pan balance. Place the other two graduated cylinders on the opposite pan. Adjust the balance screw so that the two balance. On one of the pans, add the ethanol to the water and replace the cylinder on the pan. Have students observe that the pans remain balanced. Ask students what they can infer about the mass of the water and the ethanol and the mass of the ethanol-water solution. (They are the same.) Ask students to predict the volume of the solution. (Most students will say 100 mL.) Have students observe that the volume is less than 100 mL (The final volume depends on the concentration of ethanol.) Have interested students research why the volume of the ethanol-water solution is less than the combined individual volumes of ethanol and water. (Ethanol molecules distort the liquid structure of water, making the water molecules move closer together and reducing the volume of the solution.) **LS** Visual/Logical

Teaching Key Ideas

Solutes and Solvents Point out that water is not always a solvent when it is part of a solution. A solvent is the part of the solution that has the highest concentration. A solute has lower concentration. For example, if 25 mL of ethanol is mixed with 10 mL of water, ethanol is the solvent and water is the solute. Atmospheric nitrogen, which makes up approximately 79 percent of air, is a solvent, and other atmospheric gases are solutes.

Demonstrate

Is the Mixture a Solution? You will need water and vegetable oil and at least two other liquids—one nonpolar liquid (for example, cream or lubricating oil) and one polar liquid (for example, vinegar, apple juice, or rubbing alcohol). In separate beakers, stir about 5 mL of each nonpolar and polar liquid into about 50 mL of water. Then, stir 5 mL of each nonpolar and polar liquid into 50 mL of vegetable oil. Have students observe the mixtures. Ask students: "What combinations of liquids formed solutions?" (A nonpolar liquid in a vegetable oil and a polar liquid in water will form solutions.) "How could you tell that a solution formed?" (Sample answer: The liquids did not separate into two layers.) **LS Visual**

Figure 7 Window cleaner, rubbing alcohol, and gasoline are all mixtures of liquids.

Integrating Engineering

Types of Ink Ink is a complicated mixture of substances. Some inks, such as those used in printing books and magazines, contain *pigments* that give the ink most of its color. Pigments are added to a liquid as finely ground, solid particles to form a suspension. A printing press is used to apply the ink to the paper. Then, the ink is allowed to dry.

The ink used in some ballpoint pens is different from ink used in printing. The ink in pens contains a dissolved iron salt, such as ferrous sulfate, and an organic substance called *tannic acid*. When tannic acid and the iron salt are mixed, they form a dark blue solution. This solution gives the ink its blue-black color.

Miscible liquids mix to form solutions.

Two or more liquids that form a single layer when mixed are *miscible*. Liquids can be mixed to form useful solutions, such as those shown in **Figure 7**. For example, water mixed with isopropanol makes a solution called *rubbing alcohol*, which is used to disinfect cuts and scrapes.

Chemists often have to separate miscible liquids when purifying substances. Because miscible liquids do not separate into layers, they are not as easy to separate as immiscible liquids are. One way to separate miscible liquids is by the process of *distillation*. Distillation separates miscible liquids that have different boiling points. For example, a mixture of methanol and water can be separated by distillation because methanol boils at 64.5 °C and water boils at 100.0 °C. When this mixture is heated in a distillation apparatus, the methanol boils away first, and most of the water remains.

Liquid solutions sometimes contain no water.

Many kinds of solutions that are made up of liquids mixed in another liquid do not contain water. For example, some fingernail-polish removers and paint strippers are mixtures of liquids that contain no water. Fuels such as gasoline, diesel, and kerosene are homogeneous mixtures of several liquid carbon compounds. These fuels are made from substances distilled from a mixture known as *petroleum*. Plastics are also made from some of the hydrocarbons that are obtained when petroleum is distilled.

Other states of matter can also form solutions.

Like the water in a saltwater aquarium, many common solutions are solids dissolved in liquids. However, solutes and solvents can be in any state. Vinegar is a solution that is made of two liquids—acetic acid dissolved in water. The air that you breathe is a solution of nitrogen, oxygen, argon, and other gases. Gases can also dissolve in liquids. For example, a soft drink contains carbon dioxide gas dissolved in liquid water. Air fresheners slowly give off fragrant vapor molecules that form a solution with air. The element mercury, a liquid at room temperature, dissolves in solid silver to form a solution called an *amalgam*, which can be used to fill cavities in teeth. In all of these solutions, the substance that there is the most amount of is the solvent and the substance that there is the least amount of is the solute.

✔ **Reading Check** What states of matter can be mixed with a liquid to form a solution?

Differentiated Instruction

Advanced Learners

Chromatography Chromatography is used to separate, identify, and analyze the components of mixtures, and has important forensic applications. Several types of chromatography are used under different circumstances, but many chromatography methods are based on differences in polarity. Have interested students investigate the difference between column chromatography, gas chromatography, ion chromatography, and thin layer chromatography. Then, have students present their findings to the class. **LS Verbal**

Basic Learners

The Advantages of Alloys Many students are familiar with liquid solutions, but don't recognize that solids also form solutions. Have students work individually or in small groups and choose an alloy, such as steel, brass, and bronze or alloys of various elements, including nickel, copper, tin, iron, and gold. Have students research the makeup of the alloy and its uses. Students should identify the advantages of the alloy over the use of the individual components and present their findings to the class in an oral or visual report. **LS Verbal/Logical**

How Is Crude Oil Turned into Gasoline?

REAL WORLD

The petroleum that comes out of an oil well is a complex mixture of gases, liquids, and solids. The liquid part of this mixture is known as *crude oil*. Only certain carbon compounds in crude oil can be made into gasoline, and these compounds must first be separated from the rest of the components in the oil. Distillation is a key part of the separation process.

Liquefied petroleum gas

Petrochemicals

Decreasing density and boiling point

Gasoline

Kerosene

Diesel oil

Increasing density and boiling point

Lubricating oil

Fuel oil

Crude oil

Asphalt, paraffin wax

Crude oil is heated and pumped into a large column, which has various sections. The temperature decreases in each section as the gases rise in the column. When the boiling point of a compound in the solution is greater than the temperature in a section of the column, the compound condenses and the liquid can be separated from the gases.

SCLINKS.

www.scilinks.org
Topic: Fossil Fuels
Code: HK80614

YOUR TURN

UNDERSTANDING CONCEPTS
1. Why are liquids that have lower boiling points collected at the top of the distillation column?

ONLINE RESEARCH
2. Research two other products that are obtained from crude oil. Are their boiling points higher or lower than those of the compounds that are used to make gasoline?

How Is Crude Oil Turned into Gasoline? Crude oil is a complex mixture of hydrocarbons and compounds that contain sulfur and nitrogen. Although most people think of crude oil as a thick, tarry substance, crude oil actually occurs in many forms, ranging from a liquid that has the consistency of kerosene to a solid (at room temperature) that looks like brown candle wax.

During distillation, crude oil is heated in a large closed vessel. The components that have less mass (smaller molecules) reach their boiling point first and rise high inside the distillation column. As temperature increases, the heavier components boil and then condense back to a liquid state at different levels in the distillation column. These products are captured on trays at each level and flow out of the column.

The products of crude oil are recovered based on the size of the molecules. LPG and petrochemical solvents are the liquefied form of the smallest, or lightest, molecules. These products are followed, in order of increasing molecule size, by gasoline, kerosene and jet fuels, diesel oil, lubricating oils, and the heating oil used in homes and in the boilers of ships.

The residue that does not boil during distillation contains waxes and a black mixture known as asphalt. Asphalt is mixed with stones to make pavement for roads. The waxes in the residue can be purified and used in cosmetics, in waxes and polishes for metal or wood, to waterproof cardboard or paper, and for many other applications.

Answers to Your Turn

1. Sample answer: Temperature decreases as the gases move up the distillation column. So, compounds that have lower boiling points will remain gases in the lower parts of the column. Liquid cannot be collected until the temperature in the column is low enough for the gas to condense.

2. Sample answer: Oil that is used to lubricate the engines in vehicles has a boiling point that is greater than 400 °C, which is higher than the boiling point of gasoline. Propane is used as a fuel for gas lanterns and barbeque grills. The boiling point of propane is –42 °C, which is lower than the boiling point of gasoline.

READING TOOLBOX

Visual Literacy To help students understand distillation in the separation process, have them focus on one section of the column at a time. As gases are heated, they become less dense and rise through the column. The temperature in the column decreases with height, so these components condense when they reach the section of the distillation column that is at a temperature lower than their boiling point. The asphalt and waxes never reach their boiling point, so they flow downward as hot liquid and flow out of the pipe at the bottom of the distillation column.
LS Visual

Answer to caption question
Alloys may be better for some instruments because they are harder than a pure metal is, so the instrument would not be as easily damaged.

> **Close**

Reteaching Key Ideas

Heterogeneous and Homogeneous Mixtures Discuss with the class the difference between homogeneous and heterogeneous mixtures. Ask students to name a kind of juice that illustrates each type of mixture. (heterogeneous mixture: orange juice, grapefruit juice, or any other juice that has pulp or solids; homogeneous mixture: apple juice, cranberry juice, white grape juice, or any other juice that is clear and contains no solids)
LS Logical/Verbal

Formative Assessment

Which of the following statements best describes a heterogeneous mixture?

A. A heterogeneous mixture looks uniform under a microscope. (Incorrect. A homogenous mixture looks uniform under a microscope.)

B. A heterogeneous mixture lacks uniform consistency. (Correct. A heterogeneous mixture does not have a fixed composition.)

C. A heterogeneous mixture is a solution. (Incorrect. Solutions are homogenous mixtures.)

D. A heterogeneous mixture is made up of only solids. (Incorrect. Heterogeneous mixtures can include liquids, solids, or gases.)

Figure 8 Many musical wind instruments are made of the alloy brass, which is a solid solution. **Why could it be better for a musical instrument to be made from an alloy than from a pure metal?**

alloy (AL oy) a solid or liquid mixture of two or more metals

Solids can dissolve in other solids.

Many musical instruments, such as the ones shown in **Figure 8,** are made of brass. Brass is a solution of zinc metal dissolved in copper metal. Brass is an **alloy,** a homogeneous mixture that is usually composed of two or more metals. The metals are melted to liquids and mixed. A solid solution of one metal dispersed in another metal forms when the mixture cools.

Alloys are important because they have properties that the individual metals do not have. Pure copper cannot be used to make a sturdy musical instrument because copper is too soft and bends too easily. When zinc is dissolved in copper, the resulting brass is harder than copper but can be easily shaped. Bronze, an alloy of tin in copper, resists corrosion. Many bronze sculptures made in ancient times still exist today. Not all alloys contain only metals. Some types of steel are alloys that contain the nonmetal element carbon.

Section 1 **Review**

KEY IDEAS

1. **Classify** the following mixtures as heterogeneous or homogeneous.
   a. orange juice without pulp
   b. sweat
   c. cinnamon sugar
   d. concrete

2. **Explain** how a suspension differs from a colloid.

3. **List** three examples of solutions that are not liquids.

CRITICAL THINKING

4. **Evaluating Hypotheses** You suspect that a clear liquid is actually a colloid. How would you test to see if the liquid is a colloid?

5. **Understanding Relationships** Arrange the following mixtures in order of increasing particle size: muddy water, sugar water, and egg white.

6. **Applying Concepts** Identify the solvent and solute in a solution made by dissolving a small quantity of baking soda in water.

7. **Explaining Events** A small child watches you as you stir a spoonful of sugar into a glass of clear lemon-flavored drink. The child says that she believes that the sugar went away because it seemed to disappear. How would you explain to the child what happened to the sugar, and how could you show her that you can get the sugar back?

Answers to Section Review

1. **a.** homogeneous
   b. homogeneous
   c. heterogeneous
   d. heterogeneous

2. Sample answer: The particles in a suspension are larger than those in a colloid. As a result, the particles in a suspension settle out and can be filtered out, but the particles in a colloid do not settle out and cannot be filtered out.

3. Sample answers: air, mixtures of gases used in scuba diving, dental amalgam, sterling silver, brass, bronze, and steel

4. Sample answer: I can pass light through the liquid to see if it scatters light. If it scatters light, then it is a colloid.

5. sugar water, egg white, muddy water

6. Water is the solvent and baking soda or sodium hydrogen carbonate is the solute.

7. Sample answer: I can show the child that the drink is sweet, which is evidence that the sugar is still present. I can tell the child that the sugar mixed with the water is separating into pieces so small that the pieces cannot be seen. If I allow the water to evaporate, I can show that child that the crystalline sugar reforms, although it is combined with the drink flavoring.

How Substances Dissolve

Key Ideas

> Why is water called the universal solvent?
> Why do substances dissolve?

Key Terms

polar
hydrogen bond
nonpolar

Why It Matters

Many substances, including essential minerals and oxygen, are dissolved in your blood.

S uppose that you and a friend are drinking iced tea. You add one spoonful of loose sugar to your glass of tea and stir, and all of the sugar dissolves quickly. Your friend adds a sugar cube to her tea and finds that she must stir longer than you did to dissolve all of the sugar. Why does the sugar cube take longer to dissolve? Why does sugar dissolve in water at all?

Water: A Common Solvent

Two-thirds of Earth's surface is water. The liquids that you drink are mostly water, and three-fourths of your body weight is water. **> Water is called the *universal solvent* because many substances can dissolve in water.**

Water can dissolve ionic compounds.

Water is such a good solvent because of its structure. A water molecule is made up of two hydrogen atoms that are covalently bonded to one oxygen atom. Electrons are not evenly distributed in a water molecule because oxygen atoms strongly attract electrons. The oxygen atom pulls electrons away from the hydrogen atoms and gives the hydrogen atoms a partial positive charge. The electrons are closer to the oxygen atom, so it has a partial negative charge. This uneven distribution of electrons, combined with a water molecule's bent shape, means that water molecules are **polar.** A polar molecule has partially charged positive and negative areas, which are indicated by δ+ and δ– in **Figure 1.** Water dissolves many ionic compounds because the negative side of the water molecule attracts the positive ions and the positive side of the water molecules attracts the negative ions.

polar (POH luhr) describes a molecule in which the positive and negative charges are separated

Figure 1 Water is a polar molecule because the oxygen atom strongly attracts electrons, which leaves the hydrogen atoms slightly positive.

Key Resources

 Teaching Transparencies
C21 Hydrogen Bonding
C22 Surface Area

Visual Concepts
Hydrogen Bonding
Dissolving Process
Factors Affecting the Rate of Dissolution
Like Dissolves Like

Datasheet
What Will Dissolve a Nonpolar Substance?

Science Skills Worksheet
Surface Area

Cross-Disciplinary Worksheet
Integrating Biology—Osmosis

> **Focus**

This section begins with a discussion of the structure of water molecules and the role of water in the dissolving process. The ability of a solvent to dissolve a solute is then discussed in relation to the strength of intermolecular forces. The section continues by identifying three factors that influence the speed at which a solute dissolves. Finally, the section concludes with a discussion of the effects of a solute on the freezing point and the boiling point of a solution.

Bellringer

Use the Bellringer transparency to prepare students for this section.

Demonstrate

Effects of Charge on Water Perform the following demonstration to illustrate the polarity of water. Use a plastic comb to rapidly comb someone's hair. Hold the comb near a small stream of water from a faucet or that is poured slowly from a beaker. Show students that the stream of water bends toward the comb. The comb is charged, and the partial charges of the water molecules are attracted to it. **LS Visual**

Teaching Key Ideas

Water as a Universal Solvent Have students discuss the importance of aqueous (water-based) solutions to living things. Make a list of substance that dissolve in water that might be important to a person, an animal, or a plant. (Sample answers: sugar, salt, fertilizers, pesticides, and vitamins) Why do fish rely on the ability of water to dissolve gases? (Fish use dissolved oxygen because they do not breathe air.) **LS Logical**

go.hrw.com
✳ interact online

Students can interact with the figure by going to **go.hrw.com** and typing in the keyword **HK8SOLF2.**

Demonstrate

Electrolytes and Nonelectrolytes
You will need a circuit consisting of a battery, a light bulb in a socket, and wires for leads. Connect one end of the battery to the light socket and the other end to an open lead. Connect the light socket to a second open lead to make a broken circuit. Show that pure water does not conduct an electric current by placing the ends of the two leads in distilled water. Do not allow the leads to touch. Repeat the experiment using solutions containing sodium chloride, sugar, sodium bicarbonate, and vinegar. Solutes in solutions that conduct an electric current are classified as *electrolytes* and solutes in solutions that do not conduct electric current are classified as *nonelectrolytes*. These substances, such as sugar, remain as molecules in solution. **LS Visual/Logical**

Figure 2 Water breaks apart sodium chloride crystals because water molecules pull the ions away from the crystal. Notice that the partially negative parts of the water molecules are attracted to the positive sodium ions and that the partially positive parts are attracted to the negative chloride ions.

go.hrw.com
✳ interact online
Keyword: HK8SOLF2.

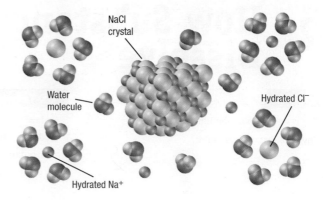

Integrating **Biology**

Cellular Diffusion Cells rely on *diffusion* to move molecules. When the concentration of a solute is greater inside a cell than outside a cell, the solute moves out of the cell through the cell membrane. But not all substances can diffuse across a cell membrane. Sodium ions and potassium ions move into and out of cells through structures called *sodium-potassium pumps*. These ions give many cells an electric charge. Nerve cells need an electric charge to send signals throughout the body.

Polar water molecules pull ionic crystals apart.

Sodium chloride, NaCl, crystals dissolve in water, as **Figure 2** shows. The partially negative oxygen atoms of water molecules attract the positively charged sodium ions at the surface of the NaCl crystal. The partially positive hydrogen atoms of water molecules attract the negatively charged chloride ions. As more water molecules attract the ions, the amount of attraction between the ions and the water molecules increases. Finally, the attraction between the ions and water molecules becomes stronger than the attraction between the sodium ions and chloride ions in the crystal. So, water molecules pull the ions away from the crystal and surround them. The entire crystal dissolves when all of the ions in the crystal are pulled into water solution.

Dissolving depends on forces between particles.

Water dissolves baking soda and many other ionic compounds in exactly the same way that water dissolves sodium chloride. The attraction of water molecules pulls the crystals apart into individual ions. But many other ionic compounds, such as silver chloride, do not dissolve in water.

The forces of attraction explain why one ionic compound dissolves in water but another one does not. An ionic compound will dissolve in water if the attraction between water molecules and the ions in the crystal is stronger than the attraction between the ions in the crystal. This explanation is true for any solvent and any solute. To dissolve a substance, the force between the solvent molecules and the particles of the substance must be greater than the force between the particles in the crystal.

Differentiated Instruction

Struggling Readers

Previewing Previewing text establishes a framework for information. If the paragraph or paragraphs beneath a heading are well written, reading the first and last sentence of this content should give a quick summary of the information. Have students read the first and last sentence under both headings on this page and relate those sentences to **Figure 2.** Ask students how an ionic substance dissolves in water. (The water exerts more force on the ions of the substance than the ions exert on one another.) **LS Visual/Verbal**

Advanced Learners

Electrolytes in the Body Aqueous solutions of electrolytes are important for the proper functioning of cells. Have interested students research and identify which electrolytes are used in sports drinks and the role of those electrolytes in the body. Then, have students make a short presentation to the class about what they learned. **LS Verbal**

Water dissolves many molecular compounds.

Water has a low molecular mass. But water is a fairly dense liquid that has a high boiling point. Water has these properties because bonding occurs between water molecules. Recall that in a water molecule, the oxygen atom pulls electrons away from the hydrogen atoms. As a result, a hydrogen atom of one water molecule and the oxygen atom of another water molecule are strongly attracted to each other. This attraction forms a **hydrogen bond.** Hydrogen bonds pull the water molecules close together.

Water dissolves many molecular compounds, such as ethanol, vitamin C, and table sugar, as **Figure 3** shows. These compounds are polar because, like water, they have hydrogen atoms bonded to oxygen. For example, the hydroxyl, –OH, group in ethanol, CH_3CH_2OH, is polar. So, the negative oxygen atom of a water molecule attracts the positive hydrogen atom of an ethanol molecule. And the positive hydrogen atom of a water molecule attracts the negative oxygen atom of an ethanol molecule. The force of attraction of these hydrogen bonds helps pull an ethanol molecule into water solution.

Hydrogen bonding is important in the dissolving of other polar molecular compounds, such as sucrose, $C_{12}H_{22}O_{11}$, as **Figure 4** shows. Water molecules form hydrogen bonds with the –OH groups in the sucrose molecule and pull the sucrose molecules away from the sugar crystal and into solution.

✔️ **Reading Check** Hydrogen bonding occurs between which atoms in water molecules?

Figure 3 As water slowly dissolves the sugar cube, streams of denser sugar solution move downward. Table sugar, or sucrose, is a molecular compound.

hydrogen bond (HIE druh juhn BAHND) the intermolecular force occurring when a hydrogen atom that is bonded to a highly electronegative atom of one molecule is attracted to two unshared electrons of another molecule

Figure 4 Hydrogen bonds form between sucrose and water. Water molecules form many hydrogen bonds with the –OH groups of a sucrose molecule. These forces pull the sucrose molecule away from the sugar crystal and into solution. **Do individual sucrose molecules break apart when they dissolve?**

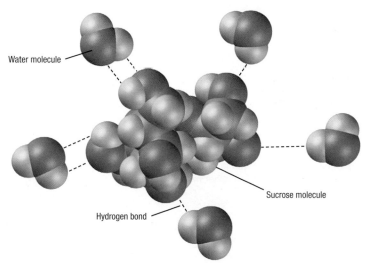

Water molecule

Sucrose molecule

Hydrogen bond

READING TOOLBOX

Reading Skills Write the first heading on the page, *Water dissolves many molecular compounds,* on the board. Before students read the page, have them write brief statements describing how water can dissolve molecular compounds, such as sugar. Finally, have students refer to these statements after they have read the page to determine whether the statements were accurate. **LS Verbal**

Science Skills

Interpreting Visuals Have students refer to **Figure 4** and count the number of –OH groups in each dissolved sucrose molecule. (Sample answer: There are at least five –OH groups because five water molecules are bound to the sucrose. [There are a total of eight –OH groups in sucrose.]) Point out that sugar easily dissolves in water because the water molecules form hydrogen bonds with the sucrose molecules and pull them into the solution. **LS Visual**

Answer to caption question
Individual sucrose molecules do not break apart when they dissolve. Instead, they are surrounded by water molecules.

MISCONCEPTION ALERT

Dissolving Substances Students may think that when any substance dissolves in a liquid, the substance undergoes a chemical change. Demonstrate that this is not always the case by dissolving sugar in a small amount of water. Then, place some of the solution in a ceramic container and place the container on a hot plate. As the water boils away, sugar crystals will form on the bottom of the container. Discuss that if the sugar had reacted chemically with the water, it would have formed a different compound. The water could not have been boiled away to leave the sugar behind. **LS Visual**

MISCONCEPTION ALERT

Universal Solvent The term *universal solvent* may lead some students to think that all substances will dissolve in water. Explain that the term is used because there are many substances that dissolve in water. But there are also substances that do not dissolve in water. Have students make a list of things that do not dissolve in water. Discuss what would happen during rainfall if water were a truly universal solvent. **LS Logical**

Nonpolar Molecules Molecules of substances such as methane (CH_4) are nonpolar because of the arrangement of the atoms that make up the molecules. Each methane molecule consists of a central carbon atom surrounded by four symmetrically arranged covalently bonded hydrogen atoms. Point out that carbon tetrachloride, CCl_4, is also a nonpolar substance. Have students predict the shape of the CCl_4 molecule. (Carbon tetrachloride is made up of a central carbon atom surrounded by four symmetrically arranged covalently bonded chlorine atoms.) **LS** **Logical/Verbal**

InquiryLab

Teacher's Notes Be sure students in the class do not have an allergy to iodine before performing this activity. Warn students that tincture of iodine stains clothing and that iodine is poisonous.

Materials per Group
• cotton swabs (3)
• ethanol
• tincture of iodine
• water

Answers to Analysis
1. Ethanol dissolved the iodine better than water did.
2. Water is more polar than ethanol is. Because iodine is nonpolar, it will dissolve better in a solvent that is less polar. Because iodine is more soluble in ethanol than water, ethanol must be less polar than water.

Figure 5 Nonpolar substances, such as oil-based paint, must be dissolved by a similar solvent. For this reason, a nonpolar solvent must be used.

nonpolar (nahn POH luhr) describes a molecule in which the centers of positive and negative charges are not separated

Academic Vocabulary
distribute (di STRIB yoot) to spread out

Like dissolves like.

A rule in chemistry is that "like dissolves like." This rule means that a solvent will dissolve substances that have molecular structures that are like the solvent's structure. For example, water is a polar molecule—it has a partially positive end and a partially negative end. So, water dissolves ions, which have charges, and other polar molecules.

Nonpolar compounds usually will not dissolve in water. Nonpolar molecules do not have partially negative and positive parts because the electrons are <u>distributed</u> evenly over the whole molecule. For example, olive oil, which is a mixture of nonpolar compounds, will not dissolve in water. The attraction between water and nonpolar molecules is less than the attraction between the nonpolar molecules. Nonpolar solvents must be used to dissolve nonpolar materials, as **Figure 5** shows. Nonpolar solvents are often distilled from petroleum.

InquiryLab   What Will Dissolve a Nonpolar Substance?

⏱ 10 min

Procedure
1. Dip a **cotton swab** in **tincture of iodine,** and make two small spots on the palm of your hand. Let the spots dry. The spots that remain are iodine.
2. Dip a **second cotton swab** in **water,** and wash one of the iodine spots with it. What happens to the iodine spot?
3. Dip a **third cotton swab** in **ethanol,** and wash the other iodine spot with it. What happens to the iodine spot?

Analysis
1. Did water or did ethanol dissolve the iodine spot better?
2. Is water more polar or less polar than ethanol? Explain your reasoning.

Differentiated Instruction

English Learners

Prefixes Point out that some prefixes, such as *non-*, *in-*, and *un-* are used to show the opposite. The word *nonpolar* has the root word *polar* and the prefix *non-*. A polar substance has positive and negative charges that are separated. A nonpolar substance does not have separated charges. Ask students what *insoluble* means. (does not dissolve) **LS** **Verbal**

The Dissolving Process

The kinetic theory of matter states that molecules are always moving. When sugar is poured into a glass of water, water molecules collide with and transfer energy to the sugar molecules at the surface of the sugar crystal. ❯ **The energy transferred from the solvent to the solute, as well as the attractive forces between the solvent and solute molecules, causes molecules at the surface of the crystal to dissolve.**

Every time that sugar molecules break away from the surface of the crystal, the sugar molecules in the layer below are exposed to the solvent. Sugar molecules keep breaking away from the surface until the crystal completely dissolves.

Solutes with a larger surface area dissolve faster.

Small pieces of a solid dissolve faster than large pieces of the same substance. Smaller pieces have more surface area that is in contact with the solute molecules. As a result, there are more collisions between the solvent and solute molecules. So, the solid dissolves faster.

As **Figure 6** shows, breaking a solid into many smaller pieces increases the total exposed surface area. If a cube is 1 cm on each edge, each face of the cube has an area of 1 cm^2. A cube has six surfaces, so the total surface area is 6 cm^2. If the large cube is cut into 1,000 cubes that are 0.1 cm on each edge, the face of each small cube has an area of 0.1 cm × 0.1 cm = 0.01 cm^2. So, each cube has a surface area of 0.06 cm^2. The total surface area of all the small cubes is 1,000 × 0.06 cm^2 = 60 cm^2, which is 10 times the surface area of the large cube.

✔ **Reading Check** Why does increasing the surface area of a solid help it dissolve faster?

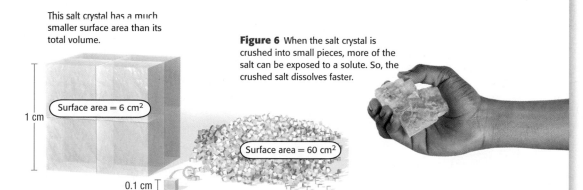

This salt crystal has a much smaller surface area than its total volume.

Figure 6 When the salt crystal is crushed into small pieces, more of the salt can be exposed to a solute. So, the crushed salt dissolves faster.

Surface area = 6 cm^2

1 cm

Surface area = 60 cm^2

0.1 cm

READING TOOLBOX

Summarizing Ideas
As you read about the dissolving process, summarize the ways in which you can make a solute dissolve faster.

READING TOOLBOX

Summarizing Ideas Answers should include:
• break into smaller pieces
• shake or stir
• heat the solvent

Demonstrate

Effect of Stirring on Dissolving You will need the following materials for this demonstration: two beakers (500 mL), a stirring plate, magnetic stirring bar, powdered drink mix and tap water.

Before conducting the demonstration, attach white paper to the back of the beakers to help students more readily see the color change that occurs. Fill each beaker with room temperature tap water. Add the magnetic stirring bar to one of the beakers. Turn on the stirring plate and adjust the rate of spinning so that a slight vortex is observed at the surface of the water. Have students predict with a show of hands in which beaker—stirred or unstirred—a powdered drink mix will dissolve more quickly. Finally, drop a small amount of powdered drink mix into each beaker. Have students observe the contents of each beaker.

Have students discuss the demonstration. In which beaker did the drink mix dissolve more quickly? (the stirred beaker) How might stirring increase solubility? (Sample answer: Stirring moves the dissolved powder away from the remaining powder so that more water molecules can interact with the solid.) **LS Visual**

Differentiated Instruction

Struggling Readers

Generalizing After reading this section, have groups determine whether each of the following statements is correct and why: "All solutions contain water." (Incorrect. Water is called a universal solvent, but it does not dissolve everything.) "Ionic compounds dissolve best in nonpolar solvents." (Incorrect. Ionic compounds dissolve best in water, which is a polar compound. Ionic compounds are highly polar compounds, so they are not likely to dissolve in nonpolar solvents.) Have students find headings, main ideas, and examples in the text to strengthen their position. **LS Verbal/Logical**

Demonstrate

Temperature and Solubility You will need a balance, beaker (150 mL), graduated cylinder (100 mL), hot plate, labels or marking pen, potassium chloride (20 g), stirrer and distilled water (100 mL).

Pour 50 mL of cold, distilled water into the beaker. Add 10 g of potassium chloride to the beaker of water. Have students time how long it takes for all of the potassium chloride to dissolve. Stir the contents of the beaker until all of the compound has dissolved. Perform the demonstration again, but this time use hot water. Ask students: "What did you observe when the potassium chloride was dissolved in cold water?" (Sample answer: The potassium chloride dissolved slowly.) "What did you observe when the potassium chloride was dissolved in hot water?" (Sample answer: The potassium chloride dissolved more quickly than it did in cold water.) "What conclusion can you make about the effect of temperature on the rate of dissolving potassium chloride in water?" (Increasing temperature increases the rate at which potassium chloride will dissolve.)
LS Visual

Stirring or shaking helps solids dissolve faster.

If you pour table sugar into a glass of water and let the glass sit, the sugar will take a long time to dissolve completely. The solid sugar is at the bottom of the glass surrounded by dissolved sugar molecules, as **Figure 7** shows. Because the dissolved sugar molecules are always moving, they will slowly *diffuse*, or spread out, throughout the solution. Until they diffuse, the dissolved sugar molecules will be near the surface of the crystal. These dissolved molecules keep water molecules from reaching the undissolved sugar. So, the molecules still in crystal will dissolve slowly.

Stirring or shaking the solution moves the dissolved sugar away from the sugar crystals. So, more water molecules can interact with the solid, also shown in **Figure 7,** and the sugar crystals dissolve faster.

Solids dissolve faster when the solvent is hot.

Solid solutes dissolve faster in a hot solvent than in a cold solvent. The kinetic theory states that when matter is heated, its particles move faster. As a result of heating, particles of solvent run into undissolved solute more often. These collisions also transfer more energy than collisions that occur when the solvent is cold. The greater frequency and energy of the collisions help "knock" undissolved solute particles away from each other and spread them throughout the solution. **Figure 8** shows the three ways to make solids dissolve faster.

SCLINKS
www.scilinks.org
Topic: Diffusion
Code: **HK80406**

Figure 7 Effect of Stirring on the Dissolving Process

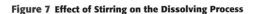

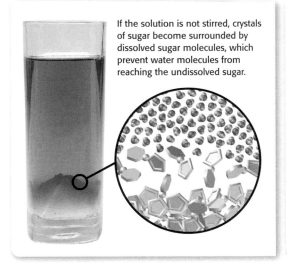

If the solution is not stirred, crystals of sugar become surrounded by dissolved sugar molecules, which prevent water molecules from reaching the undissolved sugar.

Stirring moves the dissolved sugar molecules away from the undissolved sugar, and more water molecules can reach the undissolved sugar.

Teaching Key Ideas

Attraction and Repulsion Explain that the process of dissolving, like all other chemical processes, results from attraction and repulsion among atoms, ions, and molecules. Ionic and polar substances dissolve readily in water because there is an attraction between the partial charge on a water molecule and the partial or full charge on the solute particles. Nonpolar substances dissolve in nonpolar solvents because of the strength of attraction between two nonpolar molecules. Some materials, such as soaps and detergents, have large molecules that are polar on one end and nonpolar on the other end. Ask students how a detergent might help grease dissolve in wash water. (Sample answer: The nonpolar end of the molecule is attracted to the grease, and the polar end of the molecule is attracted to the water.)
LS Verbal/Logical

Crushing the solute

Mixing the solution

Heating the solution

Figure 8 Crushing the solute, mixing the solution, or heating the solution will speed up the dissolving process.

Solutes affect the physical properties of a solution.

The boiling point of pure water is 100 °C and the freezing point is 0 °C. But if you dissolve 12 g of sodium chloride in 100 mL of water, you will find that the boiling point of the solution is increased to about 102 °C. Also, the freezing point of the solution will be lowered to about –8 °C. Many solutes increase the boiling point of a solution above that of the pure solvent. These same solutes also lower the freezing point of the solution below that of the pure solvent. The amount that the boiling point increases or the freezing point decreases depends on how many solute particles are in the solution.

The effect of a solute on freezing point and boiling point can be useful. For example, a car's cooling system often contains a mixture that is 50% water and 50% ethylene glycol, a type of alcohol. This solution acts as antifreeze in cold weather because its freezing point is about –30 °C. The solution also helps prevent boiling in hot weather because its boiling point is about 109 °C.

Section 2 Review

KEY IDEAS

1. **Explain** why water can dissolve some ionic compounds, such as ammonium chloride, NH_4Cl, as well as some molecular compounds, such as methanol.

2. **Describe** three methods that you could use to make a spoonful of salt dissolve faster in water.

CRITICAL THINKING

3. **Recognizing Relationships** Describe the relationship of attractive forces between molecules and the ability of a solvent to dissolve a substance.

4. **Predicting Outcomes** Use the rule of "like dissolves like" to predict whether the polar molecular compound glycerol is soluble in water.

5. **Applying Ideas** Explain why large crystals of coarse sea salt take longer than crystals of fine table salt to dissolve in water.

6. **Explaining Events** You make strawberry-flavored drink from water, sugar, and drink mix. You decide to freeze the mixture into ice cubes. You place an ice-cube tray filled with the drink and another tray of plain water in the freezer. Two hours later, you find that the water has frozen but the fruit drink has not. How can you explain this result?

Close

Reteaching Key Ideas

Water as a Solvent Ask students: "Why do solutes dissolve in solvents that have similar properties?" (Sample answer: Dissolving occurs when the forces that attract the particles to one another are strong.) "What types of materials dissolve easily in water?" (ionic or polar materials) "What property of water makes it a good solvent for these materials?" (the partial charges on the atoms in the water molecule)

Formative Assessment

Why is water called a universal solvent?

A. Many substances dissolve in water, including ionic and polar compounds. (Correct. Water dissolves many different materials.)

B. Water dissolves nonpolar compounds. (Incorrect. Water cannot dissolve nonpolar compounds because it is a polar compound.)

C. Water dissolves all materials regardless of temperature and amount. (Incorrect. Water dissolves many but not all substances. Additionally, temperature and amount of solute are factors.)

D. The force of water molecules on solutes is smaller than the forces between particles of the solute. (Incorrect. For dissolving to occur, the force of water molecules on the solute must be larger than the force between the molecules of solute.)

Answers to Section Review

1. Water is a polar molecule, which means that one end of the molecule has a slight positive charge and the other end of the molecule has a slight negative charge. These charged ends are attracted to opposite charges on other polar molecules, such as methanol, and to charged ions in ionic substances, such as ammonium chloride. As a result, water molecules can pull polar molecules and ions into solution.

2. Raising the temperature of the water, shaking or stirring the mixture, and breaking up the solute would increase the salt dissolution rate.

3. Solvents can dissolve a substance only if the attraction of the solvent molecules for the molecules of the substance is greater than the attraction between the molecules of the substance.

4. Sample answer: Water will dissolve glycerol because the polar water molecules attract the polar groups of glycerol and pull it into solution.

5. Sample answer: The large crystals of salt have less surface area exposed to water than the same mass of smaller crystals does. Therefore, water molecules at the surface of the smaller crystals attract more sodium and chloride ions, so they dissolve faster than large crystals do.

6. The presence of a solute lowers the freezing point below that of the pure solvent. So, the freezing point of the water and drink mix is lower than the freezing point of water alone. The drink mix is not cold enough to freeze.

Why It Matters

Blood Substitutes Have students recall that the main functions of blood are to transport oxygen and nutrients to the cells, remove carbon dioxide and waste products from the cells, and transport disease-fighting white cells and platelets throughout the body. Explain that blood is a suspension of solid substances (red blood cells, white blood cells, and platelets) in a liquid called plasma and that plasma is a water solution of dissolved nutrients.

Point out that only about one percent of the oxygen necessary for respiration is dissolved in the plasma. The remainder is bound to hemoglobin molecules in red blood cells. Unlike hemoglobin-based oxygen transport, some artificial blood substitutes use an emulsion of oxygen (up to 15%) in inert substances called perfluorocarbons to transport oxygen throughout the body.

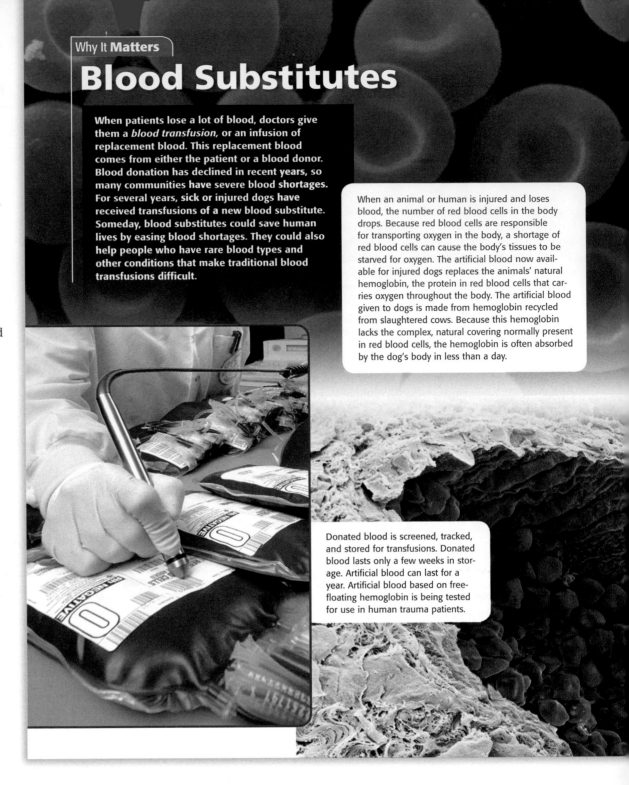

Why It Matters

Blood Substitutes

When patients lose a lot of blood, doctors give them a *blood transfusion,* or an infusion of replacement blood. This replacement blood comes from either the patient or a blood donor. Blood donation has declined in recent years, so many communities have severe blood shortages. For several years, sick or injured dogs have received transfusions of a new blood substitute. Someday, blood substitutes could save human lives by easing blood shortages. They could also help people who have rare blood types and other conditions that make traditional blood transfusions difficult.

When an animal or human is injured and loses blood, the number of red blood cells in the body drops. Because red blood cells are responsible for transporting oxygen in the body, a shortage of red blood cells can cause the body's tissues to be starved for oxygen. The artificial blood now available for injured dogs replaces the animals' natural hemoglobin, the protein in red blood cells that carries oxygen throughout the body. The artificial blood given to dogs is made from hemoglobin recycled from slaughtered cows. Because this hemoglobin lacks the complex, natural covering normally present in red blood cells, the hemoglobin is often absorbed by the dog's body in less than a day.

Donated blood is screened, tracked, and stored for transfusions. Donated blood lasts only a few weeks in storage. Artificial blood can last for a year. Artificial blood based on free-floating hemoglobin is being tested for use in human trauma patients.

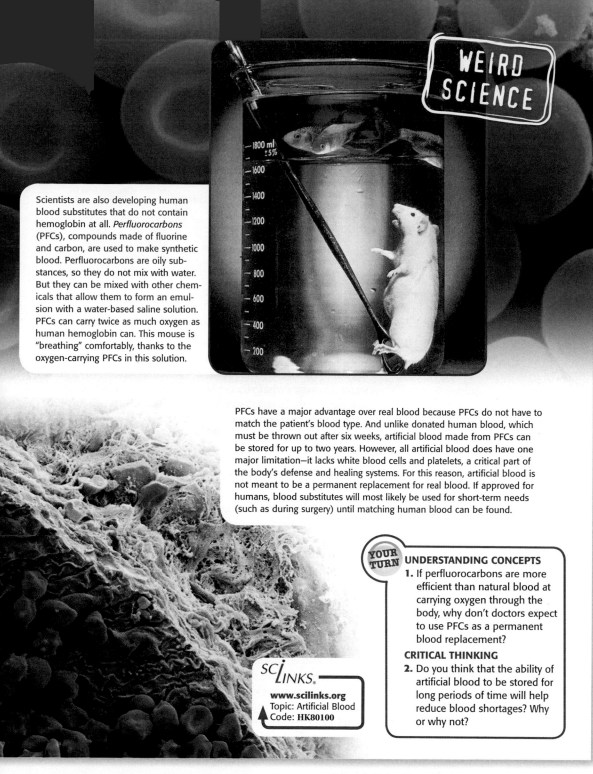

WEIRD SCIENCE

Scientists are also developing human blood substitutes that do not contain hemoglobin at all. *Perfluorocarbons* (PFCs), compounds made of fluorine and carbon, are used to make synthetic blood. Perfluorocarbons are oily substances, so they do not mix with water. But they can be mixed with other chemicals that allow them to form an emulsion with a water-based saline solution. PFCs can carry twice as much oxygen as human hemoglobin can. This mouse is "breathing" comfortably, thanks to the oxygen-carrying PFCs in this solution.

PFCs have a major advantage over real blood because PFCs do not have to match the patient's blood type. And unlike donated human blood, which must be thrown out after six weeks, artificial blood made from PFCs can be stored for up to two years. However, all artificial blood does have one major limitation—it lacks white blood cells and platelets, a critical part of the body's defense and healing systems. For this reason, artificial blood is not meant to be a permanent replacement for real blood. If approved for humans, blood substitutes will most likely be used for short-term needs (such as during surgery) until matching human blood can be found.

YOUR TURN

UNDERSTANDING CONCEPTS

1. If perfluorocarbons are more efficient than natural blood at carrying oxygen through the body, why don't doctors expect to use PFCs as a permanent blood replacement?

CRITICAL THINKING

2. Do you think that the ability of artificial blood to be stored for long periods of time will help reduce blood shortages? Why or why not?

SCLINKS.

www.scilinks.org
Topic: Artificial Blood
Code: **HK80100**

Answers to Your Turn

1. Sample answer: Artificial blood lacks other important components of blood, such as white blood cells and platelets.

2. Sample answer: Artificial blood could be used to alleviate blood shortages for situations that require short-term use of blood because the supply does not depend on people to donate blood. Also, artificial blood can be stored longer than real blood can be stored.

Solubility and Concentration

SECTION 3

Focus

This section opens with a discussion of solubility. The effect of temperature changes on the solubility of solids and gases in liquids is then introduced. Following is a discussion of various methods of quantitatively describing concentration, including molarity and the calculation of molarity from the mass of solute and the volume of the solvent.

 Bellringer

Use the Bellringer transparency to prepare students for this section.

Demonstrate

Supersaturation At least several hours prior to class, make a supersaturated solution of sodium acetate by heating 200 grams of sodium acetate in 20 mL water (use a 250 mL beaker). The supersaturated solution is not stable, so prepare extra solutions.

Explain supersaturation to the class. Ask the class to predict what will happen when a crystal of sodium acetate is added to the previously prepared and cooled supersaturated solution. Drop a small crystal of sodium acetate into the solution. The entire mass will solidify immediately because the solution is unstable. The beaker becomes warm, indicating that the crystallization is an exothermic process. The supersaturated solution can be restored by reheating in order to dissolve the solids.

Key Ideas

> What is solubility?

> What happens when you add more solute to a saturated solution?

> How do you describe how much of a solute is in a solution?

Key Terms

solubility
concentration
saturated solution
unsaturated solution
supersaturated solution
molarity

Why It Matters

The concentrations of many substances in your water supply need to be under a certain limit. For example, a small amount of fluoride in drinking water can be beneficial, but a larger amount can be harmful.

How much would you have to shake, stir, or heat the mixture of olive oil and water shown in **Figure 1** to dissolve the oil in the water? The answer is that the oil will not dissolve in the water no matter what you do. Some substances are *insoluble* in water—they do not dissolve. Other substances, such as sugar and baking soda, are *soluble* in water—they dissolve easily in water.

Solubility in Water

There is often a limit to how much of a substance will dissolve. Have you ever mixed a large amount of salt in a glass of water? You may have observed that some of the salt did not dissolve, no matter how much you stirred. Salt is soluble in water, but the amount of salt that will dissolve is limited. The maximum amount of salt that can be dissolved in 100 g of water at room temperature is 36 g, or about two tablespoons.

> **The solubility of a substance is the maximum mass of a solute that can dissolve in 100 g of solvent at a certain temperature and standard atmospheric pressure.**

Some substances, such as acetic acid, methanol, ethanol, glycerol, and ethylene glycol, are completely soluble in water. Any amount of these substances will mix with water to form a solution. Some ionic compounds, such as silver chloride, $AgCl$, are almost completely insoluble in water. Only 0.00019 g of $AgCl$ will dissolve in 100 g of water at 20 °C.

Figure 1 Olive oil and water form two layers when they are mixed. Olive oil is *insoluble* in water.

Key Resources

Teaching Transparency
TM25 Solubilities of Some Ionic Compounds

Visual Concepts
Comparing Molarity and Molality
Solution Equilibrium

Science Skills Worksheet
Percentages

Math Skills Worksheet
Molarity

Different substances have different solubilities.

The solubilities of closely related compounds can vary greatly. Compare the solubilities of the ionic compounds in **Figure 2.** Notice that all of the compounds that contain sodium also contain one other element. But sodium iodide is much more soluble than either sodium chloride or sodium fluoride.

The solubility of any substance in water depends on the strength of the forces acting between the solute particles and the strength of the forces acting between water molecules and solute particles. So, in a highly soluble substance, the forces between the solute particles are weaker than the forces between the water molecules and the solute particles. In sodium iodide, the forces between the sodium ions and iodide ions in the sodium iodide crystals are much weaker than the forces between the water molecules and the sodium and iodide ions. So, sodium iodide is more soluble than many other compounds that also contain sodium.

✓ Reading Check Why is sodium iodide so soluble?

How much of a substance is in a solution?

Not all solutions have all of the solute that can be dissolved. How would you compare a solution made with one teaspoon of salt with one made with one tablespoon of salt?

Because the amount of a substance that is dissolved in solution can vary greatly, the amount of solute that is dissolved in a given solution must be specified. A solution may be described as *weak* if only a small amount of solute is dissolved or as *strong* if a large amount of solute is dissolved. However, *weak* and *strong* do not mean the same thing to everyone. For example, the sulfuric acid solution found in automobile batteries can injure the skin. So, most people would describe the solution as strong. But a chemist knows that much stronger solutions of sulfuric acid can be prepared.

The concentration of a solution is not given by the terms *weak* and *strong*. **Concentration** is the quantity of solute that is dissolved in a given volume of solution. A chemist would describe battery acid as having a specific concentration value. A *concentrated* solution has a large amount of solute. A *dilute* solution has only a small amount of solute. However, because the terms *concentrated* and *dilute* are not quantitative, they do not give any information about the actual amount of solute in a solution.

Figure 2 Solubilities of Some Ionic Compounds in Water

Substance	Formula	Solubility in g/100 g H_2O at 20 °C
Calcium chloride	$CaCl_2$	75
Calcium fluoride	CaF_2	0.0015
Calcium sulfate	$CaSO_4$	0.32
Iron(II) sulfide	FeS	0.0006
Silver chloride	AgCl	0.000 19
Silver nitrate	$AgNO_3$	216
Sodium chloride	NaCl	35.9
Sodium fluoride	NaF	4.06
Sodium iodide	NaI	178
Sodium sulfide	Na_2S	26.3

solubility (SAHL yoo BIL uh tee) the ability of one substance to dissolve in another at a given temperature and pressure

concentration (KAHN suhn TRAY shuhn) the amount of a particular substance in a given quantity of a mixture, solution, or ore

SC*LINKS*.

www.scilinks.org
Topic: Solubility
Code: HK81421

❯ Teach

Teach Key Ideas

Solubility Have students refer to **Figure 2** and ask them the following questions: "What characteristics of each substance are given in the table?" (the substance name, chemical formula, and solubility) "How many substances are listed in the table?" (10) "What is the solubility of sodium chloride at 20 °C, and what does this value mean?" (35.9 g NaCl/100 g H_2O; 35.9 g of sodium chloride will dissolve in 100 g of water at a temperature of 20 °C) "What substance is the most soluble in water at 20 °C?" (silver nitrate) "What substance is least soluble at 20 °C?" (silver chloride)
LS Logical/Visual

Why It **Matters**

Le Châtelier's Principle and Plumping Raisins Prior to discussing this topic, obtain a few raisins and plump half of them by placing them in warm water for about 15 minutes. Have students examine the plumped and unplumped raisins and compare them. (The plumped raisins seem to have more water.) Explain to students that when a raisin is placed in water, the concentration of water within the raisin is less than the concentration of water outside the raisin. Water passes easily into the raisin, so the raisin swells. Ask students to describe when a new equilibrium will be reached. (when the rates of the water entering the raisin and the water leaving the raisin are equal) **LS** Visual

---

MISCONCEPTION ALERT

Conservation of Mass Students may believe that a solute "disappears" when in solution. Have students refer to the table in **Figure 2,** and ask them how they would prepare a saturated solution of calcium chloride using 100 g of water. (Dissolve 75 g calcium chloride in the water.) Ask students what the mass of this solution would be. (75 g + 100 g = 175 g) Remind students that the mass of a solution is equal to the combined masses of the solute and solvent. **LS** Logical

Interpreting Visuals Have students refer to **Figure 3.** Have them compare the distance between the sodium and acetate ions in the unsaturated and saturated solutions. (The ions are closer in the saturated solution.) Relate this closer proximity to the increase in the attraction between sodium and acetate ions in the solution and the reformation of crystals when more sodium acetate is added to the saturated solution, as shown in **Figure 4.** **LS** **Visual**

Teaching Key Ideas

Equilibrium in Saturated Solutions
Have students recall the concept of equilibrium. Ask students what is occurring when a chemical reaction reaches equilibrium. (The rate at which the forward reaction is taking place equals the rate at which the reverse reaction is taking place.) Ask students to write a chemical equation that identifies the two processes taking place within a solution of sodium chloride. NaCl ⇄ Na⁺ + Cl⁻ Ask students to describe the forward and reverse processes. (Sodium chloride crystals are being pulled into sodium and chloride ions in solution; sodium and chloride ions in solution are reforming crystals.) Point out that when a solution is saturated, sodium chloride is both dissolving and precipitating but the rates of the two processes are equal. **LS** **Logical/Verbal**

Academic Vocabulary

maximum (MAKS i muhm) the greatest quantity possible

saturated solution (SACH uh RAYT id suh LOO shuhn) a solution that cannot dissolve any more solute under the given conditions

unsaturated solution (uhn SACH uh RAYT id suh LOO shuhn) a solution that contains less solute than a saturated solution does and that is able to dissolve additional solute

supersaturated solution (SOO puhr SACH uh RAYT id suh LOO shuhn) a solution that holds more dissolved solute than is required to reach equilibrium at a given temperature

Saturated Solutions

The solubility of a substance is how much of that substance will dissolve in a given amount of water at a certain temperature and pressure. When you have added the <u>maximum</u> amount of solute that will dissolve in a solution, you have made a **saturated solution.** No more solute will dissolve. **➤ In a saturated solution, the dissolved solute is in equilibrium with undissolved solute. So, if you add more solute, it just settles to the bottom of the container.** To be in equilibrium means that the dissolved solute settles out of solution at the same rate that the undissolved solute dissolves.

Unsaturated solutions can become saturated.

Compare the two solutions shown in **Figure 3.** One has a white solid at the bottom, and one does not. The **unsaturated solution** of sodium acetate contains less than the maximum amount of solute that will dissolve in the solvent. If you keep adding sodium acetate to the solution, the compound dissolves until the solution becomes saturated. So, the solution will not have solid at the bottom. A solution is unsaturated as long as more solute can dissolve in it. The saturated solution in **Figure 3** has solid sodium acetate at the bottom of the beaker. No matter how much you stir, no more sodium acetate will dissolve in this saturated solution. The undissolved solid particles will sink to the bottom of the solution.

✓ Reading Check What happens when you add more solute to a saturated solution?

Figure 3 Concentration and the Dissolving Process

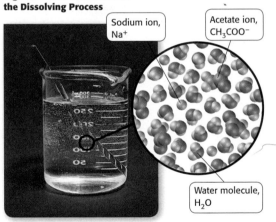

Sodium ion, Na⁺

Acetate ion, CH₃COO⁻

Water molecule, H₂O

Unsaturated Solution When more sodium acetate is added to this unsaturated solution, it can dissolve.

Saturated Solution No more sodium acetate will dissolve in this saturated solution. Any additional sodium acetate that is dissolved causes an equal amount to settle out of the solution.

Differentiated Instruction

Basic Learners

Vocabulary The terms *unsaturated* and *supersaturated* will have more meaning to students if they are related to other common usages of the term *saturated*. Ask students to describe a saturated sponge. Descriptions should mention that *saturated* refers to the greatest amount of something that normally can be contained. Once they understand *saturated*, students should be able to accurately infer the meanings of *unsaturated* and *supersaturated*. **LS** **Verbal**

Heating a saturated solution can dissolve more solute.

The solubility of most solutes increases as the temperature of the solution increases. If you heat a saturated solution of sodium acetate, more sodium acetate can dissolve until the solution becomes saturated at the higher temperature.

When the temperature of the sodium acetate solution decreases, sodium acetate crystals do not re-form. The excess solute needs a surface on which to crystallize. This solution now holds more solute than it normally would at the cooler temperature, so it is a **supersaturated solution.** Adding a small crystal of sodium acetate causes the solute to crystallize until the solution is once again saturated, as **Figure 4** shows.

Temperature and pressure affect the solubility of gases.

Soda contains carbon dioxide gas dissolved in water. Unlike solids, gases are less soluble in warmer water. So, warm soda goes flat more quickly than cold soda.

The solubility of gases also depends on pressure, as shown in **Figure 5.** Carbon dioxide is dissolved in the soda under high pressure when the bottle is sealed. When the bottle is opened, the gas pressure decreases to atmospheric pressure and the soda fizzes as the carbon dioxide comes out of solution.

Gas solubility affects scuba divers. Increased pressure underwater causes more nitrogen gas to dissolve in the blood. If the diver returns to the surface too quickly, nitrogen comes out of solution and forms bubbles in blood vessels. This condition, called the *bends*, is very painful and dangerous.

Figure 4 Adding a single crystal of sodium acetate to a supersaturated solution causes the excess sodium acetate to quickly crystallize out of the solution.

READING TOOLBOX

Summarizing Ideas
Make notes about saturated solutions by summarizing the content under the red and blue headings on these two pages.

Figure 5 Effect of Gas Pressure on Gas Solubility in Water

CO₂ under high pressure above solvent

Dissolved CO₂ molecules

Higher Pressure The pressure inside this bottle is higher than the pressure outside the bottle. Carbon dioxide gas is dissolved in water in this unopened bottle of soda.

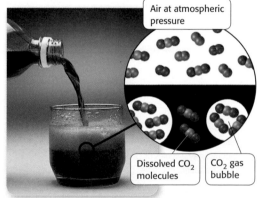

Air at atmospheric pressure

Dissolved CO₂ molecules

CO₂ gas bubble

Lower Pressure When the bottle is opened, the pressure inside the bottle decreases. Carbon dioxide gas then forms bubbles as it comes out of solution. **Will more bubbles come out of a warm soda or a cold soda?**

Why It Matters

Treating Injuries with Oxygen A tool to help heal sports injuries is hyperbaric oxygen (HBO). HBO is 100% oxygen that is delivered to the patient at pressure greater than atmospheric pressure. One of the principles of HBO therapy is that the solubility of oxygen gas in blood increases with increased gas pressure. A patient breathing pure oxygen at three times normal air pressure (equivalent to the pressure experienced by a diver at a depth of about 30 m) will have a 15-fold increase in the amount of dissolved oxygen delivered to tissues. In the treatment of an injury, the increased oxygen accelerates wound healing by promoting the growth of new capillaries in the area of the wound. Many professional sports teams use HBO therapy to rehabilitate injuries, such as sprains and injuries to soft tissues. HBO therapy is also used to treat the bends.

READING TOOLBOX

Summarizing Ideas Ask students to summarize the important points in the text about saturation and the effect of temperature and pressure on saturation. Students should note the following points: No more solute will dissolve in a saturated solution; a saturated solution is in equilibrium; temperature affects the amount of solute needed to make a saturated solution; higher pressure keeps gases dissolved; lower pressure results in the release of gases.

READING TOOLBOX

Interpreting Visuals Have students examine **Figure 5.** Ask students if there is any evidence in the photograph that a gas is dissolved in the soda in the capped bottle. (Sample answer: When considering only the photograph, the soda does not appear to contain dissolved gas because bubbles cannot be seen) Then, ask students to identify what evidence in the photo of the soda being poured into a glass leads them to believe that a soda contains a dissolved gas. (The soda formed bubbles, as evidenced by the foam at the top of the glass.) **LS Visual**

Answer to caption question
More bubbles will come out of warm soda because gas is less soluble at higher temperatures than it is at lower temperatures.

Teaching Key Ideas

Concentration Draw two one-inch squares on an overhead transparency. Place 10 large uniform dots within the first square and 20 dots within the second square. Have students indicate which square has a greater concentration of dots and discuss how they defined the term *concentration*. Ask students how they might determine the concentration of dots and express it quantitatively. (answers may include that they count the dots and express the concentration as dots per square) Tell students they will learn ways of describing solution concentrations with both words and quantities.
LS Visual/Logical

Science Skills

Ions in Sea Water Write the following values on the board:
molarity of Na^+ in sea water: 0.481 M
molarity of Cl^- in sea water: 0.560 M
Tell students that dissolved sodium chloride accounts for the sodium ions in sea water. Ask students to explain if dissolved sodium chloride in sea water accounts for all of the chloride ions. (No. If sodium chloride were the only source of chloride ions, the molarity of Na^+ and Cl^- would be the same because the chemical formula of sodium chloride, $NaCl$, shows that the ratio of the ions is 1 to 1.) Point out that sea water also contains dissolved magnesium chloride. **LS** Logical

molarity (moh LA ruh tee) a concentration unit of a solution expressed in moles of solute dissolved per liter of solution

Concentration of Solutions

The terms *concentrated, dilute, saturated,* and *unsaturated* do not reveal the quantity of dissolved solute. For example, 0.173 g of calcium hydroxide will dissolve in 100 g of water. This solution is saturated but is still dilute because so little solute is present. Scientists express the quantity of solute in a solution in several ways. ❯**One of the most common ways of expressing the concentration of a solution is molarity. Molarity** is expressed as moles of solute per liter of solution.

$$molarity = \frac{moles\ of\ solute}{liters\ of\ solution}, \text{ or } M = \frac{mol}{L}$$

A 1.0 M, which is read as "one molar," solution of NaCl contains 1.0 mol of dissolved NaCl in every 1.0 L of solution.

Math Skills Molarity

Calculate the molarity of sucrose, $C_{12}H_{22}O_{11}$, in a solution of 124 g of solute in 0.500 L of solution.

Identify	**Given:**
List the given and unknown values.	*mass of sucrose* = 124 g *volume of solution* = 0.500 L **Unknown:** *molarity*, amount of $C_{12}H_{22}O_{11}$ in 1 L of solution
Plan Write the equation for moles $C_{12}H_{22}O_{11}$ and molarity.	$moles\ C_{12}H_{22}O_{11} = \frac{mass\ C_{12}H_{22}O_{11}}{molar\ mass\ C_{12}H_{22}O_{11}}$ $molarity = \frac{moles\ C_{12}H_{22}O_{11}}{liters\ of\ solution}$
Solve Find the number of moles of $C_{12}H_{22}O_{11}$, and calculate molarity.	$molar\ mass\ C_{12}H_{22}O_{11} = 342\ g$ $moles\ C_{12}H_{22}O_{11} = \frac{124\ g}{342\ g/mol} = 0.362\ mol$ $molarity\ of\ solution =$ $\frac{0.362\ mole\ C_{12}H_{22}O_{11}}{0.500\ L\ solution} = 0.724\ M$

Practice Hint

❯ When calculating molarity, remember that molarity is moles of solute per liter of solution, not moles per liter of solvent.

❯ Problem 2: If volume is given in milliliters, you must multiply by 1 L/1,000 mL to change milliliters to liters.

Practice

1. What is the molarity of 2 mol of calcium chloride, $CaCl_2$, dissolved in 1 L of solution?

2. What is the molarity of 525 g of lead(II) nitrate, $Pb(NO_3)_2$, dissolved in 1,250 mL of solution?

For more practice, visit **go.hrw.com** and enter keyword **HK8MP**.

Math Skills

Answers to Practice
1. molarity = 2 mol $CaCl_2$/1 L solution = 2 M
2. molar mass $Pb(NO_3)_2$ = 207.2 g + 2 × (14 g + (3 × 16 g)) = 331.2 g
   moles $Pb(NO_3)_2$ = 525 g/331.2 g = 1.59 mol $Pb(NO_3)_2$
   molarity = 1.59 mol $Pb(NO_3)_2$/1.25 L solution = 1.27 M

Differentiated Instruction

Advanced Learners

Mass Percent Explain that there are several different ways to express concentration. Show students how to calculate mass percent.

$$mass\ percent = \frac{mass\ of\ solute \times 100\%}{mass\ of\ solute + mass\ of\ solvent}$$

Have students calculate the mass percent of a solution of 5 g NaCl dissolved in 95 g of water.

$$mass\ percent = \frac{5\ g\ (NaCl)}{5\ g\ (NaCl) + 95\ g\ (H_2O)}$$

$$mass\ percent = \frac{5\ g}{100\ g} \times 100\% = 0.05 \times 100\% = 5\%$$

LS Logical

Fluoride in Water

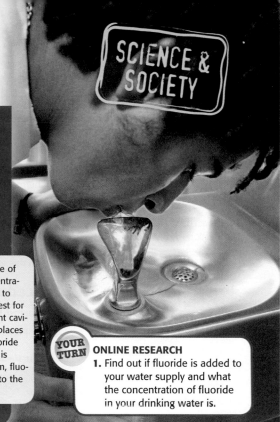

SCIENCE & SOCIETY

Fluoride ions occur naturally in drinking water. In proper concentration, these ions strengthen tooth enamel and reduce tooth decay. However, prolonged exposure to too much fluoride damages tooth enamel. The concentration of fluoride in drinking water is very small and is measured in parts per million (ppm). The amount of fluoride in most drinking water is about 1.0 ppm, or 1.0 g of fluoride per 1,000,000 g water. So, 1.0 L of water contains about 1 mg of fluoride.

Fluoride Concentration and Water Source

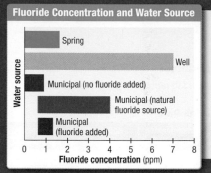

A limited range of fluoride concentration—0.7 ppm to 1.2 ppm—is best for helping prevent cavities. In many places where the fluoride concentration is below 0.7 ppm, fluoride is added to the water supply.

YOUR TURN

ONLINE RESEARCH
1. Find out if fluoride is added to your water supply and what the concentration of fluoride in your drinking water is.

Fluoride in Water A small amount of fluoride in drinking water helps build stronger teeth but too much fluoride is harmful. The human body also needs other substances in the correct amount. For example, people need to add salt and other electrolytes when they exercise and sweat because cells do not function correctly if the salt concentration is too low. However if the concentration of salt is too high, people can experience high blood pressure and other health problems.

Answer to Your Turn

1. Answers may vary. Students who do not get their water from the municipal water supply may not be able to determine the fluoride concentration in their water because it is unlikely that fluoride is added to their water.

❯Close

Reteaching Key Ideas

Saturation Have students choose a substance from **Figure 2.** Now tell them to determine the solubility of that substance in 1,000 g of water at 20 °C. (Answers may vary) Ask students: "If you put 100 grams of the substance you chose in 1,000 g of water, will a saturated or an unsaturated solution form?" "If the solution is saturated, will any solid remain undissolved?" (Calcium chloride, silver nitrate, sodium chloride, sodium iodide, and sodium sulfide will form unsaturated solutions; all other compounds will be saturated and leave material undissolved.)

Section 3 Review

KEY IDEAS

1. **Compare** the solubility of olive oil and acetic acid in water. Why is one substance more soluble than the other?

2. **Describe** how a saturated solution can become supersaturated.

3. **Express** the molarity of a solution that contains 0.5 mol of calcium acetate per 1.0 L of solution.

CRITICAL THINKING

4. **Understanding Relationships** Explain how a solution can be both saturated and dilute at the same time. Use an example from **Figure 2.**

5. **Drawing Conclusions** Determine whether sweat would evaporate more quickly if the humidity were 92% or 37%. (Hint: When the humidity is 100%, the air is saturated with dissolved water vapor.)

6. **Designing Experiments** Propose a way to determine whether a saltwater solution is unsaturated, saturated, or supersaturated.

7. **Applying Ideas** When you fill a glass with cold water from a faucet and then let the glass sit undisturbed for two hours, you will see small bubbles sticking to the glass. What are the bubbles? Why did they form?

Math Skills

8. Calculate the molarity of a solution that contains 35.0 g of barium chloride, $BaCl_2$, dissolved in 450.0 mL of solution.

Formative Assessment

What is solubility?

A. the equilibrium between dissolved solute and undissolved solute (Incorrect. This answer describes saturated solutions.)

B. the amount of solute added to a solvent (Incorrect. This answer is not specific enough to be correct.)

C. the maximum amount of a solute that will dissolve in a given quantity of solvent at a given temperature and pressure (Correct. A solvent dissolves a very specific amount of solute based on volume of solvent, temperature, and atmospheric pressure.)

D. the minimum amount of substance that can be added to a saturated solution before the solution becomes supersaturated (Incorrect. The addition of any amount of solute after a solution becomes saturated will cause the solution to become supersaturated.)

Answers to Section Review on p. 289A

ApplicationLab

Teacher's Notes

Show students how to seal the plastic bag with a twist tie without allowing the carbon dioxide gas inside the bag to escape.

Time Required

1 lab period

Ratings

EASY ——————→ HARD

Teacher Prep 🧪

Student Set-Up 🧪🧪

Concept Level 🧪🧪

Clean Up 🧪

Skills Acquired

- Collecting data
- Communicating
- Inferring
- Measuring
- Organizing and analyzing data

Scientific Methods

In this lab, students will:
- Make observations
- Analyze the results
- Draw conclusions
- Communicate results

Safety Cautions

Have students review safety guidelines before working in the lab. Students should wear safety goggles. Remind students that they should never eat or drink anything in the lab.

What You'll Do

> **Compare** the volume of carbon dioxide released from a warm soft drink with that released from a cold soft drink.

> **Draw conclusions** to relate carbon dioxide's solubility in each soft drink to the temperature of each soft drink.

What You'll Need

bags, plastic, small (2)

beaker, 1 L

ice, crushed

paper towels

soft drinks, carbonated, in plastic bottles (2)

stopwatch

tape measure, flexible, metric

thermometer

twist ties (4)

Safety

⏱ 50 min

How Temperature Affects Gas Solubility

The management at a soft-drink bottling plant wants to see if turning up the thermostat on the plant's air-conditioning system will save money. The bottling machinery was calibrated at the colder temperature. If the solubility of carbon dioxide decreases when the temperature is raised, the beverage may lose some carbonation in the bottling process. You, the lead engineer, must find out what the effect of increasing the temperature will be. To do so, you will determine the effects of temperature on the solubility of carbon dioxide, a gaseous solute, in a soft drink.

Procedure

Preparing for Your Experiment

1 Prepare a data table in your lab report similar to the one below.

Sample Data Table: Soft-Drink Data

	Temperature (°C)	Circumference of bag (cm)	Radius of bag (cm)	Volume of bag (cm³)
Room-temp soft drink				
Chilled soft drink		DO NOT WRITE IN BOOK		

Testing the Solubility of Carbon Dioxide in a Warm Soft Drink

2 Obtain a bottle of carbonated soft drink that has been stored at room temperature, and carry it to your lab table. Try not to disturb the liquid, and do not open the bottle.

3 Use a thermometer to measure the temperature in the laboratory. Record this temperature in your data table.

4 Remove the bottle's cap, and quickly place the open end of a deflated plastic bag over the bottle's opening. Seal the bag tightly around the bottle's neck with a twist tie. Begin timing with a stopwatch.

5 When the bag is almost fully inflated, stop the stopwatch. Very carefully remove the plastic bag from the bottle. Be sure to keep the bag sealed so that the carbon dioxide inside does not escape. Seal the bag tightly with another twist tie.

6 Gently mold the bag into the shape of a sphere. Measure the bag's circumference in centimeters by wrapping the tape measure around the largest part of the bag. Record the circumference in your data table.

Testing the Solubility of Carbon Dioxide in a Cold Soft Drink

7 Obtain a second bottle of carbonated soft drink that has been chilled. Place the bottle in a 1 L beaker, and pack crushed ice around the bottle. Use paper towels to dry any water on the outside of the beaker, and then carefully move the beaker to your lab table.

8 Repeat step 4. Let the second plastic bag inflate for the same length of time that the first bag was allowed to inflate. Very carefully remove the bag from the bottle as you did before. Seal the plastic bag tightly with a twist tie.

9 Wait for the bag to warm to room temperature. While you are waiting, use the thermometer to measure the temperature of the cold soft drink. Record the temperature in your data table.

10 When the bag has warmed to room temperature, repeat step 6.

Analysis

1. **Analyzing Data** Calculate the radius in centimeters of each inflated plastic bag by using the following equation. Record the results in your data table.

$$radius \text{ (in cm)} = \frac{circumference \text{ (in cm)}}{2\pi}$$

2. **Analyzing Data** Calculate the volume in cubic centimeters of each inflated bag by using the following equation. Record the results in your data table.

$$volume \text{ (in cm}^3) = \frac{4}{3}\pi \times [radius \text{ (in cm)}]^3$$

Communicating Your Results

3. **Drawing Conclusions** Compare the volume of carbon dioxide released from the two soft drinks. Use your data to explain how the solubility of carbon dioxide in a soft drink is affected by temperature.

4. **Designing Experiments** Suppose that someone tells you that your conclusion is not valid because a soft drink contains many other solutes besides carbon dioxide. How could you verify that your conclusion is correct?

Application

What would be your recommendation to the bottling-plant management, and how would you justify it?

Tips and Tricks

An alternative method of collecting the gas is to stopper the soda bottles with a one-hole stopper and collect the gas in a graduated cylinder under a bath of warm water. This method can be used to gather data in a shorter time.

Answers to Analysis

1. Answers may vary based on data collected. Check for accurate calculations.
2. Answers may vary based on data collected. Check for accurate calculations.

Answers to Communicating Your Results

3. The volume of the bag attached to the room-temperature drink is greater than the volume of the bag attached to the cold drink. This means that more carbon dioxide was released from the room-temperature drink, indicating that the solubility of carbon dioxide in the soft drink decreases as temperature increases.

4. Sample answer: I could repeat the experiment using a different solution, such as seltzer water, that contains dissolved carbon dioxide but does not contain other solutes.

Answer to Application

Sample answer: I would recommend against setting the plant's thermostat at a higher temperature because doing so would reduce the solubility of the gas in the beverage and probably cause some to be lost in the bottling process.

Key Resources

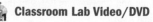

Virtual Investigation

Classroom Lab Video/DVD

Holt Lab Generator CD-ROM
Search for any lab by type, standard, difficulty level, or time. Edit any lab to fit your needs, or create your own labs. Use the Lab Materials QuickList software to customize your lab materials list.

Differentiated Datasheets
How Temperature Affects Gas Solubility

Observation Lab
Separating Substances in a Mixture

CBL™ Probeware Lab
Determining the Concentration of an Ionic Solution

Making Pie Graphs

Reteaching Key Ideas

Remind students that an alloy is a solution, not a compound. The metals in an alloy can be separated by physical means, such as heating the alloy. The metals will melt at different temperatures. Discuss with students why a jewelry manufacturer would want to use 14-karat gold instead of 24-karat gold, which is 100% gold. (The alloy has different properties than the 24-karat gold does, such as greater hardness. These characteristics may make it better for jewelry. Also, the other metals in the alloy cost less than gold does, so 14-karat gold is less expensive than 24-karat gold.) **LS** **Logical**

Answers

1. Copper is the second most abundant metal in 14-karat gold.
2.

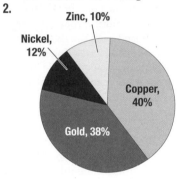

Zinc, 10%
Nickel, 12%
Copper, 40%
Gold, 38%

3. The percentage of gold in 9-karat gold is 20% less than the percentage of gold in 14-karat gold.
4. Copper is the most abundant metal by weight in 9-karat gold.
5. Nickel is in white gold, but is not in yellow gold. Silver is in yellow gold, but is not in white gold.

Problem

Often used in jewelry, 14-karat gold is an alloy that contains 58% gold by weight. The table below gives the composition of a 14-karat yellow gold alloy. Show these data in a pie graph.

Solution

❶ Make sure that all of the parts are given. Calculate percentages if necessary.	The data are already in percentages, and the numbers add up to 100%.
❷ Draw a circle that is large enough that you can see each section of the pie graph.	Silver is the smallest section. A circle about 3 cm in diameter should be large enough.
❸ Determine the size of each pie wedge. Multiply the percentage of each metal by 360°.	The size for the gold section is 360° × 0.58 = 210°. Sizes for the other sections are silver = 14°; copper = 110°; and zinc = 26°.
❹ Use a protractor to draw the sections in the circle. Color in each section with a different color.	Draw a line from the center to the edge of the circle. Measure the first section as an angle from that line (210° for gold). Repeat for each section.
❺ Label each section with the name of the category and the percentage.	The labels in the gold section are "Gold" and "58%."

Practice

Use the graph above to answer question 1.

1. What is the second most abundant metal by weight in the 14-karat gold alloy?

Use the table below to answer questions 2–5.

Percentage Composition by Weight of a 9-Karat White Gold Alloy

Metal	Weight (%)
Copper	40
Gold	38
Nickel	12
Zinc	10

Percentage Composition by Weight of a 14-Karat Yellow Gold Alloy

Metal	Weight (%)
Gold	58
Copper	31
Zinc	7.1
Silver	3.9

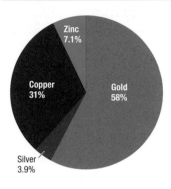

Zinc 7.1%
Copper 31%
Gold 58%
Silver 3.9%

2. The 9-karat gold is less expensive than the 14-karat gold. Create a pie graph that shows the composition of a 9-karat white gold alloy.

3. How does the amount of gold in the 9-karat white gold alloy compare to the amount of gold in the 14-karat yellow gold alloy?

4. What is the most abundant metal by weight in the 9-karat white gold alloy?

5. Which metal in the yellow gold is not in the white gold? Which metal in the white gold is not in the yellow gold?

Key Resources

📋 **Science Skills Worksheets**
SI Units and Conversions Between Them
Surface Area
Percentages

8 Summary

SUMMARY

SUPER SUMMARY

Have students connect the major concepts in this chapter through an interactive Super Summary. Visit **go.hrw.com** and type in the keyword **HK8SOLS** to access the Super Summary for this chapter.

Key Ideas	Key Terms
## Section 1 Solutions and Other Mixtures  **›Heterogeneous Mixtures** A heterogeneous mixture does not have a fixed composition. The amount of each substance in a heterogeneous mixture varies from sample to sample. (p. 259) **›Homogeneous Mixtures** A homogeneous mixture looks uniform, even when you examine it under a microscope, because the individual components are too small to be seen. (p. 263)	**suspension,** p. 260 **colloid,** p. 261 **emulsion,** p. 262 **solution,** p. 263 **solute,** p. 263 **solvent,** p. 263 **alloy,** p. 266
## Section 2 How Substances Dissolve  **›Water: A Common Solvent** Water is called the *universal solvent* because many substances can dissolve in water. Water is a polar compound. (p. 267) **›The Dissolving Process** The energy transferred from the solvent to the solute, as well as the attractive forces between the solvent and solute molecules, causes molecules at the surface of the crystal to dissolve. (p. 271)	**polar,** p. 267 **hydrogen bond,** p. 269 **nonpolar,** p. 270
## Section 3 Solubility and Concentration  **›Solubility in Water** The solubility of a substance is the maximum mass of a solute that can dissolve in 100 g of solvent at a certain temperature and standard atmospheric pressure. (p. 276) **›Saturated Solutions** In a saturated solution, the dissolved solute is in equilibrium with the undissolved solute. So, if you add more solute, it just settles to the bottom of the container. (p. 278) **›Concentration of Solutions** One of the most common ways of expressing the concentration of a solution is molarity. *Molarity* is moles of solute per liter of solution. (p. 280)	**solubility,** p. 276 **concentration,** p. 277 **saturated solution,** p. 278 **unsaturated solution,** p. 278 **supersaturated solution,** p. 279 **molarity,** p. 280

Differentiated Instruction

Alternative Assessment

Solubility Tables Have students work in small groups to make tables that describe the effect of temperature, stirring or shaking, and surface area on the solubility of solids. Students' tables should also note the effect of pressure on the solubility of gases. Encourage students to include drawings in their tables. Finally, have them share their tables with the entire class.

LS Verbal/Logical

Key Resources

⊞ **Interactive Concept Map**

▭ **Review Resources**
Concept Review Worksheets

▭ **Assessment Resources**
Chapter Tests A and B
Performance-Based Assessment

Reading Toolbox

1. Sample answers: olive oil, oil-based paint; "for example"

Using Key Terms

2. Solution a is unsaturated because the added solute dissolved. Solution b is saturated because the added solute did not dissolve.

3. An alloy is a solution because it contains particles of one or more substances, usually metals, dispersed uniformly throughout another metal. The composition of an alloy is homogeneous. Alloys are used because their properties are usually more suitable for practical applications than those of pure metals are.

4. muddy water: suspension; salt water: solution; mayonnaise: emulsion; vinegar: solution; fog: colloid; dry air: solution; cream: emulsion

5. Water is a polar compound because the hydrogen atoms have a partial positive charge and the oxygen atoms have a partial negative charge. Ethanol is also polar because it has a hydrogen atom bonded to an oxygen atom.

6. Molarity describes moles of solute per liter of solution, so there are 0.01 moles of sodium chloride per one liter of solution.

Understanding Key Ideas

7. c
8. b
9. a
10. b
11. a
12. d
13. a
14. b
15. a
16. b

READING TOOLBOX

1. **Finding Examples** List at least two examples of substances that contain nonpolar compounds given in Section 2. If a word or phrase was used to signal the example in the text, write that word or phrase next to the example in your list.

USING KEY TERMS

2. A small amount of *solute* is added to two *solutions.* In the figures below, which solution is *unsaturated?* Which solution is *saturated?* Explain your answer.

a.   **b.**

3. Explain why an *alloy* is a type of solution. Why are alloys sometimes used instead of pure metals?

4. Classify the following items as either a *suspension*, a *colloid*, an *emulsion*, or a *solution:* muddy water, salt water, mayonnaise, vinegar, fog, dry air, and cream.

5. Explain why water and ethanol are *polar* or *nonpolar* compounds.

6. The *concentration* of a sodium chloride solution is 0.01 M. How many moles of sodium chloride are in 1 L of this solution?

UNDERSTANDING KEY IDEAS

7. Which of the following mixtures is homogeneous?
   a. tossed salad   **c.** salt water
   b. soil   **d.** vegetable soup

8. The label on a bottle of medicine states, "Shake well before using." The medicine is probably a
   a. solution.   **c.** colloid.
   b. suspension.   **d.** gel.

9. Suppose that you add a teaspoon of table salt to a cool saltwater solution and stir until all of the salt dissolves. The solution you started with was
   a. unsaturated.   **c.** saturated.
   b. supersaturated.   **d.** concentrated.

10. Which of the following materials is an example of a solid dissolved in another solid?
    a. smoke   **c.** mayonnaise
    b. bronze   **d.** ice

11. The dispersed particles of a suspension are _____ than the particles of a colloid.
    a. larger   **c.** lighter
    b. smaller   **d.** less dense

12. To dissolve a substance, a solvent must attract particles of the substance more strongly than the _____ attract each other.
    a. solvent particles   **c.** ions
    b. water molecules   **d.** solute particles

13. The boiling point of a solution of sugar in water is _____ the boiling point of water.
    a. higher than   **c.** the same as
    b. lower than   **d.** not related to

14. To increase the solubility of a solid substance in a solvent, you could
    a. add more solute.   **c.** stir the solution.
    b. heat the solution.   **d.** lower the pressure.

15. A _____ solution contains as much dissolved solute as it can hold under certain conditions.
    a. saturated   **c.** supersaturated
    b. dilute   **d.** concentrated

16. Gases are more soluble in liquids when the pressure is _____ and the temperature is _____.
    a. high, high   **c.** low, high
    b. high, low   **d.** low, low

EXPLAINING KEY IDEAS

17. Why does stirring a solution help the solute dissolve faster?

18. Explain why water dissolves many ionic compounds.

INTERPRETING GRAPHICS The graph below shows how the solubilities of cadmium selenate, $CdSeO_4$, and cobalt(II) chloride, $CoCl_2$, vary with temperature. Use the graph to answer questions 19 and 20.

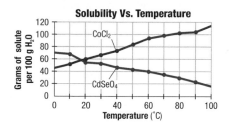

19. At what temperature is the solubility of $CdSeO_4$ equal to 40 g $CdSeO_4$/100 g H_2O?

20. Which substance has an unusual solubility trend? How is the trend unusual?

CRITICAL THINKING

21. Designing Experiments Sea water is a solution that contains many types of dissolved ions. What is the simplest way to get a clear sea-water solution from a mixture that also contains mud and sand? Explain your answer.

22. Drawing Conclusions Use the observations in the table below to decide whether each mixture is a solution, a suspension, or a colloid.

Sample	Clarity	Settles out	Scatters light
1	clear	no	yes
2	clear	no	no
3	cloudy	yes	yes
4	cloudy	no	yes

Assignment Guide

SECTION	ITEMS
1	3–4, 7–8, 10–11, 22
2	1, 5, 12–14, 17–18, 21
3	2, 6, 9, 15–16, 19–20, 23–27

Graphing Skills

23. Constructing Graphs The solubility of silver nitrate, $AgNO_3$, in water at various temperatures is given in the table below.

Temperature (°C)	Solubility of $AgNO_3$ in g $AgNO_3$/100 g H_2O
0	122
20	216
40	311
60	440
80	585

Make a graph of the solubility of $AgNO_3$. Plot temperature on the x-axis, and plot solubility on the y-axis. Answer the following questions.

a. How does the solubility of $AgNO_3$ vary with the temperature of water?

b. Estimate the solubility of $AgNO_3$ at 35 °C, at 55 °C, and at 75 °C.

c. At what temperature would the solubility of $AgNO_3$ be 512 g per 100 g H_2O?

d. Is a solution that contains 100 g $AgNO_3$ dissolved in 100 g H_2O at 10 °C saturated?

Math Skills

24. Molarity How many moles of lithium chloride, LiCl, are dissolved in 3.00 L of a 0.200 M solution of lithium chloride?

25. Molarity What is the molarity of 250 mL of a solution that contains 12.5 g of zinc bromide, $ZnBr_2$?

26. Solubility The solubility of sodium fluoride, NaF, is 4.06 g NaF/100 g H_2O at 20 °C. What mass of NaF would you have to dissolve in 1,000 g H_2O to make a saturated solution?

27. Solubility The solubility of copper(II) chloride, $CuCl_2$, at 20 °C is 73 g/100 g H_2O. Suppose that you add 50 g $CuCl_2$ to 50 g of water at 20 °C and stir until no more $CuCl_2$ dissolves. What mass of $CuCl_2$ remains undissolved at 20 °C?

Explaining Key Ideas

17. Stirring a solution helps move the dissolved solute particles away from the undissolved particles, so the solvent particles can more easily interact with the undissolved particles.

18. Water dissolves many ionic compounds because water molecules are polar. There is a strong attraction between the partially charged parts of the water molecules and the charged ions in ionic compounds.

19. about 60 °C

20. The solubility of $CdSeO_4$ is unusual because it decreases with increasing temperature.

Critical Thinking

21. Sample answer: The mixture could be filtered to obtain clear sea water because water and dissolved salts will pass through a filter, but mud and sand will not pass through the filter. It is not possible to obtain clear sea water by distillation, because only the water would boil away, leaving dissolved salts behind with sand and mud.

22. Sample 1: colloid; Sample 2: solution; Sample 3: suspension; Sample 4: colloid

Graphing Skills

23. a. The solubility of $AgNO_3$ increases with increasing temperature. Students may also note that solubility increases at a faster rate at higher temperatures.

b. 35 °C: about 285 g; 55 °C: about 410 g; and 75 °C: about 560 g

c. about 72 °C

d. The solution would be unsaturated because the solubility of silver nitrate is about 160 g per 100 g H_2O at 10 °C.

Math Skills

24. 0.200 M LiCl × 3.00 L solution = 0.600 mol LiCl

25. 12.5 g $ZnBr_2$/225 g $ZnBr_2$/mol = 0.0556 mol $ZnBr_2$; 0.0556 mol $ZnBr_2$/0.250 L — 0.222 M $ZnBr_2$

26. 4.06 g NaF/100 g $H_2O = \dfrac{x/1000\ g}{H_2O}$;

$x = 4.06$ g NaF × 1000 g H_2O/100 g H_2O = 40.6 g NaF

27. 73 g $CuCl_2$/100 g H_2O × 50 g H_2O = 36.5 g $CuCl_2$; 50 g $CuCl_2$ − 36.5 g $CuCl_2$ = 13.5 g $CuCl_2$ will remain undissolved

Standardized Test Prep

 TEST DOCTOR

Question 1 Answer B is correct. A solution appears completely uniform, even under a microscope. Answers A and C are incorrect because they describe heterogeneous mixtures, not solutions. Answer D is incorrect because a heterogeneous mixture is not uniform.

Question 2 Answer I is correct. When dissolving a gas in a liquid, lowering the temperature and raising the pressure increases solubility. Students might choose answer F or answer H if they were thinking of dissolving a solid in a liquid, in which raising the temperature increases solubility. Answer G is incorrect because low pressure reduces solubility.

Question 3 Answer C is correct. To find the correct answer, students must first multiply the concentration of 0.25 M by 2 liters, yielding 0.5 moles. This is then multiplied by the molar mass of 174 g/mole to yield an answer of 87 g of potassium sulfate.

Question 4 Full-credit answers should include the following points:
- Compound A is a polar molecule because the electric charge on the molecules is uneven.
- Compound B is a nonpolar compound because it has evenly distributed electric charge.
- Polar compounds dissolve best in polar solvents.
- Water is a polar compound.
- Compound A would dissolve more easily in water than Compound B would.

Question 5 Answer G is correct. Lowering the temperature and pressure would cause the carbon dioxide to become more like a normal gas, reducing the solubility of caffeine. Answer F is incorrect because forcing the CO_2 back through the plant material does not aid in caffeine recovery. Answer H is incorrect because the polarity of carbon dioxide is a chemical property of its atoms and cannot be changed. Answer I is incorrect because harsher solvents may be harmful to humans.

Understanding Concepts

Directions (1–3): **For each question, write on a sheet of paper the letter of the correct answer.**

1. An industrial chemist stirs some crystals into water. The resulting liquid appears completely uniform under a microscope. What is the liquid?
   - **A.** a colloid
   - **B.** a solution
   - **C.** a suspension
   - **D.** a heterogeneous mixture

2. After the lungs take in oxygen during respiration, oxygen gas is dissolved in the bloodstream. Under what conditions can the most oxygen be dissolved in the blood?
   - **F.** high blood pressure and high body temperature
   - **G.** low blood pressure and low body temperature
   - **H.** low blood pressure and high body temperature
   - **I.** high blood pressure and low body temperature

3. Potassium sulfate, K_2SO_4, has a molar mass of 174 g. If potassium sulfate is the solute in 2 L of a solution that has a concentration of 0.25 M, how many grams of potassium sulfate are in the solution?
   - **A.** 1,392 g
   - **B.** 348 g
   - **C.** 87 g
   - **D.** 43.5 g

Directions (4): **For each question, write a short response.**

4. The molecules of compound A have unevenly distributed electric charge. The molecules of compound B have evenly distributed electric charge. Which compound is more likely to dissolve easily in water? Explain your reasoning.

Reading Skills

Directions (5–6): **Read the passage below. Then, answer the questions that follow.**

SUPERCRITICAL DECAFFEINATION
One of the most common ways to remove caffeine from coffee and to preserve the flavor of the beverage is to use a solvent that dissolves the caffeine but leaves the rest of the plant material undissolved. One of the main difficulties with removing caffeine is that caffeine is a nonpolar compound. Therefore, a nonpolar solvent is required to dissolve caffeine. But most effective nonpolar solvents are poisonous to humans. Although carbon dioxide, CO_2, is a safe nonpolar compound, it is a gas under normal conditions and cannot act as a solvent for caffeine.

When both the pressure and temperature of a fluid are increased beyond a specific (or *critical*) point, a fluid has some properties of liquids and some properties of gases. Fluids under these conditions are called *supercritical fluids*. In the 1960s, coffee companies began using supercritical CO_2 to extract caffeine. The gaslike behavior of CO_2 allows its molecules to penetrate into the plant material. The liquid aspects of CO_2 allow it to dissolve caffeine molecules.

5. Once the caffeine is removed from the plant materials, how might the caffeine be recovered from the supercritical CO_2?
   - **F.** by forcing the CO_2 back through the plant materials
   - **G.** by lowering the temperature and pressure of the CO_2
   - **H.** by changing the polarity of the caffeine molecules
   - **I.** by using a harsher solvent

6. Why can't water be used to dissolve the caffeine found in coffee and tea?

Question 6 Full-credit answers should include the following points:
- The passage states that caffeine is a nonpolar compound.
- The passage states that a nonpolar solvent is required to dissolve caffeine.
- Water is a polar solvent.
- Because water is a polar solvent, it cannot dissolve nonpolar caffeine.

Question 7 Answer A is correct. Each beaker contains 500 grams of solution. The amount of sugar can be calculated by multiplying 500 g by the concentration in g of sugar per g of solution and then adding the amounts for the three beakers.

Question 8 Full-credit answers should include the following points:
- The solution that has the highest concentration, 220 g sugar per 100 g water, is the supersaturated solution,
- If additional solute is added to a supersaturated solution, crystals will likely form.

Question 9 Answer H is correct. The line in the graph curves upward, indicating that solubility increases with temperature. At 60 °C, the solubility is about 122 g/100 g H_2O. Answer F is incorrect because 88 g/100 g H_2O is solubility at 20 °C. Answer G is incorrect because 100 g/100 g H_2O is solubility at about 30 °C. Answer I is incorrect because 264 g/100 g H_2O is not shown on the graph.

Interpreting Graphics

The graphic below represents three beakers that contain 500 g of water with different amounts of sugar. One is unsaturated, one is saturated, and one is supersaturated. Use this graphic to answer questions 7–8.

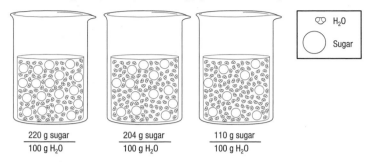

220 g sugar	204 g sugar	110 g sugar
100 g H_2O	100 g H_2O	100 g H_2O

7. How many grams of sugar are there altogether in the three cylinders?

A. 2,670 g   **C.** 534 g

B. 1,602 g   **D.** 267 g

8. Which solution would show the most dramatic results if an additional crystal of sugar were dropped into it? What would those results be?

The graph below shows how the solubility of a mystery solid in water depends on temperature. Use this graph to answer questions 9–10.

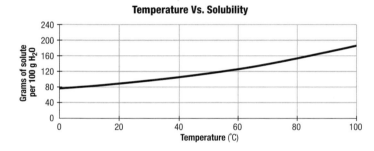

Temperature Vs. Solubility

9. The solubility of the solid is 88 g/100 g H_2O at 20 °C. What is the solubility of the substance at 60 °C?

F. 88 g/100 g H_2O **H.** 122 g/100 g H_2O

G. 100 g/100 g H_2O **I.** 264 g/100 g H_2O

10. Water normally boils at 100 °C. The scientists performing this experiment were able to measure the solubility at 100 °C because the solution was not boiling. Why was the solution not boiling at 100 °C ?

 Test Tip

To develop a short-response or extended-response answer, jot down your key ideas on a piece of scratch paper first.

Question 10 Full-credit answers should include the following points:

- The addition of a solute to a solvent increases the boiling point of the solvent.
- A solid is dissolved in water.

State Resources

 For specific resources for your state, visit **go.hrw.com** and type in the keyword **HSHSTR**.

📖 **Test Practice with Guided Reading Development**

Answers

1. B

2. I

3. C

4. Answers may vary; see Test Doctor for a detailed scoring rubric.

5. G

6. Answers may vary; see Test Doctor for a detailed scoring rubric.

7. A

8. Answers may vary; see Test Doctor for a detailed scoring rubric.

9. H

10. Answers may vary; see Test Doctor for a detailed scoring rubric.

Answers continued from p. 281

Answers to Section Review

1. Acetic acid is soluble in water, while olive oil is insoluble in water. Like water, acetic acid is polar. Olive oil is nonpolar, so it is not soluble in water.

2. The solution can be heated and additional solute dissolved in the solution. When the solution is cooled to the original temperature, it will be supersaturated.

3. $0.5 \text{ mol}/1.0 \text{ L} = 0.5 \text{ M}$

4. Some substances are only slightly soluble in water. For example, only 0.32 g of calcium sulfate dissolves in 100 g of water. Such a solution is saturated because it contains the maximum amount of solute, but the solution is still dilute because it contains only a small amount of solute per unit volume.

5. Evaporation would take place faster at 37% humidity because the solution of water vapor in air is less saturated than it is at 92% humidity.

6. Sample answer: I could add a very small amount of additional solute. If it dissolves, the solution is unsaturated. If it remains undissolved, the solution is saturated. If new crystals form in the solution, the solution is supersaturated.

7. Answers may vary. Sample answer: Gases, such as nitrogen and oxygen, from the air are dissolved in the cold water. Gas solubility decreases with increasing temperature, so the dissolved gas has come out of solution, forming bubbles as the temperature of the tap water increases.

8. $35.0 \text{ g BaCl}_2 / 208.2 \text{ g BaCl}_2/\text{mol} = 0.168 \text{ mol}; 0.168 \text{ mol} / 0.450 \text{ L} = 0.374 \text{ M}$

Acids, Bases, and Salts

	Standards	Teach Key Ideas
CHAPTER OPENER, pp. 290–292 `50 min.`		
SECTION 1 Acids, Bases, and pH, pp. 293–300 `50 min.` 〉 Acids 〉 Bases 〉 pH	UCP 1, SAI 1, SPSP 4	〉 **Bellringer Transparency** 〉 **Teaching Transparencies** TM26 Some Common Acids • C23 pH Scale • TM27 Some Common Bases 〉 **Visual Concepts** Acids • Common Acids • Bases • pH • pH Range for Common Substances
SECTION 2 Reactions of Acids with Bases, pp. 302–306 `50 min.` 〉 Acid-Base Reactions 〉 Salts	PS 3a, PS 3c, UCP 2, UCP 3	〉 **Bellringer Transparency** 〉 **Teaching Transparency** C24 Neutralization Reaction
SECTION 3 Acids, Bases, and Salts in the Home, pp. 307–313 `50 min.` 〉 Cleaning Products 〉 Personal-Care and Food Products	PS 3a, PS 3c, UCP 5, SAI 1	〉 **Bellringer Transparency** 〉 **Visual Concept** Antacid

See also PowerPoint® Resources

Chapter Review and Assessment Resources

SE Science Skills: Finding Reputable Sources, p. 316
SE Chapter Summary, p. 317
SE Chapter Review, pp. 318–319
SE Standardized Test Prep, pp. 320–321
☐ Concept Review Worksheets ■
☐ Chapter Tests A and B ■
Holt Online Assessment

CHAPTER
Fast Track *To shorten instruction because of time limitations, omit Section 3 and the chapter lab.*

Basic Learners
TE Food Labels, p. 294
TE Salt, p. 304
TE Reading Skills, p. 309
☐ Science Skills Worksheets
☐ Differentiated Datasheets A for Labs and Activities ■
☐ Study Guide A ■

Advanced Learners
TE pH of Blood, p. 298
TE Barium Sulfate, p. 305
TE New Medicines, p. 311
☐ Cross-Disciplinary Worksheets
☐ Differentiated Datasheets C for Labs and Activities ■

Key

SE Student Edition
TE Teacher's Edition

📁 Chapter Resource File
📓 Workbook
📖 Transparency

💿 CD or CD-ROM
* Datasheet or blackline master available

■ Also available in Spanish

All resources listed below are also available on the Teacher's One-Stop Planner.

Why It Matters	Hands-On	Skills Development	Assessment
Build student motivation with resources about high-interest applications.	**SE Inquiry Lab** Acid-Base Reaction, p. 291* ■	**TE Reading Toolbox** Assessing Prior Knowledge, p. 290 **SE Reading Toolbox** p. 292	📁 **Pretest** ■
TE Acid Safety, p. 294 **SE Acid Rain**, p. 301	**TE Demonstration** Tangy Taste of Acids, p. 293 **SE Inquiry Lab** Which Household Products Are Acidic and Which Are Basic? p. 296* ■ **TE Demonstration** A Natural pH Indicator, p. 299 📁 **CBL™ Probeware Lab** Determining the Concentration of an Acid Solution	**TE Science Skills** Interpreting Visuals, p. 294 **TE Science Skills** Interpreting Tables, p. 295 **SE Reading Toolbox** Cause-and-Effect Map, p. 296 **TE Reading Toolbox** Visual Literacy, p. 298 **SE Math Skills** Determining pH, p. 299 **TE Math Skills** Adding Exponents, p. 299	**TE Reteaching Key Ideas** Acids and Bases Review, p. 300 **TE Formative Assessment**, p. 300 📁 **Spanish Assessment** * ■ 📁 **Section Quiz** ■
TE Sodium Chloride, p. 305 📁 **Cross-Disciplinary Worksheet** Integrating Health—Preventing Heartburn and Indigestion	**TE Demonstration** Spectator Ions, p. 302 **TE Demonstration** Modeling a Neutralization Reaction, p. 304 **SE Skills Practice Lab** Quantities in an Acid-Base Reaction, pp. 314–315* ■ 📁 **Observation Lab** Investigating Acids and Bases	**TE Reading Toolbox** Word Meanings, p. 303 **SE Graphing Skills** Interpreting Titration Curves, p. 304 **SE Reading Toolbox** Everyday Words Used in Science, p. 305 **TE Science Skills** Naming Compounds, p. 305	**TE Reteaching Key Ideas** Neutralization Reactions, p. 306 **TE Formative Assessment**, p. 306 📁 **Spanish Assessment** * ■ 📁 **Section Quiz** ■
SE How Does Soap Remove Grease? p. 308 **TE Color-Safe Bleaches**, p. 310 **TE Acid-Base Reactions at Home**, p. 310 📁 **Cross-Disciplinary Worksheets** Connection to Social Studies—Detergents: Helpful or Harmful? • Integrating Biology—A Balance in the Body • Real World Applications—Car Batteries • Real World Applications—Cooking with Baking Powder	**TE Demonstration** Making Soap, p. 307 **SE Quick Lab** Detergents, p. 309* ■ **SE Inquiry Lab** What Does an Antacid Do? p. 312* ■	**TE Reading Toolbox** Using Words in Science, p. 311 **TE Science Skills** Interpreting Visuals, p. 311 **SE Reading Toolbox** Cause-and-Effect Map, p. 312	**TE Reteaching Key Ideas** Acids, Bases, and Salts at Home, p. 313 **TE Formative Assessment**, p. 313 📁 **Spanish Assessment** * ■ 📁 **Section Quiz** ■

See also Lab Generator

See also Holt Online Assessment Resources

Resources for Differentiated Instruction

English Learners
TE Properties of Acids and Bases, p. 297
TE Focus on Concepts, p. 304
📁 Differentiated Datasheets A, B, and C for Labs and Activities ■
📓 Study Guide A ■

Struggling Readers
TE Taking Notes, p. 295
TE Important Words, p. 310
📓 Interactive Reader

Special Education Students
TE Comparing Acids and Bases, p. 296
TE Making Models, p. 308

Alternative Assessment
TE Concept Mapping, p. 317

CHAPTER 9 Acids, Bases, and Salts

Overview

This chapter discusses the characteristics of acids and bases and the relationship between acid and base concentration and pH. Neutralization reactions and the formation of salts are introduced. Students also learn the household uses of acids, bases, and salts.

READING TOOLBOX

Assessing Prior Knowledge Students should understand the following concepts:
• moles
• ions
• writing formulas
• bonding
• chemical reactions
• chemical equations

MISCONCEPTION ALERT

Science education research has identified the following misconceptions about acids.

• Students believe that the primary activity of acids is "eating something away," and use this concept to explain and categorize all acid reactions. (The reactivity of acids depends on the strength and concentration of the acid. Point out that oranges, tomato juice, and sour candies contain acids. Use the foods and food labels to support your point.)

• Students believe that "strong acids" are always more caustic than "weak acids" regardless of concentration. (A concentrated solution of acetic acid—the weak acid in vinegar—can burn skin, but a dilute solution of phosphoric acid, a strong acid, is a component of some carbonated beverages. Bring in a carbonated beverage to support this point. Ask students to read various labels, identify the acids in the foods, and research whether the acids are strong or weak.)

Chapter Outline

❶ Acids, Bases, and pH
Acids
Bases
pH

❷ Reactions of Acids with Bases
Acid-Base Reactions
Salts

❸ Acids, Bases, and Salts in the Home
Cleaning Products
Personal-Care and Food Products

Why It Matters

Carbon dioxide dissolves in water to form an acid. This acid can then react to make a salt. This salt, calcium carbonate, will precipitate out of the water and, over millions of years, form limestone structures, such as these ice-covered rock terraces in Yellowstone National Park.

Chapter Correlations   National Science Education Standards

The following correlations show the National Science Standards that relate to this chapter. For the full text of the standards, see the National Science Education Standards at the front of the book.

PS 3a Chemical reactions occur all around us, for example in health care, cooking, cosmetics, and automobiles. (Sections 2, 3)

PS 3c A large number of important reactions involve the transfer of either electrons (oxidation/reduction reactions) or hydrogen ions (acid/base reactions) between reacting ions, molecules, or atoms. (Sections 2, 3; Skills Practice Lab: Quantities in an Acid-Base Reaction)

UCP 1 Systems, order, and organization (Section 1)

UCP 2 Evidence, models, and explanation (Section 2)

UCP 3 Constancy, change, and measurement (Section 2)

UCP 5 Form and function (Section 3)

SAI 1 Abilities necessary to do scientific inquiry (Sections 1, 3; Skills Practice Lab: Quantities in an Acid-Base Reaction)

SPSP 4 Environmental quality (Section 1)

InquiryLab ⏲ 10 min

Acid-Base Reaction

Squeeze the juice from **half of a lemon** into a **clean dish** to get about a teaspoon of juice. Add **one teaspoon of water** to the lemon juice, and stir with your finger. With a clean, dry **spoon**, add **1/2 teaspoon of baking soda,** a basic substance, to the diluted lemon juice.

Questions to Get You Started

1. Do you think that lemon juice is acidic or basic? Give reasons for your decision.

2. What happens when baking soda is added to the lemon juice?

3. What evidence do you see that a chemical reaction takes place?

InquiryLab

Teacher's Notes Emphasize that students should never taste anything in the lab, including items that would normally be considered food.

Materials per Group
- baking soda, ½ teaspoon
- dish
- lemon, one half
- teaspoon

Answers

1. Sample answer: I think lemon juice is acidic because lemons are sour.

2. Sample answer: When the lemon juice is added to baking soda, the baking soda fizzes and bubbles form.

3. Bubbles are evidence that a chemical reaction is taking place because they indicate that a gas is formed.

Key Resources

📋 **Datasheet**
Acid-Base Reaction

Science Terms

Sample answer: A base can be a head-quarters or the bottom of an object. In science, a base is a compound that increases the number of hydroxide ions in a solution.

Classification

Sample table:

Class	Defining Characteristic
strong bases	formed from metal ions and hydroxide ions
weak bases	do not contain hydroxide ions but form them in water
soaps	hydrocarbon chains that have a carboxylate group
detergents	hydrocarbon chains that have a sulfonate group; do not form scum in hard water
disinfectants	kill bacteria and viruses

Graphic Organizers

Sample cause-and-effect map:

These reading tools can help you learn the material in this chapter. For more information on how to use these and other tools, see **Appendix A.**

Science Terms

Everyday Words Used in Science Many words used in science are familiar words from everyday speech. However, the meanings of these everyday words are often different from their meanings in scientific contexts.

Your Turn Before you read this chapter, write down an informal definition of what the word *base* means to you. As you come across this word in the chapter, write the scientific definitions next to your informal definition. For each definition, write a sentence that uses the word *base* correctly.

Classification

Classifying Acids and Bases
Classification is a tool for organizing objects and ideas by grouping them into categories. Groups are classified by defining characteristics. For example, the table below shows how acids can be classified by their strength.

CLASS	DEFINING CHARACTERISTIC
strong acids	ionize completely in water
weak acids	do not ionize completely

Your Turn As you read the chapter, create a table like the one shown here for the following classes of substance: strong bases, weak bases, soaps, detergents, and disinfectants.

Graphic Organizers

Cause-and-Effect Maps You can use cause-and-effect maps to show visually how the relationships in physical processes depend on one another. To make a cause-and-effect map, follow these steps:

❶ Draw a box, and write a cause inside the box. You can have as many cause boxes as you want.

❷ Draw another box to represent an effect of the cause. You can have as many effect boxes as you want.

❸ Connect each cause box to an effect box or boxes with an arrow.

❹ If an effect is also the cause of another effect(s), you may connect the effect box to another effect box or boxes.

Your Turn As you read Section 1, complete on a separate sheet of paper the cause-and-effect map started below. Add at least two more effects.

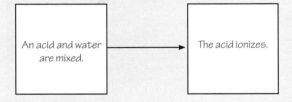

Acids, Bases, and pH

Key Ideas

❯ What are the properties of acids?

❯ What are the properties of bases?

❯ How is pH related to the concentration of hydronium ions and hydroxide ions in solution?

Key Terms

acid

indicator

electrolyte

base

pH

Why It Matters

Acid rain is a type of pollution that can have harmful effects on many parts of the environment, including animals, plants, and buildings.

❯Focus

This section describes the ionization of strong acids and the dissociation of strong bases in water. The section distinguishes between solutions of strong and weak acids and solutions of strong and weak bases. The section closes by introducing the concept of pH and relating it to the concentration of hydronium and hydroxide ions in solution.

Bellringer

Use the Bellringer transparency to prepare students for this section.

Demonstrate

Tangy Taste of Acids Have students taste samples of carbonated water (club soda) and unsweetened lemon juice. Ask students to compare these flavors with that of plain water. Be sure to differentiate this demonstration from a lab activity, in which students should never taste liquids. Explain to students that carbonated water contains carbonic acid, a weak acid that forms when carbon dioxide dissolves in water. Lemon juice has a tangy flavor because lemons contain citric acid, another weak acid. Ask students to think of other foods that have an acidic taste. (Sample answers: orange juice, lemonade, some sodas, and some candies)

LS Intrapersonal

Does the thought of eating a lemon cause your mouth to pucker? You expect that sour taste of a lemon. Eating a lime or a dill pickle may cause you to have a similar response.

Acids

Each of the foods shown in **Figure 1** tastes sour because it contains an acid. Citrus fruits, such as grapefruits, lemons, limes, and oranges, contain citric acid. Apples contain malic acid, and grapes contain tartaric acid.

When acids dissolve in water, they *ionize*, which means that they form ions. When **acids** ionize, they form hydrogen ions, H^+, which attach to water molecules to make hydronium ions, H_3O^+. These hydronium ions give acids their properties. ❯ **Acids taste sour, cause indicators to change color, and conduct electric current. They are also corrosive and can damage materials, including your skin.** Blue litmus paper contains an indicator that turns red in the presence of an acid, as **Figure 1** shows. Indicators can help you determine if a substance is acidic.

acid (AS id) any compound that increases the number of hydronium ions when dissolved in water

indicator (IN di KAYT uhr) a compound that can reversibly change color depending on conditions such as pH

Figure 1 Many fruits, such as lemons, taste sour because they contain acids. Acids, such as the citric acid in orange juice, turn blue litmus paper red.

Key Resources

 Teaching Transparencies
TM26 Some Common Acids
C23 pH Scale
TM27 Some Common Bases

Visual Concepts
Acids
Common Acids
Bases
pH
pH Range for Common Substances

Datasheet
Which Household Products Are Acidic, and Which Are Basic?

Science Skills Worksheets
Scientific Notation
Operations with Exponents
Entering Exponents

Math Skills Worksheet
Determining pH

Teaching Key Ideas

Properties of Acids Ask students how they can determine whether a food contains an acid. (Sample answer: Acids have a sour taste.) Have the class make a list on the board of foods that are acidic. (Sample answers: citrus fruits, pickles, salad dressings that contain vinegar, yogurt, sour cream, and sour candies)
LS Verbal

Science Skills

Interpreting Visuals Ask students how an acid behaves in solution. (When dissolved in water, an acid donates hydrogen ions to form hydronium ions.) Have students look at the molecular models of nitric acid and acetic acid. Ask them how the compounds HNO_3 and CH_3COOH can be classified as acids. (Both compounds transfer hydrogen ions, H^+, to water to form hydronium ions, H_3O^+.) Have students refer to **Figure 2** and **Figure 3**. Ask them to describe the evidence that indicates that nitric acid is a strong electrolyte but acetic acid is a weak electrolyte. (Sample answer: In **Figure 2,** the brightly lit bulb indicates that a strong current is moving through the circuit. Thus, the nitric acid solution is a good conductor of electrical current. In **Figure 3** the dimly lit bulb indicates little current is moving through the circuit. Thus, the acetic acid solution contains a weak electrolyte.)
LS Visual

Figure 2 Nitric acid, HNO_3, is a strong electrolyte and a strong acid because it ionizes completely in water to form hydronium ions, H_3O^+, and nitrate ions, NO_3^-.

Figure 3 Acetic acid, CH_3COOH, is a weak acid and a weak electrolyte because only a few of the molecules that are dissolved in water ionize to form hydronium ions, H_3O^+, and acetate ions, CH_3COO^-.

Strong acids ionize completely.

All acids ionize when they are dissolved in water. The ionization process shown below occurs when nitric acid is added to water. The single arrow pointing to the right shows that nitric acid ionizes completely in water.

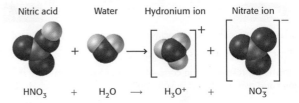

Nitric acid   Water   Hydronium ion   Nitrate ion

$$HNO_3 \;+\; H_2O \;\longrightarrow\; H_3O^+ \;+\; NO_3^-$$

When nitric acid ionizes, it forms hydronium ions and nitrate ions. These charged ions are able to move around in the solution and conduct electricity, as you see in **Figure 2.** A substance that conducts electricity when the substance is dissolved in water is an **electrolyte.**

Solutions of some acids, such as nitric acid, conduct electricity well. Nitric acid, HNO_3, is a *strong acid* because all of the molecules that are dissolved in water ionize. Other strong acids behave similarly to nitric acid when dissolved in water. A solution of sulfuric acid in water, for example, conducts electric current in car batteries. Strong acids are strong electrolytes because solutions of these acids contain as many hydronium ions as the acid can possibly form.

Weak acids do not ionize completely.

Solutions of *weak acids*, such as acetic acid, CH_3COOH, do not conduct electricity as well as nitric acid does. When acetic acid is added to water, the equilibrium represented by the reaction below is reached.

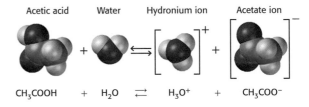

Acetic acid   Water   Hydronium ion   Acetate ion

$$CH_3COOH \;+\; H_2O \;\rightleftarrows\; H_3O^+ \;+\; CH_3COO^-$$

When acetic acid is dissolved in water, some molecules of acetic acid combine with water molecules to form ions. Many of the ions then recombine to form molecules of acetic acid. Because there are few charged ions in a solution of acetic acid, the solution does not conduct electricity very well, as **Figure 3** shows. Weak acids, such as acetic acid, are weak electrolytes.

Why It **Matters**

Acid Safety Ask students if they would ever put an acidic solution in their eyes. (Most students will respond negatively.) Ask students to describe why they would or would not put an acidic solution in their eyes. (Most students will say that acids will "eat away" and damage the eyeball.) Point out that some types of eyewash contain boric acid. Tell students that in this section they will learn that the effect of an acidic solution depends on the acid and its concentration. Caution students not to get acids in the laboratory on their skin or in their eyes.

Differentiated Instruction

Basic Learners

Food Labels Have students visit a grocery store or provide ingredient labels from up to ten food or beverage products that contain an acid in their ingredients. The students should make a list of the acids in each product and determine if the product tastes sweet, sour, or bitter. Have students review the ingredient labels from cleaning products and identify those that have ingredients that contain hydroxide. Students should list the product's hydroxide-containing ingredients. **LS** Verbal/Logical

Figure 4 Some Common Acids

Acid	Formula	Strength	Uses
Hydrochloric acid	HCl	strong	cleaning masonry; treating metal before plating or painting; adjusting the pH of swimming pools
Sulfuric acid	H_2SO_4	strong	manufacturing fertilizer and chemicals; most-used industrial chemical; the electrolyte in car batteries
Nitric acid	HNO_3	strong	manufacturing fertilizers and explosives
Acetic acid	CH_3COOH	weak	manufacturing chemicals, plastics, and pharmaceuticals; the acid in vinegar
Formic acid	HCOOH	weak	dyeing textiles; the acid in stinging ants
Citric acid	$H_3C_6H_5O_7$	weak	manufacturing flavorings and soft drinks; the acid in citrus fruits (oranges, lemons, and limes)

All of the acids used in familiar products produce hydronium ions when in water solution.

Science Skills

Interpreting Visuals Have students examine **Figure 4.** Explain that acetic, formic, and citric acid are classified as organic acids because they contain carbon. Hydrochloric, sulfuric, and nitric acids are classified as inorganic acids. Ask students if the organic acids listed in the table form strong or weak acids. Ask students which type of acid—inorganic or organic—listed in the table ionizes more completely. (Inorganic acids.) Point out that inorganic acids tend to form strong acids in solution while organic acids tend to form weak acids in solution.
LS Visual

Concentrated acid can be dangerous.

Some examples of common strong and weak acids and their uses are listed in **Figure 4**. Acids are used in many manufacturing processes and are necessary to many organisms. However, strong acids are corrosive and can damage living tissue. For example, your stomach normally contains a dilute solution of hydrochloric acid that helps you digest food, but concentrated hydrochloric acid can burn your skin.

Even weak acids are not always safe to handle. Most vinegar is a 5% solution of acetic acid in water, but concentrated acetic acid can damage the skin. The vapors are harmful to the eyes, mouth, and lungs. To be safe, always wear safety goggles, gloves, and a laboratory apron when working with acids. Never taste a chemical to determine if it is an acid.

Reading Check What precautions should you take when working with acids? (See Appendix E for answers to Reading Checks.)

Bases

Many common household substances contain bases. Like acids, bases share common properties. **❯ Bases have a bitter taste, and solutions of bases feel slippery. Solutions of bases also conduct electric current, cause indicators to change color, and can damage the skin.** When **bases** dissolve in water, they form hydroxide ions, OH^-. Some basic compounds contain hydroxide ions, but others do not. Bases that do not contain hydroxide ions react with water molecules to form hydroxide ions. The hydroxide ions cause the indicator in red litmus paper to turn blue.

Academic Vocabulary

process (PRAH SES) a set of steps, events, or changes

electrolyte (ee LEK troh LIET) a substance that dissolves in water to give a solution that conducts an electric current

base (BAYS) any compound that increases the number of hydroxide ions when dissolved in water

MISCONCEPTION ALERT

Hydrogen Atoms and Acid Strength Students might think that the more hydrogen atoms an acid has, the stronger it is. Acids that have more than one acidic hydrogen atom per molecule ionize by losing the atoms one at a time. Each hydrogen atom is more difficult to lose than the one before it because the hydrogen is being lost from a negative ion. Phosphoric acid, H_3PO_4, loses one hydrogen atom relatively easily, leaving an $H_2PO_4^-$ ion. The $H_2PO_4^-$ ion loses a hydrogen atom with more difficulty because it is negatively charged. HPO_4^{2-} ions lose their final hydrogen ion with the most difficulty. Phosphoric acid contains three acidic hydrogen atoms, but it is weaker than nitric acid, which has only one hydrogen atom, because phosphoric acid does not ionize as easily.

Differentiated Instruction

Struggling Readers

Taking Notes Provide students with self-adhesive notes. Have students read the section silently and write questions about those passages that they do not understand on the self-adhesive notes. Be sure students study figures and tables to help clarify the relevant passages. Pair students and have them discuss the passages each found difficult. If passages remain unclear, have the pair keep track of their questions for later class discussion or teacher explanation. **LS** Verbal/Interpersonal

Teaching Key Ideas

Slippery Bases Explain to students that bases feel slippery because they react with fats and oils in the skin. Weak bases, such as soap, do not harm skin, but strong bases do. Ask students to suggest a reason why drain cleaners are made of strong bases. (Sample answer: Fats and greases often clog drains. Bases react with fats, dissolving them and clearing the drain.)

InquiryLab

Teacher's Notes Have students test various acidic and basic substances including baking powder, baking soda, milk, mineral water, bleach, vinegar, soft drinks, mayonnaise, and laundry detergent.

Materials per Group
• litmus paper, red and blue
• pipets, plastic
• unknown samples, liquid, 5 mL each
• unknown samples, solid, 1 g each
• water

Answers to Analysis
1. Answers may vary depending on the substances tested. Soft drinks, white vinegar, and mayonnaise are acids and turn blue litmus paper red. Baking soda, bleach, dishwashing liquid, and laundry detergent are basic and turn red litmus paper blue.
2. Answers may vary depending on the substances tested. Tap water and sugar are neutral. They do not change the color of red or blue litmus paper.

MISCONCEPTION ALERT

Strength and Concentration
Strong bases do not always produce a large number of hydroxide ions. Calcium hydroxide is a strong base, but it does not produce a large number of hydroxide ions because of its low solubility.

InquiryLab   Which Household Products Are Acidic, and Which Are Basic? 🕐 20 min

Procedure
1. Prepare a sample of **each substance** that you will test. If the substance is a liquid, pour about 5 mL of it into a **small beaker.** If the substance is a solid, place a small amount of it in a beaker and add about **5 mL of water.** Label each beaker clearly with the name of the substance that is in the beaker.

2. Use a **disposable plastic pipet** to transfer a drop of liquid from one of the samples to **red litmus paper.** Then, transfer another drop of liquid from the same sample to **blue litmus paper.**
3. Record your observations.
4. Repeat steps 2 and 3 for each sample. Be sure to use a clean pipet to transfer each sample.

Analysis
1. Which substances are acidic? Which are basic? How did you make your determinations?
2. Which substances are not acids or bases? How did you make your determinations?

READING TOOLBOX

Cause-and-Effect Map
Draw a cause-and-effect map that shows why a solution of sodium hydroxide dissolved in water is basic.

Many common bases contain hydroxide ions.

Like strong acids, *strong bases* produce as many ions as possible when they dissolve. Strong bases are ionic compounds that contain a metal ion and a hydroxide ion. These strong bases are also known as *metal hydroxides.* When a metal hydroxide is dissolved in water, the metal ions and the hydroxide ions *dissociate,* or separate.

Sodium hydroxide, NaOH, is an example of a metal hydroxide. It is found in some drain cleaners. When sodium hydroxide dissolves, it dissociates completely. Solutions of sodium hydroxide conduct electricity well. So, like all strong bases, sodium hydroxide is a strong electrolyte. The dissociation of sodium hydroxide in water is shown below.

$$NaOH \rightarrow Na^+ + OH^-$$

Some metal hydroxides, such as calcium hydroxide and magnesium hydroxide, are not very soluble in water. However, they are still strong bases because all of the ions that do dissolve do separate. The strength of an acid or of a base does not depend on the concentration of the solution. Calcium hydroxide is used to treat soil that is too acidic. **Figure 5** lists other useful bases and shows some bases that you might find around your home.

✔ **Reading Check** Why are metal hydroxides strong bases?

READING TOOLBOX

Cause-and-Effect Map Sample cause-and-effect map:

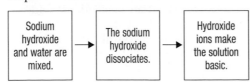

| Sodium hydroxide and water are mixed. | → | The sodium hydroxide dissociates. | → | Hydroxide ions make the solution basic. |

Differentiated Instruction

Special Education Students

Comparing Acids and Bases Draw a 3-column table on the board. Label the left column "Acids," the center column "Acids and Bases," and the right column "Bases." Ask students to fill in the diagram with details from this section. (Sample answers: Acids—have a sour flavor, react with metals; Acids and Bases—change colors of indicators, conduct electric current, have many uses; Bases—have a bitter flavor and a slippery feel) **LS** Logical/Visual

Some bases ionize in water to form hydroxide ions.

Even though molecules of ammonia, NH_3, do not contain hydroxide ions, ammonia is still a base. It forms hydroxide ions when it dissolves in water through an ionization process, which is shown below. In this process, water donates a hydrogen ion to ammonia to form an ammonium ion, NH_4^+, and leaves a hydroxide ion, OH^-, behind.

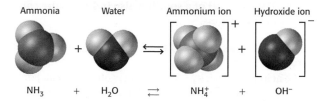

| Ammonia | | Water | | Ammonium ion | | Hydroxide ion |
| NH_3 | $+$ | H_2O | $\rightleftharpoons$ | NH_4^+ | $+$ | OH^- |

A solution of ammonia in water is a poor conductor of electricity. Only some of the ammonia molecules actually become ammonium ions when ammonia dissolves. So, an ammonia solution consists mostly of water and dissolved ammonia molecules, along with a few ammonium ions and hydroxide ions. Ammonia is a much weaker base than the metal hydroxides, which dissociate completely. Weak bases, such as ammonia, are also weak electrolytes.

Bases can be very dangerous in concentrated form. Strong bases, such as sodium hydroxide and potassium hydroxide, can be dangerous even in fairly dilute form. Bases attack living tissue very rapidly. To protect yourself when working with bases, always wear safety goggles, gloves, and a laboratory apron. If possible, work only with very dilute bases.

Figure 5 Some Common Bases

Base	Formula	Strength	Uses
Potassium hydroxide (potash)	KOH	strong	manufacturing soap; absorbing carbon dioxide from flue gases; dyeing products
Sodium hydroxide (lye)	NaOH	strong	manufacturing soap; refining petroleum; cleaning drains; manufacturing synthetic fibers
Calcium hydroxide	$Ca(OH)_2$	strong	treating acidic soil; treating lakes polluted by acid precipitation; making mortar, plaster, and cement
Ammonia	NH_3	weak	fertilizing soil; manufacturing other fertilizers; manufacturing nitric acid; making cleaning solutions
Methylamine	CH_3NH_2	weak	manufacturing dyes and medicines; tanning leather
Aniline	$C_6H_5NH_2$	weak	manufacturing dyes and varnishes; used as a solvent

These household items contain bases, so they turn red litmus paper blue.

Science Skills

Interpreting Visuals Write the chemical equation for dissociation of potassium hydroxide in solution on the board: $KOH \rightarrow K^+ + OH^-$. Ask students what process forms the hydroxide ions in solution (dissociation). Now, have students examine a molecular model for the addition of ammonia to water. Ask students to describe the role a water molecule plays in the formation of hydroxide ions when ammonia dissolves in water. (A water molecule donates a hydrogen ion to the ammonia molecule.) Ask students: What process forms ammonium ions and hydroxide ions in solution? (ionization) **LS Verbal**

Science Skills

Interpreting Tables Have students examine **Figure 5** and identify which bases listed in the table are strong bases (potassium hydroxide, sodium hydroxide, and calcium hydroxide). Ask students what ion is common to each compound (hydroxide ion). Ask what the cations in these compounds have in common. (They are all metal ions.) Point out that strong bases are also known as metal hydroxides. Have students recall that inorganic acids tend to be strong and organic acids tend to be weak. Ask students to cite information in the table to compare inorganic bases and organic bases. (With the exception of ammonia, the inorganic bases are strong bases and the organic bases are weak bases.) **LS Visual**

Differentiated Instruction

English Learners

Properties of Acids and Bases Have students work in pairs or small groups. Ensure that each English learner is paired with an English speaker. Have students brainstorm properties, examples, and uses of acids and bases. Have students use the lists to write books for younger students that explain in simple language what acids and bases are and how they are used. Ask students to create outlines and rough drafts for the books. Check these items for clarity and scientific accuracy before students finalize their books. Have the English learners translate the books into their native language alongside the English text. Encourage students to illustrate their books. Consider having students use the completed books to teach another class about acids and bases. **LS Verbal/Interpersonal**

Teaching Key Ideas

Acid and Base Definitions Most acids and bases in this chapter fit the definitions of acids and bases that Svante Arrhenius, a Swedish chemist, formulated in 1887. Arrhenius defined an acid as a substance that produces hydrogen ions in water and a base as a substance that produces hydroxide ions in water. In 1923, the Brønsted-Lowry theory, proposed by a Danish and an English chemist, defined an acid as a proton donor and a base as a proton acceptor.

Gilbert Lewis expanded the definition further by defining an acid as an electron-pair acceptor and a base as an electron-pair donor, thus including substances that do not include hydrogen.

READING TOOLBOX

Visual Literacy Have students refer to **Figure 6.** Ask students to predict the color of the pH paper for water. (The paper would be light green because the pH of water is neutral, or 7.0.) Have students explain why water has a neutral pH. (For each transfer of a hydrogen ion from one water molecule to another, one molecule ionizes to a hydronium ion and the other ionizes to a hydroxide ion. So, the concentration of hyrdronium ions and hydroxide ions remains equal.) Ask students to predict the color of the pH paper for artichokes, which have pH 5.6 (orange); rhubarb, which has a pH of 3.1 (golden-yellow); and chocolate cake, which has a pH of 7.6 (green). **LS Visual**

pH (PEE AYCH) a value that is used to express the acidity or basicity (alkalinity) of a system; each whole number on the scale indicates a tenfold change in acidity

pH

You can tell if a solution is acidic or basic by using an indicator, such as litmus paper. But to know exactly how acidic or basic a solution is, you must measure the concentration of hydronium ions, H_3O^+. **> The pH of a solution indicates its concentration of H_3O^+ ions. In solutions, the concentration of hydronium ions is related to the concentration of hydroxide ions, OH^-. The pH of a solution also indicates the concentration of OH^- ions.**

A pH value corresponds to the concentration of hydronium ions.

The acidity or basicity of a solution is often critical. For example, enzymes in your body will not work if your blood is too acidic or too basic. A pH value can tell you how acidic or basic a solution is. A pH value can even tell you if a solution is *neutral*—that is, neither an acid nor a base.

Typically, the pH values of solutions range from 0 to 14, as **Figure 6** shows. In neutral solutions, or in substances such as pure water, the pH is 7. In neutral solutions, the concentration of hydronium ions is equal to the concentration of hydroxide ions. Acidic solutions have a pH of less than 7. In acidic solutions, such as apple juice, the concentration of hydronium ions is greater than the concentration of hydroxide ions. Basic solutions have a pH of greater than 7. In basic solutions, the concentration of hydroxide ions is greater than the concentration of hydronium ions.

✓ **Reading Check** What does the pH of a solution tell you?

Figure 6 The pH of a solution is easily measured by moistening a piece of pH paper with the solution and then comparing the color of the pH paper with the color scale on the dispenser of the pH paper.

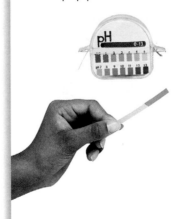

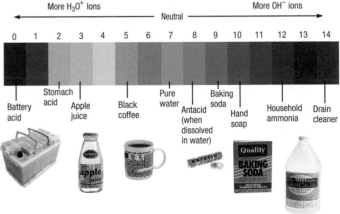

Differentiated Instruction

Advanced Learners

pH of Blood Have students research the effect on pH of dissolving carbon dioxide in water. Then, have them investigate why hyperventilation, which is breathing too rapidly and deeply, can upset the pH of the blood. Students should also explain to the class why breathing into a paper bag decreases the effects of hyperventilation on pH. Have students make a poster showing the chemical reactions involved. **LS Verbal/Visual**

You can find pH from the concentration of a strong acid.

The concentration of a substance in a solution is often described by *molarity* (M), or the number of moles of the substance per liter of solution. The hydronium ion concentration of pure water at 25 °C is 0.0000001 mol/L, or 1×10^{-7} M.

Writing the H_3O^+ concentration of a solution as a power of 10 will help you determine the pH. The pH is the negative of the power of 10 that is used to describe the concentration of H_3O^+ ions. So, the pH of pure water is 7. The pH of apple juice is about 3, so the concentration of H_3O^+ ions is 1×10^{-3} M.

You can use the concentration of a strong acid in solution to calculate the pH of the solution. In a solution, strong acids such as HCl and HNO_3 produce one hydronium ion for each particle of acid that dissolves. So, the concentration of hydronium ions in a solution of strong acid is the same as the concentration of the acid itself.

SCI LINKS.
www.scilinks.org
Topic: pH
Code: HK81129

Math Skills Determining pH

Determine the pH of a 0.0001 M solution of the strong acid HCl.

Identify
List the given and unknown values.

Given:
  concentration of HCl in solution = 0.0001 M

Unknown:
  pH

Plan
Write the molar concentration of hydroxide ions in scientific notation.

HCl is completely ionized into H_3O^+ and Cl^- ions.
concentration of H_3O^+ ions in solution = concentration of HCl in solution = 0.0001 M = 1×10^{-4} M

Solve
The pH is the negative of the power of 10 in the H_3O^+ concentration.

concentration of H_3O^+ ions = 1×10^{-4} M
$pH = -(-4) = 4$

Practice

1. Calculate the pH of a 1×10^{-4} M solution of HBr, a strong acid.
2. Determine the pH of a 0.01 M solution of HNO_3, a strong acid.
3. Nitric acid, HNO_3, is a strong acid. The pH of a solution of HNO_3 is 3. What is the concentration of the solution?

For more practice, visit **go.hrw.com** and enter keyword **HK8MP**.

Practice Hint

> If a solution contains a base, you should expect the pH to be greater than 7. If the solution contains an acid, the pH will be less than 7.

> To find the concentration of a solution of strong acid from its pH, multiply the pH value by −1. Then, use the result as a power of 10. The result is the concentration of the acid in moles per liter (mol/L).

Demonstrate

A Natural pH Indicator For this demonstration you will need an overhead projector, pipets, red cabbage juice, spot plate (24-well), and various household products (e.g. ammonia, vinegar, detergent, fruti juice, diluted drain cleaner).

Before the demonstration, prepare red cabbage juice by placing a half-head of red cabbage into a blender. Fill the blender with water and chop for one minute. Strain the liquid into a jar that has a tight-fitting lid. Start the demonstration by placing the spot plate on the overhead projector. Pipet a small amount of each of the household products into the wells on the plate. Pipet a few drops of red cabbage juice into each of the wells. Have students observe the color changes of the solutions. Copy the table below on the board and have students use it to determine the pH of each of the household products.

pH	Cabbage Juice Color
2–3	Red
3–4	Pink
4–6	Purple
6–8	Blue-Green
8–12	Green

LS Visual

Teaching Key Ideas

pH and Concentration Remind students that pH is the *negative* power of ten of the hydronium ion concentration in an acid or base. Ask students to describe what happens to the pH when the acid concentration increases. (pH decreases.) What happens to the hydroxide ion concentration when acid concentration increases? (The hydroxide ion concentration decreases) What does it mean if the pH is negative? (Hydronium ion concentration is greater than 1 M)
LS Verbal/Logical

Math Skills

Adding Exponents Illustrate the rule of adding exponents when multiplying quantities in scientific notation by using the following examples. Have students write the quantities in scientific notation as well as the answers.
- 100×10 (1000; $(1 \times 10^2) \times (1 \times 10^1) = 1 \times 10^3$)
- $1/100 \times 1/10$ (1/1000; $(1 \times 10^{-2}) \times (1 \times 10^{-1}) = 1 \times 10^{-3}$)

LS Logical

Answers to Practice
1. $pH = -(-4) = 4$
2. 0.01 M = 1×10^{-2} M; $pH = -(-2) = 2$
3. concentration = 1×10^{-3} M

❯Close

Answer to caption question

The tomato mixture is acidic because the pH meter reads a pH value of 4.0.

Reteaching Key Ideas

Acids and Bases Review Have students make an outline of this section using the headings and subheadings. Their outlines should list the information about the properties of acids and bases. When the outlines are complete, list the following properties and have students identify whether the property applies to an acid, a base, or both: pH above 7 (base), pH below 7 (acid), produces hydronium ions (acid), produces hydroxide ions (base), and can conduct electric current (both). **LS Verbal/Visual**

Formative Assessment

How does a strong acid differ from a weak acid?

A. A strong acid has a higher concentration. (Incorrect. The strength of an acid depends on its degree of ionization.)

B. A strong acid has a lower pH. (Incorrect. pH is a measure of hydronium ion concentration. The pH depends on both strength of the acid and concentration. A concentrated weak acid can have lower pH than a less concentrated strong acid does.)

C. A strong acid ionizes to a greater degree. (Correct. The strength of an acid is a measure of the degree to which it ionizes.)

D. A strong acid has more hydrogen atoms. (Incorrect. The strength of an acid depends on degree of ionization.)

Figure 7 A pH meter can measure the H_3O^+ concentration precisely. **Is the tomato mixture acidic or basic?**

Small differences in pH mean large differences in acidity.

Because pH is the negative of the power of 10 of hydronium ion concentration, small differences in pH mean large differences in the hydronium ion concentration. For example, the pH of apple juice is about 3, and the pH of coffee is about 5. This difference of two pH units means that apple juice is 10^2, or 100 times, as acidic as coffee. When antacid tablets are dissolved in water, they form a basic solution with a pH of about 8. So, coffee is about 10^3, or 1,000 times, as acidic as a solution of antacid tablets.

There is more than one way to measure pH.

There are several indicators in pH paper that change color at different pH values. A pH meter may also be used to measure pH, as **Figure 7** shows. Because ions in a solution have an electric charge, a pH meter can measure pH by determining the electric current created by the movement of the ions in the solution. If you use a pH meter properly, you can determine the pH of a solution more precisely than is possible if you use pH paper.

Section 1 Review

KEY IDEAS

1. **Explain** how a strong acid and a weak acid behave differently when each is dissolved in water.

2. **List** three properties of bases.

3. **Arrange** the following substances in order of increasing acidity: vinegar (pH = 2.8), gastric juices from inside your stomach (pH = 2.0), and a soft drink (pH = 3.4).

CRITICAL THINKING

4. **Compare and Contrast** What happens when a weak acid and a weak base ionize in water?

5. **Designing Experiments** Using litmus paper as an example, describe how you would use an indicator to find out if a solution is acidic, basic, or neutral.

6. **Forming Models** Pure water ionizes to produce hydronium ions and hydroxide ions. Write a chemical equation that shows how two water molecules can react to make these ions.

7. **Drawing Conclusions** A solution of an acid in water has a pH of 4, which is slightly acidic. Is this solution a weak acid? Explain your answer.

8. **Applying Ideas** Classify the following solutions as acidic, basic, or neutral.
   a. a soap solution, pH = 9
   b. a sour liquid, pH = 5
   c. a solution that has 4 times as many hydronium ions as hydroxide ions
   d. pure water

Math Skills

9. What is the pH of a 0.01 M solution of the strong acid $HClO_4$, perchloric acid?

10. A basic solution has a pH of 11. What is the hydronium ion concentration in this solution?

Answers to Section Review

1. A strong acid ionizes completely to form H_3O^+ ions and anions. A weak acid does not ionize completely, so some molecules of the acid reform after ionizing.

2. Bases have a bitter taste, feel slippery, and turn red litmus paper blue.

3. The pH of a solution decreases as acidity increases, so the order is soft drink, vinegar, gastric juice.

4. For both weak bases and weak acids, only a few molecules separate into ions. The ionization of a weak acid and a weak base differ in that the molecules of a weak acid ionize and the protons from the acid form hydronium ions with water molecules. The weak base causes water molecules to separate, and a proton from the water is transferred to the base molecule, forming hydroxide ions.

5. Sample answer: I would test the solution with red and blue litmus paper. If the solution turns blue litmus paper red, it is an acid. If the solution turns red litmus paper blue, it is basic. If the solution does not change the color of either type of litmus paper, it is neutral.

6. $2H_2O \rightleftharpoons H_3O^+ + OH^-$

7. Sample answer: The solution may or may not be a solution of a weak acid. It could be a weak acid, or it could be a 1×10^{-4} M solution of a strong acid, such as HCl.

Answers continued on p. 321A

Acid Rain

Normal rain has a pH of about 5.6, so it is slightly acidic. Acid rain is a type of pollution in which the precipitation has a pH that is less than 5.0. Acid rain results from emissions of sulfur dioxide, SO_2, and nitric oxide, NO, which are gases from coal-burning power plants and automobiles. The gases react with compounds in the air to form sulfuric acid, H_2SO_4, and nitric acid, HNO_3.

EYE ON THE ENVIRONMENT

Most acid rain in the United States has a pH of about 4.3. Not only does acid rain increase the acidity of lakes, streams, and soil, it also changes their chemical composition.

Acid rain has an adverse effect on plants and wildlife. It can reduce fish populations. When there are fewer fish, animals who eat the fish, such as the loon, may not find enough food to feed themselves and their young.

Acid rain can also damage human-made structures. Over time, acid rain reacts with minerals in limestone and marble, so the stone erodes.

SCiLINKS.

www.scilinks.org
Topic: Acid
    Precipitation
Code: **HK81690**

YOUR TURN **UNDERSTANDING CONCEPTS**
1. What causes acid rain?

ONLINE RESEARCH
2. Find out how acid rain affects forests, and create a poster that explains what you find.

Acid Rain The term *acid rain* is commonly used to mean the deposition of acidic components in rain, snow, fog, dew, or dry particles. Because precipitation other than rain can be acidic, the more accurate term is *acid precipitation*. Distilled water, which contains no carbon dioxide, has a neutral pH of 7. Unpolluted rain has a slightly acidic pH of 5.6 because carbon dioxide and water in the air react to form carbonic acid, a weak acid.

Acidity in rain is measured by collecting samples of rain and measuring its pH. To find the distribution of rain acidity, weather conditions are monitored and rain samples are collected at sites all over the country. The areas of greatest acidity (lowest pH values) are located in the Northeastern United States. This pattern of high acidity is caused by the large number of cities, the dense population, and the concentration of power and industrial plants in the Northeast. In addition, the prevailing wind direction brings storms and pollution to the Northeast from the Midwest, and dust from the soil and rocks in the Northeastern United States is less likely to neutralize acidity in the rain than the more alkaline dust of the deserts in the western part of the country.

Answers to Your Turn

1. Acid rain is caused by sulfur dioxide and nitric oxide gases, which are emitted by coal-burning power plants and automobiles. These gases react in the air to form sulfuric acid and nitric acid.
2. Answers may vary. Student posters should show the effect of the acidification of forest soil, the effect of acid rain on foliage, and the resulting effects on forest animals.

READING TOOLBOX

Visual Literacy Because acid rain is a form of pollution, students may think they can detect it by looking at an affected stream or lake. Have students look at the photo of a stream on this page. Point out that there is no way to determine whether the stream in the photo is acidic without measuring the pH. A stream that has a low pH does not appear to be different from a stream that has a more neutral pH. **LS Visual**

Reactions of Acids with Bases

This section opens with a discussion of chemical equations for acid-base reactions and defines a neutralization reaction and its products. It then describes titrations and the equivalence point in a neutralization reaction. The section closes with a discussion of the composition of a salt.

Bellringer

Use the Bellringer transparency to prepare students for this section.

Demonstrate

Spectator Ions For this demonstration you will need a beaker, hydrochloric acid, 6 M (1 mL), pipets (2), and sodium hydroxide, 6 M (1 mL). Allow approximately 10 minutes.

Briefly discuss with students the principles of neutralization described on this page. Pipet 1 mL each of 6 M HCl and 6 M NaOH into the beaker. Heat the beaker on a hot plate until the water evaporates. Have students observe the crystals. Ask students: What ions are in the hydrochloric acid, HCl, solution? (H_3O^+, Cl^-) What ions are in the sodium hydroxide, NaOH, solution? (Na^+, OH^-) What ions make up the crystals remaining in the beaker after the reaction? (Na^+, Cl^-) Did the sodium and chloride ions participate in the neutralization reaction? (no) What are these sodium and chloride ions called? (spectator ions)

LS Visual

Key Ideas

> What is a neutralization reaction?

> To a chemist, what exactly is a salt?

Key Terms

neutralization reaction

salt

Why It Matters

A household water softener uses a salt to remove ions from water.

Have you ever used an antacid to feel better when you have an upset stomach or heartburn? Heartburn has nothing to do with your heart. You get heartburn when your stomach's solution of hydrochloric acid, HCl, irritates the lining of your esophagus. The base in antacids reacts with the acid to reduce the acidity of the solution in your stomach.

Acid-Base Reactions

> **A neutralization reaction is the reaction between an acid and a base.** When hydrochloric acid and the base magnesium hydroxide (in an antacid, for example) are mixed, a neutralization reaction happens. As **Figure 1** shows, these types of reactions have many uses.

Neutralization is a reaction between ions.

A solution of a strong acid, such as hydrochloric acid, ionizes completely, as the following equation shows.

$$HCl + H_2O \rightarrow H_3O^+ + Cl^-$$

A solution of a strong base, such as sodium hydroxide, dissociates completely, as the following equation shows.

$$NaOH \rightarrow Na^+ + OH^-$$

If the two solutions are mixed together, the following neutralization reaction takes place.

$$H_3O^+ + Cl^- + Na^+ + OH^- \rightarrow Na^+ + Cl^- + 2H_2O$$

The Na^+ and Cl^- ions are called *spectator ions* because they are like spectators watching on the sidelines. These ions do not change during the reaction between H_3O^+ and OH^- ions. If equal concentrations and equal volumes of a strong acid and a strong base are mixed, all of the H_3O^+ and OH^- ions react to form water. So, the resulting solution is neutral.

Figure 1 Garden lime, calcium carbonate, is basic and is added to the acidic soil to increase the pH.

Key Resources

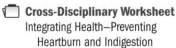 **Teaching Transparency**
C24 Neutralization Reaction

Science Skills Worksheet
Balancing Chemical Equations

Cross-Disciplinary Worksheet
Integrating Health—Preventing Heartburn and Indigestion

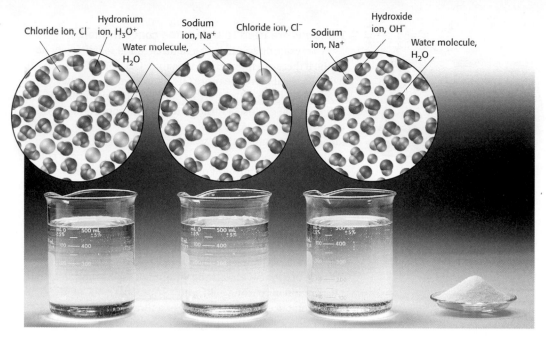

Chloride Ion, Cl⁻   Hydronium ion, H_3O^+ Sodium ion, Na^+ Chloride ion, Cl⁻   Hydroxide ion, OH⁻

Water molecule, H_2O Sodium ion, Na^+ Water molecule, H_2O

Reaction Between an Acid and a Base Reinforce the idea that a neutralization reaction occurs when an acid and a base are mixed, but the product is not always a neutral solution. Ask students: What is the pH of a neutral solution? (pH = 7) How do the pH of an acidic solution and the pH of a basic compare to pH 7? (Acid is less than 7; base is greater than 7) Have students identify the ions that affect the pH of a solution. (H_3O^+ and OH⁻) If an acid and a base are mixed and the product has more H_3O^+ ions than OH⁻ ions, how does the product pH compare to pH values of the reactants? (The pH of the product is less than 7 so it is acidic, but it is closer to 7 than the pH of the acidic reactant.) What is the pH of a solution of sodium chloride in water? (pH = 7)

go.hrw.com
✴ interact online

Students can interact with the figure by going to **go.hrw.com** and typing in the keyword **HK8ABSF2.**

Strong acids and bases react to form water and a salt.

If you do not include the spectator ions, the equation for the neutralization reaction can be written as follows.

$$H_3O^+ + OH^- \rightarrow 2H_2O$$

When an acid reacts with a base, hydronium ions react with hydroxide ions to form water. The other ions—positive ions from the base and negative ions from the acid—form an ionic compound called a **salt.** When this salt is soluble in water, such as the sodium chloride shown in **Figure 2,** the ions stay separated in solution until the water evaporates.

Neutral solutions are not always formed.

Reactions between acids and bases do not always produce neutral solutions. The pH of the final solution depends on the amounts of acid and base that are combined and on the strength of the acid and the base.

If a strong acid reacts with an equal amount of a weak base of the same concentration, the resulting solution will be acidic. Similarly, when a weak acid reacts with an equal amount of a strong base of the same concentration, the resulting solution will be basic.

✓ Reading Check What forms when a weak base and a strong acid react?

Figure 2 When a solution of HCl reacts with a solution of NaOH, the reaction produces water and leaves sodium ions and chloride ions in solution. When the water evaporates, the sodium ions and chloride ions crystallize to form pure sodium chloride.

go.hrw.com
✴ interact online
Keyword: HK8ABSF2

neutralization reaction
(NOO truh li ZAY shuhn ree AK shuhn) the reaction of the ions that characterize acids and the ions that characterize bases to form water molecules and a salt

salt (SAWLT) an ionic compound that forms when a metal atom or a positive radical replaces the hydrogen of an acid

Word Meanings Be sure students can distinguish the term *neutral* from the term *neutralization reaction. Neutral* refers to having a pH of 7. *Neutralization reaction* refers to an acid-base reaction—a chemical reaction that occurs when an acid is mixed with a base. The resulting solution of a neutralization reaction can be acidic, basic, or neutral.

Connection to Biology

Aquarium If possible, set up an aquarium of freshwater fish in the classroom. Discuss with students what factors might cause the pH of the water in the aquarium to change. Factors might include increased acidity from the carbon dioxide in the air bubbled through the tank or increased basicity from ammonia released in fish wastes. Each day, assign a student to check the pH of the water, and ask if the pH needs to be adjusted or not. If it does, have the student propose what needs to be added to the water to make the adjustment. Approve student plans before any action is taken. After approval, have the student adjust and recheck the pH.
LS Kinesthetic

Answer to caption question
The dark blue solution is basic. The indicator changes to dark blue at pH values above 7.6.

Demonstrate

Modeling a Neutralization Reaction
Label each of six large sheets of construction paper with the following: *H⁺, H⁺, Cl⁻, Na⁺, OH⁻* and *OH⁻*. Give each sheet to a student. Have students walk through the neutralization reaction of hydrochloric acid and sodium hydroxide. First, they should show HCl ionizing in water to form Cl⁻ and H_3O^+. Similarly, have students show that NaOH dissociates to form Na⁺ and OH⁻ ions. Show that the hydronium ion transfers a hydrogen ion to the hydroxide ion. As a result, two molecules of water are formed.
LS Visual/Kinesthetic

Graphing *Skills*

Answers to Practice
1. Sample answer: The solution's acidity decreases because the pH increases as more KOH is added to the solution, as indicated by the positive slope of the line in the graph.
2. Sample answer: The HCl solution had a pH of about two before the KOH was added.

Figure 3 Bromthymol blue is an indicator that changes from yellow to blue between a pH of 6.0 and 7.6. It is an ideal indicator for a titration involving a strong acid and a strong base. **Which solution is basic?**

Titrations are used to determine concentration.
The resulting solution of a neutralization reaction will be acidic if there are more H_3O^+ ions than OH⁻ ions. The solution will be basic if there are more OH⁻ ions. If you know the concentration of one of the starting solutions in a neutralization reaction, you can use a titration to find the concentration of the other solution. A *titration* is the process of adding carefully measured amounts of one solution to another solution.

In a titration, an indicator is often used that changes color when the original amount of the base in solution is equal to the amount of the acid added to the solution. The indicator *bromthymol blue* changes from yellow in acids to dark blue in bases at a pH of about 7, as **Figure 3** shows.

If the number of hydronium ions is equal to the number of hydroxide ions in a solution, the solution will be neutral. The *equivalence point* in a titration is reached when the original amount of the acid equals the amount of the base added. For the titration of a strong acid with a strong base, the equivalence point occurs at a pH of 7. For a titration of a weak base with a strong acid, the equivalence point is less than a pH of 7. The equivalence point is greater than a pH of 7 when a weak acid is titrated with a strong base.

Graphing **Skills** **Interpreting Titration Curves**

Hydrochloric acid, HCl, was titrated with potassium hydroxide, KOH. How many moles of KOH were added to reach the equivalence point?

Moles of KOH Added Vs. pH

[Graph: y-axis labeled "pH" ranging from 0 to 12; x-axis labeled "KOH added (mol)" ranging from 0 to 0.8. The titration curve rises sharply at about 0.4 mol KOH.]

❶ Locate the equivalence point on the graph.

A strong acid was titrated with a strong base. The *y*-axis indicates the pH, so the equivalence point on the titration curve has a *y*-value of 7.

❷ Read the moles of KOH from the graph.

The *x*-axis indicates how many moles of KOH were added. At pH = 7, 0.4 mol of KOH was added.

Practice

1. Does the solution's acidity increase or decrease as potassium hydroxide is added to the solution? Explain your answer.
2. What was the pH of the initial HCl solution?

Differentiated Instruction

English Learners

Focus on Concepts To reinforce students' understanding of the concepts in this section, refer them back to the Key Ideas at the beginning of the section. Have students work in pairs to create a word web or another visual representation for each Key Idea. Encourage students to be creative, and have them give oral presentations about their creations.
LS Interpersonal/Visual

Basic Learners

Salt Have pairs of students brainstorm words and phrases that they associate with the term *salt*. Have each pair compile a list of their responses. After students have finished reading this section, have them select a word or phrase from the brainstormed list and evaluate it against what they have learned. **LS** Interpersonal

Salts

When you hear the word *salt*, you probably think of white crystals that you sprinkle on food. **› To a chemist, a salt can be almost any combination of cations and anions, except hydroxides and oxides, which are bases.**

Salts have many uses.

Common table salt contains the ionic compound sodium chloride, NaCl. Most of the sodium in your diet comes from NaCl. It is widely used to season and preserve food.

As **Figure 4** shows, sodium chloride is not the only salt. Baking soda, sodium hydrogen carbonate, is another salt that you can find in your kitchen. Salts have a variety of uses, including cleaning and highway de-icing. Ceramic glazes, home water softeners, and fire extinguishers all contain salts. The chalk that is used in your classroom is one form of the salt calcium carbonate, $CaCO_3$. The walls in your house may be made of gypsum, which is calcium sulfate, $CaSO_4$. Photographic film contains the light-sensitive salts silver bromide, AgBr, and silver iodide, AgI. **Figure 5** shows how the salt barium sulfate, $BaSO_4$ is used in medical diagnosis.

Salts are rarely manufactured by neutralization reactions. Many salts, such as NaCl and $CaCO_3$, are found in mineral deposits. Underground deposits that were left when ancient seas dried up are the source of most NaCl in the United States. Other salts are produced by other chemical processes.

✓ Reading Check What are three ways that salts are used?

Figure 4 Some Common Salts

Salt	Formula	Uses
Aluminum sulfate	$Al_2(SO_4)_3$	purifying water; used in antiperspirants
Ammonium sulfate	$(NH_4)_2SO_4$	flameproofing fabric; used as fertilizer
Calcium chloride	$CaCl_2$	de-icing streets and highways; used in some kinds of concrete
Potassium chloride	KCl	treating potassium deficiency; used as table-salt substitute
Sodium carbonate	Na_2CO_3	manufacturing glass; added to wash to soften water
Sodium hydrogen carbonate	$NaHCO_3$	treating upset stomach; ingredient in baking powder; used in fire extinguishers
Sodium stearate	$NaO_2C_{18}H_{35}$	typical example of a soap; used in deodorant
Sodium lauryl sulfonate	$NaSO_3C_{12}H_{25}$	typical example of a detergent

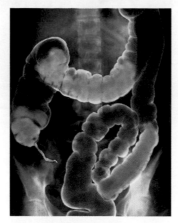

Figure 5 Barium sulfate, $BaSO_4$, is a highly insoluble salt. It can be used to block X rays. After barium sulfate coats the large intestine, the form of the intestine shows up on an X-ray image.

READING TOOLBOX

Everyday Words Used in Science
Before reading about salts, write a list of how you would use salts every day. After reading, write a new list. Compare the lists.

Teaching Key Ideas

Ionic Compounds Remind students that salts are ionic compounds and that many salts are soluble in water. Have them look at the table in **Figure 4.** Ask students: Which of the uses listed for these common salts are based on solubility in water? (Use of salt as fertilizer, for de-icing, as a table-salt substitute, for softening water, for treating an upset stomach, and as soap or detergent all require solubility in water.) **LS Visual/Verbal**

READING TOOLBOX

Everyday Words Used in Science Before reading this section, many students may think only of food and de-icing as uses for salt. Sodium chloride is used on food. Various salts, including sodium chloride, calcium chloride, and magnesium chloride, are used for de-icing roads and sidewalks. Remind students that the word *salt* has different meanings in the kitchen and in the science lab.

Science Skills

Naming Compounds Have students use library resources or the Internet to make a list of the names of all of the cations and the anions in the salts listed in the table in **Figure 4.** Point out that some anions, such as HCO_3^-, are made up of multiple atoms. (cations—aluminum, ammonium, calcium, potassium, sodium; anions—sulfate, chloride, carbonate, hydrogen carbonate, stearate, lauryl sulfonate) **LS Logical/Visual**

Differentiated Instruction

Advanced Learners

Barium Sulfate Ask students to research the use of barium sulfate ($BaSO_4$) for medical purposes and create a report that includes its uses and benefits. Additionally, you can arrange for the students to interview a medical professional who uses barium sulfate. Have the students report their findings by recording the information and playing it for the class as though the students were broadcasting for a science report on the radio. **LS Logical/Verbal**

Why It **Matters**

Sodium Chloride Most people today do not think of sodium chloride as valuable. It is inexpensive and easy to find in any kitchen or cafeteria. Rock salt is used by the ton in cold climates to melt ice on roads. However, sodium chloride is so important that it was used as money in some ancient cultures. The word *salary* comes from the use of salt as part of the pay for soldiers in the Roman army. Wars and revolutions have resulted from the need for access to salt, a necessary part of the diet of humans and many animals.

Reteaching Key Ideas

Neutralization Reactions Remind students that a neutralization reaction always has two products. Ask them the following questions: Name the products of the reaction between potassium hydroxide and sulfuric acid. (potassium sulfate and water) What compound is always a product of a neutralization reaction? (water) Are the products of a neutralization reaction acidic, basic, or neutral? (any of the three is possible depending on the strength of the reactants and their concentrations)
LS Verbal

Formative Assessment

What is the equivalence point of the titration of an acid with a base?

A. The point at which the pH is equal to 7. (Incorrect. This is only true in the case of a strong acid and a strong base.)

B. The point at which the original amount of acid equals the amount of base added. (Correct. The equivalence point is reached when the original amount of acid equals the amount of base added. The equivalence point can be basic, neutral, or acidic.)

C. The point at which the amount of base exceeds the original amount of acid. (Incorrect. Titrations are often extended beyond the point where the amounts of acid and base are equal, but the equivalence point is passed in the process.)

D. The point at which the pH reaches its minimum value. (Incorrect. When an acid is titrated, the minimum pH value occurs before base is added.)

Figure 6 Animals need salts in their diet. These butterflies can obtain salt from the dried sweat on an old sneaker. These moose can get salt by licking the salt that was used to de-ice the road.

SCLINKS.
www.scilinks.org
Topic: Salts
Code: **HK81347**

Salts are important in the body.

You often hear that a healthful diet should include potassium, sodium, calcium, magnesium, iron, phosphorus, and iodine. However, ingesting these nutrients in their elemental form, as metals, is not common and can be harmful. Instead, you get ions of these elements from minerals. Minerals contain the salts of elements that are needed by your body. All animals, including those shown in **Figure 6**, need minerals.

You probably already know that calcium ions, Ca^{2+}, are needed for strong bones and teeth, but calcium ions are also used in other parts of the body. Nerves and muscles need calcium ions to work properly. The correct proportion of potassium ions, K^+, and sodium ions, Na^+, is needed for nerve impulses to work. These ions also control how much water that your cells keep inside. Chloride ions, Cl^-, help balance the charge of these positive ions. Phosphorus, in the form of phosphate ions, PO_4^{3-}, is needed for many processes in living cells, from transportation of energy to reproduction of the genetic code.

Section 2 Review

KEY IDEAS

1. **Identify** the spectator ions in the neutralization of lithium hydroxide, LiOH, with hydrobromic acid, HBr.

2. **Identify** the two types of compounds produced by a neutralization reaction.

3. **Explain** why your body needs salts.

CRITICAL THINKING

4. **Forming Models** Write the chemical equation for the neutralization of nitric acid, HNO_3, with magnesium hydroxide, $Mg(OH)_2$, first with spectator ions and then without spectator ions.

5. **Applying Ideas** Which acid and which base could react to form the salt aluminum sulfate, $Al_2(SO_4)_3$?

6. **Drawing Conclusions** Predict whether the reaction of equal amounts of each of the following acids and bases will yield an acidic, a basic, or a neutral solution. Explain your answer for each.
   a. sulfuric acid, H_2SO_4, and ammonia, NH_3
   b. formic acid, HCOOH, and potassium hydroxide, KOH
   c. nitric acid, HNO_3, and calcium hydroxide, $Ca(OH)_2$

7. **Communicating Ideas** A classmate observes a neutralization reaction between an acid and a base. After the reaction is complete, your classmate is surprised that the resulting solution has a pH of 4 and is not neutral. What can you tell your classmate to help him understand what happened?

Answers to Section Review

1. The spectator ions are the lithium ion, Li^+, and the bromide ion, Br^-.

2. Water and a salt are produced by a neutralization reaction.

3. Sample answer: My body needs salts because salts provide metal ions, such as Ca^{2+} and K^+, that the body needs to function.

4. $Mg^{2+} + 2OH^- + 2H_3O^+ + 2NO_3^- \rightarrow Mg^{2+} + 2NO_3^- + 4H_2O$; $OH^- + H_3O^+ \rightarrow 2H_2O$

5. The Al^{3+} ion would come from the base aluminum hydroxide, $Al(OH)_3$. The sulfate ion, SO_4^{2-}, would come from the acid sulfuric acid, H_2SO_4.

6. **a.** The reaction will yield an acidic solution because sulfuric acid is a strong acid and ammonia is a weak base.

   b. The reaction will yield a basic solution because formic acid is a weak acid and potassium hydroxide is a strong base.

   c. The reaction will yield a neutral solution because nitric acid is a strong acid and calcium hydroxide is a strong base.

7. If the neutralization was done correctly, the reaction must have occurred between a strong acid and a weak base. The resulting ions combine with water in an equilibrium that yields extra hydronium ions, resulting in an acidic solution.

Acids, Bases, and Salts in the Home

Key Ideas

❯ Why are cleaning products added to water?

❯ What are some household products that contain acids, bases, and salts?

Key Terms

soap

detergent

disinfectant

bleach

antacid

Why It Matters

Without soaps and detergents, water would not remove grease or oils when you wash dishes or your face.

As you have seen, you do not find acids, bases, and salts only in a laboratory. Many items in your own home, such as soaps, detergents, shampoos, antacids, vitamins, sodas, and juices, are examples of household products that contain acids, bases, and salts.

Cleaning Products

If you work on an oily bicycle chain or eat potato chips, water alone will not remove the greasy film from your hands. ❯ **Water does not mix with grease or oil. Cleaning products improve water's ability to clean because they help water mix with oily substances.**

Soaps allow oil and water to mix.

Soap improves water's ability to clean because soap can dissolve in both oil and in water. This property of soap allows oil and water to form an emulsion that can be washed away by rinsing. For example, when you are washing your face with soap, as the girl in **Figure 1** is doing, the oil on your face is emulsified by the soapy water. When you rinse your face, the water carries away both the soap and unwanted oil to leave your face clean.

Soaps are salts of sodium or potassium and fatty acids, which have long hydrocarbon chains. The hydrocarbon chains of the soap molecules are nonpolar, so they can mix with oils. The ionic parts of the soap molecules can mix with water. Animal fats or vegetable oils react with sodium hydroxide or potassium hydroxide to make soap. The products of the reaction are soap and an alcohol called *glycerol*.

soap (SOHP) a substance that is used as a cleaner and that dissolves in water

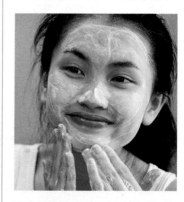

Figure 1 When you wash with soap, you create an emulsion of oil droplets spread throughout water.

Focus

The section starts with a description of soap and detergents. The section also discusses acids, bases, and salts as components of personal care products and foods.

Bellringer

Use the Bellringer transparency to prepare students for this section.

Demonstrate

Making Soap This demonstration will require a cheesecloth, ethanol (10 mL), solid vegetable shortening (25 g), sodium chloride solution (saturated, 25 mL), sodium hydroxide (1.2 g) and distilled water (30 mL).

Mix 25 g of solid vegetable shortening, 10 mL of ethanol, 1.2 g NaOH, and 5 mL of water in a 250 mL beaker. Warm the mixture on a hot plate for 15 minutes. Stir the mixture while heating. Cool the mixture in ice water. Add the rest of the water and the saturated NaCl solution to the solution. Filter the mixture using cheesecloth and press the soap into a mold to shape. Dry the soap for several days. Ask students: Which of the materials formed the soap? (NaOH and shortening) **LS Visual**

Key Resources

 Visual Concept
Antacid

 Datasheets
Detergents
What Does an Antacid Do?

Science Skills Worksheet
Classifying Items

Cross-Disciplinary Worksheets
Connection to Social Studies—
   Detergents: Helpful or Harmful?
Integrating Biology—A Balance in
   the Body
Real World Applications—Car Batteries
Real World Applications—Cooking with
   Baking Powder

How Does Soap Remove Grease?
A soap-like material found in clay cylinders during the excavation of ancient Babylon is evidence that soap making occurred as early as 2800 B.C.E. Inscriptions on the clay cylinders indicate that fats were boiled with ashes, which is a method of making soap, but do not refer to the purpose of the soap-like material.

Records show that ancient Egyptians bathed regularly. The Ebers Papyrus, a medical document from about 1500 B.C.E., describes combining animal and vegetable oils with alkaline salts to form a soap-like material used for treating skin diseases as well as for washing.

The first synthetic detergent was developed in Germany in response to a World War I-related shortage of fats for making soap. Synthetic detergents are non-soap cleaning products that are synthesized, or put together chemically, from a variety of raw materials. The discovery of detergents was also driven by the need for a cleaning agent that, unlike soap, would not combine with the mineral salts in water to form an insoluble substance known as soap curd. Today, almost all products sold for cleaning needs other than personal washing are detergents.

How Does Soap Remove Grease?

Soap is able to remove grease and oil because the cations and the negatively charged ends of the chains (–COO⁻) dissolve in water and the hydrocarbon chains dissolve in oil. Soap molecules surround oil droplets and form an emulsion with water. When you wash your hands with soap, you probably rub them together. Rubbing your hands together actually helps clean them. This action lifts most of the emulsion of grease and water into the lather, which can be rinsed into the sink.

SCI**LINKS.**
www.scilinks.org
Topic: Surfactants
Code: HK81699

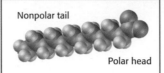

Nonpolar tail

Polar head

❶ Soap is an ionic compound. Its negative ion is a long hydrocarbon chain with a carboxylate group (–COO⁻) at one end. A positive sodium or potassium ion balances the charge of the negative ion.

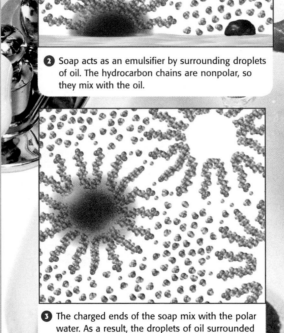

❷ Soap acts as an emulsifier by surrounding droplets of oil. The hydrocarbon chains are nonpolar, so they mix with the oil.

❸ The charged ends of the soap mix with the polar water. As a result, the droplets of oil surrounded by soap molecules stay suspended in water.

YOUR TURN

UNDERSTANDING CONCEPTS
1. Why do the hydrocarbon ends of the soap molecules mix with oils?

CRITICAL THINKING
2. Could molecules without an ionic part still work as soap does to remove oils?

Answers to Your Turn
1. Sample answer: The hydrocarbon ends of the soap are nonpolar, so they will mix with oils, which are also nonpolar.
2. Sample answer: If the molecules have a polar part that is not ionic and that would mix with water, they will work as soap does to remove oils.

Differentiated Instruction

Special Education Students

Making Models Have students make models of soap by cutting out strips of white paper and coloring one end of each strip red. Then, have students cut several small circles of white paper. Have students work in groups to arrange the strips so that the white ends are close to the circles and the red ends are as far from the circles as possible. Have students compare their arrangement to the third figure on this page.
LS Visual/Kinesthetic

Detergents have replaced soap in many uses.

As useful as soap is for cleaning, it does not work well in hard water. Hard water contains dissolved Mg^{2+}, Ca^{2+}, and Fe^{3+} ions. These cations combine with the fatty-acid anions of soap to form an insoluble salt called *soap scum*. This soap scum settles out on clothing, dishes, your skin, and your hair. The scum also makes a ring around the bathtub or sink. You can prevent this problem by using detergents instead of soap to wash clothes and dishes. Most shampoos, liquid hand soaps, and body washes contain detergents, not soap.

Detergents are salts of sodium, potassium, and sometimes ammonium. Like anions in soaps, the anions in detergents are composed of long hydrocarbon chains that have negatively charged ends. But the charged end of a detergent is a sulfonate group ($-SO_3^-$), not a carboxylate group ($-CO_2^-$). These sulfonate ions do not form insoluble salts with the ions in hard water. The hydrocarbon chains in detergents come from petroleum products rather than animal fats or plant oils.

Soaps and detergents act in the same way. The long hydrocarbon chains are soluble in oil or grease. The charged ends are soluble in water. Water molecules attract the charged sulfonate group in detergent molecules and keep the oil droplet suspended among the water molecules.

✓ Reading Check Why are detergents often used for cleaning instead of soaps?

Integrating Social Studies

Ancient Soap People have used soap for thousands of years. Ancient Egyptians took baths regularly with soap made from animal fats or vegetable oils and basic solutions of alkali-metal compounds. According to Roman legend, people discovered that the water in the Tiber River near Mount Sapo was good for washing. Mount Sapo was used for elaborate animal-sacrifice rituals, and the combination of animal fat and the basic ash that washed down the mountain made the river soapy.

detergent (dee TUHR juhnt) a water-soluble cleaner that can emulsify dirt and oil

QuickLab

Detergents

⏱ 10 min

Procedure
1. Lay some **wax paper** on a flat surface, and put a drop of **water** on it.
2. Gently touch the drop of water with the tip of a **toothpick**.
3. Now, dip the tip of the toothpick in **liquid detergent**.
4. Gently touch the drop of water with the tip of the toothpick after it has been dipped in detergent.

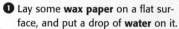
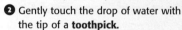

Analysis
1. Does the water wet the surface of the wax paper? How can you tell?
2. What happened to the drop of water when you touched it with the toothpick?
3. What happened to the drop of water when you touched it with the toothpick that had been dipped in detergent?
4. Based on your results, what is one way that detergents help water clean away dirt?

Teaching Key Ideas

Cleaner Sooner Clothes become cleaner if they are washed soon after they are soiled. Oils from the skin are easily removed by soaps and detergents soon after they are deposited on fabric. However, certain oils change over time, forming large molecules that tend to bond with molecules in fabric. These changes cause yellowing, especially in cotton, which is not easily removed. Discuss how detergents improve the ability of water to clean clothes before the molecules form bonds with the fabric.

QuickLab

Teacher's Notes Detergent acts as a surfactant, or wetting agent, by reducing surface tension so that the droplet will spread out on a surface. When determining if water wets a surface, students should look to see if the water beads up or if it spreads out on the surface. Students should observe that the water does not wet the surface in step 1. In step 2, nothing happens to the drop of water. In step 4, the water spreads out and the detergent allows water to better emulsify the dirt.

Materials per Group
- detergent, liquid
- dropper
- pin
- wax paper

Answers to Analysis
1. The water does not wet the surface of the wax paper because it beads up.
2. Nothing happened to the drop.
3. The water drop spreads out.
4. The detergent helps water to interact better with dirt particles.

Differentiated Instruction

Basic Learners

Reading Skills Ask student volunteers to summarize parts of the section for the class. After each summary is completed, have other students ask questions. Allow the student answering the questions to consult the text. Clarify any concepts that the student presenter is not able to address. **LS Verbal/Interpersonal**

Why It **Matters**

Color-Safe Bleaches Not all bleaches are disinfectants. Color-safe bleaches contain nonchlorine oxidizing agents and do not disinfect items. Chlorine bleaches, on the other hand, kill microorganisms but may remove color from some fabrics.

Why It **Matters**

Acid-Base Reactions at Home One result of hard water is the buildup of insoluble calcium carbonate, $CaCO_3$, on the interior of toilet bowls and other surfaces. These deposits appear as discoloration and scale and can be removed by toilet bowl cleaners, which usually contain hydrochloric acid. The reaction between the hydrochloric acid and calcium carbonate deposits produces soluble calcium and chloride ions and carbon dioxide gas, as shown in the following reaction: $2HCl + CaCO_3 \rightarrow Ca^{2+} + 2Cl^- + H_2O + CO_2$. Toilet bowl cleaners should never be used with bleach to whiten the surface of the toilet bowls. The reaction between the hydrochloric acid in the toilet bowl cleaner and the bleach yields toxic chlorine gas, as shown in the following reaction: $2HCl + NaClO \rightarrow Na^+ + Cl^- + H_2O + Cl_2$.

Figure 2 Basic solutions of ammonia can be used to clean away light grease smears, so ammonia solutions are used to clean windows.

SC**LINKS**.

www.scilinks.org
Topic: Acids and Bases
at Home
Code: HK80014

Many household cleaners contain ammonia.

Ammonia solutions are also good cleaners. Household ammonia is a solution of ammonia gas in water. Ammonia is a weak base because it ionizes only slightly in water to form ammonium ions and hydroxide ions, as shown in the reaction below. The hydroxide ions make the ammonia solution basic.

$$NH_3 + H_2O \rightleftharpoons NH_4^+ + OH^-$$

The concentration of ions is relatively low in an ammonia solution but is enough to remove fingerprints and oily smears. Many ammonia cleaners also contain alcohols, detergents, and other cleaning agents. These cleaners can be used to clean windows, such as those shown in **Figure 2.**

Bleach can eliminate stains.

A **disinfectant** is a substance that kills viruses and bacteria. Household **bleach,** a very strong disinfectant, is a basic solution of sodium hypochlorite, NaOCl. As you probably know, bleach can remove colors and stains.

Unlike soaps and detergents, bleach does not remove the substance causing the stain. Instead, bleach changes the substance to a colorless form. When mixed with water, the hypochlorite ion, ClO^-, reacts to release an oxygen atom. The oxygen atom reacts with the colored molecule and bleaches it.

If an acid is added to a bleach solution, the acid reacts with the hypochlorite ions and deadly chlorine gas is produced. For this reason, you should never mix bleach with an acid, such as vinegar. Also, ammonia and bleach should not be mixed because toxic chloramine gas, NH_2Cl, is formed.

✔ Reading Check What would happen if you were to mix vinegar with bleach?

Personal-Care and Food Products

You may not have noticed all of the substances in your home that contain acids and bases. For example, many of the clothes in your closet get their color from acidic dyes. These dyes are sodium salts of organic compounds that contain the sulfonic acid group ($-SO_3H$) or the carboxylic acid group ($-CO_2H$). If you have ever had an upset stomach because of excess stomach acid, you may have taken an antacid tablet to feel better. The antacid made you feel better because it neutralized the excess stomach acid. **》 Many healthcare, beauty, and food products in your home, in addition to cleaners, contain acids, bases, or salts.**

Teaching Key Ideas

Household Products Have students read the labels of household and personal care products to identify the ingredients. The products examined should include food, cosmetics, and cleaning supplies. Have students make a list of acids, bases, and salts among the ingredients. Ask students: "What cations and ions are common on the list?" (Accept all reasonable answers. Likely cations include sodium, potassium, aluminum, ammonium, calcium; likely anions include sulfate, phosphate, carbonate, bicarbonate, and hydroxide.) **LS Verbal**

Differentiated Instruction

Struggling Readers

Important Words Point out that writers frequently indicate important words by making them look different from the surrounding text. Ask students how the words can be made to look different. (Sample answers: bold type, italics, underline, highlighting, different color, and different font size) Have students work in pairs to make a list of words in this section that stand out because of differences in type. (soap, glycerol, detergents, disinfectant, bleach, antacids, keratin, specific, antioxidant)
LS Verbal/Interpersonal

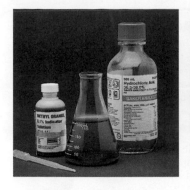
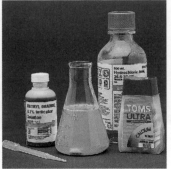

Figure 3 Stomach acid has about the same concentration of HCl as the solution in the flask in the photograph on the left. When an antacid tablet reacts with the acid, the pH increases to a less acidic level, as shown in the photograph on the right. **Why is the solution in one flask pink and the solution in the other flask orange?**

Many healthcare products are acids or bases.

In the morning before school, you may drink a glass of orange juice that contains vitamin C. Ascorbic acid is the chemical name for vitamin C, which your body needs to grow and repair bone and cartilage. Both sodium hydrogen carbonate and magnesium hydroxide (milk of magnesia) can be used as antacids. **Antacids** are basic substances that you swallow to neutralize stomach acid when you have an upset stomach. The acidic solution shown in **Figure 3** contains an indicator. When the antacid tablet is added to the acidic solution, a neutralization reaction happens. Because there are fewer hydronium ions, the pH of the solution changes. So, the color of the indicator changes from pink to orange.

Shampoos are adjusted for an ideal pH.

Shampoos can be made from soap. But if you use a soap-based shampoo and live in an area with hard water, a sticky soap scum may be left on your hair. Most shampoos are made from detergents, so they are able to remove dirt as well as most of the oil from your hair without leaving soap scum, even when they are used with hard water. Shampoo is not meant to remove all of the oil from your hair. Some oil is needed to give your hair shine and to keep it from becoming dry and brittle.

The appearance of your hair is greatly affected by the pH of the shampoo that you use. Hair looks best when it is kept at either a slightly acidic pH or very close to neutral. Hair strands are made of a protein called *keratin*. A shampoo that is too basic can cause strands of hair to swell, which gives them a dull, lifeless appearance. Shampoos are usually pH balanced—that is, they are made to be in a specific pH range. The pH of most shampoos is between 5 and 8. Shampoos that have higher pH values are better at cleaning oil from your hair. Shampoos that have lower pH values protect dry hair.

disinfectant (DIS in FEK tuhnt) a chemical substance that kills harmful bacteria or viruses

bleach (BLEECH) a chemical compound used to whiten or make lighter, such as hydrogen peroxide or sodium hypochlorite

antacid (ANT AS id) a weak base that neutralizes stomach acid

Academic Vocabulary

specific (spuh SIF ik) special to; exact

Answer to caption question
The pink solution is more acidic than the orange solution. The color of the indicator in the solution depends on the pH of the solution.

READING TOOLBOX

Using Words in Science A *buffer* protects an object from a sudden change or shock. In chemistry, buffers can dissolve moderate amounts of acids or bases without significantly changing pH. Blood must maintain a narrow pH range, and the hydrogen carbonate ion, HCO_3^-, acts as a buffer. If blood becomes too acidic, the ion acts as a base. If blood becomes too basic, the ion acts as an acid.

Science Skills

Interpreting Visuals Have students look at **Figure 3.** Explain that methyl orange, like most indicators, is a weak organic acid that changes color when it loses a proton. It appears orange in acidic solutions that have a pH between 3.1 and 4.4. It appears red in solutions that have pH values less than 3.1, and it appears yellow in solutions that have pH values above 4.4. Ask students the pH of the solution on the left (3.0 or less) and the pH of the solution on the right (between 3.1 and 4.4). Ask students why methyl orange would not be useful to differentiate water from a solution of baking soda. (Methyl orange would appear yellow in both solutions because each has a pH value greater than 4.5.) **LS Logical/Visual**

Differentiated Instruction

Advanced Learners

New Medicines Antacids work by removing acid using a neutralization reaction. Drug companies also make *proton pump inhibitors,* drugs that treat excess acid in the stomach in a different way. Have students research proton pump inhibitors to find out how they work and to compare them to antacids, such as calcium carbonate. **LS Verbal**

InquiryLab

Materials per Group

- antacid, 1 tablet
- beakers (2)
- litmus paper
- spoon
- vinegar
- water, 200 mL
- wax paper

Answers to Analysis

1. Sample answer: The antacid neutralizes the stomach acid.
2. Answers may vary. Students will likely choose the brand that neutralized the most acid.

READING TOOLBOX

Cause-and-Effect Map

Sample cause-and-effect map:

InquiryLab **What Does an Antacid Do?** ⏲ **20 min**

Procedure

❶ Pour **100 mL of water** into **one beaker.** Add **vinegar** one drop at a time while stirring. Test the solution with **litmus paper** after each drop is added. Record the number of drops that you add for the solution to turn blue litmus paper bright red.

❷ Use the back of a **spoon** to crush an **antacid tablet** to a fine powder on a piece of **wax paper.** Pour **100 mL of water** into a **second beaker,** add the powdered tablet, and stir until a suspension forms.

❸ Use litmus paper to find out whether the mixture is acidic, basic, or neutral. Record your results.

❹ Now, add vinegar to the antacid mixture. Record the number of drops that you add to cause a reaction with the antacid and turn the blue litmus paper bright red. Compare this solution with the solution that has only vinegar and water. Compare the brand of antacid that you tested with the brands of other groups.

Analysis

1. How does an antacid work to relieve the pain caused by excess stomach acid?

2. Of the brands that were tested, which brand worked best? Explain your reasoning.

READING TOOLBOX

Cause-and-Effect Map

Create a cause-and-effect map that shows why a cut apple turns brown and what happens when lemon juice is added to the apple.

Acids can be used as antioxidants.

Some cut fruits, such as the apple shown in **Figure 4,** slowly turn brown when they are exposed to air. The reason is that certain molecules in the apple react with oxygen to form brown compounds. Why does half of the apple look freshly cut? That part was coated with lemon juice shortly after the apple was cut. The citric acid in lemon juice acts as an *antioxidant* and prevents oxygen from reacting with the molecules in the apple that form the brown substances. Vitamin C, ascorbic acid, is another example of a natural antioxidant. Antioxidants work in various ways. Citric acid and vitamin C inhibit the enzyme involved in the reaction. Vitamin C also reacts with oxygen molecules before they can react with other molecules.

Figure 4 The right side of the cut apple was coated with lemon juice. Citric acid in the lemon juice kept the surface of the apple looking fresh.

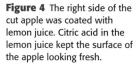

Connection to Biology

Free Radicals and Antioxidants Compounds called *oxygen-centered free radicals,* designated RO·, can damage cells at the molecular level. These substances each contain a single unpaired electron, which makes them very reactive. A free radical can easily strip away an electron from another molecule making the second molecule a free radical. This cascading effect can damage cell structures, such as the cell membrane and DNA. Antioxidants donate electrons to the free radicals before the free radicals can react with other substances in the cell. For example, the antioxidants vitamins E and C work in tandem to protect the cell membrane from damage by free radicals. Vitamin E is lipid soluble and resides within the cell membrane while vitamin C is water-soluble and exists within the cell. Vitamin E donates an electron to the free radical and becomes a free radical. Vitamin C within the cell donates an electron to the vitamin E free radical, converting the radical to vitamin E and itself becoming a radical. Within the cell, enzymes convert the vitamin C free radical to vitamin C.

Acids, bases, and salts are used in the kitchen.

Acids have many uses in the kitchen. Vinegar or citrus juices are used make acidic marinades that can tenderize meats. The acids cause the protein molecules in the meat to unravel. As a result, the meat becomes more tender.

Milk curdles if you add an acid, such as vinegar, to it. This reaction may seem undesirable, but a similar reaction occurs when yogurt is being made. Bacteria change lactose, a sugar in milk, into lactic acid. The lactic acid changes the shape of the protein casein, causing the milk to become a thick gel.

You use salts other than table salt for baking. Baking soda, or sodium hydrogen carbonate, is a salt that forms carbon dioxide gas at high temperatures. Baking soda is added to cookies so that they rise when baked. Baking powder is also used to make baked goods rise, as **Figure 5** shows. Baking powder contains baking soda and an acidic substance. When mixed in water, these compounds react to release CO_2, which makes cake batter light and fluffy and helps biscuits rise.

Bases are also used in the kitchen. Many drain cleaners contain sodium hydroxide. This strong base breaks down the grease and other organic materials that cause clogs.

Figure 5 The carbon dioxide gas released by baking powder during baking causes biscuits to rise.

Section 3 Review

KEY IDEAS

1. **Describe** how soap can dissolve in both oil and water. How does soap work with water to remove oily dirt?

2. **Explain** why soap scum might form in hard water that contains Mg^{2+} ions when soap is used instead of detergent to wash dishes.

3. **Explain** how milk of magnesia, an antacid, can reduce acidity in stomach acid.

4. **List** three acidic household substances and three basic household substances. How are the substances most often used?

CRITICAL THINKING

5. **Applying Ideas** Why does the agitation of a washing machine help a detergent clean your clothes? (Hint: Compare this motion to rubbing your hands together when you wash them.)

6. **Drawing Conclusions** Why it is not necessary for bleach to actually remove the substance that causes a stain?

7. **Analyzing Methods** Crayon companies recommend treating wax stains on clothes by spraying the stains with an oily lubricant, applying dish-washing liquid, and then washing the clothes. Explain why this treatment would remove the stain.

>Close

Reteaching Key Ideas

Acids, Bases, and Salts at Home On the board, write three headings: *Food, Cleaning,* and *Personal Care.* After reading this section, have the class brainstorm acids, bases, or salts that fall into each category. Identify each as a strong or weak acid, a strong or weak base, or a salt. Some substances, such as shampoos, may be acidic, neutral, or basic. **LS Verbal/Visual**

Formative Assessment

How do the action of soaps and detergents differ when they are used in hard water?

A. Soaps react with sodium and potassium to form a precipitate but detergents do not. (Incorrect. Soaps are sodium and potassium compounds. They precipitate with calcium and magnesium.)

B. Soaps react with calcium and magnesium to form a precipitate but detergents do not. (Correct. Soaps form a "scum" when they react with the calcium and magnesium in hard water.)

C. Detergents react with calcium and magnesium to form a precipitate but soaps do not. (Incorrect. Soaps form a "scum" when they react with the calcium and magnesium in hard water but detergents do not.)

D. Detergents react with water but soaps react with oil particles. (Incorrect. Soaps and detergents both surround nonpolar compounds with their nonpolar ends and interact with water at their polar ends.)

Answers to Section Review

1. Soap is a salt of a fatty acid. The anion consists of a hydrocarbon chain that has a carboxylate group, $-COO^-$, attached. The hydrocarbon chain is similar to the molecular structure of oil, so the hydrocarbon end of the molecule dissolves in oil, while the ionic end dissolves in water. When an oil droplet has enough hydrocarbon chains around it, the attraction between water and the carboxyl groups pulls the droplet into the water, where it can be washed away by rinsing.

2. Sample answer: Magnesium ions react with soap molecules to form an insoluble salt.

3. Sample answer: As a basic solution, milk of magnesia can neutralize stomach acid.

4. Answers may vary. Sample answers: Acidic materials could include vinegar (acetic acid), lemon juice (citric acid), Vitamin C (ascorbic acid), aspirin (acetylsalicylic acid), buttermilk or sour cream (lactic acid), acidic salts in baking powder (sodium aluminum sulfate and calcium dihydrogen phosphate), and muriatic acid (hydrochloric acid in a concentration used to clean masonry). Basic materials could include ammonia, drain cleaner made with lye (sodium hydroxide), milk of magnesia (magnesium hydroxide), other antacids (basic salts, including calcium carbonate, sodium hydrogen carbonate, and aluminum hydroxide), potash (potassium carbonate), and lime (calcium hydroxide).

Answers continued on p. 321A

Skills Practice Lab

Skills Practice

Teacher's Notes

Show students how to stir small amounts of liquids in a test tube by holding the tube at the lip with one hand and tapping the other end gently against the palm of the other hand. Neutralize both acids with the sodium hydroxide solution. Dilute with excess water, and discard in the drain. Wrap the pipets in paper toweling, and dispose of them in the trash.

Time Required

1 lab period

Lab Ratings

EASY ———————————→ HARD

Teacher Prep 🔬🔬
Student Set-Up 🔬🔬🔬
Concept Level 🔬🔬
Clean Up 🔬🔬

Skills Acquired

- Collecting data
- Communicating
- Experimenting
- Interpreting
- Measuring
- Organizing and analyzing data
- Predicting

Scientific Methods

In this lab, students will:
- Make observations
- Form a hypothesis
- Analyze the results
- Draw conclusions
- Communicate results

What You'll Do

❯ **Determine** the volume of a basic solution needed to neutralize a given volume of an acidic solution.

❯ **Analyze** the results to compare the volume of basic solution needed to neutralize a given volume of HCl solution with the volume needed to neutralize the same volume of H_2SO_4 solution.

What You'll Need

HCl solution, 0.1 M
H_2SO_4 solution, 0.1 M
NaOH solution, 0.1 M
marker
phenolphthalein indicator solution
pipets, plastic, disposable (3)
test-tube rack
test tubes (2)

Safety

Quantities in an Acid-Base Reaction

Acids and bases neutralize each other to form a salt and water. Phenolphthalein is a good indicator to use in the neutralization of a strong acid by a strong base. Phenolphthalein is a good indicator because it changes color at a pH only slightly higher than neutral. The extra amount of a base that is needed to change the color is usually too small to measure.

Procedure

Neutralizing HCl with NaOH

CAUTION: Wear an apron or lab coat to protect your clothing when working with chemicals. If a spill gets on your skin or clothing, rinse it off immediately with water for at least 5 min. Wear safety goggles and gloves when handling chemicals. If any substance gets in your eyes, immediately flush your eyes with running water for at least 15 min and notify your instructor. Always use caution when working with chemicals. Always add the base to the acid; never add the acid to the base.

1 Use the marker to write "HCl" on the bulb of one pipet. This pipet should be used only for hydrochloric acid solution. Mark a second pipet "NaOH." This pipet should be used only for sodium hydroxide solution.

2 Make a data table like the one shown.

3 Add 40 drops of 0.1 M HCl solution to a clean test tube at a steady rate. Do not let the tip of the pipet touch the sides of the test tube. Hold the long tube of the pipet with the other hand, if necessary.

4 Add 2 drops of phenolphthalein indicator to the test tube. Gently swirl the test tube to mix the liquid in the tube. Be careful not to spill or splash the liquid.

5 Note the concentrations of the HCl and NaOH solutions. Predict how many drops of NaOH solution will be required to neutralize the 40 drops of HCl. Record your prediction in the data table.

6 Add 25 drops of 0.1 M NaOH solution to the test tube. You will probably see a pink color—the color of phenolphthalein in a basic solution—develop temporarily. Remember this color. Gently swirl the test tube to mix the liquid. The pink color should disappear.

Sample Data Table: Neutralization

	Number of drops	Drops NaOH needed (predicted)	Drops NaOH needed (measured)
HCl			
H_2SO_4		DO NOT WRITE IN BOOK	

7 Add more NaOH solution to the test tube 2 drops at a time, and mix the liquids after each addition. As the pink color starts to disappear more slowly when you mix the liquids, start adding the NaOH solution 1 drop at a time, and mix the solution with each addition. When the mixture remains slightly pink after the addition of a drop and does not change within 10 s, you have reached the end of the neutralization reaction. Record in the data table the total number of drops of NaOH solution that you added.

Neutralizing H_2SO_4 with NaOH

8 Use the marker to label a third pipet "H_2SO_4." Use this pipet only for sulfuric acid solution.

9 Repeat steps 3–7, but start with 40 drops of 0.1 M H_2SO_4 solution instead of 40 drops of HCl solution. Make and record your prediction as you did in step 5.

Analysis

1. **Describing Events** Write a complete nonionic chemical equation for the reaction of HCl and NaOH. Then, write the ionic equation for the reaction without spectator ions.

2. **Describing Events** Write a complete nonionic chemical equation for the reaction of H_2SO_4 and NaOH. Then, write the ionic equation for the reaction without spectator ions.

Communicating Your Results

3. **Drawing Conclusions** In the neutralization of HCl with NaOH, how close was your predicted number of drops to the actual number of drops of NaOH solution needed? If there is a large difference, explain the reasoning that led to your prediction.

4. **Drawing Conclusions** In the neutralization of H_2SO_4 with NaOH, how close was your predicted number of drops to the actual number of drops of NaOH solution needed? If there is a large difference, explain the reasoning that led to your prediction.

Extension

Suppose that someone tries to explain your results by saying that H_2SO_4 is twice as strong an acid as HCl. How could you explain that this person's reasoning is incorrect?

Tips and Tricks

If students agitate the contents of the tube for too long a time in step 6, the mixture will change from pink back to colorless because the solution absorbs atmospheric CO_2 and becomes slightly more acidic. To save time in step 9, students may start by adding 60 drops of NaOH solution. Discrepancies between the number of drops of NaOH and HCl needed for neutralization can often be explained because students become impatient and add more base than necessary to neutralize the acid.

Answers to Analysis

1. HCl + NaOH → NaCl + H_2O; H_3O^+ + OH^- → $2H_2O$
2. H_2SO_4 + 2NaOH → Na_2SO_4 + $2H_2O$; H_3O^+ + OH^- → $2H_2O$

Answers to Communicating Your Results

3. Because both solutions are the same concentration and HCl and NaOH react in a 1:1 ratio, the number of drops of HCl and NaOH should be equal.

4. Students should infer from their experimental data and the formula of H_2SO_4 that two hydrogen ions are available from H_2SO_4. Therefore, twice as many drops of NaOH neutralize H_2SO_4.

Answer to Extension

Sample answer: I would point out that the person is confusing strength of acids with concentration of hydronium ions. The strength of an acid refers to its degree of ionization. Strong acids are completely ionized in solution. What the person is referring to as "stronger" is that, per mole of acid, sulfuric acid produces a greater concentration of H_3O^+ ions in solution than HCl does.

Key Resources

- **Virtual Investigation**
- **Classroom Lab Video/DVD**
- **Holt Lab Generator CD-ROM**
  Search for any lab by type, standard, difficulty level, or time. Edit any lab to fit your needs, or create your own labs. Use the Lab Materials QuickList software to customize your lab materials list.

- **Differentiated Datasheets**
  Quantities in an Acid-Base Reaction
- **Observation Lab**
  Investigating Acids and Bases
- **CBL™ Probeware Lab**
  Determining the Concentration of an Acid Solution

Science > Skills

Finding Reputable Sources

Looking for Useful Information Prior to looking for information on the Internet, students should ask "What source would most likely provide reliable information in this particular case? Which kind of Web site would you expect to be fair and objective?" Tell students that it is important to keep these questions in mind to identify questionable sources.

Answers to Practice

1. This is probably not a reputable source. It is a personal Web page by an 8th-grader, who is almost certainly not an expert or even an experienced researcher. The site may contain some useful information or links, however.

2. This is probably a reputable source. Although it is the site for a single faculty member, Dr. Hazard is associated with a university.

3. This might or might not be a reputable source. The Clorox Company may have first-hand information because they manufacture household products. However, they might not freely share all information about their products.

4. This is a government agency responsible for health and safety, almost certainly a reputable source.

Anyone can post ideas and information on the Internet. So, you should not believe everything that you read. Below are some tips to help you determine whether or not a Web site is a reputable source.

① **Examine the Web Address** Gather information from the site's Web address (URL).
- The domain name may tell you if a reputable business, agency, or institution created the site.
- Is the top-level domain (.com, .org, .edu, or .gov) appropriate for the information that you are seeking?
- Look for clues that indicate a personal Web site (person's name; an apparent username; or a tilde, "~"). Be cautious with the information on such sites.

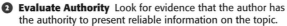

② **Evaluate Authority** Look for evidence that the author has the authority to present reliable information on the topic.
- What are the credentials of the author or institution?
- Do other cited authors or Web sites seem reputable?
- Does the site have few spelling and grammar errors?

③ **Evaluate Objectivity** Some companies, organizations, and people may benefit from making you think a particular way.
- Ask yourself what reason the author of the page may have to want you to believe the information.
- Does the language on the site have an objective tone?
- Are there links to sites that might contain other views?

④ **Check for Accuracy** Be critical of the information on a site.
- How does the information compare with what you already know?
- Is the information consistent with that on other Web sites, in books, or other publications on the topic?
- Are sources that support the information listed?

Where to look	Information
About page	who runs the Web site; mission statement (what the person's or organization's goals are)
Links; related sites	other Web sites that they would like you to visit; may or may not contain relevant information
FAQ page	frequently asked questions
publications	often a list of scholarly articles produced by the person or organization

Use the following resources to check Web Site information:
- encyclopedias
- science textbooks
- science journals and magazines

> **Practice**

Suppose that you are researching the toxicity of various household products. For each of the following Web sites, discuss why you think that the source is likely or not likely to be reputable.

1. Kenny's eighth-grade science project about household products: www.austinisd.org/~kennyken/sciproject

2. Dr. Hazard's toxicity research page: www.med.unc.edu/toxicology/faculty/hazard/toxicity

3. The Web site for a manufacturer of household chemical products: www.cloroxcompany.com

4. The Web site for the U.S. government's Occupational Safety and Health Administration: www.osha.gov

Key Resources

 Science Skills Worksheets
Scientific Notation
Operations with Exponents
Entering Exponents
Balancing Chemical Equations
Classifying Items

go.hrw.com
SUPER SUMMARY
KEYWORD: HK8ABSS

SUMMARY

Key Ideas

Key Terms

Section 1 Acids, Bases, and pH

> **Acids** Acids taste sour, cause indicators to change color, and conduct electric current. They are also corrosive and can damage materials, including your skin. (p. 293)

> **Bases** Bases have a bitter taste, and solutions of bases feel slippery. Solutions of bases also conduct electric current, cause indicators to change color, and can damage the skin. (p. 295)

> **pH** The pH of a solution indicates its concentration of H_3O^+ ions. In solutions, the concentration of hydronium ions is related to the concentration of hydroxide ions, OH^-. The pH of a solution also indicates the concentration of OH^- ions. (p. 298)

acid, p. 293
indicator, p. 293
electrolyte, p. 294
base, p. 295
pH, p. 298

Section 2 Reactions of Acids with Bases

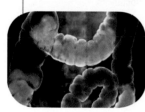

> **Acid-Base Reactions** A neutralization reaction is the reaction between an acid and a base. (p. 302)

> **Salts** To a chemist, a salt can be almost any combination of cations and anions, except hydroxides and oxides, which are bases. (p. 305)

neutralization reaction, p. 302
salt, p. 303

Section 3 Acids, Bases, and Salts in the Home

> **Cleaning Products** Water does not mix with grease or oil. Cleaning products improve water's ability to clean because they help water mix with oily substances. (p. 307)

> **Personal-Care and Food Products** Many healthcare, beauty, and food products in your home, in addition to cleaners, contain acids, bases, or salts. (p. 310).

soap, p. 307
detergent, p. 309
disinfectant, p. 310
bleach, p. 310
antacid, p. 311

SUPER SUMMARY

Have students connect the major concepts in this chapter through an interactive Super Summary. Visit **go.hrw.com** and type in the keyword **HK8ABSS** to access the Super Summary for this chapter.

Differentiated Instruction

Alternative Assessment

Concept Mapping Divide the class into groups of three to four students. Have each group use the following terms to make a concept map that compares the properties of acids and bases and lists ways to distinguish between them: *acid, base, neutral, neutralize, hydronium ions, hydroxide ions, litmus paper, salt, pH above 7, pH below 7,* and *pH 7.* Have one student from each group write their maps on the board for discussion and critique by the class. **LS** Logical/Interpersonal

Key Resources

🔲 **Interactive Concept Map**

🗂 **Review Resources**
Concept Review Worksheets

🗂 **Assessment Resources**
Chapter Tests A and B
Performance-Based Assessment

Reading Toolbox

1. dish-washing soap: detergent; laundry detergent: detergent; shampoo: detergent; liquid hand soap: detergent; and olive oil bar soap: soap

Using Key Terms

2. Sample answer: An acidic solution will turn blue litmus paper red. A basic solution will turn red litmus paper blue. A neutral solution will not cause a color change in either type of litmus paper.

3. Sample answer: Soaps and detergents are salts of acids that have a hydrocarbon chain. The hydrocarbon chain is similar to the molecular structure of oil. So, the hydrocarbon chain end of the molecule dissolves in oil, while the ionic end of the molecule dissolves in water. When an oil droplet has enough hydrocarbon chains dissolved in it, the attraction between water and the ionic groups pulls the droplet into suspension, and the oil can be washed away by rinsing.

4. Sample answer: The active substance in bleach is sodium hypochlorite. Bleach reacts with the stain, turning the stain colorless.

5. Sample answer: The fatty acid anions in soap form insoluble salts wiith Ca^{2+} and Mg^{2+}, and the salts precipitate as soap scum. If soaps were used in shampoo, this soap scum would precipitate on hair. Detergents do not form precipitates with these metal ions.

6. Sample answer: Disinfecting the work surface kills stray bacteria that could contaminate the cultures with which the microbiologist is working. Microbiologists might use bleach to clean work areas because it acts as a disinfectant, killing bacteria and other microorganisms.

7. Sample answer: Strong acids ionize completely, producing abundant ions in an aqueous solution. These ions are able to move through the solution and conduct an electric current.

READING TOOLBOX

1. **Everyday Words Used in Science** In everyday living, we sometimes use the word *soap* to refer to detergents. Identify each of the following as either a soap or a detergent: dish-washing soap, laundry detergent, shampoo, liquid hand soap, and olive oil bar soap.

USING KEY TERMS

2. Explain how you can use the *indicator* litmus, in the form of litmus paper, to determine whether a solution is acidic, basic, or neutral.

3. Explain how the molecular structure of *soaps* and *detergents* causes these substances to help water wash away oil and grease.

4. What is the active substance in *bleach*? How does this substance work to remove stains?

5. Why are most shampoos made from *detergents* rather than *soaps*?

6. Why do microbiologists often disinfect work areas before working with bacterial cultures? What might they use as a *disinfectant*?

7. Explain why a *strong acid* is also a strong *electrolyte* in solution.

8. What is a *neutralization reaction*? How might the product of a neutralization reaction have a *pH* that is less than 7?

9. How can you use the *pH* of a solution to determine how *basic* the solution is?

10. What are two ways that your body uses *salts*?

UNDERSTANDING KEY IDEAS

11. An acid produces _____ ions in solution.
    a. oxygen
    b. hydronium
    c. hydroxide
    d. sulfur

12. A base produces _____ ions in solution.
    a. oxygen
    b. hydronium
    c. hydroxide
    d. sulfur

13. What is the formula of the salt formed when a solution of nitric acid is added to a solution of calcium hydroxide?
    a. $Ca(NO_3)_2$
    b. $Ca(OH)_2$
    c. H_2O
    d. CaH

14. An antacid relieves an overly acidic stomach because antacids are
    a. acidic.
    b. neutral.
    c. basic.
    d. dilute.

15. Detergents have replaced soap in many uses because detergents
    a. are made from animal fat.
    b. do not form insoluble substances.
    c. are milder than soap.
    d. contain ammonia.

16. Which of the following ionic equations best represents a neutralization reaction?
    a. $Na + H_2O \rightarrow Na^+ + OH^- + H_2$
    b. $HNO_3 + H_2O \rightarrow H_3O^+ + NO_3^-$
    c. $2OH^- + NH_4Cl \rightarrow Cl^- + H_2O + NH_3$
    d. $OH^- + H_3O^+ \rightarrow 2H_2O$

17. An increase in the hydronium ion concentration of a solution _____ the pH.
    a. raises
    b. lowers
    c. does not affect
    d. doubles

18. Bleach removes stains by
    a. changing the color of the stain.
    b. covering the stain.
    c. removing the stain-causing substances.
    d. disinfecting the stain.

19. Which one of these materials found in the kitchen is not acidic?
    a. baking soda
    b. lemon juice
    c. vinegar
    d. vitamin C

20. Explain how the ionization of a strong acid differs from the ionization of a weak acid in a solution. Give an example of a strong acid and a weak acid. Write an equation that shows which ions form when each acid is dissolved in water.

21. If you wish to change the pH of a solution very slightly, should you add a strong acid or a weak acid? Explain your answer.

CRITICAL THINKING

22. Forming Hypotheses Baking soda, sodium hydrogen carbonate, is useful in the kitchen for baking and for absorbing odors in the refrigerator. Baking soda can also be sprinkled on a grease fire to extinguish it. How can baking soda extinguish fires?

23. Applying Ideas Insect bites hurt because the insect injects a toxin into the victim. When certain kinds of ants bite, they inject a small amount of highly irritating formic acid. Suggest a treatment that might stop an ant bite from itching or hurting.

24. Designing Experiments Suppose that your measurement of the pH of a clear solution is 3. You are asked to find out whether the solution is a very dilute solution of a strong acid or a more concentrated solution of a weak acid. Propose a method to answer the question.

25. Applying Ideas You need several grams of the solid ammonium bromide, NH_4Br, for an experiment, but you do not have any. You do, however, have a solution of hydrobromic acid, HBr, and a solution of ammonia. Suggest a way to use an acid-base reaction to make a small quantity of NH_4Br.

26. Drawing Conclusions Pure water is a poor conductor of electricity. But having any sort of plugged-in appliances near the bathtub or shower is still dangerous. Why does this danger exist? Explain your reasoning by discussing the composition of tap water.

Graphing Skills

27. Line Graphs The graph below shows how the pH of a solution changes during the course of a titration of an acid with a base. Use the graph to answer the following questions.

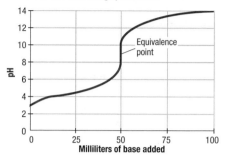

a. What is the equivalence point?
b. What is the pH at the equivalence point?
c. What is the approximate pH of the solution after 25 mL of base is added? Is the solution acidic or basic at this point?
d. Classify both the acid and the base in this neutralization reaction as either weak or strong. Explain your answer.

Math Skills

28. Determining pH What is the pH of a 0.001 M solution of hydrobromic acid, HBr, a strong acid?

29. Determining pH What is the pH of a solution that contains 0.10 mol of HCl in a volume of 100.0 L?

30. Using pH What is the molar concentration of hydronium ions in a solution with a pH of 6?

31. Determining pH The concentration of hydronium ions in a certain acid solution is 100 times the concentration of hydronium ions in a second acid solution. If the second solution has a pH of 5, what is the pH of the first solution?

---

8. Sample answer: A neutralization reaction is a reaction in which hydronium and hydroxide ions react to form water molecules and a salt. When a strong acid reacts with a weak base, there are hydronium ions left over, so the product of the reaction will be acidic and have a pH of less than 7.

9. Sample answer: A solution that has a pH greater than 7 has more hydroxide ions than hydronium ions and is basic.

10. Sample answer: The body needs Ca^{2+} ions from salts to build bones and teeth. The body uses Na^+ and K^+ ions to transmit nerve impulses.

Understanding Key Ideas

11. b
12. c
13. a
14. c
15. b
16. d
17. b
18. a
19. a

Explaining Key Ideas

20. Sample answer: Strong acids ionize completely in water to hydronium ions and the anion of the acid. Weak acids ionize only slightly in water, establishing equilibrium between ionized and non-ionized forms. For example, $HNO_3 + H_2O \rightarrow H_3O^+ + NO_3^-$ (strong acid) and $HCOOH + H_2O \rightleftharpoons H_3O^+ + HCOO^-$ (weak acid).

21. Sample answer: A weak acid would be better because it changes the pH more gradually than a strong acid does. Because of a weak acid's poor ionization, fewer hydronium ions would be added.

Critical Thinking

22. Sample answer: When heated, baking soda decomposes and releases CO_2. The CO_2 from baking soda that is applied to a fire deprives the fire of oxygen and puts the fire out.

23. Sample answer: The formic acid could be neutralized by applying a basic material, such as ammonia solution or a paste of baking soda, to the sting. A strong base would also neutralize the acid, but would also damage the skin.

Assignment Guide

Section	Items
1	2, 7, 9, 11, 12, 17, 22, 26, 28–31
2	8, 10, 13, 14, 16, 20, 21, 23–25, 27
3	1, 3–6, 15, 18, 19

24. Answers may vary: Measure the amount of base required to neutralize a sample of the solution. If the solution contains a strong acid, only a small amount of base will be needed. If the solution contains a weak acid, more base will be required for neutralization because the acid ionizes further as H_3O^+ ions react with OH⁻ ions in the base.

25. Sample answer: I would neutralize an amount of ammonia in solution with an equal amount of hydrobromic acid solution. After the water is evaporated, crystals of the salt ammonium bromide will be left behind.

Answers continued on p. 321A

Standardized Test Prep

 TEST DOCTOR

Question 1 Answer A is correct. Students might answer B if they were confusing the ion with its property of conducting electricity. They might choose C if they were confusing the ion OH⁻ (hydroxide) with the ion hydronium (H_3O^+). Students may choose D because it is a familiar term.

Question 2 Answer I is correct. A strong base will have a pH well above 7. Answer F does not describe an acid or a base because nothing can have a pH of 0. Answer G describes an acid, not a base. Answer H describes a weak base because its pH is close to 7.

Question 3 Answer D is correct. To find the correct answer, students must know that pH corresponds to the negative power of 10 for the number of moles of hydronium (H_3O^+) per liter in a given substance. The cider therefore contains 1×10^{-3} moles per liter; multiplying the molarity by 10 liters gives 1×10^{-2} moles of hydronium ions.

Question 4 Answer F is correct. The ability of a solution to conduct electricity depends on the concentration of hydronium ions in the solution. They might choose answer G if they were confusing the ions released by acids and bases. Students might choose answer H if they thought the amount of acid was more important than the strength of the acid is in determining conductivity. Students might choose answer I if they thought that stronger acids have a higher pH.

Question 5 Full-credit answers should include the following points:
- A pH of 2 corresponds to 1×10^{-2} moles of hydronium ions per liter.
- A pH of 6 corresponds to 1×10^{-6} moles of hydronium ions per liter.
- 1×10^{-2} is 10,000 (1×10^4) times greater than 1×10^{-6} is.

Question 6 Full-credit answers should include the following point:
- $H_3O^+ + OH^- \rightarrow 2H_2O$

Understanding Concepts

Directions (1–4): For each question, write on a sheet of paper the letter of the correct answer.

1. When an acid dissolves in water, which type of ion is among the products formed?
   A. hydronium   **C.** hydroxide
   B. electrolyte   **D.** antacid

2. A mystery substance is found to be a very strong base. What will its pH most likely be?
   F. 0   **H.** 8
   G. 4   **I.** 12

3. A batch of apple cider is found to have a pH of 3. How many moles of H_3O^+ are there in 10 L of the cider?
   A. 30 mol
   B. 1×10^{-30} mol
   C. 1×10^{-4} mol
   D. 1×10^{-2} mol

4. Two acidic solutions are tested for conductivity. If solution A conducts electric current much better than solution B does, what can be concluded about the two solutions?
   F. Solution A has a higher concentration of hydronium ions than solution B does.
   G. Solution A has a higher concentration of hydroxide ions than solution B does.
   H. More acid was dissolved in solution A than in solution B.
   I. The pH of solution A is higher than the pH of solution B.

Directions (5–6): For each question, write a short response.

5. How does the number of hydronium ions in 1 L of a substance with a pH of 6 compare mathematically with the number of hydronium ions in 1 L of a substance with a pH of 2?

6. Write the chemical equation that represents the reaction that takes place in every neutralization reaction.

Reading Skills

Directions (7–9): Read the passage below. Then, answer the questions that follow.

ACID RAIN

In the 1800s, the Industrial Revolution introduced large-scale manufacturing. It also introduced the widespread burning of fossil fuels. One of the negative consequences of this burning was acid rain, which remains an environmental issue to this day.

Acid rain is usually defined as any precipitation that is more acidic than normal. Ordinary precipitation tends to be slightly acidic; it ranges from a pH of about 5.6 to a pH of about 5.0. A drop in the pH of precipitation to below 5.0 usually means that pollution has entered the atmosphere and combined with other substances in the atmosphere. The resulting compounds increase the acidity of the precipitation that falls to the ground.

Coal is a fossil fuel that gives off pollutants, such as sulfur dioxide and nitrogen oxides, when burned. Other fossil fuels, such as gasoline and oil, release similar pollutants. Sulfur dioxide and nitrogen oxides dissolve very easily in water and can be carried very far by the wind. All of these compounds can increase the acidity of precipitation.

7. What is a likely pH reading for acid rain?
   A. 4   **C.** 7
   B. 6   **D.** 9

8. Which pollutants contribute to acid rain?
   F. sulfur dioxide and nitrogen oxides
   G. nitrogen and hydrogen dioxide
   H. sulfur and oxygen
   I. nitrogen oxides

9. What can individuals do to reduce the acidity of precipitation?

Question 7 Answer A is correct. The pH of acid rain is below the pH of normal rain, which is pH 5.0 to 5.6. Although answer B describes acidic rain, pH 6 is less acidic that the normal acidity of rain. Answer C describes neutral rain, which doesn't occur. Answer D indicates that students may not understand the pH scale because a pH value of 9 indicates a base, not an acid.

Question 8 Answer F is correct. According to the passage, sulfur dioxide and nitrogen oxides dissolve easily in water, lowering pH.

Question 9 Full-credit answers should include the following points:
- Individuals can reduce energy consumption, which reduces the use of fossil fuels.
- Individuals can drive less, which reduces the use of fossil fuels.

Question 10 Answer B is correct. The graph shows a neutralization reaction between an acid and a base. Students may choose answers A, C, and D because these reactions are familiar to them. However, the graph does not show these reactions.

Interpreting Graphics

The graphics below each show an acid being titrated with a base. Use these graphics to answer questions 10–11.

TITRATION CURVE

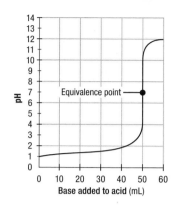
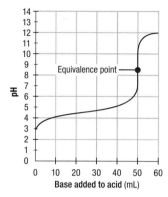

10. What type of reaction is occurring?
    - **A.** decomposition reaction
    - **B.** neutralization reaction
    - **C.** combustion reaction
    - **D.** synthesis reaction

11. Which of the graphs describes a titration in which the base is stronger than the acid? How do you know?

The graphic below shows the pH of several mystery substances. Use this graphic to answer questions 12–13.

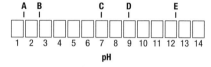

12. Which letters represent the following substances (in order): water, ammonia, battery acid, and lemon juice?
    - **F.** A, B, C, D
    - **G.** B, C, D, E
    - **H.** C, E, A, B
    - **I.** D, B, A, C

13. Which letter shows the pH of the substance that is the most basic?

Test Tip

Sometimes, only a portion of a graph or table is needed to answer a question. Focus only on the necessary information to avoid confusion.

Question 11 Full-credit answers should include the following points:
- If the base is stronger than the acid, the equivalence point is greater than 7.
- The graph on the right shows the equivalence point as pH 8.5, which is greater than 7.

Question 12 Answer H is correct. To find the correct answer, students must realize that milk is fairly neutral, ammonia is highly basic, battery acid is highly acidic, and lemon juice is somewhat acidic.

Question 13 The letter E indicates the substance with the highest pH. Other answers may indicate that students are confused about the relationship between pH and basicity.

State Resources

For specific resources for your state, visit **go.hrw.com** and type in the keyword **HSHSTR**.

📖 **Test Practice with Guided Reading Development**

Answers

1. A
2. I
3. D
4. F
5. 10,000 times greater
6. $H_3O^+ + OH^- \rightarrow 2H_2O$
7. A
8. F
9. Answers may vary; see Test Doctor for a detailed scoring rubric.
10. B
11. Answers may vary; see Test Doctor for a detailed scoring rubric.
12. H
13. letter E

Continuation of Answers

Answers continued from p. 300

8. a. basic

b. acidic

c. acidic

d. neutral

9. H_3O^+ concentration = 0.01 M = 1×10^{-2} M, so pH = –(–2) = 2

10. pH = 11, so H_3O^+ concentration = 1×10^{-11} M

Answers continued from p. 313

5. Sample answer: The agitation moves suspended oily dirt particles away from the clothing, enabling new detergent ions to reach the remaining dirt. The dirt becomes suspended in water and can be rinsed away.

6. Sample answer: Usually, bleach can decolorize the stain by oxidizing the colored substance to a colorless form.

7. Sample answer: Oil and wax are both nonpolar materials, so wax will dissolve in the oily lubricant. The nonpolar ends of the detergent molecules dissolve in the droplets of oil containing the wax, while the ionic ends dissolve in water.

Answers continued from p. 319

26. Sample answer: Pure water is a poor conductor because it contains very few ions. Tap water can contain dissolved salts of calcium and magnesium, making it much more conductive than pure water is. Soaps and detergents are also ionic salts that dissociate into ions when dissolved in water. So, the danger exists because people are almost never in contact with pure water.

Graphing Skills

27. a. The equivalence point is at 50 mL of base added.

b. The pH at the equivalence point is about 9.

c. The pH is about 4.2. The solution is acidic because the pH value is less than 7.

d. Sample answer: The pH at the equivalence point is greater than 7, which means that there are more hydroxide ions than hydronium ions in the solution. So, a weak acid was being titrated with a strong base.

Math Skills

28. As a strong acid, HBr should be completely ionized in water solution. So, the concentration of H_3O^+ ions is 0.001 M, or 1×10^{-3} M; pH = –(–3) = 3

29. Because HCl is a strong acid, the concentration of hydronium ions in the solution is the same as the molar concentration of HCl: 0.10 mol HCl ÷ 100.0 L = 0.0010 mol/L = 1×10^{-3} M H_3O^+; pH = –(–3) = 3

30. Concentration of H_3O^+ ions is $1 \times 10^{-(pH)}$ = 1×10^{-6} M

31. The hydronium ion concentration in the second solution of pH 5 is 1×10^{-5} M. So, the H_3O^+ concentration of the first solution is $100 \times (1 \times 10^{-5}) = 10^{-3}$ M; so, the pH is –(–3) = 3

Chemistry Connections Be sure students realize that the arrows show broad connections between events, but do not indicate direct cause-and-effect relationships.

Students often forget that famous scientists were people who were influenced by the social and political events of their time. Below are some events to help students connect scientists with the time period in which they lived.

Antoine Lavoisier is often considered the father of modern chemistry. He was decapitated during the French Revolution.

In addition to winning the 1954 Nobel Prize in Chemistry, Linus Pauling won the Nobel Peace Prize in 1962. Pauling was an outspoken opponent of war as well as the atmospheric testing and proliferation of nuclear weapons. In the 1950s, during the period of McCarthyism, he was accused of being a Communist. So, he was unable to get a passport for travel abroad until he won the Nobel Prize in 1954.

Rosalind Franklin used X-ray diffraction techniques to obtain the X-ray photographs of DNA while she was a research associate at King's College in London. Although she was a colleague of Maurice Wilkins, she could not eat lunch in the same dining room that he did. At the time, only men were allowed into the university's dining room. Francis Crick, James Watson, and Maurice Wilkins received the Nobel Prize in Physiology or Medicine in 1962 for their discoveries of the structure of DNA. Rosalind Franklin died of cancer in 1958 at the age 37. Thus, she was not eligible for the Nobel Prize.

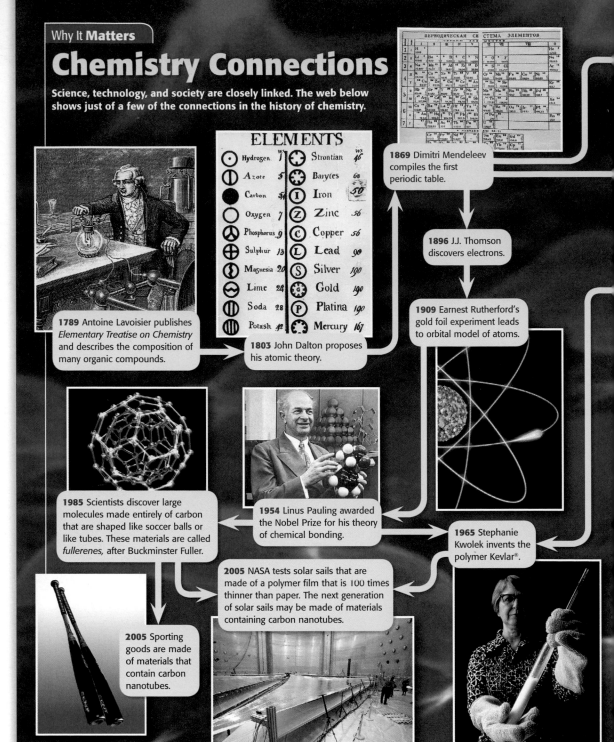

Chemistry Connections

Science, technology, and society are closely linked. The web below shows just of a few of the connections in the history of chemistry.

1869 Dimitri Mendeleev compiles the first periodic table.

1896 J.J. Thomson discovers electrons.

1789 Antoine Lavoisier publishes *Elementary Treatise on Chemistry* and describes the composition of many organic compounds.

1803 John Dalton proposes his atomic theory.

1909 Earnest Rutherford's gold foil experiment leads to orbital model of atoms.

1985 Scientists discover large molecules made entirely of carbon that are shaped like soccer balls or like tubes. These materials are called *fullerenes,* after Buckminster Fuller.

1954 Linus Pauling awarded the Nobel Prize for his theory of chemical bonding.

1965 Stephanie Kwolek invents the polymer Kevlar®.

2005 NASA tests solar sails that are made of a polymer film that is 100 times thinner than paper. The next generation of solar sails may be made of materials containing carbon nanotubes.

2005 Sporting goods are made of materials that contain carbon nanotubes.

Solar Sails Similar to the way sails harness wind energy to propel boats over water, solar sails would use photons from the sun to send vehicles through space. The pressure of reflected photons is sufficient to push a space vehicle forward in a vacuum. Solar sails would be advantageous for space missions that would cover long distances, because they would add substantially less mass to the space vehicle than traditional fuel sources would.

Remarkable Women Many famous male chemists also had talented wives. For example, Marie Lavoisier not only worked with her husband in the laboratory, she also translated many of chemistry publications from English into French for him. Fritz Haber's wife, Clara Immerwahr, was the one of the first women in Germany to receive her Ph.D. in chemistry. Linus Pauling's wife, Ava Helen, actively promoted world peace.

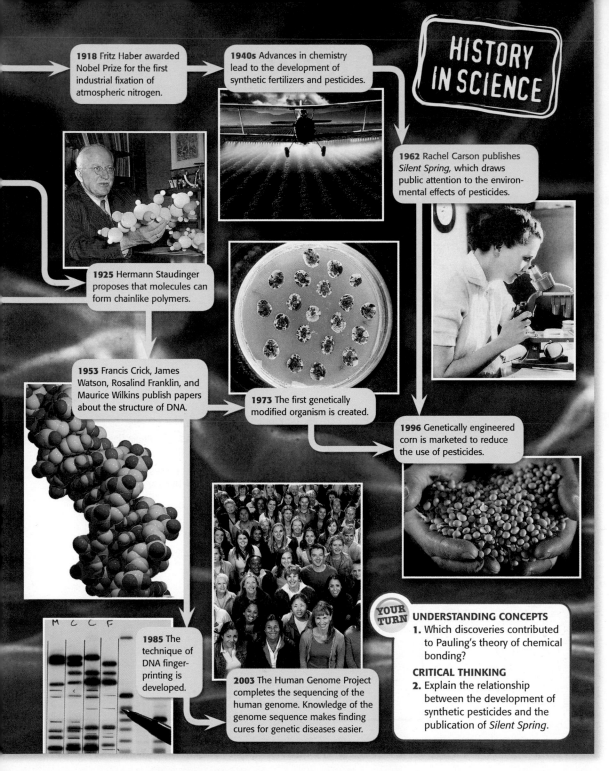

HISTORY IN SCIENCE

1918 Fritz Haber awarded Nobel Prize for the first industrial fixation of atmospheric nitrogen.

1940s Advances in chemistry lead to the development of synthetic fertilizers and pesticides.

1962 Rachel Carson publishes *Silent Spring,* which draws public attention to the environmental effects of pesticides.

1925 Hermann Staudinger proposes that molecules can form chainlike polymers.

1953 Francis Crick, James Watson, Rosalind Franklin, and Maurice Wilkins publish papers about the structure of DNA.

1973 The first genetically modified organism is created.

1996 Genetically engineered corn is marketed to reduce the use of pesticides.

1985 The technique of DNA fingerprinting is developed.

2003 The Human Genome Project completes the sequencing of the human genome. Knowledge of the genome sequence makes finding cures for genetic diseases easier.

YOUR TURN

UNDERSTANDING CONCEPTS
1. Which discoveries contributed to Pauling's theory of chemical bonding?

CRITICAL THINKING
2. Explain the relationship between the development of synthetic pesticides and the publication of *Silent Spring*.

Why It Matters

Genetically Modified Organisms A type of bacteria, E. Coli (*Escherichia coli*), was the first type of organism to be genetically modified. Recombinant DNA, DNA that is a combination of DNA from two organisms, was introduced into the bacteria cells. Similar techniques are used today to make bacteria cells that produce human insulin to treat diabetes.

READING TOOLBOX

Visual Literacy The image shown of DNA Fingerprinting shows a gel electrophoresis. The dark bands are fragments of DNA that have moved varying distances along the gel. Because DNA has a negative charge, it moves to the positive side of the gel when an electric field is applied across the gel. Smaller fragments move faster than larger fragments.

Answers to Your Turn

1. Many discoveries contributed to Pauling's theory of bonding, including the development of atomic theory, the formation of the periodic table, the discovery of electrons, and the development of the orbital model of the atom.
2. The development of synthetic pesticides led to the widespread use of pesticides. Rachel Carson published *Silent Spring* to show that the widespread use of pesticides can have harmful effects on the environment.

	Standards	Teach Key Ideas
CHAPTER OPENER, pp. 324–326 50 min.		
SECTION 1 What Is Radioactivity? pp. 327–336 50 min. ❯ Nuclear Radiation ❯ Nuclear Decay ❯ Radioactive Decay Rates	PS 1d, UCP 1, UCP 3, SAI 1, HNS 1, HNS 3	🗔 **Bellringer Transparency** 🗔 **Teaching Transparencies** TM28 Types of Nuclear Radiation • TM29 Particle Penetration • C27 Radioactive Decay of Carbon-14 💿 **Visual Concepts** Alpha, Beta, and Gamma Radiation • Comparing Alpha, Beta, and Gamma Particles • Half-Life
SECTION 2 Nuclear Fission and Fusion, pp. 337–343 50 min. ❯ Nuclear Forces ❯ Nuclear Fission ❯ Nuclear Fusion	PS 1c, UCP 1, UCP 2, UCP 3, SAI 1, ST 2	🗔 **Bellringer Transparency** 🗔 **Teaching Transparencies** C25 Chain Reaction • C26 Nuclear Fusion 💿 **Visual Concepts** Nuclear Forces • Strong Nuclear Force • Nuclear Fission • Nuclear Chain Reaction • Nuclear Fusion
SECTION 3 Nuclear Radiation Today, pp. 344–351 50 min. ❯ Where Is Radiation? ❯ Beneficial Uses of Nuclear Radiation ❯ Risks from Nuclear Radiation ❯ Nuclear Power	ST 2, SPSP 6	🗔 **Bellringer Transparency** 💿 **Visual Concepts** Radioactive Tracer • Nuclear Energy

See also PowerPoint® Resources

Chapter Review and Assessment Resources

SE Science Skills: Counting Nuclear Decay, p. 354
SE Chapter Summary, p. 355
SE Chapter Review, pp. 356–357
SE Standardized Test Prep, pp. 358–359
🗁 Concept Review Worksheets ■
🗁 Chapter Tests A and B ■
📕 Holt Online Assessment

CHAPTER
Fast Track
To shorten instruction because of time limitations, omit Section 3 and the chapter lab.

Basic Learners
TE Irène Curie, p. 332
TE Reviewing Exponents, p. 334
TE Unbalanced Forces, p. 338
TE Radioactive Foods, p. 345
🗁 Science Skills Worksheets
🗁 Differentiated Datasheets A for Labs and Activities ■
📒 Study Guide A ■

Advanced Learners
TE Radiation and Health, p. 332
TE Investigating Half-Life, p. 333
TE Graphing Half-Life, p. 335
TE Three Mile Island, p. 349
🗁 Cross-Disciplinary Worksheets
🗁 Differentiated Datasheets C for Labs and Activities ■

Key

SE Student Edition
TE Teacher's Edition

📁 Chapter Resource File
📓 Workbook
🖥 Transparency

💿 CD or CD-ROM
* Datasheet or blackline master available

■ Also available in Spanish

All resources listed below are also available on the Teacher's One-Stop Planner.

Why It Matters	Hands-On	Skills Development	Assessment
Build student motivation with resources about high-interest applications.	**SE Inquiry Lab** Radiation and Film, p. 325*■	**TE Reading Toolbox** Assessing Prior Knowledge, p. 324 **SE Reading Toolbox** p. 326	📁 **Pretest** ■

TE Effects of Radiation, p. 328 **TE Finding Neutrino Mass,** p. 331 **SE Discovering Nuclear Radiation,** p. 332 **TE Carbon Dating,** p. 335 📁 **Cross-Disciplinary Worksheets** Connection to Social Studies—A Remarkable Discovery • Connection to Language Arts—Marie Curie and the Naming of a Unit • Integrating Chemistry—Radiochemistry • Integrating Earth Science—Radioactivity Within Earth	**TE Demonstration** Detecting Radon, p. 327 **TE Demonstration** Acting Out Half-Life, p. 333 **SE Quick Lab** Modeling Decay and Half-Life, p. 335*■ **SE Skills Practice Lab** Simulating Nuclear Decay Reactions, pp. 352–353*■ 📁 **Observation Lab** Modeling Radioactive Decay with Pennies	**TE Reading Toolbox** Visual Literacy, p. 328 **SE Reading Toolbox** Analyzing Comparisons, p. 329 **TE Reading Toolbox** Identifying Preconceptions, p. 329 **TE Reading Toolbox** Visual Literacy, p. 330 **SE Math Skills** Nuclear Decay, p. 331 **SE Math Skills** Half-Life, p. 334	**TE Reteaching Key Ideas** Mass Comparisons, p. 336 **TE Formative Assessment,** p. 336 📁 **Spanish Assessment***■ 📁 **Section Quiz** ■
TE Atomic Bombs, p. 337 **TE Hideki Yukawa,** p. 338 **TE A Natural Nuclear Reactor,** p. 340 **SE The Power of Fission,** p. 343 **TE Levels of Background Radiation,** p. 344	**TE Demonstration** A Chain Reaction, p. 340 **SE Quick Lab** Modeling Chain Reactions, p. 341*■	**SE Reading Toolbox** Word Origins, p. 338 **TE Reading Toolbox** Visual Literacy, p. 339 **TE Science Skills** Graphing, p. 345 **TE Math Skills** The Sievert, p. 345	**TE Reteaching Key Ideas** Comparison T Chart, p. 342 **TE Formative Assessment,** p. 342 📁 **Spanish Assessment***■ 📁 **Section Quiz** ■
TE What Is a Rem? p. 345 **TE Radiology,** p. 346 **TE Irradiation,** p. 346 **SE How Do PET Scans Work?** p. 347 **TE Properties of Radon,** p. 348 **TE Chernobyl,** p. 349 **TE Storing Radioactive Wastes,** p. 350 📁 **Cross-Disciplinary Worksheets** Integrating Environmental Science—Environmental Radiation • Real World Applications—Radiation and Medicine • Integrating Space Science—Nuclear-Powered Space Probes • Integrating Space Science—The Life Cycle of a Star	📁 **CBL™ Probeware Lab** Determining the Effective Half-Life of Iodine-131 in the Human Body	**TE Reading Toolbox** Making Predictions, p. 346 **SE Reading Toolbox** Word Origins, p. 348 **TE Reading Toolbox** Visual Literacy, p. 349	**TE Reteaching Key Ideas** Concept Map, p. 351 **TE Formative Assessment,** p. 351 📁 **Spanish Assessment***■ 📁 **Section Quiz** ■
	See also Lab Generator		**See also Holt Online Assessment Resources**

Resources for Differentiated Instruction

English Learners
TE Making Models, p. 329
📁 Differentiated Datasheets A, B, and C for Labs and Activities ■
📓 Study Guide A ■

Struggling Readers
TE Paired Reading, p. 339
📓 Interactive Reader

Special Education Students
TE Illustrating Nuclear Decay, p. 330

Alternative Assessment
TE Fission Debate, p. 341
TE Radioactive Tracers, p. 347
TE Weighing the Risks, p. 348
TE Revising Preconceptions, p. 350
TE Predicting Reactions, p. 355

CHAPTER 10 Nuclear Changes

Overview

This chapter introduces students to radioactivity. The students will learn about the four main types of radiation. Students will also learn how to balance nuclear decay equations and calculate half-life. Nuclear fission and nuclear fusion will be explored. Students study the interaction between matter and energy and explore how chain reactions occur. Some applications of radioactivity and the associated risks will be introduced, including the use of radioactivity in medicine, as well as the benefits and drawbacks of nuclear power.

READING TOOLBOX

Assessing Prior Knowledge Students should understand the following concepts:
• scientific notation
• elements
• matter and energy
• atomic structure
• isotopes
• mass number
• atomic number

MISCONCEPTION ALERT

Science education research has identified the following misconception about nuclear change.
• Students confuse nuclear changes with chemical changes. (Both types of changes result in chemicals with different identities than the starting substances. However, nuclear changes involve changes to the protons or neutrons, while chemical changes involve changes to electron arrangement without change to nuclear particles.)

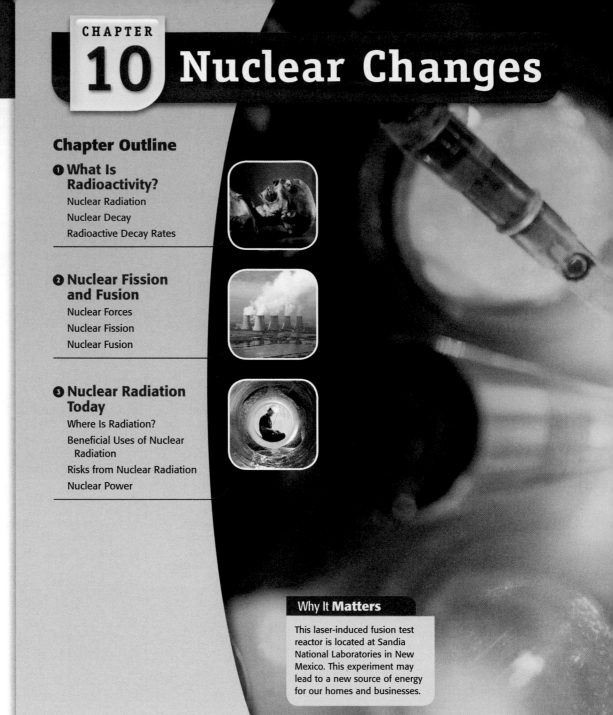

Chapter Outline

❶ What Is Radioactivity?
Nuclear Radiation
Nuclear Decay
Radioactive Decay Rates

❷ Nuclear Fission and Fusion
Nuclear Forces
Nuclear Fission
Nuclear Fusion

❸ Nuclear Radiation Today
Where Is Radiation?
Beneficial Uses of Nuclear Radiation
Risks from Nuclear Radiation
Nuclear Power

Why It Matters

This laser-induced fusion test reactor is located at Sandia National Laboratories in New Mexico. This experiment may lead to a new source of energy for our homes and businesses.

Chapter Correlations   *National Science Education Standards*

The following correlations show the National Science Standards that relate to this chapter. For the full text of the standards, see the National Science Education Standards at the front of the book.

PS 1c The nuclear forces that hold the nucleus of an atom together, at nuclear distances, are usually stronger than the electric forces that would make it fly apart. Nuclear reactions convert a fraction of the mass of interacting particles into energy, and they can release much greater amounts of energy than atomic interactions. Fission is the splitting of a large nucleus into smaller pieces. Fusion is the joining of two nuclei at extremely high temperature and pressure, and is the process responsible for the energy of the sun and other stars. (Section 2)

PS 1d Radioactive isotopes are unstable and undergo spontaneous nuclear reactions, emitting particles and/or wavelike radiation. The decay of any one nucleus cannot be predicted, but a large group of identical nuclei decay at a predictable rate. This predictability can be used to estimate the age of materials that contain radioactive isotopes. (Section 1, Skills Practice Lab: Simulating Nuclear Decay Reactions)

UCP 1 Systems, order, and organization (Sections 1, 2)

UCP 2 Evidence, models, and explanation (Section 2)

UCP 3 Constancy, change, and measurement (Sections 1, 2)

SAI 1 Abilities necessary to do scientific inquiry (Sections 1, 2; Skills Practice Lab: Simulating Nuclear Decay Reactions)

ST 2 Understandings about science and technology (Sections 2, 3)

HNS 1 Science as a human endeavor (Section 1)

HNS 3 Historical perspectives (Section 1)

SPSP 6 Science and technology in local, national, and global challenges (Section 3)

Materials per Group
- unexposed photographic film
- smoke detector
- cardboard box
- thick envelope

Answers

1. The film will show a scattering of spots on the otherwise unaffected film.
2. The spots will be more numerous near the radioactive source.

Key Resources

 Datasheet
Radiation and Film

InquiryLab ⏱ **30 min**

Radiation and Film

Obtain a sheet of **unexposed photographic film** and a new household **smoke detector** that contains a radioactive sample. Remove the detector's casing. In a **dark room,** place the film next to the smoke detector in a **cardboard box.** Close the box. On the next day, open the box in a darkened room. Place the film in a **thick envelope.** Have the film processed, and study the image on the film.

Questions to Get You Started

1. How does the image on the exposed film differ from the rest of the film?
2. How can you tell that the image is related to the radioactive source?

Word Origins

Sample table:

Type of Radiation	Named By/ When	Origin of Name
X ray	Becquerel/1896	"unknown" source of radiation
Alpha particle	Rutherford/1899	first letter of Greek alphabet
Beta particle	Becquerel/1900	second letter of Greek alphabet
Gamma ray	Villard/1900	third letter of Greek alphabet
Neutron	Chadwick/1932	"neutral subatomic particle"

Comparisons

Answers may vary. Students' tables should have several entries, with each row listing the two items being compared, a description of the similarity or difference between the things, plus a word or phrase that signals the comparison.

FoldNotes

Answers may vary. Students' Four-Corner Folds should look similar to the example shown. The four flaps should be labeled "Alpha particles," "Beta particles," "Gamma rays," and "Neutrons." Notes about each kind of nuclear radiation should be written behind the appropriate flap.

READING TOOLBOX

These reading tools can help you learn the material in this chapter. For more information on how to use these and other tools, see **Appendix A.**

Word Origins

Alpha, Beta, and Gamma Knowing the origins of science terms can give you insight into the history surrounding certain scientific discoveries. The term *radioactivity* was coined by Pierre and Marie Curie. The word was a combination of two Latin root words: *radius*, which means "beam of light," and *activus*, which means "active."

Your Turn As you learn about nuclear radiation, complete a chart like this one about the origin of the name of each type of radiation. (Some entries may need to be researched by using other sources.)

TYPE OF RADIATION	NAMED BY, WHEN NAMED	ORIGIN OF NAME
X ray	Becquerel, 1896	unknown source of radiation
Alpha particle	Rutherford, 1899	first letter of the Greek alphabet
Beta particle		
Gamma ray		
Neutron		

FoldNotes

Four-Corner Fold A four-corner fold is useful when you want to compare the characteristics of four topics.

Your Turn Make a four-corner fold by using the instructions in **Appendix A.**

1. Label the four outer flaps with the names of the four primary kinds of nuclear radiation: alpha particles, beta particles, gamma rays, and neutrons.

2. Underneath each flap, take notes about that kind of nuclear radiation.

Comparisons

Analyzing Comparisons When you are comparing two things, you describe how they are similar and how they are different. Such comparisons are signaled in language by the use of a few key words or structures. The words *like* or *unlike* can signal that a comparison is being made and can tell you whether the comparison is focused on similarities or differences. Comparative words can be formed by using the suffixes *-er* or *-est*. Comparative phrases can be formed by using the words *more* or *less*.

Your Turn As you read this chapter, fill out a table of comparisons like the one below. In the first two columns, list the two things being compared. In the third column, describe the similarity or difference that the comparison reveals. In the last column, note any words or phrases that signal the comparison. The sample entry below is for the sentence "Like alpha particles, beta particles can easily ionize other atoms."

FIRST THING	SECOND THING	SIMILARITY OR DIFFERENCE	SIGNALING WORD OR PHRASE
alpha particles	beta particles	Both can easily ionize other atoms.	like

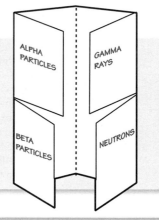

What Is Radioactivity?

Key **Ideas**

❯ What happens when an element undergoes radioactive decay?

❯ How does radiation affect the nucleus of an unstable isotope?

❯ How do scientists predict when an atom will undergo radioactive decay?

Key **Terms**

radioactive decay

nuclear radiation

alpha particle

beta particle

gamma ray

half-life

Why It **Matters**

Nuclear radiation surrounds us on Earth, but scientists did not identify nuclear radiation until a little more than 100 years ago.

Our lives are affected by radioactivity in many ways. Technology using radioactivity has helped humans detect disease, kill cancer cells, generate electricity, and design smoke detectors. However, there are also risks associated with too much nuclear radiation, so we must know where it may exist and how we can counteract it. But first, what exactly is radioactivity?

Nuclear Radiation

Certain isotopes of many elements undergo a process called radioactive decay. During **radioactive decay,** the unstable nuclei of these isotopes emit particles, or release energy, to become stable isotopes, as **Figure 1** shows. ❯ **After radioactive decay, the element changes into a different isotope of the same element or into an entirely different element.** Recall that isotopes of an element are atoms that have the same number of protons but different numbers of neutrons in their nuclei. Different elements are distinguished by having different numbers of protons.

The released energy and matter are collectively called **nuclear radiation.** Just as materials that undergo radioactive decay are changed, materials that are bombarded with nuclear radiation are also affected. These effects depend on the type of radiation and on the properties of the materials that nuclear radiation encounters. (Note that the term *radiation* can refer to light or to energy transfer. To avoid confusion, the term *nuclear radiation* will be used to describe radiation associated with nuclear changes.)

radioactive decay (RAY dee oh AK tiv dee KAY) the disintegration of an unstable atomic nucleus into one or more different nuclides

nuclear radiation (NOO klee uhr RAY dee AY shuhn) the particles that are released from the nucleus during radioactive decay

Figure 1 During radioactive decay, an unstable nucleus emits one or more particles of high-energy electromagnetic radiation.

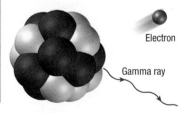

Electron

Gamma ray

❯ Focus

This section introduces students to nuclear radiation. Students learn about the four main types of radiation. They also balance equations for nuclear decay and calculate how rapidly a radioactive isotope decays.

🎧 Bellringer

Use the Bellringer transparency to prepare students for this section.

Demonstrate

Detecting Radon Explain that radon is one element that changes through radioactivity. Small amounts of radon occur naturally in the environment as a decay product of the uranium in soil. Obtain a short-term radon detection kit from a hardware store; follow its instructions. If the school has a basement, place one there in a poorly ventilated area. Allow students to observe the results. Explain that since radon forms from uranium in rocks and soil, the radon levels may be highest at the lowest part of a building. If enough radon gas is present to pose a health risk, ventilation should be increased and cracks sealed. **LS Visual**

Key Resources

 Teaching Transparencies
TM28 Types of Nuclear Radiation
TM29 Particle Penetration
C27 Radioactive Decay of Carbon-14

Visual Concepts
Alpha, Beta, and Gamma Radiation
Comparing Alpha, Beta, and Gamma Particles
Half-Life

Datasheet
Modeling Decay and Half-Life

Math Skills Worksheets
Nuclear Decay
Half-Life

Cross-Disciplinary Worksheets
Connection to Social Studies—A Remarkable Discovery
Connection to Language Arts—Marie Curie and the Naming of a Unit
Integrating Chemistry—Radiochemistry
Integrating Earth Science—Radioactivity Within Earth

Teach

Teaching Key Ideas

Nuclear Change in Elements Remind students what the numbers in the nuclear symbols represent. Then have students use the symbols in the chart to predict what will happen to a nucleus of an atom and its mass when an alpha particle is emitted and when a neutron is emitted. (When an alpha particle is emitted, the nucleus will lose two protons and two neutrons and the mass will decrease by 4. When a neutron is emitted, the nucleus will lose a neutron and the mass will decrease by 1.) **LS Verbal**

READING TOOLBOX

Visual Literacy Remind students how to interpret the symbols used in **Figure 2.** For practice, provide students with several different elements and a periodic table. Have students write similar symbols for the most common isotope of each element. For example, for phosphorus, the atomic number is 15 and the atomic mass, rounded off (mass number), is 31. The symbol for this isotope of phosphorus is $^{31}_{15}P$. **LS Visual**

SCILINKS. www.scilinks.org
Topic: Types of Radiation
Code: HK81569

Figure 2 Types of Nuclear Radiation

Radiation type	Symbol	Mass (kg)	Charge	Graphic
Alpha particle	$^{4}_{2}He$	6.646×10^{-27}	+2	
Beta particle	$^{0}_{-1}e$	9.109×10^{-31}	−1, (+1)	
Gamma ray	γ	none	0	
Neutron	$^{1}_{0}n$	1.675×10^{-27}	0	

There are different types of nuclear radiation.

Essentially, there are four types of nuclear radiation. Nuclear radiation can contain alpha particles, beta particles, gamma rays, or neutrons. Some of the properties of these types are listed in **Figure 2.** When a radioactive nucleus decays, the nuclear radiation leaves the nucleus. This nuclear radiation interacts with nearby matter. This interaction depends in part on the properties of nuclear radiation, such as charge, mass, and energy.

Alpha particles consist of protons and neutrons.

Uranium is a radioactive element that naturally occurs as three isotopes. One of its isotopes, uranium-238, undergoes nuclear decay by emitting positively charged particles. Ernest Rutherford, noted for discovering the nucleus, named this radiation *alpha* (α) *rays* after the first letter of the Greek alphabet. Later, he discovered that alpha rays were actually particles, each made of two protons and two neutrons—the same as helium nuclei. **Alpha particles** are positively charged and more massive than any other type of nuclear radiation.

Alpha particles do not travel far through materials. In fact, they barely pass through a sheet of paper. One factor that limits an alpha particle's ability to pass through matter is that it is massive compared to other subatomic particles. Because alpha particles are charged, they remove electrons from—or ionize—matter as they pass through it. This ionization causes the alpha particle to lose energy and slow further.

Reading Check **To which element is an alpha particle related?** (See Appendix E for answers to Reading Checks.)

alpha particle (AL fuh PAHRT i kuhl) a positively charged particle that consists of two protons and two neutrons and that is emitted from a nucleus during radioactive decay

beta particle (BAYT uh PAHRT i kuhl) an electron or positron that is emitted from a nucleus during radioactive decay

gamma ray (GAM uh RAY) the high-energy photon emitted by a nucleus during fission and radioactive decay

Why It Matters

Effects of Radiation When many students think of radiation, they think of its negative aspects. Emphasize to students that many positive aspects of radiation also exist. The radiation that causes sunburn on unprotected skin also keeps Earth at a temperature that can sustain life. The nuclear processes that are used in nuclear weapons also provide electricity for many places on Earth. Tell students that they will learn more about the positive and negative aspects of radiation later in the chapter. Have students investigate the effect of nuclear fission on the outcome of World War II and present their findings in a written report. **LS Visual**

Beta particles are produced from neutron decay.

Some nuclei emit a type of nuclear radiation that travels farther through matter than alpha particles do. This nuclear radiation is composed of beta particles, named after the second Greek letter, *beta* (β). **Beta particles** are often fast-moving electrons but may also be positively charged particles called *positrons*. Positrons have the same mass as electrons.

Negative particles coming from the positively charged nucleus puzzled scientists for years. However, in the 1930s, another discovery helped clear up the mystery. Neutrons, which are not charged, decay to form a proton and an electron. The electron, which has a very small mass, is then ejected at a high speed from the nucleus as a beta particle.

As **Figure 3** shows, beta particles pass through a piece of paper, but most are stopped by 3 mm of aluminum or 10 mm of wood. This greater penetration occurs because beta particles are not as massive as alpha particles. But like alpha particles, beta particles can easily ionize other atoms. As they ionize atoms, beta particles lose energy. This property prevents them from penetrating matter very deeply.

Gamma rays are high-energy electromagnetic radiation.

Unlike alpha or beta particles, gamma rays are not made of matter and do not have an electric charge. Instead, **gamma rays,** named for the third Greek letter, *gamma* (γ), are a form of electromagnetic energy. Like visible light and X rays, gamma rays consist of energy packets called *photons*. Gamma rays, however, have more energy than light or X rays do.

Although gamma rays have no electric charge, they can easily ionize matter. High-energy gamma rays can cause damage in matter. They can penetrate up to 60 cm of aluminum or 7 cm of lead. They are not easily stopped by clothing or most building materials and therefore pose a greater danger to health than either alpha or beta particles do.

Neutron radioactivity occurs in an unstable nucleus.

Like alpha and beta radiation, *neutron emission* consists of matter that is emitted from an unstable nucleus. In fact, scientists first discovered the neutron as a result of this emission.

Neutrons have no charge, and therefore they do not ionize matter as alpha and beta particles do. Because neutrons do not use their energy to ionize matter, they are able to travel farther through matter than either alpha or beta particles do. A block of lead about 15 cm thick is required to stop most fast neutrons emitted during radioactive decay.

READING TOOLBOX

Analyzing Comparisons
As you read about the different kinds of nuclear radiation, look for comparisons among them. Create a table of their similarities and differences.

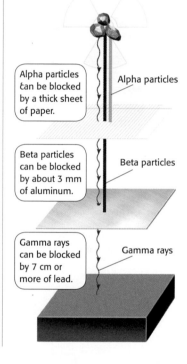

Figure 3 Different kinds of nuclear radiation penetrate different materials. **Why must both the thickness and material be specified?**

Alpha particles can be blocked by a thick sheet of paper.

Alpha particles

Beta particles can be blocked by about 3 mm of aluminum.

Beta particles

Gamma rays can be blocked by 7 cm or more of lead.

Gamma rays

READING TOOLBOX

Analyzing Comparisons Encourage students to include drawings in their charts, such as graphic depictions of each type of nuclear emission and illustrations of materials that can block these emissions.

Answer to caption question

The nuclear radiation will penetrate materials that are less dense (such as paper or wood) more deeply than materials that are more dense (such as aluminum or lead).

Teaching Key Ideas

Other Types of Radiation Tell students that the main types of radiation are discussed in the student text. However, other types exist. For example, chromium-49 decays to form vanadium-49 and what is known as a positron.

A positron (β^+) is similar to an electron except that it is positively charged. Positrons exist for an extremely short period of time because they are the antiparticles of electrons. When an electron and a positron collide, all the mass in both particles converts to energy in the form of gamma rays.

Differentiated Instruction

English Learners

Making Models Provide students with yarn, modeling clay, paper, aluminum foil, cardboard, and rulers. Have them use the materials to make a physical model of the information presented in **Figure 3.** Ask students to label each part of the model and use the model to explain the differences in the three types of radiation—alpha, beta, and gamma.
LS Kinesthetic

READING TOOLBOX

Identifying Preconceptions Write the word *radiation* on the chalkboard. Under the word, list the terms *positive* and *negative* as column heads. Have students brainstorm positive and negative perceptions that they associate with radiation. Keep a copy of the list, and use it as a discussion tool when students complete this chapter.
LS Verbal

Teaching Key Ideas

Decay of Nuclei Ask whether students are familiar with the word *decay,* indicating the breakdown of a substance, such as when food or a tooth tissue decays. Be sure students know that radioactive decay is the release of radiation by isotopes that are radioactive.

READING TOOLBOX

Visual Literacy To help students understand how nuclear decay processes are represented by equations, have them compare a nuclear equation with a chemical equation. Write the equation for the alpha decay of radium-226 on the chalkboard, and write the following chemical equation directly beneath it:

$$2H_2 + O_2 \rightarrow 2H_2O$$

Ask students: How are the two equations similar? (In both examples, the "reactants" are on the left, and the "products" are on the right. Both use an arrow to separate the terms. Both use numbers to show the quantities of items involved in the reactions.)

How are they different? (In the chemical equation, atoms are conserved. Both sides of the equation have 4 hydrogen atoms and 2 oxygen atoms. In the nuclear equation, protons and neutrons are conserved, but the atoms are not the same. The radium atom has 88 protons and emits an alpha particle with 2 protons, and thereby becomes a radon atom with 86 protons.)

LS **Logical/Verbal**

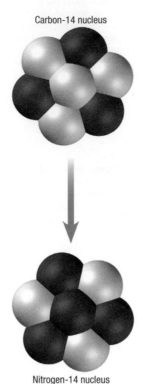

Carbon-14 nucleus

Nitrogen-14 nucleus

Beta particle (electron)

Figure 4 A nucleus that undergoes beta decay has nearly the same atomic mass afterward, but it has one more proton and one less neutron.

Nuclear Decay

Nuclear decay causes changes in the nucleus of an atom. ❯**Anytime that an unstable nucleus emits alpha or beta particles, the number of protons and neutrons changes.** An example is radium-226 (an isotope of radium with the mass number 226), which changes to radon-222 by emitting an alpha particle.

Nuclear-decay equations are similar to those used for chemical reactions. The nucleus before decay is like a reactant and is placed on the left side of the equation. The products are placed on the right side.

Gamma decay changes the energy of the nucleus.

When an atom undergoes nuclear decay and emits gamma rays, there is no change in the atomic number or the atomic mass of the element. The reason is that the number of protons and neutrons does not change. After gamma decay, the energy content of the nucleus is lower because some of its energy was taken away by the energy in the gamma ray.

The atomic number changes during beta decay.

A beta particle is not an atom and does not have an atomic number, which is the number of positive charges in a nucleus. For the sake of convenience, because an electron has a single negative charge, an electron is given an atomic number of –1 in a nuclear-decay equation. Similarly, the electron's mass is so much less than the mass of a proton or a neutron that the electron can be regarded as having a mass number of 0. The beta particle symbol, with the right mass and atomic numbers, is $_{-1}^{0}e$.

A beta-decay process occurs when carbon-14 decays to nitrogen-14 by emitting a beta particle, as **Figure 4** shows. This process can be written as follows.

$$_{6}^{14}C \rightarrow {}_{7}^{14}N + {}_{-1}^{0}e \qquad \begin{array}{l} 14 = 14 + 0 \\ 6 = 7 + (-1) \end{array}$$

In all cases of beta decay, the mass number before and after the decay does not change. The atomic number of the product nucleus, however, increases by 1, so the atom changes to a different element. During carbon-14 beta decay, a neutron changes into a proton. As a result, the positive charge of the nucleus increases by 1, and an atom of nitrogen forms.

✓ **Reading Check** How do the mass number and the atomic number change during beta decay?

Differentiated Instruction

Special Education Students

Illustrating Nuclear Decay Have students illustrate alpha decay of radium-226 visually by having them sketch the numbers of neutrons and protons in the nucleus of an atom of radium-226 before and after the nuclear change took place. Show them how to draw blocks of squares to represent tens and hundreds of particles. Then, have them use the same system to illustrate beta decay from a carbon-14 nucleus. Point out that the nucleus does not show electrons, so their picture of beta decay will not illustrate the actual beta particle. Have them label their diagrams with the nuclear equations and explain to a partner how the two visual displays are related. **LS** **Visual**

Both atomic mass and number change in alpha decay.

In alpha decay, the form of the decay equation is the same except that the symbol for an alpha particle is used. The alpha decay of radium-226 is written as follows.

$$^{226}_{88}\text{Ra} \rightarrow\ ^{222}_{86}\text{Rn} +\ ^{4}_{2}\text{He} \qquad \begin{array}{l} 226 = 222 + 4 \\ 88 = 86 + 2 \end{array}$$

The mass number of the atom before decay is 226. The mass number equals the sum of the mass numbers of the products, 222 and 4. The atomic numbers follow the same principle. The 88 protons in radium before the nuclear decay equal the 86 protons in the radon-222 nucleus and 2 protons in the alpha particle.

Academic Vocabulary

principle (PRIN suh puhl) basic law, rule, or belief

Math Skills Nuclear Decay

Actinium-217 decays by releasing an alpha particle. Write the equation for this decay process, and determine which element is formed.

Identify Write the equation with the original element on the left side and the products on the right side.	$^{217}_{89}\text{Ac} \rightarrow\ ^{A}_{Z}X +\ ^{4}_{2}\text{He}$ X = unknown product A = unknown mass Z = unknown atomic number
Plan Write math equations for the atomic and mass numbers. Rearrange the equations.	$217 = A + 4 \qquad 89 = Z + 2$ $A = 217 - 4 \qquad Z = 89 - 2$
Solve Solve for the unknown values, and rewrite the equation with all nuclei represented.	$A = 213 \qquad Z = 87$ According to the periodic table, francium has an atomic number of 87. The unknown element is therefore $^{213}_{87}\text{Fr}$. $^{217}_{89}\text{Ac} \rightarrow\ ^{213}_{87}\text{Fr} +\ ^{4}_{2}\text{He}$

Practice

Complete the following radioactive-decay equations. Identify the isotope X. Indicate whether alpha or beta decay takes place.

1. $^{12}_{5}\text{B} \rightarrow\ ^{12}_{6}\text{C} +\ ^{A}_{Z}X$

2. $^{225}_{89}\text{Ac} \rightarrow\ ^{221}_{87}\text{Fr} +\ ^{A}_{Z}X$

3. $^{63}_{28}\text{Ni} \rightarrow\ ^{A}_{Z}X +\ ^{0}_{-1}e$

4. $^{212}_{83}\text{Bi} \rightarrow\ ^{A}_{Z}X +\ ^{4}_{2}\text{He}$

For more practice, visit **go.hrw.com** and enter keyword **HK8MP**.

Practice Hint

> In all nuclear-decay problems, the atomic number of the new atom is the key to identifying the new atom.

> After determining the new atomic number, use the periodic table to find out the name of the new element.

Math Skills

Answers to Practice

1. $12 = 12 + A; A = 0$
   $5 = 6 + Z; Z = -1$
   $X = e$
   Beta decay occurs, and $^{0}_{-1}e$ is produced.

2. $225 = 221 + A; A = 4$
   $89 = 87 + Z; Z = 2$
   $X = \text{He}$
   Alpha decay occurs, and $^{4}_{2}\text{He}$ is produced.

3. $63 = A + 0; A = 63$
   $28 = Z + (-1); Z = 29$
   $X = \text{Cu}$
   Beta decay occurs, and $^{63}_{29}\text{Cu}$ is produced.

4. $212 = A + 4; A = 208$
   $83 = Z + 2; Z = 81$
   $X = \text{Tl}$
   Alpha decay occurs, and $^{208}_{81}\text{Tl}$ is produced.

Additional Examples

Have students complete the following radioactive-decay equations by identifying the nuclide X, and indicate whether alpha or beta decay takes place.

1. $^{14}_{6}\text{C} \rightarrow\ ^{A}_{Z}X +\ ^{0}_{-1}e$
   Answer: $^{14}_{7}\text{N}$, beta

2. $^{238}_{92}\text{U} \rightarrow\ ^{234}_{90}\text{Th} +\ ^{A}_{Z}X$
   Answer: $^{4}_{2}\text{He}$, alpha

3. $^{40}_{19}\text{K} \rightarrow\ ^{40}_{20}\text{Ca} +\ ^{A}_{Z}X$
   Answer: $^{0}_{-1}e$, beta

4. $^{219}_{86}\text{Rn} \rightarrow\ ^{A}_{Z}X +\ ^{4}_{2}\text{He}$
   Answer: $^{215}_{84}\text{Po}$, alpha

LS Logical

Why It Matters

Finding Neutrino Mass Some scientists are hoping to use beta decay to shed light on one of the most mysterious particles of modern physics—the neutrino. The neutrino is a fundamental particle in our universe, but we don't know much about it. Learning more about the neutrino might help scientists answer some of the most fundamental questions of modern physics today.

The neutrino, whose existence was first predicted by Wolfgang Pauli in 1931, has no electric charge and almost no mass. (Current estimates suggest that a neutrino's mass is about 10,000 times less than an electron's mass.) As a result, neutrinos are very difficult to detect and measure. Many current attempts to detect neutrinos involve elaborate set-ups, such as huge detectors in underground caves.

In 1986, scientists first observed a process that is now known as double beta decay: a nucleus emits two electrons simultaneously. Currently, scientists plan to use measurements of these double beta decay reactions to make the first measurement of the absolute mass of an electron neutrino. Have interested students find out more about neutrino detection by searching the Internet for images of the Super Kamiokande detector in Japan and other neutrino detectors.

LS Visual

▶ Teach, continued

Discovering Nuclear Radiation In 1896, the French scientist Henri Becquerel discovered that uranium gives off penetrating radiation. He tried to prove that uranium's radiation resulted from its absorbing sunlight and releasing this energy in the form of X rays. But after using uranium that had not been exposed to sunlight to expose a photographic plate, he discovered that uranium spontaneously emits radiation.

Pierre and Marie Curie used Becquerel's findings to conclude that a nuclear change takes place naturally within the uranium atoms, resulting in what they first called radioactivity.

In 1903, Marie and Pierre Curie and Henri Becquerel were jointly awarded a Nobel Prize in physics. Have students choose one of these three scientists and prepare a report. **LS** Verbal

Answers to Your Turn

1. Answers may vary. The Curies processed tons of pitchblend in a laboratory shed in order to produce less than a gram of radium chloride.

2. Answers may vary. No others have won the Nobel Prize for both chemistry and physics. John Bardeen won the Nobel Prize twice for physics, Frederick Sanger won it twice for chemistry, and Linus Pauling won one for chemistry and one for peace.

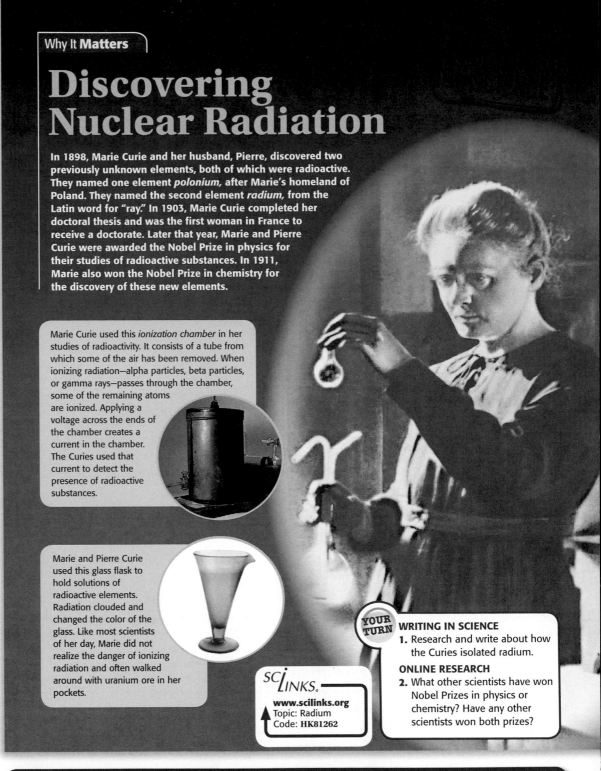

Why It Matters

Discovering Nuclear Radiation

In 1898, Marie Curie and her husband, Pierre, discovered two previously unknown elements, both of which were radioactive. They named one element *polonium,* after Marie's homeland of Poland. They named the second element *radium,* from the Latin word for "ray." In 1903, Marie Curie completed her doctoral thesis and was the first woman in France to receive a doctorate. Later that year, Marie and Pierre Curie were awarded the Nobel Prize in physics for their studies of radioactive substances. In 1911, Marie also won the Nobel Prize in chemistry for the discovery of these new elements.

Marie Curie used this *ionization chamber* in her studies of radioactivity. It consists of a tube from which some of the air has been removed. When ionizing radiation—alpha particles, beta particles, or gamma rays—passes through the chamber, some of the remaining atoms are ionized. Applying a voltage across the ends of the chamber creates a current in the chamber. The Curies used that current to detect the presence of radioactive substances.

Marie and Pierre Curie used this glass flask to hold solutions of radioactive elements. Radiation clouded and changed the color of the glass. Like most scientists of her day, Marie did not realize the danger of ionizing radiation and often walked around with uranium ore in her pockets.

SCI**LINKS.**
www.scilinks.org
Topic: Radium
Code: HK81262

YOUR TURN

WRITING IN SCIENCE
1. Research and write about how the Curies isolated radium.

ONLINE RESEARCH
2. What other scientists have won Nobel Prizes in physics or chemistry? Have any other scientists won both prizes?

Differentiated Instruction

Advanced Learners

Radiation and Health Encourage interested students to find out more about the serious health problems that resulted from Marie and Pierre Curie's work with radioactive substances. Have students report their findings by writing an obituary for both the Curies. **LS** Verbal

Basic Learners

Irène Curie Marie and Pierre Curie's daughter, Irène Curie, also won the Nobel Prize for chemistry in 1935, jointly with her husband Frédéric Joliot. Have students find out about the life and work of Irène Curie and present their findings in an oral report. **LS** Verbal

Radioactive Decay Rates

If you were asked to determine the age of a rock, you would probably not be able to do so. After all, old rocks do not look much different from new rocks. How, then, would you go about finding the rock's age? Likewise, how would a scientist find out the age of a piece of cloth found at the site of an ancient village?

One way to find the age involves radioactive decay. **❯ It is impossible to predict the moment when any particular nucleus will decay, but it is possible to predict the time required for half of the nuclei in a given radioactive sample to decay.** The time in which half of a radioactive substance decays is called the substance's **half-life.**

Half-life is a measure of how quickly a substance decays.

Different radioactive isotopes have different half-lives, as indicated in the table in **Figure 5.** Half-lives can last from nanoseconds to billions of years, depending on the stability of the isotope's nucleus.

Doctors use isotopes with short half-lives, such as iodine-131, to help diagnose medical problems. A detector follows the element as it moves through the patient's body.

Scientists can also use half-life to predict how old an object is. Geologists calculate the age of rocks by using the half-lives of long-lasting isotopes, such as potassium-40. Potassium-40 decays to argon-40, so the ratio of potassium-40 to argon-40 is smaller for older rocks than it is for younger rocks.

Figure 5 Half-Lives of Selected Isotopes

Isotope	Half-life	Nuclear radiation emitted
Thorium-219	1.05×10^{-6} s	α
Hafnium-156	2.5×10^{-2} s	α
Radon-222	3.82 days	α, γ
Iodine-131	8.1 days	β, γ
Radium-226	1,599 years	α, γ
Carbon-14	5,715 years	β
Plutonium-239	2.412×10^4 years	α, γ
Uranium-235	7.04×10^8 years	α, γ
Potassium-40	1.28×10^9 years	β, γ
Uranium-238	4.47×10^9 years	α, γ

Integrating Earth Science

Internal Furnace Earth's interior is extremely hot. One reason is that uranium and the radioactive elements produced by its decay are present in amounts of about 3 parts per million beneath the surface of Earth and their nuclear decay produces energy that escapes into the surroundings.

The long half-lives of uranium isotopes allow the radioactive decay to heat Earth for billions of years. The very large distance that this energy must travel to reach Earth's surface keeps the interior of Earth much hotter than its surface.

half-life (HAF LIEF) the time required for half of a sample of a radioactive isotope to break down by radioactive decay to form a daughter isotope

MISCONCEPTION ALERT

Radiometric Dating Students might think that all items can be dated using radioisotopes. Make sure students understand that after several half-lives, the amount of radioactive material present becomes so small that it is not measurable.

Demonstrate

Acting Out Half-Life To help students understand half-life, put all the students on one side of the room. Instruct half the students to move to the opposite side of the room and then instruct half of the remaining students to also move to the opposite side of the room. Repeat this process three or four times, with each step representing one half-life. Have one student record the number of students remaining after each half-life. The number of students in the original group represents the number of atoms of a particular isotope. When the activity is complete, have students graph the number of students remaining after each half-life. **LS Kinesthetic**

Integrating Earth Science

Radioactive Heat Emphasize to students the great amount of heat released on Earth by radioactive elements. Tell them that the radiation released by 1 g of radium during its lifetime equals the amount of energy released when thousands of kilograms of coal are burned.

Differentiated Instruction

Advanced Learners

Investigating Half-Life Give students the following equation for half-life and demonstrate how to use it to calculate the amount of substance remaining after an elapsed time given the rate of decay for a radioactive element.

$$A_f = A_i \times (\tfrac{1}{2})^{(t/t_{1/2})}$$

A_f is the amount of substance remaining after the elapsed time.

A_i is the initial amount of radioactive substance.

t is the amount of time that has elapsed.

$t_{1/2}$ is the half-life of the radioactive substance.

Have students use the equation and the information in **Figure 5** to determine the amount of carbon-14 remaining in a 100.0 mol sample after 17,145 years. (12.5 mol) **LS Logical**

Math *Skills*

Answers to Practice

1. $1 - 3/4 = 1/4$, or $1/2 \times 1/2$;
   2 half-lives; 2×8.1 days = 16 days
2. $1 - 15/16 = 1/16$, or $1/2 \times$
   $1/2 \times 1/2 \times 1/2$; 4 half-lives;
   4×3.82 days = 15.3 days
3. 13.4 billion years/4.47 billion
   years/half-life = 3 half-lives;
   $1/2 \times 1/2 \times 1/2 = 1/8 = 0.125$;
   $0.125 \times 100\% = 12.5\%$
4. $1/8 = 1/2 \times 1/2 \times 1/2$; 3 half-lives;
   87.3 years/3 half-lives =
   29.1 years/half-life

Additional Examples

1. The half-life of tritium, $^{3}_{1}\text{H}$, is
   12.3 years. How long will it take
   for 7/8 of a sample to decay?

   Answer: $1 - 7/8 = 1/8$ remains
   It will take three half-lives.
   3 half-lives $\times$ 12.3 years/half-life =
   36.9 years

2. The half-life of cobalt-60 is
   5.3 years. How much of a
   20.0 g sample will remain after
   21.2 years?

   Answer: 21.2 years/5.3 years per
   half-life = 4 half-lives.
   $20.0 \text{ g} \times 1/2 \times 1/2 \times 1/2 \times 1/2 =$
   1.25 g

   LS Logical

Math *Skills* Half-Life

Radium-226 has a half-life of 1,599 years. How long will seven-eighths of a sample of radium-226 take to decay?

Identify	**Given:**
List the given and un-known values.	half-life = 1,599 years fraction of sample decayed $= \frac{7}{8}$ **Unknown:** fraction of sample remaining = ? total time of decay = ?
Plan	fraction of sample remaining = 1 – fraction decayed = $1 - \frac{7}{8} = \frac{1}{8}$
Subtract the fraction decayed from 1 to find how much of the sample is remaining.	
Determine how much of the sample is remaining after each half-life.	amount of sample remaining after one half-life $= \frac{1}{2}$ amount of sample remaining after two half-lives $= \frac{1}{2} \times \frac{1}{2} = \frac{1}{4}$ amount of sample remaining after three half-lives $= \frac{1}{2} \times \frac{1}{2} \times \frac{1}{2} = \frac{1}{8}$
Solve	Each half-life lasts 1,599 years. total time of decay =
Multiply the number of half-lives by the time for each half-life to calculate the total time required for the radioactive decay.	3 ~~half-lives~~ $\times \dfrac{1,599 \text{ y}}{\text{half-life}} = 4,797 \text{ y}$

Practice **Hint**

➤ Make a diagram that shows how much of the original sample is left:

$1 \rightarrow 1/2 \rightarrow 1/4 \rightarrow 1/8 \rightarrow 1/16 \rightarrow \ldots$

Each arrow represents one half-life.

➤ Problems 4 and 5: You will need to work backward from the final answer to get to the time when one-half of the original sample remains.

Practice

1. The half-life of iodine-131 is 8.1 days. How long will three-fourths of a sample of iodine-131 take to decay?

2. Radon-222 is a radioactive gas with a half-life of 3.82 days. How long will fifteen-sixteenths of a sample of radon-222 take to decay?

3. Uranium-238 decays very slowly. Its half-life is 4.47 billion years. What percentage of a sample of uranium-238 will remain after 13.4 billion years?

4. A sample of strontium-90 is found to have decayed to one-eighth of its original amount after 87.3 years. What is the half-life of strontium-90?

For more practice, visit **go.hrw.com** and enter keyword **HK8MP**.

Differentiated Instruction

Basic Learners

Reviewing Exponents Some students may need to review the use of exponents before making half-life calculations. Explain that when n is the number of half-lives, $(1/2)^n$ gives the fractional part of the original substance remaining. For example, after three half-lives, $(1/2)^3$, or 1/8, of the sample is left. Have students solve the following exponents: $(1/2)^2 = ?$ (1/4), $(1/2)^4 = ?$ (1/16), $(1/2)^5 = ?$ (1/32), and $(1/2)^6 = ?$ (1/64).

LS Logical

QuickLab — Modeling Decay and Half-Life

⏱ 20 min

Procedure

❶ Place **128 pennies** in a **jar,** and place the **lid** on the jar. Shake the jar, and then pour the pennies onto a **flat work surface.**

❷ Separate pennies that are heads up from those that are tails up. Count and record the number of heads-up pennies, and set these pennies aside. Place the tails-up pennies back in the jar.

❸ Repeat the process until all of the pennies have been set aside.

Analysis

1. For each trial, divide the number of heads-up pennies set aside by the total number of pennies used in the trial. Are these ratios nearly equal to each other? What fraction are they closest to?

2. How well does this experiment model radioactive half-life?

Radioactive decay is exponential decay.

The definition of *half-life* tells us that after the first half-life of a radioactive sample has passed, half of the sample remains unchanged. After the next half-life, half of the remaining half decays, so only a quarter of the original element remains. Of that quarter, half will decay in the next half-life. Only one-eighth will then remain unchanged. This relationship is called an *exponential decay.*

A *decay curve* is a graph of the number of radioactive parent nuclei remaining in a sample as a function of time. The relationship between the fraction of carbon-14 versus time is graphed in **Figure 6.** Notice that the total number of nuclei remains constant and the number of carbon atoms continually decreases over time. As the number of carbon-14 atoms decreases, the number of nitrogen-14 atoms increases.

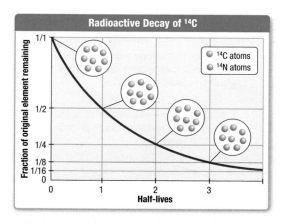

Radioactive Decay of ¹⁴C

Fraction of original element remaining vs. Half-lives

● ¹⁴C atoms
● ¹⁴N atoms

Figure 6 With each successive half-life, half of the remaining sample decays to form another element. **How much of the original element will remain after four half-lives?**

go.hrw.com
✳ **interact online**
Keyword: HK8NUCF6

QuickLab

Teacher's Notes This activity differs from an actual half-life in that eventually all the pennies are removed. Even in a small sample of a radioactive isotope, the number of atoms is so large that theoretically, some parent atoms would always remain. The number would decrease to the point that the parent atoms would not be detectable, but they would be present.

Materials per Group

• 128 pennies
• jar with a lid
• flat work surface

Answers to Analysis

1. Students should find that the ratio of heads-up pennies to the total number of pennies in the trial is approximately 1:2, or 1/2. Point out that if the actual number of atoms in a sample were considered, the ratio would be even closer to 1:2 because of the large sample size.

2. Answers may vary. The experiment models the rate of decay well. However, the scale is significantly smaller, so the numbers are not as close to 1/2 as they would be with the large numbers of atoms found in real-world samples.

Answer to caption question

After 4 half-lives, 1/16 of the original element remains.

go.hrw.com
✳ **interact online**

Students can interact with the figure by going to **go.hrw.com** and typing in the keyword **HK8NUCF6.**

Differentiated Instruction

Advanced Learners

Graphing Half-Life Have students graph their results of the Quick Lab. Graphs should show the number of remaining parent pennies on the *y*-axis and the trial number (number of half-lives) on the *x*-axis for each trial. A trial number of zero represents the starting number of pennies. Make sure student graphs show a curve with a *y*-intercept at 128 that curves downward asymptotic to the *x*-axis.
LS Logical/Visual

Why It **Matters**

Carbon Dating Have interested students investigate how carbon-14 dating was used to date the Shroud of Turin or another archeological relic. Ask a volunteer to give a class presentation with the results of his or her research. **LS** Verbal

Reteaching Key Ideas

Mass Comparisons Have students list the emissions of alpha decay, beta decay, gamma decay, and neutron emission in order from smallest to greatest mass using information in the section. (gamma decay, beta decay, neutron emission, alpha decay) **LS** **Logical**

Formative Assessment

Why is it difficult to preserve a pure sample of a radioactive element?

A. All radioactive elements eventually disappear as their atoms decay into pure energy. (Incorrect. While some energy is released as the matter changes form, the atoms of radioactive elements decay to form other elements, which are sometimes themselves radioactive.)

B. Exactly half of the atoms in a sample of a radioactive element are always a different radioactive product. (Incorrect. Only after a single half-life has taken place are exactly half the atoms in the original sample now products.)

C. At the passing of every half-life, half of the atoms in a sample of a radioactive element will become another isotope or element. (Correct. The sample would not remain pure, because its atoms would decay at an exponential rate to become atoms of a different isotope or element.)

D. Radioactive elements cannot be pure because they are always chemically combined with other radioactive elements. (Incorrect. Radioactive elements can be isolated. However, the samples decay to become mixtures of the original element and its nuclear decay product.)

Figure 7 Carbon-14 dating is used to date the remains of living things, such as this mummy of Petamenophis.

SCLINKS.

www.scilinks.org
Topic: Carbon Dating
Code: HK80218

Carbon-14 is used to date materials.

Archaeologists use the half-life of radioactive carbon-14 to date more-recent materials, such as fibers from ancient clothing, and animal or human remains, such as the mummy shown in **Figure 7**. All of these materials came from organisms that were once alive. When plants absorb carbon dioxide during photosynthesis, a tiny fraction of the CO_2 molecules contains carbon-14 rather than the more common carbon-12. While the plant, or an animal that eats plants, is alive, the ratio of the carbon isotopes remains constant.

When a plant or animal dies, it no longer takes in carbon. The amount of carbon-14 decreases through beta decay, while the amount of carbon-12 remains constant. Thus, the ratio of carbon-14 to carbon-12 decreases with time. By measuring this ratio and comparing it with the ratio in a living plant or animal, scientists can estimate how long ago the once-living organism died.

Section 1 **Review**

KEY IDEAS

1. **Identify** which of the four common types of nuclear radiation correspond to the following descriptions.
   a. an electron
   b. uncharged particle
   c. particle that can be stopped by a piece of paper
   d. high-energy electromagnetic radiation

2. **Describe** what happens when beta decay occurs.

3. **Explain** why charged particles do not penetrate matter deeply.

CRITICAL THINKING

4. **Analyzing Methods** An archaeologist finds an old piece of wood whose carbon-14 to carbon-12 ratio is one-sixteenth the ratio measured in a newly fallen tree. How old does the wood seem to be?

Math *Skills*

5. Determine the product denoted by X in the following alpha decay.

$$^{212}_{86}Rn \rightarrow {}^{A}_{Z}X + {}^{4}_{2}He$$

6. Determine the isotope produced in the beta decay of iodine-131, an isotope used to check thyroid-gland function.

$$^{131}_{53}I \rightarrow {}^{A}_{Z}X + {}^{0}_{-1}e$$

7. Calculate the time required for three-fourths of a sample of cesium-138 to decay, given that its half-life is 32.2 min.

8. Calculate the half-life of cesium-135 if seven-eighths of a sample decays in 6×10^6 years.

Answers to Section Review

1. **a.** beta
   b. neutron
   c. alpha
   d. gamma

2. A neutron decays, forming a proton and an electron. The electron is released as a beta particle.

3. They ionize the materials they pass through. Each ionization transfers energy from the alpha or beta particle to the ionized particle. Less energy means less penetration.

4. $1/16 = 1/2 \times 1/2 \times 1/2 \times 1/2$; four half-lives have passed. The old wood is 4 half-lives × 5,715 years/half-life, or 22,860 years old.

5. $212 = A + 4$, $A = 208$; $86 = Z + 2$, $Z = 84$; $X = Po$; The product is $^{208}_{84}Po$.

6. $131 = A + 0$, $A = 131$; $53 = Z + (-1)$, $Z = 54$; $X = Xe$; The product is $^{131}_{54}Xe$.

7. $1 - 3/4 = 1/4$, or $1/2 \times 1/2$, remains. Two half-lives take 2×32.2 minutes, or 64.4 minutes.

8. $1 - 7/8 = 1/8$, or $1/2 \times 1/2 \times 1/2$, remains; 6×10^6 years/3 half-lives = 2×10^6 years/half-life

Nuclear Fission and Fusion

SECTION 2

Key **Ideas**

❯ What holds the nuclei of atoms together?

❯ What is released when the nucleus of a heavy atom is split?

❯ What happens when the nuclei of small atoms are joined?

Key **Terms**

fission

nuclear chain reaction

critical mass

fusion

Why It **Matters**

Nuclear fission can be controlled and used to generate electricity.

I n 1939, German scientists Otto Hahn and Fritz Strassman conducted experiments in the hope of forming heavy nuclei. Hahn and Strassman bombarded uranium samples with neutrons and expected that a few nuclei would capture one or more neutrons. The new elements that formed had chemical properties that the scientists could not explain.

An explanation for these results came only after the scientists' former colleague Lise Meitner and her nephew Otto Frisch read the results of the experiments. Meitner and Frisch believed that instead of making heavier elements, the uranium nuclei had split into smaller elements.

In the early 1940s, Enrico Fermi and other scientists at the University of Chicago built stacks of graphite and uranium blocks, similar to the one shown in **Figure 1.** This *nuclear pile* was used to create the first controlled nuclear fission chain reaction and to launch the Manhattan Project, which led to the creation of nuclear weapons.

Nuclear Forces

Protons and neutrons are tightly packed in the tiny nucleus of an atom. As explained in Section 1, certain nuclei are unstable and undergo decay by emitting nuclear radiation. Also, an element can have both stable and unstable isotopes. For example, carbon-12 is a stable isotope, but carbon-14 is unstable and radioactive. ❯ **The stability of a nucleus depends on the nuclear forces that hold the nucleus together. These forces act between the protons and the neutrons.**

Like charges repel, so how can so many positively charged protons fit into an atomic nucleus without flying apart?

Figure 1 This nuclear pile was used in the late 1940s and early 1950s to better understand controlled nuclear fission.

❯ Focus

This section introduces students to fission and fusion. They study examples of each and learn why small losses in mass release large amounts of energy. They also learn what a chain reaction is and how chain reactions are initiated and controlled.

🔔 Bellringer

Use the Bellringer transparency to prepare students for this section.

Why It **Matters**

Atomic Bombs One of the most controversial events of recent history is President Truman's decision to drop atomic bombs on two Japanese cities during World War II. A single atomic bomb was dropped on Hiroshima on August 6, 1945; a second was dropped on Nagasaki three days later. Japan surrendered to the Allied forces less then one month afterward.

Scientists whose discoveries played a role in the development of the bomb were personally affected by the events of World War II. Albert Einstein, for example, faced Nazi persecution in Germany before fleeing to the United States. Einstein, who had been a fervent pacifist before the rise of Nazism in Germany, was instrumental in urging President Roosevelt to fund the research that produced the bomb. Lise Meitner, who offered the first explanation of nuclear fission (with her nephew Otto Frisch), was also forced to leave Nazi Germany. She fled to Switzerland in 1938.

Key Resources

 Teaching Transparencies
C25 Chain Reaction
C26 Nuclear Fusion

🔘 **Visual Concepts**
Nuclear Forces
Strong Nuclear Force
Nuclear Fission
Nuclear Chain Reaction
Nuclear Fusion

📁 **Datasheet**
Modeling Chain Reactions

READING TOOLBOX

Word Origins Originally, scientists called the nuclear force that counter-balanced the electric repulsion of positively charged protons in the nucleus "the strong force." Since the discovery of sub-atomic particles, the strong force is often known as the residual strong force.

Teaching Key Ideas

Modeling Nuclear Forces

Demonstrate the nuclear force between two protons using bar magnets. Model how like poles of magnets repel each other. Place the magnets so that the like poles are together and they touch. Wrap the rubber band tightly around them. Ask the following questions to get students thinking about nuclear forces. What part of a nucleus do the magnets represent? Explain. (protons; they repel each other) What does the rubber band represent? (a force strong enough to hold objects together even though they repel each other) **LS** Visual

Why It **Matters**

Hideki Yukawa In 1935, Hideki Yukawa, a Japanese scientist, theorized that a force exists that holds the nucleus together. He described the force as being stronger over short distances than the electrical repulsion that repels protons. He confirmed that the strong force was the result of the transfer of the predicted *meson* particle. Yukawa was awarded the Nobel Prize in 1949.

READING TOOLBOX

Word Origins
Research how the strong nuclear force was discovered. What is the origin of its name? Is there another nuclear force that is "not strong"?

Nuclei are held together by a special force.

The neutrons and protons are able to exist together in the nuclei of atoms because of the *strong nuclear force*. This force causes protons and neutrons in the nucleus to attract one another. The attraction is much stronger than the electric repulsion between protons. However, the attraction due to the strong nuclear force occurs over a very short distance, less than 3×10^{-15} m, or about the width of three protons.

Neutrons contribute to nuclear stability.

Because of the strong nuclear force, neutrons and protons in a nucleus attract other protons and neutrons. Because neutrons have no charge, they do not repel one another or the protons. However, the protons in a nucleus both repel and attract one another, as **Figure 2** shows. In stable nuclei, the attractive forces are stronger than the repulsive forces, and the element does not undergo nuclear decay.

Too many neutrons or protons can cause a nucleus to become unstable and decay.

Although a greater number of neutrons can help hold a nucleus together, there is a limit to how many neutrons that a nucleus can have. Nuclei with too many or too few neutrons are unstable and undergo decay.

Nuclei with more than 83 protons are always unstable, no matter how many neutrons that the nuclei have. These nuclei will always decay and, in the process, release large amounts of energy and nuclear radiation. Some of this released energy is transferred to the various particles ejected from the nucleus. As a result, the least massive of these particles move very fast. The rest of the energy is emitted in the form of gamma rays. The radioactive decay that takes place results in a more stable nucleus.

✔ **Reading Check** What is the maximum number of protons that can be found in a stable nucleus?

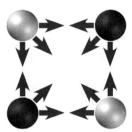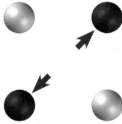

Strong nuclear force
(acts on protons and neutrons)

Electric repulsion
(acts on protons)

Figure 2 The nucleus is held together by the attractions among protons and neutrons. These forces are greater than the electric repulsion among the protons alone.

Differentiated Instruction

Basic Learners

Unbalanced Forces Have students examine the force arrows in **Figure 2.** Explain that when the forces that hold particles in a nucleus are balanced, the nucleus is stable. When the forces that hold particles in a nucleus are unbalanced, the nucleus will emit a particle. Nuclear forces, though they occur on a tiny scale, can be compared to larger forces, such as those that occur on everyday objects. For example, the forces of gravity and buoyancy on a floating object are balanced. However, if the weight of the boat is suddenly increased by a person stepping into it, the forces become unbalanced and the boat moves downward. Demonstrate balanced and unbalanced forces using a mass balance or have students pull on a rope in a tug-of-war. **LS** Visual

Nuclear Fission

The process of splitting heavier nuclei into lighter nuclei, which Hahn and Strassman observed, is called **fission.** In their experiment, uranium 235 was bombarded by neutrons. One set of products for this type of fission reaction includes two lighter nuclei, barium-140 and krypton-93, together with neutrons and energy.

$$^{235}_{92}U + ^{1}_{0}n \rightarrow ^{140}_{56}Ba + ^{93}_{36}Kr + 3^{1}_{0}n + energy$$

Notice that the products include three neutrons plus energy. Uranium-235 can also undergo fission by producing different pairs of lighter nuclei. An alternative fission of the isotope uranium-235, for example, produces strontium-90, xenon-143, and three neutrons. **> In the fission process, when the nucleus splits, both neutrons and energy are released.**

Energy is released during nuclear fission.

During fission, as **Figure 3** shows, the nucleus breaks into smaller nuclei. The reaction also releases large amounts of energy. Each dividing nucleus releases about 3.2×10^{-11} J of energy. In comparison, the chemical reaction of one molecule of the explosive trinitrotoluene (TNT) releases 4.8×10^{-18} J.

In their experiment, Hahn and Strassman determined the masses of all of the nuclei and particles before and after the reaction. They found that the overall mass had decreased after the reaction. The missing mass must have been changed into energy.

The equivalence of mass and energy observed in nature is explained by the special theory of relativity, which Albert Einstein presented in 1905. This equivalence means that matter can be converted into energy, and energy into matter, and is given by the following equation.

> **Mass-energy equation** $energy = mass \times (speed\ of\ light)^2$
> $E = mc^2$

The constant, c, is equal to 3.0×10^{8} m/s. So, the energy associated with even a small mass is very large. The mass-equivalent energy of 1 kg of matter is 9×10^{16} J, which is more than the chemical energy of 22 million tons of TNT.

Obviously, if objects around us changed into their equivalent energies, the results would be devastating. Under ordinary conditions of pressure and temperature, matter is very stable. Objects, such as chairs and tables, never spontaneously change into energy.

fission (FISH uhn) the process by which a nucleus splits into two or more fragments and releases neutrons and energy

Figure 3 When the uranium-235 nucleus is bombarded by a neutron, the nucleus breaks apart. It forms smaller nuclei, such as xenon-143 and strontium-90, and releases energy through fast neutrons.

Teaching Key Ideas

Nuclear Fission Students might think that fission in a cell and in a nucleus are identical processes because both involve splitting. The product of cell fission is two cells that are identical to each other and to the parent cell. Nuclear fission produces particles that differ from the parent atom and from each other. Have students compare and contrast illustrations of cell fission and nuclear fission. **LS Visual**

READING TOOLBOX

Visual Literacy Explain that the word *fission* means a splitting into parts. Have students examine **Figure 3** and explain why nuclear fission gets its name. (During nuclear fission, a larger atom splits into two smaller atoms.) **LS Visual**

Teaching Key Ideas

Relative Energy Students might not understand the immense difference in energies of one nucleus undergoing fission and one molecule of TNT exploding. For clarification, divide the two quantities shown in the student text:

$$\frac{3.2 \times 10^{-11}\,J}{4.8 \times 10^{-18}} = 6.7 \times 10^{6}$$

(or 6,700,000)

Explain to students that one nucleus undergoing fission releases approximately the same amount of energy as 6.7 million TNT molecules do when they explode. **LS Logical**

Differentiated Instruction

Struggling Readers

Paired Reading Pair struggling readers with strong readers. Have each pair of students take turns reading the section of text about the mass-energy equation. One student should read the paragraph out loud and the other student should summarize what it means. Encourage each pair of students to produce notes summarizing what they have learned from their reading. **LS Interpersonal/Verbal**

Demonstrate

A Chain Reaction For this demonstration you will need 8 matches, a ring stand, and tape. Starting at the top of the ring stand, use tape to attach the matches so that the heads of the matches form a vertical row along the stand support. Light the bottom match. Have students explain their observations. (Each match supplied enough energy to the next match to light it.) Ask how this demonstration is a model of a nuclear chain reaction. (Just as each match supplies energy to the next match, each neutron emitted in one fission reaction causes another fission reaction.) **Safety Caution:** Work in a well-ventilated area. Have a spray bottle with water available to extinguish the matches. **LS Visual**

Visual Literacy Have students examine **Figure 4** and make a concept map that summarizes what happens when a chain reaction occurs. Maps should start with a neutron hitting a uranium-235 atom, which then splits into barium-140 and krypton-93 atoms. Three other neutrons are released and each neutron hits another uranium-235 atom. **LS Visual**

www.scilinks.org
Topic: Fission
Code: HK80580

Academic Vocabulary

trigger (TRIG uhr) to begin or cause something to start

Figure 4 A nuclear chain reaction may be triggered by a single neutron.

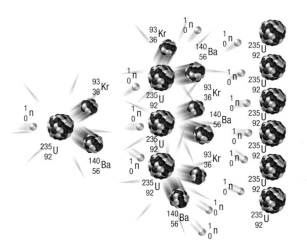

Energy is released when nuclei form.

When the total mass of any nucleus is measured, the mass is less than the individual masses of the neutrons and protons that make up the nucleus. This missing mass is referred to as the *mass defect*. What happens to the missing mass? Einstein's equation provides an explanation—the mass changes into energy. However, the mass defect of a nucleus is very small.

Another way to think about mass defect is to imagine constructing a nucleus by bringing individual protons and neutrons together. During this process, a small amount of mass changes into energy, as described by $E = mc^2$.

Neutrons released by fission can start a chain reaction.

Have you ever played marbles with a lot of marbles in the ring? When one marble is shot into the ring, the resulting collisions cause some of the marbles to scatter. Some nuclear reactions are similar—one reaction <u>triggers</u> another.

A nucleus that splits when it is struck by a neutron forms smaller product nuclei. These smaller nuclei need fewer neutrons to be held together. Therefore, excess neutrons are emitted. One of these neutrons can collide with another large nucleus, triggering another nuclear reaction that releases more neutrons. This process starts a **nuclear chain reaction,** which is a continuous series of nuclear fission reactions.

When Hahn and Strassman continued experimenting, they discovered that each dividing uranium nucleus, on average, produced between two and three additional neutrons. Therefore, two or three new fission reactions could be started from the neutrons that were ejected from one reaction.

If each of these 3 new reactions produces 3 additional neutrons, a total of 9 neutrons become available to trigger 9 additional fission reactions. From these 9 reactions, a total of 27 neutrons are produced, which set off 27 new reactions, and so on. You can probably see from **Figure 4** how the reaction of uranium-235 nuclei would very quickly result in an uncontrolled nuclear chain reaction. Therefore, the ability to create a chain reaction partly depends on the number of neutrons released during each fission reaction.

✔ Reading Check What causes a nuclear chain reaction?

Why It **Matters**

A Natural Nuclear Reactor Mother Nature created the first nuclear reactor on Earth some two billion years ago. The Oklo uranium deposits in Gabon, Africa, divided in a fission process and sustained a chain reaction that lasted hundreds of thousands of years. Have students find out more about the natural nuclear reactor in Gabon and present their findings in an oral report. **LS Verbal**

Modeling Chain Reactions

 10 min

Procedure

❶ To model a fission chain reaction, you will need a **small wooden building block** and a **set of dominoes.**

❷ Place the building block on a **table or counter.** Stand one domino upright in front of the block and parallel to one of its sides. Stand two more dominoes vertically, parallel, and symmetrical to the first domino.

❸ Continue this process until you have used all of the dominoes and have created a triangular shape, as shown here.

❹ Gently push the first domino away from the block so that it falls and hits the second group. Note that more dominoes fall with each step.

Analysis

1. Use Newton's first law of motion to explain your results.

QuickLab

Teacher's Notes Encourage students to try other domino arrangements to model chain reactions. For example, they could arrange dominoes in a chain that continually branches, so that one domino falling in the first step causes 16 dominoes to fall in the fifth step. If possible, use a video camera to tape the chain reaction, and play the footage back at slow speed. If students arranged their dominoes in branches, have them use the video to examine which domino caused each branch to fall.

Materials per Group
- small wooden building block
- set of dominoes

Answer to Analysis

1. Newton's first law states that an object at rest tends to stay at rest unless acted upon by an unbalanced force. When one domino falls onto others, it exerts an unbalanced force, causing the other dominoes to fall.

Teaching Key Ideas

Chain Reactions Have students list examples of non-nuclear chain reactions that they come in contact with daily. (Answers may vary. For example, one person tells another a secret, that person tells two other people, each of them tells two others, and the information chain continues.)
LS Verbal

Chain reactions can be controlled.

Energy produced in a controlled chain reaction can be used to generate electricity. Particles released by the splitting of the atom strike other uranium atoms and split them. The particles that are given off split still other atoms. A chain reaction is begun, which gives off energy that is used to heat water. The superheated water then transfers energy into a heat exchanger filled with water that is used to make steam. The steam then rotates a turbine to generate electricity. Energy released by the chain reaction changes the atomic energy into thermal energy, which ends up as electrical energy.

The chain-reaction principle is also used in making a nuclear bomb. Two or more masses of uranium-235 are contained in the bomb. These masses are surrounded by a powerful chemical explosive. When the explosive is detonated, all of the uranium is pushed together to create a *critical mass.* The **critical mass** refers to the minimum amount of a substance that can undergo a fission reaction and can also sustain a chain reaction. If the amount of fissionable substance is less than the critical mass, a chain reaction will not continue. Fortunately, the concentration of uranium-235 in nature is too low to start a chain reaction naturally. Almost all of the escaping neutrons are absorbed by the more common and more stable isotope uranium-238.

In nuclear power plants, control rods are used to regulate fission by slowing the chain reaction. In nuclear bombs, reactions are not controlled, and almost pure pieces of the element uranium-235 or plutonium of a precise mass and shape must be brought together and held together with great force. These conditions are not present in a nuclear reactor.

nuclear chain reaction (NOO klee uhr CHAYN ree AK shuhn) a continuous series of nuclear fission reactions

critical mass (KRIT i kuhl MAS) the minimum mass of a fissionable isotope that provides the number of neutrons needed to sustain a chain reaction

Differentiated Instruction

Alternative Assessment

Fission Debate Have students prepare for a debate about which is a better way to generate electricity: fossil fuels or nuclear fission. Ask them to use library materials and the Internet to learn about the pros and cons of each method. Then set aside 20 minutes for a class debate. Afterwards, ask students to choose a side and write a paper convincing an opponent of the benefits of his or her choice. Remind students that a successful position paper discusses both the pros and cons of an issue, explaining how the cons can be addressed.
LS Interpersonal/Verbal

Teaching Key Ideas

Containing Fusion One of the most difficult problems with nuclear fusion is containing the reaction. For the reaction to occur, it must happen at temperatures of approximately 10^8 °C. Because plasma consists of charged particles, some success has been achieved by containing the reaction within a magnetic field. However, the moving, charged particles produce new magnetic fields that interfere with the containing magnetic field.

❯ Close

Reteaching Key Ideas

Comparison T Chart Have students compare and contrast fission and fusion using a T chart. Have students brainstorm mnemonic devices that will help them keep track of these two types of nuclear reactions. **LS** Logical/Verbal

Formative Assessment

What is the difference between fission and fusion?

A. Fusion produces power in nuclear power plants, while fission produces energy in the sun. (Incorrect. The opposite is true. Fission produces power in nuclear power plants, while fusion produces energy in the sun.)

B. The overall process of fission absorbs energy, while the overall process of fusion produces energy. (Incorrect. Both nuclear reactions produce energy.)

C. In fission, one nucleus splits into two or more smaller fragments, while in fusion, two or more small nuclei combine. (Correct. Fission involves a large nucleus splitting apart into smaller nuclei, while fusion involves smaller nuclei colliding to produce larger nuclei.)

D. Fission involves changes in the numbers of electrons of an atom, while fusion involves changes in the numbers of the protons and neutrons. (Incorrect. Both involve changes in the numbers of nuclear particles, protons and neutrons.)

Nuclear Fusion

Obtaining energy from the fission of heavy nuclei is not the only nuclear process that produces energy. ❯ **Energy can be obtained when very light nuclei are combined to form heavier nuclei.** This type of nuclear process is called **fusion.**

In stars, including the sun, energy is produced primarily when hydrogen nuclei combine, or fuse together, and release tremendous amounts of energy. However, a large amount of energy is needed to start a fusion reaction. The reason is that all nuclei are positively charged and repel one another with the electric force. Energy is required to bring the hydrogen nuclei close enough to one another that the repulsive electric force is overcome by the attractive strong nuclear force. In stars, the extreme temperatures provide the energy needed to bring hydrogen nuclei together.

Four hydrogen atoms combine in the sun to make a helium atom and high-energy gamma rays. This nuclear fusion of hydrogen happens in a three step process that involves two isotopes of hydrogen: ordinary hydrogen, ^1_1H, and deuterium, ^2_1H, as **Figure 5** shows.

fusion (FYOO zhuhn) the process in which light nuclei combine at extremely high temperatures, forming heavier nuclei and releasing energy

www.scilinks.org
Topic: Fusion
Code: HK80629

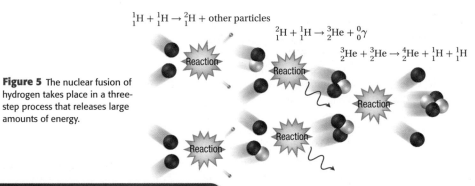

$$^1_1H + ^1_1H \rightarrow ^2_1H + \text{other particles}$$

$$^2_1H + ^1_1H \rightarrow ^3_2He + ^0_0\gamma$$

$$^3_2He + ^3_2He \rightarrow ^4_2He + ^1_1H + ^1_1H$$

Figure 5 The nuclear fusion of hydrogen takes place in a three-step process that releases large amounts of energy.

Section 2 Review

KEY IDEAS

1. **Explain** why most isotopes of elements that have a high atomic number are radioactive.

2. **Indicate** whether the following are fission or fusion reactions.

   a. $^1_1H + ^2_1H \rightarrow ^3_2He + \gamma$

   b. $^1_0n + ^{235}_{92}U \rightarrow ^{146}_{57}La + ^{87}_{35}Br + 3^1_0n$

   c. $^{21}_{10}Ne + ^4_2He \rightarrow ^{24}_{12}Mg + ^1_0n$

   d. $^{208}_{82}Pb + ^{58}_{26}Fe \rightarrow ^{265}_{108}Hs + ^1_0n$

3. **Predict** whether the total mass of a nucleus of an atom of $^{56}_{26}Fe$ is greater than, less than, or equal to the combined mass of the 26 protons and 30 neutrons that make up the nucleus. If the masses are not equal, explain why.

CRITICAL THINKING

4. **Predicting Outcomes** Suppose that a nucleus captures two neutrons and decays to produce one neutron. Is this process likely to produce a chain reaction? Explain your reasoning.

Answers to Section Review

1. The strong force acts over such a small distance that large nuclei are difficult to hold together. These unstable nuclei undergo nuclear reactions that produce nuclei that are more stable.

2. **a.** fusion
   b. fission
   c. fusion
   d. fusion

3. The total mass of the nucleus is less than the combined mass of the protons and neutrons that make up the nucleus because some of the mass is destroyed and converted into energy according to $E = mc^2$. The missing mass is known as the *mass defect.*

4. A continued (critical) chain reaction will not occur. Each step of this reaction requires more neutrons than the previous reaction releases.

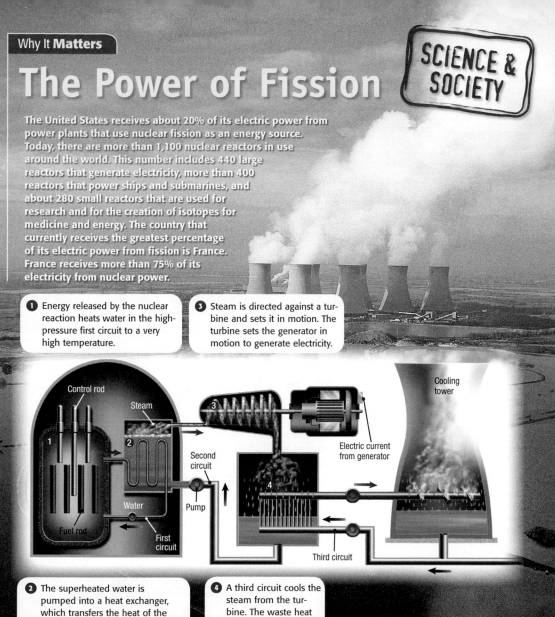

Why It **Matters**

The Power of Fission

SCIENCE & SOCIETY

The United States receives about 20% of its electric power from power plants that use nuclear fission as an energy source. Today, there are more than 1,100 nuclear reactors in use around the world. This number includes 440 large reactors that generate electricity, more than 400 reactors that power ships and submarines, and about 280 small reactors that are used for research and for the creation of isotopes for medicine and energy. The country that currently receives the greatest percentage of its electric power from fission is France. France receives more than 75% of its electricity from nuclear power.

1 Energy released by the nuclear reaction heats water in the high-pressure first circuit to a very high temperature.

3 Steam is directed against a turbine and sets it in motion. The turbine sets the generator in motion to generate electricity.

Control rod

Steam

Cooling tower

1

2

3

Second circuit

Electric current from generator

Water

Pump

4

Fuel rod

First circuit

Third circuit

2 The superheated water is pumped into a heat exchanger, which transfers the heat of the first circuit to the second circuit. Water in the second circuit flashes into high-pressure steam.

4 A third circuit cools the steam from the turbine. The waste heat is released from the cooling tower in the form of steam.

YOUR TURN

UNDERSTANDING CONCEPTS
1. What do nuclear power plants and other electric power plants have in common?

CRITICAL THINKING
2. How would using three circuits help the environment?

SCI LINKS.

www.scilinks.org
Topic: Nuclear Energy
Code: HK81047

Why It **Matters**

The Power of Fission The isotope uranium-235 is a common fuel for nuclear fission reactors. Uranium-235 represents only about 0.7 percent of naturally occurring uranium on Earth. Most of the rest is uranium-238, which naturally undergoes a series of radioactive decay reactions to become lead. While uranium-235 also undergoes natural alpha decay, in nuclear reactors, it undergoes induced fission. In induced fission, when uranium-235 nuclei are bombarded with neutrons, they undergo fission, each nucleus producing two smaller nuclei and a variable number of neutrons. The following equations describe a few of the nuclear reactions that can take place.

$$^{235}_{92}\text{U} + ^{1}_{0}n \rightarrow ^{142}_{56}\text{Ba} + ^{92}_{36}\text{Kr} + 2^{1}_{0}n + \text{energy}$$

$$^{235}_{92}\text{U} + ^{1}_{0}n \rightarrow ^{140}_{54}\text{Xe} + ^{92}_{38}\text{Sr} + 4^{1}_{0}n + \text{energy}$$

$$^{235}_{92}\text{U} + ^{1}_{0}n \rightarrow ^{134}_{54}\text{Xe} + ^{100}_{38}\text{Sr} + 2^{1}_{0}n + \text{energy}$$

$$^{235}_{92}\text{U} + ^{1}_{0}n \rightarrow ^{140}_{56}\text{Ba} + ^{93}_{36}\text{Kr} + 3^{1}_{0}n + \text{energy}$$

$$^{235}_{92}\text{U} + ^{1}_{0}n \rightarrow ^{145}_{57}\text{La} + ^{88}_{35}\text{Br} + 3^{1}_{0}n + \text{energy}$$

Each neutron ejected by these reactions can induce another fission reaction, propelling the nuclear chain reaction that heats the water in the power plant. Have students examine these equations and compare them to the illustration in **Figure 4** of a nuclear chain reaction. **LS** Visual

Answers to Your Turn
1. Energy is used to produce steam which moves a turbine that generates electricity.
2. Answers may vary.

Nuclear Radiation Today

> Focus

This section explores some of the beneficial applications of radiation. Students also learn about some of the risks associated with nuclear radiation. They study the benefits and drawbacks of producing electricity with nuclear fission, as well as the possibility of using nuclear fusion as a future energy source.

Bellringer

Use the Bellringer transparency to prepare students for this section.

Why It **Matters**

Levels of Background Radiation

Explain that although there are small variations in background radiation levels at different locations, the average levels in the United States and around the world are in the same general range. However, due to high concentrations of radioactive minerals in the soil, a few areas in Brazil, China, and India have much higher levels. For example, the background radiation in certain black sand beaches of Brazil is almost 400 times greater than the normal level in the United States. Have students find out other sources of radiation they are exposed to every day. (Answers may vary and may include terrestrial radiation, cosmic radiation, and radiation from food, smoke detectors, X rays, and televisions.)  **Verbal**

Key **Ideas**

> Where are we exposed to radiation?

> What are some beneficial uses of nuclear radiation?

> What factors determine the risks of nuclear radiation?

> How is the energy produced by nuclear fission used?

Key **Terms**

background radiation

rem

radioactive tracer

Why It **Matters**

Radioactive tracer elements are used in medical diagnostic procedures such as positron emission tomography.

Y ou may be surprised to learn that you are exposed to some form of nuclear radiation every day. Some forms of nuclear radiation are beneficial. Others present some risks. This section will discuss both the benefits and the possible risks of nuclear radiation.

Where Is Radiation?

Nuclear radiation is all around you. The form of nuclear radiation that arises naturally is called **background radiation.** **> We are continually exposed to radiation from natural sources, such as the sun, soil, rocks, and plants.** More than 80% of the radiation that we are exposed to comes from natural sources, such as those shown in **Figure 1.** The living tissues of most organisms are adapted to survive these low levels of natural nuclear radiation. Human-made sources, such as computer monitors, smoke detectors, and X rays, account for at least 20% of our everyday exposure.

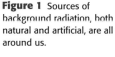

background radiation (BAK GROWND RAY dee AY shuhn) the nuclear radiation that arises naturally from cosmic rays and from radioactive isotopes in the soil and air

rem (REM) the quantity of ionizing radiation that does as much damage to human tissue as 1 roentgen of high-voltage X rays does

Figure 1 Sources of background radiation, both natural and artificial, are all around us.

Key Resources

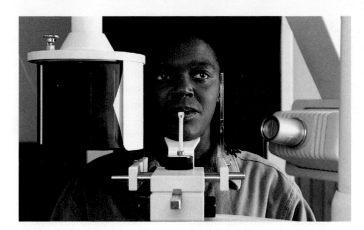

Radiation is measured in units of rems.

Levels of radiation absorbed by the human body are measured in **rems** or millirems (1 rem = 1,000 millirems). Typical exposure for an X ray at the dentist's office, shown in **Figure 2,** is about 1 millirem.

In the United States, many people work in occupations that involve nuclear radiation. Nuclear engineering, health physics, radiology, radiochemistry, X-ray technology, and other nuclear medical technology all involve nuclear radiation. A safe limit for these workers has been set at 5,000 millirems per year, in addition to natural background exposures.

Exposure varies from one location to another.

People in the United States receive varying amounts of natural radiation. Those at higher elevations receive more exposure to nuclear radiation from space than people do at lower elevations. People in areas with many rocks have higher nuclear radiation exposure than people do in areas without many rocks. Because of large differences both in elevation and background radiation sources, exposure varies greatly from one location to another, as **Figure 3** illustrates.

Some activities add to the amount of nuclear radiation exposure.

Another factor that affects levels of exposure is participation in certain activities. **Figure 4** shows actual exposure to nuclear radiation for just a few activities. Other activities besides those listed in this table also add to the amount of nuclear radiation exposure. All activities that add nuclear radiation to the air will affect everyone in the area around these activities.

Figure 3 Radiation Exposure per Location

Location	Radiation exposure (millirems/year)
Tampa, FL	63.7
Richmond, VA	64.1
Las Vegas, NV	69.5
Los Angeles, CA	73.6
Portland, OR	86.7
Rochester, NY	88.1
Wheeling, WV	111.9
Denver, CO	164.6

Figure 4 Radiation Exposure per Activity

Activity	Radiation exposure (millirems/ year)
Smoking 1 1/2 packs of cigarettes per day	8,000
Flying for 720 hours (airline crew)	267
Inhaling radon from the environment	360
Giving or receiving medical X rays	100

>Teach

Science Skills

Graphing Have students use the Internet or library sources to find the average level of radiation exposure in their area. Ask them to also find other values for comparison, such as the highest and lowest levels in the United States and in the world. Then ask them to create a bar graph that illustrates these comparisons. They could also include some average values for other U.S. cities (given in **Figure 3**). Remind them that all values must have the same units for an accurate comparison. **LS** Logical/Visual

Why It Matters

What Is a Rem? Rem stands for **r**oentgen **e**quivalent in **m**an. Wilhelm Conrad Roentgen was a German physicist who discovered X rays in 1895. One rem is the amount of radiation that causes the same effect on a human being as a given amount of X rays. Have students do research to find out more about the rem and other measurement units associated with radioactivity, such as the gray, the rad, and the sievert. **LS** Logical

Differentiated Instruction

Basic Learners

Radioactive Foods Natural radioactivity is all around us—in the air we breathe, in the rocks and soil that make up our planet, and even in the foods we eat. All foods have small amounts of radioactivity. The most common radioactive elements found in foods are potassium-40, radium-226, and uranium-238. Have students do research to find out what kinds of foods contain potassium-40. (Answers may vary. Some foods that contain potassium-40 are bananas, brazil nuts, carrots, white potatoes, red meat, and lima beans.) **LS** Logical

Math *Skills*

The Sievert Explain that another unit of measurement of radiation doses is the sievert (Sv). One sievert equals 100 rem. In fact, the sievert is the derived unit recommended by SI for measuring the biological effects of radiation. Have students make the following conversions.

1. 150 rem = ? Sv (1.5)

2. 235 Sv = ? rem (23,500)

3. 412 mrem = ? rem (0.412)

4. 32 mrem = ? Sv (0.00032)

LS Logical

READING TOOLBOX

Making Predictions Before students read about some of the beneficial uses of radiation, have them list as many applications of nuclear radiation as they can think of. After they read these pages, ask if they learned about any applications that were not on their lists. Have students add these items to their lists, writing a brief explanation of each one. You may also want to ask students to conduct research about any applications on their list that were not discussed in the text. **LS Verbal**

Teaching Key Ideas

Medical Tracers An example of a medical radioactive tracer is technetium-99m, a special form of the isotope technetium-99. Technetium-99m (called metastable technetium-99) emits gamma rays and has a half-life of 6 hours.

Why It Matters

Radiology Have a radiologist speak to the class on how tracers are used to diagnose certain health problems and why certain radioactive materials are used as tracers and others are not. Also, have the radiologist discuss which health problems are treated with radiation.

Figure 5 In a smoke alarm, a small amount of alpha-emitting isotope detects smoke particles in the air.

radioactive tracer (RAY dee oh AK tiv TRAYS uhr) a radioactive material that is added to a substance so that its distribution can be detected later

Figure 6 Research farms use radioactive tracers to reveal water movement and other biochemical processes.

Beneficial Uses of Nuclear Radiation

Radioactive substances have a wide range of applications. In these applications, nuclear radiation is used in a controlled way to take advantage of its effects on other materials. **> Some common applications of nuclear radiation include medical diagnosis and treatment, smoke detectors, manufacturing, and agriculture.**

Smoke detectors help save lives.

Small radioactive sources are present in smoke alarms, such as the one shown in **Figure 5.** These sources release alpha particles, which are charged, to produce an electric current. Smoke particles in the air reduce the flow of the current. The drop in current sets off the alarm when even small levels of smoke are present.

Nuclear radiation is used to detect diseases.

The digital computer, ultrasound scanning, CT scanning, PET, and magnetic resonance imaging (MRI) have combined to create a variety of diagnostic imaging techniques. Using these procedures, doctors can view images of parts of the organs and can detect dysfunction or disease.

Radioactive tracers are short-lived isotopes that tend to concentrate in affected cells and are used to locate tumors. Tracers are widely used in medicine.

Nuclear radiation therapy is used to treat cancer.

Radiotherapy is treatment that uses controlled doses of nuclear radiation for treating diseases such as cancer. For example, certain brain tumors can be targeted with small beams of gamma rays.

Radiotherapy treats thyroid cancer by using an iodine isotope. Treatment of leukemia also uses radiotherapy. The defective bone marrow is first killed with a massive dose of nuclear radiation and then replaced with healthy bone marrow from a donor.

Agriculture uses radioactive tracers and radioisotopes.

On research farms, such as the one shown in **Figure 6,** radioactive tracers in flowing water can show how fast water moves through the soil or through stems and leaves of crops. Tracers help us understand biochemical processes in plants. Radioisotopes are chemically identical with other isotopes of the same element. Because of that similarity, they can be substituted in chemical reactions. Radioactive forms of the element are then easily located with sensors.

Teaching Key Ideas

Agricultural Application of Radioisotopes A solution of phosphate, containing radioactive phosphorus-32, is injected into the root system of a plant. Phosphorus-32 behaves identically to phosphorus-31, which is the more common and non-radioactive form of the element. Therefore, the two isotopes of phosphorus are used by the plant in the same way. Movement of the radioactive phosphorus-32 throughout the plant can be followed by an instrument like a Geiger counter. The information that is obtained helps scientists to understand the detailed mechanism of how plants utilize phosphorus to grow and to reproduce.

Why It Matters

Irradiation Tell students that another beneficial use of nuclear radiation is the irradiation of food. Because irradiation kills bacteria, irradiated food requires fewer chemicals to keep fresh. Some foods are irradiated by gamma rays from cobalt-60 or cesium-137 to retard spoilage. Irradiation is FDA approved and most commonly used on fruits, vegetables, and spices. Students might think that such foods become radioactive. Point out that irradiated food is not radioactive and is safe to eat. Have students find examples of irradiated foods at the supermarket and report back to the class. **LS Intrapersonal**

How Do PET Scans Work?

REAL WORLD

Positron emission tomography (PET) is a medical procedure that can be used to study how a patient's body is functioning. PET scans can help doctors detect medical problems, such as cancer and heart disease. These scans can show changes in biological processes earlier than changes in anatomy are visible by using other procedures, such as CAT scans and MRIs.

❶ Patients receiving a PET scan are injected with a radioactive tracer that is attached to a natural body compound, such as glucose.

❷ After 30 to 45 minutes, patients are taken to the PET scanner. They must lie very still while the detectors record the emission of energy from the injected radioactive materials.

❸ Because living tissues use glucose for energy, different colors on the computer screen correspond to the different levels of function in the body.

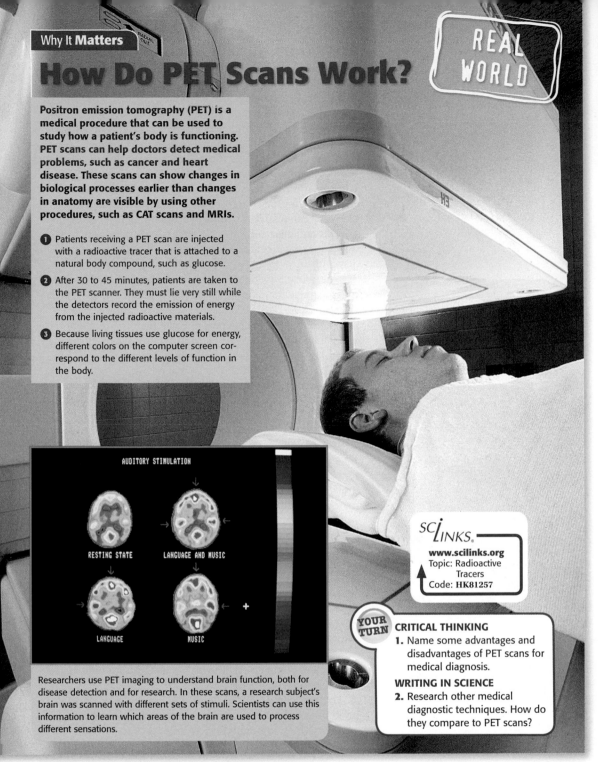

AUDITORY STIMULATION

RESTING STATE

LANGUAGE AND MUSIC

LANGUAGE

MUSIC

Researchers use PET imaging to understand brain function, both for disease detection and for research. In these scans, a research subject's brain was scanned with different sets of stimuli. Scientists can use this information to learn which areas of the brain are used to process different sensations.

SCI**LINKS**.

www.scilinks.org
Topic: Radioactive Tracers
Code: HK81257

YOUR TURN

CRITICAL THINKING
1. Name some advantages and disadvantages of PET scans for medical diagnosis.

WRITING IN SCIENCE
2. Research other medical diagnostic techniques. How do they compare to PET scans?

Why It **Matters**

How Do PET Scans Work? Nuclear medicine is the use of radioactive materials for the diagnosis and treatment of patients, as well as for the study of disease. Nuclear medicine uses radioactive tracers to study physiology rather than anatomy. The reason this is important is that biochemical and physiological changes occur in disease before anatomical changes can be identified. The techniques used in nuclear medical procedures, such as PET scans, are non-invasive and usually require no more than an intravenous injection. Have students choose a specific procedure in nuclear medicine and give an oral report on how it is used.
LS Verbal

Answers to Your Turn
1. Sample answer: PET scans allow doctors to detect medical problems without conducting invasive surgery.
2. Answers may vary. Some other medical diagnostic techniques include X rays, CAT scans, MRIs, and biopsies.

Differentiated Instruction

Alternative Assessment

Radioactive Tracers Ask students to write a short paragraph explaining why the half-life of a medical radioactive tracer is so important. (The half-life of a medical radioactive tracer must be long enough to reach its destination and be detected, but short enough to minimize the length of time healthy cells are exposed to radiation. Paragraphs might include the effects on the human body if either of these requirements is not met.) **LS** Logical/Verbal

READING TOOLBOX

Word Origins The word *ionization* comes from the root word *ion,* which means "goer" because ions were first discovered as charged particles that went towards a cathode or an anode depending on their charge. The word *dosimeter* comes from the root words *dose* and *-meter,* and thus means a "device measuring doses."

Teaching Key Ideas

Symptoms of Radiation Sickness
The initial symptoms of radiation sickness are nausea, vomiting, diarrhea, and fatigue. Later symptoms include headaches, shortness of breath, chest pains, loss of hair, hemorrhaging, inflammation of the mouth and throat, and darkening of skin. Have students research the treatments available for people suffering from radiation sickness. (Treatments of symptoms include analgesics to relieve pain and blood transfusions to relieve anemia.) **LS** Verbal

READING TOOLBOX

Word Origins
What are the origins of the words *ionization* and *dosimeter*? Do these words have root words from other languages? If so, what are the meanings of those root words?

Figure 7 A dosimeter contains a piece of film that detects radiation in the environment. Dosimeters help indicate exposure to ionizing radiation.

Risks from Nuclear Radiation

Although nuclear radiation has many benefits, there are also risks, because nuclear radiation interacts with living tissue. Alpha and beta particles, as well as gamma rays and X rays, can change the number of electrons in the molecules of living materials. This process is known as *ionization*. Ionized molecules may form substances that are harmful to life.

> **The risk of damage from nuclear radiation depends on both the type and the amount of radiation exposure.** The effects of low levels of nuclear radiation on living cells are so small that they may not be detected. However, studies have shown a relationship between exposure to high levels of nuclear radiation and cancer. Cancers associated with high-dose exposure include leukemia and breast, lung, and stomach cancers.

The ability to penetrate matter differs among different types of nuclear radiation. A layer of clothing or an inch of air can stop alpha particles. Beta particles are lighter and faster than alpha particles. Beta particles can penetrate a fraction of an inch in solids and liquids and can travel several feet in air. Several feet of material may be required to protect you from high-energy gamma rays.

High levels of nuclear radiation can cause radiation sickness.

Radiation sickness is an illness that results from excessive exposure to nuclear radiation. This sickness may occur from a single massive exposure, such as a nuclear explosion, or repeated exposures to very high nuclear radiation levels. Individuals who work with nuclear radiation must protect themselves with shields and special clothing. People who work in radioactive areas wear *dosimeters*, devices for measuring the amount of nuclear radiation exposure. **Figure 7** shows one example of a dosimeter.

High concentrations of radon gas can be hazardous.

Colorless and inert, *radon gas* is produced by the radioactive decay of the uranium-238 present in soil and rock. Radon gas emits alpha and beta particles and gamma rays. Tests have shown a correlation between lung cancer and high levels of exposure to radon gas, especially for smokers. Some areas have higher radon levels than others do. Tests for radon gas in buildings are widely available.

High concentrations of radon-222 in homes or offices can be eliminated by sealing cracks in foundations or by installing vents that draw air out of the building.

Why It Matters

Properties of Radon Radon is a noble gas, so it is only found uncombined in nature. Because it is heavier than air, it collects in basements and underground structures. Radon readily dissolves in water, so it can be found in groundwater, natural springs, and soil. Have students make an informative brochure that describes radon's properties and safety precautions associated with environmental radon. Students might also research where in the U.S. radon has been found to be a problem and how, when found, it is remediated. **LS** Verbal/Visual

Differentiated Instruction

Alternative Assessment

Weighing the Risks Tell students that technological advances involve a trade-off between anticipated benefits and risks. Weighing the benefits and risks accurately requires a scientific understanding of the technology in question. Have students write a paper explaining why the beneficial uses of radiation are worth the associated risks. Encourage them to use specific examples. **LS** Intrapersonal

Figure 8 Nuclear reactors such as this one are used over much of the world to generate electricity. **What are some advantages to nuclear power?**

Answer to caption question

Nuclear power does not produce gaseous pollutants and has significantly more energy available in its natural reserves than coal and oil.

Nuclear Power

Nuclear reactors, such as the one shown in **Figure 8,** are used in dozens of countries to generate electricity. ❯**Energy produced from fission is used to provide electrical energy to millions of homes and businesses.** There are many advantages to this source of energy. There are also disadvantages.

Nuclear fission has both advantages and disadvantages.

One advantage of nuclear fission is that it does not produce gaseous pollutants. Also, there is much more energy in the known uranium reserves than in the known reserves of coal and oil.

In nuclear fission reactors, energy is produced when a controlled fission reaction is triggered in uranium-235. However, the products of fission reactions are often radioactive isotopes. Therefore, serious safety concerns must be addressed. Radioactive products of fission must be handled carefully so that they do not escape into the environment and release nuclear radiation.

Another safety <u>issue</u> involves the safe operation of the nuclear reactors in which the controlled fission reaction is carried out. A nuclear reactor must be equipped with many safety features. The reactor requires considerable shielding and must meet very strict safety requirements. Thus, nuclear power plants are expensive to build.

✔️ **Reading Check** How do energy reserves for uranium compare to those of coal and oil?

SCLINKS.

www.scilinks.org
Topic: Nuclear Power
Code: HK81052

Academic Vocabulary

issue (ISH oo) a point of debate

Why It **Matters**

Chernobyl On April 26, 1986, the operators of a nuclear reactor at Chernobyl, Ukraine, improperly managed the water coolant levels. Overheating and an explosion resulted in radioactive materials being blown high into the air. Thirty-one people died soon after the accident, and hundreds more have suffered long-term damage to their health from radiation exposure.

Some people cite this accident as an argument against nuclear power, but proper safety precautions could have prevented the disaster. Had the explosion occurred in a containment vessel, such as that required for any nuclear power plant in the United States, no nuclear materials would have escaped into the environment. Have students write a script for a mock news report that details the events surrounding the Chernobyl accident. **LS Verbal**

Differentiated Instruction

Advanced Learners

Three Mile Island On March 28, 1979, failures in cooling water pumps at a nuclear power plant on Three Mile Island near Middletown, Pennsylvania caused the nuclear pellets of one nuclear reactor to overheat, leading to a meltdown of the reactor core. Though no deaths or injuries resulted from the accident, it gravely affected public concern for nuclear reactor management. Have students find out more about the accident at Three Mile Island and the impact it has had on Americans' feelings about nuclear power. **LS Verbal**

READING TOOLBOX

Visual Literacy Explain that nuclear power plants often have cooling towers with a distinct hyperboloid shape, as shown in **Figure 8.** The cooling towers help return hot waste water to more moderate temperatures. Explain that the shape of the cooling tower allows builders to construct the strongest tower possible with fewer materials. The strength of the hyperboloid prevents the tall and wide cooling towers from collapsing in strong winds.

Teaching Key Ideas

Containing Nuclear Waste To strengthen their understanding of the issues involved in the containment and disposal of nuclear waste, have students visit government Web sites and report their findings to the class. **LS Verbal**

Integrating Space Science

Formation of Elements In regular fusion reactions in stars, elements lighter than and including iron are formed. Elements heavier than iron are not formed because they consume instead of release energy when they form. When fuel in the star is spent, the star collapses, ending in a tremendous explosion called a supernova. Supernovas release enough energy to produce elements heavier than iron. Have students make an informative poster that describes how supernovas form. **LS Visual**

Why It **Matters**

Storing Radioactive Wastes Nuclear power poses an environmental problem because radioactive waste is generated that must be safely stored for thousands of years. The question is this: What type of storage is safe? In the United States, some leaders have proposed storing waste deep under Yucca Mountain in Nevada. The consequences of this storage method are not fully understood. Have students research various places that could be used for safe storage of nuclear wastes and present their findings in a visual display. **LS Visual**

Figure 9 Storage facilities for nuclear waste must be designed to contain radioactive materials safely for thousands of years.

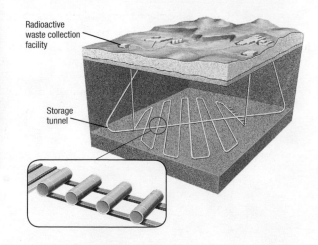

Radioactive waste collection facility

Storage tunnel

Integrating **Space Science**

Element Factory All heavy elements, from cobalt to uranium, are made when massive stars explode. The pressure that is produced in the explosion causes nearby nuclei to fuse, in some cases, more than once.

The explosion carries the newly created elements into space. These elements later become parts of new stars and planets. The elements of Earth are believed to have formed in the outer layers of an exploding star.

Nuclear waste must be safely stored.

Besides the expense that occurs during the life of a nuclear power plant is the expense of storing radioactive materials, such as the fuel rods used in the reactors. After their use, they must be placed in safe facilities that are well shielded, as **Figure 9** shows. These precautions are necessary to keep nuclear radiation from leaking out and harming living things. The facilities must also keep nuclear radiation from contacting groundwater.

Ideal places for such facilities are sparsely populated areas that have little water on the surface or underground. These areas must also be free from earthquakes.

Nuclear fusion releases large quantities of energy.

The sun uses the nuclear fusion of hydrogen atoms; this fusion results in larger helium atoms. Solar energy can be captured by solar panels or other means to provide energy for homes and businesses. Another option that holds some promise as an energy source is controlled nuclear fusion.

Some scientists estimate that 1 kg of hydrogen in a fusion reactor could release as much energy as 16 million kg of burning coal. The fusion reaction itself releases very little waste or pollution.

Because fusion requires that the electric repulsion between protons be overcome, these reactions are difficult to produce in the laboratory. However, scientists are conducting many experiments in the United States, Japan, and Europe to learn how people can exploit fusion to create a clean source of power that uses fuels extracted from ordinary water.

Differentiated Instruction

Alternative Assessment

Revising Preconceptions Have students review the list of ideas about radiation that they created in the **Reading Toolbox: Identifying Preconceptions** at the beginning of the chapter. Discuss each item, evaluating whether each one is accurate and in the correct category of positive or negative. Have students adjust items based on what they learned about radiation in this chapter. They should use the text to justify any changes. **LS Verbal**

Nuclear fusion also has advantages and disadvantages.

The most attractive feature of fusion is that the fuel for fusion is abundant. Hydrogen is the most common element in the universe, and it is plentiful in many compounds on Earth, such as water. Earth's oceans could provide enough hydrogen to meet current world energy demands for millions of years.

Practical fusion-based power, illustrated by the concept drawing in **Figure 10,** is far from being a reality. Fusion reactions have some drawbacks. They can produce fast neutrons, a highly energetic and potentially dangerous form of nuclear radiation. Because shielding material in the reactor would have to be replaced periodically, the expense of operating a fusion power plant would still be high. Lithium can be used to slow down these neutrons, but lithium is chemically reactive and rare, so its use is impractical.

Research on nuclear fusion is still in its infancy. Successful experiments are just beginning. Who can say what the future may hold? Perhaps future scientists will find the answers to the nagging questions that plague the government today concerning the perfect fuel for U.S. citizens.

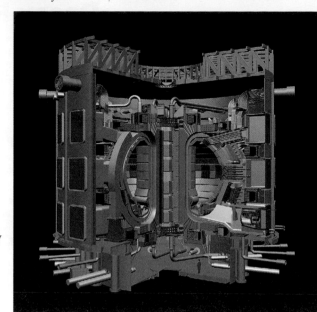

Figure 10 The ITER experimental nuclear fusion research reactor will be built in France.

> **Close**

Reteaching Key Ideas

Concept Map Have students make a concept map that organizes the following concepts: exposure to radiation, measuring radiation, benefits of radiation, risks from radiation. Have them use their concept maps to quiz each other on section material. **LS Visual**

Formative Assessment

Why must products of nuclear fission be stored safely?

A. They can burn in air. (Incorrect. While some may burn in air, their danger comes from their radioactivity and not their flammability.)

B. Many are radioactive. (Correct. Products of fission are radioactive isotopes that could release nuclear radiation into the environment.)

C. Many can be made into nuclear weapons. (Incorrect. Nuclear weapons are made from the same original radioactive substances that cause nuclear fission and not from the products of the reaction.)

D. They can revert back to their original form. (Incorrect. While the products of fission are often also radioactive, they cannot naturally change back to the radioactive elements that formed them.)

Section 3 Review

KEY IDEAS

1. **List** three sources of background radiation.
2. **Identify** three activities that add to background radiation under normal circumstances.
3. **Describe** how smoke detectors use alpha particles and what sets off the alarm.
4. **Explain** how radioactive tracers help locate tumors.
5. **Describe** three factors that contribute to how much damage is done to living tissue by radiation.
6. **Identify** some of the advantages and disadvantages of using nuclear energy.

CRITICAL THINKING

7. **Compare and Contrast** What are the benefits and risks of radiation therapy?
8. **Inferring Conclusions** Explain why it is important to use low levels of nuclear radiation for detection and treatment of disease.
9. **Drawing Conclusions** Why is the testing of buildings for radon gas levels important?
10. **Making Predictions** Suppose that uranium-238 could undergo fission as easily as uranium-235 does. Predict how that situation would change the advantages and disadvantages of fission reactors.

Answers to Section Review

1. Sun, heat, soil, water, plants, and air.
2. Sample Answer: smoking, flying, inhaling radon from environment, giving or receiving medical X rays, etc.
3. Radioactive sources in smoke detectors release alpha particles, which produce an electric current. Smoke particles reduce the flow of the current. The drop in current sets off the alarm when small levels of smoke are present.
4. Radioactive tracers are absorbed by tumors.
5. Type, duration, and amount of radiation exposure
6. Advantages: Nuclear energy does not produce gaseous pollutants and has significantly more energy available in nature than the process of burning coal or oil. Disadvantages: The products of nuclear reactions are often harmful radioactive isotopes, and nuclear reactors are expensive to build because of the safety requirements needed to control a fission reaction.
7. Radiation therapy enables doctors to treat cancer by targeting and exposing tumors to radiation. High doses of radiotherapy may harm healthy tissue.
8. Risks of high levels of nuclear radiation include cancers and radiation sickness.
9. Exposure to high levels of radon gas has been linked to lung cancer.
10. Advantages might include that fuel would be more abundant, thus lowering expense. The relative radioactivity and usefulness of waste products would need to be evaluated.

Time Required

1 lab period

Ratings

EASY ——————————— HARD

Teacher Prep 🧪🧪

Student Set-Up 🧪

Concept Level 🧪🧪🧪

Clean Up 🧪

Skills Acquired

- Classifying
- Collecting data
- Communicating
- Identifying/Recognizing patterns
- Interpreting
- Measuring
- Organizing and analyzing data

Scientific Methods

In this lab, students will:
- Make observations
- Analyze the results
- Draw conclusions
- Communicate results

Tips and Tricks

Some students may have difficulty understanding the concept of probability. Begin the lab with the following activity to illustrate the concept of probability.

Have each student write his or her name on a strip of paper. Collect all the strips and place them in a container. Ask students how likely it is that his or her name will be picked if someone were to draw a name from the container.

What You'll Do

❯ **Simulate** the decay of radioactive isotopes by throwing a set of dice, and observe the results.

❯ **Graph** the results to identify patterns in the amounts of isotopes present.

What You'll Need

cup, paper, large, with plastic lid

dice (10)

pencil

tape, masking

Simulating Nuclear Decay Reactions

In this lab, you will simulate the decay of lead-210 into its isotope lead-206. This decay of lead-210 into lead-206 occurs in a multistep process. Lead-210, $^{210}_{82}Pb$, first decays into bismuth-210, $^{210}_{83}Bi$, which then decays into polonium-210, $^{210}_{84}Po$, which finally decays into the isotope lead-206, $^{206}_{82}Pb$.

Procedure

Modeling Isotope Decay

❶ On a sheet of paper, prepare a data table as shown below. Leave room to add extra rows at the bottom, if necessary.

Sample Data Table: Dice Rolls Modeling Isotope Decay

Throw #	Number of dice representing each isotope			
	$^{210}_{82}Pb$	$^{210}_{83}Bi$	$^{210}_{84}Po$	$^{206}_{82}Pb$
0 (start)	10	0	0	0
1				
2		DO NOT WRITE		
3		IN BOOK		
4				

❷ Place all 10 dice in the cup. Each die represents an atom of $^{210}_{82}Pb$, a radioactive isotope.

❸ Put the lid on the cup, and shake the cup a few times. Then, remove the lid, and spill the dice. In this simulation, each throw represents a *half-life*.

❹ All of the dice that land with *1, 2,* or *3* up represent atoms of $^{210}_{82}Pb$ that have decayed into $^{210}_{83}Bi$. The remaining dice still represent $^{210}_{82}Pb$ atoms. Separate the two sets of dice. Count the dice, and record the results in your data table.

❺ To keep track of the dice representing the decayed atoms, you will make a small mark on them. On a die, the faces with *1, 2,* and *3* share a corner. With a pencil, draw a small circle or loop around this shared corner. This die represents the $^{210}_{83}Bi$ atoms.

❻ Put all the dice back in the cup, shake them, and roll them again. In a decay process, there are two possibilities: some atoms decay, and some do not. See the table "Guide to Isotope Decay" to help track your results.

Guide to Isotope Decay

Isotope type	Decays into	Signs of decay	Identifying the atoms in column 2
$^{210}_{82}\text{Pb}$	$^{210}_{83}\text{Bi}$	Unmarked dice land on *1*, *2*, or *3*.	Mark $^{210}_{83}\text{Bi}$ by drawing a circle around the corner where faces *1*, *2*, and *3* meet.
$^{210}_{83}\text{Bi}$	$^{210}_{84}\text{Po}$	Dice with one loop land on *1*, *2*, or *3*.	Draw a circle around the corner where faces *4*, *5*, and *6* meet.
$^{210}_{84}\text{Po}$	$^{206}_{82}\text{Pb}$	Dice with two loops land on *1*, *2*, or *3*.	Put a small piece of masking tape over the two circles.
$^{206}_{82}\text{Pb}$	Decay ends		

Sorting the Isotopes That Decayed

7 After the second throw, you have three types of atoms. Sort the dice into three sets.

 a. The first set consists of dice with a circle drawn on them that landed with *1*, *2*, or *3* facing up. These dice represent $^{210}_{83}\text{Bi}$ atoms that have decayed into $^{210}_{84}\text{Po}$.

 b. The second set consists of two types of dice: the dice with one circle that did not land on *1*, *2*, or *3* (undecayed $^{210}_{83}\text{Bi}$) and the unmarked dice that landed with *1*, *2*, or *3* facing up (representing the decay of original $^{210}_{82}\text{Pb}$ into $^{210}_{83}\text{Bi}$).

 c. The third set includes unmarked dice that did not land with *1*, *2*, or *3* facing up. These dice represent the undecayed $^{210}_{82}\text{Pb}$ atoms.

8 For your third throw, put all of the dice back into the cup. After the third throw, some of the $^{210}_{84}\text{Po}$ will decay into the stable isotope $^{206}_{82}\text{Pb}$. After this and each additional throw, do the following: separate the different types of atoms in groups, count the atoms in each group, record your data in your table, and mark the dice to identify each isotope. Use the table above as a guide.

9 Continue throwing the dice until all of the dice have indicated decay into $^{206}_{82}\text{Pb}$, which is a stable isotope.

Analysis

1. **Describing Events** Write nuclear-decay equations for the nuclear reactions modeled in this lab.

2. **Graphing Data** In your lab report, prepare a graph like the one shown here. Using a different color or symbol for each atom, plot the data for all four atoms on the same graph.

Communicating Your Results

3. **Drawing Conclusions** What do your results suggest about how the amounts of $^{210}_{82}\text{Pb}$ and $^{206}_{82}\text{Pb}$ on Earth are changing over time?

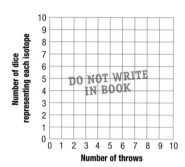

DO NOT WRITE IN BOOK

Number of dice representing each isotope / Number of throws

Extension

$^{210}_{82}\text{Pb}$ is continually produced through a series of nuclear decays that begin with $^{238}_{92}\text{U}$. Does this information cause you to modify your answer to item 3? Explain.

Answers to Analysis

1. $^{210}_{82}\text{Pb} \rightarrow {}^{210}_{83}\text{Bi} + {}^{0}_{-1}\text{e}$
 $^{210}_{83}\text{Bi} \rightarrow {}^{210}_{84}\text{Po} + {}^{0}_{-1}\text{e}$
 $^{210}_{84}\text{Po} \rightarrow {}^{206}_{82}\text{Pb} + {}^{4}_{2}\text{He}$

2. Students' graphs will vary. The graphs will depend on the results of throwing 10 dice (governed by probability) as described in the lab. A graph of the sample data in Data Table 1 is shown below.

Data Table 1

Throw	$^{210}_{82}\text{Pb}$	$^{210}_{83}\text{Bi}$	$^{210}_{84}\text{Po}$	$^{206}_{82}\text{Pb}$
0	10	0	0	0
1	6	4	0	0
2	3	5	2	0
3	2	3	4	1
4	0	4	3	3
5	0	2	4	4
6	0	0	3	7
7	0	0	2	8
8	0	0	0	10

Answer to Communicating Your Results

3. Lead-210 decays into lead-206. The amount of lead-210 gradually decreases, while lead-206 increases. Eventually, the amount of lead-210 remaining will be negligible.

Answer to Extension

If lead-210 is continually produced through the decay of uranium-238, then the overall amount of lead-210 will not necessarily decrease. This depends on how much new lead-210 is produced in a given time and how much lead-210 decays into lead-206.

Key Resources

Virtual Investigation

Classroom Lab Video/DVD

Holt Lab Generator CD-ROM
Search for any lab by type, standard, difficulty level, or time. Edit any lab to fit your needs, or create your own labs. Use the Lab Materials QuickList software to customize your lab materials list.

Differentiated Datasheets
Simulating Nuclear Decay Reactions

Observation Lab
Modeling Radioactive Decay with Pennies

CBL™ Probeware Lab
Determining the Effective Half-Life of Iodine-131 in the Human Body

Math Skills

Calculating Nuclear Decay Review with students how to convert percentages into fractions. Explain that percentages are fractions with 100 as the denominator. Explain that nuclear decay problems involving percentages follow the same steps as the problems involving fractions from earlier in the chapter.

Answers to Practice
1. 1/8
2. 3
3. The sample does not decay completely until the last atom decays, which can take many half-lives.

Counting Nuclear Decay

Technology

Math

Scientific Methods

Graphing

Problem

In a sample of francium-223, 93.75% of the sample has undergone radioactive decay. Francium-223 has a half-life of 22 min.

a. What fraction of francium-223 remains in the sample?

b. How many half-lives did it take for the sample to decay?

c. How long did the sample take to decay?

Solution

Identify

List all given and unknown values.

Given:

percentage of sample decayed = 93.75%

half-life = 22 min

Unknown:

a. *fraction of sample remaining*

b. *n = number of half-lives*

c. *time of decay*

Plan

a. Subtract the fraction decayed from 1 to find the amount of sample remaining.

b. Determine how many multiples of 1/2 are in the fraction of sample remaining.

c. Multiply the number of half-lives by the half-life to find the time of decay.

a. *fraction of sample remaining =*
$$1 - fraction\ of\ sample\ decayed =$$
$$1 - \frac{percentage\ of\ sample\ decayed}{100}$$

b. $\left(\frac{1}{2}\right)^n = fraction\ of\ sample\ remaining$

c. *time of decay = n × half-life*

Solve

Substitute the given values into the equation, calculate the unknown quantities, and solve.

a. *fraction of sample remaining =*
$$1 - \frac{93.75}{100} = 1 - 0.9375 = 0.0625 = \frac{1}{16}$$

b. $\frac{1}{16} = \left(\frac{1}{2}\right) \times \left(\frac{1}{2}\right) \times \left(\frac{1}{2}\right) \times \left(\frac{1}{2}\right) = \left(\frac{1}{2}\right)^4$

number of half-lives = n = 4

c. *time of decay = 4 × 22 min = 88 min*

Practice

1. What fraction of iodine-132 remains if 87.5% has undergone radioactive decay?

2. How many half-lives are required for the sample to decay?

3. Iodine-132 has a half-life of 2.3 h. How long does the sample take to decay completely?

go.hrw.com
SUPER SUMMARY
KEYWORD: HK8NUCS

SUMMARY

Key Ideas

Section 1 What Is Radioactivity?

❯ **Nuclear Radiation** After radioactive decay, elements change into different isotopes of the same element or into entirely different elements. (p. 327)

❯ **Nuclear Decay** Anytime an unstable nucleus emits alpha or beta particles, the number of protons and neutrons changes. (p. 330)

❯ **Radioactive Decay Rates** The time required for half of a sample of radioactive material to decay is its half-life. (p. 333)

Section 2 Nuclear Fission and Fusion

❯ **Nuclear Forces** The stability of a nucleus depends on the nuclear forces that hold the nucleus together. These forces act between the protons and the neutrons. (p. 337)

❯ **Nuclear Fission** Nuclear fission takes place when a large nucleus divides into smaller nuclei. Energy is released in the process. (p. 339)

❯ **Nuclear Fusion** Energy is released when light nuclei are combined to form heavier nuclei. (p. 342)

Section 3 Nuclear Radiation Today

❯ **Where Is Radiation?** We are continually exposed to radiation from natural sources, such as the sun, soil, rocks, and plants. (p. 344)

❯ **Beneficial Uses of Nuclear Radiation** Applications of nuclear radiation include medical diagnosis and treatment, smoke detectors, and agriculture. (p. 346)

❯ **Risks from Nuclear Radiation** The risk of damage from nuclear radiation depends on both the type and the amount of radiation exposure. (p. 348)

❯ **Nuclear Power** Energy produced from fission is used to provide electrical energy to millions of homes and businesses. (p. 349)

Key Terms

radioactive decay, p. 327

nuclear radiation, p. 327

alpha particle, p. 328

beta particle, p. 329

gamma ray, p. 329

half-life, p. 333

fission, p. 339

nuclear chain reaction, p. 340

critical mass, p. 341

fusion, p. 342

background radiation, p. 344

rem, p. 345

radioactive tracer, p. 346

SUPER SUMMARY

Have students connect the major concepts in this chapter through an interactive Super Summary. Visit **go.hrw.com** and type in the keyword **HK8NUCS** to access the Super Summary for this chapter.

Differentiated Instruction

Alternative Assessment

Predicting Reactions Show students an illustration of a hypothetical radioactive nucleus with 5 protons and 7 neutrons. Have students identify the isotope and write its chemical symbol. ($^{12}_{5}B$) Then have students write a nuclear equation to show what would happen if the nucleus underwent beta decay. ($^{12}_{5}B \rightarrow ^{12}_{6}C + ^{0}_{-1}e$) Finally, have students draw an illustration of the resulting nucleus similar to your original illustration. **LS** **Visual**

Key Resources

🔲 **Interactive Concept Map**

📋 **Review Resources**
Concept Review Worksheets

📋 **Assessment Resources**
Chapter Tests A and B
Performance-Based Assessment

Reading Toolbox

1. Answers may vary. Students' Four-Corner Folds should look similar to the example on the Reading Toolbox page and in Appendix A. Under the four flaps should be descriptions of the four following topics: nuclear fission, nuclear fusion, benefits of nuclear radiation, and risks of nuclear radiation.

Using Key Terms

2. An alpha particle is a helium nucleus with a charge of +2 and is only slightly penetrating. A beta particle is an electron and is moderately penetrating. A gamma ray is high-energy, penetrating radiation. Neutron emission occurs during fission and is more penetrating than alpha particles, beta particles, or gamma rays.

3. Beta particles come from decayed neutrons.

4. Gamma rays have no mass because they are a form of electromagnetic energy and are not made of matter.

5. No; the half-life of the tracer must be long enough to reach its destination and still be detected.

6. Enough of the radioactive substance must be present for fission to release enough neutrons to cause other nuclei to undergo fission in a continuing process.

7. Background radiation is radiation that arises naturally from cosmic rays and from radioactive isotopes in the soil and in the air.

8. The energy in stars is produced when hydrogen nuclei fuse together and result in the release of tremendous amounts of energy.

Understanding Key Ideas

9. d   10. b   11. d
12. c   13. c   14. a
15. b   16. a   17. b

Explaining Key Ideas

18. Radioactivity can increase atomic number, decrease it, or leave it unaffected. It can either decrease mass number or not affect it.

CHAPTER 10 Review

READING TOOLBOX

1. **Four-Corner Fold** Create a four-corner fold as described in Appendix A. Under two of the flaps, describe (1) nuclear fission and (2) nuclear fusion. Under the other two flaps, describe (3) some beneficial uses of nuclear radiation and (4) some risks of nuclear radiation.

USING KEY TERMS

2. Describe the main differences between the four principal types of nuclear radiation: *alpha particles, beta particles, gamma rays,* and *neutron emission.*

3. Where do *beta particles* come from?

4. Why do *gamma rays* have no mass at all?

5. Would a substance with a one-second *half-life* be effective as a *radioactive tracer*?

6. For the nuclear *fission* process, how is *critical mass* important in a *nuclear chain reaction*?

7. What is *background radiation*, and what are its sources?

8. How does nuclear *fusion* account for the energy produced in stars?

UNDERSTANDING KEY IDEAS

9. When a heavy nucleus decays, it may emit any of the following except
   a. alpha particles.   c. gamma rays.
   b. beta particles.   d. X rays.

10. A neutron decays to form a proton and a(n)
   a. alpha particle.   c. gamma ray.
   b. beta particle.   d. emitted neutron.

11. After three half-lives, _____ of a radioactive sample remains.
   a. all   c. one-third
   b. one-half   d. one-eighth

12. Carbon dating can be used to measure the age of each of the following except
   a. a 7,000-year-old human body.
   b. a 1,200-year-old wooden statue.
   c. a 2,600-year-old iron sword.
   d. a 3,500-year-old piece of fabric.

13. The strong nuclear force
   a. attracts protons to electrons.
   b. holds molecules together.
   c. holds the atomic nucleus together.
   d. attracts electrons to neutrons.

14. The process in which a heavy nucleus splits into two lighter nuclei is called
   a. fission.   c. alpha decay.
   b. fusion.   d. a chain reaction.

15. The amount of energy produced during nuclear fission is related to
   a. the temperature in the atmosphere during nuclear fission.
   b. the masses of the original nuclei and the particles released.
   c. the volume of the nuclear reactor.
   d. the square of the speed of sound.

16. Which condition is *not* necessary for a chain reaction to occur?
   a. The radioactive sample must have a short half-life.
   b. The neutrons from one split nucleus must cause other nuclei to divide.
   c. The radioactive sample must be at critical mass.
   d. Not too many neutrons must be allowed to leave the radioactive sample.

17. Which of the following is *not* a use for radioactive isotopes?
   a. as tracers for diagnosing disease
   b. as an additive to paints to increase durability
   c. as a way to treat forms of cancer
   d. as a way to study biochemical processes in plants

EXPLAINING KEY IDEAS

18. How does nuclear decay affect the atomic number and mass number of a nucleus that changes after undergoing decay?

19. What are two factors that cause alpha particles to lose energy and travel less distance than neutrons travel?

20. The nuclei of atoms are made of protons and neutrons. Every atomic nucleus larger than that of hydrogen has as least two positively charged protons. Why do the nuclei remain intact instead of being broken apart by the repulsion of their electric charges?

21. The amount of nuclear radiation exposure absorbed by the human body is measured in rems. How does the amount of exposure in rems per year in Denver, Colorado, compare with the amount that has been set as a safe limit for workers in occupations with relatively high radiation exposure? Explain your answer.

22. How can a radioactive tracer be used to locate tumors?

CRITICAL THINKING

23. Compare and Contrast Describe the similarities and differences between atomic electrons and beta particles.

24. Identifying Functions Why do people working around radioactive waste in a radioactive storage facility wear badges that contain strips of photographic film?

25. Drawing Conclusions Why would carbon-14 not be a good choice to use in household smoke detectors?

26. Predicting Outcomes Would an emitter of alpha particles be useful in measuring the thickness of a brick? Explain your answer.

Graphing Skills

27. Graphing Data The first 20 elements on the periodic table have stable nuclei composed of equal numbers of protons and neutrons. Create a graph on which you plot these elements based on the number of protons (*x*-axis) and neutrons (*y*-axis) they contain.

28. Graphing Data Extend your graph of the first 20 elements to include the other elements on the periodic table. What happens to the graph? What does this indicate about the stability of a nucleus?

29. Interpreting Graphics Using a graphing calculator or computer graphing program, create a graph for the decay of iodine-131, which has a half-life of 8.1 days. Use the graph to answer the following questions.
a. Approximately what percentage of the iodine-131 has decayed after 4 days?
b. Approximately what percentage of the iodine-131 has decayed after 12.1 days?
c. What fraction of iodine-131 has decayed after 2.5 half-lives have elapsed?

Math Skills

30. Nuclear Decay Bismuth-212 undergoes a combination of alpha and beta decays to form lead-208. Depending on which decay process occurs first, different isotopes are temporarily formed during the process. Identify these isotopes by completing the equations given below.

a. $^{212}_{83}\text{Bi} \rightarrow {}^{A}_{Z}\text{X} + {}^{4}_{2}\text{He}$
$^{A}_{Z}\text{X} \rightarrow {}^{208}_{82}\text{Pb} + {}^{0}_{-1}e$

b. $^{212}_{83}\text{Bi} \rightarrow {}^{A}_{Z}\text{X} + {}^{0}_{-1}e$
$^{A}_{Z}\text{X} \rightarrow {}^{208}_{82}\text{Pb} + {}^{4}_{2}\text{He}$

31. Half-Life Health officials are concerned about radon levels in homes. The half-life of radon-222 is 3.82 days. If a sample of gas contains 4.38 μg of radon-222, how much will remain in the sample after 15.2 days?

Assignment Guide

Section	Items
1	2–4, 9–12, 18, 19, 23, 26, 29–31
2	6, 8, 13–15, 20, 27, 28
3	1, 5, 7, 16, 17, 21, 22, 24, 25

31. 15.2 days × 1 half-life/3.82 days = about 4 half-lives
$1/2 \times 1/2 \times 1/2 \times 1/2 = 1/16$
$1/16 \times 4.38 \ \mu g = 0.274 \ \mu g$

19. Alpha particles travel less distance than neutrons because they are massive and charged.

20. The nuclear force that holds the protons together in the nucleus is stronger than the electrical repulsion that pushes them apart.

21. The average amount of radiation exposure in Denver, Colorado is 164.6 millirems per year. This average is much lower than the safe limit set for workers in high-radiation jobs, which is 5,000 millirems per year.

22. Some radioactive tracers tend to concentrate in tumors and thus can be used to locate these tumors with radiation detectors.

Critical Thinking

23. They are alike in mass and amount of charge. Beta particles, however, can have either negative or positive charge while atomic electrons are always negative. Beta particles possess more energy and are not part of a particular atom.

24. Where radioactivity strikes the film, it becomes exposed. The amount and pattern of exposure indicate the amount of radiation exposure.

25. Carbon-14 decays by emitting beta particles, which are more penetrating than the alpha particles emitted by the isotopes usually used in smoke detectors. Alpha particles penetrate the air less easily than beta particles and are therefore able to detect a change in the current of the air more quickly.

26. No. Alpha particles are relatively slow, have a large mass, and can be stopped by a sheet of paper. Therefore, they will not penetrate a brick.

Graphing Skills

27. Graphs should be a straight line extending from the zero point to somewhere in the upper right corner of the graph. Point out to the students that this graph represents a direct relationship.

28. Graphs should begin to curve upward from the slope formed by the original graph. As atoms become larger, it takes more neutrons to keep the nucleus stable.

29. Graphs may vary. One possibility is to graph number of half-lives on the *x*-axis and percentage of sample remaining on the *y*-axis.
a. 4 days/8.1 days/half-life = 0.494 half-lives; 29%
b. 64.5%
c. 82%

Math Skills

30. a. $^{212}_{83}\text{Bi} \rightarrow {}^{208}_{81}\text{Tl} + {}^{4}_{2}\text{He}$
$^{208}_{81}\text{Tl} \rightarrow {}^{208}_{82}\text{Pb} + {}^{0}_{-1}e$
b. $^{212}_{83}\text{Bi} \rightarrow {}^{212}_{84}\text{Po} + {}^{0}_{-1}e$
$^{212}_{84}\text{Po} \rightarrow {}^{208}_{82}\text{Pb} + {}^{4}_{2}\text{He}$

Standardized Test Prep

 TEST DOCTOR

Question 1 Answer B is correct. To find the correct answer, students must realize that in beta decay, the mass number does not change and the atomic number changes by one. They must also understand that electrons have so little mass that they are given a mass number of 0 in radioactive decay equations.

Question 2 Answer F is correct. To find the correct answer, students must calculate that after 40 years, $40 \div 10 = 4$ half-lives have passed. After each half-life, the amount decreases by half, and thus, $(((100 \div 2) \div 2) \div 2) \div 2 = 6.25$ g remain.

Question 3 Answer C is correct. Other answers indicate that students do not realize that beta particles have almost no mass and that a neutron is converted to a proton in beta decay.

Question 4 Full-credit answers should include the following points:
- The correct symbol for uranium-238 is $^{238}_{92}U$.
- The correct symbol for thorium-234 is $^{234}_{90}Th$.
- The correct symbol for an alpha particle is $^{4}_{2}He$.
The equation is $^{238}_{92}U \rightarrow \ ^{234}_{90}Th + \ ^{4}_{2}He$ because the mass number of uranium less the mass number of an alpha particle is $238 - 4 = 234$, which gives the mass number of the thorium isotope.

Question 5 Full-credit answers should include the following points:
- The strong nuclear force binds protons and neutrons together.
- At the very short distances between particles in a nucleus, the strong nuclear force is stronger than the electromagnetic force.

Question 6 Answer I is correct. Other answers indicate that the students do not realize that positrons (as well as electrons) are also beta particles.

Understanding Concepts

Directions (1–3): **For each question, write on a sheet of paper the letter of the correct answer.**

1. The beta-decay equation for the decay of cesium–137 into an isotope of barium is

$$^{137}_{55}Cs \rightarrow \ ^{X}_{Y}Ba + \ ^{Z}_{-1}e$$

What are the correct values for X, Y and Z?
   - **A.** 136, 55, 1
   - **B.** 137, 56, 0
   - **C.** 68, 56, 69
   - **D.** 69, 54, 68

2. The half-life of a particular radioactive isotope is 10 years. If you begin with 100 g of the substance, how much will be left after 40 years?
   - **F.** 6.25 g
   - **G.** 12.5 g
   - **H.** 25 g
   - **I.** 60 g

3. What happens to an atom's mass number and atomic number after the atom emits a beta particle?
   - **A.** Both the mass number and the atomic number increase by 1.
   - **B.** The atomic number does not change, but the mass number decreases by 1.
   - **C.** The mass number does not change, but the atomic number increases by 1.
   - **D.** Both the mass number and the atomic number decrease by 1.

Directions (4–5): **For each question, write a short response.**

4. In a particular case of alpha decay, an isotope of uranium, U, with a mass number of 238 and an atomic number of 92 emits an alpha particle and transforms into thorium, Th, which has an atomic number of 90. Write the equation for this decay process.

5. Why doesn't a nucleus full of protons fly apart because of electric repulsion?

Reading Skills

Directions (6–7): **Read the passage below. Then, answer the questions that follow.**

POSITRON

Like an electron, a positron has very little mass; however, an electron has an electric charge of –1, and a positron has an electric charge of +1. Scientists theorize that for every kind of particle, there is an antiparticle, which has the same mass but an opposite electric charge.

There are at least two ways in which positrons can be generated. One way is beta decay. In the most common form of beta decay, a neutron in the nucleus of an isotope is converted to a proton, and a beta particle is emitted in the form of an electron. This form of beta decay is properly called *beta minus decay*. In certain isotopes, however, the mirror image of this process, called *beta plus decay*, takes place: a proton is converted to a neutron, and a beta particle with a positive charge is emitted. This beta particle is a positron.

Another way that positrons can be created is for a photon to collide with a charged particle (such as an alpha particle) with a great amount of energy. The collision can result in the simultaneous creation of an electron and a positron from the energy of the photon, in a process called *pair production*.

6. What are the two types of beta particles?
   - **F.** protons and electrons
   - **G.** positrons and photons
   - **H.** electrons and photons
   - **I.** positrons and electrons

7. Which has greater mass, a positron or a photon? Explain.

Question 7 Full-credit answers should include the following points:
- A positron has a greater mass than a photon.
- Photons are electromagnetic energy and have no mass.
- Although a positron has very little mass, it still has more mass than a photon, which has none.

Question 8 Answer B is correct. Other answers indicate that students do not know that during beta decay, a neutron decays to become a proton and emits a beta particle.

Question 9 Answer H is correct. Students might answer F or G if they did not realize that adding a proton changed the atomic number and therefore the type of element, or I if they did not realize that only an electron is lost, so the mass number would stay the same.

Question 10 Full-credit answers should include the following points:
- The correct symbol for carbon-14 is $^{14}_{6}C$.
- The correct symbol for nitrogen-14 is $^{14}_{7}N$.
- The correct symbol for a beta particle is $^{0}_{-1}e$.
- $^{14}_{6}C \rightarrow \ ^{14}_{7}N + \ ^{0}_{-1}e$

Interpreting Graphics

The graphic below shows the radioactive decay of carbon-14. Use this graphic to answer questions 8–10.

RADIOACTIVE DECAY OF CARBON-14

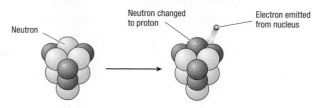

8. What type of nuclear reaction is depicted in the diagram?
   A. alpha decay
   B. beta decay
   C. fission
   D. fusion

9. What isotope is created by this process?
   F. carbon-14
   G. carbon-12
   H. nitrogen-14
   I. nitrogen-13

10. Write the equation that describes this process.

One way to measure how much of a radioactive isotope is present is to make a count of how many times per second a particle of radiation is emitted. This count is called an *activity count*. The graphic below shows the change in the activity count for a particular isotope over a period of 24 days. Use this graphic to answer questions 11–12.

ACTIVITY VS. TIME

11. What is the half-life of the isotope?
    A. 40 days
    B. 24 days
    C. 12 days
    D. 6 days

12. Assuming that this quantity of isotope had been decaying at the same rate that is shown in the graph for weeks before the measuring began, what would the activity count have been 12 days before day 0?

Test Tip

Try to figure out the answer to a question before you look at the choices. Then, compare your answer with each answer choice. Choose the answer that most closely matches your own.

Answers

1. B
2. F
3. C
4. Answers may vary; see Test Doctor for a detailed scoring rubric.
5. Answers may vary; see Test Doctor for a detailed scoring rubric.
6. I
7. Answers may vary; see Test Doctor for a detailed scoring rubric.
8. B
9. H
10. Answers may vary; see Test Doctor for a detailed scoring rubric.
11. D
12. Answers may vary; see Test Doctor for a detailed scoring rubric.

Question 11 Answer D is correct. To find the correct answer, students must determine how long it takes the number of activity counts per second to decrease by half. Since they begin at 80, are 40 at 6 days and then 20 at 12 days, the half-life of the isotope is 6 days.

Question 12 Full-credit answers should include the following points:
- 6 days before the graph begins the amount would have been twice that at day 0, or 160 activity counts per second.
- 6 days before that, the amount would have been twice 160, or 320 activity counts per second.

State Resources

For specific resources for your state, visit **go.hrw.com** and type in the keyword **HSHSTR**.

Test Practice with Guided Reading Development

Physics

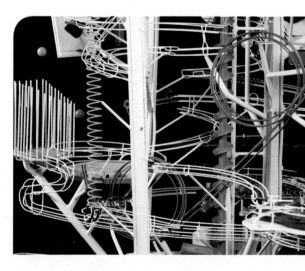

CHAPTER OPENER, pp. 362–364

`50 min.`

	Standards	Teach Key Ideas

SECTION 1 Measuring Motion, pp. 365–371 `50 min.`

> Observing Motion
> Speed and Velocity
> Calculating Speed
> Graphing Motion

Standards: UCP 2, UCP 3, SAI 2

Teach Key Ideas:
- Bellringer Transparency
- Teaching Transparencies TM30 Distance-Time Graph • TM31 Resultant Velocity • P1 Distance Vs. Displacement
- Visual Concepts Motion • Speed • Equation for Average Speed • Velocity

SECTION 2 Acceleration, pp. 372–377 `50 min.`

> Acceleration and Motion
> Calculating Acceleration
> Graphing Accelerated Motion

Standards: UCP 2, UCP 3, SAI 2, ST 2

Teach Key Ideas:
- Bellringer Transparency
- Teaching Transparencies TM32 Acceleration and Speed Graphs • P2 Changing Speed to Accelerate
- Visual Concepts Acceleration • Equation for Average Acceleration • Centripetal Acceleration • Graphical Representations of Acceleration • Final Velocity with Constant Uniform Acceleration

SECTION 3 Motion and Force, pp. 380–385 `50 min.`

> Fundamental Forces
> Balanced and Unbalanced Forces
> The Force of Friction
> Friction and Motion

Standards: PS 4a, PS 4c, PS 4d, SAI 1, SAI 2, ST 2

Teach Key Ideas:
- Bellringer Transparency
- Teaching Transparency P3 Frictional Forces and Acceleration
- Visual Concepts Force • Direction of the Friction Force • Friction • Types of Friction • Ways to Reduce or Increase Friction

See also PowerPoint® Resources

Chapter Review and Assessment Resources

SE Science Skills: Graphing Motion, p. 388
SE Chapter Summary, p. 389
SE Chapter Review, pp. 390–391
SE Standardized Test Prep, pp. 392–393
▢ Concept Review Worksheets ■
▢ Chapter Tests A and B ■
go.hrw.com Holt Online Assessment

CHAPTER Fast Track *To shorten instruction because of time limitations, omit the chapter lab.*

Basic Learners
TE Describing Motion, p. 367
TE Balanced and Unbalanced Forces, p. 381
▢ Science Skills Worksheets
▢ Differentiated Datasheets A for Labs and Activities ■
▢ Study Guide A ■

Advanced Learners
TE Illustrating Acceleration, p. 373
TE Roller Coaster Design, p. 374
TE Interviewing an Investigator, p. 378
▢ Cross-Disciplinary Worksheets
▢ Differentiated Datasheets C for Labs and Activities ■

Key

SE Student Edition
TE Teacher's Edition

📁 Chapter Resource File
📓 Workbook
🎞 Transparency

💿 CD or CD-ROM
* Datasheet or blackline master available

■ Also available in Spanish

All resources listed below are also available on the Teacher's One-Stop Planner.

Why It Matters	Hands-On	Skills Development	Assessment
Build student motivation with resources about high-interest applications.	**SE Inquiry Lab** Motion on Motion, p. 363* ■	**TE Reading Toolbox** Assessing Prior Knowledge, p. 362 **SE Reading Toolbox** p. 364	📁 Pretest ■
TE Speed and Exercise, p. 366 **TE Speed and Film,** p. 369 📁 **Cross-Disciplinary Worksheets** Real World Applications—Hiking in Yellowstone • Connections to Fine Arts—The Motions of Dance • Integrating Health—Energy Costs of Walking and Running • Integrating Biology—Speedy Dinosaurs? • Integrating Mathematics—Instantaneous Rates of Change • Connection to Social Studies—An Expanding City	**TE Demonstration** Observing Motion, p. 365 **SE Quick Lab** Measuring Speed, p. 368* ■ 📁 **Observation Lab** Testing Reaction Time	**TE Reading Toolbox** Visual Literacy, p. 366 **TE Science Skills** Distance Versus Displacement, p. 366 **TE Reading Toolbox** Visual Literacy, p. 367 **SE Math Skills** Velocity, p. 369 **SE Reading Toolbox** Everyday Words Used in Science, p. 370 **SE Graphing Skills** Calculating Slope, p. 370	**TE Reteaching Key Ideas** Concept Map, p. 371 **TE Formative Assessment,** p. 371 📁 Spanish Assessment* ■ 📁 Section Quiz ■
TE Automobile Acceleration, p. 374 **TE Particle Accelerators,** p. 375 **TE Space Acceleration Measurement System,** p. 376 **SE Accident Reconstruction,** pp. 378–379 📁 **Cross-Disciplinary Worksheet** Integrating Mathematics—Jesse Owens in the 100-Meter Dash	**TE Demonstration** Acceleration, p. 372 **TE Demonstration** Centripetal Acceleration, p. 373	**TE Science Skills** Vocabulary, p. 373 **SE Math Skills** Acceleration, p. 375 **SE Reading Toolbox** Describing Space and Time, p. 376 **SE Graphing Skills** Graphing Acceleration, p. 376 **TE Science Skills** Graphing Acceleration Two Ways, p. 376 **TE Reading Toolbox** Visual Literacy, p. 379	**TE Reteaching Key Ideas** Acceleration Chart, p. 377 **TE Formative Assessment,** p. 377 📁 Spanish Assessment* ■ 📁 Section Quiz ■
TE Forces in Molecules, p. 382 **SE How Do Brakes Work?** p. 383 **TE Speed Skating,** p. 384 📁 **Cross-Disciplinary Worksheets** Real World Applications—Designing Race Cars • Connection to Language Arts—Friction in Fiction	**TE Demonstration** Forces, p. 380 **SE Quick Lab** Friction, p. 384* ■ **SE Application Lab** Static, Sliding, and Rolling Friction, pp. 386–387* ■ 📁 **CBL™ Probeware Lab** Static and Kinetic Friction	**SE Reading Toolbox** Tri-Fold, p. 382 **TE Reading Toolbox** Visual Literacy, p. 383	**TE Reteaching Key Ideas** Connecting Ideas, p. 385 **TE Formative Assessment,** p. 385 📁 Spanish Assessment* ■ 📁 Section Quiz ■
	See also Lab Generator		**See also Holt Online Assessment Resources**

Resources for Differentiated Instruction

English Learners
TE Building with Force, p. 381
📁 Differentiated Datasheets A, B, and C for Labs and Activities ■
📓 Study Guide A ■

Struggling Readers
TE Decoding Word Problems, p. 369
TE Comparing Summary to the Text, p. 382
📓 Interactive Reader

Special Education Students
TE Calculating Average Speed, p. 368
TE Friction, p. 383

Alternative Assessment
TE Tracking Speed, p. 370
TE Observing Acceleration, p. 374
TE Helpful and Unwanted Friction, p. 384
TE Analyzing Motion, p. 389

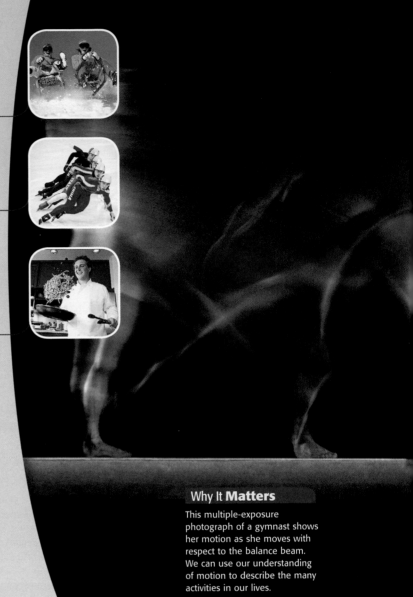

CHAPTER 11

Overview

This chapter covers motion, speed, velocity, and acceleration. Students learn how to calculate speed and acceleration and learn to interpret both distance-time graphs and speed-time graphs. The concept of force is also introduced, including balanced and unbalanced forces and the force of friction.

READING TOOLBOX

Assessing Prior Knowledge Students should understand the following concept:
• units of measurement

MISCONCEPTION ALERT

Science education research has identified the following misconception about motion and friction.
• A common misconception is that friction is a force that occurs between solids only.
Do the following demonstration to help students overcome this misconception. Fill a fish tank or a large container with water. Ask a student volunteer to put his or her hand in the water and move it from one end of the tank to the other with the palm facing forward. As the student moves the hand ask the student the following questions: "What do you feel as you move your hand?" (I feel a force pushing on my hand.) "What is exerting the force on your hand?" (the water) "On what part of your hand do you feel the force?" (on my palm) "Where do you feel the force when you move your hand backward through the water?" (on the back of my hand) After completing the demonstration, explain to the students that force felt by the volunteer was the force of friction between the water and the hand. Also explain that forces always act in a certain direction.

Chapter Outline

❶ Measuring Motion
Observing Motion
Speed and Velocity
Calculating Speed
Graphing Motion

❷ Acceleration
Acceleration and Motion
Calculating Acceleration
Graphing Accelerated Motion

❸ Motion and Force
Fundamental Forces
Balanced and Unbalanced Forces
The Force of Friction
Friction and Motion

Why It Matters

This multiple-exposure photograph of a gymnast shows her motion as she moves with respect to the balance beam. We can use our understanding of motion to describe the many activities in our lives.

Chapter Correlations   National Science Education Standards

The following correlations show the National Science Standards that relate to this chapter. For the full text of the standards, see the National Science Education Standards at the front of the book.

PS 4a Objects change their motion only when a net force is applied. (Section 3)

PS 4c The electric force is a universal force that exists between any two charged objects. (Section 3)

PS 4d Between any two charged particles, electric force is vastly greater than the gravitational force. (Section 3)

UCP 2 Evidence, models, and explanation (Sections 1, 2)

UCP 3 Constancy, change, and measurement (Sections 1, 2)

SAI 1 Abilities necessary to do scientific inquiry (Application Lab: Static, Sliding, and Rolling Friction)

SAI 2 Understandings about scientific inquiry (Sections 1–3)

ST 2 Understandings about science and technology (Sections 2, 3)

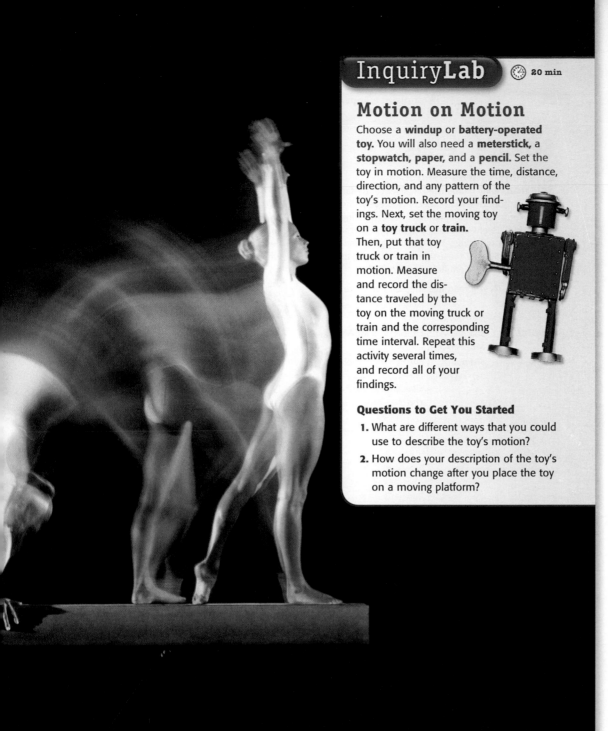

InquiryLab ⏱ 20 min

Motion on Motion

Choose a **windup** or **battery-operated toy.** You will also need a **meterstick,** a **stopwatch, paper,** and a **pencil.** Set the toy in motion. Measure the time, distance, direction, and any pattern of the toy's motion. Record your findings. Next, set the moving toy on a **toy truck** or **train.** Then, put that toy truck or train in motion. Measure and record the distance traveled by the toy on the moving truck or train and the corresponding time interval. Repeat this activity several times, and record all of your findings.

Questions to Get You Started

1. What are different ways that you could use to describe the toy's motion?

2. How does your description of the toy's motion change after you place the toy on a moving platform?

InquiryLab

Teacher's Notes The second part of the activity introduces the concept of a frame of reference. The first object's speed could be determined relative to the second object (the toy truck or train) or relative to the ground.

Materials per Group
- meterstick
- paper
- pencil
- stopwatch
- toy truck or train
- toy, windup or battery-operated

Answers

1. Answers could include the following: Descriptions of patterns and repetitions of motion, the initial direction and changes in direction, and changes in speed. Students may also use the meterstick and stopwatch to find the speed of the toy.

2. Sample answer: I could describe the motion of the toy relative to the moving platform or the motion of the toy relative to the ground. The motion of the toy relative to the ground is a combination of the motion of the toy relative to the platform and the motion of the platform.

Key Resources

📁 **Datasheet**
Motion on Motion

💿 **Interactive Tutor**
Disc Two, Module 9: Speed and Acceleration

Science Terms

Sample table:

WORD	EVERYDAY MEANING	SCIENTIFIC MEANING
velocity	speed	the speed of an object in a particular direction
acceleration	increase in speed	the rate at which velocity changes over time; an object accelerates if its speed, direction, or both change

Describing Space and Time

Sample answers: in the Space column: left, up, forward, in a circle, on a curved path, next to the door; in the Time column: in 1997, for the whole race, for several days, in 72 s, in 5.00 h, after 1 s, 1.5 s later

FoldNotes

Answers may vary. Some concepts that students may write on their tri-fold include motion, speed, velocity, acceleration, force, and friction.

These reading tools can help you learn the material in this chapter. For more information on how to use these and other tools, see **Appendix A.**

Science Terms

Everyday Words Used in Science
Many words used in science are familiar words from everyday speech. However, when these words are used in science, their meanings are often different from or are more precise than the everyday meanings. You should pay attention to the definitions of these words so that you use them correctly in scientific contexts.

Your Turn As you read this chapter, complete the table below.

WORD	EVERYDAY MEANING	SCIENTIFIC MEANING
speed	the act of moving fast	the distance an object travels divided by the time interval over which the motion occurs
velocity	speed	
acceleration	an increase in speed	

Describing Space and Time

Words and Phrases Describing the motion of objects involves describing changes in both space and time. Paying attention to language that describes space and time can help you recognize when and what kind of motion is described.

For example, if a bicycle is moving at 15 m/s, the bicycle will move a certain distance in space (15 m) in a given amount of time (1 s).

Your Turn As you read this chapter, make a two-column list like the one below on a separate sheet of paper. Add words or phrases that describe space and time.

SPACE (POSITION, SHAPE, DIRECTIONS)	TIME
in a straight line	one day
north	

FoldNotes

Tri-Fold FoldNotes are a fun way to help you learn and remember ideas that you read. FoldNotes help you organize concepts and see the "big picture." Tri-folds can help you remember the definitions or equations that go with the terms that you learn.

Your Turn Make a tri-fold, following the instructions in **Appendix A.**

1. Label the first column "Term/Quantity," the second column "Definition/Equation," and the third column "Notes."
2. Add new terms or new physical quantities to the first column.
3. Write the definition and the equation in the second column.
4. Write additional notes, such as the units, in the third column.

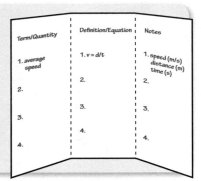

Measuring Motion

Key Ideas

❯ How is a frame of reference used to describe motion?

❯ What is the difference between speed and velocity?

❯ What do you need to know to find the speed of an object?

❯ How can you study speed by using graphs?

Key Terms

motion
frame of reference
displacement
speed
velocity

Why It Matters

Rescue workers can use the last-known velocity of a lost airplane to determine where to look for survivors.

We are surrounded by moving things. From a car moving in a straight line to a satellite traveling in a circle around Earth, objects move in many ways. In everyday life, motion is so common that it seems very simple. But describing motion scientifically calls for careful use of definitions.

Observing Motion

You may think that the **motion** of an object is easy to detect—just look at the object. But you really must observe the object in relation to other objects that stay in place, called *reference points*. A **frame of reference** is used to describe the motion of an object relative to these reference points. The trees in the background in **Figure 1** can be used as a frame of reference to describe the motion of the snowboarder.

❯ **When an object changes position with respect to a frame of reference, the object is in motion.** You can describe the direction of an object's motion with a reference direction, such as north, south, east, west, up, or down.

Distance measures the path taken.

In addition to knowing direction, you need to know how far an object moves if you want to correctly describe its motion. To measure distance, you measure the length of the path that the object took. For example, if you start at your home and drift around your neighborhood, changing directions a few times, a string that follows your path would be as long as the distance you traveled.

motion–(MOH SHUHN)–an object's change in position relative to a reference point

frame of reference–(FRAYM UHV REF uhr uhns)–a system for specifying the precise location of objects in space and time

Figure 1 In this multiple-exposure photograph, the trees can provide a frame of reference.

 Focus

This section begins by defining and discussing motion. Next, students learn about distance versus displacement, average speed, instantaneous speed, and velocity. They also learn how to read a distance-time graph and how to calculate speed and velocity.

Bellringer

Use the Bellringer transparency to prepare students for this section.

Demonstrate

Observing Motion Start walking around the room and ask students how they know that you are moving. (Accept all answers.) Then, stop moving and instruct students to close their eyes. While the students' eyes are closed, quietly move to another location in the room. Tell students to open their eyes and ask if you've moved and how they know that you moved. (Sample answer: You used to be next to your desk and now you aren't.) Next, ask students if Earth is moving and how they know that it is moving. (Accept all answers.) Ask students how early astronomers learned that Earth is moving. (Astronomers saw that the positions of the sun and the stars changed and realized that the motion of Earth caused those changes.) Finally, lead a discussion about detecting motion. Help students understand that motion is observed when an object changes position in relation to a frame of reference.
LS Visual

Key Resources

 Teaching Transparencies
TM30 Distance-Time Graph
TM31 Resultant Velocity
P1 Distance Vs. Displacement

Visual Concepts
Motion
Speed
Equation for Average Speed
Velocity

Datasheet
Measuring Speed

Science Skills Worksheet
Slope of a Line

Math Skills Worksheet
Velocity

Cross-Disciplinary Worksheets
Real World Applications—Hiking in Yellowstone
Connections to Fine Arts—The Motions of Dance
Integrating Health—Energy Costs of Walking and Running
Integrating Biology—Speedy Dinosaurs?
Integrating Mathematics—Instantaneous Rates of Change
Connection to Social Studies—An Expanding City

Teaching Key Ideas

Frames of Reference and Motion
Explain to students that anything near a moving object can be used as a frame of reference for describing motion. The chalkboard in a classroom can be a frame of reference for anything in the room. A tree outside can be a frame of reference for a bird flying by. Further explain that motion can sometimes be described by using more than one frame of reference. For example, a person sitting on a bus is not moving in relation to the seats in the bus, but the person is moving in relation to the ground. Ask students to describe other frames of reference. (Sample answers: A train station is a frame of reference for a train. A city is a frame of reference for an airplane.) **LS** **Verbal**

READING TOOLBOX

Visual Literacy Explain to students that the photos in **Figure 3** are arranged from the slowest to the fastest. The distance between the photos is not proportional to the difference in the speeds. **LS** **Visual**

Science Skills

Distance Versus Displacement Use the following questions to help students distinguish between distance and displacement: Which should you use when calculating how many gallons of gas you will need for a road trip? (distance) Which does the saying "as the crow flies" refer to? (displacement) **LS** **Verbal**

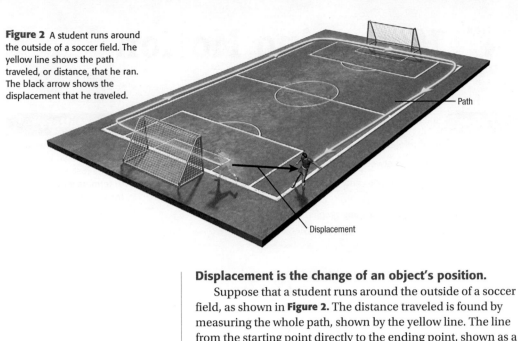

Figure 2 A student runs around the outside of a soccer field. The yellow line shows the path traveled, or distance, that he ran. The black arrow shows the displacement that he traveled.

Path

Displacement

Displacement is the change of an object's position.

Suppose that a student runs around the outside of a soccer field, as shown in **Figure 2.** The distance traveled is found by measuring the whole path, shown by the yellow line. The line from the starting point directly to the ending point, shown as a black arrow, is called the **displacement**.

Distance measures how far an object moves along a path. Displacement measures how far it is between the starting and ending points. Displacement is often shorter than the distance traveled, unless the motion is all in a straight line.

The direction of a displacement must also be given. The distance between your home and school may be 12 blocks, but that information does not tell whether you are going toward or away from school. Displacement must always indicate the direction, such as 12 blocks *toward school.*

✓ **Reading Check** What is the difference between distance and displacement? (See Appendix E for answers to Reading Checks.)

Figure 3 We encounter a wide range of speeds in our everyday life.

Person walking
1.4 m/s

Wheelchair racer
7.3 m/s

Galloping horse
19 m/s

Speed and Velocity

You know from experience that some objects move faster than others. **Speed** describes how fast an object moves. The speed for some everyday objects is shown in **Figure 3**, and the distance versus time of the objects is graphed in **Figure 4**.

Sometimes, you may need to know the direction in which an object is moving. In 1997, a 200 kg lion escaped from a zoo in Florida. A helicopter crew was able to guide searchers on the ground by reporting the lion's **velocity**, which is its speed and direction of motion. The lion's velocity may have been reported as 4.5 m/s to the north or 2.0 km/h toward the highway. Without knowing the direction of the lion's motion, searchers could not have predicted its position. **〉 Speed tells us how fast an object moves, and velocity tells us both the speed and the direction that the object moves.**

Velocity is described relative to a reference point.

The direction of motion can be described in different ways, such as east, west, south, or north of a fixed point. Or it can be an angle from a fixed line. Direction is described as positive or negative along the line of motion. So, if a body is moving in one direction, it has positive velocity. If it is moving in the opposite direction, it has negative velocity. By convention, up and right are usually positive, and left and down are negative.

Combined velocities determine the resultant velocity.

If you are riding in a bus traveling east at 15 m/s, you and all the other passengers are traveling at a velocity of 15 m/s east relative to the street. But suppose that you stand up and walk at 1 m/s toward the back of the bus. Are you still moving at the same velocity as the bus relative to the street? No, but your new velocity can be easily calculated. Your new velocity is equal to 15 m/s east + (–1 m/s east) = 14 m/s east.

displacement (dis PLAYS muhnt) the change in position of an object

speed (SPEED) the distance traveled divided by the time interval during which the motion occurred

velocity (vuh LAHS uh tee) the speed of an object in a particular direction

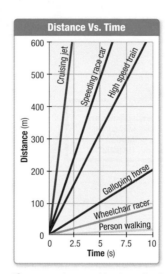

Figure 4 When an object's motion is graphed by plotting distance on the *y*-axis and time on the *x*-axis, the slope of the graph is speed.

High-speed train
67 m/s

Speeding race car
96 m/s

Cruising jet
257 m/s

Teaching Key Ideas

How are Speed and Velocity Different? Help students distinguish between speed and velocity by describing a car moving at constant speed as it rounds a curve. The speed remains constant, but its velocity has changed because the direction in which the car is moving has changed. Point out that cars have *speedometers*, not "velocitometers."

READING TOOLBOX

Visual Literacy Ask students to look at **Figure 4**. Ask students the following questions: How do you calculate the slope of a line? (change in y/ change in *x*, or rise/run) Which line has the greatest slope? (cruising jet) Which has the least slope? (walking person) What would a slope of zero represent? (a speed of zero, or an object at rest) Does each line graph represent an object traveling at a constant speed, or are the speeds changing? How can you tell? (All of the objects are traveling at a constant speed. I know this because for any given object, the line representing its motion is straight: equal changes in time correspond to equal changes in distance.) **LS** Visual

Differentiated Instruction

Basic Learners

Describing Motion Research shows that very few students grasp the subtleties of describing motion during their first exposure to ideas such as speed, velocity, and acceleration. The definitions of average speed, average velocity, and average acceleration are deceivingly simple. But the idea of speed at a particular moment (instantaneous speed) involves sophisticated mathematical ideas. To help students grasp the concept of speed, first introduce constant motion. The definition of constant motion—an object covering equal distances in equal amounts of time—naturally motivates the concept of speed. Describing non-constant motion—an object that does not cover equal distances in equal intervals of time—provides the motivation to develop the concept of average speed. You may also point out that one way to think about instantaneous speed is that it describes the distance an object *would* go if it were to travel at that speed for a certain amount of time. **LS** Verbal

Teacher's Notes Students can line up their dominoes along the edge of the meterstick to ensure that the dominoes are in a straight line.

Materials per Group
• dominoes, 25
• meterstick
• stopwatch

Answers to Analysis
1. Answers may vary.
2. Putting dominoes very close together and putting them very far apart both lead to slower average speed. The average speed is fastest when the distance between the dominoes is about half the length of a domino. Students will likely find that the results do not confirm their predictions. They will probably have predicted that placing the dominoes very close together would increase the average speed.

Teaching Key Ideas

Calculating Speed To help students remember what measurements are needed to calculate the speed of an object, tell them to think about the units for speed. Students are probably most familiar with the unit of miles per hour (mph). Explain to students that the word *per* means "divided by," so *miles per hour* means mi/h. Then, explain that speed is always calculated by dividing a distance (miles) by a time (hours). Ask students to name other possible units for speed. (Sample answers: m/s, km/h, cm/day, mi/year) **LS** **Logical**

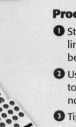

QuickLab

Measuring Speed

🕙 **10 min**

Procedure
❶ Stand up **25 dominoes** in a straight line. Try to keep equal spacing between the dominoes.

❷ Use a **meterstick** to measure the total length of your row of dominoes, and record the length.

❸ Tip over the first domino. Use a **stopwatch** to time how long it takes for all of the dominoes to fall.

❹ Repeat steps 1–3 several times using smaller and larger distances between the dominoes.

Analysis
1. To calculate the average speed for each trial, divide the total distance by the time that it takes the dominoes to fall.

2. How did the spacing between dominoes affect the average speed? Is this the result that you expected?

SC*L*INKS.

www.scilinks.org
Topic: Measuring Motion
Code: **HK80927**

Figure 5 A sledder's average speed can be determined by timing the rider on a set course.

Calculating Speed

Speed describes distance traveled over a specified time. **>To calculate speed, you must measure two quantities: the distance traveled and the time it took to travel that distance.** The SI unit for speed is meters per second (m/s).

When an object covers equal distances in equal amounts of time, it is moving at a *constant speed*. For example, if a train has a constant speed of 67 m/s, the train moves a length of 67 m every second.

Average speed is calculated as distance divided by time.

Most objects do not move at a constant speed but change speed from one instant to another. One way to make it easier to describe the motion of an object is to use *average speed*. Average speed is the distance traveled by an object divided by the time the object takes to travel that distance.

| ▶ **Average speed** | | $speed = \frac{distance}{time} \qquad v = \frac{d}{t}$ |

Suppose that a sledder, such as one shown in **Figure 5,** moves 132 m in 18 s. By putting the time and distance into the formula above, you can calculate her average speed.

$$v = \frac{d}{t} = \frac{132 \text{ m}}{18 \text{ s}} = 7.3 \text{ m/s}$$

The sledder's average speed over the length is 7.3 m/s. But she probably did not travel at this speed for the whole race. Her pace may have been slower near the start of the race and faster near the bottom of the hill.

✔ **Reading Check** How do you calculate average speed?

Differentiated Instruction

Special Education Students

Calculating Average Speed Have students conduct partner runs. Choose a 6 m path of floor with tiles that can be counted, or create "tiles" with duct tape. Mark the start with duct tape. Have student partners stand side-by-side and link their arms. One pair at a time, have students "run" down the path as quickly as possible. For each pair, record the seconds the run takes. Have students calculate average speed (tiles/seconds) for each pair. **LS** **Kinesthetic**

Instantaneous speed is the speed at a given time.

You could find the sledder's speed at any given point in time by measuring the distance traveled in a shorter time interval. The smaller the time interval, the more accurate the measurement of speed will be. Speed measured in an infinitely small time interval is called *instantaneous speed*. Although it is impossible to measure an infinitely small time interval, some devices measure speed over very small time intervals. Practically speaking, a car's speedometer gives the instantaneous speed of the car.

Academic Vocabulary

interval (IN tuhr vuhl) a space between objects, units, points, or states

Math *Skills* Velocity

Metal stakes are sometimes placed in a glacier to help measure the glacier's movement. For several days in 1936, Alaska's Black Rapids glacier surged as swiftly as 89 m per day down the valley. Find the glacier's velocity in m/s. Remember to include direction.

Identify	**Given:**
List the given and the unknown values.	*time, t* = 1 day
	distance, d = 89 m down the valley
	Unknown:
	velocity, v = ? (m/s and direction)

Plan	To find the velocity in meters per second, convert the time to seconds.
a. Perform any necessary conversions.	$t = 1 \text{ day} = 24 \text{ h} \times \dfrac{60 \text{ min}}{1 \text{ h}} \times \dfrac{60 \text{ s}}{1 \text{ min}}$
	$t = 86{,}400 \text{ s} = 8.64 \times 10^4 \text{ s}$
b. Write the equation for speed.	$speed = \dfrac{distance}{time} = \dfrac{d}{t}$

Solve	$v = \dfrac{d}{t} = \dfrac{89 \text{ m}}{8.64 \times 10^4 \text{ s}}$
Insert the known values into the equation, and solve.	(For velocity, include direction.)
	$v = 1.0 \times 10^{-3}$ m/s down the valley

Practice

1. Find the velocity in meters per second of a swimmer who swims 110 m toward the shore in 72 s.
2. Find the velocity in meters per second of a baseball thrown 38 m from third base to first base in 1.7 s.
3. Calculate the displacement in meters that a cyclist would travel in 5.00 h at an average velocity of 12.0 km/h to the southwest. Remember to include direction.

For more practice, visit **go.hrw.com** and enter the keyword **HK8MP**.

Practice **Hint**

> When a problem requires you to calculate velocity, you can use the speed equation. Remember to specify direction.

> Problem 3: The speed equation can be rearranged to isolate distance on the left side of the equation. First, multiply both sides by t.

$$v = \frac{d}{t}$$
$$v \times t = \frac{d}{t} \times t$$
$$vt = d$$
$$d = vt$$

Be sure to rearrange the equation before you substitute numbers for v, d, or t.

> You can use the distance form of the equation to find displacement. Remember to specify direction when you solve for displacement.

Why It Matters

Speed and Film The technology for creating motion pictures was developed when a way was invented to photograph live action many times per second. The photo frames are played very rapidly. In regular films, 24 frames per second are projected to produce the perception of continuous motion. Ask students what they would see if a film was projected faster or slower than 24 frames per second. (Sample answer: If the film were projected faster, the motion seen on the screen would be smoother. If the film were projected slower, the motion might not appear to be continuous.) **LS Logical**

Math *Skills*

Answers to Practice

1. $v = \dfrac{d}{t} = \dfrac{110 \text{ m}}{72 \text{ s}} = 1.5$ m/s toward shore

2. $v = \dfrac{d}{t} = \dfrac{38 \text{ m}}{1.7 \text{ s}} = 22$ m/s toward first base

3. $d = vt = 12.0$ km/h $\times$ 5 h = 60.0 km

   $(60.0 \text{ km})(1{,}000 \text{ m/km}) = 6.00 \times 10^4$ m

Additional Examples
Suppose that a lion moves due east at different speeds so that it travels 25 km in 4.0 hours. What is the lion's average speed? What is its average velocity?
Answer: average speed: 6.2 km/h = 1.7 m/s; average velocity: 6.2 km/h east = 1.7 m/s east
What would the lion's average velocity be if it traveled 15 km due north in 2 hours and 15 minutes?
Answer: 6.7 km/h north = 1.9 m/s north
LS Logical

Differentiated Instruction

Struggling Readers

Decoding Word Problems Readers often have difficulty understanding word problems. Explain that the equation

$$speed = \frac{distance}{time}$$

is read "speed is equal to distance divided by time." Then, use a sample word problem to show students how to identify the numbers that correspond to the variables *distance* and *time*. Finally, show students how to solve the equation by using the numbers in the word problem. Provide more word problems for practice. **LS Logical/Verbal**

Teaching Key Ideas

Studying Speed with a Graph Put the following data for a runner on the board.

Time (s)	Position (m)
0	0
10	20
20	30
30	30

Ask students to make a line graph of the data. Have them determine during which time interval the runner is moving faster (0 s to 10 s), moving slower (10 s to 20 s), and standing still (20 s to 30 s). Then ask them to explain the relationship between the slope of the line and the runner's speed. (The steeper the slope of the line, the faster the runner moves.)
LS Logical

Graphing *Skills*

Answers to Practice

1. The red line has a larger slope.
slope $= \dfrac{16\text{ m}}{4\text{ s}} = 4$ m/s

2. The green line has the smallest slope. The object represented by the green line is moving with the slowest speed, the object represented by the blue line is moving with the next slowest speed, and the object represented by the red line is moving with the fastest speed.

READING TOOLBOX

Everyday Words Used in Science
The words *independent* and *dependent* are used to describe variables in equations. What do these words mean in everyday speech? What do they mean in a scientific context?

Graphing Motion

You can investigate the relationship between distance and time in many ways. You can use mathematical equations and calculations. ❯ **You can plot a graph showing distance on the vertical axis and time on the horizontal axis.** Whichever method you use, you measure either distance or, if you know the direction, displacement and the time interval during which the distances or displacements take place.

Motion can be studied using a distance vs. time graph.

In a distance vs. time graph, the distance covered by an object is noted at equal intervals of time. As a rule, line graphs are made with the *x*-axis (horizontal axis) representing the independent variable and the *y*-axis (vertical axis) representing the dependent variable. Time is the independent variable because time will pass whether the object moves or not. Distance is the dependent variable because the distance depends upon the amount of time that the object is moving.

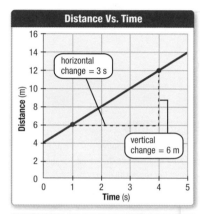

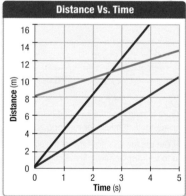

Graphing *Skills* **Calculating Slope**

The slope of a straight line equals the vertical change divided by the horizontal change. Determine the slope of the blue line shown in the top distance vs. time graph.

❶ Choose two points that you will use to calculate the slope.

Point 1:
time, t = 1 s and
distance, d = 6 m
Point 2:
t = 4 s and *d* = 12 m

❷ Calculate the vertical change and the horizontal change.

vertical change = 12 m − 6 m = 6 m
horizontal change = 4 s − 1 s = 3 s

❸ Divide the vertical change by the horizontal change.

$slope = \dfrac{6\text{ m}}{3\text{ s}} = 2$ m/s

Practice

1. Visually compare the red line with the blue line in the bottom distance vs. time graph. Which line has a larger slope? Calculate the slope of the red line.

2. Which of the three lines on the bottom graph has the smallest slope? What are the relative speeds of the objects represented by the three lines?

READING TOOLBOX

Everyday Words Used in Science To help students think about the everyday meanings of *independent* and *dependent*, instruct students to think about phrases such as "work independently" and "that depends on." Then, ask students what the independent variable in a graph is (a variable that can't be controlled). Finally, ask students what the dependent variable in a graph depends on (the independent variable). **LS** Verbal

---

Differentiated Instruction

Alternative Assessment

Tracking Speed Ask students to keep track of their speed the next time they are in a car. They should use a watch or stopwatch to measure time intervals, and note the speedometer reading every 5 seconds for a period of about a minute. (They may wish to create a data table before beginning this activity.) Ask them to use their data to plot line graphs of speed vs. time. Have them note where each graph represents the car's speed increasing (positive slope), decreasing (negative slope), and remaining constant (zero slope). **LS** Kinesthetic/Visual

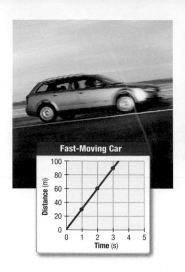

Fast-Moving Car

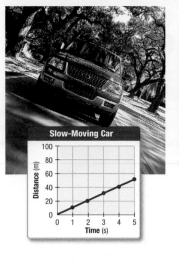

Slow-Moving Car

Car with Changing Speed

Figure 6 When an object's motion is graphed by plotting distance on the y-axis and time on the x-axis, the slope of the graph is speed. **What is the average speed of each car?**

The slope of a distance vs. time graph equals speed.

For a car moving at a constant speed, the distance vs. time graph is a straight line. **Figure 6** shows three cars moving at different speeds. The speed of each car can be found by calculating the slope of the line. The slope of any distance vs. time graph gives the speed of the object. Notice that the distance vs. time graph for the fast-moving car is steeper than the graph for the slow-moving car.

A car stopped at a stop sign has a speed of 0 m/s. Its position does not change as time goes by. So, the distance vs. time graph of a resting object is a flat line with a slope of zero. The third graph in **Figure 6** shows a car with changing speed. Between 2 s and 3 s, the car is stopped and the graph is flat.

Section 1 Review

KEY IDEAS

1. **Explain** the relationship between motion and frame of reference.

2. **Identify** the following measurements as speed or velocity.
   a. 88 km/h
   b. 9 m/s to the west
   c. 18 m/s down
   d. 10 m/s

3. **Describe** the measurements necessary to find the average speed of a high school track athlete.

4. **Determine** the unit of a caterpillar's speed if you measure the distance in centimeters (cm) and the time it takes to travel that distance in minutes (min). How would you graph the data?

CRITICAL THINKING

5. **Identifying Relationships** Imagine that you could ride a baseball that is hit hard enough for a home run. If the baseball is your frame of reference, what does the Earth appear to do?

Math Skills

6. How much time does it take for a student running at an average speed of 5.00 m/s to cover a distance of 2.00 km?

Close

Reteaching Key Ideas

Concept Map Ask students to make a concept map by using the following terms: *motion, frame of reference, displacement, speed,* and *velocity*. Tell students to think about the Key Ideas of this section when building their concept maps. **LS Verbal/Visual**

Formative Assessment

What is the difference between speed and velocity?

A. Speed is distance divided by time and velocity is displacement divided by time. (Incorrect. The numerical value of both speed and velocity are calculated by dividing distance by time.)

B. Velocity includes direction and speed does not. (Correct. Velocity is speed in a particular direction.)

C. Speed is measured in m/s and velocity is measured in km/h. (Incorrect. Both speed and velocity can be measured by any unit that is equal to a distance unit divided by a time unit.)

D. The speed of an object is always constant. The velocity of an object can change. (Incorrect. Both speed and velocity can change. The term *constant speed* refers to a specific condition and does not imply that the speed of any object cannot change.)

Answers to Section Review

1. When an object changes position with respect to a frame of reference, the object is in motion.

2. a. speed
   b. velocity
   c. velocity
   d. speed

3. Measure the distance that the athlete travels, and the time required to travel that distance.

4. cm/min; Time would be graphed on the horizontal axis and distance would be graphed on the vertical axis.

5. Earth appears to recede below you for a distance equal to the height of the baseball above Earth. Earth also appears to travel backwards for the distance the baseball travels and at the speed at which the baseball travels.

6. 2 km = 2,000 m
   $$t = \frac{d}{v} = \frac{2,000 \text{ m}}{5 \text{ m/s}} = 4.00 \times 10^2 \text{ s or 6.67 min}$$

SECTION
2
Acceleration

Focus

This section discusses what acceleration is and how to calculate and graph acceleration on a speed-line graph.

 Bellringer

Use the Bellringer transparency to prepare students for this section.

Demonstrate

Acceleration You will need a marble, inclined plane, tape, stopwatch, meter stick, protractor, and metal or glass cup. Have a student release the marble from the top of the plane. Observe the motion of the marble. Discuss the locations of lowest speed (top) and highest speed (bottom). Repeat at a different angle and have students compare the two trials.

Add quantitative values by timing the runs. Place a tape marker near the top of the plane to serve as a start line. Use a cup at the end of the plane as a sound cue for stopping the stopwatch. Measure the length of the plane. Have students record the time and angle measurements for several trials. **LS Visual/Logical**

Answer to caption question
Speed increases by 5 m/s.

go.hrw.com
✳ interact online

Students can interact with the figure by going to **go.hrw.com** and typing in the keyword **HK8MOTF1.**

SECTION 2 Acceleration

Key Ideas

> What changes when an object accelerates?

> How do you calculate the acceleration of an object moving in a straight line?

> How can a graph be used to find acceleration?

Key Terms

acceleration

Why It Matters

Acceleration is calculated by reconstructionists investigating automobile accidents.

Imagine that you are a race-car driver. You push on the accelerator. The car goes forward, moving faster and faster. As you come up to a curve in the track, you remove your foot from the accelerator to make the turn. In both situations, your velocity changes. When you increase speed, your velocity changes. Your velocity also changes if you decrease speed or if your motion changes direction.

Acceleration and Motion

Recall that velocity has both a speed and a direction. Like velocity, *acceleration* has a value and a direction. **> When an object undergoes acceleration, its velocity changes.** Positive acceleration is in the same direction as the motion and increases velocity.

Acceleration can be a change in speed.

Suppose you start moving south on your bicycle and speed up as you go, as shown in **Figure 1.** Every second, your velocity increases by 1 m/s. After 1 s, your velocity is 1 m/s south. After 2 s, your velocity is 2 m/s south. Your velocity after 5 s is 5 m/s south. Your acceleration can be stated as an increase of one meter per second per second (1 m/s/s) or 1 m/s^2 south.

acceleration (ak SEL uhr AY shuhn) the rate at which velocity changes over time; an object accelerates if its speed, direction, or both change

Figure 1 You are accelerating whenever your speed changes. This cyclist's speed increases by 1 m/s every second. **How much does his speed change in 5 s?**

go.hrw.com
✳ interact online
Keyword: HK8MOTF1

Key Resources

Teaching Transparencies
TM32 Acceleration and Speed Graphs
P2 Changing Speed to Accelerate

Visual Concepts
Acceleration
Equation for Average Acceleration
Centripetal Acceleration
Graphical Representations of
  Acceleration
Final Velocity with Constant Uniform
  Acceleration

Science Skills Worksheet
Rates of Change

Math Skills Worksheet
Acceleration

Cross-Disciplinary Worksheet
Integrating Mathematics—Jesse Owens
  in the 100-Meter Dash

Figure 2 These skaters accelerate when changing direction, even if their speed does not change.

Acceleration can also be a change in direction.

Besides being a change in speed, acceleration can be a change in direction. The skaters in **Figure 2** are accelerating because they are changing direction. Why is changing direction considered to be an acceleration? Acceleration is defined as the rate at which velocity changes with time. Velocity includes both speed and direction, so an object accelerates if its speed, direction, or both change. This idea leads to the strange but correct conclusion that you can constantly accelerate while never speeding up or slowing down.

Uniform circular motion has centripetal acceleration.

If you move at a constant speed in a circle, even though your speed is never changing, your direction is always changing. So, you are always accelerating. The moon is constantly accelerating in its orbit around Earth. A motorcyclist who rides around the inside of a large barrel is constantly accelerating. When you ride a Ferris wheel at an amusement park, you are accelerating. All these examples have one thing in common—change in direction as the cause of acceleration.

Are you surprised to find out that as you stand still on Earth's surface, you are accelerating? You are not changing speed, but you are moving in a circle as Earth revolves. An object moving in a circular motion is always changing its direction. As a result, its velocity is always changing, even if its speed does not change. The acceleration that occurs in circular motion is known as *centripetal acceleration*. Another example of centripetal acceleration is shown in **Figure 3**.

Reading Check Describe the motion of a person who is standing still on Earth's surface.

SCLINKS

www.scilinks.org
Topic: Acceleration
Code: HK80007

Figure 3 The blades of these windmills are constantly changing direction as they travel in a circle, so centripetal acceleration is occurring.

> **Teach**

Teaching Key Ideas

Changes in Direction Students may wonder why a change in direction is considered to be an acceleration. At this point, emphasize that because velocity involves both magnitude and direction, a change in either is a change in velocity, or acceleration. You can return to this concept when students study Newton's laws. According to Newton's second law, force is proportional to acceleration. Any object experiencing a net force—such as a satellite in orbit around Earth acted upon by the force of gravity—must accelerate.

Science Skills

Vocabulary Some students may associate a negative acceleration with the term *deceleration*. In this book, acceleration can be either positive or negative. Speeding up is a positive acceleration, while slowing down is a negative acceleration.

Demonstrate

Centripetal Acceleration Take students outside and demonstrate the circular motion of a ball twirled at the end of a string. As you twirl the ball, ask students, "Is this ball changing speed?" (no) "Is this ball changing direction as I twirl it?" (yes) "Is this ball accelerating?" (yes) "What kind of acceleration is taking place?" (centripetal acceleration) "How would this ball move if I were to let go of the string?" (The ball would fly in a straight line.) Make sure students are out of the way, then release the ball so students can see that it does move in a straight line. **LS Kinesthetic**

Differentiated Instruction

Advanced Learners

Illustrating Acceleration You can use a slow-motion "strobe" example on the chalkboard to illustrate acceleration. Draw a horizontal line labeled "distance" across the bottom of the board with equally-marked intervals. First, in a horizontal row across the top of the board, illustrate zero acceleration. To do this, draw a car in several positions, with equal spaces (distances) between each position. Beneath this example, in a second row, illustrate an accelerating car. For this example, each successive distance interval should be longer than the previous interval. Tell students to imagine that each "snapshot" image was taken after equal time intervals. Ask students if either or both cars are accelerating, and have them explain their answer. (The car in the first row is not accelerating because it covers equal distances in equal times; this car has a uniform velocity. The car in the second row is accelerating because it covers successively more distance in equal time intervals.) **LS Visual**

Teaching Key Ideas

Calculating Acceleration Tell students that some acceleration problems give only one numerical value for velocity to use in the calculation. Explain to students that they must read the problem carefully to determine the other value of velocity to use. For example, if an object starts at rest, its initial velocity is zero. Similarly, if an object comes to a stop, its final velocity is zero. Students should also learn to look for word clues such as "twice as fast" and "half the original speed."

Why It **Matters**

Automobile Accelerations Have students conduct research to find out the time period (in seconds) in which different kinds of cars can accelerate from 0 to 60 mi/h. Students should include a variety of models in their research, such as full-size cars, compact cars, trucks, SUVs, gas-electric hybrids, and sports cars. Ask them to create a bar graph to compare their data. Then, ask students to hypothesize why cars accelerate at different rates. Also ask students why having a car that can accelerate quickly is useful. **LS Logical**

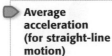

Integrating Mathematics

In the 17th century, both Sir Isaac Newton and Gottfried Leibniz studied acceleration and other rates of change. Independently, each created *calculus*, a branch of mathematics that allows for describing rates of change of a quantity such as velocity.

Calculating Acceleration

To find the acceleration of an object moving in a straight line, you need to measure the object's velocity at different times. **❯ The average acceleration over a given time interval can be calculated by dividing the change in the object's velocity by the time over which the change occurs.** The change in an object's velocity is symbolized by Δv.

Average acceleration (for straight-line motion)	$acceleration = \dfrac{final\ velocity - initial\ velocity}{time}$ $a = \dfrac{\Delta v}{t}$

If the acceleration is small, the velocity is increasing very gradually. If the acceleration is large, the velocity is increasing more rapidly. A person can accelerate at about 2 m/s², whereas a sports car can accelerate at 7.2 m/s².

In this book, for straight-line motion, a positive acceleration always means that the object's velocity is increasing—the object is speeding up. Negative acceleration means that the object's velocity is decreasing—the object is slowing down.

Acceleration is the rate at which velocity changes.

The person in **Figure 4** is slowing down on a bicycle. He starts at a speed of 5.5 m/s and slows to 1.0 m/s over a time of 3.0 s. The change in speed, Δv, is 1.0 m/s – 5.5 m/s = –4.5 m/s. The change in speed is negative because he is slowing down. The equation above can be used to find average acceleration:

$$a = \frac{1.0\ \text{m/s} - 5.5\ \text{m/s}}{3.0\ \text{s}} = -1.5\ \text{m/s}^2$$

In science, acceleration describes any change in velocity, not just "speeding up." When you slow down, your acceleration is negative because it is opposite the direction of motion.

✔ **Reading Check** How can you tell if an object is speeding up or slowing down?

Figure 4 Average acceleration can be calculated when you know the initial speed, final speed, and the time over which the acceleration takes place.

Differentiated Instruction

Advanced Learners

Roller Coaster Design Group students in pairs and have each group apply the idea of acceleration to the design of roller coasters. Students should research a particular roller coaster and create a drawing or diagram of its features. Have them describe the motion of the roller coaster in terms of its velocity and acceleration. **LS Interpersonal/Visual**

Alternative Assessment

Observing Acceleration Ask students to look around in their daily lives for examples of acceleration. Have them make a list of at least 10 examples that they observe. Also have students find a few examples of objects in motion that have zero acceleration. Then, ask students to classify each example of acceleration as an increase in speed, a decrease in speed, a change in direction, or a combination. You may also wish to have students list the examples in the approximate order of least to greatest acceleration. **LS Logical**

Acceleration is negative when slowing down.

When the driver pushes on the gas pedal in a car, the car speeds up. The acceleration is in the direction of the motion and therefore is positive. When the driver pushes on the brake pedal, the acceleration is opposite the direction of motion. The car slows down, and its acceleration is negative. When the driver turns the steering wheel, the velocity changes because the car is changing direction.

Math Skills — Acceleration

A flowerpot falls off a second-story windowsill. The flowerpot starts from rest and hits the sidewalk 1.5 s later with a velocity of 14.7 m/s. Find the average acceleration of the flowerpot.

Identify
List the given and unknown values.

Given:
time, $t = 1.5$ s
initial velocity, $v_i = 0$ m/s
final velocity, $v_f = 14.7$ m/s down
Unknown:
acceleration, $a = ?$ m/s^2 (and direction)

Plan
Write the equation for acceleration.

$$acceleration = \frac{final\ velocity - initial\ velocity}{time}$$
$$a = \frac{v_f - v_i}{t}$$

Solve
Insert the known values into the equation, and solve.

$$a = \frac{v_f - v_i}{t} = \frac{14.7\ \text{m/s} - 0\ \text{m/s}}{1.5\ \text{s}}$$
$$a = \frac{14.7\ \text{m/s}}{1.5\ \text{s}} = 9.8\ \text{m/s}^2\ \text{down}$$

Practice

1. Natalie accelerates her skateboard along a straight path from 0 m/s to 4.0 m/s in 2.5 s. Find her average acceleration.

2. A turtle swimming in a straight line toward shore has a speed of 0.50 m/s. After 4.0 s, its speed is 0.80 m/s. What is the turtle's average acceleration?

3. Find the average acceleration of a northbound subway train that slows down from 12 m/s to 9.6 m/s in 0.8 s.

4. Mai's car accelerates at an average rate of 2.6 m/s^2. How long will it take her car to speed up from 24.6 m/s to 26.8 m/s?

5. A cyclist travels at a constant velocity of 4.5 m/s westward and then speeds up with a steady acceleration of 2.3 m/s^2. Calculate the cyclist's speed after accelerating for 5.0 s.

For more practice, visit **go.hrw.com** and enter keyword **HK8MP**.

Practice Hint

▸ When a problem asks you to calculate acceleration, you can use the acceleration equation.

$$a = \frac{\Delta v}{t}$$

To solve for other variables, rearrange it as follows.

▸ Problem 4: To isolate t, first multiply both sides by t.

$$a \times t = \frac{\Delta v}{t} \times t$$
$$\Delta v = at$$

Next, divide both sides by a.

$$\frac{\Delta v}{a} = \frac{at}{a}$$
$$t = \frac{\Delta v}{a}$$

▸ Problem 5: Rearrange the acceleration equation to isolate final velocity.

$$v_f = v_i + at$$

History Connection

One of the scientists who first described motion quantitatively was Galileo Galilei. Galileo was born in Italy in 1564 and lived until 1642. Ask students to use the library or the Internet to find out what famous English writer was born the same year as Galileo. (William Shakespeare) Ask them to speculate and conduct research to find out about what historical and political forces in Europe at that time might have encouraged both the sciences and the humanities. **LS Verbal**

Math Skills

Answers to Practice

1. $\dfrac{4.0\ \text{m/s} - 0\ \text{m/s}}{2.5\ \text{s}} = 1.6\ \text{m/s}^2$ along her path

2. $\dfrac{0.80\ \text{m/s} - 0.50\ \text{m/s}}{4.0\ \text{s}} = 0.075\ \text{m/s}^2$ toward the shore

3. $\dfrac{9.6\ \text{m/s} - 12\ \text{m/s}}{0.8\ \text{s}} = -3\ \text{m/s}^2$ north $= 3\ \text{m/s}^2$ south

4. $t = \dfrac{\Delta v}{a} = \dfrac{26.8\ \text{m/s} - 24.6\ \text{m/s}}{2.6\ \text{m/s}^2} = 0.85$ s

5. $v_f = v_i + at = 4.5\ \text{m/s} + (2.3\ \text{m/s}^2 \times 5.0\ \text{s}) = 16$ m/s

Additional Examples

A car accelerates from 0 m/s to 45 m/s northward in 15 s. What is the acceleration of the car?
Answer: 3.0 m/s^2 northward
After reaching 45 m/s, the car slows down to 0 m/s in 10.0 s. What is the acceleration of the car?
Answer: 4.5 m/s^2 southward (or -4.5 m/s^2 northward)
LS Logical

Why It Matters

Particle Accelerators Some of today's physicists use particle accelerators to learn about the fundamental particles that make up our universe. The most powerful accelerator in the world is the Tevatron at Fermilab in Batavia, Illinois. The Tevatron is a 4-mile-long underground ring in which protons and other particles are accelerated to incredible speeds, and then put into collisions against one another. Scientists study these collisions to learn about the fundamental particles of matter and about conditions in the very early universe.

Some of this theoretical research has practical applications as well. For example, Magnetic Resonance Imaging (MRI) is a technique used in medicine to image the inside of the human body. The powerful superconducting magnets used in MRI technology were first developed in the 1970s for Fermilab's Tevatron. Have students research particle accelerators or MRI technology and make a poster to show what they learned.
LS Visual

Teaching Key Ideas

Slope and Acceleration Be sure that students understand that acceleration can be calculated as the slope of a straight line on a speed-time graph but cannot be calculated as the slope of a straight line on a distance-time graph. The slope of a line on a distance-time graph is equal to speed. Explain to students that they can remember which slope yields which value by looking at the units of the variables that are graphed. In a speed-time graph, the units on the vertical axis are m/s and the units on the horizontal axis are m. So, the units of the slope are (m/s)/s or m/s².

READING TOOLBOX

Describing Space and Time
Struggling students should try to redraw the graph of distance versus time on the next page. Tell them that their drawing should show an object traveling a certain distance (space) and an object that shows time, such as a stopwatch. More advanced learners should attempt to redraw a speed versus time graph and should come up with a creative way of showing varying speed in a drawing. **LS** **Visual**

Graphing **Skills**

Practice answers on p. 393A

READING TOOLBOX

Describing Space and Time
Words are not the only way to describe space and time. Redraw one of the graphs in this section to show how the graph is used to describe space and time.

Academic Vocabulary

constant (KAHN stuhnt) a quantity whose value does not change

---

Graphing Accelerated Motion

You have learned that an object's speed can be determined from a distance vs. time graph of its motion. You can also find acceleration by making a speed vs. time graph. Plot speed on the vertical axis and time on the horizontal axis.

A straight line on a speed vs. time graph means that the speed changes by the same amount over each time interval. This is called *constant acceleration.* **> The slope of a straight line on a speed vs. time graph is equal to the acceleration.**

You can look at a speed vs. time graph and easily see if an object is speeding up or slowing down. A line with a positive slope represents an object that is speeding up. A line with a negative slope represents an object that is slowing down.

Graphing **Skills** **Graphing Acceleration**

A bus traveling on a straight road at 20 m/s uniformly slows to a stop over 20 s. The bus remains stopped for 20 s, then accelerates at a rate of 1.5 m/s² for 10 s, and then continues at a constant speed. Graph speed vs. time for 60 s. What is the bus's final speed?

❶ Determine the x-axis and the y-axis of your graph.	The x-axis will indicate time, t, measured in s. The y-axis will indicate speed, v, measured in m/s.
❷ Starting from the origin, graph each section of the motion.	**A.** The bus begins at $t = 0$ s and $v = 20$ m/s. The next point is $t = 20$ s and $v = 0$ m/s. Connect these points. **B.** Draw a horizontal line from $t = 20$ s to $t = 40$ s at $v = 0$ m/s. **C.** Starting at $t = 40$ s and $v = 0$ m/s, draw a line with a slope of 1.5 m/s². **D.** Draw a horizontal line from $t = 50$ s to $t = 60$ s at $v = 15$ m/s.
❸ Read the graph to find the final speed.	At time, $t = 60$ s, the speed is 15 m/s.

Speed Vs. Time

Practice

1. A car accelerates from a stop at a rate of 2 m/s² for 20 s, then continues at a constant speed for 40 s. Graph the speed vs. time of the car. What is the car's speed at 10 s? What is its final speed?

2. A train traveling at 30 m/s takes 60 s to slow to a complete stop. Assume that the train's acceleration is constant as it moves down the track. Graph the speed vs. time of the train for 80 s. What is the slope of the graph at 30 s?

Science **Skills**

Graphing Acceleration Two Ways Give students a data table with increasing speeds. For example: 3 m/s, 6 m/s, 9 m/s, 12 m/s corresponding to the times 1 s, 2 s, 3 s, 4 s. Ask students to create both a speed–time graph and a distance–time graph. Discuss the differences between the two graphs. **LS** **Logical**

Why It Matters

Space Acceleration Measurement System NASA has developed an acceleration measurement and recording system called the Space Acceleration Measurement System, or SAMS II. SAMS II can measure, condition, and record low-gravity accelerations for microgravity experiments in space. It can be used with up to three separate experiments simultaneously. By June of 1998, SAMS II had been used on over 20 shuttle missions, as well as on the MIR space station. Ask interested students to research an experiment that used SAMS II and give an oral report on their findings. **LS** **Verbal**

Speed Vs. Time

Distance Vs. Time

Acceleration can be seen on a distance vs. time graph.

Imagine that one of the riders in **Figure 5** is slowing uniformly from 10.0 m/s to a complete stop over a period of 5.0 s. A speed vs. time graph of this motion is a straight line with a negative slope. This straight line indicates that the acceleration is constant. You can find the acceleration by calculating the slope of the line.

$$a = \frac{0.0 \text{ m/s} - 10.0 \text{ m/s}}{5.0 \text{ s}} = -2.0 \text{ m/s}^2$$

Thus, the rider's speed decreases by 2.0 m/s each second.

The distance vs. time graph, also shown in **Figure 5,** is not a straight line when the rider's velocity is not constant. This curved line indicates that the object is under acceleration.

Figure 5 The rate of velocity change is acceleration, which is positive when speeding up and negative when slowing down.

www.scilinks.org
Topic: Graphing Speed, Velocity, Acceleration
Code: **HK80687**

Section 2 Review

KEY IDEAS

1. **Explain** why circular motion includes continuous acceleration even when the speed does not change.

2. **Identify** the straight-line accelerations below as either speeding up or slowing down.
   a. 5.7 m/s²
   b. −29.8 m/s²
   c. −2.43 m/s²
   d. 9.8 m/s²

3. **Graph** the velocity vs. time from 0 s to 10 s of a car that accelerates from a standstill at a constant rate of 1.5 m/s².

CRITICAL THINKING

4. **Interpreting Data** Joshua skates in a straight line at a constant speed for 1 min, then begins going in circles at the same rate of speed, and finally begins to increase speed. When is he accelerating? Explain your answer.

Math Skills

5. What is the final speed of a skater who accelerates at a rate of 2.0 m/s² from rest for 3.5 s?

6. Graph the velocity of a car accelerating at a uniform rate from 7.0 m/s to 12.0 m/s in 2.0 s. Calculate the acceleration.

Answers to Section Review

1. Circular motion is an acceleration because the velocity is changing. Velocity includes both speed and direction. When an object moves in a circle, its direction is changing.

2. a. speeding up
   b. slowing down
   c. slowing down
   d. speeding up

3. Sample graph:

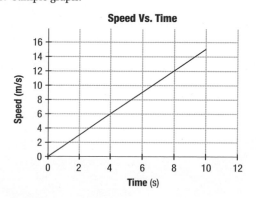

Speed Vs. Time

Answers continued on p. 393A

> **Close**

Reteaching Key Ideas

Acceleration Chart Have students make a two-column chart. In the first column, students should list examples of acceleration. In the second column, students should write how the velocity changed in each example. For example, students could write "walking around a corner" in the first column, and "change in direction" in the second column. **LS Logical**

Formative Assessment

Which of the following is NOT an example of acceleration?

A. a plane taking off (Incorrect. A plane taking off is increasing its speed and changing direction when it lifts off the ground. Therefore, the plane is accelerating)

B. a person walking 1.5 m/s along a winding path (Incorrect. The person's speed is not changing, but the person's direction is changing. Therefore, the person is accelerating.)

C. a car driving 88 km/h on a straight highway (Correct. Neither the speed nor the direction of the car are changing, so the car is not accelerating.)

D. a bicyclist stopping at a stop sign (Incorrect. The speed of the bicyclist is decreasing, so the bicyclist is accelerating.)

Accident Reconstruction Technology is advancing the science of accident reconstruction in many ways. For example, EDRs were first installed in cars to help improve the deployment of airbags. But now EDRs are designed to record a wide variety of data including the speed of a car before an accident, if the brakes were applied, if the passengers were wearing seatbelts, and if the car's lights were on.

Accident investigators may also use lasers to survey an accident scene to obtain very accurate measurements of distances at the scene. Lasers are also used to scan the vehicles involved in an accident. Scanning the vehicles gives investigators crush data, which allows them to determine the force of impact.

Accident investigators also use computers to create realistic, three-dimensional models and animations of accidents. These can be studied from any angle and help investigators understand what happened during an accident.

Accident Reconstruction

Evidence collected from the scene of an accident can be used to learn about the accident. Accident investigators apply physics formulas to find out important information, such as the speed of a vehicle at the time the brakes were applied. A good accident investigator combines information from many sources, including skid marks, vehicle damage, and witness statements. The investigator must come up with a theory that matches all of the evidence.

1 Accident investigators measure the skid distance at the accident or determine it from accident photographs.

Using Skid Marks
Skid marks occur when a vehicle is moving but the tires are not rolling. The marks are created from the heat between the tires and the road that is caused by friction. Skid marks can be used to find the change in speed from the time the brakes were applied.

Differentiated Instruction

Advanced Learners

Interviewing an Investigator Interested students can interview an accident investigator from your local police department. Students should ask the investigator about what he or she does at an accident scene, what sort of data is collected, and what kinds of technology is used in an investigation. Students should present what they learn in a poster or an oral report. Alternately, you can invite an accident investigator to give a talk to your students in class.
LS Interpersonal

FORENSICS

② Investigators calculate the coefficient of friction between the road surface and the tires. This coefficient depends on the type of tire and road conditions.

③ The skid distance and the coefficient of friction are then used to calculate the speed of the car at the time of the wreck.

Accelerometers

Investigators use a device called an *accelerometer* to measure acceleration. The investigator sets up conditions like those during the accident, using a similar vehicle and road surface. The coefficient of friction depends on many factors, such as the weight of the vehicle, the type of tires, and the condition of the road—whether wet, dry, or icy. The accelerometer results are used to estimate the coefficient of friction between the road surface and the tires.

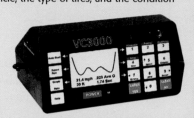

Event Data Recorders

Some auto makers are now installing devices called *Event Data Recorders* (EDRs) in cars. EDRs in automobiles are similar to the "black boxes" in airplanes. EDRs measure the change in speed over time during a crash. In other words, they measure acceleration. EDRs are especially useful in situations in which the change in speed is hard to estimate with traditional techniques.

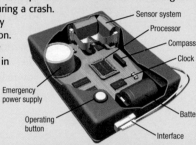

Sensor system
Processor
Compass
Clock
Emergency power supply
Battery
Operating button
Interface

YOUR TURN

UNDERSTANDING CONCEPTS
1. As soon as the brakes are applied, a car begins to slow down. Although the car's speed is decreasing, this is still an example of acceleration. Explain why.

CRITICAL THINKING
2. Why is it important to collect forensic evidence and witness accounts as soon as possible after an accident?

READING TOOLBOX

Visual Literacy As students look at the photo on these pages, ask them to list all the details they see relating to the accident and the accident investigation. (Answers may vary.) Explain to students that the details that they can see in the photo are only a small part of the data that an accident investigator must collect. Also tell students that the accident investigator began working at the scene soon after the accident happened. This fact can be observed from the photo because emergency vehicles are still at the scene and because the spill from the truck has not been cleaned up. Finally, tell students that an accident investigator must work quickly and carefully to collect all the important data because the roadway must be cleared for regular traffic. Once the accident is cleared, much of the data needed for the investigation will no longer be available.
LS Visual

Answers to Your Turn
1. Acceleration is any change in velocity. When a car slows down, its velocity is decreasing, so it is accelerating.
2. Forensic evidence must be collected as soon as possible because some evidence may be moved or tampered with if left alone and some of the evidence, such as skid marks, may disappear or fade over time. Witness accounts must be collected as soon as possible because people can easily forget details or begin remembering things incorrectly.

SECTION 3

> Focus

This section begins by defining force and identifying the four fundamental forces of nature. Students learn how to distinguish between balanced and unbalanced forces. Students study friction, including static and kinetic, and the relationship between friction and motion.

Bellringer

Use the Bellringer transparency to prepare students for this section.

Demonstrate

Forces Show several examples of objects that have forces acting on them and ask students to identify the forces. For example, you can show an object hanging on a string (gravity and the force of the string pulling up), a magnet on a metal object (magnetic force and gravity), a book on a desk (gravity and the force of the desk on the book). You can also have students pull a rope in opposite directions or push on each other's hands. Tell students that there are two forces that they cannot observe directly and these forces are called the *strong nuclear force* and the *weak nuclear force*.
LS Visual

Answer to caption question

The force of gravity is acting on Earth and the moon. ("Gravity acts on every object that has mass" is also an acceptable answer.)

SECTION 3 Motion and Force

Key **Ideas**

> What do scientists identify as the fundamental forces of nature?

> What happens when there is a net force acting on an object?

> What force always opposes motion?

> Why is friction sometimes necessary?

Key **Terms**

force
friction
static friction
kinetic friction

Why It **Matters**

The force of friction is essential to making automobile brakes work properly—and essential to making a car move forward.

You often hear the word *force* used in everyday conversation: "Our basketball team is an awesome force!" But what exactly is a force? In science, **force** is defined as any action that can change the state of motion of an object.

Fundamental Forces

Scientists identify four *fundamental forces* in nature.
> **These forces are the force of gravity, the electromagnetic force, the strong nuclear force, and the weak nuclear force.** The strong and weak nuclear forces act only over a short distance, so you do not experience them directly in everyday life. The force of gravity, as shown in **Figure 1,** is a force that you feel every day. Other everyday forces, such as friction, are a result of the electromagnetic force.

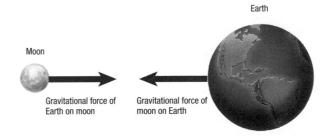

Figure 1 The force of gravity is one of the four fundamental forces in the universe. **On what objects does the force of gravity act?**

Key Resources

 Teaching Transparency
P3 Frictional Forces and Acceleration

 Visual Concepts
Force
Direction of the Friction Force
Friction
Types of Friction
Ways to Reduce or Increase Friction

 Datasheet
Friction

 Cross-Disciplinary Worksheets
Real World Applications—Designing
    Race Cars
Connection to Language Arts—Friction
    in Fiction

Fundamental forces vary in strength.

The <u>fundamental</u> forces vary widely in strength and the distance over which they act. The strong nuclear force holds together the protons and neutrons in the nuclei of atoms and is the strongest of all the forces. However, it is negligible over distances greater than the size of an atomic nucleus. The gravitational and electromagnetic forces act over longer distances. The electromagnetic force is about 1/100 the strength of the strong force. The gravitational force is very much weaker than the electromagnetic force. Consider a proton and an electron in an atom. The electromagnetic force is about 10^{40} times as great as the gravitational force between them!

Forces can act through contact or at a distance.

If you push a cart, the cart moves. When you catch a ball, it stops moving. These pushes and pulls are examples of *contact forces.* There is another class of forces—called *field forces*—that do not require that the objects touch each other. The attraction of gravity or the repulsion between two north poles of a magnet are examples of field forces. Both contact and field forces can cause an object to move or to stop moving.

Balanced and Unbalanced Forces

Suppose that you and your friends need to move a heavy sofa, as shown in **Figure 2.** Will you push from opposite sides of the sofa, or will you both push in the same direction? The *net force,* the combination of all of the forces acting on the sofa, determines if the sofa will change its motion. **❯ Whenever there is a net force acting on an object, the object accelerates in the direction of the net force.** An object will not accelerate if the net force acting on it is zero.

Academic Vocabulary

fundamental (FUHN duh MENT'l) basic

force (FAWRS) an action exerted on a body in order to change the body's state of rest or motion; force has magnitude and direction

Figure 2 When two forces acting on the same object are unequal, the forces are unbalanced. A change in motion occurs in the direction of the greater force.

Force

Acceleration

Force

❯Teach

Teaching Key Ideas

Fundamental Forces Make a table on the chalkboard to compare the four fundamental forces. In the first column of the table, list the names of the four forces and write the following headings at the top of the other columns: Where observed, Strength, and Other information. Ask students to help you complete the table. Once the table is filled in, have students copy the information into their notebooks. **LS Verbal**

MISCONCEPTION ALERT

Forces on Objects Students may believe that when an object is at rest, no forces are acting on the object. To help students overcome this misconception, attach a strong spring scale to a very heavy object and invite a volunteer to try to lift or pull the object with a single finger. Have the other students in the class observe the spring scale as the volunteer is pulling. Ask the students if they think the volunteer is exerting a force on the object. (yes) Ask how they know that this is so. (because the scale shows a nonzero reading) Ask the volunteer if he or she is exerting a force. (yes) Then ask, "If there is a force on the object, then why isn't the object moving?" (because the forces on the object are balanced) **LS Logical**

Differentiated Instruction

English Learners

Building with Force Have students work in groups to build a house of cards by using a deck of playing cards. Have students take notes while doing the activity. Then, ask students to write a paragraph about their construction observations. Instruct them to use their notes to identify the forces acting on their house of cards.
LS Interpersonal

Basic Learners

Balanced and Unbalanced Forces Instruct pairs of students to face each other, stand with feet together, hold hands and lean apart. Ask students what forces they are feeling. (Sample answers: a pulling force on their hands, gravity, and an upward force from the floor) Ask students if the forces on them are balanced when they are in that position. (yes) What would happen if the forces were not balanced? (A change in motion would occur; one person would fall forward and the other person would fall backward.)
LS Kinesthetic

Tri-Fold As students work on their FoldNotes, ask them to think of a situation in which balanced forces are preferred over unbalanced forces and a situation in which unbalanced forces are preferred. Then, have students write a description of these situations in the third column of their FoldNotes. (Sample answers: Balanced forces are preferred over unbalanced forces when building a house of cards. Unbalanced forces are preferred over balanced forces when riding on a roller coaster.)

Teaching Key Ideas

Net Force on an Object Because the direction of a force is important, the description of a force includes both a size and direction, just like velocity and acceleration. To emphasize the importance of direction, pose the following question to students: What is the net (or total) force acting on a piano if two students are each putting a force of 100 N on it? After a brief discussion, draw two scenarios on the board. The first scenario should show two forces (drawn as arrows) acting on an object in the same direction. The net force in this case would be 200 N in the direction of the forces. The second scenario should show the forces acting in opposite directions. The net force in this case would be 0 N. Finally, explain to students that the piano in the first scenario would accelerate, but the piano in the second scenario would not. **LS Logical**

Tri-Fold
Create a tri-fold. Write "balanced forces" and "unbalanced forces" in the first column. In the second column, define these terms. In the third column, create a sketch that illustrates each concept.

Figure 3 Energy provided by friction causes this match to ignite.

Balanced forces do not change motion.

When the forces applied to an object produce a net force of zero, the forces are balanced. Balanced forces do not cause an object at rest to start moving. Furthermore, balanced forces do not cause a change in the motion of a moving object.

Many objects have only balanced forces acting on them. For example, a light hanging from the ceiling does not move up or down, because the force due to tension in the cord pulls the light up and balances the force of gravity pulling the light down. A hat resting on your head is also an example of balanced forces.

Unbalanced forces do not cancel completely.

Suppose that two students push against an object on one side and only one student pushes against the object on the other side. If the students are all pushing with the same force, there is an unbalanced force: two students pushing against one student. Because the net force on the object is greater than zero, the object will accelerate in the direction of the greater force.

What happens if forces act in different directions that are not opposite to each other? In this situation, the combination of forces acts like a single force on the object and causes acceleration in a direction that combines the directions of the applied forces. If you push a box to the east and your friend pushes the box to the north, the box will accelerate in a northeasterly direction.

✔ **Reading Check** What happens when an unbalanced force acts on an object?

The Force of Friction

Imagine a car that is rolling along a flat, evenly paved street. Experience tells you that the car will keep slowing down until it finally stops. This steady change in the car's speed gives you a hint that a force must be acting on the car. The unbalanced force that acts against the car's direction of motion is **friction.** ❯ **The force of friction always opposes the motion.**

Friction occurs because the surface of any object is rough. The rubbing together of two rough surfaces creates heat. The heat from friction causes the match in **Figure 3** to strike. Surfaces that look or feel very smooth are really covered with microscopic hills and valleys. When two surfaces are touching, the hills and valleys of one surface stick to the hills and valleys of the other surface.

Friction and Motion Discuss that the force of static friction is a reaction force and that static frictional forces do not exist if there is no opposing force. Push on a heavy piece of furniture, but do not move it. Explain that when you push forward on the object, static friction acts in the backward direction and opposes the motion of the object. Further explain that if you stop pushing the object, the frictional force stops. Then, push on a wheeled chair or cart. Allow students to see that when you stop pushing on the wheeled object, the object will slow down and stop because of friction. Discuss that friction opposes the motion of moving objects and nonmoving objects. **LS Visual**

Struggling Readers

Comparing Summary to the Text Comparing written materials provides students with opportunities to examine details. Write a summary, leaving out important details. Then, have students compare the text and the summary and make a list of the missing details. For example, you can write a summary of this section leaving out the terms *force* and *friction*, and omitting descriptions about forces in opposite directions and balanced forces. If students need a hint for how to find missing information, tell them to look at the boldface words and heads to identify the main ideas. **LS Verbal**

Static friction is greater than kinetic friction.

The friction between surfaces that are stationary is called **static friction.** The friction between moving surfaces is called **kinetic friction.** Because of forces between the molecules on the two surfaces, the force required to make a stationary object start moving is usually greater than the force necessary to keep it moving. In other words, static friction is usually greater than kinetic friction.

Not all kinetic friction is the same.

There are different kinds of kinetic friction. The type of friction depends on the motion and the nature of the objects. For example, when objects slide past each other, the friction that occurs is called *sliding friction*. If a rounded object rolls over a flat surface, the friction that occurs is called *rolling friction*. Rolling friction is usually less than sliding friction.

friction (FRIK shuhn) a force that opposes motion between two surfaces that are in contact

static friction (STAT ik FRIK shuhn) the force that resists the initiation of sliding motion between two surfaces that are in contact and at rest

kinetic friction (ki NET ik FRIK shuhn) the force that opposes the movement of two surfaces that are in contact and are moving over each other

How Do Brakes Work?

REAL WORLD

Automobile brakes rely on the force of friction to slow down a moving car and bring it to a stop. Two common types of brakes are typically found in modern cars: *disc brakes* and *drum brakes*. Disc brakes are frequently used to stop the front wheels of a car. To make brakes work properly, the system requires *leverage, hydraulic force,* and *friction.*

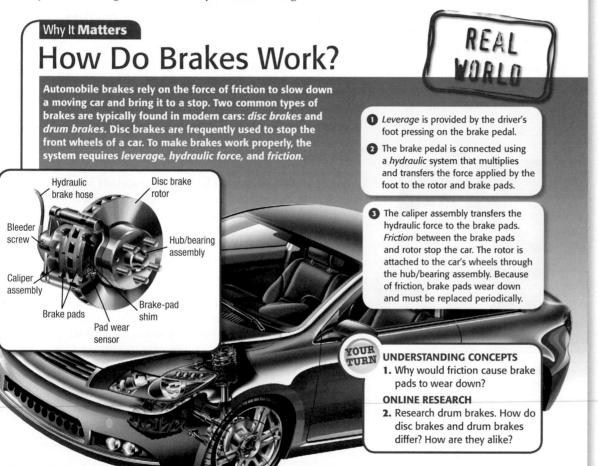

Hydraulic brake hose
Disc brake rotor
Bleeder screw
Hub/bearing assembly
Caliper assembly
Brake pads
Brake-pad shim
Pad wear sensor

❶ *Leverage* is provided by the driver's foot pressing on the brake pedal.

❷ The brake pedal is connected using a *hydraulic* system that multiplies and transfers the force applied by the foot to the rotor and brake pads.

❸ The caliper assembly transfers the hydraulic force to the brake pads. *Friction* between the brake pads and rotor stop the car. The rotor is attached to the car's wheels through the hub/bearing assembly. Because of friction, brake pads wear down and must be replaced periodically.

YOUR TURN

UNDERSTANDING CONCEPTS
1. Why would friction cause brake pads to wear down?

ONLINE RESEARCH
2. Research drum brakes. How do disc brakes and drum brakes differ? How are they alike?

How Do Brakes Work? The antilock braking system (ABS) is a special kind of braking mechanism that is found in some cars. These systems are designed to keep the wheels of a car from locking up and skidding in certain situations. By preventing skidding, an ABS helps a car stop faster and allows the driver to continue to steer and control the car. Every ABS has a computer that can sense an unusual braking condition, such as a rapid deceleration. The ABS is triggered, and the system rapidly increases and decreases the pressure on the brakes. This mimics the effect of pumping the brake pedal, but at a much faster rate. When you are driving in a car that has an ABS, you should not pump the brake pedal because doing so will interfere with the system. Instead, you should hold the brake pedal down firmly until the ABS stops and you are in complete control of the car.

READING TOOLBOX

Visual Literacy Have students study the enlarged diagram of the brake system and ask them what they think is the function of each labeled part. (Accept all reasonable answers. The function of some parts may be difficult for students to recognize.) Then, ask students why they think a pad wear sensor is necessary. (Sample answer: Friction between the brake pads and the rotor stop the car. This friction can cause the brake pads to wear down. The sensor monitors the condition of the pads and indicates when the pads need to be replaced.) **LS Visual**

Differentiated Instruction

Special Education Students

Friction This activity helps explain friction, a difficult concept for students who have language delays. Cut two 30 × 30 cm squares each of satin fabric, denim fabric, and sandpaper. Have a student cover each hand with satin fabric and rub his or her hands together. Repeat with denim, then with sandpaper. Discuss how the pieces of satin have very little friction, the pieces of denim have a little more friction, and the pieces of sandpaper have a lot of friction. **LS Kinesthetic**

Answers to Your Turn

1. Friction between the brake pads and the rotors causes the material that makes up the pad to rub off.
2. Answers may vary. Sample answer: Drum brakes differ from disc brakes because they have brake shoes that push outward against the drum to stop the wheel. Drum brakes and disc brakes are similar because they both use friction to stop a wheel from turning and because they both wear out over time.

Teacher's Notes Make sure that students always place the same side of the wooden block against the table. You may wish to paint or mark one side of each block and then tell students to keep that side pointing upward.

Materials per Group
• cup, plastic
• hook
• marbles, 50
• paper, notebook, 1 sheet
• sandpaper, 1 sheet
• string
• table
• waxed paper, 1 sheet
• wood, block

Answers to Analysis
1. no
2. More marbles were needed to move the block as the roughness of the surface increased.

Teaching Key Ideas

Helpful and Unwanted Friction After reading this page and the next page, discuss helpful and unwanted examples of friction with students. The text mentions a few examples of each. Ask students to list additional examples of both helpful and unwanted effects of friction. Then, ask students to describe ways that helpful friction can be increased.
LS Verbal

QuickLab   **Friction**   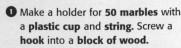 20 min

Procedure
❶ Make a holder for **50 marbles** with a **plastic cup** and **string**. Screw a **hook** into a **block of wood**.
❷ Place the wood on top of a sheet of **waxed paper** lying on a **table**. Hook the string on the block, and hang the empty cup over the edge.
❸ Add marbles to the cup until the block of wood begins to move.
❹ Repeat the process using different surfaces, such as **sandpaper, notebook paper,** and the bare table.

Analysis
1. Is the number of marbles needed to start moving the block the same for each type of surface?
2. Relate the number of marbles used in each trial to the roughness of the surface.

SCLINKS.
www.scilinks.org
Topic: Force and Friction
Code: HK80601

Figure 4 A nonstick skillet has a coating that lowers the friction between the pan and the food.

Friction and Motion

Without friction, the tires of a car would not be able to push against the ground and move the car forward, the brakes would not be able to stop the car, and you would not even be able to grip the steering wheel to turn it. Without friction, a car is useless. Friction between your pencil and your paper is necessary for the pencil to leave a mark. Without friction, you would slip and fall whenever you tried to walk. **> Friction is necessary for many everyday tasks to work correctly.**

Unwanted friction can be lowered.

It is sometimes desirable to lower unwanted friction. One way to lower friction is to use low-friction materials, such as nonstick coatings on cooking pans, as shown in **Figure 4.**

Another way to reduce friction is to use *lubricants,* substances that are applied to surfaces to lower the friction between them. Some examples of common lubricants are motor oil, wax, and grease. The air that comes out of the tiny holes of an air-hockey table also acts as a lubricant.

Helpful friction can be increased.

Helpful friction is increased by making surfaces rougher. For example, sand scattered on icy roads keeps cars from skidding. Baseball players sometimes wear textured batting gloves to increase the friction between their hands and the bat so that the bat does not slide or fly out of their hands.

Friction is also greater if the force pushing the surfaces together is increased. Your homework will not blow away if you put a heavy rock on top of it. The added mass of the rock increases friction between the paper and the ground.

Why It Matters

Speed Skating Tell students that the sport of ice racing has been transformed by modern materials and suit and helmet designs that minimize air resistance, and by skate designs that minimize friction. Put students into groups of three. Ask each group to use the library or Internet to research ways that technology has been applied to speed skating. Each group should make a short presentation to the class with the results.
LS Verbal

Differentiated Instruction

Alternative Assessment

Helpful and Unwanted Friction Have half of the students in the class draw a comic strip showing a situation where friction is helpful. Have the other students draw a comic strip showing a situation where friction is unwanted. Ask student volunteers to share their comic strips with the class. **LS** Visual

Cars could not move without friction.

What causes a car to move? As a car's wheels turn, they push against the road. As a reaction, the road pushes forward on the car. Without friction between the tires and the road, the tires would not be able to push against the road and the car would not move forward.

The force pushing the car forward must be greater than the force of friction that opposes the car's motion, as shown in **Figure 5.** Because of friction, a constant force must be applied to a car just to keep it moving at the same speed. Friction also affects objects that are not moving. When a truck is parked on a hill and its brakes are set, friction opposes the force of gravity down the hill and stops the truck from sliding.

Figure 5 Frictional Forces and Acceleration

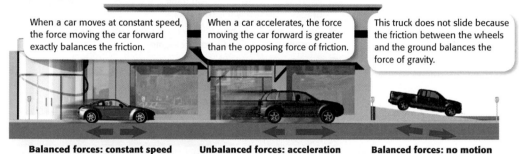

When a car moves at constant speed, the force moving the car forward exactly balances the friction.

When a car accelerates, the force moving the car forward is greater than the opposing force of friction.

This truck does not slide because the friction between the wheels and the ground balances the force of gravity.

Balanced forces: constant speed   Unbalanced forces: acceleration   Balanced forces: no motion

Section 3 Review

KEY IDEAS

1. **List** the fundamental forces of nature.

2. **Describe** a situation in which unbalanced forces are acting on an object. What is the net force on the object, and how does the net force change the motion of the object?

3. **Identify** the type of friction in each situation described below.
   a. Two students are pushing a box that is at rest.
   b. The box pushed by the students is now sliding.
   c. The students put rollers under the box and push it forward.

4. **Explain** why driving on a road requires friction. How could you increase friction on an icy road?

CRITICAL THINKING

5. **Understanding Relationships** Describe three ways to decrease the force of friction between two surfaces that are moving past each other.

6. **Analyzing Ideas** When you wrap a sandwich in plastic food wrap to protect it, you must first unroll the plastic wrap from the container and then wrap the plastic around the sandwich. In both steps, you encounter friction. In each step, is friction helpful or not? Explain your answer.

7. **Interpreting Data** The force pulling a truck downhill is 2,000 N. What is the amount of static friction acting on the truck if the truck does not move?

❭ Close

Reteaching Key Ideas

Connecting Ideas Ask students to summarize the key ideas of this section. (Answers may vary. Be sure that students can answer the questions listed on the first page of this section.) Then, ask students to explain how balanced and unbalanced forces are related to static and kinetic friction. (Sample answer: When static friction exists between two objects, the forces on the objects are balanced. When kinetic friction exists between two objects the forces on the objects are unbalanced.) **LS Verbal**

Formative Assessment

What happens when a net force acts on an object?

A. The motion of the object does not change. (Incorrect. A net force on an object always causes the motion of the object to change.)

B. The speed of the object always increases. (Incorrect. An object always accelerates when a net force acts on it, but the acceleration can be an increase or decrease of speed or a change in direction.)

C. The object's direction of motion will always change. (Incorrect. The object's direction of motion may change but it does not have to change.)

D. The object accelerates in the direction of the net force. (Correct. An object always accelerates in the direction of the net force. The acceleration can be a change in speed or direction or both.)

Answers to Section Review

1. gravity, electromagnetic force, weak nuclear force, and strong nuclear force

2. Answers may vary: A baseball falling to Earth is an example of a situation involving unbalanced forces. The net force is the force of gravity combined with kinetic friction. The net force causes the baseball to fall toward Earth.

3. a. static friction
   b. kinetic friction
   c. rolling friction

4. Friction between the tires and the road enables the tires to push against the road and vice versa so that the car experiences a net force and moves forward or makes a turn. To increase friction on an icy road, you could put salt or sand on the road.

5. Sample answer: Lubricate the surfaces; smooth the surfaces; place ball bearings between the surfaces.

6. When unrolling the plastic wrap, friction between your hand and the wrap is helpful, because it enables you to pull the wrap; but the friction between the two parts of the wrap is harmful, because it slows the flow of the wrap. When wrapping the sandwich, friction between edges of the plastic is helpful, because it keeps the plastic sticking to itself.

Answers continued on p. 393A

ApplicationLab

Teacher's Notes

If the spring scale is not very sensitive, students may record a force of zero for rolling friction. Encourage students to discuss whether this is realistic and what would be causing them to get such a result. You may want to provide more sensitive spring scales for steps 10 and 11 to avoid this problem. Textbooks should be covered with paper to provide an even sliding surface and to protect the book covers. Also make sure tabletops are clean and smooth.

Time Required

1 lab period

Lab Ratings

Teacher Prep 🧪

Student Set-Up 🧪

Concept Level 🧪🧪

Clean Up 🧪

Skills Acquired

- Collecting data
- Experimenting
- Inferring
- Measuring
- Organizing and analyzing data
- Predicting

Scientific Methods

In this lab, students will:
- Ask questions
- Test a hypothesis
- Analyze the results
- Draw conclusions
- Communicate results

Application Lab

What You'll Do

❯ **Predict** which type of friction force—static, sliding, or rolling—will be greatest and which will be smallest.

❯ **Measure** the static, sliding, and rolling friction when pulling a textbook across a table.

❯ **Apply** your results by describing how friction affects objects being pulled across a surface.

What You'll Need

rods, wooden (or metal) (4)

scissors

spring scale

string

textbook

Safety

Static, Sliding, and Rolling Friction

Current car brakes make use of static friction. As an engineer in the research and development department of a car manufacturing company, you have been asked to find out if a different approach to brakes might work better. To do so, you will investigate the circumstances under which friction is maximized.

Procedure

Preparing for Your Experiment

❶ Which type of friction do you think is the largest force: static, sliding, or rolling? Which is the smallest?

❷ Form a hypothesis by writing a short paragraph that answers the question above. Explain your reasoning.

❸ Prepare a data table like the one shown below. **CAUTION:** Secure loose clothing, and remove dangling jewelry. Do not wear open-toed shoes or sandals in the lab.

Sample Data Table: Friction Measurements

	Static friction (N)	Sliding friction (N)	Rolling friction (N)
Trial 1			
Trial 2			
Trial 3		DO NOT WRITE IN BOOK	
Average			

Collecting Data and Testing the Hypothesis

❹ Cut a piece of string, and tie it in a loop that fits inside a textbook. Hook the string to the spring scale as shown.

❺ To measure the static friction between the book and the table, pull the spring scale very slowly. Gradually increase the force with which you pull on the spring scale until the book starts to slide across the table. Pull very gently. If you pull too hard, the book will start lurching and you will not get accurate results.

❻ Practice pulling the book as in step 5 several times until you can pull back smoothly. On a smooth trial, note the largest force that appears on the scale before the book starts to move. Record this result in your data table as static friction in Trial 1.

❼ Repeat step 6 two more times, and record the results in your data table as Trials 2 and 3.

Safety Cautions

Have students review safety guidelines before working in the lab. Remind students not to wear jewelry or open-toed shoes in the lab. Jewelry can get caught in the spring scale, and falling books can pose a hazard to unprotected feet. Also remind students to be cautious when using scissors.

8 After the textbook begins to move, you can determine the sliding friction. Start pulling the book as in step 5. Once the book starts to slide, continue applying just enough force to keep the book sliding at a slow, constant speed. Practice this several times. On a smooth trial, note the force that appears on the scale as the book is sliding at a slow, constant speed. Record this force in your data table as sliding friction in Trial 1.

9 Repeat step 8 two times, and record the results as Trials 2 and 3 in your data table.

10 Place two or three rods under the textbook to act as rollers. Make sure the rods are evenly spaced. Place another rod in front of the book so that the book will roll onto it. Pull the spring scale slowly so that the book rolls across the rods at a slow, constant speed. Practice this several times, repositioning the rods each time. On a smooth trial, note the force that appears on the scale as the book is moving at a slow, constant speed. Record this force in your data table as rolling friction.

11 Repeat step 10 two times, and record the results in your data table.

Analysis

1. **Organizing Data** For each type of friction, add the results of the three trials and divide by 3 to get an average. Record these averages in your data table.

2. **Analyzing Data** Which of the three types of friction was the largest force, on average?

3. **Analyzing Data** Which of the three types of friction was the smallest force, on average?

Communicating Your Results

4. **Drawing Conclusions** Did your answers to Analysis questions 2 and 3 agree with the hypotheses you made before collecting data? If not, explain how your results differed from what you predicted.

5. **Evaluating Methods** In each trial, the force that you measured was actually the force that you were exerting on the spring scale. This force was, in turn, exerted on the book. Why could you assume that this force was equal to the force of friction in each case?

Application

If the car manufacturer that you work for wants to develop an innovative braking system, should it be based on a kind of friction different from that used in existing braking systems? Explain.

Answer to Application

No; static friction produces the greatest frictional force, so the most optimal braking system will make use of static friction.

Tips and Tricks

For best results, students should keep spring scales parallel to the table as they pull. They should also pull as gently and gradually as possible; quick pulls will give incorrect readings.

Your spring scales may or may not show force in units of newtons. The data table calls for forces in units of newtons. Students do not learn about units of force in this chapter. You may tell students to leave off units until they study force units. The units used are not important, as the purpose of the lab is to compare the relative values for different types of friction.

Answers to Analysis

1. Answers may vary based on data. The correct answers should be the averages of the three trials for each of the three types of friction.
2. Students should find that static friction is the largest force.
3. Students should find that rolling friction is the smallest force.

Answers to Communicating Your Results

4. Answers may vary based on the initial predictions and results. Students should explain why their results might have differed from their predictions.
5. Because the book is moving at a constant speed (or at rest), the forces on the book are balanced. Therefore, the force that the spring scale exerts on the book is equal to the force of friction.

Key Resources

 Virtual Investigation

 Classroom Lab Video/DVD

 Holt Lab Generator CD-ROM
Search for any lab by type, standard, difficulty level, or time. Edit any lab to fit your needs, or create your own labs. Use the Lab Materials QuickList software to customize your lab materials list.

 Differentiated Datasheets
Static, Sliding, and Rolling Friction

 Observation Lab
Testing Reaction Time

 CBL™ Probeware Lab
Static and Kinetic Friction

Reteaching Key Ideas

Interpreting Graphs Tell students that the shape of a distance versus time graph can provide qualitative information about velocity and acceleration. Review the following concepts with students: A horizontal line indicates zero velocity and acceleration, a straight line with a positive slope has positive velocity and zero acceleration, and a straight line with a negative slope has negative velocity and zero acceleration. A curved line indicates non-zero acceleration. **LS** **Visual**

Answers to Practice

1. The graph indicates an increase in distance during all time intervals prior to 22.5 s. After 22.5 s, the distance remains constant.

2. Time is the independent variable; distance is the dependent variable. As the time increases, the distance increases.

3. 8.0 m/s; from $t = 15.0$ s to $t = 17.5$ s; 0 m/s

4. 45.0 m; The runner has stopped moving after 22.5 s, as indicated by the horizontal line. It may therefore be inferred that the run is over at 22.5 s.

5. All such graphs have a positive slope, indicating an increase in distance with time regardless of changes in speed.

6. For objects A and B, the graph indicates an increasing speed. For object C, the graph indicates a constant speed.

7. Object B has the greatest acceleration. Object C is not accelerating.

Graphing Motion

Problem

The graph shown here contains data about a runner. What information is being graphed? What can be determined from the graph about the runner's speed? Is the speed constant during the run? Explain.

Solution

① Examine the graph. Determine what the *x*-axis and *y*-axis are to find out what is being graphed.	The *x*-axis is time, measured in seconds. The *y*-axis is distance, measured in meters. This is a graph of the runner's distance from some arbitrary starting point as a function of time.
② Speed is equal to the slope of a distance vs. time graph.	The runner's average speed at various times can be determined from the graph.
③ A horizontal line indicates zero speed and acceleration. A straight line has a constant speed and zero acceleration.	The slope of the graph is different at different times. The runner's speed is not constant but varies from time to time.

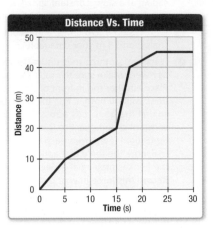

Practice

Use the graph above to answer questions 1–5.

1. Does the graph indicate an increase or decrease in distance during different time intervals? Explain.

2. Identify the independent and dependent variables. What is the relationship between the two variables?

3. What is the runner's maximum speed? During what time interval does the runner reach this speed? What is the runner's minimum speed?

4. What is the total distance traveled by the runner? What trend suggests that this is the total distance run even though the graph continues?

5. How is this graph similar to any graph showing distance traveled in a single direction over a given time interval?

Use the table below to make a graph. Use the graph to answer questions 6–8.

Time (s)	Speed of A (m/s)	Speed of B (m/s)	Speed of C (m/s)
0	0.0	0.0	22.5
5	12.5	16.5	22.5
10	25.0	33.0	22.5

6. For each object (A, B, C), does the graph indicate an increase, decrease, or no change in speed?

7. Which object has the greatest acceleration? Which object is not accelerating?

8. Could you graph the same data on a distance vs. time graph? Explain.

Answers continued

8. Yes, the data could be graphed on a distance vs. time graph. To do so, you would have to calculate the distance traveled based on the speed that each object is moving.

Key Resources

📁 **Science Skills Worksheets**
Slope of a Line
Rates of Change

go.hrw.com
SUPER SUMMARY
KEYWORD: HK8MOTS

SUMMARY

SUPER SUMMARY

Have students connect the major concepts in this chapter through an interactive Super Summary. Visit **go.hrw.com** and type in the keyword **HK8MOTS** to access the Super Summary for this chapter.

Key **Ideas**

Key **Terms**

Section 1 Measuring Motion

❯ **Observing Motion** When an object continuously changes position in comparison to a reference point, the object is in motion. (p. 365)

❯ **Speed and Velocity** Speed tells us how fast an object moves, and velocity tells us both the speed and the direction that the object moves. (p. 367)

❯ **Calculating Speed** Average speed is calculated as distance divided by time. (p. 368)

❯ **Graphing Motion** A distance vs. time graph of an object moving at constant speed is a straight line. The slope of the line is the object's speed. (p. 370)

motion, p. 365
frame of reference,
 p. 365
displacement, p. 366
speed, p. 367
velocity, p. 367

Section 2 Acceleration

❯ **Acceleration and Motion** Acceleration is a change in an object's velocity. Accelerating means speeding up, slowing down, or changing direction. (p. 372)

❯ **Calculating Acceleration** The average acceleration can be calculated by dividing the change in the object's velocity by the time over which the change occurs. (p. 374)

❯ **Graphing Accelerated Motion** The slope of a line on a velocity vs. time graph gives you the value of the acceleration. (p. 376)

acceleration, p. 372

Section 3 Motion and Force

❯ **Fundamental Forces** Scientists describe four fundamental forces in nature: the force of gravity, the electromagnetic force, the strong nuclear force, and the weak nuclear force. (p. 380)

❯ **Balanced and Unbalanced Forces** If there is a net force acting on an object, the object accelerates in the direction of the net force. (p. 381)

❯ **The Force of Friction** Friction is a force that opposes motion between the surfaces of objects. (p. 382)

❯ **Friction and Motion** Friction is necessary for many everyday tasks to work correctly. (p. 384)

force, p. 380
friction, p. 382
static friction, p. 383
kinetic friction, p. 383

Differentiated Instruction

Alternative Assessment

Analyzing Motion Organize students into small groups and give each group a remote-controlled car or another toy that can move on its own. Instruct students to design an experiment to find the maximum accelera-tion of the toy. Students will need to find the top speed of the toy and then determine how much time is needed for the toy to accelerate from rest to the top speed. Then, have students draw a diagram of their toy that explains how the forces acting on the toy cause it to move.
LS **Kinesthetic/Visual**

Key Resources

🖧 **Interactive Concept Map**

📁 **Review Resources**
 Concept Review Worksheets

📁 **Assessment Resources**
 Chapter Tests A and B
 Performance-Based Assessment

Reading Toolbox

1. Sample answer: Scientific: The *friction* between the road surface and the tire allow the automobile to move. Non-scientific: *Friction* between the two students caused them to argue while working on a science activity.

Using Key Terms

2. both; The speed is 30 m/s, and the velocity is 30 m/s westward.

3. The reference frame defines the starting, ending, and comparison points.

4. Distance is the length of the path that you travel even if you change direction. Displacement is the straight-line distance between the starting point and the ending point.

5. Uniform circular motion is motion at constant speed in a circle.

6. Static means "not moving" (stationary) and kinetic means "moving." Static friction is greater than kinetic friction, because when two surfaces are not moving past each other, the irregularities in one surface can stick to the irregularities of the other surface more easily than when the surfaces are in motion.

Understanding Key Ideas

7. b

8. a

9. c

10. a

11. b

12. b

13. a

14. d

READING TOOLBOX

1. Everyday Words Used in Science The word *friction* can be used metaphorically in a nonscientific context. For example, *friction* can mean "conflict," as between two people. Write two sentences, one using the scientific meaning of *friction* and another using the word in a nonscientific way.

USING KEY TERMS

2. State whether 30 m/s westward represents a *speed*, a *velocity*, or both.

3. Why is identifying the *frame of reference* important in describing motion?

4. What is the difference between *distance* and *displacement*?

5. What is *uniform circular motion?*

6. How do *static friction* and *kinetic friction* differ from each other?

UNDERSTANDING KEY IDEAS

7. If you jog for 1 h and travel 10 km, 10 km/h describes your
   a. momentum.
   b. average speed.
   c. displacement.
   d. acceleration.

8. An object's speed is a measure of
   a. how fast the object is moving.
   b. the object's direction.
   c. the object's displacement per unit of time.
   d. All of the above

9. Which of the quantities below represents a velocity?
   a. 25 m/s
   b. 10 km/min
   c. 15 mi/h eastward
   d. 3 mi/h

10. A car travels a distance of 210 mi in exactly 4 h. The driver calculates that he traveled 52.5 mi/h. Which of the following terms most nearly describes his calculation?
   a. average speed
   b. instantaneous speed
   c. instantaneous acceleration
   d. displacement

11. Which of the following is *not* accelerated motion?
   a. a ball being juggled
   b. a woman walking at 2.5 m/s along a straight road
   c. a satellite circling Earth
   d. a braking cyclist

INTERPRETING GRAPHICS Use the graphs below to answer questions 12–14.

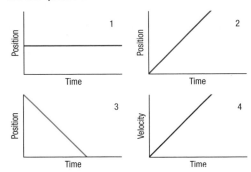

12. Which graph represents an object moving with a constant positive velocity?
   a. 1   **c.** 3
   b. 2   **d.** 4

13. Which graph represents an object at rest?
   a. 1   **c.** 3
   b. 2   **d.** 4

14. Which graph represents an object moving with constant positive acceleration?
   a. 1   **c.** 3
   b. 2   **d.** 4

EXPLAINING KEY IDEAS

15. At the end of a game, a basketball player on the winning team throws the basketball straight up as high as he can throw it. What is the basketball's velocity at the top of its path?

16. A book is sitting still on your desk. Are the forces acting on the book balanced or unbalanced? Explain.

17. Bob straps on his in-line skates and pushes himself down a hill. At the bottom of the hill, he slowly rolls to a stop. When is he accelerating?

CRITICAL THINKING

18. **Interpreting Data** A baseball is hit straight up at an initial velocity of 30 m/s. If the ball has a negative acceleration of about 10 m/s², how long does the ball take to reach the top of its path?

19. **Understanding Relationships** What can you conclude about the forces acting on an object traveling in uniform circular motion?

20. **Interpreting Data** When you drive, you will sometimes have to decide in a brief moment whether to stop for a yellow light. Discuss the variables that you must consider in making your decision. Use the concepts of force, acceleration, and velocity in your discussion.

21. **Identifying Relationships** What are some of the ways that competitive swimmers can decrease the amount of friction or drag between themselves and the water through which they are swimming? How does each method work to decrease friction?

Math Skills

22. **Velocity** Simpson drives his car with an average velocity of 85 km/h eastward. How long will it take him to drive 560 km on a perfectly straight highway?

23. **Acceleration** A driver is traveling eastward on a dirt road when she spots a pothole ahead. She slows her car from 14.0 m/s to 5.5 m/s in 6.0 s. What is the car's acceleration?

24. **Acceleration** How long will it take a cyclist with an acceleration of –2.50 m/s² to bring a bicycle with an initial forward velocity of 13.5 m/s to a complete stop?

Graphing Skills

25. The graphs below describe the motion of four different balls—a, b, c, and d. Use the graphs to determine whether each ball is accelerating, sitting still, or moving at a constant velocity.

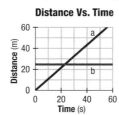
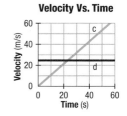

26. A rock is dropped from a bridge, and the distance it travels and the speed at which it is falling are measured every second until it hits the water. The data are shown in the chart below. Make two graphs of the data: a distance vs. time graph and a velocity vs. time graph. Use your graphs to answer the following questions.
   a. What shape is the distance vs. time graph? Explain.
   b. What shape is the velocity vs. time graph? Explain.
   c. Use the velocity vs. time graph to determine the rock's acceleration.

Time	Distance traveled	Downward speed
0 s	0 m	0 m/s
1 s	5 m	10 m/s
2 s	20 m	20 m/s
3 s	45 m	30 m/s

Assignment Guide	
Section	**Items**
1	2–4, 7–10, 12–13, 15, 22
2	5, 11, 14, 17–18, 23–26
3	1, 6, 16, 19–21

Graphing Skills

25. Objects *a* and *d* are moving with constant velocity; object *b* is at rest; object *c* is moving with constant acceleration.

26. **a.** The distance vs. time graph is curved because the rock is speeding up. The distance traveled in each succeeding time interval is bigger than the distance traveled in the preceding time interval.

   b. The velocity vs. time graph is a straight line because the rock speeds up by the same amount in each time interval.

   c. 10 m/s² downward

Explaining Key Ideas

15. 0 m/s

16. The forces acting on the book are balanced. If the forces were not balanced, the book would not be sitting still.

17. He is accelerating both when going down the hill and when slowing to a stop.

Critical Thinking

18. Velocity at the top of the path is 0 m/s.

   $t = \Delta v/a =$
   $(0 \text{ m/s} - 30 \text{ m/s})/{-10} \text{ m/s}^2 = 3 \text{ s}$

19. An object traveling in uniform circular motion must be accelerating, so there must be a net force. The acceleration is centripetal—toward the center of the circle—so the net force causing the centripetal acceleration must also be toward the center of the circle.

20. Answers may vary. Some of the variables include the length of time the light is yellow, the force that can be applied by the brakes, the force that can be applied with the engine, the distance to the intersection when the light turns yellow, and the width of the intersection. To stop successfully, the brakes must provide enough force for negative acceleration to give zero velocity before the intersection is entered. To get through the intersection safely, the engine must apply enough force to travel the distance to the intersection plus the width of the intersection before the light turns red.

21. Answers should involve streamlining (e.g., shaving heads, wearing bathing caps, wearing a helmet similar to racing bike helmets) and/or lubrication.

Math Skills

22. $t = \dfrac{d}{v} = \dfrac{560 \text{ km}}{85 \text{ km/h}} = 6.6 \text{ h}$

23. $a = \dfrac{5.5 \text{ m/s} - 14.0 \text{ m/s}}{6.0 \text{ s}} = \dfrac{-8.5 \text{ m/s}}{6.0 \text{ s}}$
   $= -1.4 \text{ m/s}^2 \text{ eastward}$

24. $t = \dfrac{\Delta v}{a} = \dfrac{v_f - v_i}{a}$
   $= \dfrac{0 \text{ m/s} - 13.5 \text{ m/s}}{-2.50 \text{ m/s}^2} = 5.4 \text{ s}$

Standardized Test Prep

Standardized Test Prep

 TEST DOCTOR

Question 1 Answer C is correct. Answer A describes something that can change an object's motion but does not describe the object's motion. Answer B relates to a change in an object's velocity, not a constant velocity as given in the question. Answer D refers to how far an object has moved, not how fast it is moving.

Question 2 Answer I is correct. Answers F and G are forces that oppose motion. Answer H does not cause change in motion.

Question 3 Answer A is correct. Average acceleration is found by taking the difference of the final and initial velocities and dividing that difference by the elapsed time. Answer B reflects adding the velocities instead of subtracting. Answer C comes from dividing the elapsed time by the sum of the velocities. Answer D is the result of dividing the elapsed time by the difference in velocities.

Question 4 Full-credit answers should include the following points:
- Kinetic friction causes negative acceleration (opposes motion).
- The less kinetic friction that is exerted on a bowling ball, the more speed the ball will retain on its way down the bowling lane.
- The faster the ball, the more pins it is likely to knock down.

Question 5 Full-credit answers should include the following points:
- The slope of the graph is equal to distance divided by time.
- Distance divided by time gives the beetle's average speed crossing the driveway.

Question 6 Answer G is correct. When the shoe slips, the frictional force changes from static friction to kinetic friction. Kinetic friction is always less than static friction, so the force exerted in the opposite direction (forward) decreases. Answer F indicates not knowing the difference between static and kinetic friction. Answers H and I indicate that a student misunderstands the direction of the force exerted by friction.

Understanding Concepts

Directions (1–3): For each question, write on a sheet of paper the letter of the correct answer.

1. A meteorologist describes a tropical storm as traveling northwest at 50 mi/h. Which attribute of the storm's motion has the meteorologist described?
   - **A.** force
   - **B.** acceleration
   - **C.** velocity
   - **D.** displacement

2. Which of the following must be applied to move an object at rest, such as a large rock?
   - **F.** static friction
   - **G.** kinetic friction
   - **H.** balanced forces
   - **I.** unbalanced forces

3. A fish swimming at a constant speed of 0.5 m/s suddenly notices a shark appear behind it. Five seconds later, the fish is swimming in the same direction at a speed of 2.5 m/s. What was the fish's average acceleration?
   - **A.** 0.4 m/s^2
   - **B.** 0.6 m/s^2
   - **C.** 1.7 m/s^2
   - **D.** 2.5 m/s^2

Directions (4–5): For each question, write a short response.

4. Bowling lanes are made as smooth as possible in order to minimize kinetic friction. Why is this desirable in a bowling lane?

5. Two amateur entomologists are observing the movement of a beetle traveling in a straight line across a driveway. Every 10 s, they measure the distance that the beetle has traveled. Afterward, they create a graph of the beetle's motion, with distance on the *y*-axis and time on the *x*-axis. What does the slope of their graph represent?

Reading Skills

Directions (6–7): Read the passage below. Then, answer the questions that follow.

MOVING BY FRICTION

Friction is usually thought of as interfering with motion, but there are many sorts of movement that depend on friction. When any two surfaces move against each other, friction exerts force in a direction opposite to the direction of push. Runners use the energy in their leg muscles to push backward on the ground with one foot. The ground forces their body forward. If not for the friction between the running shoes and the ground, their feet would slip backward against the ground instead.

The friction between two surfaces before they move is called static friction. After the two surfaces begin moving against each other, the frictional force lessens; the force is then called kinetic friction. Once a runner's foot begins to slip, the frictional force decreases, as does the force exerted on the runner in the opposite direction—toward the finish line! Runners need friction to move forward.

6. When a runner's shoe slips against the ground, what is the effect on the net force affecting the runner?
   - **F.** The net force pushing the runner forward increases.
   - **G.** The net force pushing the runner forward decreases.
   - **H.** The net force pushing the runner toward the ground increases.
   - **I.** The net force pushing the runner toward the ground decreases.

7. A runner decides to get new running shoes because the old ones are slipping too much against the ground. What should the runner look for in a new pair of shoes?

Question 7 Full-credit answers should include the following points:
- More friction is needed between the running shoe and the ground.
- Because the bottom of the shoes touches the ground, the bottom of the new shoes needs to be different from the bottom of the old shoes to increase the friction between the shoes and the ground.
- The bottom of the shoes may be improved by having a rougher surface, having cleats, or being less worn out.

Question 8 Answer B is correct. Students calculate how long it takes each event to occur. For answers A and B, students find the relative velocity between the two cycles by finding the

difference between their given velocities, and then divide the starting distance between the two cycles by the relative velocity. Answers C and D, students would divide the distance between the cycle and the finish line by the cycle's velocity. The time to each event is as follows: Answer A, 40 s; Answer B, 13 s; Answer C, 20 s; Answer D, 20 s.

Question 9 Answer G is correct. Students find the relative velocity between Cycle A and the other cycles, by taking the difference between their given velocities. The greatest difference is between Cycle A and Cycle D, so Cycle D appears to be moving the fastest toward Cycle A. Other answers may indicate that the distance between two moving objects is related to their relative velocity, which is not true.

Interpreting Graphics

The graphic below shows four motorcycle racers on the last 800 m of a track. Use this graphic to answer questions 8 and 9.

SPEED AND LOCATION OF FOUR MOTORCYCLES

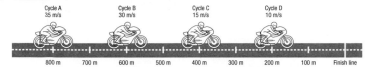

8. Assuming that each motorcycle continues to travel toward the finish line at the given constant velocity above, which event will occur first?
   A. Cycle A passes Cycle B.   **C.** Cycle B crosses the finish line.
   B. Cycle B passes Cycle C.   **D.** Cycle D crosses the finish line.

9. From Cycle A's frame of reference, which cycle or cycles are moving toward Cycle A the fastest?
   F. Cycle B appears to be moving the fastest.
   G. Cycle D appears to be moving the fastest.
   H. Cycles B and D appear to be moving at the same speed.
   I. All three cycles appear to be moving at the same speed.

The graph below shows how long it took for two vehicles to stop from a speed of 30 m/s. Use the graph below to answer questions 10 and 11.

SPEED VS. TIME FOR TWO VEHICLES

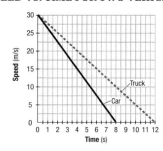

10. What can we conclude from the graph about the car and the truck?
    A. The truck's final velocity is greater than the car's.
    B. The car's final velocity is greater than the truck's.
    C. The truck's acceleration has greater absolute value than the car's.
    D. The car's acceleration has greater absolute value than the truck's.

11. If the slope of the two lines remained the same, how long would it take each vehicle to coast to a stop from an initial velocity of 100 mph?

Question 10 Answer D is correct. An answer of A or B indicates confusion with velocity and acceleration. Answer C may be equating a longer deceleration time with greater acceleration, when the opposite is true.

Question 11 Full-credit answers should include the following points:
- The car would take 27 s to coast to a stop and the truck would take 40 s.
- The slope of each line must be calculated, which equals the negative acceleration of each vehicle.
- Students need to use the slopes in the equation $y = mx + b$ where b is equal to 100 m/s and y is equal to 0 m/s.

Answers

1. C
2. I
3. A
4. Answers may vary; see Test Doctor for a detailed scoring rubric.
5. Answers may vary; see Test Doctor for a detailed scoring rubric.
6. G
7. Answers may vary; see Test Doctor for a detailed scoring rubric.
8. B
9. G
10. D
11. Answers may vary; see Test Doctor for a detailed scoring rubric.

Test Tip

When several questions refer to the same graph or table, answer the questions that you are most sure of first.

State Resources

For specific resources for your state, visit **go.hrw.com** and type in the keyword **HSHSTR**.

 **Test Practice with Guided Reading Development**

Continuation of Answers

Answers to Practice

1. Sample graph:

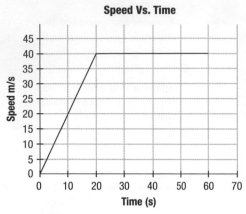

Speed Vs. Time

20 m/s; 40 m/s

2. Sample graph:

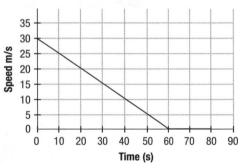

Speed Vs. Time

–0.5 m/s²

Answers continued from p. 377

4. He is accelerating both when he is going in circles at the same rate of speed and when he is increasing speed. One involves a change in direction, while the other involves a change in speed. Both speed and direction are a part of velocity, and any change of velocity is acceleration.

5. $v_f = v_i + at = 0 + (2.0 \text{ m/s}^2)(3.5 \text{ s}) = 7.0 \text{ m/s}$

6. 2.5 m/s² is the acceleration. The graph should be a straight line from 7.0 m/s at the 0 s line of time to 12 m/s at the 2.0 s line of time (with time on the horizontal axis and speed on the vertical axis).

Answers continued from p. 385

7. If there is no acceleration, the net force is zero. The force of static friction is equal to, but in the opposite direction of the force pulling the truck downhill: 2,000 N uphill.

CHAPTER PLANNER 12 Forces

		Standards	Teach Key Ideas
CHAPTER OPENER, pp. 394–396	50 min.		
SECTION 1 Newton's First and Second Laws, pp. 397–402 ❯ Newton's First Law ❯ Newton's Second Law	50 min.	PS 4a, UCP 1, UCP 2, UCP 3, SAI 2, ST 2, HNS 3	▨ **Bellringer Transparency** ▨ **Teaching Transparency** P4 Newton's Second Law ◉ **Visual Concepts** Newton's First Law • Newton's Second Law • Force
SECTION 2 Gravity, pp. 403–410 ❯ Weight and Mass ❯ Law of Universal Gravitation ❯ Free Fall ❯ Projectile Motion	50 min.	PS 4b, UCP 1, UCP 2, SAI 2	▨ **Bellringer Transparency** ▨ **Teaching Transparencies** TM33 Law of Universal Gravitation • TM34 Projectile Motion • P5 Terminal Velocity • P6 Two Motions Cause Orbiting ◉ **Visual Concepts** Law of Universal Gravitation • Equation for Newton's Universal Law of Gravitation • Gravity and Orbit • Projectile Motion • Free Fall • Comparing Mass and Weight
SECTION 3 Newton's Third Law, pp. 412–417 ❯ Action and Reaction Forces ❯ Momentum ❯ Conservation of Momentum	50 min.	PS 4a, UCP 1, UCP 2, SAI 1, SAI 2, ST 2, HNS 3	▨ **Bellringer Transparency** ▨ **Teaching Transparency** TM35 Rocket Propulsion ◉ **Visual Concepts** Newton's Third Law • Momentum • Equation for Momentum • Momentum and Collisions • Equation for Conservation of Momentum • Action and Reaction Forces • Acceleration and Gravity

See also PowerPoint® Resources

Chapter Review and Assessment Resources

SE Science Skills: Rearranging Equations, p. 420
SE Chapter Summary, p. 421
SE Chapter Review, pp. 422–423
SE Standardized Test Prep, pp. 424–425
▢ Concept Review Worksheets ■
▢ Chapter Tests A and B ■
▧ Holt Online Assessment

CHAPTER
Fast Track *To shorten instruction because of time limitations, omit the chapter lab.*

Basic Learners
TE Performing Magic, p. 398
TE The Direction of Gravity, p. 405
▢ Science Skills Worksheets
▢ Differentiated Datasheets A for Labs and Activities ■
▢ Study Guide A ■

Advanced Learners
TE Terminal Velocity, p. 407
TE Crumple Zones, p. 415
▢ Cross-Disciplinary Worksheets
▢ Differentiated Datasheets C for Labs and Activities ■

Key

SE Student Edition
TE Teacher's Edition

📁 Chapter Resource File
📖 Workbook
🖨 Transparency

💿 CD or CD-ROM
* Datasheet or blackline master available

■ Also available in Spanish

All resources listed below are also available on the Teacher's One-Stop Planner.

Why It Matters	Hands-On	Skills Development	Assessment
Build student motivation with resources about high-interest applications.	**SE Inquiry Lab** Earth's Attraction, p. 395*■	**TE Reading Toolbox** Assessing Prior Knowledge, p. 394 **SE Reading Toolbox** p. 396	📁 **Pretest** ■
SE How Do Airbags Work? p. 399 📁 **Cross-Disciplinary Worksheets** Science and the Consumer—Car Seat Safety • Integrating Mathematics—Using Force Diagrams	**TE Demonstration** Inertia, p. 397 **SE Quick Lab** Newton's First Law, p. 398*■ 📁 **CBL™ Probeware Lab** Determining Your Acceleration on a Bicycle	**TE Reading Toolbox** Visual Literacy, p. 399 **SE Reading Toolbox** Two-Column Notes, p. 400 **TE Science Skills** Intrepreting Equations, p. 400 **SE Math Skills** Newton's Second Law, p. 401	**TE Reteaching Key Ideas** Newton's Laws, p. 402 **TE Formative Assessment,** p. 402 📁 **Spanish Assessment***■ 📁 **Section Quiz** ■
TE Astronaut Health, p. 404 **TE Apparent Weightlessness,** p. 406 **TE Parachutes,** p. 407 **TE Escape Velocity,** p. 408 **SE Black Holes,** p. 411 📁 **Cross-Disciplinary Worksheets** Integrating Biology—Blood Pressure in Space • Connection to Social Studies—The Great Plague and Isaac Newton • Integrating Space Science—Gravity and the Planets • Integrating Biology—How Fish Maintain Neutral Buoyancy	**TE Demonstration** Gravity, p. 403	**SE Reading Toolbox** Signal Words, p. 406 **TE Reading Toolbox** Visual Literacy, p. 407 **TE Reading Toolbox** Everyday Terms with Scientific Meanings, p. 408 **TE Reading Toolbox** Concept Maps, p. 409 **TE Reading Toolbox** Visual Literacy, p. 411	**TE Reteaching Key Ideas** Projectile Motion, p. 410 **TE Formative Assessment,** p. 410 📁 **Spanish Assessment***■ 📁 **Section Quiz** ■
📁 **Cross-Disciplinary Worksheets** Integrating Technology—Hydraulic Lift Force • Connection to Fine Arts—Momentum of Line in Art • Real World Applications—Driving Safely	**TE Demonstration** Magnets, p. 412 **SE Quick Lab** Action and Reaction Forces, p. 414*■ **SE Inquiry Lab** Building a Catapult, pp. 418–419*■ 📁 **Observation Lab** Observing the Conservation of Momentum	**SE Reading Toolbox** Two-Column Notes, p. 414 **SE Math Skills** Momentum, p. 415 **TE Reading Toolbox** Visual Literacy, p. 416	**TE Reteaching Key Ideas** Flash Cards, p. 417 **TE Formative Assessment,** p. 417 📁 **Spanish Assessment***■ 📁 **Section Quiz** ■

See also Lab Generator

See also Holt Online Assessment Resources

Resources for Differentiated Instruction

English Learners

TE Newton's Three Laws of Motion, p. 413
📁 Differentiated Datasheets A, B, and C for Labs and Activities ■
📖 Study Guide A ■

Struggling Readers

TE Paired Summarizing, p. 398
📖 Interactive Reader

Special Education Students

TE Newton Demonstrations, p. 400
TE Mass Judgments, p. 406

Alternative Assessment

TE Isaac Newton, p. 401
TE Applying Newton's Laws, p. 421

CHAPTER 1

Overview

This chapter covers Newton's first and second laws of motion, including problem-solving with the second law. It also discusses the law of universal gravitation, free fall, and projectile motion. Finally, the chapter explores Newton's third law of motion and also covers momentum.

READING TOOLBOX

Assessing Prior Knowledge Students should understand the following concepts:
- mass
- acceleration
- balanced and unbalanced forces

MISCONCEPTION ///ALERT\\\

Science education research has identified the following misconceptions about forces and free fall.
- Students believe that when there is no motion, there is no force. Students characterize equilibrium as the result of the strongest forces winning and believe that all forces cease to act at equilibrium. (Static systems contain opposing forces that continue to act although there is no motion.)
- Students believe that heavier objects fall faster, and some students are unable to identify how air resistance affects the rate of falling objects. (Acceleration due to gravity alone is the same for all objects. Variations are due to air resistance, which is a function of the object's density and shape.)

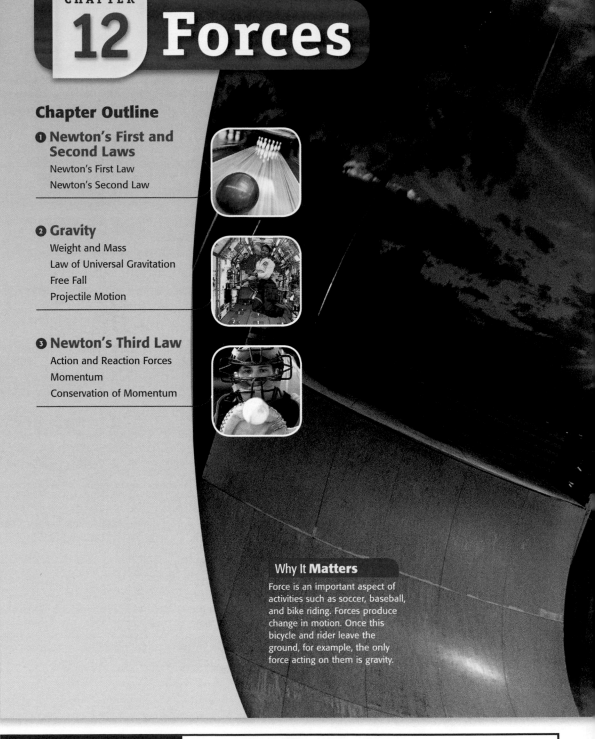

CHAPTER 12 Forces

Chapter Outline

❶ Newton's First and Second Laws
Newton's First Law
Newton's Second Law

❷ Gravity
Weight and Mass
Law of Universal Gravitation
Free Fall
Projectile Motion

❸ Newton's Third Law
Action and Reaction Forces
Momentum
Conservation of Momentum

Why It **Matters**

Force is an important aspect of activities such as soccer, baseball, and bike riding. Forces produce change in motion. Once this bicycle and rider leave the ground, for example, the only force acting on them is gravity.

Chapter Correlations   *National Science Education Standards*

The following correlations show the National Science Standards that relate to this chapter. For the full text of the standards, see the National Science Education Standards at the front of the book.

PS 4a Objects change their motion only when a net force is applied. Laws of motion are used to calculate precisely the effects of forces on the motion of objects. The magnitude of the change in motion can be calculated using the relationship F = ma, which is independent of the nature of the force. Whenever one object exerts force on another, a force equal in magnitude and opposite in direction is exerted on the first object. (Sections 1, 3)

PS 4b Gravitation is a universal force that each mass exerts on any other mass. The strength of the gravitational attractive force between two masses is proportional to the masses and inversely proportional to the square of the distance between them. (Section 2)

UCP 1 Systems, order, and organization (Sections 1–3)

UCP 2 Evidence, models, and explanation (Sections 1–3)

UCP 3 Constancy, change, and measurement (Section 1)

SAI 1 Abilities necessary to do scientific inquiry (Inquiry Lab: Building a Catapult)

SAI 2 Understandings about scientific inquiry (Sections 1–3)

ST 2 Understandings about science and technology (Sections 1, 3)

HNS 3 Historical perspectives (Sections 1, 3)

Teacher's Notes Do not allow students to use hollow balls for this activity. (Solid balls act more nearly like ideal point masses. Hollow thin-walled balls roll differently and do not behave ideally.) The weight of the balls is not important. The closer the board is to vertical, the faster the balls will accelerate.

Materials per Group
• balls, different masses, (2)
• board
• stopwatch

Answers

1. Sample answer: The balls crossed the finish line at the same instant, so the balls were rolling at the same speed.
2. Sample answer: The angle of the board affected the motion of the balls. The mass of the balls did not affect their motion.

Key Resources

Datasheet
Earth's Attraction

InquiryLab ⏱ 10 min

Earth's Attraction

You can investigate Earth's pull on objects by using a **stopwatch**, a **board**, and **two balls** of different masses. Set one end of the board on a stack of books and the other end on the floor. Mark a point on the floor across the room to be the finish line. Time each ball as it rolls down the board to the finish line. Then, several more times, roll both balls down the board at different angles. Adjust the angle by changing the number of books under the end of the board.

Questions to Get You Started

1. Does the heavier ball move faster, move more slowly, or move at the same speed as the lighter one?

2. What factors do you think may have affected the motion of the two balls?

FoldNotes

Students' key-term folds should look similar to the example shown and should contain definitions for each of the key terms from the chapter (*inertia, weight, free fall, terminal velocity, projectile motion,* and *momentum.*)

Cause and Effect

Answers may vary. Students should create three-column tables. For each row, the first column should identify a cause, and the second column should identify an effect of that cause. The third column should include words and phrases that signal the cause and effect relationship. Some cause-and-effect pairs may have no explicit signals.

Note Taking

Answers may vary. Students' notes should appear similar to the example shown. The key ideas should be reflective of the key ideas in Section 1, but they do not need to be identical to the Key Ideas listed at the beginning of the section.

READING TOOLBOX

These reading tools can help you learn the material in this chapter. For more information on how to use these and other tools, see **Appendix A.**

FoldNotes

Key-Term Fold The key-term fold can help you learn the key terms from this chapter.

Your Turn Create a key-term fold, as described in **Appendix A.**

① Write one key term from the Summary page on the front of each tab.

② As you read the chapter, write the definition for each term under its tab.

③ Use this FoldNote to study the key terms.

inertia
weight
free fall
terminal velocity
projectile motion
momentum

Cause and Effect

Signal Words Certain words or phrases can serve as signals of cause and effect relationships. Such signals are called *cause and effect markers.*

CAUSE MARKERS
cause
affect
produce
as a result of
due to
because

EFFECT MARKERS
therefore
thus
as a result
is an effect of
results from
consequently

Your Turn Complete the table of cause and effect markers that are in this chapter.

CAUSE	EFFECT	MARKER(S)
Inertia	You appear to slide toward the side of a car	Because

Note Taking

Two-Column Notes Two-column notes can help you learn the Key Ideas from each section.

- The Key Ideas are in the left column.
- In your own words, write detailed notes and examples in the right column.

Your Turn Complete the two-column notes for Section 1, adding another row for each Key Idea.

KEY IDEA #1: What makes an object speed up, slow down, or change directions?	• Objects change their state of motion only when a net force is applied. • When there is no net force, an object does not change its state of motion. • For example, if there were no friction, a bowling ball would keep rolling forever. It would not stop.

Newton's First and Second Laws

Key Ideas

> What makes an object speed up, slow down, or change directions?

> What determines how much an object speeds up or slows down?

Key Terms

inertia

Why It Matters

Newton's second law of motion helps explain how air bags have saved lives.

Every change in motion that you observe or feel is caused by a force. Sir Isaac Newton (1642–1727), a British scientist, described the relationship between motion and force in three laws that we now call *Newton's laws of motion*. Newton's laws apply to a wide range of motion—a caterpillar crawling on a leaf, a person riding a bicycle, or a rocket moving in space.

Newton's First Law

If you start your book sliding across a rough surface, such as carpet, the book soon comes to rest. On a smooth surface, such as ice, the book will slide much farther. Because there is less frictional force between the ice and the book, the smaller force must act over a longer time before the book stops. Without friction, the book would keep sliding. This is an example of Newton's first law, which is stated as follows.

Newton's first law	An object at rest remains at rest and an object in motion maintains its velocity unless it experiences a net force.

> **Objects change their state of motion only when a net force is applied.** A book sliding on carpet comes to rest because friction acts on the book. If no net force acted on the book, the book would continue moving with the same velocity.

Objects tend to maintain their state of motion.

If you have ever bowled, you know that a bowling ball, such as the one shown in **Figure 1,** will continue moving down the alley until it comes in contact with the bowling pins. In fact, if the alley were <u>infinitely</u> long and frictionless, the ball would keep rolling on and on! In the real world, friction (an outside force) will eventually cause the ball to stop.

Figure 1 A bowling ball in motion tends to remain in motion unless acted on by an outside force. **Why is it difficult to start a bowling ball moving?**

Academic Vocabulary

infinite (IN fuh nit) without limits

SECTION 1

❯ Focus

In this section, students learn Newton's first law of motion, also called the law of inertia, and they learn that mass is a measure of inertia. Next, students study and apply Newton's second law of motion $(F = ma)$.

🔔 Bellringer

Use the Bellringer transparency to prepare students for this section.

Demonstrate

Inertia You will need a toy dump truck, a small doll, and a textbook. Set the doll in the back of the truck. Place the truck and the book on a flat surface, with the truck facing the book. Give the truck a push toward the book. When the truck hits the book and stops, the doll will fly out. Ask students to explain this event in terms of inertia. (Since the doll and truck are in motion, they both have a tendency to stay in motion until experiencing an unbalanced force. The book exerts an unbalanced force on the truck; the truck stops. This force does not affect the doll, so the doll continues moving and flies out of the truck.) **LS Visual**

Key Resources

 Teaching Transparency
P4 Newton's Second Law

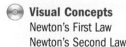 **Visual Concepts**
Newton's First Law
Newton's Second Law
Force

Datasheet
Newton's First Law

Math Skills Worksheet
Newton's Second Law

Cross-Disciplinary Worksheets
Science and the Consumer—Car Seat
Safety
Integrating Mathematics—Using Force
Diagrams

Teacher's Notes In step 2, students should observe the coin fall into the glass. The coin may move slightly sideways with the card. If students are having difficulty, emphasize that they must flick the card very quickly. Make sure that students understand that in step 3, the coin should not fall into the glass; it should remain resting on the card. The force of friction caused the coin to move sideways with the card.

Materials per Group
• coin
• glass
• index card

Answer to Analysis

1. In step 2, the coin fell into the cup because it tended to stay at rest when the card was moved. In step 3, the coin moved with the card because of friction.

Teaching Key Ideas

Newton's First Law Ask students: "If you are sitting on your bike on level ground, what do you need to do to make it move?"(pedal) "If you are coasting on your bike, what do you need to do to make the bike stop?" (apply the brakes) Explain to students that to change the motion of the bike—either to speed it up or slow it down—requires force because the bike's tendency is to keep still if it is still, and to keep moving if it is moving. **LS Logical**

Newton's First Law

🕐 **10 min**

Procedure

❶ Set an **index card** over a **glass.** Put a **coin** on top of the card.

❷ With your thumb and forefinger, quickly flick the card sideways off the glass. Observe what happens to the coin. Does the coin move with the index card?

❸ Repeat step 1. This time, slowly pull the card sideways, and observe what happens to the coin.

Analysis

1. Use Newton's first law of motion to explain your results.

---

inertia (in UHR shuh) the tendency of an object to resist a change in motion unless an outside force acts on the object

Figure 2 This backward-facing car seat stops the forward motion of the baby and distributes the force of the stop over the baby's whole body.

Inertia is related to an object's mass.

Inertia is the tendency of an object at rest to remain at rest or, if moving, to continue moving at a constant velocity. All objects resist changes in motion, so all objects have inertia. An object that has a small mass, such as a baseball, can be accelerated by a small force. But accelerating an object whose mass is larger, such as a car, requires a much larger force. Thus, mass is a measure of inertia. An object whose mass is small has less inertia than an object whose mass is large does.

Newton's first law of motion is often summed up as follows: Matter resists any change in motion. Because this property of matter is called *inertia,* Newton's first law is sometimes called the *law of inertia.*

✔ **Reading Check** How is inertia related to mass? (See Appendix E for answers to Reading Checks.)

Seat belts and car seats provide protection.

Because of inertia, you appear to slide toward the side of a car when the driver makes a sharp turn. You continue in the same direction while the car makes the turn. Inertia is also the reason that a plane, car, or bicycle cannot stop instantaneously. There is always a time lag between the moment the brakes are applied and the moment the car comes to rest.

When the car that you are riding in comes to a stop, your seat belt and the friction between you and the seat stop your forward motion. They provide the unbalanced backward force that is needed to bring you to a stop as the car stops.

Babies are placed in backward-facing car seats, as shown in **Figure 2.** When this kind of car seat is used, the force that is needed to bring the baby to a stop is safely spread out over the baby's whole body.

Differentiated Instruction

Basic Learners

Performing Magic A magician who pulls a tablecloth out from under a table set with dishes—without moving or breaking the dishes —is taking advantage of the dishes' inertia. Ask students to perform this magic trick at home. Instruct them to start with a single, non-breakable dish and to use caution. If a student is able to master the trick, have him perform it for the class with non-breakable dishes. Make sure that students are seated at a safe distance. Ask a volunteer to explain how inertia is involved in the demonstration. **LS Kinesthetic**

Struggling Readers

Paired Summarizing Have students work in groups, reading one section at a time, taking turns summarizing main ideas and details aloud; other students should check summaries for essential information. For homework, students should outline their sections. At the next class, groups should revise and combine summaries to create one study guide on Newton's laws. Groups can exchange and compare outlines and vote on the best one. **LS Verbal/Interpersonal**

How Do Air Bags Work?

REAL WORLD

Air bags are standard equipment in every new automobile sold in the United States. In a collision, air bags explode from a compartment to cushion the passenger's head. By decreasing the acceleration of a passenger's head and body during a crash, an air bag reduces the force acting on the passenger and makes injuries less likely. Air bags are credited with saving more than 5,000 lives between 1986 and 2000.

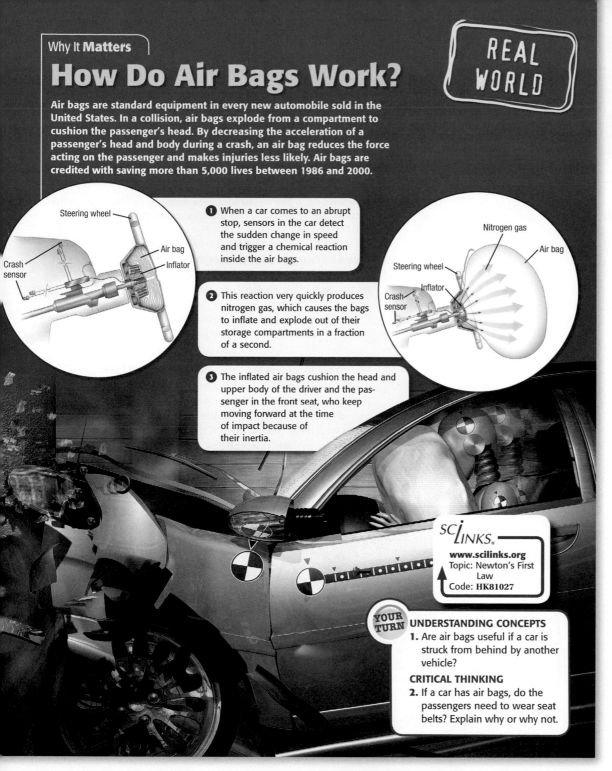

Steering wheel
Crash sensor
Air bag
Inflator

❶ When a car comes to an abrupt stop, sensors in the car detect the sudden change in speed and trigger a chemical reaction inside the air bags.

❷ This reaction very quickly produces nitrogen gas, which causes the bags to inflate and explode out of their storage compartments in a fraction of a second.

❸ The inflated air bags cushion the head and upper body of the driver and the passenger in the front seat, who keep moving forward at the time of impact because of their inertia.

Nitrogen gas
Air bag
Steering wheel
Inflator
Crash sensor

SCI LINKS.

www.scilinks.org
Topic: Newton's First Law
Code: HK81027

YOUR TURN

UNDERSTANDING CONCEPTS

1. Are air bags useful if a car is struck from behind by another vehicle?

CRITICAL THINKING

2. If a car has air bags, do the passengers need to wear seat belts? Explain why or why not.

How Do Air Bags Work? The key to an air bag's success during a crash is the speed at which it inflates. Inside the bag is a gas generator that contains the compounds sodium azide, potassium nitrate, and silicon dioxide. At the moment of a crash, an electronic sensor in the vehicle detects the sudden decrease in speed. The sensor sends a small electric current to the gas generator, providing the energy needed to start the chemical reaction.

The force that triggers the inflation of an air bag is approximately the same as that of hitting a solid barrier head-on at 20 km/h. The chemicals sodium azide and potassium nitrate react to form nontoxic, nonflammable nitrogen gas, which inflates the bag. (Several toxic chemicals are also formed, but they quickly react with other substances to make them less hazardous.) The rate at which the reaction occurs is very fast. In 0.04 s—less than the blink of an eye—the gas formed in the reaction inflates the bag. By filling the space between the person and the car's dashboard, the air bag protects the person from injury.

READING TOOLBOX

Visual Literacy Students may have difficulty interpreting the rapid series of events that cause an air bag to inflate. Ask students to describe what happens in each step in the illustration. If possible, have a volunteer sketch the steps on the board and use force arrows to identify the forces involved. **LS Visual**

Answers to Your Turn

1. Sample Answer: No, if your car is struck from behind, your body moves toward the seat back and not toward the dashboard, where the air bag is located.

2. Sample answer: Yes. Passengers still need to wear seatbelts because an air bag is only a supplementary restraint system.

Two-Column Notes Have students read silently the text under the heading *Newton's Second Law,* including the Math Skills example. Students should take two-column notes on the passage. If students are having difficulty with the passage, group them together in pairs. Have each pair of students review their notes and discuss the parts of the passage that they found difficult. **LS Verbal**

Science Skills

Interpreting Equations Use simple examples to explore Newton's second law conceptually. For example, ask: "What happens to acceleration when the force doubles and the mass remains constant?" (acceleration doubles) "What happens when the force is halved?" (acceleration is halved) These questions illustrate that force is proportional to acceleration. Use similar questions to show that force is inversely proportional to mass. **LS Logical**

Answer to caption question
The acceleration of the sled would be greater if the force acting on the sled were larger.

Two-Column Notes
Create two-column notes for Newton's second law. Put the Key Idea in the left column, and add details and examples in your own words in the right column.

Figure 3 Because the left sled has a smaller mass than the right sled does, the same force gives the left sled a greater acceleration. **How would the acceleration of the right sled change if the force were larger?**

Newton's Second Law

Newton's first law describes what happens when no net force is acting on an object: the object either remains at rest or keeps moving at a constant velocity. What happens when the net force is not zero?

When the net force is not zero, Newton's second law applies. Newton's second law describes the effect of an unbalanced force on the motion of an object. This law can be stated as follows.

| Newton's second law | The unbalanced force acting on an object equals the object's mass times its acceleration. |

❯ **Net force is equal to mass times acceleration. The unbalanced force on an object determines how much an object speeds up or slows down.** Newton's second law can also be written as a mathematical equation.

> **Newton's second law** $\quad net\ force = mass \times acceleration$
> $F = ma$

For equal forces, a larger mass accelerates less.

Consider the difference between the two photos shown in **Figure 3.** The students on the left are pushing a sled with nobody on it. In contrast, the students on the right are pushing a sled with three people on it. If the students push with the same force in each case, the first sled will have a greater acceleration because its mass is smaller than the mass of the second sled. This is an example of Newton's second law.

Greater acceleration · Smaller mass · Equal forces

Lesser acceleration · Larger mass

Overcoming Friction Students may believe that applying any force to an object will cause the object to accelerate. In the real world of weight and friction, a constant force is required to keep an object moving at a constant velocity. This force, however, is balanced by the opposite force of friction, so no unbalanced force is acting on the object. To demonstrate this idea, hook a spring scale to a chair or student desk and pull the object across the floor. Show that the force required to keep the object moving at constant velocity is relatively constant, depending on the uniformity of the floor surface. **LS Visual**

Special Education Students

Newton Demonstrations Physical involvement helps many students learn more effectively. Organize the class into three groups. Ask each group to demonstrate one of Newton's three laws of motion as a pantomime. **LS Kinesthetic**

Force is measured in newtons.

Newton's second law can be used to derive the SI unit of force, the newton (N). One newton is the force that gives a mass of one kilogram an acceleration of one meter per second squared:

$$1 \text{ N} = 1 \text{ kg} \times 1 \text{ m/s}^2$$

The pound (lb) is sometimes used as a unit of force. One newton is equal to 0.225 lb. Conversely, 1 lb equals 4.45 N.

✓ Reading Check Name two units of force.

www.scilinks.org
Topic: Newton's Laws of Motion
Code: HK81028

Math Skills Newton's Second Law

Zoo keepers lift a stretcher that holds a sedated lion. The total mass of the lion and stretcher is 175 kg, and the upward acceleration of the lion and stretcher is 0.657 m/s². What force is needed to produce this acceleration of the lion and the stretcher?

Identify
List the given and unknown values.
	Given:
	   mass, m = 175 kg
	   acceleration, a = 0.657 m/s²
	Unknown:
	   force, F = ? N

Plan Write the equation for Newton's second law.	*net force = mass × acceleration* $F = ma$
Solve Insert the known values into the equation, and solve.	$F = 175 \text{ kg} \times 0.657 \text{ m/s}^2$ $F = 115 \text{ kg} \times \text{m/s}^2 = 115 \text{ N}$

Practice

1. What net force is needed to accelerate a 1.6×10^3 kg automobile forward at 2.0 m/s²?

2. A baseball accelerates downward at 9.8 m/s². If the gravitational force is the only force acting on the baseball and is 1.4 N, what is the baseball's mass?

3. A sailboat and its crew have a combined mass of 655 kg. If a net force of 895 N is pushing the sailboat forward, what is the sailboat's acceleration?

4. The net forward force on the propeller of a 3.2 kg model airplane is 7.0 N. What is the acceleration of the airplane?

For more practice, visit **go.hrw.com** and enter keyword **HK8MP**.

Practice Hint

▸ When a problem requires you to calculate the unbalanced force on an object, you can use Newton's second law ($F = ma$).

▸ Problem 2: The equation for Newton's second law can be rearranged to isolate mass on the left side as follows.

$$F = ma$$

Divide both sides by *a*.

$$\frac{F}{a} = \frac{m\cancel{a}}{\cancel{a}}$$
$$m = \frac{F}{a}$$

▸ Problem 3: To isolate acceleration on the left, you need to rearrange the equation. Be sure to rearrange the equation before substituting numeric values for *F* and *a*.

Teaching Key Ideas

Newton's Second Law Students may benefit from a concrete example of the relationships between force, mass, and acceleration. Ask students: "Do people who race bicycles use heavy bikes or light bikes?" (They use light bikes.) "Why?" (Because if the same force is applied to a light bike and a heavy bike, the light bike will accelerate faster.) Likewise, explain to students that a stronger rider of the same mass can cause a bike to accelerate faster than a weak rider can. **LS Logical**

Math Skills

Answers to Practice

1. $F = ma = (1.6 \times 10^3 \text{ kg})(2.0 \text{ m/s}^2) = 3.2 \times 10^3 \text{ N}$

2. $m = F/a = (1.4 \text{ N}/9.8 \text{ m/s}^2) = 0.14 \text{ kg}$

3. $a = F/m = 895 \text{ N}/655 \text{ kg} = 1.37 \text{ m/s}^2$ in the direction of the force

4. $a = F/m = 7.0 \text{ N forward}/3.2 \text{ kg} = 2.2 \text{ m/s}^2$ forward

Additional Examples

A 1,200 kg car has a force of 1,500 N from the engine pushing it forward. The car also has a combined frictional force of 1,100 N pushing it backward. What is the acceleration of the car? (Hint: You will need to calculate the net force first.)
Answer: 0.33 m/s² forward
If the driver eases up on the gas pedal, the frictional force remains the same, and the engine is exerting a force of only 950 N, what is the new acceleration?
Answer: –0.13 m/s² forward = 0.13 m/s² backward (The car is slowing down.)
LS Logical

Differentiated Instruction

Alternative Assessment

Isaac Newton It is generally accepted that Isaac Newton was one of the greatest scientists in history. In addition to his work with forces, he made significant advancements in mathematics, astronomy, and other branches of physics. Have students research some aspect of his life or work. Possible topics include: his studies of light and color, his invention of calculus, his personal history, or his personality and character. Ask each student to prepare a brief presentation for the class. **LS Verbal**

MISCONCEPTION ALERT

Mass versus Weight The introduction of the pound as a unit of force may bring up the issue of weight. Remind students that mass and weight are not the same. In the SI system, mass is measured in kilograms, and weight—a force—is measured in newtons. The weight of an apple is about 1 newton. Tell students they will learn more about weight in this section, when they study gravity.

› Close

Reteaching Key Ideas

Newton's Laws Have students create a concept map for Newton's first and second laws. Instruct them to include all of the following terms in their maps: Newton's first law, inertia, mass, unbalanced force, balanced force, Newton's second law, acceleration, newtons. **LS Verbal**

Formative Assessment

You wear a seatbelt in a car to hold you in your seat in the event of a crash. Which of the following is the reason you would continue moving without a seatbelt when the car stopped suddenly?

A. inertia (Correct. Because you were an object in motion, you tend to stay in motion unless some unbalanced force stops you.)

B. acceleration (Incorrect. When a car stops suddenly, your tendency is not to accelerate but to remain moving at the same rate as before. Review Newton's second law.)

C. friction (Incorrect. A seatbelt holds you in place because, if a car stops suddenly, friction cannot keep you in your seat. Review Newton's first law.)

D. velocity (Incorrect. Velocity is a measure of distance over time. Review Newton's second law.)

Lesser acceleration Lesser force

Greater acceleration Greater force

Figure 4 For a given mass, a larger force causes a greater acceleration.

Acceleration depends on force and mass.

So far, we have talked about Newton's second law in terms of force. The second law can also be given in terms of acceleration:

| Newton's second law | The acceleration of an object is directly proportional to the net force on the object and inversely proportional to the object's mass. |

The mathematical version of this form of the law is as follows.

| ▷ Newton's second law | $acceleration = \dfrac{net\ force}{mass}$
 $a = \dfrac{F}{m}$ |

For example, the mass of the car shown in **Figure 4** is the same in both photos. When the masses are the same, a greater force causes a greater acceleration.

Section 1 Review

KEY IDEAS

1. **State** Newton's first law of motion in your own words. Give an example that illustrates the law.

2. **List** two examples of Newton's second law of motion.

CRITICAL THINKING

3. **Applying Ideas** Explain how the law of inertia relates to seat belt safety.

4. **Drawing Conclusions** Determine whether each example below is a case of Newton's first law or Newton's second law.
   a. a skydiver accelerating toward the ground
   b. a skydiver falling with constant velocity
   c. a skydiver on the ground at rest

5. **Making Predictions** Predict what will happen in the following situations. (Hint: Use Newton's laws.)
   a. A car traveling on an icy road comes to a sharp bend.
   b. A car traveling on an icy road has to stop quickly.

Math › Skills

6. What is the acceleration of a boy on a skateboard if the net force on the boy is 15 N? The total mass of the boy and the skateboard is 58 kg.

7. What is the mass of an object if a force of 34 N produces an acceleration of 4.0 m/s²?

Answers to Section Review

1. Answers may vary. Students should say in their own words that an object at rest remains at rest and an object in motion maintains its velocity unless it experiences an unbalanced force. They should then give an example of this law.

2. Answers may vary. Sample answer: a student pushing a piano across a floor, an apple falling from a tree

3. Answers may vary. Sample answer: When you have on a seatbelt and the vehicle stops suddenly, the seatbelt applies a force that stops you and keeps you from continuing forward, as inertia keeps you in motion after the car has stopped.

4. **a.** Newton's second law
   b. Newton's first law
   c. Newton's first law

5. **a.** The car may be unable to turn. Newton's first law states that the object (car) will continue to travel in a straight line unless an unbalanced force acts on the object. Since the road is icy, the friction between the tires and the ice may not be large enough to turn the car.
   b. The car will slide for the same reasons in (a). Also, Newton's second law states that acceleration is proportional to force. Since the friction force is much smaller on an icy road, the negative acceleration ("deceleration") is much smaller.

6. $a = F/m = 15 \text{ N}/58 \text{ kg} = 0.26 \text{ m/s}^2$ forward

7. $m = F/a = 34 \text{ N}/4 \text{ m/s}^2 = 8.5 \text{ kg}$

Gravity

Key Ideas

> How are weight and mass related?

> Why do objects fall to the ground when dropped?

> What is the relationship between free-fall acceleration and mass?

> Why does a projectile follow a curved path?

Key Terms

weight

free fall

terminal velocity

projectile motion

Why It Matters

Even though we can't see black holes, we know where they might be by measuring how they attract mass nearby.

Have you ever seen a movie about the Apollo astronauts walking on the moon? When they tried to walk on the lunar surface, they bounced all over the place! Why does the astronaut wearing a massive spacesuit in **Figure 1** bounce around so easily on the moon? The answer is that gravity is not as strong on the moon as it is on Earth.

Weight and Mass

The force on an object due to gravity is called **weight.** On Earth, your weight is simply the amount of gravitational force exerted on you by Earth. The *free-fall acceleration* near a massive object is a constant acceleration that all masses near that object experience. Near Earth's surface, the free-fall acceleration, *g,* is about 9.8 m/s^2. You can use $F = ma$ (Newton's second law) to calculate a body's weight. **> Thus, weight is equal to mass times free-fall acceleration.** Mathematically, this relationship is as follows:

> **Weight** | $weight = mass \times free\text{-}fall\ acceleration$
> $w = mg$

Weight is measured in newtons.

Because weight is a force, the SI unit of weight is the newton (N). A small apple weighs about 1 N on Earth. A typical textbook, which has a mass of about 2,250 g, has a weight of 2.25 kg × 9.8 m/s^2 = 22 N on Earth.

weight (WAYT) a measure of the gravitational force exerted on an object

Figure 1 Because gravity on the moon is less than gravity on Earth, the Apollo astronauts bounced as they walked on the moon's surface.

> Focus

In this section, students study gravitational force and the law of universal gravitation, free-fall acceleration, the difference between mass and weight, terminal velocity, and projectile motion.

Bellringer

Use the Bellringer transparency to prepare students for this section.

Demonstrate

Gravity Fill a round balloon with air and let it rest freely on your open hand. Ask: "What force is keeping this balloon on my hand?" (gravity) Explain to students that all objects in the universe attract each other through the force of gravity. In this case, the balloon and the Earth are attracting each other, but your hand is preventing the balloon's fall. Let the balloon fall to the floor, and draw on the board the path of the balloon. Next, place the balloon on your hand once more and tap the balloon so it moves off your hand horizontally and falls to the floor. Ask: "Does gravity still affect the balloon when it is in motion?" (yes) Draw the path of the balloon on the board again, using arrows to illustrate the forces acting on the balloon. **LS Visual**

Key Resources

 Teaching Transparencies
TM33 Law of Universal Gravitation
TM34 Projectile Motion
P5 Terminal Velocity
P6 Two Motions Cause Orbiting

 Visual Concepts
Law of Universal Gravitation
Equation for Newton's Universal Law of Gravitation
Gravity and Orbit
Projectile Motion
Free Fall
Comparing Mass and Weight

Science Skills Worksheet
Equations Involving a Constant

Cross-Disciplinary Worksheets
Integrating Biology—Blood Pressure in Space
Connection to Social Studies—The Great Plague and Isaac Newton
Integrating Space Science—Gravity and the Planets
Integrating Biology—How Fish Maintain Neutral Buoyancy

Teaching Key Ideas

Mass and Weight Use a pan balance to take the mass of a common object. Ask students: "Would a pan balance work the same on the moon as on earth?" (yes) "Why?" (because a pan balance measures mass) Show students that the gravitational force of the planet would act equally on the object on the pan and the counterweights used to measure the mass. Show students a spring scale to help them understand the difference between mass and weight. **LS Visual**

Answers to Integrating Space Science

Earth: 570 N
Venus: 520 N
Mars: 210 N
Neptune: 640 N

Why It Matters

Astronaut Health In the reduced gravity of space, astronauts lose bone and muscle mass, even after a very short time. These effects happen more gradually on Earth as people age. Scientists are interested in studying the effects of microgravity so they can find ways to counteract them in space and on Earth. Have interested students investigate how scientists are preventing the loss of bone mass in astronauts that travel in space. **LS Logical**

Answer to caption question

The elephant has thicker legs because it weighs much more than the flamingo, which has thin legs.

Integrating Space Science

Planets in our solar system have different masses and different diameters. Therefore, each planet has its own unique value for *g*. Find the weight of a 58 kg person on the following planets:

 Earth, where
$g = 9.8$ m/s^2

 Venus, where
$g = 8.9$ m/s^2

 Mars, where
$g = 3.7$ m/s^2

 Neptune, where
$g = 11.0$ m/s^2

Figure 2 Elephants and flamingos have quite different legs because one animal weighs much more than the other. **How has their weight affected the shape of the animals' legs?**

Weight is different from mass.

Mass and weight are easy to confuse. Although mass and weight are directly proportional to one another, they are not the same. Mass is a measure of the amount of matter in an object. Weight is the gravitational force that an object experiences because of its mass.

The weight of an object depends on the gravitational force at the location, so moving an object may change its weight. For example, a 66 kg astronaut weighs 66 kg × 9.8 m/s^2 = 650 N (about 150 lb) on Earth. On the moon's surface, where *g* is only 1.6 m/s^2, the astronaut would weigh 66 kg × 1.6 m/s^2, which equals only 110 N (about 24 lb). The astronaut's mass remains the same everywhere, but his or her weight changes as the gravitational force acting on the astronaut changes in each place.

✓ Reading Check What is the difference between weight and mass?

Weight influences shape.

Gravitational force affects the shapes of living things. On land, large animals need strong skeletons to support their mass against the force of gravity. Tall trees need rigid trunks to support their mass. **Figure 2** shows the difference between the legs of a very heavy land animal and those of a much smaller bird. The more massive elephant has a much larger skeleton to support it larger weight. In contrast, the bird has a much smaller mass and can support its weight on long, thin legs.

MISCONCEPTION ///ALERT

Mass and Weight Some students believe that the "felt weight" of an object is a property of the object, and mass is something that "presses down." Review the definition of mass with students, then discuss the concept of weight. Emphasize that weight is proportional to mass, but mass and weight are not the same. When free-fall acceleration changes, mass (the measure of matter in an object) does not change, but weight does change because weight = mass × free fall acceleration.

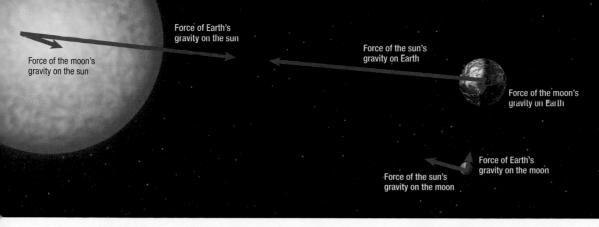

Force of the moon's gravity on the sun

Force of Earth's gravity on the sun

Force of the sun's gravity on Earth

Force of the moon's gravity on Earth

Force of Earth's gravity on the moon

Force of the sun's gravity on the moon

Teaching Key Ideas

The Law of Universal Gravitation On the *Apollo 15* mission, astronaut David Scott released a hammer and a feather on the moon at precisely the same moment. Ask students to hypothesize about what happened in the experiment based on their knowledge of free-fall acceleration. (Because there is no air resistance on the moon, the hammer and feather fell with the same acceleration and hit the moon at the same instant.)
LS Logical

Teaching Key Ideas

Falling Objects and Locomotion Students are probably well aware that dropped objects fall. But remind them that walking and running both make use of this same principle. To take a step, humans lean forward and begin to fall. Reaching out with one leg to prevent the fall allows us to move forward. Walking is just a series of prevented falls. Watching a baby learn to walk helps further illustrate this.

Real-World Connection

Armstrong on the Moon For your discussion of gravity, rent and play the video of Neil Armstrong's first step on the moon during the *Apollo 11* mission.

Math Connection

Universal Gravitation Equation The symbol *G* in the universal gravitation equation is a constant, sometimes called the *constant of universal gravitation*. Scientists have used experiments to determine the value of *G*: 6.674×10^{-11} N•m²/kg².

Law of Universal Gravitation

For thousands of years, two of the most puzzling questions were "Why do objects fall toward Earth?" and "What keeps the planets in motion in the sky?" Newton understood that these two questions have the same answer.

❯**All objects in the universe attract each other through the force of gravity.** The same force that causes objects to fall to Earth controls the motion of planets in the sky.

Newton stated his observations on gravity in a law known as the *law of universal gravitation*, given by the following equation.

Universal gravitation equation	$F = G\dfrac{m_1 m_2}{d^2}$

This equation says that gravitational force increases as one or both masses increase. It also says that gravitational force decreases as the distance between two masses increases. The symbol *G* in the equation is a constant.

All matter is affected by gravity.

Whether two objects are very large or very small, there is a gravitational force between them. When one object is very massive, as Earth is, the force is easy to detect. The force exerted by something that has a small mass, such as a paper clip, however, is not noticeable. Yet no matter how small or how large an object is, it exerts this force on every other object, as shown in the Earth-moon-sun system in **Figure 3.** The force of gravity between two masses is easier to understand if you consider it in two parts: (1) the size of the masses and (2) the distance between the masses.

Figure 3 The force of gravity acts between all objects in the universe. For example, the moon is affected by the gravity of both Earth and the sun. (The force arrows shown here are not drawn to scale.)

Integrating **Biology**

Blood Pressure Gravity plays a role in your body. Blood pressure, for example, is affected by gravity. Therefore, when you are standing, your blood pressure will be greater in the lower part of your body than in the upper part. Doctors and nurses take your blood pressure on your arm at the level of your heart to see what your blood pressure is likely to be at your heart.

Differentiated Instruction

Basic Learners

The Direction of Gravity Every force acts in a specific direction. Ask students: "What is the direction of the force of gravity?" (Many students will say: "down.") Display a globe. Point to Australia and ask what "down" means there. Continue with other places. Develop the idea that, regardless of location, the force of Earth's gravity is always toward the center of the Earth.
LS Visual

MISCONCEPTION ///ALERT\\\

Gravity Some students think of gravity as "holding," or as something "that keeps things from floating away." Students also think that gravity is not present in space. Another common misconception is that gravity stops acting on an object when an object is at rest. Ask specific questions to target these misconceptions, such as "Can gravity occur in space?" (Gravity is everywhere: Earth's gravity keeps the moon in its orbit; the sun's gravity keeps Earth in orbit.) and "Does gravity act on an object on Earth's surface?" (Yes. There are equal and opposite forces of gravity between Earth and objects at rest on it.)

Apparent Weightlessness Many students will have experienced a temporary sensation of weightlessness in an elevator or on a roller coaster. This experience is similar to what an astronaut experiences in space. As a rollercoaster car begins descending at the acceleration of gravity, there is no gravitational force holding the passengers in their seats. This causes the sensation of weightlessness. In reality, rollercoaster passengers have weight—that is why they fall rapidly toward Earth! Ask students if they know of other experiences of a sensation of weightlessness. (Riding on a swing or riding in a car over a bump can also provide the experience.)

READING TOOLBOX

Signal Words Students should make a three-column note that includes the left-hand column labeled *Cause,* the middle column labeled *Effect* and the right-hand column labeled *Markers.* As students read, have them identify the signal words that indicate a cause and effect relationship.

READING TOOLBOX

Signal Words Locate the signal words on this page that indicate a cause and effect relationship. Use a table with 3 columns to record causes, effects, and their markers.

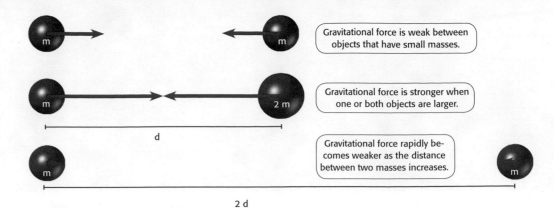

Gravitational force is weak between objects that have small masses.

Gravitational force is stronger when one or both objects are larger.

Gravitational force rapidly becomes weaker as the distance between two masses increases.

Figure 4 Arrows indicate the gravitational force between objects. The length of an arrow indicates the strength of the force.

Gravitational force increases as mass increases.

Gravity is the reason that an apple falls from a tree. When an apple's stem breaks, the apple falls down because the gravitational force between Earth and the apple is much greater than the gravitational force between the apple and the tree. The relationship between mass and gravitational force is shown in **Figure 4.**

Imagine an elephant and a cat. Because the elephant has a larger mass than the cat does, the gravitational force between the elephant and Earth is greater than the gravitational force between the cat and Earth. Thus, picking up a cat is much easier than picking up an elephant! Gravitational force also exists between the cat and the elephant, but it is very weak because the cat's mass and the elephant's mass are so much smaller than Earth's mass.

✔ **Reading Check** How does mass affect gravitational force?

Gravitational force decreases as distance increases.

Gravitational force depends on the distance between two objects. When calculating the gravitational force between two large objects, use the distance between the objects' centers. As **Figure 4** shows, if the distance between the two balls is doubled, the gravitational force between them decreases to one-fourth its original value. If the distance is tripled, the gravitational force decreases to one-ninth its original value.

Gravitational force is weaker than other types of forces because the gravitational constant, *G,* is a very small number. When the masses are very large, however, the gravitational force will be strong enough to hold the planets, stars, and galaxies together.

Differentiated Instruction

Special Education Students

Mass Judgments Gather 15 or 20 different-sized, solid-mass items, such as marbles, books, or heavy backpacks. Randomly pair the items. Select two pairs. Ask students which of the two pairs has greater gravitational force. Continue until all pairs are addressed. Then, choose two items and ask a volunteer to choose two other items that have more or less gravitational force. **LS** **Kinesthetic**

Free Fall

When Earth's gravity is the only force acting on an object, the object is said to be in **free fall.** Free-fall acceleration is directed toward the center of Earth. **❯ In the absence of air resistance, all objects falling near Earth's surface accelerate at the same rate regardless of their mass.**

Why do all objects have the same free-fall acceleration? Newton's second law states that acceleration depends on both force and mass. A heavy object has a greater gravitational force than a light object does. However, it is harder to accelerate a heavy object than a light object because the heavy object has more mass.

Free-fall acceleration is constant because of the law of universal gravitation.

Let's look again at the universal gravitation equation. The constant G does not change at any location. Near the surface of Earth, two other values are nearly constant. The distance, d, is about equal to the radius of Earth at or near the surface of Earth. The first mass, m_1, is the mass of Earth. Using these values, we can calculate the free-fall acceleration of an object.

Near the surface of Earth, the only variable in the gravity equation is m_2, the mass of the object near Earth. Thus, we can calculate the weight of an object by using Newton's gravitation equation.

Air resistance can balance weight.

Both air resistance and gravity act on objects moving through Earth's atmosphere. A falling object stops accelerating when the force of air resistance becomes equal to the gravitational force on the object (the weight of the object), as **Figure 5** shows. The reason is that the air resistance acts in the opposite direction to the weight. When air resistance and weight are equal, the object stops accelerating and reaches its maximum velocity, which is called **terminal velocity.**

When sky divers start a jump, their parachutes are closed and they are accelerated toward Earth by the force of gravity. As their velocity increases, the force that they experience increases because of air resistance. When air resistance and the force of gravity are equal, sky divers reach a terminal velocity of about 320 km/h (200 mi/h). But when they open their parachutes, the increased air resistance slows them down. Eventually, they reach a new terminal velocity of several kilometers per hour, which allows them to land safely.

free fall (FREE FAWL) the motion of a body when only the force of gravity is acting on the body

terminal velocity (TUHR muh nuhl vuh LAHS uh tee) the constant velocity of a falling object when the force of air resistance is equal in magnitude and opposite in direction to the force of gravity

Figure 5 When a sky diver reaches terminal velocity, the force of gravity is balanced by air resistance.

READING TOOLBOX

Visual Literacy Have students examine **Figure 5.** Ask: "Because the forces of air resistance and gravity are balanced, is the sky-diver at rest? Use Newton's laws to explain your answer." (According to Newton's first law, an object will maintain a state of rest or motion if an unbalanced force does not act on it. Although the forces of air resistance and gravity are balanced, the skydiver remains in motion.) **LS** **Logical/Visual**

Why It Matters

Parachutes The parachute is a great practical application of the use of air resistance to balance weight. For years, scientists have speculated that jet planes could benefit from carrying a safety parachute. If the jet engines no longer operated, the chute would deploy, and the aircraft would fall to Earth at a controlled rate. A safety parachute is currently available for small personal aircraft and has already saved lives. NASA is currently working with private companies to design a parachute for larger planes. Ask students: "What would be one difference between a parachute used for a person and a parachute used to slow the fall of a plane?" (The parachute for the plane would be much larger.) **LS** **Logical**

Differentiated Instruction

Advanced Learners

Terminal Velocity The acceleration due to gravity is the same for all objects, regardless of weight (disregarding air resistance). Ask students to explain whether terminal velocity for an object falling in air depends on the object's weight. (Yes. Terminal velocity is the point where air resistance equals weight, so if weight changes, a different amount of air resistance will be needed to balance the force of gravity. Therefore, a different terminal velocity will be achieved.) **LS** **Logical**

MISCONCEPTION ALERT

Falling Objects and Air Resistance Many students believe that heavier objects fall faster than lighter objects, and some may have trouble identifying the effects of air resistance on falling objects. Use discussion questions and the examples in this section to address this misconception.

Everyday Terms with Scientific Meanings The word *orbit* is used in many different contexts. Tell students that in astronomy, it can be used as a noun and a verb, and it also has several other related meanings. Have students write a sentence using each of the word's meanings in astronomy. Then have them use a dictionary to find out as many other meanings as possible. As an extension, have students speculate about the relationships between the various meanings that they find. **LS** Verbal

Connection to Space Science

Artificial Satellites An artificial satellite's orbit is an example of projectile motion. Divide students into groups and ask each group to prepare a presentation about artificial satellites. Instruct each group to include a visual aid with their presentation, such as a poster or a transparency page. Presentation topics could include the following: different satellite orbits, uses of satellites, early satellite experiments, details about a particular satellite, or the *International Space Station*. **LS** Visual/Verbal

go.hrw.com
✳ interact online

Students can interact with the figure by going to **go.hrw.com** and typing in the keyword **HK8FORF7**.

Figure 6 In the orbiting space shuttle, which is in free fall, astronauts experience apparent weightlessness.

Figure 7 Two motions combine to form projectile motion.

go.hrw.com
✳ interact online
Keyword: HK8FORF7

Astronauts in orbit are in free fall.

Why do astronauts appear to float inside a space shuttle? Are they "weightless" in space? You may have heard that objects are weightless in space, but this statement is not true. Very far from any galaxies or other massive objects, gravitational force is very weak. But one cannot be truly weightless anywhere in the universe.

Astronauts in orbit are actually quite near Earth and are certainly not weightless. However, astronauts in orbit experience *apparent weightlessness* because they are in free fall. The astronauts and the vehicle in which they are traveling are falling toward Earth with the same acceleration.

✓ Reading Check Why do astronauts in orbit seem weightless?

Projectile Motion

The orbit of the space shuttle around Earth is an example of *projectile motion*. **Projectile motion** is the curved path followed by an object that is thrown, launched, or otherwise projected near the surface of Earth. The motions of leaping frogs, thrown balls, and arrows shot from a bow are examples of projectile motion. **❯ Projectile motion has two components—horizontal and vertical. When the two motions are combined, they form a curved path**.

The two components of projectile motion are independent; that is, they do not affect each other. In other words, the downward acceleration due to gravity does not change a projectile's horizontal motion, and the horizontal motion does not affect the downward motion.

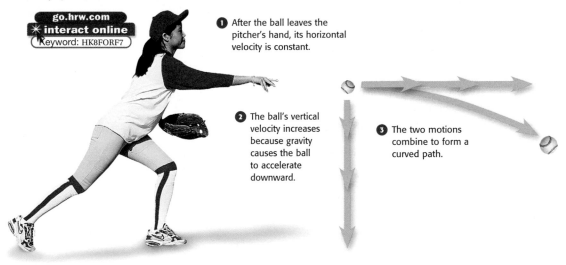

1 After the ball leaves the pitcher's hand, its horizontal velocity is constant.

2 The ball's vertical velocity increases because gravity causes the ball to accelerate downward.

3 The two motions combine to form a curved path.

Escape Velocity Escape velocity is the speed and direction that an object must travel to escape another body's gravitational attraction. If a rocket launched from Earth does not attain escape velocity, it will fall back to Earth in projectile motion or orbit Earth. Because the force of gravity is proportional to mass, the escape velocity of different planets varies. For example, Jupiter has a greater escape velocity than Earth because Jupiter has much more mass than Earth. Ask students: "Is the escape velocity from the moon greater or less than the escape velocity of Earth?" (The escape velocity from the moon is less.) "Why?" (Because the mass of the moon is less than the mass of Earth.) **LS** Logical

Struggling Readers

Modifying Words Students may be confused about the difference between "weightlessness" and "apparent weightlessness." Point out that the word *apparent* is an adjective that modifies the word *weightless*. Ask students to explain the difference between "the apparent winner" and "the winner." (The apparent winner may not have won, but seems to have won. The winner has definitely won.) Encourage students to look for modifiers. For each one they find, they should explain the impact of the modifier and write down other examples of how that modifier is used. **LS** Verbal

Projectile motion has a horizontal component.

As **Figure 7** shows, when you throw a ball, your hand and arm exert a force on the ball that makes the ball move forward. This force gives the ball its horizontal motion. Horizontal motion is motion that is perpendicular, or at a 90° angle, to Earth's gravitational force.

After you have thrown a ball, no horizontal forces are acting on the ball (if air resistance is ignored). So, the horizontal <u>component</u> of velocity of the ball is constant after the ball leaves your hand. Ignoring air resistance, when it is small, allows one to simplify projectile motion.

Projectile motion also has a vertical component.

The movement of a ball is affected not only by horizontal motion but also by vertical motion. If not affected by gravitational acceleration, the ball would continue moving in a straight line and never fall. When you throw a ball, gravity pulls it downward, which gives the ball vertical motion.

In the absence of air resistance, gravity on Earth pulls objects that are in projectile motion downward with an acceleration of 9.8 m/s², just as it pulls down all falling objects. **Figure 8** shows that the downward accelerations of a thrown object and a falling object are identical.

Because objects in projectile motion accelerate downward, you should aim above a target if you want to hit the target with a thrown or propelled object. For example, if you aim an arrow directly at a bull's-eye, the arrow will strike below the center of the target rather than the middle.

Academic Vocabulary

component (kuhm POH nuhnt) a part of something

projectile motion (proh JEK tuhl MOH shuhn) the curved path that an object follows when thrown, launched, or otherwise projected near the surface of Earth

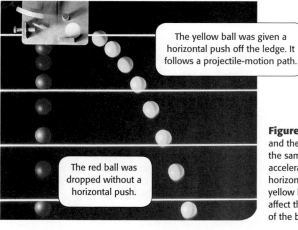

The yellow ball was given a horizontal push off the ledge. It follows a projectile-motion path.

The red ball was dropped without a horizontal push.

Figure 8 The red ball and the yellow ball have the same downward acceleration. The horizontal motion of the yellow ball does not affect the vertical motion of the ball.

Teaching Key Ideas

Projectile Motion Use Newton's thought experiment to help students understand how an orbiting space station is an example of projectile motion. Newton imagined a cannon on top of a tall mountain. When the cannon is fired, the cannonball has projectile motion, and it eventually falls to Earth. The greater the cannonball's speed, the more distance it travels before hitting the ground. Draw a few examples of this scenario on the board. Ask students to describe what would eventually happen when the cannonball's speed reached a high enough value. (Remind them that this is a thought experiment, and the scenario is hypothetical.) (Students should realize that if the cannonball's speed were great enough, it would continually "fall" around Earth. In other words, the cannonball would be in orbit around Earth. An object orbiting Earth is an example of projectile motion.)
LS Verbal

READING TOOLBOX

Concept Maps Students should make a concept map that describes projectile motion. If students are struggling with this task, prompt them with the following sentence: "Projectile motion is a curved path that results when an object's horizontal velocity is affected by gravitational attraction, which pulls the object downward."
LS Visual/Logical

Connection to Space Science

Microgravity When an object such as a satellite or a space station is in free fall around Earth, a condition of microgravity is said to exist. According to NASA, the term *microgravity* refers to "a condition of free fall within a gravitational field in which the weight of an object is reduced compared to its weight at rest on Earth." Although astronauts in microgravity are not weightless, they appear to be weightless because they are falling around Earth at the same rate as the objects around them.

Reteaching Key Ideas

Projectile Motion Have students explain how the projectile motion of a thrown baseball is similar to a satellite's motion in orbit. Students should also explain how the motions are different. Ask students why a thrown baseball does not orbit Earth. Students can use illustrations to explain their responses.
LS Logical/Visual

Formative Assessment

The planet Mercury is less massive than Earth. Your mass on Mercury would be

A. less than your mass on Earth. (Incorrect. Mass remains constant. Review the definitions of the terms *weight* and *mass*.)

B. the same as your mass on Earth. (Correct. Mass is constant. Your mass anywhere is the same. Review the material under the heading, "Weight and Mass.")

C. greater than your mass on Earth. (Incorrect. Mass is constant. Review the material under the heading, "Weight and Mass.")

D. unrelated to your mass on Earth. (Incorrect. An object's mass is the same everywhere, so the mass of any object on Earth is identical to its mass on Mercury. Review the material under the heading, "Weight and Mass.")

Orbiting is projectile motion.

An object is said to be orbiting when it is traveling in a circular or nearly circular path around another object. When a spaceship orbits Earth, it is moving forward but it is also in free fall toward Earth. **Figure 9** shows how these two motions combine to cause orbiting. Because of free fall, the moon stays in orbit around Earth, and the planets stay in orbit around the sun.

Figure 9 Forward motion and free-fall motion combine to form an orbit around Earth or another massive body.

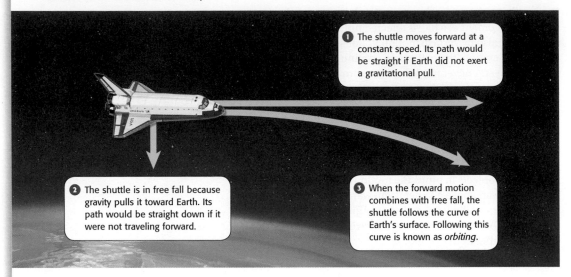

❶ The shuttle moves forward at a constant speed. Its path would be straight if Earth did not exert a gravitational pull.

❷ The shuttle is in free fall because gravity pulls it toward Earth. Its path would be straight down if it were not traveling forward.

❸ When the forward motion combines with free fall, the shuttle follows the curve of Earth's surface. Following this curve is known as *orbiting*.

Section 2 Review

KEY IDEAS

1. **Explain** why your weight would be less on the moon than on Earth even though your mass would not change.

2. **State** the law of universal gravitation, and use examples to explain how changes in mass and changes in distance affect gravitational force.

3. **Explain** why free-fall acceleration near Earth's surface is constant.

4. **Name** the two components that make up orbital motion, and explain why objects stay in orbit.

CRITICAL THINKING

5. **Making Inferences** Explain why the gravitational acceleration of any object near Earth is the same no matter what the mass of the object is.

Math *Skills*

6. The force between a planet and a spacecraft is 1 million newtons. If the spacecraft moves to half of its original distance from the center of the planet, what will the force be?

Answers to Section Review

1. The moon's mass is much smaller than Earth's mass. Since the force of gravitational attraction between two objects depends on the mass of both objects, the force of gravitational attraction between you and the moon would therefore be smaller than the force between you and Earth.

2. Sample answer: The law of universal gravitation says that the force of gravitational attraction is proportional to the attracting masses and inversely proportional to the square of the distance between the masses. If you make the mass of one or both of the attracting masses larger, then the force will be larger. (Weight on Jupiter is larger than weight on Earth because the mass of Jupiter is so much larger than the mass of Earth.)

The gravitational attraction between Earth and a satellite gets smaller as the satellite moves farther away from Earth.

3. Near Earth's surface, the distance between the object that is falling and the center of Earth does not change very much. Also, the mass of Earth is constant. Thus, the force given by the law of universal gravitation depends only on the mass of the object that is falling.

4. Orbital motion has two components—horizontal and vertical. Horizontal motion propels the object forward, and vertical free fall pulls the object downward toward the center of gravity of the larger mass.

Answers continued on p. 425A

Black Holes

A black hole is an object in space that has a huge amount of mass packed into a relatively small volume. For example, a black hole 10 times as massive as the sun would have a radius of only 30 km.

Because of its great mass, a black hole has a very strong gravitational force. In fact, this force is so powerful that it crushes any matter that falls into the black hole to the point that the matter has almost no volume. Objects that enter a black hole can never get out. Not even light can escape from a black hole.

How Black Holes Form

Scientists think that black holes form from dying stars. The death of a star is a massive explosion called a *supernova*. The remaining mass of the star contracts under its own gravity into a dense core.

Sagittarius A* is a supermassive black hole at the center of our galaxy. Scientists suspect that there is a black hole at the center of every galaxy in the universe.

This artist's conception shows a disk of material orbiting a black hole. Such disks provide indirect evidence of black holes within our own galaxy.

SCiLINKS®
www.scilinks.org
Topic: Black Holes
Code: HK80174

YOUR TURN

UNDERSTANDING CONCEPTS
1. How does mass relate to the powerful gravitational force of a black hole? (Hint: Think of Newton's law of gravitation.)

CRITICAL THINKING
2. How might scientists detect and locate black holes?

Answers to Your Turn
1. Sample Answer: Black holes are extremely massive and very dense. A black hole's mass exerts a very strong gravitational force.
2. Sample answer: Because light cannot escape a black hole, scientists cannot see them directly. However, scientists can observe the effects of black holes on other nearby objects.

Black Holes Black holes are objects that are so massive that the speed required to escape their gravitational pull is greater than the speed of light. Einstein determined that no mass can travel at or greater than the speed of light. As a result, no mass can escape the gravitational pull of a black hole. Even light cannot travel fast enough to escape a black hole!

Scientists think that there may be a supermassive black hole at the center of most galaxies. Scientists do not know how the black holes at the center of galaxies are created. However, astronomers have calculated that the size of central black holes is proportional to the total mass of stars in a galaxy. This data suggests that the growth of galaxies is closely related to the growth of black holes at their center and that super massive black holes may cause the formation of galaxies.

READING TOOLBOX

Visual Literacy Students may have trouble understanding the illustrations and captions on this page. Explain that the image of Sagittarius A* was made by a very sensitive space-borne X-ray telescope called the *Chandra Observatory*. The image shown was made during a two-week period in which Sagittarius A* produced several X-ray bursts. Because the bursts happened relatively quickly, scientists hypothesize that they occurred near the event horizon of the black hole. Have students find other images of Sagittarius A* or other objects thought to contain black holes and share them with the class. **LS Visual**

SECTION
3

Newton's Third Law

> **Focus**

In the first part of this section, students learn about Newton's third law, also called the law of action and reaction. Next, they study momentum, including problem solving with momentum and the conservation of momentum. The section concludes with a discussion of rocket propulsion and additional examples of action/reaction pairs.

 Bellringer

Use the Bellringer transparency to prepare students for this section.

Demonstrate

Magnets Use two identical horseshoe magnets and an overhead projector to demonstrate Newton's third law. Place the two magnets close together on the overhead projector, with the like poles facing one another. Release the magnets at the same moment, and have students observe their motion and final positions. The magnets should move away from one another and come to rest in a symmetrical pattern.

LS Visual

Key Ideas

> What happens when an object exerts a force on another object?

> How do you calculate the momentum of an object?

> What is the total momentum after objects collide?

Key Terms

momentum

Why It Matters

Newton's third law explains how rockets lift off the ground and maintain acceleration in space.

When you kick a soccer ball, as shown in **Figure 1,** you notice the effect of the force exerted by your foot on the ball. The ball experiences a change in motion. Is the force that moves the ball the only force present? Do you feel a force acting on your foot?

Action and Reaction Forces

The moment that you kick the ball, the ball exerts an equal and opposite force on your foot. The force exerted on the ball by your foot is called the *action force,* and the force exerted on your foot by the ball is called the *reaction force.* This pair of forces gives an example of Newton's third law of motion, also called the *law of action and reaction.*

Newton's third law	For every action force, there is an equal and opposite reaction force.

> **When one object exerts a force on a second object, the second object exerts a force equal in size and opposite in direction on the first object.**

Forces always occur in pairs.

Action and reaction forces are applied to different objects. These forces are equal and opposite. The action force acts on the ball, and the reaction force acts on the foot. Action and reaction force pairs are present even when there is no motion. For example, when you sit on a chair, your weight pushes down on the chair. The force of your weight is the action force. The chair pushing back up with a force equal to your weight is the reaction force.

Reaction force

Action force

Figure 1 According to Newton's third law, the foot and the soccer ball exert equal and opposite forces on each other.

Key Resources

Teaching Transparency
TM35 Rocket Propulsion

Visual Concepts
Newton's Third Law
Momentum
Equation for Momentum
Momentum and Collisions
Equation for Conservation of
 Momentum
Action and Reaction Forces
Acceleration and Gravity

Datasheet
Action and Reaction Forces

Science Skills Worksheets
Ordering Multiple Operations
Rearranging Algebraic Equations

Math Skills Worksheet
Momentum

Cross-Disciplinary Worksheets
Integrating Technology—Hydraulic
 Lift Force
Connection to Fine Arts—Momentum of
 Line in Art
Real World Applications—Driving Safely

The action force is the swimmer pushing the water backward.

The reaction force is the water pushing the swimmer forward.

Forces in a force pair do not act on the same object.

Newton's third law states that forces happen in pairs. In other words, every force is part of a force pair made up of an action force and a reaction force. Although the forces are equal and opposite, they do not cancel each other because they act on different objects. In the example shown in **Figure 2,** the swimmer's hands and feet exert the action force on the water. The water exerts the reaction force on the swimmer's hands and feet. Note that action and reaction forces occur at the same time. But the action and reaction forces never act on the same object.

✔ **Reading Check** Why don't the forces in a force pair cancel each other?

Equal forces don't always have equal effects.

Another example of an action-reaction force pair is shown in **Figure 3.** If you drop a ball, the force of gravity pulls the ball toward Earth. This force is the action force exerted by Earth on the ball. But the same force of gravity also pulls Earth toward the ball. That force is the reaction force exerted by the ball on Earth.

It is easy to see the effect of the action force—the ball falls to Earth. Why don't you notice the effect of the reaction force—Earth is pulled upward? Remember Newton's second law: an object's acceleration is equal to the force applied to the object divided by the object's mass. The force applied to Earth is equal to the force applied to the ball. However, Earth's mass is much larger than the ball's mass. Thus, compared with the ball's acceleration, Earth's acceleration is almost undetectable.

Figure 2 The two forces in a force pair act on different objects. In this example, the action force acts on the water, and the reaction force acts on the swimmer.

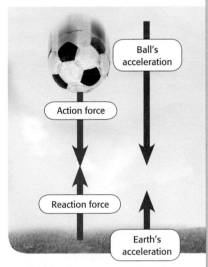

Ball's acceleration

Action force

Reaction force

Earth's acceleration

Figure 3 Earth accelerates toward the ball as the ball accelerates toward Earth. (The acceleration arrows are not drawn to scale.) **Why is Earth's acceleration so much smaller than the ball's?**

⟩Teach

Teaching Key Ideas

Newton's Third Law After students read about Newton's third law, use the classic horsecart problem as an example of this key idea. If a horse pulls a cart with a certain horizontal force, the cart exerts an equal and opposite force on the horse. Challenge students to explain how the cart accelerates. (Students should realize that the action and reaction forces are acting on different objects. So, although the forces are equal and opposite, they do not cancel.) Ask a student volunteer to draw separate force diagrams for the horse and cart to emphasize this point. (In addition to action/reaction pair, the diagrams may include the force of friction between the horse's feet and the ground, and the friction between the cart wheels and the ground. The net force on the horse and the cart should be shown to be in the forward direction.) **LS** Verbal

Answer to caption question

Earth's acceleration is smaller than the ball's acceleration because Earth has much more mass than the ball.

Differentiated Instruction

English Language Learners

Newton's Three Laws of Motion Have students work in small groups. Tell each group to choose one of Newton's three laws of motion. Have groups try to explain the laws in their own words. Then, have each group create activities or draw illustrations to demonstrate how their law works. Have each group present their ideas to the class. **LS** Interpersonal

MISCONCEPTION ///ALERT\\\

Action/Reaction Forces Do Not Cancel Emphasize that the equal but opposite forces in Newton's third law act on different objects. As A acts on B, B acts on A. Action/reaction forces never cancel out because they act on different objects. The only situation in which forces could cancel out (add up to zero) would be if they acted on the same object.

QuickLab

Teacher's Notes If students have difficulty with question 1, encourage them to list the forces acting on each object separately. For example, the forces acting on the middle spring scale are the scale's weight, the downward pull of the 2 kg mass, and the upward pull of the top spring scale.

Materials per Group
• mass, 2 kg
• spring scales (2)

Answers to Analysis

1. The reaction forces that correspond with each force are the upward force on the Earth from the mass of the spring scale, the upward force on the 2 kg mass, and the downward pull on the top spring scale.

2. Students should be able to determine that the reading on the top spring scale should be the weight of the 2 kg mass plus the weight of the other spring scale. The reading on the bottom spring scale should be the weight of the 2 kg mass. Because the bottom spring scale is pulling down on the top spring scale with a force equal to its weight plus the weight of the 2 kg mass, the top scale must exert an upward force on the bottom scale that is equal to the weight of the bottom scale plus the 2 kg mass.

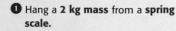

QuickLab — Action and Reaction Forces
 10 min

Procedure

❶ Hang a **2 kg mass** from a **spring scale**.

❷ Observe and record the reading on the spring scale.

❸ While keeping the mass connected to the first scale, link a **second spring scale** to the first. The first spring scale and the mass should hang from the second spring scale, as the photograph shows.

❹ Observe and record the readings on each spring scale.

Analysis

1. What are the action and reaction forces in the spring scale–mass system that you have constructed?

2. How did the readings on the two spring scales in step 4 compare? Explain how this experiment demonstrates Newton's third law.

momentum (moh MEN tuhm) a quantity defined as the product of the mass and velocity of an object

READING TOOLBOX

Two-Column Notes After reading this page and the next, take two-column notes on the key idea of momentum. Write down the key idea in the first column, and add detailed notes and examples in the second column.

Momentum

If a small car and a large truck are moving with the same velocity and the same braking force is applied to each vehicle, the truck takes more time to stop than the car does. Likewise, a fast-moving car takes more time to stop than a slow-moving car of the same mass does. The large truck and the fast-moving car have more **momentum** than the small car and the slow-moving car do. Momentum is a property of all moving objects. ❱ **For movement along a straight line, momentum is calculated by multiplying an object's mass and velocity.**

Momentum equation	$momentum = mass \times velocity$ $p = mv$

In the SI, momentum is expressed in kilograms times meters per second (kg•m/s). Like velocity, momentum has direction. An object's momentum and velocity are in the same direction.

Momentum increases as mass and velocity increase.

The momentum equation states that for a given velocity, the greater the mass of an object, the greater the momentum of the object. A tractor-trailer truck has much more momentum than a sports car moving at the same speed does. The momentum equation also states that the faster an object is moving, the greater the momentum of the object. If an object is not moving, its momentum is zero.

✓ **Reading Check** To what two quantities is momentum proportional?

READING TOOLBOX

Two-Column Notes Two-column notes can be used to learn and review details of specific concepts. On their paper, have students label the left-hand column *Key Ideas* and then write all key ideas for the concept momentum. Label the right-hand column *Supporting Details* and have students write the supporting details along with any examples that illustrate momentum.

Teaching Key Ideas

Calculating Momentum Remind students that momentum is directly proportional to mass and to velocity. This allows them to do some quick mental calculations that can help them check answers that they write down. Offer the following example: When does a car have more momentum, traveling at 30 km/hr or 90 km/hr? (90 km/hr) How much more momentum will it have at 90 km/hr? (3 times as much) **LS Logical**

Force is related to change in momentum.

To catch a baseball, you must apply a force on the ball to make the ball stop moving. When you force an object to change its motion, you force it to change its momentum. In fact, you are changing the momentum of the ball over a period of time.

As the period of time of the momentum's change becomes longer, the force needed to cause this change in momentum becomes smaller. So, if you pull your glove back while you are catching a ball, as shown in **Figure 4,** you increase the time for changing the ball's momentum. Increasing the time causes the ball to put less force on your hand. As a result, the sting to your hand is less than it would be otherwise.

Figure 4 Moving the glove back during the catch increases the time of the momentum's change. **How does this movement change the force?**

Math **Skills**

Answers to Practice

1. $p = mv$
   a. $(75\ kg)(16\ m/s) = 1{,}200\ kg{\cdot}m/s$ forward
   b. $(135\ kg)(16.2\ m/s) = 2{,}190\ kg{\cdot}m/s$ north
   c. $(5.0\ kg)(72\ m/s) = 360\ kg{\cdot}m/s$ eastward
   d. $(48.5\ kg)(0\ m/s) = 0\ kg{\cdot}m/s$
2. $v = (p/m) = (5\ kg\ m/s)/0.8\ kg = 6\ m/s$ forward

Additional Examples
An athlete with a mass of 73.0 kg runs with a constant forward velocity of 1.50 m/s. What is the athlete's momentum?
Answer: 110 kg•m/s forward (rounded to correct significant figures)
If a car with a mass of 925 kg has the same momentum as the athlete, what is the car's speed?
Answer: 0.119 m/s
LS **Logical**

Math Skills Momentum

Calculate the momentum of a 6.00 kg bowling ball moving at 10.0 m/s down the alley toward the pins.

Identify	**Given:**
List the given and unknown values.	mass, $m = 6.00\ kg$ velocity, $v = 10.0\ m/s$ **Unknown:** momentum, $p = ?\ kg \cdot m/s$ *(and direction)*
Plan	momentum = mass × velocity $p = mv$
Write the equation for momentum.	
Solve	$p = mv = 6.00\ kg \times 10.0\ m/s$ $p = 60.0\ kg \cdot m/s$ *(toward the pins)*
Insert the known values into the equation, and solve.	

www.scilinks.org
Topic: Momentum
Code: HK80988

Practice

1. Calculate the momentum of the following objects:
   a. a 75 kg speed skater moving forward at 16 m/s
   b. a 135 kg ostrich running north at 16.2 m/s
   c. a 5.0 kg baby on a train moving eastward at 72 m/s
   d. a 48.5 kg passenger seated on a train that is stopped
2. Calculate the velocity of a 0.8 kg kitten with a forward momentum of 5 kg • m/s.

For more practice, visit **go.hrw.com** and enter keyword **HK8MP.**

Practice **Hint**

❯ When a problem requires that you calculate velocity when you know momentum and mass, you can use the momentum equation.

❯ Problem 2: You may rearrange the momentum equation to isolate velocity on the left side:

$$v = \frac{p}{m}$$

Differentiated Instruction

Advanced Learners

Crumple Zones Most modern cars are designed so that, upon impact, the hood and trunk of the car will absorb the force and crumple under the passenger compartment. Just as in the baseball glove example, as the car crumples it absorbs the force over a longer period of time, perhaps reducing the effects of the impact on the passengers. Have interested students investigate the crumple zones built into cars and how they contribute to auto safety. Students can prepare a brief report or a computer presentation explaining what they have learned. **LS** **Verbal**

Teaching Key Ideas

Momentum You can use a toy called "Newton's cradle" to demonstrate the conservation of momentum. Newton's cradle—a common office toy—consists of five or seven steel balls suspended from a horizontal bar, hanging close enough together that the balls are touching when they are at rest. If a ball from one side is picked up and then released, a ball from the other side flies out, and the motion continues back and forth. If two balls are used, two balls move on the other side, and so on. Show students what happens when you pick up one, two, and three balls, and discuss how the toy demonstrates the conservation of momentum. You can also discuss the demonstration by identifying action/reaction forces. **LS Kinesthetic**

READING TOOLBOX

Visual Literacy The student text discusses rocket propulsion in terms of action and reaction forces. Ask students to use the illustration of a rocket on this page to explain how rocket propulsion is an example of the conservation of momentum. (When the rocket is at rest, the momentum of the rocket/fuel system is zero. When combustion occurs, the gases move downward. The rocket moves in the opposite direction with a velocity that keeps the total momentum zero.) **LS Visual**

Academic Vocabulary

predict (pree DIKT) to tell in advance

Conservation of Momentum

Imagine that two cars of different masses moving with different velocities collide head on. The momentum of the cars after the collision can be predicted. This prediction can be made because momentum is always conserved, or, in other words, always remains constant. Some momentum may be transferred from one car to the other, but the total momentum remains the same. This principle is known as the *law of conservation of momentum.*

Law of conservation of momentum	The total amount of momentum in an isolated system is conserved.

❯ **The total momentum of two or more objects after a collision is the same as it was before the collision.** In some cases, cars bounce off each other and move in opposite directions. If the cars stick together after a collision, they will move in the direction of the car that had the greater momentum initially.

Why It **Matters**

How Do Rockets Work?

REAL WORLD

Rockets are made in various sizes and designs, but the basic principle of each rocket is the same. The outward push of the hot gases through the nozzle is matched by an equal push in the opposite direction on the combustion chamber. This push accelerates the rocket forward.

Hydrogen

Oxygen

Combustion chamber

Gases push the rocket forward.

Conservation of Momentum
Together, the rocket and fuel form a system. The change in the fuel's momentum as it exits must be matched by an equal change in the rocket's momentum in the opposite direction. Thus, the total momentum of the system stays the same.

Newton's Third Law
The upward push on the rocket equals the downward push on the exhaust gases. These two forces form an action-reaction pair.

The rocket pushes the gases backward.

YOUR TURN

WRITING IN SCIENCE
1. Some people think that rockets work because flowing hot gases push against the atmosphere. If this were true, rockets could not travel through space. Write a paragraph to explain why.

MISCONCEPTION ALERT

Force Pairs Students sometimes have difficulty identifying the reaction force in a force pair. Use the illustration of the rocket on this page to help them see how pairs of forces interact. To emphasize that action/reaction force pairs are everywhere, remind students that *every* action force has a reaction force. This is not always obvious because in some cases, the effects of one of the forces in the pair are not easily visible, especially if the mass of one of the objects is so large that the acceleration produced by the force is not easily observable.

Answer to Your Turn

1. Answers may vary. Students should use Newton's third law to explain how rockets can accelerate in space.

Figure 5 Some of the cue ball's momentum is transferred to the billiard ball during a collision.

Momentum is conserved in collisions.

When a moving object hits a second object, some or all of the momentum of the first object is transferred to the second object. Imagine hitting a billiard ball with a cue ball such that the billiard ball starts moving, as **Figure 5** shows. During a collision with a billiard ball, the cue ball transfers some of its momentum to the billiard ball. Anytime two or more objects interact, they may exchange momentum, but the total momentum of the system always stays the same.

Newton's third law explains conservation of momentum. In a game of pool, the cue ball hits the billiard ball with a force—the action force. The equal but opposite force exerted by the billiard ball on the cue ball is the reaction force.

Section 3 Review

KEY IDEAS

1. **State** Newton's third law of motion, and give an example that shows how this law works.

2. **Describe** how momentum is calculated.

3. **Explain** what the law of conservation of momentum means, and give an example.

CRITICAL THINKING

4. **Evaluating Models** Which of the following models explains why the action and reaction forces don't cancel each other when a soccer ball is kicked?
   a. The force of the player's foot on the ball is greater than the force of the ball on the player's foot.
   b. The forces do not act on the same object.
   c. The reaction force happens after the action force.

5. **Identifying Examples** List the action and reaction forces in three force pairs. Do not use examples from the chapter.

6. **Applying Ideas** The forces exerted by Earth and a skier become an action-reaction force pair when the skier pushes the ski poles against Earth. Explain why the skier accelerates while Earth does not seem to move at all. (Hint: Think about the math equation for Newton's second law of motion for each of the forces.)

Math › Skills

7. Calculate the momentum of a 1 kg ball that is moving eastward at 12 m/s.

❯ Close

Reteaching Key Ideas

Flash Cards Have students review the Key Ideas in this section by making flash cards for each Key Idea. On the front side of each index card, students should copy the Key Idea question as it appears at the beginning of the section. Then, have students find an answer for each Key Idea question and write the answer on the back of the corresponding card. Students can use these flash cards as a study aid for the Chapter Review. **LS Intrapersonal**

Formative Assessment

The mass of a ball is 2 kg. The ball is moving at 5 m/s. What is the momentum of the ball?

A. 7 kg•m/s (Incorrect. You have added the mass and the velocity. To calculate momentum, multiply mass by velocity.)

B. 10 kg•m/s (Correct. To calculate momentum, multiply mass by velocity.)

C. 2.5 kg•m/s (Incorrect. You have divided velocity by mass. To calculate momentum, multiply mass by velocity.)

D. 3 kg•m/s (Incorrect. You have subtracted mass from velocity. To calculate momentum, multiply mass by velocity.)

Answers to Section Review

1. Newton's third law states that anytime one object applies a force to a second object, the second object applies a force on the first object that is equal in size and opposite in direction. For example, when you sit in a chair, you push down on the chair (action force), and the chair pushes up on you (reaction force).

2. Momentum is mass × velocity.

3. The law of conservation of momentum says that in any system or group of objects, the momentum will not change if a net outside force does not act on the system or group of objects.

4. b

5. Answers may vary. They can include any action-reaction force pairs, such as fingers and keyboard (on computer or piano, etc.), cheese and cheese cutter, person and floor, etc.

6. The forces exerted by Earth and a skier are an action-reaction force pair because Earth exerts an equal and opposite force on the skier as the skier had exerted on Earth. Since $F = ma$ and F is equal for both, the smaller mass of the skier (when compared to the mass of Earth) will mean the skier's acceleration away from Earth will be very much greater than Earth's unnoticeable acceleration away from the skier.

7. $p = mv = (1.0 \text{ kg})(12 \text{ m/s}) = 12 \text{ kg•m/s}$ eastward

Time Required
1 lab period

Ratings

EASY ———————————— HARD

Teacher Prep 🧪🧪

Student Set-Up 🧪🧪

Concept Level 🧪🧪🧪

Clean Up 🧪🧪

Skills Acquired
- Collecting data
- Communicating
- Designing experiments
- Experimenting
- Identifying/Recognizing patterns
- Inferring
- Interpreting
- Measuring
- Organizing and analyzing data

Scientific Methods
In this lab, students will:
- Make observations
- Form a hypothesis
- Analyze the results
- Draw conclusions
- Communicate results

Safety Cautions
Remind students to review all safety cautions and icons before beginning this lab activity. Pick up any marbles, pins, or other materials that fall on uncarpeted floors immediately. This helps prevent slips and falls. Give students plenty of space to do this lab.

Inquiry Lab

50 min

Building a Catapult

Catapults have been used for centuries to throw objects great distances. According to Newton's third law of motion (whenever one object exerts a force on a second object, the second object exerts an equal and opposite force on the first), when an object is launched, something must also happen to the catapult. In this activity, you will build a simple catapult that will allow you to observe the effects of Newton's third law of motion and the law of conservation of momentum.

Asking a Question
According to Newton's third law of motion, how will the motion of an object shot from a catapult compare with the motion of the catapult?

Building the Catapult
1. Glue the cardboard rectangles together to make a stack of three. Let the glue dry for 5–10 min.
2. Push two of the pushpins into the cardboard stack near the corners at one end, as shown below. These pushpins will be the anchors for the rubber band.
3. Make a small loop of string.
4. Put the rubber band through the loop of string, and then place the rubber band over the two pushpin anchors. The rubber band should be stretched between the two anchors with the string loop in the middle.
5. Pull the string loop toward the end of the cardboard stack opposite the end with the anchors, and fasten the loop in place with the third pushpin.

What You'll Do
> **Construct** a simple catapult.
> **Predict** how Newton's third law of motion will affect a catapult and an object shot from the catapult.

What You'll Need
cardboard rectangles,
  10 cm × 15 cm (3)
glue
marble
meterstick
pushpins (3)
rubber band
scale
scissors
straws, plastic (6)
string

Safety

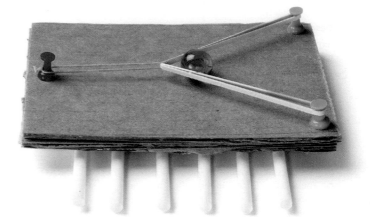

Forming and Testing a Hypothesis

6 Weigh and record the mass of the catapult and the marble. Consider the operation of the catapult in light of Newton's third law of motion, and form a hypothesis about how the motion of a marble shot from the catapult will compare with the motion of the catapult.

Designing Your Experiment

7 With your lab partner(s), decide how you will test your hypothesis.

8 In your lab report, list each step you will perform in your experiment. (Hint: Use the scissors to cut the string as well as the straws to lay your catapult on.)

Performing Your Experiment

9 Have your teacher approve your plan, and carry out your experiment.

Analysis

1. **Identifying Relationships** Which has more mass, the marble or the catapult?

2. **Describing Events** What happened to the catapult when the marble was launched?

3. **Describing Events** How far did the marble fly before it landed? Did the catapult move as far as the marble did?

Communicating Your Results

4. **Drawing Conclusions** Explain, in terms of Newton's third law of motion, why the marble and the catapult moved as they did.

5. **Explaining Events** If the forces that made the marble and the catapult move apart are equal, why didn't the marble and the catapult move apart the same distance? Suggest two contributing factors.

6. **Applying Concepts** Using the law of conservation of momentum, explain why the marble and the catapult moved in opposite directions after the launch.

Extension

How would you modify the catapult if you wanted to keep it from moving backward as far as it did, while still having it rest on straws? Using items that you can find in the classroom, design a catapult that will move backward less than the one originally designed.

Answers to Analysis

1. Answers will depend on the type of marble and the type of cardboard. It is likely that the catapult will have more mass.
2. The catapult moved backward.
3. Answers may vary, depending on the mass of the marble, the type of cardboard, and the size of the straws.

Answers to Communicating Results

4. The catapult moved backward as a result of Newton's third law. The catapult exerted a force on the marble that made it move forward. The marble exerted an equal and opposite force on the catapult, making it move backward.
5. More friction acts on the cardboard because it is in contact with the straws. Some students may also note that the marble and the cardboard have different masses. The acceleration of each is different as expressed in Newton's second law.
6. Because the initial momentum of the system is 0 kg•m/s, the catapult has to move backward with a momentum equal to that of the marble moving forward. The momenta of the catapult and marble have to be in opposite directions so they will cancel out.

Answers to Extension

Accept all reasonable designs.

Key Resources

 Virtual Investigation

 Classroom Lab Video/DVD

 Holt Lab Generator CD-ROM
Search for any lab by type, standard, difficulty level, or time. Edit any lab to fit your needs, or create your own labs. Use the Lab Materials QuickList software to customize your lab materials list.

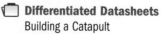 **Differentiated Datasheets**
Building a Catapult

Observation Lab
Observing the Conservation of Momentum

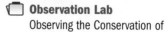 **CBL™ Probeware Lab**
Determining Your Acceleration on a Bicycle

Reteaching Key Ideas

Net Forces and Acceleration

Remind students that net acceleration describes the change in the velocity of an object as a result of unbalanced forces. There is an acceleration associated with each force in an equation. The net acceleration is the result of the cancellation of forces and results in the motion that is observed. In problems where more than one force or acceleration value is given, students must determine whether these values are in the same or opposite direction to each other. Students can then add or subtract the values accordingly. **LS** **Logical**

Answers to Practice

1. 4.5 m/s^2 to the east
2. 3.5 m/s^2 in a backward direction (deceleration)
3. $a_{net} = (F_1 - F_2)/m = (11.0 \text{ N} - 8.4 \text{ N}) / 2.2 \text{ kg} = 1.2 \text{ m/s}^2$

Rearranging Equations

Technology

Math

Scientific Methods

Graphing

Problem

A car's engine exerts a force of 1.5×10^4 N in the forward direction, while friction exerts an opposing force of 9.0×10^3 N. If the car's mass is 1.5×10^3 kg, what is the magnitude of the car's net acceleration?

Solution

Identify

List all given and unknown values.

Given:

forward force, $F_1 = 1.5 \times 10^4$ N

opposing force, $F_2 = 9.0 \times 10^3$ N

mass, $m = 1.5 \times 10^3$ kg

Unknown:

acceleration, $a = ?$ m/s^2

Diagram:

Plan

a. Use Newton's second law, and rearrange for acceleration.

b. Because the given forces act in different directions, subtract to find the net force, F.

c. Combine the two equations.

a. $F = ma$

$a = \dfrac{F}{m}$

b. $F = F_1 - F_2$

c. $a = \dfrac{F}{m} = \dfrac{F_1 - F_2}{m}$

Solve

Substitute the given values into the equation, and solve.

$a = \dfrac{F_1 - F_2}{m} = \dfrac{(1.5 \times 10^4 \text{ N}) - (9.0 \times 10^3 \text{ N})}{1.5 \times 10^3 \text{ kg}}$

$a = \dfrac{6.0 \times 10^3 \text{ N}}{1.5 \times 10^3 \text{ kg}} = \dfrac{6.0 \times 10^3 \text{ kg} \cdot \text{m/s}^2}{1.5 \times 10^3 \text{ kg}} = 4.0 \text{ m/s}^2$

Practice

1. A car has a mass of 1.50×10^3 kg. If the net force acting on the car is 6.75×10^3 N to the east, what is the car's acceleration?

2. A bicyclist slows with a force of 3.5×10^2 N. If the bicyclist and bicycle have a total mass of 1.0×10^2 kg, what is the acceleration?

3. Roberto and Laura study across from each other at a wide table. Laura pushes a 2.2 kg book toward Roberto with a force of 11.0 N straight ahead. If the force of friction opposing the movement is 8.4 N, what is the magnitude and direction of the book's acceleration?

Key Resources

 Science Skills Worksheets

Equations Involving a Constant

Ordering Multiple Operations

Rearranging Algebraic Equations

go.hrw.com
SUPER SUMMARY
KEYWORD: HK8FORS

SUMMARY

Key Ideas

Section 1 Newton's First and Second Laws

❯ **Newton's First Law** Objects change their state of motion only when a net force is applied. (p. 397)

❯ **Newton's Second Law** The unbalanced force acting on an object determines how much an object speeds up or slows down. It equals the object's mass times its acceleration, or $F = ma$. (p. 400)

Section 2 Gravity

❯ **Weight and Mass** Weight is equal to the force of gravity on an object and is proportional to an object's mass. Mathematically: $w = mg$. (p. 403)

❯ **Law of Universal Gravitation** Objects fall to the ground when dropped because all objects in the universe attract each other through the force of gravity. (p. 405)

❯ **Free Fall** In the absence of air resistance, all objects near Earth's surface accelerate at the same rate, regardless of their mass. (p. 407)

❯ **Projectile Motion** Projectile motion has two components—horizontal and vertical. When the two motions are combined, they form a curved path. (p. 408)

Section 3 Newton's Third Law

❯ **Action and Reaction Forces** When one object exerts a force on a second object, the second object exerts a force equal in size and opposite in direction on the first object. (p. 412)

❯ **Momentum** For movement along a straight line, momentum is calculated by multiplying an object's mass by its speed. (p. 414)

❯ **Conservation of Momentum** The total momentum of two or more objects after they collide is the same as it was before the collision. (p. 416)

Key Terms

inertia, p. 398

weight, p. 403
free fall, p. 407
terminal velocity, p. 407
projectile motion, p. 408

momentum, p. 414

SUPER SUMMARY

Have students connect the major concepts in this chapter through an interactive Super Summary. Visit **go.hrw.com** and type in the keyword **HK8FORS** to access the Super Summary for this chapter.

Differentiated Instruction

Alternative Assessment

Applying Newton's Laws Ask students to find examples of forces in their daily lives. Ask them to make a list of at least three examples. For each example, instruct them to write a paragraph explaining how any or all of Newton's laws can be used to analyze the forces involved. Students may wish to use force diagrams to supplement their written explanations. **LS Intrapersonal**

Key Resources

⊟ **Interactive Concept Map**

▢ **Review Resources**
Concept Review Worksheets

▢ **Assessment Resources**
Chapter Tests A and B
Performance-Based Assessment

Reading Toolbox

1. Sample answers: The bowling ball had more inertia than the table-tennis ball. An object in free fall is only affected by the force of gravity. Falling objects reach terminal velocity because air resistance eventually balances acceleration due to gravity. A thrown baseball is an example of a projectile in motion. Momentum is the product of an object's mass and its velocity.

Using Key Terms

2. Inertia is the behavior of matter that defines mass in the laws of motion. It is important because inertia resists the effects of a net force. The more mass or inertia an object has, the smaller the acceleration for a given net force.

3. The wrestler will weigh less on the moon than he does on Earth, because the *force* exerted on him will be different at these locations. Since he has the same *mass* in both places, his *weight* will depend on the acceleration due to *gravity* at each location. The moon causes a much smaller acceleration due to *gravity,* so the wrestler will weigh less there.

4. As a skydiver jumps from a plane, *gravity* pulls her downward. *Air resistance* pushes upward against the downward motion. The skydiver accelerates downward until the force of *air resistance* equals the downward force of *gravity.* Then the skydiver stops accelerating and falls downward at a constant speed. This is called *terminal velocity.*

5. The ball on the far right will undergo a *collision* with the four stationary balls. *Conservation of momentum* requires that the ball on the far left will rise to a height equal to that at which the ball on the far right started.

Understanding Key Ideas

6. c
7. d
8. a
9. b
10. b

READING TOOLBOX

1. **Key-Term Fold** Use the FoldNote that you made at the beginning of the chapter to study the key terms for this chapter. See if you know all of the definitions. When you have reviewed the terms, use each term in a sentence.

USING KEY TERMS

2. What is *inertia,* and why is it important in the laws of motion?

3. A wrestler weighs in for the first match on the moon. Will the athlete weigh more or less on the moon than he does on Earth? Explain your answer by using the terms *weight, mass, force,* and *gravity.*

4. Describe a skydiver's jump from the airplane to the ground. In your answer, use the terms *air resistance, gravity,* and *terminal velocity.*

INTERPRETING GRAPHICS The photo below shows part of a Newton's cradle. Study the photo and use it to answer question 5.

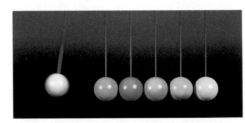

5. What will happen next? Explain by using the terms *collision* and *conservtion of momentum.*

UNDERSTANDING KEY IDEAS

6. The first law of motion applies to
   a. only objects that are moving.
   b. only objects that are not moving.
   c. all objects, whether moving or not.
   d. no object, whether moving or not.

7. Newton's first law of motion states any of the following except
   a. an object at rest remains at rest unless it experiences an unbalanced force.
   b. an object in motion maintains its velocity unless it experiences an unbalanced force.
   c. an object will tend to maintain its motion unless it experiences an unbalanced force.
   d. an object will tend to maintain its motion unless it experiences a balanced force.

8. A measure of inertia is an object's
   a. mass.   c. velocity.
   b. weight.   d. acceleration.

9. Automobile seat belts are necessary for safety because of a passenger's
   a. weight.   c. speed.
   b. inertia.   d. gravity.

10. Suppose you are pushing a car with a certain net force. If you then push with twice the net force, the car's acceleration
    a. becomes four times as much.
    b. becomes two times as much.
    c. stays the same.
    d. becomes half as much.

11. Any change in an object's velocity is caused by
    a. the object's mass.
    b. the object's direction.
    c. a balanced force.
    d. an unbalanced force.

12. An object's acceleration is never
    a. directly proportional to the net force.
    b. inversely proportional to the object's mass.
    c. in the same direction as the net force.
    d. in the opposite direction as the net force.

13. Gravitational force between two masses _____ as the masses increase and rapidly _____ as the distance between the masses increases.
    a. increases, increases
    b. decreases, decreases
    c. decreases, increases
    d. increases, decreases

EXPLAINING KEY IDEAS

14. What is the difference between free fall and weightlessness?

INTERPRETING GRAPHICS The graph below shows the velocity of a bicycle over time. Use the graph below to answer questions 15 and 16.

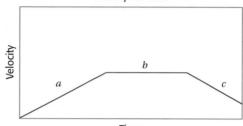

Velocity Vs. Time

15. Determine whether the acceleration is positive, negative, or zero for each segment.

16. Where is the net force on the bicycle zero?

CRITICAL THINKING

17. Applying Concepts What happens to the gravitational force between two objects if their masses do not change but the distance between them becomes four times as much?

18. Analyzing Ideas There is no gravity in outer space. Write a paragraph explaining whether this statement is true or false.

19. Making Predictions How will acceleration change if the mass being accelerated is multiplied by three but the net force is reduced to half?

20. Applying Knowledge For each pair, determine whether the objects have the same momentum. If the objects have different momentums, determine which object has more momentum.
   a. a car and train that have the same velocity
   b. a moving ball and a still bat
   c. two identical balls moving at the same speed in opposite directions

Assignment Guide	
SECTION	**ITEMS**
1	2, 6, 7, 8, 9, 10, 11, 12, 13, 15, 17, 19, 21, 24
2	3, 4, 14, 18, 22
3	1, 5, 16, 20, 23

Math Skills

21. Newton's Second Law A student tests the second law of motion by accelerating a block of ice at a rate of 3.5 m/s². If the ice has a mass of 12.5 kg, what force must the student apply to the ice?

22. Weight A bag of sugar has a mass of 2.26 kg. What is its weight in newtons on the moon, where the acceleration due to gravity is one-sixth of that on Earth? (Hint: On Earth, $g = 9.8$ m/s².)

23. Momentum Calculate the momentum of the following objects:
   a. a 65 kg skateboarder moving forward at the rate of 3 m/s
   b. a 20 kg toddler in a car traveling west at the rate of 22 m/s
   c. a 16 kg penguin at rest

Graphing Skills

24. Line Graphs An experiment is done using a lab cart. Varying forces are applied to the cart and measured while the cart is accelerating. Each force is applied in the same direction as the movement of the cart. The following data are obtained from the experiment.

Trial	Acceleration (m/s²)	Applied force (N)
1	0.70	0.35
2	1.70	0.85
3	2.70	1.35
4	3.70	1.85
5	4.70	2.35

   a. Graph the data in the table. Place acceleration on the x-axis and applied force on the y-axis.
   b. Recall that $F = ma$. What does the line on the graph represent?
   c. Use your graph to determine the mass of the lab cart.

Graphing Skills

24. a. Sample graph:

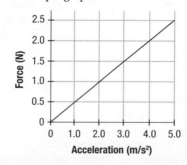

   b. The slope of the line represents mass.
   c. From $F = ma$, and using numbers from the table, we learn that mass = 0.50 kg.

Explaining Key Ideas

14. Free fall literally means falling freely. Falling straight down is free fall. An object in orbit falls freely toward Earth but is also propelled forward. The combination of those two motions is what keeps the object in orbit. Because we experience our weight by pressing against Earth or an object supported by Earth, when we fall freely, we don't feel our weight. We feel "weightless." However, weightless actually means that there is no force of gravity acting. (Weight is the force of gravity acting on an object.) So there's no such thing as actual weightlessness. Weight of objects that are very far from any other objects is very small, but it is not zero.

15. segment *a*: positive acceleration; segment *b*: zero acceleration; segment *c*: negative acceleration

16. The net force is zero in segment *b* because the acceleration is zero there.

Critical Thinking

17. The gravitational force between the two objects would become 1/16 as much.

18. The student should explain that the statement is false. Even in space, objects exert gravitational force on each other.

19. The acceleration will be 1/6 what it was.

20. a. train
   b. ball
   c. equal

Math Skills

21. $F = ma = 12.5$ kg $\times$ 3.5 m/s² = 44 N

22. $w = mg/6 = (2.26$ kg $\times$ 9.8 m/s²)/6 = 3.7 N

23. $p = mv$
   (65 kg)(3.0 m/s forward) = 195 kg•m/s forward
   (20.0 kg)(22 m/s west) = 440 kg•m/s west
   (16 kg)(0 m/s) = 0 kg•m/s

 **TEST DOCTOR**

Question 1 Answer C is correct. Students might answer A if they thought the bills experienced more static friction due to their greater area, B if they thought that heavier objects fell faster than light ones, or D if they thought the Earth exerted a magnetic pull on metal coins.

Question 2 Answer G is correct. Remind students who answer this question incorrectly that an object's mass never changes, but an object's weight is dependent on the mass of the planet or satellite the object is on.

Question 3 Answer A is correct. Objects only travel at a constant velocity if no net force is acting on them. Students might answer B if they thought that net force was equal to velocity divided by mass, C if they thought that net force was equal to mass divided by velocity, or D if they thought that net force was mass times velocity and they also counted the wrong number of zeros.

Question 4 Answer H is correct. Students who select other answers should review the definition of terminal velocity.

Question 5 Full-credit answers should include the following points:
• The forward motion of the moon combines with the downward pull of gravity.
• The resulting path forms an orbit around Earth.
Students struggling with this idea should review the section on orbits and projectiles in motion.

Question 6 3,600 N. The answer is arrived at by first finding the average acceleration, by dividing the difference in velocities by the amount of time. 60 m/s $\div$ 5 = 12 m/s^2. That acceleration is then multiplied by the mass to find the net force. 12 m/s^2 × 300 kg = 3,600 kg•m/s^2 = 3,600 N. Students struggling with this question may have simply found the acceleration and neglected to multiply by the mass. Remind students it takes two calculations to find this answer.

Understanding Concepts

Directions (1–4): **For each question, write on a sheet of paper the letter of the correct answer.**

1. After a bank customer cashes a check, some of the money received accidentally slips from the customer's hands. What force causes the bills to hit the ground later than the coins do?
   A. static friction
   B. gravity
   C. air resistance
   D. magnetism

2. If the nickel and iron at the Earth's core were suddenly replaced with cotton candy, what would happen to the mass and weight of the objects on the Earth's surface?
   F. Their mass and weight both increase.
   G. Their mass would stay the same and their weight would decrease.
   H. Their mass would decrease and their weight would increase.
   I. Neither their mass nor weight change.

3. A truck with a mass of 2,000 kg is traveling at a constant velocity of 40 m/s. What is the net force acting upon the truck?
   A. 0.0 N
   B. 0.02 N
   C. 50 N
   D. 800 N

4. A high-altitude balloonist at an altitude of 15,000 m drops an instrument package. When does the package reach terminal velocity?
   F. as it begins to fall
   G. as it matches the speed of the plane
   H. as it stops accelerating from air resistance
   I. as it impacts the Earth's surface

Directions (5–6): **For each question, write a short response.**

5. Explain why the moon does not fly off into space in a straight line nor plummet directly toward the Earth's surface.

6. A racing motorcycle with a mass of 300 kg accelerates from 0 to 60 m/s in 5 seconds. How much force is acting on the motorcycle?

Reading Skills

Directions (7–8): **Read the passage below. Then, answer the questions that follow.**

A REGULAR VISITOR

A microgravity environment is one in which the apparent weight of an object is much less than its weight on Earth. The term *microgravity* is used instead of weightlessness because every object has some weight, though that weight may be so minuscule as to be undetectable. Because every object in the universe exerts a gravitational pull on every other object, every object possesses weight.

Microgravity occurs whenever an object is in free fall. Scientists achieve microgravity environments in a number of ways. Drop towers and research aircraft provide it for up to 20 s. The Shuttle and the International Space Station can provide it for months.

A rocket ship that is accelerating by firing its rockets cannot provide microgravity. Even if the rocket is accelerating uniformly, force is applied to the rocket by the gas escaping out the back. This force must be transferred to each part of the ship through either pressure or tension, and thus weightlessness is not experienced.

7. When the Shuttle is orbiting, it is in constant motion around the Earth. Why isn't this motion experienced as weight?
   A. There is no net force acting on the Shuttle.
   B. The Shuttle's mass is not large enough to exert a measurable gravitational pull.
   C. The Earth is exerting the same pull on both the Shuttle and its passengers.
   D. The Earth is too far away to have a measurable gravitational effect.

8. Why can the Shuttle provide microgravity only after it achieves orbit?

Question 7 Answer A is correct. Students might answer B if they thought the experience of weight could only arise from the mass of the orbiting vehicles, C if they thought that weight was transferred through the vehicles, or D if they misunderstood the distance at which Earth's gravity becomes negligible.

Question 8 Full-credit answers should include the following points:
• Prior to achieving orbit, the Shuttle is accelerating.
• Acceleration is causing a net force.
• Net force is transferred through the Shuttle to the objects within it.

Question 9 Answer C is correct. The answer is found by multiplying the mass of each object by its velocity at 1 second.
Bicycle: 12 kg × 5 m/s = 60 kg•m/s
Falling rock: 2 kg × 20 m/s = 40 kg•m/s
Bowling ball: 6 kg × 10 m/s = 60 kg•m/s
Students struggling with this question should review the formula for determining momentum.

Question 10 Answer H is correct. Because the other two objects are each moving at a constant velocity at 3 seconds, the bowling ball is the only object with net force acting on it. Students struggling with this question may benefit from reviewing the concept of net force.

Interpreting Graphics

The following graph charts the speeds of three objects in motion. Use this graph to answer questions 9 and 10.

SPEED VS. TIME FOR FALLING OBJECTS

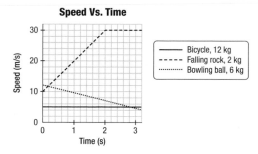

Speed Vs. Time

9. At the 1 s mark, which objects have equal momentum?
   A. the bicycle and the rock
   B. the rock and the bowling ball
   C. the bowling ball and the bicycle
   D. All three objects have the same momentum.

10. At the 3 s mark, which object or objects have a net force acting on them?
    F. the bicycle   **H.** the bowling ball
    G. the rock   **I.** the bicycle and the bowling ball

The following graphic shows a long jumper making a jump from west to east. Use this graphic to answer questions 11 and 12.

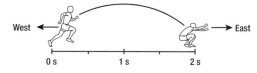

11. In what direction or directions is the net force acting on the jumper between 0.5 s and 2 s?
    A. first up and to the east, then down and to the west
    B. first up and to the east, then down and to the east
    C. up and to the east
    D. down and to the west

12. When the long jumper jumps, Earth exerts a force that moves him up and to the east. Since there is a reaction force exerted on Earth, why doesn't Earth move the same distance down and to the west?

Question 11 Answer D is correct. After the initial push off the ground, the only forces acting on the jumper are gravity (down) and air resistance (west). Students struggling with this question should diagram the forces involved, and notice that gravity and air resistance are the forces acting after the jumper leaves the ground.

Question 12 Full-credit answers should include the following points:
- The acceleration of an object equals the force that acts upon it, divided by the mass.
- The mass of the Earth is so great that the opposite force to that which accelerates the jumper up into the air has an extremely small effect on the Earth.

Answers

1. C
2. G
3. A
4. H
5. Answers may vary; see Test Doctor for a detailed scoring rubric.
6. 3,600 N
7. A
8. Answers may vary; see Test Doctor for a detailed scoring rubric.
9. C
10. H
11. D
12. Answers may vary; see Test Doctor for a detailed scoring rubric.

Test Tip

Pay attention to your time limit. If you begin to run short on time, quickly read the remaining questions and answer those that are the easiest for you.

State Resources

For specific resources for your state, visit **go.hrw.com** and type in the keyword **HSHSTR**.

📖 **Test Practice with Guided Reading Development**

Continuation of Answers

Answers continued from p. 410

5. Answers may vary, but they should state something similar to the following: Newton's second law shows that acceleration depends on both force and mass. A heavier object experiences a greater gravitational force than a lighter object (as you can see from the law of universal gravitation). But a heavier object is also harder to accelerate because it has more mass. The extra mass of the heavy object exactly compensates for the additional gravitational force. Since $F = ma$ (or $a = F/m$), if F is increased at the same rate as m, then a remains the same.

6. The force of gravity is inversely proportional to the square of distance. Since the distance is made twice as close, the force of gravity will be four times as great (the square of 2), or 4 million N.

Why It Matters

Lighting Designer This career requires a combination of technical scientific knowledge and creativity. Lighting designers must be both innovative and practical, and they need excellent communication skills. In theater and film productions, lighting designers may work closely with directors to create a specific mood for each scene or environment. Many lighting designers also handle the technical aspects of setting up and running the lights.

Careers Using Physics

When you think of a physicist, you might think of a scientist who studies subatomic particles or neutron stars. Actually, there are hundreds of careers in which people use physics. Whether designing buildings, engineering movie stunts, or lighting up a rock show, people use physics to get the job done. The careers discussed here are just a few examples of careers that use physics.

Lighting Designer

Lighting designers apply their knowledge of light and optics to light up architectural displays, movie sets, theater productions, and concerts. Lights such as lasers, strobes, and high-intensity projectors are used at concerts. Lighting designers also filter white light sources and combine the resulting colors of light to match a particular song. The movement of the filters and the lights is controlled precisely by motors. Because timing is essential, computers are used to control the light changes. The next time you see a light display or concert, think of how physics helped light up the show!

Architect

To design buildings, architects must understand many aspects of physical science. For example, architects must know how to calculate the weight and stress that a building's walls can bear. To make such calculations, architects often use computer-modeling programs that incorporate data about the weight and strength of various materials. Architects must understand the physics of heat transfer to be able to design houses that are comfortable to live in. For example, architects use the thickness and thermal conductivity of a building material to calculate the material's thermal resistance.

Fab Technician

Have you ever thought about all of the steps that are needed to make a computer chip? Manufacturing computer chips requires knowledge of physics and a high degree of precision. Building a computer chip is similar to printing a series of extremely detailed photographs on a silicon wafer. Fab technicians need to know how to use specialized equipment to create the circuit patterns on the chips, to measure the tiny dimensions of the pattern, and to test the circuits to make sure that they work properly.

Robotics Engineer

The introduction of the first commercially successful housecleaning robot in 2002 demonstrated that robots are becoming parts of our lives. Robotics engineers work in a wide variety of fields. They may invent assistive devices for the disabled or develop rovers to explore the surface of Mars. Robotics engineers must design reliable, efficient machines that accomplish specific tasks. Knowledge of the mechanics of movement and of electrical circuits, motors, and simple machines are essential to designing robots that can move, sense, and respond to their environment.

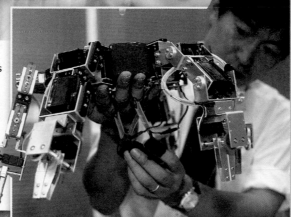

READING TOOLBOX

Visual Literacy The robot shown here is a rescue robot. A sensor that is attached to one of the limbs allows the robot to probe disaster areas in search of trapped people. Researchers around the world are working to develop rescue robots that rely on a variety of technologies, including microphones, cameras, and thermal cameras. The hope is that these robots can someday be used to search disaster sites that are too dangerous for rescue workers and search dogs.

Windsmith

Wind turbines are as tall as a football field is long, and their blades can be larger than the wings of a 747 jet. Wind turbines are the fastest growing source of renewable energy in the world, and each one requires regular maintenance. Windsmiths are people who operate and maintain the wind turbines on a wind farm. Wind turbines convert the work done by moving air into electrical energy, and in some places, they spin almost continuously throughout the year. Therefore, a wind turbine's moving parts can wear quickly. To ensure that wind turbines are operating at peak efficiency, windsmiths use knowledge of physical science to maintain the mechanical, electrical, and hydraulic systems that enable wind turbines to produce electricity.

Why It Matters

Video Game Programmer Today's complex video games are often developed by a variety of programmers with different specialties. Programmers may specialize in areas such as physics simulation, artificial intelligence, three-dimensional graphics, sound, or game play. Many programming jobs request a bachelor's degree in mathematics, physics, or computer science. Programmers often learn many of their skills on the job.

Video Game Programmer

Imagine that your job was to crash cars, blow things up, and help people dive off the tops of buildings—in the virtual world of video games! Increasingly, video games are programmed using the principles of Newtonian physics. To simulate the behavior of objects in the natural world, programmers must calculate inertia, friction, velocity, and wind resistance. Integrating principles of physical science into video games makes virtual car races and flight simulators more realistic. Physics is so important to video games that dedicated physics processing chips, which perform millions of calculations per second, are built into video game consoles.

YOUR TURN

UNDERSTANDING CONCEPTS
1. Describe how understanding physics plays an important role in two of the careers described on these pages.

CRITICAL THINKING
2. Why would an architect calculate a material's thermal resistivity?

SCLINKS

www.scilinks.org
Topic: Careers in Physics
Code: HK81246

Answers to Your Turn

1. Sample answer: An architect must have thorough knowledge of the principles of force and materials so that the structures that are designed will be as stable as possible. A video game designer must understand the dynamics of moving objects so that the action simulated in game play will be as realistic as possible.

2. When designing a house, architects must know the thermal resistivity of materials used in the house to be sure that the house is adequately insulated. As a result, the temperature inside the house can be controlled without excessive heating or air conditioning, which would waste resources and be expensive to maintain.

		Standards	Teach Key Ideas
CHAPTER OPENER, pp. 428–430	50 min.		

SECTION 1 Work, Power, and Machines, pp. 431–437 *(50 min.)*
> What Is Work?
> Power
> Machines and Mechanical Advantage

UCP 1, UCP 2, UCP 3, SAI 2

- Bellringer Transparency
- Visual Concepts Work • Power • Equation for Mechanical Advantage

SECTION 2 Simple Machines, pp. 438–443 *(50 min.)*
> What Are Simple Machines?
> The Lever Family
> The Inclined Plane Family
> Compound Machines

UCP 1, UCP 2, UCP 3

- Bellringer Transparency
- Teaching Transparencies P7 Levers • P8 Pulleys
- Visual Concepts Overview of Simple Machines • Lever • Pulley • Wheel and Axle • Inclined Plane • Wedge • Screws • Compound Machine

SECTION 3 What Is Energy? pp. 444–452 *(50 min.)*
> Energy and Work
> Potential Energy
> Kinetic Energy
> Other Forms of Energy

PS 1c, PS 3b, PS 5a, PS 5b, PS 6a, UCP 1, UCP 2, UCP 3, SAI 2

- Bellringer Transparency
- Teaching Transparency Pg Kinetic Energy Graph
- Visual Concepts Types of Energy • Potential Energy • Kinetic Energy

SECTION 4 Conservation of Energy, pp. 453–461 *(50 min.)*
> Energy Transformations
> The Law of Conservation of Energy
> Efficiency of Machines

PS 5a, PS 5b, UCP 1, UCP 2, UCP 3, SAI 1, ST 2, SPSP 3

- Bellringer Transparency
- Teaching Transparency Ph Energy Graphs
- Visual Concepts Conservation of Mechanical Energy • Mechanical Efficiency • Laws of Conservation of Energy

See also PowerPoint® Resources

Chapter Review and Assessment Resources

SE Science Skills: Making Measurements and Observations, p. 464
SE Chapter Summary, p. 465
SE Chapter Review, pp. 466–467
SE Standardized Test Prep, pp. 468–469
☐ Concept Review Worksheets ■
☐ Chapter Tests A and B ■
Holt Online Assessment

CHAPTER
Fast Track   *To shorten instruction because of time limitations, omit Section 2 and the chapter lab.*

Basic Learners
TE Everyday Levers, p. 439
TE Acrostic, p. 442
TE Algebra and Kinetic Energy, p. 448
TE Types of Energy, p. 456
TE Efficiency Equation, p. 459
☐ Science Skills Worksheets
☐ Differentiated Datasheets A for Labs and Activities ■
☐ Study Guide A ■

Advanced Learners
TE Simple Machines, p. 442
TE Potential and Kinetic Changes, p. 447
TE Accounting for Energy, p. 456
TE Perpetual Motion Machines, p. 460
☐ Cross-Disciplinary Worksheets
☐ Differentiated Datasheets C for Labs and Activities ■

Key

SE Student Edition
TE Teacher's Edition

📁 Chapter Resource File
📓 Workbook
📠 Transparency

💿 CD or CD-ROM
* Datasheet or blackline master available

■ Also available in Spanish

All resources listed below are also available on the Teacher's One-Stop Planner.

Why It Matters	Hands-On	Skills Development	Assessment
Build student motivation with resources about high-interest applications.	**SE** Inquiry Lab Kitchen Tools, p. 429* ■	**TE** Reading Toolbox Assessing Prior Knowledge, p. 428 **SE** Reading Toolbox p. 430	📁 Pretest ■
TE Electric Power, p. 434 **SE** What Machines Are Used on Bicycles? p. 435 📁 Cross-Disciplinary Worksheet Integrating Biology—Muscles and Work	**TE** Demonstration Work and Machines, p. 431 **TE** Demonstration Measuring the Force of Gravity, p. 432 **SE** Quick Lab Power Output, p. 433* ■	**SE** Math Skills Work, p. 432 **TE** Reading Toolbox Word Problems, p. 432 **SE** Math Skills Power, p. 434 **TE** Reading Toolbox Visual Literacy, p. 435 **SE** Math Skills Mechanical Advantage, p. 436	**TE** Reteaching Key Ideas Writing Questions, p. 437 **TE** Formative Assessment, p. 437 📁 Spanish Assessment* ■ 📁 Section Quiz ■
TE Are All Machines Simple? p. 440 **TE** Wheelchair Ramps, p. 441 📁 Cross-Disciplinary Worksheet Social Studies Connection—The Pyramids	**TE** Demonstration Pulleys, p. 438 **SE** Quick Lab A Simple Inclined Plane, p. 441* ■	**SE** Reading Toolbox Concept Map, p. 439 **TE** Reading Toolbox Visual Literacy, p. 440	**TE** Reteaching Key Ideas Flash Cards, p. 443 **TE** Formative Assessment, p. 443 📁 Spanish Assessment* ■ 📁 Section Quiz ■
TE Potential Energy in Food, p. 446 **TE** Energy Equivalence, p. 450 **TE** Energy Pyramids, p. 451 **SE** Energy Stored in Plants, p. 451 📁 Cross-Disciplinary Worksheets Connection to Language Arts—The Concept of Energy • Real World Applications—Calories and Nutrition • Integrating Chemistry—Chemical Reactions	**TE** Demonstration What Is Energy? p. 444 📁 Observation Lab Exploring Work and Energy	**SE** Math Skills Potential Energy, p. 446 **SE** Math Skills Kinetic Energy, p. 448 **SE** Reading Toolbox Mathematical Language, p. 447 **TE** Science Skills Kinetic Energy, p. 448 **SE** Reading Toolbox Approximations in Science, p. 449	**TE** Reteaching Key Ideas Key Idea Teams, p. 451 **TE** Formative Assessment, p. 451 📁 Spanish Assessment* ■ 📁 Section Quiz ■
TE The First Rollercoasters, p. 454 **SE** How Do Engineers Use Conservation of Energy? p. 458 **TE** Increasing Efficiency, p. 460 📁 Cross-Disciplinary Worksheets Integrating Environmental Science—Understanding the Conservation of Energy • Integrating Technology—Batteries and Emerging Technology	**TE** Demonstration Storing Energy, p. 453 **SE** Quick Lab Energy Transfer, p. 454* ■ **SE** Inquiry Lab Is Energy Conserved by a Pendulum? p. 457* ■ **SE** Skills Practice Lab Energy of a Rolling Ball, pp. 462–463* ■	**TE** Reading Toolbox Visual Literacy, p. 454 **SE** Graphing Skills Graphing Mechanical Energy, p. 455 **TE** Reading Toolbox Visual Literacy, p. 455 **SE** Math Skills Efficiency, p. 460	**TE** Reteaching Key Ideas Five Points, p. 461 **TE** Formative Assessment, p. 461 📁 Spanish Assessment* ■ 📁 Section Quiz ■

See also Lab Generator

See also Holt Online Assessment Resources

Resources for Differentiated Instruction

English Learners
TE Pictorial Representations, p. 440
📁 Differentiated Datasheets A, B, and C for Labs and Activities ■
📓 Study Guide A ■

Struggling Readers
TE Create a Table, p. 449
📓 Interactive Reader

Special Education Students
TE Note Cards, p. 448

Alternative Assessment
TE Research, p. 433
TE Law of Conservation, p. 434
TE Pulley System, p. 440
TE Open and Closed Systems, p. 457

Overview

This chapter covers work, power, and the mechanical advantage of machines. This chapter then explores the six simple machines and relates work to energy, and distinguishes between different forms of energy. Finally, energy transformations, the conservation of energy, and the efficiency of machines are covered.

READING TOOLBOX

Assessing Prior Knowledge Students should understand the following concepts:

• speed
• velocity
• forces
• gravity
• mass versus weight

MISCONCEPTION ///ALERT\\\

Science education research has identified the following misconceptions about work and energy.

• Students often use force and work interchangeably. (Work is force multiplied by distance. Energy is the capacity to do work.)

• Some students think energy is only associated with inanimate objects, or only with humans, or that it is a fluid, ingredient, or fuel. (Energy is the ability to change or move matter. Because people and inanimate objects are made of matter, people and objects can both be moved or changed, and so both can have energy or be affected by energy.)

• The idea of energy conservation is counter-intuitive to many students. (Energy does not appear out of nowhere, and doesn't disappear. All the energy in a system can be accounted for.)

CHAPTER 13 Work and Energy

Chapter Outline

❶ Work, Power, and Machines
What Is Work?
Power
Machines and Mechanical Advantage

❷ Simple Machines
What Are Simple Machines?
The Lever Family
The Inclined Plane Family
Compound Machines

❸ What Is Energy?
Energy and Work
Potential Energy
Kinetic Energy
Other Forms of Energy

❹ Conservation of Energy
Energy Transformations
The Law of Conservation of Energy
Efficiency of Machines

Why It **Matters**

This whimsical sculpture created by artist George Rhoads is called an *audiokinetic sculpture*. Kinetic, potential, and sonic energy are in constant interplay in this piece of art.

Chapter Correlations *National Science Education Standards*

The following correlations show the National Science Standards that relate to this chapter. For the full text of the standards, see the National Science Education Standards at the front of the book.

PS 1c Nuclear reactions convert a fraction of the mass of interacting particles into energy, and they can release much greater amounts of energy than atomic interactions. Fission is the splitting of a large nucleus into smaller pieces. Fusion is the joining of two nuclei at extremely high temperature and pressure, and is the process responsible for the energy of the sun and other stars. (Section 3)

PS 3b Chemical reactions may release or consume energy. Light can initiate many chemical reactions such as photosynthesis. (Section 3)

PS 5a The total energy of the universe is constant. Energy can be transferred by collisions in chemical and nuclear reactions, by light waves and other radiations, and in many other ways. However, it can never be destroyed. (Sections 3, 4)

PS 5b All energy can be considered to be either kinetic energy, which is the energy of motion; potential energy, which depends on relative position; or energy contained by a field, such as electromagnetic waves. (Sections 3, 4; Skills Practice Lab: Energy of a Rolling Ball)

PS 6a Waves, including sound and seismic waves, waves on water, and light waves, have energy and can transfer energy when they interact with matter. (Section 3)

UCP 1 Systems, order, and organization (Sections 1–4)

UCP 2 Evidence, models, and explanation (Sections 1–4)

UCP 3 Constancy, change, and measurement (Sections 1–4)

SAI 1 Abilities necessary to do scientific inquiry (Section 4, Skills Practice Lab: Energy of a Rolling Ball)

SAI 2 Understandings about scientific inquiry (Sections 1, 3)

ST 2 Understandings about science and technology (Section 4)

SPSP 3 Natural resources (Section 4)

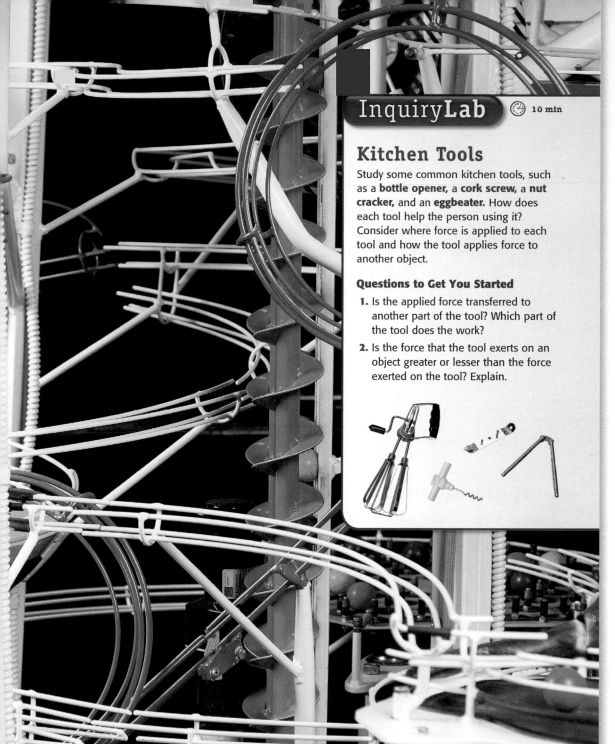

InquiryLab ⏱ 10 min

Kitchen Tools

Study some common kitchen tools, such as a **bottle opener,** a **cork screw,** a **nut cracker,** and an **eggbeater.** How does each tool help the person using it? Consider where force is applied to each tool and how the tool applies force to another object.

Questions to Get You Started

1. Is the applied force transferred to another part of the tool? Which part of the tool does the work?

2. Is the force that the tool exerts on an object greater or lesser than the force exerted on the tool? Explain.

InquiryLab

Teacher's Notes Materials that can be substituted for the ones listed include a crowbar, a drill bit, a pair of pliers, and a hand drill.

Materials per Group
• bottle opener
• cork screw
• nutcracker
• eggbeater

Answers

1. Answers may vary depending on the tools chosen for the lab, but in all simple machines, the applied force is transferred to another part of the tool.

2. Answers may vary depending on the tools chosen for the lab, but in these simple machines, the output force is greater than the input force.

Key Resources

📁 **Datasheet**
Kitchen Tools

💿 **Interactive Tutor**
Disc Two, Module 10: Work

Science Terms

Answers may vary. Power is the rate at which work is done. The term *efficiency* is commonly used to mean to do something without much wasted effort. To scientists, efficiency is a quantity usually expressed as a percentage that measures the ratio of useful work output to work input.

Word Problems

Student charts may vary slightly, but should reflect the following: The value of *F* is 5,200 N. The distance is told in the phrase, "lift a girder 25 meters." The variable representing work in the equation is "*W*."

Graphic Organizers

Answers may vary. The concept map may be read as a long sentence, such as, "Simple machines are divided into the lever family, which includes levers, pulleys and a wheel and axle, and inclined planes, which includes wedges, ramps, and the outer edge of a screw."

READING TOOLBOX

These reading tools can help you learn the material in this chapter. For more information on how to use these and other tools, see **Appendix A.**

Science Terms

Everyday Words Used in Science

Many words used in science are familiar from everyday speech. However, when these words are used in science, their meanings are often different from or more precise than the everyday meanings. Pay special attention to the definitions of such words so that you use the words correctly in scientific contexts.

Your Turn As you read this chapter, complete a table like the one below.

WORD	EVERYDAY MEANING	SCIENTIFIC MEANING
work	a job; to do labor	the transfer of energy to a body when a force causes the body to move
power	physical strength	
efficiency		

Word Problems

Mathematical Language Word problems describe science or math problems in words. To solve a word problem, you need to translate the language of words to the language of equations, mathematical symbols, variables, and numbers.

Your Turn Complete a table like the one below for the following word problem.

A crane uses an average force of 5,200 N to lift a girder 25 m. How much work does the crane do on the girder?

PHRASE	VARIABLE	VALUE
uses an average force of 5,200 N	force, *F*	
	distance, *d*	25 m
How much work		unknown

Graphic Organizers

Concept Maps A concept map is a diagram that helps you see relationships between the key ideas and categories of a topic. To construct a concept map, do the following:

1. Select a main concept for the map.
2. List all of the other related concepts.
3. Build the map by arranging the concepts according to their importance under the main concept. Add linking words to give meaning to the arrangement of concepts.

Your Turn Make a concept map for Section 2 using this as a start.

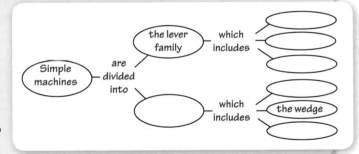

430   CHAPTER 13 Work and Energy

1 Work, Power, and Machines

Key Ideas

❯ How is work calculated?

❯ What is the relationship between work and power?

❯ How do machines make work easier?

Key Terms

work

power

mechanical advantage

Why It Matters

We use many types of simple machines to repair other machines, such as bikes and cars.

SECTION 1

❯Focus

This section introduces work and the specific conditions in which work is done. Power, the rate at which work is done, is also discussed. The section concludes with a discussion of the mechanical advantage of various simple machines.

Bellringer

Use the Bellringer transparency to prepare students for this section.

Demonstrate

Work and Machines Show students the bottom of a clean, empty steel can (such as a can used for coffee or vegetables). Ask students: "Without machines, what would I need to do to put a hole in the bottom of this can?" (Students will probably say that making the hole would take a lot of work.) Next, take out a can opener (the kind that is a lever) and gently make a hole in the bottom of the can. Ask students: "Why can I easily make a hole in the can with a can opener?" (Answers may vary.) Tell students that the can opener helps because it is a machine—a lever—that that multiplies the force put into it. Explain that this section explores what work is, and how we use machines to make work easier.

LS Verbal

Answer to caption question

No, work is zero when an object is stationary.

If you needed to change a flat tire, you would use a car jack to lift the car. Machines—from complex ones such as cars to relatively simple ones such as car jacks, hammers, and ramps—help people to get things done every day.

What Is Work?

Imagine trying to lift the front of a car without using a jack. You could exert a lot of force without moving the car at all. Exerting all that force may seem like hard work. In science, however, the word *work* has a very specific meaning.

Work is done only when force is applied to an object and the object moves in the same direction as the applied force. ❯ **Work is calculated by multiplying the force by the distance over which the force is applied.** The force used to calculate work must be applied in the direction of the object's motion.

❯ **Work equation**	$work = force \times distance$ $W = Fd$

Work is zero when an object is not moving.

If you are trying to lift a car, you might apply a large force, but if the distance that the car moves is equal to zero, the work done on the car is also equal to zero. However, once the car moves even a small amount, you have done some work on it. You could calculate how much by multiplying the force that you have applied by the distance that the car moves. The weightlifter in **Figure 1** is applying a force to the barbell as she holds the barbell over her head, but the barbell is not moving. Is she doing any work on the barbell?

work (WUHRK) the transfer of energy to an object by the application of a force that causes the object to move in the direction of the force

Figure 1 This weightlifter is holding a barbell over her head. **Is she doing any work on the barbell?**

Key Resources

Visual Concepts
Work
Power
Equation for Mechanical Advantage

Datasheet
Power Output

Science Skills Worksheet
Equations with Three Parts

Math Skills Worksheets
Work
Power
Mechanical Advantage

Cross-Disciplinary Worksheet
Integrating Biology—Muscles and Work

Word Problems Students struggling with this activity may benefit from working on the board. Write the text of this page and the Math Skills word problem on the board. Assign a different color to each variable in the equation *W*, *F*, and *d*. Have students use the appropriate colored pens or chalk to circle the phrases from the text that align with each variable. Students should then be able to fill in their charts easily.

Demonstrate

Measuring the Force of Gravity You will need a spring scale, a length of string, and a textbook.

Step 1 Hang the book from the scale with string. Have students note the scale reading. Is there a force acting on the book? (Yes, gravity pulls down and the spring exerts an upward force.) Is work being done on the book? (No, because the book's displacement is zero.)

Step 2 Now lift the book (using the scale) about 1 m at a constant velocity. Does the scale reading change? (Yes, at the beginning and the end of the motion) Is work being done on the book? (Yes, because a force moves the book through a distance.)

Step 3 Now hold the scale at shoulder height and carry the book at a constant speed across the room. Does the reading on the scale change? (No) Is work being done on the book? (No, because the motion is perpendicular to the force.) **LS Visual**

READING TOOLBOX

Word Problems As you read through the practice problems on this page, create a table showing the variable to which each phrase corresponds and the value given for each variable.

Practice Hint

❯ Problem 4: To use the work equation, you must use units of newtons for force and units of meters for distance. To convert from mass to force (weight), use the definition of weight:

$$w = mg$$

where *m* is the mass in kilograms and *g* = 9.8 m/s². The force in the work equation is equal to the value of the weight.

Math Skills

Answers to Practice
1. $W = (5,200 \text{ N})(25 \text{ m}) = 1.3 \times 10^5 \text{ J}$
2. $W = (1 \text{ N})(1 \text{ m}) = 1 \text{ J}$
3. $W = (125 \text{ N})(14.0 \text{ m}) = 1,750 \text{ J}$
4. $W = (1,200 \text{ kg})(9.8 \text{ m/s}^2)(0.50 \text{ m}) = 5,900 \text{ J}$

Work is measured in joules.

Because work is calculated as force times distance, it is expressed in newtons times meters (N • m). This combination of SI units is also called *joules* (J). One joule is equal to one kilogram times meter squared per second squared:

$$1 \text{ N} \bullet \text{m} = 1 \text{ J} = 1 \text{ kg} \bullet \text{m}^2/\text{s}^2$$

Because all of these units are equivalent, when solving a particular problem, you can choose which unit to use. Substituting equivalent units will often help you cancel out other units in a problem.

You do about 1 J of work when you lift an apple, which weighs about 1 N, from your arm's length down at your side to the top of your head, a distance of about 1 m.

Math *Skills* Work

Imagine a father playing with his daughter by lifting her repeatedly in the air. How much work does he do with each lift if he lifts her 2.0 m and exerts an average force of 190 N?

Identify	**Given:**
List the given and unknown values.	*force, F* = 190 N *distance, d* = 2.0 m **Unknown:** *work, W* = ? J
Plan	$work = force \times distance$
Write the equation for work.	$W = Fd$
Solve	$W = 190 \text{ N} \times 2.0 \text{ m} =$
Insert the known values into the equation, and solve.	$380 \text{ N} \bullet \text{m} = 380 \text{ J}$

Practice

1. A crane uses an average force of 5,200 N to lift a girder 25 m. How much work does the crane do on the girder?

2. An apple weighing 1 N falls a distance of 1 m. How much work is done on the apple by the force of gravity?

3. A bicycle's brakes apply 125 N of frictional force to the wheels as the bike moves 14.0 m. How much work do the brakes do?

4. A mechanic uses a hydraulic lift to raise a 1,200 kg car 0.50 m off the ground. How much work does the lift do on the car?

For more practice, visit **go.hrw.com** and enter keyword **HK8MP**.

Teaching Key Ideas

How is Work Calculated? Students may confuse the scientific meaning of *work* with the common, everyday meaning. In order to clarify the proper scientific meaning, point out that when used in the scientific sense, *work* is always done *by* a force, *on* an object, changing the motion of the object. Have students come up with sentences using *work* in both the common sense and the scientific sense. **LS Verbal**

Power Output

⏱ 20 min

Procedure

❶ Use a **scale** to determine your weight in newtons. If your scale measures in pounds, multiply your weight by 4.45 N/lb.

❷ With a classmate, use a **stopwatch** to time how long each of you takes to walk quickly up the **stairs.** Record your results.

❸ Use a **meterstick** to measure the height of one step in meters. Multiply by the number of steps to calculate the height of the stairway.

❹ Multiply your weight in newtons by the height of the stairs in meters to find the work that you did in joules.

❺ To express your power in watts, divide the work done in joules by the time in seconds that you took to climb the stairs.

Analysis

1. How would your power output change if you walked up the stairs faster?

2. What would your power output be if you climbed the stairs in the same amount of time while carrying a stack of books weighing 20 N?

3. Why did you use your weight as the force in the work equation?

Power

Running up a flight of stairs does not require more work than walking up slowly does, but running is more exhausting than walking. The amount of time that a given amount of work takes is an important <u>factor</u> when you consider work and machines. The quantity that measures work in relation to time is **power.** ❯ **Power is the rate at which work is done, or how much work is done in a given amount of time.**

| ▷ **Power equation** | $power = \dfrac{work}{time}$ $P = \dfrac{W}{t}$ |

Running a given distance takes less time than walking the same distance does. How does reducing the time in the power equation change the power if the work done stays the same?

Power is measured in watts.

The SI unit used to express power is the watt (W). One watt is the amount of power needed to do one joule of work in one second. It is about equal to the power needed to lift an apple over your head in 1 s. Do not confuse the symbol for work, *W*, which is italic, with the symbol for the watt, W. You can tell which one is meant from the context and by the use of italics.

✅ **Reading Check** What is the SI unit for power? (See Appendix E for answers to Reading Checks.)

power (POW uhr) a quantity that measures the rate at which work is done or energy is transformed

Academic Vocabulary

factor (FAK tuhr) a condition or event that brings about a result

---

Teacher's Notes Do not ask students to disclose their weight to the class. Instruct students not to run on the stairs as well as to emphasize that this is not a contest.

Materials per Group
- scale
- stopwatch
- stairs
- meter stick

Answers to Analysis

1. Your power output would be greater if you walked up the stairs faster.

2. Answers may vary depending on data. Answer should be slightly larger than the power output calculated in item 5 of the procedure.

3. Students are lifting themselves up the stairs against the force of gravity. The gravitational force is equivalent to their weight.

Teaching Key Ideas

Work and Power Use the following analogy to help students understand the difference between work and power. Consider a summer lawn-mowing job. If you have to mow 30 lawns in one month, you could mow six lawns each day and finish in five days, or mow one lawn each day and take the entire month. The total number of mowed lawns (30) is the same, but the rate is different (either 6 per day or 1 per day). Ask students what is analogous to the total number of lawns mowed (work) and to the rate of mowing (power). **LS Verbal**

Differentiated Instruction

Alternative Assessment

Research The unit of power is called the watt, named for the Scottish scientist, James Watt. Have interested students research the life and discoveries of James Watt. (James Watt (1736–1819) was a Scottish inventor who played an important role in the development of the steam engine. Watt was born in Greenock, Scotland in 1736. Although he did not invent the steam engine, as is commonly stated, his contributions—which dramatically improved its efficiency—were fundamental to its development.

Inventions on his first patent of 1769 included a separate condensing chamber for the steam engine (which prevented huge amounts of steam loss), oil lubrication, and cylinder insulation. He later developed a steam indicator to measure the amount of steam pressure in an engine.

Watt also made contributions to other fields throughout his lifetime. In addition to his physical science work, he conducted surveys of canal routes as a civil engineer. He also invented an adaptor for telescopes to aid in distance measuring. Watt died in England in 1819.)

Math Skills

1. $P = W/t = 3{,}960$ J $/ 60.0$ s $= 66.0$ W
2. **a.** $P = W/t = [(565$ N$)(3.25$ m$)]/$
   12.6 s $= 146$ W
   b. $P = [(565$ N$)(3.25$ m$)]/10.5$ s $=$
   175 W

Additional Examples

A student lifts a 12 N textbook 1.5 m in 1.5 s and carries the book 5 m across the room in 7 s.

a. How much work does the student do on the textbook?
Answer: 18 J

b. What is the power output of the student?
Answer: 12 W

Find the work and power used in the following cases:

a. A 43 N force is exerted through a distance of 2.0 m over a time of 3.0 s.
Answer: $W = 86$ J, $P = 29$ W

b. A 43 N force is exerted through a distance of 3.0 m over a time of 2.0 s.
Answer: $W = 130$ J, $P = 65$ W

LS Logical

Answer to caption question

The structure of a jack allows the user to apply less force at any given moment.

Math Skills Power

Lifting an elevator 18 m takes 100 kJ. If doing so takes 20 s, what is the average power of the elevator during the process?

Identify	**Given:**
List the given and unknown values.	work, $W = 100$ kJ $= 1 \times 10^5$ J time, $t = 20$ s Distance is not needed.
	Unknown:
	power, $P = ?$ W
Plan	
Write the equation for power.	$power = \dfrac{work}{time}$ $P = \dfrac{W}{t}$
Solve	
Insert the known values into the equation, and solve.	$P = \dfrac{1 \times 10^5 \text{J}}{20 \text{ s}} = 5 \times 10^3$ J/s $P = 5 \times 10^3$ W $P = 5$ kW

Practice Hint

> Problem 2: To calculate power, first use the work equation to calculate the work done in each case.

Practice

1. While rowing across the lake during a race, John does 3,960 J of work on the oars in 60.0 s. What is his power output in watts?

2. Anna walks up the stairs on her way to class. She weighs 565 N, and the stairs go up 3.25 m vertically.
   a. If Anna climbs the stairs in 12.6 s, what is her power output?
   b. What is her power output if she climbs the stairs in 10.5 s?

For more practice, visit **go.hrw.com** and enter keyword **HK8MP**.

Figure 2 A jack makes lifting a car easy by multiplying the input force. **How does a jack spread out the work over a large distance?**

Machines and Mechanical Advantage

Which is easier, lifting a car by hand or lifting the car with a jack? Obviously, using a jack, shown in **Figure 2**, takes less effort. But you may be surprised to learn that both methods require the same amount of work. The jack makes the work easier by allowing you to apply less force at any given moment. **> Machines help do work by changing the size of an input force, the direction of the force, or both.** Machines redistribute the work that we put into them and can change the direction of an input force. Machines can also make the force greater by decreasing the distance over which the force is applied. This process is often called *multiplying the force*.

✓ **Reading Check** How do machines make work easier?

Why It Matters

Electric Power Most utility companies bill customers in units of kilowatt-hours, which is actually a unit of energy, not power. One kilowatt-hour, which equals 3,600,000 joules, is the amount of energy used at the rate of one kilowatt (1,000 W, or 1,000 J/s) over a time period of one hour (1,000 J/s × 3,600 s/h × 1 h = 3,600,000 J). Ask your local power company for an anonymous sample power bill and have students determine the average number of kilowatt-hours used each day by the client being billed. Also have students convert this value to joules.
LS Logical

Differentiated Instruction

Alternative Assessment

Law of Conservation The idea that different forces can do the same amount of work is one way of introducing the law of conservation of energy. The law is implicit throughout this chapter, but it is not stated explicitly until Section 4. Ask students to write a paragraph explaining how energy transferred to objects by work is conserved in machines. Be sure they give special attention to how changes in force and displacement, the factors affecting work, vary so that energy is conserved. **LS** Verbal

---

What Machines Are Used on Bicycles?

Bicycles consist of many mechanical components. Many tools, each of which is some kind of machine, are used to maintain and repair bicycles. Each tool provides a mechanical advantage—by multiplying or changing the direction of the applied force—and makes working on bicycles much easier than it would be otherwise.

Tire lever

A tire lever is used to pry the tire from its rim.

Air pump

An air pump compresses air to increase the pressure in the tires.

Allen wrenches

A wrench changes the direction of an applied force.

This bicyclist can use several simple machines to attach the back wheel to the bicycle. He is using a wrench to change the direction of the force from his hand to turn a nut onto a bolt.

YOUR TURN

SUMMARIZING INFORMATION

1. What other tools are used to work on a bicycle? What is each tool used to do?

APPLYING CONCEPTS

2. When climbing a steep hill, would you want a larger or a smaller bicycle gear?

Answers to Your Turn

1. Other tools include pliers (grabbing and holding) a screwdriver (turning screws), and cable cutters (used for cutting cable).
2. You would want a large mechanical advantage, and therefore a large gear, climbing a hill.

Why It Matters

What Machines Are Used on Bicycles? The mechanical advantage of a bicycle can permit humans to travel very quickly, tow tremendous amounts of weight, and even fly. In 1959, industrialist Henry Kremer established a prize of $95,000 to be awarded to the first person who could demonstrate sustained, maneuverable, human-powered flight. Almost 20 years later Dr. Paul B. MacCready and Dr. Peter B. S. Lissaman, designed the Gossamer Condor, a radical new kind of aircraft made of ultra-lightweight materials that would be pedaled like a bicycle. They chose Bryan Allen who was an experienced hang glider pilot and bicycle racer to be the pilot of the new aircraft.

On August 23, 1977, Allen flew the Condor through a figure-8 course and over two hurdles covering a total distance of 1.35 miles in the air to claim the prize. The Gossamer Condor is now housed at the Smithsonian National Air and Space Museum.

READING TOOLBOX

Visual Literacy Students may be confused by the concept that there are machines on a bicycle and machines used to fix bicycles. Have struggling students make a chart that categorizes the machines that allow a bike to have mechanical advantage in transportation, and the machines that allow someone to repair a bike. **LS Visual**

Teaching Key Ideas

Machines Make Work Easier

Emphasize to students that machines do not increase the quantity of work that one can do. Given a specific amount of work to be done, a machine takes advantage of the fact that force and distance are inversely proportional. Either one can be increased by decreasing the other.

As an example, you can use the equation $W = F \times d$ to show that a longer distance implies a smaller force for the same amount of work. For instance, to lift a 225 N box into the back of a truck that is 1.00 m off the ground requires 225 J of work. If you lift the box straight up into the truck, the force needed is 225 N, but if you use a 3.00 m ramp, the force needed is only 75 N (ignoring friction).

Math Skills

Answers to Practice

1. MA = input distance/output distance = 6.0 m/1.5 m = 4.0
2. output force = (MA)(input force) = (5.2)(15 N) = 78 N

Additional Examples

A mover uses a pulley system with a mechanical advantage of 10.0 to lift a piano 3.5 m. Disregarding friction, how far must the mover pull the rope?
Answer: 35 m
A person pushes a 950 N box up an incline. If the person exerts a force of 350 N along the incline, what is the mechanical advantage of the incline?
Answer: 2.7
LS Logical

mechanical advantage (muh KAN i kuhl ad VANT ij) a quantity that expresses how much a machine multiplies force or distance

www.scilinks.org
Topic: Mechanical
Advantage
Code: **HK80928**

Practice **Hint**

> The mechanical advantage equation can be rearranged to isolate any of the variables on the left.

> Problem 2: Rearrange the equation to isolate output force on the left.

> When rearranging, use only the part of the full equation that you need.

Mechanical advantage is an important ratio.

A ramp makes doing work easier by multiplying the force that is applied. Scientists and engineers use a number that describes how much the force or distance is multiplied by a machine. This number, called the **mechanical advantage,** is defined as the ratio between the output force and the input force. It is also equal to the ratio between the input distance and the output distance if friction is ignored.

> **Mechanical advantage equation** | $$\text{mechanical advantage} = \frac{\text{output force}}{\text{input force}} = \frac{\text{input distance}}{\text{output distance}}$$

A machine that has a mechanical advantage greater than one multiplies the input force. Such a machine can help you move or lift a heavy object, such as a car or a box of books. A machine that has a mechanical advantage of less than one does not multiply force but increases distance and speed.

Math Skills Mechanical Advantage

Calculate the mechanical advantage of a ramp that is 5.0 m long and 1.5 m high.

Identify List the given and unknown values.	**Given:** input distance = 5.0 m output distance = 1.5 m **Unknown:** mechanical advantage = ?
Plan Write the equation for mechanical advantage.	We need only the distance part of the full equation: $$\text{mechanical advantage} = \frac{\text{input distance}}{\text{output distance}}$$
Solve Insert the known values, and solve.	$$\text{mechanical advantage} = \frac{5.0 \text{ m}}{1.5 \text{ m}} = 3.3$$

Practice

1. Find the mechanical advantage of a ramp that is 6.0 m long and 1.5 m tall.

2. Alex pulls on the handle of a claw hammer with a force of 15 N. If the hammer has a mechanical advantage of 5.2, how much force is exerted on the nail in the claw?

For more practice, visit **go.hrw.com** and enter keyword **HK8MP.**

Teaching Key Ideas

Work, Power, and Machines Use the following activity to assess students' progress:
Write the terms and definitions at right on the board in two columns. Ask students to match each term with the correct description. Then, ask students to give the equation and the SI unit for each term.

left column:

1. work (c; force × distance; joules)
2. power (b; work/time; watts)
3. mechanical advantage (a; output force/input force; no units)

right column:

a. the amount that a machine multiplies force or distance

b. the rate at which work is done

c. what is done when a force makes an object move

LS Logical

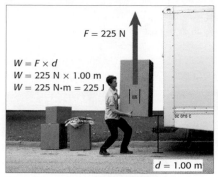

$F = 225$ N

$W = F \times d$
$W = 225$ N $\times$ 1.00 m
$W = 225$ N·m $= 225$ J

$d = 1.00$ m

When lifting a box straight up, a mover applies a large force over a short distance.

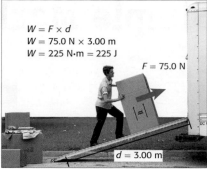

$W = F \times d$
$W = 75.0$ N $\times$ 3.00 m
$W = 225$ N·m $= 225$ J

$F = 75.0$ N

$d = 3.00$ m

When using a ramp to lift the box, the mover applies a smaller force over a longer distance.

Figure 3 Lifting a box directly onto a truck and pushing the box up a ramp require the same amount of work.

Different forces can do the same amount of work.

Compare the amount of work required to lift a box onto the bed of a truck with the amount of work required to push the same box up a ramp. When the mover shown in **Figure 3** lifts the box straight up, he applies 225 N of force over a short distance. Using the ramp, he applies a smaller force over a longer distance. But the work done is the same in both cases.

Both a car jack and a loading ramp make doing work easier by increasing the distance over which force is applied. Both allow the same amount of work to be done by decreasing the force while increasing the distance.

Section 1 Review

KEY IDEAS

1. **Define** *work* and *power*. How are work and power related?

2. **Determine** if work is being done in the following situations:
   a. lifting a spoonful of soup to your mouth
   b. holding a large stack of books motionless over your head
   c. letting a pencil fall to the ground

3. **Describe** how a ramp can make lifting a box easy without changing the amount of work being done.

CRITICAL THINKING

4. **Applying Concepts** Both a short ramp and a long ramp reach a height of 1 m. Which ramp has a greater mechanical advantage?

Math *Skills*

5. How much work is done by a person who uses a horizontal force of 25 N to move a desk 3.0 m?

6. A bus driver applies a force of 55.0 N to the steering wheel, which in turn applies 132 N of force to the steering column. What is the mechanical advantage of the steering wheel?

7. A 400 N student climbs up a 3.0 m ladder in 4.0 s.
   a. How much work does the student do?
   b. What is the student's power output?

8. An outboard engine on a boat can do 1.0×10^6 J of work in 50.0 s. Calculate its power in watts. Convert your answer to horsepower (1 hp $= 746$ W).

> **Close**

Reteaching Key Ideas

Writing Questions Have students write out the equations for work, power, and mechanical advantage. Have each student write two questions addressing each equation. Have students answer their own questions, and then swap their questions with another student. Students should try to answer those questions. Students are responsible for helping each other understand how to answer the questions.
LS Interpersonal

Formative Assessment

How do jacks make lifting a car easier?

A. Jacks reduce the amount of force needed to lift cars off the ground. (Incorrect. The amount of force needed to lift the car off the ground is constant. Review the section on mechanical advantage.)

B. Jacks increase the amount of input force a person can exert. (Incorrect. Machines do not work by changing the ability of the person exerting the force. Review the section on mechanical advantage.)

C. Jacks spread the amount of output force over a greater distance. (Correct. Because a jack spreads the force over a greater distance, it allows you to exert less force at any given moment.)

D. Jacks reduce the mass of the car. (Incorrect. Machines do not alter the mass of objects. Review the section on mechanical advantage.)

Answers to Section Review

1. Work is the quantity of energy transferred by a force applied to an object that moves in the direction of the force. Power is a quantity that measures the rate at which work is done. Power equals work divided by time.

2. **a.** yes
   b. no
   c. yes (by gravity)

3. A ramp allows the use of a smaller input force exerted over a longer distance, so that work is unchanged.

4. The long ramp has a greater mechanical advantage than the short ramp.

5. $W = 75$ J

6. $MA = 2.40$

7. **a.** $W = 1,200$ J
   b. $P = 300$ W

8. $P = 2.0 \times 10^4$ W (27 hp)

›Focus

This section discusses each of the six simple machines in detail, and then describes the characteristics of compound machines.

 Bellringer

Use the Bellringer transparency to prepare students for this section.

Demonstrate

Pulleys You will need two masses (75 g and 100 g), three pulleys (2 fixed, 1 free), a ring stand with a horizontal clamp, and string. Tell students that this section will discuss the way simple machines make work easier. Use this demonstration to show students how a pulley works.

Step 1 Arrange the free pulley and one fixed pulley as shown in **Figure 3.** Attach the other fixed pulley to the clamp, and thread over it the string from beneath the free pulley.

Step 2 Attach the 100 g mass to the bottom of the free pulley and the 75 g mass to the string's free end. Hold the masses in place and ask students what they think will happen when you let go.

Step 3 Release the masses. The 75 g mass should fall and the 100 g mass should rise, showing that a lighter mass can lift a heavier mass with the help of simple machines.

LS Visual

Simple Machines

Key **Ideas**

› What are the six types of simple machines?

› What are the two principal parts of all levers?

› How does using an inclined plane change the force required to do work?

› What simple machines make up a pair of scissors?

Key **Terms**

simple machine

compound machine

Why It **Matters**

A simple machine, such as a ramp, makes work easier by reducing the force required to do work.

Can you pop the cap off of a bottle of soda by using just your fingers? You probably can't, especially if the bottle doesn't have a screw cap! Instead, you use a bottle opener. Similarly, you don't use the palm of your hand to drive a nail into a block of wood. Instead, you use a hammer. These simple machines make doing work easier.

What Are Simple Machines?

The most basic machines are called **simple machines.** Other machines are either modifications of simple machines or combinations of several simple machines.

Figure 1 shows examples of the six kinds of simple machines. › **The six types of simple machines are the simple lever, the pulley, the wheel and axle, the simple inclined plane, the wedge, and the screw.** Simple machines are divided into two families: the *lever family* and the *inclined plane family.*

simple machine (SIM puhl muh SHEEN) one of the six basic types of machines, which are the basis for all other forms of machines

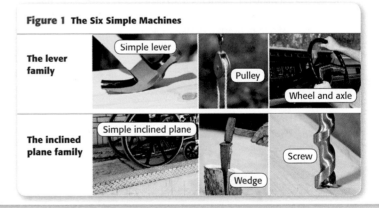

Figure 1 The Six Simple Machines

The lever family: Simple lever, Pulley, Wheel and axle

The inclined plane family: Simple inclined plane, Wedge, Screw

---

Key Resources

Teaching Transparencies
P7 Levers
P8 Pulleys

Visual Concepts
Overview of Simple Machines
Lever
Pulley
Wheel and Axle
Inclined Plane
Wedge
Screws
Compound Machine

Datasheet
A Simple Inclined Plane

Cross-Disciplinary Worksheet
Connection to Social Studies—The Pyramids

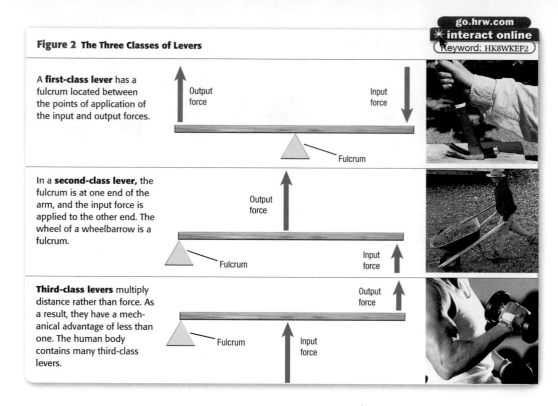

Figure 2 The Three Classes of Levers

go.hrw.com
✳ interact online
Keyword: HK8WKEF2

A **first-class lever** has a fulcrum located between the points of application of the input and output forces.

Output force

Input force

Fulcrum

In a **second-class lever,** the fulcrum is at one end of the arm, and the input force is applied to the other end. The wheel of a wheelbarrow is a fulcrum.

Output force

Fulcrum

Input force

Third-class levers multiply distance rather than force. As a result, they have a mechanical advantage of less than one. The human body contains many third-class levers.

Output force

Fulcrum

Input force

The Lever Family

Imagine using a claw hammer to pull out a nail. As you pull on the handle of the hammer, the head of the hammer turns around the point where the hammer meets the wood. The force applied to the handle is transferred to the claw on the other end of the hammer. The claw hammer is a lever. ❯ **All levers have a rigid *arm* that turns around a point called the *fulcrum*.** The input force is multiplied or redirected into an output force.

Levers are divided into three classes.

Levers are divided into three classes depending on the locations of the fulcrum, the input force, and the output force, as **Figure 2** shows. First-class levers, such as the claw hammer, are the most common kind of lever. A pair of pliers is made of two first-class levers joined together.

Wheelbarrows, nutcrackers, and hinged doors are examples of second-class levers. A person's forearm is an example of a third-class lever. The biceps muscle, which is attached to the bone near the elbow, contracts a short distance to move the hand a large distance.

READING TOOLBOX

Concept Maps
Using *levers* for the main concept, create a simple concept map. Include the words *fulcrum, input force,* and *output force* in the map.

› Teach

Teaching Key Ideas

Six Types of Simple Machines Have students examine the chapter opener photographs and identify as many simple machines in the kinetic sculptures as they can. Students may refer to **Figure 1** for examples of the six simple machines. ⓛⓢ **Visual**

Teaching Key Ideas

Key Parts of Levers Figure 2 shows the three classes of levers. Ask students: "For each of the three examples, where is force input and where is force output? Do the levers multiply force or increase distance on the output side?" (Second-class levers always multiply force, third-class levers always increase distance, and first-class levers may either multiply force or increase distance.) ⓛⓢ **Visual**

go.hrw.com
✳ interact online

Students can interact with the figure by going to **go.hrw.com** and typing in the keyword **HK8WKEF2**.

READING TOOLBOX

Concept Map Remind students that concept maps are made of both concepts and linking terms. The concepts and linking terms should read as a sentence. Remind students that many valid concept maps can be made using the same terms.

Differentiated Instruction

Special Education Students

Everyday Levers Many students may not have used a claw hammer or crowbar. Show students other common levers such as a teeter-totter or a see-saw. Ask students: "How can a larger person and a small person use a teeter-totter or a see-saw together?" (The larger person must sit nearer to the fulcrum than the smaller person.) Tell students that by shifting the fulcrum nearer to the larger person, the smaller person increased his or her mechanical advantage and needs less input force to lift the larger person. ⓛⓢ **Intrapersonal**

READING TOOLBOX

Visual Literacy Explain that in the second and third parts of **Figure 3,** the pulley's mass adds to the overall weight. In these cases, the input force would have to be greater than 75 N and 50 N by small amounts. Much of the rope's weight is evenly distributed on either side of the stationary pulley. Explain that in most cases, the weight of the rope and pulleys is much smaller than the weight of the load, and can be ignored.

Answer to caption question

The wheel turns the axle directly in a fixed-wheel machine. When the wheel turns, the axle also turns.

Why It Matters

Wheelchair Ramps Without ramps and other accommodations, accessing public buildings is difficult for people in wheelchairs. Ask students why good wheelchair ramps provide a long gradual inclined surface rather than a short steep surface. (Sample answer: Good ramps are long and have a gradual slope because a long gradual ramp requires less force than a short steep ramp. A ramp that requires less force to use permits people in wheelchairs access with less strain.) **LS** **Logical**

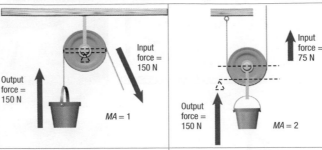

Figure 3 The Mechanical Advantage of Pulleys

Output force = 150 N   Input force = 150 N   *MA* = 1

When a 150 N weight is lifted by using a single, fixed pulley, the weight must be fully supported by the rope on each side of the pulley. This kind of pulley has a mechanical advantage of one.

Input force = 75 N   Output force = 150 N   *MA* = 2

When a moving pulley is used, the load is shared by two sections of rope pulling upward. The input force supports only half of the weight. This pulley system has a mechanical advantage of two.

Input force = 50 N   Output force = 150 N   *MA* = 3

In this arrangement of multiple pulleys, all of the sections of rope are pulling up against the downward force of the weight. This arrangement gives an even higher mechanical advantage.

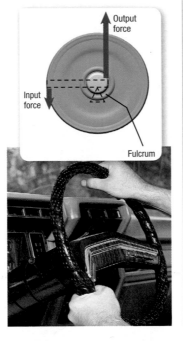

Figure 4 A wheel and axle is in the lever family of simple machines. **How does a wheel and axle differ from a pulley?**

Output force

Input force

Fulcrum

Pulleys are modified levers.

A pulley is another kind of simple machine in the lever family. You may have used a pulley to lift things, such as a flag on a flagpole or a sail on a boat.

Figure 3 shows how a pulley is like a lever. The point in the middle of a pulley is like the fulcrum of a lever. The rest of the pulley behaves like the rigid arm of a first-class lever. Because the length from the fulcrum is the same on both sides of a fixed pulley, this kind of pulley has a mechanical advantage of one—it simply changes the direction of the force.

Using moving pulleys or more than one pulley at a time can increase the mechanical advantage, as **Figure 3** also shows. Multiple pulleys are sometimes combined into a single unit called a *block and tackle.*

✓ Reading Check What is the mechanical advantage of a single, fixed pulley?

A wheel and axle is a lever connected to a shaft.

The steering wheel of a car is another kind of simple machine: a wheel and axle. A wheel and axle is made of a lever or a pulley (the wheel) connected to a shaft (the axle), as shown in **Figure 4.** When the wheel is turned, the axle also turns. When a small input force is applied to the steering wheel, the force is multiplied to become a large output force applied to the steering column, which turns the front wheels of the car. Screwdrivers and cranks are other everyday wheel-and-axle machines.

Differentiated Instruction

English Learners

Pictorial Representations Using **Figure 4,** ask students to create a poster or bulletin board showing the six simple machines in the lever and inclined plane families. Students can use cut-out pictures or their own drawings to show their understanding of the different types of machines. If possible, the students can tour the school building and take pictures or list machines in each category they find. Additionally, they can add the category of compound machines. **LS** **Visual**

Alternative Assessment

Pulley System Have students read the explanation of how the pulley at left in **Figure 3** is like a first-class lever with the fulcrum in the middle. Tell students that the middle pulley is like a second-class lever. Have students discuss this. Next tell students that in pulley systems, the mechanical advantage may be found by simply counting the number of weight-supporting ropes. Ask students to find the mechanical advantage of all three pulley systems in **Figure 3** (1, 2, 3). **LS** **Logical**

QuickLab

A Simple Inclined Plane

 10 min

Procedure

❶ Make an inclined plane out of a **board** and a stack of **books**.

❷ Tie a **string** to an object that is heavy but has low friction, such as a metal **toy car** or a **roll of wire**. Use the string to pull the object up the plane.

❸ Still using the string, try to lift the object straight up through the same distance.

Analysis

1. Which action required more force?

2. Which action required more work?

The Inclined Plane Family

Imagine that you need to load a piano into a moving van. Which will <u>require</u> more force: lifting the piano directly into the van or rolling the piano up a ramp? A ramp, such as the one in **Figure 5**, is an inclined plane, another kind of simple machine. ❭ **Pushing an object up an inclined plane requires less input force than lifting the same object does.**

The same amount of work must be done whether you lift something straight up or push it up a ramp. When you push an object up a ramp, you apply a force in the direction parallel to the ramp over the length of the ramp. When you lift something straight up, the force applied is perpendicular to the ground.

Pushing an object up a long, gradual ramp takes less force than pushing the object up a short, steep ramp. The mechanical advantage of an inclined plane is equal to the length of the inclined plane divided by the height to which the load is lifted.

Academic Vocabulary

require (ri KWIER) to need

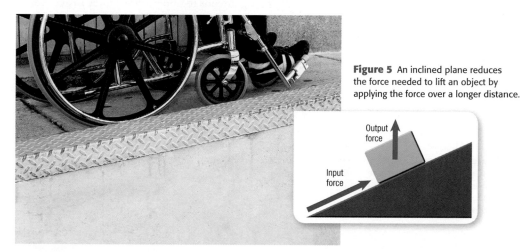

Figure 5 An inclined plane reduces the force needed to lift an object by applying the force over a longer distance.

Social Studies Connection

Archimedes' Machines Archimedes was a Greek mathematician (287 BCE–212 BCE) of Syracuse, Sicily. Although his first love was pure mathematics, he also figured out how to use simple machines in a variety of practical applications. In response to a challenge by the King, Archimedes developed a system of levers and pulleys to launch a heavy ship. The King was astonished to see the fully-loaded ship glide into the water with a simple pull of a rope.

Later, when the Romans were attacking Syracuse, Archimedes designed machines to defend the city. He made cranes that would pick up Roman ships and smash them against rocks. He also created catapults to hurl huge stones at ships and soldiers.

The Romans were forced to withdraw, but they eventually gained control by starving the citizens. The Roman leader Marcellus ordered his men to "Spare that mathematician" but, tragically, Archimedes was killed. Encourage interested students to find out more about the life, death, and scientific contributions of Archimedes.

QuickLab

Teacher's Notes The object used in this activity can be any heavy rolling object (such as a wheeled dynamics cart) or simply a heavy object with low friction. A roll of wire with string tied through the hollow shaft so that the roll moves freely when dragged up the ramp will work well.

Materials per Group

• board
• stack of books
• string
• heavy object with low friction

Answers to Analysis

1. Lifting the object straight up requires more force than dragging it up the ramp.

2. The work done is the same in either case, if friction is ignored.

Teaching Key Ideas

Inclined Plane Changes Force An inclined plane changes the force required to lift an object by applying the force over a greater distance. Students may be familiar with the curved ramps used in sports such as skateboarding. These ramps have a constantly changing slope. Ask students: Is the force needed to push an object up a flat ramp constant or variable? (constant) Is the force needed to push an object up a curved skateboard ramp constant or variable? (variable) Where on the ramp is the most and least force required? (More force is required at the top when the ramp is steep, and less is required at the bottom when the ramp's slope is low.) **LS** Logical

Teaching Key Ideas

Compound Machines Many common levers, such as scissors (first-class), nutcrackers (second-class), and tweezers (third-class), are actually compound machines combining two levers together. Ask students to look for everyday examples of both single and compound (double) levers. Have students add their examples to a list on the chalkboard, noting the class of the lever and whether the lever is single or double. Have other students check the classifications for accuracy. (Sample responses: hammer claw, first-class, single; see-saw, first-class, single; scissors, first-class, double; pliers, first-class, double; wheelbarrow, second-class, single; bottle opener, second-class, single; nutcracker, second-class, double; fishing rod, third-class, single; tweezers, third-class, double; tongs, third-class, double.) **LS Intrapersonal**

Answer to caption question

A screw is an inclined plane wrapped around a cylinder. On the drill bit, the cutting edge is the inclined plane and the core or shaft of the bit is the cylinder.

Figure 6 A wedge turns a downward force into two forces directed out to the sides.

Input force

Output force

Integrating Social Studies

The ancient Egyptians built dozens of large stone pyramids as tombs for the bodies of kings and queens. The largest one is the pyramid of Khufu at Giza, or the Great Pyramid. It is made of more than 2 million blocks of stone. These blocks have an average weight of 2.5 tons, and the largest blocks weigh 15 tons. These blocks were lifted by using long inclined planes.

A wedge is a modified inclined plane.

When an ax blade or a splitting wedge hits a piece of wood, it pushes through and breaks apart the wood, as shown in **Figure 6.** An ax blade is an example of a wedge, another kind of simple machine in the inclined plane family. A wedge is formed of two inclined planes placed back to back. Using a wedge is like pushing a ramp instead of pushing something up a ramp. A wedge turns a single downward force into two forces directed out to the sides. Some kinds of wedges, such as nails, are used as fasteners.

A screw is an inclined plane wrapped around a cylinder.

A kind of simple machine that you probably use often is a screw. The threads on a screw look like a spiral inclined plane. In fact, a screw is an inclined plane wrapped around a cylinder. Like pushing something up a ramp, tightening a screw with gently sloping threads requires a small force to act over a long distance. Tightening a screw with steeper threads requires more force over less distance. A drill bit, such as the one shown in **Figure 7,** is another example of a screw. Jar lids are screws that people use every day. Spiral staircases are also everyday screws.

✓ Reading Check What are two examples of a modified inclined plane?

Figure 7 If you could unwind a screw, you would see that it is an inclined plane wrapped around a cylinder. **How is a drill bit like a screw?**

Differentiated Instruction

Basic Learners

Acrostic Ask students to create an acrostic they can use as a memory aid for the six simple machines. Use the following example (or create one of your own) to give students the idea: **L**ouis **P**lank **W**as an **I**nteresting, **W**itty **S**cholar. (**L**ever, **P**ulley, **W**heel and axle, **I**nclined plane, **W**edge, **S**crew)

Tell students to create their own example because they will probably remember their own words better than an acrostic written by someone else. Also remind them that they can list the machines in any order. **LS Verbal**

Advanced Learners

Simple Machines Have students list the two families of simple machines and the type of simple machines that belong to each family. Then have students describe the characteristics of a compound machine.

1. Lever family: levers, pulleys, and wheel-and-axle machines
2. Inclined plane family: inclined planes, wedges, and screws
3. A compound machine is any machine made up of two or more simple machines.

LS Logical

Compound Machines

Many devices that you use every day are made of more than one simple machine. A **compound machine** is a machine that combines two or more simple machines. **A pair of scissors, for example, uses two first-class levers joined at a common fulcrum; each lever arm has a wedge that cuts into the paper.** Most car jacks use a lever in combination with a large screw.

Bicycles and cars are compound machines. How many simple machines can you identify in the bicycle shown in **Figure 8?** How many can you identify in a car?

compound machine (KAHM POWND muh SHEEN) a machine made of more than one simple machine

Brake lever

Gears

Figure 8 A bicycle is made of many simple machines.

Reteaching Key Ideas

Flash Cards Have students make flashcards—one for each type of simple machine. Students should make a card for each type of lever and pulley. On one side students can diagram the machine, and show force arrows. On the other side, students can explain how the machine makes work easier, and provide examples of each machine. **LS Visual**

Formative Assessment

How does an inclined plane change the force required to do work?

A. The inclined plane reduces the distance over which the force is applied. (Incorrect. An inclined plane does not reduce the distance, but increases the distance over which the force is applied.)

B. The inclined plane increases the distance over which the force is applied. (Correct. By distributing the force over a greater area, an inclined plane allows you to use less force at any given moment.)

C. The inclined plane reduces the mass of the object being moved. (Incorrect. The mass remains constant.)

D. The inclined plane reduces the amount of force needed to move an object. (Incorrect. The amount of force is constant.)

Section 2 Review

KEY IDEAS

1. **List** the six types of simple machines.

2. **Identify** the kind of simple machine represented by each of the following examples:
   a. a drill bit
   b. a skateboard ramp
   c. a boat oar

3. **Describe** how a lever can increase the force applied without changing the amount of work being done.

4. **Explain** why pulleys are in the lever family.

CRITICAL THINKING

5. **Making Predictions** Can an inclined plane have a mechanical advantage of less than one? Explain.

6. **Interpreting Graphics** Study the lever drawn here. To which class of levers does this lever belong? Where is the output force?

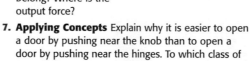

Input force

7. **Applying Concepts** Explain why it is easier to open a door by pushing near the knob than to open a door by pushing near the hinges. To which class of levers does a door belong?

8. **Identifying Functions** Think of a compound machine that you use every day, and identify the simple machines that make it up.

Answers to Section Review

1. lever, pulley, wheel and axle, inclined plane, wedge, screw

2. **a.** screw
   b. inclined plane
   c. lever

3. A lever can increase the force without increasing the work done, because the output force will be exerted through a smaller distance.

4. The middle of the pulley is the fulcrum; the wheel of the pulley is like a lever-arm extended into a circle. Pulleys are different from ordinary levers because you can change the location of the fulcrum of a lever.

5. If the MA were 1, the plane would be as long as it is tall. Because you cannot travel a distance shorter than the actual height you need to lift an object, you cannot build an inclined plane with a MA less than 1.

6. second class lever; between the fulcrum and the input force

7. A door is normally a second-class lever. Pushing near the knob is easier because the input distance is longer. If you push near the hinges, the input arm is shorter than the output arm, and the door becomes a third-class lever, with an MA of less than 1.

Answers continued on p. 469A

SECTION 3

> ## Focus

This section begins by relating energy and work. Students then will learn how to identify and calculate potential and kinetic energy. The section concludes with a discussion of several examples of nonmechanical energy.

Bellringer

Use the Bellringer transparency to prepare students for this section.

Demonstrate

What is Energy? In front of the class squeeze a spring until it's closed. Ask the class: When does the spring have energy, when it's relaxed or compressed? (The spring has more energy when it's compressed.) Where does the energy come from? (The energy is input by a human hand squeezing.) How did the hand get the energy to squeeze? (The energy is from food.) Where did the food get the energy? (The energy is from the sun.) Tell students that this section will discuss energy transfers such as the energy from the sun that eventually was transferred to the spring.
LS Verbal

SECTION 3 What Is Energy?

Key Ideas

> What is the relationship between energy and work?

> Why is potential energy called *energy of position*?

> What factors does kinetic energy depend on?

> What is nonmechanical energy?

Key Terms

energy

potential energy

kinetic energy

mechanical energy

Why It Matters

Some of the energy that reaches Earth from the sun is stored in plants. This energy is converted to work by the animals that consume plants.

The world around us is full of energy. Energy exists in many forms. A lightning bolt has electrical energy. A flashlight battery has chemical energy. A moving bicycle has mechanical energy. A rock sitting still on top of a mountain also has mechanical energy, simply because it could move downhill! We harness various forms of energy to power tools and machines, from flashlights to submarines.

Energy and Work

A moving object has **energy** associated with its motion. The mallet that the person in **Figure 1** is swinging has energy. When the mallet hits the lever, the mallet's energy is transferred to the puck, the puck rises to strike the bell, and the bell releases energy into the air as sound. Work has been done. **> Whenever work is done, energy is transformed or is transferred from one system to another system.** In fact, one definition of *energy* is "the ability to do work."

Energy is measured in joules.

Although work is done only when an object experiences a change in its position or its motion, energy can be present in an object or a system that is at rest. The energy in an object can be calculated whether the object is in motion or at rest. The transfer of energy from one object or system to another, such as the transfer of energy from the puck to the bell in **Figure 1,** can be measured by how much work is done on the receiving object. Because energy is the ability to do work, measurements of energy and work are expressed in the same units—joules.

Figure 1 The moving mallet has energy and can do work on the puck. The transfer of energy causes the puck to rise against gravity and ring the bell.

Key Resources

Teaching Transparency
TM36 Kinetic Energy Graph

Visual Concepts
Types of Energy
Potential Energy
Kinetic Energy

Science Skills Worksheet
Squares and Square Roots

Math Skills Worksheet
Gravitational Potential Energy
Kinetic Energy

Cross-Disciplinary Worksheets
Connection to Language Arts—The Concept of Energy
Real World Applications—Calories and Nutrition
Integrating Chemistry—Chemical Reactions

Potential Energy

When you stretch a rubber band, you do work. The energy used to stretch the rubber band is stored until you release the rubber band. When you release the rubber band, it flies from your hand. But where is the energy between the time you stretch the rubber band and the time you release the rubber band?

A stretched rubber band stores energy in a form called **potential energy.** ❯ **Potential energy (*PE*) is sometimes called *energy of position* because it results from the relative positions of objects in a system.** Any object that is stretched or compressed to increase or decrease the distance between its parts has potential energy that is called *elastic potential energy.* Stretched bungee cords and compressed springs have elastic potential energy.

Imagine that you are at the top of the first hill of the roller coaster shown in **Figure 2.** Your position above the ground gives you energy that could potentially do work as you move toward the ground. Any system of two or more objects separated by a vertical distance has potential energy that results from the gravitational attraction between the objects. This kind of stored energy is called *gravitational potential energy.*

✔ **Reading Check** What kind of energy does a stretched rubber band have?

Gravitational potential energy depends on both mass and height.

An apple at the top of a tree has more gravitational potential energy with respect to the Earth than an apple of the same size on a lower branch does. But if two apples of different masses are at the same height, the heavier apple has more gravitational potential energy than the lighter one does.

Because it is caused by the force of gravity, gravitational potential energy near Earth depends on both the mass of the object and the height of the object relative to Earth's surface.

> ❯ **Gravitational potential energy equation**
> $grav. PE = mass \times free\text{-}fall\ acceleration \times height$
> $PE = mgh$

Notice that *mg* is the weight of the object in newtons, which is equal to the force on the object due to gravity. So, like work, gravitational potential energy is calculated by multiplying force and distance.

Figure 2 This roller coaster car has gravitational potential energy. This energy results from the gravitational attraction between the car and Earth.

energy (EN uhr jee) the capacity to do work

potential energy (poh TEN shuhl EN uhr jee) the energy that an object has because of the position, shape, or condition of the object

www.scilinks.org
Topic: Potential Energy
Code: HK81197

❯Teach

Teaching Key Ideas

Work and Energy When defining energy as the ability to do work, point out that an acceptable definition for work is the transfer of mechanical energy from one object (or system) to another. When a force is applied through a distance, work is done by one object on another object. The energy to do the work comes from the first object, and is transferred to the second object. Energy transfer and conservation of energy will be discussed in Section 4 in more detail, but the idea may be introduced here.

Teaching Key Ideas

Energy of Position *Potential energy* is a term that encompasses many types of energy. Other forms of potential energy include elastic, chemical, electrical, and magnetic. These may seem like very different concepts to students, but all forms of potential energy deal with position. Just as gravitational potential energy depends on distances between masses, elastic potential energy depends on the elongation of elastic materials. Chemical potential energy depends on bonds (position) between atoms within molecules. Electrical potential energy depends on distances between charged particles, and magnetic potential depends on the orientation of magnetic particles in a magnetic field.

READING TOOLBOX

Reading for Differences Help students read for differences. These differences will help students understand the relationships between concepts. For example, *gravitational potential energy* is different from *weight* because height is taken into account. The equation for gravitational potential energy is really weight, *mg,* times height, *h.* This is also a measurement of the work that the gravitational field would do on an object if it were to fall through a certain distance (the height).

Math Skills

Answers to Practice

1. **a.** $PE = mgh = (1{,}200 \text{ kg})$
   $(9.8 \text{ m/s}^2)(42 \text{ m}) = 4.9 \times 10^5 \text{ J}$
   b. $PE = (65 \text{ kg})(9.8 \text{ m/s}^2)$
   $(8{,}800 \text{ m}) = 5.6 \times 10^6 \text{ J}$
   c. $PE = (0.52 \text{ kg})(9.8 \text{ m/s}^2)$
   $(550 \text{ m}) = 2.8 \times 10^3 \text{ J}$
2. $h = PE/mg = 8.0 \text{ J}/[(0.055 \text{ kg})$
   $(9.8 \text{ m/s}^2)] = 15 \text{ m}$
3. $m = PE/gh = 3{,}400 \text{ J}/[(9.8 \text{ m/s}^2)$
   $(6.0 \text{ m})] = 58 \text{ kg}$

Additional Examples

A spider has 0.080 J of gravitational potential energy as it reaches the halfway point climbing up a 2.8 m wall. What is the potential energy of the spider at the top of the wall? (**HINT:** You do not need to find the mass first.)

Answer: 0.16 J

A 0.50 g leaf falls from a branch 4.0 m off the ground to a bird's nest 2.5 m off the ground. How much gravitational potential energy did the leaf lose?

Answer: 7.4×10^{-3} J

LS Logical

Height is relative.

The value for h in the equation for gravitational potential energy is often measured from the ground. But in some cases, a different height may be more important. For example, if an apple were about to fall into a bird's nest on a branch below the apple, the apple's height above the nest would be used to calculate the apple's potential energy with respect to the nest.

Math Skills Potential Energy

A 65 kg rock climber ascends a cliff. What is the climber's gravitational potential energy at a point 35 m above the base of the cliff?

Identify	**Given:**
List the given and unknown values.	*mass, m* = 65 kg *height, h* = 35 m *free-fall acceleration, g* = 9.8 m/s² **Unknown:** *gravitational potential energy,* *PE* = ? J
Plan	*grav. PE = mass × free-fall acceleration* × *height*
Write the equation for gravitational potential energy.	$PE = mgh$
Solve	$PE = (65 \text{ kg})(9.8 \text{ m/s}^2)(35 \text{ m})$
Insert the known values into the equation, and solve.	$PE = 2.2 \times 10^4 \text{ kg} \cdot \text{m}^2/\text{s}^2 = 2.2 \times 10^4 \text{ J}$

Practice Hint

▸ Problem 2: The gravitational potential energy equation can be rearranged to isolate height on the left.

$$mgh = PE$$

Divide both sides by *mg,* and cancel.

$$\frac{\cancel{mg}h}{\cancel{mg}} = \frac{PE}{mg}$$

$$h = \frac{PE}{mg}$$

▸ Problem 3: Rearrange the equation to isolate mass on the left.

▸ When solving all of these problems, use $g = 9.8 \text{ m/s}^2$.

Practice

1. Calculate the gravitational potential energy of the following:
   a. a 1,200 kg car at the top of a hill that is 42 m high
   b. a 65 kg climber on top of Mount Everest (8,800 m high)
   c. a 0.52 kg bird flying at an altitude of 550 m

2. A science student holds a 55 g egg out a window. Just before the student releases the egg, the egg has 8.0 J of gravitational potential energy with respect to the ground. How high is the student's arm above the ground, in meters? (Hint: Convert the mass to kilograms before solving.)

3. A diver has 3,400 J of gravitational potential energy after climbing up onto a diving platform that is 6.0 m above the water. What is the diver's mass in kilograms?

For more practice, visit **go.hrw.com** and enter keyword **HK8MP**.

Why It Matters

Potential Energy in Food Whenever we eat food, we are supplying our bodies with energy. The body constantly uses that energy to perform actions and to stay alive, for example to breathe and to pump blood. A person who exercises regularly needs more calories of energy each day than someone who is inactive. In fact, each individual has a daily caloric requirement based on their size and activity level. The daily requirements listed in nutrition labels on food are for a person who needs 2,000 calories per day, but many individuals actually need more or less than this average value.

If someone eats more calories than their daily requirement, the body stores the extra energy in the form of fat. The energy—which is now in the form of potential energy—can be used at a later time when it is needed. Losing body fat requires using up this potential energy by using more calories than are taken in every day. This is best accomplished by a combination of calorie reduction and exercise. Have interested students study nutritional information provided by fast food restaurants and create a computer presentation on what they learn. **LS** Verbal

Kinetic Energy

Once an object begins to move, it has the ability to do work. Consider an apple that falls from a tree. The apple can do work when it hits the ground or lands on someone's head. The energy that an object has because it is moving is called **kinetic energy.**

The kinetic energy (KE) of an object depends on the object's mass. A bowling ball can do more work than a table-tennis ball if both balls are moving at the same speed. The kinetic energy of the object also depends on the object's rate of acceleration. An apple that is falling at 10 m/s can do more work than an apple that is falling at 1 m/s. In fact, the kinetic energy of a moving object depends on the square of the object's speed. **❯ Kinetic energy depends on both the mass and the speed of an object.**

> **Kinetic energy equation** $\quad kinetic\ energy = \frac{1}{2} \times mass \times speed\ squared$
>
> $$KE = \frac{1}{2}mv^2$$

Figure 3 shows a graph of kinetic energy versus speed for a snowboarding student who has a mass of 50 kg. Notice that kinetic energy is expressed in joules. Because kinetic energy is calculated by using mass and speed squared, kinetic energy is expressed in kilograms times meter squared per second squared (kg • m^2/s^2), which is equivalent to joules.

✔ **Reading Check** What are the SI units for kinetic energy?

Figure 3 A small increase in speed causes a large increase in kinetic energy. Kinetic energy varies as the speed squared. **How would the kinetic energy of this snow boarder change if he were wearing a heavy backpack?**

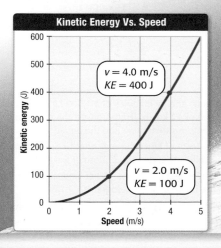

Kinetic Energy Vs. Speed

$v = 4.0$ m/s
$KE = 400$ J

$v = 2.0$ m/s
$KE = 100$ J

kinetic energy (ki NET ik EN uhr jee) the energy of an object due to the object's motion

READING TOOLBOX

Mathematical Language
Mathematical language is often used to describe physical quantities. What is meant by the phrase *speed squared*? Can you find other examples of mathematical language in this section?

Teaching Key Ideas
Kinetic Energy Kinetic energy, like all other kinds of energy, is an ability to do work. Kinetic energy is probably the most obvious form of energy. If students have had problems grasping energy, now is a good time to reinforce the concept. When you think of an "energetic" person, you may think of someone who moves around a lot. Something moving has, by nature of its motion, an ability to do work.

READING TOOLBOX

Visual Literacy Have students examine the graph in **Figure 3.** The graph shows kinetic energy versus speed for a snowboarder weighing 50 kg. Point out that as the speed increases, the kinetic energy increases rapidly. This happens because kinetic energy depends on the square of the speed. The curve on this graph is half of a parabola. **LS Visual**

MISCONCEPTION ALERT

Kinetic Energy and Momentum Some students may confuse kinetic energy and momentum. For those students, write the equations for momentum and for kinetic energy side-by-side. Have students consider how they are similar and how they are different. (Both quantities depend on mass and velocity, but kinetic energy has a more sensitive dependence on velocity because of the squared quantity.)

Differentiated Instruction

Advanced Learners
Potential and Kinetic Changes Have students write a brief paragraph describing the changes in potential and kinetic energy in a roller coaster as it sits motionless at the top of a rise, then begins rolling down the rise until it reaches the bottom. (At the top of the rise, the energy is all *PE* based on the coaster's height. As it starts rolling down the hill, its height decreases, so it loses *PE*. At the same time, its speed increases, so it gains *KE*. At the bottom of the hill, *KE* is at a maximum, and its *PE* has run out.) **LS Verbal**

READING TOOLBOX

Mathematical Language Speed squared means multiplying the number that quantifies the speed by itself. If the speed is 10 km/s, the speed squared would be 10 km/s × 10 km/s = 100 km^2/s^2. Other examples of mathematical language are "equation," "multiply," and "take the square root."

Math › Skills

Answers to Practice

1. $v = (42 \text{ km/h})(1{,}000 \text{ m/km})$
$(1 \text{ h}/3{,}600 \text{ s}) = 12 \text{ m/s}$
$KE = (1/2)(1{,}500 \text{ kg})(12 \text{ m/s})^2 =$
$1.1 \times 10^5 \text{ J}$
2. $v = \sqrt{2 \text{ KE/m}}$
$= \sqrt{[(2)(190 \text{ J})]/35 \text{ kg}} = 3.3 \text{ m/s}$
3. $m = 2 \text{ KE}/v^2 = [(2)(16 \text{ J})]/$
$(2.0 \text{ m/s})^2 = 8.0 \text{ kg}$

Additional Examples
A 2 kg ball and a 4 kg ball are travel-ing at the same speed. If the kinetic energy of the 2 kg ball is 5 J, what is the kinetic energy of the 4 kg ball? (**HINT:** You do not have to solve for the speed.)
Answer: (10 J)

A 2.0 kg ball has 4.0 J of kinetic energy when traveling at a certain speed. What is the kinetic energy of the ball when traveling at twice the original speed? (**HINT:** You do not have to solve for the original speed.)
Answer: (16 J)
LS Logical

www.scilinks.org
Topic: Kinetic Energy
Code: HK80833

Kinetic energy depends on speed more than it depends on mass.

You may have heard that car crashes are more dangerous at speeds above the speed limit than at the speed limit. The kinetic energy equation provides a scientific reason. In the kinetic energy equation, speed is squared, so a small change in speed causes a large change in kinetic energy. Because a car has much more kinetic energy at high speeds, it can do much more work—and thus much more damage—in a collision.

Atoms and molecules have kinetic energy.

Atoms and molecules are always moving. Therefore, these tiny particles have kinetic energy. The motion of particles is related to temperature. The higher the kinetic energy of the atoms and molecules in an object is, the higher the object's temperature is.

Math › Skills Kinetic Energy

What is the kinetic energy of a 44 kg cheetah running at 31 m/s?

Practice Hint

› Problem 2: Rearrange the kinetic energy equation to isolate speed on the left. First, write the equation for kinetic energy.

$$\frac{1}{2} mv^2 = KE$$

Multiply both sides by $\frac{2}{m}$.

$$\left(\frac{2}{m}\right) \times \frac{1}{2} mv^2 = \left(\frac{2}{m}\right) \times KE$$

$$v^2 = \frac{2KE}{m}$$

Take the square root of each side.

$$\sqrt{v^2} = \sqrt{\frac{2KE}{m}}$$

$$v = \sqrt{\frac{2KE}{m}}$$

› Problem 3: Rearrange the kinetic energy equation to isolate mass on the left:

$$m = \frac{2KE}{v^2}$$

Identify List the given and unknown values.	**Given:** *mass, m* = 44 kg *speed, v* = 31 m/s **Unknown:** *kinetic energy, KE* = ? J
Plan Write the equation for kinetic energy.	$kinetic\ energy = \frac{1}{2} \times mass \times speed\ squared$ $KE = \frac{1}{2} mv^2$
Solve Insert the known values into the equation, and solve.	$KE = \frac{1}{2}(44 \text{ kg})(31 \text{ m/s})^2$ $KE = 2.1 \times 10^4 \text{ kg} \cdot \text{m}^2/\text{s}^2 = 2.1 \times 10^4 \text{ J}$

Practice

1. Calculate the kinetic energy in joules of a 1,500 kg car that is moving at a speed of 42 km/h. (Hint: Convert the speed to me-ters per second before substituting into the equation.)
2. A 35 kg child has 190 J of kinetic energy after he sleds down a hill. What is the child's speed at the bottom of the hill?
3. A bowling ball traveling 2.0 m/s has 16 J of kinetic energy. What is the mass of the bowling ball in kilograms?

For more practice, visit **go.hrw.com** and enter keyword **HK8MP**.

Differentiated Instruction

Special Education Students
Note Cards Using note cards, ask students to label each card with a different form of energy. Have them include at least five different forms of energy in their note cards. On the back of each card, ask students to write a definition of each type of energy and list examples of how the energy is used. Any additional information, such as equations, may be added to the note cards. These cards may be used as study tools and to show understanding of the section.
LS Visual

Basic Learners
Algebra and Kinetic Energy Rearranging the kinetic energy equation involves working with squares and square roots. Ask an algebra teacher to visit your class to review these concepts with students. The Practice Hint shows students how to solve the equation for velocity and also gives them the equation rearranged to isolate mass.

Other Forms of Energy

An apple that is falling from a tree has both kinetic and potential energy. The sum of the kinetic energy and the potential energy in a system is called **mechanical energy.** Mechanical energy can also be thought of as the amount of work that something can do because of its kinetic and potential energies.

An apple can give you energy when you eat it. What form of energy is that? In almost every system, there are hidden forms of energy that are related to the arrangement of atoms that make up the objects in the system.

❯ **Energy that lies at the level of the atom is sometimes called *nonmechanical energy.*** However, a close look at the different forms of energy in a system reveals that in most cases, nonmechanical forms of energy are just special forms of either kinetic or potential energy.

Chemical reactions involve potential energy.

Chemical energy is a kind of potential energy. In a chemical reaction, bonds between atoms break apart. When the atoms form new bonds, a different substance is formed. Both the formation of bonds and the breaking of bonds involve changes in energy. The amount of *chemical energy* in a substance depends in part on the relative positions of the atoms in the substance.

Reactions that release energy decrease the potential energy in a substance. For example, when a match is struck, as shown in **Figure 4,** the release of stored energy from the match head produces light and a small explosion of hot gas.

✔ **Reading Check** What does chemical energy depend on?

Living things get energy from the sun.

Where does the lightning bug shown in **Figure 5** get the energy to glow? Where do you get the energy you need to live? The energy comes from food. When you eat a meal, you eat plants, animals, or both. Animals also eat plants, other animals, or both. Plants and algae do not need to eat, because they get their energy directly from sunlight.

Plants use *photosynthesis* to turn the energy in sunlight into chemical energy. This energy is stored in sugars and other organic molecules that make up cells in living tissue. Thus, when you eat a meal, you are really eating stored energy. When your body needs energy, some organic molecules are broken down through respiration. Respiration releases the energy your body needs in order to live and do work.

mechanical energy (muh KAN i kuhl EN uhr jee) the amount of work an object can do because of the object's kinetic and potential energies

Figure 4 When a match is struck, the chemical energy stored inside the head of the match is released as light and heat.

Figure 5 A lightning bug produces light through an efficient chemical reaction in its abdomen. Over 95% of the chemical energy is converted to light. **What other plants and animals produce light?**

Teaching Key Ideas

Nonmechanical Energy The distinction between mechanical energy and nonmechanical energy is vague by nature. Nonmechanical energy is often called "internal energy," also a vague concept. In most cases, nonmechanical energy can be reduced to some kind of mechanical energy (for instance, the kinetic energy of atoms in a gas as the basis for thermal energy). For each type of energy introduced in the next few pages, discuss how it can also be considered as either kinetic or potential energy.

Science Skills

Approximations in Science Explain to students that the practice of considering only major effects and ignoring small effects is a very common practice in science. As students read this page they may ask how scientists can consider some energy to be nonmechanical at some times and not at others. Explain that scientists are often trying to investigate one aspect of a thing in isolation from other things.

Answer to caption question

Some fish, bacteria, and fungi can all produce light.

Differentiated Instruction

Struggling Readers

Creating a Table Students who struggle with the reading on this page may benefit from creating a table that illustrates the differences between mechanical energy and nonmechanical energy. The table should include a column that names examples of each kind of energy. **LS** **Visual**

MISCONCEPTION ALERT

What is Energy? Students commonly believe that energy is a fluid, an ingredient, or a fuel. Emphasize that energy is not a material substance. The definition of energy as the ability to do work may seem vague to some students; remind them that the amount of energy associated with an object or system can be precisely quantified, as for example with the *KE* and *PE* equations they have learned in this section.

Teaching Key Ideas

Nuclear Energy Understanding non-mechanical energy can be difficult, but nuclear energy can be especially difficult to grasp. Tell students to imagine a large water balloon filled almost to the breaking point. You have to carry a balloon like that very carefully because the slightest bump will cause it to break. Now have students imagine two smaller water balloons that are not as full. There is still a large amount of flexibility in the balloon. Large nuclei are like an overfilled water balloon. The balloon (strong nuclear forces that hold the nucleus together) is stretched to the breaking point. When a nucleus undergoes fission, it splits into smaller nuclei, where the nuclear forces are not "stretched" as much. The energy that is released is the difference in the energy required to hold the nuclei together. It takes less energy to contain two small nuclei than it does to contain one very large one.

MISCONCEPTION
///ALERT

Effects of Energy It may not be clear to many students that forms of energy such as light, chemical, and sound energy can make things happen. Point out that sunlight is energy plants use to grow. Use other examples on these pages to make the effects of energy clearer. For example, chemical energy makes a match burn.

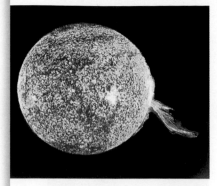

Figure 6 The nuclei of atoms contain enormous amounts of energy. The sun is fueled by nuclear fusion reactions in its core.

The sun gets energy from nuclear reactions.

The sun, shown in **Figure 6,** not only gives energy to living things but also keeps our whole planet warm and bright. And the energy that reaches Earth from the sun is only a small portion of the sun's total energy output. How does the sun produce so much energy?

The sun's energy comes from nuclear fusion, a kind of reaction in which light atomic nuclei combine to form a heavier nucleus. This nuclear energy is a kind of potential energy stored by the forces holding subatomic particles together in the nuclei of atoms.

Nuclear power plants use a different process, called *nuclear fission,* to release nuclear energy. In fission, a single large nucleus is split into two or more smaller nuclei. In both fusion and fission, small quantities of mass are converted into large quantities of energy.

Energy can be stored in fields.

The lights and appliances in your home are powered by another form of energy, electrical energy. Electrical energy results from the location of charged particles in an *electric field.* An electric field is similar to a gravitational field. Certain places have high *electric potential,* while others have low electric potential. When electrons move from an area of higher electric potential to an area of lower electric potential, they gain energy. Moving electrons also create magnetic fields, which can do work to power a motor. Electrons moving through the air between the ground and a cloud cause the lightning shown in **Figure 7.**

Figure 7 Electrical energy is derived from the flow of charged particles, as in a bolt of lightning or in a wire. We can harness electricity to power appliances in our homes.

Why It Matters

Energy Equivalence A piece of toast with butter contains about 315,000 J of chemical energy. This is enough energy for the following tasks:
- running a car for 7 seconds (at 80 km/h)
- jogging for 6 minutes
- bicycling for 10 minutes
- walking quickly for 15 minutes
- sleeping for 1½ hours
- using a 60 W light bulb for 1½ hours

Ask students how long each task could be performed with the energy from 230 Cal energy bar. (running a car: 21 seconds; jogging: 18 minutes; bicycling: 30 minutes; walking quickly: 45 minutes; sleeping: 4½ hours; using a 60-watt light bulb: 4½ hours)
As an extension, have students plot these values on a bar graph to visually compare the amount of time different tasks can be performed with a given amount of energy. **LS Logical**

Energy Stored in Plants

REAL WORLD

The sun floods Earth with a large amount of energy in the form of *electromagnetic radiation*. Nature has a unique way to store this energy from the sun. Green plants, algae, and some kinds of bacteria convert solar energy into chemical potential energy through the process of *photosynthesis*. Photosynthesis is a set of chemical reactions that use solar energy, carbon dioxide, and water to produce carbohydrates and oxygen. Chemical reactions in the bodies of animals and humans on Earth convert carbohydrates into work and thermal energy.

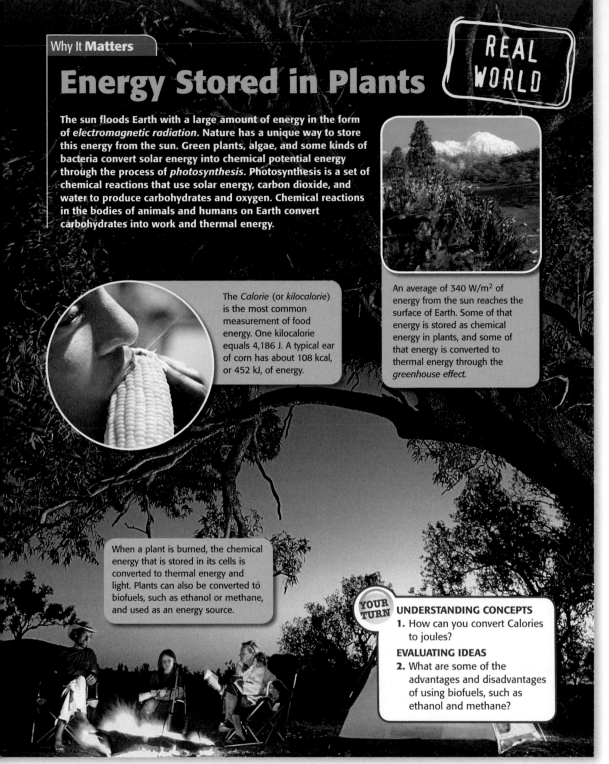

The *Calorie* (or *kilocalorie*) is the most common measurement of food energy. One kilocalorie equals 4,186 J. A typical ear of corn has about 108 kcal, or 452 kJ, of energy.

An average of 340 W/m² of energy from the sun reaches the surface of Earth. Some of that energy is stored as chemical energy in plants, and some of that energy is converted to thermal energy through the *greenhouse effect*.

When a plant is burned, the chemical energy that is stored in its cells is converted to thermal energy and light. Plants can also be converted to biofuels, such as ethanol or methane, and used as an energy source.

YOUR TURN

UNDERSTANDING CONCEPTS
1. How can you convert Calories to joules?

EVALUATING IDEAS
2. What are some of the advantages and disadvantages of using biofuels, such as ethanol and methane?

Energy Stored in Plants Plants and other organisms that store the energy from the sun as chemical energy are called *producers*. Other organisms, such as animals, which eat producers for energy, are called *consumers*. Consumers also eat the consumers that eat the plants, in a progression that ecologists call an *energy pyramid*. Each time an organism in the energy pyramid is consumed, the organism passes the energy stored in its body to the organism that eats it. However, not all the energy an organism has consumed is passed on. Most of the energy—about 90 percent of it—is used to build and maintain the body of the organism. So, only 10 percent of the energy consumed or produced at one level of an energy pyramid is passed on to the next.

READING TOOLBOX

Visual Literacy Have students list all the organisms and parts of organisms on the page. (Students should remember that people and plants are organisms.) Ask students: Which of the organisms have stored energy? (all of them) Where did the organisms in the pictures get energy? (The plants get energy from the sun. The people get energy from the foods they eat). **LS Visual**

Answers to Your Turn

1. The conversion factor is 4,186 J per Calorie (kilocalorie)
2. Advantages include: Biofuels are renewable and cleaner burning than fossil fuels. Disadvantages include: Can't yet meet demand, and still produce greenhouse gasses.

›Close

Reteaching Key Ideas

Key Idea Teams In teams of four, have each student become an expert on 1 Key Idea from the section opener. Have students use their books and class notes to answer the question posed by the key idea in writing. After students have answered the question, they should explain their answer to the group. Students can take turns explaining all the key ideas. **LS Interpersonal**

Answer to caption question

Light carries energy, so blocking light prevents light from carrying energy to shaded areas.

Formative Assessment

What happens to an object when work is done to it?

A. The object experiences a change of motion or position. (Correct. Work causes an object to move. If the object was already moving, work causes that motion to change.)

B. The object's kinetic energy always increases. (Incorrect. If an object were in motion and work were done to put the object at rest, then the object would have less kinetic energy after the work was done.)

C. The object's potential energy always increases. (Incorrect. Work can sometimes reduce an object's potential energy.)

D. The object's potential energy changes to kinetic energy. (Incorrect. Work can sometimes increase an object's potential energy.)

Figure 8 Electromagnetic waves carry energy from the sun to Earth. **Why is it cooler in the shade than in the sun?**

Light can carry energy across empty space.

Consider a bright summer day at a beach such as the one shown in **Figure 8.** Is it hotter where light is shining directly on the sand or under the shade of the umbrella? You might guess, correctly, that a seat in the direct sunlight is hotter. The reason is that light carries energy.

Light energy travels from the sun to Earth across empty space in the form of *electromagnetic waves*. Electromagnetic waves are made of electric and *magnetic fields,* so light energy is another example of energy stored in a field. You will learn more about light and waves in another chapter.

Section 3 Review

KEY IDEAS

1. **List** three forms of energy.
2. **Explain** how energy differs from work.
3. **Explain** the difference between potential energy and kinetic energy.
4. **Determine** what form or forms of energy apply to each of the following situations, and specify whether each form is mechanical or nonmechanical:
   a. a flying disk moving through the air
   b. a hot cup of soup
   c. a wound clock spring
   d. sunlight
   e. a boulder sitting at the top of a cliff

CRITICAL THINKING

5. **Applying Concepts** Water storage tanks are usually built on towers or placed on hilltops. Why?

6. **Analyzing Ideas** Name one situation in which gravitational potential energy might be useful, and name one situation in which it might be dangerous.

Math › Skills

7. Calculate the gravitational potential energy of a 93.0 kg sky diver who is 550 m above the ground.
8. What is the kinetic energy of a 0.02 kg bullet that is traveling 300 m/s? Express your answer in joules.
9. Calculate the kinetic or potential energy in joules for each of the following situations:
   a. A 2.5 kg book is held 2.0 m above the ground.
   b. A 15 g snowball is moving through the air at 3.5 m/s.
   c. A 35 kg child is sitting at the top of a slide that is 3.5 m above the ground.
   d. An 8,500 kg airplane is flying at 220 km/h.

Answers to Section Review

1. Answers may include: kinetic energy, potential energy (gravitational or elastic), mechanical energy, nonmechanical energy, chemical energy, electrical energy, nuclear energy, light energy.

2. Energy is the ability to do work. Or when work is done, energy is transferred from one object to another.

3. Potential energy is energy due to position. Kinetic energy is the energy of motion.

4. **a.** gravitational *PE* and *KE* (both mechanical)
   b. kinetic energy of the molecules (nonmechanical), chemical energy of the molecules (nonmechanical)

c. elastic potential energy, kinetic energy as the spring unwinds (both mechanical)

d. light energy (nonmechanical)

e. gravitational *PE* (mechanical)

5. Storing the water up high gives the water gravitational potential energy, so the water will naturally flow out of the tank if needed.

6. The water tank in item 5 is a case where gravitational *PE* is useful. Gravitational *PE* is dangerous to people hanging from the side of a cliff or building.

7. $PE = mgh = (93.0 \text{ kg})(9.8 \text{ m/s}^2)(550 \text{ m}) = 5.0 \times 10^5 \text{ J}$

Answers continued on page 469A

Conservation of Energy

Key Ideas

❯ How does energy change?

❯ What is the law of conservation of energy?

❯ How much of the work done by a machine is actually useful work?

Key Terms

efficiency

Why It Matters

Hydroelectric power plants use conservation of energy to generate the electricity that you use every day.

❯ Focus

In this section, students learn about energy transformations and the law of energy conservation. The section concludes with a discussion of the efficiency of machines.

🔊 Bellringer

Use the Bellringer transparency to prepare students for this section.

Demonstrate

Storing Energy Hold a basketball in front of you. Ask: What kind of energy is this basketball storing? (gravitational potential energy) Drop a basketball and let it bounce a few times. Ask students: What kind of energy does the ball gain as it falls? (kinetic energy) When does the basketball gain potential energy again? (as it bounces upward) What happens to that potential energy? (It changes to kinetic energy when the ball falls again.) Why doesn't the ball just keep bouncing forever? (The ball loses energy in the forms of heat, friction, and sound energy.) Tell students that in this chapter, they will explore how energy changes form.
LS Verbal

Answer to caption question

The forms of energy seen on a roller coaster include work put into the roller coaster and stored as gravitational potential energy, kinetic energy, and heat energy.

Imagine that you are sitting in the front car of a roller coaster, such as the one shown in **Figure 1.** A conveyor belt pulls the car slowly up the first hill. When you reach the crest of the hill, you are barely moving. Then, you go over the edge and start to race down the hill. You speed faster and faster until you reach the bottom of the hill. The wheels are roaring along the track. You continue to move up, down, and around through smaller humps, twists, and turns. Finally, you climb another hill almost as big as the first, drop down again, and coast to the end of the ride.

Energy Transformations

In the course of a roller coaster ride, energy changes form many times. You may not have noticed the conveyor belt at the beginning, but in terms of energy input, the conveyor belt is the most important part of the ride. All of the energy required for the whole ride comes from work done by the conveyor belt as it lifts the cars and the passengers up the first hill.

The energy from that initial work is stored as gravitational potential energy at the top of the first hill. After that point, most of the energy goes through a series of transformations, or changes, turning into kinetic energy and then back into potential energy.

A small quantity of the stored energy is transferred to the wheels as heat and to the air as vibrations that make a roaring sound. ❯ **Energy readily changes from one form to another.** But whatever forms the energy takes during a transformation, the total amount of energy always remains the same.

Figure 1 The Kingda Ka roller coaster, located in New Jersey, takes riders up 139 m and allows them to drop at near free-fall acceleration. **What forms of energy propel a roller coaster car?**

Key Resources

 Teaching Transparency
TM37 Energy Graphs

Visual Concepts
Conservation of Mechanical Energy
Mechanical Efficiency
Law of Conservation of Energy

Datasheets
Energy Transfer
Is Energy Conserved in a Pendulum

Science Skills Worksheet
Percentages

Math Skills Worksheet
Efficiency

Cross-Disciplinary Worksheets
Integrating Environmental Science—
  Understanding the Conservation of
  Energy
Integrating Technology—Batteries and
  Emerging Technology

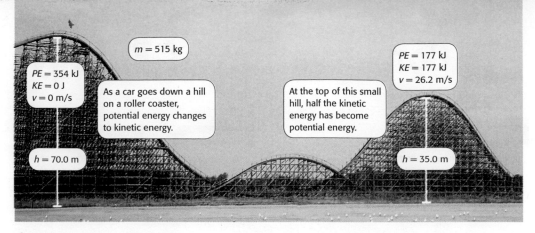

$m = 515$ kg

$PE = 354$ kJ
$KE = 0$ J
$v = 0$ m/s

As a car goes down a hill on a roller coaster, potential energy changes to kinetic energy.

$h = 70.0$ m

At the top of this small hill, half the kinetic energy has become potential energy.

$PE = 177$ kJ
$KE = 177$ kJ
$v = 26.2$ m/s

$h = 35.0$ m

Figure 2 The energy of a roller coaster car changes from potential energy to kinetic energy and back again many times during a ride.

Teaching Key Ideas

Energy Changing Form Point out to students that in a world with no friction, the exchange of energy—from potential to kinetic and back again—could go on forever. In the real world, some energy is converted to friction as the car rolls along the track, so the roller coaster could not continue forever without some energy input (such as that provided by the motor that pulls the cars up the first hill).

READING TOOLBOX

Visual Literacy Figure 2 shows diagrams of two different hills on a roller coaster. Walk students through the energy quantities, which are generated by the equations learned in Section 3. What assumption is made in each diagram about the energy of the roller-coaster car? (The total mechanical energy of the car at a later time is equal to the total mechanical energy of the car at any earlier time. This is based on the law of conservation of energy.) **LS Logical**

QuickLab ⏱ 10 min

Energy Transfer

❶ Flex a piece of **thick wire** or part of a **coat hanger** back and forth about 10 times with your hands.

❷ After flexing the wire, cautiously touch the part of the wire where you bent it.

❸ How does the wire feel? What happened to the energy you put into it? Did you do work?

QuickLab

Teacher's Notes Caution students to avoid flexing the wire too many times, as it may break or heat up enough to cause burns.

Materials per Group
• thick wire or part of a coat hanger

Answer
3. The wire feels hot. This is because the mechanical energy involved in moving the wire is transformed into kinetic energy of atoms in the wire. The wire is displaced by a force during the flexing, so work is done on the wire.

Potential energy can become kinetic energy.

Compare the energy of a roller coaster car at the top of a hill with the car's energy at the bottom of a hill. As **Figure 2** shows, almost all of the energy of the roller coaster car is potential energy at the top of a tall hill. The potential energy slowly changes to kinetic energy as the car accelerates down the hill. At the bottom of the lowest hill, the car has the most kinetic energy and the least potential energy.

Notice that the system has the same total amount of energy whether the car is at the top or the bottom of the hill. All of the gravitational potential energy at the top changes to kinetic energy as the car goes down the hill. When the car reaches the lowest point, the system has no potential energy left. If all of the energy were to remain as mechanical energy, then the increase in kinetic energy would exactly equal the decrease in potential energy.

✓ **Reading Check** Where on a roller coaster is the potential energy the least?

Kinetic energy can become potential energy.

When the car is at the lowest point on the roller coaster, its energy is almost all kinetic. This kinetic energy can do the work to carry the car up another hill. As the car climbs the hill, the car slows down and its kinetic energy decreases. Where does that energy go? Most of it turns back into potential energy.

At the top of a smaller hill, the car will still have some kinetic energy, along with some potential energy. The kinetic energy will carry the car forward over the top of the next hill. Of course, the roller coaster car cannot climb a hill that is taller than the first hill without an extra boost. The car does not have enough energy.

Social Studies Connection

The First Roller Coasters Though common roller coasters are a good example of energy transfer, the principle of changing potential to kinetic energy can be shown on every surface. In fact, the first roller coasters were giant ice slides made in Russia. The first of these ice slides, which was in St. Petersburg, consisted of a 70-foot wooden frame packed with watered-down snow that turned into ice. The sleds were made of two-foot ice blocks with seats carved into them. Because ice has a low coefficient of friction, the ice "cars" easily slid down the ice slide. The seats were lined with straw or fur for insulation.

Mechanical energy can change to other forms of energy.

If changes from potential energy to kinetic energy and back again were always complete, then balls would always bounce back to the same height from which they were dropped and cars on roller coasters could keep gliding forever. When a ball bounces on the ground, not all of its kinetic energy changes to elastic potential energy. Some of the kinetic energy compresses the air around the ball, which makes a sound, and some of the kinetic energy makes the ball, the air, and the ground a little warmer. As **Figure 3** shows, each time the ball bounces, it loses some mechanical energy.

Likewise, a moving roller coaster car loses mechanical energy as it rolls, because of friction and air resistance. This energy does not just disappear, though. Some of it increases the temperature of the track, the car's wheels, and the air. Some of the energy compresses the air and causes a roaring sound. Often, when energy seems to disappear, it is really just changing to a nonmechanical form.

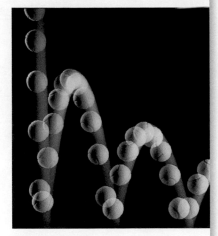

Figure 3 Each time a tennis ball bounces, some of its mechanical energy changes to nonmechanical energy.

SCiLINKS.
www.scilinks.org
Topic: Energy Transformations
Code: HK80517

Graphing ⟩ **Skills**

Graphing Mechanical Energy

The bar graph shown here presents data about a roller coaster car. What variables are plotted? Identify the dependent and independent variables. What does the legend tell you about this graph?

Identify Study the axes and legend to determine the variables.	Location is the variable on the *x*-axis. Two variables are plotted on the *y*-axis: kinetic and potential energy.
Plan Consider the relationship between the variables.	The independent variable is location, because the car's kinetic energy and potential energy change with location.
Solve Examine the legend and how it relates to the graph.	The legend indicates that the car's mechanical energy consists of both kinetic energy and potential energy.

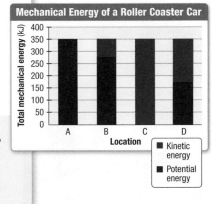

Mechanical Energy of a Roller Coaster Car

■ Kinetic energy
■ Potential energy

Practice

1. At which location does the car have the greatest potential energy? At which location does the car have the least potential energy?
2. Given the data in this graph, can you calculate the car's speed?
3. What does this graph show about the relationship between potential energy and kinetic energy?

Teaching Key Ideas

Understanding Energy Transfers The flight of a ball can help illustrate energy transfers. On the board, draw the flight of a ball thrown from one person to another. This should be drawn as an inverted parabola. Ask students to identify where the ball has the maximum kinetic energy (at the bottom on either side of the curve) and where the ball has the maximum potential energy (at the top). Point out to students that the ball they have just drawn on the board does not have 0 J *KE* at the top, because it is traveling sideways as well as up and down. Therefore, the ball still has some *KE* at the top. If it did not, it would fall straight down, because there would be no energy at the top of the path to carry the ball sideways. **LS** **Visual**

Graphing ⟩ **Skills**

Answers to Practice

1. position A; position C
2. No; you cannot calculate the speed because the mass of the roller coaster car is not given.
3. This graph demonstrates that as kinetic energy increases, potential energy decreases and that as kinetic energy decreases, potential energy increases. In other words, the sum of the kinetic and potential energies does not change.

Demonstrate

Bouncing Balls You will need several different types of balls (super ball, tennis ball, racquet ball, squash ball, steel ball bearing, ball made of clay, etc.) Allow 10 minutes.

Rotating through all the types of balls, hold two at a time approximately 1 m above the floor or a desk. Drop the balls simultaneously. Lead a discussion about why each ball bounces to a different height. Discuss the energy conversions mentioned in the text. Ask students to hypothesize about the "disappearance" of the energy. Explain to students that each ball has a different ability to store elastic potential energy—the super ball is very elastic, while the ball of clay is definitely not. Students should be able to conclude that some energy is converted to other forms in the collision with the floor or table. Lead students to the realization that some energy is released as sound, and some is stored internally as the temperature of the ball rises. **LS** **Visual**

Teaching Key Ideas

Conservation of Energy Students may confuse the conservation of energy law with the kind of energy conservation that is important to ecologists and environmentalists. They are related but not the same. Conservationists want to preserve energy in a useable form. Most energy technologies are inefficient, and after the energy has been used, it is no longer useful. (For example, once gasoline is burned, the energy has been used to move the car, heat the tires and road, and so on.)

MISCONCEPTION ALERT

Energy Transformations Many students believe that energy transformations involve only one form of energy at a time. The transformation from kinetic to thermal energy is especially hard to visualize. Point out that both types of energy involve motion; the first is on a large scale, such as motion of a bending wire, and the second is on a molecular scale, such as the motion of atoms in the wire.

When fireworks explode, potential energy is converted to many other forms of energy: kinetic energy, sound, light, and heat.

Midway through its path, the rocket has both potential and kinetic energy.

Figure 4 When it is on the ground, the fireworks rocket has chemical potential energy.

The Law of Conservation of Energy

In our study of machines, we saw that the work done on a machine is equal to the work that it can do. Similarly, in our study of the roller coaster, we found that the energy present at the beginning of the ride is present throughout the ride and at the end of the ride even though the energy changes form.

These simple observations are based on one of the most important principles in science—the law of conservation of energy. Here is the law in its simplest form.

Law of conservation of energy	Energy cannot be created or destroyed.

❯ **In other words, the total amount of energy in the universe never changes, although energy may change from one form to another.** Energy never disappears, but it does change form.

Energy does not appear or disappear.

Energy cannot be created from nothing. Imagine a girl jumping on a trampoline. If her second bounce is higher than her first bounce, we must conclude that she added energy to her bounce by doing work with her legs. Whenever the total energy in a system increases, the increase must be due to energy that enters the system.

Mechanical energy can change to nonmechanical energy through chemical reactions, air resistance, and other factors. Some of the energy in a system may leak out into the surrounding environment. When fireworks explode in a burst of heat, light, and sound, as shown in **Figure 4,** the conversion of energy is spectacular!

Thermodynamics describes energy conservation.

Energy can be transferred as work or as heat. For example, when you lift a ball, you give the ball potential energy. When you sand wood, the wood gets warm and energy is transferred as heat. ❯ **For any system, the net change in energy equals the energy transferred as work and as heat.** When no energy is transferred as heat or as work, mechanical energy is conserved. This form of the law of energy conservation is called the *first law of thermodynamics.*

Energy has many forms and can be found almost everywhere. Accounting for all of the energy in a given case can be complicated. To make studying a case easier, scientists often limit their view to a small area or a small number of objects. These boundaries define a system.

Differentiated Instruction

Advanced Learners

Accounting for Energy Many examples in the chapter so far have assumed "ideal" circumstances, disregarding friction and air resistance. However, once the idea that mechanical energy can change to nonmechanical energy is introduced, deviations from the ideal in "real world" situations can be explained. After they have finished reading this page, have students return to earlier examples in the chapter to consider realistic energy transfer from them. Have them write a few paragraphs about a given example, accounting for as much of the "lost" energy as possible. **LS Verbal**

Basic Learners

Types of Energy Ask struggling students if they have ever seen a fireworks display. Have them describe what they see and hear when a rocket is sent up. Students will probably know the rocket travels up, and bursts into a shower of light and sound. Use **Figure 4** to help students understand kinetic, potential and chemical energy. Draw the entire flight of the rocket on the board. Have students identify all the kinds of energy at each point in the rocket's path. **LS Intrapersonal**

Systems may be open, closed or isolated.

A system in which energy and matter are exchanged with the surroundings is an *open* system. If energy, but not matter, is exchanged, the system is *closed*. An *isolated* system is one in which neither energy nor matter is exchanged. Imagine a beaker of water over a burner. If you considered only the flow of energy as the water was heated, it might seem like a closed system. But matter in the form of water vapor leaves the beaker, especially if the water is boiling. Thus, it is an open system.

Very few real-world systems are isolated systems. Most systems are open. Earth itself might be considered a closed system because its limited exchange of matter with outer space could be <u>ignored</u>. However, Earth receives energy from the sun that is reradiated to space. So Earth is not an isolated system.

✓ Reading Check What is the difference between an open system and a closed system?

Academic Vocabulary

ignore (ig NAWR) to refuse to notice

InquiryLab
Is energy conserved by a pendulum?

 30 min

Procedure

❶ Hang a **pendulum bob** from a **string** in front of a **chalkboard** or a **white board.** On the board, draw the diagram shown in the photograph below. Use a **meterstick** and a **level** to make sure the horizontal line is parallel to the ground.

❷ Pull the pendulum ball back to the "X." Make sure that everyone is out of the way. Release the pendulum. Mark how high the pendulum swings on the other side in the first swing.

❸ Let the pendulum swing back and forth several times. How many swings does the pendulum make before the ball noticeably fails to reach its original height?

❹ Stop the pendulum, and hold it again at the "X." Get another student to place the eraser end of a **pencil** on the intersection of the horizontal and vertical lines. Again, make sure that everyone, especially your helper, is out of the way.

❺ Release the pendulum again. This time, its motion will be altered halfway through the swing as the string hits the pencil. How high does the pendulum swing now? Why?

❻ Place the pencil at different heights along the vertical line. How is the motion of the pendulum affected? If you put the pencil down close enough to the arc of the pendulum, the pendulum will do a loop around the pencil. Explain why.?

Analysis

1. Use the law of conservation of energy to explain your observations in steps 2–6.

2. If you let the pendulum swing long enough, it will start to slow down and will not rise to the line anymore. Has the system lost energy? Where did the energy go?

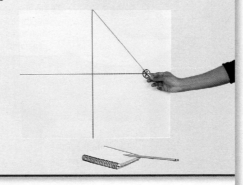

Differentiated Instruction

Alternative Assessment

Open and Closed Systems Have students think of different systems (just about anything can be considered a system). For each idea, ask what boundaries define the system. Is the system open or closed? (Almost all systems are open to some degree.) If open, where does energy come into and leak out of the system? Ask each student to choose an open system to diagram. Diagrams should illustrate the system boundaries and should also show places where energy comes in and out of the system. **LS Logical**

Demonstrate

Open or Closed? In lab and a safe distance from students, boil a beaker of water over a hot plate or gas flame. Ask students: What is happening in this system? (The beaker is being heated by the hot plate or flame.) Is this an open system or a closed system? (It's an open system, because energy is being added to the beaker and then the energy is creating steam that leaves the beaker and enters the air of the room.) Explain to students that very few energy systems are truly closed, and that most energy systems on Earth are open, because it is very difficult to prevent all energy from flowing into or out of any system. **LS Visual**

InquiryLab

Teacher's Notes Attach the string and hooks or nails before students arrive. Try to make sure that the string is far enough from the wall that the plumb bob and string do not rub against anything as they swing.

Materials per Group
- chalkboard or white board
- level
- meter stick
- pendulum bob
- string, 1 m

Answers to Analysis

1. The bob's *PE* at the beginning is converted into *KE* at the bottom of the swing. The *KE* at the bottom is converted back into *PE* as the bob rises. When the pencil is low enough, the bob cannot rise enough to convert all *KE* into *PE,* so the bob continues to travel, looping over the pencil.

2. The energy of the pendulum is lost to friction between the string and hook, and very slightly to air friction. This causes the string and nail to heat up and the air to move, respectively.

Why It **Matters**

How Do Engineers Use Conservation of Energy? When students think of dams and hydropower, they probably think of the large-scale operations that generate tremendous amounts of power. But these same principles also can be used on much smaller scales to generate electricity: Flowing water can move a turbine to generate electricity.

In fact, home owners with a creek or a stream can generate substantial power without even building a dam, because even without a dam, a flowing creek is converting potential energy into kinetic energy, that can spin a turbine and change in to electrical energy. To be useful for hydropower, the creek must have enough water flow and vertical drop to turn the small turbine. The greater the flow and the vertical drop, the more electricity can be created.

The start-up costs of building a micro-hydro power pant can be substantial, but in many cases homeowners can generate more power than they can use, and then sell power to a local power company. Have interested students investigate building a micro-hydro power station, and create a computer presentation to share what they learn with the class. **LS Logical**

Why It **Matters**

How Do Engineers Use Conservation of Energy?

REAL WORLD

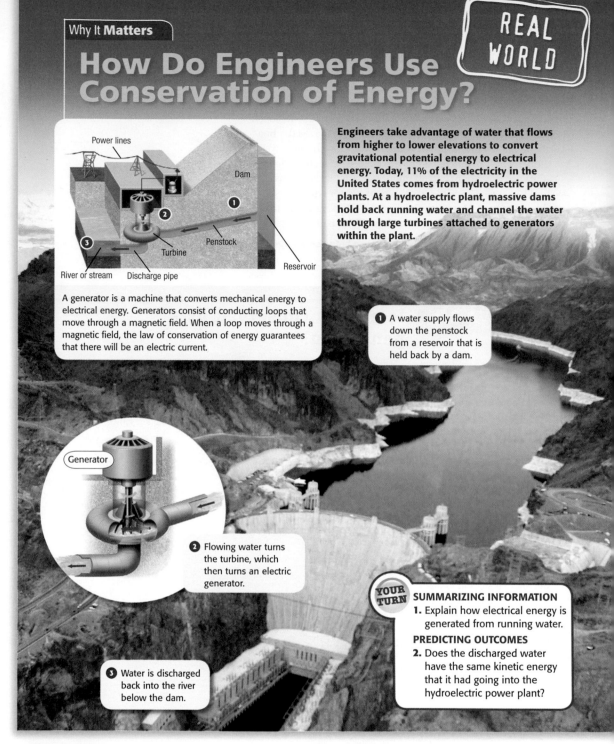

A generator is a machine that converts mechanical energy to electrical energy. Generators consist of conducting loops that move through a magnetic field. When a loop moves through a magnetic field, the law of conservation of energy guarantees that there will be an electric current.

Engineers take advantage of water that flows from higher to lower elevations to convert gravitational potential energy to electrical energy. Today, 11% of the electricity in the United States comes from hydroelectric power plants. At a hydroelectric plant, massive dams hold back running water and channel the water through large turbines attached to generators within the plant.

① A water supply flows down the penstock from a reservoir that is held back by a dam.

② Flowing water turns the turbine, which then turns an electric generator.

③ Water is discharged back into the river below the dam.

YOUR TURN

SUMMARIZING INFORMATION
1. Explain how electrical energy is generated from running water.

PREDICTING OUTCOMES
2. Does the discharged water have the same kinetic energy that it had going into the hydroelectric power plant?

READING TOOLBOX

Visual Literacy Ask students: Is a hydroelectric dam, like the one shown on this page, an open system or a closed system? (open). Where does the energy come from to make the electricity? (from the potential energy of the water behind the dam) Where does water get the potential energy? (from the water flowing to the dam) What are some ways that water flows to a river? (rainfall and snowmelt) What provides the energy to evaporate water into the atmosphere? (the sun) So, what is the original source of energy for hydropower? (the sun)

Answers to Your Turn
1. Water falls, turning a turbine, the turbine turns conducting loops. As the loops move through a magnetic field, they produce an electric current.
2. No, some of the kinetic energy was converted to electrical energy.

Efficiency of Machines

If you use a pulley to raise a sail on a sailboat like the one in **Figure 5,** you have to do work against the force of friction in the pulley. You also must lift the added weight of the rope and the hook connected to the sail. As a result, only some of the energy that you transfer to the pulley is available to raise the sail. **❯ Only a portion of the work done by any machine is** *useful* **work— that is, work that the machine is designed or intended to do.**

Not all of the work done by a machine is useful work.

Because of friction and other factors, only some of the work done by a machine is applied to the task at hand. The machine also does some incidental work that does not serve any intended purpose. There is a difference between the total work and the useful work done by a machine.

Even though all of the work done on a machine has some effect on the output work that the machine does, the output work may not be in the form that you expect. For example, because of friction, some of the energy applied to the pulley to lift the sail is transferred as heat that warms the pulley. This warming is not a desired effect. The amount of useful work might decrease slightly more if the pulley squeaks, because some energy is "lost" as it dissipates into forces that vibrate the pulley and the air to produce the squeaking sound.

✔ Reading Check What are some of the ways that energy is "lost" in machines?

Efficiency is the ratio of useful work out to work in.

The **efficiency** of a machine is a measure of how much useful work a machine can do. Efficiency is defined as the ratio of useful work output to total work input.

Efficiency equation

$$efficiency = \frac{useful\ work\ output}{work\ input}$$

Efficiency is usually expressed as a percentage. To change an answer found by using the efficiency equation into a percentage, multiply the answer by 100 and then add the percent sign (%).

A machine that is 100% efficient would produce exactly as much useful work as the work done on the machine. Because every machine has some friction, no machine is 100% efficient. The useful work output of a machine never equals—and certainly cannot exceed—the work input.

Figure 5 The pulleys on a sailboat, like all machines, are less than 100% efficient.

efficiency (e FISH uhn see) a quantity, usually expressed as a percentage, that measures the ratio of useful work output to work input

Why It Matters

Energy Guide Labels In the United States, consumers can easily determine the relative efficiency of many common appliances, including refrigerators, freezers, clothes washers, dishwashers, and room air conditioners. All they need to do is consult the mandatory yellow *EnergyGuide* label placed on appliances by the manufacturers. These labels indicate the lowest and highest amounts of average yearly energy use for appliances of this type. The energy use for the appliance in question is indicated on this scale. This shows consumers the relative efficiency of the appliance.

For example, a clothes washer label might show that washers of this type use from 312 kW•h/y to 1,306 kW•h/y, with the washer in question operating at 860 kW•h/y. Thus, this washing machine's efficiency is about average. The *EnergyGuide* labels also show the approximate yearly operating cost for the appliance. (The labels became mandatory in the 1970s; appliances made before then do not have the labels.) Ask interested students to visit a store to compare the efficiency of different models of the same appliance. Have them create a chart or graph to share with the class. **LS Logical**

Differentiated Instruction

Basic Learners

Efficiency Equation Students struggling with the efficiency equation may benefit from a review of ratios. It may also help to show them efficiency in their real lives. For example, a batting average is just an efficiency equation. A batting average shows the number of hits a batter gets divided by all of his or her attempts. Ask: "What is the batting average for a batter who had 5 hits in 10 attempts at bat?" (0.500) **LS Logical**

Teaching Key Ideas

Useful Work Compare the last sentence on this page with the following phrase from the subsection in Section 1 titled *Machines and Mechanical Advantage*: "Therefore, a machine allows the same amount of work to be done . . ." How can these both be true? (The law of conservation of energy requires that the energy that goes into the machine does not disappear, although it may change form. If the energy changes form, it may no longer be in a useful form.) **LS Verbal**

Why It Matters

Increasing Efficiency Even though perpetual motion machines are impossible, reducing friction and air resistance has increased the efficiency of many machines we use. Cars, planes, high-speed trains, and ships have all benefited from careful designs that reduce drag. Reduced drag allows the machines to use less fuel, and consequently make less pollution. Ask students: "What tools would help scientists decrease a car's air resistance?" (a computer model or a wind tunnel.) **LS** **Logical**

Answer to caption question

Perpetual motion is impossible because it is impossible to build a system that has absolutely no friction and air resistance, and every system needs energy input.

Math Skills

Answers to Practice

1. *efficiency* = (1,800 J)/(2,400 J) = 0.75 or 75%
2. *work input* = *useful work output/ efficiency* = 1,200 J /0.25 = 4,800 J
3. *useful work output* = (*efficiency*)(*work input*) = (0.375)(125 J) = 46.9 J

Additional Examples

How much work must you do using a pulley that has an efficiency of 65 percent to raise a 120 N box up to a 3.0 m shelf? (**Hint:** First solve for the work done on the box.)
Answer: 550 N

If you improve the efficiency of the pulley to 85 percent by oiling it, how much work would you have to do?
Answer: 420 J
LS **Logical**

Figure 6 Theoretically, a perpetual motion machine could keep going forever without any energy loss or energy input. **Why is a perpetual motion machine impossible?**

Practice Hint

> The efficiency equation can be rearranged to isolate any of the variables on the left.
> Problem 2: Rearrange the efficiency equation to isolate work input on the left side.
> Problem 3: Rearrange the efficiency equation to isolate useful work output.
> When using these rearranged forms to solve the problems, you will have to plug in values for efficiency. When doing so, do not use a percentage. Instead, convert the percentage to a decimal by dropping the percent sign and dividing by 100.

Perpetual motion machines are impossible.

A machine designed to keep going forever without any input of energy is shown in **Figure 6**. Such a theoretical machine is called a *perpetual motion machine*. Many clever inventors have devoted a lot of time and effort to designing such a machine. But a perpetual motion machine could work only in the absence of friction and air resistance, a condition not found in this world.

Math Skills — Efficiency

A sailor uses a rope and an old, squeaky pulley to raise a sail that weighs 140 N. He finds that he must do 180 J of work on the rope to raise the sail by 1 m. (He does 140 J of work on the sail.) What is the efficiency of the pulley? Express your answer as a percentage.

Identify List the given and unknown values.	**Given:** $work\ input = 180\ J$ $useful\ work\ output = 140\ J$ **Unknown:** $efficiency = ?\ \%$
Plan Write the equation for efficiency.	$efficiency = \dfrac{useful\ work\ output}{work\ input}$
Solve Insert the known values into the equation, and solve.	$efficiency = \dfrac{140\ J}{180\ J} = 0.78$ To express this number as a percentage, multiply by 100 and add the percent sign (%). $efficiency = 0.78 \times 100 = 78\%$

Practice

1. Alice and Jim calculate that they must do 1,800 J of work to push a piano up a ramp. However, because they must also overcome friction, they actually must do 2,400 J of work. What is the efficiency of the ramp?
2. It takes 1,200 J of work to lift a car high enough to change a tire. How much work must be done by the person operating the jack if the jack is 25% efficient?
3. A windmill has an efficiency of 37.5%. If a gust of wind does 125 J of work on the blades of the windmill, how much output work can the windmill do as a result of the gust?

For more practice, visit **go.hrw.com** and enter keyword **HK8MP**.

Differentiated Instruction

Advanced Learners

Perpetual Motion Machines Have students research some of the ideas people have had throughout history for perpetual motion machines. Remind them that perpetual motion machines are not possible, because some energy always transfers out of a system. With this in mind, ask each student to choose a particular example to illustrate on poster board. Display students' posters around the classroom. **LS** **Verbal**

Machines need energy input.

Because energy always leaks out of a system, a machine such as the solar car in **Figure 7** needs at least a small amount of energy input to keep going. But new technologies, from magnetic trains to high-speed microprocessors, reduce the amount of energy that leaks from systems so that energy can be used as efficiently as possible.

Figure 7 This solar electric car converts solar energy to electrical energy and converts electrical energy to mechanical energy and work.

Section 4 Review

KEY IDEAS

1. **List** three cases in which potential energy becomes kinetic energy and three cases in which kinetic energy becomes potential energy.

2. **State** the law of conservation of energy in your own words. Give an example of a situation that you have either encountered or know about in which the law of conservation of energy is demonstrated.

3. **Explain** why machines are never 100% efficient.

4. **Describe** the rise and fall of a thrown basketball by using the concepts of kinetic energy and potential energy.

CRITICAL THINKING

5. **Creative Thinking** Using what you have learned about energy transformations, explain why the driver of a car has to continuously apply pressure to the gas pedal in order to keep the car cruising at a steady speed, even on a flat road. Does this situation violate the law of conservation of energy? Explain.

6. **Applying Knowledge** Use the concepts of kinetic energy and potential energy to describe the motion of a child on a swing. Why does the child need a push from time to time?

Math Skills

7. When you do 100 J of work on the handle of a bicycle pump, the pump does 40 J of work pushing the air into the tire. What is the efficiency of the pump?

8. A river does 6,500 J of work on a water wheel every second. The wheel's efficiency is 12%.
   a. How much work in joules can the axle of the wheel do?
   b. What is the power output of the wheel in 1 s?

9. John is using a pulley to lift the sail on his sailboat. The sail weighs 150 N, and he must lift it 4.0 m.
   a. How much work must be done on the sail?
   b. If the pulley is 50% efficient, how much work must John do on the rope to lift the sail?

› Close

Reteaching Key Ideas

Five Points Have students write down the three key ideas for this section, leaving space beneath each key idea. Under each idea, have students write five important points or examples that illustrate the key idea. Have students exchange their papers with a partner, and then have each partner explain the five points or examples chosen.
LS Interpersonal

Formative Assessment

When you kick a soccer ball, some of the energy is transferred to the ball as kinetic energy. What happens to the rest of the energy?

A. Some of the energy of the kick is transformed into chemical energy of the ball. (Incorrect. No chemical change takes place when a soccer ball is kicked.)

B. Some of the energy of the kick is destroyed. (Incorrect. Energy cannot be destroyed.)

C. Some of the energy from the kick is transformed into heat energy and sound energy that leave the system. (Correct. Most of the energy is transferred to the ball, but some of the energy changes form—becoming heat and sound which flow from the ball into the area around the ball.)

D. Some of the energy becomes electrical energy. (Incorrect. Electrical energy is made using magnetic fields and conducting materials.)

Answers to Section Review

1. *PE* to *KE*: a falling ball, anything rolling downhill, a pendulum on the downswing; *KE* to *PE*: a rising ball, anything rolling uphill, a pendulum on the upswing

2. Energy can neither be created nor destroyed. In a swinging pendulum, energy is constantly transformed from potential to kinetic energy and back again. In all of these transformations, the total mechanical energy remains the same.

3. Friction prevents machines from being 100 percent efficient.

4. The player throws the ball, giving it *KE*. The ball begins to rise and slow down as *KE* is transformed into *PE* due to gravity. At its peak, the ball has maximum *PE*, then begins to fall, transforming *PE* into *KE*.

5. The driver must keep transferring potential energy from the gas to the kinetic energy of the car to make up for the losses due to friction within the car's mechanisms, between the tires and the road, and due to wind resistance. This does not violate the law of conservation of energy because mechanical energy is transformed into nonmechanical forms.

Answers continued on p. 469A

Skills Practice

Energy of a Rolling Ball

Raised objects have gravitational potential energy. Moving objects have kinetic energy. In this lab, you will find out how these two kinds of energy are related in a system in which a ball rolls down a ramp.

Time Required

1 lab period

Ratings

EASY ——————→ HARD

Teacher Prep 🧪

Student Set-Up 🧪🧪

Concept Level 🧪🧪

Clean Up 🧪

Skills Acquired

- Collecting data
- Communicating
- Identifying/Recognizing patterns
- Interpreting
- Measuring
- Organizing and analyzing data

Scientific Methods

In this lab, students will:
- Make observations
- Analyze the results
- Draw conclusions
- Communicate results

Safety Cautions

The balls used for the experiment could cause trip and fall hazards. Be sure that students use a catch box at the end of the ramp.

Objectives

> **Measure** the height, distance traveled, and time interval for a ball rolling down a ramp.

> **Calculate** the ball's potential energy at the top of the ramp and its kinetic energy at the bottom of the ramp.

> **Analyze** the results to find the relationship between potential energy and kinetic energy.

Materials

balance
board, at least 90 cm (3 ft) long
box
golf ball, racquet ball, or handball
masking tape
meterstick
stack of books, at least 45 cm high
stopwatch

Procedure

Preparing for Your Experiment

❶ On a blank sheet of paper, prepare a table like the one shown below.

Sample Data Table: Potential Energy and Kinetic Energy

	Height 1	Height 2	Height 3
Mass of ball (kg)			
Length of ramp (m)			
Height of ramp (m)			
Time ball traveled, first trial (s)			
Time ball traveled, second trial (s)			
Time ball traveled, third trial (s)			
Average time ball traveled (s)	DO NOT WRITE IN BOOK		
Average speed of ball (m/s)			
Final speed of ball (m/s)			
Final kinetic energy of ball (J)			
Initial potential energy of ball (J)			
Initial *PE* – Final *KE* (J)			

❷ Measure the mass of the ball, and record it in your table.

❸ Place a strip of masking tape across the board close to one end, and measure the distance from the tape to the opposite end of the board. Record this distance in the row labeled "Length of ramp."

❹ Make a catch box by cutting out one side of a box.

❺ Make a stack of books approximately 15 cm high. Build a ramp like the one shown in the photograph by setting the taped end of the board on top of the books. Place the other end of the board in the catch box. Measure the vertical height of the ramp at the tape, and record this value in your table in the row labeled "Height of ramp."

Making Time Measurements

6 Place the ball on the ramp at the tape. Release the ball, and use a stopwatch to measure how long the ball takes to travel to the bottom of the ramp. Record the time in your table.

7 Repeat step 6 two times, and record the results in your table. After three trials, calculate the average travel time, and record it in your table.

8 Using a stack of books that is approximately 30 cm high, repeat steps 5–7. Using a stack that is approximately 45 cm high, repeat the steps again.

Analysis

1. Analyzing Data Calculate the average speed of the ball by using the following equation:

$$average\ speed = \frac{length\ of\ ramp}{average\ time\ ball\ traveled}$$

Multiply the average speed by 2 to obtain the final speed of the ball, and record the final speed.

2. Analyzing Data Calculate the final kinetic energy of the ball by using the equation below. Record this value in your table.

$$KE = \frac{1}{2} \times mass\ of\ ball \times (final\ speed)^2$$

$$KE = \frac{1}{2}\ mv^2$$

3. Analyzing Data Calculate and record the initial potential energy of the ball by using the following equation:

$$grav.\ PE = mass\ of\ ball \times (9.8\ m/s^2) \times height\ of\ ramp$$

$$PE = mgh$$

Communicating Your Results

4. Making Comparisons For each of the three heights, compare the ball's potential energy at the top of the ramp with the ball's kinetic energy at the bottom of the ramp.

5. Drawing Conclusions How did the values for the ball's potential and kinetic energy change as the height of the ramp was increased?

Extension

Suppose that you perform this experiment and find that the values for kinetic energy are always just a little less than the values for potential energy. Did you do the experiment wrong? Why or why not?

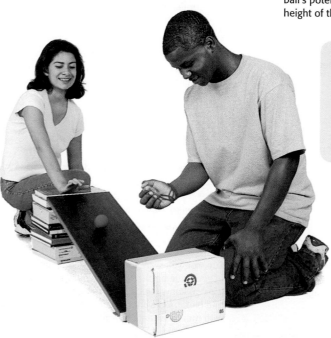

Before the lab, review the law of conservation of energy with students and discuss the concepts of kinetic and potential energy. Give students examples such as a speeding car or a skydiver for kinetic energy and a coconut in a tree or a book on the edge of a desk for potential energy. Explain to students that they may have some difficulty obtaining precise measurements of the time it takes the ball to roll down the ramp. Have the students try the experiment a few times to decide on their best method for timing.

Answers to Analysis

1. Answers may vary. All answers should be between 0.25 m/s and 0.35 m/s for the ramp heights used in the experiment.

2. Answers may vary. Unreasonable answers should be checked for errors in calculation.

3. Answers may vary. Answers should all be less than 1.0 J.

Answers to Communicating Your Results

4. The gravitational potential energy at the top and the kinetic energy at the bottom should be nearly the same.

5. The higher the ramp, the greater the potential and kinetic energies.

Sample Data Table
Potential Energy and Kinetic Energy

	Height 1	Height 2	Height 3
Mass of ball (kg)	0.045	0.045	0.045
Length of ramp (m)	1.513	1.513	1.513
Height of ramp (m)	0.28	0.445	0.583
Time ball traveled, first trial (s)	1.59	1.31	1.09
Time ball traveled, second trial (s)	1.62	1.28	1.06
Time ball traveled, third trial (s)	1.56	1.25	1.04
Average time ball traveled (s)	1.59	1.28	1.06
Final speed of ball (m/s)	1.90	2.36	2.86
Final kinetic energy of ball (J)	0.081	0.125	0.184
Initial potential energy of ball (J)	0.123	0.196	0.257

Key Resources

Virtual Investigation

Classroom Lab Video/DVD

Holt Lab Generator CD-ROM
Search for any lab by type, standard, difficulty level, or time. Edit any lab to fit your needs, or create your own labs. Use the Lab Materials QuickList software to customize your lab materials list.

Differentiated Datasheets
Energy of a Rolling Ball

Observation Lab
Exploring Work and Energy

CBL™ Probeware Lab
Determining Which Ramp is More Efficient

Making Measurements and Observations

Technology

Math

> Scientific Methods

Graphing

Reteaching Key Ideas

Observing Simple Machines Remind students that they probably used simple machines long before they understood how the machine saved them effort. Even small children use simple machines. Tricycles, doll carriages, toy hammers, and ramps for toy cars are all machines that save work. Ask students if, when they were kids, they ever chose to ride a bike to a friend's house? (Students probably did.) Ask students why they might choose to ride a bike instead of walk. (it's faster, or easier) This decision represents an early kind of scientific observation: Students knew that the machine could help them move more efficiently. **LS Intrapersonal**

Answers to Practice

1. Sample answer: Step 1: I think that I can reach 30 mph by the time I've ridden a city block. By that time, I'm traveling almost as fast as the cars. Step 2: I would need a speedometer on the bike to measure speed. I would use a stopwatch to measure how much time it took me to go from rest to 30 mph. I would measure in seconds on the stopwatch, to a precision of hundredths of a second. Step 3: I would do 10 trials and take an average. Step 4: I would ride the same flat stretch of road each time.

2. Sample answer: I would do this with observations. I would have both line up at one end of the block and race to the other end. I would be at the other end to observe who reached the end first.

Observations and measurements are at the heart of science. We get *qualitative* information about the physical world with observations, and we gather *quantitative* information with measurements.

❶ Start with General Observations
Science starts with observations. Observations help you to form questions and hypotheses that you can test. Write down all your observations and measurements in a notebook. Detailed records help you to remember what you did and saw and help others to reproduce the work.

- Observation: Mom fills up the tank of her pickup truck more often than Dad fills up his compact car.
- Observation: Both Mom and Dad drive about the same amount.
- Hypothesis: Dad's car has better gas mileage than Mom's truck.

❷ Plan Measurements and Choose Instruments
Decide what measurements are necessary to test your hypothesis. Choose the instruments you will need for the measurements. You should also plan for any calculations you will need to make. It is often useful to create a data table to record your measurements.

- Measurements: distance traveled and fuel used
- Instruments: odometers of vehicles; meters on gas pumps
- Calculations:
  $$\text{mileage} = \frac{\text{distance traveled}}{\text{fuel used}}$$

❸ Make Multiple Measurements
If possible, make multiple measurements, and then calculate an average.

- Record 10 fills for each vehicle.
- Add all 10 mileage values for each vehicle, then divide by the total gas used.

❹ Avoid Measurement Pitfalls
Try to keep all variables constant except for those you are testing. Be careful to avoid errors when reading instruments. Read any available instructions on calibrating and reading instruments properly.

- Use the same grade of gasoline in both cars.
- Always fill the tank until the pump stops itself.
- If possible, use the same gas pump every time.

Practice

1. Suppose you want to find out how long it takes you to accelerate from rest to a speed of 30 miles per hour on your bicycle. Work through the steps above to plan this measurement.

2. Suppose you want to compare the cycling speeds of your little brother and your little sister. You want to know which one can ride a distance of one block in the shortest time. Would you do this with measurements or with observations? Explain.

Key Resources

📁 **Science Skills Worksheets**
Equations with Three Parts
Squares and Square Roots
Percentages

go.hrw.com
SUPER SUMMARY
KEYWORD: HK8WKES

SUMMARY

Key Ideas

Section 1 Work, Power, and Machines

> **What Is Work?** Work is done when a force causes an object to change its motion or position. (p. 431)

> **Power** Power is the rate that work is done. (p. 433)

> **Machines and Mechanical Advantage** Machines change the size and/or direction of forces. (p. 434)

Section 2 Simple Machines

> **What Are Simple Machines?** The lever, pulley, wheel and axle, inclined plane, wedge, and screw are simple machines. (p. 438)

> **The Lever Family** Levers have a rigid arm. (p. 439)

> **The Inclined Plane Family** Inclined planes turn a small input force into a large output force. (p. 441)

> **Compound Machines** Compound machines are made of two or more simple machines. (p. 443)

Section 3 What Is Energy?

> **Energy and Work** Whenever work is done, energy is transformed or transferred. (p. 444)

> **Potential Energy** Potential energy results from the relative positions of objects in a system. (p. 445)

> **Kinetic Energy** Kinetic energy depends on both mass and speed. (p. 447)

> **Other Forms of Energy** Nonmechanical energy occurs on the level of atoms. (p. 449)

Section 4 Conservation of Energy

> **Energy Transformations** Energy readily changes from one form to another. (p. 453)

> **The Law of Conservation of Energy** Energy can never be created or destroyed. (p. 456)

> **Efficiency of Machines** A machine can't do more work than the work required to operate it. (p. 459)

Key Terms

work, p. 431
power, p. 433
mechanical advantage, p. 436

simple machine, p. 438
compound machine, p. 443

energy, p. 444
potential energy, p. 445
kinetic energy, p. 447
mechanical energy, p. 449

efficiency, p. 459

SUMMARY

SUPER SUMMARY

Have students connect the major concepts in this chapter through an interactive Super Summary. Visit **go.hrw.com** and type in the keyword **HK8WKES** to access the Super Summary for this chapter.

Differentiated Instruction

Alternative Assessment

Knowledge Master Organize students into small groups (no more than 4). Each group is responsible for writing questions along with the answers for the end of the chapter review game. Students should use their books, class notes, and previous questions from other class activities. Questions should include key ideas from the chapter. **LS** Interpersonal

Key Resources

⊞ **Interactive Concept Map**

🗂 **Review Resources**
Concept Review Worksheets

🗂 **Assessment Resources**
Chapter Tests A and B
Performance-Based Assessment

Reading Toolbox

1. Answers may vary. Work used in the scientific sense should imply a force acting on an object and changing the object's motion, while work in other contexts may have other meanings.

Using Key Terms

2. **a.** PE
b. KE
c. PE

3. Energy is the ability to do work. Doing work is transferring or transforming energy. Work is exerting a force through a distance to change the motion, and thus the energy, of an object. An object that has energy has the ability to exert a force through a distance. The rate of changing energy, or work, per unit time is power.

4. Answers may vary. Students may say that electrical energy supplies the power for computers, light bulbs, air conditioners, refrigerators, and many other appliances and machines, and that light energy provides plants with the energy that is converted by photosynthesis into the chemical energy that sustains living things.

5. wheel and axle, wedge, lever

Understanding Key Ideas

6. c
7. a
8. c
9. c
10. d
11. c
12. d
13. a
14. b

READING TOOLBOX

1. Write one sentence using the word *work* in the scientific sense, and write another sentence using the word in a nonscientific sense. Explain the difference in the meaning of *work* in the two sentences.

USING KEY TERMS

2. For each of the following, state whether the system contains primarily *kinetic energy* or *potential energy*:
a. a stone in a stretched slingshot
b. a speeding race car
c. water above a hydroelectric dam

3. How is *energy* related to *work, force,* and *power*?

4. List several examples that show how *electrical energy* and *light energy* are useful to you.

5. Name three *simple machines* that make up a can opener, which is a *compound machine*.

UNDERSTANDING KEY IDEAS

6. _____ is defined as force times distance.
a. Power
b. Energy
c. Work
d. Potential energy

7. The quantity that measures how much a machine multiplies force is called
a. mechanical advantage.
b. leverage.
c. efficiency.
d. power.

8. The unit that represents 1 J of work done each second is the
a. power.
b. newton.
c. watt.
d. mechanical advantage.

9. Which of the following phrases describes a situation in which potential energy is *not* changed into kinetic energy?
a. an apple falling from a tree
b. a dart being shot from a spring-loaded gun
c. the string of a bow being pulled back
d. a creek flowing downstream

10. _____ is determined by both mass and velocity.
a. Work
b. Power
c. Potential energy
d. Kinetic energy

11. Energy that does not involve the large-scale motion or the position of objects in a system is called
a. potential energy.
b. mechanical energy.
c. nonmechanical energy.
d. conserved energy.

12. A machine cannot
a. change the direction of a force.
b. multiply or increase a force.
c. redistribute work.
d. increase the total amount of work done.

13. A machine that has a mechanical advantage of less than one
a. increases speed and distance.
b. multiplies force.
c. increases output force.
d. reduces distance and speed.

14. Which of these statements describes the law of conservation of energy?
a. No machine is 100% efficient.
b. Energy is neither created nor destroyed.
c. The energy resources of Earth are limited.
d. The energy of a system is always decreasing.

15. Use the law of conservation of energy to explain why the work output of a machine can never exceed the work input.

16. If a machine cannot multiply the amount of work, what is the advantage of using a machine?

17. You are trying to pry the lid off a paint can by using a screwdriver, but the lid will not budge. Should you try using a shorter screwdriver or a longer screwdriver? Explain.

18. Many fuels come from fossilized plant and animal matter. How is energy stored in these fuels? How do you think that energy got into the fuels in the first place?

19. Analyzing Information If a bumper car triples its speed, how much more work can it do on a bumper car at rest? (Hint: Use the equation for kinetic energy.)

20. Drawing Conclusions You are attempting to move a large rock by using a long lever. Will the work you do on the lever be greater than, the same as, or less than the work the lever does on the rock? Explain your answer.

21. Predicting Outcomes You are designing a roller coaster ride in which a car will be pulled to the top of a hill and then will be released to roll freely down the hill and up again toward the top of the next hill. The next hill is twice as high. Will your design be successful? Explain.

22. Applying Knowledge In two or three sentences, explain the force-distance trade-off that occurs when a machine is used to make work easier. Use the lever as an example of one type of trade-off.

Graphing Skills

23. Interpreting Graphics The diagram below shows five points on a roller coaster.

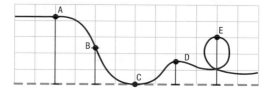

a. List the points in order from the point where the car has the greatest potential energy to the point where the car has the least potential energy.

b. Now, list the points in order from the point where the car has the greatest kinetic energy to the point where the car has the least kinetic energy.

c. How do your two lists relate to each other?

Math Skills

24. You and two friends apply a force of 425 N to push a piano up a 2.0 m long ramp.
  a. Work How much work, in joules, has been done when you reach the top of the ramp?
  b. Power If you make it to the top in 5.0 s, what is your power output in watts?
  c. Mechanical Advantage If lifting the piano straight up requires 1,700 N of force, what is the mechanical advantage of the ramp?

25. A crane uses a block and tackle to lift a 2,200 N flagstone to a height of 25 m.
  a. Work How much work is done on the flagstone?
  b. Efficiency The crane's hydraulic motor does 110 kJ of work on the cable in the block and tackle. What is the efficiency of the block and tackle?
  c. Potential Energy When the flagstone is 25 m above the ground, what is its potential energy?

Assignment Guide

Section	Items
1	1, 6, 8, 13, 15, 18, 19, 21, 23
2	5, 7, 12, 16
3	2, 3, 4, 11, 17, 20, 22
4	9, 3, 14, 24

Math Skills

24. a. $W = 425 \times 2.0 \text{ m} = 850 \text{ J}$
  b. $P = 850 \text{ J}/5.0 \text{ s} = 170 \text{ W}$
  c. $MA = 1{,}700 \text{ N}/425 \text{ N} = 4.0$

25. a. $W = 2{,}200 \text{ N} \times 25 \text{ m} = 55{,}000 \text{ J}$ (or 55 kJ)
  b. *efficiency* $= 55 \text{ kJ}/110 \text{ kJ} = 0.50$ (or 50%)
  c. $PE = 425 \text{ N} \times 25 \text{ m} = 55 \text{ kJ}$

Explaining Key Ideas

15. Because energy cannot be created, the machine can only put out an amount of work equal to or less than the energy within the machine, which is equal to or less than the work input.

16. The advantage of using a machine lies in its ability to redistribute work by changing the direction of an input force or changing the distance over which the force is applied.

17. You should use a longer screwdriver. The output length remains the same (the distance from the fulcrum to the output force), but the input length increases with a longer screwdriver, creating a larger mechanical advantage and therefore a larger output force.

18. chemical energy; Light (solar) energy was converted into chemical energy through photosynthesis.

Critical Thinking

19. nine times

20. The work done on the lever will be greater than the work done on the rock by the lever, because some energy is dissipated or "lost" as nonmechanical energy every time energy is transferred from one object to another.

21. No, the design will not be successful, because the car will not have enough kinetic energy to climb a hill that is taller than the first one, without receiving an additional input of energy.

22. Because work equals force multiplied by distance, machines can be used to decrease or increase force by changing the distance over which the force is applied. A second-class lever, for example, multiplies input force by decreasing the distance over which the work occurs, whereas a third-class lever, decreases input force by increasing distance.

Graphing Skills

23. a. A, E, B, D, C
  b. C, D, B, E, A
  c. The lists are identical, except in reverse order.

Standardized Test Prep

TEST DOCTOR

Question 1 Answer C is correct. Students might answer A if they thought the two sides of a lever directed forces out to the sides, B if they thought the downward pressure on a screw was only directed outward on two sides instead of all the way around, or D if they thought the two sides of a pulley directed forces out to the sides.

Question 2 Answer G is correct. Students must first convert the mass to kilograms (0.0025 kg), then multiply this value by the free-fall acceleration of Earth (9.8 m/s^2) and the height (350 m) to obtain 8.575 joules. Students answering F or I may have converted the mass of the penny to kg incorrectly.

Question 3 Answer B is correct. Remind struggling students that photosynthesis is a chemical process by which most organisms on Earth directly or indirectly obtain energy.

Question 4 Answer I is correct. Students must multiply force times distance to find the amount of work. Answers F and H indicate that the student does not know the correct unit of work; answers F and G indicate that the student believed dividing force by distance was the way to find the amount of work.

Question 5 40 m/s. Students must rearrange the equation $KE = 1/2mv^2$ to the formula $2KE/m = v^2$. $2(200,000)/250 = 1,600 = v^2$, so $v = 40$ m/s.

Question 6 37 J. Students must multiply the mass of the rock by the free-fall acceleration of Mars by the distance lifted.

Question 7 Answer D is correct. Have struggling students return to the passage and find the paragraph that mentions simple machines in its opening sentence. Students can underline the machines discussed in the paragraph.

Understanding Concepts

Directions (1–4): For each question, write on a sheet of paper the letter of the correct answer.

1. What type of simple machine turns a downward force into two forces directed out to the sides?
   A. lever   **C.** wedge
   B. screw   **D.** pulley

2. The mass of a penny is 2.5 g. If the penny is held out a window on one of the upper floors of the Empire State Building, 350 m off the ground, what is the gravitational potential energy of the penny with respect to the ground?
   F. 0.875 J   **H.** 140 J
   G. 8.575 J   **I.** 875 J

3. What type of potential energy is stored within food and used by the consumer of the food?
   A. elastic energy
   B. chemical energy
   C. mechanical energy
   D. gravitational energy

4. A veterinarian picks up a small dog from the floor and places it on the operating table. If the dog weighs 80 N and the operating table is 1.25 m high, how much work does the veterinarian do?
   F. 64 W   **H.** 100 W
   G. 64 J   **I.** 100 J

Directions (5–6): For each question, write a short response.

5. If a motorcycle with a mass of 250 kg has a kinetic energy of 200,000 J, what is the motorcycle's speed in m/s?

6. The pull of gravity (g) on Mars is 3.7 m/s^2. If an astronaut on Mars lifts a 10 kg rock 1 m off the ground, just to see what's under it, how much work has the astronaut performed?

Reading Skills

Directions (7-9): Read the passage below. Then, answer the questions that follow.

PYRAMID POWER

One of the most ancient and amazing architectural creations in the world is the Great Pyramid of Egypt. This structure consists of several million rectangular blocks, each weighing an average of 2.5 tons.

The pyramid was assembled by using simple machines. Ramps made of wood, rock, and mud were most likely used to raise the blocks. Although the slope of a single ramp would be too steep to move such heavy objects, the workers may have used a series of smaller ramps.

Another possibility is that the gigantic blocks were moved by using a pulley connected to a counterweight set on a sloping ramp on the other side of the Pyramid. When the counterweight was set, it would be attached to a heavy block and released. The lowering of the counterweight would raise the massive block.

7. What two simple machines may have been used to construct the Great Pyramid?
   A. lever and pulley
   B. lever and inclined plane
   C. pulley and wedge
   D. pulley and inclined plane

8. 100 workers pull a 3 ton block to 100 m high using a ramp with a mechanical advantage of 4. With each heave, each worker does 50 J of net work. How many heaves will it take for the workers to pull the block all the way up the ramp? (Note: 1 ton = 8,896 newtons.)
   F. 14 heaves   **H.** 1,335 heaves
   G. 134 heaves   **I.** 13,344 heaves

9. Why would a long series of gradual ramps be better than one short, steep ramp for moving heavy blocks of stone?

Question 8 Answer G is correct. Students must first convert the weight of the block from 3 tons to 26,688 N. Divide that by the mechanical advantage of 4 to get the force required to move the block up the ramp: 6,672 N. Then multiply by the height the block will be lifted, for a total amount of work of 667,200 J. That figure is then divided by the product of 100 workers doing 50 J of useful work each, or 5,000 J per heave, for a total of 133.44 heaves.

Question 9 Full-credit answers should include the following points:
- The longer the ramp, the greater the mechanical advantage it conveys.
- Mechanical advantage equals input distance divided by output distance.

Question 10 Answer D is correct. Students might answer A if they mistook the fulcrum for the weight, B if they misunderstood the path of the pendulum, or C if they were confusing gravitational potential energy with kinetic energy.

Question 11 Answer H is correct. Students might answer F if they mistook the fulcrum for the weight, G if they misunderstood the path of the pendulum, or I if they were confusing gravitational potential energy with kinetic energy.

Question 12 Answer B is correct. Students must know that the gravitational potential energy equals the maximum kinetic energy from the fall and that kinetic energy equals $1/2mv^2$. At point B, 100 J $= 1/2m(10)^2$, so $m = 2$ kg.

Interpreting Graphics

The following diagram shows the complete arc of one swing of a pendulum. Use this diagram to answer questions 10–11.

ARC OF A PENDULUM

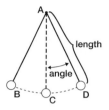

10. Where does the pendulum weight have the greatest gravitational potential energy?

A. A **C.** C

B. A and C **D.** B and D

11. Where does the pendulum weight have the greatest kinetic energy?

F. A **H.** C

G. A and C **I.** B and D

On a distant planet, an extraterrestrial fruit falls from a tree. We know the gravitational potential energy of the alien fruit at point A and its velocity at point B. Use this graphic to answer questions 12–13.

FREE FALL ON AN ALIEN PLANET

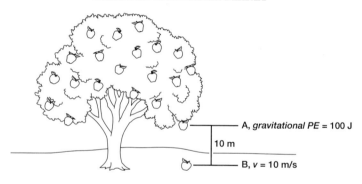

A, *gravitational PE = 100 J*

10 m

B, *v = 10 m/s*

12. What is the mass of the alien fruit?

A. 1 kg **C.** 5 kg

B. 2 kg **D.** 10 kg

13. What is the free-fall acceleration of the alien planet?

Question 13 5 m/s². Students must rearrange grav. $PE = mgh$ to $g = $ grav. $PE/mh = $ 100 J/(2 kg × 10 m) = 5 m/s².

Test Tip

Test questions may not be arranged in order of increasing difficulty. If you are unable to answer a question, mark it and move on to another question.

State Resources

For specific resources for your state, visit **go.hrw.com** and type in the keyword **HSHSTR**.

 Test Practice with Guided Reading Development

Answers:

1. C

2. G

3. B

4. I

5. 40 m/s

6. 37 J

7. D

8. G

9. Answers may vary; see Test Doctor for a detailed scoring rubric.

10. D

11. H

12. B

13. 5 m/s²

Continuation of Answers

Answers continued from p. 443

8. Answers may vary. A pencil sharpener, for example, is a compound machine that consists of a couple of screws (the blades to sharpen the pencil), wedges (the edges of those blades), and a wheel and axle (the crank).

Answers continued from p. 452

8. $KE = \frac{1}{2}mv^2 = (1/2)(0.02 \text{ kg})(300 \text{ m/s})^2 = 900 \text{ J}$

9. **a.** $PE = mgh = (2.5 \text{ kg})(9.8 \text{ m/s}^2)(2.0 \text{ m}) = 49 \text{ J}$

   b. $KE = \frac{1}{2}mv^2 = (1/2)(0.015 \text{ kg})(3.5 \text{ m/s})^2 = 0.092 \text{ J}$

   c. $PE = mgh = (35 \text{ kg})(9.8 \text{ m/s}^2)(3.5 \text{ m}) = 1{,}200 \text{ J}$

   d. $KE = \frac{1}{2}mv^2 = (1/2)(8{,}500 \text{ kg})[(220 \text{ km/h})(1{,}000 \text{ m/km})(1 \text{ h}/3{,}600 \text{ s})]^2 = 1.6 \times 10^7 \text{ J}$

Answers continued from p. 461

6. A child on a swing undergoes energy transformations from maximum *PE* at the top (both sides) to maximum *KE* at the bottom and back to maximum *PE* at the top of the opposite side. The child needs a push every now and then to make up for the energy lost to friction between the rope and the support, as well as some energy lost to air resistance.

7. *efficiency* = *useful work output/work input* = $(40 \text{ J})/(100 \text{ J}) = 0.4$ or 40%

8. **a.** *useful work output* = *(efficiency)(work input)* = $(0.12)(6{,}500 \text{ J}) = 780 \text{ J}$

   b. $P = W/t = 780 \text{ J}/1 \text{ s} = 780 \text{ W}$

9. **a.** $W = Fd = (150 \text{ N})(4.0 \text{ m}) = 6.0 \times 10^2 \text{ J}$

   b. *work input* = *useful work output/efficiency* = $6.0 \times 10^2 \text{ J}/0.50 = 1{,}200 \text{ J}$

		Standards	Teach Key Ideas

CHAPTER OPENER, pp. 470–472 — 50 min.

SECTION 1 Temperature, pp. 473–479 — 50 min.

> Temperature and Energy
> Temperature Scales
> Relating Temperature to Energy Transfer

Standards: PS 5b, PS 5c, UCP 1, UCP 2, UCP 3, SAI 1, SAI 2

Teach Key Ideas:
- Bellringer Transparency
- Teaching Transparency P9 Temperature Scales
- Visual Concepts Temperature • Temperature and Temperature Scale • Temperature Scales • Measuring Temperature • Temperature and Heat • Heat

SECTION 2 Energy Transfer, pp. 480–489 — 50 min.

> Methods of Energy Transfer
> Conductors and Insulators
> Specific Heat

Standards: PS 5b, PS 5d, PS 6a, UCP 3, UCP 4, SAI 1, SAI 2, ST 2

Teach Key Ideas:
- Bellringer Transparency
- Teaching Transparencies TM38 Specific Heats • TM39 Temperature Energy Graph • P10 Conduction and Convection
- Visual Concepts Comparing Convection, Conduction, and Radiation • Electrical Conductors and Insulators • Equation for Specific Heat Capacity

SECTION 3 Using Heat, pp. 490–493 — 50 min.

> Laws of Thermodynamics
> Heat Engines

Standards: PS 5a, PS 5d, UCP 3, UCP 4, ST 2

Teach Key Ideas:
- Bellringer Transparency
- Teaching Transparency P11 Internal Combustion Engine

See also PowerPoint® Resources

Chapter Review and Assessment Resources

SE Science Skills: Solving Problems, p. 496
SE Chapter Summary, p. 497
SE Chapter Review, pp. 498–499
SE Standardized Test Prep, pp. 500–501
☐ Concept Review Worksheets ■
☐ Chapter Tests A and B ■
Holt Online Assessment

CHAPTER FastTrack To shorten instruction because of time limitations, omit Section 3 and the chapter lab.

Basic Learners

TE Interpreting Visuals, p. 476
TE Temperature Versus Energy, p. 486
TE Life Without Heating or Cooling, p. 489
☐ Science Skills Worksheets
☐ Differentiated Datasheets A for Labs and Activities ■
☐ Study Guide A ■

Advanced Learners

TE Graphing, p. 475
TE Message in a Bottle, p. 483
TE History of Heating and Cooling, p. 488
☐ Cross-Disciplinary Worksheets
☐ Differentiated Datasheets C for Labs and Activities ■

Key

SE	Student Edition
TE	Teacher's Edition

📁 Chapter Resource File
📓 Workbook
📦 Transparency

💿 CD or CD-ROM
* Datasheet or blackline master available

■ Also available in Spanish

All resources listed below are also available on the Teacher's One-Stop Planner.

Why It Matters	Hands-On	Skills Development	Assessment
Build student motivation with resources about high-interest applications.	**SE Inquiry Lab** Color and Temperature, p. 471* ■	**TE Reading Toolbox** Assessing Prior Knowledge, p. 470 **SE Reading Toolbox** p. 472	📁 **Pretest** ■
TE Bridges and Roads, p. 474 **TE Solar System Temperatures**, p. 477 **TE Burns**, p. 478 📁 **Cross-Disciplinary Worksheets** Integrating Space Science—Starlight, Star Heat • Integrating Health—Skin Temperature	**TE Demonstration** Boiling Water, p. 473 **SE Quick Lab** Sensing Hot and Cold, p. 474* ■ **TE Demonstration** Building a Thermometer, p. 476 **SE Inquiry Lab** Temperature and Energy, p. 478* ■ 📁 **Observation Lab** Energy Transfer and Specific Heat	**SE Reading Toolbox** Word Families, p. 475 **TE Math Skills** Understanding Formulas, p. 475 **SE Math Skills** Temperature-Scale Conversion, p. 477	**TE Reteaching Key Ideas** How a Thermometer Works, p. 479 **TE Formative Assessment,** p. 479 📁 **Spanish Assessment*** ■ 📁 **Section Quiz** ■
TE Popping Popcorn, p. 482 **SE Why Does the Wind Blow?** p. 483 **TE Superconductors**, p. 484 **SE How Are Homes Heated and Cooled?** pp. 488–489 **TE Cooling System**, p. 489 📁 **Cross-Disciplinary Worksheets** Integrating Earth Science—Land and Sea Breezes • Connection to Social Studies—Early Central Heating • Connection to Social Studies—The Little Ice Age • Integrating Biology—Hibernation and Torpor	**TE Demonstration** Energy Transfer in Boiling Water, p. 480 **SE Inquiry Lab** Absorption of Radiated Heat, p. 482* ■ **SE Quick Lab** Conductors and Insulators, p. 484* ■ **SE Inquiry Lab** Conduction of Heat by Metals, pp. 494–495* ■	**TE Reading Toolbox** Visual Literacy, p. 481 **TE Reading Toolbox** Visual Literacy, p. 483 **SE Reading Toolbox** Comparison Table, p. 485 **TE Science Skills** Graphing, p. 485 **SE Math Skills** Specific Heat, p. 486 **TE Reading Toolbox** Visual Literacy, p. 488	**TE Reteaching Key Ideas** Designing a Solar Cooker, p. 487 **TE Formative Assessment,** p. 487 📁 **Spanish Assessment*** ■ 📁 **Section Quiz** ■
TE Perpetual Motion Machines, p. 491 **TE Energy Efficiency**, p. 491 **TE Benjamin Thompson, Count Rumford**, p. 492 📁 **Cross-Disciplinary Worksheets** Integrating Environmental Science—Thermal Pollution • Real World Applications—Appliance Energy Use and Cost	**TE Demonstration** Reviewing Conservation of Energy, p. 490	**SE Reading Toolbox** Flowchart, p. 492	**TE Reteaching Key Ideas** Heat Engines and Thermodynamics, p. 493 **TE Formative Assessment,** p. 493 📁 **Spanish Assessment*** ■ 📁 **Section Quiz** ■

See also Lab Generator

See also Holt Online Assessment Resources

Resources for Differentiated Instruction

English Learners
TE Recognizing Roots, p. 474
📁 Differentiated Datasheets A, B, and C for Labs and Activities ■
📓 Study Guide A ■

Struggling Readers
TE Reviewing Vocabulary, p. 481
📓 Interactive Reader

Special Education Students
TE Understanding Terms, p. 484
TE Comparing Entropy, p. 491

Alternative Assessment
TE Designing a Habitat, p. 478
TE Conductors and Insulators in the Kitchen, p. 485
TE Heat and Temperature Collage, p. 497

Overview

This chapter covers temperature and heat, including temperature scale conversions. It also explores methods of energy transfer (conduction, convection, and radiation) and conductors and insulators. Students also learn how to use specific heat in calculations. Finally, this chapter explains the laws of thermodynamics and how heat engines work.

READING TOOLBOX

Assessing Prior Knowledge Students should understand the following concepts:
• units of measurement
• mass
• matter
• energy
• conservation of energy

MISCONCEPTION
///ALERT

Science education research has identified the following misconceptions about temperature and heat.
• Students do not recognize the distinctions between temperature and heat. To help students overcome this misconception, lead a discussion about a large ice block and a small ice cube. Explain that the two samples of ice are at the same temperature, but the large ice block can absorb much more heat before melting than the ice cube can. This is because *temperature* is a measure of the *average* thermal energy throughout an object, whereas *heat* is a measure of the *total* thermal energy in an object.

CHAPTER 14 Heat and Temperature

Chapter Outline

❶ **Temperature**
  Temperature and Energy
  Temperature Scales
  Relating Temperature to
    Energy Transfer

❷ **Energy Transfer**
  Methods of Energy Transfer
  Conductors and Insulators
  Specific Heat

❸ **Using Heat**
  Laws of Thermodynamics
  Heat Engines

Why It Matters

We want to keep our houses at a comfortable temperature and to do so as cheaply as possible. The white and red areas on this thermogram show where energy, as heat, is escaping from a house. These areas show where the house needs to be better insulated so that heating energy is not wasted.

Chapter Correlations   *National Science Education Standards*

The following correlations show the National Science Standards that relate to this chapter. For the full text of the standards, see the National Science Education Standards at the front of the book.

PS 5a The total energy of the universe is constant. As these [energy] transfers occur, the matter involved becomes steadily less ordered. (Section 3)

PS 5b All energy can be considered to be either kinetic energy, which is the energy of motion; potential energy, which depends on relative position; or energy contained by a field, such as electromagnetic waves. (Sections 1, 2)

PS 5c Heat consists of random motion and the vibrations of atoms, molecules, and ions. The higher the temperature, the greater the atomic or molecular motion. (Section 1)

PS 5d Everything tends to become less organized and less orderly over time. Thus, in all energy transfers, the overall effect is that the energy is spread out uniformly. Examples are the transfer of energy from hotter to cooler objects by conduction, radiation, or convection and the warming of our surroundings when we burn fuels. (Sections 2, 3)

PS 6a Waves, including sound and seismic waves, waves on water, and light waves, have energy and can transfer energy when they interact with matter. (Section 2)

UCP 1 Systems, order, and organization (Section 1)

UCP 2 Evidence, models, and explanation (Section 1)

UCP 3 Constancy, change, and measurement (Sections 1–3)

UCP 4 Evolution and equilibrium (Sections 2, 3)

SAI 1 Abilities necessary to do scientific inquiry (Sections 1, 2; Inquiry Lab: Conduction of Heat by Metals)

SAI 2 Understandings about scientific inquiry (Sections 1, 2)

ST 2 Understandings about science and technology (Sections 2, 3)

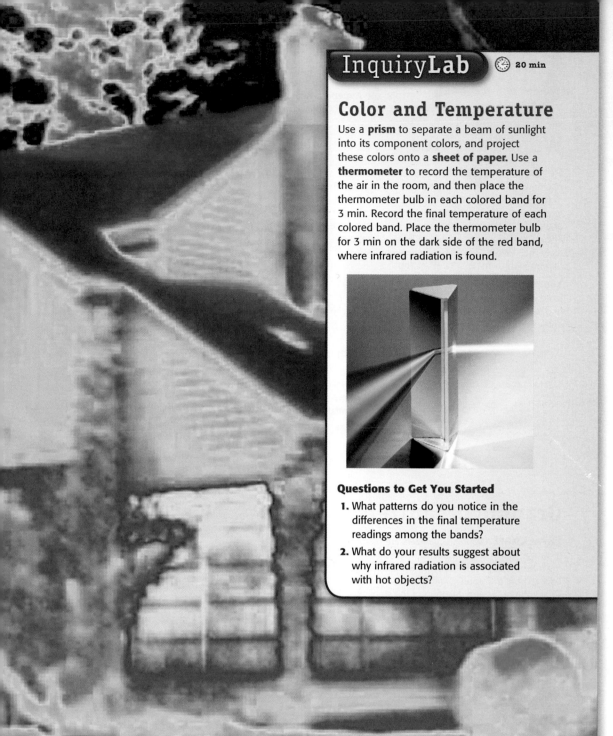

InquiryLab ⏱ 20 min

Color and Temperature

Use a **prism** to separate a beam of sunlight into its component colors, and project these colors onto a **sheet of paper.** Use a **thermometer** to record the temperature of the air in the room, and then place the thermometer bulb in each colored band for 3 min. Record the final temperature of each colored band. Place the thermometer bulb for 3 min on the dark side of the red band, where infrared radiation is found.

Questions to Get You Started

1. What patterns do you notice in the differences in the final temperature readings among the bands?

2. What do your results suggest about why infrared radiation is associated with hot objects?

InquiryLab

Teacher's Notes This activity will work best with a sheet of white paper.

Materials per Group
- paper, white, 1 sheet
- prism
- thermometer

Answers

1. I found that the temperature of the color bands increases, moving from violet (the coolest) to red (the hottest).

2. Infrared radiation, which is past the red part of the visible spectrum, must be associated with hot objects because it carries a lot of heat.

Key Resources

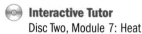 **Datasheet**
Color and Temperature

Interactive Tutor
Disc Two, Module 7: Heat

READING TOOLBOX

Word Families

Sample table:

WORD	ROOT	PREFIX OR SUFFIX	DEFINITION
ther-mometer	therm-	-meter	an instrument that measures and indicates temperature
thermo-stat	therm-	-stat	a device that controls the temperature in a building
thermal conduc-tion	therm-		the transfer of energy as heat through a material
thermo-dynam-ics	therm-	-dynam-ics	science that deals with the way heat acts
thermal energy	therm-		the kinetic energy of a substance's atoms

Comparisons

Answers may vary. Students' tables should have several entries, with each row listing two or more things being compared, plus a word or phrase that signals the comparison.

Graphic Organizers

Students' flow charts should show the following four steps in the cycle: intake stroke, compression stroke, power stroke, and exhaust stroke. The chart may start with any one of these steps, but the steps should proceed in the order given in the chapter, connecting the steps with arrows from the prior step to the subsequent step.

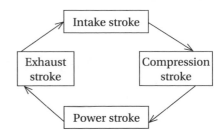

These reading tools can help you learn the material in this chapter. For more information on how to use these and other tools, see **Appendix A.**

Word Families

Prefixes and Suffixes What do you think of when you hear the word *thermal*? You may think of the word *thermos* or perhaps the phrase *thermal blanket*. The noun *thermal* means "a current of warm air." What do these words or phrases have in common? They are related to heat or temperature. These words or phrases have a common root, *thermo-*, which means "heat" or "hot."

Your Turn On a separate sheet of paper, start a table like the one below. As you read the chapter, find words that contain the root *thermo-* and make entries in the table for them.

WORD	ROOT	PREFIX OR SUFFIX	DEFINITION
thermometer	thermo-	-meter	a device that measures temperature

Graphic Organizers

Flow Chart Graphic Organizers are drawings that you can make to help you organize the concepts that you learn. A flow chart is a Graphic Organizer that shows the order and direction of the steps in a process.

Your Turn As you read Section 3, create your own flow chart for the cycle of an internal-combustion engine. At right is an example to get you started.

Comparisons

Comparison Table When you are comparing two things, you can describe how they are similar or how they are different.

- Often, a comparison describes one thing as *greater than* or *less than* another thing in some way.
- A single comparative word can also be used to make comparisons. Comparative words use the suffixes *-er* or *-est*.
- Comparative phrases may use the words *more* or *less*.

Your Turn As you read this chapter, fill out a comparison table like the one below. Each row of the table should list the things being compared and the word or phrase that indicates a comparison.

FIRST THING	COMPARISON WORD OR PHRASE	SECOND THING
air near the equator	hotter than	air near the poles

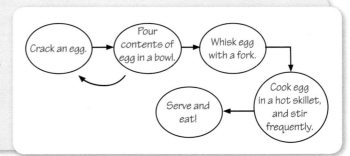

Temperature

Key Ideas

❯ What does temperature have to do with energy?

❯ What three temperature scales are commonly used?

❯ What makes things feel hot or cold?

Key Terms

temperature

thermometer

absolute zero

heat

Why It Matters

We control temperatures for many reasons, such as keeping ourselves comfortable.

In this section, students learn how temperature is related to kinetic energy. They also learn how to convert between Fahrenheit, Celsius, and Kelvin scales and about the transferring of energy.

🔔 Bellringer

Use the Bellringer transparency to prepare students for this section.

Demonstrate

Boiling Water This demonstration requires dry ice, a beaker, water, a hot plate, and a thermometer. Before class begins, place the beaker on the hot plate. Be sure that the hot plate is turned off and that the plug or power light is not visible. Fill the beaker halfway with water and add dry ice. Place the thermometer in the water. When students enter the class, the water should be bubbling as if boiling. **Safety Caution:** Do not handle dry ice with bare hands. Use gloves and/or tongs. Ask students to observe the beaker, write their observations, and write down their guesses of the water's temperature. Have a student read the thermometer. Then, lead a discussion on the importance of using instruments to make observations. **LS Visual**

When you touch the hood of an automobile, you sense how hot or cold the car is. In everyday life, we sometimes call this feeling of hot or cold the *temperature* of an object. However, the words *hot* and *cold* serve only as rough indicators of temperature. Temperature itself is closely related to energy.

Temperature and Energy

People use **temperature** readings, such as the ones shown in **Figure 1,** to make many kinds of decisions every day. You check the temperature of the air outside to decide what to wear. To find out if a roasting turkey is done, a cook checks its temperature. You take your temperature to find out if you are ill. In all these cases, what is actually being measured is kinetic energy. ❯ **The temperature of a substance is proportional to the average kinetic energy of the substance's particles.**

temperature (TEM puhr uh chuhr) a measure of how hot (or cold) something is; specifically, a measure of the average kinetic energy of the particles in an object

Figure 1 Many decisions are made based on temperature.

Key Resources

🗄 Teaching Transparency
P9 Temperature Scales

💿 Visual Concepts
Temperature
Temperature and Temperature Scale
Temperature Scales
Measuring Temperature
Temperature and Heat
Heat

📋 Datasheets
Sensing Hot and Cold
Temperature and Energy

📋 Math Skills Worksheet
Temperature-Scale Conversion

📋 Cross-Disciplinary Worksheets
Integrating Space Science—Starlight, Star Heat
Integrating Health—Skin Temperature

Teacher's Notes To extend this activity, have students predict which objects in the room will feel cool and which objects will feel warm.

Materials per Group
• cardboard
• metal
• plastic
• plastic foam
• rock
• thermometer strip
• wood

Answers

1. Sample answer: The wood felt warmest to me. All the materials had the same temperature.

2. Sample answer: Some materials felt warmer because energy from my hand was not transferred to those materials very quickly. My hand was not a good thermometer because I thought the objects were at different temperatures even though all of them had the same temperature.

Teaching Key Ideas

Average Kinetic Energy Speed and kinetic energy are related, so temperature and average particle speed are related. If the temperature is high, the particles on average are moving quickly. If the temperature is low, the particles on average are moving slowly. Discuss this simple relationship with students. It will help them understand many of the effects associated with temperature differences and temperature changes. **LS Logical**

QuickLab **Sensing Hot and Cold** ⏱ 20 min

Procedure

❶ Gather small pieces of the following materials: **metal, wood, plastic foam, rock, plastic,** and **cardboard.** Allow the materials to sit untouched on a table for a few minutes.

❷ For each of the materials, put the palms of your hands on the material until you can tell how cool or warm it feels. List the materials in order from coolest to warmest.

❸ Place a **thermometer strip** on the surface of each material. Record the temperature of each material.

Analysis

1. Which material felt the warmest to your hands? Which material had the highest temperature?

2. Why do you think some materials felt warmer than others? Was your hand a good thermometer? Explain.

All particles have kinetic energy.

All particles in a substance are constantly moving. Like all moving objects, each particle has kinetic energy. Temperature is related to the kinetic energy of particles.

As the average kinetic energy of the particles in an object increases, the object's temperature increases. The particles in a hot car hood move faster than particles in a cool car hood because the hot particles have more kinetic energy. But how do we measure the temperature of an object? It is impossible to find the kinetic energy of every particle in an object and calculate their average energy. Actually, there is a very simple way to measure temperature directly.

✔ **Reading Check** How is the temperature of a substance related to the kinetic energy of the particles in the substance? (See Appendix E for answers to Reading Checks.)

Common thermometers rely on expansion.

To measure temperature, we use a simple physical property of substances: Most substances expand when their temperatures increase. **Thermometers,** such as the one shown in **Figure 2,** use the expansion of liquids such as mercury or colored alcohol to measure temperature. These liquids expand as their temperature increases and contract as their temperature falls.

As the temperature rises, the particles in the liquid inside a thermometer gain kinetic energy and move faster. With this increased motion, the particles in the liquid move farther apart. So, the liquid expands and rises up the narrow tube.

thermometer (thuhr MAHM uht uhr) an instrument that measures and indicates temperature

Figure 2 This thermometer uses the expansion of a liquid, colored alcohol in this case, to indicate changes in temperature.

Why It Matters

Bridges and Roads Because most substances expand when their temperature increases, bridges and roads are built to account for this expansion when the weather gets hotter. Expansion joints are built between sections of the road to prevent it from breaking when the road expands. Give students bimetallic strips and have them experiment with heating and cooling the strip. Ask students to describe the behavior of the strip in terms of thermal expansion. Be sure that students use tongs and wear heat-resistant gloves when heating the strip. **LS Kinesthetic**

Differentiated Instruction

English Learners

Recognizing Roots Help students remember the meanings of the words *expansion* and *expand* by discussing the prefix *ex-*. Ask students to list other words that start with *ex-*. (Sample answers may include exit, extra, excel, exoskeleton, and explosion.) Then, ask students to describe what the prefix *ex-* means. (Sample answers may include out, outside, and beyond.) Finally, discuss what happens when a substance expands. (Sample answer: The substance gets bigger or goes outside of its original boundaries.) **LS Verbal**

Thermostats rely on the expansion of different metals.

Most metals also expand when heated and contract when cooled. This turns out to be a useful property in making thermometers that are part of household appliances.

The thermometer inside a thermostat is based on the expansion of metal, as shown in **Figure 3.** The thermometer contains a coil made from two different metal strips pressed together. Both strips expand and contract at different rates as the temperature changes. As the temperature falls, the coil unwinds and moves the pointer to the new temperature mark. As the temperature rises, the coil winds up and moves the pointer in the opposite direction.

Temperature Scales

Suppose you hear someone say that it is 37 degrees outside. How do you know whether to wear a sweater or a T-shirt? On the Fahrenheit temperature scale, 37 degrees is just above freezing. But on the Celsius scale, this temperature would mean that it is very hot outside! **> The Fahrenheit, Celsius, and Kelvin temperature scales are commonly used for different applications in different parts of the world.**

The Fahrenheit and Celsius scales are two different temperature scales.

The units on the Fahrenheit scale are called *degrees Fahrenheit* (°F). On the Fahrenheit scale, water freezes at 32 °F and boils at 212 °F.

Most countries other than the United States use the Celsius scale. This scale is also the one that is widely used in science. The Celsius scale gives a value of 0 °C to the freezing point of water and a value of 100 °C to the boiling point of water at standard atmospheric pressure. The difference between these two points is divided into 100 equal parts, called *degrees Celsius* (°C).

One degree Celsius is equal to 1.8 degrees Fahrenheit. Also, the temperature at which water freezes differs for the two scales by 32 degrees. To convert from one scale to the other, use one of the following formulas.

Fahrenheit-Celsius conversion equations	Fahrenheit temperature = (1.8 × Celsius temperature) + 32.0
	$T_F = 1.8T_C + 32.0$
	Celsius temperature = $\dfrac{\text{Fahrenheit temperature} - 32.0}{1.8}$
	$T_C = \dfrac{T_F - 32.0}{1.8}$

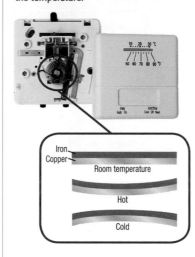

Figure 3 Inside a thermostat, a coil made of two different metal strips expands and contracts in response to the temperature.

Iron
Copper
Room temperature
Hot
Cold

READING TOOLBOX

Word Families
The word *thermostat* begins with the root *therm-*. What do you think the root *stat-* means, based on what the root *therm-* means and what a thermostat does?

Teaching Key Ideas

Temperature Scales Draw two horizontal number lines on the chalkboard, one above the other. At the left end of the lines, draw a vertical line and write "Water Freezes." At the right end, draw another vertical line and write "Water Boils." Label the top line "°F" and the bottom line "°C." Label the left end of the top line "32" and the bottom line "0." Label the right ends "212" and "100." Show students that the temperatures mean the same thing, but they have different units, like 2.54 cm and 1 inch. Also point out that there are 180 spaces in between water freezing and boiling on the top line, but there are only 100 spaces on the bottom line. That means that a °C must be 1.8 times as big as a °F.

Finally, introduce students to the Kelvin temperature scale and explain to them that the interval between units on the Kelvin scale is the same size as the interval between degrees on the Celsius scale. Draw and label another horizontal number line to represent the Kelvin scale. Refer students also to **Figure 4** on the next page. **LS Visual**

READING TOOLBOX

Word Families *Answer: -stat* means stabilizing or static. Ask students to think of other words that contain the root *-stat*. (Sample answers may include static, static electricity, static friction, hemostat, statute, and statistic.) Then ask students how the words are related to the meaning of the root *-stat*. (Answers may vary.) **LS Verbal**

Differentiated Instruction

Advanced Learners

Graphing Tell students that there is a linear relationship between the Celsius and Fahrenheit scales. Then, have them use the freezing and boiling points of water (0° C/32 °F and 100 °C/212 °F) to draw a line graph of °F versus °C. Ask students to determine the slope of the line graph (1.8/1) and the *y*-intercept (32°). Students can use their graphs to convert between the two scales. Also ask students to find the equation of the line. (Use the equation $y = mx + b$, where m = slope and b — *y*-intercept, $y = 1.8x + 32$.) **LS Logical**

Math Skills

Understanding Formulas Show students the origin of the factor 1.8 in the Fahrenheit-to-Celsius conversions.
100 °C temperature change = 180 °F temperature change; therefore, 1 °C = (180/100) °F = 1.8 °F **LS Logical**

Demonstrate

Building a Thermometer Allow 30 minutes for this demonstration. **Safety Caution:** Wear goggles and an apron. Be sure to carry out this demonstration at a sufficient distance from students to protect against any glass breakage.

Materials
• ring stand
• Bunsen burner
• 500 mL flask
• roughly 8 in. long glass tube
• stopper with one hole (stopper should fit the flask)
• water trough

Step 1 Cover the open end of the flask with the stopper containing the glass tube. Invert the flask through the ring on the ring stand.

Step 2 The length of the glass tube inside the flask should be less than 1/2 in. Place the other end of the glass tube in the trough of water.

Step 3 Build a temperature scale as long as the length of the glass tube, using an arbitrary unit. Ask students to help you name the unit.

Step 4 Using the Bunsen burner, gently heat the glass vessel until a few bubbles escape from the trough. Stop heating at this point. As the air inside the flask cools down, the water level in the glass tube will increase.

Step 5 Point out that the temperature scale you just created allows you to quantify the temperature.
LS Visual

Answer to caption question
On the Kelvin temperature scale, all temperatures are positive, but the scales for Fahrenheit and Celsius show both positive and negative values for temperature.

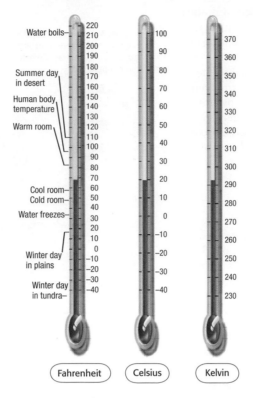

Fahrenheit   Celsius   Kelvin

Figure 4 Temperature can be converted from one of the three temperature scales—Fahrenheit, Celsius, and Kelvin—to another. **How does the Kelvin scale differ from the other two temperature scales?**

absolute zero (AB suh LOOT ZIR oh) the temperature at which molecular energy is at a minimum (0 K on the Kelvin scale or −273.15 °C on the Celsius scale)

The Kelvin scale is based on absolute zero.

You have probably heard of negative temperatures, such as those reported on very cold winter days in the northern United States and Canada. Remember that temperature is a measure of the average kinetic energy of the particles in an object. Even far below 0 °C, these particles are still moving, so they have some kinetic energy. But how low can the temperature fall? The theoretically lowest temperature is −273.15 °C and is called **absolute zero.** At a temperature of absolute zero, the kinetic energy of an object would be zero.

Some recent experiments have reached temperatures that are very close to absolute zero. Matter behaves very differently at these extremely low temperatures. Absolute zero can never be reached, however, because particles never completely stop moving.

Absolute zero is the basis for the Kelvin temperature scale. On this scale, 0 kelvin, or 0 K, is absolute zero. Because the theoretically lowest temperature is given a value of zero, there are no negative temperature values on the Kelvin scale. The Kelvin scale is used in many fields of science, especially those involving low temperatures. The three temperature scales are compared in **Figure 4.**

One kelvin is equal to one degree on the Celsius scale. The only difference between the two scales is the way that *zero* is defined. To approximate any temperature in kelvins, just add 273 to the same temperature in degrees Celsius. The equation for this conversion is given below.

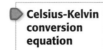 **Celsius-Kelvin conversion equation**

Kelvin temperature = Celsius temperature + 273

$$T_K = T_C + 273$$

Reading Check What is the difference between the Celsius and Kelvin temperature scales?

Differentiated Instruction

Basic Learners

Interpreting Visuals Write three or four Fahrenheit temperatures on the board. Have students use **Figure 4** to determine the approximate Celsius and Kelvin equivalents. Possible choices are 98.6 °F (body temperature), 70 °F (room temperature), 32 °F (water's freezing point), and −40 °F (the same value on the Celsius scale). **LS** Visual

Temperature-Scale Conversion

The highest temperature ever recorded in Earth's atmosphere was 57.8 °C at Al-Aziziyah, Libya, in 1922. Express this temperature in degrees Fahrenheit and in kelvins.

Identify	**Given:**
List the given and unknown values.	$T_C = 57.8\,°C$ **Unknown:** $T_F = ?\,°F,\ T_K = ?\,K$
Plan Write down the equations for temperature conversions.	$T_F = 1.8T_C + 32.0$ $T_K = T_C + 273$
Solve Insert the known values into the equations, and solve.	$T_F = (1.8 \times 57.8) + 32.0$ $= 104 + 32.0 = 136\,°F$ $T_K = 57.8 + 273 = 331\,K$

Practice

1. Express these temperatures in degrees Fahrenheit and in kelvins.
   a. the boiling point of liquid hydrogen (–252.87 °C)
   b. the temperature of a winter day at the North Pole (–40.0 °C)
   c. the melting point of gold (1,064 °C)

2. Make the necessary conversions to complete the table below.

Example	Temp. (°C)	Temp. (°F)	Temp. (K)
Air in a typical living room	21	?	?
Metal in a running car engine	?	?	388
Liquid nitrogen	–196	?	?
Air on a summer day in the desert	?	110	?

3. Use **Figure 4** to determine which of the following is a likely temperature for ice cubes in a freezer.
   a. 20 °C   c. 20 K
   b. –4 °F   d. 100 K

4. Use **Figure 4** to determine which of the following values is closest to the normal temperature of the human body.
   a. 50 °C   c. 98 °C
   b. 75 °F   d. 310 K

For more practice, visit **go.hrw.com** and enter keyword **HK8MP**.

Integrating Space Science

Temperatures in Space
Astronomers measure a wide range of temperatures in the universe, from the cold of deep space to the heat of stars. All objects produce different types of electromagnetic waves depending on their temperature. By identifying the distribution of wavelengths that an object radiates, astronomers can estimate the object's temperature. The sun gives off electromagnetic radiations at many wavelengths. Light received from the sun indicates that the temperature of the sun's surface is 6,000 K. And the temperature at the center of the sun is 15,000,000 K!

www.scilinks.org
Topic: Temperature Scales
Code: **HK81506**

Math Skills

Answers to Practice

1. **a.** $1.8(-252.87) + 32.0 = -423.17\,°F$
      $-252.87 + 273 = 20.13\,K$
   b. $1.8(-40.0) + 32.0 = -40.0\,°F$
      $-40.0 + 273 = 233\,K$
   c. $1.8(1064) + 32.0 = 1947\,°F$
      $1064 + 273 = 1337\,K$

2. $1.8(21) + 32 = 70\,°F$
   $21 + 273 = 294\,K$
   $388 - 273 = 115\,°C$
   $1.8(115) + 32.0 = 239\,°F$
   $1.8(-196) + 32.0 = -321\,°F$
   $-196 + 273 = 77\,K$
   $\dfrac{(110.0 - 32.0)}{1.8} = 43\,°C$
   $43 + 273 = 316\,K$

3. b
4. d

Social Studies Connection

Temperature Scales The Kelvin scale is named after the British physicist Lord Kelvin (1824–1907). The Fahrenheit scale is named after the German physicist Gabriel Fahrenheit (1686–1736). The Celsius scale is named for the Swedish astronomer Anders Celsius (1701–1744). The Celsius scale was originally called the centigrade scale because there are 100 degrees between the freezing and boiling points of water. In Latin, *centi* means "100" and *gradus* means "degree."

Why It Matters

Solar System Temperatures Have the students create a table of the planets in our solar system, comparing the temperature of each planet with the classroom's temperature. Record the table on the board or on an overhead transparency. Develop some general principles that can guide the students to classify which planets are "hotter" or "colder." General principles that should be suggested to students are the distance of a planet from the sun and the type of atmosphere of the planet.

As an extension, have students graph the relationship between the temperature of the planets and their distance from the sun. For a dramatic effect, you could prepare a large wall-sized graph on butcher paper or a bulletin board, using a cutout thermometer for the *y*-axis of the graph, and have students plot the points using cutouts of the planets. **LS Logical**

Teaching Key Ideas

Feeling Energy Transfers Display several objects that are at different temperatures, such as an ice cube, a cup of warm water, and a piece of metal at room temperature. Invite students to touch the objects and describe how the objects feel. Explain to students that objects feel hot or cold to them because of a transfer of energy. The ice and the metal feel cold because energy is transferred away from the students' hands to the objects. But the water feels warm because energy is transferred from the water to the students' hands. **LS Kinesthetic**

InquiryLab

Teacher's Notes Be sure that students wear heat-resistant gloves during this activity. The washers used within a single group should be the same size.

Materials per Group
- beaker
- cups, plastic-foam, 2
- hot plate
- string, 2 pieces
- thermometer
- washers, metal, 40
- water, cool

Answers to Analysis
1. the cup with 30 washers
2. One cup reached a higher temperature because more metal (30 washers as opposed to 10 washers) can transfer more energy.
3. The fact that more washers resulted in a higher temperature in the water shows that temperature changes depend on the amount of energy transferred.

Relating Temperature to Energy Transfer

When you touch a piece of ice, it feels very cold. When you step into a hot bath, the water feels very hot. Clasping your hands together usually produces neither sensation. These three cases can be explained by comparing the temperatures of the two objects that are making contact with each other. When two objects that are at different temperatures are touching, energy will be <u>transferred</u> from one to the other. ❯ **The feeling associated with temperature difference results from energy transfer**. Imagine that you are holding a piece of ice. The temperature of ice is lower than the temperature of your hand. Therefore, the molecules in the ice move slower than the molecules in your hand. As the molecules on the surface of your hand collide with those on the surface of the ice, energy is transferred from your hand to the ice. As a result, the molecules in the ice speed up, and their kinetic energy increases. This process causes the ice to melt.

Academic Vocabulary

transfer (TRANS fuhr) to carry or cause to pass from one thing to another

InquiryLab — Temperature and Energy ⏱ 30 min

Procedure
1. Tie **10 metal washers** on one piece of **string** and **30 identical washers** on another piece of string.
2. Fill a **beaker** two-thirds full with **water.** Lower the washers into the beaker. (Let enough string hang out such that you can safely remove the washers later.) Set the beaker on a **hot plate.**
3. Heat the water to boiling.
4. Put **50 mL of cool water** in **two plastic-foam cups.** Use a **thermometer** to measure and record the initial temperature of the water in each cup.
5. When the water in the beaker has boiled for about 3 min, remove the group of 30 washers.
6. Gently shake any water off the washers, and quickly place them into one of the plastic-foam cups. Observe the change in temperature of the cup's water. Record the highest temperature reached.
7. Repeat steps 5 and 6, this time removing the 10 washers and placing them in the other cup.

Analysis
1. Which cup's water reached the higher temperature?
2. Both cups had the same starting temperature. Both sets of washers started at 100 °C. Why did one cup reach a higher final temperature?
3. What general principle does this result illustrate about the relationship between temperature changes and energy changes?

Why It Matters

Burns The painful sensation of a burn is caused by a rapid transfer of energy. Burns are usually caused by touching a very hot object, but burns can also be caused by touching a very cold object. When you touch a hot object, energy flows from the object into your skin cells very rapidly, causing damage. When you touch a very cold object, energy transfers from your skin into the object, also resulting in tissue damage. Lead a discussion with students on how to prevent burns and how to treat burns if they occur. **LS Intrapersonal**

Differentiated Instruction

Alternative Assessment

Designing a Habitat Some animals, like lizards and frogs, do not have an internal mechanism to regulate their body temperature. Lizards and frogs bask in the sun to increase their body temperature by absorbing energy as heat. When it is very cold outside, these animals become inactive because they do not have a lot of extra energy to spend. Have students learn more about lizards and frogs and then ask them to design an indoor, caged habitat that would be suitable for a pet lizard or frog. Students may also build the habitat if materials are available. **LS Kinesthetic**

Temperature changes indicate an energy transfer.

The energy transferred between the particles of two objects, because of a temperature difference between the two objects, is called **heat.** This transfer of energy is always from something at a higher temperature to something at a lower temperature. As **Figure 5** shows, if you hold a glass of ice water in your hands, energy will be transferred as heat from your hand to the glass. But if you hold a cup of hot tea, energy will be transferred as heat from the cup to your hand.

Because temperature is a measure of the average kinetic energy of internal particles, you can use temperature to predict the direction in which energy will be transferred. Internal kinetic energy will be transferred as heat from the warmer object to the cooler object. The reason is that rapidly moving particles will always transfer the energy of their motion to particles that are not moving as rapidly. So, when energy is transferred from the hot water in the cup to your skin, the temperature of the water falls while the temperature of your skin rises.

When two materials that are at very different temperatures touch, the energy transfer between them happens quickly at first. The greater the difference in the temperatures of the two objects, the faster the energy will be transferred as heat. But when both your skin and the cup in your hand approach the same temperature, energy is transferred more slowly from the cup to your skin.

heat (HEET) the energy transferred between objects that are at different temperatures

Figure 5 The direction in which energy is transferred between your hand and whatever it is touching determines whether your hand feels hot or cold.

Section 1 Review

KEY IDEAS

1. **Define** *absolute zero* in terms of the kinetic energy of particles.

2. **Predict** which molecules will move faster on average: water molecules in hot soup or water molecules in iced lemonade.

3. **Describe** the relationship between temperature and energy.

4. **Predict** whether a greater amount of energy will be transferred as heat between 1 kg of water at 10 °C and a freezer at −15 °C or between 1 kg of water at 60 °C and an oven at 65 °C.

CRITICAL THINKING

5. **Applying Concepts** Consider two samples of water: Lake Michigan and a cup of boiling water. Which has a higher average kinetic energy? Which has a higher total kinetic energy?

Math Skills

6. Convert the temperature of the air in a room air-conditioned to 20.0 °C to equivalent temperatures on the Fahrenheit and Kelvin scales.

7. The coldest outdoor temperature ever recorded was −128.6 °F in Vostok, Antarctica. Convert this temperature to degrees Celsius and kelvins.

Answers to Section Review

1. Absolute zero is the temperature at which particles have theoretically zero kinetic energy.

2. The higher temperature of the hot soup means that the water molecules in the soup will move faster on average than the water molecules in iced lemonade.

3. Temperature is a measure of the average kinetic energy of particles of a substance. The higher the kinetic energy of particles is, the higher the temperature is.

4. More energy will be transferred between water at 10 °C and a freezer at −15 °C because the temperature difference is greater.

5. A cup of boiling water has a higher temperature and thus higher average kinetic energy than Lake Michigan has, but Lake Michigan has more total kinetic energy (and thus more heat) because it has more particles.

6. $1.8(20.0) + 32.0 = 68.0$ °F

   $20 + 273 = 293$ K

7. $(-128.6 - 32.0)/1.8 = -89.2$ °C

   $-89.2 + 273 = 184$ K

❯ Close

Reteaching Key Ideas

How a Thermometer Works Have students write an explanation of how a thermometer works. Tell students that their explanations should discuss the relationship between temperature and energy, temperature scales, and energy transfer. Students may include diagrams in their explanation if they wish.
LS Verbal

Formative Assessment

You could comfortably wear a short-sleeved shirt outside when the temperature is

A. 30 °C (Correct. 30 °C is the temperature of a warm summer day.)

B. 30 °F (Incorrect. 30 °F is below the freezing point of water and is the temperature of a cold winter day.)

C. 30 K (Incorrect. 30 K is very cold and is close to absolute zero.)

D. −30 K (Incorrect. The kelvin scale does not include negative temperatures.)

SECTION 2

Energy Transfer

>Focus

In this section, students learn about conduction, convection, and radiation; conductors and insulators; and problem solving with specific heat.

Bellringer

Use the Bellringer transparency to prepare students for this section.

Demonstrate

Energy Transfer in Boiling Water Fill a beaker with water and place it on the hot plate. Place a metal spoon and a wooden spoon in the water and bring the water to a boil. Have students observe the setup and ask the following questions:

1. Which spoon is safe to touch? (the wooden spoon)
2. Why is one spoon cool and the other hot? (Metal conducts heat, so it will be hot. Wood conducts heat poorly, so it will not be hot.)
3. Where are all the energy transfers occurring? (The hot plate heats the beaker, the beaker heats the water, and the water heats both spoons. The steam escapes into the air, heating up the air around it.)

LS Visual

Key Ideas

> How does energy transfer happen?
> What do conductors and insulators do?
> What makes something a good conductor of heat?

Key Terms

thermal conduction

convection

convection current

radiation

specific heat

Why It Matters

Energy transfer is a crucial factor that governs global wind patterns, which mariners use to navigate safely.

While water is being heated for your morning shower, your breakfast food is cooking. In the freezer, water in ice trays becomes solid after the freezer cools the water to 0 °C. Outside, the morning dew evaporates soon after light from the rising sun strikes it. These examples are ways that energy transfers from one object to another.

Methods of Energy Transfer

> **Heat energy can be transferred in three ways: conduction, convection, and radiation.** Roasting marsh-mallows around a campfire, as **Figure 1** shows, provides an opportunity to experience each of these three ways.

Figure 1 Ways of Transferring Energy

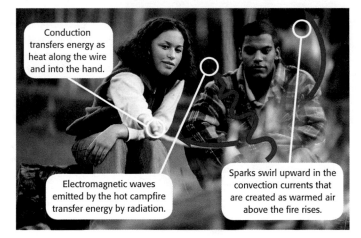

Conduction transfers energy as heat along the wire and into the hand.

Electromagnetic waves emitted by the hot campfire transfer energy by radiation.

Sparks swirl upward in the convection currents that are created as warmed air above the fire rises.

Key Resources

Teaching Transparencies
TM38 Specific Heats
TM39 Temperature Energy Graph
P10 Conduction and Convection

Visual Concepts
Comparing Convection, Conduction, and Radiation
Electrical Conductors and Insulators
Equation for Specific Heat Capacity

Datasheets
Absorption of Radiated Heat
Conductors and Insulators

Math Skills Worksheet
Specific Heat

Cross-Disciplinary Worksheets
Integrating Earth Science—Land and Sea Breezes
Connection to Social Studies—Early Central Heating
Connection to Social Studies—The Little Ice Age
Integrating Biology—Hibernation and Torpor

Figure 2 Conduction

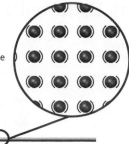
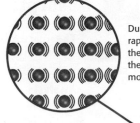

Before conduction takes place, the average kinetic energy of the particles in the metal wire is the same throughout.

During conduction, the rapidly moving particles in the wire transfer some of their energy to slowly moving particles nearby.

Conduction occurs between objects in direct contact.

Imagine that you place a marshmallow on one end of a wire made from a metal coat hanger. Then, you hold the other end of the wire while letting the marshmallow cook over the campfire flame. Soon, the end of the wire that you are holding gets warmer. This transfer of energy as heat through the wire is an example of **thermal conduction.**

Conduction takes place when objects that are in direct contact are at unequal temperatures. It also takes place between particles within an object. The energy transferred from the fire to the atoms in the wire causes the atoms to vibrate rapidly. As **Figure 2** shows, when these rapidly vibrating atoms collide with slowly vibrating atoms, energy is transferred as heat all along the wire and to your hand.

Convection results from the movement of warm fluids.

While roasting your marshmallow, you may notice that sparks from the fire rise and begin to swirl. They are following the movement of air away from the fire. The air close to the fire becomes hot and expands, so the space between the air particles increases. As a result, the air becomes less dense and moves upward, carrying its extra energy with it, as **Figure 3** shows. The rising warm air is forced upward by cooler, denser air. The cooler air then expands and rises as it is heated by the fire. Eventually, the rising hot air cools, contracts, becomes denser, and sinks. Energy transfer resulting from the movement of warm fluids is **convection.**

Convection is possible only in fluids. Most fluids are liquids or gases. The cycle of a heated fluid that rises and then cools and falls is called a **convection current.** The heating and cooling of a room involves convection currents. Warm air expands and rises from vents near the floor. It cools and contracts near the ceiling and then sinks back to the floor. In this way, all of the air in the room gets heated.

thermal conduction (THUHR muhl kuhn DUHK shuhn) the transfer of energy as heat through a material

convection (kuhn VEK shuhn) the movement of matter due to differences in density that are caused by temperature variations

convection current (kuhn VEK shuhn KUHR uhnt) any movement of matter that results from differences in density; may be vertical, circular, or cyclical

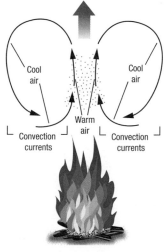

Figure 3 During convection, energy is carried away by a heated fluid that expands and rises above cooler, denser fluids.

> **Teach**

READING TOOLBOX

Visual Literacy Have students examine **Figure 3.** Have them brainstorm explanations for why you can put your hand close to the side of a candle flame and not get burned while putting your hand above the flame will burn your hand. Much of the candle's energy is transferred by convection as hot air rises. Therefore, the air next to the flame is not as hot as the air above the flame. **LS Visual**

Teaching Key Ideas

Convection A convection current is generated when a layer of fluid becomes hot and rises as it becomes less dense. Suppose a glass tube containing water is heated by putting a flame next to the top portion of the water layer. Ask the students if energy transfer will occur by convection, causing the bottom layer of water to get hot. (No, the hot water will remain at the top because it is less dense than cold water.) **LS Logical**

Differentiated Instruction

Struggling Readers

Reviewing Vocabulary Have students make flashcards to help them learn the important terms in this section. Give students index cards or instruct students to cut notebook paper into fourths or eighths. Tell students to write one highlighted or italicized term on one side of each card. On the other side of the cards, students should write a definition for the term in their own words or draw diagrams that explain the term. Students can use the flashcards to test one another's knowledge of the vocabulary. **LS Verbal**

InquiryLab

Teacher's Notes You may want to have students bring cans from home, but be sure each group gets two cans that are matched in size. If you decide to use sunlight, try to take students outside, since the glass in the classroom windows will reflect or absorb the infrared and ultraviolet light. If you go outside, you will need stopwatches. If you use lamps, try to use 100 W bulbs.

Materials per Group
- cans, empty, soup, 2
- lamp
- paint, black
- thermometer
- water, cool

Answers to Analysis
1. Both sets of data should show an increase in the temperature of the water.
2. The black can should absorb more energy.
3. The starting temperature of the water, the volume of the water, the distance of each can from the light, and the size of each can were controlled variables in the experiment.
4. Black absorbs more energy, which is why solar heating panels are often black.
5. In winter, a black car would absorb wanted energy, and in summer, a white or silver car would reflect unwanted energy.

InquiryLab Absorption of Radiated Heat ⏱ 30 min

Procedure
1. Obtain **two empty soup cans,** and remove the labels. Paint the inside and outside of one soup can with **black paint.**
2. Pour **50 mL of cool water** into each can.
3. Place a **thermometer** in each can, and record the temperature of the water in each can at the start. Leave the thermometers in the cans. Aim a bright **lamp** at the cans, or place them in sunlight.
4. Record the temperature of the water in each can every 3 min for at least 15 min.

Analysis
1. Prepare a graph. Label the *x*-axis "Time" and the *y*-axis "Temperature." Plot your data for each can of water.
2. The water in which can absorbed more radiation?
3. Which variables in the lab were controlled (unchanged throughout the experiment)? How did the controlled variables help you obtain valid results?
4. Use your results to explain why panels used for solar heating are often painted black.
5. Based on your results, what color would you want your car to be in the winter? in the summer? Justify your answer.

---

radiation (RAY dee AY shuhn) the energy that is transferred as electromagnetic waves, such as visible light and infrared waves

Figure 4 Heat as infrared radiation is visible in this thermogram. The warmest parts of the dog are white, and the coolest parts are dark blue.

Radiation does not require physical contact between objects.

As you stand close to a campfire, you can feel its warmth. This warmth can be felt even when you are not in the path of a convection current. The fire emits energy in the form of *electromagnetic waves,* which include infrared radiation, visible light, and ultraviolet rays. Energy that is transferred as electromagnetic waves is called **radiation.** When the molecules in your skin absorb this energy, the average kinetic energy of these molecules—and thus the temperature of your skin—increases.

All hot objects give off infrared radiation, which is electromagnetic waves at a frequency lower than that of visible light. The warmer an object is, the more infrared radiation it gives off. The image of the dog in **Figure 4** shows the areas of the dog that are warmer (white and red) and the areas that are cooler (black and blue).

Radiation differs from conduction and convection in that it does not involve the movement of matter across space. Only electromagnetic waves carry radiation. Radiation is therefore the only way that energy can be transferred through a vacuum, such as outer space. Much of the energy that we receive from the sun is transferred by radiation.

✔ **Reading Check** How does radiation differ from conduction and convection?

Why It Matters

Popping Popcorn Cooking popcorn is a familiar example of energy transfer, as well as a dramatic example of what happens when water rapidly undergoes a phase change to become steam. The hard kernels absorb energy until, at a high temperature, superheated water inside the kernel suddenly turns to steam and rushes outward, and the kernels burst open to form popcorn. Have students do experiments with popcorn kernels to find ways that would prevent the kernels from popping. (Poking holes in the kernels with a thumbtack or drying the kernels in sunlight will prevent kernels from popping.) **LS Kinesthetic**

Why Does the Wind Blow?

As Earth rotates, the sun's rays heat up the part of Earth facing the sun. This differential heating causes convection, in which cooler air or water moves to replace warmer air or water. Convection affects global wind and ocean-current patterns. Mariners have known about and taken advantage of these patterns for centuries.

REAL WORLD

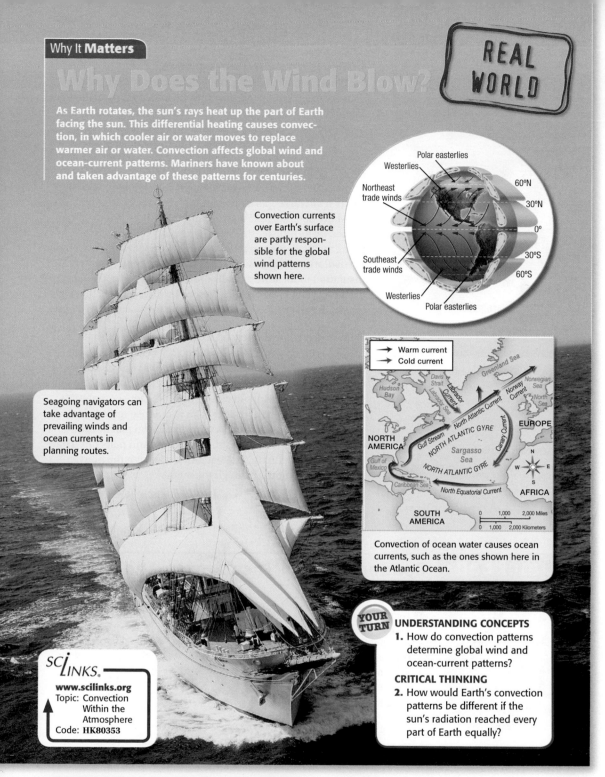

Convection currents over Earth's surface are partly responsible for the global wind patterns shown here.

Polar easterlies
Westerlies
Northeast trade winds
Southeast trade winds
Westerlies
Polar easterlies
60°N
30°N
0°
30°S
60°S

Seagoing navigators can take advantage of prevailing winds and ocean currents in planning routes.

→ Warm current
→ Cold current

Greenland Sea
Davis Strait
Hudson Bay
Labrador Current
Norwegian Sea
North Sea
Norway Current
North Atlantic Current
Gulf Stream
NORTH ATLANTIC GYRE
EUROPE
NORTH AMERICA
Sargasso Sea
Canary Current
Gulf of Mexico
NORTH ATLANTIC GYRE
Caribbean Sea
North Equatorial Current
AFRICA
SOUTH AMERICA

0   1,000   2,000 Miles
0   1,000   2,000 Kilometers

Convection of ocean water causes ocean currents, such as the ones shown here in the Atlantic Ocean.

SC/LINKS.
www.scilinks.org
Topic: Convection Within the Atmosphere
Code: HK80353

YOUR TURN

UNDERSTANDING CONCEPTS
1. How do convection patterns determine global wind and ocean-current patterns?

CRITICAL THINKING
2. How would Earth's convection patterns be different if the sun's radiation reached every part of Earth equally?

Why Does the Wind Blow? The electromagnetic waves from the sun provide energy, causing the temperature of our planet to increase. It is often assumed that the temperature of the atmosphere rises because of the direct energy transfer between the electromagnetic waves and the air molecules. In fact, very little energy is absorbed by the air molecules as the electromagnetic waves pass through the atmosphere. First, the electromagnetic waves transfer energy to the ground, raising its temperature. The hot ground then transfers energy to the layer of air next to the ground by conduction. The hot ground also produces infrared radiation, which travels upward in the air. The infrared radiation is mostly absorbed by water vapor and CO_2 in the air. Convection currents are then generated in the air, rise up, and transfer energy to subsequent layers of the atmosphere.

READING TOOLBOX

Visual Literacy Tell students that convection currents in Earth's atmosphere form large, circular patterns called *convection cells* that surround Earth. These convection cells are pictured in the diagram of Earth shown, as large loops above Earth's surface. Ask students to do research to find out why convection cells in the atmosphere are separated by pressure belts about every 30° of latitude. **LS Logical**

Differentiated Instruction

Advanced Learners

Message in a Bottle Have students research whether a bottle tossed off the coast of the United States could travel to Europe or Africa. Students should find where in the United States the bottle must be thrown and where it will land. Ask students to draw a map showing the path that the bottle will most likely follow and identifying the currents responsible for the bottle's motion. **LS Visual**

Answers to Your Turn

1. Convection patterns determine global wind and ocean patterns by the movement of warm air or warm water toward areas of cool air or cool water.
2. If the same amount of the sun's radiation reached every part of Earth, there would be no global convection patterns.

Teaching Key Ideas

Conductors and Insulators Some texts refer to materials that readily allow energy transfer between objects at different temperatures as *thermal conductors* and those that do not as *thermal insulators*. Materials that are good conductors of electricity are often good thermal conductors as well. For example, most metals are both electrical and thermal conductors. Conversely, many electrical insulators are also thermal insulators. Discuss the relationship between thermal and electrical conductors and insulators with your students. Then challenge students to think of a substance that is a poor electrical conductor but a good thermal conductor. (Sample answer: pure (deionized) water)

LS **Verbal**

QuickLab

Teacher's Notes After completing the activity, you may want to have students brainstorm ways to improve the accuracy of the activity, such as using thermometers or using materials of uniform thickness and shape.

Materials per Group
- bowl
- ice cubes
- flatware utensils, made of different materials

Answer to Analysis

1. Sample answer: The metal spoon became cold soonest. Different materials of which the utensils are made and different widths of the utensils would cause differences in the results.

Figure 5 A well-insulated coat can keep in body heat even in cold temperatures.

Academic Vocabulary
conduct (kuhn DUHKT) to be able to carry

Conductors and Insulators

When you are cooking, the pan must <u>conduct</u> energy to heat the food, but the handle must be insulated from the heat so that you can hold the handle. If you are using conduction to increase the temperature of a substance, you must use materials through which energy can be quickly transferred as heat. Cooking pans are usually made of metal because energy passes quickly between the particles in most metals. ⟩ **A *conductor* is a material through which energy can be easily transferred as heat.**

Many people avoid wasting energy. Energy is most often wasted by its transfer through the roof or walls of a house. Using an insulator can reduce energy transfer. ⟩ **An *insulator*, or insulation, is a material that transfers energy poorly.** Insulation in the attic or walls of a house helps keep energy from escaping. Insulation in warm clothing, such as that shown in **Figure 5,** keeps energy as heat from leaving the body.

Heat energy is transferred through particle collisions.

Gases are very poor heat conductors because their particles are so far apart. Much less energy per volume can be transferred through a gas than through a solid or a liquid, whose particles are much closer together. Denser materials usually conduct energy better than less dense materials do. Metals tend to conduct energy very well, and plastics conduct energy poorly. For this reason, metal pots and pans often have plastic handles. Energy as heat moves through the plastic slower than it moves through the metal.

✓ **Reading Check** What makes a material a good conductor?

QuickLab Conductors and Insulators ⏱ 10 min

Procedure

❶ For this activity, you will need **several flatware utensils.** Each one should be made of a different material, such as **stainless steel, aluminum,** and **plastic.** You will also need a **bowl** and **ice cubes.**

❷ Place the ice cubes in the bowl. Place an equal length of each utensil under the ice.

Analysis

1. After the utensils have been in the ice for 30 s, briefly touch each utensil at the same distance from the ice. Which utensil feels coldest? Which differences between the utensils might account for the different results? Explain.

Why It **Matters**

Superconductors At very low temperatures, certain substances lose all their resistance to electric current and become electrical *superconductors*. The temperature at which a substance becomes a superconductor is close to absolute zero. For example, aluminum becomes a superconductor at 1.2 K. Scientists are trying to develop materials that superconduct at normal temperatures. Some possible uses for superconductors are the storage and transmission of energy, medical magnetic resonance imaging (MRI), and magnetic-levitation trains. Encourage interested students to learn how magnetic-levitation trains work and make a poster to illustrate how they levitate. **LS** **Visual**

Differentiated Instruction

Special Education Students

Understanding Terms Ask students to fold a piece of paper in half vertically. Label one side of the paper "Conductors" and the other side "Insulators." Under each term, write a definition. Using information from the chapter, students can list materials that are good conductors of energy and poor conductors (insulators). Discussion in small groups about the practical uses of these materials would help students understand the concept. **LS** **Interpersonal**

Specific Heat

You have probably noticed that a metal spoon, such as the one shown in **Figure 6,** becomes hot when placed in a cup of hot liquid. And you may have noticed that a spoon made of a different material, such as plastic, does not become hot as quickly. The difference between the final temperatures of the two spoons depends on whether the spoons are good conductors or good insulators. ❯ **What makes a substance a good or poor conductor depends in part on how much energy is required to change the temperature of the substance by a certain amount.**

Specific heat describes how much energy is required to raise an object's temperature.

Not all substances behave the same way when they absorb energy. For example, a metal spoon left in a metal pot becomes hot seconds after the pot is placed on a hot stovetop burner. The reason is that a small amount of energy is enough to raise the spoon's temperature by a lot. However, if you place a wooden spoon that has the same mass as the metal spoon in the same pot, that same amount of energy produces a much smaller temperature change in the wooden spoon.

For all substances, specific heat is a characteristic physical property, which is represented by c. In this book, the **specific heat** of any substance is the amount of energy required to raise the temperature of 1 kg of that substance by 1 K.

Some values for specific heat are given in **Figure 7.** These values are in units of joules per kilogram times kelvin (J/kg•K). Thus, each value is the amount of energy in joules needed to raise the temperature of 1 kg of the substance by exactly 1 K.

Figure 7 Values of Specific Heat at 25 °C

Substance	c (J/kg•K)	Substance	c (J/kg•K)
Water (liquid)	4,186	Copper	385
Ethanol (liquid)	2,440	Iron	449
Ammonia (gas)	2,060	Silver	234
Steam	1,870	Mercury	140
Aluminum	897	Gold	129
Carbon (graphite)	709	Lead	129

Figure 6 The spoon's temperature increases rapidly because of the spoon's low specific heat.

READING TOOLBOX

Comparison Table
To help you understand specific heat, make a comparison table. Compare the amount of heat it takes to raise the temperature of some of the substances listed on this page.

specific heat (spuh SIF ik HEET) the quantity of heat required to raise a unit mass of homogenous material 1 K or 1 °C in a specified way given constant pressure and volume

Teaching Key Ideas

Specific Heat and Conductors Have students examine **Figure 7.** Point out that the numbers in the chart represent how much energy is required to raise the temperature of 1 kg of the substance by 1 K (or 1 °C). Have students make a list ranking the substances from the ones that absorb energy the easiest to the one that absorbs the least energy. Then, ask students to describe the relationship between specific heat and the ability to conduct thermal energy. **LS Logical**

READING TOOLBOX

Comparison Table Students' tables should show that more heat is required to raise the temperature of substances that have high specific heats.

Science Skills

Graphing Have students prepare a graph of the following data (1 kg sample) with energy on the y-axis and the temperature change on the x-axis. Have advanced students calculate the slope (140 J/kg•K) and use **Figure 7** to determine the substance.

Energy (J)	Temperature change (K)
700	5
1400	10
2100	15
2800	20
3500	25

LS Logical

Differentiated Instruction

Alternative Assessment

Conductors and Insulators in the Kitchen Ask students to examine and list 10 items of cookware in their kitchens at home. Lists could include kitchen appliances, pots and pans, cooking utensils, and dishes. Instruct students to write down all of the materials each item is made of, and then ask them to classify the materials as conductors or insulators. If an item is made up of more than one material, for example a metal pan with a plastic handle, students should be sure to list and classify each material separately. **LS Intrapersonal**

MISCONCEPTION ALERT

Rate of Energy Transfer When one substance feels colder than another, is it because the first substance has a lower temperature? Actually, the difference is in the rate at which each item transfers energy. For example, a tile floor might feel colder to bare feet than a rug in the same room. This is because the tile, which is a better thermal conductor than the rug, readily absorbs the heat from the feet.

Integrating Earth Science

Specific Heat and Sea Breezes The movement of sea breezes described in the student page holds true on a local level. Many other factors affect the direction of the wind: convection currents on a global scale, weather disturbances such as thunderstorms or hurricanes, the size of the landmass and water mass, etc.

Teaching Key Ideas

Specific Heat Tell students the specific heat is the "price" to raise the temperature of 1 kg of a substance. Water changes its "price" as the temperature of water changes. At 20 °C, water's specific heat is 4181 J/kg•K, while its specific heat changes to 4196 J/kg•K at 80 °C.

Math Skills

Answers to Practice

1. energy = (449 J/kg•K)(0.755 kg) (403 K – 283 K) = 40,700 J

2. energy = (4186 J/kg•K)(0.225 kg) (35 °C – 5 °C) = 28,000 J

Additional Examples

Identify an unknown substance with a mass of 0.455 kg that absorbs 6.33×10^3 J, in which a temperature change of 15.5 °C is observed.
Answer: aluminum
What temperature change would copper experience under the same conditions as those above (same mass and energy)?
Answer: 36.1 °C or 36.1 K
LS Logical

Specific Heat and Sea Breezes
Sea breezes result from convection currents in the coastal air and from differences in the specific heats of water and land. During the day, the temperature of the land increases more than that of the ocean water, which has a larger specific heat. Thus, the temperature of the air over land increases more than the temperature of air over the ocean. As a result, the warm air over the land rises, and the cool ocean air moves inland to replace the rising warm air. At night, the temperature of the land drops below that of the ocean, and the breezes reverse direction.

Specific heat can be used to figure out how much energy it takes to raise an object's temperature.

Because specific heat is a ratio, it can be used to predict the effects of temperature changes for masses other than 1 kg. For example, if 4,186 J is required to raise the temperature of 1 kg of water by 1 K, twice as much energy, 8,372 J, will raise the temperature of 2 kg of water by 1 K. About 25,120 J will be required to raise the temperature of the 2 kg of water by 3 K. This relationship is described by the equation below.

> **Specific heat equation** | energy = specific heat × mass × temperature change
> energy = $cm\Delta T$

The specific heat of a substance can change slightly with changes in pressure and volume. However, the problems in this chapter will assume that specific heat does not change.

Math Skills Specific Heat

How much energy must be transferred as heat to 200 kg of water in a bathtub to raise the water's temperature from 25 °C to 37 °C?

Identify List the given and unknown values.	**Given:** $\Delta T = 37 \,°C - 25 \,°C = 12 \,°C = 12$ K $\Delta T = 12$ K $m = 200$ kg $c = 4{,}186$ J/kg•K **Unknown:** *energy* = ? J
Plan Write down the specific heat equation from this page.	energy = $cm\Delta T$
Solve Substitute values of specific heat, mass, and temperature change, and solve.	energy = $\left(\dfrac{4{,}186 \text{ J}}{\text{kg•K}}\right) \times (200 \text{ kg}) \times (12 \text{ K})$ energy = 10,000,000 J = 1.0×10^4 kJ

Practice

1. How much energy is needed to increase the temperature of 755 g of iron from 283 K to 403 K?

2. How much energy must a refrigerator absorb from 225 g of water to decrease the temperature of the water from 35 °C to 5 °C?

For more practice, visit **go.hrw.com** and enter keyword **HK8MP**.

Differentiated Instruction

Basic Learners

Temperature Versus Energy This assignment will help students distinguish between temperature and energy. Write the following experiment on the chalkboard, and ask students to write a paragraph explaining the results.
Experiment: Two beakers are each filled with 10 ice cubes. A small amount of boiling water is poured into *Beaker A,* and a large amount of boiling water (at the same temperature) is poured into *Beaker B.* Only 3 of the ice cubes in *Beaker A* melt, while all 10 of the cubes in *Beaker B* melt. Since the water was at the same temperature, why didn't the same number of ice cubes melt in each beaker? (Although the boiling water poured into both beakers had the same temperature, *Beaker B* received more energy than *Beaker A* because much more water was poured into it. Thus, more energy was transferred to the ice cubes, and all of the ice cubes were able to melt. In *Beaker A,* there was only enough energy to melt some of the ice cubes.) **LS** Visual

Heat raises an object's temperature or changes the object's state.

The graph in **Figure 8** represents what happens to water over a range of temperatures as energy is added. At 0 °C, the water is at first in the solid state (ice). A certain amount of energy per kilogram is required to melt the ice. While the ice is melting, the temperature does not change. The same is true when water is at 100 °C and is boiling. Energy is required to pull liquid molecules apart. While the water is boiling, energy added to the water is used in changing the water to a gas. While water is changing to a gas, the temperature does not change. For any substance, added energy either raises its temperature or changes its state, not both at the same time.

Figure 8 Energy put into a substance either raises the substance's temperature or changes the substance's state. **As energy is added to water, what is happening during the times that temperature does not change?**

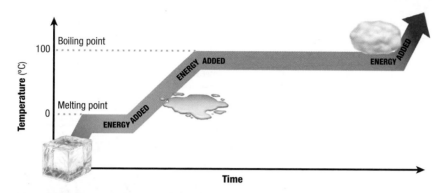

Section 2 **Review**

KEY IDEAS

1. **Describe** how energy is transferred by conduction, convection, and radiation.

2. **Predict** whether the hottest part of a room will be near the ceiling, in the center, or near the floor, given that there is a hot-air vent near the floor. Explain your reasoning.

3. **Explain** why there are temperature differences on the moon's surface even though there is no atmosphere present.

CRITICAL THINKING

4. **Applying Concepts** Explain why cookies baked near the turned-up edges of a cookie sheet receive more energy than those baked near the center do.

Math Skills

5. How much energy would be absorbed by 550 g of copper that is heated from 24 °C to 45 °C? (Hint: Refer to **Figure 7**.)

6. A 144 kg park bench made of iron sits in the sun, and its temperature increases from 25 °C to 35 °C. How many kilojoules of energy does the bench absorb? (Hint: Refer to **Figure 7**.)

7. Suppose that a car's radiator contains 2.0 kg of water. The water absorbs energy from the car engine. In the process, the water's temperature increases from 298 K to 355 K. How much energy did the water absorb?

> ## ❯Close

Reteaching Key Ideas

Designing a Solar Cooker Have students design a solar cooker that can cook a hotdog. Tell students to think about methods of energy transfer, conductors and insulators, and specific heat as they design their cookers. Students' designs should be safe to handle as well as effective at cooking. A well-designed cooker should be able to collect solar radiation, have parts made from an insulating material that can be safely touched to adjust the cooker, and may have metal prongs made from a metal that has a low specific heat that can help cook a hotdog from the inside by conduction. **LS Logical**

Answer to caption question

The state is changing, that is, water is changing from a liquid to a gas.

Formative Assessment

Energy from the sun is transferred to Earth by

A. conduction. (Incorrect. Conduction involves direct contact. The sun and Earth are not in contact.)

B. convection. (Incorrect. Convection results from the movement of fluids. No fluids exist in space.)

C. radiation. (Correct. Radiation is the only way that energy can be transferred through the vacuum of space.)

D. reflection. (Incorrect. Reflection is not a method of energy transfer.)

Answers to Section Review

1. Energy transfer by conduction involves direct contact. Higher-energy molecules transfer energy to lower-energy molecules. Energy transfer by convection involves the movement of the higher-energy molecules from one place to another. Energy transfer by radiation involves the emission and absorption of electromagnetic waves.

2. The hottest part of the room should be near the ceiling because hot air rises.

3. The temperature differences on the moon's surface are due to two factors. One is the varying composition of the moon's surface. The other factor is the location of the spot, whether it is in the sun or covered by shade.

4. The cookies near the turned-up edge receive conduction energy from the cookie sheet, just as the cookies in the middle do. However, those near the edge also receive energy from air convection currents and radiation from the side.

5. energy = (385 J/kg•K)(0.55 kg)(45 °C − 24 °C) = 4,400 J

6. energy = (449 J/kg•K)(144 kg)(35 °C − 25 °C) (1 kJ/1000 J) = 650 kJ

7. energy = (4186 J/kg•K)(2 kg)(355 K − 298 K) = 4.8×10^5 J

How Are Homes Heated and Cooled?
Solar-heating systems heat a building by using an approach similar to that of a basking reptile. A solar collector uses panels to gather energy radiated from the sun. This energy is used to heat water, which can be pumped through a device called a *heat exchanger,* as shown in the image in the top right of this page. This type of solar heating system is called an *active solar-heating system.*

Another type of solar heating system is the *passive solar-heating system.* Ask students to learn more about passive solar heating systems. Then, have students draw diagrams that show how passive solar-heating systems work. **LS Visual**

READING TOOLBOX

Visual Literacy The image at the bottom left of the page is a schematic of a central heating system. A central heating system has a furnace that burns coal, fuel oil, or natural gas. The energy released in the furnace is transferred as heat to water, steam, or air as indicated by the blue arrows. The hot water, steam, or hot air is then moved to each room through pipes or ducts as indicated by the small red arrows. Because the temperature of the pipe is higher than that of the air, energy is transferred as heat to the air in the room. The large arrows in the image show the movement of air throughout the central heating system. The red arrows shown traveling up the thin pipe show the movement of carbon dioxide exhaust.

How Are Homes Heated and Cooled?

People tend to be most comfortable when the temperature of the air around them is in the range of 21 °C to 25° C (70 °F to 77 °F). To raise the indoor temperature on colder days, one must use a heating system to transfer energy into a room's air. Most heating systems use a source of energy to raise the temperature of a substance such as air or water. In cooling systems, energy is transferred as heat from one substance to another, which leaves the first substance at a lower temperature. Cooled or heated air circulates throughout a home by convection currents. For the temperature of a home to be effectively regulated, heating and cooling units must be designed to make the best use of the flow of heat energy by convection.

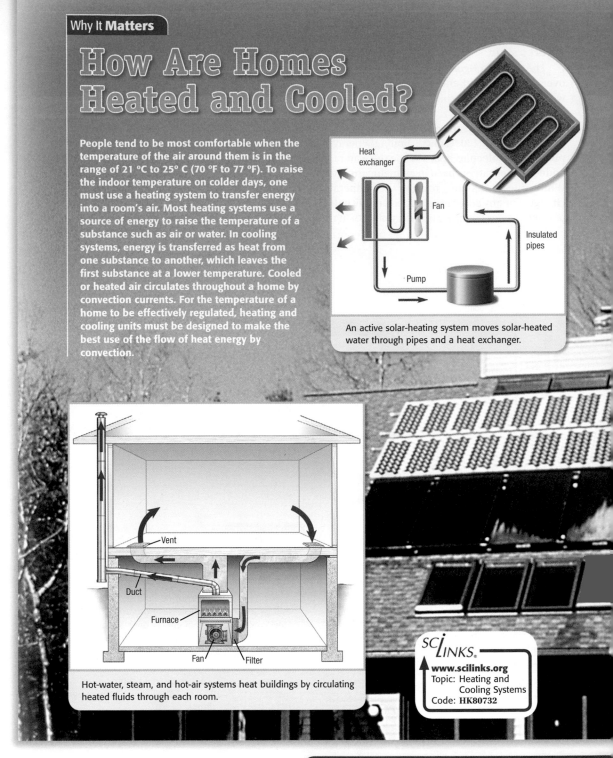

An active solar-heating system moves solar-heated water through pipes and a heat exchanger.

Hot-water, steam, and hot-air systems heat buildings by circulating heated fluids through each room.

SCLINKS.
www.scilinks.org
Topic: Heating and Cooling Systems
Code: HK80732

Differentiated Instruction

Advanced Learners

History of Heating and Cooling Have students research the history of a modern heating or cooling system, such as air conditioners or refrigerators. Instruct them to draw timelines of the major events in the development of their chosen systems. Then, have students find out what other historical events were happening around the same times and ask them to include these events in their timelines for context. **LS Verbal**

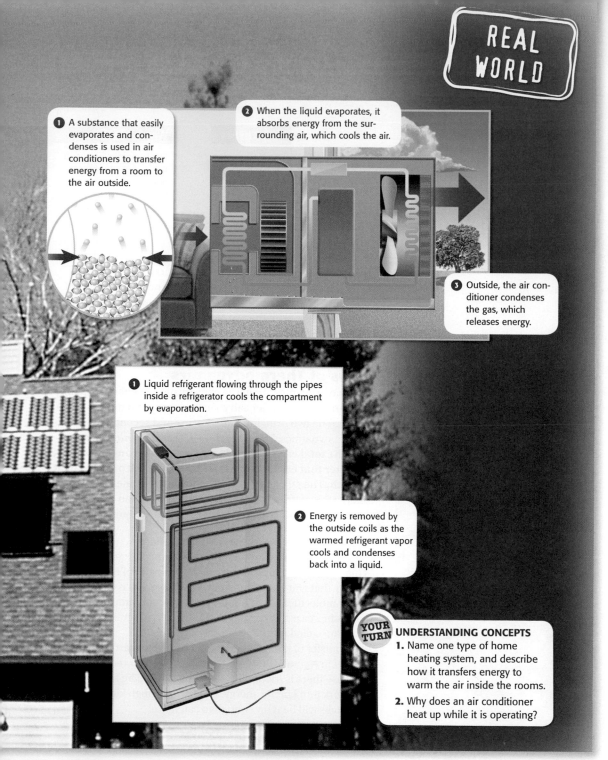

REAL WORLD

❶ A substance that easily evaporates and condenses is used in air conditioners to transfer energy from a room to the air outside.

❷ When the liquid evaporates, it absorbs energy from the surrounding air, which cools the air.

❸ Outside, the air conditioner condenses the gas, which releases energy.

❶ Liquid refrigerant flowing through the pipes inside a refrigerator cools the compartment by evaporation.

❷ Energy is removed by the outside coils as the warmed refrigerant vapor cools and condenses back into a liquid.

YOUR TURN

UNDERSTANDING CONCEPTS

1. Name one type of home heating system, and describe how it transfers energy to warm the air inside the rooms.

2. Why does an air conditioner heat up while it is operating?

Why It Matters

Cooling System A refrigerator is an example of a cooling system. A refrigerator lowers the temperature of the air and the food inside it. But because the first law of thermodynamics requires energy to be conserved, the energy inside the refrigerator must be transferred to the air outside the refrigerator. If you place your hand near the rear or base of a refrigerator, you will feel warm air being discharged. Much of the energy in this air was removed from inside the refrigerator. Ask students to explain why they cannot cool a room by leaving a refrigerator door open. (The energy removed by the refrigerator from the room air will be transferred back to the room at the back of the refrigerator.) **LS** **Logical**

Answers to Your Turn

1. Sample answer: A hot-water heating system circulates hot water to pipes throughout a house, and heat energy thus circulates from the pipes to the air in the house's rooms.

2. An air conditioner heats up while the coolant gas absorbs the heat energy from the room's air.

Differentiated Instruction

Basic Learners

Life Without Heating or Cooling Ask students to imagine what life would be like without a particular heating or cooling system. Have them write short stories set in times before their chosen systems were invented or before they were in common use. For example, a student who researched the history of air conditioning could write about a family visiting a movie theater with air conditioning for the first time. **LS** **Verbal**

SECTION 3

❯ Focus

In this section, students will learn about the first and second laws of thermodynamics and will learn how an internal combustion heat engine works.

🔊 Bellringer

Use the Bellringer transparency to prepare students for this section.

Demonstrate

Reviewing Conservation of Energy
Complete the following activity before beginning this section: Ask students to rub their hands together very quickly and describe what they feel. (Sample answer: My hands started to feel warmer.) Ask students if they created energy by rubbing their hands together. (Sample answer: No, energy cannot be created or destroyed by normal means.) Then ask students what caused their hands to feel warmer. (Sample answer: The kinetic energy from rubbing my hands was converted to thermal energy.) Finally, tell students that the first law of thermodynamics is an application of the law of conservation of energy. **LS Logical**

SECTION 3 Using Heat

Key Ideas
❯ What happens to heat energy when it is transferred?
❯ What do heat engines do?

Key Terms
entropy
heat engine

Why It Matters
Heat engines are used to do important work, such as running automobiles.

Heating a house in the winter, cooling an office building in the summer, or preserving food throughout the year is possible because of machines that transfer energy as heat from one place to another. An air conditioner does work to remove energy as heat from the warm air inside a room and then transfers the energy to the warmer air outside the room.

Laws of Thermodynamics

Two principles about the conservation of energy explain how an air conditioner can transfer energy and make a room cooler. The two principles are the first and second laws of thermodynamics. ❯ **The *first law of thermodynamics* states that the total energy used in any process is conserved, whether that energy is transferred as a result of work, heat, or both.** The *second law of thermodynamics* states that the energy transferred as heat always moves from an object at a higher temperature to an object at a lower temperature.

Work can increase average kinetic energy.

When you rub your hands together, they become warmer. This process is an example of *work,* a transfer of energy. The energy that you transfer to your hands by work is transferred to the molecules of your hands, and the temperature of your hands increases. Processes in which energy is transferred by work are called *mechanical processes.*

Transfer of kinetic energy can be used to start a fire, as shown in **Figure 1.** Rubbing two sticks together requires work, because there is friction between the sticks. The friction turns the work into kinetic energy. If there is enough kinetic energy, the sticks will heat up enough to catch fire.

Figure 1 Kinetic energy can be used to start a fire.

Key Resources

 Teaching Transparency
P11 Internal Combustion Engine

 Cross-Disciplinary Worksheets
Integrating Environmental Science—
  Thermal Pollution
Real World Applications—Appliance
  Energy Use and Cost

The disorder of a system tends to increase.

According to the second law of thermodynamics, a system left to itself tends to move from a state of higher energy to a state of lower energy. Many highly ordered states, such as the state of the house of cards shown in **Figure 2,** are high-energy states. This means that you have to put a lot of energy into the cards to get them to that state. A high-energy state can very easily become a lower-energy state. For this reason, just a nudge will cause a house of cards to crash to the floor. In the science of thermodynamics, the measure of the disorder of a system is called **entropy.** Over time, in any given system left to itself, the entropy of that system will tend to increase.

You can do work on a system to decrease its entropy. But the second law of thermodynamics states that if you do work on a system, the total entropy of a larger system will increase. For example, the sun's energy enables plants to make sugars from smaller molecules. The result is an increase in order and therefore a decrease in entropy. But the total energy that the sun gives off represents a huge increase in entropy. So, the entropy of the larger system increases.

✔ Reading Check What does the second law of thermo- dynamics state about the energy state of a system left to itself?

Usable energy decreases in all energy transfers.

When energy can be easily transformed and transferred to do work, such as heating a room, we say that the energy is in a usable form. After this transfer, the same amount of energy exists, according to the law of conservation of energy. But because of an increase in entropy, less of this energy is in a form that can be used.

The energy used to increase the temperature of the water in the tank of a hot-water heater should ideally stay in the hot water. However, keeping some energy from being transferred as heat to parts of the tank and its surroundings is impossible. The amount of usable energy decreases even in the most efficient heating systems.

Because of conduction and radiation, some energy is lost to the tank's surroundings, such as the air and nearby walls. Cold water in the pipes that feed into the hot-water heater also draws energy from some of the hot water in the tank. When energy from electricity is used to heat water in the tank, some of the energy is used to increase the temperature of the water heater itself. In general, the amount of usable energy always decreases whenever energy is transferred or transformed.

Figure 2 A house of cards falling is an example of an increase in entropy. **How can you tell that the cards in the first picture are in a high-energy state?**

entropy (EN truh pee) a measure of the randomness or disorder of a system

> **Teach**

Teaching Key Ideas

Loss of Useful Energy Point out to students that transferring energy is like pouring water from one cup into another, then another, etc. Each time you pour the water into a new cup, some leftover water remains in the "empty" cup. Even if you hold the cup upside down and wait, some of the water still remains in the "empty" cup. Each time you pour water into a cup, the amount of water will decrease.

Answer to caption question

The cards in the first picture are highly ordered, and this indicates a high-energy state.

Why It **Matters**

Energy Efficiency Energy-efficient heating and cooling systems are able to maintain more usable energy than less energy-efficient systems. Discuss with students the importance of efficient heating and cooling systems in both economic and environmental terms. Point out that in addition to an energy-efficient system, energy use can also be reduced by having good insulation in the walls and ducts. For example, leaks in duct systems can cost hundreds of dollars a year. Temperature regulation can also make a significant difference: Turning down a thermostat 10% to 15% for eight hours each night in winter can reduce the year's energy bills by 10%. Lead a discussion about ways that students and their families can save energy in their homes. **LS Interpersonal**

Differentiated Instruction

Special Education Students

Comparing Entropy Help students understand the concept of entropy by asking them to draw before-and-after pictures of objects that change from having low entropy to having higher entropy. Tell students that the two photos of the house of cards in **Figure 2** are examples of such before-and-after images. Other possible images could include a whole egg and a broken egg, a container of marbles and a spilled container of marbles, and a stack of papers and scattered papers.

Why It **Matters**

Perpetual Motion Machines A perpetual motion machine is a machine that would produce all the energy it needs to run. Therefore, a perpetual motion machine could run forever without any additional energy. However, perpetual motion machines cannot exist because they would violate the first and second laws of thermodynamics. Have students design a candidate perpetual motion machine. Then have students explain where energy may be lost to cause the machine to stop working. **LS Logical**

Teaching Key Ideas

Parts of an Internal Combustion Engine Help students understand how internal combustion engines work by giving them more information about the parts of the engine discussed.

Crank shaft The crank shaft turns the piston's up-and-down motion into a circular motion.

Spark plug The spark plug supplies the spark that ignites the air-fuel mixture so that combustion can occur.

Valves The intake and exhaust valves open at the proper time to let in air and fuel and to let out exhaust. Both valves are closed during compression and combustion so that the combustion chamber is sealed.

Piston A piston is a piece of metal shaped like the cylinder but smaller in diameter than the cylinder. It moves up and down inside the cylinder.

Combustion chamber The combustion chamber is the area where compression and combustion take place. As the piston moves up and down, the size of the combustion chamber changes.

LS **Verbal**

READING TOOLBOX

Flowchart Be sure that students' flowcharts indicate that the steps an automobile cylinder goes through are part of a continuing cycle. Therefore, the flowcharts should somehow connect the first step shown in **Figure 4** to the last step.

LS **Visual**

---

heat engine (HEET EN juhn) a machine that transforms heat into mechanical energy, or work

Academic Vocabulary

internal (in TUHR nuhl) taking place inside

READING TOOLBOX

Flow Chart
Create a flow chart that outlines the steps that an automobile cylinder goes through in a complete cycle.

Heat Engines

> **In a heat engine, chemical energy is converted to mechanical energy through the process of combustion.** Internal-combustion engines and external-combustion engines are the two main types of heat engines. They are named for the place where combustion occurs—inside the engine or outside the engine. Engines in cars and trucks are internal-combustion engines. A steam engine is an external-combustion engine.

Internal-combustion engines burn fuel inside the engine.

In an <u>internal</u>-combustion engine, fuel burns in cylinders within the engine. There are pistons inside the cylinders, as shown in **Figure 3.** Up-and-down movements, or strokes, of the pistons cause the crankshaft to turn. The motion of the crankshaft is transferred to the wheels of the car or truck.

Most automobile engines are four-stroke engines. In these engines, four strokes take place for each cycle of the piston. The four strokes are called *intake, compression, power,* and *exhaust* strokes. In the power stroke, a spark plug ignites the fuel.

Diesel engines are also internal-combustion engines, but they work differently. A diesel engine has no spark plugs. Instead, the fuel-air mixture is compressed so much that it becomes hot enough to ignite without a spark.

Internal-combustion engines always generate heat.

In an internal-combustion engine, only part of the chemical energy is converted to mechanical energy. As engine parts move, friction and other forces cause much of the energy to be lost to the atmosphere as heat. An internal-combustion engine becomes so hot that a cooling system must be used to cool the engine.

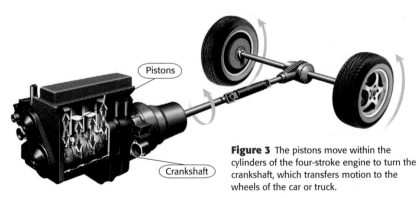

Pistons

Crankshaft

Figure 3 The pistons move within the cylinders of the four-stroke engine to turn the crankshaft, which transfers motion to the wheels of the car or truck.

Why It Matters

Benjamin Thompson, Count Rumford Benjamin Thompson, Count Rumford (1753–1814) was a physicist who made an early connection between work and heat. At the time, most scientists believed that heat was a fluid called *caloric.* While supervising cannon boring at a military workshop in Munich, Rumford noticed that the boring produced a great deal of heat in a brass gun and its metal shavings. He conducted a number of experiments with the cannon borer. He found that the friction between two metallic surfaces produced a constant stream of heat in all directions without any sign of lessening, even over a long period of time. His observa-

tions could not be explained by the caloric theory, and, after eliminating all other variables, Rumford came to the conclusion that heat is simply a form of motion.

It took some time for Rumford's idea of heat to gain acceptance. Rumford also made many practical innovations during his lifetime, including central heating, thermal underwear, the smokeless chimney, the kitchen oven, and the pressure cooker. Ask students to do research to find out how a pressure cooker works. Then have students modify a recipe for use in a pressure cooker. (Recipes should indicate that a shorter cooking time is needed.) **LS** **Logical**

Automobile engines use carburetors or fuel injectors.

The four-stroke cycle of an engine with a carburetor is illustrated in **Figure 4.** A *carburetor* is another part of the engine, in which liquid gasoline becomes vaporized.

Some engines have fuel injectors instead of carburetors. In some fuel-injected engines, only air enters the cylinder during the intake stroke. During the compression stroke, fuel vapor is injected directly into the compressed air in the cylinder. The other steps are the same as in an engine with a carburetor.

Figure 4 The Four Strokes of an Automobile Cylinder

go.hrw.com
✳ **interact online**
Keyword: HK8HTMF4

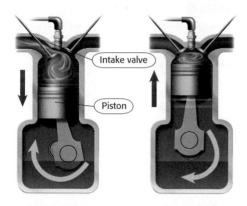
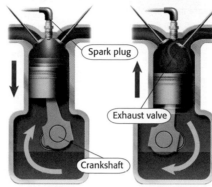

In the *intake* stroke, a mixture of fuel vapor and air is brought into the cylinder from the carburetor as the piston moves downward.

In the *compression* stroke, the piston moves up and compresses the fuel-air mixture.

In the *power* stroke, the spark plug ignites the mixture, which expands quickly and moves the piston down to turn the crankshaft.

The *exhaust* stroke takes place when the piston moves up again and forces the waste products to move out of the exhaust valve.

Section 3 Review

KEY IDEAS

1. **Restate** the first two laws of thermodynamics in your own words.
2. **Describe** what happens over time to the disorder of a system left to itself.
3. **Define** the term *entropy* in your own words.
4. **Name** the two types of heat engines.
5. **Relate** the output of energy from a heat engine to the energy put into the heat engine, considering the second law of thermodynamics.

CRITICAL THINKING

6. **Applying Concepts** Give an example of work that you can do to transfer kinetic energy. Explain, in terms of the first two laws of thermodynamics, what happens to that energy.
7. **Explaining Events** Describe each of the strokes of an automobile engine. Explain how the spark-plug ignition of compressed gas results in work done by the engine.
8. **Analyzing Processes** If you clean up your room, its order increases. According to the second law of thermodynamics, what else must happen?

go.hrw.com
✳ **interact online**

Students can interact with the figure by going to **go.hrw.com** and typing in the keyword **HK8HTMF4.**

❯Close

Reteaching Key Ideas

Heat Engines and Thermodynamics
Lead a discussion with students to review the first and second laws of thermodynamics. Also discuss the function of heat engines. Finish your discussion by asking students to describe how the first and second laws of thermodynamics are observed in an internal combustion engine.

Formative Assessment

During which stroke of a four-stroke engine is chemical energy converted into mechanical energy?

A. the intake stroke (Incorrect. Fuel vapor is brought into the cylinder during the intake stoke.)

B. the compression stroke (Incorrect. The fuel-air mixture is compressed during the compression stroke.)

C. the power stroke (Correct. The fuel-air mixture reacts by combustion during the power stroke. The mixture expands and pushes the piston down, thereby changing chemical energy into mechanical energy.)

D. the exhaust stoke (Incorrect. Waste products are moved out of the cylinder during the exhaust stroke.)

Answers to Section Review

1. Sample answer: The first law of thermodynamics states that energy from heat always goes somewhere rather than being created or destroyed. The second law of thermodynamics states that heat always tends to go from an area of high temperature to an area of low temperature.

2. The disorder of a system will increase over time if the system is left to itself.

3. Sample answer: Entropy is the amount of randomness in a region.

4. The two types of heat engines are the internal combustion engine and the external combustion engine.

5. The second law of thermodynamics requires that the output energy of a heat engine always be less than the energy put into it.

6. Sample answer: I transfer kinetic energy when I pedal my bicycle. The first law of thermodynamics states that none of that energy is destroyed. According to the second law of thermodynamics, some of the energy gets transferred to the bicycle and turns the wheels, while some of it turns into heat.

7. Students' drawings should resemble **Figure 4** on this page. The spark plug ignition uses electrical energy to convert the chemical energy of gas into mechanical energy, which is also called *work*.

8. Since cleaning up my room increased the room's order, an increase of disorder elsewhere must be the result.

🕐 50 min

Teacher's Notes

The wires used in this lab should be bare, solid rather than braided, and made of the same metal. Copper wires of various diameters are available in electronics stores, electrical supply stores, and hardware stores. Select candleholders that are designed to catch wax drips.

Time Required

1 lab period

Ratings

EASY ———————→ HARD

Teacher Prep
Student Set-Up 🧪🧪
Concept Level 🧪🧪🧪
Clean Up 🧪

Skills Acquired

- Collecting data
- Communicating
- Designing experiments
- Experimenting
- Identifying/recognizing patterns
- Inferring
- Interpreting
- Measuring
- Organizing and analyzing data
- Predicting

Scientific Methods

In this lab, students will:
- Make observations
- Ask a question
- Analyze the results
- Draw conclusions
- Communicate results

What You'll Do

❯ **Develop** a plan to measure how quickly energy is transferred as heat through a metal wire.

❯ **Compare** the speed of energy conduction in metal wires of different thicknesses.

What You'll Need

caliper or metric ruler

candle

clothespin

lighter or matches

newspaper or other covering to catch hot wax

stopwatch

wires, metal, of various thicknesses, each about 30 cm long (3)

Safety

Conduction of Heat by Metals

Metals are typically very good conductors of energy. In this lab, you will test wires of different thicknesses to see whether the thickness of a metal wire affects the wire's ability to conduct energy as heat.

Asking a Question

How does the thickness of a metal wire affect the wire's ability to conduct energy as heat?

Investigating Conduction in Wires

❶ Obtain three wires of different thicknesses. Clip a clothespin on one end of one of the wires. Lay the wire and attached clothespin on the lab table. Spread some newspaper or other covering below the wire to catch any extra hot wax.

❷ Light the candle. **CAUTION:** Tie back long hair, and confine loose clothing. Never reach across an open flame. To avoid burning yourself, always use the clothespin to hold the wire as you heat and move the wire. Remember that the wires will be hot for some time after they are removed from the flame.

❸ Hold the lighted candle above the middle of the wire, and tilt the candle slightly so that some of the melted wax drips onto the middle of the wire.

❹ Wait a couple of minutes for the wire and dripped wax to cool completely. The dripped wax will harden and form a small ball. Using the clothespin to hold the wire, place the other end of the wire in the candle's flame. When the ball of wax melts, remove the wire from the flame and place it on the lab table.

Forming and Testing a Hypothesis

❺ Think about what caused the wax on the wire to melt. Form a hypothesis about whether a thick wire will conduct energy more quickly or more slowly than a thin wire.

Designing Your Experiment

❻ With your lab partner(s), decide how you will use the materials available in this lab activity to compare the speed of conduction in three wires of different thicknesses.

❼ In your lab report, list each step that you will perform in your experiment.

❽ Have your teacher approve your plan before you carry out your experiment.

Sample Data Table: Heat Conductivity for Copper Wire				
	Wire diameter (mm)	Time to melt wax (s)		
		Trial 1	Trial 2	Trial 3	Average time
Wire 1	1.0	39.1	37.8	38.4	38.4
Wire 2	1.5	35.0	36.1	34.8	35.3
Wire 3	2.0	34.0	33.3	30.9	32.7

Performing Your Experiment

9 After your teacher approves your plan, you can carry out your experiment.

10 Prepare a data table that is similar to the sample data table.

11 Record in your table how many seconds the ball of wax on each wire takes to melt. Perform three trials for each wire. Allow the wires to cool to room temperature between trials.

Sample Data Table: Conductivity

	Wire diameter (mm)	Time to melt wax (s)		
		Trial 1	Trial 2	Trial 3
Wire 1				
Wire 2				
Wire 3				

Analysis

1. **Analyzing Data** Measure the diameter of each wire that you tested. If the diameter is listed in inches, convert it to millimeters by multiplying by 25.4. If the diameter is listed in mils, convert it to millimeters by multiplying by 0.0254. In your data table, record the diameter of each wire in millimeters.

2. **Analyzing Data** Calculate the average time required to melt the ball of wax for each wire. Record your answers in your data table.

3. **Graphing Data** Plot the data in your lab report in the form of a graph like the one shown. On your graph, draw the line or smooth curve that best fits the points.

Time to Melt Wax Versus Diameter of Wire

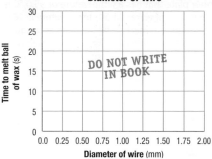

DO NOT WRITE IN BOOK

Communicating Your Results

4. **Drawing Conclusions** Based on your graph, which conducts energy more quickly: a thick wire or a thin wire?

5. **Justifying Conclusions** Suppose that someone tells you that your conclusion is valid only for the particular metal that you tested. Without doing further experiments, how can you argue that your conclusion is valid for other metals, too?

Extension

When roasting a large cut of meat, some cooks insert a metal skewer into the meat to make the inside cook more quickly. What difference would the thickness of the skewer make in this case? Explain.

Tips and Tricks

Students should control all variables except for wire diameter. A distance from the end of the wire that is consistent among the three wires and across the three trials should be specified. The end of each wire should be held in the same part of the flame, so the temperature measured at the end will be the same for all wires. The wax balls on the wires should be close to the same size and be the same distance from the flame. If the thinnest wires are too flexible, students may hold both ends of the wire (with two clamps or clothespins) and heat the wire somewhere between the clamps.

Safety Cautions

Clothespins can be a fire hazard. As an alternative, wires can be strung between two test-tube clamps on ring stands or lab supports. Be sure students always use a clamp or clothespin to hold the wire as it heats. Remind students that the wires will be hot for some time after they are removed from the flame.

Answers to Analysis

1. Answers may vary. See sample data.
2. Answers may vary. See sample data.
3. See sample graph. Results may vary, but times should be greater for smaller-diameter wires. The line that best fits the data points should decrease as the diameter of the wire increases.

Answers continued on p. 501A

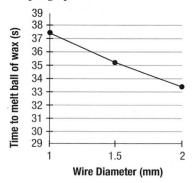

Sample graph:

Key Resources

 Virtual Investigation

 Classroom Lab Video/DVD

 Holt Lab Generator CD-ROM
Search for any lab by type, standard, difficulty level, or time. Edit any lab to fit your needs, or create your own labs. Use the Lab Materials QuickList software to customize your lab materials list.

 Differentiated Datasheets
Conduction of Heat by Metals

 Observation Lab
Energy Transfer and Specific Heat

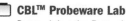 **CBL™ Probeware Lab**
Determining the Better Insulator for Your Feet

Reteaching Key Ideas

Energy Conservation Because the energy transferred as heat is not specifically called for in solving the problem, students can use the principle of energy conservation to equate $c_{plate}m_{plate}\Delta T_{plate}$ with $c_{water}m_{water}\Delta T_{water}$. This applies the important principle that the energy leaving the plate must be transferred to other matter, in this case the water. **LS Logical**

Answers to Practice

1. $energy = (4{,}186 \text{ J/kg•K})(3.0 \text{ kg})$
   $(27.1 \text{ °C} - 26.0 \text{ °C}) = 1{,}400 \text{ J}$
   $c_{plate} = (1{,}400 \text{ J})/(1.5 \text{ kg})$
   $(95.0 \text{ °C} - 27.1 \text{ °C}) = 137 \text{ J/kg•K}$
2. $energy = (280 \text{ J/kg•K})(1.5 \text{ kg})$
   $(95.0 \text{ °C} - 35.0 \text{ °C}) = 25{,}000 \text{ J}$
   $mass_{water} = (25{,}000 \text{ J})/$
   $[(4{,}186 \text{ J/kg•K})(35.0 \text{ °C} - 29.0 \text{ °C})]$
   $= 0.99 \text{ kg}$

Science › Skills

Temperature Conversions Remind students that when they calculate the temperature difference, the magnitude of a degree Celsius is identical to the magnitude of a kelvin. Thus, the difference between two Celsius temperatures can be expressed in kelvins, and vice versa. Have students convince themselves of this by taking the difference between two Celsius temperatures (for instance, 45 °C and 14 °C). Then have them express these in kelvins using the Celsius-Kelvin Conversion Formula (45 + 273 and 14 + 273). By taking the difference, the conversion factors 273 cancel out, so that $\Delta T = 31 \text{ °C} = \Delta T = 31 \text{ K}$. **LS Logical**

Solving Problems

Problem

A dinner plate that has a temperature of 95.0 °C is placed in a container of water whose temperature is 26.0 °C. The final temperature reached by the plate and water is 28.2 °C. The mass of the plate is 1.5 kg, and the mass of the water is 3.0 kg. What is the plate's specific heat? First calculate the energy transferred as heat to the water, which is the same as the energy transferred from the plate. Then rearrange the equation to calculate the plate's specific heat.

Solution

Identify

List all the given and unknown values. Note that a change of temperature is the same whether expressed in degrees Celsius or kelvins.

The first step for this type of problem is to calculate the temperature changes.

Given:

$temperature\ change\ of\ plate\ (\Delta T_{plate}) =$
  $95.0 \text{ °C} - 28.2 \text{ °C} = 66.8 \text{ °C} = 66.8 \text{ K}$
$temperature\ change\ of\ water\ (\Delta T_{water}) =$
  $28.2 \text{ °C} - 26.0 \text{ °C} = 2.2 \text{ °C} = 2.2 \text{ K}$
$mass\ of\ plate\ (m_{plate}) = 1.5 \text{ kg}$
$mass\ of\ water\ (m_{water}) = 3.0 \text{ kg}$
$specific\ heat\ of\ water\ (c_{water}) = 4{,}186 \text{ J/kg•K}$

Unknown:

$specific\ heat\ of\ plate\ (c_{plate})\ \text{in J/kg•K}$

Plan

Write down the specific heat equation, and then rearrange it to calculate the specific heat of the plate.

$energy = cm\Delta T = c_{water}m_{water}\Delta T_{water}$
$= c_{plate}m_{plate}\Delta T_{plate}$

$c_{plate} = \dfrac{energy}{m_{plate}\Delta T_{plate}}$

Solve

Find the energy transferred, and then calculate the specific heat of the plate.

$energy = \left(\dfrac{4{,}186 \text{ J}}{\text{kg•K}}\right) \times (3.0 \text{ kg}) \times (2.2 \text{ K}) = 2.8 \times 10^4 \text{ J}$

$c_{plate} = \dfrac{2.8 \times 10^4 \text{ J}}{1.5 \text{ kg} \times 66.8 \text{ K}} = \dfrac{2.8 \times 10^4 \text{ J}}{1.0 \times 10^2 \text{ kg•K}} = 280 \text{ J/kg•K}$

Practice

1. Suppose that in the example problem, the final temperature of the plate and water was 27.1 °C. Calculate what the specific heat of the plate would have been in that case.

2. Suppose that in the example problem, the water's initial temperature was 29.0 °C and the final temperature of the plate and water was 35.0 °C. If the plate is the same, what is the water's mass?

go.hrw.com
SUPER SUMMARY
KEYWORD: HK8HTMS

SUMMARY

Key **Ideas**	Key **Terms**

Section 1 Temperature

❯ **Temperature and Energy** The temperature of a substance is proportional to the average kinetic energy of the substance's particles. (p. 473)

❯ **Temperature Scales** The Fahrenheit, Celsius, and Kelvin temperature scales are commonly used for different applications in different parts of the world. (p. 475)

❯ **Relating Temperature to Energy Transfer** The feeling associated with temperature difference results from energy transfer. (p. 478)

temperature, p. 473
thermometer, p. 474
absolute zero, p. 476
heat, p. 479

Section 2 Energy Transfer

❯ **Methods of Energy Transfer** Energy can be transferred in three ways: conduction, convection, and radiation. (p. 480)

❯ **Conductors and Insulators** A conductor is a material through which energy can be easily transferred. An insulator is a material that transfers energy poorly. (p. 484)

❯ **Specific Heat** What makes a substance a good or poor conductor depends in part on how much energy is required to change the temperature of the substance by a certain amount. (p. 485)

thermal conduction, p. 481
convection, p. 481
convection current, p. 481
radiation, p. 482
specific heat, p. 485

Section 3 Using Heat

❯ **Laws of Thermodynamics** The first law of thermodynamics states that the total energy used in any process is conserved, whether that energy is transferred as a result of work, heat, or both. (p. 491)

❯ **Heat Engines** In a heat engine, chemical energy is converted to mechanical energy through the process of combustion. (p. 492)

entropy, p. 491
heat engine, p. 492

SUPER SUMMARY

Have students connect the major concepts in this chapter through an interactive Super Summary. Visit **go.hrw.com** and type in the keyword **HK8HTMS** to access the Super Summary for this chapter.

Differentiated Instruction

Alternative Assessment

Heat and Temperature Collage Have students make a collage by using images cut out from magazines that illustrate the topics covered in this chapter. Have students label each image with a brief description of how the image relates to the chapter. Tell students that they should have at least one image for each Key Idea in the chapter. **LS** Visual

Key Resources

⊡ **Interactive Concept Map**

🗀 **Review Resources**
Concept Review Worksheets

🗀 **Assessment Resources**
Chapter Tests A and B
Performance-Based Assessment

Answers to Chapter Review

1. Sample table:

First thing	Comparison word or phrase	Second Thing
Insulators	conduct heat better than	conductors
Insulators	have a higher specific heat than	conductors
Insulators	are usually denser than	conductors

Using Key Terms

2. A thermometer using the Kelvin scale would have "0" set at absolute zero, while a thermometer using the Celsius scale would have "0" set at the freezing point of water.

3. Warm, moist air rises up as it approaches the mountains. As the air rises, it cools. The cool, dry air continues over the mountain and sinks down the other side toward the desert, creating a downdraft.

4. Metal is a conductor with a low specific heat, so pouring a hot beverage in a metal cup would make the cup hot also. This cup would be unpleasant to hold. A china cup is a better insulator with a higher specific heat, so it will not become hot as rapidly.

5. The dark clothing absorbs energy transferred from the sun by radiation.

6. The amount of entropy in books on a library shelf is lower than the entropy of books that are randomly piled.

Understanding Key Ideas

7. b
8. c
9. a
10. d
11. d
12. a
13. d

CHAPTER 14 Review

READING TOOLBOX

1. Comparison Table Make a comparison table that gives three ways in which insulators differ, or are likely to differ, from conductors.

USING KEY TERMS

2. How would a *thermometer* that measures temperatures on the Kelvin scale differ from one that measures temperatures on the Celsius scale?

3. Explain how *convection currents* form downdrafts in deserts near tall mountain ranges, as shown in the figure below.

4. Use the differences between a *conductor* and an *insulator* and the concept of *specific heat* to explain whether you would rather drink a hot beverage from a metal cup or from a china cup.

5. If you wear dark clothing on a sunny day, the clothing will become hot after a while. Explain why by using the concept of *radiation*.

6. Describe how the amount of *entropy* compares between the books on a library shelf and books in a pile in a library return bin.

UNDERSTANDING KEY IDEAS

7. The temperature at which the particles of a substance would have no kinetic energy is
   a. 2,273 K. **c.** 0 °C.
   b. 0 K. **d.** 273 K.

8. Temperature is proportional to the average kinetic energy of particles in an object. Thus, an increase in temperature results in a(n)
   a. increase in mass.
   b. decrease in average kinetic energy.
   c. increase in average kinetic energy.
   d. decrease in mass.

9. The type of energy transfer that takes place between objects in direct contact is
   a. conduction.
   b. convection.
   c. contraction.
   d. radiation.

10. A type of energy transfer that can occur in empty space is
   a. convection.
   b. contraction.
   c. conduction.
   d. radiation.

11. A material made of _____ would be a very good conductor of energy.
   a. air
   b. liquid
   c. wood
   d. metal

12. Of the following substances, which is the poorest conductor of energy?
   a. air
   b. liquid
   c. wood
   d. metal

13. The amount of usable energy decreases
   a. only when systems are used for heating.
   b. only when systems are used for cooling.
   c. only if a heating or cooling system is poorly designed.
   d. whenever energy is transferred.

EXPLAINING KEY IDEAS

14. Explain how the common thermometer works by expansion. What expands, and how does that expansion indicate the temperature?

15. If two objects that have different temperatures come into contact, what will happen to their temperatures after several minutes?

16. If you bite into a piece of hot apple pie, the pie filling might burn your mouth but the crust, at the same temperature, will not. Explain why.

CRITICAL THINKING

17. **Applying Concepts** Why do the metal shades of desk lamps have small holes at the top?

18. **Analyzing Processes**
Glass can conduct some energy. Double-pane windows consist of two plates of glass separated by a small layer of insulating air. Explain why a double-pane window prevents more energy from escaping from a house than a single-pane window does.

19. **Applying Concepts** Explain why the back part of window-unit air conditioners always hangs outside. Why can't the entire air conditioner be in the room?

20. **Identifying Patterns** In one southern state, the projected yearly costs for heating a home are $463 if a heat pump is used, $508 if a natural-gas furnace is used, and $1,220 if electric radiators are used. Find out from your local utility company what the projected yearly costs for the three heating systems are in your area. Make a table that compares the costs of the three systems.

21. **Inferring Relationships** Considering specific heat only, indicate which would make a better coolant for car engines: water ($c = 4{,}186$ J/kg·K) or ethanol ($c = 2{,}440$ J/kg·K). Explain why.

Graphing Skills

22. **Interpreting Graphics** The graph shown here gives the monthly cost of heating a certain house over the course of one year. What seasonal patterns are represented in the graph? Explain the patterns in the graph based on the first law of thermodynamics.

Heating Costs

Math Skills

23. **Temperature-Scale Conversion** A piece of dry ice, solid CO_2, has a temperature of −78 °C. What is its temperature in kelvins and in degrees Fahrenheit?

24. **Temperature-Scale Conversion** The temperature in deep space is thought to be about 3 K. What is 3 K in degrees Celsius and in degrees Fahrenheit?

25. **Specific Heat** It takes 3,190 J to increase the temperature of a 0.400 kg sample of glass from 273 K to 308 K. What is the specific heat for this type of glass?

26. **Specific Heat** A vanadium bolt gives up 1,124 J of energy as its temperature drops 25 K. If its mass is 93 g, what is its specific heat?

27. **Specific Heat** An aluminum baking sheet ($c = 897$ J/kg·K) whose mass is 225 g absorbs 2.4×10^4 J from an oven. If its temperature was initially 25 °C, what will its temperature be after it is heated in the oven?

Explaining Key Ideas

14. The liquid in a thermometer expands when its temperature rises; the greater the expansion, the higher the temperature reading from the thermometer.

15. Their temperatures will become closer to each other than they were at the start.

16. The pie filling would feel hotter because it has a higher specific heat; it is also a better heat conductor than the crust.

Critical Thinking

17. The small holes at the top of the metal lamp shades are to allow heat to escape, since the metal of the lamp shade will get very hot because of its high conductivity.

18. The layer of air between the two panes is a very good insulator, so more heat is prevented from escaping through the window than if there were only a single pane of glass.

19. The air conditioner must exhaust some energy. If the air conditioner were contained entirely within the room, the exhaust energy would also be in the room, transferring the exchanged heat back into the room.

20. Answers may vary, based on factors such as the current price of natural gas. Students should find that heat pumps, which are basically reverse air conditioners, tend to be efficient.

21. Considering just specific heat, water would be better because it has a higher specific heat. For a certain amount of water or ethanol, the water would absorb more energy from the engine per degree of temperature change.

Graphing Skills

22. The graph shows that the cost of heating the house is higher for the colder months and highest in the winter. The trend shown in the graph above is explained by the first law of thermodynamics because more heat will escape from the house during the colder months than during the warmer months.

Assignment Guide	
SECTION	**ITEMS**
1	2, 7–8, 14, 24
2	1, 3–5, 9–12, 16–18, 21, 25–28
3	6, 13, 15, 19–20, 22–23

Math Skills

23. $-78 + 273 = 195$ K
$1.8(-78) + 32.0 = -108.4$ °F

24. $3 - 273 = -270$ °C
$1.8(-270) + 32.0 = -454$ °F

25. $c = 3{,}190$ J/[(0.400 kg)(308 K − 273 K)] = 228 J/kg·K

26. $c = 1124$ J/[(93 g)(1 kg/1000 g)(25 K)] = 480 J/kg·K

27. $\Delta T = (2.4 \times 10^4$ J)/[(897 J/kg·K)(0.225 kg)]
$\Delta T = 120$ K = 120 °C
$T_f - 25$ °C = 120 °C
$T_f = 145$ °C

TEST DOCTOR

Question 1 Answer D is correct. Remind students that energy transfer by conduction and convection require matter and matter does not exist in space. Therefore, answers A and B are incorrect. Insulation is not a method of energy transfer, so answer C is incorrect.

Question 2 Answer F is correct. Students may answer G if they forgot that temperature increases as the average kinetic energy of the particles in matter increases. Students may answer H if they think that the energy release is in the form of particles of matter. Students may answer I if they imagine that the iron bar is melting from the heat.

Question 3 Answer C is correct. Remind students that energy cannot be created or destroyed by normal means, so answers A and D are not correct. Remind students that energy lost in an engine is not useful and therefore cannot be used to decrease entropy. Therefore, answer B is incorrect.

Question 4 The specific heat equation is energy = (specific heat) × (mass) × (temperature change). A change in 1 °C is equal to a change in 1 K. 140 J/kg•K × 2 kg × 1 K = 280 J

Question 5 Full-credit answers should include the following points:
• All materials expand when heated.
• If the rate of expansion of a material increases, the material will expand more as it is heated.
• A mercury thermometer would have to be longer and the distance between degree marks would have to increase going up the thermometer because its volume would increase more with every degree change in temperature.

Question 6 Answer H is correct. Students who select choices F and G may believe that the size of the ocean alone is what contributes to its major role in shaping Earth's climate. Students who select choice I may have forgotten that water has a low conductivity.

Understanding Concepts

Directions (1–3): For each question, write on a sheet of paper the letter of the correct answer.

1. What method of transferring energy carries energy from the sun to Earth?
   A. conduction
   B. convection
   C. insulation
   D. radiation

2. A certain amount of energy is added to an iron bar. Afterward, the iron bar glows white-hot and gives off energy both as light and heat. What does this energy release indicate about the particles of iron in the bar?
   F. They have high kinetic energy.
   G. They have low kinetic energy.
   H. They are being emitted from the bar.
   I. They are changing phase.

3. What happens to the energy that is not used when an engine is less than 100% efficient?
   A. It is destroyed during combustion.
   B. It is used to decrease entropy.
   C. It is converted to heat.
   D. It is converted to matter.

Directions (4–5): For each question, write a short response.

4. Mercury has a specific heat of 140 J/kg·K. How much energy is required to raise the temperature of 2 kg of mercury by 1 °C?

5. If the rate of expansion of mercury increased as it was heated, in what way would mercury thermometers have to be different so that the same temperature range could be accurately read from them?

Reading Skills

Directions (6–7): Read the passage below. Then, answer the questions that follow.

CLIMATE IS ALL ABOUT THE OCEANS
The high specific heat of the ocean plays a central role in shaping Earth's climate. Earth's atmosphere cannot store as much energy as the oceans can. The heat energy that can be stored in the entire atmosphere can be stored in a layer of the ocean just 3.2 m deep.

The specific heat of dry land is less than 25% that of sea water. The land surface also has a low conductivity. As a result, only the top 2 m or so of the land typically plays an active role in energy storage and release. Therefore, land plays a much smaller role in the storage of energy than the ocean does.

Major ice sheets, such as those over Antarctica and Greenland, have a large mass. Ice has a higher heat conductivity than land does, but as on land, the transfer of energy as heat occurs primarily through conduction. The key difference between ice and water is that energy as heat can transfer through water by convection because water is a fluid. Convection can occur faster than conduction, so ice sheets and glaciers do not play a major role in energy storage and transfer.

6. Which characteristic makes the ocean play such a major role in shaping Earth's climate?
   F. the mass of the ocean
   G. the area of the ocean
   H. the specific heat of the ocean
   I. the conductivity of the ocean

7. Summarize how energy as heat is transferred through different parts of Earth's surface by conduction and convection.

Question 7 Full-credit answers should include the following points:
• Conduction of heat occurs through Earth's solid surface.
• Convection occurs through the ocean.

Question 8 Answer B is correct. Although energy from the fire is also transferred by radiation, the illustration demonstrates the process of heat transfer by the motion of fluid particles, known as convection.

Question 9 Answer I is correct. Answer F is not correct because fire is not a material that is in contact with anything; no transfer of heat by conduction is occurring. Answer G is not correct because the illustration is representing convec-

tion and the question asks for a different form of energy transfer. Answer H is not a form of energy transfer.

Question 10 Answer B is correct. Students who miss this question should be reminded colder air is denser than warmer air is. Students should also be reminded that less dense materials rise and denser materials descend. Therefore, colder air descends during convection.

Interpreting Graphics

The graphic below shows energy transfer above a campfire. Use this graphic to answer questions 8–10.

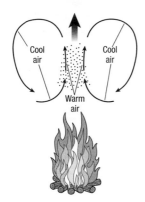

8. What form of energy transfer is represented by this illustration?
   - **A.** conduction
   - **B.** convection
   - **C.** insulation
   - **D.** radiation

9. In what form of energy transfer other than the form represented by this illustration does the fire participate?
   - **F.** conduction
   - **G.** convection
   - **H.** insulation
   - **I.** radiation

10. Which of the following principles of energy transfer causes the flow of air shown in the illustration to be circular?
    - **A.** Warmer air descends.
    - **B.** Cooler air descends.
    - **C.** Warm air and cool air are attracted to each other.
    - **D.** Warm air and cool air tend to repel each other.

Test Tip

If you find a particular question difficult, put a light pencil mark beside it and keep working. (Do not write in this book.) As you answer other questions, you may find information that helps you answer the difficult question.

Answers

1. D
2. F
3. C
4. 280 J
5. Answers may vary; see Test Doctor for a detailed scoring rubric.
6. H
7. Answers may vary; see Test Doctor for a detailed scoring rubric.
8. B
9. I
10. B

State Resources

For specific resources for your state, visit **go.hrw.com** and type in the keyword **HSHSTR**.

📖 **Test Practice with Guided Reading Development**

Continuation of Answers

Answers continued from p. 495

Answers to Communicating Your Results

4. Thicker wires conduct energy more quickly than thinner wires.
5. Metals have the common property of conducting energy well, so it follows that a thicker wire of any metal will conduct energy more quickly than a thinner wire of that metal.

Answer to Extension

A thicker skewer will conduct heat energy more quickly than a thin skewer, so the meat will cook faster.

	Standards	**Teach Key Ideas**
CHAPTER OPENER, pp. 502–504 `50 min.`		

SECTION 1 Types of Waves, pp. 505–513   `50 min.`

> What Is a Wave?
> Vibrations and Waves
> Transverse and Longitudinal Waves
> Surface Waves

Standards: PS 5a, PS 5b, PS 6a, PS 6b, UCP 1, UCP 2, UCP 3

Teach Key Ideas:
- Bellringer Transparency
- Teaching Transparencies TM40 Simple Harmonic Motion • TM41 Transverse Wave • TM42 Longitudinal Wave • P12 Wave Model • P13 Wave Water Motion
- Visual Concepts Formation and Movement of Ocean Waves • Electromagnetic Waves • Tsunami • Transverse Wave • Longitudinal Wave

---

SECTION 2 Characteristics of Waves, pp. 514–523   `50 min.`

> Wave Properties
> Wave Speed
> The Doppler Effect

Standards: PS 2e, PS 5a, PS 6a, UCP 1, UCP 3, SAI 1, SAI 2, ST 2, SPSP 5

Teach Key Ideas:
- Bellringer Transparency
- Teaching Transparency P14 Frequency
- Visual Concepts Characteristics of a Wave • Wave Properties • Wave Period of Ocean Waves • Equation for the Speed of a Wave • Doppler Effect and Sound

---

SECTION 3 Wave Interactions, pp. 524–529   `50 min.`

> Reflection, Diffraction, and Refraction
> Interference
> Standing Waves

Standards: UCP 1, UCP 3

Teach Key Ideas:
- Bellringer Transparency
- Teaching Transparency TM43 Interference
- Visual Concepts Reflection • Diffraction • Refraction • Comparing Constructive and Destructive Interference • Standing Wave

See also PowerPoint® Resources

Chapter Review and Assessment Resources

SE Science Skills: Graphing Waves, p. 532
SE Chapter Summary, p. 533
SE Chapter Review, pp. 534–535
SE Standardized Test Prep, pp. 536–537
📁 Concept Review Worksheets ■
📁 Chapter Tests A and B ■
 Holt Online Assessment

Basic Learners
TE Remembering Symbols, p. 519
📁 Science Skills Worksheets
📁 Differentiated Datasheets A for Labs and Activities ■
📁 Study Guide A ■

Advanced Learners
TE Bikes: Function and Form, p. 510
TE Gathering More Information, p. 516
TE Seismic Waves, p. 518
📁 Cross-Disciplinary Worksheets
📁 Differentiated Datasheets C for Labs and Activities ■

CHAPTER Fast Track   *To shorten instruction because of time limitations, omit Section 3 and the chapter lab.*

Key
SE Student Edition
TE Teacher's Edition

📁 Chapter Resource File
📓 Workbook
📦 Transparency

💿 CD or CD-ROM
* Datasheet or blackline master available

■ Also available in Spanish

All resources listed below are also available on the Teacher's One-Stop Planner.

Why It Matters	Hands-On	Skills Development	Assessment
Build student motivation with resources about high-interest applications.	**SE Inquiry Lab** Making Waves, p. 503* ■	**TE Reading Toolbox** Assessing Prior Knowledge, p. 502 **SE Reading Toolbox** p. 504	📁 **Pretest** ■
TE Earthquakes, p. 506 **TE Tsunamis—Deep and Shallow,** p. 507 **SE How Does Mountain-Bike Suspension Work?** p. 510 📁 **Cross-Disciplinary Worksheets** Connection to Engineering—Wave Energy • Science and the Consumer—Bicycle Design and Shock Absorption	**TE Demonstration** Do the Wave, p. 505 **TE Demonstration** Harmonic Motion, p. 508 **SE Quick Lab** Particle Motion in a Wave, p. 509* ■ **SE Quick Lab** Polarization, p. 511* ■ **TE Demonstration** Longitudinal Waves in Air, p. 512	**SE Reading Toolbox** Classification, p. 507 **TE Reading Toolbox** Visual Literacy, p. 509	**TE Reteaching Key Ideas** Wave Examples, p. 513 **TE Formative Assessment,** p. 513 📁 **Spanish Assessment*** ■ 📁 **Section Quiz** ■
TE Elephant Sounds, p. 516 **SE How Are Good Surfing Waves Formed?** p. 517 **TE Elasticity,** p. 520 **TE Visible Light,** p. 521 **TE Speed of Light,** p. 521 📁 **Cross-Disciplinary Worksheets** Connection to Language Arts—Writing a Plan for Wave Observation • Integrating Technology—Radio Waves • Integrating Earth Science—Earthquake Waves	**TE Demonstration** Properties of Waves, p. 514 **SE Quick Lab** Wave Speed, p. 520* ■ **TE Demonstration** Doppler Effect, p. 522 **SE Skills Practice Lab** Transverse Waves, pp. 530–531* ■ 📁 **Observation Lab** Creating and Measuring Standing Waves	**TE Reading Toolbox** Visual Literacy, p. 516 **TE Reading Toolbox** Visual Literacy, p. 517 **SE Math Skills** Wave Speed, p. 519 **TE Reading Toolbox** Visual Literacy, p. 521 **SE Reading Toolbox** Outlining, p. 522	**TE Reteaching Key Ideas** Connecting Ideas, p. 523 **TE Formative Assessment,** p. 523 📁 **Spanish Assessment*** ■ 📁 **Section Quiz** ■
TE Diamonds and Refraction, p. 527 **TE Color by Interference,** p. 528 📁 **Cross-Disciplinary Worksheets** Integrating Math—Bending Light Waves to Magnify • Connection to Architecture—Architectural Acoustics	**TE Demonstration** Showing Reflection, p. 524 **TE Demonstration** Beats and Tuning, p. 528 📁 **CBL™ Probeware Lab** Tuning a Musical Instrument	**SE Reading Toolbox** Outlining, p. 528 **TE Reading Toolbox** Visual Literacy, p. 528	**TE Reteaching Key Ideas** Wave Interactions Table, p. 529 **TE Formative Assessment,** p. 529 📁 **Spanish Assessment*** ■ 📁 **Section Quiz** ■

See also Lab Generator

See also Holt Online Assessment Resources

Resources for Differentiated Instruction

English Learners
TE Outline, p. 509
TE Surfing Jargon, p. 517
📁 Differentiated Datasheets A, B, and C for Labs and Activities ■
📓 Study Guide A ■

Struggling Readers
TE Vocabulary Practice, p. 506
TE Honing Reading Skills, p. 525
📓 Interactive Reader

Special Education Students
TE Make a Wave, p. 511
TE Making a Model, p. 515

Alternative Assessment
TE Simple Harmonic Motion, p. 508
TE Transverse and Longitudinal Waves, p. 512
TE Chuck Yeager and the Speed of Sound, p. 520
TE Wave Review, p. 522
TE Wave Phenomena, p. 525
TE Standing Waves on a Rope, p. 526
TE Making Waves, p. 533

Overview

This chapter covers waves and vibrations and distinguishes between different wave types. The chapter then explores wave characteristics such as amplitude, wavelength, frequency, and period. Students also calculate wave speed and learn about the Doppler effect. The chapter finally discusses wave behaviors and interactions.

READING TOOLBOX

Assessing Prior Knowledge Students should understand the following concepts:
• interactions of matter and energy
• motion
• force
• work
• forms of energy
• energy transformations

MISCONCEPTION ///ALERT\\\

Science education research has identified the following misconception about waves: The motion of the medium (e.g., the water in a water wave) is frequently confused with the motion of the wave itself.

Have students complete the following activity to help them overcome this misconception. Tell students to put about 2 cm of water into a pie pan or another shallow pan and then place a small piece of cork or plastic foam in the water. Then, tell students to try to move the cork to the side of the pan by tapping the water with the end of a pencil using only an up-and-down motion. After students have time to experiment with making waves, lead a discussion about what they observed. Help students understand that the cork did not move to the side of the pan because the medium of a wave and anything in the medium does not travel with the wave.

LS Kinesthetic

Chapter Outline

❶ Types of Waves
What Is a Wave?
Vibrations and Waves
Transverse and Longitudinal Waves
Surface Waves

❷ Characteristics of Waves
Wave Properties
Wave Speed
The Doppler Effect

❸ Wave Interactions
Reflection, Diffraction, and Refraction
Interference
Standing Waves

Why It Matters
This award-winning photo—shown here upside down—was taken by a high school student. Reflected light waves create a mirror image of the landscape in the lake.

Chapter Correlations   *National Science Education Standards*

The following correlations show the National Science Standards that relate to this chapter. For the full text of the standards, see the National Science Education Standards at the front of the book.

PS 2e Solids, liquids, and gases differ in the distances and angles between molecules or atoms and therefore the energy that binds them together. In solids the structure is nearly rigid; in liquids molecules or atoms move around each other but do not move apart; and in gases molecules or atoms move almost independently of each other and are mostly far apart. (Section 2)

PS 5a Energy can be transferred by collisions in chemical and nuclear reactions, by light waves and other radiations, and in many other ways. (Sections 1, 2)

PS 5b All energy can be considered to be either kinetic energy, which is the energy of motion; potential energy, which depends on relative position; or energy contained by a field, such as electromagnetic waves. (Section 1)

PS 6a Waves, including sound and seismic waves, waves on water, and light waves, have energy and can transfer energy when they interact with matter. (Sections 1, 2)

PS 6b Electromagnetic waves result when a charged object is accelerated or decelerated. Electromagnetic waves include radio waves (the longest wavelength), microwaves, infrared radiation (radiant heat), visible light, ultraviolet radiation, x-rays, and gamma rays. (Section 1)

UCP1 Systems, order, and organization (Sections 1–3)

UCP 2 Evidence, models, and explanation (Section 1)

UCP 3 Constancy, change, and measurement (Sections 1–3)

SAI 1 Abilities necessary to do scientific inquiry (Section 2, Skills Practice Lab: Transverse Waves)

SAI 2 Understandings about scientific inquiry (Section 2)

ST 2 Understandings about science and technology (Section 2)

SPSP 5 Natural and human-induced hazards (Section 2)

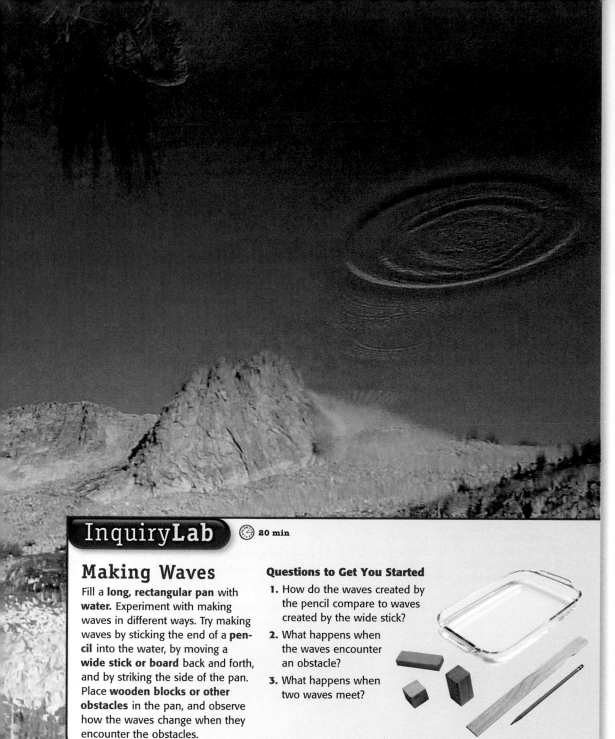

Teacher's Notes Rectangular
9×13 in. baking pans are a good
size for this lab. The water in the
pans should be 2 to 3 cm deep.

Materials per Group
- blocks, wooden or other obstacles
- pan, long, rectangular
- pencil
- stick or board, wide
- water

Answers

1. The waves created by the pencil
   are smaller than the waves created
   by the wide stick.
2. When the waves encounter an
   obstacle, they pass around it.
3. When two waves encounter each
   other, they pass through each
   other and keep going in their
   original directions.

Key Resources

 **Datasheet**
   Making Waves

Interactive Tutors
   Disc Two, Module 12: Frequency and
      Wavelength
   Disc Two, Module 14: Refractions

InquiryLab ⏱ 20 min

Making Waves

Fill a **long, rectangular pan** with
water. Experiment with making
waves in different ways. Try making
waves by sticking the end of a **pencil** into the water, by moving a
wide stick or board back and forth,
and by striking the side of the pan.
Place **wooden blocks or other
obstacles** in the pan, and observe
how the waves change when they
encounter the obstacles.

Questions to Get You Started

1. How do the waves created by
   the pencil compare to waves
   created by the wide stick?
2. What happens when
   the waves encounter
   an obstacle?
3. What happens when
   two waves meet?

Word Parts

1. Sample answer: Diffraction is a change in the direction of a wave when the wave meets an obstacle or an edge. Refraction is the bending of a wave as it passes from one medium to another. Both diffraction and refraction cause the path of a wave to change suddenly, which may cause the path of the wave to appear broken.

2. Sample answer: Other words with the root *fract-* include *fraction* (a part, especially a part of a whole number), *fracture* (to break), and *infraction* (the breaking of a rule).

Classification

Sample table:

Wave type	Basis for classification	Examples
Mechanical waves	Require a medium	Waves on a pond, sound waves, seismic waves
Electromagnetic waves	Do not require a medium	Visible light, radio waves
Transverse waves	Particle motion is perpendicular to wave travel	"The Wave" in a stadium, a wave on a rope
Longitudinal waves	Particle motion is parallel to wave travel	A wave on a spring, sound waves

---

READING TOOLBOX

These reading tools can help you learn the material in this chapter. For more information on how to use these and other tools, see **Appendix A.**

Word Parts

Root Words Many scientific words are made up of word parts derived from Latin and Greek. You can unlock the meaning of an unfamiliar science term by analyzing its word parts. **Appendix A** contains a list of many word parts and their meanings. A root word from two key terms in this chapter is shown below.

ROOT	SOURCE	MEANING
fract	Latin verb frangere	"to break"

Your Turn

❶ After you have read Section 3, write out the definitions of *diffraction* and *refraction*. Explain why it is appropriate that these terms contain a root meaning "to break."

❷ Make a list of other words that contain the same root, then write the definitions of those words. Use a dictionary if you need to.

Classification

Types of Waves Classification is a logical tool for organizing the many things and ideas in our world. Classification involves grouping things into categories.

> **Example:** In the classification of states of matter, *liquids* are defined as substances that can easily change shape but have a fixed volume.

Your Turn In Section 1, you will learn about different kinds of waves. As you learn about these wave types, make a table with three columns. In the first column, list the wave types. In the second column, describe the basis for classification for each wave type. In the third column, list examples of each wave type.

Note Taking

Outlining Taking notes in outline form can help you see how information is organized in a chapter. You can use your outline notes to review the chapter before a test.

Your Turn As you read through this chapter, make notes about the chapter in outline form. An example from Section 1 is shown on the right to help you get started. You can find more information about outlines in **Appendix A.**

> I. TYPES OF WAVES
> A. What Is a Wave?
> 1. A wave is a disturbance that carries energy through matter or space.
> 2. Most waves travel through a medium.
> a. Waves that require a medium are called mechanical waves.
> b. Sound waves are mechanical waves. Air is a common medium for sound waves.

Note Taking

Answers may vary. Student outlines should approximate the guidelines shown on the student page and discussed in detail in Appendix A. The top-level ideas (Roman numerals) may correspond to section titles, the next level (capital letters) may correspond to the main headings, then the next level (numerals) may correspond to subheads, and the last level (lowercase letters) may correspond to details within each subhead.

Types of Waves

Key **Ideas**

❯ What does a wave carry?

❯ How are waves generated?

❯ What is the difference between a transverse wave and a longitudinal wave?

❯ How do the particles in ocean waves move?

Key **Terms**

medium

mechanical wave

electromagnetic wave

transverse wave

longitudinal wave

crest

trough

Why It **Matters**

Shock absorbers in mountain bikes minimize vibrations to help the biker stay in control. Vibrations are closely related to waves.

❯ Focus

In this section, students learn what waves are and how they transfer energy. They also learn how to distinguish between electromagnetic and mechanical waves and between transverse and longitudinal waves. Students also find out how particles move in ocean waves.

🔊 Bellringer

Use the Bellringer transparency to prepare students for this section.

When you throw a stone into a pond, ripples form on the surface of the water. Ripples are a type of *wave*. In this section, you will learn about different types of waves.

What Is a Wave?

A leaf floating on water, such as the one shown in **Figure 1,** will bob up as a wave passes by. After the wave passes, the leaf will drop back close to its original position. Likewise, individual drops of water are lifted up when a wave passes and then drop back close to their resting places. They do not travel with the wave. If leaves and drops of water do not move along with a wave as the wave passes, then what does move along with the wave? Energy does. ❯ **A wave is a disturbance that carries energy through matter or space.**

Demonstrate

Do the Wave First, have your students do "the wave" in the classroom a few times. Then ask them the following questions: "How was the wave you made like other waves?" (Sample answer: Our wave moved up-and-down like a water wave.) "How was the wave you made unlike other waves?" (Sample answer: Energy didn't travel from one person to another in our wave.)
LS Kinesthetic/Logical

❯ Teach

Answer to caption question
The wave carries energy.

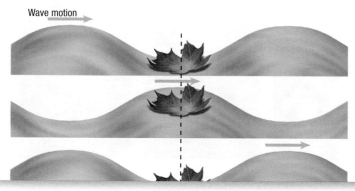

Wave motion

Figure 1 This leaf moves up and down as the wave passes by. **What does the wave carry?**

Key Resources

Teaching Transparencies
TM40 Simple Harmonic Motion
TM41 Transverse Wave
TM42 Longitudinal Wave
P12 Wave Model
P13 Wave Water Motion

Visual Concepts
Formation and Movement of Ocean Waves
Electromagnetic Waves
Tsunami
Transverse Wave
Longitudinal Wave

Datasheets
Particle Motion in a Wave
Polarization

Cross-Disciplinary Worksheets
Connection to Engineering—Wave Energy
Science and the Consumer—Bicycle Design and Shock Absorption

Teaching Key Ideas

Waves Carry Energy Review the definition of the term *energy* with your students. (Energy is the ability to do work.) Ask students to name different forms of energy. (Sample answers may include kinetic energy, thermal energy, potential energy, and chemical energy.) Finally, ask them to give examples showing that waves carry energy. (Sample answers: A boat gains kinetic energy when it bobs up and down on a water wave. Objects gain thermal energy when they absorb electromagnetic waves and warm up.) **LS** **Verbal**

Demonstrate

Watching Waves For the following demonstration you will need a shallow clear baking dish, a wooden dowel (cut to dish width), overhead projector, and wood scraps and corks.

Step 1 Put about 3 cm of water in the pan and place it on the overhead projector.

Step 2 Make waves by holding the dowel along the surface of the water and moving it up and down at a consistent frequency. You can also make circular waves with the end of the dowel.

Step 3 Have students observe how the waves reflect off the walls of the pan or off pieces of wood placed in the water. Also demonstrate the motion of corks floating on the surface.

www.scilinks.org
Topic: Waves
Code: HK81641

medium (MEE dee uhm) a physical environment in which phenomena occur

mechanical wave (muh KAN i kuhl WAYV) a wave that requires a medium through which to travel

electromagnetic wave (ee LEK troh mag NET ik WAYV) a wave that consists of oscillating electric and magnetic fields, which radiate outward at the speed of light

Figure 2 Mechanical waves require a medium, but electromagnetic waves do not.

Most waves travel through a medium.

Ripples in a pond, such as the ones shown in **Figure 2,** are disturbances that travel through water. The sound you hear from your stereo is a disturbance that travels in waves through air. Earthquakes are disturbances that travel in *seismic waves,* waves that travel through Earth.

In each of these examples, waves involve the movement of some kind of matter. The matter through which a wave travels is called the **medium**. For waves on a pond, water is the medium. For sound from a stereo, air is the medium. And for earthquakes, Earth itself is the medium.

Waves that require a medium are called **mechanical waves.** Most waves are mechanical waves. The only waves that do not require a medium are electromagnetic waves.

Electromagnetic waves do not require a medium.

The laser lights shown in **Figure 2** are an example of electromagnetic waves. **Electromagnetic waves** consist of changing electric and magnetic fields in space. Electromagnetic waves do not require a medium. For instance, light can travel from the sun to Earth across empty space.

Visible light waves are just one type of electromagnetic wave. Radio waves, such as those that carry signals to your radio or television, are also electromagnetic waves. Other kinds of electromagnetic waves will be introduced in later chapters.

✔️ **Reading Check** **Are light waves mechanical waves?** (See Appendix E for answers to Reading Checks.)

Mechanical waves

Electromagnetic waves

Why It **Matters**

Earthquakes Seismic waves carried through Earth's crust happen when tectonic plates shift against one another suddenly. This phenomenon is known as an earthquake. Fault lines are places on Earth's surface where tectonic plates meet. Locations on Earth that are near fault lines may be subject to small or large earthquakes. Show students a map of recent earthquakes from the United States Geological Survey Web site (www.usgs.gov) and ask them to calculate the location of fault lines in the United States. **LS** **Logical/Visual**

Differentiated Instruction

Struggling Readers

Vocabulary Practice This section contains many key terms that may be unfamiliar to students. Have students make a vocabulary practice device by folding a sheet of paper lengthwise in half. Then, have students make tabs in the paper by cutting from one edge of the paper to the center fold. Tell students to write a key term from this section on the front of each of the tabs. Finally, instruct students to write the definitions for the terms under the appropriate tabs. Students can use this device to quiz themselves or one another. **LS** **Verbal**

Figure 3 This image of a tsunami was created by the Japanese artist Hokusai in 1830.

Waves transfer energy.

Energy is the ability to exert a force over a certain distance, or to do *work*. We know that waves carry energy because they can do work. For example, water waves can do work on a leaf or on a boat. Sound waves can do work on your eardrum.

The bigger the wave is, the more energy it carries. A wave caused by dropping a stone in a pond may carry enough energy to move a leaf up and down several centimeters. A cruise ship moving through the ocean may create waves big enough to move a fishing boat up and down a few meters.

Figure 3 shows a woodblock print of a *tsunami,* a huge ocean wave that is caused by an earthquake. A tsunami may be as high as 30 m—taller than a 10-story building—when it reaches shore. Such a wave carries enough energy to cause a lot of damage to coastal towns. Normal ocean waves do work on the shore, too; their energy breaks up rocks into tiny pieces to form sandy beaches.

Energy may spread out as a wave travels.

If you stand next to the speakers at a rock concert, the sound waves may damage your ears. But if you stand 100 m away, the sound of the rock band is harmless. Why?

Think about the waves created when a stone falls into a pond. The waves spread out in circles that get bigger as the waves move farther from the center. Each of these circles, called a *wave front,* carries the same amount of energy. But in the larger circles, the energy is spread out over a larger area. When sound waves travel in air, the waves spread out in spheres. As the waves travel outward, the spherical wave fronts get bigger, so the energy spreads out over a larger volume.

Classification
Waves are classified in different ways. As you read this section, list two ways in which waves are classified, and give examples of each type of wave.

Academic Vocabulary

sphere (SFIR) a three-dimensional surface whose points are equally distant from the center; a globe

Social Studies Connection

Draw students' attention to **Figure 3.** People who live on Pacific islands, such as Japan, or in Pacific Coast countries, have great respect for the power of tsunamis. These tidal waves occur more frequently around the Pacific than in other oceans because of earthquakes and underwater volcanic activity associated with the movement of the continental plates in that region.

Why It **Matters**

Tsunamis—Deep and Shallow It may surprise students to know that if they were on a ship in the deep part of the ocean when a tidal wave passed, it would cause only a smooth rise and fall of a few inches. When that energy becomes concentrated in shallow water, it will produce a fearsome tsunami. Show students videos or news reports of the tsunami that struck Asia on December 26, 2004. Then, lead a discussion about the destructive effects of tsunamis and the need for tsunami warning systems. **LS Interpersonal**

Classification When students learn to classify waves, be sure they understand that any single wave can be grouped by using both classification systems. So a wave can be both a mechanical wave and a transverse wave. Students should also know that electromagnetic waves are always transverse waves, but that mechanical waves can be transverse waves, longitudinal waves, or surface waves. **LS Verbal**

Teaching Key Ideas

Spherical Wave Fronts Mechanical waves spread out through the medium evenly and spherically from the source if the source is open to the medium in all directions. If the source, such as a speaker, is pointed in a particular direction, the sound waves will spread spherically but will be stronger in the direction the speaker points.

Teaching Key Ideas

Vibrations and Waves Invite students who play instruments to bring their instruments to class. Have each student perform a short piece with his or her instrument. Then, instruct students to work in small groups to find the vibrating object that produces the sound of each instrument. (Sample answers: Cellos have vibrating strings, clarinets have vibrating reeds, and drums have vibrating skins.) **LS** **Musical**

Demonstrate

Harmonic Motion You will need a spring with a support, and a mass.
Step 1 Set up a demonstration of the system illustrated in **Figure 4.**
Step 2 Demonstrate the up-and-down vibration (oscillation) of the mass when it is pulled down or pushed up from its resting position.
Step 3 Draw a set of *x*- and *y*-axes on the board. Extend the *x*-axis out to the right and label it "Elapsed time." Label the *y*-axis "Displacement." Zero on the *y*-axis represents the resting position of the mass.
Step 4 Set the mass in motion and walk along the board to the right at a steady pace while reproducing the up-and-down motion of the mass with chalk. The resulting curve should be a sine curve that describes the harmonic motion of the weight. Point out that any vibration can be graphed in this way.

Answer to caption question

No, the total mechanical energy is conserved.

www.scilinks.org
Topic: Vibrations and Waves
Code: **HK81604**

Vibrations and Waves

When a singer sings a note, vocal cords in the singer's throat move back and forth. That motion makes the air in the throat vibrate, which creates sound waves that eventually reach your ears. The vibration of the air in your ears causes your eardrums to vibrate. The motion of the eardrum triggers a series of electrical pulses to your brain, and your brain interprets these electrical pulses as sounds.

Waves are related to vibrations. **> Most waves are caused by vibrating objects.** The sound waves produced by a singer are caused by vibrating vocal cords. Electromagnetic waves may be caused by vibrating charged particles. In the case of a mechanical wave, the particles in the medium through which the wave passes vibrate, too.

✓ Reading Check What is the source of most waves?

The mechanical energy of a vibrating mass-spring system changes form.

A mass hanging on a spring is shown in **Figure 4.** If the mass is pulled down slightly and released, it will begin to move up and down around its original resting position.

When the mass is pulled away from its resting place, the mass-spring system gains elastic potential energy. The spring exerts a force that pulls the mass back toward its original position. **Figure 4** shows the changes in energy that occur as the spring moves up and down. Although the form of the energy changes, the total amount of mechanical energy does not change (if losses due to friction are ignored).

Whenever the spring is expanded or compressed, it exerts a force that moves the mass back to the original resting position. Thus, the mass bounces up and down, or vibrates. This type of vibration is called *simple harmonic motion*.

Figure 4 When a mass hanging on a spring is disturbed from rest, it starts to vibrate up and down about its original position. **Does the total amount of mechanical energy change?**

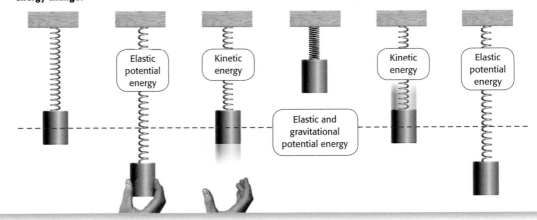

Differentiated Instruction

Alternative Assessment

Simple Harmonic Motion Have students apply the principles of simple harmonic motion to a playground swing. After studying **Figure 4,** ask them to draw a swing at four different points of one cycle (up in one direction, back through the starting point, and up in the other direction, back through the starting point). Tell them to disregard friction and assume that the swing is in motion the entire time. Have them label the illustrations *A, B, C,* and *D.* For each, have students list whether potential and kinetic energy are at maximum or minimum. Have students make a single graph of displacement (from the starting point) versus time. Finally, ask students what type of potential energy is involved in this example. (At *A* and *C,* potential energy is maximum and kinetic energy is minimum. At *B* and *D,* kinetic energy is maximum and potential energy is minimum. The graph is a sine curve. The high and low points correspond to *A* and *C,* and the curve crosses the horizontal axis at *B* and *D.* The potential energy is gravitational potential energy.) **LS** **Visual**

Figure 5 A wave can pass through a series of masses on springs. The masses act like the particles in a medium.

A wave can pass through a series of vibrating objects.

Imagine a series of masses and springs tied together in a row, such as the series shown in **Figure 5.** If you pull down on a mass at the end of the row, that mass will begin to vibrate. As the mass vibrates, it pulls on the mass next to it and causes that mass to vibrate. The energy in the vibration of the first mass, which is a combination of kinetic energy and elastic potential energy, is transferred to the second mass-spring system. In this way, the disturbance that started with the first mass travels down the row. This disturbance is a wave that carries energy from one end of the row to the other.

If the first mass were not connected to the other masses, it would keep vibrating on its own. However, because it transfers its energy to the second mass, it slows down and returns to its resting position sooner than it would if it were free. A vibration that fades out as energy is transferred from one object to another is called *damped harmonic motion.*

READING TOOLBOX

Visual Literacy Figure 5 shows a simple model of wave motion in a medium. Have students look at the top part of the figure and predict what will happen when the person lets go of the first mass. Ask for a volunteer to draw a picture on the board to show the class's prediction. (The diagram should show a "wave" traveling across the masses.) Ask students: "What will happen when the wave reaches the end of the series?" (The wave will be reflected.)
LS Visual

QuickLab

Teacher's Notes Be sure students do not stretch the spring enough to permanently deform it. A metal spring toy is preferable to a plastic one.

Materials per Group
- ribbon, colored
- spring

Answers to Analysis
1. In step 3, the ribbon moved from the resting position to one side, then to the other side, and finally, back to the resting position. In step 4, the ribbon moved from the resting position, then forward, then backward, and finally, back to the resting position.
2. Sample answer: I know that energy is passing along the spring because the energy was able to set matter in motion along the length of the spring. The energy came from the motion (vibration) of the hand holding the spring.

QuickLab

Particle Motion in a Wave 20 min

Procedure
❶ Ask a partner to hold one end of a **spring.** Take the other end, and stretch it out along a smooth floor.

❷ Have another person tie a small piece of **colored ribbon** to a coil near the middle of the spring. The ribbon will help you compare particle motion with wave motion.

❸ Swing your end of the spring from side to side to start a wave traveling along the spring. Observe the motion of the ribbon as the wave passes by.

❹ Take a section of the spring, and bunch it together. Release the spring to create a different kind of wave traveling along the spring. Observe the motion of the ribbon as this wave passes by.

Analysis
1. How would you describe the motion of the ribbon in step 3? How would you describe the motion of the ribbon in step 4?

2. How can you tell that energy is passing along the spring? Where does that energy come from?

Differentiated Instruction

English Learners

Outline Students can create a basic outline of the chapter by first listing the chapter headings. Under each heading, students will find key terms in bold lettering. Key terms should be listed under the heading where they are found.

I. Types of Waves
  A. What is a Wave?
    1. wave

B. Most waves travel through a medium
  1. medium
  2. mechanical waves

C. Light does not require a medium
  1. electromagnetic waves

This basic outline can be used as a study guide for individuals or small groups of students.
LS Verbal

How Does Mountain-Bike Suspension Work? Like mountain bikes, cars and trucks have systems in place to absorb vibrations that are caused by bumps in the road. These systems include springs attached to each wheel and devices called *shock absorbers.* Shock absorbers are fluid-filled tubes that turn the simple harmonic motion of the springs into a dampened harmonic motion. In a dampened harmonic motion, each cycle of stretch and compression of the spring is much smaller than the previous cycle. Ask students to learn about different arrangements of springs and shock absorbers in cars and trucks. Students can also learn how the front suspension systems on mountain bikes work. Students should make diagrams of their chosen systems. **LS** **Logical/Visual**

Answers to Your Turn

1. The damper dissipates the energy, which damps the vibration.

2. Having suspension systems in both the front and the rear will make the ride smoother and give the biker more control.

Why It **Matters**

How does mountain-bike suspension work?

REAL WORLD

Mountain bikers often ride over rough terrain. Good suspension systems keep bikers from being jolted by every bump in the road and smooth their landings when they jump. Many of today's mountain bikes have suspension systems in both the front and the rear. The diagrams below show how a rear suspension system works.

Spring

Damper

1 A suspension system has two parts, the spring and the damper. Together, these parts form a shock absorber. The spring compresses when the bike hits a bump.

2 The damper is an oil-filled device that dissipates the energy in the spring. Without a damper, the spring would continue vibrating in simple harmonic motion. Instead, the spring quickly returns to its rest position.

SCI**LINKS**.

www.scilinks.org
Topic: Shock Absorbers
Code: **HK81698**

YOUR TURN

UNDERSTANDING CONCEPTS
1. How do shock absorbers prevent a mountain bike from continually bouncing?

CRITICAL THINKING
2. Why is it useful to have both front and rear suspension systems on a mountain bike?

Differentiated Instruction

Advanced Learners

Bikes: Function and Form Ask students to bring different types of bikes to class, preferably at least one mountain bike, one racing/road bike, and one BMX bike. Ask students to analyze the difference between the bikes in terms of the function of the bikes. Then have students make a table that lists features of the bikes in one column and lists the reasons why the bikes have those particular features in the second column. **LS** **Logical**

Wave particles move like masses on springs.

If you tie one end of a rope to a doorknob, pull the rope straight, and then rapidly move your hand up and down once, you will generate a single wave, as **Figure 6** shows. As the wave moves along the rope, each ribbon moves up, down, and back to its starting point. The motion of each part of the rope is like the vibrating motion of a mass hanging on a spring. As one part of the rope moves, it pulls on the part next to it. In this way, a wave passes along the length of the rope.

Transverse and Longitudinal Waves

Particles in a medium can vibrate either up and down or back and forth. Waves are often classified according to the direction in which the particles in the medium move as a wave passes by. ❭ **A transverse wave is a wave in which the wave motion is perpendicular to the particle motion. A longitudinal wave is a wave in which the wave motion is parallel to the particle motion.**

Transverse waves have perpendicular motion.

When a crowd does "the wave" at a sporting event, people stand up and raise their arms as the wave reaches their part of the stadium. The wave travels around the stadium, but the individual people move straight up and down. This wave motion is similar to the wave motion in the rope in **Figure 6.** In these cases, the motion of the "particles"—the people in the crowd or the points on the rope—is perpendicular to the motion of the wave as a whole. Waves in which the motion of the particles is perpendicular to the motion of the wave are called **transverse waves.**

Electromagnetic waves are another example of transverse waves. The changing electric and magnetic fields that make up an electromagnetic wave are perpendicular to each other and to the direction in which the wave travels.

✓ **Reading Check** What is one example of a transverse wave?

The points along the rope vibrate up and down.

The wave travels to the right.

QuickLab ⏱ 10 min

Polarization

❶ Polarizing filters block all light waves except for those waves that vibrate in a certain direction. Look through **two polarizing filters** at once, and note your observations.

❷ Now, rotate one filter by 90°, and look again. What do you observe this time?

❸ Do your observations support the idea that light is a transverse wave? Explain your answer.

transverse wave (TRANS vuhrs WAYV) a wave in which the particles of the medium move perpendicularly to the direction the wave is traveling

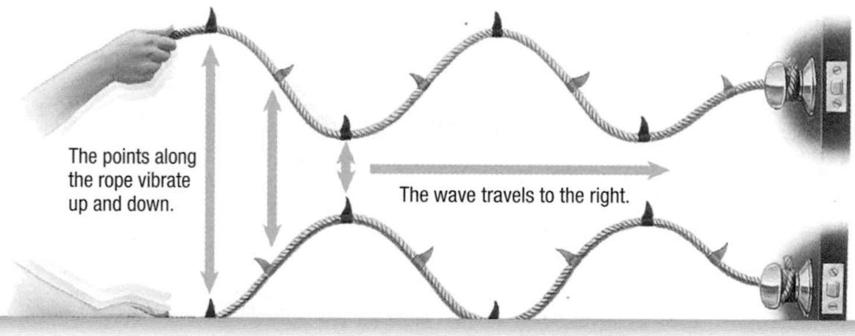

Figure 6 As a wave passes along this rope, the ribbons move up and down as the wave moves to the right. **Why is this situation an example of a transverse wave?**

go.hrw.com
✱ interact online
Keyword: HK8WAVF6

QuickLab

Teacher's Notes The planes of vibration of electromagnetic waves in a beam of light are oriented randomly around an axis passing along the direction of the motion of the light. A polarizing filter allows only electromagnetic waves of a single orientation to pass through. As a result, the light is dimmed as it passes through the filter.

Materials per Group
• polarizing filters, 2

Answers

2. When the polarizing filters are aligned, the second filter will not dim the light much further. When the slits are perpendicular, almost all of the light may be blocked.

3. Yes. A polarizing filter allows light waves of only one orientation to pass through. If a second polarizing filter is held so that its slits are perpendicular to the slits in the first polarizing filter, the light waves that passed through the first filter cannot pass through the second filter because they have the wrong orientation.

Answer to caption question

This is a transverse wave because the particles move up and down while the wave travels to the right. Thus, the particle motion is perpendicular to the wave motion.

go.hrw.com
✱ interact online

Students can interact with the figure by going to **go.hrw.com** and typing in the keyword **HK8WAVF6.**

Differentiated Instruction

Special Education Students

Make a Wave Make the activity shown in **Figure 6** come alive for all the students in these two ways:

1. Prepare a rope as shown, tie it to a doorknob, and create the wave as shown.

2. Using squirt glue or fabric paint, draw the wavy rope and the points on a piece of thick cardboard. When the glue or paint dries, let students who are visually impaired feel the raised path so they can understand the concepts.

LS Kinesthetic

Connection to Chemistry

A Matter of Attraction The transfer of energy by transverse mechanical waves depends on the attraction or bonds of the molecules of matter to one another so that the motion of one particle is easily transferred to the next. This explains why transverse waves in nature occur commonly in the condensed states of matter—solid and liquid—but seldom in gases.

Teaching Key Ideas

Longitudinal and Transverse To help students remember the difference between longitudinal waves and transverse waves, write the following mnemonic phrase on the board, "Particles in LONGitudinal waves vibrate aLONG the wave." Also remind students that the root *trans-* means "across" and that particles in transverse waves vibrate across the wave. **LS** Verbal

Demonstrate

Longitudinal Waves in Air For this demonstration you will need a source of amplified music connected to a raw speaker about 5 inches in diameter (or a mounted speaker with an exposed cone).
Step 1 Play music and speech through the speaker and invite students to gently touch the vibrating cone.
Step 2 Ask students to explain what happens to the air when the speaker cone moves forward (the cone pushes air molecules closer together, causing a compression) and when the speaker cone moves backward (the cone pulls air molecules farther apart, causing a rarefaction).
LS Logical

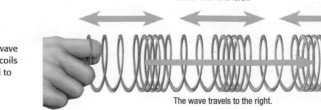

Figure 7 As a longitudinal wave passes along this spring, the coils move back and forth, parallel to the direction of the wave.

The points along the spring vibrate back and forth.

The wave travels to the right.

longitudinal wave (LAHN juh TOOD'n uhl WAYV) a wave in which the particles of the medium vibrate parallel to the direction of wave motion
crest (KREST) the highest point of a wave
trough (TRAWF) the lowest point of a wave

Figure 8 Transverse waves have crests and troughs, while longitudinal waves have compressions and rarefactions.

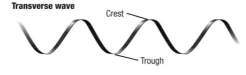

Transverse wave

Crest

Trough

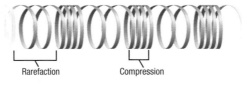

Longitudinal wave

Rarefaction

Compression

Longitudinal waves have parallel motion.

Suppose you attach a long, flexible spring to a doorknob, grab one end, and move your hand back and forth. You will see a wave travel along the spring, as shown in **Figure 7.** As the wave passes along the spring, a ribbon tied to one of the spring's coils would move back and forth, parallel to the direction in which the wave travels. Waves that cause the particles in a medium to vibrate parallel to the direction of wave motion are called **longitudinal waves.**

Sound waves are an example of longitudinal waves that we encounter every day. Sound waves traveling in air compress and expand the air in bands. Molecules in the air move backward and forward, parallel to the direction in which the sound waves travel.

✓ Reading Check **What is the difference between a transverse wave and a longitudinal wave?**

Waves have crests and troughs or compressions and rarefactions.

Look at the transverse wave in **Figure 8.** The high points of a transverse wave are called **crests.** The low points of a transverse wave are called **troughs.** Now look at the longitudinal wave in **Figure 8.** This wave does not have crests and troughs because the particles move back and forth instead of up and down. If you look closely at a longitudinal wave in a spring, you will see a moving pattern of areas where the coils are bunched up alternating with areas where the coils are stretched out. The crowded areas are called *compressions*. The stretched-out areas are called *rarefactions*.

Differentiated Instruction

Alternative Assessment
Transverse and Longitudinal Waves
Step 1 Ask students to draw diagrams that model transverse and longitudinal waves.
Step 2 Have students draw lines between the two kinds of waves, connecting corresponding parts (crest to compression and trough to rarefaction).
Step 3 Students should then describe the motion of the medium as each type of wave passes through it. **LS** Visual

Surface Waves

Unlike the examples of waves discussed so far, waves on the ocean or in a swimming pool are not simply transverse waves or longitudinal waves. Water waves are an example of *surface waves*.

❯ **The particles in a surface wave move both perpendicularly and parallel to the direction in which the wave travels.** Surface waves occur at the boundary between two different mediums, such as water and air.

Follow the motion of the beach ball shown in **Figure 9** as a wave passes by. The wave is traveling from left to right. At first, the ball is in a trough. As the crest approaches, the ball moves to the left (parallel to the wave) and upward (perpendicularly to the wave). When the ball is near the crest, it starts to move to the right. Once the crest has passed, the ball starts to fall back downward and then to the left. The up-and-down motions combine with the side-to-side motions to produce a circular motion overall.

Particles in surface waves move, as the beach ball does, in an ellipse. (A circle is a special case of an ellipse.) The motion of the beach ball helps make visible the motion of the particles (water molecules) in a surface wave.

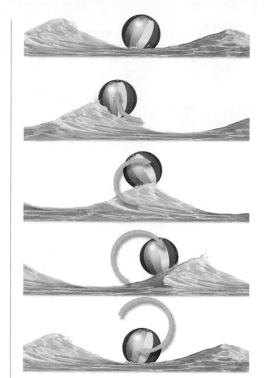

Figure 9 Ocean waves are surface waves at the boundary between air and water.

Section 1 **Review**

KEY IDEAS

1. **Identify** the mediums for the following waves:
   a. ripples on a pond
   b. the sound waves from a stereo speaker
   c. seismic waves
   d. waves on a spring
   e. ocean waves

2. **Name** the one kind of wave that does not require a medium.

3. **Describe** the motion of a mass vibrating on a spring. How does this motion relate to wave motion? What is the source of the wave?

4. **Explain** the difference between transverse waves and longitudinal waves. Give an example of each type of wave.

5. **Draw** a transverse wave and a longitudinal wave. Label a crest, a trough, a compression, and a rarefaction.

6. **Describe** the motion of a water molecule on the surface of the ocean as a wave passes by.

CRITICAL THINKING

7. **Applying Concepts** Describe a situation that demonstrates that water waves carry energy.

8. **Making Inferences** Sometimes, people at a sports event do "the wave" across a stadium. Is "the wave" really an example of a wave? Why or why not?

9. **Drawing Conclusions** Why can supernova explosions in space be seen but not heard on Earth?

Answers to Section Review

1. **a.** water
   b. air
   c. Earth's crust and interior
   d. the spring
   e. water

2. Electromagnetic (light) waves

3. The mass vibrates up and down from a low point to a high point. Particles in a medium vibrate like masses on springs when a wave passes.

4. In a transverse wave, particles in the medium move back and forth at right angles to the direction the wave is moving. A wave along a rope is a transverse wave. In a longitudinal wave, particles in the medium move back and forth in the same direction the wave is moving. A sound wave is a longitudinal wave.

5. Student diagrams should show a transverse wave with a crest and a trough labeled and a longitudinal wave with a compression and a rarefaction labeled.

6. The wave causes the molecule to move up and down as well as forward and backward at the same time. This combination causes the molecule to move in an elliptical path.

Answers continued on p. 537A

Teaching Key Ideas

Surface Waves Tell students that waves in the ocean are only one example of surface waves. Certain types of seismic waves are also surface waves. *Love waves* cause rock to move side-to-side and perpendicular to the direction in which the waves are traveling. *Rayleigh waves* cause the ground to move with an elliptical, rolling motion. Waves in the ocean are similar to Rayleigh seismic waves. **LS** Verbal

❯ Close

Reteaching Key Ideas

Wave Examples Have students brainstorm as many examples of waves as they can. For each example, have them identify how the wave was generated and state whether the wave is a transverse, longitudinal, or surface wave. **LS** Logical

Formative Assessment

Waves transfer

A. matter. (Incorrect. Although some waves travel through matter, the matter does not travel with a wave.)

B. energy. (Correct. All waves transfer energy through matter or space.)

C. vibrating particles. (Incorrect. A wave is made up of vibrating particles, but the wave does not transfer the particles.)

D. water. (Incorrect. Water is a medium through which waves can travel, but, like all media, water does not travel with the wave.)

SECTION
2
Characteristics of Waves

Focus

This section introduces many of the terms used to describe wave characteristics: amplitude, wavelength, period, and frequency. Students learn about the relationship between wavelength, frequency, and wave speed. The section concludes with a discussion of the Doppler effect.

Bellringer

Use the Bellringer transparency to prepare students for this section.

Demonstrate

Properties of Waves Tie a rope to a doorknob or to the back of a chair. Hold the end of the rope and move it up-and-down at a constant speed to create a transverse wave. While you are making the wave, ask students what you can do to change how the wave looks. (Sample answers: Move the end of the rope faster. Move the end of the rope farther up-and-down.) Change how you move the rope according to each student response and ask students how the waveform changed. (Sample answers: The waves were not as long. The waves were taller.) Explain to students that the properties of waves that they saw changing have special names and that they will be learning about their properties in this section. **LS** Visual

Key Ideas

❯ What are some ways to measure and compare waves?

❯ How can you calculate the speed of a wave?

❯ Why does the pitch of an ambulance siren change as the ambulance rushes past you?

Key Terms

amplitude

wavelength

period

frequency

Doppler effect

Why It Matters

Surfers observe characteristics of ocean waves to determine when and where the conditions are best for surfing.

If you have spent any time at the beach or on a boat, you have probably observed many properties of waves. Sometimes the waves are very large; other times they are smaller. Sometimes they are close together, and sometimes they are farther apart. How can these differences be described and measured in more detail?

Wave Properties

In this section, you will learn about several wave properties, including amplitude, wavelength, period, and frequency. ❯ **Amplitude and wavelength are measurements of distance. Period and frequency are measurements based on time.** These four properties are useful for describing and comparing waves.

Amplitude measures the amount of particle vibration.

The greatest distance that particles are displaced from their normal resting positions is called the **amplitude** of the wave. In a transverse wave, the amplitude is the distance from the rest position to a crest or to a trough. The amplitude of a transverse wave is illustrated in **Figure 1**.

The simplest transverse waves have similar shapes no matter how big they are or what medium they travel through. An ideal transverse wave has the shape of a *sine curve*. A sine curve looks like an *S* lying on its side. Waves that have the shape of a sine curve are called *sine waves*. The wave illustrated in **Figure 1** is an example of a sine wave. Although many waves are not perfect sine waves, their shapes can be approximated by the graph of a sine curve.

Amplitude

Rest position

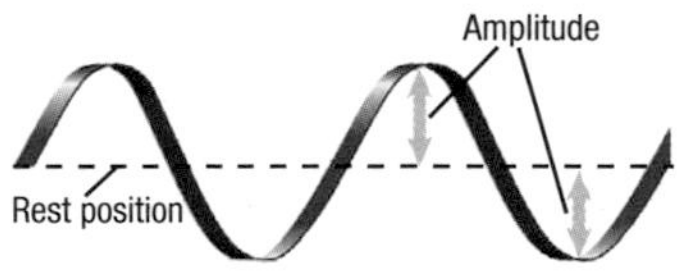

Figure 1 The amplitude of a transverse wave is measured from the rest position to the crest or the trough.

Key Resources

 Teaching Transparency
P14 Frequency

Visual Concepts
Characteristics of a Wave
Wave Properties
Wave Period of Ocean Waves
Equation for the Speed of a Wave
Doppler Effect and Sound

Datasheet
Wave Speed

Math Skills Worksheet
Wave Speed

Cross-Disciplinary Worksheets
Connection to Language Arts—Writing a Plan for Wave Observation
Integrating Technology—Radio Waves
Integrating Earth Science—Earthquake Waves

Transverse wave

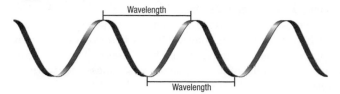

Longitudinal wave

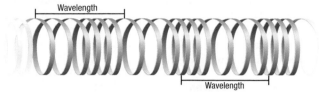

Figure 2 Wavelength is the distance between two identical points on a wave. **Does the distance between crests equal the distance between troughs?**

Wavelength is the distance between two equivalent parts of a wave.

The crests of ocean waves at a beach may be separated by several meters, while ripples in a pond may be separated by only a few centimeters. The distance from one crest to the next crest, or from one trough to the next trough, is called the **wavelength.** In a longitudinal wave, the wavelength is the distance between two compressions or between two rarefactions. More generally, the wavelength is the distance between any two successive identical parts of a wave. **Figure 2** shows the wavelengths of a transverse wave and a longitudinal wave.

Not all waves have a single wavelength that is easy to measure. For instance, most sound waves have a complicated shape, so the wavelength can be difficult to determine. When used in equations, wavelength is represented by the Greek letter lambda, λ. Because wavelength is a distance measurement, it is expressed in the SI unit, meters.

✔ **Reading Check** How is the wavelength of a longitudinal wave measured?

Amplitude and wavelength tell you about energy.

Earthquake waves can cause serious damage, as **Figure 3** shows. The larger the amplitude of a wave is, the more energy it carries. The waves of destructive earthquakes have greater amplitudes, and therefore more energy, than the waves of minor earthquakes. The wavelength of a wave is also related to the wave's energy: The shorter the wavelength of a wave is, the more energy it carries.

amplitude (AM pluh TOOD) the maximum distance that the particles of a wave's medium vibrate from their rest position

wavelength (WAYV LENGKTH) the distance from any point on a wave to an identical point on the next wave

Figure 3 In 1989, portions of the Cypress Freeway in Oakland, California collapsed during a major earthquake.

>**Teach**

Answer to caption question
Yes, the distance between crests is equal to the distance between troughs.

Teaching Key Ideas
Exploring Wave Properties Provide students with yarn and tape. Have them use the yarn to construct a transverse wave similar to the ones on these two pages. Ask them to increase the amplitude of the wave while keeping the frequency constant. (Students will need excess yarn for this step.) Have them explain what increasing the amplitude represents. Then, have them change the frequency, and ask them what happened to the wavelength when they changed the frequency. (The wavelength decreased with an increase in frequency, and it increased with a decrease in frequency.) **LS Kinesthetic**

Demonstrate

Representing Sound Waves Explain to students that oscilloscopes can be used to show sound waves as transverse waves. Strike a tuning fork and hold it near the microphone of the oscilloscope to produce a sine wave on the screen. Tell students that sound waves and electrical signals can be represented as transverse waves when, in fact, neither is a transverse wave. When showing a sound wave as a transverse wave, the crests of the wave correspond to compressions and the troughs of the wave correspond to rarefactions.

Differentiated Instruction

Special Education Students
Making a Model Using **Figure 2,** students can create a model that illustrates the characteristics of a wave. Have students first form the shape of the wave using pipe cleaners or string and then glue their wave to a piece of cardboard. Have students label the following: wavelength, crest, trough, and amplitude. This model can be used as a study guide by covering the labels and asking students to recall which wave characteristic is hidden.
LS Kinesthetic

> Teach, continued

Teaching Key Ideas

Period and Frequency To help students understand the inverse relationship between wave period and wave frequency, try this analogy. Suppose you are at a railroad crossing waiting for a freight train to pass. All of the boxcars are the same length, and you find that 120 cars pass in 5 minutes. Calculate the period and frequency at which the cars pass.
($T = 2.5$ s; $f = 0.4$ cars per second)
LS Logical

Why It **Matters**

Elephant Sounds Elephants communicate with low-frequency sounds that humans cannot hear. Their low-frequency calls travel much further than higher-frequency sounds. Under the right conditions, an elephant call can carry over thirty kilometers or more! Ask students to learn what other animals communicate with low-frequency sounds. (Sample answers may include blue whales, finback whales, hippopotamuses, or rhinoceroses.)
LS Verbal

READING TOOLBOX

Visual Literacy Figure 4 shows a boy floating in an inner tube as a wave passes by. Each successive image shows the wave crests one second later than the previous image. Have students determine the frequency and period of this wave.
($T = 2$ s; $f = 0.5$ Hz) **LS** Visual

Academic Vocabulary

successive (suhk SES iv) following one after the other; consecutive

period (PIR ee uhd) in physics, the time that it takes a complete cycle or wave oscillation to occur

frequency (FREE kwuhn see) the number of cycles or vibrations per unit of time; also the number of waves produced in a given amount of time

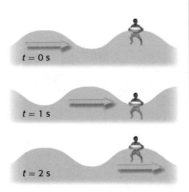

$t = 0$ s

$t = 1$ s

$t = 2$ s

Figure 4 A person floating in an inner tube can determine the period and frequency of the waves by counting the number of seconds that pass between wave crests.

The period is a measurement of the time it takes for a wave to pass a given point.

If you swim out into the ocean until your feet can no longer touch the bottom, your body will be free to move up and down as waves come into shore. As your body rises and falls, you can count the number of seconds between two <u>successive</u> wave crests.

The time required for one complete vibration of a particle in a medium—or of one rise and fall of a swimmer in the ocean—is called the **period** of the wave. The period is also the time required for one full wavelength of a wave to pass a certain point. In equations, the period is represented by the symbol *T*. Because the period is a time measurement, it is expressed in the SI unit, seconds.

Frequency is a measurement of the vibration rate.

If you were floating in an inner tube, like the person shown in **Figure 4,** you could count the number of crests that passed by in a certain time, say, in one minute. The number of wavelengths that pass a point in a given time interval is called the **frequency** of a wave. Frequency also refers to how rapidly vibrations occur in the medium, at the source of the wave, or both.

The symbol for frequency is *f*. The SI unit for frequency is hertz (Hz). (This unit is named after Heinrich Hertz, the scientist who experimentally demonstrated, in 1888, the existence of electromagnetic waves.) Hertz units measure the number of vibrations per second. One vibration per second is 1 Hz, two vibrations per second is 2 Hz, and so on. You can hear sounds with frequencies as low as 20 Hz and as high as 20,000 Hz. At 20,000 Hz, there are 20,000 compressions hitting your ear every second.

The frequency and the period of a wave are related.

The more vibrations that are made in a second, the less time each vibration takes. In other words, the frequency is the inverse of the period.

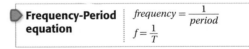

Frequency-Period equation $frequency = \dfrac{1}{period}$
$f = \dfrac{1}{T}$

In **Figure 4,** a wave crest passes the inner tube every 2 s, so the period is 2 s. The frequency can be found by using the frequency-period equation above: $f = 1/T = 1/2$ s $= 0.5$ Hz.

✔ **Reading Check** How are frequency and period related?

Differentiated Instruction

Advanced Learners

Gathering More Information Some students have a natural curiosity that drives them to want to know information beyond the textbook. Ask some of these students to research examples of jobs where a person would need to figure out amplitude, wavelength, frequency, or wave speed. **LS** Verbal

How Are Good Surfing Waves Formed?

Storms on the ocean usually create large waves. Often, the waves die out at sea. But if a storm is strong enough, the waves may crash into each other, and combine their energies. The resulting waves can travel all the way to shore and provide enjoyment for surfers.

REAL WORLD

Three main factors affect the magnitude of surfing waves: the speed of the wind (*wind velocity*), the surface area of the ocean affected by the wind (*fetch*), and the time that the wind blows over the area (*duration*). Surfers check weather forecasts—and sometimes even satellite data–to see which storms will create good surfing opportunities.

YOUR TURN

CRITICAL THINKING

1. What vertical forces act on a surfer?

2. If a surfer accelerates forward while riding a wave, are the horizontal forces balanced?

SCiLINKS.

www.scilinks.org
Topic: Ocean Waves
Code: HK81066

How are Good Surfing Waves Formed? Ask students if they have observed waves breaking at the beach. When a wave approaches the shore, its height increases as the water depth decreases. The crests become peaked, and the wave loses stability. Eventually, the speed of the crest exceeds the speed of the wave, and the wave "breaks." The steepness of the ocean floor determines how the waves break. When the floor is very steep, the waves roll onto the beach before actually breaking. These waves—called *surging breakers*—are the most destructive. A moderately steep slope produces *plunging breakers,* a favorite of surfers. Plunging breakers have a characteristic curl at the top of the crest. Gentle slopes produce *spilling breakers,* which break far from the shore. Foam slides down the surface as these waves slowly approach the shore. Show students videos of various kinds of breaking waves and ask them to identify each one. **LS** Visual

READING TOOLBOX

Visual Literacy The surfboard shown in the images is a shortboard, or a thruster. Shortboards are generally between 6 to 8 feet in length and are more maneuverable than other kinds of surfboards but are more difficult to ride. Encourage interested students to make a diagram that compares the features of shortboards and longboards. **LS** Visual

---

Differentiated Instruction

English Learners

Surfing Jargon Tell students that people involved in some sports, such as surfing, use special terms and phrases to describe features of their sport. Often words that mean one thing in everyday English mean something different in sports jargon. Have students make a table of words used in surfing. The table should list the meaning of the word in everyday English and the meaning of the word in surfing jargon. **LS** Verbal

Answers to Your Turn

1. gravitational force and buoyancy
2. No, the horizontal forces are not balanced while the surfer is accelerating. According to Newton's second law, an acceleration is caused by a net (unbalanced) force.

Teaching Key Ideas

Wave Speed Equations When students are solving wave speed problems, they may have difficulty knowing which wave speed equation to use. Tell students that they should always examine the units of the values given in the problem to help them decide on the correct equation to use. The final units of wave speed should always be a distance divided by a time. So if a unit in the problem is a time unit, students should use $v = \lambda/T$, and if a unit is Hz, students should use $v = \lambda \times f$. **LS Logical**

Demonstrate

Wave Speed Use a ripple tank or shallow baking dish to show differences in wave speed. Adjust the water depth for the best effect. The speed of water waves changes in shallow water. Place a block with a large horizontal surface in the tank so that it is submerged less than 1 cm. Students will observe that the ripples change speed as they pass over the block. **LS Visual**

Integrating Earth Science

Seismic Waves Earthquakes create waves, called *seismic waves,* that travel through Earth. There are two main types of seismic waves, *P waves* (primary waves) and *S waves* (secondary waves). P waves are longitudinal waves that can travel through solids and liquids. S waves are transverse waves that can travel only through solids. P waves travel faster than S waves, so they always move ahead of S waves. S waves move more slowly, but they carry more energy than P waves.

Figure 5 By observing the frequency and wavelength of waves passing a pier, you can calculate the speed of the waves.

Wave Speed

Imagine watching water waves as they move past a post of a pier such as the one in **Figure 5.** If you count the number of crests passing the post for 10 s, you can determine the frequency of the waves. If you measure the distance between crests, you can find the wavelength of the waves. But how can you know the speed of the waves? **❯ The speed of a wave is equal to wavelength divided by period, or to frequency multiplied by wavelength.**

✔ **Reading Check** What are two ways to calculate wave speed?

Wave speed equals wavelength divided by period.

The speed of a moving object is found by dividing the distance the object travels by the time it takes the object to travel that distance. This calculation is shown in the following equation:

$$speed = \frac{distance}{time} \qquad v = \frac{d}{t}$$

If SI units are used for distance and time, speed is expressed as meters per second (m/s). The *wave speed* is simply how fast a wave moves, or, more precisely, how far the wave travels in a certain amount of time. To calculate wave speed, use the wavelength as the distance traveled, and the period as the amount of time it takes the wave to travel a distance of one wavelength.

 Wave speed equation | $wave\ speed = \dfrac{wavelength}{period} \qquad v = \dfrac{\lambda}{T}$

Differentiated Instruction

Advanced Learners

Seismic Waves P waves and S waves travel through Earth from the focus of an earthquake. Because P and S waves travel at different speeds, seismologists can use the time interval between the arrivals of the two kinds of waves to locate the epicenter of an earthquake. This time interval is called the *lag time.* Have students make a poster that shows how lag times and the process of triangulation are used to find the epicenter of an earthquake. **LS Logical**

Wave speed equals frequency times wavelength.

Because period is the inverse of frequency, dividing by the period is equivalent to multiplying by the frequency. Therefore, the speed of a wave can also be calculated by multiplying the wavelength by the frequency.

> **Wave speed equation**
> $wave\ speed = frequency \times wavelength$
> $v = f \times \lambda$

For example, suppose waves passing by a post of a pier have a frequency of 0.4 Hz and a wavelength of 10 m. The waves in this case have a wave speed of 0.4 Hz × 10 m = 4 m/s.

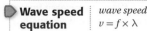 **Math Skills** Wave Speed

The string of a piano that produces the note middle C vibrates with a frequency of 262 Hz. If the sound waves produced by this string have a wavelength in air of 1.30 m, what is the speed of the sound waves?

Identify	**Given:**
List the given and unknown values.	$frequency, f = 262$ Hz $wavelength, \lambda = 1.30$ m **Unknown:** $wave\ speed, v = ?$ m/s
Plan	$v = f \times \lambda$
Write the equation for wave speed.	
Solve	$v = 262$ Hz $\times\ 1.30$ m
Insert the known values into the equation, and solve.	$v = 341$ m/s

Practice

1. The average wavelength in a series of ocean waves is 15.0 m. A wave crest arrives at the shore on average every 10.0 s, so the frequency is 0.100 Hz. What is the average speed of the waves?

2. Green light has a wavelength of 5.20×10^{-7} m. The speed of light is 3.00×10^8 m/s. Calculate the frequency of green light waves with this wavelength.

3. The speed of sound in air is about 340 m/s. What is the wavelength of a sound wave with a frequency of 220 Hz (on a piano, the A below middle C)?

For more practice, visit **go.hrw.com** and enter keyword **HK8MP**.

Practice **Hint**

> Problem 2: The wave speed equation can be rearranged to isolate frequency in the following way:

$$v = f \times \lambda$$

Divide both sides by λ.

$$\frac{v}{\lambda} = \frac{f \times \cancel{\lambda}}{\cancel{\lambda}}$$

$$f = \frac{v}{\lambda}$$

> Problem 3: In this problem, you will need to rearrange the equation to isolate wavelength.

Math Skills

Answers to Practice
1. $v = f \times \lambda$
   $v = 0.100$ Hz $\times\ 15.0$ m $= 1.50$ m/s
2. $f = v/\lambda$
   $f = (3.00 \times 10^8$ m/s$)/$
   $(5.20 \times 10^{-7}$ m$) = 5.77 \times 10^{14}$ Hz
3. $\lambda = v/f$
   $\lambda = (340$ m/s$)/(220$ Hz$) = 1.5$ m

Additional Examples
The speed of sound in dry air at 40 °C is 355 m/s. The speed at 0 °C is 331 m/s. Will a sound of a given frequency have a longer or shorter wavelength at 40 °C than at 0 °C?
Answer: Longer because the waves will be farther apart as the speed is greater.
Calculate the frequency of microwaves that have a wavelength of 0.0085 m and a speed of 3.00×10^8 m/s.
Answer: 3.5×10^{10} Hz
The speed of sound in seawater is 1,530 m/s at 25 °C. A sonar device emits a pulse of sound of 922 Hz. What is the wavelength of sound at this frequency in seawater? If an echo from the sonar device returns 4.76 s after the pulse is sent, how deep is the object that reflected the sonar?
Answer: 1.66 m; 3,640 m in depth
LS Logical

Differentiated Instruction

Basic Learners
Remembering Symbols Some students may have difficulty remembering that the symbol λ refers to wavelength. Remind students that λ is the Greek letter *lambda* and that it corresponds to the letter L in the English alphabet. Students can then remember that $\lambda = L =$ length = wavelength. **LS Verbal**

MISCONCEPTION ALERT

Wave Properties Students confuse independent properties of waves, such as amplitude, frequency, and wave speed. Some students believe that a rapid vibration will always produce a large amplitude and a fast wave speed. Emphasize that wave speed depends on the medium. A vibration in air will produce a different wave speed than the same vibration in water. Temperature also affects wave speed. Sound travels faster through hot air than through cool air. Amplitude is related to the sound's loudness, and does not directly relate to wave speed.

Teacher's Notes You may also use the setup from the second Demonstrate in Section 1.

Materials per Group
- dowel, wooden, 3 cm diameter or thicker
- pan, rectangular
- water

Answer to Analysis

1. Students should observe that the velocity of the waves stays the same because it is determined by the medium. Waves of higher frequency will have shorter wavelengths, and waves of lower frequency will have longer wavelengths.

Why It Matters

Elasticity The speed of sound in a material depends on the elasticity of the material. Elasticity is the tendency of a material to restore itself or "bounce back" after being deformed by an external force. A sound wave is a compression wave, so it is reasonable that a material that quickly bounces back from a compression can transmit sound at a high velocity.

Very elastic materials include steel, glass, and aluminum. Lead, however, is much less elastic by comparison because it bounces back less quickly. The speed of sound in lead is about one-third the speed of sound in steel. Materials thought of as elastic, such as rubber, actually have relatively poor elasticity with respect to sound.

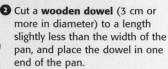

QuickLab **Wave Speed** ⏱ 10 min

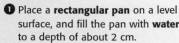

Procedure

❶ Place a **rectangular pan** on a level surface, and fill the pan with **water** to a depth of about 2 cm.

❷ Cut a **wooden dowel** (3 cm or more in diameter) to a length slightly less than the width of the pan, and place the dowel in one end of the pan.

❸ Move or roll the dowel back and forth slowly, and observe the length of the wave generated.

❹ Now move the dowel back and forth faster (to increase frequency), and observe the wavelength.

Analysis

1. Do the waves always travel at the same speed in the pan?

The speed of a wave depends on the medium.

Sound waves can travel through air. If they couldn't, you would not be able to have a conversation with a friend or hear music from a radio across the room. Because sound travels very fast in air (about 340 m/s), you don't notice a time delay in most situations.

Sound waves travel three to four times faster in water than they do in air. If you swim with your head underwater, you may hear certain sounds very clearly. Dolphins, such as those shown in **Figure 6,** use sound waves to communicate with one another over long distances underwater.

Sound waves travel even faster in solids than they do in air or in water. Sound waves have speeds 15 to 20 times as fast in rock or metal as in air. If someone strikes a long steel rail with a hammer at one end, you might hear two bangs at the other end. The first sound, which has traveled through the steel rail itself, reaches you shortly before the second sound, which has traveled through the air.

The speed of a wave depends on the medium. In a given medium, though, the speed of waves is constant; it does not depend on the frequency of the wave. No matter how fast you shake your hand up and down to create waves on a rope, the waves will travel at the same speed. Shaking your hand faster just increases the frequency and decreases the wavelength.

Figure 6 Dolphins use sound waves to communicate with one another. **Does sound in water travel faster or slower than sound in air?**

Answer to caption question
Sound travels faster in water than it travels in air.

Differentiated Instruction

Alternative Assessment

Chuck Yeager and the Speed of Sound Chuck Yeager was the first person to travel faster than the speed of sound. Have students research Yeager's historic supersonic flight and find out how he was able to break the sound barrier. Students should write a report of what they learned. (Students should learn that Yeager flew a plane at a speed of 293 m/s at an altitude of 12,000 m above sea level. Students should also note that the temperature of the air at that altitude was so low that the speed of sound was only 290 m/s.) **LS Verbal**

Kinetic theory explains differences in wave speed.

The arrangement of particles in a medium determines how well waves travel through it. Solids, liquids, and gases have different degrees of organization at the particle level.

In gases, the molecules are far apart and move around randomly. A molecule must travel through a lot of empty space before it bumps into another molecule. Waves don't travel as fast in gases as they do in solids and liquids.

In liquids, such as water, the molecules are much closer together than they are in gases, and they are free to slide past one another. Molecules in a liquid can be compared to vibrating masses on springs that are so close together that the masses rub against each other. In the case of masses on springs, vibrations are transferred easily from one mass to the next. In the case of a liquid, vibrations are transferred easily from one molecule to another. As a result, waves travel faster in liquids than they do in gases. For example, sound waves travel faster through water than they do through air.

In solids, molecules are closer yet, and are bound tightly to each other. Molecules in a solid can be compared to vibrating masses that are glued together. When one mass starts to vibrate, all the others also start to vibrate almost immediately. As a result, waves travel very quickly through most solids.

✓ **Reading Check** Why does sound travel faster in solids than it does in liquids or in gases?

Light has a finite speed.

When you flip a light switch, light seems to fill the room instantly. However, light does take time to travel from place to place. All electromagnetic waves in empty space travel at the same speed, known as the *speed of light*. The speed of light in empty space is 3.00×10^8 m/s (186,000 mi/s). This value is a constant that is often represented by the symbol c. Light travels more slowly when it has to pass through a medium such as air or water.

Our eyes can detect light with frequencies ranging from about 4.3×10^{14} Hz to 7.5×10^{14} Hz. Light in this range is called *visible light*. The differences in frequency in visible light account for the differences in color that we see in **Figure 7**. Electromagnetic waves also exist in a range of frequencies that we cannot see directly. The full range of light at different frequencies and wavelengths is called the *electromagnetic spectrum*. Because the speed of light is constant, you can use the wave speed equation ($f \times \lambda = c$) to find frequency if you know wavelength, or vice versa.

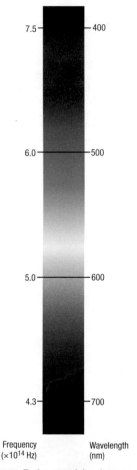

Frequency (×10^14 Hz)   Wavelength (nm)

Figure 7 The part of the electromagnetic spectrum that we can see is called visible light. **How does frequency change as wavelength increases?**

READING TOOLBOX

Visual Literacy Have students examine **Figure 7.** Ask students to formulate a general statement comparing the wavelengths and frequencies at the red and violet extremes of the visible spectrum. (Sample answer: The radiation at the violet end of the spectrum has the shortest wavelengths and the highest frequencies. Radiation at the red end has the longest wavelengths and the lowest frequencies.) **LS Visual**

Why It Matters

Visible Light Help students understand that visible light does not have special properties when compared to other electromagnetic waves. In addition, visible light makes up only a tiny fraction of the entire electromagnetic spectrum. Ask students to find out how other types of electromagnetic waves are used. (Sample answers: Radio waves transmit radio and TV signals. Microwaves cook food in microwave ovens. X rays are used to make images of bones.) **LS Logical**

Answer to caption question
Frequency decreases as wavelength increases. The product, which equals wave speed, remains constant.

Why It Matters

Speed of Light Although light requires no medium for transmission, it does interact with matter that it passes through by slowing down somewhat, depending on the material. For example, light slows down from 3.00×10^8 m/s to around 2.25×10^8 m/s when it enters water. The speed of light in diamond is only about 40% the speed of light in air. Ask students why light slows down when it enters a solid or a liquid, but sound waves speed up. (Light is absorbed by the molecules of the solid or liquid, and then re-emitted. Sound travels faster in solids and liquids than in air because it requires a medium, and solids and liquids are denser than air.)

Demonstrate

Doppler Effect The following materials are needed for the demonstration: a strong mesh bag, battery-powered alarm clock and 1 m of heavy cord.

Step 1 Adjust the clock to start the alarm. Place the clock in a mesh bag tied securely to a sturdy cord about 1 m long.

Step 2 Swing the bag containing the clock in a circle over your head. To hear the changes in pitch, students should stand just below the plane of the circle. Do not allow students to stand in the plane in case the bag or cord should break. If necessary, add mass to the bag to slow the circular motion.

READING TOOLBOX

Outlining If students are struggling with their outlines, suggest that they use the head structure in the text as a skeleton for their outlines. The title of the section should be the main group (I); the red heads should be the first subgroup (A, B, C, etc.); and the blue heads should be the next subgroup (1, 2, 3, etc.).

The Doppler Effect

Imagine that you are standing on a corner as an ambulance rushes by. As the ambulance passes, the sound of the siren changes from a high pitch to a lower pitch. Why?
❯ **Motion between the source of waves and the observer creates a change in observed frequency.** In the case of sound waves, motion creates a change in pitch.

Pitch is determined by the frequency of sound waves.

The *pitch* of a sound, how high or low it is, is determined by the frequency at which sound waves strike the eardrum in your ear. A high-pitched sound is caused by sound waves of high frequency. As you know from the wave speed equation, frequency and wavelength are also related to the speed of a wave.

Suppose you could see the sound waves from the ambulance siren when the ambulance is at rest. You would see the sound waves traveling out from the siren in spherical wave fronts, as shown in **Figure 8.** The distance between two successive wave fronts represents the wavelength of the sound waves. When the sound waves reach your ears, they have a frequency equal to the number of wave fronts that strike your eardrum each second. That frequency determines the pitch of the sound that you hear.

READING TOOLBOX

Outlining
Create an outline using the main ideas from this section. Include all key ideas, key terms, and red and blue topic headings. Use the outline to review the material.

Figure 8 The Doppler Effect

When an ambulance is not moving, the sound waves produced by the siren spread out in spheres. The frequency of the waves is the same at all locations.

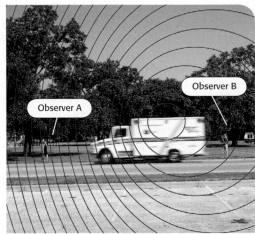

When an ambulance is moving, the sound waves produced by the siren are closer together in front and farther apart behind. Observer A hears a higher-pitched sound than Observer B hears.

Teaching Key Ideas

The Doppler Effect Reinforce the idea that the pitch of sound you hear depends entirely on the frequency at which compressions strike the eardrum, even if the source of vibration is at a higher or lower frequency. Emphasize that the frequency of vibration of the sound source remains constant. However, the waves are pushed closer together ahead of the moving vehicle and stretched farther apart behind it. Also stress the point that the speed of the waves does not change; it is determined by the nature of the medium.

Differentiated Instruction

Alternative Assessment

Wave Review Have students draw examples of two transverse waves, making the second wave have a higher frequency and lower amplitude than the first. Ask students to label wavelength and amplitude on the two waves. Ask students to explain the nature of a sound wave and how it travels through matter (as compressions and rarefactions). Also ask them what measure constitutes wavelength in a sound wave (distance between compressions or rarefactions). **LS Visual**

Figure 9 This Doppler radar dome receives radio waves that have been sent out and then reflected back by rain, snow, and hail. The observed frequency shifts help meteorologists track storms.

Frequency changes when the source of waves is moving.

If an ambulance is moving toward you, the sound waves from the siren are compressed in the direction of motion, as shown in **Figure 8.** Between the time that one sound wave and the next sound wave are emitted, the ambulance moves forward. The distance between wave fronts is shortened, though the wave speed remains the same. As a result, the sound waves reach your ear at a higher frequency; they sound higher-pitched than they would if the ambulance were at rest.

Conversely, if an ambulance is moving away from you, the frequency at which the waves reach your ear is less, and you hear the sound of the siren at a lower pitch than you would if the ambulance were at rest. This change in the observed frequency of a wave is called the **Doppler effect.** This effect can result from the motion of the source or the observer or both. The Doppler effect occurs for light waves and for other types of waves as well. The Doppler effect can be used to track storms, as **Figure 9** shows.

SC*i*LINKS.

www.scilinks.org
Topic: Doppler Effect
Code: HK80424

Doppler effect (DAHP luhr e FEKT) an observed change in the frequency of a wave when the source or observer is moving

Real-World Connection

Observing the Doppler Effect Ask students to relate experiences in which they heard the Doppler effect, such as along highways, at airports, or near railroad tracks. Ask students to explain the characteristic sound that allows you to identify an auto race on TV, even if you can't see the picture. Consider having students use an audio recorder or a video camera to record examples of the Doppler effect.

❯ Close

Reteaching Key Ideas

Connecting Ideas Have students create a concept map by using the boldface and italicized terms from this section. Be sure that students' concept maps illustrate this section's key ideas. **LS Verbal**

Formative Assessment

Which of the following wave properties is never used in a wave speed calculation?

A. amplitude (Correct. The amplitude of a wave is not related to the speed of the wave.)

B. frequency (Incorrect. Frequency is used in calculations for wave speed that use the equation $v = f \times \lambda$.)

C. period (Incorrect. Period is used in calculations for wave speed that use the equation $v = \lambda / T$.)

D. wavelength (Incorrect. Wavelength is used in all calculations of wave speed.)

Section 2 **Review**

KEY IDEAS

1. **Draw** a sine curve, and label a crest, a trough, and the amplitude.

2. **Describe** how the frequency and period of a wave are related.

3. **Explain** why sound waves travel faster in liquids or solids than in air.

4. **Describe** the Doppler effect, and explain why it occurs.

CRITICAL THINKING

5. **Identifying Relationships** What happens to the wavelength of a wave when the frequency of the wave is doubled but the wave speed stays the same?

6. **Applying Concepts** Imagine you are waiting for a train to pass at a railroad crossing. Will the train whistle have a higher pitch as the train approaches you or after it has passed you by?

Math ❭ Skills

7. A wave along a guitar string has a frequency of 440 Hz and a wavelength of 1.5 m. What is the speed of the wave?

8. The speed of sound in air is about 340 m/s. What is the wavelength of sound waves produced by a guitar string vibrating at 440 Hz?

9. The speed of light is 3×10^8 m/s. What is the frequency of microwaves with a wavelength of 1 cm?

Answers to Section Review

1. Students' drawings should show a sine wave with labels for crest, trough, and amplitude.

2. Frequency and period are the inverse of each other.

3. Sound travels faster in liquids and solids than in air because the particles in those media are closer together than those in air.

4. The Doppler effect is an observed change in frequency. It occurs because there is relative motion between the source of the waves and the observer.

5. The wavelength is halved.

6. The whistle's pitch will sound higher as the train approaches and will become lower as the train passes.

7. $v = f \times \lambda$

$v = (440\ \text{Hz})(1.5\ \text{m}) = 660\ \text{m/s}$

8. $\lambda = v/f$

$\lambda = 340\ \text{m/s}/440\ \text{Hz} = 0.77\ \text{m}$

9. $f = v/\lambda$

$f = 3 \times 10^8\ \text{m/s}/0.01\ \text{m} = 3 \times 10^{10}\ \text{Hz}$

Wave Interactions

❯Focus

This section covers wave behaviors and interactions. Students learn about reflection, diffraction, refraction, and constructive and destructive interference. They also learn how interference can create standing waves.

Bellringer

Use the Bellringer transparency to prepare students for this section.

Demonstrate

Showing Reflection Attach one end of a rope to a doorknob. Tell students that you are going to make a wave on the rope and ask them to predict what will happen to the wave when it reaches the end of the rope. (Sample answers: The wave will stop. The wave will come back in the other direction.) Make a single pulse by moving your hand up and down once and then holding the rope straight but not taut so that the wave pulse can travel down the rope and reflect back to your hand. Ask students to describe what they saw. (Some students may notice that the pulse is inverted after reflection.) Explain to students that the wave reflected after it hit a barrier (the doorknob) and that other kinds of waves also undergo reflection when they hit a barrier. **LS** Visual

❯Teach

Answer to caption question
This is an example of reflection.

Key Ideas

> How do waves behave when they hit a boundary, when they pass around an edge or opening, and when they pass from one medium to another?

> What happens when two or more waves are in the same location?

> How does a standing wave affect the medium in which it travels?

Key Terms

reflection
diffraction
refraction
interference
constructive interference
destructive interference
standing wave

Why It Matters

Wave interactions make it possible to see your reflection in a mirror, to hear sounds from a nearby room, and to see colorful patterns on soap bubbles.

Have you ever seen a landscape reflected in a still lake? This reflection occurs because of the way waves interact with their environment and with other waves. You will learn about wave interactions in this section.

Reflection, Diffraction, and Refraction

When waves are moving through a continuous medium or through space, they may move in straight lines like waves on the ocean, spread out in circles like ripples on a pond, or spread out in spheres like sound waves in air. But what happens when a wave meets an object? And what happens when a wave passes into another medium? ❯ **When a wave meets a surface or a boundary, the wave bounces back. When a wave passes the edge of an object or passes through an opening, the wave bends. A wave also bends when it passes from one medium to another at an angle.**

Reflection occurs when a wave meets a boundary.

When light waves strike a shiny surface, they reflect off the surface. **Reflection** is simply the bouncing back of a wave when it meets a surface or boundary. The reflection of light waves can create a mirror image of a landscape when they hit the surface of a lake. Other types of waves reflect, too. When water waves hit the side of a boat, they are reflected. **Figure 1** shows another example of the reflection of water waves.

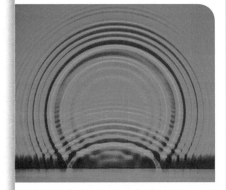

Figure 1 These water waves bounce back when they hit the surface. **What wave behavior does this illustrate?**

Key Resources

 Teaching Transparency
TM43 Interference

 Visual Concepts
Reflection
Diffraction
Refraction
Comparing Constructive and
Destructive Interference
Standing Wave

Cross-Disciplinary Worksheets
Integrating Mathematics—Bending
Light Waves to Magnify
Connection to Architecture—
Architectural Acoustics

Figure 2 Diffraction

Waves bend when they pass the edge of an obstacle.

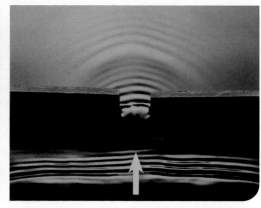

When they pass through an opening, waves bend around both edges.

Diffraction is the bending of waves around an edge.

If you stand outside the doorway of a classroom, you may be able to hear the sound of voices inside the room. But if the sound waves cannot travel in a straight line to your ear, how are you able to hear the voices?

When waves pass the edge of an object, they spread out as if a new wave were created there. The same effect occurs when waves pass through an opening, such as an open window or a door. In effect, the waves bend around an object or opening. This bending of waves as they pass an edge is called **diffraction.** The amount of diffraction of a wave depends on its wavelength and on the size of the barrier or opening. Diffraction is the reason that shadows never have perfectly sharp edges.

The photograph on the left in **Figure 2** shows waves passing around a block in a tank of water. Before they reach the block, the waves travel in a straight line. After they pass the block, the waves near the edge bend and spread out into the space behind the block. This is an example of diffraction.

The photograph on the right in **Figure 2** shows two blocks placed end to end with a small gap between them. Water waves bend around the two edges and spread out as they pass through the opening. Sound waves passing through a door behave in the same way. Because sound waves spread out into the space beyond the door, a person who is near the door on the outside can hear sounds from inside the room.

✓ Reading Check What is one example of diffraction?

SCI
LINKS.

www.scilinks.org
Topic: Reflection,
Refraction,
Diffraction
Code: **HK81284**

reflection (ri FLEK shuhn) the bouncing back of a ray of light, sound, or heat when the ray hits a surface that it does not go through

diffraction (di FRAK shuhn) a change in the direction of a wave when the wave finds an obstacle or an edge, such as an opening

❯ Teach, *continued*

Teaching Key Ideas

Reflection and Diffraction Lead a discussion with your students about reflection and diffraction. Tell students that these wave interactions are two ways that waves can change direction. Students may understand reflection better because they are more familiar with the effects of reflection. Ask students to list real-world examples of waves reflecting. (Sample answers may include seeing an image in a mirror or water waves bouncing back from the side of a bathtub.) Tell students that diffraction is not as uncommon as they may think. Discuss how sound waves diffract around corners and how waves in the ocean diffract around rocks and jetties. **LS Verbal**

MISCONCEPTION //ALERT\\\

Bending Waves Caution students that the word *bend,* when applied to light waves, seldom means that they bend in a curving path like a highway. In diffraction and refraction, it refers to light waves changing direction abruptly.

Differentiated Instruction

Struggling Readers

Honing Reading Skills Have students read the material on reflection, diffraction, and refraction, one topic at a time. After each topic, ask for volunteers to summarize each phenomenon, giving particular attention to what happens to the waves and the conditions that are necessary to make the waves happen. **LS Verbal**

Alternative Assessment

Wave Phenomena Ask students to draw diagrams showing reflection, refraction, and diffraction of waves. Students do not need to draw waves but simply sketch the geometry of each phenomenon. Tell them to label each of the diagrams clearly as to which phenomenon it represents. Students should also label the objects and boundaries involved and use arrows to show the direction of wave travel both before and after the encounter between the waves and the objects. **LS Visual**

Teaching Key Ideas

Refraction and Frequency Tell students that refraction is a third way that waves can bend. Refracted waves bend because part of a wave begins to travel at a different speed before the rest of the wave does. Students may think that as a wave enters a different medium and its speed changes, its frequency also changes. Be sure students understand that when a wave changes speed, its wavelength changes, but its frequency remains the same. Frequency is dependent on the source, not on the medium.

Answer to caption question

This is an example of refraction.

Demonstrate

Observing Reflection and Refraction For this demonstration you will need an aquarium tank (5 or 10 gal) or other large transparent container, milk, mirror, and a laser pointer or focusing flashlight. Allow about 5 minutes.

Step 1 Fill the aquarium with water. Add several drops of milk to the water and stir.

Step 2 Demonstrate refraction by directing the laser beam straight down into the water and then moving it in an arc to change the angle at which the beam enters the water. Students will be able to see the beam bend toward the normal (vertical) as it enters the water.

Step 3 Demonstrate reflection by placing the small mirror on the bottom of the tank.

Figure 3 Because light waves bend when they pass from one medium to another, this spoon looks like it is in two pieces. **What is this phenomenon called?**

refraction (ri FRAK shuhn) the bending of a wave front as the wave front passes between two substances in which the speed of the wave differs

interference (IN tuhr FIR uhns) the combination of two or more waves that results in a single wave

constructive interference (kuhn STRUHK tiv IN tuhr FIR uhns) a superposition of two or more waves that produces an intensity equal to the sum of the intensities of the individual waves

destructive interference (di STRUHK tiv IN tuhr FIR uhns) a superposition of two or more waves that produces an intensity equal to the difference of the intensities of the individual waves

Waves can also bend by refraction.

Why does the spoon in **Figure 3** look as though it is broken into two pieces? This strange appearance results from the bending of light waves. The bending of waves when they pass from one medium into another is called **refraction**. All waves are refracted when they pass from one medium to another at an angle.

Light waves which reflect from the top of the spoon handle pass straight through the glass and the air to your eyes. But the light waves which reflect from the bottom part of the spoon start out in the water, then pass through the glass, then pass through the air to your eyes. Each time the waves enter a new medium, they bend slightly because of a change in wave speed. The waves reflected from the bottom part of the spoon reach your eyes from a different angle than the waves reflected from the top of the spoon handle. Because one set of light waves is reaching your eyes from one direction, and another set of light waves is reaching your eyes from a different direction, the spoon appears to be broken.

✓ Reading Check How is refraction different from diffraction?

Interference

What would happen if you and another person tried to walk through the exact same space at the same time? You would run into each other. Material objects, such as human bodies, cannot share space with other material objects. Waves, however, can share space with other waves. **❯ When several waves are in the same location, they combine to produce a single, new wave that is different from the original waves.** This interaction is called **interference**. **Figure 4** shows interference occurring as water waves pass through each other. Once the waves have passed through each other and moved on, they will return to their original shapes.

Figure 4 Interference patterns form when water waves pass through each other.

Differentiated Instruction

Alternative Assessment

Standing Waves on a Rope Students can experience standing waves and observe the basics of harmonics and resonance.

Step 1 Have two students stand about 5 m apart holding a rope or piece of rubber tubing between them.

Step 2 Ask one student to make the entire rope vibrate in a single standing wave by moving the end up and down continuously.

Step 3 After students get the rhythm of this vibration, tell them to make the rope vibrate in two segments, with a node in the middle. They

will discover that this will happen only at twice the frequency of the previous wave.

Step 4 Ask students to find the next higher natural frequency of the rope. This will occur at three times the original frequency, and the rope will exhibit a standing wave of three parts with two nodes.

Step 5 Have students suggest ways to make the rope vibrate at different frequencies. Point out that the rope is a model for a string on a violin, guitar, piano, or other stringed instrument.

LS Kinesthetic

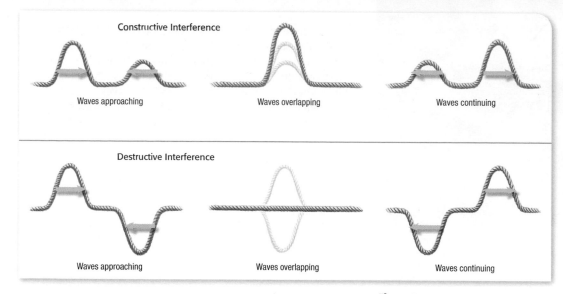

Constructive Interference

Waves approaching   Waves overlapping   Waves continuing

Destructive Interference

Waves approaching   Waves overlapping   Waves continuing

Constructive interference increases amplitude.

When the crest of one wave overlaps the crest of another wave, the waves reinforce each other, as the top image in **Figure 5** shows. Think about what happens at the particle level. Suppose the crest of one wave moves a particle up 4 cm from its original position, and the crest of another wave moves the particle up 3 cm.

When these waves overlap, the result is a wave whose amplitude is the sum of the amplitudes of the two individual waves. The particle moves up 4 cm because of one wave and 3 cm because of the other, for a total displacement of 7 cm. This phenomenon is called **constructive interference**.

Destructive interference decreases amplitude.

When the crest of one wave meets the trough of another wave, the resulting wave has a smaller amplitude than the larger of the two waves. This phenomenon is called **destructive interference**.

To understand how destructive interference works, imagine the following scenario between two waves. Suppose the crest of one wave has an amplitude of 4 cm, and the trough of the other wave has an amplitude of 3 cm. If the crest and trough overlap, a new wave will be formed with an amplitude of just 1 cm. When destructive interference occurs between two waves that have the same amplitude, the waves may completely cancel each other out, as the lower image in **Figure 5** shows.

Figure 5 Waves can interfere constructively or destructively. **What condition is required for complete destructive interference?**

Integrating **Architecture**

Dead Spots You might have experienced destructive interference in an auditorium or a concert hall. As sound waves reflect from the walls, there are places, known as *dead spots*, where the waves interfere destructively and cancel each other out. Dead spots are produced by the interaction of sound waves coming directly from the stage with waves reflected off the walls. To prevent dead spots, architects design concert halls so that the dimensions are not simple multiples of each other. They also try to avoid smooth, parallel walls in the design. Irregularities in the wall and ceiling tend to reduce the direct reflections of waves and the resulting interference.

Teaching Key Ideas

Interference The word *interference* may have a negative connotation to some students. As a result, they may think that interfering waves always have negative effects on one another. Emphasizing the words *reinforcement* and *cancellation* can help convey the idea that interference can have both positive and negative results. **LS Verbal**

Answer to caption question

The waves must match in amplitude and frequency, and the crests of one wave must exactly overlap the troughs of the other.

Why It **Matters**

Diamonds and Refraction The angle at which a light wave refracts when entering a new medium depends on the indices of refraction of the original medium and new medium. The index of refraction is the ratio of the speed of light in a vacuum to the speed of light in a particular medium. Diamonds have a particularly high index of refraction, which is partly responsible for a diamond's brilliance or sparkle. Gem cutters try to cut diamonds so that light that enters the diamond will refract and reflect inside the diamond and will eventually exit out the top of the diamond. Have students do research to find how the index of refraction can be used to distinguish between real diamonds and fake diamonds. **LS Logical**

Teaching Key Ideas

Standing Waves in Stringed Instruments Tell students that standing waves occur in many different kinds of musical instruments. With a stringed instrument, such as a guitar or a violin, pressing down a string before plucking it creates a node at that point. The location of the node effectively determines the pitch of the note. Invite students who play string instruments to bring their instruments to class. Have students look at the strings as a note is played to see the standing waves formed on the strings. (Standing waves are easier to see on larger instruments, so cellos and double basses are ideal for this activity.) Ask the instrument players to play a harmonic and challenge the other students to find the nodes on the string. **LS Kinesthetic**

Outlining Some learners may benefit from filling in blanks of a partially completed outline. Construct an outline of this section and then remove key words and phrases. Make copies of the incomplete outline and have students fill in the missing information as they read the section.

Demonstrate

Beats and Tuning Ask two or more students who play instruments to demonstrate beats and the techniques of tuning. They can do this by playing the same note initially out of tune with each other, then "splitting the difference" until they are in tune with each other.

Visual Literacy In **Figure 7,** sound waves that are interfering to produce beats are shown as transverse waves. Remind students that sound waves are actually longitudinal waves, but the image uses transverse waves for clarity.

Answer to caption question
The amplitude is greatest at t_2.

Figure 6 The colorful swirls on a bubble result from the constructive interference of some light waves and the destructive interference of other light waves.

Outlining
Create an outline that covers the material in this section. Be sure to include all of the key ideas. Also include supporting ideas, examples, and key terms.

Figure 7
When two waves of slightly different frequencies interfere with each other, they produce beats. **When is the amplitude of the resultant wave greatest?**

Interference of light waves creates colorful displays.

You can see a rainbow of colors when oil is spilled onto a watery surface. Soap bubbles, like the ones shown in **Figure 6,** have reds, blues, and yellows on their surfaces. The colors are due to interference patterns between light waves.

When light waves strike a soap bubble, some waves bounce off the outside of the bubble and travel directly to your eye. Other light waves travel into the thin shell of the bubble, bounce off the inner side of the bubble's shell, then travel back through the shell, into the air, and to your eye. These waves travel farther than the waves reflected directly off the outside of the bubble. At times the two sets of waves are out of phase with each other. They interfere constructively at some frequencies (colors) and destructively at other frequencies (colors). The result is a swirling rainbow effect.

Interference of sound waves produces beats.

The sound waves from two tuning forks of slightly different frequencies will interfere with each other as shown in **Figure 7.** The compressions and rarefactions of their respective sound waves will arrive at your ear at different rates.

When compressions from the two tuning forks arrive at your ear at the same time, constructive interference occurs, and the sound is louder. A short time later, a compression from one and a rarefaction from the other arrive together. Destructive interference occurs, and a softer sound is heard. Within the overall sound, you hear a pattern of alternating loud and soft sounds, called *beats*.

Piano tuners listen for beats between a tuning fork of known frequency and a string on a piano. By adjusting the tension in the string, the tuner can change the pitch (frequency) of the string's vibration. When no beats are heard, the string is vibrating at the same frequency as the tuning fork.

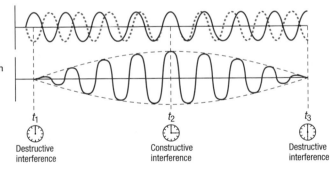

t_1
Destructive interference

t_2
Constructive interference

t_3
Destructive interference

Why It Matters

Color by Interference Other examples of color in nature may be attributed to light interference rather than colored pigments. Ask students to give examples of where they have seen colors similar to those in soap bubbles. These colors are typically jewel-like colors that we associate with the term *iridescent.* Students may think of thin oil slicks they see after a rain or the colors of liquid-crystal thermometers that you press to the forehead. The colors on the wings of butterflies and moths and the colors of many beetles' shells are produced by interference. Interference also produces colors in bird feathers, as in the tail of a peacock.

Standing Waves

Suppose you send a wave through a rope tied to a wall at the other end. The wave is reflected from the wall and travels back along the rope. If you continue to send waves down the rope, the waves that you make will interfere with those waves that reflect off the wall and travel back toward you, to form *standing waves*.

A **standing wave** results from interference between a wave and its reflected wave. **>A standing wave causes the medium to vibrate in a stationary pattern that resembles a loop or a series of loops.** Although it appears as if one wave is standing still, in reality two waves are traveling in opposite directions. **Figure 8** shows standing waves that were captured with strobe photography.

Standing waves have nodes and antinodes.

Each loop of a standing wave is separated from the next loop by points that have no vibration, called *nodes*. Nodes lie at the points where the crests of the original waves meet the troughs of the reflected waves. Nodes are points of complete destructive interference. The top wave in **Figure 8** has a node at each end.

Midway between the nodes lie points of maximum vibration, called *antinodes*. Antinodes form where the crests of the original waves line up with the crests of the reflected waves so that complete constructive interference occurs. The top wave in **Figure 8** has a single antinode in the middle.

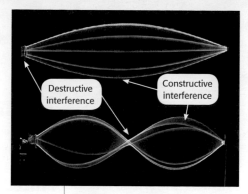

Destructive interference

Constructive interference

Figure 8 These photos of standing waves were captured using a strobe light that flashes different colors at different times. **How many nodes and antinodes does each wave have?**

standing wave (STAN ding WAYV) a pattern of vibration that simulates a wave that is standing still

Answer to caption question
The first wave has two nodes and one antinode. The second wave has three nodes and two antinodes.

>Close

Reteaching Key Ideas

Wave Interactions Table On the board, make a table with three columns and six rows. Fill in the first row with "Wave interaction," "Cause," and "Effect." Fill in the first column with "Reflection," "Refraction," "Diffraction," "Interference," and "Standing waves." Call on different students to fill in the different spaces in the table, indicating what causes each wave interaction and what effect each has on a wave. **LS Logical**

Formative Assessment

Standing waves involve all of the following wave interactions EXCEPT

A. constructive interference. (Incorrect. Constructive interference occurs at the antinodes of a standing wave.)

B. destructive interference. (Incorrect. Destructive interference occurs at the nodes of a standing wave.)

C. diffraction. (Correct. Diffraction is not involved in the formation of standing waves.)

D. reflection. (Incorrect. Reflection happens at the ends of a standing wave. The waves traveling on a string reflect back and forth along the string and combine by interference.)

Section 3 Review

KEY IDEAS

1. **Describe** what may happen when ripples on a pond encounter a large rock in the water.

2. **Explain** why you can hear two people talking even after they walk around a corner.

3. **Name** the conditions required for two waves to interfere constructively.

4. **Name** the conditions required for two waves on a rope to interfere completely destructively.

5. **Explain** why colors appear on the surface of a soap bubble.

6. **Draw** a standing wave, and label the nodes and antinodes.

CRITICAL THINKING

7. **Applying Concepts** Imagine that you and a friend are trying to tune the lowest strings on two different guitars to the same pitch. Explain how you could use beats to determine if the strings are tuned to the same frequency.

8. **Drawing Conclusions** Determine the longest possible wavelength of a standing wave on a string that is 2 m long.

Answers to Section Review

1. The waves will reflect off of the rock.

2. Sound waves diffract when they pass the edge of a barrier, spreading into the medium beyond the barrier.

3. The waves must be in the same place, and the crest of one wave must overlap the crest of the other.

4. The waves must match in amplitude and frequency, and the crests of one wave must exactly overlap the troughs of the other.

5. When light strikes a bubble, some light reflects off the outer surface of the bubble, while other light passes through the thickness of the bubble membrane and reflects off the inner surface. The two sets of reflected waves interfere. Some wavelengths are reinforced while others are canceled, producing colors.

6. Student drawings should show a standing wave with the nodes and antinodes labeled.

7. Decide which guitar will be used as the standard pitch. Pluck the strings of both guitars and listen for beats as the tones fade. Adjust the tension of the string on the second guitar until no beats are heard.

8. The longest possible wavelength is twice the length of the string, 4 m.

Teacher's Notes

Review Section 2 *Characteristics of Waves* with students before beginning this lab.

You may want to prepare the cups before students perform the lab. Have students perform a trial run before doing the actual experiment to make sure the flow of sand from the cup is sufficient.

If students want to change the length of the pendulum, make sure the strings are still tied securely to the ringstand.

Time Required

1 lab period

Ratings

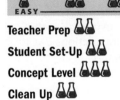

EASY ———————————————→ HARD

Teacher Prep 🧪🧪
Student Set-Up 🧪🧪
Concept Level 🧪🧪🧪
Clean Up 🧪🧪

Skills Acquired

- Collecting data
- Constructing models
- Experimenting
- Identifying/recognizing patterns
- Interpreting
- Measuring
- Organizing and analyzing data
- Predicting

Scientific Methods

In this lab, students will:
- Form a hypothesis
- Analyze the results
- Draw conclusions

Skills Practice

What You'll Do

❯ **Create** sine curves by pulling paper under a sand pendulum.
❯ **Measure** the amplitude, wavelength, and period of transverse waves using sine curves as models.
❯ **Form a hypothesis** about how changes to the experiment may change the amplitude and wavelength of the sine curve.
❯ **Calculate** frequency and wave speed using your measurements.

What You'll Need

cup, paper or plastic-foam
meterstick
small nail
ring stand or other support
sand, colored
stopwatch
string and scissors
tape, masking
white paper, about 30-cm-wide rolls

Safety

Transverse Waves

You can model transverse waves by making a pendulum out of a cup that drops colored sand onto paper. In this lab, you will investigate variations in wave characteristics by making variations in the pendulum.

Procedure

Making Sine Curves with a Sand Pendulum

❶ Review the discussion in Section 2 of this chapter on the use of sine curves to represent transverse waves.

❷ On a blank sheet of paper, prepare a table like the one below.

Sample Data Table: Characteristics of Transverse Waves

Length along paper = 1 m	Time (s)	Average wavelength (m)	Average amplitude (m)
Curve 1			
Curve 2		DO NOT WRITE IN BOOK	
Curve 3			

❸ Use a small nail to poke a small hole in the bottom of a paper or plastic-foam cup. Also punch two holes on opposite sides of the cup near the rim. Tie strings of equal length through the upper holes. Make a pendulum by tying the strings from the cup to a ring stand or other support. Clamp the stand down at the end of a table. Cover the bottom hole with a large piece of tape, then fill the cup with sand.

❹ Unroll some of the paper, and mark off a length of 1 m using a dotted line at each end. Then roll the paper back up, and position the paper under the pendulum.

❺ Remove the tape over the hole. Start the pendulum swinging as your lab partner pulls the paper perpendicular to the cup's swing. Another lab partner should loosely hold the paper roll. Try to pull the paper in a straight line with a constant speed. The sand should trace an approximation of a sine curve, as shown in the photograph.

❻ As your partner pulls the paper under the pendulum, start the stopwatch when the sand trace reaches the first dotted line. When the sand trace reaches the second dotted line (marking the length of 1 m), stop the watch. Record the time in your table.

❼ When you are finished making the curve, stop the pendulum and cover the hole in the bottom of the cup. (You may want to temporarily move the sand to another container before retaping the cup.) Be careful not to jostle the paper; if you do, your trace may be erased. You may want to tape the paper down.

8 For the part of the curve between the dotted lines, measure the distance from the first crest to the last crest, then divide that distance by the total number of crests. Record your answer in the table under "Average wavelength."

9 For the same part of the curve, measure the vertical distance between the first crest and the first trough, between the second crest and the second trough, and so on. Add the distances together, and divide by two. Then, divide by the number of distances you measured. Record your answer in the table under "Average amplitude."

Designing Your Experiment

10 With your lab partners, form a hypothesis about how to make two additional sine curve traces: one with an average wavelength different from that of the first trace, and one with an average amplitude different from that of the first trace.

11 In your lab report, write down your plan for changing these two factors. Before you carry out your experiment, your teacher must approve your plan.

Performing Your Experiment

12 After your teacher approves your plan, carry out your experiment. For each curve, measure and record the time, the average wavelength, and the average amplitude.

13 After each trace, return the sand to the cup and roll the paper back up.

Analysis

1. Analyzing Data For each of your three curves, calculate the average speed at which the paper was pulled by dividing the length of 1 m by the time measurement. This is equivalent to the speed of the wave that the curve models or represents.

2. Analyzing Data For each curve, use the wave speed equation to calculate average frequency.

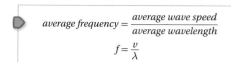

$$average\ frequency = \frac{average\ wave\ speed}{average\ wavelength}$$
$$f = \frac{v}{\lambda}$$

Communicating Your Results

3. Drawing Conclusions What factor did you change to alter the average wavelength of the curve? Did your plan work? If so, did the wavelength increase or decrease?

4. Drawing Conclusions What factor did you change to alter the average amplitude? Did your plan work?

Extension

To determine the period of each of the wave traces you made, divide the time by the number of wavelengths in one meter. Then determine the frequency of each wave. **Hint:** What is the relationship between period and frequency?

Answer to Extension

To calculate the period, first divide 1 m by the wavelength to find the number of wavelengths per meter, then divide the time elapsed in seconds by the number of wavelengths. The frequency is the inverse of the period and is found by dividing 1 by the period.

Answers to Analysis

1. Students should calculate the average speed of the paper by dividing the length measurement by the time measurement.

2. Students should use the wave speed equation to calculate the average frequency. Another way to calculate frequency is to count the number of times the cup swings back and forth during a 10 s interval. Divide the number of swings by 10 to calculate the average period of the pendulum. Then use the frequency-period equation to calculate the frequency of the wave.

   The frequency will be close to the same in every case, unless the length of the pendulum was changed. (A pendulum of given length has a more or less fixed period. Increasing the length increases the period.)

Answers to Communicating Your Results

3. To make a curve with a different average wavelength, students should have pulled the paper at a different average speed and/or have changed the frequency of the pendulum (by altering the length of the pendulum).

4. To make a curve with a different average amplitude, students should have changed the initial displacement of the pendulum (so it swings through a smaller or larger arc).

Key Resources

 Virtual Investigation

 Classroom Lab Video/DVD

 Holt Lab Generator CD-ROM
Search for any lab by type, standard, difficulty level, or time. Edit any lab to fit your needs, or create your own labs. Use the Lab Materials QuickList software to customize your lab materials list.

 **Differentiated Datasheets**
Transverse Waves

 **Observation Lab**
Creating and Measuring Standing Waves

 **CBL™ Probeware Lab**
Tuning a Musical Instrument

Graphing Waves

Graphing

Graphing › Skills

Understanding Graphs To help students understand the graphs, draw three or four transverse waves on the board, each showing a wave at different moments. Indicate that each graph is like a snapshot of the wave taken at different times. Point out that if the graphs could be stacked, the time axis would be at a right angle to the chalkboard.

Answers to Practice

1. a line graph
2. time; distance
3. amplitude and period; amplitude and wavelength
4. $T = 0.02$ s, amplitude $= 5$ cm, $\lambda = 40$ cm
5. $f = 5 \times 10^1$ Hz; $v = 2.00 \times 10^3$ cm/s $= 20.0$ m/s
6. One graph describes the change in the wave with time, while the other describes its motion through the medium. The first graph depicts how a single point on the wave ($x =$ constant) changes its transverse position with time; the second graph depicts how the motion of the wave in the x-direction appears at a single moment ($t =$ constant).
7. The amplitude of this graph is 3.00 cm, and its wavelength is 2.5 cm.

Problem

The graphs below show the behavior of a single transverse wave. Study the graphs, and answer the following questions.

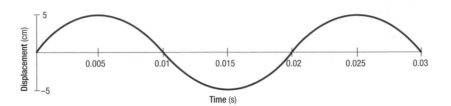

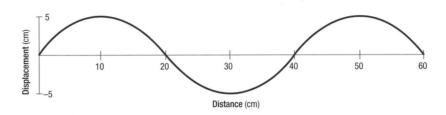

Practice

Use the graphs to answer questions 1–6.

1. What type of graph are the graphs shown here?
2. What variable is described in the x-axis of the first graph? What variable is described in the x-axis of the second graph?
3. What information about the wave is indicated by the first graph? What information is indicated by the second graph?
4. Determine from the graphs the period, the amplitude, and the wavelength of the wave.
5. Using the frequency-period equation, calculate the frequency of the wave. Use the wave speed equation to calculate the speed of the wave.
6. Why are both graphs needed to provide complete information about the wave?

Use the data table to complete question 7.

7. Plot the data given in the table shown here. From the graph, calculate the wavelength and the amplitude of the wave.

x-axis (cm)	y-axis (cm)
0	0.93
0.25	2.43
0.50	3.00
0.75	2.43
1.00	0.93
1.25	−0.93
1.50	−2.43
1.75	−3.00
2.00	−2.43
2.25	−0.93
2.50	0.93
2.75	2.43
3.00	3.00

go.hrw.com
SUPER SUMMARY
KEYWORD: HK8WAVS

SUMMARY

SUPER SUMMARY

Have students connect the major concepts in this chapter through an interactive Super Summary. Visit **go.hrw.com** and type in the keyword **HK8WAVS** to access the Super Summary for this chapter.

Key Ideas

Section 1 Types of Waves

> **What Is a Wave?** A wave is a disturbance that carries energy through matter or space. (p. 505)

> **Vibrations and Waves** Most waves are caused by vibrating objects. (p. 508)

> **Transverse and Longitudinal Waves** A transverse wave is a wave in which the wave motion is perpendicular to the particle motion. A longitudinal wave is a wave in which the wave motion is parallel to the particle motion. (p. 511)

> **Surface Waves** The particles in a surface wave move both perpendicularly and parallel to the direction in which the wave travels. (p. 513)

Section 2 Characteristics of Waves

> **Waves Properties** Wave properties include amplitude, wavelength (λ), period (T), and frequency (f). (p. 514)

> **Wave Speed** The speed of a wave is equal to wavelength divided by period, or to frequency multiplied by wavelength: $v = \lambda/T = f \times \lambda$. (p. 518)

> **The Doppler Effect** Motion between the source of waves and the observer creates a change in observed frequency. (p. 522)

Section 3 Wave Interactions

> **Reflection, Diffraction, and Refraction** When a wave meets a surface or a boundary, the wave bounces back. When a wave passes the edge of an object or passes through an opening, the wave bends. A wave also bends when it passes from one medium to another at an angle. (p. 524)

> **Interference** When several waves are in the same location, they combine to produce a single wave that is different from the original waves. (p. 526)

> **Standing Waves** A standing wave causes the medium to vibrate in a stationary pattern that resembles a loop or a series of loops. (p. 529)

Key Terms

medium, p. 506
mechanical wave, p. 506
electromagnetic wave, p. 506
transverse wave, p. 511
longitudinal wave, p. 512
crest, p. 512
trough, p. 512

amplitude, p. 514
wavelength, p. 515
period, p. 516
frequency, p. 516
Doppler effect, p. 523

reflection, p. 524
diffraction, p. 525
refraction, p. 526
interference, p. 526
constructive interference, p. 527
destructive interference, p. 527
standing wave, p. 529

Differentiated Instruction

Alternative Assessment

Making Waves Give pairs of students a coiled spring toy and have each pair sit 1 to 2 m apart on the floor with the toy stretched between the two students. Ask students to use the springs to show the following things: transverse waves, longitudinal waves, changes in wavelengths, changes in amplitudes, changes in frequencies, reflection, interference, and standing waves. After students have worked out each task, invite student pairs to take turns demonstrating the tasks to the class.
LS Interpersonal/Kinesthetic

Key Resources

- **Interactive Concept Map**

- **Review Resources**
  Concept Review Worksheets

- **Assessment Resources**
  Chapter Tests A and B
  Performance-Based Assessment

Reading Tool Box

1. Answers may vary. Sample answer: *flect* is from the Latin verb *flectere,* which means "to bend." When a wave reflects off a surface, its path is bent. Other words that contain this root include *deflect, flex, flexible, inflection,* and *reflex.*

Using Key Terms

2. The amplitude of a wave is half the vertical distance between the crest and the trough.

3. Waves bend due to refraction when they pass from one medium to another. Waves bend due to diffraction when they pass an edge or an opening.

4. Beats occur when sound waves from different sources vibrate at different frequencies. When compressions in the two waves arrive at a listener's ear at the same time, constructive interference occurs, creating a loud beat. When the compression from one wave and the rarefaction from the other arrive together, destructive interference occurs, and a soft beat is heard. When no beats are heard, the waves are vibrating at the same frequency.

5. Mechanical waves involve the movement of matter. Electromagnetic waves do not require a material medium.

6. To cause a longitudinal wave in a rod, you would strike the end of the rod, along the axis of the rod. To cause a transverse wave, you would strike the rod at right angles to its axis.

7.

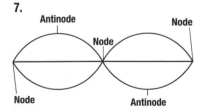

Understanding Key Ideas

8. c
9. a
10. c
11. c
12. c
13. d

READING TOOLBOX

1. **Root Words** The word *reflection* contains the root *flect.* Use a dictionary to find the origin and meaning of this root, and explain why it is appropriate that the word *reflection* contains this root. Then, list at least three other words that contain the root.

USING KEY TERMS

2. How would you describe the *amplitude* of a wave using the words *crest* and *trough*?

3. Explain the difference between waves bending due to *refraction* and *diffraction*.

4. How do beats help determine whether two sound waves are of the same *frequency*? Use the terms *constructive interference* and *destructive interference* in your answer.

5. How is an *electromagnetic wave* different from a *mechanical wave*?

6. You have a long metal rod and a hammer. How would you hit the metal rod to create a *longitudinal wave*? How would you hit it to create a *transverse wave*?

7. Draw a picture of a *standing wave,* and label a *node* and an *antinode*.

UNDERSTANDING KEY IDEAS

8. A wave is a disturbance that transmits
   a. matter.
   b. particles.
   c. energy.
   d. a medium.

9. The speed of a wave depends on the
   a. medium.
   b. frequency.
   c. amplitude.
   d. wavelength.

10. Most waves are caused by
    a. velocity.
    b. amplitude.
    c. a vibration.
    d. earthquakes.

11. A sound wave is an example of
    a. an electromagnetic wave.
    b. a transverse wave.
    c. a longitudinal wave.
    d. a surface wave.

12. In an ocean wave, the molecules of water
    a. move perpendicularly to the direction of wave travel.
    b. move parallel to the direction of wave travel.
    c. move in ellipses.
    d. don't move at all.

13. Half the vertical distance between the crest and the trough of a wave is called the
    a. frequency.
    b. crest.
    c. wavelength.
    d. amplitude.

14. The number of waves passing a given point per unit of time is called the
    a. frequency.
    b. wave speed.
    c. wavelength.
    d. amplitude.

15. The combining of waves as they meet is known as
    a. a crest.
    b. noise.
    c. interference.
    d. the Doppler effect.

16. The Greek letter λ is often used to represent a wave's
    a. period.
    b. wavelength.
    c. frequency.
    d. amplitude.

EXPLAINING KEY IDEAS

17. Imagine you are shaking the end of a rope to create a series of waves. What will you observe if you begin shaking the rope more quickly?

18. Describe the changes in elastic potential energy and kinetic energy that occur when a mass vibrates on a spring.

19. Use the kinetic theory to explain the difference in wave speed in solids, liquids, and gases.

CRITICAL THINKING

20. **Making Inferences** A friend standing 2 m away strikes two tuning forks—one at a frequency of 256 Hz and the other at 240 Hz—at the same time. Which sound will reach your ear first? Explain your answer.

21. **Analyzing Relationships** When you are watching a baseball game, you may hear the crack of the bat a short time after you see the batter hit the ball. Why does this happen? (**Hint:** Consider the relationship between the speed of sound and the speed of light.)

22. **Applying Concepts** You are standing on a street corner, and you hear a fire truck approaching. As the fire truck gets closer to you, does the pitch of the siren increase, decrease, or stay constant? Explain.

23. **Drawing Conclusions** If you yell or clap your hands while standing at the edge of a large rock canyon, you may hear an echo a few seconds later. Explain why this happens.

24. **Applying Concepts** A piano tuner listens to a tuning fork vibrating at 440 Hz to tune a string of a piano. He hears beats between the tuning fork and the piano string. Is the string in tune? Explain your answer.

25. **Making Observations** Describe how you interact with waves during a typical school day. Document the types of waves you encounter. Document also how often you interact with each type of wave. Decide whether some types of waves are more important in your life than others.

26. **Evaluating Information** A new car is advertised as having antinoise technology. The manufacturer claims that inside the car any sounds are negated. Evaluate the possibility of such a claim. What would have to be created to cause destructive interference with any sound in the car? Do you believe that the manufacturer's claim is correct?

Graphing Skills

27. **Making Graphs** Draw a sine curve, and label its crest, trough, and amplitude.

28. **Interpreting Graphs** The wave shown in the figure below has a frequency of 25.0 Hz. Find the following values for this wave:
    a. amplitude   c. speed
    b. wavelength   d. period

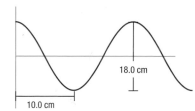

10.0 cm
18.0 cm

29. **Interpreting Graphs** For each image below, draw the wave that results from interference between the two waves.

a.   b.

Math Skills

30. **Wave Speed** Ocean waves are hitting a beach at a rate of 2.0 Hz. The distance between wave crests is 1.5 m. Calculate the speed of the waves.

31. **Wavelength** The frequencies of radio waves range from approximately 3.00×10^5 Hz to 3.00×10^7 Hz. What is the range of wavelengths of these waves? Use 3.00×10^8 m/s as the speed of electromagnetic waves.

32. **Frequency** The note A above middle C on a piano emits a sound wave with wavelength 0.7750 m. What is the frequency of the wave? Use 341.0 m/s as the speed of sound in air.

Explaining Key Ideas

17. If the rope is shaken more quickly, the wave speed will remain constant; the frequency will increase; and the wavelength will decrease.

18. When a mass is pulled away from its resting place, the mass-spring system will gain elastic potential energy. As the spring moves back to its original position, the elastic potential energy changes to kinetic energy, and the mass moves beyond its original resting place. At the top of its motion, the mass loses its kinetic energy but gains elastic potential energy and gravitational potential energy. The mass moves downward again, and the cycle repeats.

19. Kinetic theory states that different states of matter are due to different degrees of organization at the particle level. Since molecules are far apart in gases, one molecule must travel through a lot of empty space before it bumps into another molecule, and thus waves travel relatively slowly in gases. In liquids, molecules are closer together so that vibrations are transferred more quickly than they are in gases, and wave speed increases. Waves speed is fastest in solids, where molecules are close together and bound to one another.

Critical Thinking

20. Both sounds will reach your ear at the same time. The speed of sound in a given medium is constant.

21. You see the bat strike the ball before you hear the crack of the bat because the speed of light is much faster than the speed of sound. The light from the bat reaches your eyes almost instantly, but the sound takes a discernible, although small, time to reach your ears.

Assignment Guide	
SECTION	**ITEMS**
1	5, 8, 10–12, 18, 25
2	2, 6, 9, 13–14, 16–17, 19–22, 27–28, 30–32
3	1, 3–4, 7, 15, 23–24, 26, 29

22. As a fire truck approaches, the pitch of the siren is higher than it would be if the fire truck were at rest. However, the pitch of the truck does not change noticeably until the fire truck is passing right in front of you, when the pitch rapidly drops. In fact, as the truck approaches, the pitch from the siren is always dropping to some degree because you are standing at the side of the road.

23. You hear an echo because the sound waves you produced by clapping or shouting have reflected off the walls of the canyon and returned to your ears.

Answers continued on p. 537A

Standardized Test Prep

 TEST DOCTOR

Question 1 Answer C is correct. To find the correct answer, students must divide the wavelength of 7.5 m by the period of 5 seconds to find the speed of the waves.

Question 2 Answer F is correct. Students may answer G if they had not correctly visualized the waves described in the question. Answers H and I indicate that students may not understand the mechanics of two interfering waves being added to form a resulting wave.

Question 3 Answer B is correct. Students may answer A if they divided the wavelength by the wave's height. Students may answer C if they found half the wavelength instead of half the wave's height. Students may answer D if they used the difference between the wavelength and the wave's height.

Question 4 Taking the inverse of the frequency to find the period gives the correct answer, which is 1×10^{-9} seconds per cycle.

Question 5 Full-credit answers should include the following points:
• The pitch the motorcyclist hears is higher.
• The pitch rises due to the Doppler effect.
If students say the pitch is lower, then they probably misunderstand the relation between motion and sound waves that results in the Doppler effect.

Question 6 Full-credit answers should include the following points:
• The particles in a solid are closer together and more tightly bound to one another than in a a liquid or gas.
• Waves propagate faster through a solid medium.

Question 7 Answer F is correct. Students may answer G if they were confusing Doppler radar with the Doppler effect. Students may answer H if they thought the Doppler effect was tied to acceleration or may answer I if they did not realize that light travels at a constant speed.

Understanding Concepts

Directions (1–3): **For each question, write on a sheet of paper the letter of the correct answer.**

1. A wave pool at a water amusement park has a machine at one end that generates regular waves that are 7.5 m long. At the other end, waves crest over the side every 5 s. How fast are the waves traveling?
   - **A.** 0.2 m/s
   - **B.** 0.67 m/s
   - **C.** 1.5 m/s
   - **D.** 37.5 m/s

2. Two waves that have exactly the same wavelength, frequency, and amplitude are occupying the same space. If the second wave follows exactly half a wavelength behind the first, what is true of the resulting wave?
   - **F.** The resulting wave has zero amplitude.
   - **G.** The resulting wave has twice the amplitude of the original waves.
   - **H.** The resulting wave has zero wavelength.
   - **I.** The resulting wave has a wavelength twice as long as the original waves.

3. A sine wave measures 12 cm from the top of the crest to the bottom of the trough, and 30 cm from the top of one crest to the top of the next. What is the amplitude of the wave?
   - **A.** 2.5 cm
   - **B.** 6 cm
   - **C.** 15 cm
   - **D.** 18 cm

Directions (4–6): **For each question, write a short response.**

4. Many home computers have a frequency of over 1 GHz, meaning 1×10^9 cycles per second. What is the period of a 1 GHz computer?

5. A motorcyclist approaches an outdoor concert. How does the pitch that the motorcyclist hears from the concert differ from the pitch that a stationary listener at the concert hears?

6. Why do waves tend to travel faster through a solid medium than through a liquid or a gas?

Reading Skills

Directions (7–8): **Read the passage below. Then answer the questions that follow.**

THE DOPPLER EFFECT IN SPACE

The Doppler effect is defined as a change in the wavelength (or frequency) of waves, as a result of motion of either the source or the receiver of the waves. If the source of the waves and the receiver are approaching each other (because of the motion of either or both), the frequency of the waves will increase and the wavelength will be shortened. As a result, sounds will become higher pitched and light will appear bluer. If the sender and receiver are moving apart, sounds will become lower pitched and light will appear redder.

In astronomy, the Doppler effect is used to measure the velocity and rotation of stars and galaxies. Both blue shifts and red shifts are observed for various objects, indicating relative motion both toward and away from Earth. The Doppler effect also explains the red shifts of distant galaxies. These shifts indicate that distant galaxies are moving away from us and from each other.

7. If light from a celestial object is observed to shift towards the blue end of the spectrum, what conclusion can be drawn?
   - **F.** The object is moving toward Earth.
   - **G.** The object is reflecting radio waves emanating from the Earth.
   - **H.** The velocity of the object is increasing.
   - **I.** The velocity of the light emanating from the object is decreasing.

8. If two trains are moving down the same track, in the same direction and at the same speed, and the train in front blows its whistle, will the passengers in the rear of the second train experience the Doppler effect? Why or why not?

Question 8 Full-credit answers should include the following points:
• The two trains are traveling with the same velocity, so they are not moving in relation to each other.
• The passengers on the rear train will not experience the Doppler effect when the first train blows it whistle.

Question 9 Answer A is correct. To answer this question correctly, students must note that the two interfering waves are in phase so no destructive interference will happen.

Question 10 Answer G is correct. Other answers indicate that students are not properly visualizing the wave addition.

Question 11 All of them have the same wavelength. If students answer *frequency* or *period*, they may mistakenly believe that the *x*-axis denotes time instead of distance.

Question 12 Answer C is correct. At some places along the *x*-axis, the amplitudes of the waves are both positive or both negative, resulting in constructive interference; at some places, the amplitude of one wave is positive and the other negative, resulting in destructive interference.

Interpreting Graphics

The following two graphs each describe two waves and the resultant wave that occurs when the original two waves interfere with each other. Use these graphs to answer questions 9–11.

Graph A

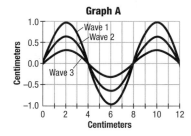

Graph B

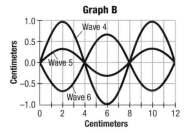

9. In Graph A, "Wave 1" is the resultant wave. What type of interference is shown in Graph A?

   A. constructive
   B. partial destructive
   C. complete destructive
   D. constructive and destructive

10. In Graph B, which wave is the resultant wave?

   F. Wave 4
   G. Wave 5
   H. Wave 6
   I. This cannot be determined.

11. What characteristic do all six of these waves have in common?

The following graph describes two waves. Use this graph to answer questions 12–13.

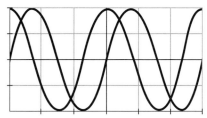

12. If these waves interfere with each other, what will result?

   A. constructive interference
   B. destructive interference
   C. constructive interference in some places and destructive interference in others
   D. neither constructive nor destructive interference

13. The two waves have identical amplitudes. What else would they have in common if the x-axis were in units of time? What else would they have in common if the x-axis were in units of distance?

Test Tip

Take a few minutes at the end of the test period to review your answers.

Question 13 Full-credit answers should include the following points:
- If the x-axis referred to time, the waves would have the same period and frequency.
- If the x-axis referred to distance, the waves would have the same wavelength.

State Resources

For specific resources for your state, visit **go.hrw.com** and type in the keyword **HSHSTR**.

Test Practice with Guided Reading Development

Answers

  1. C
  2. F
  3. B
  4. 1×10^{-9} seconds per cycle.
  5. Answers may vary; see Test Doctor for a detailed scoring rubric.
  6. Answers may vary; see Test Doctor for a detailed scoring rubric.
  7. F
  8. Answers may vary; see Test Doctor for a detailed scoring rubric.
  9. A
  10. G
  11. All have the same wavelength.
  12. C
  13. Answers may vary; see Test Doctor for a detailed scoring rubric.

Continuation of Answers

Answers continued from p. 513

7. Answers may vary. Students should cite any instance in which waves move objects from their positions. Examples include tsunamis, beach erosion during storms, and waves destroying waterfront buildings in a hurricane.

8. Sample answer: This is not a real wave because energy is not transmitted from one person to the next; the people stand up and down on their own.

9. Light does not require a medium through which to travel, so it is transmitted through space. Sound, however, requires a medium, so it cannot be transmitted through space.

Answers continued from p. 535

24. If beats are heard, the string is not in tune. The string and the tuning fork vibrate at slightly different frequencies. As a result, the two sounds interfere constructively and destructively in succession. These successive reinforcements and cancellations are heard as beats. When the frequencies are exactly equal, no beats are heard.

25. Students will probably think of sound waves, visible light waves, and maybe water waves. Encourage them to look at the entire electromagnetic spectrum, including infrared light, microwaves, and radio waves.

26. Ask students to consider how they would listen to music if the antinoise device canceled all interior noise. They should consider the effect of such cancellation on safety. Students may be interested in exploring the current status of these devices and which cars have them. The technology is called Active Noise Reduction (ANR).

Graphing Skills

27.

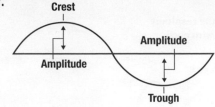

28. a. 9 cm = 0.09 m

b. 20.0 cm = 0.200 m

c. $v = f \times \lambda$
$v = (25.0 \text{ Hz}) \times (0.200 \text{ m})$
$v = 5.00$ m/s

d. $T = 1/f = 1/25.0$ Hz
$T = 0.0400$ s

29. Left: Drawings should have three crests (high points) and two troughs (low points) and be twice as large (tall) as the waves shown.
Right: Drawings should show a straight line (the waves completely cancel each other).

Math Skills

30. $v = f \times \lambda$
$v = (2.0 \text{ Hz}) \times (1.5 \text{ m})$
$v = 3.0$ m/s

31. $\lambda = v/f = (3.00 \times 10^8 \text{ m/s})/$
$(3.00 \times 10^5 \text{ Hz}) = 1.00 \times 10^3$ m

$\lambda = v/f = (3.00 \times 10^8 \text{ m/s})/$
$(3.00 \times 10^7 \text{ Hz}) = 1.00 \times 10^1$ m

λ range $= 1.00 \times 10^1$ m to 1.00×10^3 m

32. $f = v/\lambda = (341.0 \text{ m/s})/$
$(0.7750 \text{ m}) = 440.0$ Hz

Why It **Matters**

Physics Connections Be sure students realize that the arrows show broad connections between events, but do not indicate direct cause-and-effect relationships.

Famous scientists are shaped by and help to shape the world around them. The examples below will help students to connect scientists to the social and political events of the time in which they lived.

Benjamin Franklin was involved in the writing of the Declaration of Independence and the United States Constitution. He was also very interested in improving his community. He was a printer by trade and published the *Pennsylvania Gazette* and *Poor Richard's Almanack*. In 1731, he founded a public library in Philadelphia that allowed people to borrow books; this idea was rare at the time. He also founded the first volunteer firefighting company in the United States—The Union Fire Company.

Thomas Edison invented many devices other than the incandescent light bulb, such as the phonograph and the motion picture camera. These inventions helped to shape the ways we entertain ourselves today.

Before becoming President, Dwight D. Eisenhower was a Supreme Commander of the Allies in Europe during World War II.

Why It **Matters**

Physics Connections

Science, technology, and society are closely linked. The web below shows just a few of the connections in the history of physics.

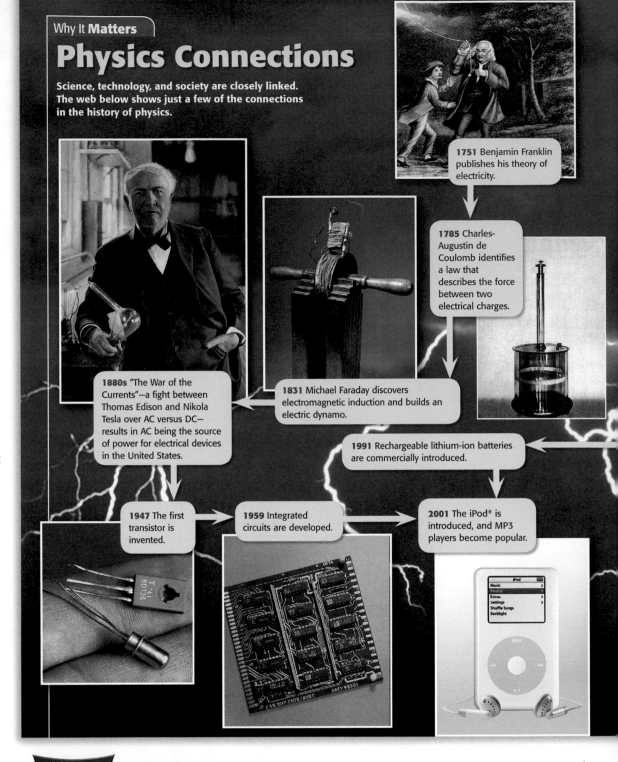

1751 Benjamin Franklin publishes his theory of electricity.

1785 Charles-Augustin de Coulomb identifies a law that describes the force between two electrical charges.

1880s "The War of the Currents"—a fight between Thomas Edison and Nikola Tesla over AC versus DC—results in AC being the source of power for electrical devices in the United States.

1831 Michael Faraday discovers electromagnetic induction and builds an electric dynamo.

1991 Rechargeable lithium-ion batteries are commercially introduced.

1947 The first transistor is invented.

1959 Integrated circuits are developed.

2001 The iPod® is introduced, and MP3 players become popular.

READING TOOLBOX

Visual Literacy Coulomb used a torsion balance like the one shown here to demonstrate his inverse square law of electric force. Inside the balance, two small spheres are fixed to the ends of a light horizontal rod. One sphere is charged and then brought near another charged object. The electric force between the two objects causes the rod to rotate. The angle of rotation provides a quantitative measure of the electric force.

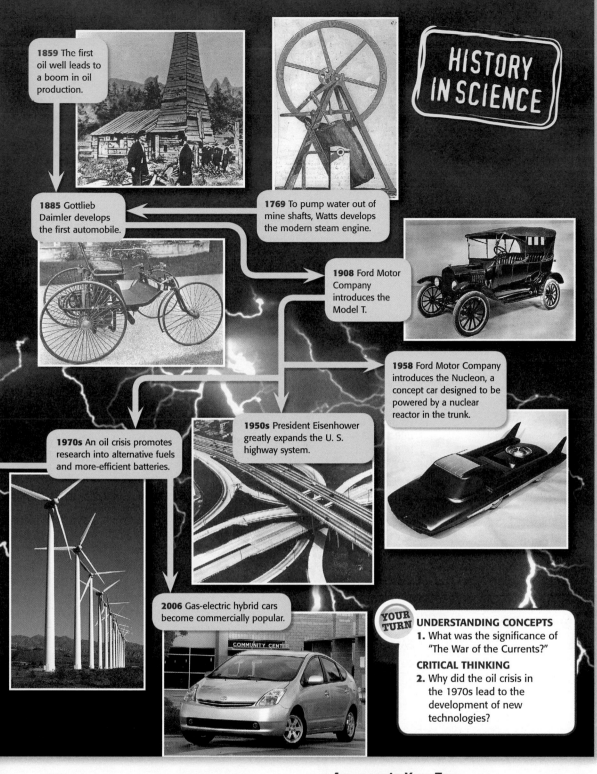

1859 The first oil well leads to a boom in oil production.

1769 To pump water out of mine shafts, Watts develops the modern steam engine.

1885 Gottlieb Daimler develops the first automobile.

HISTORY IN SCIENCE

1908 Ford Motor Company introduces the Model T.

1958 Ford Motor Company introduces the Nucleon, a concept car designed to be powered by a nuclear reactor in the trunk.

1950s President Eisenhower greatly expands the U. S. highway system.

1970s An oil crisis promotes research into alternative fuels and more-efficient batteries.

2006 Gas-electric hybrid cars become commercially popular.

YOUR TURN

UNDERSTANDING CONCEPTS
1. What was the significance of "The War of the Currents?"

CRITICAL THINKING
2. Why did the oil crisis in the 1970s lead to the development of new technologies?

Why It Matters

Transistors The size of the first mass-produced transistor was about 1.25 cm. These transistors were made from the semiconductor germanium, not silicon. In 1954, about 1 million of these transistors were produced. They were used in hearing aids and in transistor radios.

Integrated circuits connect transistors and other electronic components on the same piece of semiconductor crystal. Jack Kilby won the Nobel Prize in Physics in 2000 for his involvement in the invention of the integrated circuit.

A microprocessor is a type of integrated circuit. In 1971, the first microprocessor contained a little more than 2,000 transistors. In 2006, one microprocessor in a desktop computer could contain nearly 300 million transistors—almost 300 times as many transistors as were produced in 1954. The transistors on modern microprocessors are so small that about 10 million of them could fit in an area of 1 mm^2.

Why It Matters

The Ford Nucleon A concept car is a prototype car that is designed to showcase a new style or technology. The Nucleon, a 3/8 scale model, was developed during the beginning of the atomic age. Many concept cars (including the Nucleon) are never actually manufactured or produced. A model of the Nucleon can be seen at the Henry Ford Museum in Detroit, Michigan.

Answers to Your Turn

1. Sample answer: "The War of the Currents" resulted in AC current being used as the main type of current that delivers power in the United States. So, when I plug a device into a wall socket, it is powered by AC current.
2. The oil crisis made oil scarcer and increased the price of oil. As a result, cheaper fuels were desirable.

CHAPTER PLANNER 16 Sound and Light

		Standards	Teach Key Ideas

CHAPTER OPENER, pp. 540–542 — 50 min.

SECTION 1 Sound, pp. 543–551 — 50 min.
> Properties of Sound
> Musical Instruments
> Hearing and the Ear
> Ultrasound and Sonar

Standards: PS 2e, PS 6a, UCP 1, UCP 5, SAI 1, ST 2

Teach Key Ideas:
- Bellringer Transparency
- Teaching Transparency P15 The Ear
- Visual Concepts Speed of Sound • Sound Intensity and Decibel Level • Pitch

SECTION 2 The Nature of Light, pp. 552–559 — 50 min.
> Waves and Particles
> The Electromagnetic Spectrum

Standards: PS 6a, PS 6b, UCP 1, UCP 2, UCP 3, SAI 2, ST 2, HNS 1, HNS 2, HNS 3

Teach Key Ideas:
- Bellringer Transparency
- Teaching Transparencies TM44 Wave Frequency and Photon Energy • E18 Electromagnetic Spectrum
- Visual Concepts The Dual Nature of Light • Energy of a Photon • Electromagnetic Spectrum

SECTION 3 Reflection and Color, pp. 560–565 — 50 min.
> Reflection of Light
> Mirrors
> Seeing Colors

Standards: UCP 1, UCP 2, SAI 1

Teach Key Ideas:
- Bellringer Transparency
- Teaching Transparencies TM45 Law of Reflection • TM46 Flat Mirror
- Visual Concepts Reflection • Law of Reflection • Comparing Real and Virtual Images • Additive Color Mixing

SECTION 4 Refraction, Lenses, and Prisms, pp. 566–573 — 50 min.
> Refraction of Light
> Lenses
> Dispersion and Prisms

Standards: UCP 1, UCP 5, SAI 1, ST 2

Teach Key Ideas:
- Bellringer Transparency
- Teaching Transparencies P16 Refraction • P17 The Eye
- Visual Concepts Refraction • Dispersion of Light • Converging and Diverging Lenses • Parts of the Human Eye

See also PowerPoint® Resources

Chapter Review and Assessment Resources

- **SE** Science Skills: Using Fractions, p. 576
- **SE** Chapter Summary, p. 577
- **SE** Chapter Review, pp. 578–579
- **SE** Standardized Test Prep, pp. 580–581
- Concept Review Worksheets ■
- Chapter Tests A and B ■
- Holt Online Assessment

CHAPTER Fast Track To shorten instruction because of time limitations, omit Section 3 and the chapter lab.

Basic Learners
- **TE** Speeds of Sound, p. 544
- **TE** Sound Levels, p. 545
- **TE** Law of Reflection, p. 563
- Science Skills Worksheets
- Differentiated Datasheets A for Labs and Activities ■
- Study Guide A ■

Advanced Learners
- **TE** Music and Math, p. 547
- **TE** Benefits and Drawbacks of Cell Phones, p. 559
- **TE** Mirror Height, p. 562
- **TE** Index of Refraction, p. 567
- **TE** Vision Problems, p. 569
- Cross-Disciplinary Worksheets
- Differentiated Datasheets C for Labs and Activities ■

Key

SE Student Edition
TE Teacher's Edition

📁 Chapter Resource File
📓 Workbook
🖨 Transparency

💿 CD or CD-ROM
* Datasheet or blackline master available

■ Also available in Spanish

All resources listed below are also available on the Teacher's One-Stop Planner.

Why It Matters	Hands-On	Skills Development	Assessment
Build student motivation with resources about high-interest applications.	**SE Inquiry Lab** Colors in White Light, p. 541* ■	**TE Reading Toolbox** Assessing Prior Knowledge, p. 540 **SE Reading Toolbox** p. 542	📁 **Pretest** ■
TE Elephant Sounds, p. 546 **TE Cochlear Implants,** p. 549 **SE What Are Sonograms?** p. 550	**TE Demonstration** Loudness and Pitch, p. 543 **SE Quick Lab** Sound in Different Mediums, p. 544* ■ **SE Quick Lab** Frequency and Pitch, p. 547* ■ **SE Inquiry Lab** How Can You Amplify the Sound of a Tuning Fork? p. 548* ■ **TE Demonstration** Showing Waves with a Stroboscope, p. 548	**TE Reading Toolbox** Visual Literacy, p. 545 **TE Reading Toolbox** Visual Literacy, p. 546 **SE Reading Toolbox** Mnemonics, p. 549 **TE Reading Toolbox** Visual Literacy, p. 550	**TE Reteaching Key Ideas** Retracing the Process of Sound and Hearing, p. 551 **TE Formative Assessment,** p. 551 📁 **Spanish Assessment*** ■ 📁 **Section Quiz** ■
TE The Radio Spectrum, p. 556 **SE How Do Cell Phones Work?** p. 559 📁 **Cross-Disciplinary Worksheet** Real World Applications—How Does Sunscreen Work?	**TE Demonstration** Two-Slit Experiment, p. 552	**TE Reading Toolbox** Visual Literacy, p. 553 **SE Reading Toolbox** Booklet, p. 554 **TE Reading Toolbox** Visual Literacy, p. 554	**TE Reteaching Key Ideas** Comparing Models, p. 558 **TE Formative Assessment,** p. 558 📁 **Spanish Assessment*** ■ 📁 **Section Quiz** ■
📁 **Cross-Disciplinary Worksheet** Integrating Space Science—The Refracting Telescope at Yerkes	**TE Demonstration** Adding Colors, p. 560 **SE Quick Lab** Curved Mirror, p. 563* ■ **SE Quick Lab** Filtering Light, p. 564* ■	**TE Reading Toolbox** Visual Literacy, p. 561 **SE Reading Toolbox** Prefixes, p. 562	**TE Reteaching Key Ideas** What Happens to Light? p. 565 **TE Formative Assessment,** p. 565 📁 **Spanish Assessment*** ■ 📁 **Section Quiz** ■
TE Eyeglass Lenses, p. 568 **SE Detecting Counterfeit Money,** pp. 572–573	**TE Demonstration** Refraction, p. 566 **SE Quick Lab** Water Prism, p. 570* ■ **TE Demonstration** Dispersion, p. 570 **SE Application Lab** Lenses and Images, pp. 574–575* ■	**TE Reading Toolbox** Visual Literacy, p. 567 **TE Reading Toolbox** Visual Literacy, p. 569 **SE Reading Toolbox** Booklet, p. 571 **TE Reading Toolbox** Visual Literacy, p. 573	**TE Reteaching Key Ideas** Reviewing Refraction, p. 571 **TE Formative Assessment,** p. 571 📁 **Spanish Assessment*** ■ 📁 **Section Quiz** ■

See also Lab Generator

See also Holt Online Assessment Resources

Resources for Differentiated Instruction

English Learners
TE Pitch Versus Volume, p. 546
TE Learning Prefixes, p. 555
TE Vocabulary, p. 568
📁 Differentiated Datasheets A, B, and C for Labs and Activities ■
📓 Study Guide A ■

Struggling Readers
TE Summarizing, p. 553
TE Distinguishing Words, p. 563
📓 Interactive Reader

Special Education Students
TE Feeling Vibrations, p. 544
TE Sunscreen and SPF, p. 557

Alternative Assessment
TE Instruments of Other Cultures, p. 547
TE Comparing Frequency and Intensity, p. 548
TE The Newton-Huygens Debate, p. 554
TE Electromagnetic Wave Applications, p. 556
TE Making a Periscope, p. 561
TE Brochure, p. 572
TE Comparing Concepts, p. 577

Overview

This chapter covers sound, including the properties of sound, musical instruments, the human ear, and ultrasound and sonar. Next, it explores the wave and particle properties of light and the electromagnetic spectrum. It also covers the reflection of light, including mirrors, and explains how we see colors. Finally, the chapter covers the refraction of light, including the use of lenses in microscopes, telescopes, and the human eye. The chapter concludes with a discussion of dispersion and prisms.

READING TOOLBOX

Assessing Prior Knowledge Students should understand the following concepts:
• electrons
• structure of atoms
• energy transformation
• types of waves
• relationship of vibrations and waves
• reflection
• diffraction
• interference
• standing waves
• waves and energy

MISCONCEPTION ///ALERT

Science education research has identified the following misconception about sound.
• Students believe that sound cannot travel through solids and liquids, but can travel through a vacuum and space. (To demonstrate that sound travels through solids, ask students to place an ear against their desktop and then tap the desk with their finger. To demonstrate that sound cannot travel through a vacuum, place a wind-up alarm clock inside a sealed jar. Use a vacuum pump to remove the air from the bell jar as the alarm clock rings. Students should hear the sound of the alarm clock fade as a vacuum is formed inside the jar.)

CHAPTER 16 Sound and Light

Chapter Outline

❶ Sound
Properties of Sound
Musical Instruments
Hearing and the Ear
Ultrasound and Sonar

❷ The Nature of Light
Waves and Particles
The Electromagnetic Spectrum

❸ Reflection and Color
Reflection of Light
Mirrors
Seeing Colors

❹ Refraction, Lenses, and Prisms
Refraction of Light
Lenses
Dispersion and Prisms

Why It Matters
The properties of sound and light waves affect how we experience our surroundings. The properties of light can explain both the colors of the car lights and the colors of the road signs on this busy highway system.

Chapter Correlations   *National Science Education Standards*

The following correlations show the National Science Standards that relate to this chapter. For the full text of the standards, see the National Science Education Standards at the front of the book.

PS 2e In solids the structure is nearly rigid; in liquids molecules or atoms move around each other but do not move apart; and in gases molecules or atoms move almost independently of each other and are mostly far apart. (Section 1)

PS 6a Waves, including sound and seismic waves, waves on water, and light waves, have energy and can transfer energy when they interact with matter. (Sections 1, 2)

PS 6b Electromagnetic waves include radio waves (the longest wavelength), microwaves, infrared radiation (radiant heat), visible light, ultraviolet radiation, x-rays, and gamma rays. The energy of electromagnetic waves is carried in packets whose magnitude is inversely proportional to the wavelength. (Section 2)

UCP 1 Systems, order, and organization (Sections 1–4)

UCP 2 Evidence, models, and explanation (Sections 2, 3)

UCP 3 Constancy, change, and measurement (Section 2)

UCP 5 Form and function (Sections 1, 4)

SAI 1 Abilities necessary to do scientific inquiry (Sections 1, 3, 4)

SAI 2 Understandings about scientific inquiry (Section 2)

ST 2 Understandings about science and technology (Sections 1, 2, 4)

HNS 1 Science as a human endeavor (Section 2)

HNS 2 Nature of scientific knowledge (Section 2)

HNS 3 Historical perspectives (Section 2)

InquiryLab ⏱ 20 min

Colors in White Light

Your teacher will give you a **spectroscope** or instructions for making one. Turn on an **incandescent light bulb.** Look at the light bulb through your spectroscope. Write a description of what you see. Then, repeat the procedure with a **fluorescent light bulb.** Again, describe what you see.

Questions to Get You Started

1. Compare your observations of the incandescent light bulb and your observations of the fluorescent light bulb.

2. Both kinds of bulbs produce white light. What did you learn about white light by using the spectroscope?

3. Light from a flame is yellowish but is similar to white light. What do you think you would see if you used a spectroscope to look at light from a flame?

InquiryLab

Teacher's Notes The instructions for making a spectroscope are as follows.

1. Cut a narrow slit in the center of a piece of black construction paper. Tape the paper to one end of a paper-towel tube. The paper should cover the opening of the tube.

2. Look through the open end of the tube at an incandescent light bulb. If no light passes through the slit in the paper, make the slit a little wider.

3. Hold a diffraction grating against the open end of the tube. Look at the light bulb through the grating. Make sure the slit in the paper is vertical.

4. Rotate the diffraction grating until you see colors inside the tube to the left and right sides of the slit. Tape the diffraction grating to the tube in this position.

Materials per Group
- light bulb, incandescent
- light bulb, fluorescent
- spectroscope

Answers

1. When I looked at the incandescent light I saw a continuous spectrum of colors on the sides of the spectroscope tube. When I looked at the fluorescent light I saw a spectrum of colors, but some bands were bright and others were faint.

2. White light is made up of many colors of light.

3. I would expect to see more colors

Key Resources

🗀 **Datasheet**
Colors in White Light

Word Parts

Sample table:

WORD	ROOT	DEFINITION
ultrasound	sound	beyond the range of human hearing (beyond 20 kHz)
ultraviolet	violet	beyond the violet end of the visible spectrum
infrared	red	below the red end of the visible spectrum

Mnemonics

Sample answer: **R**ed **o**striches **y**odel for **g**reat **b**ig **v**ittles.

FoldNotes

Answers may vary. Students' Booklets should look similar to the example shown. The front of the Booklet should be labeled "Sound." The booklet should contain notes about Section 1.

These reading tools can help you learn the material in this chapter. For more information on how to use these and other tools, see **Appendix A.**

Word Parts

Prefixes Analyzing the parts of a science term can help you figure out the meaning of the word. Some word parts and their meanings are listed in **Appendix A.**

Prefixes are used in front of word roots to modify the meaning of the word root. Two prefixes that are used in this chapter are listed below.

- *ultra-* means "beyond" or "extremely"
- *infra-* means "below"

Your Turn As you read this chapter, make a table like the one started below that lists each word that contains the prefix *ultra-* or *infra-*, the root of the word, and the word's definition.

WORDS WITH THE PREFIX *ULTRA-* OR *INFRA-*

WORD	ROOT	DEFINITION
infrasound	sound	sound below the range of human hearing (below 20 Hz)
ultrasound		

Mnemonics

Colors of the Spectrum A mnemonic device can help you remember related words. Although the electromagnetic spectrum is continuous, the colors in the visible part can be divided into six main colors—red, orange, yellow, green, blue, and violet. One way to remember these colors and their order is by using a made-up name, such as the one below, as a mnemonic device.

> **ROY G BiV**

Note that the letter "i" is added so that you can pronounce the last name.

Your Turn Practice saying the name above to help yourself learn and remember the colors of the visible spectrum and the order of the colors. Make up a sentence with words that start with these letters to create another type of mnemonic device.

FoldNotes

Booklet FoldNotes can help you remember ideas that you learn as you read. You can use a booklet to organize the details of a main topic in the chapter.

Your Turn Make a booklet by following the instructions in **Appendix A.**

1. Label the front of the booklet "Sound."
2. Label each of the pages of the booklet with one of the red headings from Section 1.
3. Take notes from Section 1 on the appropriate page of the booklet.

SOUND

```
MISCONCEPTION
///ALERT\\\
```

Colors of the Spectrum Some students may have learned that the spectrum contains seven main colors. Discuss that indigo is no longer considered one of the main colors in the visible spectrum. The seven colors were defined by Sir Isaac Newton, who used a prism to separate the colors in visible light. He defined seven colors to parallel the seven main notes on a musical scale.

Sound

Key Ideas

❯ What are the characteristics of sound waves?

❯ How do musical instruments make sound?

❯ How do ears help humans hear sound waves?

❯ How are the reflections of sound waves used?

Key Terms

sound wave

pitch

infrasound

ultrasound

resonance

sonar

Why It Matters

Sound waves are responsible for much more than the sounds we hear. They are used to create images of the human body that are used in medicine.

SECTION 1

❯Focus

In this section, students relate properties of sound to wave characteristics. The section also covers musical instruments, the human ear, and applications of ultrasound and sonar.

Bellringer

Use the Bellringer transparency to prepare students for this section.

Demonstrate

Loudness and Pitch Borrow a practice piano that you can take to your classroom on rollers. If a piano is not available, use an acoustic guitar or other musical instruments. First, demonstrate differences in loudness using notes of the same pitch. Use a sound level meter to reinforce the judgment of students. Then, demonstrate difference in pitch. Students may be able to see that the lowest string of a guitar vibrates with noticeably lower frequency than the highest string. Having students touch the strings lightly as they vibrate will also help convey this idea. **LS Musical**

When you listen to your favorite musical group, you hear a variety of sounds. Although these sounds come from different sources, they are all longitudinal waves that are produced by vibrating objects. Musical instruments and stereo speakers make sound waves in the air.

Properties of Sound

The head of a drum vibrates up and down when a drummer hits it. Each time the drumhead moves upward, it compresses the air above it. When the head moves back down, it leaves a small region of air that has a lower pressure. A series of compressions and rarefactions is created in the air as the drumhead moves up and down repeatedly, as **Figure 1** shows.

Sound waves, such as those created by a drum, are longitudinal waves caused by vibrations. The particles of air in these waves vibrate in the same direction the waves travel. ❯**Sound waves are caused by vibrations and carry energy through a medium.** All sound waves are made by vibrating objects that cause the surrounding medium to move. In air, the waves spread out in all directions away from the source. When sound waves from the drum reach your ears, the waves cause your eardrums to vibrate.

sound wave (SOWND WAYV) a longitudinal wave that is caused by vibrations and that travels through a material medium

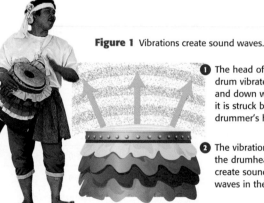

Figure 1 Vibrations create sound waves.

❶ The head of a drum vibrates up and down when it is struck by the drummer's hand.

❷ The vibrations of the drumhead create sound waves in the air.

Key Resources

Teaching Transparency
P15 The Ear

Visual Concepts
Speed of Sound
Sound Intensity and Decibel Level
Pitch

Datasheets
Sound in Different Mediums
Frequency and Pitch
How Can You Amplify the Sound of a
    Tuning Fork?
Echoes and Distance

Science Skills Worksheet
Equations Involving a Constant

Teacher's Notes The utensil should not be one with parts that rattle. Use hard kite string. Students should wrap the string near their fingertips and try to arrange the string so that the last loop before the downward part passes over the ends of their fingers ensuring that the string is pushed against their ears. Heavier objects, such as wrenches and oven racks make the loudest sounds. Try striking with a soft object such as a rubber stopper.

Materials per Group
• spoon or other utensil
• string, 1–2 m

Answers to Analysis
1. The sound that I heard through the string was louder. It was a ringing, bell-like sound.
2. Sound travels better through the string. The sound was louder.
3. The sound waves that reached my ear through the string were more intense than the sound waves that traveled through air. The intensity was due to sound waves traveling faster through solids than gases.

Teaching Key Ideas

Sources of Sound Some students believe that sound can be produced without any materials. Ask students to name examples of sounds, and write them in a column on the board. Have students determine the source of the sound. Write these next to each example. Use these examples to illustrate that all sounds can be traced back to a vibrating source. **LS** **Logical**

QuickLab Sound in Different Mediums ⏱ 10 min

Procedure
❶ Tie a **spoon** or other utensil to the middle of a 1 to 2 m length of **string**.
❷ Wrap the loose ends of the string around your index fingers, and place your fingers against your ears.
❸ Swing the spoon so that it strikes a **tabletop**.

Analysis
1. Compare the volume and quality of the sound received through the string with the volume and quality of the sound received through the air.
2. Does sound travel better through the string or through the air? Explain.
3. Explain your results.

Academic Vocabulary

transmit (trans MIT) to send from one place to another

SCI**LINKS**.
www.scilinks.org
Topic: Properties of Sound
Code: HK81233

The speed of sound depends on the medium.

If you stand near a drummer, you may think that you hear the sound from the drum at the same time that the drummer's hand strikes the drum head. Sound waves travel very fast. The speed of sound in air at room temperature is about 346 m/s.

The speed of a sound wave depends on the temperature and the material through which the wave travels, as **Figure 2** shows. The speed of sound in a medium depends on how quickly the particles <u>transmit</u> the motion of the sound waves. The molecules in a gaseous medium, such as air, are farther apart than the particles in a solid or liquid are, so sound waves travel slower in air. Gas molecules move faster and collide more frequently at high temperatures than at low temperatures, so sound waves travel faster at high temperatures.

In a liquid or solid, the particles are much closer together than in a gas, so the vibrations are transferred more rapidly from one particle to the next. However, some solids, such as rubber, dampen vibrations so that sound does not travel well. Materials like rubber can be used for soundproofing.

Figure 2 Speed of Sound in Various Mediums

Medium	Speed of sound (m/s)	Medium	Speed of sound (m/s)
Gases		**Liquids at 25 °C**	
Air (0 °C)	331	Water	1,490
Air (25 °C)	346	Sea water	1,530
Air (100 °C)	386	**Solids**	
Helium (0 °C)	972	Copper	3,813
Hydrogen (0 °C)	1,290	Iron	5,000
Oxygen (0 °C)	317	Rubber	54

Differentiated Instruction

Special Education Students

Feeling Vibrations Make sure students understand the word *vibration*. Borrow a drum from the band room. Place the drum on its side. Have two or three students hold their hands on the bottom of the drum. Firmly hit the top of the drum several times. Ask students if they can feel the vibrations. Repeat with students' hands at the edge. Ask students if they can feel the hit any more "loudly" when their hands are on the top of the drum. **LS** **Kinesthetic**

Basic Learners

Speeds of Sound Using **Figure 2,** have students rearrange the speed of sound in various materials from fastest to slowest. Ask students what materials could be used for soundproofing the classroom. You may also ask students to explain, in writing, orally, or dictated, why sound waves travel faster in one material than another. **LS** **Logical/Visual**

Loudness is determined by intensity.

How do the sound waves change when you increase the volume on your stereo or television? The *loudness* of a sound depends partly on the energy contained in the sound waves. The *intensity* of a sound wave describes the rate at which a sound wave transmits energy through a given area of a medium. Intensity depends on the amplitude of the sound wave and your distance from the source of the sound. The greater the intensity of a sound is, the louder the sound will seem.

However, a sound that has twice the intensity of another sound does not seem twice as loud. Humans perceive loudness on a logarithmic scale. So, a sound seems twice as loud when its intensity is 10 times the intensity of another sound.

The quietest sound a human can hear is the threshold of hearing. The *relative intensity* of a sound is found by comparing the intensity of a sound with the intensity at the threshold of hearing. Intensity is measured in units called *decibels*, dB. An increase in intensity of 10 dB means a sound seems about twice as loud. A few common sounds and their decibel levels are shown in **Figure 3.**

The quietest sound a human can hear is 0 dB. A sound of 120 dB is at the threshold of pain, so sounds louder than this can hurt your ears and give you headaches. Extensive exposure to sounds above 120 dB can cause permanent deafness.

✓ **Reading Check** What determines the intensity of a sound wave? (See Appendix E for answers to Reading Checks.)

Figure 3 Sound intensity is measured on a logarithmic scale of decibels. **How many times louder than a cat purring will a normal conversation seem?**

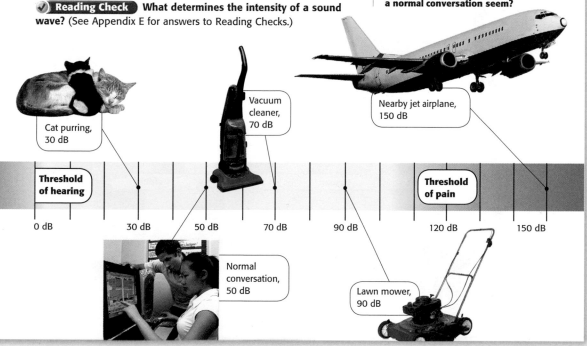

Cat purring, 30 dB

Vacuum cleaner, 70 dB

Nearby jet airplane, 150 dB

Normal conversation, 50 dB

Lawn mower, 90 dB

Threshold of hearing

Threshold of pain

0 dB 30 dB 50 dB 70 dB 90 dB 120 dB 150 dB

READING TOOLBOX

Visual Literacy Figure 3 shows the decibel levels of several common sounds. Have students examine the figure. Discuss with students: What is the decibel level of normal conversation? (50 dB) What is the level of a vacuum cleaner? (70 dB) How many times louder would a vacuum cleaner sound than a normal conversation? (four times as loud; an increase of 10 dB makes a sound seem twice as loud.) **LS** **Visual**

Answer to caption question
A normal conversation should seem about four times as loud as a cat purring.

MISCONCEPTION ALERT

Loudness Some students believe that hitting an object harder will change the pitch of the sound. This actually affects the amplitude, and thus the intensity or loudness of the sound. The pitch depends on the frequency of the vibration, which is not affected by how hard an object is struck. Use a drum to demonstrate the relationship between loudness and how hard the drum is struck. **LS** **Musical**

Differentiated Instruction

Basic Learners

Sound Levels If you have or can borrow a sound level meter, let students measure the intensity of various sounds around school. Have them take note of the decibel (dB) scale on the meter. These meters are inexpensive and available at local electronic stores. **LS** **Kinesthetic**

READING TOOLBOX

Visual Literacy Have students examine **Figure 4.** Ask students which of these mammals can hear the highest sounds? (dolphins) Which can hear the lowest? (elephants) Do the hearing ranges of mammals overlap? (yes) What frequency of sounds can be heard by all of the mammals shown? (70 Hz to 12,000 Hz) **LS** Visual

Why It Matters

Elephant Sounds Several years ago, scientist Katherine Payne of Cornell University discovered that elephants can make and hear sounds having pitches well below the range of human hearing, which ends at about 20 Hz. She found that elephants in the wild communicate over long distances with these sounds, which were in the range of 6 to 18 Hz. Few objects or materials can absorb the energy of sound waves of these frequencies, so the sounds can be heard by other elephants long distances away. Encourage interested students to learn more about elephant communication. Have students summarize their research in a poster to display in the classroom. **LS** Visual

pitch (PICH) a measure of how high or low a sound is perceived to be, depending on the frequency of the sound wave

infrasound (IN fruh SOWND) slow vibrations of frequencies lower than 20 Hz

ultrasound (UHL truh SOWND) any sound wave with frequencies higher than 20,000 Hz

Pitch is determined by frequency.

Pitch is a measure of how high or low a sound is and depends on the sound wave's frequency. A high-pitched sound is made by something vibrating rapidly, such as a violin string or air in a flute. A low-pitched sound is made by something vibrating slowly, such as a cello string or the air in a tuba.

In other words, high-pitched sounds have high frequencies, and low-pitched sounds have low frequencies. Trained musicians are capable of detecting subtle differences in frequency, even a change as slight as 2 Hz.

Humans hear sound waves in a limited frequency range.

The human ear can hear sounds from sources that vibrate as slowly as 20 vibrations per second (20 Hz) and as rapidly as 20,000 Hz. Any sound that has a frequency below the range of human hearing is **infrasound.** Any sound that has a frequency above the range of human hearing is **ultrasound.** Many animals can hear frequencies of sound outside the range of human hearing, as **Figure 4** shows.

Reading Check What are the upper limit and the lower limit of frequencies that humans can hear?

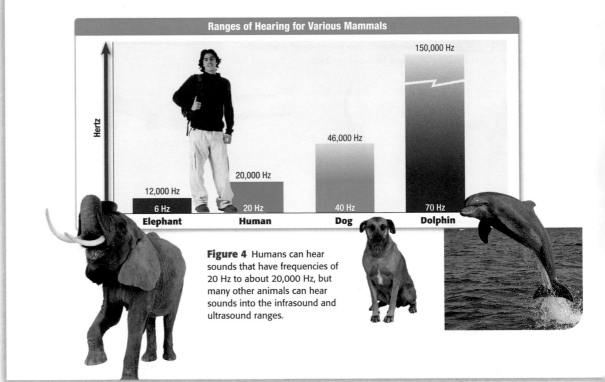

Figure 4 Humans can hear sounds that have frequencies of 20 Hz to about 20,000 Hz, but many other animals can hear sounds into the infrasound and ultrasound ranges.

Differentiated Instruction

English Learners

Pitch Versus Volume Students unfamiliar with musical terms may confuse the idea of high and low pitch with loud and soft sounds. All students should understand these words before proceeding. Also, students should understand that the words *fast* and *slow*—when applied to vibration—refer to the frequency, or "oftenness," of the back and forth movement.

Musical Instruments

Musical instruments, from deep-sounding tubas to twangy banjos, come in a wide variety of shapes and sizes and produce a wide variety of sounds. But musical instruments can be grouped into a small number of categories based on how they make sound. ❯ **Most instruments produce sound through the vibration of strings, air columns, or membranes.**

Musical instruments rely on standing waves.

When you pluck the string of a guitar, as **Figure 5** shows, particles in the string vibrate. Sound waves travel out to the ends of the string and then reflect back toward the middle. These vibrations cause a standing wave on the string. The two ends of the string are called *nodes,* and the middle of the string is called an *antinode.*

You can change the pitch by placing your finger on the string anywhere on the guitar's neck. A shorter length of string vibrates more rapidly, and the standing wave has a higher frequency. The resulting sound has a high pitch.

Standing waves can exist only at certain wavelengths on a string. The primary standing wave on a vibrating string has a wavelength that is twice the length of the string. The frequency of this wave, which is also the frequency of the string's vibrations, is called the *fundamental frequency.*

All musical instruments use standing waves to produce sound. The standing waves that form on the head of a drum are shown in **Figure 5.** In a flute, standing waves form in the column of air inside the flute. Opening or closing holes in the flute body changes the length of the air column, which changes the wavelength and frequency of the standing waves.

QuickLab ⏱ 10 min

Frequency and Pitch

❶ Hold one end of a **flexible metal or plastic ruler** on a **desk** with about half of the ruler hanging off the edge. Bend the free end of the ruler, and then release it. Can you hear a sound?

❷ Try changing the position of the ruler so that less hangs over the edge. How does the change in position change the sound produced?

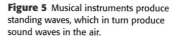
Figure 5 Musical instruments produce standing waves, which in turn produce sound waves in the air.

Vibrations on a guitar string produce standing waves on the string.

Vibrations on a drum head produce standing waves on the head.

QuickLab

Teacher's Notes Be sure that students do not bend the rulers too far. They should not cause the metal rulers to be permanently bent or cause the plastic rulers to break. Have students relate their observations to the idea of pitch.

Materials per Group
• desk
• ruler, flexible metal or plastic

Answers
1. Sample answer: Yes, I can hear the sound.
2. When less of the ruler vibrates, the ruler is vibrating at a higher frequency, so the sound has a higher pitch.

Teaching Key Ideas

Fundamental Frequency To explain how standing waves relate to fundamental frequency, point out that any object, when disturbed, will vibrate at certain natural frequencies that are characteristic of that object. Certain objects vibrate better than others and produce sounds of recognizable pitch. Ask students to name objects that fit into this category. (Responses may include bells, stretched strings, xylophone bars (metal), marimba bars (wood), crystal glassware.)

Differentiated Instruction

Advanced Learners

Music and Math A musical interval (two notes played together) can sound either consonant (harmonious or pleasing) or dissonant (inharmonious or harsh). In many consonant intervals, there is a whole-number ratio between the two frequencies, for example the octave (2:1), the perfect fifth (3:2), and the major third (5:4). Many dissonant intervals have irrational ratios. Encourage students to learn more about the relationship between mathematics and music and to share their results with the class.
LS Logical

Alternative Assessment

Instruments of Other Cultures Ask students to research instruments from other cultures. Students may wish to focus on the instruments of one culture, or on one general type of instrument. Ask them to design a sales brochure or catalog for the instruments they learn about, including illustrations, information about what the instruments sound like and how the sounds are produced, and comparisons to familiar instruments. **LS Visual**

InquiryLab

Teacher's Notes You should provide each group with at least one pair of forks of the same frequency. If you have a hollow resonance box, you may include it along with blocks of wood, metal bars, and so on. Caution students not to strike the tuning forks against anything hard. Dents and dings will eventually make a tuning fork useless. Tuning forks may be activated with a rubber stopper if rubber blocks are not available. Students can also get the second fork to vibrate by touching the bases of both forks simultaneously to a resonant surface.

Materials per Group
- block, rubber
- objects, wood or metal
- tuning forks, 2 of the same frequency and at least 1 of a different frequency

Answers to Analysis
1. Sample answer: The objects, such as desktops, boxes, tabletops, and sheets of poster board, were made of hard, thin materials and had a relatively large surface area.
2. Yes, this works when using two tuning forks with the same pitch.
3. Sample answer: Yes, if I touch the base of a ringing tuning fork to a resonant object and then touched a tuning fork of the same frequency to the object, the second tuning fork starts vibrating.
4. They both ring with the same frequency, or pitch.

InquiryLab — How Can You Amplify the Sound of a Tuning Fork?

 20 min

Procedure

1. Activate a **tuning fork** by striking the tongs of the fork against a **rubber block.**

2. Touch the base of the tuning fork to various **wood or metal objects.** Listen for any changes in the sound of the tuning fork.

3. Activate the fork again. Then, try touching the base of the tuning fork to the bases of other tuning forks. Make sure that the tines of the forks are free to vibrate and are not touching anything.

4. If you find two tuning forks that resonate with each other, try activating one and holding it near the tines of the other one.

Analysis

1. What are some characteristics of the objects that helped to amplify the sound of the tuning fork in step 2?

2. In step 3, could you make another tuning fork start vibrating by touching it with the base of your tuning fork?

3. In step 4, could you make another tuning fork vibrate without touching it with your tuning fork?

4. What is the relationship between the frequencies of the tuning forks that resonate with each other in steps 3 and 4?

resonance (REZ uh nuhns) a phenomenon that occurs when two objects naturally vibrate at the same frequency

Instruments use resonance to amplify sound.

When you pluck a guitar string, you can feel that the bridge and the body of the guitar vibrate. These vibrations, which are a response to the vibrating string, are called *forced vibrations.* The body of the guitar has *natural frequencies,* which are the specific frequencies at which it is most likely to vibrate.

The sound produced by the guitar will be loudest when the forced vibrations cause the body of the guitar to vibrate at a natural frequency. This effect is called resonance. When **resonance** occurs, both the string and the guitar body are vibrating at the same frequency, which amplifies the sound. The guitar body has a larger area than the string and is in contact with more molecules in the air. So, the guitar body is better at transferring the vibrations to the air than the string is.

The natural frequency of an object depends on the object's shape, size, mass, and the material from which the object is made. Complex objects such as guitars have many natural frequencies, so they resonate well at many pitches. However, some musical instruments, such as an electric guitar, do not resonate well and must be amplified electronically.

✔ **Reading Check** Why does resonance amplify a sound?

Demonstrate

Showing Waves with a Stroboscope If your school has an adjustable strobe lamp, show students the standing wave on a vibrating string of a guitar. Adjust the strobe until students can see that the string vibrates not only in one segment but in two or more at the same time. A bright flashlight shining through the blades of a fan is a makeshift substitute, but the fan's speed must be continuously adjustable.

Differentiated Instruction

Alternative Assessment

Comparing Frequency and Intensity Have students use common objects or musical instruments to demonstrate the following:
- two sounds of different intensities but the same frequency; two sounds of different frequencies but about the same intensity
- two sounds of different pitches but about the same amplitude; two sounds of different amplitudes but the same pitch
- two sounds of different wavelengths but the same amplitude

LS Kinesthetic/Musical

Hearing and the Ear

How do you hear waves and interpret them as different sounds? **❱ The human ear is a sensitive organ that senses vibrations in the air, amplifies them, and then transmits signals to the brain.** In some ways, the process of hearing is the reverse of the process by which a drum head makes a sound. In the ear, sound waves cause membranes to vibrate.

Vibrations pass through three regions in the ear.

Your ear is divided into three regions—outer, middle, and inner—as **Figure 6** shows. Sound waves travel through the fleshy part of your outer ear and down the ear canal. The ear canal ends at the eardrum, a thin, flat piece of tissue. The vibrations pass from the eardrum through the three small bones of the middle ear—the hammer, the anvil, and the stirrup. The vibrations cause the stirrup to strike a membrane at the opening of the inner ear, which sends waves through the spiral-shaped cochlea.

Resonance occurs in the inner ear.

The cochlea contains a long, flexible membrane called the *basilar membrane.* Different parts of this membrane vibrate at different natural frequencies. So, a wave of a particular frequency causes a specific part of the basilar membrane to vibrate. Hair cells near that part of the membrane then stimulate nerve fibers that send an impulse to the brain. The brain interprets this impulse as a sound that has a specific frequency and intensity.

READING TOOLBOX

Mnemonics
Create a sentence to help you remember the parts of the ear (eardrum, anvil, hammer, stirrup, and cochlea). The words in the sentence should begin with the letters *E, A, H, S,* and *C.*

SCI LINKS.
www.scilinks.org
Topic: The Ear
Code: HK80440

Teaching Key Ideas
How the Human Ear Works
Figure 6 shows the different parts of the ear. As students read the description of vibrations passing through the ear, have them follow the path of the vibrations in the figure. Then, ask students the following questions: What is the function of the outer ear? (to collect sound waves and direct them into the ear canal) What do the bones in the middle ear do? (The three bones act as levers to increase the size of vibrations.) What happens in the inner ear? (vibrations are converted into electrical signals for the brain to interpret) **LS Visual**

READING TOOLBOX

Mnemonics Students can also include other parts of the ear, such as *pinna* and *ear canal,* in their mnemonic sentence. Encourage students to make a sentence that keeps the order of the parts correct. Sample answer: **E**ach **h**amster **a**te **s**everal **c**arrots. **LS Verbal**

go.hrw.com
✳ interact online

Students can interact with the figure by going to **go.hrw.com** and typing in the keyword **HK8SALF6.**

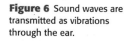

Figure 6 Sound waves are transmitted as vibrations through the ear.

go.hrw.com
✳ interact online
Keyword: HK8SALF6

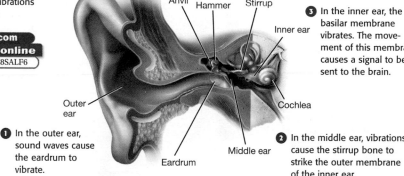

Anvil   Hammer   Stirrup

Inner ear

❸ In the inner ear, the basilar membrane vibrates. The movement of this membrane causes a signal to be sent to the brain.

Cochlea

Outer ear

Eardrum   Middle ear

❶ In the outer ear, sound waves cause the eardrum to vibrate.

❷ In the middle ear, vibrations cause the stirrup bone to strike the outer membrane of the inner ear.

Why It Matters

Cochlear Implants Since the late 1980s, scientists around the world have used cochlear implants in over 70,000 people. While hearing aids merely amplify sound, cochlear implants actually bypass damaged parts of the inner ear, thereby restoring some level of hearing to people with profound deafness. Although the implants cannot fully restore hearing, they provide enough benefit to drastically improve the recipient's ability to communicate fluently in verbal conversation. The recipient of a cochlear implant wears a microphone in a hearing case behind the ear, and a sound processor about the size of a personal radio on a belt or in a pocket. The microphone picks up sounds and send them to the processor, which selects and arranges the sounds. A transmitter converts these sounds to electrical signals, which are sent to electrodes implanted in the cochlea and then to the brain. Researchers are currently working to improve hearing for cochlear-implant recipients and to find additional candidates for the use of this new technology.

Teaching Key Ideas

Echolocation Animals such as bats, dolphins, and beluga whales use echolocation to find food and to locate objects in their path. An animal that uses echolocation sends out sound waves. The sound waves reflect off objects and are heard by the animal as an echo. The time needed for the echo to reach the animal lets the animal know how far away an object is.

Why It **Matters**

What Are Sonograms? In addition to sonograms and sonar, there are many other medical and non-medical uses for ultrasound. Have interested students choose an application to research, and ask them to write a report with their findings. Discuss the following with students to give them some starting points for topic ideas. Kidney stones can be disintegrated with frequencies between 20,000 Hz and 30,000 Hz. Tumors have been treated by ultrasound beams from outside the body. The beams come to a focus at the site of the tumor and kill the tissue by heating it. Students may also look into some of the dangers of the misuse of ultrasound. In addition to heating, some frequencies can cause cells to disintegrate. In nonmedical applications, ultrasound can be used to locate hairline fractures in metal support beams and machinery. High-intensity ultrasonic waves passing through a liquid-filled tank are used to clean jewelry, dentures, or small machinery placed in the tank. **LS** Verbal

Ultrasound and Sonar

If you shout over the edge of a rock canyon, the sound may be reflected by the rock walls. If the reflected sound reaches your ears, you will hear an echo. ❯ **Reflected sound waves are used to determine distances and to create images.**

Some ultrasound waves are reflected at boundaries.

Ultrasound waves have frequencies greater than 20,000 Hz. At high frequencies, ultrasound waves can travel through most materials. But some sound waves are reflected when they pass from one type of material into another. The number of waves reflected depends on the density of the materials at each boundary. The reflected waves from different boundary surfaces can be made into a computer image called a *sonogram*.

Ultrasound is used to see inside the human body because it does not harm living cells. For one to see the details in a sonogram, the wavelengths of the ultrasound must be slightly smaller than the smallest parts of the object being viewed. The higher the frequency of a wave is, the shorter the wave's wavelength is. Sound waves that have a frequency of 15,000,000 Hz have a wavelength of less than 1 mm when they pass through soft tissue. So, in a sonogram, you would be able to see details that are about 1 mm in size.

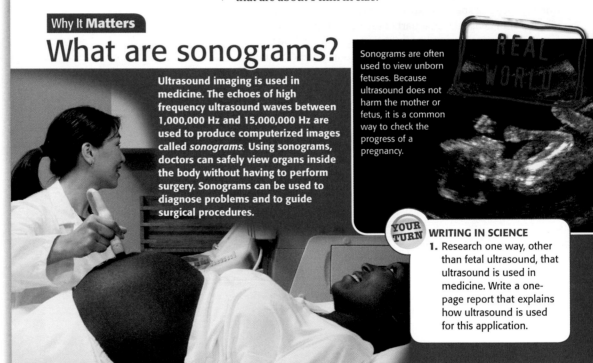

Why It **Matters**
What are sonograms?

Ultrasound imaging is used in medicine. The echoes of high frequency ultrasound waves between 1,000,000 Hz and 15,000,000 Hz are used to produce computerized images called *sonograms*. Using sonograms, doctors can safely view organs inside the body without having to perform surgery. Sonograms can be used to diagnose problems and to guide surgical procedures.

Sonograms are often used to view unborn fetuses. Because ultrasound does not harm the mother or fetus, it is a common way to check the progress of a pregnancy.

YOUR TURN

WRITING IN SCIENCE
1. Research one way, other than fetal ultrasound, that ultrasound is used in medicine. Write a one-page report that explains how ultrasound is used for this application.

Answer to Your Turn
1. Answers may vary. Examples of applications may include the use of ultrasound to do diagnostic imaging such as an echocardiogram, or to find gallstones or certain types of tumors.

READING TOOLBOX

Visual Literacy The image of the fetus is an example of a sonogram. Ask students to compare the sonogram to a photograph. (Sample answer: The sonogram is more grainy than a photograph. The sonogram is monochromatic and photographs are usually in color.) Explain to students that sonograms are harder to "read" than regular photographs. Tell students that ultrasound technicians and doctors must receive special training to learn how to read sonograms properly. **LS** Visual

Sonar is used to locate objects underwater.

How can a person on a ship measure the distance to the ocean floor, which may be thousands of meters from the water's surface? **Sonar** is a system that uses reflected sound waves for measurement and can measure large distances.

Using sonar, distance can be determined by measuring the time it takes for sound waves to be reflected from a surface. A sonar device on a ship sends a pulse of sound downward and measures the time, t, that it takes for the sound to be reflected back to the device from the ocean floor. The distance, d, can be calculated by using a form of the speed equation that solves for distance, using the average speed of sound in water, v.

$$d = vt$$

Because the sound waves travel to a surface and back to the device, the measured time must be divided by two to obtain the distance from the device to the surface. Fisherman and researchers can use sonar to detect fish. If a school of fish passes under the ship, the sound pulse will be reflected back much sooner than the sound from the ocean floor. Submarines can also be detected using sonar.

Ultrasound works very well in sonar systems because the waves can be focused into narrow beams and can be directed more easily than other sound waves. Bats use reflected ultrasound to navigate in flight and to locate insects for food.

QuickLab ⏱ 10 min

Echoes and Distance

1. Stand outside in front of a **large wall,** and clap your hands. Do you hear an echo?

2. Use a **stopwatch** to measure the time that passes between the time you clap your hands and the time you hear the echo.

3. The speed of sound in air is about 340 m/s. Use the approximate time from step 2 and the speed equation to estimate the distance to the wall.

sonar (SOH NAHR) **so**und **n**avigation **a**nd **r**anging, a system that uses acoustic signals and echoes to determine the location of objects or to communicate

QuickLab

Teacher's Notes Have students work in pairs so that one student can handle the stopwatch as the other student claps. Tell students to count to three and clap and start the stopwatch simultaneously.

Materials per Group
• stopwatch

Answers
1. Sample answer: Yes, I heard an echo.
2. Sample answer: It took 1.2 s for the sound to return.
3. Sample answer: $d = vt =$ $(340 \text{ m/s} \times 1.2 \text{ s})/2 = 204 \text{ m}$

❯ Close

Reteaching Key Ideas

Retracing the Process of Sound and Hearing Ask students what the first step is in sound production. (a vibration) Have a student draw a very simple sketch of this on the board. Then, ask students what happens to the sound. (Sound waves are carried through a medium.) Have another student draw a very simple sketch of this process on the board. Then, ask students what happens to the sound once it reaches your ear. (It is funneled by the outer ear, magnified by the middle ear, and changed into electrical signals by the inner ear.) Have another student draw a sketch of this process on the board.
LS Visual/Verbal

Section 1 Review

KEY IDEAS

1. **Identify** two factors that affect the speed of sound.

2. **Explain** why sound travels slower in air than in water.

3. **Distinguish** between infrasound and ultrasound.

4. **Determine** which two properties of a sound wave change when pitch gets higher.

5. **Determine** which two properties of a sound wave change when a sound gets louder.

CRITICAL THINKING

6. **Analyzing Information** Your friend tells you that a clap of thunder has a sound intensity of about 130 dB, so it is almost twice as loud as a vacuum cleaner. Explain whether or not your friend is correct.

7. **Applying Ideas** Why does an acoustic guitar generally sound louder than an electric guitar without an electronic amplifier sounds?

8. **Inferring Relationships** On a piano keyboard, the C5 key has a frequency that is twice the frequency of the middle C key. Is the string that vibrates to make the sound waves for the C5 key shorter or longer than the middle C string? Explain your reasoning.

9. **Describing Events** You hear a phone ring. Describe the process that occurs in your ear that results in sound waves from the phone being translated into nerve impulses that are sent to the brain.

10. **Analyzing Methods** To create sonograms, why are ultrasound waves used instead of audible sound waves?

Formative Assessment

In general, the speed of sound is fastest in

A. solids. (Correct. The particles of matter are closest together in solids, so vibrations of sound waves travel through solids the fastest. However some solids, such as rubber, dampen vibrations.)

B. liquids. (Incorrect. Although the particles in liquids are close together, sound generally travels faster in solids than in liquids.)

C. gases. (Incorrect. The particles of gases are far apart, so vibrations do not travel through gases as quickly as they do through liquids and solids.)

D. vacuums. (Incorrect. Sound cannot travel in vacuums.)

Answers to Section Review

1. Sample answers: State of matter, nature of the medium, and temperature affect the speed of sound.

2. In water, the molecules are packed closer together; in air the molecules are farther apart and collide less often than in water.

3. Infrasound refers to sounds that are below the range of human hearing (frequencies lower than 20 Hz). Ultrasound refers to sounds above the range of human hearing (frequencies higher than 20,000 Hz)

4. When pitch gets higher, the frequency increases and the wavelength decreases.

Answers continued on p. 581A

SECTION
2

The Nature of Light

SECTION 2

❯Focus

In this section, students learn about the wave and particle characteristics of light. They also study the electromagnetic spectrum in detail, including the relationship of energy to frequency and applications of electromagnetic waves in communication, medicine, and other areas.

Bellringer

Use the Bellringer transparency to prepare students for this section.

Demonstrate

Two-Slit Experiment Obtain a helium-neon laser and a two-slit plate (sometimes called a *Cornell plate*) to reproduce the experiment shown in **Figure 1.** Show students that the light from the laser forms a single dot when it shines directly onto a wall, but forms a wide pattern of light and dark spots when it passes through the double slits. Explain to students that diffraction and interference of light waves produces the pattern that they see.
LS Visual

Key **Ideas**	Key **Terms**	Why It **Matters**
❯ How do scientific models describe light? ❯ What does the electromagnetic spectrum consist of?	photon intensity radar	Cell phones use radio waves, not sound waves, to send signals.

Most of us see and feel light almost every moment of our lives. We even feel the warmth of the sun on our skin, which is an effect of infrared light. We are very familiar with light, but how much do we understand about what light really is?

Waves and Particles

It is difficult to describe all of the properties of light with a single scientific model. ❯ **The two most common models describe light either as a wave or as a stream of particles.**

Light produces interference patterns as water waves do.

In 1801, the English scientist Thomas Young devised an experiment to test the nature of light. He passed a beam of light through two narrow openings and then onto a screen on the other side of the openings. He found that the light produced a striped pattern on the screen, like the pattern in **Figure 1.** This striped pattern is an interference pattern that is formed when waves interfere with each other.

Figure 1 Light can produce an interference pattern.

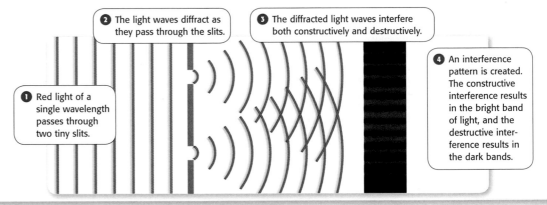

❷ The light waves diffract as they pass through the slits.

❸ The diffracted light waves interfere both constructively and destructively.

❶ Red light of a single wavelength passes through two tiny slits.

❹ An interference pattern is created. The constructive interference results in the bright band of light, and the destructive interference results in the dark bands.

Key Resources

Teaching Transparencies
TM44 Wave Frequency and
     Photon Energy
E18 Electromagnetic Spectrum

Visual Concepts
The Dual Nature of Light
Energy of a Photon
Electromagnetic Spectrum

Cross-Disciplinary Worksheet
Real World Applications—How Does
     Sunscreen Work?

Light can be modeled as a wave.

Because the light in Young's experiment produced interference patterns, Young concluded that light consists of waves. The model of light as a wave is still used today to explain many of the basic properties of light and light's behavior.

This model describes light as transverse waves that do not require a medium in which to travel. Light waves are also called *electromagnetic waves* because they consist of changing electric and magnetic fields. The transverse waves produced by these fields can be described by their amplitude, wavelength, and frequency.

The wave model of light explains how light waves interfere with one another. It also explains why light waves may reflect when they meet a mirror, refract when they pass through a lens, and diffract when they pass through a narrow opening.

The wave model cannot explain some observations.

In the early part of the 20th century, physicists began to realize that some observations could not be explained by the wave model of light. For example, when light strikes a piece of metal, electrons may fly off the metal's surface. Experiments show that in some cases, dim, blue light may knock some electrons off a metal plate, while very bright, red light cannot knock off any electrons, as **Figure 2** shows.

According to the wave model, very bright, red light has more energy than dim, blue light has because the waves in bright light have greater amplitude than the waves in dim light. But this energy difference does not explain how blue light can knock electrons off the plate while red light cannot.

Light can be modeled as a stream of particles.

One way to explain the effects of light striking a metal plate is to assume that the energy of the light is contained in small packets. A packet of blue light carries enough energy to knock an electron off the plate, but a packet of red light does not. Bright, red light contains many packets, but no single packet has enough energy to knock an electron off the plate.

In the particle model of light, these packets, or units of light, are called **photons.** A beam of light is a stream of photons. Photons are considered particles, but they are not like ordinary particles of matter. Photons do not have mass. They are like little bundles of energy. Unlike the energy in a wave, the energy in a photon is located in a specific area.

> ✓ **Reading Check** What can the particle model of light explain that the wave model cannot explain?

Figure 2 The particle model of light can explain some effects that the wave model cannot explain.

Bright, red light cannot knock electrons off this metal plate.

Dim, blue light can knock electrons off the plate. The wave model of light cannot explain this effect, but the particle model can.

photon (FOH TAHN) a unit or quantum of light

> **Teach**

Teaching Key Ideas

Particle versus Wave Isaac Newton believed that light is made up of tiny particles, which he called *corpuscles.* He published this theory in his book *Optics* in 1704. One of Newton's contemporaries, Christiaan Huygens, argued that light is a wave. Both Newton and Huygens offered convincing evidence, and the subject was a matter of great debate. Later experiments (such as Young's double-split experiment) seemed to verify Huygens' theory, which became widely accepted by scientists until Einstein proposed his photon theory in 1905. Einstein did not dispute the wave nature of light, but argued that in some cases, a particle model is more useful.

READING TOOLBOX

Visual Literacy To help students understand the photon concept pictured in **Figure 2,** have them visualize a brick wall being struck by streams of thousands of ping-pong balls. No single ball has enough kinetic energy to chip the bricks. Then imagine the same wall being struck at the same speed by only a few steel bolts. Even though just a few strike the wall, each has enough energy to break chips out of the bricks. The many ping-pong balls represent bright red light and the few bolts represent dim blue light. The brightness of light corresponds to the number of photons striking a surface per unit of time, and the color of light corresponds to the energy per photon.

Differentiated Instruction

Struggling Readers

Summarizing The speed of light and the wave-particle duality of light are fundamental ideas of science. To help students grasp these concepts, proceed in a stepwise fashion by having students read the subheadings under "Waves and Particles" one at a time. At the end of each subsection, stop and ask for volunteers to summarize that part. After the student finishes, ask students whether they agree on the summary given. If not, ask for other volunteers to offer their insights. **LS Verbal**

READING TOOLBOX

Booklet One way that students can make their booklets more useful is to number the pages and then cross-reference them. For example, on the page that describes which phenomena are explained by the wave model of light, students may write the number of the page that describes which phenomena are explained by the particle model.

Teaching Key Ideas

Accepting Two Models Some students may have difficulty understanding or accepting the idea of using two models of light. Tell students that scientists often use two or more models to represent the same phenomenon. Discuss some examples of more familiar dual models, such as maps and globes to represent the surface of Earth and the Bohr model and the electron-cloud model of the atom. Help students see that some models are useful in certain circumstances and other models are useful at different times.

Answer to caption question

The frequency increases as wave energy increases.

SCiLINKS.
www.scilinks.org
Topic: Properties of Light
Code: HK81227

READING TOOLBOX

Booklet
Create a booklet, and label the cover "Models of light." Label half of pages inside the booklet "Wave model" and the other half of the pages "Particle model." Write details about each model on the appropriate pages of your booklet.

Figure 3 The energy of photons of light is related to the frequency of electromagnetic waves. **What happens to the frequency of the waves as the energy increases?**

The model of light used depends on the situation.

Light can be modeled as either waves or particles. Which model is correct? The success of any scientific theory depends on how well the theory can explain various observations. Some effects, such as the interference of light, are more easily explained with the wave model. Other effects, such as light knocking electrons off a metal plate, are better explained by the particle model. The particle model also easily explains how light can travel across empty space without a medium.

Most scientists currently accept both the wave model and the particle model of light. The model they use depends on the situation that they are studying. Some scientists think that light has a *dual nature,* which means that light can behave both as waves and as particles. In many cases, using either the wave model or the particle model of light gives good results.

The energy of light is proportional to frequency.

Whether modeled as a particle or as a wave, light is also a form of energy. Each photon of light can be thought of as carrying a small amount of energy. The amount of this energy is proportional to the frequency of the corresponding electromagnetic wave, as **Figure 3** shows.

A photon of red light, for example, carries an amount of energy that corresponds to the frequency of waves in red light, 4.5×10^{14} Hz. Ultraviolet photons have about twice as much energy as red light photons. So, the frequency of ultraviolet waves is about twice the frequency of red light waves. Likewise, a photon that has half the energy of red light, a photon of infrared light, corresponds to a wave that has half the frequency of a wave of red light.

Type of wave	Wavelength	Wave frequency	Photon energy
Infrared 	1.33×10^{-6} m	2.25×10^{14} Hz	1.5×10^{-19} J
Visible light 	6.67×10^{-7} m	4.5×10^{14} Hz	3.0×10^{-19} J
Ultraviolet 	3.33×10^{-7} m	9.0×10^{14} Hz	6.0×10^{-19} J

READING TOOLBOX

Visual Literacy Use **Figure 3** to remind students that light color relates to the energy per photon. In the wave model, color relates to frequency, as pointed out in the next subsection. Therefore, frequency and energy per photon correspond to each other.

Differentiated Instruction

Alternative Assessment

The Newton-Huygens Debate Have students research the arguments used by Newton and Huygens for their theories of light. Ask them to assess the validity of the arguments, and evaluate which arguments still hold today and which have been overturned by our modern understanding of light. **LS Logical**

The speed of light depends on the medium.

In a vacuum, all light travels at the same speed and is represented by the variable *c*. The speed of light is very fast, about 3×10^8 m/s (about 186,000 mi/s). There is no known entity in the universe that is faster than light.

Light travels through transparent media, such as air, water, and glass. When light passes through a medium, however, the light travels slower than it does in a vacuum. **Figure 4** shows the speed of light in several mediums.

The brightness of light depends on intensity.

Reading near a lamp that has a 100 W bulb is easier than reading near a lamp that has a 60 W bulb. A 100 W bulb is brighter than a 60 W bulb and helps you see. The quantity that measures the amount of light illuminating a surface is **intensity.** Intensity depends on the number of photons per second, or power, that pass through a certain area of space.

The intensity of light decreases as distance from the light source increases because the light spreads out in spherical wave fronts. Imagine a series of spheres centered on a source of light, as **Figure 5** shows. As light spreads out from the source, the number of photons or the power passing through a given area on a sphere decreases. So, the light is dimmer for an observer farther from the light source than for an observer closer to the light source.

✓ **Reading Check** What does the intensity of light depend on?

Figure 4 Speed of Light in Various Mediums

Medium	Speed of light ($\times 10^8$ m/s)
Vacuum	2.997925
Air	2.997047
Ice	2.29
Water	2.25
Quartz	2.05
Glass	1.97
Diamond	1.24

intensity (in TEN suh tee) the rate at which energy flows through a given area of space

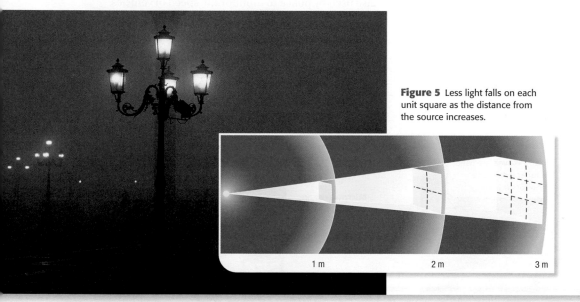

Figure 5 Less light falls on each unit square as the distance from the source increases.

1 m   2 m   3 m

Teaching Key Ideas

Speed of Light Unlike sound, which travels better in liquids and solids than in air, light travels more slowly as the density of the medium increases. When light passes through a medium, it encounters the many atoms that make up the medium. If light hits an atom, the light is scattered, which takes a very small amount of time. As light passes through the empty space between atoms in the medium, the light moves at its full speed of 3.0×10^8 m/s. The speed of light in the medium is really an average speed that takes into account the scattering of the light as it encounters atoms.

READING TOOLBOX

Visual Literacy The speed of light in air is slower than the speed of light in a vacuum, but the difference is very small, as students can see in **Figure 4.** The speed of light in a diamond is less than half the speed of light in a vacuum, but still on the same order of magnitude ($\times 10^8$ m/s).

Differentiated Instruction

English Learners

Learning Prefixes Tell students that the prefix *photo-* means "relating to light." Ask students to brainstorm a list of words that begin with *photo-*. Then, have them write definitions of the words and describe how the words relate to light. **LS Verbal/Visual**

Teaching Key Ideas

Electromagnetic Spectrum Remind students that radiation in other parts of the electromagnetic spectrum is qualitatively no different from visible light. However, our eyes are sensitive to the frequencies in the visible spectrum. The unique properties mentioned in the text depend less on the nature of the radiation and more on the way the radiation interacts with matter. Emphasize the continuity of the visible spectrum by pointing out that it consists not only of red, orange, yellow, green, blue, and violet, but all intermediate colors as well.

READING TOOLBOX

Visual Literacy Figure 6 shows the different parts of the electromagnetic spectrum. Ask students: Which end of the spectrum has higher frequency? (Frequency increases toward the right side of the spectrum.) Which end of the spectrum has longer wavelengths? (Wavelength increases toward the left side of the spectrum.) Which end of the spectrum has higher energy? (The right side has higher energy; the energy of electromagnetic waves is proportional to frequency.) **LS Visual**

www.scilinks.org
Topic: Electromagnetic Spectrum
Code: HK80482

radar (RAY DAHR) **ra**dio **d**etection and **r**anging, a system that uses reflected radio waves to determine the velocity and location of objects

Figure 6 The Electromagnetic Spectrum

The Electromagnetic Spectrum

Light fills the air and space around us. Our eyes can detect light waves that have wavelengths of 400 nm (violet light) to 700 nm (red light). But the visible spectrum is only a small part of the electromagnetic spectrum, as **Figure 6** shows. We live in a sea of electromagnetic waves that range from radio waves given off by TV stations to the sun's ultraviolet waves.

› The electromagnetic spectrum consists of waves at all possible energies, frequencies, and wavelengths. Although all electromagnetic waves are similar in certain ways, each part of the electromagnetic spectrum has unique properties. Many modern technologies, including radar guns and cancer treatments, use electromagnetic waves.

Radio waves are used in communications and radar.

Radio waves are the longest waves in the electromagnetic spectrum and have wavelengths from tenths of a meter to thousands of meters. This part of the electromagnetic spectrum includes TV signals, and AM and FM radio signals.

Air traffic control towers at airports use radar to find the locations of aircraft. **Radar** is a system that uses radio waves to find the locations of objects. Antennas at the control tower emit radio waves. The radio waves bounce off the aircraft and return to a receiver at the tower. Many airplanes are equipped with special radios called *transponders*. These radios receive a signal from the tower and send a new signal back to the tower. This signal gives the plane's location and elevation. Radar is also used by police to monitor the speed of vehicles.

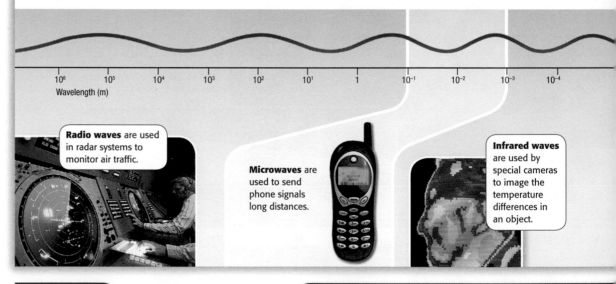

Radio waves are used in radar systems to monitor air traffic.

Microwaves are used to send phone signals long distances.

Infrared waves are used by special cameras to image the temperature differences in an object.

Why It **Matters**

The Radio Spectrum The frequencies at which radio and television stations broadcast in the United States are assigned by the Federal Communications Commission (FCC). In fact, the FCC has assigned frequencies for all devices that use radio waves, including garage door openers, radio controlled toys, and baby monitors. Have students research how the FCC has divided the radio-wave spectrum and make a poster showing what they learned.

Differentiated Instruction

Alternative Assessment

Electromagnetic Wave Applications Have students research electromagnetic wave applications. Ask each student to focus on one application that is not discussed in the student text. Have them prepare a poster that illustrates the application, including how it works, what type of electromagnetic waves are used, and why that type works best. Display student posters around the classroom. **LS Verbal/Visual**

Microwaves are used in cooking and communication.

Electromagnetic waves that have wavelengths in the range of centimeters are known as *microwaves*. Microwaves are used to carry telecommunication signals over long distances. Space probes use microwaves to transmit signals back to Earth.

Microwaves are reflected by metals and are easily transmitted through air, glass, paper, and plastic. However, the water, fat, and sugar molecules in food all absorb microwaves. The absorbed microwaves can cook food. Microwaves can travel about 3 to 5 cm into most foods. They are absorbed as they go deeper into food. The energy from the absorbed waves causes water and other molecules to rotate. The energy of these rotations spreads throughout the food and warms it.

Infrared light can be felt as warmth.

Electromagnetic waves that have wavelengths slightly longer than wavelengths of red visible light are in the *infrared* (IR) part of the spectrum. Infrared light from the sun warms you. Infrared light from heat lamps is used to keep food warm.

Devices and photographic film that are sensitive to infrared light can reveal images of objects. An infrared sensor can measure the heat energy that objects radiate. These data can then be used to create images that show temperature variations. Remote infrared sensors on weather satellites can record temperature changes in the atmosphere and track the movement of clouds. Many computers can detect infrared signals from external devices, such as a computer mouse.

Reading Check Name three devices that use infrared light.

Academic Vocabulary

detect (dee TEKT) to discover the presence of something

Real-World Connection

Microwave Ovens Although microwaves are reflected by metals, powdered metals absorb a significant amount of microwaves and become very hot. This technology is used in packaging microwavable foods. A paper or plastic sheet containing metal powder becomes hot and browns or fries the food.

Teaching Key Ideas

Dividing the Electromagnetic Spectrum Be sure students understand that the division point between microwaves and radio waves is arbitrarily set, as are other division points on the electromagnetic spectrum. There is no significant difference between the waves on either side of a division point. The exception is visible light, which is limited by the eye's sensitivity.

Teaching Key Ideas

Energy and Penetrating Power Reiterate the connection between color and energy by pointing out that ultraviolet light can damage cells because of the high energy of its photons, which also gives it penetrating ability. Call students' attention to the fact that X rays lie just beyond the ultraviolet part of the spectrum and have enough penetrating power to pass completely through the body. Also point out that X rays are even more damaging to cells than UV rays of the same intensity.

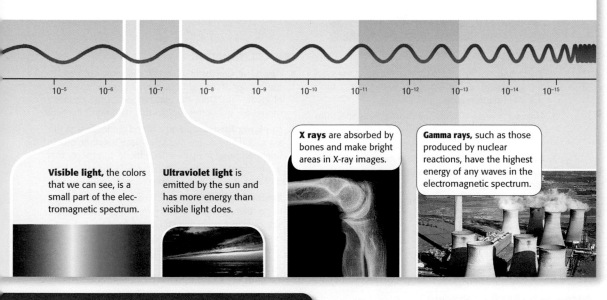

10⁻⁵   10⁻⁶   10⁻⁷   10⁻⁸   10⁻⁹   10⁻¹⁰   10⁻¹¹   10⁻¹²   10⁻¹³   10⁻¹⁴   10⁻¹⁵

Visible light, the colors that we can see, is a small part of the electromagnetic spectrum.

Ultraviolet light is emitted by the sun and has more energy than visible light does.

X rays are absorbed by bones and make bright areas in X-ray images.

Gamma rays, such as those produced by nuclear reactions, have the highest energy of any waves in the electromagnetic spectrum.

Differentiated Instruction

Special Education Students

Sunscreen and SPF Have students examine labels from different kinds of sunscreen, and develop a chart listing the different kinds and the SPF for each. By using information from the chapter, have students add a column to their chart that describes the effects on the skin that can be avoided when each kind of sunscreen is used. Students should also be able to explain why a person can still get a sunburn on a cloudy day. **LS Logical/Visual**

Reteaching Key Ideas

Comparing Models Have students make a two-column chart that compares the wave model of light and the particle model of light. Tell students to include evidence supporting both models in their chart. Also have students describe how the electromagnetic spectrum is arranged in both models. (In the wave model, the electromagnetic spectrum is arranged by wavelength and frequency. In the particle model, the electromagnetic spectrum is arranged by photon energy.)
LS Logical/Visual

Formative Assessment

Photon energy increases as

A. wavelength increases. (Incorrect. As the wavelength of light increases, the photon energy decreases.)

B. intensity decreases. (Incorrect. The energy of light does not depend on intensity. As the intensity of light decreases, the brightness of the light decreases.)

C. frequency increases. (Correct. Photon energy is directly proportional to frequency. As the frequency of light increases, photon energy increases.)

D. frequency decreases. (Incorrect. Photon energy is directly proportional to frequency. As the frequency of light decreases, photo energy decreases.)

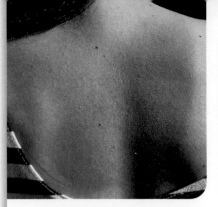

Figure 7 We cannot see ultraviolet light, but it can still damage the skin. Sunscreens protect skin by absorbing or blocking ultraviolet light before it reaches the skin.

Sunlight contains ultraviolet light.

The invisible light that lies just beyond violet light falls into the *ultraviolet* (UV) part of the spectrum. Ultraviolet light has higher energy and shorter wavelengths than visible light does. Although humans cannot see UV light, many insects can see it.

Nine percent of the energy emitted by the sun is ultraviolet light. Earth's atmosphere, in particular the *ozone layer,* absorbs much of this UV light. The UV light that makes it through the ozone layer has enough energy that some of the energy can pass through thin layers of clouds. As a result, you can get a sunburn, as **Figure 7** shows, on overcast days.

X rays and gamma rays are used in medicine.

Beyond the ultraviolet part of the spectrum are waves called *X rays*, which have higher energy and shorter wavelengths than ultraviolet waves do. X rays have wavelengths less than 10^{-8} m. *Gamma rays* are the electromagnetic waves with the highest energy and have wavelengths shorter than 10^{-10} m.

An X-ray image of bones is made by passing X rays through the body. Most of them pass right through, but a few are absorbed by bones and other tissues. The X rays that pass through the body to a photographic plate produce an image.

X rays are useful tools for doctors, but they can also be dangerous. Both X rays and gamma rays have very high energies, so they may kill living cells or turn them into cancer cells. However, gamma rays can also be used to treat cancer by killing the diseased cells.

Section 2 Review

KEY IDEAS

1. **State** one piece of evidence that supports the wave model of light and one piece of evidence that supports the particle model of light.

2. **Name** the regions of the electromagnetic spectrum from the shortest wavelengths to the longest wavelengths.

3. **Determine** which photons have more energy, those associated with microwaves or those associated with visible light.

4. **Determine** which band of the electromagnetic spectrum has the following:
   a. the lowest frequency   **c.** the most energy
   b. the shortest wavelength   **d.** the least energy

CRITICAL THINKING

5. **Applying Concepts** A certain molecule can absorb the energy of red light but cannot absorb the energy of green light. Does the wave model or the particle model of light better explain this statement? Explain.

6. **Applying Ideas** You and a friend are looking at the stars, and you notice two stars close together, one bright and one fairly dim. Your friend comments that the bright star emits much more light than the dimmer star. Is your friend correct? Explain your answer.

7. **Evaluating Conclusions** You and a friend decide to go hiking on a cloudy day. Your friend claims that she does not need any sunscreen because the sun is not shining. What is wrong with her reasoning?

Answers to Section Review

1. Answers may vary. Interference, reflection, and refraction support the wave model. The fact that blue light can knock electrons off a metal plate while red light cannot (the photoelectric effect) supports the particle model.

2. The regions of the electromagnetic spectrum from shortest to longest wavelength are gamma rays, X rays, ultraviolet light, visible light (from violet to red), infrared light, microwaves, and radio waves.

3. Photons of visible light have higher energy than photons associated with microwaves because their frequency is greater.

4. **a.** Radio waves have the lowest frequency.
   b. Gamma rays have the shortest wavelength.
   c. Gamma rays have the most energy.
   d. Radio waves have the least energy.

5. The particle model of light explains this better than the wave model because only certain packets of energies are absorbed.

6. He may be wrong because there is no way to judge. The star that appears brighter may actually emit less light but be much closer than the dimmer star.

7. Ultraviolet light from the sun has enough energy to make it through clouds, so it could still cause a sunburn.

How do cell phones work?

If you looked inside of a cellular phone, you would find a small radio wave transmitter/receiver, or *transceiver*. Cellular phones communicate with one of an array of antennas mounted on towers or tall buildings. The area covered by each antenna is called a *cell*. As the user moves from one cell to another, the phone switches to communicate with the antenna in that cell. As long as the phone is not too far from a cellular antenna, the user can make and receive calls. The antenna is connected to a base station, which is also a transceiver. The base station sends the call to the mobile telephone switching office, which routes the call.

REAL WORLD

5 The base station sends a signal to your friend's phone.

3 Depending on its destination, the call is routed through a wire cable, fiber-optic cable, microwave towers, or communication satellites.

4 The telephone signal arrives at another switching office and is sent to a base station near your friend.

2 The call is sent to the mobile telephone switching office (MTSO).

1 Your telephone call is picked up by the nearest cell phone tower.

SC**L**INKS.
www.scilinks.org
Topic: Telephone Technology
Code: HK81499

YOUR TURN

UNDERSTANDING CONCEPTS
1. When you place a call on a cellular phone, where is the first place that the radio signal goes?
ONLINE RESEARCH
2. Research the development of the cellular phone and the timeline of the history of this development.

How Do Cell Phones Work? Students may be surprised to learn that the cell covered by each antenna is approximately only 26 km^2—a circular area that has a radius of approximately 3 km. So if a person in a moving car is using a cell phone, the antenna that handles the call changes frequently. Ask students to learn why dividing an area into relatively small cells is advantageous. Have students write what they learn in a one-page paper. **LS** Verbal

READING TOOLBOX

Visual Literacy The diagram on this page shows how a signal travels from one cell phone to another. In the diagram, the signal is shown as waves traveling from one component to another in a single path. Be sure students understand that the signals sent out by certain components, such as the cell phone and the base stations, are actually sent out in all directions.

Answers to Your Turn
1. The signal from my phone goes to the nearest cell phone tower first.
2. Answers may vary.

Differentiated Instruction

Advanced Learners
Benefits and Drawbacks of Cell Phones
Organize students into two teams and ask the teams to debate the benefits and drawbacks of cell phones. Randomly assign which team will argue the benefits and which team will argue the drawbacks. Give the teams a few days to do research and to organize their arguments. Then, have the teams debate orally in class.
LS Verbal/Interpersonal

SECTION 3

Reflection and Color

> Focus

This section begins with the law of reflection. Next, students learn how flat and concave mirrors form virtual and real images. The section concludes with a discussion of color, including why objects appear as different colors and how colors can be added or subtracted.

 Bellringer

Use the Bellringer transparency to prepare students for this section.

Demonstrate

Adding Colors Cover one lens of a high-intensity flashlight with a green filter and a second flashlight lens with a red filter. In a darkened room, turn the "green" light on, and shine it on a white sheet, white wall, or overhead screen. Turn the "red" light on, and shine it on a different area of the screen. Ask the students what colors they see. Ask students to predict what color they will see if you overlap the green and red light. The students will probably answer "brown." Overlap the two colors. (Yellow will appear.) **LS Visual**

Answer to caption question

The light is focused into the large box in front of the mirror. (Teacher's Note: The large box is a large furnace.)

Key Ideas

> How do objects interact with incoming light?

> How can you see an image in a mirror?

> Why do we see colors?

Key Terms

light ray

virtual image

real image

Why It Matters

An object's color comes from the light that is reflected by the object.

You may be used to thinking about light bulbs, candles, and the sun as objects that send light to your eyes. But all of the other objects that you see, including this book, also send light to your eyes. Otherwise, you would not be able to see them.

Light from the sun differs from light from a book. The sun emits its own light. The light from a book is light that is given off by the sun or a lamp and that then bounces off the book.

Reflection of Light

Mirrors, such as those on the solar collector shown in **Figure 1,** reflect almost all incoming light. **> Every object reflects some light and absorbs some light.** The way light is reflected depends on the surface of the object. Because of the way mirrors reflect light, you can see an image of yourself in a mirror.

Light can be modeled as a ray.

It is useful to use another model for light, the light ray, to describe reflection, refraction, and many other ways light behaves. A **light ray** is an imaginary line running in the direction that the light travels. The direction of the light ray is the same as the direction of wave travel in the wave model of light or as the path of photons in the particle model of light.

Light rays do not represent a full picture of the complex nature of light but are good for showing how light will behave in many cases. The study of light in cases in which light behaves like a ray is called *geometrical optics*. Using light rays, one can trace the path of light in geometrical drawings called *ray diagrams*.

✓ Reading Check What are two behaviors of light that light rays are used to model?

light ray (LIET RAY) a line in space that matches the direction of the flow of radiant energy

Figure 1 This solar collector in the French Pyrenees uses mirrors to reflect and focus light. **Where is the light focused?**

Key Resources

Teaching Transparencies
TM45 Law of Reflection
TM46 Flat Mirror

Visual Concepts
Reflection
Law of Reflection
Comparing Real and Virtual Images
Additive Color Mixing

Datasheets
Curved Mirror
Filtering Light

Cross-Disciplinary Worksheet
Integrating Space Science—The
Refracting Telescope at Yerkes

Rough surfaces reflect light rays in many directions.

Many of the surfaces that we see every day, such as paper, wood, cloth, and skin, reflect light but do not appear shiny. When a beam of light is reflected, the path of each light ray in the beam changes from its initial direction to another direction. If a surface is rough, light striking the surface will be reflected at all angles, as **Figure 2** shows. This reflection of light into random directions is called *diffuse reflection*.

Smooth surfaces reflect light rays in one direction.

When light hits a smooth surface, such as a polished mirror, the light does not reflect diffusely. Instead, all of the light hitting a mirror from one direction is reflected together into a single, new direction, as the bottom of **Figure 2** shows.

The new direction of the light rays is related to the old direction in a definite way. The angle of the light rays reflecting off the surface, called the *angle of reflection*, is the same as the angle of the light rays striking the surface, called the *angle of incidence*. This equality of angles is the *law of reflection*.

Law of reflection	The angle of incidence equals the angle of reflection.

Both of these angles are measured from a line that is perpendicular to the surface at the point where the light hits the surface. This line is called the *normal*. **Figure 3** shows a ray diagram that illustrates how the law of reflection works.

Figure 2 Surfaces affect how light is reflected.

Light rays that are reflected from a rough surface are reflected in many directions.

Light rays that are reflected from a smooth surface are reflected in the same direction.

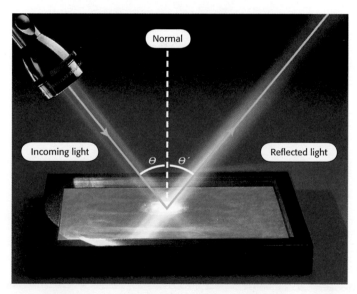

Figure 3 When light hits a surface, the angle of incidence (θ) equals the angle of reflection (θ').

SCiLINKS

www.scilinks.org
Topic: Reflection
Code: HK81282

Teach

READING TOOLBOX

Visual Literacy Explain that the small arrows on the rays in **Figure 2** indicate direction of travel. Point out that in both cases, the incoming light rays are parallel. After reflecting from the rough surface, the rays are no longer parallel, but the rays reflected from the smooth surface remain parallel.

Demonstrate

Angles of Reflection You will need an aquarium (5 or 10 gal), milk, small mirror, aluminum foil, laser pointer, transparent plastic protractor, concave mirror, and a convex mirror.

Step 1 Fill the aquarium about two-thirds full with water. Add three drops of milk to the water, and stir. Shine the laser into the water to see if the beam is visible. Add more milk as needed.

Step 2 Simulate the first image in **Figure 2** with the shiny side of crumpled aluminum foil and the second image in **Figure 2** with a flat mirror lying at the bottom of the tank.

Step 3 Demonstrate the angles of incidence and reflection with the flat mirror on the bottom of the tank. Move the light source to achieve various angles to show the validity of the law of reflection. Tape a transparent protractor to the outside of the tank to measure angles.

Continued on the next page

Differentiated Instruction

Alternative Assessment

Making a Periscope Organize students into groups. Give each group a shoebox, two small hand mirrors, some modeling clay, and a pair of scissors. Have students cut a 3 cm hole on the left side of each end of the box (so the holes will not be directly opposite each other). Then, tell students to arrange the mirrors inside of the box with the modeling clay in such a way that someone can look straight into one hole and see out of the other hole. Ask students to explain how this device works.
LS Logical/Interpersonal

Teaching Key Ideas

Reflection and Absorption Take your students outside on a sunny day. Find a shiny object that is in the sun, such as a school bus with windows or metal mailbox. Ask students what happens to the sunlight that hits the object. Students should recognize that light reflects off the object. Tell students that they can see a reflection in the object because light reflects off it and that any "glare" they see is reflected light. Help students understand that light is also absorbed by the object. Have students touch the object and tell them that the object feels warm because of the light energy it absorbed. **LS** Kinesthetic/Verbal

Demonstrate

Continued from previous page

Step 4 Place the convex ("wide-angle") mirror at the bottom of the tank. Shine the laser pointer vertically downward onto the mirror, and move it from side to side over the mirror. Rays will reflect increasingly outward as you move the beam in any direction away from the center of the mirror. Reverse the rays by shining the beam onto the mirror from many different angles. Ask students why this type of mirror is called a wide-angle mirror.

Step 5 Place a concave mirror at the bottom of the tank. Again, shine the beam straight down at the mirror, and move it back and forth. Students will observe that all of the rays reflect inward through a common point. Use two beams if you can to show that they cross at a common point no matter where the beams strike the mirror.

Step 6 Place both mirrors in the tank and adjust a flashlight to produce a straight beam. Shine the beam into the mirrors. Students will see the light spread from the convex mirror and focus to a point from the concave mirror.

READING TOOLBOX

Prefixes Have students write other words that start with *re-* to help them determine the meaning of the prefix. (Sample answers: return, rebound, react, recoil) Then, ask students what *re-* means. (Sample answer: *Re-* means back.) **LS Verbal**

READING TOOLBOX

Prefixes The word *reflection* contains the prefix *re-*. What is the meaning of this prefix? How can it help you understand the word *reflection*?

virtual image (VUHR choo uhl IM ij) an image from which light rays appear to diverge, even though they are not actually focused there; a virtual image cannot be projected on a screen

real image (REE uhl IM ij) an image that is formed by the intersection of light rays; a real image can be projected on a screen

Figure 4 Flat mirrors create virtual images.

Mirrors

When you look into a flat mirror, you see an image of yourself that appears to be behind the mirror. You see a twin or copy of yourself standing on the other side of the glass, but your image is flipped from left to right. You also see a whole room, a whole world of space beyond the mirror. **> Mirrors reflect light as described by the law of reflection, and this light reaches your eyes. The type of image you perceive depends on the type of mirror.**

Flat mirrors form virtual images by reflection.

The ray diagram in **Figure 4** shows the path of light rays striking a flat mirror. When a light ray is reflected by a flat mirror, the angle at which it is reflected is equal to the angle of incidence, as described by the law of reflection.

When the reflected rays reach your eyes, your eyes sense light coming from certain directions. Your brain interprets the light as if it traveled in straight lines from an object to your eyes. So, you perceive an image of yourself behind the mirror.

Of course, there is not actually a copy of you behind the mirror. The image that you see, called a **virtual image,** results from the apparent path of the light rays, not an actual path. The virtual image appears to be as far behind the mirror as you are in front of the mirror.

✓ Reading Check Why is the image that a flat mirror creates called a *virtual image*?

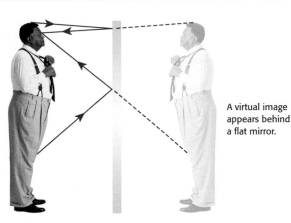

A virtual image appears behind a flat mirror.

A ray diagram shows where the light actually travels as well as where you perceive that it has come from.

Differentiated Instruction

Advanced Learners

Mirror Height Have students use what they know about reflection to explain why a plane mirror must be at least half a person's height for the person to see his or her full image in the mirror. Have students use diagrams or mirrors in their explanations. (Note: The mirror should be hung so that the top of the mirror is midway between the top of the person's head and his or her eyes.) (The angle of incidence equals the angle of reflection, so a person can see the top of his or her head by looking at a point on the mirror halfway between his or her eyes and the top of his or her head. A person can see his or her feet by looking at a point on the mirror halfway between his or her eyes and feet. Together, these two images add up to half the person's height) **LS Logical/Visual**

Curved Mirror

⏱ 10 min

Procedure

❶ Observe the reflection of a **short pencil** in the inner part of a **large, stainless steel spoon.**

❷ Slowly move the spoon closer to the pencil. Note any changes in the appearance of the pencil's reflection.

❸ Repeat steps 1 and 2 by using the other side of the spoon as the mirror.

Analysis

1. Which side of the spoon is a concave mirror? Which side is a convex mirror?

2. What differences in the reflected images did you observe?

3. How does distance affect an object's image in concave and convex mirrors?

Curved mirrors can distort images.

If you have ever looked into the passenger's side mirror on a car or a dressing table mirror, you have used a curved mirror. The images created by these mirrors are <u>distorted</u> so that they are smaller or larger than the real object.

Curved mirrors create images by reflecting light according to the law of reflection. But because the surface is not flat, the line perpendicular to the mirror (the normal) points in different directions for different parts of the mirror.

Mirrors that bulge out are called *convex mirrors*. Convex mirrors, such as that on the passenger's side of the car shown in **Figure 5,** make images appear smaller than they actually are. Indented mirrors are called *concave mirrors*. Some concave mirrors magnify objects so that the image created is larger than the object.

Concave mirrors can create real images.

Concave mirrors are used to focus reflected light. A concave mirror can form one of two kinds of images. It may form a virtual image behind the mirror or a real image in front of the mirror. When light rays from an object are focused onto a small area, a **real image** forms.

If a piece of paper is placed at the point where the light rays come together, the real image appears on the paper. If you placed a piece of paper behind a mirror where the virtual image seemed to appear, you would not see the image on the paper. This example shows the primary difference between a real and a virtual image. Light rays exist at the point where the real image appears. A virtual image appears to exist in a certain place, but no light rays exist there.

Academic Vocabulary

distort (di STAWRT) to change the natural appearance of something

Figure 5 Images formed by a convex mirror are smaller than the original object.

Teacher's Notes This experiment works best with a large spoon that is very shiny and that has a large radius of curvature.

Materials per Group
• pencil, short
• spoon, large, stainless steel

Answers to Analysis

1. The front side of the spoon curves inward and is the concave mirror. The back side of the spoon curves outward and is a convex mirror.

2. The image in the concave part of the spoon was small and upside down, except when the pencil was very close to the spoon. The image was smaller than the pencil in the convex part of the spoon.

3. Answers may vary. In the concave part of the spoon, the image of the pencil was larger than the pencil when the pencil was very close to the mirror. As the distance between the pencil and the concave mirror increased, the image inverted and became smaller than the actual pencil. For the convex mirror, the image was always right side up and smaller, and the image became smaller the farther the pencil was from the spoon.

Teaching Key Ideas

Images in Mirrors The ray diagram in **Figure 4** does not show every light ray involved in producing the image. One ray from the knee and one ray from the top of the head are shown as they reflect off the surface and to the eye of the observer. The dotted lines represent the straight-line paths that your brain calculates the rays have taken.

Differentiated Instruction

Struggling Readers

Distinguishing Words Help students understand the difference between the terms *concave* and *convex*. Have students draw items with concave and convex parts and write the terms *concave* and *convex* as parts of the drawings in place of concave and convex lines. For example, a student might draw a crescent moon where one section of the inner edge is replaced with the term *concave* and one section of the outer edge is replaced with the term *convex*. **LS Verbal/Visual**

Basic Learners

Law of Reflection Give students a diagram of a plane mirror with three rays of light approaching it at different angles. Have them draw the resulting reflected rays. Evaluate to see if students understand the law of reflection. Repeat with a concave mirror, but have the rays parallel to each other and the middle ray striking the exact center of the mirror. (The reflected rays should meet at a common point. The ray in the center is reflected straight back along the same path.) **LS Visual**

QuickLab

Teacher's Notes You may be able to obtain used but still functioning filters from your school's theater department.

Materials per Group
• filters, colored, 4

Answers

1–2. Answers may vary depending on the filters used and the objects being viewed. Sample answer: When I looked through the yellow filter, the color of the object changed. Objects looked more yellow, and some objects looked darker.

3. Answers may vary. When I combined the yellow and the blue filter, the objects looked greener and some objects appeared to be darker. The colors of the objects were different than when I looked at them through a single filter because each filter absorbs certain wavelengths of light, so those wavelengths are subtracted out from what I see. Fewer colors pass through two combined filters than through one filter.

4. When I look through all of the filters at once, the objects are very dark and have very little color.

QuickLab 20 min

Filtering Light

❶ Look through one of **four colored filters**—red, blue, yellow, or green—at an object across the room. Describe the object's color.

❷ Repeat step 1 with each one of the filters.

❸ Look at the same object through two filters placed together. Describe the object's color. Why does the object's color differ from the color when one filter is used?

❹ Place the red, blue, and yellow filters together, and look at the same object. Describe what you see. Why do you see this?

Figure 6 A Rose in White and Red Light

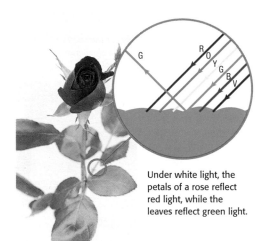

Under white light, the petals of a rose reflect red light, while the leaves reflect green light.

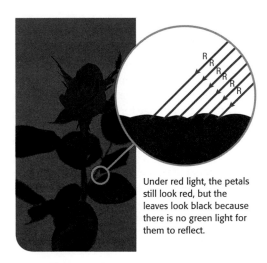

Under red light, the petals still look red, but the leaves look black because there is no green light for them to reflect.

Seeing Colors

❯ **The colors that you perceive depend on the wavelengths of visible light that reach your eyes.** When you see light that has a wavelength of about 550 nm, your brain interprets the light as *green*. If the light comes from the direction of a leaf, then you will think that the leaf is green.

A leaf does not emit light. And in the darkness of night, you may not be able to see the leaf at all. The leaf reflects green light from another light source.

Objects have the color of the wavelengths they reflect.

If you pass the light from the sun through a prism, the prism separates the light into a rainbow of colors. White light from the sun actually contains light that has all of the wavelengths in the visible region of the electromagnetic spectrum.

When white light strikes a leaf, as **Figure 6** shows, the leaf reflects light that has a wavelength of about 550 nm, which corresponds to the color green. The leaf absorbs light at other wavelengths, so those wavelengths are not reflected. When the light reflected from the leaf enters your eyes, your brain interprets the light as *green*. When you look through a transparent object, such as a color filter, you see the color of the light that passes through the filter. A green filter transmits green light and absorbs other colors of light.

Likewise, the petals of a red rose reflect red light and absorb other colors. So, the petals appear to be red. If you view a rose and its leaves under red light, as **Figure 6** shows, the petals will appear red but the leaves will appear black.

Teaching Key Ideas

Color Perception When the brain receives signals from certain combinations of photoreceptor cells in the retina, it interprets them as the color green. These receptors are three kinds of cone cells, one each for red, green, and blue. Be sure students understand that there is nothing inherently green about electromagnetic waves in one part of the visible spectrum. "Green" is just the way our brains interpret certain signals.

MISCONCEPTION ////ALERT\\\\

Colors of Light Most students believe that white light is colorless and pure, and that a color filter adds color to a white beam. These students have trouble understanding that white light is actually a mixture of colored light. You can show students a prism separating white light into a rainbow of colors to dispel this misconception.

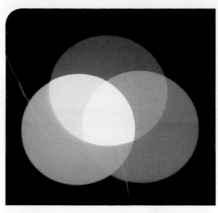

Red, green, and blue lights can combine to produce yellow, magenta, cyan, or white lights.

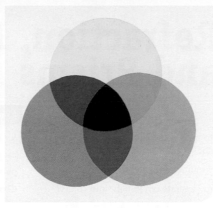

Yellow, magenta, and cyan filters can be combined to produce red, green, blue, or black.

Answer to caption question
The center of the lights is white because all of the colors in light combine to form white light. The center of the filters is black because filters subtract out light, so no light is getting through, and black is the absence of light.

Mixtures of colors produce other colors.

Most of the colors that we see are not pure colors. They are mixtures of primary colors. Televisions and computer monitors display many colors by combining light of the *additive primary colors*—red, green, and blue. Mixing light of two of these colors can produce the secondary colors yellow, cyan, and magenta, as shown on the left of **Figure 7.** Mixing light of the three additive primary colors makes white light.

Because pigments and filters absorb light, the opposite effect happens when they are mixed. The *subtractive primary colors*—yellow, cyan, and magenta—can be combined to create red, green, and blue, as shown in the right of **Figure 7.** If filters or pigments of all three colors are combined in equal proportions, all visible light is absorbed. No light gets to your eyes, so you see black. Black is not a color. It is the absence of color.

Figure 7 Colors combine to produce other colors. **Why is the center of the lights white and the center of the filters black?**

›Close

Reteaching Key Ideas

What Happens to Light? Gather a variety of objects such as mirrors, a colored T-shirt, an orange, white paper, and black patent-leather shoes. Ask students to describe what happens to the light that strikes the object. Students should recognize that all the objects reflect and absorb light. They should also note that some objects reflect light diffusely and some objects reflect objects normally (non-diffusely). Students should be able to explain why objects appear to be different colors. **LS** Logical/Visual

Formative Assessment

Which kind of mirror can create real images?

A. a flat mirror (Incorrect. Flat mirrors can form only virtual images.)

B. a concave mirror (Correct. Concave mirrors can form real images and virtual images.)

C. a convex mirror (Incorrect. Convex mirrors can form only virtual images.)

D. a diffuse mirror (Incorrect. Diffuse mirror is not a type of mirror.)

Section 3 Review

KEY IDEAS

1. **List** three examples of the diffuse reflection of light.
2. **Describe** the law of reflection in your own words.
3. **Draw** a ray diagram that represents a light reflecting off of a flat surface to illustrate the law of reflection.
4. **Discuss** how reflection from objects that appear blue differs from objects that appear yellow.
5. **Explain** why a plant may look green in sunlight but black under red light.

CRITICAL THINKING

6. **Analyzing Information** A friend says that only mirrors and other shiny surfaces reflect light. Explain what is wrong with this reasoning.
7. **Applying ideas** How does a flat mirror form a virtual image?
8. **Forming Models** A convex mirror can be used to see around the corner of a hallway. Draw a simple ray diagram that illustrates how this works.

Answers to Section Review

1. Examples may include bicycle reflectors, clothing, and paper. Almost anything that is visible, except a direct source of light, reflects light. Only polished surfaces, such as mirrors, reflect light non-diffusely.

2. Sample answer: The law of reflection states that the angle of the reflected light ray is equal to the angle of the incoming light ray.

3. Ray diagrams should resemble the diagram for reflection from a smooth surface in **Figure 2.** The angle of incidence should approximately equal the angle of reflection.

4. Blue objects reflect blue light and absorb colors in the rest of the visible spectrum. Yellow objects reflect yellow light and absorb other colors.

5. A green leaf reflects green light. Light from the sun contains all colors, so the leaf looks green. Red light contains no green, so the leaf reflects no light and appears black.

6. You see all objects by light reflected from them. Therefore, anything you can see, except for direct sources of light, reflects light.

7. Light that reaches your eyes from the mirror comes from in front of the mirror. However, because the path of the rays goes through the mirror, you see an image that appears to be behind the mirror.

8. Diagrams should show how reflected light is directed outward by a convex mirror.

SECTION 4

>Focus

This section discusses the refraction of light as it passes between mediums. Students also learn about lenses and how they function in microscopes and the human eye. The section also covers dispersion and prisms.

Bellringer

Use the Bellringer transparency to prepare students for this section.

Demonstrate

Refraction You can demonstrate refraction using an aquarium (5 or 10 gal) or other large transparent container, milk, a small mirror, a laser pointer or focusable flashlight, and two dusty chalkboard erasers. Fill the aquarium about two-thirds full with water. Add three drops of milk to the water, and stir. Shine the laser into the water to see if the beam is visible. Add more milk as needed. Shine the laser into the water at about a 30° angle from the normal. Hold the erasers over the aquarium and gently tap them together. Let students observe how the light ray bends as it enters the water. Shine the laser from various different angles to show students how the path of the light ray in the water depends on the angle at which the light strikes the water's surface.

Refraction, Lenses, and Prisms

> **Key Ideas**
> > What happens to light when it passes from one medium to another medium?
> > What happens when light passes through a lens?
> > How can a prism separate white light into colors?

> **Key Terms**
> lens
> magnification
> prism
> dispersion

> **Why It Matters**
> Your eyes contain lenses that bend and focus light to allow you to see objects around you.

Light travels in straight lines through empty space. But we also see light that passes through various media, such as air, water, or glass. The direction of a light wave may change when the light passes from one medium into another.

Refraction of Light

> **Light waves bend, or refract, when they pass from one transparent medium to another.** Light bends when it changes mediums because the speed of light differs in each medium. If light meets the boundary of two mediums at an angle to the normal, as in **Figure 1,** the light changes direction.

When light moves from a material in which its speed is high to a material in which its speed is lower, such as from air to glass, the ray is bent toward the normal. If light moves from a material in which its speed is low to one in which its speed is higher, the ray is bent away from the normal.

Figure 1 Light waves can change direction.

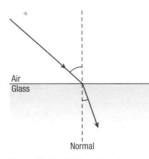

The path of a light ray bends toward the normal when the light ray moves from air into glass.

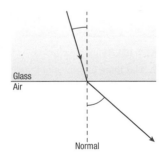

The path of a light ray is bent away from the normal when the ray passes from glass into air.

Key Resources

 Teaching Transparencies
P16 Refraction
P17 The Eye

 Visual Concepts
Refraction
Dispersion of Light
Converging and Diverging Lenses
Parts of the Human Eye

 Datasheet
Water Prism

Science Skills Worksheets
Angles and Degrees
The Area of a Circle

Refraction makes objects appear to be in different positions.

When a cat looks at a fish underwater, the cat perceives the fish as closer than it actually is, as the ray diagram in the top of **Figure 2** shows. On the other hand, when the fish looks at the cat above the surface, the fish perceives the cat as farther than it really is, as **Figure 2** also shows.

The images that the cat and the fish see are virtual images like the images that form behind a mirror. The light rays that pass from the fish to the cat bend away from the normal when they pass from water to air. But the cat's brain interprets the light as if it traveled in a straight line, and thus the cat sees a virtual image. Similarly, the light from the cat to the fish bends toward the normal as it passes from the air into water, which causes the fish to see a virtual image.

✓ **Reading Check** Why does the fish seem closer than it is?

Refraction in the atmosphere creates mirages.

Have you ever seen what looks like water on the road on a hot, dry summer day? If so, then you may have seen a *mirage* like the one shown in **Figure 3.** A mirage is a virtual image that is caused by refraction of light in the atmosphere.

The air temperature affects the speed at which light travels. When light from the sky passes into the layer of hot air just above the asphalt on a road, the light refracts and bends upward away from the road. This refraction creates a virtual image of the sky coming from the direction of the road. Your mind may assume that a reflection was caused by water.

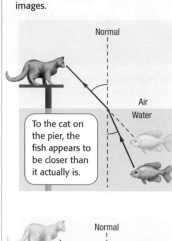

Figure 2 Refraction creates virtual images.

To the cat on the pier, the fish appears to be closer than it actually is.

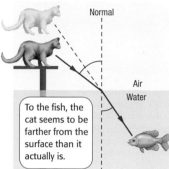

To the fish, the cat seems to be farther from the surface than it actually is.

Figure 3 A mirage is produced when light bends as it passes through air at different temperatures.

> **Teach**

Teaching Key Ideas

Light Refraction Steering bulldozers and tanks is analogous to light refraction. Ask students if they have ever steered a track-driven vehicle. A tracked vehicle changes direction by the driver either applying a brake to slow down the track on one side or by speeding up the track on the other side (or both actions for sharp turns). Another analogy is making a turn while rowing a boat.

READING TOOLBOX

Visual Literacy Figure 2 on this page, like **Figure 4** in Section 3, shows both light rays and dotted lines. The dotted lines show the perceived, or apparent, path of the light rays. Ask students whether the images in the figure are virtual images or real images. (They are virtual images.) **LS Visual**

Life Science Connection

Archerfish and Refraction
Archerfish *(Toxotes jaculator)* have the ability to correct for the refraction of light between air and water, and they have the ability to judge the distance to their prey. Archerfish knock insects and other small prey from overhanging vegetation by spitting jets of water at them. Archerfish have a groove in the roof of their mouth. When the tongue is pressed against the groove and the gills are squeezed shut, a jet of water is produced. These fish can hit prey more than 1.5 m away.

Differentiated Instruction

Advanced Learners

Index of Refraction The index of refraction for a medium is calculated by dividing the speed of light in a vacuum by the speed of light in the medium. When light moves from a medium with a lower index to one with a higher index, light rays bend toward the normal. Conversely, when it moves from a higher to a lower index, light rays bend away from the normal. Have students use a reference source to find the speed of light in various mediums and ask them to calculate the index of refraction for each medium. Then, have students determine whether light will bend toward or away from the normal for different combinations of mediums. Remind them that the higher the index, the more the light bends. **LS Logical**

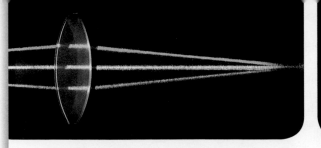

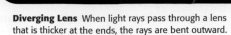

Converging Lens When light rays pass through a lens that is thicker at the middle, the rays are bent inward.

Diverging Lens When light rays pass through a lens that is thicker at the ends, the rays are bent outward.

Figure 4 The way the surface of a lens curves affects how light rays bend as the rays pass through the lens.

❯Teach, *continued*

Teaching Key Ideas

Using Converging Lenses Give each pair of students a magnifying lens. Tell students to use the lens to look at an object. First, tell students to use the lens to see an image that is larger than the object. Have students draw diagrams showing the relative positions of their eye, the magnifying lens, and the object. Then, challenge students to use the lens to see an image that is smaller than the object. Ask them to draw a diagram for this situation, too. Tell students that the larger image is a virtual image and the smaller image is a real image. **LS Kinesthetic/Visual**

Why It **Matters**

Eyeglass Lenses Students can determine the correction in eyeglasses with the following tests. Hold the lens horizontally above a page of type, and move the lens back and forth. If the lens is converging (used to correct farsightedness), the type will seem to move opposite the direction that the lens moves. With a diverging lens (for nearsightedness), the type seems to move in the same direction as the lens moves. If a lens has correction for astigmatism, rotating the lens over the type will cause the type to distort as the lens turns. **LS Kinesthetic**

lens (LENZ) a transparent object that refracts light waves such that they converge or diverge to create an image

magnification (MAG nuh fi KAY shuhn) the increase of an object's apparent size by using lenses or mirrors

Figure 5 A magnifying glass makes a large virtual image of a small object.

Lenses

You may not realize that you use the refraction of light every day. Human eyes, as well as cameras, contact lenses, eyeglasses, and microscopes, contain parts that bend light.

Light traveling at an angle through a thin, flat medium is refracted twice—once when it enters the medium and again when it reenters the air. So, the position of a light ray that exits the medium is shifted, but the light ray is still parallel to the original light ray. However, if the medium has a curved surface, the exiting rays will not be parallel to the original ray.

❯**When light passes through a medium that has a curved surface, a lens, the light rays change direction.** Each light ray strikes the surface of the curved surface at a slightly different angle, so angles at which the rays are bent differ. The effects of a *converging lens* and a *diverging lens* on light rays are shown in **Figure 4**. A converging lens bends light inward. This type of lens can create either a virtual image or a real image, depending on the distance from the lens to the object. A diverging lens bends light outward and can create only a virtual image.

✔ **Reading Check** Which type of lens can create a real image?

Lenses can magnify images.

A magnifying glass is a familiar example of a converging lens. A magnifying glass reveals details that you would not usually be able to see, such as the small parts of the flower in **Figure 5**. The large image that you see through the lens is a virtual image. **Magnification** is any change in the size of an image compared with the size of the object. Magnification can produce an image that is larger than the object.

If you hold a magnifying glass over a piece of paper in bright sunlight, you can see a real image of the sun on the paper. By adjusting the height of the lens above the paper, you can focus the light rays together into a small area, called the *focal point*. At the focal point, the image of the sun may contain enough energy to eventually set the paper on fire.

Differentiated Instruction

English Learners

Vocabulary The words *converge* and *diverge* derive from the Latin verb *vergere*, "to slant, slope, or incline." The prefix *con-* means "together," and the prefix *di-* means "apart." Thus, a converging lens slants light rays together, and a diverging lens slants light rays apart.

Microscopes use multiple lenses.

A compound light microscope, shown in **Figure 6,** uses multiple lenses to provide greater magnification than a single magnifying glass can. The objective lens is closest to the object and forms a large, real image of the object. The eyepiece then acts like a magnifying glass and creates a larger virtual image that you see when you look through the microscope.

The eye depends on refraction and lenses.

Without refraction of light, you would not be able to see at all. The way a human eye bends light, which is shown in **Figure 7,** is similar to the way a simple camera operates. Light enters a camera through a large lens, which focuses the light into an image on the film at the back of the camera.

Light first enters the eye through a transparent tissue called the *cornea.* The cornea is responsible for 70% of the refraction of light in the eye. After the cornea, light passes through the *pupil.* Then, light travels through the *lens,* which is composed of fibers. The curvature of the lens determines how much the lens refracts light. Muscles can adjust the curvature of the lens until an image is focused on the *retina.*

The retina is composed of tiny, light-sensitive structures called *rods* and *cones.* When light strikes the rods and cones, signals are sent to the brain where they are interpreted as images. Most cones are in the center of the retina, and most rods are on the outer edges. The cones are responsible for color vision, but they respond only to bright light. Therefore, you cannot see color in very dim light. The rods are more sensitive to dim light but cannot resolve details well. So, you can glimpse faint movements from the corners of your eyes.

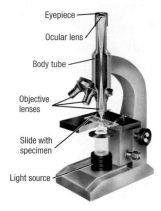

Figure 6 A compound light microscope uses several lenses to produce a highly magnified image.

Figure 7 Eyes focus light.

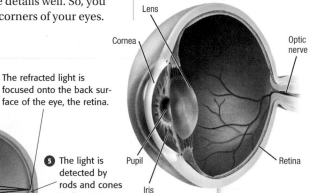

❸ Light is refracted again by the lens, which is made up of transparent fibers.

❹ The refracted light is focused onto the back surface of the eye, the retina.

❷ Light passes through a hole in the colorful iris known as the pupil.

❺ The light is detected by rods and cones in the retina.

❶ The cornea is a transparent membrane that covers the eye and refracts light.

❻ The optic nerve carries signals to the brain.

Labels on Figure 7: Lens, Cornea, Optic nerve, Pupil, Iris, Retina

READING TOOLBOX

Visual Literacy Figure 6 shows that light from a point on the specimen is focused to a point somewhere inside the body tube. If a screen were placed at this point, a small image of the specimen would appear on it. However, a real image can be viewed without a screen. A magnifying lens—the eyepiece—at the top of the tube lets you view a magnified image of the already-magnified real image inside the tube. A telescope works in the same way as a microscope, except that the objective lens is large to capture a lot of light, and it brings light to a focus much farther from the lens.

MISCONCEPTION ALERT

The Eye Lens Some students were probably taught in the past that the lens of the eye is solely responsible for forming an image on the retina. Help them overcome this error by calling their attention to the fact that the curved cornea is a lens too. The lens is important, because muscles change its curvature to adjust the focus for nearby and distant objects. Some students may be interested in exploring the use of surgery to reshape the cornea to correct vision defects that would otherwise be corrected by contact lenses or eyeglasses.

Differentiated Instruction

Advanced Learners

Vision Problems Encourage interested students to learn why certain vision problems occur. For example, students can find out what causes nearsightedness, farsightedness, and colorblindness. Have students summarize their research in a poster that they can present to the class. **LS Verbal/Visual**

Demonstrate

Nearsighted and Farsighted Projector To simulate normal vision, have students focus an image from an overhead projector onto a screen. Then, to simulate a nearsighted eye, have students increase the distance between the projector and the screen. The image becomes blurry because it is focused in front of the screen. Then, have students move the projector closer to the screen than it was originally. This simulates farsightedness: the image is now focused behind the screen, making the image blurry. **LS Visual**

Demonstrate

Dispersion For this demonstration you will need an aquarium, prism, slide projector, and a focusable halogen flashlight.

Step 1 Darken the room for this demonstration. Focus the flashlight to produce a beam that does not diverge. Shine the beam through a prism, as shown in **Figure 8.** Arrange the prism and beam so that a light spectrum appears on a light-colored wall or on white paper.

Step 2 Fill the aquarium with clear water. Shine the projector beam through the side of the tank so that it refracts, as shown in the diagram below. Arrange the aquarium so that a bright spectrum falls on a light-colored wall. You will need to adjust the lens of the projector to produce the narrowest possible beam. If you do not get a good spectrum, place a sheet of aluminum foil with a 1/8-inch wide vertical slit over the projector lens. This should produce a narrow beam. You may have to adjust the placement of the projector for best results.

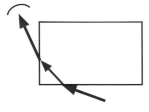

Spectrum

Looking down from above

QuickLab ⏱ **10 min**

Water Prism

❶ Fill a **shallow dish** with about 3 cm of **water.**

❷ Place a **flat mirror** in the tray so that about half of the mirror is under the water. The mirror should be placed at an angle and should lean against the side of the dish.

❸ Use a **white piece of paper** to capture the **sunlight** that is reflected by the mirror. Change the distance of the paper from the mirror and the angle of the paper until you see colors in the reflection. What colors do you see?

❹ Why are the colors of the reflected sunlight separated by the water?

prism (PRIZ uhm) in optics, a system that consists of two or more plane surfaces of a transparent solid at an angle with each other

dispersion (di SPUHR zhuhn) in optics, the process of separating a wave (such as white light) of different frequencies into its individual component waves (the different colors)

www.scilinks.org
Topic: Refraction
Code: HK81285

Dispersion and Prisms

A **prism,** such as the one in **Figure 8,** can separate white light into its component colors. Water droplets in the air can also separate the color in white light to produce a rainbow. **❯ A prism can separate the colors of light because the speeds of light waves traveling through the medium depend on the wavelengths of light.**

Different colors of light are refracted by different amounts.

Light waves of all wavelengths travel at the same speed $(3.0 \times 10^8 \text{ m/s})$ in a vacuum. But when a light wave travels through a medium, the speed of the light wave depends on the light wave's wavelength. The colors in the visible spectrum, in order of longest to shortest wavelength, are red, orange, yellow, green, blue, and violet. In the visible spectrum, violet light has the shortest wavelength and travels the slowest. Red light has the longest wavelength and travels the fastest.

Because violet light travels slower than red light, violet light bends more than red light when it passes from one medium to another. When white light passes from air to the glass in the prism, violet bends the most and red bends the least. When the light exits the prism, the light is separated into the colors in the visible spectrum. This effect in which light separates into different colors because of differences in wave speed is called **dispersion.**

Figure 8 A prism separates white light into its component colors.

White light enters the prism.

In the light exiting the prism, the colors are separated. Notice that violet light is bent more than red light.

QuickLab

Teacher's Notes If you cannot use sunlight for this lab, a bright light, such as a flashlight, may be used. If you use an artificial light source, you should have the students cut a slit in a piece of cardboard or black construction paper and shine the light through the slit.

Materials per Group
• dish, shallow
• mirror, flat
• paper, white, 1 sheet
• sunlight
• water

Answers

3. Answers may vary depending on quality of reflection. Sample answer: I see red, orange, yellow, green, blue, and violet.

4. When light travels through the water, the wavelengths of visible light travel at different speeds. Red light travels fastest and is bent the least, and violet travels the slowest and is bent the most. As a result, the colors are dispersed, or spread out.

Figure 9 Sunlight is dispersed and reflected by water droplets to form a rainbow.

Rainbows are caused by dispersion and reflection.

Rainbows, such as the one in **Figure 9,** may form any time that water droplets are in the air. When sunlight strikes a droplet of water, the light is dispersed into different colors as it passes from the air into the water. If the angle at which the refracted light rays meet the back surface of the water droplet is small enough, the rays can be reflected. Some of the light will reflect back through the droplet. The light disperses further when it passes out of the water back into the air.

When light finally leaves the droplet, violet light emerges at an angle of 40°, red light emerges at 42°, and the other colors are in between these angles. We see light from many droplets as arcs of color, which form a rainbow. Only the red light from droplets higher in the air and only the violet light from lower droplets reaches your eyes. So, the colors of a rainbow are separated in space.

READING TOOLBOX

Booklet
Create a booklet you can use to compare mirrors, lenses, and prisms. Label the cover "Mirror, Lenses, and Prisms." Label the first two pages "Mirrors," the next two pages "Lenses," and the last two pages "Prisms."

READING TOOLBOX

Booklet Remind students to review Section 3 when working on the pages for mirrors. Be sure students note which light interaction (reflection or refraction) is caused by each object.

❯ Close

Reteaching Key Ideas

Reviewing Refraction Give groups a converging lens, a diverging lens, a prism, and a bright flashlight. Instruct students to experiment with their materials and then work together to draw diagrams that show and explain how refraction affects the light that passes through the prism and the lenses.
LS Interpersonal/Visual

Section 4 **Review**

KEY IDEAS

1. **Draw** a ray diagram that shows the path of light when the light travels from air into glass.

2. **Describe** how a mirage is formed.

3. **Explain** how a simple magnifying glass works.

4. **Explain** why light is dispersed by a prism.

CRITICAL THINKING

5. **Explaining Events** How does your eye focus light on the retina?

6. **Applying Ideas** A spoon partially immersed in a glass of water may appear to be bent. Is the image of the spoon in the water a real image or a virtual image?

7. **Forming Conclusions** In the dispersed light that exits a glass prism, green light is closer to violet light than yellow light is. Does green light or yellow light travel faster through the glass prism?

8. **Applying Ideas** If light traveled at the same speed in raindrops as it does in air, could rainbows exist? Explain your reasoning.

Formative Assessment

Which of the following correctly describes the path of light as it passes from air into a glass prism and then back into air?

A. The light will bend toward the normal as it passes into the prism and then bend away from the normal as it passes back into air. (Correct. During refraction, light bends toward the normal when passing into a medium.)

B. The light will bend away from the normal as it passes into the prism and then bend toward the normal as it passes back into air. (Incorrect. The speed of light in air is higher than the speed of light in glass.)

C. The light will bend away from the normal as it passes into the prism and then bend away from the normal as it passes back into air. (Incorrect. When light enters a new medium, it will refract either toward or away from the normal. When light exits the medium, it will refract in the opposite direction.)

D. The light will bend toward the normal as it passes into the prism and then will not bend when it passes back into air. (Incorrect. The speed of light is different in air from that in glass, so refraction should happen when light passes from air to glass and when light passes from glass to air.)

Answers to Section Review on p. 581A

Why It **Matters**

Detecting Counterfeit Money Tell students that the newly designed bills have other distinctive features. For example, each of the new bill denominations is shaded with different colors. The $10 bill is shaded with orange, yellow, and red; the $20 bill is shade with green, peach, and blue; and the $50 bill is shaded with red and blue. Also, the security threads in the bills are placed in different locations and glow different colors when viewed under ultraviolet light. The security thread in the $10 bill is located to the right of the portrait and glows orange. The security thread in the $20 bill is located on the far left of the portrait and glows green. The security thread in the $50 bill is located very close to the right side of the portrait and glows yellow. Ask students why these features are useful. (Sample answer: The shading in the bills makes it easier for people to tell the difference between different denominations and makes it more difficult to counterfeit the bills. Varying the location and behavior of the security thread makes it easy to identify counterfeit bills by placing the bills under ultraviolet light.) **LS** **Logical**

Why It **Matters**

Detecting Counterfeit Money

You might think that high-quality photocopiers, scanners, and printers would make it easy to print fake money. However, newer 10, 20, and 50 dollar bills have security features that cannot be duplicated by an ink-jet printer. The United States Treasury introduced a redesigned 10 dollar bill in 2006. This bill, along with 20 and 50 dollar bills, was updated to include security features that make counterfeit money harder to make and easier to detect. Several of the security features depend on how light interacts with the paper and inks used to make money. These features include a security thread, a watermark, and features that are printed using color-shifting ink.

A plastic strip known as a security thread is embedded in the paper. If you hold the bill up to the light and look to the right of the portrait of Alexander Hamilton, you will be able to see the words *USA TEN* printed on the thread. This strip glows orange when the bill is held under ultraviolet light.

It may be obvious that more colors are used in the new bills. But if you look closely at a bill, you will notice that the patterns are made by very fine lines. The colors appear darker where the lines are more closely spaced. The bills even include text, called *microprinting*, that you cannot read without a magnifying lens. The fine patterns and microprinting make it hard for counterfeiters to reproduce the quality of the printing on real money.

Have you ever left a dollar bill in your pocket and found that it is still in one piece after it has been through the washing machine? If money were printed on regular paper, it would have fallen apart. All paper money is printed on special paper made from linen and cotton, which is known as rag paper. This paper is very thin and does not feel like other papers. Counterfeiters cannot buy this paper. It is made only for the U.S. government.

Differentiated Instruction

Alternative Assessment

Brochure Have students make brochures that teach people how to identify counterfeit money. Students should include information they learned in this feature and information that they gather through research. Encourage students to distribute their brochures to small business owners in your area. **LS** **Visual**

Color-shifting ink is used to print the number 10 in the lower right of the bill. This ink contains metal particles that reflect light. Only certain wavelengths make it out of the ink to produce the color you see. The other light waves destructively interfere with one another. The light waves that you see also depend on the angle of the light. When you tilt the bill, you see a different color. The color on the new bills shifts from copper to green.

FORENSICS

If you hold the bill up to the light and look in the white oval, you will see another image of Alexander Hamilton. This image is a watermark. The image is not created with ink. It is part of the paper. The thickness of the paper is varied to make a watermark. Less light comes through the thicker parts of the paper, which creates an image that is darker than the surrounding area. The watermark can be seen through both sides of the paper.

YOUR TURN

UNDERSTANDIING CONCEPTS

1. If you tilt a 10 dollar bill, what should you see change?

CRITICAL THINKING

2. Suppose counterfeiters use paper that is similar to the paper that the government uses to print money. Do you think that they would be able to successfully make fake money? Explain your reasoning.

SCI**LINKS**

www.scilinks.org
Topic: Printing Processes
Code: HK81700

READING TOOLBOX

Visual Literacy Instruct students to study the image on these pages and compare it to an older version of the $10 bill. If older versions of the $10 bill are hard to find, have students compare the image to $1 or older $5 bills which should be easier to find. (A new design for the $5 bill will be issued in early 2008.) Ask students to make a list of differences between the appearance of the older bills and the appearance of the redesigned bills. (Sample answers: The portraits in the older bills are smaller and in an oval. Older bills do not have watermarks or color variations. Newer bills have a large number in the lower right corner on the back.) **LS** **Visual**

Answers to Your Turn

1. The color of the 10 in the lower right corner will shift from copper to green.

2. Sample answer: I do not think that they would be able to successfully counterfeit money because the paper would need to have the watermark and the security thread embedded in it. Also, they would need to find a source of the color-shifting ink and a way to print the special ink.

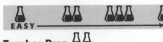
Time Required
1 lab period

Lab Ratings
EASY ————————→ HARD

Teacher Prep &&
Student Set-Up &&
Concept Level &&&
Clean Up &

Skills Acquired
- Collecting data
- Communicating
- Interpreting
- Measuring
- Organizing and analyzing data

Scientific Methods
In this lab, students will:
- Make observations
- Analyze the results
- Draw conclusions
- Communicate results

Tips and Tricks
A 15 W bulb works well for the experiments. Each setup can accommodate 2–3 students.

In step 4, a partially darkened room produces a closer approximation of f. As a result, the students may have some difficulty measuring the actual size of the image in step 7.

Emphasize the relationship between f measured in step 1 and $\frac{1}{f}$ calculated in the analysis of the results.

Application Lab

What You'll Do
> **Observe** images formed by a convex lens.
> **Measure** the distance of objects and images from the lens.
> **Analyze** your results to determine the focal length of the lens.

What You'll Need
cardboard screen, 10 cm × 20 cm
convex lens, 10 cm to 15 cm focal length
lens holder
light box with light bulb
meterstick
ruler, metric
screen holder
supports for meterstick

Safety
◆

⚙ 50 min

Lenses and Images
As an optical engineer for a camera company, you have been given a lens for which your job is to figure out the focal length. Based on the specifications you obtain by doing an experiment, a new model of camera will be designed that uses that lens.

Procedure
Preparing for Your Experiment
❶ The shape of a lens determines the size, position, and types of images that it may form. When parallel rays of light from a distant object pass through a converging lens, they come together to form an image at a point called the *focal point*. The distance from this point to the lens is called the *focal length*. In this experiment, you will find the focal length of a lens. Then, verify this value by forming images, measuring distances, and using the lens formula below.

$$\frac{1}{d_o} + \frac{1}{d_i} = \frac{1}{f}$$

where d_o = object distance,

   d_i = image distance, and

   f = focal length

❷ On a clean sheet of paper, make a data table like the one shown.

❸ Set up the equipment as illustrated in the figure below. Make sure the lens and screen are securely fastened to the meterstick.

Determining Focal Length
❹ Stand about 1 m from a window, and point the meterstick at a tree, parked car, or similar object. Slide the screen holder along the meterstick until a clear image of the distant object forms on the screen. Measure the distance between the lens and the screen in centimeters. This distance is very close to the focal length of the lens that you are using. Record this value at the top of your data table.

Safety Cautions
Students should be cautioned that the light bulb will become hot to the touch during the course of the lab. Only devices that are UL-listed should be used. The condition of the wiring and adequate grounding should be checked prior to use.

Sample Data: Objects, Lenses, and Images								
Focal length of lens: 10.2 cm	Object distance do (cm)	Image distance di (cm)	$\frac{1}{d_o}$	$\frac{1}{d_i}$	$\frac{1}{d_o} + \frac{1}{d_i}$	$\frac{1}{f}$	Size of object (mm)	Size of image (mm)
Trial 1	22.0	18.2	0.045	0.055	0.100	0.100	19	16
Trial 2	20.4	21.6	0.049	0.046	0.095	0.095	19	18
Trial 3	16.5	28.0	0.061	0.036	0.097	0.097	19	32

Sample Data Table: Objects, Lenses, and Images

Focal length of lens, f: _____ cm	Object distance, d_o (cm)	Image distance, d_i (cm)	$\frac{1}{d_o}$	$\frac{1}{d_i}$	$\frac{1}{d_o} + \frac{1}{d_i}$	$\frac{1}{f}$	Size of object (mm)	Size of image (mm)
Trial 1								
Trial 2		DO NOT WRITE IN BOOK						
Trial 3								

Forming Images

5 Set up the equipment as illustrated in the figure. Place the lens more than twice the focal length from the light box.

6 Move the screen along the meterstick until a clear image forms. Record the distance from the light to the lens, d_o, and the distance from the lens to the screen, d_i, in centimeters as Trial 1 in your data table. Also, record the height of the object and of the image in millimeters. The object in this case may be either the filament of the light bulb or a cut-out shape in the light box.

7 For Trial 2, place the lens exactly twice the focal length from the object. Slide the screen along the stick until a clear image is formed, as in step 6. Record the distances from the screen and the sizes of the object and image as you did in step 6.

8 For Trial 3, place the lens at a distance from the object that is greater than the focal length but less than twice the focal length. Adjust the screen, and record the measurements as you did in step 7.

Analysis

1. **Analyzing Data** Perform the necessary calculations to complete your data table.

2. **Analyzing Data** How does $\frac{1}{d_o} + \frac{1}{d_i}$ compare with $\frac{1}{f}$ in each of the three trials?

Communicating Results

3. **Drawing Conclusions** If the object distance is greater than the image distance, how will the size of the image compare with the size of the object?

Application

Does the lens that you tested conform to the lens equations for image formation? If a camera that contained this lens was made, what would the minimum length of the camera have to be? Explain your answer.

Answers to Analysis

1. Results may vary. See sample data table.

2. The value of $\frac{1}{d_o} + \frac{1}{d_i}$ is generally very close to the value of $\frac{1}{f}$.

Answer to Communicating Your Results

3. If the object distance is greater than the image distance, the image will be smaller than the object.

Answer to Application

Yes, the experiments showed that the lens forms images according to the standard lens equations. The minimum length of the camera would have to be the focal length of the lens, plus whatever additional space is needed for the camera housing and other components that would go behind the camera's image-capturing mechanism.

Key Resources

 Virtual Investigation

 Classroom Lab Video/DVD

 Holt Lab Generator CD-ROM
Search for any lab type, standard, difficulty level, or time. Edit any lab to fit your needs, or create your own labs. Use the Lab Material QuickList software to customize your lab materials list.

 Datasheet
Lenses and Images

 Observation Lab
Mirror Images

 CBL™ Probeware Lab
Choosing a Pair of Sunglasses

Reteaching Key Ideas

Energy Conservation To help students visualize the variation of intensity with the square of distance, have them think in terms of energy conservation. Have them consider a light that is at the center of several clear spheres. Each sphere has a slightly greater radius (1 m, 2 m, 3 m, etc.). If the amount of energy the light emits each second (its power) is constant, the amount of energy that must go through each sphere each second must be the same. Because the surface area of the sphere through which the light passes increases as it moves further from the source, a smaller fraction of energy passes through each unit of area on each sphere. The surface area of each sphere is proportional to the square of its radius (the distance from the light), and so for an observer at a point on each sphere, the light's intensity decreases with the square of the distance to the light.

Answers to Practice

1. $I = \dfrac{100.0 \text{ W}}{4 \times \pi \times (1.00 \text{ m}^2)} = 7.96 \text{ W/m}^2$;

   $\dfrac{7.96}{0.318} = 25$ times greater

2. $I = \dfrac{3.85 \times 10^{26} \text{ W}}{4 \times \pi \times (1.50 \times 10^{11})^2} =$

   $1.36 \times 10^3 \text{ W/m}^2$

3. $15.0 \text{ W/m}^2 = \dfrac{3.85 \times 10^{26} \text{ W}}{4 \times \pi \times x^2}$

   $1.88 \times 10^2 \text{ W/m}^2 \times x^2 =$

   $3.85 \times 10^{26} \text{ W}$

   $x = \sqrt{2.04 \times 10^{24} \text{ m}^2} = 1.43 \times 10^{12} \text{ m}$

   $\dfrac{1.43 \times 10^{12}}{1.5 \times 10^{11}} = 9.53$ times larger

Problem

The intensity of light at a distance, r, from a source with power output, P, is described by the following equation:

$$intensity = \frac{power}{4\pi \, (distance)^2} = \frac{P}{4\pi r^2}$$

What is the intensity of a 100.0 W light bulb at a distance of 5.00 m from the light bulb?

Solution

Identify

List all given and unknown values.

Given:

   $power \, (P) = 100.0 \text{ W}$

   $distance \, (r) = 5.00 \text{ m}$

Unknown:

   $intensity \, (\text{W/m}^2)$

Plan

Write down the equation for intensity.

Given:

   $intensity = \dfrac{P}{4\pi r^2}$

Solve

Solve for intensity.

a. To evaluate an equation that is written as a fraction, first evaluate the top and the bottom parts of the fraction separately.

b. Then, divide the top number by the bottom number to get the final answer.

a. $intensity = \dfrac{100.0 \text{ W}}{4 \times \pi \times (5.00 \text{ m})^2}$

   $intensity = \dfrac{100.0 \text{ W}}{4 \times 3.14 \times 25 \text{ m}^2}$

b. $intensity = \dfrac{100.0 \text{ W}}{314 \text{ m}^2} = 0.318 \text{ W/m}^2$

Because a watt (W) is the amount of power required to do 1 joule (J) of work in 1 s, 0.318 J of energy pass through each square meter of area at a distance of 5.00 m from the light bulb each second.

Practice

1. What is the intensity of the 100.0 W light bulb at a distance of 1.00 m from the light bulb? How many times greater is the intensity at 1.00 m than the intensity at 5.00 m?

2. The total power output of the sun is equal to 3.85×10^{26} W. What is the intensity of sunlight at a distance of 1.50×10^{11} m (the average distance of Earth from the sun) from the sun?

3. When the sun is directly above the clouds that form the surface of Saturn, the intensity of sunlight on the surface is 15.0 W/m². What is the distance from the sun to Saturn? How many times larger is the distance between the sun and Saturn than the distance between the sun and Earth?

Technology

 Math

Scientific Methods

Graphing

Key Resources

 Science Skills Worksheets
Equations Involving a Constant
Angles and Degrees
The Area of a Circle

Key Ideas

Section 1 Sound

> **Properties of Sound** Sound waves are caused by vibrations and carry energy through a medium. (p. 543)

> **Musical Instruments** Most instruments produce sound through the vibrations of strings, air columns, or membranes. (p. 547)

> **Hearing and the Ear** The human ear is a sensitive organ that senses vibrations in the air and amplifies them. (p. 549)

> **Ultrasound and Sonar** Reflected sound waves are used to determine distances and to create images. (p. 550)

Section 2 The Nature of Light

> **Waves and Particles** The two most common models describe light either as a wave or as a stream of particles. (p. 552)

> **The Electromagnetic Spectrum** The electromagnetic spectrum consists of waves at all possible energies, frequencies, and wavelengths. (p. 556)

Section 3 Reflection and Color

> **Reflection of Light** Every object reflects some light and absorbs some light. (p. 560)

> **Mirrors** Mirrors reflect light as described by the law of reflection, and this light reaches your eyes. The type of image you perceive depends on the type of mirror. (p. 562)

> **Seeing Colors** The colors that you perceive depend on the wavelengths of visible light that reach your eyes. (p. 564)

Section 4 Refraction, Lenses, and Prisms

> **Refraction of Light** Light waves bend, or refract, when they pass from one transparent medium to another. (p. 566)

> **Lenses** When light passes through a medium with a curved surface, a lens, the light rays change direction. (p. 568)

> **Dispersion and Prisms** A prism can separate the colors of light because the speeds of light waves traveling through the medium depend on the wavelengths of light. (p. 570)

Key Terms

sound wave, p. 543
pitch, p. 546
infrasound, p. 546
ultrasound, p. 546
resonance, p. 548
sonar, p. 551

photon, p. 553
intensity, p. 555
radar, p. 556

light ray, p. 560
virtual image, p. 562
real image, p. 563

lens, p. 568
magnification, p. 568
prism, p. 570
dispersion, p. 570

SUMMARY

SUPER SUMMARY

Have students connect the major concepts in this chapter through an interactive Super Summary. Visit **go.hrw.com** and type in the keyword **HK8SALS** to access the Super Summary for this chapter.

Differentiated Instruction

Alternative Assessment

Comparing Concepts Have students make a three-column table that compares sound and light. The title of the first column should be "Property, Interaction, or Concept," the second column should be "Sound," and the third column should be "Light." For example, on one row of the table students may write: "type of wave" in the first column, "longitudinal" in the second column, and "transverse" in the third column. **LS Logical**

Key Resources

⊟ **Interactive Concept Map**

▢ **Review Resources**
Concept Review Worksheets

▢ **Assessment Resources**
Chapter Tests A and B
Performance-Based Assessment

Reading Toolbox

1. Answers may vary. Sample answer: *son:* sonogram, sonic; *phot:* photon, photograph

Using Key Terms

2. Both amplitude and intensity are directly related to the energy of sound waves. The more energy the waves contain, the louder the sound is.

3. Pitch is the way the brain interprets the frequency of a sound wave. Higher frequency corresponds to higher pitch, and lower frequency corresponds to lower pitch.

4. When a guitar string is plucked, it vibrates in standing waves, producing a fundamental pitch. Resonance in the body of the guitar at the frequencies produced by the strings moves more air and thus amplifies the sound.

5. A clarinet is not likely to have the same fundamental frequency as a saxophone because they are different lengths, so the frequencies at which the columns of air inside the instruments vibrate will differ.

6. Infrasonic waves occur below the range of human hearing. Ultrasonic waves occur above the human hearing range.

7. Sonar is a system that uses reflected sound waves to determine the distance to objects, whereas radar is a system that uses reflected radio waves to determine distance. Sonar would be useful on a boat to determine water depth. Radar can be used by air traffic controllers to determine the location of incoming and outgoing planes.

8. When you view a virtual image, you are seeing light rays that only appear to be coming from the location of the image. Examples include a reflection in a flat mirror and the enlarged image seen through a magnifying glass. When you view a real image, you are seeing light rays actually coming from the location of the image. A real image can be projected on a screen. Examples are projected movies and the images formed in the tubes of microscopes and telescopes.

CHAPTER 16 Review

READING TOOLBOX

1. **Word Roots** The word root *son* or *sono* means "sound," and the root *phot* or *photo* means "light." For each of the roots, list two words that contain the root. Define the words in your list.

USING KEY TERMS

2. How is the loudness of a sound related to *amplitude* and *intensity*?

3. How is the *pitch* of a sound related to the sound's *frequency*?

4. Explain how a guitar produces sound by using the terms *standing waves* and *resonance.*

5. Explain why you would not expect a clarinet to have the same *fundamental frequency* as a saxophone.

6. Describe *infrasound* and *ultrasound*, and explain why humans cannot hear these waves.

7. Define *sonar* and *radar*. State their differences and their similarities, and describe a situation in which each system would be useful.

8. Explain how a *virtual image* differs from a *real image*. Give an example of each type of image.

9. Explain why a leaf may appear green in white light but black in red light. Use the following terms in your answer: *wavelength* and *reflection*.

10. What happens to light after it passes through a *converging lens* and after is passes through a *diverging lens*?

UNDERSTANDING KEY IDEAS

11. Relative intensity of sound is measured in units that have the symbol
    a. dB.　　　c. J.
    b. Hz.　　　d. V.

12. Sound waves travel faster through liquid water than through air because
    a. water is hotter than air.
    b. water is less dense than air.
    c. the particles of the liquid transfer energy better than the particles in a gas.
    d. the particles in the liquid vibrate more than the particles in a gas.

13. A flat mirror forms an image that is
    a. smaller than the object.
    b. larger than the object.
    c. virtual.
    d. real.

14. Microwaves are higher in energy than
    a. radio waves.　　　c. gamma rays.
    b. visible light.　　　d. X rays.

15. Light can be modeled as
    a. reflection and refraction.
    b. a stream of particles called *photons*.
    c. rays that travel in a curved path.
    d. sound waves.

16. In the eye, most of the refraction of light is done by the
    a. lens.　　　c. rods and cones.
    b. pupil.　　　d. cornea.

17. The energy of a photon is proportional to
    a. the amplitude of a wave.
    b. the wavelength of a wave.
    c. the frequency of a wave.
    d. the speed of light.

18. When white light passes through a prism, the light is separated into the colors in the visible spectrum because
    a. the prism reflects the light.
    b. the prism filters the light.
    c. the wavelengths of light travel at different speeds in the prism.
    d. the wavelengths of light increase in the prism.

EXPLAINING KEY IDEAS

19. Describe the anatomy of the human ear, and explain how the ear senses vibrations.

20. Draw a figure that illustrates what happens when light rays hit a rough surface and what happens when they hit a smooth surface. Explain how your illustration demonstrates diffuse reflection and the law of reflection.

21. How can an object appear bigger under a magnifying glass?

22. Describe how you can make red, green, blue, and black paint with a paint set that contains only yellow, magenta, and cyan paint.

CRITICAL THINKING

23. Applying Ideas A guitar has six strings, each tuned to a different pitch. What, other than the length of the strings, determines the pitch of the strings? (**Hint:** Think about what will affect the frequency at which the string vibrates.)

24. Drawing Conclusions By listening to an orchestra, how can you determine that the speed of sound is the same for all frequencies?

25. Analyzing Methods Sonar devices on ships use a narrow ultrasonic beam for determining depth. Why would a wider beam be used to locate fish?

26. Predicting Outcomes Imagine laying this page flat on a table and then standing a mirror upright at the top of the page. Using the law of reflection, draw the image of each of the following letters of the alphabet in the mirror.

A B C F W T

27. Forming Hypotheses Why is white light not dispersed into a spectrum when it passes through a flat pane of glass such as a window?

28. Understanding Relationships People who are *colorblind* are unable to see at least one of the primary colors. What part of the eye do you think is not working in colorblind people?

Assignment Guide	
SECTION	**ITEMS**
1	2–6, 11–12, 19, 23–25, 29–30
2	1, 7, 14–15, 17, 31–32
3	9, 13, 20, 22, 26, 28
4	8, 10, 16, 18, 21, 27

Graphing Skills

29. Line Graphs As a ship travels across a lake, a sonar device on the ship sends out downward pulses of ultrasound and detects the reflected pulses. The table below gives the ship's distance from the shore and the time for each pulse to return to the ship.

Distance from shore (m)	Time to receive pulse ($\times 10^{-2}$ s)
100	1.7
120	2.0
140	2.6
150	3.1
170	3.2
200	4.1
220	3.7
250	4.4
270	5.0
300	4.6

a. Use the speed of sound in water to calculate the depth of the lake at each distance from shore.

b. Construct a graph of the depth of the lake as a function of distance from the shore. Mark the maximum and minimum depth.

Math Skills

30. Sonar Calculate the distance to the bottom of a lake when a ship using sonar receives the reflection of a pulse in 0.055 s.

31. Electromagnetic Waves Using the speed of light, calculate the wavelength of radio waves from an AM radio station that is broadcasting at 1,200 kHz. (**Hint:** The wave speed equation is $v = f \times \lambda$.)

32. Electromagnetic Waves Waves that make up green light have a wavelength of about 550 nm. Use the wave speed equation and the speed of light to find their frequency.

Critical Thinking

23. The frequency of vibration of a string will also depend on the mass of the string, the material from which it is made, and the tension, or tightness, of the string.

24. Different instruments in the orchestra will transmit sound at different frequencies, because each instrument has its unique fundamental frequency. However, the sounds of the different instruments reach my ears at the same time, suggesting that the speed of sound is at least approximately the same at all frequencies.

Answers continued on p. 581A

9. The leaf appears green because it reflects green light and absorbs other wavelengths. Red light contains no green wavelengths, so the leaf can reflect no light and appears black.

10. A converging lens bends light inward, while a diverging lens bends light outward.

Understanding Key Ideas

11. a
12. c
13. c
14. a
15. b
16. d
17. c
18. c

Explaining Key Ideas

19. Sound waves are funneled through the outer ear down the ear canal to the eardrum, which vibrates. These vibrations pass through the anvil, hammer, and stirrup of the middle ear to a membrane at the opening of the inner ear. The waves then pass through the cochlea, which contains the basilar membrane. Hairs near the membrane stimulate nerve fibers that send impulses to the brain.

20. Figures should resemble the drawings in **Figure 2** of Section 3. Diffuse reflection occurs when light strikes a rough surface sending light rays in random directions. When light hits a smooth surface, all the light rays reflect off the surface at the same angle. The law of reflection, which states that the angle of incidence equals the angle of reflection, applies in both cases but is more clearly observed when light reflects off a smooth surface.

21. A magnifying glass is a converging lens and can create a virtual image that is larger than the object.

22. Paints are subtractive pigments. Red paint can be made by combining yellow and magenta. Green paint can be made by combining yellow and cyan. Blue paint can be made by combining magenta and cyan. Black paint can be made by combining yellow, magenta, and cyan.

Standardized Test Prep

Standardized Test Prep

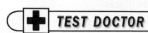

TEST DOCTOR

Question 1 Answer B is correct. Students must know that for every 10 dB increase, the perceived loudness of a sound doubles. Therefore, the sound of vacuum cleaner would be 10 dB less than the sound of the garbage disposal, or 70 dB. If students answer A, they have divided by 2. If they answer C, they added 10 db. If they answer D, they multiplied by 2.

Question 2 Answer H is correct. Students that answered F thought there were bones in the outer ear. If they answered G, they confused the ear canal with the middle ear. I reflected confusion that the cochlea has 3 bones.

Question 3 Answer B is correct. Other answers indicate that students do not know that ultrasound refers to frequencies higher than humans can hear, or that frequency is measured in Hz.

Question 4 Answer F is correct. Other answers indicate that students cannot distinguish by name between the optical interactions that occur when light strikes a surface.

Question 5 Full-credit answers should include the following points:
- The surface will appear to be black.
- The only color of light that will be striking it is green.
- No light will be reflected because the surface does not reflect green light.
- The absence of light appears as the color black.

Question 6 Full-credit answers should include the following points:
- Radar and sonar are both devices that radiate energy waves and detect them bouncing back off distant objects.
- Sonar uses sound waves.
- Radar uses electromagnetic waves (radio waves).

Question 7 Full-credit answers should include the following points:
- Sound is likely to travel faster on a hot day.

Understanding Concepts

Directions (1-4): For each question, write on a sheet of paper the letter of the correct answer.

1. A family notices that the garbage disposal in the sink sounds twice as loud as the vacuum cleaner does. If the sound of the garbage disposal is 80 dB, about how loud is the vacuum cleaner?
   - **A.** 40 dB
   - **B.** 70 dB
   - **C.** 90 dB
   - **D.** 160 dB

2. A medical student is examining a model of the ear. Where should the student look to find the hammer, anvil, and stirrup?
   - **F.** in the outer ear
   - **G.** in the ear canal
   - **H.** in the middle ear
   - **I.** in the cochlea

3. What sounds can an ultrasound system, such as sonar, detect that the human ear cannot?
   - **A.** sounds greater than 150 dB
   - **B.** sounds greater than 20,000 Hz
   - **C.** sounds traveling faster than 400 m/s
   - **D.** sounds traveling through a medium that is denser than air

4. Light striking a pane of glass passes through the glass, but the angle of the light changes while inside the pane of glass. What is this change called?
   - **F.** refraction
   - **G.** reflection
   - **H.** incidence
   - **I.** diffusion

Directions (5-7): For each question, write a short response.

5. A surface reflects all colors of light except for green. A light filter that allows only green light to pass through is placed between a light source and the surface. What color or colors will the surface appear to be under the filter?

6. How are radar and sonar alike? How are they different?

7. Is sound likely to travel faster through the air on a very cold day or on a very hot day? Why?

Reading Skills

Directions (8-9): Read the passage below. Then, answer the questions that follow.

STIMULATING EMISSIONS

Today, there is an astonishing variety of uses for lasers, from CD players to surgery. Lasers are beams of focused and concentrated light. The word *laser* began as an acronym for *Light Amplification by the Stimulated Emission of Radiation.*

Laser light is created by first adding energy to a chamber that contains certain types of atoms. Elements in the noble gas family work well for lasers. This addition of energy is the stimulation. The energy is absorbed by electrons in the atoms, which causes the electrons to jump to a higher energy level. At this point, the atoms are in an excited state. They can return to their original energy level by losing the energy they gained. When the electrons return to their original energy level, the lost energy is emitted as photons. This energy is the radiation referred to in the acronym.

The emitted photons can then strike other atoms that are in an excited state and cause them to emit photons in turn. The new photons are aimed in the same direction as the original photons. When mirrors are placed in certain positions within the chamber, the photons bounce back and forth many times and multiply, or amplify, the intensity of the photon emissions.

8. What optical effect is responsible for the amplification referred to in the acronym *laser*?
   - **A.** refraction
   - **B.** reflection
   - **C.** dispersion
   - **D.** diffusion

9. What happens when a photon strikes an atom that is in an excited state?

- Air molecules collide more frequently at higher temperatures and transfer energy more efficiently.

Question 8 Answer B is correct. Reflection caused by mirrors in the laser chamber causes the amplification of light emission.

Question 9 Full-credit answers should include the following points:
- The atom in an excited state emits a photon.
- The new photon is aimed in the same direction as the original photon.

Question 10 Answer I is correct. Students must know that red is the color of visible light with the lowest frequency and the longest wavelength. Knowing that infrared has a lower frequency than visible light might provide a clue, as would the order of colors in a rainbow.

Question 11 Answer C is correct. Students must know that gamma rays have the highest frequency in the electromagnetic spectrum.

Question 12 Full-credit answers should include the following points:
- Wavelength and frequency in waves are inversely proportional.
- As the wavelengths of electromagnetic waves increase, their frequencies decrease.

Interpreting Graphics

The diagram below shows the electromagnetic spectrum, and various ranges of the spectrum are labeled. Use the diagram to answer questions 10–12.

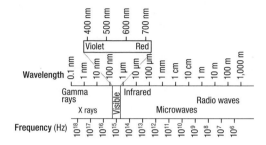

10. What is the wavelength of red light?
  F. about 7 m
  G. about 70 nm
  H. about 5 μm
  I. about 700 nm

11. Which of the following statements about gamma rays is true?
  A. They have a frequency of 10^{16} Hz.
  B. They have less energy than X rays have.
  C. They have more energy than X rays have.
  D. They have wavelengths that are greater than 10 nm.

12. As the wavelengths of electromagnetic waves increase, what happens to the frequency of the waves?

The diagram below shows a ray of light being reflected by two mirrors, which are aligned in parallel. Use this diagram to answer questions 13–14.

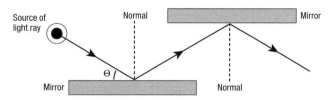

13. If angle θ is 40°, what is the angle of reflection on the second mirror?
  F. 40°
  G. 50°
  H. 90°
  I. 130°

14. Are either the first or second reflections diffuse reflections? Explain.

Test Tip

Carefully read the instructions, the question, and the answer options before choosing the answer.

Answers

1. B
2. H
3. B
4. F
5. Answers may vary; see Test Doctor for a detailed scoring rubric.
6. Answers may vary; see Test Doctor for a detailed scoring rubric.
7. Answers may vary; see Test Doctor for a detailed scoring rubric.
8. B
9. Answers may vary; see Test Doctor for a detailed scoring rubric.
10. I
11. C
12. Answers may vary; see Test Doctor for a detailed scoring rubric.
13. G
14. Answers may vary; see Test Doctor for a detailed scoring rubric.

Question 13 Answer G is correct. To find the correct answer, students must realize that because the normal is perpendicular to the reflective surface, the angle of incidence will be 90° minus the angle between the light ray and the mirror. Therefore, the angle of incidence (and, therefore, the angle of reflection) in the first reflection is 50°.

Question 14 Full-credit answers should include the following points:
• Diffuse reflections come from rough surfaces.
• The light ray in the diagram is reflecting off mirrors which are smooth.
• Neither reflection is a diffuse reflection.

State Resources

For specific resources for your state, visit go.**hrw**.com and type in the keyword **HSHSTR**.

📖 **Test Practice with Guided Reading Development**

Continuation of Answers

Answers continued from p. 551

5. When a sound gets louder, the amplitude and intensity of the sound wave increase.

6. The sound from a vacuum cleaner has a sound intensity of about 70 dB, so my friend is incorrect. A sound that has an intensity of 130 dB is 60 dB more intense than the sound of a vacuum. A difference in 10 dB means the sound is about twice as loud, so the thunder will seem about 64 (2^6, or $2 \times 2 \times 2 \times 2 \times 2 \times 2$) times as loud as a vacuum cleaner.

7. The acoustic guitar is constructed so that the hollow body vibrates in resonance with the string. Electric guitars usually have a solid body that vibrates very little.

8. The string of the C5 key will be shorter than the string of the middle C key. A shorter string will vibrate faster, so it will have a higher frequency and therefore a higher pitch.

9. When the phone rings, the sound travels to my outer ear and makes my eardrum vibrate. The vibrations of the eardrum cause the hammer, anvil, and stirrup bones in the middle ear to vibrate. The vibrating stirrup bone strikes the membrane at the opening of the inner ear and sends vibrations through the cochlea. In the cochlea, parts of the basilar membrane vibrate in response to the frequencies made by the phone. This stimulates nearby hair cells, which sends a signal to my brain. My brain interprets the frequency and intensity of the sound, and I recognize that the phone is ringing.

10. Ultrasound vibrations travel easily through tissue, but audible waves do not.

Answers to Section Review from p. 571

1. Diagrams should resemble the diagram in **Figure 1** in which the ray is bending towards the normal as it passes from air into glass.

2. A mirage is formed when light bends as it passes through air with different temperatures and forms a virtual image.

3. A magnifying lens refracts light rays from an object near the lens so that the light from points on the object appear to be coming from points that are farther apart. This produces an enlarged virtual image.

4. The speed at which light travels through a prism depends on the wavelength of the light. Light traveling at different speeds is bent at different angles, so the wavelengths are spread out when they exit a prism.

5. A light ray is first refracted as it passes into the cornea of the eye. From there it passes through the pupil and then on to the lens. The lens refracts the light further so that light is focused on the retina, forming a real image.

6. a virtual image

7. The yellow light travels faster than green light does. Violet light travels the slowest through a prism, so if yellow light is the farther away from violet, it must travel faster than green light.

8. No, rainbows are a result of the dispersion of colors, which is caused by refraction. Refraction results from the change in the speed of light as it passes from one medium to another. If light traveled the same speed in water as in air, no refraction would occur.

Answers continued from p. 579

25. A wider beam is used to locate fish because the fisherman does not know where the fish are, and a wider beam has a better chance of hitting a fish.

26. Student drawings should resemble the following: ∀ B C Ⱦ Ɯ ⊥

27. It is dispersed slightly as it refracts when entering the glass. However, when it emerges, it is refracted in exactly the opposite way and is recombined into white light.

28. Colors are perceived primarily by the cones of the eye. On the retina, there is one set of cones for red light, one set for green light, and one set for blue light. Different types of colorblindness are caused by of one or more of these sets of cones not working.

Graphing Skills

29. a.

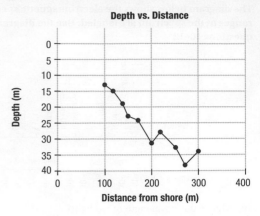

Depth vs. Distance

b. Students should mark the minimum depth at 100 m from shore and the maximum depth at 270 m from shore.

Math Skills

30. 0.055 s × 1,490 m/s = 82 m; 82 m / 2 = 41 m

31. $\lambda = v / f = 3.0 \times 10^8$ m/s / 1,200,000 Hz = 250 m

32. $f = v / \lambda = 3.0 \times 10^8$ m/s / 550×10^{-9} m = 5.5×10^{14} Hz

CHAPTER PLANNER 17 Electricity

	Standards	Teach Key Ideas

CHAPTER OPENER, pp. 582–584 — 50 min.

SECTION 1 Electric Charge and Force,
pp. 585–592 — 50 min.
- > Electric Charge
- > Transfer of Electric Charge
- > Electric Force

Standards: PS 1a, PS 4c, PS 4d, PS 5d, UCP 1, SAI 1, ST 2, HNS 1, HNS 3

Teach Key Ideas:
- Bellringer Transparency
- Teaching Transparencies TM47 Point Charges • TM48 Electric Fields • P18 Induced Charges • P19 Charging by Contact
- Visual Concepts Electric Charge • Characteristics of Electric Charge • Electrical Conductors and Insulators • Charging by Contact • Electric Fields and Test Charges

SECTION 2 Current, pp. 593–599 — 50 min.
- > Voltage and Current
- > Electrical Resistance

Standards: PS 6d, UCP 1, UCP 3, SAI 1

Teach Key Ideas:
- Bellringer Transparency
- Teaching Transparency TM49 Electric Potential Energy
- Visual Concepts Electrical Potential Energy • Battery

SECTION 3 Circuits, pp. 600–607 — 50 min.
- > What Are Circuits?
- > Series and Parallel Circuits
- > Electrical Energy and Electric Power
- > Fuses and Circuit Breakers

Standards: UCP 1, UCP 2, SAI 1, ST 2

Teach Key Ideas:
- Bellringer Transparency
- Teaching Transparencies TM50 Circuit and Diagram • P20 Series and Parallel
- Visual Concepts Electric Circuit • Schematic Diagram and Common Symbols • Resistors in Series • Resistors in Parallel • Equation for Electric Power • Fuse

See also PowerPoint® Resources

Chapter Review and Assessment Resources

- **SE** Science Skills: Learning Internet Terminology, p. 610
- **SE** Chapter Summary, p. 611
- **SE** Chapter Review, pp. 612–613
- **SE** Standardized Test Prep, pp. 614–615
- Concept Review Worksheets ■
- Chapter Tests A and B ■
- Holt Online Assessment

Basic Learners
- **TE** Electron Transfer, p. 589
- **TE** Inverse Square Law, p. 591
- **TE** Building Reading Skills, p. 603
- Science Skills Worksheets
- Differentiated Datasheets A for Labs and Activities ■
- Study Guide A ■

Advanced Learners
- **TE** Types of Lightning, p. 587
- **TE** Variable Resistors, p. 597
- **TE** Writing Computer Programs, p. 604
- Cross-Disciplinary Worksheets
- Differentiated Datasheets C for Labs and Activities ■

CHAPTER Fast Track To shorten instruction because of time limitations, omit Section 3 and the chapter lab.

Key

SE Student Edition
TE Teacher's Edition

📁 Chapter Resource File
📖 Workbook
📽 Transparency

💿 CD or CD-ROM
* Datasheet or blackline master available

■ Also available in Spanish

All resources listed below are also available on the **Teacher's One-Stop Planner.**

Why It Matters	Hands-On	Skills Development	Assessment
Build student motivation with resources about high-interest applications.	**SE Inquiry Lab** A Simple Circuit, p. 583* ■	**TE Reading Toolbox** Assessing Prior Knowledge, p. 582 **SE Reading Toolbox** p. 584	📁 Pretest ■
SE Benjamin Franklin, p. 587 **TE Helicopters,** p. 589 📁 **Cross-Disciplinary Worksheets** Connection to Social Studies—Incandescent Light Bulbs • Integrating Biology—Electric Eels	**TE Demonstration** Electroscope, p. 585 **SE Quick Lab** Charging Objects, p. 590* ■	**TE Reading Toolbox** Visual Literacy, p. 587 **TE Reading Toolbox** Visual Literacy, p. 588 **SE Reading Toolbox** Word Families, p. 591 **TE Reading Toolbox** Visual Literacy, p. 591	**TE Reteaching Key Ideas** Charging Objects, p. 592 **TE Formative Assessment,** p. 592 📁 Spanish Assessment* ■ 📁 Section Quiz ■
TE Resistor Color Codes, p. 597 📁 **Cross-Disciplinary Worksheets** Science and the Consumer—Battery Issues • Integrating Chemistry—Rechargeable Ni-Cd Batteries • Real World Applications—Electric Shock: Caution!	**TE Demonstration** Potential Difference, p. 593 **SE Quick Lab** Using a Lemon as a Cell, p. 595* ■ **SE Inquiry Lab** How Can Materials Be Classified by Resistance? p. 598* ■ 📁 **CBL™ Probeware Lab** How the Length of a Conductor Affects Resistance	**TE Reading Toolbox** Visual Literacy, p. 594 **SE Reading Toolbox** Analogies, p. 595 **SE Math Skills** Resistance, p. 597	**TE Reteaching Key Ideas** Building on an Analogy, p. 599 **TE Formative Assessment,** p. 599 📁 Spanish Assessment* ■ 📁 Section Quiz ■
TE Circuits and Technology, p. 601 **TE Holiday Lights,** p. 603 **SE Miniaturization of Circuits,** p. 604 **TE Energy Use in Home Appliances,** p. 605 📁 **Cross-Disciplinary Worksheet** Integrating Health—Recording Electricity in the Brain	**TE Demonstration** Building Closed Circuits, p. 600 **SE Skills Practice Lab** Constructing Electric Circuits, pp. 608–609* ■ 📁 **Observation Lab** Converting Wind Energy Into Electricity	**TE Reading Toolbox** Visual Literacy, p. 601 **TE Reading Toolbox** Visual Literacy, p. 604 **SE Reading Toolbox** Tri-Fold, p. 605 **SE Math Skills** Electric Power, p. 606	**TE Reteaching Key Ideas** Drawing Circuits, p. 607 **TE Formative Assessment,** p. 607 📁 Spanish Assessment* ■ 📁 Section Quiz ■

See also Lab Generator

See also Holt Online Assessment Resources

Resources for Differentiated Instruction

English Learners
TE Prediction Guide, p. 588
TE Common Words, p. 596
📁 Differentiated Datasheets A, B, and C for Labs and Activities ■
📖 Study Guide A ■

Struggling Readers
TE Reading Organizer, p. 594
TE Reading Skills, p. 601
📖 Interactive Reader

Special Education Students
TE Classifying Materials, p. 598
TE Visualizing Current, p. 602

Alternative Assessment
TE Graphing Force and Distance, p. 590
TE Electrical Potential Energy, p. 594
TE Maglev Trains, p. 598
TE Ground Fault Interrupters, p. 606
TE Concept Mapping, p. 611

CHAPTER 17 Electricity

CHAPTER 17 Electricity

Overview

This chapter starts by covering electric charge, the electric force, and electric fields. Then, students study electric current and related concepts, including potential difference, resistance, and the classification of materials as conductors, insulators, semiconductors, and superconductors. Finally, they learn about electric circuits, including schematic diagrams, series and parallel circuits, electrical power, and fuses and circuit breakers.

READING TOOLBOX

Assessing Prior Knowledge Students should understand the following concepts:
• scientific notation
• atomic structure
• force
• acceleration
• potential energy

MISCONCEPTION ///ALERT\\\

Science education research has identified the following misconception about electricity.
• Students believe that current flowing through a battery grows weaker with distance, and that a bulb farther away from a battery will be dimmer than one that is closer. (Relatively short differences in distance will not affect the performance of a circuit.) To overcome this misconception, have students experiment with a D-cell, a flashlight bulb, and wires of several lengths. Show students how to assemble a simple circuit and tell them to determine what happens when they change the length of wire connecting the D-cell and the light bulb. Students will find that increasing the length of wire within reasonable limits does not affect the performance of the circuit. **LS Kinesthetic/Logical**

Chapter Outline

❶ Electric Charge and Force
  Electric Charge
  Transfer of Electric Charge
  Electric Force

❷ Current
  Voltage and Current
  Electrical Resistance

❸ Circuits
  What Are Circuits?
  Series and Parallel Circuits
  Electrical Energy and Electric Power
  Fuses and Circuit Breakers

Why It **Matters**

A Tesla coil creates a very large voltage that can be discharged as an impressive electrical arc. Nicola Tesla used his invention to study the electrical nature of Earth and its atmosphere.

Chapter Correlations   *National Science Education Standards*

The following correlations show the National Science Standards that relate to this chapter. For the full text of the standards, see the National Science Education Standards at the front of the book.

PS 1a The electric force between the nucleus and electrons holds the atom together. (Section 1)

PS 4c The electric force is a universal force that exists between any two charged objects. Opposite charges attract while like charges repel. The strength of the force is proportional to the charges, and, as with gravitation, inversely proportional to the square of the distance between them. (Section 1)

PS 4d Most observable forces such as those exerted by a coiled spring or friction may be traced to electric forces acting between atoms and molecules. (Section 1)

PS 5d All energy can be considered to be either kinetic energy, which is the energy of motion; potential energy, which depends on relative position; or energy contained by a field, such as electromagnetic waves. (Section 1)

PS 6d In some materials, such as metals, electrons flow easily, whereas in insulating materials such as glass they can hardly flow at all. Semiconducting materials have intermediate behavior. At low temperatures some materials become superconductors and offer no resistance to the flow of electrons. (Section 2)

UCP1 Systems, order, and organization (Sections 1–3)

UCP 2 Evidence, models, and explanation (Section 3)

UCP 3 Constancy, change, and measurement (Section 2)

SAI 1 Abilities necessary to do scientific inquiry (Sections 1, 2; Skills Practice Lab: Constructing Electric Circuits)

ST 2 Understandings about science and technology (Sections 1, 3)

HNS 1 Science as a human endeavor (Section 1)

HNS 3 Historical perspectives (Section 1)

Teacher's Notes Be sure that batteries and bulbs used are functioning properly before doing this activity. If students have difficulty building their circuit, tell them to study the inside of the flashlight and use the wires or foil to mimic the arrangement of the wires inside the flashlight.

Materials per Group
• battery, D-cell
• flashlight
• foil, aluminum
• wire, electrical

Answers
1. The bulb should light up when you connect the bottom of the bulb to one terminal of the battery and the side of the bulb's base to the other terminal of the battery. This configuration makes a closed circuit including the battery.
2. The bulb will not light under any other configuration. Other configurations will not work because they are not closed circuits or the circuit does not include the battery.

Key Resources

📁 **Datasheet**
A Simple Circuit

💿 **Interactive Tutors**
Disc One, Module 8: Batteries and Cells
Disc Two, Module 15: Force Between Charges

InquiryLab ⏱ 20 min

A Simple Circuit

You can investigate electricity by using the parts of a simple **flashlight.** Use the **bulb** and **battery** from a flashlight and some **wire** or **aluminum foil** to make the bulb light. Try connecting the light bulb to the battery in several different ways.

Questions to Get You Started

1. Which method caused the bulb to light? Why did that method work?
2. Which method did not cause the bulb to light? Why didn't that method work?

Word Families

Sample answers:

electric power the rate at which electrical energy is converted into other forms of energy

electric field the space around a charged object in which another charged object experiences an electric force

electric circuit a set of electrical components connected such that they provide one or more complete paths for the movement of charges

Analogies

Sample table:

ANALOGY PHRASE	ITEM 1	ITEM 2
like	energy	electric charge is never created or destroyed
is similar	an object will fall from a region of higher to lower gravitational potential energy	charges will move from the side with a higher electrical potential energy to the side with a lower electrical potential energy
equal to	one volt per ampere	one ohm

FoldNotes

Answers may vary. KWL notes should be similar in form to the example shown. Make sure that students fill in the "Learned" column after they have read the relevant passages in the chapter.

READING TOOLBOX

These reading tools can help you learn the material in this chapter. For more information on how to use these and other tools, see **Appendix A.**

Word Families

Electric You will soon learn many new terms containing the words *electric* or *electrical*. These new terms use *electric* in the same way—meaning "pertaining to electricity." Here are some familiar words that you will see again in this chapter.

TERM	DEFINITION
energy	the capacity to do work
power	the rate at which work is done
field	a region of space in which a force operates
circuit	a closed loop

Your Turn Combine each of the words in the chart with *electric* or *electrical*, and write your own definition of the new term. Here is an example to get you started:

electrical energy: the capacity to do work using electricity

Analogies

Comparisons Analogies compare two things that may seem quite different. Analogies can make an unfamiliar idea easier to understand by linking it to something more familiar. Certain phrases help us spot analogies.

WORD OR PHRASE	HOW IT IS USED
just as	Turning a corner is acceleration, just as speeding up is.
is similar/ equal to	Force is equal to mass times acceleration.
act like/is like	A screw is like an inclined plane wrapped around a cylinder.

Your Turn Complete a table that is similar to this one as you come across analogies in this chapter.

ANALOGY PHRASE	ITEM 1	ITEM 2
just as	a ball will roll downhill	a negative charge will move away from another negative charge

FoldNotes

Tri-Fold KWL notes can help you start thinking about the subject matter before you read. KWL stands for "what I **K**now, what I **W**ant to know, and what I **L**earned." KWL notes also help you relate new ideas to those you already know. This can help make new ideas easier to understand.

Your Turn Create a tri-fold FoldNote. In the left column, labeled "Know," write what you know about electricity. In the center column, labeled "Want to know," write what you want to know. As you read the chapter, write in the final column, labeled "Learned," what you learn about electricity.

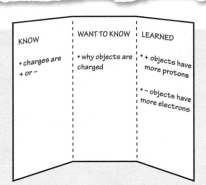

SECTION 1

Electric Charge and Force

Key Ideas

❯ What are the different kinds of electric charge?

❯ How do materials become charged when rubbed together?

❯ What force is responsible for most everyday forces?

Key Terms

electric charge

electrical conductor

electrical insulator

electric force

electric field

Why It Matters

We consider electrons to be *negative* because of a guess made by Benjamin Franklin. Almost all of the technology that you use is based on controlling the flow of electrons.

When you speak into a telephone, the microphone in the handset changes your sound waves into electrical signals. Light shines in your room when you flip a switch. And if you step on a pin with bare feet, your nerves send messages back and forth between your brain and your muscles so that you react quickly. Electric pulses moving through your nerve cells carry these messages.

Electric Charge

You have probably noticed that after running a plastic comb through your hair on a dry day, the comb attracts strands of your hair. It might even attract small bits of paper. Maybe you have reached for a doorknob after walking across a rug and received a shock, as **Figure 1** shows. You receive a shock because your body picks up electric charge as your shoes move across the carpet. Although you may not notice these charges when they are spread throughout your body, you notice them as they pass from your finger to the metal doorknob. You experience this movement of charges as a little tingle or perhaps a sharp snap.

Electric charge is an electrical property of matter. ❯ **An object can have a *negative* charge, a *positive* charge, or no charge at all.** Positive and negative electric charges are said to be opposite, because an object with an equal amount of positive and negative charge has no net charge. Like energy, electric charge is never created or destroyed. Conservation of charge is one of the fundamental laws of nature.

electric charge (ee LEK trik CHAHRJ) an electrical property of matter that creates electric and magnetic forces and interactions

Figure 1 Electric charge can jump from your body to a doorknob. **What kind of floor is likely to cause the buildup of electric charge?**

Key Resources

 Teaching Transparencies
TM47 Point Charges
TM48 Electric Fields
P18 Induced Charges
P19 Charging by Contact

Visual Concepts
Electric Charge
Characteristics of Electric Charge
Electrical Conductors and Insulators
Charging by Contact
Electric Fields and Test Charges

Datasheet
Charging Objects

Cross-Disciplinary Worksheets
Connection to Social Studies—
  Incandescent Light Bulbs
Integrating Biology—Electric Eels

SECTION 1

❯Focus

In this section students learn how pairs of charges repel and attract. Next, students learn how objects become charged and how charges move within objects. The section ends with a discussion of electric force and electric fields.

Bellringer

Use the Bellringer transparency to prepare students for this section.

Demonstrate

Electroscope For this demonstration, you will need 2 pith balls, string, PVC pipe 6 inches long, wool, aluminum pipe, and plastic cling wrap.

Step 1 Construct an electroscope by attaching each pith ball to a piece of string with a plastic hook or other fastening device. Then, hang the pith balls so they touch.

Step 2 Rub the PVC pipe with the wool. Touch the charged PVC pipe to the pith balls. The charged pith balls will repel each other.

Step 3 Discharge the pith balls by touching them to a faucet.

Step 4 Rub the aluminum with the plastic, giving the aluminum a positive charge. Then, touch the aluminum to the pith balls. The balls will again repel each other.
LS Visual

Answer to caption question

A carpeted floor is likely to cause a buildup of electric charge

Teaching Key Ideas

Kinds of Charges Review the structure of the atom with your students. Draw a model of a carbon atom on the board. The model should have 6 protons and 6 neutrons making up the nucleus and have 6 electrons moving around the nucleus. Drawing a Bohr model will help students see the position of the electrons more easily. Use the model to explain how objects can gain electrons to become negatively charged or lose electrons to become positively charged. Emphasize that protons and neutrons are never gained or lost under ordinary conditions.

Figure 2 If you rub a balloon across your hair on a dry day, both the balloon and your hair become electrically charged.

The balloon and hair are oppositely charged and attract each other.

These two charged balloons have the same charge and repel each other.

www.scilinks.org
Topic: Static Electricity
Code: HK81451

Like charges repel, and opposite charges attract.

One way to observe charge is to rub a balloon back and forth across your hair. You may find that the balloon is attracted to your hair, as **Figure 2** shows. If you rub two balloons across your hair and then gently bring them near each other, also shown in **Figure 2,** the balloons will push away from, or repel, each other.

After this rubbing, the balloons and your hair have some kind of charge on them. Your hair is attracted to the balloon, yet the two balloons are repelled by each other. This demonstration shows that there are different kinds of charges—the kind on the balloons and the kind on your hair.

The two balloons must have the same kind of charge because each became charged in the same way. Because the two charged balloons repel each other, we see that like charges repel each other. However, the balloon and your hair did not become charged in the same way, and they are attracted to each other. The reason is that unlike charges attract one another.

✓ Reading Check How do electric charges affect each other? (See Appendix E for answers to Reading Checks.)

Electric charge depends on an imbalance of protons and electrons.

All matter, including you, is made of atoms. Atoms, in turn, are made up of even smaller building blocks—electrons, protons, and neutrons. Electrons are negatively charged, protons are positively charged, and neutrons have no charge.

Objects are made up of an enormous number of neutrons, protons, and electrons. Whenever there is an imbalance in the number of protons and electrons in an atom, molecule, or other object, the object has a net electric charge. The difference in the numbers of protons and electrons determines an object's electric charge. Negatively charged objects have more electrons than protons. Positively charged objects have fewer electrons than protons.

The SI unit of electric charge is the *coulomb* (C). The electron and the proton have exactly the same amount of charge, 1.6×10^{-19} C. Electrons and protons are oppositely charged—a proton has a charge of $+1.6 \times 10^{-19}$ C, and an electron has a charge of -1.6×10^{-19} C. An object with a charge of -1.0 C has 6.25×10^{18} excess electrons. Because the amount of electric charge on an object depends on the number of protons and electrons, the net electric charge of a charged object is always an exact multiple of 1.6×10^{-19} C.

Teaching Key Ideas

Charged Objects You can use the triboelectric series to determine the charge on two objects that are rubbed together. When two materials are rubbed together, the material that is closer to the positive end of the series charges positively, and the material that is closer to the negative end charges negatively.

Triboelectric Series

Become Positive	Become Negative
glass	hard rubber
nylon	nickel and copper
wool	brass and silver
silk	synthetic rubber
aluminum	Orlon™
paper	Saran™
Remain Neutral	polyethylene
cotton	Teflon™
steel	silicone rubber

Benjamin Franklin

HISTORY IN SCIENCE

Benjamin Franklin (1706–1790) first suggested the terms *positive* and *negative* for the two types of charge. At the age of 40, Franklin was a successful printer and journalist. He saw some experiments on electricity and was so fascinated by them that he began to devote much of his time to experimenting. Franklin was the first person to realize that lightning is a huge electric discharge, or spark. He invented the first lightning rod, for which he became famous. He also flew a kite into thunderclouds—at great risk to his life—to collect charge from them. During and after the Revolutionary War, Franklin gained fame as a politician and statesman.

Benjamin Franklin used a kite to gather charges from a cloud during a thunderstorm. In a very dangerous experiment, he was able to gather charges on a key tied to the kite string and let the charges jump to his knuckles.

After convincing himself that lightning was indeed a form of electricity, Franklin used that knowledge to design the lightning rod, a simple conducting rod used to direct lightning strikes away from homes and buildings to the ground.

SCILINKS
www.scilinks.org
Topic: Benjamin Franklin
Code: HK80159

YOUR TURN

WRITING IN SCIENCE
1. Franklin is credited with much work in addition to his groundbreaking electricity experiments. Prepare a presentation in the form of a skit, story, or computer program about his work on fire departments, public libraries, or post offices.

WRITING IN SCIENCE
2. One of Franklin's other technological achievements was the invention of the Franklin stove. Research this stove, and write a brochure explaining the benefits of this stove to prospective customers of Franklin's time.

Why It **Matters**

Benjamin Franklin When Franklin started writing about his experiments on electricity, he found that he needed to invent words to describe his research. Some of the words coined by Franklin include *positively, negatively, battery, charge,* and *conductor*. Surprisingly, Franklin, a prolific writer, did not write about his experiment with the kite and the key. However, the details of the experiment were precisely described by Joseph Priestley, a British chemist who is credited with discovering oxygen. Encourage interested students to research the scientific work done by Franklin or Priestley and make a poster of what they learn. **LS** Visual

READING TOOLBOX

Visual Literacy The image of the lightning near the house shows the lightning and the bottom of the cloud are negatively charged. Tell students that during a thunderstorm, water droplets, ice, and air move inside storm clouds. As a result, negative charges build up, often at the bottom of the clouds. Positive charges often build up at the top of the clouds, but that part of the clouds is not shown in the diagram.

Differentiated Instruction

Advanced Learners

Types of Lightning Lightning comes in several different shapes and forms. Ball, forked, sheet, and bead lightning are a few examples. Have students research the many forms of lightning. Encourage them to be creative in the presentation of their results. Ask them to include photographs, if possible. **LS** Logical/Visual

Answers to Your Turn

1. Students' presentations may include the following information: As Philadelphia's Postmaster, Franklin made many improvements, including speeding up domestic and foreign delivery by hiring more couriers. In 1731, he founded the Philadelphia Library, America's first circulating library. In 1736, he organized the Union Fire Company of Philadelphia, the world's first volunteer fire department.
2. Sample answer: The Franklin stove has metal baffles, which increase its heating efficiency. The Franklin was placed in the middle of the room being heated, allowing it to radiate heat in all directions and allowing more efficient convection than a fireplace in the wall.

Teaching Key Ideas

Charging Objects Have students inflate 2 balloons and tie a 50 cm length of string to each one. Tell one student to grasp the end of a string in each hand. Instruct another student to rub one of the balloons with a wool cloth about 10 times. Students should then allow the balloons to hang freely. Ask students to share their observations. (The balloons move toward each other.) Then, have students rub both balloons with the cloth and observe what happens. (The balloons, which now have the same charge, move away from each other.) Ask students how the balloons became charged. (Rubbing caused electrons to move from the cloth to the balloons.)
LS Kinesthetic

Answer to caption question

Insulation around the wires prevents charges from leaking into the surroundings. If there were no insulation, you could get a shock by touching the wires.

Visual Literacy Have students look at **Figure 4,** and ask them what will happen to the doorknob when the negatively charged rod is removed. (There will no longer be an induced charge on the two sides of the doorknob; it will be electrically neutral.)
LS Visual

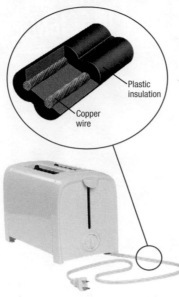

Figure 3 Appliance cords are made of metal wire surrounded by plastic insulation. **How does this insulation make the appliance safer to use?**

electrical conductor (ee LEK tri kuhl kuhn DUHK tuhr) a material in which charges can move freely

electrical insulator (ee LEK tri kuhl IN suh LAYT uhr) a material in which charges cannot move freely

Transfer of Electric Charge

Protons and neutrons are relatively fixed in the nucleus of the atom, but the outermost electrons can easily move from one atom to another. **When different materials are rubbed together, electrons can be transferred from one material to the other.** The direction in which the electrons are transferred depends on the materials.

Conductors allow charges to flow; insulators do not.

Have you ever noticed that the electrical cords attached to appliances, such as the toaster shown in **Figure 3,** are plastic? These cords are not plastic all the way through, however. The center of an electrical cord is made of thin copper wires. Cords are layered in this way because of the electrical properties of each material.

Materials such as the copper in cords are called **electrical conductors.** Conductors allow electric charges to move freely. The plastic in the cord, however, does not allow the electric charges to move freely. Materials that do not transfer charge easily are called **electrical insulators.** Cardboard, glass, silk, and plastic are insulators. Charges in the electrical cord attached to an appliance can move through the conducting center but cannot escape through the surrounding insulator.

Charges can move within uncharged objects.

The charges in a neutral conductor can be redistributed without actually changing the overall charge of the object. **Figure 4** shows a negatively charged rubber rod brought close to, but not touching, a metal doorknob. The electrons in the doorknob are repelled by the rod and move away. As a result, the part of the doorknob closest to the rod is positively charged. The part of the doorknob farthest from the rod is negatively charged. The total charge on the doorknob will still be zero, but the opposite sides will have an *induced* charge.

Figure 4 A negatively charged rod brought near a metal doorknob induces a positive charge on the side of the doorknob closest to the rod and a negative charge on the side farthest from the rod.

Differentiated Instruction

English Learners

Prediction Guide Before students read the passage about friction, conduction, and induction, ask them to explain what they think these terms mean and to think of an example of each term. Then, have them evaluate their responses after reading these pages. **LS Verbal**

Figure 5 Electric Charging by Contact

go.hrw.com
✳ interact online
Keyword: HK8ELEF5

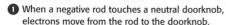

❶ When a negative rod touches a neutral doorknob, electrons move from the rod to the doorknob.

❷ The transfer of electrons to the metal doorknob gives the doorknob a net negative charge.

Objects can be charged by contact.

The transfer of electrons from one object to another can charge objects. For example, when a negatively charged rubber rod touches a neutral object, such as the doorknob shown in **Figure 5,** some electrons move from the rod to the doorknob. The doorknob then has a net negative charge. The rubber rod still has a negative charge, but its charge becomes smaller. Objects charged by touching a charged object to a neutral object are said to be charged by *contact.*

If a positively charged rod were to touch a neutral doorknob, electrons would move from the doorknob into the positively charged rod. The doorknob would then have a net positive charge, and the net charge on the rod would again be decreased.

Objects can be charged by friction.

When you slide across a fabric car seat, some electrons are transferred between your clothes and the car seat. Depending on the types of materials involved, the electrons can be transferred from your clothes to the seat or from the seat to your clothes. One material gains electrons and becomes negatively charged, and the other loses electrons and becomes positively charged. This is an example of *charging by friction.*

Have you ever pulled clothes out of the dryer and had them stick together? They stick together because of *static electricity.* Your clothes are charged by friction as they rub against each other inside the dryer, and the electric charge builds up on the clothes. Static electricity can damage sensitive electronics when it discharges quickly through them.

✔ **Reading Check** What causes static electricity?

Integrating Biology

Charges and Living Organisms
Atoms or molecules with a net electric charge are known as *ions*. All living cells contain ions. Most cells also need to be bathed in solutions of ions to stay alive. As a result, most living things are fairly good conductors.

Dry skin can be a good insulator. But if your skin gets wet, it becomes a conductor and charge can move through your body more easily. So, there is a greatly increased risk of electrocution when your skin is wet.

---

go.hrw.com
✳ interact online

Students can interact with the figure by going to **go.hrw.com** and typing in the keyword **HK8ELEF5.**

Teaching Key Ideas

Representing Charge Remind students that the charges shown in **Figures 4** and **5** do not show all of the protons and electrons in the doorknobs. For example, in the second image in **Figure 5,** there are many atoms with equal numbers of protons and electrons that are not shown. The negative charges that are shown illustrate that the doorknob has an overall negative charge. It would be impossible to show all of the charges due to the enormous number of atoms present even in very small objects. **LS Visual**

Why It Matters

Helicopters When helicopters are flying, the propellers rub across the air many times per second. If the humidity is low, the friction can charge the propeller blades, which in turn charge the entire helicopter. For this reason, the electronics of the helicopter must be insulated from the outer skin of the helicopter so that they cannot be burned out by this built-up charge. When the helicopter lands, the excess charge goes into the ground and the helicopter becomes neutral. When the helicopter is flying in humid air, the helicopter continually discharges into the atmosphere.

Differentiated Instruction

Basic Learners

Electron Transfer Do the following demonstration to help students visualize the transfer of electrons between objects. Hold up a chalk eraser saturated with dust. Tell the class that the eraser represents a negatively charged object, the chalk particles represent electrons, and the (clean) board represents an uncharged object. Wipe the board with the eraser. Students will observe the "electron trail" that the chalk leaves behind. **LS Visual**

Teacher's Notes To avoid the possible spread of lice, you may instruct students to rub the comb with a piece of wool cloth instead of using the comb in their hair.

Materials per Group
• comb, plastic
• paper, tissue

Answers to Analysis

1. The plastic comb and the tissue paper are insulators.
2. Negative charges are transferred from my hair to the comb making the comb negatively charged. When the comb is held near the tissue paper, molecules in the tissue paper are polarized, producing an induced positive charge on the surface nearest the comb and an induced negative charge on the surface farthest from the comb. As a result, the pieces of tissue paper are electrically attracted to the comb.
3. If I held the comb near my hair, my hair would be attracted to the comb.

Answer to caption question

A stream of water is deflected when a charged object is nearby because water molecules are polarized.

QuickLab — Charging Objects

⏱ 20 min

Procedure

1. Tear a **sheet of tissue paper** into small pieces, and pile the pieces on a table.
2. Use a **plastic comb** to vigorously comb your hair.
3. Use the comb to pick up the pieces of tissue.

Analysis

1. Are the plastic comb and tissue paper conductors or insulators?
2. What happens to the charges in the comb, tissue, and your hair?
3. What would happen if you held the comb near your hair?

Figure 6 Rubbing a balloon with wool induces a negative charge on the balloon. The balloon can then deflect a stream of water. **What property of water causes this movement to occur?**

A surface charge can be induced on insulators.

How can a negatively charged comb pick up pieces of neutral tissue paper? The electrons in tissue paper cannot move about freely because the paper is an insulator. But when a charged object is brought near an insulator, the positions of the electrons within the individual molecules of the insulator change slightly. One side of a molecule will be slightly more positive or negative than the other side. This *polarization* of the atoms or molecules of an insulator produces an induced charge on the surface of the insulator. Molecules of water are polarized and respond easily to charged objects, such as the balloon shown in **Figure 6.**

Electric Force

The attraction of tissue paper to a negatively charged comb and the repulsion of two similarly charged balloons are examples of **electric force.** Such pushes and pulls between charges are all around you. For example, a table feels solid, even though its atoms contain mostly empty space. The electric force between the electrons in the table's atoms and your hand is strong enough to prevent your hand from going through the table. ❯ **The electric force at the atomic and molecular levels is responsible for most of the everyday forces that we observe, such as the force of a spring and the force of friction.**

The electric force is also responsible for effects that we cannot see. It is part of what holds atoms together. The bonding of atoms to form molecules is also due to the electric force. The electric force plays a part in the interactions among molecules, such as the proteins and other building blocks of our bodies. Without the electric force, life itself would be impossible.

Differentiated Instruction

Alternative Assessment

Graphing Force and Distance The table shows the distance between two positively or negatively charged objects and the electric force between them. Have students graph the data to see the shape of the curve that describes the interaction between charges. Using their graphs, students should be able to predict the force when the distance is 6 mm. (about 6.75 N)

LS Visual

Distance (mm)	Force (N)
1	243
3	27
5	10
7	5
9	3

Electric force depends on charge and distance.

The electric force between two charged objects varies depending on the amount of charge on each object and the distance between them. The electric force between two objects is proportional to the product of the charges on the objects. If the charge on one object is doubled, the electric force between the objects will also be doubled, as long as the distance between the objects remains the same.

The electric force is also inversely proportional to the square of the distance between two objects. For example, if the distance between two charges is doubled, the electric force between them decreases to one-fourth its original value. If the distance between two small charges is quadrupled, the electric force between them decreases to one-sixteenth its original value.

✓ **Reading Check** On what factors does electric force depend?

Electric force acts through a field.

As described earlier, electric force does not require that objects touch. How do charges interact over a distance? One way to model this property of charges is with the concept of an electric field. An **electric field** always exists in the space around a charged particle. Any other charged particle in that field will experience an electric force. This force is due to the electric field associated with the first charged particle.

One way to show an electric field is by drawing *electric field lines*. Electric field lines point in the direction of the electric force on a positive charge. Electric field lines near isolated charges are shown in **Figure 7.** Because two positive charges repel each other, the electric field lines around a positive charge point outward. In contrast, the electric field lines around a negative charge point inward.

electric force (ee LEK trik FAWRS) the force of attraction or repulsion on a charged particle that is due to an electric field

electric field (ee LEK trik FEELD) the space around a charged object in which another charged object experiences an electric force

READING TOOLBOX

Word Families
Go back to the definitions that you created earlier for terms containing the word *electric*. How do they compare to the formal definitions found on this page?

Figure 7 Electric Field Lines near an Isolated Charge

A positive charge placed in the electric field due to a positive charge would be pushed away.

A positive charge placed in the electric field due to a negative charge would be pulled in.

Teaching Key Ideas
Drawing Electric Field Lines
Students may have difficulty remembering that the electric field points in the direction of the electric force on a positive charge. Draw a positive test charge at the location of the electric field. The electric field will point in the direction that this positive charge would move. Negatively charged particles will move in the opposite direction of the electric field.

READING TOOLBOX

Word Families As an extension, ask students to list other words or phrases that contain *electric* or *electrical*. (Sample answers: electric circuit, electric blanket, electric fence, electrical outlet, or electrical engineer) Have students brainstorm definitions for these words as a class. **LS Verbal**

READING TOOLBOX

Visual Literacy Figure 7 shows the electric fields for a positive source charge and a negative source charge. Ask students what can be concluded about the charges by comparing the electric field lines. (Because the number of field lines from the positive charge is equal to the number of field lines approaching the negative charge, the charges must be equal in magnitude. The field lines also show that the first charge is positive because they are pointing away from the charge. Because the field lines point toward the second charge, they show that the charge is negative.) **LS Visual**

Differentiated Instruction

Basic Learners

Inverse Square Law The relationship between electric force and distance behaves according to the inverse square law. Some students may have difficulty thinking about the inverse square law abstractly. To help these students understand, use real numbers to illustrate the relationship. Write the following on the board, "$64 \div x^2 = ?$" Then, tell students to solve the problem with x equal to 2, 4, and 8. Write down each problem and answer so that students can see the numbers. Finally, ask students to describe how the answer changes as the value for x changes. **LS Logical**

Reteaching Key Ideas

Charging Objects Have students draw a step-by-step series of sketches that show how two neutral objects become charged by friction. The last drawing of the series should show the electric field lines between the charged objects. Tell students that their sketches should be well labeled, should explain how charges are transferred, and should explain how the electric force acts on the objects after they are charged. **LS Visual**

Formative Assessment

Clothes in a dryer sometimes become charged by _____.

A. contact (Incorrect. Charging by contact happens when a charged object touches a neutral object. The clothes in the dryer all start as neutral objects.)

B. friction (Correct. The clothes in a dryer rub against each other and the charges from some clothes are transferred to other clothes.)

C. induction (Incorrect. Charging by induction happens when a charged object is held close to a neutral object and causes charges in the neutral object to redistribute.)

D. insulation (Incorrect. Insulation is not a method of charging objects.)

Figure 8 Electric Field Lines near Two Charges

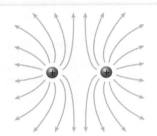

The electric field lines for two positive charges located near each other show the repulsion between the charges.

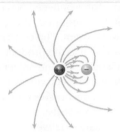

Half of the field lines starting on the positive charge end on the negative charge because the positive charge is twice as large as the negative charge.

Electric field lines never cross one another.

You can see from **Figure 8** that the electric field near two charges can also be drawn. The field lines near two positive charges point away from each other, and show that the positive charges repel each other. At a great distance from the charges, the electric field looks like that of a single charge with a charge of +2.

Field lines can show both the direction of an electric field and the relative strength of each charge. The electric field lines near two charges—one positive charge and one negative charge—will show a different pattern. When the positive charge is two times as large as the negative charge, only half of the electric field lines that leave the positive charge end at the negative charge.

Section 1 Review

KEY IDEAS

1. **Describe** the interaction between two like charges. Is the interaction the same between two unlike charges?

2. **Categorize** the following objects as conductors or insulators:
   a. copper wire
   b. your body when your skin is wet
   c. a plastic comb

3. **Explain** how the electric force between two positive charges changes under the following conditions:
   a. the distance between the charges is tripled
   b. the amount of one charge is doubled

CRITICAL THINKING

4. **Classifying** Identify the electric charge of each of the following atomic particles: a proton, a neutron, and an electron.

5. **Using Graphics** Diagram what will happen if a positively charged rod is brought near the following:
   a. a metal washer
   b. a plastic disk

6. **Interpreting Graphics** What missing electric charge would produce the electric field shown in this diagram?

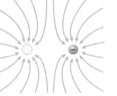

Answers to Section Review

1. Like charges repel each other. No, two unlike charges attract each other.

2. **a.** conductor
   b. conductor
   c. insulator

3. **a.** The force will become one-ninth as large as the original force.
   b. The force will double.

4. proton—positive; neutron—neutral, no charge; electron—negative

5. **a.** The drawing should show negative charges on the side of the metal washer nearest the rod and positive charges on the side of the washer farthest from the rod.

   b. The drawing should show "polarized molecules" with the side of each "molecule" nearest the rod negative and the side farthest from the rod positive.

6. a negative charge of equal amount

SECTION 2 Current

Key Ideas

❯ How are electrical potential energy and gravitational potential energy similar?

❯ What causes electrical resistance?

Key Terms

electrical potential energy

potential difference

cell

electric current

resistance

Why It Matters

Once started, current will flow forever in a loop of superconducting material. Modern MRI machines, which help identify health problems, contain superconducting magnets.

W hen you wake up in the morning, you reach up and turn on the light switch. The light bulb is powered by moving charges. How do charges move through a light bulb? What causes the charges to move?

Voltage and Current

Gravitational potential energy of a ball depends on the relative position of the ball, as **Figure 1** shows. A ball rolling downhill moves from a position of higher gravitational potential energy to one of lower gravitational potential energy. An electric charge also has potential energy—**electrical potential energy**—that depends on its position in an electric field.

❯ **Just as a ball will roll downhill, a negative charge will move away from another negative charge.** The movement is the result of the first negative charge's electric field. The electrical potential energy of the moving charge decreases because the electric field does work on the charge.

You can do work on a ball to move it uphill. As a result, the ball's gravitational potential energy increases. In the same way, a force can push a charge in the opposite direction of the electric force. As a result, the electrical potential energy associated with the charge's relative position increases.

electrical potential energy
(ee LEK tri kuhl poh TEN shuhl
EN uhr jee) the ability to move an electric charge from one point to another

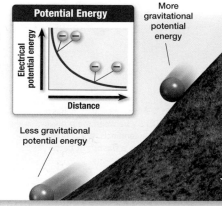

Potential Energy

Electrical potential energy

Distance

More gravitational potential energy

Less gravitational potential energy

Figure 1 The gravitational potential energy of a ball decreases as the ball rolls downhill. Similarly, the electrical potential energy between two like charges decreases as the distance between the charges increases.

SECTION 2

❯ Focus

This section covers current and many related concepts, including electrical potential energy, potential difference, batteries, electric current, and resistance. Students also learn how materials can be classified as conductors, insulators, semiconductors, or superconductors.

Bellringer

Use the Bellringer transparency to prepare students for this section.

Demonstrate

Potential Difference Borrow a Van de Graaf generator from the physics teacher. You will also need a small, tube-shaped fluorescent light bulb. Turn on the generator and allow it to build up a charge. The fluorescent tube can be taped to the end of a meterstick for better visibility. Hold the tube near the generator so that it points out radially, but do not touch the ball of the generator. Turn the lights off in the room. There will be a potential difference across the tube, and it will light up slightly. Tell students they will learn about potential difference in this section.

Safety Caution: Use a plastic fluorescent tube cover to protect students from possible shattering glass. Be careful to discharge the generator before touching it. **LS** Visual

Key Resources

Teaching Transparency
TM49 Electric Potential Energy

Visual Concepts
Electrical Potential Energy
Battery

Datasheets
Using a Lemon as a Cell
How Can Materials Be Classified by Resistance?

Math Skills Worksheet
Resistance

Cross-Disciplinary Worksheets
Science and the Consumer—Battery Issues
Integrating Chemistry—Rechargeable Ni-Cd Batteries
Real World Applications—Electric Shock: Caution!

SECTION 2 Current   593

Teaching Key Ideas

Electrical Potential Energy Be sure students understand that electrical potential energy is also high between two positive charges that are close together. So, the following statement is also true: "Just as a ball will roll downhill, a positive charge will move away from another positive charge." Tell students that the graph in **Figure 1** on the previous page will look the same whether the two charges shown are both negative or both positive. **LS** Logical

READING TOOLBOX

Visual Literacy Have students look at **Figure 2,** and ask them when the electrical potential energy would be the lowest for an electron in the electric field due to a positively charged object. (It would be lowest when the electron and positively charged object are very close together.) **LS** Visual

Answer to caption question
The voltage across a flashlight battery is usually 1.5 V.

Figure 2 Electrical Potential Energy and Relative Position

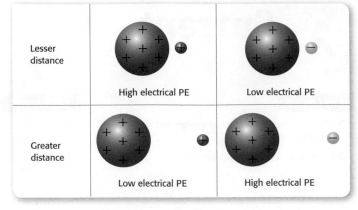

Lesser distance	High electrical PE	Low electrical PE
Greater distance	Low electrical PE	High electrical PE

Academic Vocabulary

convert (kuhn VUHRT) to change from one form to another

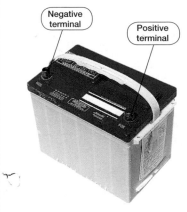

Negative terminal
Positive terminal

Figure 3 A typical car battery has a voltage of 12 V between the positive and negative terminals. **What is the voltage across a flashlight battery?**

Potential difference is measured in volts.

The electrical potential energy (PE) changes with distance between two charges, as **Figure 2** shows. For a repulsive force—that between two like charges—electrical potential energy increases as the charges move closer to each other. The opposite holds for the attractive force between unlike charges.

Usually, it is more practical to consider potential difference than electrical potential energy. **Potential difference** is the change in the electrical potential energy of a charged particle divided by its charge. This change occurs as a charge moves from one place to another in an electric field.

The SI unit for potential difference is the *volt* (V), which is equivalent to one joule per coulomb (1 J/C). For this reason, potential difference is often called *voltage*.

✔ **Reading Check** What is another common name for potential difference?

There is a voltage across the terminals of a battery.

The potential difference, or voltage, across the two ends, or *terminals,* of a battery ranges from about 1.5 V for a small battery to about 12 V for a car battery, such as the one shown in **Figure 3.** Most batteries are *electrochemical* **cells**—or groups of connected cells—that convert chemical energy into electrical energy. A common cell has a potential difference of 1.5 V between the positive and negative terminals.

Electrochemical cells contain an *electrolyte*, a solution that conducts electricity, and two *electrodes*, each a different conducting material. These cells can be dry cells or wet cells. Dry cells, such as those used in flashlights, contain a pastelike electrolyte. Wet cells, such as those used in almost all car batteries, contain a liquid electrolyte.

Differentiated Instruction

Alternative Assessment

Electrical Potential Energy Ask students to write a paragraph describing how the electrical potential energy of a charged object depends on the object's position relative to another charged object. (Sample answer: If two charged objects repel each other, the electrical potential energy will be greatest when the objects are near each other. If two charged objects attract each other, the electrical potential energy will be greatest when they are far apart.) **LS** Verbal

Struggling Readers

Reading Organizer Have students read the first three pages of this section and then organize the ideas presented in an outline. The outline should be organized in terms of the details presented for each heading. **LS** Verbal

A voltage sets charges in motion.

When a flashlight is switched on, the terminals of the battery are connected through the light bulb. This connection creates a voltage across the filament of the light bulb. This voltage makes the charges move from the side with a higher electrical potential energy to the side with a lower electrical potential energy. In other words, charges begin to move. This movement is similar to an object falling from a region of higher to lower gravitational potential energy.

Current is the rate of charge movement.

The **electric current** is the rate at which the charges move through the wire. The SI unit of current is the *ampere* (A). One ampere equals 1 C of charge moving past a point in 1 s.

A battery is a *direct current* source because the charges always move from one terminal to the other in the same direction. Current can be made up of positive, negative, or a combination of both positive and negative charges. In metals, moving electrons make up the current. In gases and many chemical solutions, current is the result of both positive and negative charges in motion.

A negative charge moving in one direction has the same effect as a positive charge moving in the opposite direction. *Conventional current* is the current made of positive charge that would have the same effect as the actual motion of charge in the material. So, the direction of current is *opposite* to the direction that electrons move.

potential difference (poh TEN shuhl DIF uhr uhns) the voltage difference in potential between two points in a circuit

cell (SEL) a device that produces an electric current by converting chemical or radiant energy into electrical energy

electric current (ee LEK trik KUHR uhnt) the rate at which charges pass through a given point

READING TOOLBOX

Analogies
As you read about electric current, look for analogies. Create a table or appropriate FoldNote. Record the analogy phrase and the two items that are compared.

READING TOOLBOX

Analogies If students don't understand how to fill in the analogy FoldNote, ask them to brainstorm some everyday analogies. Show students how these would be written in the FoldNote. Sample table:

Analogy phrase	Item 1	Item 2
like	the bicyclist rides	the wind
acted like	the person who won the lottery	a kid in candy store

QuickLab

Teacher's Notes It is important that the electrodes are inserted as deeply as possible into the lemon so that there is maximum contact between the metal and the lemon juice. If zinc is not available, use magnesium. Any fruit with an acidic juice, such as an orange or grapefruit, will work. Potatoes will also work.

Materials per Group
- copper, strip
- different metals, strips
- galvanometer
- lemon
- knife
- wire, insulated copper
- wire strippers
- zinc, strip

Answers to Analysis
1. Answers may vary depending on the metals used as electrodes. Larger electrodes will produce greater current. Consult an electrochemical series to determine which pair of electrodes should produce the greatest current.
2. Answers may vary.

QuickLab Using a Lemon as a Cell

⏱ 20 min

Procedure

❶ Using a **knife,** make two parallel cuts 6 cm apart along the middle of a **juicy lemon.** Insert a **copper strip** into one of the cuts and a **zinc strip** of the same size into the other.

❷ Cut two equal lengths of **insulated copper wire.** Use **wire strippers** to remove the insulation from both ends of each wire. Connect one end of each wire to one of the terminals of a **galvanometer.**

❸ Touch the free end of one wire to the copper strip in the lemon. Touch the free end of the other wire to the zinc strip. Record the galvanometer reading for the zinc-copper cell.

❹ Replace the strips of copper and zinc with equally sized **strips of different metals.** Record the galvanometer readings for each pair of electrodes.

Analysis

1. Which pair of electrodes resulted in the largest current?

2. Construct a table of your results.

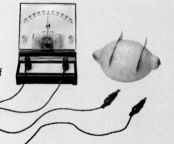

Earth Science Connection

Lightning Lightning is the flow of charge from a cloud to Earth, from Earth to a cloud, or between clouds. In the first situation, negative charges build up in the cloud. As the charge increases, an electric field forms between Earth and the cloud. When the potential difference between the cloud and the ground is great enough, the air acts as a conductor. At that point, the lightning strikes the closest point on the ground, delivering up to 1 million joules of electrical energy. If a house is hit by lightning, the electrical charges flow through any metal material throughout the house until the charges reach Earth. Lightning can explode brick walls and concrete and start fires. Have students work in groups to create informative pamphlets on lightning safety. The pamphlets should include information on why lightning is dangerous and what a person should do or not do during a thunderstorm.
LS **Verbal/Interpersonal**

Teaching Key Ideas

Modeling Resistance Tell students that a wire made from a material that has a low resistance is like an empty pipe. Water can flow easily through an empty pipe. But a wire made from a material that has a high resistance is like a pipe filled with gravel. Water can still flow through the pipe, but it is slowed down by friction between the water and the gravel.

Historical Connection

Electrical Lighting The first commercially viable incandescent light bulb was made by Thomas Edison on October 21, 1879. Between October 21 and December 31, Edison and his crew worked day and night to construct the huge number of components necessary for a complete electric lighting system—including wires, insulators, bulb sockets, and connectors. This electrical system was then used for the first public demonstration of electrical lighting on New Year's Eve in 1879. Have interested students do research on Edison and the contributions he made to science. Students can write and perform a skit to present what they learn to the class. **LS Verbal/Interpersonal**

resistance (ri ZIS tuhns) the opposition presented to the current by a material or device

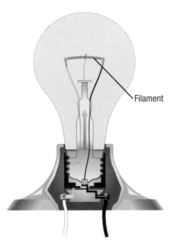

Filament

Figure 4 When current flows in the tungsten filament of a light bulb, the bulb converts electrical energy to heat and light.

Electrical Resistance

Electrical appliances that you plug into a standard outlet are designed for the same voltage: 120 V. But different appliances have different power ratings. For example, light bulbs may be dim 40 W bulbs or bright 100 W bulbs. These bulbs use different amounts of power because they have different currents in them. The difference in current between these bulbs is due to their resistance. **⟩ Resistance is caused by internal friction, which slows the movement of charges through a conducting material.** Because measuring the internal friction directly is difficult, resistance is defined by a relationship between the voltage across a conductor and the current through it.

The resistance of the *filament* of a light bulb, such as the one shown in **Figure 4,** determines how bright the bulb will be. The filament of a 40 W light bulb has a higher resistance than the filament of a 100 W light bulb.

Resistance can be calculated if current and voltage are known.

You have probably noticed that electrical devices such as televisions or stereos become warm after they have been on for a while. As moving electrons collide with the atoms of the material, some of the *kinetic energy* of the electrons is transferred to the atoms. This energy transfer causes the atoms to vibrate, and the material warms up. In most materials, some of the kinetic energy of electrons is lost as heat.

A conductor's resistance indicates how much the motion of charges within it is resisted because of collisions. Resistance is found by dividing the voltage across the conductor by the current.

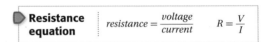

⟩ **Resistance equation** $\quad resistance = \dfrac{voltage}{current} \qquad R = \dfrac{V}{I}$

This equation is also commonly called *Ohm's law.* The SI unit of resistance is the ohm (Ω), which is equal to one volt per ampere. If a voltage of 1 V across a conductor produces a current of 1 A, then the resistance of the conductor is 1 Ω.

A *resistor* is a special type of conductor used to control current. Every resistor is designed to have a specific resistance. For example, for any applied voltage, the current in a 10 Ω resistor is half the current in a 5 Ω resistor.

✓ **Reading Check** What is another name for the resistance equation?

Differentiated Instruction

English Learners

Common Words Have students make lists of new words from this chapter that have common word parts. For example, one list could be *conduct, conductor, semiconductor,* and *superconductor.* Then, have students write sentences that explain how the words differ. (Sample answer: A conductor conducts current all the time but a semiconductor conducts current only under certain conditions.) **LS Verbal**

Math Skills — Resistance

The headlights of a typical car are powered by a 12 V battery. What is the resistance of the headlights if they draw 3.0 A of current when they are turned on?

Identify
List the given and unknown values.

Given:
current, $I = 3.0$ A
voltage, $V = 12$ V
Unknown:
resistance, $R = ?\ \Omega$

Plan
Write the equation for resistance.

$resistance = \dfrac{voltage}{current}$
$R = \dfrac{V}{I}$

Solve
Insert the known values into the equation, and solve.

$R = \dfrac{V}{I} = \dfrac{12\ V}{3.0\ A}$
$R = 4.0\ \Omega$

Practice

1. Find the resistance of a portable lantern that uses a 24 V power supply and draws a current of 0.80 A.

2. The current in a resistor is 0.50 A when connected across a voltage of 120 V. What is the resistance of the resistor?

3. The current in a video game is 0.50 A. If the resistance of the game's circuitry is 12 Ω, what is the voltage of the battery?

4. A 1.5 V battery is connected to a small light bulb that has a resistance of 3.5 Ω. What is the current in the bulb?

For more practice, visit **go.hrw.com** and enter keyword **HK8MP**.

Practice Hint

❯ When a problem requires you to calculate the resistance of an object, you can use the resistance equation $R = V/I$.

❯ Problem 3: The resistance equation can be rearranged to isolate voltage on the left in the following way:
$$R = \dfrac{V}{I}$$
Multiply both sides by I.
$$IR = \dfrac{V\cancel{I}}{\cancel{I}}$$
$$V = IR$$

❯ Problem 4: You will need to rearrange the equation to isolate current on the left.

Math Skills

Answers to Practice

1. $R = \dfrac{V}{I} = \dfrac{24V}{0.80A} = 3.0 \times 10^1\ \Omega$

2. $R = \dfrac{V}{I} = \dfrac{120V}{0.50A} = 2.4 \times 10^2\ \Omega$

3. $V = IR = (0.50\ A)(12\ \Omega) = 6.0\ V$

4. $I = \dfrac{V}{R} = \dfrac{(1.5\ V)}{(3.5\ \Omega)} = 0.43\ A$

Additional Examples

A battery-operated CD player uses 12 V from the wall socket and draws a current of 2.5 A. Calculate the resistance of the CD player.

Answer: $R = \dfrac{V}{I} = \dfrac{12V}{2.5A} = 4.8\ \Omega$

A light bulb has a resistance of 12 Ω. It is attached to a battery that has a voltage of 24 V. Calculate the current in the light bulb.

Answer: $I = \dfrac{V}{R} = (24\ V) / (12\ \Omega) = 2.0\ A$

LS Logical

Conductors have low resistance.

Whether or not charges will move in a material depends partly on how tightly electrons are held in the atoms of the material. A good conductor is any material in which electrons can flow easily under the influence of an electric field. Metals, such as the copper found in wires, are some of the best conductors because electrons can move freely throughout them. Certain metals, conducting alloys, or carbon can be used in resistors. When you flip the switch on a flashlight, the light seems to come on immediately. But the electrons do not travel that rapidly. The electric field, however, is directed through the conductor at almost the speed of light when a voltage source is connected to the conductor.

Differentiated Instruction

Advanced Learners

Variable Resistors The resistance of electrical circuits is not always fixed. This can be demonstrated by changing the volume control on a portable stereo. The volume control is an example of a variable resistor. Ask students to speculate how a variable resistor works based on their knowledge of resistance. Have students think of other devices that also have variable resistors. (Responses could include indoor light-dimmer switches and electric oven controls. Most variable resistors work by varying the length of high-resistance wire that a current must pass through.) **LS** Logical

Why It Matters

Resistor Color Codes Resistors have three colored bands that signify their resistance. The first two bands are read as digits, and the third band is the multiplier. For example, the color red represents the digit 2 and the multiplier 100. So, 3 red bands would represent 22 multiplied by 100, or 2,200 Ω. Resistors can also have a fourth band, which indicates whether the resistance value is accurate within 5%, 10%, or 20%. If the example resistor were accurate within 5%, its resistance is actually between 2,090 and 2,310 Ω. Give groups of students a variety of resistors and a table for decoding the bands and ask the groups to determine the resistance of each resistor. **LS** Logical

InquiryLab

Teacher's Notes Students should be careful not to touch both terminals of the battery or touch any two conductors connected to those terminals.

Materials per Group
- alligator clips, 2
- base holder
- battery, 6 V
- bulb, flashlight
- cardboard, strip
- chalk, piece
- cork, strip
- dowel, wooden
- hooks, metal, 2
- key, brass
- nail, aluminum
- nail, iron
- spoon, plastic
- stirring rod, glass
- wire, copper
- wire leads, 3
- small wood, block

Answers to Analysis
1. The conductivity tester lights up.
2. The iron nail, copper wire, aluminum nail, and brass key were good conductors. The glass stirring rod, wooden dowel, chalk, cardboard, plastic utensil, and cork were poor conductors.
3. Good conductors have low resistance and allow charges to pass through, while good insulators have high resistance.

InquiryLab

How Can Materials Be Classified by Resistance?

⏱ **30 min**

Procedure
❶ Construct a conductivity tester. First, screw **two metal hooks** into a **block of wood.**

❷ Create a circuit using **three wire leads** with **alligator clips,** a **6 V battery,** and a **flashlight bulb** in a **base holder,** as the diagram shows.

❸ Collect some or all of the following materials to test: a **glass stirring rod,** an **iron nail,** a **wooden dowel,** a **copper wire,** a **piece of chalk,** a **strip of cardboard,** a **plastic spoon,** an **aluminum nail,** a **brass key,** and a **strip of cork.**

❹ Test the conductivity of the materials by laying each object, one at a time, across the hooks of the conductivity tester.

Analysis
1. What happens to the conductivity tester if the material is a good conductor?
2. Which materials were good conductors? Which materials were poor conductors?
3. Explain your results in terms of resistance.

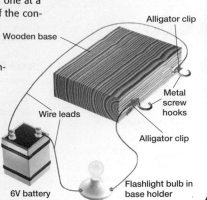

SC**I**LINKS.
www.scilinks.org
Topic: Semiconductors and Insulators
Code: HK81377

Figure 5 Most electronic devices contain conductors, insulators, and semiconductors.

Insulators have high resistance.
Insulators have a high resistance to charge movement. For this reason, insulating materials are used to prevent electric current from flowing in directions other than the desired direction. The plastic coating around the copper wire of an electrical cord is an example of an insulator. This coating keeps the current from escaping into the floor or into your body.

Most electrical sockets are wired with three connections: two current-carrying wires and a *ground* wire. The ground wire is literally connected to the ground. The ground wire conducts any excess charge to Earth, where it spreads safely over the planet.

Semiconductors conduct under certain conditions.
Semiconductors belong to a third class of materials that have electrical properties between those of insulators and conductors. In their pure state, semiconductors are insulators. The controlled addition of specific atoms of other materials as impurities greatly increases a semiconductor's ability to conduct electric charge.

Silicon and germanium are two common semiconductors. Electronic devices, such as the computer board shown in **Figure 5,** are usually made of conductors, insulators, and semiconductors.

Differentiated Instruction

Alternative Assessment
Maglev Trains Have students research the Japanese or German Maglev trains and write a report summarizing their results. These Maglev trains levitate on a magnetic field provided by superconducting electromagnets. Have students discuss whether Maglev trains would be practical in the United States. **LS Verbal**

Special Education Students
Classifying Materials Obtain circuit boards from old computers or partially dismantled broken electronic devices. Ask students to examine the parts of the circuit boards or the devices and identify which parts are conductors and which parts are insulators. Ask students to explain their classification and to explain why conductors are needed in certain places but insulators are needed in others. **LS Logical**

Some materials can become superconductors.

Some metals and compounds have zero resistance when their temperature falls below a *critical temperature*. These types of materials are called *superconductors*. Metals such as niobium, tin, and mercury and some metal compounds containing barium, copper, and oxygen become superconductors below their respective critical temperatures. The critical temperature depends on the material and ranges from less than −272 °C (−458 °F) to as high as −123 °C (−189 °F). The search continues for a material that is superconducting at room temperature.

Once a current is established in a superconductor, the current continues even if the applied voltage is removed. In fact, steady currents in superconducting loops have been observed to continue for many years without any signs of stopping. This feature makes such materials useful for a wide variety of applications.

One useful application of these materials is in superconducting magnets. These magnets are strong enough to levitate commuter trains, such as the one shown in **Figure 6,** above the tracks. As a result, the friction that would exist between the tracks and a normal train is eliminated. These magnets are also being studied for storing energy.

Figure 6 This train uses superconducting magnets to float above the tracks.

Section 2 Review

KEY IDEAS

1. **Describe** the motion of charges from one terminal of a battery to the other through a flashlight.

2. **Identify** which of the following could produce a current:
   a. a wire connected across a battery's terminals
   b. two electrodes in a solution of positive and negative ions
   c. a salt crystal whose ions cannot move
   d. a sugar-water mixture

CRITICAL THINKING

3. **Making Predictions** Predict which way a positive charge will move between two positions of different electrical potential energy, one high and one low.
   a. from low to high
   b. from high to low
   c. back and forth between high and low

4. **Identifying Variables** What quantities are needed to calculate an object's resistance?

5. **Classifying** Classify the following materials as conductors or insulators: wood, paper clip, glass, air, paper, plastic, steel nail, and rubber.

6. **Inferring Conclusions** Recent discoveries have led some scientists to hope that a material will be found that is superconducting at room temperature. Why would such a material be useful?

Math Skills

7. If the current in a certain resistor is 6.2 A and the voltage across the resistor is 110 V, what is the resistance of the resistor?

8. If the voltage across a flashlight bulb is 3 V and the bulb's resistance is 6 Ω, what is the current through the bulb?

> **Close**

Reteaching Key Ideas

Building on an Analogy Review the analogy between electrical potential energy and gravitational potential energy with students. Ask students how the analogy can be extended to describe current and resistance. (Sample answer: The rate at which balls roll down a hill is similar to a current. Placing objects such as rocks on the side of the hill to prevent balls from rolling downhill as quickly is similar to increasing resistance.)
LS Logical

Formative Assessment

Which of the following arrangements would have the highest electrical potential energy?

A. A large positive charge close to a large negative charge (Incorrect. A positive charge near a negative charge will have a low electrical potential energy.)

B. A large positive charge close to a small negative charge (Incorrect. A positive charge near a negative charge will have a low electrical potential energy.)

C. A large positive charge far away from small positive charge (Incorrect. A positive charge far away from another positive charge will have a low electrical potential energy.)

D. A large positive charge close to a large positive charge (Correct. A positive charge near another positive charge will have a high electrical potential energy.)

Answers to Section Review

1. Electrons move away from the negative terminal of the battery and travel through the filament in the light bulb. They heat the filament, causing it to give off light. The electrons then travel toward the positive terminal of the battery.

2. a, b

3. b

4. To calculate resistance, you need to know the voltage across the object and the current.

5. wood—insulator
   paper clip—conductor
   glass—insulator
   air—insulator
   paper—insulator
   plastic—insulator
   steel nail—conductor
   rubber—insulator

6. Such a material would enable people to use devices that rely on extremely efficient conductors of electricity (such as Maglev trains) without having to cool the conducting material to extremely cold temperatures.

7. $R = V/I = 110\ \text{V}/6.2\ \text{A} = 18\ \Omega$

8. $I = V/R = 3\ \text{V}/6\ \Omega = 0.5\ \text{A}$

Circuits

›Focus

In this section, students learn what electric circuits are, how they are represented by schematic diagrams, and how they can be classified as series or parallel. They also learn how to use voltage and current to calculate electric power. The section concludes with a discussion of fuses and circuit breakers.

Bellringer

Use the Bellringer transparency to prepare students for this section.

Demonstrate

Building Closed Circuits Ask students to read the first three pages of this section before class. Draw different basic circuit diagrams having 4, 5, or 6 light bulbs on the board. Have groups of students wire these diagrams using a 6 V battery, wire connectors with alligator clips on the ends, and lights cut off of a set of holiday lights. Ask students why the circuits they built are called *closed circuits.* (The circuits form a complete path and include a source of voltage.) Then, ask students what they could do to open their circuit. (Disconnect one of the wires so that the path is broken.) Ask students to predict what would happen if the circuit were not closed. (No charge would flow and the bulbs would not light.) Then have students open the circuit to test their prediction.

 Visual/Logical

Key **Ideas**

› What is a closed circuit?

› What are the two ways that devices can be connected in a circuit?

› What happens to the energy that charges have in a circuit?

› Why is an overloaded circuit dangerous?

Key **Terms**

electric circuit

schematic diagram

series circuit

parallel circuit

electric power

fuse

circuit breaker

Why It **Matters**

The electric circuits used to make computers have changed and have become much smaller over the years. The first computers took up large rooms, but computers today can be held in the palm of your hand.

Think about how you get a flashlight bulb to light. Would the bulb light if it were not fully screwed into its socket? Would it light if it were connected to only one side of a battery? What elements are necessary to make the bulb light?

What Are Circuits?

When plug and wires connect an electrical outlet to a string of light bulbs, as **Figure 1** shows, electric charges have a complete path to follow. Together, the bulb, electrical outlet, and wires form an **electric circuit.** In this circuit, the outlet is the source of voltage. Because of the voltage of the outlet, charges move through the wires and bulbs from one side of the outlet to the other.

In other words, there is a closed-loop path for electrons to follow. Because charges are moving, there is a current in the circuit. ›**The conducting path produced when a load, such as a string of light bulbs, is connected across a source of voltage is called a *closed circuit*.** Without a complete path and a source of voltage, there is no charge flow and therefore no current. When there is no complete path, the circuit is called an *open circuit.*

If a bulb is connected to a battery, the inside of the battery is part of the closed path of current through the circuit. The voltage source, whether a battery or an outlet, is always part of the conducting path of a closed circuit.

Figure 1 When a string of light bulbs is plugged into an electrical outlet, the voltage across the plug prongs generates a current that lights the bulbs.

Key Resources

 Teaching Transparencies
TM50 Circuit and Diagram
P20 Series and Parallel

Visual Concepts
Electric Circuit
Schematic Diagram and Common
    Symbols
Resistors in Series
Resistors in Parallel
Equation for Electric Power
Fuse

 Math Skills Worksheet
Electric Power

Cross-Disciplinary Worksheet
Integrating Health—Recording
    Electricity in the Brain

Switches interrupt the flow of charges in a circuit.

A device called a *switch* can be added to a circuit, as **Figure 2** shows. You use a switch to open and close a circuit, as you have probably done many times. The switches on your walls at home are used to turn lights on and off. When you flip a light switch, you either close or open the circuit to turn a light on or off.

The switch shown in **Figure 2** is a *knife switch*. The metal bar is a *conductor*. When the bar is touching both sides of the switch, the circuit is closed. Electrons can move through the bar to reach the other side of the switch and light the bulb. If the metal bar on the switch is lifted, the circuit is open. Then, there is no current, and the bulb does not glow.

✓ Reading Check What is the purpose of a switch in a circuit?

Schematic diagrams are used to represent circuits.

Suppose that you want to describe to someone the contents and connections in the light bulb and battery shown in **Figure 3.** How might you draw each element? Could you use the same representations of the elements to draw a more complex circuit?

A diagram that depicts the construction of an electric circuit or apparatus is called a **schematic diagram. Figure 3** shows how the battery, wires, and light bulb can be drawn as a schematic diagram. The symbols that are used in this figure can be used to describe any other circuit that has a battery and one or more bulbs. All electrical devices, from toasters to computers, can be described by schematic diagrams.

Figure 2 When added to the circuit, a switch can be used to open and close the circuit. **Is this switch open or closed?**

electric circuit (ee LEK trik SUHR kit) a set of electrical components connected such that they provide one or more complete paths for the movement of charges

schematic diagram (skee MAT ik DIE uh GRAM) a graphical representation of a circuit that uses lines to represent wires and different symbols to represent components

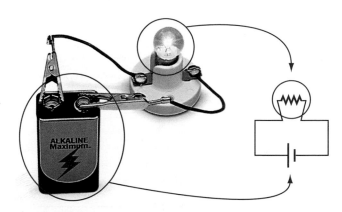

Figure 3 The connections between the light bulb and battery can be represented by symbols. This type of illustration is called a *schematic diagram*.

Differentiated Instruction

Struggling Readers

Reading Skills Have students read the first three pages of this section and write out a summary of the ideas on these pages. Ask for a volunteer to read his or her summary. The class, as listeners, should ask for clarification of parts of the passage once the "reteller" has finished. All students may consult the text during the clarification process. **LS Verbal**

❯Teach

Answer to caption question
The switch in the circuit is closed.

READING TOOLBOX

Visual Literacy Students should recognize that the straight-line symbols connecting the battery symbol with the bulb symbol in **Figure 3** represent not only the wires but also all parts of the conducting connection between the bulb and battery. Ask the students to list the parts of the photo symbolized by the black straight lines in **Figure 3**. (The black lines symbolize the conducting path provided by the wires, clips, and socket.) **LS Visual**

Why It Matters

Circuits and Technology Have the computer and technology teacher come into class and lecture on the use of electrical circuits in technology. The teacher can discuss the different uses of basic analog circuits and digital circuits as well as the historical development of electrical circuits. Encourage students to ask the teacher questions about technology and circuits.

Teaching Key Ideas

Fluid Model Many teachers use a fluid model of electric voltage. In this model, charges moving due to potential difference are analogous to water moving to a level of lower gravitational potential energy. Wires are analogous to horizontal pipes, and resistors are analogous to water wheels, which transform the energy to another form. Batteries and generators act like pumps in that they lift water upward, increasing its potential energy.

Technology Connection

Mercury Switches Mercury is the only metal that is a liquid at room temperature. Some switches make use of mercury in what is called a rocker switch. When the switch is rocked in one direction, the liquid mercury flows downhill and will cover two electrodes. Because mercury is a conductor, it makes an electrical connection with these two electrodes and closes the circuit. When the switch is rocked in the opposite direction, the liquid flows in the opposite direction and moves off the electrodes. This breaks the connection between the electrodes and opens the circuit, stopping charges from flowing.

www.scilinks.org
Topic: Electric Circuits
Code: HK80471

Schematic diagrams use standard symbols.

As **Figure 4** shows, each element used in a piece of electrical equipment is represented by a symbol that reflects the element's construction or function. For example, the symbol in the schematic diagram that represents an open switch resembles the knife switch shown in the corresponding photograph. Any circuit can be drawn by using a combination of these and other, more complex schematic-diagram symbols.

✓ **Reading Check** What are used to draw schematic diagrams?

Figure 4 Schematic-Diagram Symbols

Component	Symbol used in this book	Explanation
Wire or conductor		Wires that connect elements are conductors.
Resistor		Resistors are shown as wires with multiple bends. These bends indicate resistance to a straight path.
Light bulb		The winding of the filament indirectly indicates that the light bulb is a resistor, something that impedes the movement of electrons or the flow of charge.
Battery or other direct current source		The difference in line height indicates a voltage between positive and negative terminals of the battery. The taller line represents the positive terminal of the battery.
Switch	Open — Closed	The small circles indicate the two places where the switch makes contact with the wires. Most switches work by breaking only one of the contacts, not both.

Differentiated Instruction

Special Education Students

Visualizing Current Give students a chance to "see" the idea of the flow and interruption of current. Place several books end-to-end about 2 cm from the wall. Roll a small ball (about the size of a ping-pong or golf ball) down the indented path created by the space between the book and the wall. Ask students to notice how the ball can roll from the first book to the last book. Explain that electric charges in a circuit also move freely. Then, ask a student to watch until the ball has started rolling and then pull out a book at about the halfway point. When the ball reaches the point where the book is missing and falls into the opening, point out that the pulling out of the book is similar to the flipping of a switch in an electric circuit because the continuous path is broken, causing the current to stop. **LS** **Visual**

Series and Parallel Circuits

Most circuits in everyday use contain more than one element. Usually, two or more devices—such as appliances or light bulbs—are connected in a circuit. **❯ Electrical devices can be connected as a series circuit so that the voltage is divided among the devices. They can also be connected as a parallel circuit so that the voltage is the same across each device.** A more complex circuit will contain combinations of both series and parallel components.

Series circuits have a single path for current.

When appliances or other devices are connected in a series circuit, as **Figure 5** shows, they form a single pathway for charges to flow. Charges cannot build up or disappear at a point in a circuit. For this reason, the amount of charge that enters one device in a given time interval equals the amount of charge that exits that device in the same amount of time. Because there is only one path for a charge to follow when devices are connected in series, the current in each device is the same. Even though the current in each device is the same, the resistances may be different. Therefore, the voltage across each device in a series circuit can be different.

If one element along the path in a series circuit is removed, the circuit will not work. For example, if either of the light bulbs in **Figure 5** were removed, the other one would not glow. The series circuit would be open. Several kinds of breaks may interrupt a series circuit. An open switch, a burned-out light bulb, a cut wire, or any other interruption can cause the whole circuit to fail.

Parallel circuits have multiple paths for current.

When devices are connected in parallel rather than in series, the voltage across each device is the same. The current in each device does not have to be the same. Instead, the sum of the currents in all of the devices equals the total current. **Figure 6** shows a simple parallel circuit. The two lights are connected to the same points. The electrons leaving one end of the battery can pass through either bulb before returning to the other terminal. If one bulb has less resistance, more charge moves through that bulb because the bulb offers less opposition to the movement of charges.

Even if one of the bulbs in the circuit shown in **Figure 6** were removed, charges would still move through the other loop. Thus, a break in any path in a parallel circuit does not interrupt the flow of electric charge in the other paths.

series circuit (SIR eez SUHR kit) a circuit in which the parts are joined one after another such that the current in each part is the same

parallel circuit (PAR uh LEL SUHR kit) a circuit in which the parts are joined in branches such that the potential difference across each part is the same

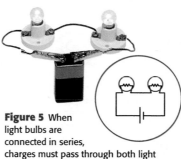

Figure 5 When light bulbs are connected in series, charges must pass through both light bulbs to complete the circuit.

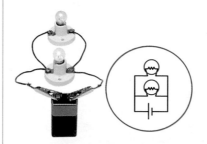

Figure 6 When light bulbs are connected in parallel, charges have more than one path to follow. The circuit can be complete even if one light bulb burns out.

Teaching Key Ideas

Series and Parallel Give groups of students three flashlight bulbs with bases, wires, and a 9 V battery. Have students wire a series circuit using all three bulbs and a parallel circuit using all three bulbs. Ask students to compare the brightness of the bulbs in the two circuits. (The bulbs will be brighter in the parallel circuit.) Then, instruct students to create other circuits using the materials and draw schematic diagrams of each circuit. Students may use any number of bulbs in their circuits. Finally, challenge students to build a single circuit that has bulbs in series and in parallel. (Students should wire two bulbs in parallel and then wire the third bulb in series.)
LS Kinesthetic

Why It **Matters**

Holiday Lights When holiday lights became popular in the 1970s, they were usually sold in strands of 48 bulbs. Each strand had 48 2.5-volt lights wired into a series circuit. Since the lights were wired in series, a single burned-out bulb opened the circuit and caused the entire strand to go dark. Today, most holiday lights have a combination of series and parallel circuits. For strands with 100 or 150 lights, groups of 50 lights connected in series are wired together in parallel. Ask students to do research to find out what change has been made to prevent a single burned-out bulb from causing the entire strand to go dark. (Modern bulbs contain an internal shunt wire below the light bulb filament. If a bulb burns out, the shunt wire activates, allowing current to continue flowing through the circuit.) **LS Logical**

Differentiated Instruction

Basic Learners

Building Reading Skills Pair students and have them read the section on series circuits. One student should be the "reteller" and the other should be the "listener." The listener should not interrupt unless there is a portion of the summary that requires clarification. The reteller may consult the text during his or her summary. The listener should then state any inaccuracies or omissions, and the students should work together to refine the summary. The students should then change roles and read the section on parallel circuits.
LS Interpersonal

Why It **Matters**

Miniaturization of Circuits ENIAC belonged to what is referred to as the "first generation" of computers. The "second generation" of computers, used from about 1950 to 1964, were computers in which solid-state components replaced the vacuum tubes and high-level computer languages were first used. The invention of the integrated circuit marked the beginning of the "third generation" of computers. The "fourth generation" of computers, comprised of computers that contain microprocessors, are still in use today. Have students research the "fifth generation" of computers to find out how they are different from computers in previous generations. Students can summarize their research in a poster or an oral report. **LS Logical/Visual**

READING TOOLBOX

Visual Literacy Instruct students to study the three smaller photos on this page and ask them what features are common to these computers. (Sample answers: They each have a keyboard or keys. They each have a screen. They each have a central processing unit (CPU).) Then, ask students why each of the common features is a necessary component of computers. (Sample answers: Keys or a keyboard is necessary for people to enter information for the computer to process or for giving the computer commands to execute. A screen is necessary for receiving output from the computer. A CPU is the "brains" of the computer.) **LS Visual**

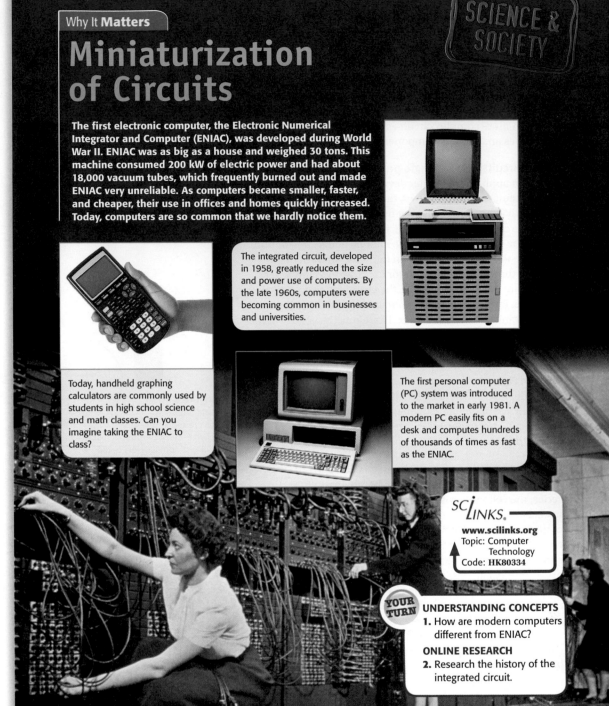

SCIENCE & SOCIETY

Why It **Matters**

Miniaturization of Circuits

The first electronic computer, the Electronic Numerical Integrator and Computer (ENIAC), was developed during World War II. ENIAC was as big as a house and weighed 30 tons. This machine consumed 200 kW of electric power and had about 18,000 vacuum tubes, which frequently burned out and made ENIAC very unreliable. As computers became smaller, faster, and cheaper, their use in offices and homes quickly increased. Today, computers are so common that we hardly notice them.

The integrated circuit, developed in 1958, greatly reduced the size and power use of computers. By the late 1960s, computers were becoming common in businesses and universities.

Today, handheld graphing calculators are commonly used by students in high school science and math classes. Can you imagine taking the ENIAC to class?

The first personal computer (PC) system was introduced to the market in early 1981. A modern PC easily fits on a desk and computes hundreds of thousands of times as fast as the ENIAC.

SCILINKS.
www.scilinks.org
Topic: Computer Technology
Code: HK80334

YOUR TURN

UNDERSTANDING CONCEPTS
1. How are modern computers different from ENIAC?

ONLINE RESEARCH
2. Research the history of the integrated circuit.

Answers to Your Turn

1. Modern computers are smaller, faster, cheaper, and more reliable than ENIAC was.
2. Accept all reasonable responses. Student's answers should include the contributions made by Jack Kilby and Robert Noyce and may include information on how integrated circuits are made.

Differentiated Instruction

Advanced Learners

Writing Computer Programs Have students learn how to write simple programs in a computer language such as BASIC. Challenge students to create a program that will use one of the equations in this chapter to do calculations. **LS Logical**

Electrical Energy and Electric Power

Many of the devices that you use on a daily basis, such as a flashlight or a toaster, require *electrical energy* to run. The energy for these devices may come from a battery or from a power plant miles away.

When a charge moves in a circuit, the charge loses energy. ❯ **Some of this energy is <u>transformed</u> into useful *work*, such as the turning of a motor, and some is lost as heat.** The rate at which electrical energy is changed to other forms of energy is called **electric power.** Electric power is calculated by multiplying the total current, I, by the voltage, V, in a circuit.

 **Electric power equation**	$power = current \times voltage$ $P = IV$

If you combine the electric power equation with the resistance equation, $V = IR$, you can calculate the power lost, or *dissipated*, by a resistor.

$$P = I(IR) = I^2R = \frac{V^2}{R}$$

Earlier in this text, you learned that *power* is the rate at which work is done. The same is true for electric power; electric power is the rate at which electrical work is done.

The SI unit for power is the watt.

Most light bulbs are labeled in terms of watts (W). The amount of heat and light given off by a bulb is related to the power rating. For example, a typical desk lamp uses a 60 W bulb. A typical hair dryer is rated at about 1,800 W.

In terms of energy, 1 W is equal to 1 J/s. A watt is also equal to 1 A × 1 V. Another common unit of power is the kilowatt (kW). One kilowatt is equal to 1,000 W.

Electric companies measure energy in kilowatt-hours.

Power companies charge for energy, not power, used in the home. The unit of energy that power companies use to track consumption of energy is the kilowatt-hour (kW•h). One kilowatt-hour is the energy delivered in 1 h at the rate of 1 kW. In SI units, 1 kW•h = 3.6×10^6 J.

Depending on where you live, the cost of energy ranges from 5 to 20 cents per kilowatt-hour. Power companies use electric meters, such as the one shown in **Figure 7,** to determine how much electrical energy is consumed over a certain time interval.

electric power (ee I FK trik POW uhr) the rate at which electrical energy is converted into other forms of energy

Academic Vocabulary

transform (trans FAWRM) to change form

 READING TOOLBOX

Tri-Fold
Create a tri-fold FoldNote. Label the columns "Current," "Voltage," and "Resistance." Describe in words and equations how power depends on each quantity.

Figure 7 An electric meter records the amount of energy consumed.

Why It **Matters**

Energy Use in Home Appliances Determine the power ratings for a few large appliances, such as a refrigerator, an air conditioner, or an electric heater. Bring a household electric-company bill (optional) and a few small appliances to class, such as a toaster, a clock/radio, and a hand-held vacuum cleaner. Look for a label on the back or bottom of each appliance. Record the power rating, which is given in units of watts (W). Use the billing statement to find the cost of energy per kilowatt-hour.

Put students into groups. Ask the students in each group to calculate the cost of running each appliance for 1 hour. Then have them estimate how many hours a day each appliance is used, and calculate the monthly cost of using each appliance based on their estimate. After students have finished, compare the estimates from each group. **Safety Caution:** Unplug appliances and use caution when handling electrical equipment. **LS Logical/Interpersonal**

Teaching Key Ideas

Energy Transformations Ask students to brainstorm a list of electrical devices that they have in their homes. (Sample answers: lamp, electric fan, washing machine, and television) Then, ask students what happens to the energy of charges that move through the circuits that contain the electrical devices. (Sample answer: In an electric fan, some of the energy is used to turn the fan blades and some of the energy is lost as heat.) Be sure that students understand that some energy is lost as heat in every circuit. **LS Logical**

READING TOOLBOX

Tri-Fold Tell students that this tri-fold will not be used to take KWL notes like the tri-fold created at the beginning of the chapter. Instead, this tri-fold will be used to group information about current, voltage, and resistance into separate columns.

Math *Skills*

Answers to Practice

1. $P = IV = (29\text{ A})(120\text{ V}) = 3.5 \times 10^3\text{ W}$

2. $P = IV = (2.6 \times 10^{-3}\text{ A})(6.0\text{ V}) = 1.6 \times 10^{-2}\text{ W}$

3. $I = \dfrac{P}{V} = \dfrac{320\text{ W}}{120\text{ V}} = 2.7\text{ A}$

4. $V = \dfrac{P}{I} = \dfrac{590\text{ W}}{5.0\text{ A}} = 1.2 \times 10^2\text{ V}$

Additional Examples

A certain electrical motor needs a 9.0 V battery to operate and has a power output of 1.6 W. Calculate the current in the motor.

Answer: $I = \dfrac{P}{V} = \dfrac{1.6\text{ W}}{9.0\text{ V}} = 0.18\text{ A}$

A single solar panel for home use puts out 550 W of electrical power. If the electrical current produced by this panel is 4.2 A, calculate the voltage generated by the panel.

Answer: $V = \dfrac{P}{I} = \dfrac{550\text{ W}}{4.2\text{ A}} = 1.3 \times 10^2\text{ V}$

LS **Logical**

Teaching Key Ideas

Circuit Safety Instruct students to work in groups to design circuit safety pamphlets that can be given to people in your community. The pamphlets should explain how circuits can become overloaded and warn of the dangers of overloaded circuits. The pamphlets should also give instructions on how to prevent overloading circuits and instructions on how to change fuses and reset circuit breakers.

LS **Interpersonal**

Practice **Hint**

> Problem 3: The electric power equation can also be rearranged to isolate current on the left in the following way:

$$P = IV$$

Divide both sides by *V*.

$$\dfrac{P}{V} = \dfrac{I\cancel{V}}{\cancel{V}}$$

$$I = \dfrac{P}{V}$$

> Problem 4: You will need to rearrange the equation to isolate voltage on the left.

Math *Skills* **Electric Power**

When a hair dryer is plugged into a 120 V outlet, the hair dryer has a 9.1 A current in it. What is the hair dryer's power rating?

Identify List the given and unknown values.	**Given:** *voltage,* $V = 120$ V *current,* $I = 9.1$ A **Unknown:** *electric power,* $P = ?$ W
Plan Write the equation for electric power.	*power = current × voltage* $P = IV$
Solve Insert the known values into the equation, and solve.	$P = (9.1\text{ A})(120\text{ V})$ $P = 1.1 \times 10^3$ W

Practice

1. An electric space heater draws 29 A of current when plugged into a 120 V outlet. What is the power rating of the heater?

2. A graphing calculator uses a 6.0 V battery and draws 2.6×10^{-3} A of current. What is the power rating of the calculator?

3. A color television has a power rating of 320 W. How much current is in the television when it is connected across 120 V?

4. The current in the heating element of an iron is 5.0 A. If the iron dissipates 590 W of power, what is the voltage across the iron?

For more practice, visit **go.hrw.com** and enter keyword **HK8MP**.

Figure 8 These fuses are typical for modern electronic devices. The one on the left has been overloaded and is "blown."

Fuses and Circuit Breakers

If many devices are connected across an electrical outlet, the overall resistance of the circuit is lowered. As a result, the electrical wires carry more than a safe level of current, and the circuit is said to be *overloaded.* **> The high currents in overloaded circuits can cause fires.**

Worn insulation on wires can also be a fire hazard. If a wire's insulation wears down, two wires may touch and create an alternative pathway for current, or a *short circuit.* The lower resistance greatly increases the current in the circuit. Short circuits can be very dangerous. Fuses, such as the ones shown in **Figure 8,** and circuit breakers can reduce the danger and the threat to sensitive electronic devices.

Differentiated Instruction

Alternative Assessment

Ground Fault Interrupters Ground Fault Circuit Interrupters and Ground Fault Interrupters are mounted in electrical outlets and in certain appliances to prevent electrocution. GFCIs and GFIs are usually installed in the kitchen, bathroom, and outdoor outlets. They function by comparing the current in both wires of a socket. If there is a difference in current, the device opens the circuit within a few milliseconds. If you were to touch a bare wire, the device would detect the change in current and open the circuit; you would get only a small shock. Some circuit breakers are equipped with a GFI. Have students draw diagrams that explain how GFCIs and GFIs work. **LS** **Visual**

Fuses melt to prevent circuit overloads.

To prevent overloading in circuits, fuses are connected in series along the supply path. A **fuse** is a ribbon of wire that has a low melting point. If the current in the line becomes too large, the fuse melts and the circuit is opened.

Fuses "blow out" when the current in the circuit reaches a certain level. For example, a 20 A fuse will melt if the current in the circuit exceeds 20 A. A blown fuse is a sign that a short circuit or a circuit overload may exist somewhere in your home. It is wise to find out what made a fuse blow out before replacing it.

Circuit breakers open circuits with high current.

Many homes are equipped with circuit breakers, such as those shown in **Figure 9,** instead of fuses. A **circuit breaker** uses a magnet or *bimetallic strip*, a strip with two different metals welded together, that responds to current overload by opening the circuit. The circuit breaker acts as a switch. As you would for blown fuses, you should determine why the circuit breaker opened the circuit. Unlike fuses, circuit breakers can be reset by turning the switch back on.

A *ground fault circuit interrupter* (GFCI) is a special kind of electrical outlet that acts as a small circuit breaker. These special outlets are often found in bathrooms and kitchens, where water is used near electricity.

Figure 9 Many homes have a panel of circuit breakers such as these. **Are the circuits on each switch wired in series or in parallel? Why?**

fuse (FYOOZ) an electrical device that contains a metal strip that melts when current in the circuit becomes too great

circuit breaker (SUHR kit BRAYK uhr) a switch that opens a circuit automatically when the current exceeds a certain value

Answer to caption question
A circuit breaker is wired in series along the supply path of each circuit. When overloaded, the breaker will open and stop the current in the entire circuit.

❯ Close

Reteaching Key Ideas

Drawing Circuits Have students draw schematic diagrams of a series circuit and a parallel circuit. Each circuit should include at least two bulbs, one battery, and one switch. Identify each part of the circuit with a label and its function. **LS** **Logical**

Formative Assessment

A circuit contains two light bulbs, a battery, and one switch. When the switch is open light bulb 1 is lit, but light bulb 2 is not lit. Which of the following must be true?

A. The switch is wired in parallel to both light bulbs. (Incorrect. If the switch were in parallel to both bulbs, opening the switch would not affect either light bulb and both would be lit.)

B. The switch is wired in series to both light bulbs. (Incorrect. If the switch were in series to both bulbs, neither bulb would be lit when the switch is open.)

C. The switch and light bulb 1 are wired in series and are wired in parallel to light bulb 2. (Incorrect. If the switch were open in this arrangement, light bulb 2 would be lit and light bulb 1 would not be lit.)

D. The switch and light bulb 2 are wired in series and are wired in parallel to light bulb 1. (Correct. Opening the switch would prevent light bulb 2 from lighting and not affect light bulb 1.)

Section 3 Review

KEY IDEAS

1. **Identify** the number of and types of elements in this schematic diagram.

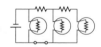

2. **Describe** the advantage of using a parallel arrangement of decorative lights rather than a series arrangement.

3. **Demonstrate** how to calculate power if you are given the voltage and resistance in a circuit.

4. **Contrast** how a fuse and a circuit breaker work to prevent overloading in circuits.

CRITICAL THINKING

5. **Making Predictions** Predict whether a fuse will work successfully if it is connected in parallel with the device it is supposed to protect.

6. **Applying Ideas** Draw a schematic diagram with four lights in parallel.

7. **Predicting Outcomes** Draw a schematic diagram of a circuit with two light bulbs in which you could turn off either light and still have a complete circuit. (Hint: You will need to use two switches.)

Math ❯ Skills

8. When a VCR is connected across a 120 V outlet, the VCR has a 0.33 A current in it. What is the power rating of the VCR?

9. A 40 W light bulb and a 75 W light bulb are in parallel across a 120 V outlet. Which bulb has the greater current in it?

Answers to Section Review

1. battery = 1, switch = 1, resistor = 2, light bulb = 3

2. In a parallel arrangement, if one light burns out, the rest will still keep working. In a series arrangement, if one burns out, all of the lights will stop working.

3. Power is equal to the current times the voltage in the circuit. $P = IV$

4. Fuses melt when the current exceeds their current rating, while circuit breakers break the connection when the current exceeds their current rating. Circuit breakers can also be reset and reused.

5. If a fuse is attached in parallel, it will not protect the intended device because even if the fuse blows out, there will still be current in the device.

6.

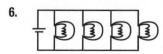

7.

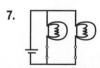

Answers continued on p. 615A

Skills Practice Lab

Teacher's Notes

Use a 100 Ω and a 200 Ω resistor. Most new batteries will have 1.55–1.6 V. Battery holders that have tabs or wires attached to the positive and negative terminals will make it easier for students to connect the batteries in a circuit. To connect components, students may use miniature test leads with spring clips at each end, or wires approximately 10 cm long with small alligator clips soldered to each end. The test leads attached to the multimeter should also have alligator clips at their ends.

Time Required

1 lab period

Lab Ratings

EASY ——————————→ HARD

Teacher Prep 🧪
Student Set-Up 🧪🧪
Concept Level 🧪🧪🧪
Clean Up 🧪🧪

Skills Acquired

- Experimenting
- Recognizing patterns
- Inferring
- Interpreting
- Measuring
- Organizing and analyzing data
- Predicting

Scientific Methods

In this lab, students will:
- Make observations
- Analyze the results
- Draw conclusions
- Communicate results

Skills Practice

Lab

What You'll Do

> **Construct** parallel and series circuits.
> **Predict** voltage and current by using the resistance law.
> **Measure** voltage, current, and resistance.

What You'll Need

battery, dry-cell
battery holder
multimeter
resistors (2)
tape, masking
wires, connecting (5)

Safety

Constructing Electric Circuits

The current that flows through an electric circuit depends on voltage and resistance. All these factors are dependent on one another. In this lab, you will make circuits using different configurations of resistors and batteries to see how the voltage and current depend on them.

Procedure

Preparing for Your Experiment

1. In this laboratory exercise, you will use an instrument called a *multimeter* to measure voltage, current, and resistance. Your teacher will demonstrate how to use the multimeter to make each type of measurement.

2. As you read the steps listed below, refer to the diagrams for help making the measurements. Write down your predictions and measurements in your lab notebook. **CAUTION:** Handle the wires only where they are insulated.

Circuits with a Single Resistor

3. Using the multimeter, measure the resistance in ohms of one of the resistors. Write the resistance on a small piece of masking tape, and tape it to the resistor. Repeat for the other resistor.

4. Use the resistance equation, $R = V/I$, to predict the current in amps that will be in a circuit consisting of one of the resistors and one battery. (Hint: You must rearrange the equation to solve for current.)

5. Test your prediction by building the circuit. Do the same for the other resistor.

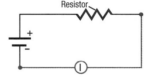

Circuits with Two Resistors in Series

6. Measure the total resistance across both resistors when they are connected in series.

Safety Cautions

Warn students to be careful not to short the batteries. The resistors may become warm during the lab. Check students' circuits before the final connection is made.

7 Using the total resistance that you measured, predict the current that will be in a circuit consisting of one battery and both resistors in series. Test your prediction.

8 Using the current that you measured, predict the voltage across each resistor in the circuit that you just built. Test your prediction.

Circuits with Two Resistors in Parallel

9 Measure the total resistance across both resistors when they are connected in parallel.

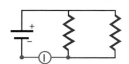

10 Using the total resistance that you measured, predict the total current that will be in an entire circuit consisting of one battery and both resistors in parallel. Test your prediction.

11 Predict the current that will be in each resistor individually in the circuit that you just built. Test your prediction.

Analysis

1. **Describing Events** If you have a circuit consisting of one battery and one resistor, what happens to the current if you double the resistance?

2. **Describing Events** What happens to the current if you add a second, identical battery in series with the first battery?

3. **Describing Events** What happens to the current if you add a second resistor in parallel with the first resistor?

Communicating Your Results

4. **Drawing Conclusions** Suppose that you have a circuit consisting of one battery plus a 10 Ω resistor and a 5 Ω resistor in series. Which resistor will have the greater voltage across it?

5. **Drawing Conclusions** Suppose that you have a circuit consisting of one battery plus a 10 Ω resistor and a 5 Ω resistor in parallel. Which resistor will have more current in it?

Extension

Suppose that someone tells you that you can make the battery in a circuit last longer by adding more resistors in parallel. Is this statement correct? Explain your reasoning.

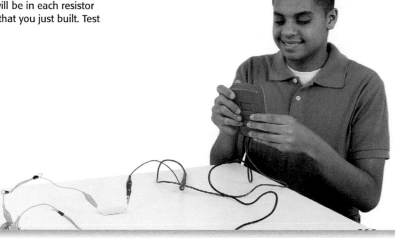

Tips and Tricks

Test batteries before the lab. Show students that they must connect the meter's leads *across* a component (in parallel) to measure voltage or resistance, and they must open up a circuit and insert the meter *into* the circuit (in series) to measure current. Make sure students understand how to switch the multimeter from one mode to another (voltmeter, ammeter, ohmmeter). Also make sure students know to start with the highest range and then switch to progressively lower ranges (smaller units) if the multimeter is not auto-ranging.

Procedure

Review how current and voltage throughout a circuit depend on values of the resistances and whether the resistors are arranged in series or in parallel. Remind students that current is the same everywhere throughout a series circuit, while the voltage across each element depends on the element's resistance. The voltage across each element is the same in a parallel circuit, but the total current is the sum of the currents in each element.

Tell students that there is also an internal resistance of the battery and a small amount of resistance due to the connecting wires. Note that the internal resistance of the battery can be used to explain discrepancies between the predicted and observed results.

Disposal Information

Discharged batteries should be taken to hazardous waste disposal.

Answers to Procedure

3. The resistances should be about 100 Ω and 200 Ω.

4. $I = \frac{V}{R} = (1.5\ V)/(100\ \Omega) = 0.015$ A in the 100 Ω circuit

   $I = \frac{V}{R} = (1.5\ V) / (200\ \Omega) = 0.0075$ A in the 200 Ω circuit

5. About 0.015 A should be in the 100 Ω circuit and 0.0075 A should be in the 200 Ω circuit.

6. The total resistance should be about 300 Ω.

7. $I = \frac{V}{R} = (1.5\ V) / (300\ \Omega) = 0.005$ A. The total current should be about 0.005 A.

Answers continued on p. 615A

Key Resources

- **Virtual Investigation**
- **Classroom Lab Video/DVD**
- **Holt Lab Generator CD-ROM**
  Search for any lab by type, standard, difficulty level, or time. Edit any lab to fit your needs, or create your own labs. Use the Lab Materials QuickList software to customize your lab materials list.

- **Differentiated Datasheets**
  Constructing Electric Circuits
- **Observation Lab**
  Converting Wind Energy into Electricity
- **CBL™ Probeware Lab**
  How the Length of a Conductor Affects Resistance

Learning Internet Terminology

Science Skills

Science Skills

Learning HTML Have students learn to write simple HTML code. Several HTML tutorials exist on the Internet and there are also many books on the subject. Then, instruct students to build a Web page using word processing software. Tell students that their Web page should have text in different font sizes and font colors, should have a photo embedded in it, and should contain at least one hyperlink to a different Web page.
LS Logical

Answers to Practice

1. HTML (Hypertext Markup Language)
2. a Web browser (or browser)
3. Answers may vary. Sample answer: text, graphics, hyperlinks
4. A Web page is a single HTML document, while a Web site is a group of linked documents under a single domain.

Knowing the basic terms associated with the Internet and its use can help you understand how the Internet works and how you can use it more effectively.

Term	Definition
Internet	a worldwide, decentralized network of computers that can communicate with one another
World Wide Web (www or "the Web")	part of the Internet consisting of linked documents that allow the combined presentation of text, graphics, sounds, and other media
TCP/IP (Transmission Control Protocol/Internet Protocol)	the primary communications protocol used by computers on the Internet
URL (Uniform Resource Locator)	a unique address for every file on the Web; for example, http://go.hrw.com/gopages/index.html
domain name	the part of a URL that tells the logical or sometimes geographical location of a computer on the Internet (in the example URL, go.hrw.com is the domain name)
HTML (Hypertext Markup Language)	the language behind all documents on the Web; allows areas of text or images to be hyperlinks to other files
hyperlink (or link)	a URL embedded in an HTML document; clicking on that part of the document allows you to connect to that URL; often appears as underlined text
Web page	a single HTML document
Web site	a group of linked documents under a single domain name
Web browser (or browser)	software that allows you to view HTML and other documents on the World Wide Web
plug-in	a program that allows a browser to handle files other than HTML files
search engine	a Web site used to search for files on the Web
keyword	a word used in a search by a search engine
bookmark or favorite	a URL stored in a browser so that you can return to it later
cookie	text put on your computer by a Web site; contains information that the Web site can use when you return to that site
spam	unwanted e-mail messages, usually in mass mailings
instant messaging or chat	interactive communication in which users send short messages back and forth in real time (with little delay)

Practice

1. In what language are most files on the World Wide Web written?
2. What kind of program is used for viewing files on the Web?
3. Name three kinds of elements that could appear on a Web page.
4. What is the difference between a Web page and a Web site?

go.hrw.com
SUPER SUMMARY
KEYWORD: HK8ELES

Key Ideas

Section 1 Electric Charge and Force

❯ **Electric Charge** An object can have a negative charge, a positive charge, or no charge at all. Like charges repel; unlike charges attract. (p. 585)

❯ **Transfer of Electric Charge** When different materials are rubbed together, electrons can be transferred from one material to the other. (p. 588)

❯ **Electric Force** The electric force at the atomic and molecular levels is responsible for most of the everyday forces that we observe, such as the force of a spring and the force of friction. (p. 590)

Section 2 Current

❯ **Voltage and Current** Just as a ball will roll downhill, a negative charge will move away from another negative charge. (p. 593)

❯ **Electrical Resistance** Resistance is caused by internal friction, which slows the movement of charges through a conducting material. (p. 596)

Section 3 Circuits

❯ **What Are Circuits?** The conducting path produced when a load, such as a string of light bulbs, is connected across a source of voltage is called a *closed circuit*. (p. 600)

❯ **Series and Parallel Circuits** Electrical devices can be connected either as a series circuit, so that the voltage is divided among the devices, or as a parallel circuit, so that the voltage is the same across each device. (p. 603)

❯ **Electrical Energy and Electric Power** Electrical energy is transformed into useful work, such as the turning of a motor, and some is lost as heat. (p. 605)

❯ **Fuses and Circuit Breakers** The high currents in overloaded circuits can cause fires. (p. 606)

Key Terms

electric charge, p. 585
electrical conductor, p. 588
electrical insulator, p. 588
electric force, p. 590
electric field, p. 591

electrical potential energy, p. 593
potential difference, p. 594
cell, p. 594
electric current, p. 595
resistance, p. 596

electric circuit, p. 600
schematic diagram, p. 601
series circuit, p. 603
parallel circuit, p. 603
electric power, p. 605
fuse, p. 607
circuit breaker, p. 607

SUPER SUMMARY

Have students connect the major concepts in this chapter through an interactive Super Summary. Visit **go.hrw.com** and type in the keyword **HK8ELES** to access the Super Summary for this chapter.

Differentiated Instruction

Alternative Assessment

Concept Mapping Instruct students to make a concept map that contains all the Key Terms from this chapter. Tell students to make sure that the connecting words that they use fully explain the relationship between the terms. Also tell students to incorporate the Key Ideas from this chapter in their concept maps. **LS Verbal**

Key Resources

🔲 **Interactive Concept Map**

📂 **Review Resources**
Concept Review Worksheets

📂 **Assessment Resources**
Chapter Tests A and B
Performance-Based Assessment

Reading Toolbox

1. Electrical resistance is actually caused by the friction on moving charges. Both resistance and friction cause a loss of energy as heat. Resistance takes place within a conductor, while friction is usually thought of as occurring between two surfaces in relative motion.

Using Key Terms

2. As a positive charge moves toward a negatively charged object, the charge's kinetic energy increases and its electrical potential energy decreases. The electric field due to the negatively charged object does work on the positive charge.

3. Resistance is caused by internal friction, which slows the movement of charges through a material. Resistance is measured by dividing the voltage across a conductor by the current.

4. Due to the potential difference across the wire, there is a current in the wire. The wire is made of a conductor covered with an insulator. The insulator prevents the current from leaking to the surroundings.

5. You can ground an electrical appliance by running a conducting wire between the object and the ground.

6. Check student drawings for accuracy. In a series circuit, every charge must travel through every component in the circuit. In a parallel circuit, there is more than one conducting path for charges to move through. As a charge moves through the circuit, it may travel through any one of the complete paths.

7. The bulbs are probably connected in a series circuit because if one element in a series circuit is not working, the circuit will be open and will not work.

READING TOOLBOX

1. **Comparisons** Electrical resistance is sometimes explained by saying that it is like friction for electric current. Describe how resistance and friction are alike and how they may be different.

USING KEY TERMS

2. Explain the energy changes involved when a positive charge moves because of a nearby, negatively charged object. Use the terms *electrical potential energy, work,* and *kinetic energy* in your answer.

3. What causes *resistance* in an electric circuit? How is resistance measured?

4. How do charges move through an insulated wire connected across a battery? Use the terms *potential difference, electric current, electrical conductor,* and *electrical insulator* in your answer.

5. How would you *ground* an electrical appliance?

6. Contrast the movement of charges in a *series circuit* and in a *parallel circuit*. Use a diagram to aid in your explanation.

7. If a string of lights goes out when one of the bulbs is removed, are the lights probably connected in a *series circuit* or a *parallel circuit*? Explain your answer.

8. Explain the difference between a *fuse* and a *circuit breaker*. If you were designing a circuit for a reading lamp, would you include a fuse, a circuit breaker, or neither? Explain your answer.

UNDERSTANDING KEY IDEAS

9. If two charges attract each other,
   a. both charges must be positive.
   b. both charges must be negative.
   c. the charges must be different.
   d. the charges must be the same.

10. The electric force between two objects depends on all of the following *except*
   a. the distance between the objects.
   b. the electric charge of the first object.
   c. the way that the two objects became electrically charged.
   d. the electric charge of the second object.

11. In the figure below,
   a. the positive charge is greater than the negative charge.
   b. the negative charge is greater than the positive charge.
   c. both charges are positive.
   d. both charges are negative.

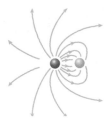

12. In order to produce a current in a cell, the terminals must
   a. have a potential difference.
   b. be exposed to light.
   c. be in a liquid.
   d. be at two different temperatures.

13. An electric current does *not* exist in
   a. a closed circuit.
   b. a series circuit.
   c. a parallel circuit.
   d. an open circuit.

14. Which of the following can help prevent a circuit from overloading?
   a. a resistor
   b. a switch
   c. a galvanometer
   d. a fuse

EXPLAINING KEY IDEAS

INTERPRETING GRAPHICS The schematic diagrams below represent four different circuits. Use the diagrams to answer question 15.

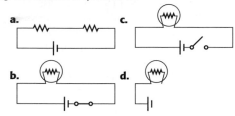

15. Which of the diagrams represent circuits that cannot have current in them as drawn?

16. Describe the characteristics of the electric field due to a single positive charge. How does the electric field of a negative charge differ?

17. Compare and contrast conductors, super-conductors, semiconductors, and insulators.

18. Explain how fuses and circuit breakers are used to prevent circuit overload.

CRITICAL THINKING

19. Making Comparisons The gravitational force is always attractive, and the electric force is both attractive and repulsive. What accounts for this difference?

20. Understanding Relationships Why is charge usually transferred by electrons? Which materials transfer electrons most easily? In what situations can positive charge move?

21. Designing Systems How many ways can you connect three light bulbs and a battery in a circuit? Draw a schematic diagram of each circuit.

22. Applying Knowledge At a given voltage, which light bulb has the greater resistance, a 200 W light bulb or a 75 W light bulb? Explain.

Graphing Skills

23. The graph below shows how electrical potential energy changes as the distance between two charges changes. Is the second charge positive or negative? Explain.

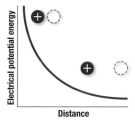

Math Skills

24. Electric Force Electric force is directly proportional to the product of the charges and inversely proportional to the square of the distance between them. If q_1 and q_2 are the charges on two objects and d is the distance between them, which of the following represents the electric force, F, between them?

a. $F \alpha \dfrac{q_1 q_2}{d}$ **c.** $F \alpha \dfrac{d^2}{q_1 q_2}$

b. $F \alpha \dfrac{q_1 q_2}{d^2}$ **d.** $F \alpha \dfrac{(q_1 q_2)^2}{d}$

25. Resistance A potential difference of 12 V produces a current of 0.30 A in a piece of copper wire. What is the resistance of the wire?

26. Resistance What is the voltage across a 75 Ω resistor with 1.6 A of current?

27. Electric Power A portable cassette player uses 3.0 V (two 1.5 V batteries in series) and has 0.33 A of current. What is its power rating?

28. Electric Power Find the current in a 2.4 W flashlight bulb powered by a 1.5 V battery.

Assignment Guide

Section	Items
1	9–11, 16, 19–20, 24
2	1–4, 12, 17, 23, 25–26
3	5–8, 13–15, 18, 21–22, 27–28

22. $R = V^2/P = V^2/(200\ \text{W})$; $R = V^2/P = V^2/(75\ \text{W})$; The 75 W bulb has a greater resistance. Alternatively, students may argue that a dimmer bulb (75 W) has a greater resistance than a brighter bulb (200 W) does.

Graphing Skills

23. The second charge is positive. The electrical potential energy is high when two like charges are close together, as shown in the graph.

Answers continued on p. 615A

8. A fuse is an electrical device that melts when current in a circuit becomes too great, whereas a circuit breaker is a switch that opens a circuit when the current becomes too great. In designing a circuit for a reading lamp, a circuit breaker would work better than a fuse because a circuit breaker can be reset after it has opened an overloaded circuit.

Understanding Key Ideas

9. c

10. c

11. a

12. a

13. d

14. d

Explaining Key Ideas

15. Neither c nor d can have current in them as drawn. Both a and b can have current.

16. The electric field of a positive charge extends outward from the charge. The electric field of a negative charge points inward toward the charge.

17. Conductors easily conduct electricity; they have a low resistance. Superconductors have zero resistance below a certain temperature. Semiconductors conduct electricity when "doped" with certain elements. Insulators do not easily conduct electricity; they have high resistance.

18. Fuses and circuit breakers create an open circuit when the current becomes too high.

Critical Thinking

19. Masses are always positive, while charges can be either positive or negative.

20. Protons are trapped in the nucleus and cannot escape. As a result, electrons are the only subatomic particles that can be transferred. Metals transfer electrons most easily. In gases and certain chemical solutions, current can be the result of positive charge movement.

21. four (ignoring the position of the battery and as long as the light bulbs are identical): all in series, all in parallel, two in parallel in series with the third, two in series in parallel with the third.

TEST DOCTOR

Question 1 Answer A is correct. To find the correct answer, students must divide the number of coulombs by the number of seconds in 5 minutes. 7,500 C ÷ (5 min × 60 s/min) = 25 C/s = 25 A. If students answer B or C, they do not know that the basic unit of electrical current is the ampere. If they answer D, they have multiplied 7,500 by 5.

Question 2 Answer G is correct. To find the correct answer, students must multiply the current by the voltage to find the power output. 120 V × 0.5 A = 60 V•A = 60 W. If students answer F or H, they do not know that the basic unit of electrical power is the watt. If they answer I, they have divided 120 by 0.5.

Question 3 Answer C is correct. Other answers indicate that students do not know that when devices or resistors are connected in parallel, the voltage across each is identical.

Question 4 220 V. To answer this question, students must multiply the horsepower by the power of the engine in watts (5 hp × 746 W/hp = 3,730 W), and divide the wattage by the current (3,730 W ÷ 17 A = 220 V).

Question 5 Full-credit answers should include the following points:
• Circuit breakers do not need to be replaced.
• Circuit breakers can be switched back on.
• Fuses need to be replaced.

Question 6 Full-credit answers should include the following points:
• Resistors must be made out of material that does not conduct electricity well.
• Copper conducts electricity very well.

Question 7 Answer D is correct. To find the answer, students must learn from the passage that each cell produces 0.5 V, and understand that when the cells are connected in series, their voltages are added. A minimum of 96 cells in a single

Understanding Concepts

Directions (1–3): For each question, write on a sheet of paper the letter of the correct answer.

1. Over a period of 5 min, 7,500 C is found to have traveled past a particular point in a circuit. How much current must have been flowing through the circuit?
- **A.** 25 A
- **B.** 1,500 V
- **C.** 7,500 V
- **D.** 37,500 A

2. If 0.5 A is flowing through a household light bulb and the bulb is plugged into a 120 V outlet, what is the bulb's power output?
- **F.** 0.5 Ω
- **G.** 60 W
- **H.** 120 Ω
- **I.** 240 W

3. To cool a microprocessor, an engineer designs a circuit with a battery and four tiny fans. If the voltage across each fan must be identical, how should the circuit be designed?
- **A.** The circuit should resemble a circle made of a single wire, with the battery and two fans in a series.
- **B.** There should be at least one fuse or circuit breaker for each fan.
- **C.** The fans should be connected in parallel in the circuit.
- **D.** Each fan must offer the same amount of resistance.

Directions (4–6): For each question, write a short response.

4. Before the adoption of SI units, the power output of some engines was measured in horsepower. One horsepower is equal to approximately 746 W. If a 5.0 horsepower engine is putting out 17 A of current, what is the voltage of the circuit?

5. Why are circuit breakers preferable to fuses?

6. Why aren't resistors made from copper?

Reading Skills

Directions (7–8): Read the passage below. Then, answer the questions that follow.

TURNING LIGHT INTO ELECTRICITY
On a clear day, sunlight strikes Earth's surface with an intensity of approximately 1,000 W/m². If all of that energy could be collected and transformed into electricity, there would be more than enough to run all the homes and businesses on the planet. At this point, the most efficient solar cells in existence capture only about 15% of the energy of sunlight, or approximately 150 W/m².

Solar cells can be constructed in a variety of shapes and sizes. Individual cells, regardless of their size, always produce a voltage of about 0.5 V. However, larger cells produce more current, and therefore more power (measured in W), because power is current times voltage. When multiple solar cells are connected in series, their voltages are added, but the current remains the same. When solar cells are connected in parallel, their current is added, but the voltage remains the same. Solar panels consist of a grid of cells, some connected in series and some in parallel, so that both voltage and current can be raised to useful levels.

7. A particular solar panel has a potential difference of 48 V. What is the minimum number of solar cells the panel could have?
- **A.** 12
- **B.** 24
- **C.** 48
- **D.** 96

8. A solar panel measuring 15 m by 10 m is operating at the maximum efficiency currently possible. If the panel has a potential difference of 225 V, how much current is the panel producing?
- **F.** 100 W
- **G.** 100 A
- **H.** 150 W
- **I.** 150 A

series would be needed to add up to 48 V. If students chose any other answer, ask them first to identify the voltage of each cell (0.5 V), then to reread to find out how the voltage can be higher (cells can be connected in series). Then ask how many 0.5 V cells would be needed to add up to 48 V (96).

Question 8 Answer G is correct. To find the correct answer, students must first find the number of square meters the panel occupies; 15 m × 10 m = 150 m². Students must learn from the passage that the maximum possible efficiency is 150 W per square meter, and multiply that the area of the solar panel by 150 W/m² to get the total power output of the panel. 150 m² ×

150 W/m² = 22,500 W. The total wattage is then divided by the potential difference of 225 V to get 100 A.

Question 9 Answer A is correct. To find the correct answer, students must see bulb A is in series with all the other bulbs in the circuit. Students should recognize that if any other bulb burns out, part of the circuit will still remain closed. If students choose any other answer, have them cover the bulb they chose, then try to find a path for the charge to flow in the circuit.

Question 10 Answer I is correct. If students choose any other answer, they may have the definitions of series circuits and parallel circuits backwards.

Interpreting Graphics

The schematic diagram below depicts an electrical circuit. Use this schematic to answer questions 9–11.

LIGHT BULB CIRCUIT

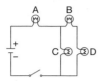

9. Which bulb burning out would mean that no current could flow through the circuit?
   - **A.** bulb A
   - **B.** bulb B
   - **C.** bulb C
   - **D.** bulb D

10. Which bulbs are connected in parallel with each other?
    - **F.** Bulb A is connected in parallel with bulb C.
    - **G.** Bulb B is connected in parallel with bulb D.
    - **H.** Bulb A is connected in parallel with bulbs B and D.
    - **I.** Bulb C is connected in parallel with bulbs B and D.

11. What must change in the circuit for the bulbs to light?

The following graphic displays the resistance graphs of two thermistors. Use this graphic to answer questions 12–13.

RESISTANCE VS. TEMPERATURE

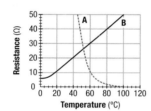

12. At approximately what temperature do the two thermistors experience the same resistance?
    - **A.** 0 °C
    - **B.** 50 °C
    - **C.** 100 °C
    - **D.** The two thermistors never experience the same resistance.

13. Which of the two thermistors is more likely to be made of platinum wire? Which is more likely to be made of manganese oxide?

Test Tip

If using a graph to answer a question, read the graph's title and the labels on the axes. For graphs that show a change in some variable over time, keep in mind that the steepness and direction of a curve indicate the relative rate of change at a given point in time.

Question 11 Full-credit answers should include the following point:
- Indicate that the circuit must be closed.

Question 12 Answer B is correct. To find the correct answer, students must observe where the two graphs cross, and note the corresponding value for temperature on the x-axis.

Question 13 Full-credit answers should include the following points:
- The thermistor represented by graph B is more likely to be made of platinum wire.
- The thermistor represented by graph A is more likely to be made of manganese oxide.

State Resources

For specific resources for your state, visit **go.hrw.com** and type in the keyword **HSHSTR**.

📖 **Test Practice with Guided Reading Development**

Answers
1. A
2. G
3. C
4. 220 V or 2.2×10^2 V.
5. Answers will vary; see Test Doctor for a detailed scoring rubric.
6. Answers will vary; see Test Doctor for a detailed scoring rubric.
7. D
8. G
9. A
10. I
11. Answers will vary; see Test Doctor for a detailed scoring rubric.
12. B
13. Answers will vary; see Test Doctor for a detailed scoring rubric.

Continuation of Answers

Answers continued from p. 607
8. $P = IV = (9.5 \text{ A})(120\text{V}) = 1.1 \times 10^3 \text{ W}$

9. $I = P/V = 40 \text{ W}/120 \text{ V} = 0.3 \text{ A}$

$I = P/V = 75 \text{ W}/120 \text{ V} = 0.62 \text{ A}$

The 75 W bulb has more current in it.

Answers continued from p. 609
8. $V = IR = (0.005 \text{ A})(100 \text{ }\Omega) = 0.5 \text{ V}$. The voltage should be about 0.5 V across the 100 Ω resistor. $V = IR = (0.005 \text{ A})(200 \text{ }\Omega) = 1.0 \text{ V}$. The voltage should be about 1.0 V across the 200 Ω resistor.

9. The total resistance should be about 67 Ω.

10. $I = \dfrac{V}{R} = (1.5 \text{ V}) / (67 \text{ }\Omega) = 0.022 \text{ A}$. The total current should be about 0.022 A.

11. $I = \dfrac{V}{R} = (1.5 \text{ V}) / (100 \text{ }\Omega) = 0.015 \text{ A}$. About 0.015 A should be in the 100 Ω resistor.

$I = \dfrac{V}{R} = (1.5 \text{ V}) / (200 \text{ }\Omega) = 0.075 \text{ A}$.

About 0.0075 A should be in the 200 Ω resistor.

Answers to Analysis

1. The current will be half as much as the original currnet.
2. the total current will be double the original current.
3. The total current will increase.

Answers to Communicating Your Results

4. The 10 Ω resistor will have the greater voltage across it.
5. The 5 Ω resistor will have more current in it.

Answer to Extension

No, adding more resistors will increase the amount of current in the circuit, which will drain the battery more quickly.

Answers continued from p. 613
Math Skills

24. b

25. $R = V/I = (12 \text{ V})/(0.30 \text{ A}) = 4.0 \times 10^1 \text{ }\Omega$

26. $V = IR = (1.6 \text{ A})(75 \text{ }\Omega) = 1.2 \times 10^2 \text{ V}$

27. $P = IV = (0.33 \text{ A})(3.0 \text{ V}) = 0.99 \text{ W}$

28. $I = P/V = (2.4 \text{ W})/(1.5 \text{ V}) = 1.6 \text{ A}$

	Standards	**Teach Key Ideas**

CHAPTER OPENER, pp. 616–618   `50 min.`

SECTION 1 Magnets and Magnetic Fields, pp. 619–625   `50 min.`

> Magnets
> Magnetic Fields
> Earth's Magnetic Field

Standards: PS 5b, UCP 1, UCP 2, SAI 1, SAI 2

Teach Key Ideas:
- Bellringer Transparency
- Teaching Transparency TM51 Magnetic Field
- Visual Concepts Magnetic Materials • Magnetic Poles • Magnetic Field • Earth's Magnetic Field

---

SECTION 2 Magnetism from Electric Currents, pp. 626–631   `50 min.`

> Electromagnetism
> Electromagnetic Devices

Standards: PS 4e, UCP 1, SAI 1, ST 2, HNS 1

Teach Key Ideas:
- Bellringer Transparency
- Teaching Transparencies P21 Electric Motor • TM52 Right-Hand Rule • TM53 Solenoid • TM54 Galvanometer • P21 Electric Motor
- Visual Concepts Right-Hand Rule for a Current-Carrying Wire • Solenoid • Galvanometer

---

SECTION 3 Electric Currents from Magnetism, pp. 632–639   `50 min.`

> Electromagnetic Induction
> The Electromagnetic Force
> Transformers

Standards: PS 4e, PS 5a, PS 5b, PS 6b, UCP 2, SAI 1, ST 1, ST 2, HNS 1

Teach Key Ideas:
- Bellringer Transparency
- Teaching Transparencies P22 AC Generator • P23 Induced Current • P24 How Transformers Change Voltage
- Visual Concepts Ways of Inducing a Current in a Circuit • Function of a Generator • Electromagnetic Waves • Transformer

See also PowerPoint® Resources

Chapter Review and Assessment Resources

- **SE** Science Skills: Making Predictions, p. 642
- **SE** Chapter Summary, p. 643
- **SE** Chapter Review, pp. 644–645
- **SE** Standardized Test Prep, pp. 646–647
- ☐ Concept Review Worksheets ■
- ☐ Chapter Tests A and B ■
- 📀 Holt Online Assessment

CHAPTER Fast Track *To shorten instruction because of time limitations, omit the chapter lab.*

Basic Learners

- **TE** Levitating Magnets, p. 620
- **TE** Magnetic Domains, p. 621
- **TE** Interpreting Diagrams, p. 636
- ☐ Science Skills Worksheets
- ☐ Differentiated Datasheets A for Labs and Activities ■
- 📖 Study Guide A ■

Advanced Learners

- **TE** Comparing Forces, p. 621
- **TE** Electric Motors, p. 630
- ☐ Cross-Disciplinary Worksheets
- ☐ Differentiated Datasheets C for Labs and Activities ■

Key

SE Student Edition
TE Teacher's Edition

📁 Chapter Resource File
📓 Workbook
* Datasheet or blackline master available
📖 Transparency

💿 CD or CD-ROM

■ Also available in Spanish

All resources listed below are also available on the Teacher's One-Stop Planner.

Why It Matters	Hands-On	Skills Development	Assessment
Build student motivation with resources about high-interest applications.	**SE Inquiry Lab** Magnetic Levitation, p. 617* ■	**TE Reading Toolbox** Assessing Prior Knowledge, p. 616 **SE Reading Toolbox** p. 618	📁 **Pretest** ■
TE Ceramic Magnets, p. 620 **SE Earth's Changing Magnetic Field,** p. 625 📁 **Cross-Disciplinary Worksheet** Connection to Social Studies—The Natural Forces and Laws of Compasses	**TE Demonstration** Creating a Magnet, p. 619 **SE Quick Lab** Magnetic Poles, p. 621* ■ **TE Demonstration** Shapes of Magnetic Fields, p. 622 📁 **Observation Lab** Constructing and Using a Compass	**TE Reading Toolbox** Word Families, p. 620 **SE Reading Toolbox** Double-Door FoldNote, p. 623	**TE Reteaching Key Ideas** Navigation Using Magnetic Fields, p. 624 **TE Formative Assessment,** p. 624 📁 **Spanish Assessment*** ■ 📁 **Section Quiz** ■
SE Airport Security, p. 629 **TE Particle Accelerators,** p. 630 📁 **Cross-Disciplinary Worksheet** Integrating Chemistry—Molecular Magnetism	**SE Quick Lab** Electromagnet, p. 628* ■ **TE Demonstration** Magnetic Force on a Current Loop, p. 628 📁 **CBL™ Probeware Lab** Testing Magnets for an Electric Motor	**TE Reading Toolbox** Concept Map, p. 627 **SE Reading Toolbox** Cause and Effect, p. 631	**TE Reteaching Key Ideas** Electric Motors, p. 631 **TE Formative Assessment,** p. 631 📁 **Spanish Assessment*** ■ 📁 **Section Quiz** ■
TE Tethered Satellites, p. 633 **SE How Do Electric Guitars Work?** p. 635 **TE Wire Taps,** p. 637 📁 **Cross-Disciplinary Worksheet** Integrating Technology—Magnetic Resonance Imaging	**TE Demonstration** Faraday's Law, p. 632 **SE Inquiry Lab** Can You Demonstrate Electromagnetic Induction? p. 633* ■ **TE Demonstration** Mechanical Energy to Electrical Energy, p. 634 **TE Demonstration** Alternating Current, p. 636 **SE Inquiry Lab** Making a Better Electromagnet, pp. 640–641* ■	**TE Reading Toolbox** Visual Literacy, p. 634 **TE Reading Toolbox** Interpreting Visuals, p. 635 **SE Reading Toolbox** Cause and Effect, p. 636	**TE Reteaching Key Ideas** Group Study, p. 639 **TE Formative Assessment,** p. 639 📁 **Spanish Assessment*** ■ 📁 **Section Quiz** ■

See also Lab Generator

See also Holt Online Assessment Resources

Resources for Differentiated Instruction

English Learners
TE Letter Writing, p. 638
📁 Differentiated Datasheets A, B, and C for Labs and Activities ■
📖 Study Guide A ■

Struggling Readers
TE Right-Hand Rule, p. 627
📓 Interactive Reader

Special Education Students
TE Exploring Magnetism, p. 622
TE Voltage Variations, p. 634

Alternative Assessment
TE Generators, p. 638
TE Electromagnetic Devices, p. 643

Overview

This chapter begins with a discussion of magnets, magnetic force, magnetic fields, and compasses. It then explores how electric currents can produce magnetic fields, and discusses galvanometers, electric motors, and stereo speakers. Electromagnetic induction and Faraday's law are also explained so that students can learn how generators and transformers work.

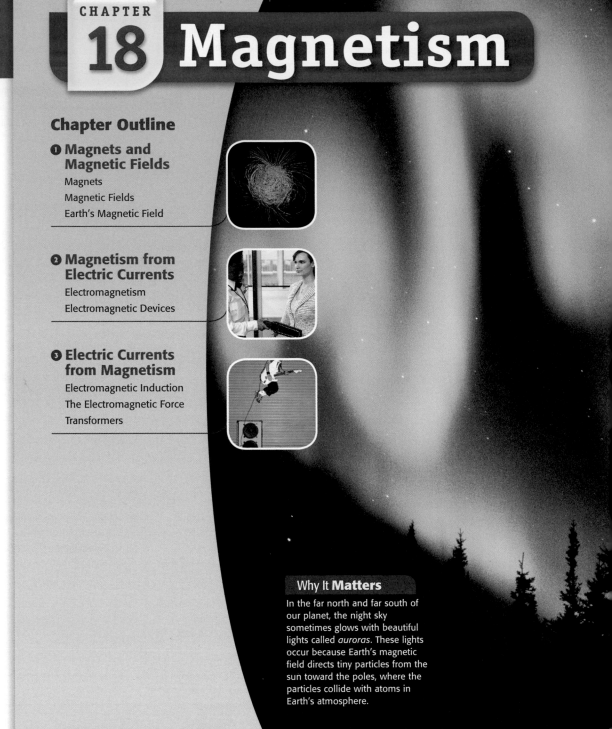

CHAPTER 18 Magnetism

Chapter Outline

❶ Magnets and Magnetic Fields
Magnets
Magnetic Fields
Earth's Magnetic Field

❷ Magnetism from Electric Currents
Electromagnetism
Electromagnetic Devices

❸ Electric Currents from Magnetism
Electromagnetic Induction
The Electromagnetic Force
Transformers

Why It Matters
In the far north and far south of our planet, the night sky sometimes glows with beautiful lights called *auroras*. These lights occur because Earth's magnetic field directs tiny particles from the sun toward the poles, where the particles collide with atoms in Earth's atmosphere.

READING TOOLBOX

Assessing Prior Knowledge Students should understand the following concepts:
• charged particles
• electromagnetic waves
• electric current
• electric fields
• circuits

MISCONCEPTION ALERT

Science education research has identified the following misconceptions about magnetism.
• Students believe that the size of a magnet determines its strength. (The strength of a magnet depends on the alignment of magnetic domains within the magnet.)
• Students believe that anything metal will be attracted to a magnet. (Many metals, for example copper and aluminum, are not attracted to magnets.)
• Students guess that magnetism will pass through paper, but not through wood, books, and similar materials. (Magnetism is a field force, like gravity, and can pass through solid materials.)
• Students believe that only magnets produce magnetic fields, and that magnetic fields only exist outside the magnet in two-dimensional lines. (Electric currents can produce magnetic fields. Magnetic fields exist outside the magnet in three dimensions.)

Chapter Correlations   *National Science Education Standards*

The following correlations show the National Science Standards that relate to this chapter. For the full text of the standards, see the National Science Education Standards at the front of the book.

PS 4e Electricity and magnetism are two aspects of a single electromagnetic force. Moving electric charges produce magnetic forces, and moving magnets produce electric forces. These effects help students to understand electric motors and generators. (Sections 2, 3)

PS 5a Energy can be transferred by collisions in chemical and nuclear reactions, by light waves and other radiations, and in many other ways. However, it can never be destroyed. (Section 3)

PS 5b All energy can be considered to be either kinetic energy, which is the energy of motion; potential energy, which depends on relative position; or energy contained by a field, such as electromagnetic waves. (Sections 1, 3)

PS 6b Electromagnetic waves include radio waves (the longest wavelength), microwaves, infrared radiation (radiant heat), visible light, ultraviolet radiation, x-rays, and gamma rays. (Section 3)

UCP 1 Systems, order, and organization (Sections 1, 2)

UCP 2 Evidence, models, and explanation (Sections 1, 3)

SAI 1 Abilities necessary to do scientific inquiry (Sections 1, 2; Inquiry Lab: Making a Better Electromagnet)

SAI 2 Understandings about scientific inquiry (Section 1)

ST 1 Abilities of technological design (Inquiry Lab: Making a Better Electromagnet)

ST 2 Understandings about science and technology (Sections 2, 3)

HNS 1 Science as a human endeavor (Sections 2, 3)

InquiryLab ⏱ 20 min

Magnetic Levitation

You can use **two ring-shaped magnets** and a **pencil** to see levitation in action. First, use a **scale** to find the mass of each magnet. Record the masses. Drop one of the magnets over the end of the pencil so that the magnet rests on your hand. Now, drop the other magnet over the end of the pencil. If the magnets are oriented correctly, the second magnet will levitate above the first. If the magnets attract, remove the second magnet, flip it over, and drop it over the end of the pencil.

Questions to Get You Started

1. How much magnetic force is necessary to levitate the magnet?
2. How does the force between the magnets change when you flip one of the magnets over?

InquiryLab

Teacher's Notes The top magnet will levitate if the magnets' north poles are next to each other or if the south poles are next to each other. If the north and south poles are next to each other, the magnets will be attracted, and the top magnet will not levitate.

Materials per Group
- magnets, ring-shaped (2)
- pencil

Answers

1. The magnetic force must be equal to the force of gravity (weight) of the upper magnet.
2. The force changes direction (from repulsive to attractive, or vice versa) when one of the magnets is flipped.

Key Resources

📁 **Datasheets**
Magnetic Levitation

💿 **Interactive Tutor**
Disc Two, Module 17: Magnetic Field of a Wire

Word Parts

Sample table:

WORD	ROOT	WHAT IT MEASURES
altimeter	alti-	altitude
speedometer	speed-	speed
galvanometer	galvan- (Named for Luigi Galvani who discovered that electric current passes through nerves and muscles)	current
ammeter	am- (Named for Andre-Marie Ampere, one of the discoverers of electro-magnetism)	current (SI unit)
voltmeter	volt- (Named for Alessandro Volta, inventor of the battery)	potential difference

Cause and Effect

Answers may vary. Students should list cause-and-effect relationships from sentences in Sections 2 and 3 and should note the cause-and-effect markers when they exist in those sentences.

FoldNotes

Answers may vary. Students' double-door folds should look similar to the example shown. Notes about Section 2 should be behind the door labeled "Magnetism from Electric Currents," and notes about Section 3 should be behind the door labeled "Electric Currents from Magnetism."

These reading tools can help you learn the material in this chapter. For more information on how to use these and other tools, see **Appendix A.**

Word Parts

Suffixes The word *meter* often refers to an instrument used for measuring, such as a *parking meter*. The word *meter* is also used as a suffix. An instrument's name is often a root plus *–meter*. The root identifies what the instrument measures. For example, an *altimeter* measures altitude. If the root ends in a consonant, an *o* can be added. So, the suffix becomes *–ometer,* as in *speedometer*.

Your Turn As you read this chapter, note words that use the suffix *–meter*. Use words from this chapter to continue a table like the one shown here. Many of the root words are derived from the names of scientists. Note the connection that each scientist has to what is being measured.

WORD	ROOT	WHAT IT MEASURES
altimeter	alti	altitude
speedometer	speed	speed

Cause and Effect

Signal Words Certain words or phrases can signal cause-and-effect relationships. Words and phrases that signal causes include

- *produce*
- *as a result of*
- *because*

Words and phrases that signal effects include

- *therefore*
- *results from*
- *consequently*

Sentences can also express cause-and-effect relationships without using explicit markers.

Your Turn In Sections 2 and 3 of this chapter, you will read about cause-and-effect relationships between electricity and magnetism. Complete a table like this one of cause-and-effect pairs.

CAUSE	EFFECT	MARKER(S)
bolt of lightning	the direction of a compass needle changes	(none)

FoldNotes

Double-Door Fold FoldNotes are a fun way to help you learn and remember ideas that you encounter as you read. FoldNotes help you organize concepts and see the "big picture."

Your Turn Following the instructions in **Appendix A,** make a double-door fold. Label the first door "Magnetism from Electric Currents" and the second door "Electric Currents from Magnetism." Take notes about Section 2 behind the first door, and take notes about Section 3 behind the second door.

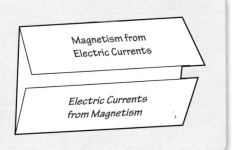

Magnets and Magnetic Fields

Key Ideas

❯ What happens when the poles of two magnets are brought close together?

❯ What causes a magnet to attract or repel another magnet?

❯ How is Earth's magnetic field oriented?

Key Terms

magnetic pole
magnetic field

Why It Matters

Earth's magnetic field has reversed direction in its geologic history and may reverse again in the future, which will affect all compasses on Earth.

Magnets are often used to attach papers or photos to a refrigerator door. But magnets are also used in many devices, such as motors, VCRs, and medical-imaging machines. Some home alarm systems use the simple magnetic attraction between a piece of iron and a magnet to alert homeowners that a window or door has been opened.

Magnets

Magnets got their name from a region of Magnesia, which is now part of present-day Greece. The first lodestones, which are naturally occurring magnetic rocks, were found in this region almost 3,000 years ago. A lodestone, shown in **Figure 1,** is composed of an iron-based mineral called *magnetite*.

You know that like electric charges repel each other and that the attraction between two opposite charges gets stronger as those charges are brought closer together. A similar situation exists for **magnetic poles,** points that have opposing magnetic properties.

All magnets have at least one pair of poles, a *north pole* and a *south pole*. The poles of magnets exert a force on each other. ❯ **Two like poles repel each other. Two unlike poles attract each other.** Thus, the north pole of one magnet will repel the north pole of another magnet. But the north pole of one magnet will attract the south pole of another magnet.

It is impossible to isolate a magnet's south pole from the magnet's north pole. If a magnet is cut into two or more pieces, each piece will still have two poles. No matter how small the pieces of a magnet are, each piece still has both a north pole and a south pole.

magnetic pole (mag NET ik POHL) one of two points, such as the ends of a magnet, that have opposing magnetic qualities

Figure 1 A naturally occurring magnetic rock, called a lodestone, will attract a variety of iron objects.

>Focus

In the first part of this section, students learn what magnets are. Next they study magnetic fields and learn how compasses work. The section concludes with a discussion of Earth's magnetic field.

🔊 Bellringer

Use the Bellringer transparency to prepare students for this section.

Demonstrate

Creating a Magnet For this demonstration you will need a bar magnet, an iron nail, and paper clips. Magnetize the nail with the bar magnet by rubbing the magnet on the end of the nail. Rub the nail in only one direction, and do not change direction. If you rub back and forth in two directions, the nail will not become magnetized. Have a student rub the magnet on the nail 10 times and then determine how many paper clips the nail will lift. Next, rub the nail 10 more times and see how many paper clips the nail will lift. If you continue to rub the nail, the magnetic force will increase. At some point, additional rubbing with the bar magnet will not increase the strength of the magnetized nail. Lead a discussion with students on the magnetizability of certain materials.
 Kinesthetic/Visual

Key Resources

 Teaching Transparency
TM51 Magnetic Field

💿 **Visual Concepts**
Magnetic Materials
Magnetic Poles
Magnetic Field
Earth's Magnetic Field

📁 **Datasheets**
Magnetic Poles
Magnetic Field of a File Cabinet

📁 **Cross-Disciplinary Worksheet**
Connection to Social Studies—The Natural Forces and Laws of Compasses

Word Families Write the words *magnet* and *magnetic field* on the chalkboard. Ask students to come up with words or phrases that relate to magnets and magnetic fields. Have students suggest potential applications of magnetic fields in industry and in daily life. Students should write down their ideas if they need clarification. **LS Verbal**

Earth Science Connection

Magnetite Magnetite, Fe_3O_4, is a lustrous black magnetic mineral that occurs in crystals with a cubic structure. It is one of the important ores of iron and is a common constituent of igneous and metamorphic rocks. It is found in Norway, Sweden, the Urals, and various parts of the United States. One variety of magnetite—lodestone—has been noted for its natural magnetism since antiquity.

Why It **Matters**

Ceramic Magnets Some permanent magnets are made out of ceramic materials, such as barium or strontium ferrite. These magnets can be extremely strong, are resistant to demagnetization, and are inexpensive, but they are also extremely brittle. Ceramic magnets must be machined before they are magnetized. Then they can be magnetized in the desired direction. These magnets are used for a wide range of applications from motors and cellular phones to toys.

SC LINKS.
www.scilinks.org
Topic: Properties of Magnets
Code: HK81229

Figure 2 When a magnet is dipped into a bucket of nails, the magnet can pick up a chain of nails. Each nail in the chain is temporarily magnetized by the nail above it.

Some materials can be made into permanent magnets.

Some substances, such as lodestones, are magnetic all of the time. These magnets are called *permanent magnets*. You can change any piece of iron, such as a nail, into a magnet by stroking the iron several times with a magnet. Placing a piece of iron near a strong magnet will also change the iron into a magnet. After a time, the iron becomes magnetic and remains that way even if the strong magnet is removed.

Although a magnetized piece of iron is called a *permanent* magnet, its magnetism can be weakened or even removed. Heating or hammering a magnetic object can reduce its magnetic properties.

Some materials retain their magnetism better than others do. Scientists classify materials as either magnetically *hard* or magnetically *soft*. Iron is a soft magnetic material. A piece of iron is easily magnetized, but it also tends to lose its magnetic properties easily. Hard magnetic materials, such as cobalt and nickel, are difficult to magnetize. However, these materials do not lose their magnetism easily.

✔ **Reading Check** **What can you do to decrease the magnetism of a soft magnetic material?** (See Appendix E for answers to Reading Checks.)

Magnets exert magnetic forces on each other.

As **Figure 2** shows, a magnet that is dipped into a bucket of nails will often pick up several nails. As soon as a nail touches the magnet, the nail itself acts as a magnet and attracts other nails. More than one nail is lifted because each nail in the chain becomes temporarily magnetized and exerts a *magnetic force* on the nail below.

The iron nails are a soft magnetic material. So, the temporary magnetism disappears when the chain of nails is no longer touching the magnet. Sometimes, the nails remain slightly magnetized after the chain is no longer in contact with the permanent magnet. However, the nails will eventually return to their unmagnetized state.

The length of the chain of nails is limited. The length depends on the ability of the nails to become magnetized and on the strength of the magnet. The greater the distance between a nail and the magnet, the weaker the nail's magnetic force. Eventually, the magnetic force between the two lowest nails is not strong enough to overcome the force of gravity. In other words, the bottom nail weighs too much to stay attached, so it falls.

Magnets Some students believe that anything metal will be attracted to a magnet. Show students some examples to dispel this misconception. Use a bar magnet and a variety of metal objects, including some that are attracted to the magnet and others that are not attracted.

Differentiated Instruction

Basic Learners

Levitating Magnets Ring magnets can be placed on a pencil so that they will levitate. Place many ring magnets on a pencil so that they all repel each other. Notice that the spacing between magnets gradually decreases as you go from top to bottom. This is because the bottom magnet must support the weight of all the levitated magnets, while the middle magnet must support only half the weight. Turn the pencil 90° so that it is parallel to the ground. The gaps between magnets are equal because each magnet exerts the same amount of force when the pencil is horizontal. **LS Kinesthetic**

QuickLab Magnetic Poles ⏱ 10 min

Procedure

❶ Use **strips of tape** to cover the pole markings at both ends of a **bar magnet**.

❷ Tie a **piece of string** to the center of the magnet, and suspend the magnet from a **support stand**.

❸ Use another **bar magnet** to determine the north pole and the south pole of the hanging magnet.

Analysis

1. What happens when you bring one pole of your magnet near each end of the hanging magnet?

2. After you have decided the identity of each pole, remove the tape to check. Could you have determined the north pole and the south pole of the hanging magnet if you had covered the poles of both magnets?

Magnetic Fields

Try holding a magnet and moving its south pole toward the south pole of a magnet that can move freely. Do not let the magnets touch. The magnet that you are not holding moves away from the other one. A force is being exerted on the freely moving magnet even though the magnets never touch.

Because it acts at a distance, a magnetic force is a field force. You should already be familiar with other forces that act at a distance. For example, gravitational forces and the force between electric charges act at a distance. A **magnetic field** is a region where a magnetic force can be detected. ❯ **Magnets repel or attract each other because of the interaction of their magnetic fields.**

Magnets are sources of magnetic fields.

A magnetic field surrounds any magnetized material. Some magnetic fields are stronger than others. The strength of a magnetic field depends on the material the magnet is made of and on how much the material has been magnetized.

Moving charges create magnetic fields. An atom has magnetic properties because of the movement of the electrons within the atom. In most materials, such as copper and aluminum, the magnetic fields of the individual atoms cancel each other out. These materials are not magnetic.

In materials such as iron, nickel, and cobalt, groups of atoms tend to create larger groups of atoms called *magnetic domains*. These groups of atoms all line up the same way and form small, magnetized regions within the material. When an external magnetic field is applied near this material, the small regions align and increase the magnetic field of the material.

magnetic field (mag NET ik FEELD) a region where a magnetic force can be detected

Integrating Social Studies

Finding North With the invention of iron ships and steel ships in the late 1800s, it became necessary to develop a nonmagnetic compass. The *gyrocompass*, a device containing a spinning loop, was the solution. Because of inertia, the gyrocompass always points toward Earth's geographic North Pole, regardless of which way the ship turns.

QuickLab

Teacher's Notes The string should be tied so that the magnet will be balanced and hang parallel to the ground. A small piece of tape will keep the string from moving while the magnet is suspended. Be sure you perform this experiment away from metal objects like metal cabinets and faucets, which may attract the magnet.

Materials per Group
• bar magnets (2)
• tape
• string
• support stand

Answers to Analysis

1. When one pole of the hand-held magnet is brought near one end of the suspended magnet, it moves away from the pole. When the same pole of the hand-held magnet is brought near the other end of the suspended magnet, it moves closer to the pole.

2. If left alone, the hanging magnet would align itself with Earth's magnetic field, with its N pole pointing north. Using this fact, you could determine the unknown poles of both magnets.

Teaching Key Ideas

Magnetic Fields and Field Lines Students think the poles of a magnet are named for the geographic North and South Poles of Earth. Point out that the N pole of a magnet is actually the "north-seeking pole." Many students believe that magnetic field lines show the direction in which the magnet will push another magnet. The magnetic field lines indicate how a second magnet will align itself in the magnetic field of the first magnet.

Differentiated Instruction

Advanced Learners

Comparing Forces Some students might think that the forces exerted by gravity, by electric charges, and by magnets are identical. Have students write a few paragraphs that compare and contrast these three forces. Be sure students include both similarities and differences in their paragraphs. For example, one similarity is that all three forces act at a distance. One difference is that electric and magnetic forces can be attractive or repulsive, while the force of gravity is always an attractive force. **LS Verbal**

Basic Learners

Magnetic Domains Repeat the demonstration of magnetizing a nail. Have students use the discussion of magnetic domains to explain what happens in this demonstration. (When the magnet is rubbed on the iron nail, the domains in the iron become aligned, and the iron becomes magnetic. The overall magnetic field increases as more domains became aligned.) Ask students what would happen to the nail if it were dropped after being rubbed by the magnet. (Some domains would lose their alignment, and the nail's magnetic field would weaken.) **LS Verbal/Logical**

Shapes of Magnetic Fields For this demonstration you will need two bar magnets, a horseshoe magnet, iron filings, a blank transparency, and an overhead projector. Set the two bar magnets about 4 cm apart, aligned with opposite poles facing each other on the overhead projector, and lay a blank transparency over the magnets. Sprinkle the iron filings onto the transparency. Repeat the demonstration using the horseshoe magnet. Ask students to speculate about why the patterns look different. **LS Visual**

Life Science Connection

Magnetic Fields in Animal Navigation Ask a biology teacher to come into the class to discuss the use of magnetic fields in animal navigation. *Aquaspirillum magnetotacticum,* a bacteria, was the first organism found to use magnetic fields to navigate. There has also been a great deal of research with bees as well as with birds. Have students research different migratory animals and present a poster on how the animals use magnetic fields in navigation. **LS Verbal**

Answer to caption question

Magnetic field lines seem to travel from the north pole to the south pole.

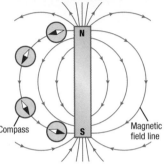

Figure 3 The magnetic field of a bar magnet can be traced with a compass. **In which direction do magnetic field lines seem to travel?**

www.scilinks.org
Topic: Magnetism
Code: **HK80900**

Magnetic field lines can be used to represent magnetic fields.

Electric field lines are often used to represent an electric field. Similarly, magnetic field lines can be used to represent the magnetic field of a bar magnet. These field lines always form closed loops.

In the photograph of the magnet in **Figure 3**, small pieces of iron are used to show the field around the bar magnet. The field also exists within the magnet and continues farther away from the magnet. The greater the distance between the magnetic field and the magnet, the weaker the magnetic field is. As is the case with electric field lines, magnetic field lines that are close together indicate a strong magnetic field. Field lines that are farther apart indicate a weaker field. So, you can tell from **Figure 3** that a magnet's field is strongest near its poles.

Magnetic field lines always form closed loops.

As the drawing in **Figure 3** shows, a compass can be used to analyze the direction of a magnetic field. A compass is a magnet suspended on top of a pivot so that the magnet can rotate freely. You can make a simple compass by using a piece of string to hang a bar magnet from a support. Simply tie the string to the magnet's midpoint and the support.

By convention, magnetic field lines begin at the north pole of a magnet and end at the south pole of the magnet. However, magnetic field lines do not really have a beginning or end. They always form closed loops. In a permanent magnet, the field lines actually continue within the magnet itself to form the loops. (Note: These lines are not shown in the illustration.)

✔ **Reading Check** In a bar magnet, where do magnetic field lines begin and where do they end?

Compasses align with Earth's magnetic field.

If it is not near another strong magnet, a compass will align with Earth's magnetic field like iron filings aligning with a bar magnet's field. The compass points in the direction that lies along, or is *tangent* to, the magnetic field line at a given point.

Sailors used lodestones to make the first compasses. The sailors would place a lodestone on a small plank of wood that was floating in calm water. Then, they would watch the wood as it turned and pointed toward the north star. Thus, sailors could gauge their direction even during the day, when stars are not visible. Later, sailors found that a steel or iron needle rubbed with lodestone acted in the same manner. By convention, the pole of a magnet that points north is painted red.

MISCONCEPTION ALERT

Magnetic Field Lines Some students believe that magnetic field lines are two-dimensional. Be sure students realize that although the field lines are represented two-dimensionally on the page, the magnetic field actually acts in three dimensions all around a magnet. You can use a compass and a magnet to illustrate this. Show how the field acts on the compass, not just in a single plane around the magnet, but above and below the magnet as well.

Differentiated Instruction

Special Education Students

Exploring Magnetism To help students understand the difference between materials that are attracted to magnets and those that are not, give students a magnet and ask them to discover materials in the classroom that are attracted to magnets. Have students create two lists of objects, one list of objects that are attracted to magnets and the other list of objects that are not. Discuss the materials of which the objects in each category are made. **LS Kinesthetic/Verbal**

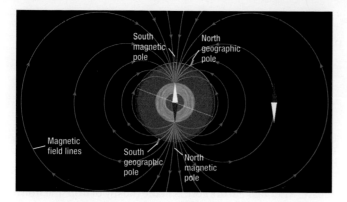

Figure 4 Earth's Geographic and Magnetic Poles

Teaching Key Ideas

Earth's Magnetic Field The orientation of Earth's magnetic field, shown in **Figure 4,** can be confusing for many students. Emphasize that the N and S poles of a magnet are named for the geographical poles they point to. Discuss that the geographic poles and magnetic poles are not on the same axis.

Earth's Magnetic Field

Earth's magnetic poles are not in the same place as its geographic poles, as **Figure 4** shows. **❯ Earth's magnetic field lines run from geographic south to geographic north.** The pole in Antarctica is actually a magnetic north pole, and the pole in northern Canada is a magnetic south pole. For historical reasons, the poles of magnets are named for the geographic pole to which they point. Thus, the end labeled *N* is the "north-seeking" pole of the magnet, and the end labeled *S* is the "south-seeking" pole of the magnet.

Earth's magnetic field has both direction and strength. If you were to move northward along Earth's surface and you had a compass whose needle could point up and down, the needle of the compass would slowly tilt forward. At a point in northeastern Canada, the needle would point straight down. This point is one of Earth's magnetic poles. There is an opposite magnetic pole in Antarctica.

READING TOOLBOX

Double-Door FoldNote
Create a double-door FoldNote. Label the first door "Earth's North Pole" and the second door "Earth's South Pole." Take notes about these topics behind each door.

READING TOOLBOX

Double-Door FoldNote Notes under Earth's North Pole may include: located in Canada, a magnetic south pole, a place where a compass needle points straight down. Notes under Earth's South Pole may include: located in Antarctica, a magnetic north pole, a place where a compass needle points straight down.

QuickLab

Magnetic Field of a File Cabinet

🕐 10 min

Procedure

❶ Stand in front of a **metal file cabinet,** and hold a **compass** face up and parallel to the ground.

❷ Move the compass from the top of the cabinet to the bottom to see if the direction in which the compass needle points changes. If the direction in which the needle points changes, the cabinet is magnetized.

Analysis

1. Can you explain what might have caused the file cabinet to become magnetized? Remember that Earth's magnetic field lines run not only horizontally to Earth's surface but also up and down.

2. Can you find other objects in your classroom that have become magnetized by Earth's magnetic field?

QuickLab

Teacher's Notes If you are performing this lab in class, test the file cabinet before the lab. Possible substitutes include iron flagpoles and iron fence posts such as those around tennis courts. Remind students that Earth's magnetic field has both a vertical and horizontal component. The file cabinet is magnetized by the vertical component. Have them try to find an object that has been magnetized by the horizontal component of Earth's magnetic field.

Materials per Group
• compass
• metal file cabinet

Answers to Analysis

1. The file cabinet becomes magnetized due to prolonged exposure to Earth's magnetic field. The amount of magnetization that occurs is dependent upon the kind of metal from which the cabinet is made. If the cabinet is aluminum, it will not be magnetic at all. If the cabinet is steel, it is slightly magnetic and therefore causes the compass needle to be deflected.

2. Answers may vary. Some may include metal book shelves or desks.

❯Close

Reteaching Key Ideas

Navigation Using Magnetic Fields
Have students speculate how the magnetic particles in the tissues of animals might detect where on Earth the animals are located. They should think about how the direction and strength of Earth's magnetic field changes in different parts of the planet. Encourage students to use illustrations in their responses.
LS Logical/Visual

Formative Assessment

What happens if you cut a magnet in half?

A. You get one magnet with only a north pole and one with only a south pole. (Incorrect. It is impossible to separate a magnet's north pole from its south pole.)

B. You get two smaller magnets, each one with its own north and south poles. (Correct. No matter how small the pieces a magnet is cut into, each piece will always have a north pole and a south pole.)

C. You get two unmagnetized pieces. (Incorrect. Cutting a magnet does not remove its magnetism. Hitting a magnetic material with a hammer can cause it to lose its magnetism.)

D. You get one magnet with two north poles and one magnet with two south poles. (Incorrect. Magnets always have one north pole and one south pole.)

Figure 5 Birds may use Earth's magnetic field to guide them during migration.

The source of Earth's magnetism is not yet fully understood.

The source of Earth's magnetism is a topic of scientific debate. Although Earth's core is made mostly of iron, the iron in the core is too hot to retain any magnetic properties. Instead, many researchers believe that the circulation of ions or electrons in the liquid layer of Earth's core may be the source of the magnetism. Others believe Earth's magnetism is due to a combination of several factors.

The sun also has a magnetic field and ejects charged particles into space. Earth's magnetic field deflects most of these particles so that the charged particles enter Earth's atmosphere only near the magnetic poles. Collisions between these particles and atoms in Earth's atmosphere cause the Northern and Southern lights.

For years, scientists have speculated that some birds, such as the geese in **Figure 5,** use Earth's magnetic field to guide their migrations. Magnetic particles that seem to have a navigational role have been found in the tissues of migrating animals, such as birds, bees, and fish.

Section 1 Review

KEY IDEAS

1. **Determine** whether the magnets will attract or repel each other in each of the following cases.

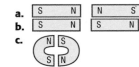

2. **Illustrate** the magnetic field around a permanent magnet.

3. **Describe** the direction in which a compass needle points in Australia.

CRITICAL THINKING

4. **Interpreting Graphics** Which orientation of the compass needles in the figure below correctly describes the direction of the bar magnet's magnetic field at the given location?

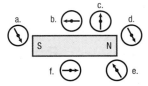

5. **Applying Concepts** The north pole of a magnet points toward the geographic North Pole, yet like poles repel. Explain this seeming discrepancy.

Answers to Section Review
1. **a.** repel
   b. attract
   c. attract
2. Students' illustrations should resemble **Figure 3.**
3. The compass needle would point north.
4. a, b
5. The north pole of a magnet is attracted to Earth's magnetic south pole, which is near the geographic North Pole.

Earth's Changing Magnetic Field

Earth's magnetic field has decreased in strength by about 10% in the past 150 years. This change suggests that Earth's magnetic field may be heading toward a magnetic field reversal—a 180° change in direction. Earth's magnetic field has changed direction throughout geologic time. Evidence of more than 20 reversals in the last 5 million years is preserved in the magnetization of ocean-floor rocks. To explain how this change is possible, some scientists propose that a *geodynamo* may be the source of Earth's magnetic field.

WEIRD SCIENCE

This computer simulation of a geodynamo represents one possible model of Earth's magnetic field. The orange field lines point outward (as does a magnetic north pole), and the blue field lines point inward.

After running the geodynamo model for a long time, the computer simulation shows that the field undergoes a magnetic field reversal. Computer models such as this one help scientists understand the behavior of Earth's magnetic field.

A history of Earth's magnetic field is recorded in the volcanic rocks on the floor of Earth's oceans. Scientists collect samples using a core sampler, such as the one shown here, at a number of locations on the ocean floor near mid-ocean ridges.

YOUR TURN

UNDERSTANDING CONCEPTS

1. What evidence suggests that Earth is heading toward a magnetic field reversal?

ONLINE RESEARCH

2. Research the mid-ocean ridges. What do their magnetic patterns say about the history of Earth's continents?

SC**LINKS**

www.scilinks.org
Topic: Earth's Magnetic Field
Code: **HK80448**

Earth's Changing Magnetic Field

Evidence of Earth's changing magnetic field is well-observed in seafloor rocks along the Mid-Atlantic Ridge. As fresh basalt emerges at spreading centers in the seafloor, magnetic materials in the liquid magma align with Earth's magnetic field, recording the polarity of Earth at the time the rock is formed. Symmetrical patterns of polarity are observed on either side of the ridge because plate movement moves rock away from the ridge on both sides. The most recent reversal of Earth's magnetic field happened about 780,000 years ago.

The Geodynamo Model, a computer simulation, was developed in the early 1990's by Gary Glatzmaier at the University of California, Santa Cruz and Paul Roberts of the University of California, Los Angeles. It simulates Earth with a solid inner core that rotates slightly faster than Earth's surface. This generates a magnetic field around Earth that is very similar to the observed magnetic field. The simulation was run simultaneously on two super computers. The model has a time step of 15 days and spans millions of years.

Answers to Your Turn

1. Earth's magnetic field has decreased in strength in the last 150 years.

2. Magnetic patterns in the mid-ocean ridges show that the Pacific Ocean is decreasing in size, while the Atlantic Ocean is growing. This means that the Americas are moving closer toward Asia and away from Europe and Africa.

SECTION
2

Magnetism from Electric Currents

> Focus

In this section, students learn how electric currents produce magnetic fields and what causes magnetism. Then they apply these concepts to galvanometers, electric motors, and stereo speakers.

Bellringer

Use the Bellringer transparency to prepare students for this section.

Demonstrate

Electromagnet For this demonstration you will need a 6 V battery, a spool of insulated wire, a compass, and 2 ring stands. First, make a large coil of wire, perhaps 1 ft in diameter. Use many loops around the coil so that the magnetic field is strong. An easy way to make the coil is to wrap the wire around a soccer ball or basketball. Use a ring stand to hold the loop off the table. The loop should be oriented perpendicular to the ground and with its axis in a direction other than north-south. Attach the wire to the battery so that a current is going through the loop, creating a magnetic field at its center. Place the compass at the center of the loop and turn the circuit on and off. The compass needle should move when the circuit is activated. The compass does not need to be at the exact center; however, that is where the magnetic field is the strongest. Use the compass to trace the magnetic field around the loop.

Key Ideas

> What happens to a compass near a wire that is carrying a current?

> Why are electric motors useful?

Key Terms

solenoid
electromagnet
electric motor
galvanometer

Why It Matters

Because magnetic fields are created by electric currents, metal detectors used by airport security guards are able to detect metal.

During the 18th century, people noticed that lightning could momentarily change the direction of a compass needle. They also noticed that iron pans sometimes became magnetized during lightning storms. These observations suggested a relationship between electricity and magnetism, but the relationship was not understood until 1820.

Electromagnetism

In 1820, Hans Christian Oersted, a Danish science teacher, first experimented with the effects of an electric current on the needle of a compass. He found that moving electric charges produce magnetism. After class, Oersted showed some of his students that when a compass is brought near a wire carrying a current, the compass needle is deflected from its usual north-south orientation.

The apparatus shown in **Figure 1** uses compasses to reveal the magnetic field near a current-carrying wire. When no current is in the wire, all of the needles will point in the same direction—that of Earth's magnetic field. **> When the wire carries a strong, steady current, all of the compass needles move to align with the magnetic field created by the electric current.** If the current is reversed, each needle will point in the opposite direction.

The direction that the compass needles are pointing in **Figure 1** suggests that the magnetic field around a current-carrying wire forms a circle around the wire. Each needle points in a direction tangent to a circle centered at the wire.

Figure 1 When a wire carries a current, the magnetic field induced by the current forms concentric circles around the wire.

Key Resources

Teaching Transparencies
P21 Electric Motor
TM52 Right-Hand Rule
TM53 Solenoid
TM54 Galvanometer

Visual Concepts
Right-Hand Rule for a Current-Carrying Wire
Solenoid
Galvanometer

Datasheet
Electromagnet

Cross-Disciplinary Worksheet
Integrating Chemistry—Molecular Magnetism

The right-hand rule is used to find the direction of the magnetic field produced by a current.

Is the direction of a wire's magnetic field clockwise or counterclockwise? Repeated measurements have suggested an easy way to predict the direction of a field. This method is summarized by the *right-hand rule.*

Right-hand rule	If you hold a wire in your right hand and point your thumb in the direction of the positive current, the direction that your fingers curl is the direction of the magnetic field.

The right-hand rule is illustrated in **Figure 2.** The right hand grasps the wire while the thumb points in the direction of the current. The fingers encircle the wire, and the fingertips point in the direction of the magnetic field—counterclockwise when viewed from the top. If the direction of the current were from the top to the bottom of the page, the thumb would point downward, and the magnetic field would run clockwise. *Remember: Never grasp or touch an uninsulated wire connected to a power source. You could be electrocuted.*

✔ **Reading Check** When using the right-hand rule, you should point your thumb in which direction?

Solenoids and bar magnets have similar magnetic fields.

As you have learned, the magnetic field of a current-carrying wire exerts a force on a compass needle. This force causes the needle to turn in the direction of the wire's magnetic field. However, this force is very weak for a small current. Increasing the current in the wire is one way to increase the force, but large currents can be fire hazards. Wrapping the wire into a coil is a safer way to create a stronger magnetic field, as **Figure 3** shows. This device is called a **solenoid.**

In a solenoid, the magnetic field of each loop of wire adds to the strength of the magnetic field of any neighboring loops. The result is a strong magnetic field similar to the magnetic field produced by a bar magnet. Like a magnet, a solenoid has a north and south pole.

Current

Magnetic field

Figure 2 You can use the right-hand rule to find the direction of the magnetic field near a wire that is carrying a current.

solenoid (SOH luh NOYD) a coil of wire with an electric current in it

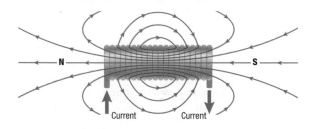

N   S
Current   Current

Figure 3 The magnetic field of a solenoid resembles the magnetic field of a bar magnet.

> **Teach**

READING TOOLBOX

🔗 **Concept Map** Have students read this section and then organize the ideas presented in the form of a concept map or other reading organizer. The organization can be in terms of the order presented in the chapter or in terms of detailed characteristics listed for each idea. **LS Verbal**

Teaching Key Ideas

Compass Near A Wire Ask students to think about what will happen to the needle on a compass as you move the compass away from a current-carrying wire. Have them draw a picture of the magnetic field around a cross-section of a current-carrying wire, showing concentric circles that are closer together near the wire and farther apart farther from the wire. Students should understand that the compass will align tangent to a circle around the wire when the compass is closer to the wire and the magnetic field is stronger, but that it will begin to align with the magnetic field of Earth as it moves away from the wire and the magnetic field due to the wire becomes weaker. **LS Visual/Logical**

Differentiated Instruction

Struggling Readers

Right-Hand Rule Have students practice using the right-hand rule by confirming that the direction of the magnetic field shown in **Figure 3** is correctly drawn for the solenoid. Ask them which end of the solenoid would be the N pole if the current were reversed. (the right side) **LS Visual**

Teacher's Notes The electromagnet will work better if the wire is wound very tightly together. **Safety Caution:** The wires will get hot. Students should use heat-resistant gloves to handle the electromagnet. Be sure students disconnect the battery after making their observations.

Materials per Group
- battery, 6 V
- compass
- nail, iron or steel, large
- wire, insulated, 1 m

Answers to Analysis
1. an electromagnet—the coil of wire is the solenoid, and the nail is the magnetic core
2. The direction of the compass needle reverses when the current is reversed because the charges move in the opposite direction.
3. Drop the nail several times, or hit the nail sharply with a hammer.

QuickLab Electromagnet

🕐 **20 min**

Procedure
1. Wind **1 m of insulated wire** around a **large iron or steel nail.**
2. Remove the insulation from the ends of the wire. Hold the insulated wire so that the ends touch the terminals of a **6 V lantern battery.**
3. Move a **compass** toward the nail.
4. Flip the battery around so that the current is reversed. Bring the compass near the same part of the nail.

Analysis
1. What type of device have you produced? Explain your answer.
2. What happened to the compass needle after you reversed the direction of the current? Explain your observation?
3. After you detach the coil from the cell, what can you do to make the nail nonmagnetic?

---

electromagnet (ee LEK troh MAG nit) a coil that has a soft iron core and that acts as a magnet when an electric current is in the coil

Academic Vocabulary

device (di VIES) a piece of equipment made for a specific use

---

The strength of a solenoid can be increased.

The strength of the magnetic field of a solenoid depends on the number of loops of wire and the amount of current in the wire. In particular, more loops or more current can create a stronger magnetic field.

The strength of a solenoid's magnetic field can also be increased by inserting a rod made of a magnetic metal, such as iron, through the center of the coils. The resulting <u>device</u> is called an **electromagnet.** The magnetic field of the solenoid causes the rod to become a magnet as well. Then, the magnetic field of the rod adds to the coil's field and thus creates a magnet that is stronger than the solenoid alone.

✓ **Reading Check** What relationship does the number of loops of wire in a solenoid have to the strength of a solenoid?

Moving charges cause magnetism.

The movement of charges is the cause of all magnetism. But what charges are moving in a bar magnet? Negatively charged electrons moving around the nuclei of atoms make magnetic fields. Atomic nuclei also have magnetic fields because protons move within the nuclei. Each electron has a property called *electron spin,* which also produces a tiny magnetic field.

In most cases, the various sources of magnetic fields in an element cancel out and leave the atom essentially nonmagnetic. However, not all of the fields cancel in some materials, such as iron, nickel, and cobalt. Thus, the magnetism of the uncanceled fields in these materials combines to make the materials magnetic overall.

Magnetic Force on a Current Loop
Materials: a strong horseshoe magnet, a wire, two ring stands and supports, and a variable DC power supply. Lay the magnet on its side so that one pole is above the other. Connect the wire to the power supply, and support the wire so that it passes through the center of the poles of the magnet. Turn on the power supply, and gradually increase the current in the wire until the wire is forced to one side. Ask students what will happen if the direction of the current is reversed. (The wire will move in the opposite direction.) Reverse the connections to the power supply and repeat the demonstration. **LS Visual**

Real-World Connection

Industrial Electromagnets Electromagnets are used in many different industries. Perhaps their best-known use is for lifting junk cars at a junkyard. These electromagnets are suspended at the end of a crane. Large currents are used to power the electromagnet so that its magnetic field is strong enough to lift a car off the ground. Heavy-duty electromagnets are also used to lift machine parts that are being cast in foundries. After parts have been cast, they must cool in their molds. Once they solidify, but before they are completely cool, they must be removed from the mold for additional processing. Electromagnets are needed for this because the parts are still too hot to touch.

Airport Security

Before traveling on an airplane, you are required to pass through a metal detector on your way to the gate. You may also be asked to submit to a sweep with a hand-held metal detector. Metal detectors make use of electromagnetism. Most airport metal detectors use a system called *pulse induction* (PI). These systems consist of a power supply, a sensor circuit, and a coil of metal through which a current can pass.

❶ Short pulses of current are passed through the coil at a rate of about 100 pulses per second. Each pulse creates a short-lived magnetic field that quickly collapses.

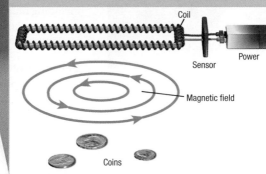

Coil
Sensor
Power
Magnetic field
Coins

❷ When a metal object passes through the metal detector or a hand-held detector passes near a metal object, an opposite magnetic field is induced in the metal object.

❸ When it detects the opposing magnetic field, the sensor activates a light or sound that signals the operator of the metal detector.

YOUR TURN

UNDERSTANDING CONCEPTS
1. Does the field induced in the metal object increase or decrease the pulsed field?

WRITING IN SCIENCE
2. Choose another device used in airport security, and describe how this device works.

Why It Matters

Airport Security In most airport metal detectors, one side of the arch contains both a coil and a detector. A short, strong burst of current is pulsed through the coil creating a magnetic field. After the burst of current, the magnetic field reverses direction and then collapses, resulting in an electrical spike. The spike produces a second current in the coil called the reflected pulse. If there are no large metal objects in the metal detector, the reflected pulse lasts about 30 microseconds. When a metal object passes through the PI detector, a magnetic field is induced in the object. This magnetic field increases the time required for the reflected pulse to disappear. For example, if a reflected pulse lasts significantly longer than 30 microseconds, the detector signals that metal is present. PI detectors typically sample between 25 and 1,000 times per second.

It may help to use an analogy of producing echoes to explain this phenomenon. If someone yells in a room with few hard surfaces, the sound waves quickly disappear. When someone yells into a room with many hard surfaces, the sound waves bounce around, producing an echo. Metal passing through a PI detector acts in the same way as a hard surface does, increasing the time that the magnetic field persists.

Answers to Your Turn

1. increases
2. Answers may vary. Topics may include explosives detectors, surveillance cameras, and X-ray machines used to scan luggage. The CAPPS II system is a new biometric system that uses fingerprints and retinal scans to verify passenger lists.

Demonstrate

Galvanometers Your science department may have a demonstration galvanometer with clear sides. Otherwise, remove the case of a galvanometer. The meter portion is typically screwed into a plastic case with four small screws. Often the back portion of the meter is clear, and the internal parts can be seen. Remove the meter from the case and show it to students. Hook the meter to a small 1.5 V battery and show students the coils of wire being deflected.

Why It **Matters**

Particle Accelerators CERN, the Center for European Nuclear Research, studies subatomic particles. This is done by accelerating charged particles to speeds near the speed of light and then smashing them into other particles. Large wire coils are used to generate strong magnetic fields that help accelerate and steer the particles. Have students research this or another particle accelerator and make a poster showing the dimensions of the accelerator and labeling its key parts. **LS Visual**

Answer to caption question

If the current is reversed, the meter moves in the opposite direction.

Figure 4 A blow-dryer is one example of an everyday device that uses an electric motor.

electric motor (ee LEK trik MOHT uhr) a device that converts electrical energy into mechanical energy

galvanometer (GAL vuh NAHM uht uhr) an instrument that detects, measures, and determines the direction of a small electric current

www.scilinks.org
Topic: Electromagnets
Code: **HK80484**

Electromagnetic Devices

Many modern devices, such as blow-dryers and stereo speakers, make use of the magnetic field produced by coils of current-carrying wire. Devices such as the blow-dryer shown in **Figure 4,** are able to function because the coils inside the devices work as motors.

Electric motors are machines that convert electrical energy into mechanical energy. **A motor can perform mechanical work when it is attached to an external device.** Electric motors are used in many devices around your home, including many toys. Larger motors are found in washing machines and clothes dryers, and simple motors can be found in common household fans.

Galvanometers detect current.

Galvanometers are devices that are used to measure current. The basic construction of a galvanometer is shown in **Figure 5.** In all cases, a galvanometer detects current, or the movement of charges in a circuit.

A galvanometer consists of a coil of insulated wire wrapped around an iron core that can rotate between the poles of a permanent magnet. When the galvanometer is attached to a circuit, a current exists in the coil of wire. The coil and iron core act as an electromagnet and produce a magnetic field. This magnetic field interacts with the magnetic field of the surrounding permanent magnet. The resulting forces turn the core, which moves a needle along a scale.

A galvanometer can be used with other circuit elements to function as an *ammeter,* which measures current, or as a *voltmeter,* which measures voltage.

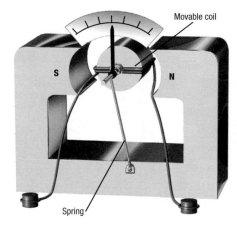

Figure 5 When there is current in the coil of a galvanometer, magnetic repulsion between the coil and the magnet causes the coil to twist. **How does the direction of the motion change if the current is reversed?**

Real-World Connection

Electromagnetic Keys Many hotels now use electromagnetic card keys instead of traditional keys. Within the door lock mechanism are small solenoids with many loops. These solenoids read the magnetic signature on a key to determine whether the lock should unlock. The same kind of reader is also used in ATMs and credit card reading machines.

Differentiated Instruction

Advanced Learners

Electric Motors Use small electric motors whether they work or not. Remove the outer casing with a pair of pliers. Let students investigate the inner components. Students will see the wire coils, the permanent magnets in the casing, and the brushes and commutator. Ask students to draw the inner components and to write a paragraph describing what happens during one rotation of the coil. **LS Visual**

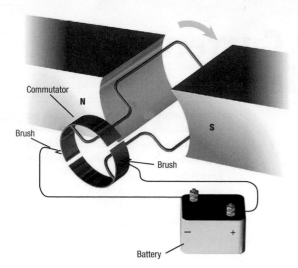

Figure 6 In an electric motor, the current in the coil produces a magnetic field that interacts with the magnetic field of the surrounding magnet and thus causes the coil to turn.

Motors use a commutator to spin in one direction.

The arrow in **Figure 6** shows how the coil of wire in a motor turns when a current is in the wire. Unlike the coil in a galvanometer, the coil in an electric motor keeps spinning. A device called a *commutator* is used to make the current change direction every time the flat coil makes a half revolution. This commutator is two half rings of metal. Devices called *brushes* connect the commutator to the wires from the battery. Because of the slits in the commutator, charges must move through the coil of wire to reach the opposite half of the ring.

So, the magnetic field of the coil changes direction as the coil spins. In this way, the coil is repelled by both the north and south poles of the magnet surrounding it. Because the current keeps reversing, the loop rotates in one direction. If the current did not keep changing direction, the loop would simply bounce back and forth in the magnetic field until the force of friction caused the loop to come to rest.

READING TOOLBOX

Cause and Effect
Many factors influence how a motor works. As you read this page and the previous page, look for multiple causes and multiple effects that enable a motor to turn.

READING TOOLBOX

Cause and Effect Sample table:

CAUSE	EFFECT
current in coil	magnetic field
magnetic field of wire	wire spins
slits in commutator	change direction of current
reversal of current	wire rotates in one direction

❯ Close

Reteaching Key Ideas

Electric Motors Have students trace the path of electric charge through the motor in **Figure 6.** Discuss: In which direction does the magnetic field of the loop point as the loop is oriented in the figure? If you consider the loop as simulating a bar magnet, how would this bar magnet be oriented? How would the magnetic field of the surrounding magnets affect such a bar magnet?
LS Visual/Kinesthetic

Section 2 Review

KEY IDEAS

1. **Describe** the shape of a magnetic field produced by a straight wire that is carrying a current.

2. **Determine** the direction in which a compass needle will point when the compass is held above a wire carrying positive charges that are moving west.

3. **Explain** how galvanometers and electric motors function.

CRITICAL THINKING

4. **Predicting Outcomes** Predict whether a solenoid suspended by a string could be used as a compass.

5. **Analyzing Ideas** A friend claims to have built a motor by attaching a shaft to the core of a galvanometer and removing the spring. Can this motor rotate through a full rotation? Explain your answer.

Formative Assessment

What components make up an electromagnet?

A. a coiled wire (Incorrect. A coiled wire can only act as an electromagnet if it carries a current.)

B. two half loops of metal attached to two brushes (Incorrect. Two half loops of metal make a commutator. Brushes connect wires to the commutator in an electric motor)

C. a current-carrying solenoid with an iron core (Correct. An electromagnet is a coiled wire surrounding an iron core. The iron core increases the magnetic strength of the solenoid.)

D. a straight current-carrying wire (Incorrect. A straight current-carrying wire simply produces a magnetic field.)

Answers to Section Review

1. It is in the shape of concentric rings with the wire at the center.

2. The direction of the compass needle is north.

3. Both a galvanometer and an electric motor consist of a coil of insulated wire wrapped around an iron core that spins between the poles of a permanent magnet. When attached to a circuit, the coil and core act as an electromagnet, producing a magnetic field that causes the core to rotate. In a galvanometer, the core just deflects to one side or the other. In an electric motor, a commutator causes the current to alternate directions, which in turn causes the core to continue spinning in one direction.

Answers continued on p. 647A

›Focus

In this section, students learn what conditions are required for electromagnetic induction. Next, they apply this concept to generators. They also learn how transformers change voltage across power lines.

Bellringer

Use the Bellringer transparency to prepare students for this section.

Demonstrate

Faraday's Law Set up two magnets about two inches apart with their N and S poles adjacent, as shown in **Figure 1.** Ask students to speculate about what might happen when a loop of wire moves through the magnetic field. Attach two ends of a loop of wire to a galvanometer. Pass the loop of wire through the space between the magnets. Explain that an electric current is induced, which exists as long as the magnetic field is changing relative to the wire.
LS Visual/Verbal

›Teach

Teaching Key Ideas

Wire Loop in a Magnetic Field Have students look at **Figure 1.** Ask them to state the condition required for current to exist in the loop in the figure. (There must be relative motion between the loop and the magnetic field.)

Answer to caption questions
Current will flow through the lamp.

Key **Ideas**

› What happens when a magnet is moved into or out of a coil of wire?

› How are electricity and magnetism related?

› What are the basic components of a transformer?

Key **Terms**

electromagnetic induction

generator

alternating current

transformer

Why It **Matters**

Many common devices, such as electric guitars and speakers, rely on electromagnetic induction to function.

Electric power plants convert mechanical energy—usually the movement of water or steam—into electrical energy. How can electrical energy be generated from mechanical energy?

Electromagnetic Induction

In 1831, Michael Faraday discovered that a current can be produced by pushing a magnet through a coil of wire. This happens without a battery or other source of voltage. › **Moving a magnet into and out of a coil of wire causes charges in the wire to move.** The process of creating a current in a circuit by changing a magnetic field is called **electromagnetic induction.** Electromagnetic induction is so fundamental that it has become one of the laws of physics—*Faraday's law*.

Faraday's law	An electric current can be produced in a circuit by changing the magnetic field crossing the circuit.

Consider the loop of wire moving between the two magnetic poles in **Figure 1.** As the loop moves into and out of the magnetic field of the magnet, a current is *induced* in the circuit. As long as the wire continues to move into or out of the field in a direction that is not parallel to the field, an induced current will exist in the circuit.

Rotating the circuit or changing the strength of the magnetic field will also induce a current in the circuit. In each case, a changing magnetic field is passing through the loop. You can use the concept of magnetic field lines to predict whether a current will be induced. A current will be induced if the number of field lines that pass through the loop changes.

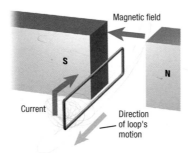

Magnetic field

S

N

Current

Direction of loop's motion

Figure 1 When the loop moves into or out of the magnetic field, a current is induced in the wire. **What happens if the loop is rotated between the magnets?**

Key Resources

 Teaching Transparencies
P22 AC Generator
P23 Induced Current
P24 How Transformers Change Voltage

Visual Concepts
Ways of Inducing a Current in a Circuit
Function of a Generator
Electromagnetic Waves
Transformer

Datasheet
Can You Demonstrate Electromagnetic Induction?

Cross-Disciplinary Worksheet
Integrating Technology—Magnetic Resonance Imaging

Electromagnetic induction obeys conservation of energy.

Although electromagnetic induction may seem to create energy from nothing, it does not. Electromagnetic induction does not violate the law of conservation of energy. Pushing a loop through a magnetic field requires work. The greater the magnetic field, the stronger the force required to push the loop through the field. The energy required for this work comes from an outside source, such as your muscles pushing the loop through the magnetic field. So, electromagnetic induction produces electrical energy, but energy is required for electromangetic induction to occur.

The magnetic force acts on moving electric charges.

A charged particle moving in a magnetic field will experience a force in a direction that is at right angles to the direction of the magnetic field lines. This magnetic force is zero when the charge moves in the same direction as the magnetic field lines. The force is at its maximum value when the charge moves perpendicularly to the field. As the angle between the charge's direction and the direction of the magnetic field decreases, the force on the charge also decreases. This force also acts on a wire that is carrying a current.

Academic Vocabulary

violate (VIE uh LAYT) to fail to keep

electromagnetic induction (ee LEK troh mag NET ik in DUHK shuhn) the process of creating a current in a circuit by changing a magnetic field

Teach, *continued*

Why It **Matters**

Tethered Satellites A tethered satellite is a satellite connected to a spacecraft through a long cable called a tether. As the tether moves through Earth's magnetic field, the charges in the tether experience a force due to the magnetic field and try to move to one end of the tether. This motion produces a voltage across the tether. The tether can then be used as an energy source. A tethered satellite may be able to generate more than 1 A of current.

NASA conducted the first test of a tethered satellite in 1992. The Space Shuttle Atlantis released a spherical satellite with a 21-km long tether into space. Unfortunately, the tethered satellite jammed on the reel, and could not be deployed further. NASA conducted a second test in 1996 with the Space Shuttle Columbia. This time, the tether broke after deployment, and the satellite drifted away. However, before the break, the satellite generated 3,500 volts and up to 0.5 amps of current. So the mission did meet its objective by demonstrating that tethered satellites can use Earth's magnetic field to generate electric current.

InquiryLab — Can You Demonstrate Electromagnetic Induction?

⏱ **30 min**

Procedure

1. Connect each end of a **hollow-core wire coil,** or **solenoid,** to a **galvanometer,** as shown in the photo.
2. Any current induced in the solenoid will pass through the galvanometer. For each of the following motions, record the direction in which the galvanometer needle points and the amount by which it moves.
3. Insert the north pole of a **bar magnet** into the solenoid.
4. Pull the magnet out of the solenoid.
5. Turn the magnet around, and move the south pole into and out of the solenoid.
6. Vary the speed of your motion.
7. Use **two magnets,** and hold them alongside each other so that like poles are touching.

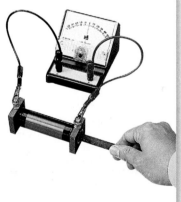

Analysis

1. What evidence indicates that a changing magnetic field induces a current? What happens if you do not move the magnet at all?
2. Compare the current induced by a south pole with the current induced by a north pole.
3. What two observations show that more current is induced if the magnetic field changes rapidly?
4. How does the amount of current induced depend on the strength of the magnetic field?

InquiryLab

Teacher's Notes Students who finish early can be challenged to try to produce a steady current or a highly variable one by moving the magnet in different ways.

Materials per Group
- bar magnets (2)
- galvanometer
- solenoid
- wire leads, insulated (2)

Answers to Analysis

1. As the magnet moves in and out of the solenoid, the galvanometer needle deflects. This means that a current is induced in the solenoid when the magnetic field in the solenoid changes. When the magnet does not move, no current is induced.
2. The current is in opposite directions when the different poles are used.
3. Pushing or pulling the magnet rapidly causes a large deflection.
4. The induced current is greater when the magnetic field is stronger.

READING TOOLBOX

Visual Literacy Have students use **Figure 2** to explain why a current is not induced in a loop that is moving parallel to a magnetic field. (There is only a magnetic force on a charge moving perpendicularly to the direction of the magnetic field.) **LS Visual**

go.hrw.com
★ interact online

Students can interact with the figure by going to **go.hrw.com** and typing in the keyword **HK8MAGF2.**

Demonstrate

Mechanical Energy to Electrical Energy For this demonstration you will need a hand crank generator, a light bulb, and a socket. Use the generator to light up a light bulb. This demonstrates that different types of energy can be converted into electrical energy. Talk through the different energy conversions in the process: chemical energy in your muscles is converted into kinetic energy to make your hand crank the motor. This kinetic energy is converted into electrical energy when a magnet or coil rotates inside the generator. The magnetic field through the wire loop generates an electrical current. In the light bulb, electrical energy is converted to light. Throughout the system, some energy is lost as heat.

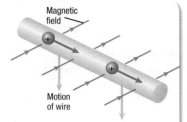

When the wire in a circuit moves perpendicularly to the magnetic field, the current induced in the wire is at a maximum.

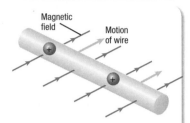

When the wire moves parallel to the magnetic field, no current is induced in the wire.

Figure 2 A current is induced in a closed circuit when the circuit moves through a magnetic field.

go.hrw.com
★ interact online
Keyword: HK8MAGF2

generator (JEN uhr AYT uhr) a machine that converts mechanical energy into electrical energy

alternating current (AWL tuhr NAYT ing KUHR uhnt) an electric current that changes direction at regular intervals (abbreviation, AC)

The magnetic force acts on wires carrying a current.

When studying electromagnetic induction, you may find it helpful to imagine the individual charges in a wire. Imagine that the wire in a circuit is a tube full of charges, as illustrated in **Figure 2.** When the wire is moving perpendicularly to a magnetic field, the force on the charges is at a maximum. In this case, a current is in the wire and circuit. When the wire is moving parallel to the field, no current is induced in the wire. Because the charges are moving parallel to the field, they experience no magnetic force.

Generators convert mechanical energy into electrical energy.

Generators are similar to motors but convert mechanical energy into electrical energy. If you expend energy to do work on a simple generator, such as the one in **Figure 3,** the loop of wire inside turns within a magnetic field and thus produces a current. For each half rotation of the loop, the current produced by the generator reverses direction. A current that changes direction at regular intervals is called an **alternating current** (AC).

The generators that produce the electrical energy that you use at home are alternating-current generators. The current supplied by the outlets in your home and in most of the world is alternating current. The glowing light bulb in **Figure 3** indicates that the coil turning in the magnetic field of the magnet creates a current. The magnitude and direction of the current that results from the coil's rotation vary depending on the orientation of the loop in the field.

✓ Reading Check **What must be done to produce a current using a generator?**

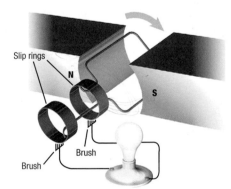

Slip rings

N

S

Brush

Brush

Figure 3 In an alternating-current generator, the mechanical energy of the loop's rotation is converted into electrical energy when a current is induced in the wire. The current lights the light bulb.

Differentiated Instruction

Special Education Students

Voltage Variations Assign three teams of students to illustrate the following:
1. Voltage is stepped up at a power plant.
2. Voltage is stepped down at a local distribution station.
3. Voltage is stepped down near homes.
LS Interpersonal/Kinesthetic

How Do Electric Guitars Work?

The word *pickup* refers to a device that "picks up" the sound of an instrument and turns that sound into an electrical signal. The most common type of electric guitar pickup uses electromagnetic induction to convert string vibrations into electrical energy. Conversely, a speaker converts an electrical signal back into sound.

Electric guitar pickups come in many styles, and a single electric guitar often has two or three kinds of pickups. One kind of pickup, the humbucker, is designed to reduce the noise, or hum, that simpler pickups make because of alternating current.

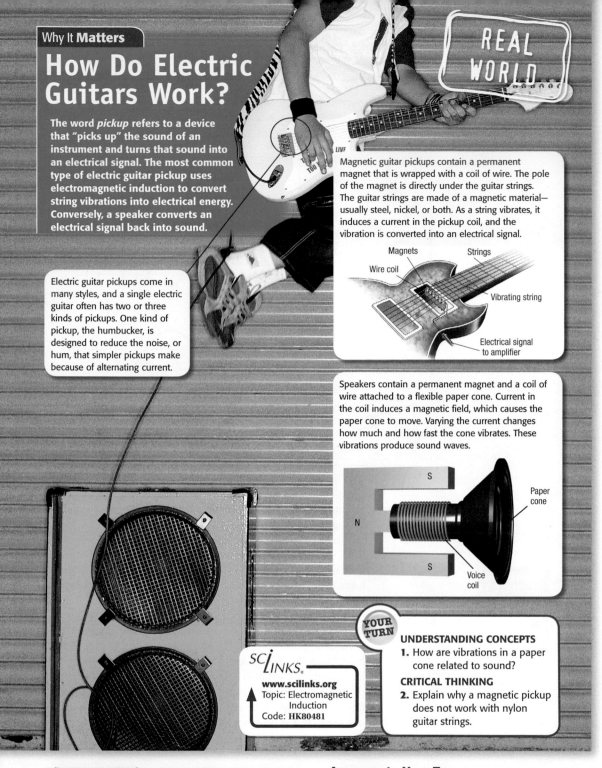

REAL WORLD

Magnetic guitar pickups contain a permanent magnet that is wrapped with a coil of wire. The pole of the magnet is directly under the guitar strings. The guitar strings are made of a magnetic material—usually steel, nickel, or both. As a string vibrates, it induces a current in the pickup coil, and the vibration is converted into an electrical signal.

Magnets
Strings
Wire coil
Vibrating string
Electrical signal to amplifier

Speakers contain a permanent magnet and a coil of wire attached to a flexible paper cone. Current in the coil induces a magnetic field, which causes the paper cone to move. Varying the current changes how much and how fast the cone vibrates. These vibrations produce sound waves.

S
N
S
Paper cone
Voice coil

SCI LINKS.
www.scilinks.org
Topic: Electromagnetic Induction
Code: HK80481

YOUR TURN

UNDERSTANDING CONCEPTS

1. How are vibrations in a paper cone related to sound?

CRITICAL THINKING

2. Explain why a magnetic pickup does not work with nylon guitar strings.

How Do Electric Guitars Work?
Electric guitars were first developed in the 1930s. They are probably the instrument that enabled rock to become a dominant musical genre and are certainly the most well-known type of instrument developed in the United States.

Similar to acoustic guitars, electric guitars have six strings that stretch from the body to the handle. The handle is lined with frets and the strings terminate on tuning pegs. However, while an acoustic guitar has a hollow body, most electric guitars have solid bodies.

Pickups are solenoids that convert the vibration of the string into an electronic signal. A large variety of pickups may be used in electric guitars. Some of the pickups are made up of a single solenoid under all six strings. Other pickups are made up of individual solenoids under each string. Some pickups are adjustable so that the height of the solenoid can be moved closer or farther from the string. In general, the closer the solenoid is to the string, the greater the current produced. Most guitars have a number of pickups throughout the body of the guitar. The signals of the pickups can be paired in different ways to produce an enormous variety of sounds.

In most guitars, the electrical circuit is rather simple. It consists of one resistor that controls the tone and a second resistor that controls the amplitude. The signal is sent to a jack that is connected to an amplifier that greatly increases the amplitude of the signal. The amplifier output is then fed to a speaker that converts the electrical signal into sound waves.

READING TOOLBOX

Interpreting Visuals In the figure of the speaker, the voice coil makes the speaker move forward and backward in a line. When a speaker is turned up too loud, it begins to move in a side-to-side direction. The speaker generates distortion in the sound, and the paper cone begins to tear, causing the speaker to buzz.

Answers to Your Turn

1. The vibrations in the paper cone produce sound waves.
2. The nylon strings are not made of a magnetic material, they will not induce a current in the pickup coil.

Demonstrate

Alternating Current For this demonstration you will need an overhead projector and a piece of colored cellophane mounted in a frame (like a 35 mm slide). This demonstration illustrates the effects of the changing cross-sectional area of a loop on induced current and shows how generators create AC. The light from the overhead projector represents a uniform magnetic field and the frame represents a wire loop. The amount of colored light that reaches the screen represents the magnetic field that passes through the wire loop, the change in which is related to the induced current. Slowly rotate the filter over the overhead projector, starting with the frame parallel to the ground, and allow changing amounts of colored light to reach the screen. Observe the changing intensity of the white light. Draw a graph of the changes in intensity. (The graph is a sine curve.) Discuss the analogy between the changing intensity and a changing current. The intensity is at a maximum (with the frame perpendicular to the light source) when the induced current would be at a minimum (when the loop is perpendicular to the magnetic field). **LS Visual**

READING TOOLBOX

Cause and Effect Causes should indicate the relative angles of the magnetic field and the direction of movement of the wire. Effects should indicate the amount of current produced.

Figure 4 Induced Current in a Generator

Position of loop	Amount of current	Graph of current versus angle of rotation
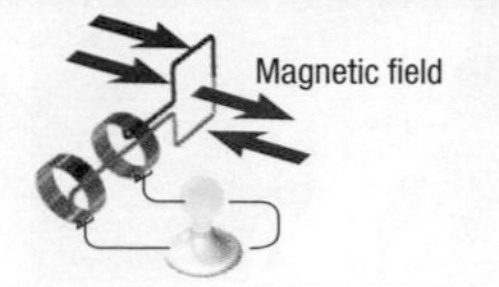 Magnetic field	zero current	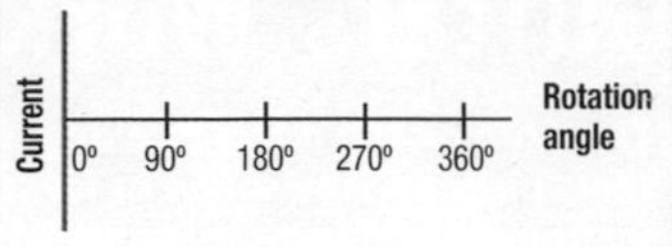 Current vs Rotation angle, 0° 90° 180° 270° 360°
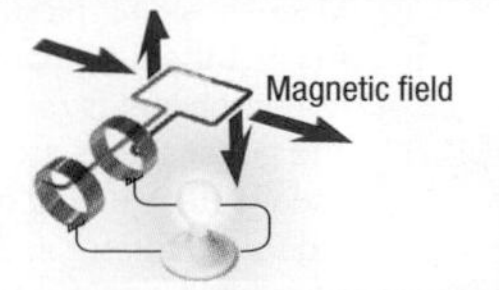 Magnetic field	maximum current	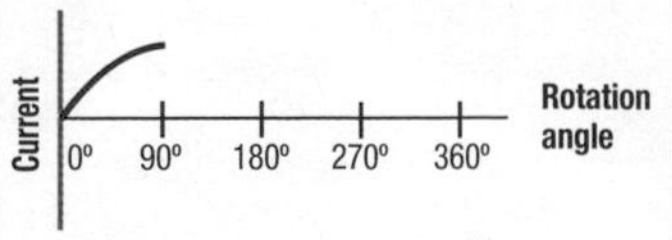 Current vs Rotation angle, 0° 90° 180° 270° 360°
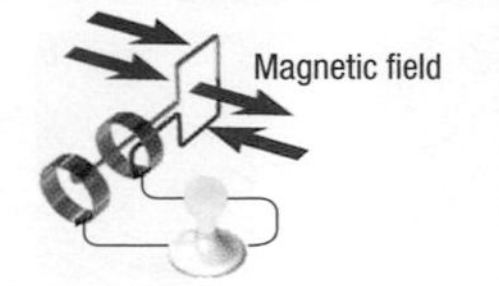 Magnetic field	zero current	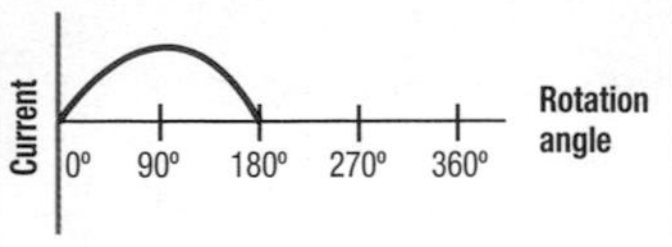 Current vs Rotation angle, 0° 90° 180° 270° 360°
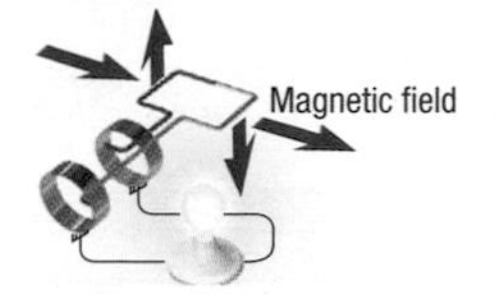 Magnetic field	maximum current (opposite direction)	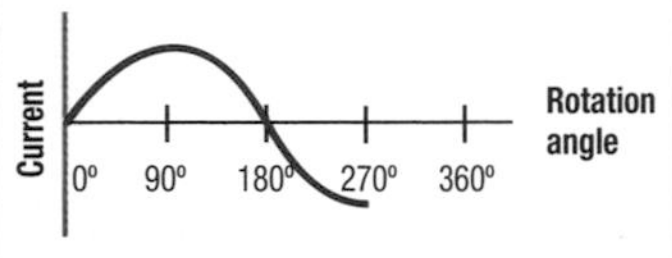 Current vs Rotation angle, 0° 90° 180° 270° 360°
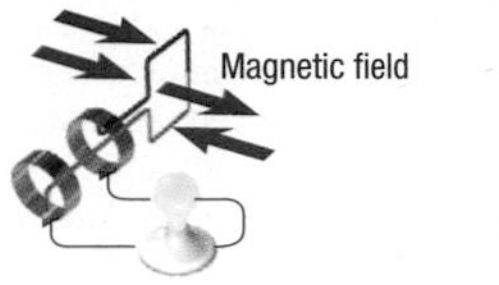 Magnetic field	zero current	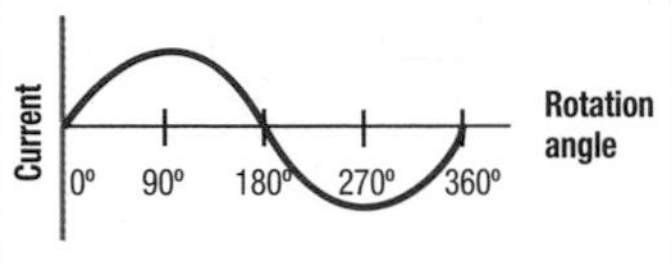 Current vs Rotation angle, 0° 90° 180° 270° 360°

READING TOOLBOX

Cause and Effect
As you read this page, look for cause-and-effect markers. Make a two-column table or appropriate FoldNote, and label the columns "Cause" and "Effect." Fill the table with information that you learn about induced current.

The amount of current produced by an AC generator changes with time.

Study the diagrams in **Figure 4.** When the loop is perpendicular to the field, the current is zero. Recall that a charge moving parallel to a magnetic field experiences no magnetic force. This is the case here. The charges in the wire experience no magnetic force, so no current is induced in the wire.

As the loop turns, the current increases until it reaches a maximum. When the loop is parallel to the field, charges on either side of the wire move perpendicularly to the magnetic field. Thus, the charges experience the maximum magnetic force, and the current is large. Current decreases as the loop rotates. When the loop is perpendicular to the magnetic field again, the current once again reaches zero. As the loop continues to rotate, the direction of the current reverses.

Differentiated Instruction

Basic Learners

Interpreting Diagrams Have students work in pairs and use **Figure 4** to describe the changing magnetic field through the wire loop and the force on charged particles as the loop rotates in the magnetic field. **LS Interpersonal**

Generators produce the electrical energy that you use in your home.

Large power plants use generators to convert mechanical energy into electrical energy. The mechanical energy used in a commercial power plant comes from a variety of sources. One of the most common sources is running water. Dams are built to harness the kinetic energy of falling water. Water is forced through small channels at the top of a dam. As the water falls to the base of the dam, it turns the blades of large turbines. The turbines are attached to a core wrapped with many loops of wire that rotate within a strong magnetic field. The end result is electrical energy.

Coal power plants use the energy from burning coal to make steam that eventually turns the blades of turbines. Other sources of energy are nuclear power (fission), wind power, geothermal power, and solar power.

Some mechanical energy is always lost as waste heat, and resistance in the wires of the generator reduces the electrical energy that is available. Many power plants are not very efficient. Methods of producing energy that are more efficient and safer are constantly being sought.

Reading Check What are three sources of mechanical energy used by power plants to produce electrical energy?

The Electromagnetic Force

So far, you have learned that moving charges produce magnetic fields and that changing magnetic fields cause electric charges to move. **❯ Electricity and magnetism are two aspects of a single force, the electromagnetic force.**

The energy that results from the electromagnetic force is electromagnetic energy. Light is a form of electromagnetic energy. Visible light travels as electromagnetic waves, or *EM waves,* as do other forms of radiation, such as radio signals and X rays. As **Figure 5** shows, EM waves are made up of oscillating electric and magnetic fields that are perpendicular to each other. This is true of any type of EM wave regardless of the frequency.

Both the electric and magnetic fields in an EM wave are perpendicular to the direction in which the wave travels. So, EM waves are transverse waves. As an EM wave moves along, the changing electric field generates the magnetic field. The changing magnetic field generates the electric field. Because each field regenerates the other, EM waves are able to travel through empty space.

Integrating Biology

Biomagnets Many types of bacteria contain magnetic particles of iron oxide and iron sulfide. Encased in a membrane within the cell, these particles form a magnetosome. The magnetosomes in a bacterium spread out in a line and align with Earth's magnetic field. As the cell uses its flagella to swim, it travels along a north-south axis. Recently, magnetite crystals have been found in human brain cells, but the role that these particles play remains uncertain.

SCILINKS®

www.scilinks.org
Topic: Generators
Code: HK80643

Figure 5 An electromagnetic wave consists of electric and magnetic field waves that are at right angles.

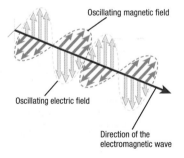

Oscillating magnetic field

Oscillating electric field

Direction of the electromagnetic wave

Demonstrate

Measuring Energy For this demonstration you will need a small electrical motor, a galvanometer, some string, various weights, a ring stand, and a test-tube clamp. Attach the motor to the ring stand with the test-tube clamp. Raise it to the highest position. Put something heavy on top of the ring stand base to keep it from falling over. The shaft of the motor should hang over the edge of the table. Tape or glue the end of the string to the shaft of the motor and wind it around the shaft. Tie a small mass to the string. The mass should be heavy enough so that, when released, the weight of the mass will cause the motor to turn. Attach the galvanometer. Release the weight and record the reading of the galvanometer when the mass reaches the floor or some fixed position. Repeat the experiment with different weights. Discuss the energy transformations involved.

Teaching Key Ideas

The Electromagnetic Force Review the section on fundamental forces in the chapter on motion. Ask students to name the four fundamental forces. (force of gravity, electromagnetic force, weak nuclear force, strong nuclear force) Ask students to give examples of other forces that are actually caused by electromagnetic force. (Examples include: electric force, magnetic force, the force of friction.) Explain that even contact forces are only apparently due to contact. At the atomic scale, matter almost never touches other matter, but instead just gets very close until electromagnetic forces come into play. **LS** Logical

Why It Matters

Wire Taps Telephone wire taps are possible because the current in the wires that are carrying the conversation produces a magnetic field. Coils are placed near the telephone wire to measure the fluctuations in this magnetic field. The pattern of changes in the magnetic field is converted to another current (a current is induced in the coil by the changing magnetic field), which is converted to sound by a speaker, reproducing the telephone conversation. Fiber-optic cables cannot be tapped in this way because they do not produce an external magnetic field.

Demonstrate

DC Transformer For this demonstration you will need an iron loop, a 9 V battery, a knife switch, a flashlight bulb in a holder, and two wires about 1 m in length. Set up the primary side of the transformer before class by connecting the battery and the switch in series with one of the wires coiled around one side of the iron loop. The primary coil should have 50 turns. Set up the secondary coil with 25 turns on the opposite side of the iron loop. Connect the flashlight bulb to the secondary coil. In class, demonstrate this step-down transformer by momentarily closing the switch and then opening it again. Have students discuss the transfer of energy that occurs in this situation. Close the switch and keep it closed. Have students note the behavior of the bulb. Discuss the brief illumination and fading of the bulb with students. Lead students to consider the concept of changing current. Again, open the switch and note the illumination. Ask students what kind of current could be used to keep the bulb continually lit. (alternating current) **LS Visual**

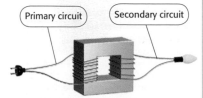

Figure 6 A transformer uses the alternating current in the primary circuit to induce an alternating current in the secondary circuit.

transformer (trans FAWRM uhr) a device that increases or decreases the voltage of alternating current

Transformers

You may have seen metal cylinders on power line poles in your neighborhood. These cylinders hold devices called **transformers**, devices that increase or decrease the voltage of alternating current. **>In its simplest form, a transformer consists of two coils of wire wrapped around opposite sides of a closed iron loop.** In the transformer shown in **Figure 6**, one wire is attached to a source of alternating current, such as a power outlet, and is called the *primary circuit*. The other wire is attached to an appliance, such as a lamp, and is called the *secondary circuit*.

When there is current in the primary circuit, this current creates a changing magnetic field in the primary coil that magnetizes the iron core. The changing magnetic field of the iron core then induces a current in the secondary coil. The direction of the current in the secondary coil changes every time the direction of the current in the primary coil changes.

Transformers can increase or decrease voltage.

The voltage induced in the secondary circuit of a transformer depends on the number of loops, or *turns*, in the coil, as shown in **Figure 7**. In *step-up transformers,* the primary coil has fewer turns than the secondary coil does. In this case, the voltage across the secondary coil is greater than the voltage across the primary coil. In *step-down transformers,* the secondary coil has fewer loops than the primary coil does. The voltage across the secondary circuit is lower than the voltage across the primary circuit.

Figure 7 How Transformers Change Voltage

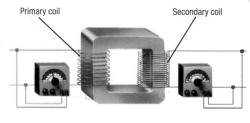

In a step-up transformer, the primary coil has fewer loops than the secondary coil does. The voltage in the secondary coil must be higher than the voltage in the primary coil.

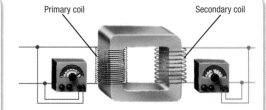

In a step-down transformer, the primary coil has more loops than the secondary coil does. The voltage in the secondary coil must be lower than the voltage in the primary coil.

Differentiated Instruction

Alternative Assessment

Generators There are many different types of power generation techniques. Assign groups of students different generation techniques to research. Have each group prepare a presentation that includes how the technique works; a diagram of the system; and information on fuel, power output, cost, and environmental impact. **LS Interpersonal/Visual**

English Learners

Letter Writing Ask students to write letters to power plants in the area inquiring about the source of mechanical energy and the generators used by the plant. If Internet access is available, they may be able to find the power plant's website to obtain information. E-mail contact with the power plants may also result in additional information. Have students write their findings out in a short report. **LS Verbal**

Transformers must obey the law of conservation of energy.

Transformers may seem to provide something—more voltage—for nothing. But they do not. The power output of the secondary coil is, at best, equal to the power input to the primary coil. One cannot get more electrical energy per unit of time, or power, out of the transformer than one puts into it. For this reason, the current in the secondary coil of a step-up transformer is always less than the current in the primary coil.

Real transformers are not perfectly efficient. Some of the energy that is put into a transformer is lost as heat because of resistance in the coils. The power lost increases quickly as current increases. To decrease loss and maximize the energy that is delivered, power companies use a high voltage and a low current when transferring power over long distances.

Transformers are used in the transfer of electrical energy.

Step-up and step-down transformers are used in the transmission of electrical energy from power plants to homes and businesses. A step-up transformer is used at or near a power plant to increase the voltage to about 120,000 V. This high voltage limits the loss of energy that the resistance of the transmission wires causes. Then, step-down transformers like the ones in **Figure 8** are used near homes to reduce the voltage to about 120 V. This low voltage is much safer to use in homes.

Figure 8 Step-down transformers like the ones shown here are used to reduce the voltage across power lines. **What is the advantage of using a lower voltage within homes?**

Teaching Key Ideas

Transformers Voltages are transformed down near homes and businesses with step-down transformers on utility poles, like the one shown in **Figure 8,** and at substations. Have students locate transformers or substations in their neighborhood or around the school. In areas with underground wiring, the transformers may be installed on the ground.

Answer to caption question
Lower voltage is safer to use in a home.

❯Close

Reteaching Key Ideas

Group Study Have students pair up and review the key ideas for the section. Have them copy the questions onto a sheet of paper and then find the answers in the section. The team can make sure that both members understand the key ideas, and the answers can be used to study for the Chapter Review.
LS Interpersonal/Verbal

Formative Assessment

A _____ can increase or decrease voltage.
A. generator (Incorrect. A generator produces electrical energy.)
B. solenoid (Incorrect. A solenoid is a coil of wire with a current running through it that produces a magnetic field.)
C. galvanometer (Incorrect. A galvanometer measures current.)
D. transformer (Correct. Depending on the number of loops in the primary and secondary coils of a transformer, it can increase or decrease voltage.)

Section 3 Review

KEY IDEAS

1. **Identify** which of the following will not increase the current induced in a wire loop moving through a magnetic field.
   a. increasing the strength of the magnetic field
   b. increasing the speed of the wire
   c. rotating the loop until it is perpendicular to the field

2. **Explain** how hydroelectric power plants use moving water to produce electricity.

3. **Explain** how electricity and magnetism are related to one another.

4. **Determine** whether the following statement describes a step-up transformer or a step-down transformer: The primary coil has 7,000 turns, and the secondary coil has 500 turns.

CRITICAL THINKING

5. **Making Predictions** For each of the following actions, predict the movement of the needle of a galvanometer attached to a coil of wire. Assume that the north pole of a bar magnet has been inserted into the coil, which causes the needle to deflect to the right.
   a. pulling the magnet out of the coil
   b. letting the magnet rest in the coil
   c. thrusting the south pole of the magnet into the coil

6. **Determining Cause and Effect** A spacecraft orbiting Earth contains a coil of wire. An astronaut measures a small current in the coil even though the coil is not connected to a battery and the spacecraft does not contain any magnets. What is causing the current?

Answers to Section Review

1. c
2. The moving water rotates a turbine. The turbine is attached to a core wrapped with many loops of wire that rotates within a magnetic field. Alternating current is induced in the wire loop as it turns.
3. A changing electric field induces a magnetic field and a changing magnetic field induces an electric field.
4. a step down transformer
5. **a.** The needle will be deflected to the left.
   b. The needle will fall back to the zero reading because the magnetic field is no longer changing.
   c. The needle will be deflected to the left.
6. As the spacecraft orbits, the coil encounters a change in both the strength and orientation of Earth's magnetic field, inducing a current in the coil.

InquiryLab

Time Required
1 lab period

Lab Ratings

EASY ——————————————→ HARD

Teacher Prep 🍶🍶
Student Set-Up 🍶🍶
Concept Level 🍶🍶🍶
Clean Up 🍶🍶

Skills Acquired
- Collecting data
- Designing experiments
- Inferring
- Interpreting
- Measuring
- Organizing and analyzing data
- Predicting

Scientific Methods
In this lab, students will:
- Make observations
- Ask a question
- Form a hypothesis
- Make predictions
- Test a hypothesis
- Analyze the results
- Draw conclusions
- Communicate results

Safety Cautions
Safety goggles and heat-resistant gloves must be worn at all times. Instruct students on the safe use of the wire strippers. Warn students to be careful not to short the batteries. Do not let metal rods roll on the floor; they create a slip hazard. Students should wash their hands after the lab and avoid touching their eyes.

Inquiry

Lab

What You'll Do
- **Build** several electromagnets.
- **Determine** how many paper clips each electromagnet can lift.
- **Analyze** your results to identify the features of a strong electromagnet.

What You'll Need
batteries, D-cell (2)
battery holders (2)
electrical tape
metal rods (1 iron, 1 tin, 1 aluminum, and 1 nickel)
paper clips, small (1 box)
wire, extra-insulated
wire, insulated, thick, 1 m long
wire, insulated, thin, 1 m long
wire stripper

Safety

Making a Better Electromagnet

In a Quick Lab earlier in this chapter, you made an electromagnet by using batteries and a wire coil. In this lab, you will experiment with the characteristics that make an electromagnet stronger.

Asking a Question
What combination of various batteries, wires, and metal rods will make the strongest electromagnet?

Building an Electromagnet
1. Review the basic steps in making an electromagnet by looking at the Quick Lab in Section 2.
2. On a blank sheet of paper, prepare a data table like the one shown in this activity.
3. Wind the thin wire around the thickest metal core. Carefully pull the core out of the center of the thin wire coil. Using the thick wire, repeat the steps above. You now have two wire coils that can be used to make electromagnets. **CAUTION:** Handle the wires only where they are insulated.

Forming and Testing a Hypothesis
4. Think about the following, and predict the features that the strongest electromagnet would have.
   a. Which metal rod would make the best core?
   b. Which of the two wires would make a stronger electromagnet?
   c. How many coils should the electromagnet have?
   d. Should the batteries be connected in series or in parallel?

Answers to Analysis
1. Answers will depend on the diameter of the copper conductor in each wire, the thickness of each wire's insulation, and the number of coils made with each wire. A larger-diameter conductor can carry more current, but a thinner wire (conductor plus insulator) allows more coils to be made. Both effects increase the strength of an electromagnet.
2. The iron and nickel cores should make the strongest electromagnets. The sources of magnetic fields in the atoms of these metals do not cancel each other out, as they do in most materials. As a result, they have the most magnetism.

Sample Data Table: Differences in Electromagnets

Electromagnet number	Wire (thick or thin)	No. of coils	Core (iron, tin, alum., or nickel)	Batteries (series or parallel)	No. of paper clips lifted
1					
2					
3		DO NOT WRITE IN BOOK			
4					
5					
6					

Designing Your Experiment

5 With your lab partners, decide how you will determine the features that combine to make a strong electromagnet.

6 In your lab report, list each step you will perform in your experiment.

Performing Your Experiment

7 After your teacher approves your plan, carry out your experiment. You should test all four metal rods, both thicknesses of wire, and both battery connections (series and parallel). Count the number of coils of wire in each electromagnet that you build.

8 Record your results in your data table.

Analysis

1. **Explaining Events** Which wire made a stronger electromagnet: the thick wire or the thin wire? How can you explain this result?

2. **Explaining Events** Which metal cores made the strongest electromagnets? Why?

3. **Explaining Events** Could your electromagnet pick up more paper clips when the batteries were connected in series or when they were connected in parallel? Explain why.

Communicating Your Results

4. **Drawing Conclusions** What combination of wire, metal core, and battery connection made the strongest electromagnet?

Extension

Suppose someone tells you that your conclusion is invalid because each time you tested a magnet on the paper clips, the paper clips became more and more magnetized. How could you show that your conclusion is valid?

Tips and Tricks

Review the construction of an electromagnet with the students before beginning the activity. Discuss the parts of an electromagnet (the solenoid and metal core) and their functions in an electromagnet. Remind the students that the strength of the magnetic field produced by a solenoid increases with increasing current in the solenoid and with the number of coils. Review the relationship between current, voltage, and resistance. Remind students that a thin wire will have a greater resistance than a thick wire. Encourage them to discuss how the diameter of a wire will affect how many times it can be wound around a core. Also review series and parallel circuits. Ask students to draw schematic diagrams for two batteries and a resistor in series and in parallel. Have them trace the path of a charge through each circuit and discuss the energy changes involved.

Procedure

Students should propose a systematic testing procedure, changing only one variable (wire thickness, type of metal core, or battery connection) from one test to the next.

Disposal Information

The metal cores can be kept for future use. The wire can be unwound and stored. The batteries should be tested. Discharged batteries should be taken to hazardous waste disposal.

---

3. Accept all reasonable answers. Sample answer: The electromagnet picked up more paper clips with the batteries connected in series. With a series connection, the voltages of the two batteries add together. A larger voltage produces a greater current in the wire, making the magnetic field stronger.

Answer to Communicating Your Results

4. The strongest electromagnet should have resulted from using the iron or nickel core, the series arrangement of batteries, and the thicker wire (as long as the difference in number of coils for the thin and thick wires is small).

Answers continued on p. 647A

Key Resources

⊚ **Virtual Investigation**

▣ **Classroom Lab Video/DVD**

⊚ **Holt Lab Generator CD-ROM**
Search for any lab by type, standard, difficulty level, or time. Edit any lab to fit your needs, or create your own labs. Use the Lab Materials QuickList software to customize your lab materials list.

📁 **Differentiated Datasheets**
Making a Better Electromagnet

📁 **Observation Lab**
Constructing and Using a Compass

📁 **CBL™ Probeware Lab**
Testing Magnets for an Electric Motor

Making Predictions

Reteaching Key Ideas

Transformers Show students a step-up transformer in which the primary coil has a single loop with a voltage of 5 V and the secondary coil has two loops. Ask students to write down observations about the set-up. Attach a voltmeter across the primary coil, then across the secondary coil. Have students add the voltmeter readings to their observations. Have students form a hypothesis about how the secondary coil changes the voltage. (Sample answer: The voltage in the first coil is multiplied by the number of coils in the secondary coil.) Then have them make predictions about what might happen if you changed the secondary coil so that it had four loops. (If the hypothesis is true, the voltage would be about 20 V. If the hypothesis is false, the voltage will not be close to 20 V.) Finally, increase the number of loops in the secondary coil to 4 so students can see if their hypotheses are true or false. **LS Kinesthetic/Logical**

Answers to Practice

1. **a.** If the hypothesis is true, the needle of the compass will point toward the south pole of the magnet and away from the north pole. **b.** If the hypothesis is false and the reverse is true, the needle of the compass will point toward the north pole of the magnet and way from the south pole.
2. Answers may vary, but should not be too far from 125 (125 ± 25).

One of the main goals of science is to explain the nature of the world around us. Another important goal is to allow us to predict—with a reasonable degree of confidence and accuracy—what will happen in the future. Predictions based on hypotheses help scientists design experiments. Predictions based on established scientific laws or theories help scientists apply science to solve real-world problems.

Technology
Math
Scientific Methods
Graphing

❶ Predictions Based on Hypotheses
- A hypothesis is formed from observations that you have made or data that you have collected.
- After you have a hypothesis, you should make two kinds of predictions: one that states what will happen if the hypothesis is true and one that states what will happen if the hypothesis is not true.
- These predictions can help you plan how to test the hypothesis.

- Observations: Magnets stick to a metal refrigerator door, but not to a door made of wood or plastic.
- Hypothesis: Magnets are attracted to any kind of metal, but not to anything else.
- Predictions if hypothesis is true: (1) I will not be able to find a metal to which a magnet will not stick and (2) I will not be able to find a nonmetal to which a magnet will stick.
- Predictions if hypothesis is NOT true: (1) I will be able to find a metal to which a magnet will not stick and (2) I will be able to find a nonmetal to which a magnet will stick.

❷ Predictions Based on Established Theories
- After a hypothesis has been tested and confirmed repeatedly by many scientists, the hypothesis can be accepted as a scientific law or as part of a theory. You can then use this theory to make further predictions.
- You can use equations to make precise, quantitative predictions.
- You can extrapolate, or continue the trend suggested by past known data, using graphs to obtain quantitative predictions.

- Established scientific law: Observations of sunspots (dark patches on the surface of the sun) have shown that the spots grow and fade in an 11-year cycle.
- Fact: The last time the sunspot cycle was at a maximum was in 2001.
- Prediction: The next time the cycle will be at a maximum will be around 2012.

Practice

1. Suppose that you want to test the hypothesis that Earth's North Pole is like the south pole of a bar magnet. Predict how a compass will behave around a bar magnet if (a) the hypothesis is true and (b) the hypothesis is not true.

2. The "sunspot number" is an index that is used to measure the amount of sunspot activity on a given day. Use the Internet to research the sunspot cycle for the sun. Predict what the peak sunspot number will be in 2023.

go.hrw.com
SUPER SUMMARY
KEYWORD: HK8MAGS

SUMMARY

Key Ideas

Key Terms

Section 1 Magnets and Magnetic Fields

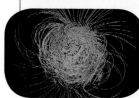

> **Magnets** All magnets have two poles that cannot be isolated. Like poles repel each other, and unlike poles attract each other. (p. 619)

> **Magnetic Fields** Magnets repel or attract each other because of the interaction of their magnetic fields. (p. 621)

> **Earth's Magnetic Field** Earth's magnetic field lines run from geographic south to geographic north. The magnetic north pole is in Antarctica, and the magnetic south pole is in northern Canada. (p. 623)

magnetic pole, p. 619
magnetic field, p. 621

Section 2 Magnetism from Electric Currents

> **Electromagnetism** When a wire carries a strong, steady current, the needles of any compasses nearby move to align with the magnetic field created by the electric current. (p. 626)

> **Electromagnetic Devices** A motor can perform mechanical work when it is attached to an external device. Electric motors convert electrical energy into mechanical energy. (p. 630)

solenoid, p. 627
electromagnet, p. 628
electric motor, p. 630
galvanometer, p. 630

Section 3 Electric Currents from Magnetism

> **Electromagnetic Induction** Moving a magnet into and out of a coil of wire causes charges in the wire to move. A current is produced in a circuit by a changing magnetic field. (p. 632)

> **The Electromagnetic Force** Electricity and magnetism are two aspects of a single force, the electromagnetic force. Electromagnetic waves consist of magnetic and electric fields oscillating at right angles to each other. (p. 637)

> **Transformers** A transformer consists of two coils or wire wrapped around opposite sides of a closed iron loop. In a transformer, the magnetic field produced by a primary coil induces a current in a secondary coil. (p. 638)

electromagnetic induction, p. 632
generator, p. 634
alternating current, p. 634
transformer, p. 638

SUPER SUMMARY

Have students connect the major concepts in this chapter through an interactive Super Summary. Visit **go.hrw.com** and type in the keyword **HK8MAGS** to access the Super Summary for this chapter.

Differentiated Instruction

Alternative Assessment

Electromagnetic Devices Organize students into small groups and have them research one of the following electromagnetic devices: a hair dryer, a doorbell, or a tape recorder. Have them put together a short (about 5 minute) presentation of how electromagnetism is used in the device, using drawings or diagrams where appropriate. **LS Interpersonal/Verbal**

Key Resources

⊟ **Interactive Concept Map**

🗁 **Review Resources**
Concept Review Worksheets

🗁 **Assessment Resources**
Chapter Tests A and B
Performance-Based Assessment

Reading Toolbox

1. A magnetometer is an instrument for measuring the strength of magnetic fields.

Using Key Terms

2. The magnetic field of Earth points from the magnetic N pole in Antarctica to the magnetic S pole in northern Canada. The N pole of a compass needle is attracted to Earth's magnetic S pole and ends up pointing to the north.

3. A magnetic compass aligns with Earth's magnetic field and points in the direction that lies along the magnetic field toward Earth's magnetic S pole, near the geographic north pole. Using a magnetic compass is useful for determining location relative to Earth's magnetic poles. However, the magnetic fields of other objects may interfere with the functioning of a magnetic compass.

4. A galvanometer consists of a coil of insulated wire wrapped around an iron core between the poles of a permanent magnet. When attached to a circuit, the coil and core act as an electromagnet, producing a magnetic field, which causes the core to rotate. The greater the electric current, the stronger the magnetic field and the greater the rotation. It is similar to an electric motor in that both use magnetic force to cause motion. However, unlike the coil in a galvanometer, the coil in a motor keeps spinning.

5. The commutator makes the current change direction every time the coil makes a half revolution, and thus it keeps the coil rotating in one direction.

6. Falling water can be used to generate electricity by converting the kinetic and potential energy of the water into electrical energy. This is done by having the water turn a turbine attached to a coil of wire that is inside a magnetic field, inducing a current in the wire. This is called electromagnetic induction. Electromagnetic induction is the basis of all power generators.

READING TOOLBOX

1. Suffixes The magnetometer was first designed in 1833 by Carl Friedrich Gauss, a German mathematician and scientist. A magnetometer is also sometimes called a *gaussmeter*. A gauss is also a unit for measuring the strength of magnetic fields. Given this information, what do you think a magnetometer is?

USING KEY TERMS

2. Use the terms *magnetic pole* and *magnetic field* to explain why the north pole of a compass needle points toward northern Canada.

3. Write a paragraph explaining the advantages and disadvantages of using a magnetic compass to determine direction. Use the terms *magnetic pole* and *magnetic field* in your answer.

4. How does a *galvanometer* measure electric current? How is it similar to and different from an *electric motor*?

5. What is the purpose of a *commutator* in an *electric motor*?

6. Use the terms *generator* and *electromagnetic induction* to explain how *kinetic energy* of falling water is used to generate *electrical energy*.

UNDERSTANDING KEY IDEAS

7. If the poles of two magnets repel each other,
 a. both poles must be south poles.
 b. both poles must be north poles.
 c. one pole is south and the other is north.
 d. the poles are the same type.

8. The part of a magnet where the magnetic field and forces are strongest is called a magnetic
 a. field.
 b. pole.
 c. attraction.
 d. repulsion.

9. A compass held directly below a current-carrying wire in which positive charges are moving north will point

 a. Current

 c. Current

 b. Current

 d. Current

10. An electric motor uses an electromagnet to change
 a. mechanical energy into electrical energy.
 b. magnetic fields in the motor.
 c. magnetic poles in the motor.
 d. electrical energy into mechanical energy.

11. An electric generator is a device that can convert
 a. nuclear energy into electrical energy.
 b. wind energy into electrical energy.
 c. energy from burning coal into electrical energy.
 d. All of the above

12. The process of producing an electric current by moving a magnet into and out of a coil of wire is called
 a. magnetic deduction.
 b. electromagnetic induction.
 c. magnetic reduction.
 d. electromagnetic production.

13. In a transformer, the voltage of a current will increase if the secondary circuit
 a. has more turns than the primary circuit does.
 b. has fewer turns than the primary circuit does.
 c. has the same number of turns that the primary circuit does.
 d. is parallel to the primary circuit.

7. d

8. b

9. d

10. d

11. d

12. b

13. a

EXPLAINING KEY IDEAS

14. How could you use a compass that has a magnetized needle to determine if a steel nail is magnetized?

15. What happens to the magnetic domains in a material when the material is placed in a strong magnetic field?

INTERPRETING GRAPHICS The diagram below shows a wire wrapped around a magnetic compass. Use the diagram to answer question 16.

16. Which of the following might be the purpose of the device shown here?
  a. to measure the amount of voltage across the wire
  b. to determine the direction of the current in the wire
  c. to find the resistance of the wire

17. Transformers are usually used to raise or lower the voltage across an alternating-current circuit. Can a transformer be used in a direct-current circuit? Can a transformer be used if the direct current is pulsating (turning on and off)?

CRITICAL THINKING

18. Understanding Systems Fire doors are doors that, when closed, can slow the spread of fire from room to room. In some buildings, fire doors are held open by electromagnets. Explain why electromagnets rather than permanent magnets are used.

19. Making Decisions You have two iron bars and a ball of string. One bar is magnetized, and the other is not magnetized. How can you determine which bar is magnetized?

20. Applying Technology Use your imagination and your knowledge of electromagnetism to invent a useful electromagnetic device. Use a computer-drawing program to make sketches of your invention, and write a description of how it works.

21. Applying Knowledge What do adaptors do to voltage and current? Examine the input/output information on several electrical adapters to find out. Do they contain step-up or step-down transformers?

22. Relating Concepts Research how electro-magnetism is used in containing nuclear fusion reactions. Write a report on your findings.

Graphing Skills

23. Induced Current The figure below is a graph of current versus rotation angle for the output of an alternating-current generator.
  a. At what point(s) does the generator produce no current?
  b. Is the current produced at point B less than or more than the current at points C and E?
  c. Is the current produced at point D less than or more than the current at points C and E?
  d. What does the negative value for the current at point D signify?

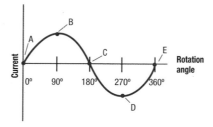

Assignment Guide

Section	Items
1	1–3, 7, 8, 14, 15, 19
2	4, 5, 9, 10, 16, 18, 20
3	6, 11–13, 17, 21–23

Graphing Skills

23. a. A, C, E
  b. more
  c. more
  d. Current at D is moving in the opposite direction to current at B.

Explaining Key Ideas

14. If a steel nail is magnetized, then the compass needle will point to the S end of the nail. As you move the compass from one end of the nail to the other, the compass should rotate to align with the nail's magnetic field. If it does not rotate, the nail is not magnetized.

15. The magnetic domains align with the external magnetic field.

16. b

17. Usually, a transformer would not work if DC current were used; however, it would work if the current were turned off and on repeatedly.

Critical Thinking

18. Electromagnets are used so that the doors can be closed automatically in the event of a fire.

19. Hang each of the bars from its midpoint using string. The magnetized bar will rotate and align itself with Earth's magnetic field.

20. Check students' drawings. They may include a combination of the following: a source of a magnetic field, wire loops, solenoids, electromagnets, and a voltage source.

21. Adapters change the voltage and the current to different levels in order to power electrical devices. Most adapters contain step-down transformers because they reduce household AC to a lower voltage.

22. The plasmas used in nuclear fusion reactions have extremely high temperatures, usually more than 100,000,000 °C, so they cannot be contained in a vessel. Because plasmas are made up of charged particles (atomic nuclei and electrons), they can be contained by magnetic fields.

Standardized Test Prep

Standardized Test Prep

 TEST DOCTOR

Question 1 Answer C is correct. Using the right-hand rule, your thumb should point straight down. Answers A and B may indicate confusion between electrical current and magnetic field. Answer D may indicate confusion about how to use the right-hand rule.

Question 2 Answer G is correct. It is the only choice that uses the suffix *-meter,* which indicates that it is used to measure something. The other choices all use electromagnetism, but they are not used for measuring it.

Question 3 Answer C is correct. Answers A and B indicate confusion regarding electromagnetic induction. Answer D indicates confusion of the right-hand rule.

Question 4 Answer G is correct. When the loop of wire is perpendicular—90° or 270°—to the magnetic poles, the most current will be generated. Choices F, H, and I indicate that the loop is parallel with the poles.

Question 5 Full-credit answers should include the following point:
• A compass needle at the geographic north pole will point toward the magnetic pole in Canada.

Question 6 Full-credit answers should include the following points:
• A solenoid is a coil of wires.
• An electromagnet is made by placing a rod made of iron inside the coils of a solenoid.

Question 7 Full-credit answers should include the following points:
• Ferric oxide powder-coated plastic strips and steel wires are magnetizable.
• Ferric oxide powder-coated tape and steel wires were used in recording devices.

Question 8 Full-credit answers should include the following point:
• The sound worsened after it was replayed.

Question 9 Full-credit answers should include the following points:

Understanding Concepts

Directions (1–4): **For each question, write on a sheet of paper the letter of the correct answer.**

1. A straight vertical wire is carrying an electric current. Positive charges are flowing straight down. What is the direction of the magnetic field generated by the wire as viewed from above?
   A. straight up
   B. straight down
   C. clockwise
   D. counterclockwise

2. What type of device is used to measure the current in an electromagnet?
   F. an electric motor
   G. a galvanometer
   H. a generator
   I. a solenoid

3. A charged particle is moving through a magnetic field. In which direction is the particle moving when the magnetic force acting on the particle is at its greatest?
   A. in the same direction as the magnetic field lines
   B. in the opposite direction from the magnetic field lines
   C. at right angles to the magnetic field lines
   D. clockwise around the magnetic field lines

4. In an AC generator, a loop of wire rotates between two magnetic poles. At what angle(s) of rotation relative to the magnet does the loop generate the most current?
   F. 0° and 180°   H. 180°
   G. 90° and 270°   I. 360°

Directions (5–6): **For each question, write a short response.**

5. How would a compass located precisely at the Earth's geographic north pole behave?

6. What is the difference between a solenoid and an electromagnet?

Reading Skills

Directions (7–10): **Read the passage below. Then, answer the questions that follow.**

GETTING IT ON TAPE

Magnetic tape consists of a thin plastic strip bonded to a coating of ferric oxide powder. The ferric oxide, Fe_2O_3, makes the tape magnetizable. Early tape recorders were first developed in Germany and Britain. The first tape recorder used by the British Broadcasting Corporation in 1932 was a huge machine. It used steel razor tape that was 3 mm wide and 0.08 mm thick. The tape had to be run at 90 m/min, so the length of tape required for a half-hour program was nearly 3 km long, and a full reel had a mass of 25 kg. Furthermore, the quality of the sound experienced considerable degradation in the recording and playback process.

Higher-quality sound recording was developed in Germany during the late 1930s. During World War II, the Allies became aware of German radio broadcasts that seemed to be recorded. However, the audio quality and duration of the recordings were far greater than Allied technology would allow. At the end of the war, the Allies captured a number of German Magnetophon recorders from Radio Luxembourg, and commercial-quality magnetic recording entered the English-speaking world.

7. How is a tape coated with Fe_2O_3 similar to a steel wire?

8. Was the sound of a British recording during World War II better or worse after the recording was played?

9. The Allies captured recording devices called *magnetophons*. Why is this name appropriate?

10. Why would bringing audiotape near a powerful magnet be a bad idea?

• The prefix *magneto-* refers to magnetism and the magnetophon relied on magnetism to make recordings.
• The *-phon* part of the word indicates sound and the magnetophon made recordings of sound.

Question 10 Full-credit answers should include the following points:
• Ferric oxide powder is bound to the tape. Sound signals are converted to magnetic signals and are recorded on the tape.
• If a magnet is brought near the tape, the particles of powder realign to reflect the direction of the magnetic field lines, erasing the recorded sound signal.

Question 11 Answer A is correct. Identify the direction of the current, which is from point E to point F. Use the right-hand rule. Wrapping a right hand around the wire results in fingers moving into the page at point X. Answer C indicates the direction of current. Answer B indicates confusion about using the right-hand rule.

Question 12 Answer I is correct. The current flows from the north pole toward the south pole: from point D to point B. Answer G indicates confusion about the flow of current. Answers F and H indicate a misunderstanding of the polarity of an electromagnet.

Interpreting Graphics

The diagram below shows an electric circuit that includes a solenoid. Use this diagram to answer questions 11–12.

ELECTRIC CIRCUIT WITH SOLENOID

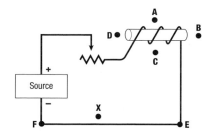

11. What is the direction of the magnetic field at point X due to the current in section EF?
- **A.** into the page
- **B.** out of the page
- **C.** to the left
- **D.** to the right

12. To which point is the north pole of the solenoid the closest?
- **F.** A
- **G.** B
- **H.** C
- **I.** D

The following graphic shows four bar magnets and the magnetic fields that they generate. Use this graphic to answer questions 13–14.

MAGNETIC FIELD OF TWO PAIRS OF BAR MAGNETS

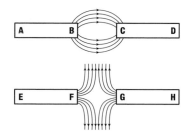

13. Suppose that A and E are the north poles of their magnets. What other points have a north polarity?
- **A.** B and G
- **B.** C and H
- **C.** D and G
- **D.** D and H

14. Which two magnets could combine their magnetic fields into one long magnet without being rotated? What would happen to their poles?

Test Tip

When using an illustration that has labels to answer a question, read the labels carefully, and then check that the answer you choose matches your interpretation of the labels.

Answers

1. C
2. G
3. C
4. G
5. Answers may vary; see Test Doctor for a detailed scoring rubric.
6. Answers may vary; see Test Doctor for a detailed scoring rubric.
7. Answers may vary; see Test Doctor for a detailed scoring rubric.
8. Answers may vary; see Test Doctor for a detailed scoring rubric.
9. Answers may vary; see Test Doctor for a detailed scoring rubric.
10. Answers may vary; see Test Doctor for a detailed scoring rubric.
11. A
12. I
13. B
14. Answers may vary; see Test Doctor for a detailed scoring rubric.

Question 13 Answer B is correct. The top two magnets are attracted to each other. This means that B must be a south pole and C a north pole. The bottom two magnets repel each other. F and G are both south poles and H is a north pole.

Question 14 Full-credit answers should include the following points:
- The top pair of magnets can combine to form one long magnet.
- If you put two magnets together by attaching north and south poles, they combine into one long magnet and the two poles in the center lose their polarity.

State Resources

For specific resources for your state, visit **go.hrw.com** and type in the keyword **HSHSTR**.

📔 **Test Practice with Guided Reading Development**

Continuation of Answers

Answers continued from p. 631

4. A solenoid suspended by a string could be used as a compass. The magnetic field of the solenoid would align itself with the magnetic field of Earth, just as a bar magnet would.

5. No, because of the lack of a commutator.

Answers continued from p. 641

Answer to Extension

Answers may vary. To account for the magnetism of the paper clips, students could determine how many paper clips stick to each electromagnet when the batteries are disconnected. They could also use a different set of paper clips for each electromagnet design that they test.

Reference

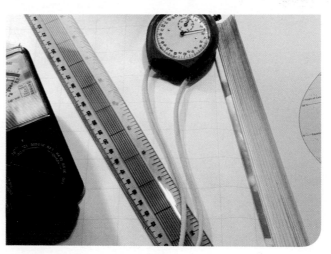

649

READING
TOOLBOX

This page summarizes the types of Reading Toolbox activities and how to use them. Assign students these activities—found on the third page of each chapter, in the margins of the student pages, and in the wrap of the Teacher's Edition—to reinforce student understanding of key concepts in the text.

Reading Toolbox Overview

Science textbooks can be hard to read because you have to learn new words and new ideas. The Reading Toolbox page at the beginning of each chapter in this book contains tools that can help you get the most out of your reading. Each of the sections on these pages is designed to help you analyze words, language, or ideas.

Analyzing Words

Analyzing Words tools will help you learn and understand specific words or phrases in a chapter.

- **FoldNotes** The key-term fold will help you learn the key terms in the chapter. Instructions for making a key-term fold are on page 656.

- **Science Terms** This tool will help you understand how the common meanings of words can differ from the scientific meanings. A table of everyday words used in science can be found on pages 668–669.

- **Word Parts** If you understand the meanings of the prefixes, suffixes, or word roots, you can understand many science terms. A table of word parts used in science terms is on pages 666–667.

- **Word Origins** Learning the origin of words and phrases used in science can help you remember the word.

- **Word Families** Because similar words can be grouped together into word families, understanding one word can help you understand all of the words in the family.

Analyzing Language

Analyzing Language tools will help you discover connections between ideas and specific kinds of language.

- **Analogies, Comparisons, and Cause and Effect** These tools help you understand the relationship between various words and phrases.

- **Generalizations, Making Predictions, Frequency, and Finding Examples** These tools help you identify language that can key you into when generalizations or predictions are being made, how often something occurs, and when an example is being used.

- **Fact, Hypothesis, or Theory?; Describing Time and Space; Reading Equations; and Word Problems** These tools can help you understand language that is used to describe science concepts and mathematical language.

- **Classification** This tool will help you understand how language is used to organize items.

- **Mnemonics** A mnemonic is a useful study tool to help you remember related words.

Analyzing Ideas

Analyzing Ideas tools will help you organize ideas and create materials that you can use to study.

- **Note Taking** These tools are various methods for taking notes while you read. For details about note-taking methods, see pages 651–655.

- **FoldNotes** There are various types of FoldNotes that you can make to help you learn information. Instructions for making FoldNotes can be found on pages 656–659.

- **Graphic Organizers** These tools are a visual way of showing relationships between ideas. Information on how to create various types of graphic organizers can be found on pages 660–665.

Note Taking

It is important to organize the information that you learn while you are reading a chapter so that you can use those notes to study for your tests. There are many ways to take notes. Each of these note-taking methods is a way to create a clear summary of the key points that you will need to remember for exams.

Comparison Table

A comparison table is useful when you want to compare the characteristics of two or more topics in science. Organizing information in a table helps you compare several topics at one time. In a table, all topics are described in terms of the same list of characteristics, which helps you make a thorough comparison.

❶ **Create Table** Draw as many columns and rows as you need to compare the topics of interest, as shown below.

❷ **Identify Topics** In the top row, write the topics that you want to compare.

❸ **Identify Characteristics** In the left-column, write the general characteristics that you want to compare. As you read the chapter, fill in the characteristics for each topic in the appropriate boxes.

	Solid	Liquid	Gas	Plasma
Definite volume	yes	yes	no	no
Definite shape	yes	no	no	no
Possible changes of state	melting, sublimation	freezing, evaporation	condensation	

Practice

1. Make a comparison table to compare apples, oranges, and broccoli. Compare the following characteristics: color, shape, fruit or vegetable, and vitamins contained.

Answer to Practice

1. Sample table:

	Apples	Oranges	Broccoli
Color	red, green	orange	dark green
Shape	round	round	irregular
Fruit/vegetable	fruit	fruit	vegetable
Vitamins	Vitamin A, Vitamin C	Vitamin A, Vitamin C	Vitamin A, Vitamin C

Outlining

Outlining is one of the most widely used methods for taking notes. A well-prepared outline can be an effective tool for understanding, comprehending, and achieving success on tests. Most outlines follow the same structure. This textbook is organized in such a way that you can easily outline the important ideas in a chapter or section.

1 List Main Ideas List main ideas or topics first. Each topic can be a section title and is listed after a Roman numeral.

2 Add Major Points Add major points that give you important information about the topic. Each major point will appear in red type in the section. You should add the points to your outline following capitalized letters.

3 Add Subpoints Add subpoints that describe or explain the major points. The first subpoint should be the key idea that appears in bold after the red heading in the chapter. The blue headings that appear after the red main topic can be used as other subpoints. Subpoints should be added after numerals in your outline.

4 Include Supporting Details Finally, add supporting details for each subpoint. Pick important details from the text that follow the blue sentences. Add the details to your outline following lower-case letters.

I. The Nature of Chemical Reactions

  A. Chemical Reactions
      1. Chemical reactions occur when substances undergo chemical changes to form new substances.
      2. Chemical reactions rearrange atoms.
          a. Products and reactants contain the same types of atoms.
          b. Mass is always conserved in chemical reactions.

Practice

1. Outline one of the sections in the chapter that you are currently covering in class.

Answer to Practice

1. Answers will depend on the chapter being covered, but answers should follow the basic outline format.

Pattern Puzzles

You can use pattern puzzles to help you remember information in the correct order. Pattern puzzles are not just a tool for memorization. They can also help you better understand a variety of scientific processes, from the steps used to solve a mathematical conversion to the procedure used to write a lab report. Pattern puzzles are useful tools to practice and to review before tests. They also work very well in problem solving.

❶ **Write Steps** In your own words, write down the steps of a process on a sheet of paper. Write one step per line, and do not number the steps. You should divide longer steps into two or three shorter steps.

❷ **Separate Steps** Cut the sheet of paper into strips with only one step per strip of paper. Shuffle the strips of paper so that they are out of sequence.

❸ **Reorganize Steps** Place the strips in their proper sequence. Confirm the order of the process by checking your text or your class notes.

How to convert an amount of a substance to mass

- List the given and unknown information.

- Look at the periodic table to determine the molar mass of the substance.

- Write the correct conversion factor to convert moles to grams.

- Multiply the amount of substance by the conversion factor.

- Solve the equation, and check your answer.

- Write the correct conversion factor to convert moles to grams.

- List the given and unknown information.

- Solve the equation, and check your answer.

- Look at the periodic table to determine the molar mass of the substance.

- Multiply the amount of substance by the conversion factor.

Practice

1. Create a pattern puzzle that describes the steps that you take during one of your favorite activities (for example, baking cookies, writing a short story, playing a song on the guitar, or scoring a soccer goal). See if a friend can put the pieces of your puzzle in the correct order.

Answer to Practice
1. Answers may vary.

Summarizing

Summarizing is a simple method of taking notes in which you restate what you read in your own words. A summary is simply a brief restatement of a longer passage. Summarizing is a useful way to take notes because it helps you focus on the most important ideas. You can use your notes when you are reviewing for a test so that you can study all of the main points without having to reread the entire chapter.

❶ **Identify Main Ideas** Identify the main idea in a paragraph by reading completely through the paragraph. Sometimes, the first or last sentence of a paragraph states the main idea directly. Key-idea sentences may also be used as the main idea.

❷ **Create Summary Statement** Write a short statement that expresses the main idea. It is best to use complete sentences. You can use abbreviations as long as you will remember later what they mean. You may be able to summarize more

than one paragraph in a single statement. In other cases, you may need more than one sentence to summarize a paragraph. Skip a couple of lines, and then repeat these first two steps for each paragraph in the section or chapter that you are reading.

❸ **Include Additional Notes** Add important notes or facts in the lines in between your summary statements. Read the text in Section 2 of Chapter 12 that follows the heading" Weight is different from mass." The heading, "Weight is different from mass," is too simple to be a summary statement because it does not tell you *how* weight and mass are different. On the other hand, you don't need to include any of the information about the astronaut in your summary. A good summary for this text is given below.

Mass is the amount of matter in an object. Weight is the gravitational force on an object due to its mass.

Mass is the same everywhere, but weight changes with location.

Practice

1. Summarize the first paragraph of this page.

Answer to Practice

1. Summary notes should restate the main ideas of a passage in the students' own words.

Two-Column Notes

Two-column notes can be used to learn and review definitions of vocabulary terms or details of specific concepts. One strategy for using two-column notes is to organize main ideas and their details. The two-column method of review is great for preparing for quizzes or tests. Cover the information in the right-hand column with a sheet of paper, and after reciting what you know, uncover the notes to check your answers.

❶ Make Table Divide a blank sheet of paper into two columns. Label the left-hand column "Main idea" and the right-hand column "Detail notes."

❷ Identify Main Ideas Identify the main ideas. Key ideas are listed at the beginning of each section. However, you should decide which ideas to include in your notes. Key words can include boldface terms as well as any other terms that you may have trouble remembering. Questions may include those that the author has asked or any questions that your teacher may have asked during class.

❸ Add Main Ideas In the right-hand column, write the main ideas as questions, key words, or a combination of both. The table below shows some of the main ideas from the first section of Chapter 1, "Introduction to Science."

❹ Create Detail Notes Do not copy ideas from the book or waste time writing in complete sentences. Summarize your ideas using by phrases that are easy to understand and remember. Decide how many details you need for each main idea, and include that number to help you focus on the necessary information.

❺ Include Detail Notes Write the detail notes in the right-hand column. Be sure to list as many details as you designated in the main-idea column.

Main idea	Detail notes
Branches of science (4 important details)	• natural science—how nature works • three main branches—biological science, physical science, Earth science • physical science—physics and chemistry • branches of science overlap (biochemistry)
Scientific theory (4 important details)	• tested experimentally • possible explanation • explains a natural event • used to predict

Practice

1. Make your own two-column notes using the periodic table. Include in the details the symbol and the atomic number of each of the following elements.

   a. neon   **c.** copper   **e.** lead
   b. oxygen   **d.** calcium   **f.** sodium

Answer to Practice

1. Sample table:

Main Idea	Detail Notes
Neon (2 important details)	• Symbol—Ne • Atomic number—10
Oxygen (2 important details)	• Symbol—O • Atomic number—8
Copper (2 important details)	• Symbol—Cu • Atomic number—29
Calcium (2 important details)	• Symbol—Ca • Atomic number—20
Lead (2 important details)	• Symbol—Pb • Atomic number—82
Sodium (2 important details)	• Symbol—Na • Atomic number—11

FoldNotes

FoldNotes are a useful study tool that you can use to organize concepts. One FoldNote focuses on a few main concepts. By using a FoldNote, you can learn how concepts fit together. FoldNotes are designed to make studying concepts easier so that you can remember the ideas for tests.

Key-Term Fold

A key-term fold is useful for studying definitions of key terms in a chapter. Each tab can contain a key term on one side and its definition on the other. Use the key-term fold to quiz yourself on the definitions of the key terms in a chapter.

1 Fold a **sheet of lined notebook paper** in half from left to right.

2 Using **scissors,** cut along every third line from the right edge of the paper to the center fold to make tabs.

Booklet

A booklet is a useful tool for taking notes as you read a chapter. Each page of the booklet can contain a main topic from the chapter. Write details of each main topic on the appropriate page to create an outline of the chapter.

1 Fold a **sheet of paper** in half from left to right. Then, unfold the paper.

2 Fold the sheet of paper in half again from the top to the bottom. Then, unfold the paper.

3 Refold the sheet of paper in half from left to right.

4 Fold the top and bottom edges to the center crease.

5 Completely unfold the paper.

6 Refold the paper from top to bottom.

7 Using **scissors,** cut a slit along the center crease of the sheet from the folded edge to the creases made in step 4. Do not cut the entire sheet in half. Unfold the paper.

8 Fold the sheet of paper in half from left to right. While holding the bottom and top edges of the paper, push the bottom and top edges together so that the center collapses at the center slit. Fold the four flaps to form a four-page book.

Double-Door Fold

A double-door fold is useful when you want to compare the characteristics of two topics. The double-door fold can organize characteristics of the two topics side by side under the flaps. Similarities and differences between the two topics can then be easily identified.

❶ Fold a **sheet of paper** in half from the top to the bottom. Then, unfold the paper.

❷ Fold the top and bottom edges of the paper to the center crease.

Four-Corner Fold

A four-corner fold is useful when you want to compare the characteristics of four topics. The four-corner fold can organize the characteristics of the four topics side by side under the flaps. Similarities and differences between the four topics can then be easily identified.

❶ Fold a **sheet of paper** in half from top to bottom. Then, unfold the paper.

❷ Fold the top and bottom of the paper to the crease in the center of the paper.

❸ Fold the paper in half from side to side. Then, unfold the paper.

❹ Using **scissors,** cut the top flap creases made in step 3 to form four flaps.

Layered Book

A layered book is a useful tool for taking notes as you read a chapter. The four flaps of the layered book can summarize information into four categories. Write details of each category on the appropriate flap to create a summary of the chapter.

❶ Lay one **sheet of paper** on top of **another sheet.** Slide the top sheet up so that 2 cm of the bottom sheet is showing.

❷ Holding the two sheets together, fold down the top of the two sheets so that you see four 2 cm tabs along the bottom.

❸ Using a **stapler,** staple the top of the FoldNote.

Pyramid

A pyramid provides a unique way for taking notes. The three sides of the pyramid can summarize information into three categories. Use the pyramid as a tool for studying information in a chapter.

❶ Place a **sheet of paper** in front of you. Fold the lower left-hand corner of the paper diagonally to the opposite edge of the paper.

❷ Cut off the tab of paper created by the fold (at the top).

❸ Open the paper so that it is a square. Fold the lower right-hand corner of the paper diagonally to the opposite corner to form a triangle.

❹ Open the paper. The creases of the two folds will have created an X.

❺ Using **scissors,** cut along one of the creases. Start from any corner, and stop at the center point to create two flaps. Use **tape** or **glue** to attach one of the flaps on top of the other flap.

Table Fold

A table fold is a useful tool for comparing the characteristics of two or three topics. In a table fold, all topics are described in terms of the same characteristics so that you can easily make a thorough comparison.

❶ Fold a **piece of paper** in half from the top to the bottom. Then, fold the paper in half again.

❷ Fold the paper in thirds from side to side.

❸ Unfold the paper completely. Carefully trace the fold lines by using a pen or pencil.

Tri-Fold

A tri-fold is a useful tool that helps you track your progress. By organizing the chapter topic into what you know, what you want to know, and what you learn, you can see how much you have learned after reading a chapter.

① Fold a piece a paper in thirds from the top to the bottom.

② Unfold the paper so that you can see the three sections. Then, turn the paper sideways so that the three sections form vertical columns.

③ Trace the fold lines by using a **pen** or **pencil.** Label the columns "Know," "Want," and "Learn."

Three-Panel Flip Chart

A three-panel flip chart is useful when you want to compare the characteristics of three topics. The three-panel flip chart can organize the characteristics of the three topics side by side under the flaps. Similarities and differences between the three topics can then be easily identified.

① Fold a **piece of paper** in half from the top to the bottom.

② Fold the paper in thirds from side to side. Then, unfold the paper so that you can see the three sections.

③ From the top of the paper, cut along each of the vertical fold lines to the fold in the middle of the paper. You will now have three flaps.

Two-Panel Flip Chart

A two-panel flip chart is useful when you want to compare the characteristics of two topics. The two-panel flip chart can organize the characteristics of the two topics side by side under the flaps. Similarities and differences between the two topics can then be easily identified.

① Fold a **piece of paper** in half from the top to the bottom.

② Fold the paper in half from side to side. Then, unfold the paper so that you can see the two sections.

③ From the top of the paper, cut along the vertical fold line to the fold in the middle of the paper. You will now have two flaps.

Graphic Organizers

Graphic Organizers are a way to draw or map concepts. Graphic Organizers can show simply how concepts are connected, when steps occur in a process, or how events are related. When you outline a concept using Graphic Organizers, you will understand the concept better and have a study tool that you can use later.

Concept Map

Concept maps are useful when you are trying to identify how several ideas are connected to a main concept. Concept maps may be based on vocabulary terms or on main topics from the text. As you read about science, look for terms that can be organized in a concept map.

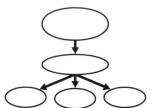

How to Make a Concept Map

❶ **Main Ideas** Identify main ideas from the text. Write the ideas as short phrases or single words.

❷ **Main Concepts** Select a main concept. Place this concept at the top or center of a piece of paper.

❸ **More Ideas** Place other ideas under or around the main concept based on their relationship to the main concept. Draw a circle around each idea.

❹ **Connections** Draw lines between the concepts. Add linking words to connect the ideas.

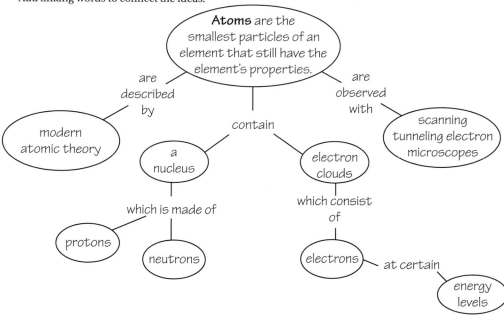

Flow Chart

Science is full of processes. A flow chart shows the steps that a process takes to get from one point to another point. Timelines and cycles are examples of the kinds of information that can be organized well in a flow chart. As you read, look for information that is described in steps or in a sequence, and draw a process chart that shows the progression of the steps or sequence.

How to Make a Flow Chart

1 Box First Step Draw a box. In the box, write the first step of a process or cycle.

2 Add Next Step Under the box, draw another box, and draw an arrow to connect the two boxes. In the second box, write the next step of the process.

3 Add More Steps Continue adding boxes until each step of the process or cycle is written in a box. For cycles only, draw an arrow to connect the last box and the first box.

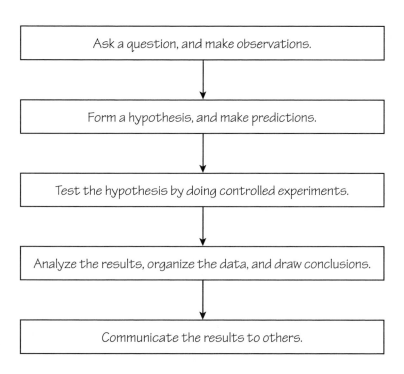

Ask a question, and make observations.

Form a hypothesis, and make predictions.

Test the hypothesis by doing controlled experiments.

Analyze the results, organize the data, and draw conclusions.

Communicate the results to others.

Chain-of-Events Chart

When to Use a Chain-of-Events Chart

A chain-of-events chart is similar to a flow chart. A chain-of-events chart shows the order in which steps occur. As you read, look for information that occurs in a sequence, and draw a chain-of-events chart that shows the order of the sequence.

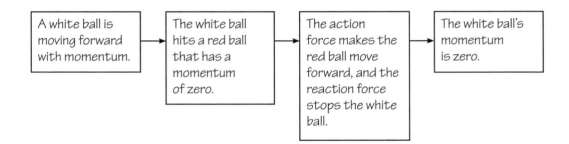

How to Make a Chain-of-Events Chart

1 **Box First Event** Draw a box. In the box, write the first event of a chain of events.

2 **Add Next Event** Draw another box to the right of the first box. Draw an arrow to connect the two boxes. In the second box, write the next event in the timeline.

3 **Add More Events** Continue adding boxes until each step of the chain of events is written in a box.

A white ball is moving forward with momentum. → The white ball hits a red ball that has a momentum of zero. → The action force makes the red ball move forward, and the reaction force stops the white ball. → The white ball's momentum is zero.

Cause-and-Effect Map

A cause-and-effect map is a useful tool for illustrating a specific type of scientific process. Use a cause-and-effect map when you want to describe how, when, or why one event causes another event. As you read, look for events that are either causes or results of other events, and draw a cause-and-effect map that shows the relationships between the events.

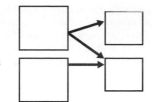

How to Make a Cause-and-Effect Map

❶ **Cause Box** Draw a box, and write a cause in the box. You can have as many cause boxes as you want. The diagram shown here is one example of a cause-and-effect map.

❷ **Effect Boxes** Draw another box to the right of the cause box to represent an effect. You can have as many effect boxes as you want. Draw arrows from each cause box to the appropriate effect boxes.

❸ **Descriptions** In the cause boxes, explain the process that makes up the cause. In the effect boxes, write a description of the effect or details about the effect.

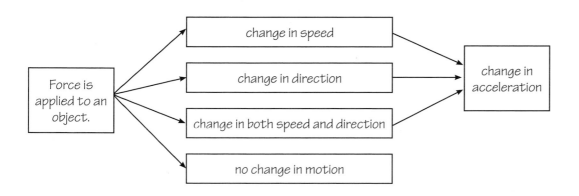

Spider Map

A spider map is an effective tool for classifying the details of a specific topic in science. A spider map divides a topic into ideas and details. As you read about a topic, look for the main ideas or characteristics of the topic. Within each idea, look for details. Use a spider map to organize the ideas and details of each topic.

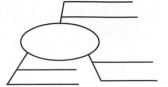

How to Make a Spider Map

1 **Main Topic** Write the main topic in the center of your paper. Draw a circle around the topic.

2 **Main Ideas** From the circle, draw legs to represent the main ideas or characteristics of the topic. Draw as many legs as you want. Write an idea or characteristic along each leg.

3 **Details** From each leg, draw horizontal lines. As you read the chapter, write details about each idea on the idea's horizontal lines. To add more details, make the legs longer and add more horizontal lines.

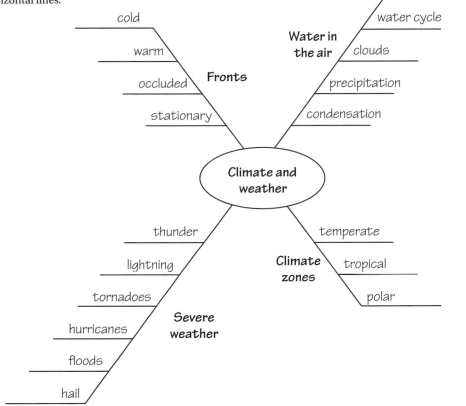

Venn Diagram

A Venn diagram is a useful tool for comparing two or three topics in science. A Venn diagram shows which characteristics that the topics share and which characteristics are unique to each topic. Venn diagrams are ideal when you want to illustrate relationships in a pair or small group of topics. As you read, look for topics that have both shared and unique characteristics, and draw a Venn diagram that shows how the topics are related.

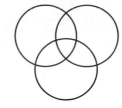

How to Make a Venn Diagram

❶ Circles Draw overlapping circles. Draw one circle for each topic, and make sure that each circle partially overlaps the other circles.

❷ Main Topics In each circle, write a topic that you want to compare with the topics in the other circles.

❸ Shared Characteristics In the areas of the diagram where circles overlap, write the characteristics that the topics in the overlapping circles share.

❹ Unique Characteristics In the areas of the diagram where circles do not overlap, write the characteristics that are unique to the topic of the particular circle.

Physical properties

- can be observed or measured without changing the identity of a substance

- color, odor, mass, volume, weight, density, strength, flexibility, magnetism, and electrical conductivity

- help describe and define matter

- can be characteristic properties

Chemical properties

- describe matter based on its ability to change into new matter that has different properties

- cannot always be observed

- reactivity, including flammability

Understanding Word Parts

Many scientific words are made up of parts based on the Greek and Latin languages. Understanding the meaning of the parts will help you understand the meaning of the scientific words. The tables here provide definitions and examples of prefixes, roots, and suffixes that you may see in this textbook.

Prefix	Definition	Example
bio-	life	**biochemistry** the study of the matter of living things
co-	with; together	**covalent bond** a bond formed when atoms share one or more pairs of electrons
com-	with; together	**compound** a substance made up of atoms of two or more different elements joined by chemical bonds
counter-	opposite; contrary to	**counterclockwise** in a direction opposite to that in which the hands of a clock move
dis-	away; in different directions	**displace** to move out of place; to move away from
endo-	in; within	**endothermic reaction** a chemical reaction that requires energy input
exo-	outside; external	**exothermic reaction** a chemical reaction in which energy is released to the surroundings as heat
infra-	below; beneath	**infrared** describes electromagnetic radiation with energy that is less than, or just below, the red end of the visible spectrum
ir-	not	**irregular galaxy** a small galaxy that has no identifiable shape and that contains a great amount of dust and gas
iso-	equal	**isotope** an atom that has the same number of protons (or the same atomic number) as other atoms of the same element do but that has a different number of neutrons (and thus a different atomic mass)
non-	not	**nonmetal** an element that conducts heat and electricity poorly and that does not form positive ions in an electrolytic solution; not a metal
retro-	backward	**retrograde rotation** the clockwise, or backward, spin of a planet or moon as seen from above the planet's North Pole
super-	above; over	**supernova** a gigantic, or oversized, explosion in which a massive star collapses and throws its outer layers into space
trans-	across; through	**transmission** the passing of light or another form of energy through matter
ultra-	beyond; exceedingly	**ultraviolet** a band of electromagnetic radiation that has wavelengths that are shorter than the wavelengths of violet light; beyond violet
uni-	one	**universe** the sum of all space, matter, and energy that exist, that have existed in the past, and that will exist in the future; the sum of all things as one unit

Word root	Definition	Example
astr	star	**astronomy** the scientific study of the universe
flamm	to burn; flame	**flammability** the ability of a substance to burn
ject	to throw	**projectile motion** the curved path that an object follows when thrown, launched, or otherwise projected near the surface of Earth
mer	part	**polymer** a large molecule that is formed by more than five monomers, or small units; a molecule made of many parts
phot	light	**photon** a unit or quantum of light
poly	many	**polyatomic ion** an ion made of two or more atoms
solute	to free; to loosen	**solubility** the ability of one substance to dissolve when in contact with another substance at a given temperature and pressure; as the substance dissolves, each of its particles becomes free from the surrounding particles
spec	to look	**spectrum** the band of colors produced when white light passes through a prism
therm	heat	**thermal conduction** the transfer of energy as heat through a material
thesis	proposition	**hypothesis** a testable idea or explanation that leads to scientific investigation
vapor	gaseous form of any substance	**evaporation** the change of state from a liquid to a gas

Suffix	Definition	Example
-cule	little	**molecule** the smallest unit of a substance that can exist by itself and retain all of the substance's chemical properties
-gram	thing written	**schematic diagram** a graphical representation of a circuit that uses lines to represent wires and different symbols to represent components
-ic	pertaining to	**periodic** describes something that occurs or repeats at regular intervals; pertaining to periods
-ion	the act of	**compression** a force that is exerted when matter is pushed or squeezed together; the act of squeezing
-meter	to measure	**thermometer** an instrument that measures and indicates temperature
-nomy	the science of	**astronomy** the scientific study of the universe
-oid	resembling	**metalloids** elements that have properties of both metals and nonmetals; they resemble metals more than nonmetals do
-scope	an instrument for seeing or observing	**telescope** an instrument that collects light from the sky and concentrates it for better observation

Everyday Words Used in Science

Scientific words may have common meanings that you already know. Understanding the difference between everyday meanings and scientific meanings will help you develop a scientific vocabulary. The table here provides common and scientific meanings for words that you will see in this textbook.

Word	Common meaning	Scientific meaning
base	the lowest part	any compound that increases the number of hydroxide ions when dissolved in water
catalyst	something that causes change	a substance that changes the rate of a chemical reaction without being consumed or changed significantly
cell	a small room, as in a prison	in electricity, a device that produces an electric current by converting chemical or radiant energy into electrical energy
concentration	the act of focusing one's attention on something	the amount of a particular substance in a given quantity of a mixture or solution
condensation	the droplets of liquid on the outside of a glass or window	the change of state from a gas to a liquid
conservation	protection of something	conservation of mass—mass cannot be created or destroyed in ordinary chemical or physical changes
element	a fundamental constituent part	a substance that cannot be separated or broken down into simpler substances by chemical means
energy	the ability to be active	the capacity to do work
fluid	smooth; graceful (for example, fluid movement)	a nonsolid state of matter in which the atoms or molecules are free to move past each other, as in a gas or liquid
force	violence used to compel a person or thing	an action exerted on a body in order to change the body's state of rest or motion; force has magnitude and direction
friction	conflict between people who have opposing views	a force that opposes motion between two surfaces that are in contact
gas	short for *gasoline;* a liquid fuel used by vehicles, such as cars and buses	a form of matter that does not have a definite volume or shape
gravity	seriousness (for example, the gravity of the situation)	a force of attraction between objects that is due to their masses and that decreases as the distance between the objects increases
group	a number of people gathered together	a vertical column of elements in the periodic table; elements in a group share chemical properties
inertia	resistance to change	the tendency of an object to resist a change in motion unless an outside force acts on the object
mass	a quantity of material that has an unspecified shape	a measure of the amount of matter in an object

Word	Common meaning	Scientific meaning
matter	a subject of concern or topic of discussion	anything that has mass and takes up space
medium	a measurement that is intermediate between small and large	a physical environment in which phenomena occur
model	a miniature representation of a larger object	a pattern, plan, representation, or description designed to show the structure or workings of an object, system, or concept
mole	a small, brown, permanent mark on the skin; a small mammal that burrows underground	the SI base unit used to measure the amount of a substance whose number of particles is the same as the number of atoms of carbon in exactly 12 g of carbon-12
motion	movement	an object's change in position relative to a reference point
organic	describes an organism or object that is produced without the use of synthetic drugs, fertilizers, or hormones	describes a covalently bonded compound that contains carbon, excluding carbonates
period	a punctuation mark used to indicate the end of a sentence	in chemistry, a horizontal row of elements in the periodic table
phase	a distinguishable stage in a cycle	in astronomy, the change in the illuminated area of one celestial body as seen from another celestial body
pressure	the burden of mental stress	the amount of force exerted per unit area of a surface
product	something available for sale (for example, a computer product)	a substance that forms in a chemical reaction
reaction	a response to a stimulus	the process by which one or more substances change to produce one or more different substances
revolution	the overthrow of one government and the substitution of that government with another (for example, the American Revolution)	the motion of a body that travels around another body in space; one complete trip along an orbit
solution	the answer to a problem	a homogeneous mixture throughout which two or more substances are uniformly dispersed
star	a person who is highly celebrated in a particular field	a large celestial body that is composed of gas and that emits light
table	a piece of furniture that has a flat, horizontal surface	an orderly arrangement of data
theory	an assumption based on limited knowledge	a system of ideas that explains many related observations and is supported by a large body of evidence acquired through scientific investigation
volume	a measure of how loud a sound is	a measure of the size of a body or region in three-dimensional space
work	a job; a task to be done	the transfer of energy to a body by the application of a force that causes the body to move in the direction of the force

Math Skills

Fractions

Fractions represent numbers that are less than 1. In other words, fractions are a way of using numbers to represent a part of a whole. For example, if you have a pizza with 8 slices and you eat 2 of the slices, you have 6 out of the 8 slices, or $\frac{6}{8}$, of the pizza left. The top number in the fraction is called the *numerator*. The bottom number is called the *denominator*.

There are special rules for adding, subtracting, multiplying, and dividing fractions. **Figure 1** summarizes these rules.

Figure 1 Basic Operations for Fractions

Rule and example		
Multiplication	$\left(\frac{a}{b}\right)\left(\frac{c}{d}\right) = \frac{ac}{bd}$	$\left(\frac{2}{3}\right)\left(\frac{4}{5}\right) = \frac{8}{15}$
Division	$\frac{a}{b} \div \frac{c}{d} = \frac{\left(\frac{a}{b}\right)}{\left(\frac{c}{d}\right)} = \frac{ad}{bc}$	
	$\frac{2}{3} \div \frac{4}{5} = \frac{\left(\frac{2}{3}\right)}{\left(\frac{4}{5}\right)} = \frac{(2)(5)}{(3)(4)} = \frac{10}{12}$	
Addition and subtraction	$\frac{a}{b} \pm \frac{c}{d} = \frac{ad \pm bc}{bd}$	
	$\frac{2}{3} - \frac{4}{5} = \frac{(2)(5) - (3)(4)}{(3)(5)} = -\frac{2}{15}$	

Percentages

Percentages are the same as other fractions except that in a percentage the whole (or the number in the denominator) is considered to be 100. Any percentage, $x\%$, can be read as x out of 100. For example, if you completed 50% of an assignment, you completed $\frac{50}{100}$, or $\frac{1}{2}$, of the assignment.

Percentages can be calculated by dividing the part by the whole. Your calculator displays a decimal value when it solves a division problem that has an answer that is less than 1. The decimal value can be written as a fraction. For example, 0.45 can be written as the fraction $\frac{45}{100}$.

An easy way to calculate a percentage is to divide the part by the whole and then multiply by 100. This multiplication moves the decimal point two positions to the right and gives you the number that would be over 100 in a fraction. So, $0.45 = 45\%$.

Try this example:

> You scored 73 out of 92 problems on your last exam. What was your percentage score?

First, divide the part by the whole to get a decimal value. The fraction $\frac{73}{92} = 0.7935$, which is equal to $\frac{79.35}{100}$.

Then, multiply by 100 to find the percentage: $0.7935 \times 100 = 79.35\%$.

Practice

1. The molar mass of the oxygen atom in a water molecule is 16.00 g/mol. A water molecule has a total molar mass of 18.01 g/mol. What percentage of the mass of water is made up of oxygen?

2. A candy bar contains 14 g of fat. The total fat contains 3.0 g of saturated fat and 11 g of unsaturated fat. What percentage of the fat is saturated? What percentage is unsaturated?

Practice

1. Perform the following calculations:

   a. $\frac{7}{8} + \frac{1}{3} =$ c. $\frac{7}{8} \div \frac{1}{3} =$

   b. $\frac{7}{8} \times \frac{1}{3} =$ d. $\frac{7}{8} - \frac{1}{3} =$

Math *Skills*

Answers to Practice

1. a. $\frac{29}{24}$ or $1\frac{5}{24}$

   b. $\frac{7}{24}$

   c. $\frac{21}{8}$ or $2\frac{5}{8}$

   d. $\frac{13}{24}$

Math *Skills*

Answers to Practice

1. 88.84%
2. saturated fat: 21%
   unsaturated fat: 79%

Exponents

An exponent is a number that is a superscript to the right of another number. The best way to explain how an exponent works is with an example. In the value 5^4, 4 is the exponent on 5. The number with its exponent means that 5 is multiplied by itself 4 times.

$$5^4 = 5 \times 5 \times 5 \times 5 = 625$$

Exponent are powers.

You will frequently hear exponents referred to as *powers*. Using this terminology, one could read the above equation as *five to the fourth power equals 625*. Keep in mind that any number raised to the zero power is equal to 1. Also, any number raised to the first power is equal to itself:

$$5^1 = 5$$

Figure 2 summarizes the rules for dealing with exponents.

Figure 2 Rules for Dealing with Exponents

	Rule	Example
Zero power	$x^0 = 1$	$7^0 = 1$
First power	$x^1 = x$	$6^1 = 6$
Multiplication	$(x^n)(x^m) = x^{(n+m)}$	$(x^2)(x^4) = x^{(2+4)} = x^6$
Division	$\dfrac{x^n}{x^m} = x^{(n-m)}$	$\dfrac{x^8}{x^2} = x^{(8-2)} = x^6$
Exponents that are fractions	$x^{1/n} = \sqrt[n]{x}$	$4^{1/3} = \sqrt[3]{4} = 1.5874$
Exponents raised to a power	$(x^n)^m = x^{nm}$	$(5^2)^3 = 5^6 = 15,625$

Roots are the opposite of exponents.

The symbol for a square root is $\sqrt{}$. The value underneath this symbol is equal to a number times itself. It is also possible to have roots other than the square root. For example, $\sqrt[3]{x}$ is a cube root, which means that if you multiply some number, n, by itself 3 times, you will get the number x, or $x = n \times n \times n$.

We can turn our example of $5^4 = 625$ around to solve for the fourth root of 625.

$$\sqrt[4]{625} = 5$$

Taking the nth root of a number is the same as raising that number to the power of $1/n$. Therefore, $\sqrt[4]{625} = 625^{1/4}$.

Use a calculator to solve exponents and roots.

You can solve problems involving exponents and roots easily by using a scientific calculator. Many calculators have dedicated keys for squares and square roots. But what do you do if you want to find other powers, such as cubes and cube roots? Most scientific calculators have a key with a caret symbol, (^), that is used to enter exponents. If you type in "5^4" and hit the equals sign or the enter key, the calculator will display the answer 625.

Many scientific calculators have a key with the symbol $\sqrt[x]{}$ that you can use to enter roots. When using this key, enter the root first. To solve the problem of the fourth root of 625, you would type "4 $\sqrt[x]{}$ 625," and the calculator would return the answer 5. If your calculator does not have the root key, you may be able to enter the root as a fraction if your calculator has a key that allows you to enter fractions. In this case you would use the exponent key and the fraction key to enter "625^$\frac{1}{4}$." If your calculator does not have a fraction key, you can enter the decimal equivalent of the fractional exponent to find the root. Instead of entering $\frac{1}{4}$ as the exponent, enter "625^0.25," because 0.25 is equal to $\frac{1}{4}$.

Practice

1. Perform the following calculations:

a. $9^1 =$

b. $(3^3)^5 =$

c. $\dfrac{2^8}{2^2} =$

d. $(14^2)(14^3) =$

e. $11^0 =$

f. $6^{1/6} =$

Math Skills

Answers to Practice

1. a. $9^1 = 9$

b. $(3^3)^5 = 3^{15} = 14,348,907$

c. $2^8/2^2 = 2^{(8-2)} = 2^6 = 64$

d. $(14^2)(14^3) = 14^{(2+3)} = 14^5 = 537,824$

e. $11^0 = 1$

f. $6^{1/6} = \sqrt[6]{6} = 1.348$

Order of Operations

Use the following phrase to remember the correct order for long mathematical problems: *Please Excuse My Dear Aunt Sally*. This phrase stands for "Parentheses, Exponents, Multiplication, Division, Addition, Subtraction." **Figure 3** summarizes these rules.

Figure 3 Order of Operations

Step	Operation
1	**Parentheses** Simplify groups inside parentheses. Start with the innermost group, and work out.
2	**Exponents** Simplify all exponents.
3	**Multiplication and Division** Perform multiplication and division in order from left to right.
4	**Addition and Subtraction** Perform addition and subtraction in order from left to right.

Try the following example:

$$4^3 + 2 \times [8 - (3 - 1)] = ?$$

❶ Simplify the operations inside parentheses. Begin with the innermost parentheses:

$$(3 - 1) = 2$$
$$4^3 + 2 \times [8 - 2] = ?$$

Move on to the next-outer brackets:

$$[8 - 2] = 6$$
$$4^3 + 2 \times 6 = ?$$

❷ Simplify all exponents:

$$4^3 = 64$$
$$64 + 2 \times 6 = ?$$

❸ Perform multiplication:

$$2 \times 6 = 12$$
$$64 + 12 = ?$$

❹ Solve the addition problem:

$$64 + 12 = 76$$

Practice

1. $2^3 \div 2 + 4 \times (9 - 2^2) =$
2. $\dfrac{2 \times (6 - 3) + 8}{4 \times 2 - 6} =$

Geometry

Shapes are a useful way to model many objects and substances studied in science. For example, many of the properties of a wheel can be understood by using a perfect circle as a model.

Therefore, knowing how to calculate the area or the volume of certain shapes is a useful skill in science. Equations for the area and volume of several geometric shapes are provided in **Figure 4.**

Figure 4 Geometric Areas and Volumes

Geometric shape	Useful equations
Rectangle	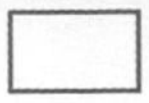 $area = lw$
Circle	 $area = \pi r^2$ $circumference = 2\pi r$
Triangle	 $area = \frac{1}{2}bh$
Sphere	$surface\ area = 4\pi r^2$ $volume = \frac{4}{3}\pi r^3$
Cylinder	 $volume = \pi r^2 h$
Rectangular box	 $surface\ area = 2(lh + lw + hw)$ $volume = lwh$

Practice

1. A cylinder has a diameter of 14 cm and a height of 8 cm. What is the cylinder's volume?
2. Calculate the surface area of a 4 cm cube.
3. Will a sphere with a volume of 76 cm³ fit in a rectangular box that is 7 cm × 4 cm × 10 cm?

Math *Skills*

Answers to Practice

1. $2^3 \div 2 + 4 \times (9 - 2^2) =$
   $8 \div 2 + 4 \times (9 - 4) =$
   $8 \div 2 + 4 \times 5 =$
   $4 + 20 = 24$

2. $\dfrac{2 \times (6 - 3) + 8}{4 \times 2 - 6} =$

   $\dfrac{2 \times 3 + 8}{4 \times 2 - 6} =$

   $\dfrac{6 + 8}{8 - 6} =$

   $\dfrac{14}{2} = 7$

Math *Skills*

Answers to Practice

1. $r = \dfrac{14\ cm}{2} = 7\ cm$

   $volume\ of\ cylinder = \pi r^2 h$
   $\pi(7\ cm)^2(8\ cm) = 1{,}232\ cm^3$

2. $surface\ area = 2(lh + lw + hw) =$
   $2[(4\ cm)^2 + (4\ cm)^2 + (4\ cm)^2] =$
   $2[16\ cm^2 + 16\ cm^2 + 16\ cm^2] =$
   $2[48\ cm^2] = 96\ cm^2$

3. $volume\ of\ sphere = \dfrac{4}{3}\pi r^3 = 76\ cm^3$
   $r^3 = 18\ cm^3$
   $r = 2.6\ cm$
   $diameter\ of\ sphere = r \times 2 = 5.2\ cm$
   The box must be at least 5.2 cm in each dimension for the sphere to fit. The box has one dimension that is too small for the sphere to fit.

Algebraic Rearrangements

Often in science, you will need to determine the value of a variable from an equation written as an algebraic expression.

Algebraic expressions contain constants and variables. *Constants* are numbers that you know and that do not change, such as 2, 3.14, and 100. *Variables* are represented by letters, such as *x, y, a,* and *b*. Variables in equations are unspecified quantities and are also called the *unknowns*.

An algebraic expression contains one or more of the four basic mathematical operations: addition, subtraction, multiplication, and division. Constants, variables, or terms made up of both constants and variables can be involved in the basic operations.

Solve for the variable.

To find the value of some variable, you need to simplify the expression by rearranging the equation. Ideally, after you have finished rearranging the equation, you will end up with a simple equation that tells you the value of the variable.

To get from a complicated equation to a simpler one, you need to isolate the variable on one side of the equation. You can do so by performing the same operations on both sides of the equation until the variable is alone. Because both sides of the equation are equal, if you do the same operation on both sides of the equation, the results will still be equal.

Look at the following simple problem:

$$8x = 32$$

In this equation, you need to solve for the variable *x*. You can add, subtract, multiply, or divide anything to or from one side of an equation as long as you do the same thing to the other side of the equation. In this case, we need to get rid of the 8 so that the *x* is by itself. If we divide both sides by 8, we have this equation:

$$\frac{8x}{8} = \frac{32}{8}$$

The 8s on the left side of the equation cancel each other out, and the fraction $\frac{32}{8}$ can be reduced to give the whole number 4.

$$x = 4$$

Next, consider the following equation:

$$x + 2 = 8$$

Remember that you can add or subtract the same quantity from each side. To isolate *x*, you need subtract 2 from each side:

$$x + 2 - 2 = 8 - 2$$
$$x + 0 = 6$$
$$x = 6$$

Now, consider one more equation:

$$-3(x - 2) + 4 = 29$$

One way to solve this more complicated expression is to follow the order of operations in reverse order to isolate *x*. First, subtract the 4.

$$-3(x - 2) + 4 - 4 = 29 - 4$$
$$-3(x - 2) = 25$$

Now, divide by –3.

$$\frac{-3(x - 2)}{-3} = \frac{25}{-3}$$

$$x - 2 = -8.3$$

Now, only the expression that was inside the parentheses remains on the left side of the equation. You can find the value of *x* by adding 2 to both sides of the equation.

$$x - 2 + 2 = -8.3 + 2$$
$$x = -6.3$$

Practice

1. Rearrange each of the following equations to give the value of the variable indicated with a letter:

   a. $8x - 32 = 128$

   b. $6 - 5(4a + 3) = 26$

   c. $-2(3m + 5) = 14$

   d. $\left[8\frac{(8 + 2z)}{32} \right] + 2 = 5$

   e. $\frac{(6b + 3)}{3} - 9 = 2$

Math *Skills*

Answers to Practice

1. **a.** $8x - 32 = 128$
   $8x - 32 + 32 = 128 + 32$
   $8x = 160$
   $x = \frac{160}{8} = 20$

   b. $6 - 5 \times (4a + 3) = 26$
   $6 - 6 - 5 \times (4a + 3) = 26 - 6$
   $-5 \times (4a + 3) = 20$
   $\frac{-5 \times (4a + 3)}{-5} = \frac{20}{-5}$
   $4a + 3 = -4$
   $4a + 3 - 3 = -4 - 3$
   $4a - 7$
   $a = -1.75$

c. $-2 \times (3m + 5) = 14$
$\frac{-2 \times (3m + 5)}{-2} = \frac{14}{-2}$
$(3m + 5) = -7$
$3m + 5 - 5 = -7 - 5$
$3m = -12$
$m = -4$

d. $\left| 8\frac{(8 + 2z)}{32} \right| + 2 = 5$
$\left| 8\frac{(8 + 2z)}{32} \right| + 2 - 2 = 5 - 2$
$8\frac{(8 + 2z)}{32} = 3$
$8\frac{(8 + 2z)}{32} \times 32 = 3 \times 32$
$8(8 + 2z) = 96$
$8\frac{(8 + 2z)}{8} = \frac{96}{8}$

$8 + 2z = 12$
$8 + 2z - 8 = 12 - 8$
$2z = 4$
$z = 4$

e. $\frac{(6b + 3)}{3} - 9 = 2$
$\frac{(6b + 3)}{3} - 9 + 9 = 2 + 9$
$\frac{(6b + 3)}{3} = 11$
$\frac{(6b + 3)}{3} \times 3 = 11 \times 3$
$6b + 3 = 33$
$6b + 3 - 3 = 33 - 3$
$6b = 30$
$\frac{6b}{6} = \frac{30}{6}$
$b = 5$

Scientific Notation

Often, scientists deal with very large or very small quantities. For example, in one second, about 3,000,000,000,000,000,000 electrons' worth of charge pass through a standard light bulb; and the ink required to make the dot over an *i* in this textbook has a mass of about 0.000000001 kg.

Obviously, it is very time-consuming to read and write such large and small numbers. It is also easy to lose track of the zeros and make an error when doing calculations with numbers that have many zeros. Powers of the number 10 are used to keep track of the zeros in large and small numbers. Numbers that are expressed as some power of 10 multiplied by another number with only one digit to the left of the decimal point are said to be written in *scientific notation*.

Use exponents to write large numbers.

Study the positive powers of 10 shown in the chapter entitled "Introduction to Science." The number of zeros corresponds to the exponent to the right of the 10. The number for 10^4 is 10,000; it has 4 zeros.

But how can you use the powers of 10 to simplify large numbers such as the number of electron-sized charges passing through a light bulb? The number 3,000,000,000,000,000,000 can be written as $3 \times 1,000,000,000,000,000,000$. To write the large number as an exponent, count the zeros—there are 18 zeros. Therefore, the exponent is 10^{18}. So, 3,000,000,000,000,000,000 can be expressed as 3×10^{18} in scientific notation.

Use exponents to write small numbers.

Now, you know how to simplify really large numbers, but how do you simplify really small numbers, such as 0.000000001? To simplify numbers that are less than 1, use negative exponents.

Next, study the negative powers of 10. To determine the exponent that you need to use, count the number of decimal places that you must move the decimal point to the right so that only one digit is to the left of the decimal point. To simplify the mass of the ink in the dot on an *i*, 0.000000001 kg, you must move the decimal point 9 decimal places to the right for the numeral 1 to be on the left side of the decimal point. In scientific notation, the mass of the ink is 1×10^{-9} kg.

Use scientific notation to write any number.

Values that have more than one nonzero number can also be written using scientific notation. For example, 5,943,000,000 is 5.943×10^9 when expressed in scientific notation. The number 0.0000832 is 8.32×10^{-5} when expressed in scientific notation.

When you use scientific notation in calculations, follow the rules for using exponents in calculations. When you multiply two numbers expressed in scientific notation, add the exponents, as shown below.

$$(4 \times 10^5) \times (2 \times 10^3) = [(4 \times 2) \times 10^{(5+3)})] = 8 \times 10^8$$

When you divide two numbers expressed in scientific notation, subtract the exponents.

The order of magnitude is the power of 10.

When a number is expressed in scientific notation, you can easily determine the order of magnitude of the number. For numbers less than 5, the order of magnitude is the power of 10 when the number is written in scientific notation. For numbers greater than 5, the order of magnitude is the power of 10 to which the number would be rounded. For example, in the number 5.943×10^9, the order of magnitude is 10^{10}, because 5.943 rounds to another 10, and 10 times 10^9 is 10^{10}.

The order of magnitude can be used to help quickly estimate your answers. Simply perform the operations required, but instead of using numbers, use the orders of magnitude. Your final answer should be within two orders of magnitude of your estimate.

Practice

1. Rewrite the following values using scientific notation:
   a. 12,300,000 m/s
   b. 0.0000000000045 kg
   c. 0.0000653 m
   d. 55,432,000,000,000 s
   e. 273.15 K
   f. 0.00062714 kg

Math Skills

Answer to Practice

1. a. 1.23×10^7 m/s
   b. 4.5×10^{-12} kg
   c. 6.53×10^{-5} m
   d. 5.5432×10^{13} s
   e. 2.7315×10^2 K
   f. 6.2714×10^{-4} kg

SI

One of the most important parts of scientific research is being able to communicate your findings to other scientists. Today, scientists need to be able to communicate with other scientists all around the world. They need a common language in which to report data. If you do an experiment in which all of your measurements are in pounds and you want to compare your results to those of a French scientist whose measurements are in grams, you will need to convert all of your measurements. For this reason, the *Système International d'Unités*, or SI, was created in 1960.

You are probably accustomed to measuring distance in inches, feet, and miles. Most of the world, however, measures distance in centimeters (cm), meters (m), and kilometers (km). The meter is the official SI unit for measuring distance. **Figure 5** lists the SI units for some common measurements.

Prefixes are used to indicate quantities.

Notice that centi*meter* and kilo*meter* each contain the word *meter*. When dealing with SI units, you frequently use the base unit, in this case the meter, and add a prefix to indicate that the quantity that you are measuring is a multiple of that unit. Most SI prefixes indicate multiples of 10. For example, the centimeter is 1/100 of a meter. Any SI unit with the prefix *centi-* will be 1/100 of the base unit. A centigram is 1/100 of a gram.

Figure 5 Some SI Units

Quantity	Unit name	Symbol
Length	meter	m
Mass	kilogram	kg
Time	second	s
Temperature	kelvin	K
Amount of substance	mole	mol
Electric current	ampere	A
Pressure	pascal	Pa
Volume	cubic meters	m^3

Figure 6 Some SI Prefixes

Prefix	Symbol	Exponential factor
giga-	G	10^9
mega-	M	10^6
kilo-	k	10^3
hecto-	h	10^2
deka-	da	10^1
deci-	d	10^{-1}
centi-	c	10^{-2}
milli-	m	10^{-3}
micro-	μ	10^{-6}
nano-	n	10^{-9}
pico-	p	10^{-12}
femto-	f	10^{-15}

How many meters are in a *kilo*meter? The prefix *kilo-* indicates that the unit is 1,000 times the base unit. A kilometer is equal to 1,000 meters. Multiples of 10 make dealing with SI values much easier than values such as feet or gallons. To convert from feet to miles, you must remember a large conversion factor, 1.893939×10^{-4} miles per foot. To convert from kilometers to meters, you need to look only at the prefix to know that you will multiply by 1,000.

Figure 6 lists possible prefixes and their meanings. When working with a prefix, simply take the unit symbol and add the prefix symbol to the front of the unit symbol. For example, the symbol for *kilometer* is written "km."

> **Practice**
>
> 1. Convert each value to the requested units:
>   a. 0.035 m to decimeters
>   b. 5.24 m^3 to cubic centimeters
>   c. 13,450 g to kilograms

Math *Skills*

Answer to Practice

1. a. 0.35 dm
   b. 5.24×10^6 cm^3
   c. 13.45 kg

Significant Figures

Significant figures indicate the precision of a value. You can use the rules in the following list to determine the number of significant figures in a reported value. After you have reviewed the rules, use **Figure 7** to check your understanding of the rules. Cover up the second column of the table, and try to determine how many significant figures each number has.

You can use a few rules to determining the number of significant figures in a measurement.

1 All nonzero digits are significant.

Example **1,246** (four significant figures, shown in red)

2 Any zeros between significant digits are also significant.

Example **1,206** (four significant figures)

3 If the value does not contain a decimal point, any zeros to the right of a nonzero digit are not significant.

Example **1,2**00 (two significant figures)

4 Any zeros to the right of a significant digit and to the left of a decimal point are significant.

Example **1,200.** (four significant figures)

5 If a value has no significant digits to the left of a decimal point, any zeros to the right of the decimal point and to the left of a nonzero digit are not significant.

Example 0.00**12** (two significant figures)

6 If a measurement is reported that ends with zeros to the right of a decimal point, those zeros are significant.

Example 0.**1200** (four significant figures)

If you are adding or subtracting two measurements, your answer can have only as many decimal positions as the value with the least number of decimal places. The final answer in the following problem has five significant figures. It has been rounded to two decimal places because 0.04 g has only two decimal places.

$$134.050 \text{ g}$$
$$\underline{-0.04 \text{ g}}$$
$$134.01 \text{ g}$$

Figure 7 Significant Figures

Measurement	Number of significant figures	Rule
12,345	5	1
2,400 cm	2	3
305 kg	3	2
2,350. cm	4	4
234.005 K	6	2
12.340	5	6
0.001	1	5
0.002450	4	5 and 6

When you multiply or divide measurements, your final answer can have only as many significant figures as the value with the least number of significant figures. Examine the following multiplication problem.

$$12.0 \text{ cm}^2$$
$$\underline{\times 0.04 \text{ cm}}$$
$$0.5 \text{ cm}^3$$

The final answer has been rounded to one significant figure because 0.04 cm has only one. When performing both types of operations (addition/subtraction and multiplication/division), round the result after you complete each type of operation, and round the final result.

Practice

1. Determine the number of significant figures in each of the following measurements:
   a. 65.04 mL   **c.** 0.007504 kg
   b. 564.00 m   **d.** 1,210 K

2. Perform each of the following calculations, and report your answer with the correct number of significant figures and units:
   a. 0.004 dm + 0.12508 dm
   b. 340 m ÷ 0.1257 s
   c. 40.1 kg × 0.2453 m^2
   d. 1.03 g − 0.0456 g

Math Skills

Answer to Practice

1. **a.** 4
   b. 5
   c. 4
   d. 3

2. **a.** 0.004 dm + 0.12508 dm =
   0.12908 dm = 0.129 dm
   b. $\dfrac{340 \text{ m}}{0.1257 \text{ s}} =$
   2,704.852824 m/s = 2,700 m/s
   c. 40.1 kg × 0.2453 m² =
   9.83653 kg•m² = 9.84 kg•m²
   d. 1.03 g − 0.0456 g
   0.9844 g = 0.98 g

Graphing Skills

Line Graphs

Usually, in laboratory experiments, you will control one variable and see how changes in that variable affect another variable. Line graphs can show these relationships clearly. Suppose that you want to determine the rate of a plant's growth by measuring the growth of a plant over time. In this experiment, you would control the time intervals at which the plant height is measured. Thus, time is the *independent variable*. The change in the height of the plant that you measure depends on the time interval that you choose. So, plant height is the *dependent variable*. The table in **Figure 8** shows some sample data from an experiment that measured the rate of plant growth.

When you make a line graph, always plot the independent variable on the *x*-axis. For the plant-height experiment, the axis will be labeled "Time (days)." Remember to include the units in your axis label. Pick a range for your graph that is just large enough to enter all of your data points. From the data in **Figure 8,** you can see that plant height was measured over 35 days. Therefore, the *x*-axis should have a range of 0 days to 35 days.

Plot the dependent variable on the *y*-axis. In this case, the *y*-axis is labeled "Plant height (cm)" and has a range from 0 cm to 5 cm.

When you draw the axes for your graph, you want to use as much of the available space as possible. You should label the grid marks for each axis at intervals that evenly divide up the data range. In the graph in **Figure 9,** the *y*-axis has grid marks at intervals of 1, and the *x*-axis has grid marks at intervals of 5. Notice that the interval of the grid marks on the *x*-axis is not the same interval at which the data were measured.

Think of your graph as a grid with lines running horizontally from the *y*-axis and vertically from the *x*-axis. To plot a point, find the *x*-value for that point on the *x*-axis. Follow the vertical line from the *x*-axis until it intersects the horizontal line from the *y*-axis at the corresponding *y*-value. At the intersection of these two lines, place your point. After you have plotted all of your data points, connect each point with a straight line. **Figure 9** shows a line graph of the data in **Figure 8.**

Figure 8 Data for Plant Growth Versus Time

Time (days)	Plant height (cm)
0	1.43
7	2.16
14	2.67
21	3.25
28	4.04
35	4.67

Figure 9 Line Graph for Plant Growth Versus Time

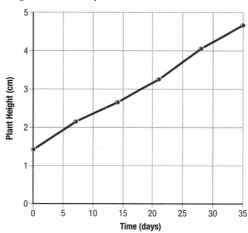

Practice

1. Create a line graph of the data below.

Time (days)	Plant height (cm)
0	1.46
7	2.67
14	3.89
21	4.82

2. Compare the graph you made with **Figure 9.** What can you conclude about the two groups of plants?

Graphing Skills

Different Kinds of Graphs Be sure that students understand that not all graphs are alike. Each type of graph has its strengths and showcases certain aspects of a data set. A line graph shows trends over a continuous range. Bar graphs work well to show the relationship between data organized in categories. Pie graphs easily show proportions making up a whole.

Graphing Skills

Answers to Practice

1. Answers may vary. The axes of the graph should show units and be clearly labeled. The four points should be plotted on the graph with lines connecting consecutive points.
2. The plants in the graph from item 1 grew faster than those represented in Figure 9.

Scatter Plots

Some groups of data are best represented in a graph called a *scatter plot*. Scatter plots are often used to find trends, or general patterns, in data. A scatter plot is similar to a line graph. The data points are plotted on the graph that has an *x*-axis and a *y*-axis, but each point is not connected with a line. Instead, a straight best-fit line is drawn through the data points to show the overall trend. A best-fit line is a single, smooth line that represents all of the data points without necessarily going through all of them. To find a best-fit line,

pick a line that is equidistant from as many data points as possible. Examine the graph in **Figure 10.**

If we connected all of the data points with lines, the lines would create a zigzag pattern. It would be hard to see the general pattern in the data. But if we find a best-fit line, we can see a trend more clearly. The trend in a scatter plot depends on the data. The best-fit line in **Figure 11** shows that magazine subscriptions increased.

If you pick two points on the best-fit line, you can estimate the line's slope. The slope will tell you the average rate of increase in magazine subscriptions. By using the dotted lines in **Figure 11,** you can estimate the data point for 1940 as 18 magazine subscriptions per 1,000 households and for 1960 as 42 magazine subscriptions per 1,000 households. The slope is (42 subscriptions – 18 subscriptions) divided by (1960 – 1940). The slope tells you that there is an increase of 24 subscriptions per 1,000 households every 20 years.

Figure 10

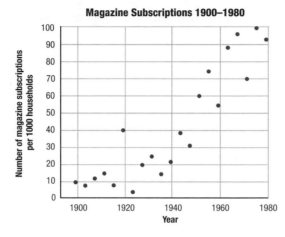

Figure 11

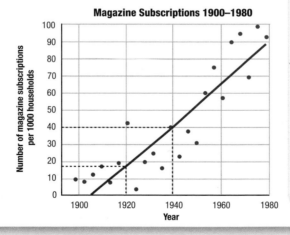

Practice

1. Create a scatter plot, and draw a best-fit line for the data below.

Year	Magazine subscriptions per 1,000 households
1918	17
1931	15
1942	42
1954	36
1967	64
1980	73
1992	60
2008	70

2. What does the best-fit line represent?

3. If these data are from a different city than the data in **Figure 11,** what conclusions could you draw about the two cities?

Graphing *Skills*

Answers to Practice

1. Answers may vary. The axes of the graphs should show units and be clearly labeled. The points from the data table should be plotted and a straight fit line drawn through the middle of the points.

2. The line represents an average number of magazine subscriptions, and how the average changed over time.

3. The city represented in item 1 had an average of more magazine subscriptions per 1,000 households, but the rate of change was about the same.

Bar Graphs

Bar graphs should be used for noncontinuous data. They make it easy to compare data quickly when you have one value for multiple items. You can see from **Figure 12** that Jupiter has the largest radius and Mercury has the smallest radius. You could easily arrange the planets in order of size.

Figure 12

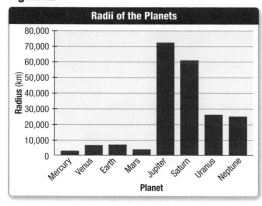

The data are represented accurately in **Figure 13,** but you cannot draw conclusions quickly. Remember that when you create a graph, you want the graph to be as clear as possible. The same data are graphed in **Figure 14,** but the range and scale of the *y*-axis are smaller than they are in **Figure 13.** The trend in the data is much easier to see in **Figure 14.**

Figure 14

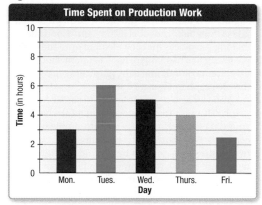

Choosing the scale of a bar graph will make identifying trends in the data easier. Examine **Figure 13** below.

Figure 13

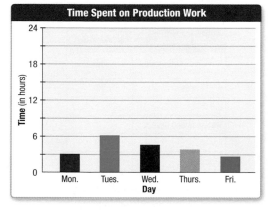

Practice

1. Which day of the week is most productive, according to **Figure 14**?

2. Which day of the week is least productive, according to **Figure 14**?

3. Using the following data, create an easily readable bar graph.

Fiscal period	Money spent (in millions)
First quarter	89
Second quarter	56
Third quarter	72
Fourth quarter	41

Graphing Skills

Answers to Practice

1. Tuesday
2. Friday
3. Answers may vary. Students' graphs should be easy to interpret and have clearly labeled axes.

Pie Graphs

Pie graphs are an easy way to visualize how parts make up a whole. Often, pie graphs are made from percentage data, such as the data in **Figure 15.**

To create a pie graph, begin by drawing a circle. Because percentages represent parts of 100, imagine dividing the circle into 100 equal parts. Then, you need to figure out how much of the pie each part takes up. It is easiest to start with the largest piece. To graph the data in **Figure 15,** you would start with the data for oxygen. Half of the circle equals 50 parts, so you know that 46% will be slightly less than half of the pie. Shade a piece that is less than half, and label it "Oxygen." Continue making pie pieces for each element until the entire pie graph has been filled. Each element should be a different color to make the graph easy to read as the pie graph in **Figure 16** shows.

You can also use a protractor to construct a pie graph. This method is especially helpful when your data cannot be converted into simple percentages. First, convert the percentages to degrees by dividing each number by 100 and multiplying that result by 360. Next, draw a circle, and make a vertical mark across the top of the circle. Use a protractor to measure the largest angle from your table. Mark this angle along the circumference. For example, 32.9% would be 118° because 32.9/100 = 0.329 and 0.329 × 360 = 118.

To create the next pie piece, measure a second angle from the second mark to make a third mark along the circumference. Continue measuring the angles for each segment until all of your slices are measured. Draw lines from the marks to the center of the circle, and label each slice.

Figure 16 Composition of Earth's Crust

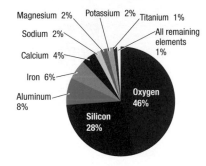

Figure 15 Composition of Earth's Crust

Element	Percentage of Earth's crust
Oxygen	46%
Silicon	28%
Aluminium	8%
Iron	6%
Calcium	4%
Sodium	2%
Magnesium	2%
Potassium	2%
Titanium	1%
All remaining elements	1%

Practice

1. Use the data below to make a pie graph.

Kind of land use	Percentage of total land
Grassland and rangeland	29
Wilderness and parks	13
Urban	7
Wetlands and deserts	4
Forest	30
Cropland	17

2. If humans use half of forests and grasslands, as well as all croplands and urban areas, how much of the total land do humans use?

Graphing Skills

Answers to Practice

1. Answers may vary. Students' graphs should have approximately the correct portion of the pie allotted to each kind of land use, and the graph should be clearly labeled and easy to interpret.

2. Slightly more than half of the total land (53.5%).

Technology Skills

Using Search Engines

The World Wide Web is filled with information on almost any topic imaginable. Search engines make it possible to sort through this vast amount of information to find what you need.

A search engine is software that you use to search for Web pages by using keywords. Some search engines let you search huge databases that cover large portions of the Web. Other search engines may search a limited but more focused range of pages, such as the pages on a single Web site or journal articles in a specific subject area.

Although the scope of search engines may differ, most search engines work in a similar way. For example, consider Scirus, a search engine that searches for scientific information. You can access Scirus by entering the Web address *www.scirus.com* into the address bar of your Web browser, as **Figure 17** shows.

Figure 17 Address Bar of Web Browser

Once you are on the Scirus home page, you will see a search box. To find information on a specific topic, type into the search box keywords that you think are most likely to target the web pages about that topic. Then, click on the Search button to start the search. For example, if you are researching black holes, you would type the keywords "black hole." The search engine will return a list of pages containing those keywords. You can then click on the links to visit the pages that seem most promising for your research goals.

Use the help pages to improve your searches.

Although all search engines work in a similar way, they are all slightly different. To make your searches more effective on a particular site, look at the site's help page or advanced search page for helpful tips and advanced search options.

If you search a broad topic, you may get too many Web sites in your search results. The help page or advanced search page can also help you determine the best way to narrow your search so that you will find a more manageable number of Web sites. For example, these pages may allow you to select other keywords to include or exclude from your search, tell you where to look for the keywords on Web pages, and tell you what types of Web sites to include in the search. Suppose that you wanted to find only Web pages that contain information about neutrinos and black holes. You could use the advanced search page to help narrow your results, as **Figure 18** shows.

Figure 18 Advanced Search Page

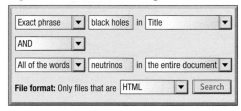

Check the reliability of Web sites.

When you visit a site to find factual information, remember to check the source of the information. Anyone can post information on the Internet, but the information does not have to be correct. Usually, government and educational institutions are reliable sources of information; personal Web sites may not contain accurate information.

Practice

1. Use an Internet search engine to find information about gamma rays. List three Web sites, and discuss how reliable each one might be.

Answer to Practice

1. Answers may vary. Students should consider the source of the Web site when discussing the site's reliability.

How Search Engines Work

Most search engines rely on Boolean logic. Boolean logic uses three words—*AND, OR,* and *NOT*—to define the relationships between topics. These three words, known as *Boolean operators*, can be used to make very effective searches.

Use the AND operator to find multiple terms.

When you use the AND operator between two search terms, both of the terms must be present in the results. For example, to find Web pages that contain both the words *work* and *power,* you would enter both search terms, as **Figure 19** shows. The shaded area of the Venn diagram in **Figure 19** represents the results of this search.

Figure 19 Search Results Using AND

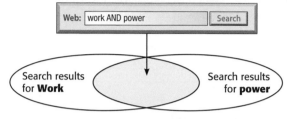

Note that the AND operator is in all capital letters. Some search engines require that you use all capital letters to distinguish the operators from the search terms.

Use the OR operator to find either term.

When you use the OR operator between two search terms, the results should show pages that contain either one or both of the terms. If you use the OR operator, your search result will have more Web pages, as the shaded area in **Figure 20** shows.

Figure 20 Search Results Using OR

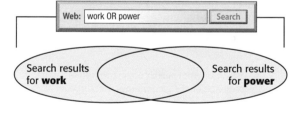

Use the NOT operator to exclude a term.

When you use the NOT operator before a word, your search results should not contain that term. This operator will help you narrow your search by excluding a certain set of Web pages that commonly have the word of the topic that you are looking for. **Figure 21** shows a Venn diagram of the search results for the search "work NOT power."

Figure 21 Search Results Using NOT

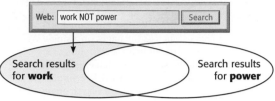

Using more than one Boolean operator will make your searches more specific. For example, to find Web sites that contain information about work and power, but not electricity, you would search "work AND power NOT electricity."

Some search engines do not support the direct use of Boolean operators. You may have to go to the advanced search page to do Boolean searches. Many advanced search pages allow you to fill in search fields that are similar to the Boolean operators, as **Figure 22** shows.

Figure 22 Search Fields and Boolean Operators

Advanced search field	Boolean operator
All of the words	AND
Any of the words	OR
None of the words	NOT

Practice

1. Write a Boolean search query to find Web pages that must contain the word *circuit* and either the word *series* or the word *parallel.*

2. Draw a Venn diagram to represent the search query that you wrote in item 1.

Answers to Practice

1. series OR parallel AND circuit
2. Answer may vary. Students' should draw three overlapping circles—one labeled *circuit,* one labeled *series,* and one labeled *parallel.* They should shade in the part of the *work* circle that overlaps with both the *series* and *parallel* circles to represent the results of their query.

Technology in the Library

Libraries are one of the best places to find highly reliable reference materials, such as encyclopedias, dictionaries, and nonfiction books. Printed materials are often subject to editing and peer review, unlike much of the information on the Internet. Libraries also have books, magazines, newspapers, and journals that may not be available on the Internet or are expensive to access.

If you do not have a specific source in mind, the best place to start your library research is the library's catalog. Most libraries now have systems for searching their catalogs by computer. So, searching the catalog is similar to using a search engine on the Web. When you are doing a library search, you should specify whether the keywords are for a subject, a title, or an author.

Once you have the results of a catalog search, you will need to know where to find the books that come up in your search results. Most libraries use one of two classification systems—the Library of Congress system or the Dewey decimal system. Whichever system your library uses, you should write down the call numbers for the books that you want to find from your catalog search. Then, use a map or directory of the library to find the books.

Both classification systems organize nonfiction books by subject, as **Figure 23** and **Figure 24** show. Most large libraries use the Library of Congress system, whereas many smaller libraries use the Dewey decimal system.

Figure 24 Library of Congress Classification System

Letter on book binding	Subject
A	General works
B	Philosophy, psychology, and religion
C–F	History
G–H	Geography and social sciences (e.g., anthropology)
J	Political science
K	Law
L	Education
M	Music
N	Fine arts
P	Literature
Q	Science
R	Medicine
S	Agriculture
T	Technology
U–V	Military and naval science
Z	Bibliography and library science

Figure 23 Dewey Decimal System

Number on book binding	Subject
000–099	General works
100–199	Philosophy and psychology
200–299	Religion
300–399	Social studies
400–499	Language
500–599	Pure sciences
600–699	Technology
700–799	Arts
800–899	Literature
900–999	History

Practice

1. What system does your school library use to classify books?
2. List three magazines or journals in your school or local library that could contain current information on scientific research.
3. Name the title and call number for a book on science.

Answers to Practice

1. Answers will depend on the system used in your library.
2. Answers may vary.
3. Answers may vary, but the call number should start with Q for the Library of Congress system or should start with a number between 500 and 599 for the Dewey Decimal System.

Scientific Methods

Scientists gain new knowledge and understanding of the natural world by using scientific methods. These methods are sometimes presented in a series of ordered steps. However, there is no single scientific method. The steps may be done in a different order, or certain steps may be repeated in some scientific investigations.

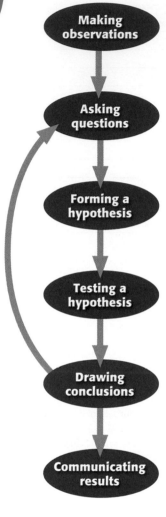

Making Observations Observing objects and events in the natural world is an important step in any scientific method. Observation is usually the starting point of any scientific study. You also make observations when doing experiments. It is important to keep detailed records of observations so that you can accurately remember them.

Asking Questions Careful observations eventually lead to questions. A good question should be specific and should serve as the focus for the entire investigation.

Forming a Hypothesis A hypothesis is a possible explanation or answer to your question. You do not know whether a hypothesis is the right answer until it is tested. You should be able to test your hypothesis to determine whether it is true or false. You should make predictions about what you think will happen if your hypothesis is true and what will happen if your hypothesis is false. These predictions can help you design an experiment to test the hypothesis.

Testing a Hypothesis Once you have a question, a hypothesis, and a set of predictions, you are ready to do an experiment to test the hypothesis. You should design your experiment to be as simple as possible, and you should consider which variables you want to control. Your design should also include plans about what instruments and materials you will use and how you will analyze the data that you collect.

Drawing Conclusions After you finish an experiment, you will determine whether your hypothesis is correct by examining your results. You may evaluate your hypothesis by seeing if your original predictions were correct. If your results do not support your hypothesis, they may lead you to ask more questions. You may need to form a new hypothesis, make new predictions, and perform a new or modified version of your experiment.

Communicating Results If you carry out an investigation that provides new information, you should publish your results. Others who read about your investigation may try to understand how you drew your conclusions. They may try your experiment to see if they get the same results or use your results to form new hypotheses and do new experiments.

Conducting Experiments

Many scientific experiments try to determine a cause-and-effect relationship—"When *A* happens, *B* happens." The *A* and the *B* in this relationship are variables, or changing quantities. The variable that you change intentionally in an experiment is called the *independent variable* and, in this case, is *A*. The *dependent variable*, *B*, changes in response to the changes in the independent variable.

Suppose that your experiment is seeking to answer the following question: "What happens to the speed of a motor when the voltage of the power supply changes?" In this case, voltage would be the independent variable, and the speed of the motor would be the dependent variable. You would change the voltage and then measure the resulting change in speed. When you graph your results, independent variables are represented on the *x*-axis, and dependent variables are represented on the *y*-axis.

Make observations in the lab.

You should write down any observations that you make during an experiment, along with any data that you collect. Record the characteristics of the materials that you use, the conditions during your experiment, any changes that occur, and anything that you think might be relevant to the experiment. These observations will help you when you are reporting your results. They can also help you figure out why your experimental results may not be what you expected. Usually, a pen is used to record your observations in a lab notebook because people reading the notes later can be sure that you did not change your notes after the experiment.

Avoid measurement pitfalls.

One common error in taking measurements results from parallax. *Parallax* is an apparent shift in position caused by a change in viewing angle. To avoid parallax errors, always line up your eyes with the part of the measurement scale that you are reading.

Another common measurement error is recording the wrong units of measurement. Always check the instrument to make sure that you know which units it uses, and record those units.

Taking Measurements

It is important to note the limits of the tools that you use to collect data. The exactness of a measurement is called *precision*, and it is determined by the instrument that you use. Precision is reflected in the number of significant figures. When you record measurements, you should use the correct number of significant figures. Usually, instruments with a digital readout give you the correct number of significant figures. So, you can record the measurement exactly as you see it on the instrument. When you need to read the measurement from a scale on an instrument, you should record as many digits as are marked on the scale and estimate one more digit beyond that.

Measure volume with a graduated cylinder.

You should use a graduated cylinder when you need precise measurements of volume.

1. Place the graduated cylinder on a flat, level surface.

2. Make sure that you are at eye level with the surface of the liquid.

3. Read the mark closest to the liquid level. Because most liquids climb slightly up the glass walls of a graduated cylinder, they produce a curved surface called a *meniscus*, shown in **Figure 25**. You should always take volume readings from the bottom of the meniscus.

Tip Holding a piece of white paper behind the graduated cylinder can make the meniscus easier to see.

Figure 25 Meniscus in a Graduated Cylinder

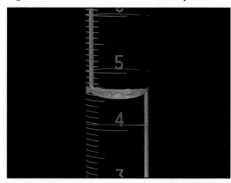

Measure mass with a balance.

A triple-beam balance, shown in **Figure 26,** can measure mass to a precision of 0.01 g.

❶ Make sure that the balance is properly "zeroed." First, make sure that the balance is on a level surface. Then, slide all of the slider weights to zero. Turn the zero adjustment knob until the pointer is in line with the zero at the center of the arrow.

❷ Place the object to be measured on the pan. **Caution:** Never place chemicals or hot objects directly on the balance pan.

❸ To determine the total mass of the object, add the readings from all three beams.

❹ Move the largest slider weight to the right along the beam until the balance tips. Then, move the slider back one notch so that the beam tips back the other way. Repeat this step for the next-largest slider weight. Then, move the smallest slider weight to the right until the pointer points to the zero on the right end.

❺ If you are measuring solid chemicals, start by putting a piece of weighing paper on the pan. Record the mass of the weighing paper. Then, place the chemical on the weighing paper. Measure the total mass of the chemical and paper. Then, subtract the mass of the paper to determine the mass of the chemical alone. You may use a similar method for measuring the mass of a liquid in a container.

Tip If you want to use a specified amount of a substance, move the sliders to the right by the amount of mass that you want to obtain. The balance will tip. Slowly add the substance until the balance points to zero.

Measure temperature with a thermometer.

Digital thermometers and bulb thermometers are often used in the lab. Bulb thermometers consist of a column of liquid—either mercury or colored alcohol—in a glass tube, as shown in **Figure 27**. As the liquid heats up, it expands, so the column of liquid rises up the tube.

❶ To measure temperature with a digital thermometer, immerse the probe in the liquid or touch it to an object. Wait for the digital read-out to stabilize, and then record the temperature. Make sure that the thermometer is set to the desired scale (Celsius or Fahrenheit).

❷ To measure temperature with a bulb thermometer, put the thermometer in the liquid to be measured. Wait for the level of colored liquid inside the thermometer to stabilize.

❸ With your eyes level with the top of the liquid inside the thermometer, take the reading on the scale next to the column of liquid. Pay attention to the scale on the thermometer. The smallest unit marked on a bulb thermometer is usually 1 °C. These markings are close together, so you can only estimate half a unit between marks, or 0.05 °C.

CAUTION A glass thermometer can break if it hits a solid object or overheats. In addition to producing broken glass, the liquid inside will spill. If a mercury thermometer should ever break, immediately notify your teacher or another adult. Let your teacher clean up the spill. Do not touch the mercury. Because mercury is a hazardous substance, mercury thermometers are rarely used in class laboratories.

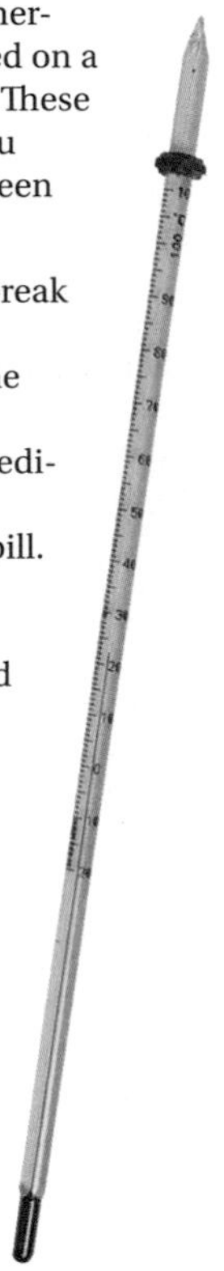

Figure 26 Triple-Beam Balance

Figure 27 Alcohol Thermometer

Communicating Scientific Results

Whether you are writing a laboratory report for your teacher or submitting a paper to a scientific journal, you should use a similar structure to report the results of an experiment. Your lab report should contain enough information so that others can use it to reproduce your experiment and compare their results to yours. Laboratory reports should contain the same basic parts.

Start with a title.

Choose a title that clearly conveys the nature of the experiment. The title could describe the subject, the hypothesis, or the result. If you are doing an experiment from a lab manual, this title could be the same as the title of the experiment given in the manual.

Include background information.

The background section should briefly explain why your experiment is important. State the question that your experiment is trying to answer. You could also include a description of the initial observations that led you to the question. Sometimes, the background section includes the basic principles that you will use when you analyze your experiment.

State your hypothesis.

This section should state your hypothesis and your predictions of what will happen if the hypothesis is true and what will happen if the hypothesis if false. Your hypothesis is what you think will happen in the experiment. Often, a hypothesis is written as an "If . . . then" statement. The independent variable, or variable that you will change, should follow the "If" in the statement. The effect on the dependent variable should follow the "then" in the statement. Suppose that you want to find out if adding salt to water changes the boiling temperature of water. You would change the amount of salt that you add to water and measure the temperature at which the water boils. So, the amount of salt would be your independent variable, and the boiling temperature would be your dependent variable. Your hypothesis statement could be "If salt is added to water, the temperature at which water boils will increase."

List your materials before you start your experiment.

To make sure that you have everything that you need for your experiment, list all of the equipment and other supplies that you use in the experiment. For experiments taken from a lab manual, these materials are usually listed in the manual.

Describe the procedure that you used.

Detailed steps that describe exactly how you did your experiment are included in the procedure. Include details about how you set up the equipment, how you took your measurements, and what analysis or calculations you did with your data after collecting it. Your description should be detailed enough that someone else could reproduce the experiment exactly as you did it. If you are doing an experiment from a lab manual, you should write the steps in your own words and note anything that you did that was different from the procedure in the manual.

Record your observations, data, and analysis.

You should list all of the data you collected and show the results of any analysis or calculations that you performed with the data. It is often useful to present data or other results using tables or graphs. Also, include any observations that you made that might be relevant to your conclusions. Some experiments in lab manuals list specific questions that you should answer in your analysis.

End the report with your conclusions.

In your conclusions, you should discuss whether or not your experiment supports your original hypothesis. Remember that your experiment may not support your hypothesis. You can still explain why you think that the experiment did not turn out the way that you expected. You can also present a new or modified hypothesis and briefly describe additional experiments that could be done if you were to continue or expand your investigation. Some experiments in lab manuals list specific questions that you should answer in your conclusions.

Figure 1 The Electromagnetic Spectrum

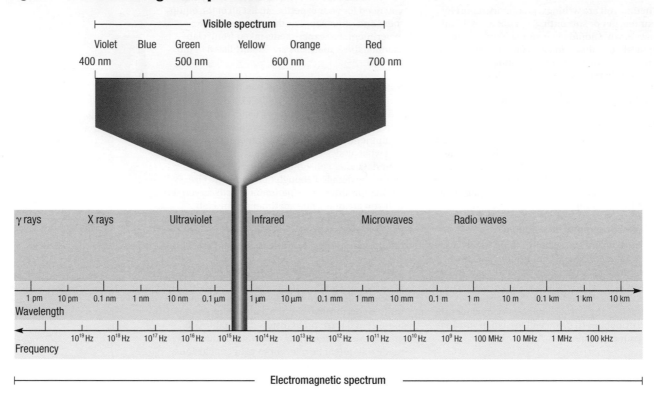

Figure 2 SI Base Units

Quantity	Unit	Symbol
Length	meter	m
Mass	kilogram	kg
Time	second	s
Temperature	kelvin	K
Electric current	ampere	A
Amount of substance	mole	mol
Luminous intensity	candela	cd

Figure 3 Other Commonly Used Units

Quantity	Unit	Symbol	Conversion
Electric charge	coulomb	C	$1\ \text{A·s}$
Temperature	degree Celsius	°C	$1\ \text{K}$
Frequency	hertz	Hz	$1/s$
Work and energy	joule	J	$\dfrac{1\ \text{kg·m}^2}{\text{s}^2} = 1\ \text{N·m}$
Force	newton	N	$1\ \dfrac{\text{kg·m}}{\text{s}^2}$
Pressure	pascal	Pa	$1\ \dfrac{\text{kg}}{\text{m·s}^2} = 1\ \dfrac{\text{N}}{\text{m}^2}$
Angular displacement	radian	rad	(unitless)
Electric potential difference	volt	V	$1\ \dfrac{\text{kg·m}^2}{\text{A·s}^3} = 1\ \dfrac{\text{J}}{\text{C}}$
Power	watt	W	$1\ \dfrac{\text{kg·m}^2}{\text{s}^3} = 1\ \dfrac{\text{J}}{\text{s}}$
Resistance	ohm	Ω	$1\ \dfrac{\text{kg·m}^2}{\text{A}^2\text{·s}^3} = 1\ \dfrac{\text{V}}{\text{A}}$

Figure 4 Densities of Various Materials

Material	Density (g/cm³)
Air, dry	1.293×10^{-3}
Aluminum	2.70
Bone	1.7–2.0
Brick, common	1.9
Butter	0.86–0.87
Carbon (diamond)	3.5155
Carbon (graphite)	2.2670
Copper	8.96
Cork	0.22–0.26
Ethanol	0.783
Gasoline	0.7
Gold	19.3
Helium	1.78×10^{-4}
Iron	7.86
Lead	11.3
Mercury	13.5336
Paper	0.7–1.15
Rock salt	2.18
Silver	10.5
Sodium	0.97
Stainless steel	8.02
Steel	7.8
Sugar	1.59
Water (at 25 °C)	0.99705
Water (ice)	0.917

Figure 5 Specific Heats

Material	c (J/kg•K)
Acetic acid (CH_3COOH)	2,070
Air	1,007
Aluminum (Al)	897
Calcium (Ca)	647
Calcium carbonate ($CaCO_3$)	818
Carbon (C, diamond)	487
Carbon (C, graphite)	709
Carbon dioxide (CO_2)	843
Copper (Cu)	385
Ethanol (CH_3CH_2OH)	2,440
Gold (Au)	129
Helium (He)	5,193
Hematite (Fe_2O_3)	650
Hydrogen (H_2)	14,304
Hydrogen peroxide (H_2O_2)	2,620
Iron (Fe)	449
Lead (Pb)	129
Magnetite (Fe_3O_4)	619
Mercury (Hg)	140
Methane (CH_4)	2,200
Neon (Ne)	1,030
Nickel (Ni)	444
Nitrogen (N_2)	1,040
Oxygen (O_2)	918
Platinum (Pt)	133
Silver (Ag)	234
Sodium (Na)	1,228
Sodium chloride (NaCl)	864
Tin (Sn)	228
Tungsten (W)	132
Water (H_2O)	4,186
Zinc (Zn)	388

Values at 25 °C and 1 atm pressure

Figure 6 Properties of the Planets

Planet	Diameter (km)	Average surface temperature (°C)	Number of moons	Atmosphere
Mercury	4,879	350	0	Essentially none
Venus	12,104	460	0	Thick: carbon dioxide, nitrogen
Earth	12,756	20	1	Nitrogen, oxygen
Mars	6,794	−23	2	Thin: carbon dioxide
Jupiter	142,984	−130	63	Hydrogen, helium, ammonia, methane
Saturn	120,536	−180	47	Hydrogen, helium, ammonia, methane
Uranus	51,118	−210	27	Hydrogen, helium, ammonia, methane
Neptune	49,528	−220	13	Hydrogen, helium, methane

Figure 7 International Weather Symbols

Current weather

Hail	△	Light drizzle		Light rain		Light snow	*
Freezing rain		Steady, light drizzle		Steady, light rain		Steady, light snow	* *
Smoke		Intermittent, moderate drizzle		Intermittent, moderate rain		Intermittent, moderate snow	
Tornado	)(	Steady, moderate drizzle		Steady, moderate rain		Steady, moderate snow	
Dust storms		Intermittent, heavy drizzle		Intermittent, heavy rain		Intermittent, heavy snow	
Fog	≡	Steady, heavy drizzle		Steady, heavy rain		Steady, heavy snow	
Thunderstorm							
Lightning	<						
Hurricane							

Cloud coverage

Clear	◯	Scattered		Four-eighths covered		Seven-eighths covered	
One-eighth Coverage		Three-eighths covered		Five-eighths covered		Overcast	●

Clouds

Low:	Stratus	—	Cumulus		Cumulonimbus calvus	
	Stratocumulus		Cumulus congestus		Cumulonimbus with anvil	
Middle:	Altostratus	∠	Altocumulus		Altocumulus castellanus	M
High:	Cirrus		Cirrostratus	2	Cirrocumulus	

Wind speed (in km/h)

Calm	◎	4–13		24–33	
1–3	—	14–23		34–40	

Figure 8 Sky Maps for the Northern Hemisphere

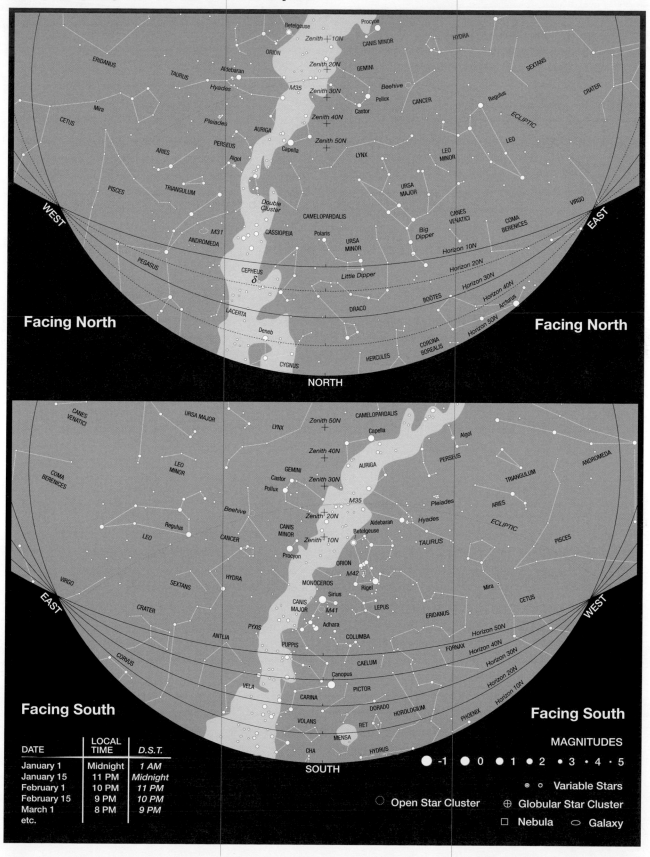

DATE	LOCAL TIME	D.S.T.
January 1	Midnight	*1 AM*
January 15	11 PM	*Midnight*
February 1	10 PM	*11 PM*
February 15	9 PM	*10 PM*
March 1	8 PM	*9 PM*
etc.		

MAGNITUDES

●−1 ● 0 ● 1 ● 2 • 3 · 4 · 5

⊚ ○ Variable Stars

○ Open Star Cluster   ⊕ Globular Star Cluster

□ Nebula   ◯ Galaxy

Figure 9 The World: Physical

ELEVATION

Feet		Meters
13,120		4,000
6,560		2,000
1,640		500
656		200
(Sea level) 0		0 (Sea level)
Below sea level		Below sea level

Ice cap

SCALE: at Equator

0   500   1,000   1,500   2,000 Miles

0   1,000   1,500 Kilometers

Projection: Mollweide

APPENDIX C

ARCTIC 80N OCEAN
North Cape
BARENTS SEA
KARA SEA
LAPTEV SEA
EAST SIBERIAN SEA
EUROPE
BALTIC SEA
Volga River
Ob River
URAL MOUNTAINS
Yenisei River
Lena River
Kolyma River
60N
SEA OF OKHOTSK
KAMCHATKA PENINSULA
Sakhalin Island
Amur River
ALTAY MOUNTAINS
ARAL SEA
Balqash Lake
Lake Baikal
BLACK SEA
CASPIAN
ASIA
GOBI
Huang He
40N
MEDITERRANEAN SEA
Tigris River
Euphrates River
PERSIAN GULF
HIMALAYAS
Chang River
SEA OF JAPAN
Hokkaido
Honshu
Shikoku
Kyushu
EAST CHINA SEA
Taiwan
Tropic of Cancer
20N
SAHARA
RED SEA
Nile River
ARABIAN PENINSULA
THAR DESERT
Indus River
Ganges River
Mekong
ARABIAN SEA
BAY OF BENGAL
PACIFIC
OCEAN
AFRICA
Sri Lanka
STRAIT OF MALACCA
SOUTH CHINA SEA
Philippine Islands
Congo River
Lake Tanganyika
Lake Victoria
MALAY PENINSULA
Borneo
Sumatra
Celebes
New Guinea
Solomon Islands
Equator 0
Java
INDIAN OCEAN
Madagascar
MOZAMBIQUE
CORAL SEA
New Hebrides
New Caledonia
Fiji Islands
20S
KALAHARI DESERT
GREAT SANDY DESERT
AUSTRALIA
Tropic of Capricorn
GREAT VICTORIA DESERT
Darling River
GREAT DIVIDING RANGE
Cape of Good Hope
TASMAN SEA
NEW ZEALAND
North Island
60S
Tasmania
South Island
ANTARCTICA
20E 40E 60E 80E 100E 120E 140E 160E

Europe
N W E S
DENMARK
Iceland
North Cape
BARENTS SEA
KARA SEA
KJÖLEN MTS.
0 250 500 750 Miles
0 250 500 750 Kilometers
Projection: Mollweide
60N
ATLANTIC OCEAN
NORTH SEA
British Isles
BALTIC SEA
Volga River
URAL MTS.
50N
Rhine R.
Danube
ALPS
Tigris R.
BAY OF BISCAY
40N
BLACK SEA
STRAIT OF GIBRALTAR
MEDITERRANEAN SEA
Crete

Figure 10 Map of Natural Resources in the United States

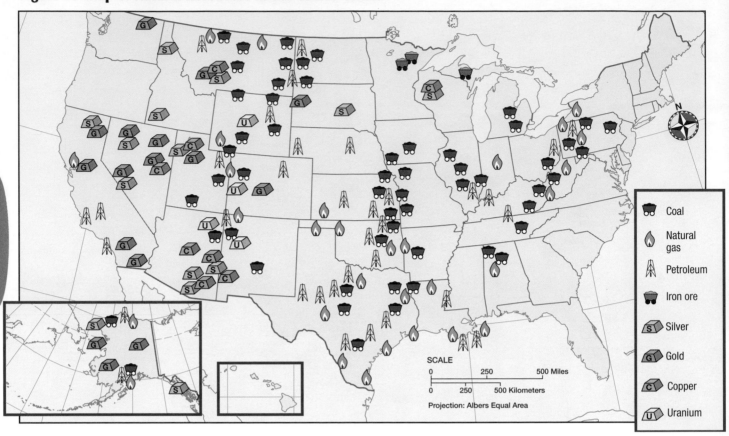

Coal	
Natural gas	
Petroleum	
Iron ore	
Silver	
Gold	
Copper	
Uranium	

SCALE

0   250   500 Miles

0   250   500 Kilometers

Projection: Albers Equal Area

Figure 11 Typical Weather Map

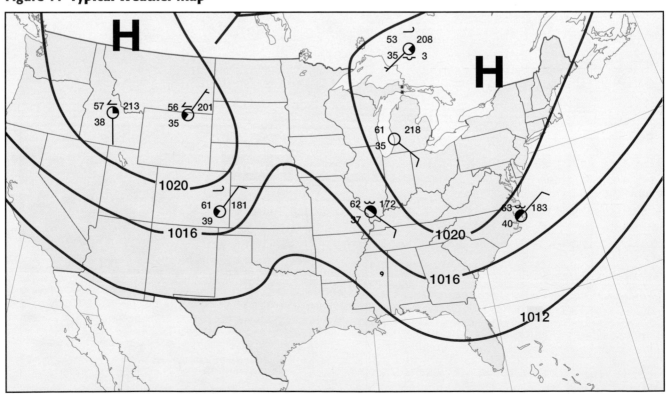

Selected Math Answers

Chapter 1
Introduction to Science

Practice, page 19
2. 1,600 g
4. 6,100 mA

Section 2 Review, page 21
10. 420 m

Practice, page 25
2. **a.** 4,500 g
b. 0.0000000199 cm

Practice, page 26
2. **a.** 5.5×10^5 cm^2
b. 6.9 g/cm^3

Section 3 Review, page 28
6. **a.** 9.20×10^7 m^2
b. 9.66×10^{-5} cm^2

Chapter Review, page 37
28. **a.** 2.6×10^{14} A•s
b. 6.42×10^{-7} m^3/s
30. **a.** 133 m^2
b. 210 L/min

Chapter 2
Matter

Practice, page 54
2. 3.26 g/cm^3

Section 2 Review, page 58
6. 1.4×10^{-4} g/cm^3

Science Skills Practice, page 68
2. 0.001 g/mm^3
4. greater; 700,000 g/m^3

Chapter Review, page 71
24. 4.5 g/cm^3
26. 61 cm^3

Chapter 3
States of Matter

Section 3 Review, page 94
8. 273 Pa

Practice, page 98
2. 200 mL

Section 4 Review, page 101
10. 3.50×10^3 L

Chapter Review, page 107
26. 5×10^3 N
28. 12 L

Chapter 4
Atoms

Section 2 Review, page 127
14. 620 g Hg
16. 51.3 mol He

Chapter Review, page 139
28. 407 g Al

Chapter 6
The Structure of Matter

Practice, page 193
2. $BeCl_2$

Practice, page 196
2. BH_3

Section 3 Review, page 196
6. H_2SO_4

Chapter Review, page 211
24. **a.** $Sr(NO_3)_2$
b. NaCN
c. $Cr(OH)_3$

Chapter 7
Chemical Reactions

Science Skills Practice, page 250
2. 323.0 g $ZnSO_4$

Chapter Review, page 253
20. $2HgO \rightarrow 2Hg + O_2$

Chapter 8
Solutions

Practice, page 280
2. 1.27 M

Section 3 Review, page 281
8. 0.374 M

Chapter Review, page 287
24. 0.600 mol LiCl
26. 40.6 g NaF

Chapter 9
Acids, Bases, and Salts

Practice, page 299
2. pH = 2

Section 1 Review, page 300
10. 1×10^{-11} M

Chapter Review, page 319
28. pH = 3
30. 1×10^{-6} M

Chapter 10
Nuclear Changes

Practice, page 331

2. $A = 4$
$Z = 2$
$X = \text{He}$
Alpha decay occurs, and ^4_2He is produced.

4. $A = 208$
$Z = 81$
$X = \text{Tl}$
Alpha decay occurs, and $^{208}_{81}\text{Tl}$ is produced.

Practice, page 334

2. 15.3 days

4. 29.1 years

Section 1 Review, page 336

6. $A = 131$
$Z = 54$
$X = \text{Xe}$
$^{131}_{54}\text{Xe}$

8. 2×10^6 years

Science Skills Practice, 354

2. 3 half-lives

Chapter Review, page 357

30. a. $^{212}_{83}\text{Bi} \rightarrow {}^{208}_{81}\text{Tl} + {}^4_2\text{He}$

$^{208}_{81}\text{Tl} \rightarrow {}^{208}_{82}\text{Pb} + {}^{\ 0}_{-1}e$

b. $^{212}_{83}\text{Bi} \rightarrow {}^{212}_{84}\text{Po} + {}^{\ 0}_{-1}e$

$^{212}_{84}\text{Po} \rightarrow {}^{208}_{82}\text{Pb} + {}^4_2\text{He}$

Chapter 11
Motion

Practice, page 369

2. 22 m/s toward first base

Section 1 Review, page 371

6. 400 s or 6.67 min

Practice, page 375

2. 0.075 m/s^2 toward the shore

4. 0.85 s

Section 2 Review, page 377

6. acceleration $= 2.5 \text{ m/s}^2$

Chapter Review, page 391

22. 6.6 h

24. 5.4 s

Chapter 12
Forces

Practice, page 401

2. 0.14 kg

4. 2.2 m/s^2 forward

Section 1 Review, page 402

6. 0.26 m/s^2 forward

Section 2 Review, page 410

6. 4,000,000 N

Practice, page 415

2. 6 m/s forward

Science Skills Practice, page 420

2. 3.5 m/s^2 in a backward direction (deceleration)

Chapter Review, page 423

22. 3.7 N

Chapter 13
Work and Energy

Practice, page 432

2. 1 J

4. 6,000 J

Practice, page 434

2. a. 146 W
b. 175 W

Practice, page 436

2. 78 N

Section 1 Review, page 437

6. MA $= 2.40$

8. 2.0×10^4 W, 27 hp

Practice, page 446

2. 15 m

Practice, page 448

2. 3.3 m/s

Section 3 Review, page 452

8. 900 J

Practice, page 460

2. work input $= 4,800$ J

Section 4 Review, page 461

8. a. useful work output $= 780$ J
b. 780 W

Chapter Review, page 467

24. a. 850 J
b. 170 W
c. 4

APPENDIX D

Chapter 14
Heat and Temperature

Practice, page 477

2. Row 1: 70 °F, 294 K
   Row 2: 115 °C, 239 °F
   Row 3: −321 °F, 77 K
   Row 4: 43 °C, 316 K

4. d

Section 1 Review, page 479

6. 68.0 °F, 293 K

Practice, page 486

2. 28,000 J (28 kJ)

Section 2 Review, page 487

6. 550 kJ

Science Skills Practice, page 496

2. 1.0 kg

Chapter Review, page 499

24. −270 °C, −454 °F

26. 480 J/kg•K

Chapter 15
Waves

Practice, page 519

2. 5.77×10^{14} Hz

Section 2 Review, page 523

8. 0.77 m

Chapter Review, page 535

30. 3.0 m/s

32. 440.0 Hz

Chapter 16
Sound and Light

Science Skills Practice, page 576

2. 1.36×10^3 W/m^2

Chapter Review, page 579

30. 41 m

32. 5.5×10^{14} Hz

Chapter 17
Electricity

Practice, page 597

2. 240 Ω

4. 0.43 A

Section 2 Review, page 599

8. 0.5 A

Practice, page 606

2. 1.6×10^{-2} W

4. 120 V

Section 3 Review, page 607

8. 40 W

Chapter Review, page 613

24. b

26. 120 V

28. 1.6 A

Answers to Reading Checks

Chapter 1
Introduction to Science

Section 1, page 7
Roentgen repeated his experiment.

Section 1, page 9
A scientific law explains how something works but does not explain why it happens. A scientific theory explains why something happens.

Section 1, page 11
Models can be pictures on paper, real objects, and mental pictures.

Section 2, page 15
No, the sequence of steps in a scientific method can vary depending on the question that you are trying to answer.

Section 2, page 16
Scientists should publish their results so the results can be reviewed by other scientists.

Section 2, page 18
SI units are used to express very small or large measurements, so that you do not have to write many zeros.

Section 3, page 23
I should use a line graph to represent data that changes continuously during an experiment.

Section 3, page 24
I should use scientific notation when working with very large or very small numbers.

Section 3, page 27
The answer should have as many significant figures as the least precise value that I am adding.

Chapter 2
Matter

Section 1, page 46
No, elements cannot be broken down into simpler substances.

Section 1, page 48
Compounds are pure substances because they have fixed compositions and definite properties.

Section 2, page 52
Answers should list five physical properties. Physical properties include shape, color, mass, odor, texture, state, melting point, boiling point, strength, hardness, density, and the ability to conduct electricity, magnetism, or heat.

Section 2, page 54
Water's density is 1.00 g/mL.

Section 2, page 56
Two chemical properties are flammability and reactivity.

Section 3, page 61
Physical changes do not change the identity of a substance, whereas chemical changes do.

Section 3, page 63
Compounds can be broken down only by chemical changes because compounds are made of atoms that are chemically combined. Mixtures can be separated by physical changes because substances in a mixture are not chemically combined.

Chapter 3
States of Matter

Section 1, page 79
Liquids do not change volume, but gases do.

Section 1, page 80
Temperature is a measure of the average kinetic energy of the particles in an object.

Section 2, page 85
Answers may vary. One example of sublimation is dry ice changing into gaseous carbon dioxide.

Section 2, page 86
The freezing and melting points are the same.

Section 3, page 91
A substance that is denser than another substance will sink in that substance, whereas a substance that is less dense will float.

Section 3, page 92
A small force is applied to a small area. This force exerts pressure on a liquid in the device. The pressure is transmitted equally to a larger area, where the pressure creates a larger force.

Section 4, page 97
Boyle's law relates pressure and volume.

Section 4, page 99
The pressure decreases.

Chapter 4
Atoms

Section 1, page 114
Dalton and Democritus both believed that atoms are the fundamental units of matter and that atoms are indivisible.

Section 1, page 117
Rutherford's results were surprising because they did not match his predictions based on Thomson's model of the atom. He expected most of the positive particles to pass straight through, but instead, several were deflected at large angles.

Section 2, page 121
The atomic number defines the element because atoms of each element always have the same number of protons but can have different numbers of neutrons.

Section 2, page 122
The isotope tritium ($A = 3$) has the most mass.

Section 2, page 125
A mole of iron contains 6.022×10^{23} iron atoms.

Section 3, page 129
In earlier atomic models, electrons were considered to be particles. In the electron-wave model, electrons act more like waves than like particles.

Section 3, page 131
An electron jumps to an excited state when it absorbs a photon.

Chapter 5
The Periodic Table

Section 1, page 146
Mendeleev left gaps in his periodic table for the new elements that he predicted would be discovered. These gaps were needed to make the patterns work out correctly.

Section 2, page 153
Group 1 and group 17 elements easily form ions because the addition or removal of a single electron creates a full outer energy level.

Section 2, page 154
The category "metals" contains the most elements, and the category "semiconductors" contains the least elements.

Section 3, page 157
Alkali metals are reactive because each atom has one valence electron that can easily be removed. Thus, they form compounds very easily.

Section 3, page 159
Answers will vary. Transition metals include gold, silver, platinum, and titanium.

Section 3, page 161
The noble gases are unreactive because their s and p orbitals are full of electrons.

Section 3, page 163
Answers will vary but could include chlorophyll, glucose, and isooctane.

Chapter 6
The Structure of Matter

Section 1, page 178
A ball-and-stick model shows bond lengths, and a space-filling model shows relative atom sizes.

Section 1, page 180
The hardness of minerals is explained by the fact that their chemical structure consists of rigid networks of bonded atoms.

Section 2, page 184
In an ionic bond, ions are held together by the attraction between their opposite charges.

Section 2, page 186
Covalently bonded atoms are held together by the sharing of electrons between the atoms.

Section 2, page 189
Parentheses are used in a chemical formula to represent the fact that a polyatomic ion acts as a single unit.

Section 3, page 192
The number of each kind of ion in a compound is determined by whatever number of those ions will give a charge of zero to the compound.

Section 3, page 194

An empirical formula shows the simplest possible ratio of atoms present in a compound.

Section 4, page 199

The shortest carbon chain with more than one possible arrangement is one with four carbon atoms; carbon chains with three or fewer carbon atoms cannot form branched chains.

Section 4, page 201

A polymer is a molecule that is a long chain of smaller molecules called *monomers*.

Section 4, page 202

You need to eat carbohydrates so your body can get the energy that it needs.

Chapter 7
Chemical Reactions

Section 1, page 221

Most of the energy that is released in a chemical reaction comes from the stored energy in chemical bonds.

Section 1, page 222

An exothermic reaction is a reaction that releases energy, and an endothermic reaction is a reaction that absorbs energy.

Section 2, page 226

Chemical equations should be balanced so that they accurately show the conservation of mass in a chemical reaction.

Section 3, page 231

Decomposition reactions are the opposite processes of synthesis reactions.

Section 3, page 233

In all single-displacement reactions, one reactant changes place with part of another reactant.

Section 3, page 235

A free radical, an atom or molecule with an unpaired electron, is very reactive because electrons tend to form pairs with each other.

Section 4, page 239

Reactions are faster at higher temperatures because molecular motion is greater at higher temperatures, so more-frequent collisions between molecules occur.

Section 4, page 241

An enzyme catalyzes biological reactions.

Section 4, page 244

When a soda bottle is opened, the pressure of the gas on top of the soda is released, so the dissolved gas in the soda can come out of solution.

Chapter 8
Solutions

Section 1, page 260

The particles will settle out of a suspension if it is left undisturbed.

Section 1, page 263

Atoms, ions, or molecules of solute are present in a solution.

Section 1, page 264

A solid, liquid, or gas can be mixed with a liquid to form a solution.

Section 2, page 269

Hydrogen bonding occurs between the hydrogen atom of one water molecule and the oxygen atom of another molecule.

Section 2, page 271

Increasing the surface area of a solid exposes more of the molecules in the solid to the solvent. So, there are more collisions between the solute and the solvent molecules, and the solid dissolves faster.

Section 3, page 277

Sodium iodide is soluble because the forces between the water molecules and the sodium ions and the iodide ions are much greater than the forces between the sodium ions and iodide ions in the crystal.

Section 3, page 278

The solute will not dissolve and will sink to the bottom of the solution.

Chapter 9
Acids, Bases, and Salts

Section 1, page 295

I should wear safety goggles, gloves, and a laboratory apron when working with acids.

Section 1, page 296

Metal hydroxides are strong bases because they dissociate completely when they dissolve in water.

Section 1, page 298

The pH of a solution tells me how acidic or basic a solution is by telling me the concentration of hydroxide ions in solution.

Section 2, page 303

Water and a salt form when an acid reacts with a base. When a weak base reacts with a strong acid, the resulting solution will be acidic.

Section 2, page 305

Answers may vary. Sample answer: Salts are used in ceramic glazes, as chalk, and as a highway de-icer.

Section 3, page 309

Detergents do not form soap scum, so they are used instead of soap.

Section 3, page 310

Chlorine gas will be produced if an acid is mixed with bleach.

Chapter 10
Nuclear Changes

Section 1, page 328

An alpha particle is the nucleus of a helium atom.

Section 1, page 330

The mass number does not change, but the atomic number increases by 1.

Section 2, page 338

The maximum number of protons in a stable nucleus is 83.

Section 2, page 340

A nuclear chain reaction is triggered by a single neutron that strikes a nucleus.

Section 3, page 349

There is more energy in the known reserves of uranium than in the known reserves of coal and oil.

Chapter 11
Motion

Section 1, page 366

Distance measures how far an object travels along a path. Displacement measures how far it is between the starting and ending points of the path.

Section 1, page 368

Average speed is calculated by dividing the distance traveled by the time it takes to travel that distance.

Section 2, page 373

Any object standing still on Earth's surface is traveling in a circle (accelerating) as Earth revolves, including people.

Section 2, page 374

A positive velocity means that an object is speeding up, and a negative velocity means that an object is slowing down.

Section 3, page 382

When an unbalanced force acts on an object, the object accelerates in the direction of the combined force.

Chapter 12
Forces

Section 1, page 398

Inertia is directly related to mass; the larger an object's mass is, the greater its inertia will be.

Section 1, page 401

The newton (N) is the SI unit of force. The pound (lb) is also used to measure force.

Section 2, page 404

Mass is a measure of how much matter is in an object; weight is a measure of the gravitational force that acts on an object. Weight depends on the gravitational force at a location, but mass does not depend on an object's location.

Section 2, page 406

Gravitational force increases as mass increases.

Section 2, page 408

Astronauts seem weightless because they are accelerating toward Earth at the same rate as their spacecraft. They are in free fall.

Section 3, page 413

Force pairs do not cancel out each other because the action and reaction forces do not act on the same object.

Section 3, page 414

Momentum is proportional to the mass and velocity of an object.

Chapter 13
Work and Energy

Section 1, page 433

The SI unit for power is the watt, which equals 1 J/s.

Section 1, page 434

Machines make work easier by either multiplying a force or changing the direction of the applied force.

Section 2, page 440

The mechanical advantage of a single fixed pulley is one.

Section 2, page 442

The wedge and the screw are both modified inclined planes.

Section 3, page 445

A stretched rubber band has elastic potential energy.

Section 3, page 447

The SI unit for kinetic energy is the joule.

Section 3, page 449

Chemical energy depends on the relative positions of the atoms in molecules.

Section 4, page 454

The potential energy on a roller coaster is smallest at the roller coaster's lowest point.

Section 4, page 457

An open system exchanges both energy and matter with the surroundings. A closed system exchanges energy, but not matter, with the surroundings.

Section 4, page 459

Energy may be lost as heat, sound, and vibrations.

Chapter 14
Heat and Temperature

Section 1, page 474

The temperature of a substance is proportional to the kinetic energy of its particles.

Section 1, page 476

The Celsius temperature scale has 0 defined as the freezing point of water, whereas the Kelvin temperature scale has 0 defined as absolute zero.

Section 2, page 482

Radiation differs from conduction and convection because radiation does not involve the movement of matter and therefore can take place in a vacuum.

Section 2, page 484

A material through which energy can be easily transferred as heat is a good conductor.

Section 3, page 491

The second law of thermodynamics states that disorder will always increase in a system left to itself.

Chapter 15
Waves

Section 1, page 506

No, light waves are not mechanical. They are electromagnetic.

Section 1, page 508

Most waves are caused by vibrating objects.

Section 1, page 511

Answers may vary. One example of a transverse wave is an electromagnetic wave.

Section 1, page 512

In a transverse wave, the wave motion and the vibrations are perpendicular. In a longitudinal wave, they are parallel.

Section 2, page 515

The wavelength can be measured from any two identical, consecutive points, such as from crest to crest.

Section 2, page 516

Period and frequency are inversely related.

Section 2, page 518

Wave speed equals wavelength divided by period, or wavelength times frequency.

Section 2, page 521

Sound waves travel faster in solids than in liquids or gases because the particles are closer together and, thus, can transfer vibrations faster.

Section 3, page 525

Answers may vary. One example of diffraction is hearing sounds from inside a room when you are standing outside the room's doorway.

Section 3, page 526

Both involve the bending of waves. Diffraction is the bending of waves around an obstacle, whereas refraction is the bending that occurs when a wave passes into a new medium.

Chapter 16
Sound and Light

Section 1, page 545

The amplitude determines the intensity of a sound wave.

Section 1, page 546

The lowest frequency that humans can hear is 20 Hz, and the highest frequency that humans can hear is 20,000 Hz.

Section 1, page 548
Resonance amplifies sound because two objects are vibrating at the same frequency.

Section 2, page 553
The particle model of light can be used to explain why blue light can knock electrons out of a metal plate but red light cannot.

Section 2, page 555
The intensity of light depends on the number of photons per second that pass through a certain area of space.

Section 2, page 557
Answers may include heat lamps, weather satellites, and computer mice, all of which use infrared light.

Section 3, page 560
Light rays are used to model reflection and refraction.

Section 3, page 562
A virtual image is the result of the apparent path of the light rays and appears to be behind the mirror.

Section 4, page 567
The fish seems closer because the light rays coming from the fish bend away from the normal when they pass from water to air. The cat sees a virtual image of the fish.

Section 4, page 567
A converging lens can create a real image.

Chapter 17
Electricity

Section 1, page 586
Like charges repel and unlike charges attract each other.

Section 1, page 589
Charging by friction causes static electricity.

Section 1, page 591
Electric force depends on charge and distance.

Section 2, page 594
Potential difference is commonly called *voltage*.

Section 2, page 596
The resistance equation is called *Ohm's law*.

Section 3, page 601
Switches are used to interrupt the electric current in a circuit.

Section 3, page 602
Standardized symbols are used to draw schematic diagrams.

Chapter 18
Magnetism

Section 1, page 620
Heating or hammering a soft magnetic material can reduce its magnetism.

Section 1, page 622
Magnetic field lines have no beginning and no ending. They always form closed loops.

Section 2, page 627
Your thumb points in the direction of the current when using the right-hand rule.

Section 2, page 628
The more loops of wire there are in a solenoid, the stronger the magnetic field is.

Section 3, page 634
You must move a closed loop of wire within a magnetic field to produce a current using a generator.

Section 3, page 637
Answers may include running water, burning coal, nuclear fission, wind, geothermal power, and solar power.

absolute zero (AB suh LOOT ZIR oh) the temperature at which molecular energy is at a minimum (0 K on the Kelvin scale or –273.15 °C on the Celsius scale) (476)

cero absoluto la temperatura a la que la energía molecular es mínima (0 K en la escala de Kelvin ó –273.15 °C en la escala de Celsius) (476)

acceleration (ak SEL uhr AY shuhn) the rate at which velocity changes over time; an object accelerates if its speed, direction, or both change (372)

aceleración la tasa a la que la velocidad cambia con el tiempo; un objeto acelera si su rapidez cambia, si su dirección cambia, o si tanto su rapidez como su dirección cambian (372)

accuracy (AK yur uh see) a description of how close a measurement is to the true value of the quantity measured (27)

exactitud término que describe qué tanto se aproxima una medida al valor verdadero de la cantidad medida (27)

acid (AS id) any compound that increases the number of hydronium ions when dissolved in water; acids turn blue litmus paper red and react with bases and some metals to form salts (293)

ácido cualquier compuesto que aumenta el número de iones de hidrógeno cuando se disuelve en agua; los ácidos cambian el color del papel tornasol a rojo y forman sales al reaccionar con bases y con algunos metales (293)

alkali metal (AL kuh LIE MET'l) one of the elements of Group 1 of the periodic table (lithium, sodium, potassium, rubidium, cesium, and francium) (157)

metal alcalino uno de los elementos del Grupo 1 de la tabla periódica (litio, sodio, potasio, rubidio, cesio y francio) (157)

alkaline-earth metal (AL kuh LIEN UHRTH MET'l) one of the elements of Group 2 of the periodic table (beryllium, magnesium, calcium, strontium, barium, and radium) (158)

metal alcalinotérreo uno de los elementos del Grupo 2 de la tabla periódica (berilio, magnesio, calcio, estroncio, bario y radio) (158)

alloy (AL oy) a solid or liquid mixture of two or more metals (266)

aleación una mezcla sólida o líquida de dos o más metales (266)

alpha particle (AL fuh PAHRT i kuhl) a positively charged particle that consists of two protons and two neutrons and that is emitted from a nucleus during radioactive decay; it is identical to the nucleus of a helium atom and has a charge of +2 (328)

partícula alfa una partícula con carga positiva que está formada por dos protones y dos neutrones y que se emite desde el núcleo durante la desintegración radiactiva; es idéntica al núcleo de un átomo de helio y tiene una carga de +2 (328)

alternating current (AWL tuhr NAYT ing KUHR uhnt) an electric current that changes direction at regular intervals (abbreviation, AC) (634)

corriente alterna una corriente eléctrica que cambia de dirección en intervalos regulares (abreviatura: CA) (634)

amino acid (uh MEE noh AS id) a compound of a class of simple organic compounds that contain a carboxyl group and an amino group and that combine to form proteins (203)

aminoácido un compuesto de una clase de compuestos orgánicos simples que contienen un grupo carboxilo y un grupo amino y que al combinarse forman proteínas (203)

amplitude (AM pluh TOOD) the maximum distance that the particles of a wave's medium vibrate from their rest position (514)

amplitud la distancia máxima a la que vibran las partículas del medio de una onda a partir de su posición de reposo (514)

antacid (ANT AS id) a weak base that neutralizes stomach acid (311)

antiácido una base débil que neutraliza el ácido del estómago (311)

atom (AT uhm) the smallest unit of an element that maintains the chemical properties of that element (46)

átomo la unidad más pequeña de un elemento que conserva las propiedades químicas de ese elemento (46)

GLOSSARY • GLOSARIO

atomic number (uh TAHM ik NUHM buhr) the number of protons in the nucleus of an atom; the atomic number is the same for all atoms of an element (121)

número atómico el número de protones en el núcleo de un átomo; el número atómico es el mismo para todos los átomos de un elemento (121)

B

background radiation (BAK GROWND RAY dee AY shuhn) the nuclear radiation that arises naturally from cosmic rays and from radioactive isotopes in the soil and air (344)

radiación de fondo la radiación nuclear que surge naturalmente de los rayos cósmicos y de los isótopos radiactivos que están en el suelo y en el aire (344)

base (BAYS) any compound that increases the number of hydroxide ions when dissolved in water; bases turn red litmus paper blue and react with acids to form salts (295)

base cualquier compuesto que aumenta el número de iones de hidróxido cuando se disuelve en agua; las bases cambian el color del papel tornasol a azul y forman sales al reaccionar con ácidos (295)

beta particle (BAYT uh PAHRT i kuhl) an electron or positron that is emitted from a nucleus during radioactive decay (329)

partícula beta un electrón o positrón que se emite desde un núcleo durante la desintegración radiactiva (329)

bleach (BLEECH) a chemical compound used to whiten or make lighter, such as hydrogen peroxide or sodium hypochlorite (310)

blanqueador un compuesto químico que se usa para blanquear o aclarar, tal como el peróxido de hidrógeno o el hipoclorito de sodio (310)

boiling point (BOYL ing POYNT) the temperature and pressure at which a liquid becomes a gas (52)

punto de ebullición la temperatura y presión a la que un líquido se transforma en gas (52)

bond angle (BAHND ANG guhl) the angle formed by two bonds to the same atom (178)

ángulo de enlace el ángulo formado por dos enlaces al mismo átomo (178)

bond length (BAHND LENGKTH) the distance between two bonded atoms at their minimum potential energy; the average distance between the nuclei of two bonded atoms (178)

longitud de enlace la distancia entre dos átomos que están enlazados en el punto en que su energía potencial es mínima; la distancia promedio entre los núcleos de dos átomos enlazados (178)

buoyant force (BOY uhnt FAWRS) the upward force that keeps an object immersed in or floating on a fluid (90)

fuerza boyante la fuerza ascendente que hace que un objeto se mantenga sumergido en un fluido o flotando en él (90)

C

carbohydrate (KAHR boh HIE drayt) a class of molecules that includes sugars, starches, and fiber; contains carbon, hydrogen, and oxygen (202)

carbohidrato una clase de moléculas entre las que se incluyen azúcares, almidones y fibra; contiene carbono, hidrógeno y oxígeno (202)

catalyst (KAT uh LIST) a substance that changes the rate of a chemical reaction without being consumed or changed significantly (240)

catalizador una sustancia que cambia la tasa de una reacción química sin ser consumida ni cambiar significativamente (240)

cell (SEL) in electricity, a device that produces an electric current by converting chemical or radiant energy into electrical energy (594)

celda en electricidad, un aparato que produce una corriente eléctrica transformando la energía química o radiante en energía eléctrica (594)

chemical bond (KEM i kuhl BAHND) the attractive force that holds atoms or ions together (177)

enlace químico la fuerza de atracción que mantiene unidos a los átomos o iones (177)

chemical change (KEM i kuhl CHAYNJ) a change that occurs when one or more substances change into entirely new substances with different properties (61)

cambio químico un cambio que ocurre cuando una o más sustancias se transforman en sustancias totalmente nuevas con propiedades diferentes (61)

chemical energy (KEM i kuhl EN uhr jee) the energy released when a chemical compound reacts to produce new compounds (221)

energía química la energía que se libera cuando un compuesto químico reacciona para producir nuevos compuestos (221)

chemical equation (KEM i kuhl ee KWAY zhuhn) a representation of a chemical reaction that uses symbols to show the relationship between the reactants and the products (225)

ecuación química una representación de una reacción química que usa símbolos para mostrar la relación entre los reactivos y los productos (225)

chemical equilibrium (KEM i kuhl EE kwi LIB ree uhm) a state of balance in which the rate of a forward reaction equals the rate of the reverse reaction and the concentrations of products and reactants remain unchanged (245)

equilibrio químico un estado de equilibrio en el que la tasa de la reacción directa es igual a la tasa de la reacción inversa y las concentraciones de los productos y reactivos no sufren cambios (245)

chemical structure (KEM i kuhl STRUHK chuhr) the arrangement of the atoms in a molecule (178)

estructura química la disposición de los átomos en una molécula (178)

circuit breaker (SUHR kit BRAYK uhr) a switch that opens a circuit automatically when the current exceeds a certain value (607)

disyuntor un interruptor que abre un circuito automáticamente cuando la corriente excede un valor determinado (607)

colloid (KAHL oyd) a mixture consisting of tiny particles that are intermediate in size between those in solutions and those in suspensions and that are suspended in a liquid, solid, or gas (261)

coloide una mezcla formada por partículas diminutas que son de tamaño intermedio entre las partículas de las soluciones y las de las suspensiones y que se encuentran suspendidas en un líquido, sólido o gas (261)

combustion reaction (kuhm BUHS chuhn ree AK shuhn) the oxidation reaction of an organic compound, in which heat is released (232)

reacción de combustión la reacción de oxidación de un compuesto orgánico, durante la cual se libera calor (232)

compound (KAHM POWND) a substance made up of atoms of two or more different elements joined by chemical bonds (47)

compuesto una sustancia formada por átomos de dos o más elementos diferentes unidos por enlaces químicos (47)

compound machine (KAHM POWND muh SHEEN) a machine made of more than one simple machine (443)

máquina compuesta una máquina hecha de más de una máquina simple (443)

concentration (KAHN suhn TRAY shuhn) the amount of a particular substance in a given quantity of a mixture, solution, or ore (277)

concentración la cantidad de una cierta sustancia en una cantidad determinada de mezcla, solución o mena (277)

condensation (KAHN duhn SAY shuhn) the change of state from a gas to a liquid (86)

condensación el cambio de estado de gas a líquido (86)

constructive interference (kuhn STRUHK tiv IN tuhr FIR uhns) a superposition of two or more waves that produces an intensity equal to the sum of the intensities of the individual waves (527)

interferencia constructiva una superposición de dos o más ondas que produce una intensidad igual a la suma de las intensidades de las ondas individuales (527)

convection (kuhn VEK shuhn) the movement of matter due to differences in density that are caused by temperature variations; can result in the transfer of energy as heat (481)

convección el movimiento de la materia debido a diferencias en la densidad que se producen por variaciones en la temperatura; puede resultar en la transferencia de energía en forma de calor (481)

convection current (kuhn VEK shuhn KUHR uhnt) any movement of matter that results from differences in density; may be vertical, circular, or cyclical (481)

corriente de convección cualquier movimiento de la materia que se produce como resultado de diferencias en la densidad; puede ser vertical, circular o cíclico (481)

covalent bond (koh VAY luhnt BAHND) a bond formed when atoms share one or more pairs of electrons (186)

enlace covalente un enlace formado cuando los átomos comparten uno o más pares de electrones (186)

crest (KREST) the highest point of a wave (512)

cresta el punto más alto de una onda (512)

critical mass (KRIT i kuhl MAS) the minimum mass of a fissionable isotope that provides the number of neutrons needed to sustain a chain reaction (341)

masa crítica la cantidad mínima de masa de un isótopo fisionable que proporciona el número de neutrones que se requieren para sostener una reacción en cadena (341)

critical thinking (KRIT i kuhl THINGK ing) the ability and willingness to assess claims critically and to make judgments on the basis of objective and supported reasons (14)

razonamiento crítico la capacidad y voluntad de evaluar declaraciones críticamente y de hacer juicios basados en razones objetivas y documentadas (14)

D

decomposition reaction (DEE kahm puh ZISH uhn ree AK shuhn) a reaction in which a single compound breaks down to form two or more simpler substances (231)

reacción de descomposición una reacción en la que un solo compuesto se descompone para formar dos o más sustancias más simples (231)

density (DEN suh tee) the ratio of the mass of a substance to the volume of the substance; commonly expressed as grams per cubic centimeter for solids and liquids and as grams per liter for gases (54)

densidad la relación entre la masa de una sustancia y su volumen; comúnmente se expresa en gramos por centímetro cúbico para los sólidos y líquidos, y como gramos por litro para los gases (54)

destructive interference (di STRUHK tiv IN tuhr FIR uhns) a superposition of two or more waves that produces an intensity equal to the difference of the intensities of the individual waves (527)

interferencia destructiva una superposición de dos o más ondas que produce una intensidad igual a la diferencia de las intensidades de las ondas individuales (527)

detergent (dee TUHR juhnt) a water-soluble cleaner that can emulsify dirt and oil (309)

detergente un limpiador no jabonoso, soluble en agua, que emulsiona la suciedad y el aceite (309)

diffraction (di FRAK shuhn) a change in the direction of a wave when the wave finds an obstacle or an edge, such as an opening (525)

difracción un cambio en la dirección de una onda cuando ésta se encuentra con un obstáculo o un borde, tal como una abertura (525)

disinfectant (DIS in FEK tuhnt) a chemical substance that kills harmful bacteria or viruses (310)

desinfectante una sustancia química que elimina bacterias dañinas o virus (310)

dispersion (di SPUHR zhuhn) in optics, the process of separating a wave (such as white light) of different frequencies into its individual component waves (the different colors) (570)

dispersión en óptica, el proceso de separar una onda que tiene diferentes frecuencias (por ejemplo, la luz blanca) de las ondas individuales que la componen (los distintos colores) (570)

displacement (dis PLAYS muhnt) the change in position of an object (366)

desplazamiento el cambio en la posición de un objeto (366)

Doppler effect (DAHP luhr e FEKT) an observed change in the frequency of a wave when the source or observer is moving (523)

efecto Doppler un cambio que se observa en la frecuencia de una onda cuando la fuente o el observador está en movimiento (523)

double-displacement reaction (DUHB uhl dis PLAYS muhnt ree AK shuhn) a reaction in which a gas, a solid precipitate, or a molecular compound forms from the apparent exchange of atoms or ions between two compounds (234)

reacción de doble desplazamiento una reacción en la que un gas, un precipitado sólido o un compuesto molecular se forma a partir del intercambio aparente de átomos o iones entre dos compuestos (234)

E

efficiency (e FISH uhn see) a quantity, usually expressed as a percentage, that measures the ratio of work output to work input (459)

eficiencia una cantidad, generalmente expresada como un porcentaje, que mide la relación entre el trabajo de entrada y el trabajo de salida (459)

electrical conductor (ee LEK tri kuhl kuhn DUHK tuhr) a material in which charges can move freely (588)

conductor eléctrico un material en el que las cargas se mueven libremente (588)

electrical insulator (ee LEK tri kuhl IN suh LAYT uhr) a material in which charges cannot move freely (588)

aislante eléctrico un material en el que las cargas no pueden moverse libremente (588)

electrical potential energy (ee LEK tri kuhl poh TEN shuhl EN uhr jee) the ability to move an electric charge from one point to another (593)

energía potencial eléctrica la capacidad de mover una carga eléctrica de un punto a otro (593)

electric charge (ee LEK trik CHAHRJ) an electrical property of matter that creates electric and magnetic forces and interactions (585)

carga eléctrica una propiedad eléctrica de la materia que crea fuerzas e interacciones eléctricas y magnéticas (585)

electric circuit (ee LEK trik SUHR kit) a set of electrical components connected such that they provide one or more complete paths for the movement of charges (600)

circuito eléctrico un conjunto de componentes eléctricos conectados de modo que proporcionen una o más rutas completas para el movimiento de las cargas (600)

electric current (ee LEK trik KUHR uhnt) the rate at which charges pass through a given point; measured in amperes (595)

corriente eléctrica la tasa a la que las cargas pasan por un punto determinado; se mide en amperes (595)

electric field (ee LEK trik FEELD) the space around a charged object in which another charged object experiences an electric force (591)

campo eléctrico el espacio que se encuentra alrededor de un objeto con carga y en el que otro objeto con carga experimenta una fuerza eléctrica (591)

electric force (ee LEK trik FAWRS) the force of attraction or repulsion on a charged particle that is due to an electric field (590)

fuerza eléctrica la fuerza de atracción o repulsión en una partícula con carga debido a un campo eléctrico (590)

electric motor (ee LEK trik MOHT uhr) a device that converts electrical energy into mechanical energy (630)

motor eléctrico un aparato que transforma la energía eléctrica en energía mecánica (630)

electric power (ee LEK trik POW uhr) the rate at which electrical energy is converted into other forms of energy (605)

potencia eléctrica la tasa a la que la energía eléctrica se transforma en otras formas de energía (605)

electrolyte (ee LEK troh LIET) a substance that dissolves in water to give a solution that conducts an electric current (294)

electrolito una sustancia que se disuelve en agua y crea una solución que conduce la corriente eléctrica (294)

electromagnet (ee LEK troh MAG nit) a coil that has a soft iron core and that acts as a magnet when an electric current is in the coil (628)

electroimán una bobina que tiene un centro de hierro suave y que funciona como un imán cuando hay una corriente eléctrica en la bobina (628)

electromagnetic induction (ee LEK troh mag NET ik in DUHK shuhn) the process of creating a current in a circuit by changing a magnetic field (632)

inducción electromagnética el proceso de crear una corriente en un circuito por medio de un cambio en el campo magnético (632)

electromagnetic wave (ee LEK troh mag NET ik WAYV) a wave that consists of oscillating electric and magnetic fields, which radiate outward at the speed of light (506)

onda electromagnética una onda que está formada por campos eléctricos y magnéticos oscilantes, que irradia hacia fuera a la velocidad de la luz (506)

electron (ee LEK TRAHN) a subatomic particle that has a negative charge (115)

electrón una partícula subatómica que tiene carga negativa (115)

element (EL uh muhnt) a substance that cannot be separated or broken down into simpler substances by chemical means; all atoms of an element have the same atomic number (46)

elemento una sustancia que no se puede separar o descomponer en sustancias más simples por medio de métodos químicos; todos los átomos de un elemento tienen el mismo número atómico (46)

empirical formula (em PIR i kuhl FAWR myoo luh) a chemical formula that shows the composition of a compound in terms of the relative numbers and kinds of atoms in the simplest ratio (194)

fórmula empírica una fórmula química que muestra la composición de un compuesto en función del número relativo y el tipo de átomos que hay en la proporción más simple (194)

emulsion (ee MUHL shuhn) any mixture of two or more immiscible liquids in which one liquid is dispersed in the other (262)

emulsión cualquier mezcla de dos o más líquidos inmiscibles en la que un líquido se encuentra disperso en el otro (262)

endothermic reaction (EN doh THUHR mik ree AK shuhn) a chemical reaction that requires energy input (222)

reacción endotérmica una reacción química que necesita una entrada de energía (222)

energy (EN uhr jee) the capacity to do work (80, 444)

energía la capacidad de realizar un trabajo (80, 444)

entropy (EN truh pee) a measure of the randomness or disorder of a system (491)

entropía una medida del grado de aleatoriedad o desorden de un sistema (491)

enzyme (EN ziem) a molecule, either protein or RNA, that acts as a catalyst in biochemical reactions (241)

enzima una molécula, ya sea una proteína o ARN, que actúa como catalizador en las reacciones bioquímicas (241)

evaporation (ee VAP uh RAY shuhn) the change of state from a liquid to a gas (85)

evaporación el cambio de estado de líquido a gas (85)

exothermic reaction (EK soh THUHR mik ree AK shuhn) a chemical reaction in which energy is released to the surroundings as heat (222)

reacción exotérmica una reacción química en la que se libera energía a los alrededores en forma de calor (222)

fission (FISH uhn) the process by which a nucleus splits into two or more fragments and releases neutrons and energy (339)

fisión el proceso por medio del cual un núcleo se divide en dos o más fragmentos y libera neutrones y energía (339)

fluid (FLOO id) a nonsolid state of matter in which the atoms or molecules are free to move past each other, as in a gas or liquid (79)

fluido un estado no sólido de la materia en el que los átomos o moléculas tienen libertad de movimiento, como en el caso de un gas o un líquido (79)

force (FAWRS) an action exerted on a body in order to change the body's state of rest or motion; force has magnitude and direction (380)

fuerza una acción que se ejerce en un cuerpo con el fin de cambiar su estado de reposo o movimiento; la fuerza tiene magnitud y dirección (380)

frame of reference (FRAYM UHV REF uhr uhns) a system for specifying the precise location of objects in space and time (365)

marco de referencia un sistema para especificar la ubicación precisa de los objetos en el tiempo y el espacio (365)

free fall (FREE FAWL) the motion of a body when only the force of gravity is acting on the body (407)

caída libre el movimiento de un cuerpo cuando la única fuerza que actúa sobre él es la fuerza de gravedad (407)

free radical (FREE RAD i kuhl) an atom or a group of atoms that has one unpaired electron (235)

radical libre un átomo o un grupo de átomos que tiene un electrón no apareado (235)

frequency (FREE kwuhn see) the number of cycles or vibrations per unit of time; *also* the number of waves produced in a given amount of time (516)

frecuencia el número de ciclos o vibraciones por unidad de tiempo; *también*, el número de ondas producidas en una cantidad de tiempo determinada (516)

friction (FRIK shuhn) a force that opposes motion between two surfaces that are in contact (382)

fricción una fuerza que se opone al movimiento entre dos superficies que están en contacto (382)

fuse (FYOOZ) an electrical device that contains a metal strip that melts when current in the circuit becomes too great (607)

fusible un aparato eléctrico que contiene una tira de metal que se derrite cuando la corriente en el circuito es demasiado elevada (607)

fusion (FYOO zhuhn) the process in which light nuclei combine at extremely high temperatures, forming heavier nuclei and releasing energy (342)

fusión el proceso por medio del cual núcleos ligeros se combinan a temperaturas extremadamente altas formando núcleos más pesados y liberando energía (342)

G

galvanometer (GAL vuh NAHM uht uhr) an instrument that detects, measures, and determines the direction of a small electric current (630)

galvanómetro un instrumento que detecta, mide y determina la dirección de una corriente eléctrica pequeña (630)

gamma ray (GAM uh RAY) the high-energy photon emitted by a nucleus during fission and radioactive decay (329)

rayo gamma el fotón de alta energía emitido por un núcleo durante la fisión y la desintegración radiactiva (329)

gas laws (GAS LAWZ) the laws that state the mathematical relationships between the volume, temperature, pressure, and quantity of a gas (97)

leyes de los gases las leyes que establecen las relaciones matemáticas entre el volumen, temperatura, presión y cantidad de un gas (97)

generator (JEN uhr AYT uhr) a machine that converts mechanical energy into electrical energy (634)

generador una máquina que transforma la energía mecánica en energía eléctrica (634)

group (GROOP) a vertical column of elements in the periodic table; elements in a group share chemical properties (150)

grupo una columna vertical de elementos de la tabla periódica; los elementos de un grupo comparten propiedades químicas (150)

H

half-life (HAF LIEF) the time required for half of a sample of a radioactive isotope to break down by radioactive decay to form a daughter isotope (333)

vida media el tiempo que se requiere para que la mitad de una muestra de un isótopo radiactivo se descomponga por desintegración radiactiva y forme un isótopo hijo (333)

halogen (HAL oh juhn) one of the elements of Group 17 of the periodic table (fluorine, chlorine, bromine, iodine, and astatine); halogens combine with most metals to form salts (162)

halógeno uno de los elementos del Grupo 17 de la tabla periódica (flúor, cloro, bromo, yodo y ástato); los halógenos se combinan con la mayoría de los metales para formar sales (162)

heat (HEET) the energy transferred between objects that are at different temperatures; energy is always transferred from higher-temperature objects to lower-temperature objects until thermal equilibrium is reached (479)

> **calor** la transferencia de energía entre objetos que están a temperaturas diferentes; la energía siempre se transfiere de los objetos que están a la temperatura más alta a los objetos que están a una temperatura más baja, hasta que se llega a un equilibrio térmico (479)

heat engine (HEET EN juhn) a machine that transforms heat into mechanical energy, or work (492)

> **motor térmico** una máquina que transforma el calor en energía mecánica, o trabajo (492)

hydrogen bond (HIE druh juhn BAHND) the intermolecular force occurring when a hydrogen atom that is bonded to a highly electronegative atom of one molecule is attracted to two unshared electrons of another molecule (269)

> **enlace de hidrógeno** la fuerza intermolecular producida por un átomo de hidrógeno que está unido a un átomo muy electronegativo de una molécula y que experimenta atracción a dos electrones no compartidos de otra molécula (269)

indicator (IN di KAYT uhr) a compound that can reversibly change color depending on conditions such as pH (293)

> **indicador** un compuesto que puede cambiar de color de forma reversible dependiendo de condiciones tales como el pH (293)

inertia (in UHR shuh) the tendency of an object to resist a change in motion unless an outside force acts on the object (398)

> **inercia** la tendencia de un objeto a resistir un cambio en el movimiento a menos que actúe una fuerza externa sobre el objeto (398)

infrasound (IN fruh SOWND) slow vibrations of frequencies lower than 20 Hz (546)

> **infrasonido** vibraciones lentas de frecuencias inferiores a 20 Hz (546)

intensity (in TEN suh tee) in physical science, the rate at which energy flows through a given area of space (555)

> **intensidad** en las ciencias físicas, la tasa a la que la energía fluye a través de un área determinada de espacio (555)

interference (IN tuhr FIR uhns) the combination of two or more waves that results in a single wave (526)

> **interferencia** la combinación de dos o más ondas que resulta en una sola onda (526)

ion (IE AHN) an atom, radical, or molecule that has gained or lost one or more electrons and has a negative or positive charge (153)

> **ion** un átomo, radical o molécula que ha ganado o perdido uno o más electrones y que tiene una carga negativa o positiva (153)

ionic bond (ie AHN ik BAHND) the attractive force between oppositely charged ions, which form when electrons are transferred from one atom to another (184)

> **enlace iónico** la fuerza de atracción entre iones con cargas opuestas, que se forman cuando se transfieren electrones de un átomo a otro (184)

isotope (IE suh TOHP) an atom that has the same number of protons (or the same atomic number) as other atoms of the same element do but that has a different number of neutrons (and thus a different atomic mass) (122)

> **isótopo** un átomo que tiene el mismo número de protones (o el mismo número atómico) que otros átomos del mismo elemento, pero que tiene un número diferente de neutrones (y, por lo tanto, otra masa atómica) (122)

kinetic energy (ki NET ik EN uhr jee) the energy of an object that is due to the object's motion (447)

> **energía cinética** la energía de un objeto debido al movimiento del objeto (447)

kinetic friction (ki NET ik FRIK shuhn) the force that opposes the movement of two surfaces that are in contact and are moving over each other (383)

> **fricción cinética** la fuerza que se opone al movimiento de dos superficies que están en contacto y se mueven una sobre la otra (383)

law (LAW) a descriptive statement or equation that reliably predicts events under certain conditions (9)

ley una ecuación o afirmación descriptiva que predice sucesos de manera confiable en determinadas condiciones (9)

length (LENGKTH) a measure of the straight-line distance between two points (21)

longitud una medida de la distancia en línea recta entre dos puntos (21)

lens (LENZ) a transparent object that refracts light waves such that they converge or diverge to create an image (568)

lente un objeto transparente que refracta las ondas de luz de modo que converjan o diverjan para crear una imagen (568)

light ray (LIET RAY) a line in space that matches the direction of the flow of radiant energy (560)

rayo luz una línea en el espacio que corresponde con la dirección del flujo de energía radiante (560)

longitudinal wave (LAHN juh TOOD'n uhl WAYV) a wave in which the particles of the medium vibrate parallel to the direction of wave motion (512)

onda longitudinal una onda en la que las partículas del medio vibran paralelamente a la dirección del movimiento de la onda (512)

magnetic field (mag NET ik FEELD) a region where a magnetic force can be detected (621)

campo magnético una región donde puede detectarse una fuerza magnética (621)

magnetic pole (mag NET ik POHL) one of two points, such as the ends of a magnet, that have opposing magnetic qualities (619)

polo magnético uno de dos puntos, tales como los extremos de un imán, que tienen cualidades magnéticas opuestas (619)

magnification (MAG nuh fi KAY shuhn) the increase of an object's apparent size by using lenses or mirrors (568)

magnificación el aumento del tamaño aparente de un objeto mediante el uso de lentes o espejos (568)

mass (MAS) a measure of the amount of matter in an object; a fundamental property of an object that is not affected by the forces that act on the object, such as the gravitational force (21)

masa una medida de la cantidad de materia que tiene un objeto; una propiedad fundamental de un objeto que no está afectada por las fuerzas que actúan sobre el objeto, como por ejemplo, la fuerza gravitacional (21)

mass number (MAS NUHM buhr) the sum of the numbers of protons and neutrons in the nucleus of an atom (121)

número de masa la suma de los números de protones y neutrones que hay en el núcleo de un átomo (121)

matter (MAT uhr) anything that has mass and takes up space (45)

materia cualquier cosa que tiene masa y ocupa un lugar en el espacio (45)

mechanical advantage (muh KAN i kuhl ad VANT ij) a number that tells how many times a machine multiplies force; it can be calculated by dividing the output force by the input force (436)

ventaja mecánica un número que dice cuántas veces una máquina multiplica una fuerza; se calcula dividiendo la fuerza de salida entre la fuerza de entrada (436)

mechanical energy (muh KAN i kuhl EN uhr jee) the amount of work an object can do because of the object's kinetic and potential energies (449)

energía mecánica la cantidad de trabajo que un objeto realiza debido a las energías cinética y potencial del objeto (449)

mechanical wave (muh KAN i kuhl WAYV) a wave that requires a medium through which to travel (506)

onda mecánica una onda que requiere un medio para desplazarse (506)

medium (MEE dee uhm) a physical environment in which phenomena occur (506)

medio un ambiente físico en el que ocurren fenómenos (506)

melting point (MELT ing POYNT) the temperature and pressure at which a solid becomes a liquid (52)

punto de fusión la temperatura y presión a la cual un sólido se convierte en líquido (52)

metal (MET'l) an element that is shiny and that conducts heat and electricity well (154)

metal un elemento que es brillante y conduce bien el calor y la electricidad (154)

metallic bond (muh TAL ik BAHND) a bond formed by the attraction between positively charged metal ions and the electrons around them (188)

enlace metálico un enlace formado por la atracción entre iones metálicos cargados positivamente y los electrones que los rodean (188)

mixture (MIKS chuhr) a combination of two or more substances that are not chemically combined (48)

mezcla una combinación de dos o más sustancias que no están combinadas químicamente (48)

molarity (moh LA ruh tee) a concentration unit of a solution expressed as moles of solute dissolved per liter of solution (280)

molaridad una unidad de concentración de una solución, expresada en moles de soluto disuelto por litro de solución (280)

mole (MOHL) the SI base unit used to measure the amount of a substance whose number of particles is the same as the number of atoms of carbon in exactly 12 g of carbon-12 (125)

mol la unidad fundamental del sistema internacional de unidades que se usa para medir la cantidad de una sustancia cuyo número de partículas es el mismo que el número de átomos de carbono en exactamente 12 g de carbono-12 (125)

molecular formula (moh LEK yoo luhr FAWR myoo luh) a chemical formula that shows the number and kinds of atoms in a molecule, but not the arrangement of the atoms (195)

fórmula molecular una fórmula química que muestra el número y los tipos de átomos que hay en una molécula, pero que no muestra cómo están distribuidos (195)

molecule (MAHL i KYOOL) a goup of atoms that are held together by chemical forces; a molecule is the smallest unit of matter that can exist by itself and retain all of a substance's chemical properties (47)

molécula un conjunto de átomos que se mantienen unidos por acción de las fuerzas químicas; una molécula es la unidad más pequeña de la materia capaz de existir en forma independiente y conservar todas las propiedades químicas de una sustancia (47)

mole ratio (MOHL RAY shee OH) the relative number of moles of the substances required to produce a given amount of product in a chemical reaction (228)

razón molar el número relativo de moles de las sustancias que se requieren para producir una cantidad determinada de producto en una reacción química (228)

momentum (moh MEN tuhm) a quantity defined as the product of the mass and velocity of an object (414)

momento una cantidad que se define como el producto de la masa de un objeto por su velocidad (414)

motion (MOH shuhn) an object's change in position relative to a reference point (365)

movimiento el cambio en la posición de un objeto respecto a un punto de referencia (365)

neutralization reaction (NOO truh li ZAY shuhn ree AK shuhn) the reaction of the ions that characterize acids (hydronium ions) and the ions that characterize bases (hydroxide ions) to form water molecules and a salt (302)

reacción de neutralización la reacción de los iones que caracterizan a los ácidos (iones hidronio) y de los iones que caracterizan a las bases (iones hidróxido) para formar moléculas de agua y una sal (302)

neutron (NOO TRAHN) a subatomic particle that has no charge and that is located in the nucleus of an atom (119)

neutrón una partícula subatómica que no tiene carga y que está ubicada en el núcleo de un átomo (119)

noble gas (NOH buhl GAS) one of the elements of Group 18 of the periodic table (helium, neon, argon, krypton, xenon, and radon); noble gases are unreactive (161)

gas noble uno de los elementos del Grupo 18 de la tabla periódica (helio, neón, argón, criptón, xenón y radón); los gases nobles son no reactivos (161)

nonmetal (nahn MET'l) an element that conducts heat and electricity poorly and that does not form positive ions in an electrolytic solution (154)

no metal un elemento que es mal conductor del calor y la electricidad y que no forma iones positivos en una solución de electrolitos (154)

nonpolar (nahn POH luhr) describes a molecule in which centers of positive and negative charge are not separated (270)

no polar término que describe una molécula en la que los centros de carga positiva y negativa no están separados (270)

nuclear chain reaction (NOO klee uhr CHAYN ree AK shuhn) a continuous series of nuclear fission reactions (340)

reacción nuclear en cadena una serie continua de reacciones nucleares de fisión (340)

nuclear radiation (NOO klee uhr RAY dee AY shuhn) the particles that are released from the nucleus during radioactive decay, such as neutrons, electrons, and photons (327)

radiación nuclear las partículas que el núcleo libera durante la desintegración radiactiva, tales como neutrones, electrones y fotones (327)

nucleus (NOO klee uhs) in physical science, an atom's central region, which is made up of protons and neutrons (118)

núcleo en ciencias físicas, la región central de un átomo, la cual está constituida por protones y neutrones (118)

O

orbital (AWR buh tuhl) a region in an atom where there is a high probability of finding electrons (129)

orbital una región en un átomo donde hay una alta probabilidad de encontrar electrones (129)

organic compound (awr GAN ik KAHM POWND) a covalently bonded compound that contains carbon, excluding carbonates and oxides (197)

compuesto orgánico un compuesto enlazado de manera covalente que contiene carbono, excluyendo a los carbonatos y óxidos (197)

oxidation-reduction reaction (AHKS i DAY shuhn ri DUHK shuhn ree AK shuhn) any chemical change in which one species is oxidized (loses electrons) and another species is reduced (gains electrons); also called *redox reaction* (237)

reacción de óxido-reducción cualquier cambio químico en el que una especie se oxida (pierde electrones) y otra especie se reduce (gana electrones); también se denomina *reacción redox* (237)

P

parallel circuit (PAR uh LEL SUHR kit) a circuit in which the parts are joined in branches such that the potential difference across each part is the same (603)

circuito paralelo un circuito en el que las partes están unidas en ramas de manera tal que la diferencia de potencial entre cada parte es la misma (603)

pascal (pas KAL) the SI unit of pressure; equal to the force of 1 N exerted over an area of 1 m^2 (symbol, Pa) (89)

pascal la unidad de presión del sistema internacional de unidades; es igual a la fuerza de 1 N ejercida sobre un área de 1 m^2 (símbolo: Pa) (89)

period (PIR ee uhd) in chemistry, a horizontal row of elements in the periodic table (150); in physics, the time that it takes a complete cycle or wave oscillation to occur (516)

período en química, una hilera horizontal de elementos en la tabla periódica (150); en física, el tiempo que se requiere para completar un ciclo o la oscilación de una onda (516)

periodic law (PIR ee AHD ik LAW) the law that states that the repeating chemical and physical properties of elements change periodically with the atomic numbers of the elements (147)

ley periódica la ley que establece que las propiedades químicas y físicas repetitivas de un elemento cambian periódicamente en función del número atómico de los elementos (147)

GLOSSARY · GLOSARIO

pH (PEE AYCH) a value that is used to express the acidity or alkalinity (basicity) of a system; each whole number on the scale indicates a tenfold change in acidity; a pH of 7 is neutral, a pH of less than 7 is acidic, and a pH of greater than 7 is basic (298)

pH un valor que expresa la acidez o la alcalinidad (basicidad) de un sistema; cada número entero de la escala indica un cambio de 10 veces en la acidez; un pH de 7 es neutro, un pH de menos de 7 es ácido y un pH de más de 7 es básico (298)

photon (FOH TAHN) a unit or quantum of light; a particle of electromagnetic radiation that has zero rest mass and carries a quantum of energy (131, 553)

fotón una unidad o quantum de luz; una partícula de radiación electromagnética que tiene una masa de reposo de cero y que lleva un quantum de energía (131, 553)

physical change (FIZ i kuhl CHAYNJ) a change of matter from one form to another without a change in chemical properties (59)

cambio físico un cambio de materia de una forma a otra sin que ocurra un cambio en sus propiedades químicas (59)

pitch (PICH) a measure of how high or low a sound is perceived to be, depending on the frequency of the sound wave (546)

altura tonal una medida de qué tan agudo o grave se percibe un sonido, dependiendo de la frecuencia de la onda sonora (546)

plasma (PLAZ muh) in physical science, a state of matter that consists of free-moving ions and electrons; a plasma's properties differ from the properties of a solid, liquid, or gas (79)

plasma en ciencias físicas, un estado de la materia que consiste en iones y electrones que se mueven libremente; las propiedades de un plasma son distintas de las propiedades de un sólido, de un líquido o de un gas (79)

polar (POH luhr) describes a molecule in which the positive and negative charges are separated (267)

polar término que describe una molécula en la que las cargas positivas y negativas están separadas (267)

polyatomic ion (PAHL ee uh TAHM ik IE ahn) an ion made of two or more atoms (189)

ion poliatómico un ion formado por dos o más átomos (189)

polymer (PAHL uh muhr) a large molecule that is formed by more than five monomers, or small units (201)

polímero una molécula grande que está formada por más de cinco monómeros, o unidades pequeñas (201)

potential difference (poh TEN shuhl DIF uhr uhns) the voltage difference in potential between two points in a circuit (594)

diferencia de potencial la diferencia de voltaje en el potencial entre dos puntos de un circuito (594)

potential energy (poh TEN shuhl EN uhr jee) the energy that an object has because of the position, shape, or condition of the object (445)

energía potencial la energía que tiene un objeto debido a su posición, forma o condición (445)

power (POW uhr) a quantity that measures the rate at which work is done or energy is transformed (433)

potencia una cantidad que mide la tasa a la que se realiza un trabajo o a la que se transforma la energía (433)

precision (pree SIZH uhn) the exactness of a measurement (26)

precisión la exactitud de una medición (26)

pressure (PRESH uhr) the amount of force exerted per unit area of a surface (89)

presión la cantidad de fuerza ejercida en una superficie por unidad de área (89)

prism (PRIZ uhm) in optics, a system that consists of two or more plane surfaces of a transparent solid at an angle with each other (570)

prisma en óptica, un sistema formado por dos o más superficies planas de un sólido transparente ubicadas en un ángulo unas respecto a otras (570)

product (PRAHD uhkt) a substance that forms in a chemical reaction (220)

producto una sustancia que se forma en una reacción química (220)

projectile motion (proh JEK tuhl MOH shuhn) the curved path that an object follows when thrown, launched, or otherwise projected near the surface of Earth; the motion of objects that are moving in two dimensions under the influence of gravity (408)

movimiento proyectil la trayectoria curva que sigue un objeto cuando es aventado, lanzado o proyectado de cualquier otra manera cerca de la superficie de la Tierra; el movimiento de objetos que se mueven en dos dimensiones bajo la influencia de la gravedad (408)

protein (PROH teen) an organic compound that is made of one or more chains of amino acids and that is a principal component of all cells (203)

proteína un compuesto orgánico que está hecho de una o más cadenas de aminoácidos y que es el principal componente de todas las células (203)

proton (PROH TAHN) a subatomic particle that has a positive charge and that is located in the nucleus of an atom; the number of protons in the nucleus is the atomic number, which determines the identity of an element (119)

protón una partícula subatómica que tiene una carga positiva y que está ubicada en el núcleo de un átomo; el número de protones que hay en el núcleo es el número atómico, y éste determina la identidad del elemento (119)

pure substance (PYOOR SUHB stuhns) a sample of matter, either a single element or a single compound, that has definite chemical and physical properties (48)

sustancia pura una muestra de materia, ya sea un solo elemento o un solo compuesto, que tiene propiedades químicas y físicas definidas (48)

R

radar (RAY DAHR) **ra**dio **d**etection **a**nd **r**anging, a system that uses reflected radio waves to determine the velocity and location of objects (556)

radar detección y exploración a gran distancia por medio de ondas de radio; un sistema que usa ondas de radio reflejadas para determinar la velocidad y ubicación de los objetos (556)

radiation (RAY dee AY shuhn) the energy that is transferred as electromagnetic waves, such as visible light and infrared waves (482)

radiación la energía que se transfiere en forma de ondas electromagnéticas, tales como las ondas de luz y las infrarrojas (482)

radioactive decay (RAY dee oh AK tiv dee KAY) the disintegration of an unstable atomic nucleus into one or more different nuclides, accompanied by the emission of radiation, the nuclear capture or ejection of electrons, or fission (327)

desintegración radiactiva la desintegración de un núcleo atómico inestable para formar uno o más nucleidos diferentes, lo cual va acompañado de la emisión de radiación, la captura o expulsión nuclear de electrones, o fisión (327)

radioactive tracer (RAY dee oh AK tiv TRAYS uhr) a radioactive material that is added to a substance so that its distribution can be detected later (346)

trazador radiactivo un material radiactivo que se añade a una sustancia de modo que su distribución pueda ser detectada posteriormente (346)

reactant (ree AK tuhnt) a substance or molecule that participates in a chemical reaction (220)

reactivo una sustancia o molécula que participa en una reacción química (220)

reactivity (REE ak TIV uh tee) the capacity of a substance to combine chemically with another substance (56)

reactividad la capacidad de una sustancia de combinarse químicamente con otra sustancia (56)

real image (REE uhl IM ij) an image that is formed by the intersection of light rays; a real image can be projected on a screen (563)

imagen real una imagen que se forma por la intersección de rayos de luz; una imagen real se puede proyectar en una pantalla (563)

reflection (ri FLEK shuhn) the bouncing back of a ray of light, sound, or heat when the ray hits a surface that it does not go through (524)

reflexión el rebote de un rayo de luz, sonido o calor cuando el rayo golpea una superficie pero no la atraviesa (524)

refraction (ri FRAK shuhn) the bending of a wavefront as the wavefront passes between two substances in which the speed of the wave differs (526)

refracción el curvamiento de un frente de ondas a medida que el frente pasa entre dos sustancias en las que la velocidad de las ondas difiere (526)

rem (REM) the quantity of ionizing radiation that does as much damage to human tissue as 1 roentgen of high-voltage X rays does (345)

rem la cantidad de radiación ionizante que produce el mismo daño a los tejidos humanos que 1 roentgen de rayos X de alto voltaje (345)

resistance (ri ZIS tuhns) in physical science, the opposition presented to the current by a material or device (596)

resistencia en ciencias físicas, la oposición que un material o aparato presenta a la corriente (596)

resonance (REZ uh nuhns) a phenomenon that occurs when two objects naturally vibrate at the same frequency; the sound produced by one object causes the other object to vibrate (548)

resonancia un fenómeno que ocurre cuando dos objetos vibran naturalmente a la misma frecuencia; el sonido producido por un objeto hace que el otro objeto vibre (548)

S

salt (SAWLT) an ionic compound that forms when a metal atom or a positive radical replaces the hydrogen of an acid (303)

sal un compuesto iónico que se forma cuando el átomo de un metal o un radical positivo reemplaza el hidrógeno de un ácido (303)

saturated solution (SACH uh RAYT id suh LOO shuhn) a solution that cannot dissolve any more solute under the given conditions (278)

solución saturada una solución que no puede disolver más soluto bajo las condiciones dadas (278)

schematic diagram (skee MAT ik DIE uh GRAM) a graphical representation of a circuit that uses lines to represent wires and different symbols to represent components (601)

diagrama esquemático una representación gráfica de un circuito, la cual usa líneas para representar cables y diferentes símbolos para representar los componentes (601)

science (SIE uhns) the knowledge obtained by observing natural events and conditions in order to discover facts and formulate laws or principles that can be verified or tested (7)

ciencia el conocimiento que se obtiene por medio de la observación natural de acontecimientos y condiciones con el fin de descubrir hechos y formular leyes o principios que puedan ser verificados o probados (7)

scientific methods (SIE uhn TIF ik METH uhdz) a series of steps followed to solve problems, including collecting data, formulating a hypothesis, testing the hypothesis, and stating conclusions (15)

métodos científicos una serie de pasos que se siguen para solucionar problemas, los cuales incluyen recopilar información, formular una hipótesis, comprobar la hipótesis y sacar conclusiones (15)

scientific notation (SIE uhn TIF ik noh TAY shuhn) a method of expressing a quantity as a number multiplied by 10 to the appropriate power (24)

notación científica un método para expresar una cantidad en forma de un número multiplicado por 10 a la potencia adecuada (24)

semiconductor (SEM i kuhn DUK tuhr) an element or compound that conducts electric current better than an insulator does but not as well as a conductor does (154)

semiconductor un elemento o compuesto que conduce la corriente eléctrica mejor que un aislante, pero no tan bien como un conductor (154)

series circuit (SIR eez SUHR kit) a circuit in which the parts are joined one after another such that the current in each part is the same (603)

circuito en serie un circuito en el que las partes están unidas una después de la otra de manera tal que la corriente en cada parte es la misma (603)

significant figure (sig NIF uh kuhnt FIG yuhr) a prescribed decimal place that determines the amount of rounding off to be done based on the precision of the measurement (26)

cifra significativa un lugar decimal prescrito que determina la cantidad de redondeo que se hará con base en la precisión de la medición (26)

simple machine (SIM puhl muh SHEEN) one of the six basic types of machines, which are the basis for all other forms of machines (438)

máquina simple uno de los seis tipos fundamentales de máquinas, las cuales son la base de todas las demás formas de máquinas (438)

single-displacement reaction (SING guhl dis PLAYS muhnt ree AK shuhn) a reaction in which one element or radical takes the place of another element or radical in a compound (233)

reacción de sustitución simple una reacción en la que un elemento o radical toma el lugar de otro elemento o radical en el compuesto (233)

soap (SOHP) a substance that is used as a cleaner and that dissolves in water (307)

jabón una sustancia que se usa como limpiador y que se disuelve en el agua (307)

solenoid (SOH luh NOYD) a coil of wire with an electric current in it (627)

solenoide una bobina de alambre que tiene una corriente eléctrica (627)

solubility (SAHL yoo BIL uh tee) the ability of one substance to dissolve in another at a given temperature and pressure; expressed in terms of the amount of solute that will dissolve in a given amount of solvent to produce a saturated solution (276)

solubilidad la capacidad de una sustancia de disolverse en otra a una temperatura y presión dadas; se expresa en términos de la cantidad de soluto que se disolverá en una cantidad determinada de solvente para producir una solución saturada (276)

solute (SAHL YOOT) in a solution, the substance that dissolves in the solvent (263)

soluto en una solución, la sustancia que se disuelve en el solvente (263)

solution (suh LOO shuhn) a homogeneous mixture throughout which two or more substances are uniformly dispersed (263)

solución una mezcla homogénea en la cual dos o más sustancias se dispersan de manera uniforme (263)

solvent (SAHL vuhnt) in a solution, the substance in which the solute dissolves (263)

solvente en una solución, la sustancia en la que se disuelve el soluto (263)

sonar (SOH NAHR) sound navigation and ranging, a system that uses acoustic signals and returned echoes to determine the location of objects or to communicate (551)

sonar navegación y exploración por medio del sonido; un sistema que usa señales acústicas y ondas de eco que regresan para determinar la ubicación de los objetos o para comunicarse (551)

sound wave (SOWND WAYV) a longitudinal wave that is caused by vibrations and that travels through a material medium (543)

onda sonora una onda longitudinal que se origina debido a vibraciones y que se desplaza a través de un medio material (543)

specific heat (spuh SIF ik HEET) the quantity of heat required to raise a unit mass of homogeneous material 1 K or 1 °C in a specified way given constant pressure and volume (485)

calor específico la cantidad de calor que se requiere para aumentar una unidad de masa de un material homogéneo 1 K ó 1 °C de una manera especificada, dados un volumen y una presión constantes (485)

speed (SPEED) the distance traveled divided by the time interval during which the motion occurred (367)

rapidez la distancia que un objeto se desplaza dividida entre el intervalo de tiempo durante el cual ocurrió el movimiento (367)

standing wave (STAN ding WAYV) a pattern of vibration that simulates a wave that is standing still (529)

onda estacionaria un patrón de vibración que simula una onda que está parada (529)

static friction (STAT ik FRIK shuhn) the force that resists the initiation of sliding motion between two surfaces that are in contact and at rest (383)

fricción estática la fuerza que se opone a que se inicie el movimiento de deslizamiento entre dos superficies que están en contacto y en reposo (383)

sublimation (SUHB luh MAY shuhn) the process in which a solid changes directly into a gas (the term is sometimes also used for the reverse process) (85)

sublimación el proceso por medio del cual un sólido se transforma directamente en un gas (en ocasiones, este término también se usa para describir el proceso inverso) (85)

substrate (SUHB STRAYT) a part, substance, or element that lies beneath and supports another part, substance, or element; the reactant in reactions catalyzed by enzymes (241)

sustrato una parte, sustancia o elemento que se encuentra debajo de otra parte, sustancia o elemento y lo sostiene; el reactivo en reacciones que son catalizadas por enzimas (241)

supersaturated solution (SOO puhr SACH uh RAYT id suh LOO shuhn) a solution that holds more dissolved solute than is required to reach equilibrium at a given temperature (279)

solución sobresaturada una solución que contiene más soluto disuelto que el que se requiere para llegar al equilibro a una temperatura dada (279)

suspension (suh SPEN shuhn) a mixture in which particles of a material are more or less evenly dispersed throughout a liquid or gas (260)

suspensión una mezcla en la que las partículas de un material se encuentran dispersas de manera más o menos uniforme a través de un líquido o de un gas (260)

synthesis reaction (SIN thuh sis ree AK shuhn) a reaction in which two or more substances combine to form a new compound (231)

reacción de síntesis una reacción en la que dos o más sustancias se combinan para formar un compuesto nuevo (231)

T

technology (tek NAHL uh jee) the application of science for practical purposes; the use of tools, machines, materials, and processes to meet human needs (8)

tecnología la aplicación de la ciencia con fines prácticos; el uso de herramientas, máquinas, materiales y procesos para satisfacer las necesidades de los seres humanos (8)

temperature (TEM puhr uh chuhr) a measure of how hot (or cold) something is; specifically, a measure of the average kinetic energy of the particles in an object (80, 473)

temperatura una medida de qué tan caliente (o frío) está algo; específicamente, una medida de la energía cinética promedio de las partículas de un objeto (80, 473)

terminal velocity (TUHR muh nuhl vuh LAHS uh tee) the constant velocity of a falling object when the force of air resistance is equal in magnitude and opposite in direction to the force of gravity (407)

velocidad terminal la velocidad constante de un objeto en caída cuando la fuerza de resistencia del aire es igual en magnitud y opuesta en dirección a la fuerza de gravedad (407)

theory (THEE uh ree) a system of ideas that explains many related observations and is supported by a large body of evidence acquired through scientific investigation (9)

teoría un sistema de ideas que explica muchas observaciones relacionadas y que está respaldado por una gran cantidad de pruebas obtenidas mediante la investigación científica (9)

thermal conduction (THUHR muhl kuhn DUHK shuhn) the transfer of energy as heat through a material (481)

conducción térmica la transferencia de energía en forma de calor a través de un material (481)

thermal energy (THUHR muhl EN uhr jee) the total kinetic energy of a substance's atoms (81)

energía térmica la energía cinética total de los átomos de una sustancia (81)

thermometer (thuhr MAHM uht uhr) an instrument that measures and indicates temperature (474)

termómetro un instrumento que mide e indica la temperatura (474)

transformer (trans FAWRM uhr) a device that increases or decreases the voltage of alternating current (638)

transformador un aparato que aumenta o disminuye el voltaje de la corriente alterna (638)

transition metal (tran ZISH uhn MET'l) one of the metals that can use the inner shell before using the outer shell to bond (159)

metal de transición uno de los metales que tienen la capacidad de usar su orbital interno antes de usar su orbital externo para formar un enlace (159)

transverse wave (TRANS VUHRS WAYV) a wave in which the particles of the medium move perpendicularly to the direction the wave is traveling (511)

onda transversal una onda en la que las partículas del medio se mueven perpendicularmente respecto a la dirección en la que se desplaza la onda (511)

trough (TRAWF) the lowest point of a wave (512)

seno el punto más bajo de una onda (512)

ultrasound (UHL truh SOWND) any sound wave with frequencies higher than 20,000 Hz (546)

ultrasonido cualquier onda de sonido que tenga frecuencias superiores a los 20,000 Hz (546)

unified atomic mass unit (YOON uh FIED uh TAHM ik MAS YOON it) a unit of mass that describes the mass of an atom or molecule; it is exactly 1/12 of the mass of a carbon atom with mass number 12 (symbol, u) (124)

unidad de masa atómica unificada una unidad de masa que describe la masa de un átomo o molécula; es exactamente 1/12 de la masa de un átomo de carbono con número de masa de 12 (símbolo: u) (124)

unsaturated solution (uhn SACH uh RAYT id suh LOO shuhn) a solution that contains less solute than a saturated solution does and that is able to dissolve additional solute (278)

solución no saturada una solución que contiene menos soluto que una solución saturada, y que tiene la capacidad de disolver más soluto (278)

valence electron (VAY luhns ee LEK trahn) an electron that is found in the outermost shell of an atom and that determines the atom's chemical properties (130)

electrón de valencia un electrón que se encuentra en la capa más externa de un átomo y que determina las propiedades químicas del átomo (130)

variable (VER ee uh buhl) a factor that changes in an experiment in order to test a hypothesis (15)

variable un factor que se modifica en un experimento con el fin de probar una hipótesis (15)

velocity (vuh LAHS uh tee) the speed of an object in a particular direction (367)

velocidad la rapidez de un objeto en una dirección dada (367)

virtual image (VUHR choo uhl IM ij) an image from which light rays appear to diverge, even though they are not actually focused there; a virtual image cannot be projected on a screen (562)

imagen virtual una imagen de la que los rayos de luz parecen divergir, aunque no están enfocados allí realmente; una imagen virtual no se puede proyectar en una pantalla (562)

viscosity (vis KAHS uh tee) the resistance of a gas or liquid to flow (94)

viscosidad la resistencia de un gas o un líquido a fluir (94)

volume (VAHL yoom) a measure of the size of a body or region in three-dimensional space (21)

volumen una medida del tamaño de un cuerpo o región en un espacio de tres dimensiones (21)

wavelength (WAYV lengkth) the distance from any point on a wave to an identical point on the next wave (515)

longitud de onda la distancia entre cualquier punto de una onda y un punto idéntico en la onda siguiente (515)

weight (WAYT) a measure of the gravitational force exerted on an object; its value can change with the location of the object in the universe (21, 403)

peso una medida de la fuerza gravitacional ejercida sobre un objeto; su valor puede cambiar en función de la ubicación del objeto en el universo (21, 403)

work (WUHRK) the transfer of energy to a body by the application of a force that causes the body to move in the direction of the force; it is equal to the product of the magnitude of the component of a force along the direction of displacement and the magnitude of the displacement (431)

trabajo la transferencia de energía a un cuerpo por medio de la aplicación de una fuerza que hace que el cuerpo se mueva en la dirección de la fuerza; es igual al producto de la magnitud del componente de una fuerza aplicada en la dirección del desplazamiento por la magnitud del desplazamiento (431)

GLOSSARY • GLOSARIO

Page references followed by *f* refer to illustrative material, such as figures and tables.

INDEX

G

galvanometers, 630, 630*f*
gamma decay, 330, 338
gamma rays, 328, 328*f,* 329
  in electromagnetic spectrum, 557*f,* 558
  from nuclear fusion, 342
  penetration of matter by, 329, 329*f,* 348
  in radiotherapy, 346
gases. *See also* **atmosphere; fluids**
  changes of state, 84*f,* 85–86, 85*f,* 86*f,* 87*f*
  heat conduction by, 484
  kinetic energy of particles in, 80, 80*f*
  lab on, 99
  laws of, 97–101, 97*f,* 99*f,* 100*f*
  in mixtures, 50, 50*f,* 96, 264
  molecules of, 181
  noble, 161, 161*f*
  pressure of, 97–99, 97*f,* 99*f,* 101
  properties of, 97
  reaction rates of, 240
  solubility in liquids, 279, 279*f,* 282–283
  as state of matter, 78, 78*f,* 79, 79*f*
  wave speed in, 521
gas grills, 198
gas laws, 97–101, 97*f,* 99*f,* 100*f*
gasoline
  burning of, 220–221, 221*f*
  isooctane in, 220–222, 220*f,* 221*f*
  separation from crude oil, 265
Gateway Arch, 29
Gay-Lussac's law, 99, 99*f*
generators, 634, 634*f,* 636–637, 636*f. See also* **electrical energy**
geodynamo, 625
geology, 8
geometrical optics, 560
geometry, 672, 672*f*
geophysics, 8
germanium, 146, 146*f*
glass, 65
glass blowing, 65
glycerol, 307
glycogen, 202
graduated cylinder, 685
grams (g), 20*f*
  converting to/from moles, 126, 126*f*
Graphic Organizers
  cause-and-effect map, 292, 663
  chain-of-events chart, 662

  concept map, 430, 660
  flow chart, 472, 661
  instructions for, 660–665
  spider map, 4, 144, 664
  Venn diagram, 665
graphs, 23–24, 677–680. *See also* **distance vs. time graph; line graphs; slope**
  bar graphs, 23, 23*f,* 455, 679
  line graphs, 23, 23*f,* 388, 677
  pie charts, 24, 24*f,* 284, 680
  scatter plots, 678
  of speed vs. time, 376–377, 377*f*
  of transverse waves, 532
gravitational constant, 405, 406, 407
gravitational potential energy, 445–446, 445*f,* 453–454, 454*f*
  electrical potential energy and, 593, 593*f,* 595
  hydroelectric power and, 458
  lab on, 462–463
gravity, 403–411. *See also* **free fall; weight**
  acting on Earth's mass, 405, 405*f,* 413, 413*f*
  of black holes, 411
  blood pressure and, 405
  distance and, 405, 406, 406*f,* 407, 445
  Earth's surface and, 403, 407, 409
  as field force, 381
  friction in opposition to, 385, 385*f*
  as fundamental force, 380, 380*f,* 381
  living things and, 404, 404*f*
  mass and, 405–406, 406*f,* 407, 445, 446
  on moon, 403, 403*f,* 404
  projectile motion and, 408, 408*f,* 409, 410*f*
  stars and, 406
  strength of, 381, 406
  sun and, 405, 405*f*
  universal law of, 10, 405–406, 405*f,* 406*f,* 407
grease, cleaning products for, 307–310, 307*f,* 310*f,* 311
greenhouse effect, 451
ground, electrical, 598
ground fault circuit interrupter, 607
ground state, 131
groups (categories)
  classification of, 4, 292, 504
  generalizations about, 144
groups (periodic table), 150
  electron arrangements in, 151, 151*f,* 152*f*
  ion formation and, 153

guitars, electric, 635
gyrocompass, 621

H

Haber process, 246–247
Hahn, Otto, 337, 339, 340
half-life, 333–336, 333*f,* 335*f*
  calculations with, 334, 354
halogens, 162, 162*f*
hard magnetic materials, 620
hard water, 309, 311
harmonic motion. *See also* **vibrations**
  damped, 509
  simple, 508
hearing, 508, 549, 549*f*
heat. *See also* **temperature**
  changes of state and, 487, 487*f*
  chemical reaction caused by, 222
  conduction of, 480–481, 480*f,* 481*f*
  conductors of, 154, 155*f,* 484–485, 494–495
  convection of, 480, 480*f,* 483
  definition of, 479
  dissolving process and, 272, 273*f,* 279
  from electric circuit, 605
  as energy transfer, 88, 456, 479, 479*f*
  from engine, 492
  from friction, 382, 382*f,* 459
  in homes, 488–489, 490, 491
  kinetic energy of particles and, 448, 490
  lab on, 482
  methods of transfer of, 480–483, 480*f,* 481*f,* 482*f*
  radiated, 482, 482*f,* 557
  second law of thermodynamics and, 490
  specific heat, 485–486, 485*f,* 496, 689
  temperature and, 84, 487, 487*f,* 490
  theories about, 9, 9*f,* 10
  as waste energy, 491
heat engines, 492–493, 492*f,* 493*f*
heating systems, 488, 491
height. *See also* **distance; length**
  gravitational potential energy and, 445–446
helium
  atoms of, 120, 120*f*
  in sun, 132
hertz (Hz), 516
Hertz, Heinrich, 516

INDEX

INDEX

INDEX

Credits

Photography

Abbreviations used
(t) top, (c) center, (b) bottom, (l) left, (r) right, (bkgd) background

Cover
© Ed Honowitz/Stone/Getty Images

Table of Contents
v (bl) Digital Vision/Getty Images; vi (tl) The Granger Collection, New York; vi (b) David Madison/Getty Images; vii (cr) TZ Aviation/Airliners.net; viii (bl) Expuesto- Nicolas Randall/Alamy; ix (tr) Bob Thomason/Getty Images/Stone; ix (b) Frans Lanting/Minden Pictures; x (bl) Tim Platt/Getty Images; xi (tr) Ted Kinsman/Photo Researchers, Inc.; xi (b) Garry Black/Masterfile; xii (tl) A. Ramey/PhotoEdit; xii (bl) Brian J. Skerry/National Geographic Image Collection; xiii (tr) © Brand X Pictures/Alamy; xiv (tr) Buzz Pictures/Alamy; xvi (b) Scott B. Rosen/HRW Photo; xvii (br) Scott B. Rosen/HRW Photo

Chapter One
2-3 (bkgd) Courtesy of Pagani Automobili, Italy; 2 (tl) © PhotoLink/PhotoDisc Red/gettyimages; 2 (cl) Sam Dudgeon/HRW; 2 (bl) Peter Van Steen/HRW; 3 (cr) Scott B. Rosen/HRW Photo; 5 (bl) Hulton Archive/Getty Images; 5 (br) Kari Marttila/Alamy; 7 (tr) AIP Emilio Segrè Visual Archives, Landé Collection; 8 (tl) © Dr. Tim Evans/SPL/Photo Researchers, Inc.; 8 (bl) Nicolas Russell/Getty Images; 8 (br) Volker Steger/Photo Researchers, Inc.; 9 (br) Sam Dudgeon/HRW; 10 (tl) © PhotoLink/PhotoDisc Red/gettyimages; 11 (tr) Kristian Hilsen/Getty Images/Stone; 11 (b) Ianni Dimitrov/Alamy; 11 (br) Courtesy Arup Photo Library; 12 (tl) NOAA; 12 (cl) NOAA; 12 (tr) NOAA; 13 (bkgd) © Ashley Cooper/CORBIS; 13 (tr) Scala/Art Resource, NY; 13 (tl) The Granger Collection, New York; 13 (cl) Scala/Art Resource, NY; 14 (bl) Scott B. Rosen/HRW Photo; 14 (bl) Scott B. Rosen/HRW Photo; 16 (br) Roger Ressmeyer/CORBIS; 17 (t) Bryan Allen/Corbis; 17 (tr) Fred A. Calvert/cold Spring Observatory/Adam Black/KPNO/AURA/NSF; 19 (tr) Hemera Technologies/Alamy; 20 (tr) Sam Dudgeon/HRW; 20 (cl) Peter Van Steen/HRW; 20 (cr) Image Copyright © Photodisc, Inc.; 20 (c) Sam Dudgeon/HRW; 20 (c) © Eyewire/gettyimages; 20 (bl) Peter Van Steen/HRW; 20 (tl) Scott B. Rosen/HRW Photo; 20 (cr) © Ragnar Schmuck/Getty Images; 20 (c) Ian M. Butterfield/Alamy; 20 (bl) PhotoDisc; 20 (br) Royalty-Free/Corbis; 20 (br) Scott B. Rosen/HRW Photo; 21 (tr) CNF, Cornell University; 22 (bl) Peter Van Steen/HRW; 24 (tl) BananaStock; 27 (tl) Sam Dudgeon/HRW; 27 (tc) Sam Dudgeon/HRW; 27 (tc) Sam Dudgeon/HRW; 27 (tr) Sam Dudgeon/HRW; 29 (bkgd) Andrea Pistolesi/Getty Images; 29 (cl) Jefferson National Expansion Memorial/National Parks Service; 29 (bl) Jefferson National Expansion Memorial/National Parks Service; 31 (b) HRW Owned; 32 (b) Scott B. Rosen/HRW Photo; 35 (tl) © PhotoLink/PhotoDisc Red/gettyimages; 35 (cl) Sam Dudgeon/HRW; 35 (bl) Peter Van Steen/HRW

Chemistry Unit Opener
41 (cl) Darren Higgins Photography; (tr) Adastra/Getty Images; (br) Edward Kinsman/Photo Researchers, Inc.

Chapter Two
42-43 (bkgd) James Caldwell/Alamy; 42 (br) Charles D. Winters/Photo Researchers, Inc.; 42 (cl) Aqua Image/Alamy; 42 (cl) Charles O'Rear/CORBIS; 43 (br) Scott B. Rosen/HRW Photo; 45 (br) Index Stock Imagery, Inc.; 46 (bl) David Muir/Masterfile; 46 (cl) Charles D. Winters/Photo Researchers, Inc.; 47 (b) David Madison/Getty Images; 48 (bl) Scott B. Rosen/HRW Photo; 49 (tl) Scott B. Rosen/HRW Photo; 49 (tl) Scott B. Rosen/HRW Photo; 50 (cr) FoodPix/Getty Images; 50 (c) Tudio Bonisolli-StockFood Munich/Stockfood America; 51 (cr) © Judith Collins/Alamy; 51 (b) Judith Collins/Alamy; 51 (br) Stockdisc Classis/Alamy; 52 (bl) © Photodisc/gettyimages; 53 (bkgd) NASA/Jet Propulsion Laboratory; 53 (cl) NASA; 53 (b) NASA/Jet Propulsion Laboratory; 55 (cr) Comstock; 55 (b) Scott B. Rosen/HRW Photo; 55 (tl) Scott B. Rosen/HRW Photo; 56 (bl) Rob Boudreau/Getty Images/Stone; 57 (bkgd) Charles Gupton/CORBIS; 57 (tl) Mauro Fermariello/Photo Researchers, Inc.; 57 (cl) Mauro Fermariello/Photo Researchers, Inc.; 57 (bl) Mauro Fermariello/Photo Researchers, Inc.; 58 (cl) Aqua Image/Alamy; 58 (c) Scott B. Rosen/HRW Photo; 58 (cr) Scott B. Rosen/HRW Photo; 59 (bc) Benelux Press/Index Stock Imagery, Inc.; 59 (bl) HRW Owned; 59 (br) Lance Schriner/HRW; 60 (cl) Sam Dudgeon/HRW; 60 (tl) Royalty Free/Corbis; 60 (tc) Charles O'Rear/CORBIS; 60 (tr) © PunchStock; 61 (bl) James Randklev/Corbis; 61 (bc) BSIP/Phototake; 61 (br) SuperStock; 62 (t) Scott B. Rosen/HRW Photo; 62 (bl) Ben Fink/FoodPix; 62 (tr) HRW Owned; 63 (br) Scott B. Rosen/HRW Photo; 63 (tr) David Buffington/Getty Images 64 (t) HRW Owned; 65 (bkgd) Steve Sant/Alamy; 65 (tl) Richard S. Huntrods; 65 (tr) Expuesto-Nicolas Randall/Alamy; 67 (r) Scott B. Rosen/HRW Photo; 69 (bl) Charles O'Rear/CORBIS; 69 (cl) Aqua Image/Alamy; 69 (tl) Charles D. Winters/Photo Researchers, Inc.; 70 (bl) Andrew Lambert Photography Photo Researchers, Inc.

Chapter Three
74-75 (bkgd) John McAnulty/CORBIS; 74 (t) Johnny Johnson/Getty Images; 74 (tl) ImageState/Alamy; 74 (cl) Royalty-Free/Corbis; 74 (bl) David R. Frazier Photolibrary, Inc./Alamy; 75 (br) Sam Dudgeon/HRW Photo; 77 (br) Royalty-Free/Corbis; 78 (t) Sam Dudgeon/HRW; 79 (t) Scott Van Osdol/HRW; 79 (b) Johnny Johnson/Getty Images; 80 (br) Tony Freeman/PhotoEdit; 80 (bc) Galen Rowell/CORBIS; 80 (bl) John Langford/HRW; 81 (tl) Scott B. Rosen/HRW Photo; 82-83 (bkgd) © PunchStock; 82 (bl) Scott Stulberg/CORBIS; 83 (r) NASA; 85 (b) Digital Vision/Punchstock; 86 (b) ImageState/Alamy; 86 (tl) Scott B. Rosen/HRW Photo; 87 (l) John Langford/HRW; 87 (cr) Tony Freeman/PhotoEdit; 87 (bc) Galen Rowell/CORBIS; 88 (l) Fancy Photography/Veer; 91 (t) Scott B. Rosen/HRW Photo; 92 (b) Royalty-Free/Corbis; 93 (b) Brian Hagiwara/FoodPix; 95 (bkgd) CORBIS; 96 (bl) W.H. Muller/Zefa/Corbis; 99 (bl) Scott B. Rosen/HRW Photo; 99 (t) David R. Frazier Photolibrary, Inc./Alamy; 100 (b) Charles D. Winters; 103 (bl) Scott B. Rosen/HRW Photo; 105 (t) Johnny Johnson/Getty Images; 105 (tl) ImageState/Alamy; 105 (bl) Royalty-Free/Corbis; 105 (b) David R. Frazier Photolibrary, Inc./Alamy

Chapter Four
110-111 (bkgd) © Eye of Science/SPL/Photo Researchers, Inc.; 110 (t) Sam Dudgeon/HRW; 110 (c) Sam Dudgeon/HRW; 110 (b) TZ Aviation/Airliners.net; 111 (b) Scott B. Rosen/HRW Photo; 113 (br) Scott B. Rosen/HRW Photo; 114 (bl) Michael Newman/Photo Edit; 115 (t) Charles D. Winters/Photo Researchers, Inc.; 115 (b) Sam Dudgeon/HRW; 118 (tr) Douglas Peebles/CORBIS; 118 (inset) CORBIS Images/HRW; 120 (t) Mira/Alamy; 122 (t) Scott B. Rosen/HRW Photo; 123 (r) GJLP/Photo Researchers, Inc.; 123 (bl) © Spencer Grant/SPL/Photo Researchers, Inc.; 125 (bc) Sam Dudgeon/HRW; 127 (t) Dynamic Graphics Group/IT Stock Free/Alamy; 129 (b) TZ Aviation/Airliners.net; 132 (c) PhotoDisc/Getty Images; 135 (r) Scott B. Rosen/HRW Photo; 137 (tl) Sam Dudgeon/HRW; 137 (cl) Sam Dudgeon/HRW; 137 (bl) TZ Aviation/Airliners.net

Chapter Five
142-143 (bkgd) Andrew Syred/Photo Researchers, Inc.; 142 (cl) Sam Dudgeon/HRW Photo; 142 (bl) PHOTOTAKE Inc./Alamy; 145 (br) Science Photo Library/Photo Researchers, Inc.; 145 (c) HRW Owned; 145 (bc) HRW Owned; 146 (b) The Granger Collection, New York; 146 (l) Richard Megna/Fundamental Photographs; 147 (b) Volvox/PictureQuest; 147 (bl) © Foodcollection/Alamy; 147 (cr) Russ Lappa/Photo Researchers, Inc.; 150 (tl) Tom Pantages Photography; 150 (tc) © Klaus Guldbrandsen/SPL/Photo Researchers, Inc.; 150 (tr) Richard Megna/Fundamental Photographs; 155 (tl) Sam Dudgeon/HRW Photo; 155 (cl) HRW Owned; 155 (tc) Sally Anderson-Bruce/HRW; 155 (c) Astrid & Hanns-Frieder Michler/Photo Researchers, Inc.; 155 (tr) Russ Lappa/Photo Researchers, Inc.; 155 (cr) Astrid & Hanns-Frieder Michler/Photo Researchers, Inc.; 156 (bl) Rob Lewine/CORBIS; 157 (br) Andrew Lambert Photography/Photo Researchers, Inc.; 157 (cr) © Andrew Lambert Photography/SPL/Photo Researchers, Inc.; 158 (bc) Richard Megna Fundamental Photographs; 158 (br) LADA/Photo Researchers, Inc.; 159 (tl) Peter Van Steen/HRW; 159 (cr) Phil Degginger/Alamy; 160 (bl) Oullette/Theroux/Publiphoto/Photo Researchers, Inc.; 161 (bc) PHOTOTAKE Inc./Alamy; 161 (b) Owaki-Kulla/CORBIS; 162 (bl) Martyn Chillmaid/Oxford Scientific; 162 (bc) Ric Frazier/Masterfile; 163 (cr) Charles D. Winters/Photo Researchers, Inc.; 163 (cl) © Imageshop/Alamy; 163 (bl) Horst Klemm/Masterfile; 165 (bkgd) Lawrence Manning/CORBIS; 165 (c) © John Maher/Index Stock Imagery, Inc.; 165 (bc) Richard T. Nowitz/CORBIS; 165 (cr) © Tetra Images/Alamy; 169 (cl) Sam Dudgeon/HRW Photo; 169 (bl) PHOTOTAKE Inc./Alamy

Chapter Six
174-175 (bkgd) Peter Arnold, Inc./Alamy; 174 (t) GC Minerals/Alamy; 174 (tl) Index Stock/Alamy; 174 (cl) Paul Silverman, Fundamental Photographs, NYC; 174 (bl) Alexander Hubrich/zefa/Corbis; 175 (br) HRW OWNED; 177 (bl) Sergio Purtell/Foca/HRW; 177 (br) Sergio Purtell/Foca/HRW; 179 (t) digitalvision/punchstock; 179 (cl) AAD Worldwide Travel Images/Alamy; 179 (bl)

nagelestock/Alamy; 180 (br) GC Minerals/Alamy; 181 (tr) Sam Dudgeon/HRW; 181 (br) Profimedia.CZ s.r.o./Alamy; 182 (l) Furnald/Gray/Getty Images; 184 (bl) Sam Dudgeon/HRW; 185 (bc) Richard Megna, Fundamental Photographs, NYC; 185 (tr) Scott B. Rosen/HRW Photo; 185 (bl) Hrw Owned; 185 (bl) Richard Megna, Fundamental Photographs, NYC; 186 (l) Leslie Garland Picture Library/Alamy; 188 (bl) Scott B. Rosen/HRW Photo; 188 (cr) Index Stock/Alamy; 192 (bc) Paul Silverman, Fundamental Photographs, NYC; 192 (br) © Andrew Lambert Photography/SPL/Photo Researchers, Inc.; 194 (br) © Getty Images; 194 (br) © Getty Images; 194 (bl) © Getty Images; 194 (bl) © Getty Images; 197 (br) Peter Van Steen/HRW; 198 (b) Justin Kase/Alamy; 200 (t) Sam Dudgeon/HRW; 200 (bl) Scott B. Rosen/HRW Photo; 201 (tr) Royalty-free/CORBIS; 202 (tr) Alexander Hubrich/zefa/Corbis; 203 (br) Scott B. Rosen/HRW Photo; 205 (bkgd) Fritz Goro/Time & Life Pictures/Getty Images; 205 (tl) Andrew Brookes/Corbis; 205 (cl) © TEK Image/SPL/Photo Researchers, Inc.; 205 (bl) © James Holmes/Cellmark Diagnostics/SPL/Photo Researchers, Inc.; 207 (br) Scott B. Rosen/HRW Photo; 209 (t) GC Minerals/Alamy; 209 (tl) Index Stock/Alamy; 209 (cl) Paul Silverman, Fundamental Photographs, NYC; 209 (bl) Alexander Hubrich/zefa/Corbis; 214-215 (bkgd) Ted Horowitz/CORBIS; 214 (tr) Gabe Palmer/CORBIS; 214 (cl) © Michael Donne/SPL/Photo Researchers, Inc.; 214 (br) Aurora/Getty Images; 215 (tr) Richard Levine/Alamy; 215 (cl) Gail Moone/CORBIS; 215 (bc) Royalty-Free/CORBIS

Chapter Seven

216-217 (bkgd) Ian Cartwright/Getty Images; 216 (t) Charles D. Winters; 216 (cl) Royalty-Free/CORBIS; 216 (cl) Royalty-Free/CORBIS; 216 (bl) Photo ITAR-TASS/Vladimir Malygin; 217 (br) Scott B. Rosen/HRW Photo; 219 (bl) Charles D. Winters; 219 (bc) Charles D. Winters; 219 (br) Charles D. Winters; 220 (br) Matt Rainey/Star Ledger/Corbis; 223 (bkgd) Jeff Rotman/Getty Images; 223 (cl) Gregory G. Dimijian/Photo Researchers, Inc.; 223 (tl) Gail Shumway/Getty Images; 223 (bl) © Ted Kinsman/SPL/Photo Researchers, Inc.; 224 (c) Dorling Kindersley/Getty Images; 225 (br) Royalty-Free/Corbis; 226 (tl) Sam Dudgeon/HRW; 228 (tl) Scott B. Rosen/HRW Photo; 229 (cr) Charlie Winters; 230 (br) Judith Haeusler/Getty Images; 231 (cr) © Paul Rapson/SPL/Photo Researchers, Inc.; 231 (br) Royalty-Free/Corbis; 231 (b) Royalty-Free/CORBIS; 232 (b) Syracuse Newspapers/Carl J. Single/The Image Works; 233 (bl) Sergio Purtell/Foca/HRW; 234 (br) Sergio Purtell/Foca/HRW; 234 (tl) Sergio Purtell/Foca/HRW; 235 (tr) Scott B. Rosen/HRW Photo; 236 (bkgd) Lester Lefkowitz/CORBIS; 236 (bl) NASA/Goddard Space Flight Center; 236 (bc) NASA/Goddard Space Flight Center; 238 (bl) StockTrek/Getty Images; 239 (tr) Sergio Purtell/Foca/HRW; 239 (cr) Sergio Purtell/Foca/HRW; 239 (br) Scott B. Rosen/HRW Photo; 240 (bl) Dorling Kindersley Limited courtesy of Science Museum, London/Corbis; 242-243 (bkgd) © Simon Fraser/SPL/Photo Researchers, Inc.; 242 (bc) Virgo/zefa/Corbis; 243 (tl) David Stoecklein/CORBIS; 243 (c) Microworks/Phototake; 244 (bl) Scott B. Rosen/HRW Photo; 244 (br) Scott B. Rosen/HRW Photo; 245 (br) SuperStock; 246 (br) Visuals Unlimited/Tom J. Ulrich; 247 (tr) Photo ITAR-TASS/Vladimir Malygin; 249 (br) Scott B. Rosen/HRW Photo; 251 (c) Charles D. Winters; 251 (tl) Royalty-Free/CORBIS; 251 (cl) Royalty-Free/CORBIS; 251 (bl) Photo ITAR-TASS/Vladimir Malygin

Chapter Eight

256-257 (bkgd) Lester Lefkowitz/CORBIS; 256 (tl) Peter Van Steen/HRW; 256 (cl) PunchStock; 256 (bl) Charlie Winters/Photo Researchers Inc.; 257 (cr) Scott B. Rosen/HRW Photo; 259 (cr) Peter Van Steen/HRW; 259 (br) Peter Van Steen/HRW; 260 (tl) Sam Dudgeon/HRW; 260 (tr) Sam Dudgeon/HRW; 260 (tl) Sam Dudgeon/HRW; 260 (tr) Sam Dudgeon/HRW; 261 (b) HRW Owned; 262 (inset) Bruce Iverson; 262 (br) Peter Van Steen/HRW; 262 (tl) Scott B. Rosen/HRW Photo; 263 (bl) Sergio Purtell/Foca/HRW; 263 (cr) Sergio Purtell/Foca/HRW; 263 (br) Sergio Purtell/Foca/HRW; 264 (tl) Scott B. Rosen/HRW Photo; 265 (bkgd) © PunchStock; 266 (t) Tim Pannell/Corbis; 267 (br) © PunchStock; 269 (tl) Richard Megna/Fundamental Photographs, New York; 270 (t) Sam Dudgeon/HRW; 270 (b) Scott B. Rosen/HRW Photo; 271 (br) Scott B. Rosen/HRW Photo; 272 (bl) Peter Van Steen/HRW; 272 (br) Peter Van Steen/HRW; 273 (tl) HRW Owned; 273 (tc) HRW Owned; 273 (tr) HRW Owned; 274-275 (bkgd) © Scimat/SPL/Photo Researchers, Inc.; 274 (bl) Lester Lefkowitz/CORBIS; 275 (cr) Black Star; 276 (br) Charlie D. Winters/Photo Researchers, Inc.; 278 (bl) Peter Van Steen/HRW; 278 (br) Peter Van Steen/HRW; 279 (tr) Charlie Winters/Photo Researchers, Inc.; 279 (bl) Charles D. Winters; 279 (br) Charles D. Winters; 279 (tr) Christina Kennedy/Getty Images; 283 (r) Scott B. Rosen/HRW Photo; 285 (t) Peter Van Steen/HRW; 285 (c) PunchStock; 285 (b) Charlie Winters/Photo Researchers, Inc.

Chapter Nine

290-291 (bkgd) Pat O'Hara/CORBIS; 290 (tl) Oliver Strewe/Getty Images; 290 (cl) CNR/Photo Researchers, Inc.; 290 (bl) © Jake Wyman/Getty Images; 291 (br) Scott B. Rosen/HRW Photo; 293 (br) Scott B. Rosen/HRW Photo; 294 (bl) Sergio Purtell/Foca/HRW; 294 (tl) Sergio Purtell/Foca/HRW; 295 (tr) Scott B. Rosen/HRW Photo; 296 (cl) John Morrison/Morrison Photography; 297 (br) Sam Dudgeon/HRW; 298 (bl) Charles D. Winters; 298 (bc) Charles D. Winters; 298 (c) Charles D. Winters; 298 (br) Charles D. Winters; 298 (r) Charles D. Winters; 298 (cl) Scott B. Rosen/HRW Photo; 298 (l) Royalty-Free/Corbis; 300 (tl) Charles D. Winters/Photo Researchers, Inc.; 301 (bkgd) © Oliver Strewe/Getty Images; 301 (tr) Ted Spiegel/CORBIS; 301 (cl) Michael S. Quinton/Getty Images; 301 (c) Sally A. Morgan; Ecoscene/CORBIS; 302 (bl) Leonard Lessin/Peter Arnold, Inc.; 303 (t) Charles D. Winters; 304 (tl) Charles D. Winters; 305 (tr) CNRI/Photo Researchers, Inc.; 305 (br) Scott B. Rosen/HRW Photo; 306 (tl) Frans Lanting/Minden Pictures; 306 (tr) David Whitten/PictureQuest; 307 (br) Bob Thomason/Getty Images/Stone; 308 (bkgd) Aaron Haupt/Photo Researchers, Inc.; 309 (bl) Scott B. Rosen/HRW Photo; 310 (tl) © Jake Wyman/Getty Images; 311 (tl) Peter Van Steen/HRW; 311 (tc) Peter Van Steen/HRW; 312 (tr) Scott B. Rosen/HRW Photo; 312 (br) Scott B. Rosen/HRW Photo; 313 (tr) Scott B. Rosen/HRW Photo; 313 (cr) Scott B. Rosen/HRW Photo; 313 (br) Scott B. Rosen/HRW Photo; 315 (br) HRW Owned; 317 (tl) Oliver Strewe/Getty Images; 317 (cl) CNR/Photo Researchers, Inc.; 317 (bl) Jake Wyman/Getty Images; 322 (tr) The Granger Collection, New York; 322 (tc) Bettmann/CORBIS; 322 (tl) The Granger Collection, New York; 322 (cr) Mike Agliolo/Photo Researchers, Inc.; 322 (c) Oxford Science Archive/Heritage-Images/The Image Works; 322 (cl) Alfred Pasieka/Photo Researchers, Inc.; 322 (bl) Getty Images; 322 (br) Courtesy of DuPont; 322 (bc) Columbus Dispatch, Craig Holman/Associated

Press, AP; 323 (tl) Albert Riethausen/Associated Press, AP; 323 (tc) Ron Sanford/CORBIS; 323 (tr) Underwood & Underwood/CORBIS; 323 (c) © NREL/US Department of Energy/SPL/Photo Researchers, Inc.; 323 (cl) © Dr. Tim Evans/SPL/Photo Researchers, Inc.; 323 (cr) Scott Olson/Getty Images/NewsCom; 323 (bl) © David Parker/SPL/Photo Researchers, Inc.; 323 (bc) Stone/Getty Images

Chapter Ten

324-325 (bkgd) Roger Ressmeyer/CORBIS; 324 (tl) Giani Dagli Orti/CORBIS; 324 (cl) Jason Hawkes/CORBIS; 324 (bl) US Department of Energy/Photo Researchers, Inc.; 325 (br) Scott B. Rosen/HRW Photo; 332 (bkgd) Bettmann/CORBIS; 332 (cl) Jean-loup Charmet/Photo Researchers, Inc.; 332 (bl) DK Limited/CORBIS; 335 (tr) Scott B. Rosen/HRW Photo; 336 (t) Giani Dagli Orti/CORBIS; 337 (br) Bettmann/CORBIS; 341 (tl) Peter Van Steen/HRW; 343 (bkgd) Jason Hawkes/CORBIS; 344 (br) SuperStock; 345 (t) Keith Brofsky; 346 (tl) Peter Van Steen/HRW; 346 (bl) Larry Lefever/Grant Heilman Photography, Inc.; 347 (bkgd) Lester Lefkowitz/CORBIS; 347 (bl) Roger Ressmeyer/CORBIS; 348 (bl) © Martyn F. Chillmaid/SPL/Photo Researchers, Inc.; 349 (tl) Colin Cuthbert/SPL/Photo Researchers, Inc.; 350 (tl) US Department of Energy/Photo Researchers, Inc.; 351 (r) ITER/Photo Researchers, Inc.; 355 (tl) Giani Dagli Orti/CORBIS; 355 (cl) Jason Hawkes/CORBIS; 355 (bl) US Department of Energy/Photo Researchers, Inc.

Physics Unit Opener

361 (cl) John McAnulty/CORBIS; (tr) James Caldwell/Alamy; (br) Andrew Syred/Photo Researchers, Inc.

Chapter Eleven

362-363 (bkgd) Adastra/Getty Images; 362 (cl) Duomo/CORBIS; 362 (bl) Mike Powell/Getty Images; 362 (tl) Josef Fankhauser/Getty Images; 363 (tr) David Muir/Masterfile; 365 (br) Sam Spurgeon; 366 (bc) Alan Levenson/Getty Images/Stone; 366 (br) Index Stock Photography, Inc.; 366 (bl) Rubberball/Jupiter Images; 367 (bc) Michael H. Dunn/Corbis Stock Market; 367 (bl) Courtesy of Amtrak; 367 (br) Thinkstock/Superstock; 368 (tl) Scott B. Rosen/HRW Photo; 368 (bl) Josef Fankhauser/Getty Images; 371 (tr) Transtock Inc./Alamy; 371 (tc) Zoomstock/Masterfile; 371 (tl) David A. Barnes/Alamy; 373 (br) © Royalty Free/Wernher Krutein/CORBIS; 373 (t) Duomo/CORBIS; 377 (t) AFP/Getty Images; 378-379 (bkgd) David Frazier/The Image Works; 379 (t) Courtesy of Vericom Computers, Inc.; 381 (bl) Scott B. Rosen/HRW Photo; 381 (br) Scott B. Rosen/HRW Photo; 382 (bl) Al Francekevich/CORBIS; 384 (tl) Scott B. Rosen/HRW Photo; 384 (bl) Mike Powell/Getty Images; 387 (b) Scott B. Rosen/HRW Photo; 389 (tl) Josef Fankhauser/Getty Images; 389 (cl) Duomo/CORBIS; 389 (bl) Mike Powell/Getty Images

Chapter Twelve

394-395 (bkgd) Duomo/CORBIS; 394 (tl) Dennis O'Clair/Getty Images; 394 (cl) NASA; 394 (bl) Brian Bailey/CORBIS; 395 (br) Scott B. Rosen/HRW Photo; 397 (br) Dennis O'Clair/Getty Images; 398 (tl) Scott B. Rosen/HRW Photo; 398 (bl) Phillip Kaake/CORBIS; 399 (bkgd) Rick Fischer/Masterfile; 400 (bl) Sam Dudgeon/HRW; 400 (br) Sam Dudgeon/HRW; 402 (tl) Sam Dudgeon/HRW; 402 (tr) Sam Dudgeon/HRW; 403 (br) NASA; 404 (br) Gavriel Jecan/Getty; 404 (bc) Jeremy Woodhouse/Getty Images; 404 (t) Royalty-Free/Corbis;

404 (tl) CORBIS; 404 (cl) Royalty Free/Corbis; 404 (bl) JPL/NASA; 407 (br) Toby Rankin/Masterfile; 408 (tl) NASA; 408 (bl) Michelle Bridwell/Frontera Fotos; 408 (b) Image Copyright © PhotoDisc, Inc./HRW; 409 (bl) Richard Megna/Fundamental Photographs; 411 (bkgd) NASA; 411 (tr) NASA; 411 (cr) NASA; 412 (t) David Madison; 412 (bl) Tim Platt/Getty Images; 413 (cr) Tim Platt/Getty Images; 414 (tl) Scott B. Rosen/HRW Photo; 415 (tr) Brian Bailey/CORBIS; 416 (bl) Digital Vision/Getty Images; 417 (t) INSADCO Photography/Alamy; 419 (b) Scott B. Rosen/HRW Photo; 421 (tl) Dennis O'Clair/Getty Images; 421 (cl) NASA; 421 (bl) Brian Bailey/CORBIS; 422 (bl) Stefan Puetz/zefa/Corbis; 426-427 (bkgd) Royalty-Free/CORBIS; 426 (tr) David Zalubowski/ Associated Press, AP; 426 (cl) Ronnie Kaufman/CORBIS; 426 (br) Lester Lefkowitz/CORBIS; 427 (tr) Reuters/ CORBIS; 427 (cl) Ed Young/CORBIS; 427 (bc) Ric Francis/Associated Press, AP

Chapter Thirteen

428-429 (bkgd) Darren Higgins Photography; 428 (t) Shawn Frederick/Getty Images; 428 (tl) SuperStock; 428 (bl) Alec Ptylowany/Masterfile; 428 (b) Altera Stefano/NASC/GAMMA; 429 (tr) Scott B. Rosen/HRW Photo; 431 (br) Mike Powell/Getty Images; 433 (tl) Scott B. Rosen/HRW Photo; 434 (bl) Shawn Frederick/Getty Images; 435 (bkgd) Reuters/Stefano Rellandini; 435 (tl) Philip Gatward (c) Dorling Kindersley; 435 (tc) photolibrary pty. ltd./NewsCom; 435 (tr) Image Farm Inc./Alamy; 437 (tl) Peter Van Steen/HRW; 437 (tr) Peter Van Steen/HRW; 438 (tl) Robert Wolf/HRW Photo; 438 (tc) Visuals Unlimited/A. J. Copley; 438 (bc) SuperStock; 438 (br) Dr. E. R. Degginger/Color-Pic, Inc.; 438 (tr) Peter Van Steen/HRW Photo; 438 (bl) Scott B. Rosen/HRW Photo; 439 (tr) Michelle Bridwell/HRW; 439 (tc) John P. Kelly/Getty Images/The Image Bank; 439 (r) Purcstock; 440 (bl) Peter Van Steen/HRW Photo; 441 (tr) Scott B. Rosen/HRW Photo; 441 (bl) Scott B. Rosen/HRW Photo; 442 (tr) SuperStock; 442 (br) Dr. E. R. Degginger/Color Pic, Inc.; 443 (tc) Peter Van Steen/HRW; 443 (tl) Peter Van Steen/HRW; 443 (tr) Peter Van Steen/HRW; 444 (bl) Pulse Productions/SuperStock/PictureQuest; 445 (tr) Richard Bannister; 447 (b) Alec Pytlowany/Masterfile; 449 (r) Royalty-Free/Corbis; 449 (br) © Darwin Dale/SPL/ Photo Researchers, Inc.; 450 (tl) NASA/Phototake; 450 (br) Steve Bloom Images; 451 (bkgd) David Trood/Getty Images; 451 (cl) Dennis MacDonald/Alamy; 452 (t) Garry Black/Masterfile; 453 (br) Six Flags/Splash News; 454 (t) Coaster Gallery/JAR Productions; 455 (tr) SuperStock; 456 (tl) P. Freytag/zefa/Corbis; 457 (br) Scott B. Rosen/ HRW Photo; 458 (bkgd) Patrick Eden/Alamy; 459 (tr) Jouanneau Thomas/CORBIS SYGMA; 460 (tl) Hank Morgan/Rainbow Inc.; 461 (c) Altera Stefano/NASC/ GAMMA; 463 (l) Peter Van Steen/HRW; 465 (t) Shawn Frederick/Getty Images; 465 (tl) SuperStock; 465 (c) Alec Pytlowany/Masterfile; 465 (b) Altera Stefano/NASC/ GAMMA; 466 (cl) Peter Van Steen/HRW; 467 (c) Scott B. Rosen/HRW Photo; 467 (c) Scott B. Rosen/HRW Photo; 467 (c) Scott B. Rosen/HRW Photo

Chapter Fourteen

470-471 (bkgd) Edward Kinsman/Photo Researchers, Inc.; 470 (tl) Phanie/Photo Researchers, Inc.; 470 (cl) Steve Mason/ Photodisc Green/Getty Images; 470 (bl) NativeStock; 471 (r) Thinkstock Images; 473 (bl) Steve Bloom Images/Alamy; 473 (bc) Michael Newman/PhotoEdit; 473 (br)

Phanie/Photo Researchers, Inc.; 474 (tl) Scott B. Rosen/HRW Photo; 474 (bl) HRW Owned; 475 (tr) Scott B. Rosen/HRW Photo; 479 (tr) Burke/Triolo Productions; 479 (cr) Deborah Ory Photography/Stockfood America; 480 (b) © Steve Mason/Photodisc Green/gettyimages; 482 (tr) Sam Dudgeon/HRW; 482 (bl) Ted Kinsman/Photo Researchers, Inc.; 483 (bkgd) Masumi Nakada/zefa/Corbis; 484 (bl) Sam Dudgeon/HRW; 484 (tl) © Brian & Cherry Alexander/Alamy; 485 (tr) Charles D. Winters; 488-489 (bkgd) Robert Perron; 490 (bl) NativeStock; 491 (tr) Guy Grenier/Masterfile; 491 (cr) Lorcan/DigitalVision/gettyimages; 495 (b) Scott B. Rosen/HRW Photo; 497 (tl) Phanie/Photo Researchers, Inc.; 497 (t) Steve Mason/Photodisc Green/Getty Images; 497 (bl) NativeStock

Chapter Fifteen

502-503 (bkgd) Courtesy of Patricia Levi; 502 (tl) Travelshots/Alamy; 502 (cl) Jim Sugar/CORBIS; 502 (bl) Michael Freeman/Bruce Coleman, Inc.; 503 (br) Scott B. Rosen/HRW Photo; 506 (br) Travelshots/Alamy; 506 (bl) SuperStock; 507 (tl) Art Resource, NY; 509 (bl) Scott B. Rosen/HRW Photo; 510 (bkgd) Davo Blair/ Alamy; 515 (br) Jim Sugar/CORBIS; 517 (bkgd) Buzz Pictures/Alamy; 517 (tl) Buzz Pictures/Alamy; 517 (cl) Buzz Pictures/Alamy; 517 (bl) Buzz Pictures/Alamy; 517 (b) Buzz Pictures/Alamy; 518 (tr) ©Joe Devenney/Getty Images/The Image Bank; 520 (tl) Scott B. Rosen/HRW Photo; 520 (br) Brian J. Skerry/National Geographic Image Collection; 522 (bl) Peter Van Steen/HRW; 522 (br) Peter Van Steen/HRW; 523 (tl) © Jim Reed/SPL/ Photo Researchers, Inc.; 523 (tr) Jim Reed/CORBIS; 524 (bl) Erich Schrempp/Photo Researchers, Inc.; 525 (tl) Richard Megna/Fundamental Photographs; 525 (tr) FP/Fundamental Photographers; 526 (tl) Peter Van Steen/HRW; 526 (br) E. R. Degginger/Color-Pic, Inc.; 528 (tl) Michael Freeman/Bruce Coleman, Inc.; 529 (tr) Richard Megna/Fundamental Photographs; 529 (tr) Richard Megna/Fundamental Photographs; 531 (b) Scott B. Rosen/HRW Photo; 533 (tl) Travelshots/Alamy; 533 (cl) Jim Sugar/CORBIS; 533 (bl) Michael Freeman/Bruce Coleman, Inc.; 538-539 (bkgd) Aaron Horowitz/CORBIS; 538 (tr) The Granger Collection, New York; 538 (cr) The Granger Collection, New York; 538 (c) The Granger Collection, New York; 538 (cl) The Granger Collection, New York; 538 (bl) © Tony Craddock/SPL/Photo Researchers, Inc.; 538 (bc) Sheila Terry/Rutherford Appleton Laboratory/Photo Researchers, Inc.; 538 (br) Getty Images; 539 (tl) Hulton Archive/Getty Images; 539 (tc) Hulton Archive/Getty Images; 539 (cl) The Granger Collection, New York; 539 (cr) The Granger Collection, New York; 539 (br) FPG/Hulton Archive/Getty Images; 539 (c) J. R. Eyerman/Time Life Pictures/Getty Images; 539 (bl) Digital Vision/Getty Images Royalty Free; 539 (bc) Toyota/Getty Images

Chapter Sixteen

540-541 (bkgd) Jose Fuste Raga/CORBIS; 540 (t) © Andrew Lambert Photography/SPL/Photo Researchers, Inc.; 540 (tl) Royalty-Free/CORBIS; 540 (cl) Swerve/ Alamy; 540 (bl) © Jeremy Woodhouse/PunchStock; 541 (cr) Scott B. Rosen/HRW Photo; 543 (bc) A. Ramey/PhotoEdit; 544 (tl) Scott B. Rosen/HRW Photo; 545 (cl) Outdoor Perspectives/Alamy; 545 (bl) Michael Newman/PhotoEdit; 545 (c) Getty Images Royalty

Free; 545 (br) Comstock Royalty Free; 545 (cr) Mint Photography/Alamy; 546 (cl) Royalty-Free/CORBIS; 546 (c) HRW Owned; 546 (bl) PhotoDisc, Inc.; 546 (br) Doug Perrine; 547 (bl) Redferns Music Picture Library/ Alamy; 547 (br) © Andrew Lambert Photography/SPL/ Photo Researchers, Inc.; 548 (cl) Scott B. Rosen/HRW Photo; 550 (br) Taxi/Getty Images; 550 (b) Blend Images/Alamy; 555 (bl) Gukenter Rossenbach/zefa/ CORBIS; 556 (br) E. R. Degginger/Animals Animals/ Earth Scenes; 556 (bl) Telegraph Colour Library/Getty Images/Taxi; 556 (bc) Don Couch/HRW Photo; 557 (bc) Ron Chapple/Getty Images/Taxi; 557 (bl) ©Royalty-Free/CORBIS; 557 (br) Royalty-Free/CORBIS; 558 (tl) Sheila Terry/Photo Researchers, Inc.; 559 (tr) Royalty-Free/CORBIS; 559 (bl) Andersen Ross/Getty Images; 560 (bl) Claude Gazuit/Photo Researchers, Inc.; 561 (bl) Richard Megna/Fundamental Photographs, New York; 562 (b) John Langford/HRW; 563 (tl) Scott B. Rosen/HRW Photo; 563 (br) Swerve/Alamy; 564 (bl) Peter Van Steen/HRW; 564 (br) Peter Van Steen/HRW; 566 (bl) Richard Megna/Fundamental Photographs; 567 (bl) © Jeremy Woodhouse/PunchStock; 568 (tl) Richard Megna/Fundamental Photographs; 568 (tr) Richard Megna/Fundamental Photographs; 568 (bl) Peter Van Steen/HRW; 570 (br) © Science Photo Library/Photo Researchers, Inc.; 571 (t) Graham French/Masterfile; 572-573 (bkgd) Scott B. Rosen/HRW Photo; 572 (c) Scott B. Rosen/HRW Photo; 572 (tr) Scott B. Rosen/HRW Photo; 572 (l) Scott B. Rosen/HRW Photo; 573 (t) Scott B. Rosen/HRW Photo; 573 (b) Scott B. Rosen/HRW Photo; 577 (t) © Andrew Lambert Photography/SPL/Photo Researchers, Inc.; 577 (tl) Royalty-Free/CORBIS; 577 (cl) Swerve/Alamy; 577 (bl) © Jeremy Woodhouse/ PunchStock

Chapter Seventeen

582-583 (bkgd) © Arthur S. Aubry/Getty Images; 582 (tl) Scott B. Rosen/HRW Photo; 582 (cl) Joseph Brignolo/Getty Images; 582 (bl) Brand X Pictures/Alamy; 583 (br) Scott B. Rosen/HRW Photo; 585 (br) Scott B. Rosen/ HRW Photo; 586 (tl) Scott B. Rosen/HRW Photo; 586 (cl) Scott B. Rosen/HRW Photo; 587 (bkgd) Douglas E. Walker/Masterfile; 587 (tr) National Portrait Gallery, Smithsonian Institution/Art Resource, NY; 587 (cl) Bettman/ CORBIS; 588 (cl) Scott B. Rosen/HRW Photo; 590 (bl) Scott B. Rosen/HRW Photo; 590 (tl) Scott B. Rosen/HRW Photo; 594 (bl) Sam Dudgeon/HRW; 595 (br) Scott B. Rosen/HRW Photo; 598 (bl) Royalty-Free/CORBIS; 599 (tr) Joseph Brignolo/Getty Images; 600 (bl) © Brand X Pictures/Alamy; 601 (bl) Sam Dudgeon/HRW; 601 (tr) Sam Dudgeon/HRW; 602 (tl) Sergio Purtell/Foca/HRW; 602 (c) Sergio Purtell/Foca/HRW; 602 (cl) Sam Dudgeon/HRW; 602 (bl) Sergio Purtell/Foca/ HRW; 602 (bc) Sergio Purtell/Foca/HRW; 603 (tc) Sergio Purtell/Foca/HRW; 603 (cr) Sam Dudgeon/HRW; 603 (br) Sam Dudgeon/ HRW; 604 (bkgd) CORBIS; 604 (c) SSPL/The Image Works; 604 (cl) Scott B. Rosen/HRW Photo; 604 (tr) Courtesy of Computer History Museum; 605 (br) Royalty-Free/CORBIS; 606 (bl) Paul Silverman/Fundamental Photographs; 607 (tr) Scott B. Rosen/HRW Photo; 609 (br) Scott B. Rosen/HRW Photo; 611 (tl) Scott B.

Rosen/HRW Photo; 611 (cl) Joseph Brignolo/
Getty Images; 611 (bl) © Brand X Pictures/
Alamy

Chapter Eighteen

616-617 (bkgd) Mike Macri/Masterfile; 616 (tl) © G.
Glatsmaaier, Los Alamos National Laboratory/P. Roberts,
UCLA/SPL/Photo Researchers, Inc.; 616 (cl) Dynamic
Graphics Group/Creatas/Alamy; 616 (bl) Tara Moore/
Getty Images; 617 (tr) Victoria Smith/HRW; 619 (br) Breck
P. Kent/Animals Animals/Earth Scenes; 620 (bl) Peter
Van Steen/HRW; 621 (tr) Scott B. Rosen/HRW Photo;
622 (tl) © Cordelia Molloy/SPL/Photo Researchers,
Inc.; 623 (bl) Scott B. Rosen/HRW Photo; 624 (tl) Tim
Davis/CORBIS; 625 (bkgd) Michael Carlowicz, Woods
Hole Oceanographic Institute; 625 (t) © G. Glatsmaaier,
Los Alamos National Laboratory/P. Roberts, UCLA/SPL/
Photo Researchers, Inc.; 625 (cr) © G. Glatzmaier, Los
Alamos National Laboratory/P. Roberts, UCLA/SPL/Photo
Researchers, Inc.; 626 (bl) Richard Megna/Fundamental
Photographs, New York; 627 (tr) Scott B. Rosen/HRW
Photo; 628 (tl) Scott B. Rosen/HRW Photo; 629
(bkgd) © PunchStock; 629 (cr) © Dynamic Graphics
Group/Creatas/Alamy; 630 (tl) Take 2 Productions/Ken
Kaminesky/CORBIS; 633 (cr) Mike Fager/HRW; 635
(bkgd) © Tara Moore/Getty Images; 639 (tr) Peter
Casolino/Alamy; 641 (br) Sam Dudgeon/HRW Photo;
643 (tl) © G. Glatsmaaier, Los Alamos National
Laboratory/P. Roberts, UCLA/SPL/Photo Researchers, Inc.;
643 (cl) Dynamic Graphics Group/Creatas/Alamy; 643
(bl) Tara Moore/Getty Images

Reference Section Opener

649 (all) Sam Dudgeon/HRW

Reference Section

685 (br) HRW Photo; 686 (bl) Sam Dudgeon/HRW; 686
(br) Scott Rosen/Bill Smith Studio

HRW Staff

The people who contributed to *Holt Science Spectrum:
Physical Science* are listed below. They represent
editorial, design, production, eMedia, marketing, and
permissions.

David Alvarado, Wesley M. Bain, Kimberly Barr, Angela
Beckmann, Cindy Brooks, Sara Buller, Becky Calhoun,
Soojinn Choi, Lorraine Cooper, Martize Cross, Eddie
Dawson, Julie Dervin, Lydia Doty, Paul Draper, Sam
Dudgeon, Sally Garland, Diana Goetting, Jessica
Gonzalez, Jevara Jackson, Simon Key, Jane A. Kirschman,
Liz Kline, Laura Likon, Jenifer Limb, Denise Mahoney,
Richard Metzger, Mercedes Newman, Micah Newman,
Cathy Paré, Jenny Patton, Peter D. Reid, Raegan
Remington, Sara Rider, Kelly Rizk, Jeff Robinson, Tara
Ross, Michelle Rumpf-Dike, Beth Sample, Kay Selke,
Angela Senicz, Chris Smith, Victoria Smith, Dawn Marie
Spinozza, Sherry Sprague, Jeff Streber, JoAnn Stringer,
Jeannie Taylor, Lindsey Thomas, Bob Tucek, Kira J.
Watkins, Aimee Wiley, Sara Zettner, Patricia Zepeda